MODERN BIOLOGY

HOLT, RINEHART AND WINSTON

A Harcourt Classroom Education Company

Austin • New York • Orlando • Atlanta • San Francisco • Boston • Dallas • Toronto • London

ACKNOWLEDGMENTS

STAFF CREDITS

Executive Editor
Susan Feldk...

Managing
Mau...
...er
...ricks

...rs
...Spinozza,
...pyediting Supervisor

...oke Fugitt

...torial Staff
Jeanne Graham

Mary Helbling

Tanu'e White

Editorial Permissions
Ann B. Farrar
Production
Eddie Dawson,
Production Manager

Electronic Publishing
Richard Chavez,
Project Coordinator

Page design:
The Quarasan Group, Inc.
Cover image:
© Manfred Danegger/Okapai/
Photo Researchers, Inc.

Design
Richard Metzger,
Design Director

David Hernandez,
Designer

Image Acquisitions
Joe London,
Director

Elaine Tate,
Art Buyer Supervisor

David Knowles,
Art Buyer

Jeannie Taylor,
Photo Research Supervisor

Bob McClellan,
Senior Photo Researcher

Elisabeth McCoy
Assistant Photo Researcher

Photo Studio
Sam Dudgeon,
Senior Staff Photographer

Victoria Smith
Staff Photographer

Media
Kim Anderson

Adriana Bardin-Prestwood

CONTRIBUTING WRITERS

I. Edward Alcamo, Ph.D.
Professor of Biology
State University of New York
Farmingdale, NY

Katy Z. Allen
Science Writer
Wayland, MA

David M. Armstrong, Ph.D.
Professor
University of Colorado
Boulder, CO

Barry Bogin, Ph.D.
Professor of Anthropology
Department of Behavioral Sciences
University of Michigan
Dearborn, MI

Curtis Chubb, Ph.D.
Blanco, TX

Linda Culp
Teacher
Thorndale High School
Thorndale, TX

Cara J. Cunningham
Teacher
Ursuline Academy of Dallas
Dallas, TX

William J. Ehmann, Ph.D.
Chair, Dept. of Environmental Science
Trinity College of Washington, D.C.
Washington, D.C.

Mark R. Feil, M.S.
Wilmington, DE

David R. Hershey, Ph.D.
Adjunct Professor, Biology/ Horticulture Dept.
Prince George's Community College
Largo, MD

Mitchell Leslie
Science Writer and Editor
Albuquerque, NM

Karel F. Liem, Ph.D.
Professor
Harvard University
Cambridge, MA

Thomas Manerchia
Teacher
Archmere Academy
Wilmington, DE

Alyson Mike
Teacher
East Valley Middle School
East Helena, MT

Patricia Mokry
Teacher
Westlake High School
Austin, TX

C. Ford Morishita
Biology Teacher
Clackamas High School
Milwaukie, OR

Patricia Morrell, Ph.D.
Assistant Professor
University of Portland
Portland, OR

William Thwaites, Ph.D.
Professor Emeritus
Biology Department
San Diego State University
San Diego, CA

Salvatore Tocci
Science Writer
East Hampton, NY

Albert C. Wartski
Biology Teacher
Chapel Hill High School
Chapel Hill, NC

Lynn Marie Wartski
Science Writer
Hillsborough, NC

Printed in the United States of America

ISBN 0-03-056541-3   1 2 3 4 5 6 7 8 048 06 05 04 03 02

CONTENTS

UNIT 3 GENETICS

UNIT 4 EVOLUTION   258

UNIT 5   ECOLOGY   356

UNIT 8 INVERTEBRATES   664

UNIT 9   VERTEBRATES   796

UNIT 10 HUMAN BIOLOGY

902

FEATURES

 internet **connect**

This textbook contains the following on-line resources to help you make the most of your science experience.

go. hrw .com

Visit **go.hrw.com** for extra help and study aids matched to your textbook. Just type in the keyword HM2 HOME.

SCILINKS NSTA

Visit **www.scilinks.org** to find resources specific to topics in your textbook. Keywords appear throughout your book to take you further.

 Smithsonian Institution® **Internet Connections**

Visit **www.si.edu/hrw** for specifically chosen on-line materials from one of our nation's premier science museums.

CNNfyi.com

Visit **www.cnnfyi.com** for late-breaking news and current events stories selected just for you.

Quick Labs

CHAPTER INVESTIGATIONS

◀ INTERACTIVE EXPLORATIONS ▶

Using CD-ROM technology, Interactive Explorations allow you to manipulate variables, collect data, and draw conclusions about biological phenomena. See pages 1090-1091 for details on how to use these unique laboratory explorations.

BIOLOGICAL PRINCIPLES

" *Our ideas are only instruments which we use to break into phenomena; we must change them when they have served their purpose, as we change a blunt lancet that we have used long enough.* **"**

Claude Bernard

Organisms living in this taiga ecosystem are adapted for dry, cold weather and reduced availability of food in winter.

DNA is responsible for transmitting genetic information to offspring.

This giant panda gets its energy by eating bamboo leaves. The Amazon water lily, above left, lives in shallow eutrophic ponds.

Red-eyed tree frog

THE SCIENCE OF LIFE

Snowy owls, Nyctea scaniaca, *live on the open tundra and build their nests on the ground. This juvenile owl hatched in a flower-filled alpine meadow.*

FOCUS CONCEPT: *Biological Themes and Processes*

As you read, take note of the recurring themes of biology and the characteristics that all organisms share.

THEMES OF BIOLOGY

Scientists estimate that 40 million species of organisms inhabit the Earth. But of these 40 million species, only about 2 million have been identified and named, and only a few thousand have been studied in any detail. Thus, much of the world of biology remains to be explored and studied. Fortunately, there are guideposts to help chart a course through this vast and fascinating world. These guideposts are the themes that unify biology. In this chapter, you will read about the unifying themes of biology that allow biologists to study the enormous diversity of life.

SECTION
1-1

OBJECTIVES

▲

List six unifying themes of biology.

●

Explain how organisms get the energy they need to survive.

■

Describe the main difference between the structure of a living thing and that of a nonliving thing.

THE STUDY OF LIFE

The first life-form probably arose on Earth more than 3.5 billion years ago. Much evidence suggests that this first **organism**—or living thing—was a single cell, too small to be seen without the aid of a microscope. For millions of years, single-celled organisms floating in the seas were the only life on Earth. No fish swam in the oceans, no birds flew through the air, and no snakes moved across the ground.

Over time, organisms changed. New kinds of organisms arose from older kinds and came to inhabit almost every region of the Earth. Today brilliantly colored birds glide through the trees of tropical rain forests. Odd-looking fish prowl the dark depths of the oceans, emitting a strange red light that helps them locate their prey. Giant sequoia trees tower hundreds of feet above the ferns growing on the forest floors. Nearly blind moles burrow their way underground searching for tiny insects to consume.

These and millions of other types of organisms form the diverse population of Earth. **Biology**—the science of life—is the study of all living things. Biology includes the study of the microscopic structure of single cells. It also includes the study of the global interactions of millions of organisms. It includes the study of the life history of individual organisms as well as the collective history of all organisms.

The science of biology is as varied as the organisms that are its subjects. (Compare the owl shown on the facing page with the algae shown in Figure 1-1.) Biology is unified by certain themes, however, that come into play no matter what organism or what kind of

FIGURE 1-1

This microscopic unicellular alga, *Eremoophaera* sp. (LM, 31×), lives in a water environment. It, together with the owl shown on the facing page, gives an indication of the great diversity found in the living world.

FIGURE 1-2

These tightly packed cells are from a thin section of human skin (LM 240×). There are many different kinds of cells in animal bodies.

 Quick Lab

Observing Homeostasis

Materials 500 mL beakers (3), wax pen, tap water, thermometer, ice, hot water, goldfish, small dip net, watch or clock with a second hand

Procedure

1. Use a wax pen to label three 500 mL beakers as follows: 27°C (80°F), 20°C (68°F), and 10°C (50°F). Put 250 mL of tap water in each beaker. Use hot water or ice to adjust the temperature of the water in each beaker to the temperature indicated on the label.

2. Put the goldfish in the beaker of 27°C water. Record the number of times the gills move in 1 minute.

3. Move the goldfish to the beaker of 20°C water. Repeat observations. Move the goldfish to the beaker of 10°C water. Repeat observations.

Analysis What happens to the rate at which gills move when the temperature changes? Why? How do gills help fish maintain homeostasis?

interaction is studied. Six major themes recur throughout this book: (1) cell structure and function, (2) stability and homeostasis, (3) reproduction and inheritance, (4) evolution, (5) interdependence of organisms, and (6) matter, energy, and organization. The paragraphs that follow will give you a brief introduction to each theme. You will get a closer look at each theme in later chapters of this book. By reflecting on these themes in your study of biology, you will recognize the patterns that connect all life-forms.

Cell Structure and Function

The cell is the basic unit of life. All organisms are made of and develop from cells. Some organisms are composed of only one cell. These organisms are called **unicellular** (YOON-uh-SEL-yoo-luhr) **organisms.** Most of the living things that you see around you are **multicellular** (MUHL-ti-SEL-yoo-luhr) **organisms.** That is, they are composed of more than one cell.

Cells are small but highly organized. They contain specialized structures that carry out the cell's life processes. There are many different kinds of cells, but all cells are similar in several ways. They are surrounded by a membrane and contain a set of instructions—in the form of genetic information—necessary for making new cell parts, as well as new cells, from the molecules the cell takes in.

Look again at Figure 1-1, and compare the unicellular organism with the cells shown in Figure 1-2. New cells produced by unicellular organisms are virtually identical to the parent unicellular organisms that produced them. In contrast, mature multicellular organisms, which also begin their lives as one cell, contain not only *many* cells but also many different *kinds* of cells. The cells of multicellular organisms underwent **differentiation.** That is, they became different from each other as they multiplied and followed the various roles supplied for them by their genetic instructions.

Stability and Homeostasis

Living things, from single cells to entire large organisms, maintain very stable internal conditions. You know that the human body operates within a very narrow temperature range, around 37°C (98.6°F). Animal bodies like yours have systems that maintain internal conditions, such as temperature, water content, and even food intake, at very stable levels. This stable level of internal conditions, called **homeostasis** (HOH-mee-oh-STAY-sis), is found in all living things, including single cells.

The seal shown in Figure 1-3 can keep its body temperature very stable in a variety of water temperatures, even in very cold water. It takes in enough food to maintain a thick layer of fat under its skin for insulation. Blood flow through the seal's body, and in its flippers, is adjusted according to the temperature of the water it swims in. Its body can conserve or release heat as needed to remain at a stable temperature.

FIGURE 1-3

The shape and composition of the body of this harp seal, *Phoca groenlandica,* together with its efficient, heat-conserving circulatory system, allow the seal to survive in water temperatures that would kill many other animals.

Reproduction and Inheritance

All organisms produce new organisms like themselves. In this process, called **reproduction,** organisms transmit hereditary information to their offspring. This hereditary information is in the form of a large molecule called deoxyribonucleic acid, or **DNA.** In multicellular organisms and in some unicellular organisms, DNA is enclosed within a structure made of membrane. In other unicellular organisms, DNA exists as a loop, like the one shown in Figure 1-4. A short segment of DNA that contains the instructions for the development of a single trait of an organism is called a **gene.**

The DNA of a cell is like a large library. It contains all of the books of instructions—genes—that the cell will ever need. In this way, the cell can make the structures and complex chemicals necessary for life. In multicellular organisms, the DNA of every body cell, even different kinds of body cells, is identical. Each cell uses certain genes from the complete set. For example, cells in your thyroid gland use the set of genes from your DNA that are instructions for making thyroid hormone. Your other body cells ignore these instructions and use only the genes appropriate to their particular functions.

In **sexual reproduction,** hereditary information from two parts of a single organism or from two organisms of the same species is combined. When an egg of a female leopard frog is fertilized by the sperm of a male leopard frog, the egg and sperm join to form a single cell. This joining produces a fertilized egg cell that contains hereditary information from both the female parent and the male parent. This cell begins a series of cell divisions to produce a new leopard frog. With each division, every new cell receives a complete copy of the same hereditary information. Thus, the new organism is composed of cells that contain complete sets of hereditary information from both of its parents.

In **asexual reproduction,** hereditary information from different organisms is not combined. For example, when a bacterium reproduces asexually, it splits in two. As a result, one cell gives rise to two cells. Each of the two cells contains an identical copy of the hereditary information from the original bacterium.

FIGURE 1-4

A loop of DNA (SEM 72,000×) contains the genetic information of the unicellular organism that it is found in. Many genes are linked in the DNA loop.

Evolution

Populations of organisms **evolve,** or change, over generations. The study of **evolution** helps us understand how the many kinds of organisms that have lived on Earth came into existence. It also explains how organisms alive today are related to those that lived in the past. It helps us understand why organisms look and behave the way they do. It provides a basis for exploring the relationships among different groups of living organisms.

Scientists suggest that a process called **natural selection** is the most important driving force in evolution. According to the theory of evolution by natural selection, organisms that have certain favorable traits are better able to successfully reproduce than organisms that lack these traits. For example, white fur is helpful in snowy environments for animals like rabbits and mice, which are prey for many other species. Obviously, an animal that is killed early in life can produce no offspring at all. The animal in Figure 1-5 has a coat that changes color as the day length changes. Thus, it can retain its camouflage during winter and summer.

Evolution by natural selection is driven in part by the competition among individuals for resources necessary for survival, such as food. Not all individuals are able to live and reproduce to the same degree. Differences among individuals of a species can affect their ability to produce offspring. Some individuals have traits that give them advantages for survival and reproduction, and they tend to pass these traits on to their offspring.

The survival of organisms with favorable traits causes a gradual change in populations of organisms over many generations. This "descent with modification" as organisms adapted to different kinds of environments is responsible for the multitude of life-forms we see today.

FIGURE 1-5

Elegant solutions to the year-round problem of predation have evolved in some animals. The very different winter and summer coats of the arctic hare, *Lepus arcticus,* help the hare avoid predators.

Interdependence of Organisms

The study of individual organisms is an important part of biology. To fully understand the biological world, however, scientists study the interactions of organisms with one another and with their environment. This branch of biology is called **ecology.** A scientist may study the ecology of a single species. This would include observing individuals of the species and their interactions with each other and their environment. Scientists may also conduct large ecological studies of environments, studying specific **ecosystems** (EK-oh-SIS-tuhmz), or environmental communities. By studying ecology, biologists have come to recognize the interdependence of organisms with their physical environment. To survive, all organisms need substances such as nutrients, water, and gases from the environment. The stability of the environment in turn depends on the healthy functioning of organisms in that environment.

Scientists now recognize the enormous effect that humans have had on environments all over the world. For thousands of years, tropical rain forests, like the one shown in Figure 1-6, have provided stable—but fragile—environments for their inhabitants. In recent years, humans have cleared vast areas of these forests by cutting and burning vegetation. Roads cross areas that were once havens for tropical organisms. What is the effect of this activity? Plant and animal species native to the forest become extinct. The typically thin topsoil layer becomes depleted of nutrients and hardened by the sun. This makes the land unsuitable for planting or reestablishment of the forest. The atmospheric oxygen that was produced by the dense vegetation is lost. It is replaced by carbon dioxide from the burning of trees. Destruction of these ancient and valuable forests could affect all life on Earth.

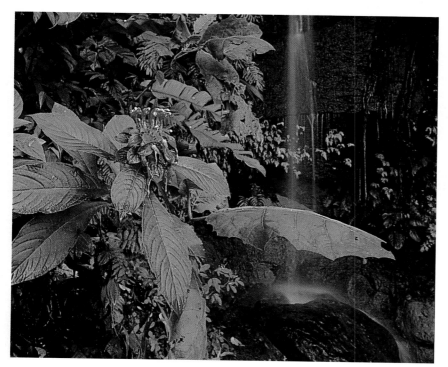

Eco ▲ Connection

Saving the Forests

Tropical rain forests, like the one shown in Figure 1-6, exist at equatorial latitudes in Central and South America, Africa, and Asia. They are lush but extremely fragile multi-storied ecosystems that support a staggering variety of life-forms. Before humans began cutting trees for timber and clearing land for farming, tropical rain forests covered about 6 million square miles on Earth. In the late 1970s, rain forests were being cleared at a rate of 29,000 square miles per year. By the early 1990s, that figure had climbed to more than 55,000 square miles per year. In less than 100 years, the rain forests may be gone.

Rain-forest products include rubber, coffee, and various kinds of fruits and nuts, as well as wood used for furniture, such as mahogany and teak, and wood used in paper manufacturing. Purchase by consumers of periodically harvested resources such as fruits, nuts, and rubber encourage responsible management of the rain forest renewable resources. Unfortunately, some paper manufacturers are very large-scale consumers of rain-forest wood. By learning about the track record of manufacturers with respect to rain-forest conservation, consumers can make more-responsible decisions about the products they use. Such awareness may help slow damage to these complex and irreplaceable ecosystems.

FIGURE 1-6

Tropical rain forests, like this one on the eastern slope of the Andes Mountains in Ecuador, support an extraordinary variety and number of plants and animals, typically on a very thin layer of fertile topsoil.

Matter, Energy, and Organization

Word Roots and Origins

photosynthesis

from the Greek *photo,* meaning "light," and *syntithenai,* meaning "to put together"

Living things have highly organized structures that must be maintained in their orderly state by a constant supply of energy. How organisms obtain, use, and transfer energy is a major topic of study in biology. Almost all the energy for life on Earth comes from the sun. Through the process of **photosynthesis** (FOH-toh-SIN-thuh-sis), plants and some types of unicellular organisms capture the energy from the sun and change it into a form of energy that can be used by living things.

Organisms that obtain their energy by making their own food, like plants, are called **autotrophs** (AWT-oh-TROHFS). Using the energy they trap from the sun, some kinds of autotrophs convert water and carbon dioxide from the environment into energy-rich substances such as sugars and starches. These substances are then used by the organisms for their own energy needs. Other kinds of autotrophs use different chemical processes to get energy. Autotrophs may be consumed and used as an energy source by other living things. **Heterotrophs** (HET-er-oh-TROHFS) are organisms that must take in food to meet their energy needs. Heterotrophs include all animals and fungi as well as many unicellular organisms and a few plant species. Because they cannot make their own food, heterotrophs must consume autotrophs, other heterotrophs, or both for their energy needs.

FIGURE 1-7

Many nonliving things, like this salt crystal (LM 55×), have a very organized structure but do not display the degree of organization and complexity found in living things.

In living things, complex chemicals are broken down. Their parts are then reassembled into chemicals and structures needed by the organism. Living things are set apart by their complexity. Even a simple, small organism, such as the alga shown in Figure 1-1, is far more complex than a nonliving thing, such as the mineral that appears in Figure 1-7. The mineral has an organized molecular and crystalline structure. However, the multitude of different molecular structures found in the alga are much more complex and varied than anything found outside the living world.

SECTION 1-1 REVIEW

1. List six unifying themes of biology.

2. How do organisms produce offspring like themselves?

3. What are two of the driving forces behind the process of natural selection?

4. Why are rain forests considered fragile environments that are vulnerable to permanent destruction?

5. How do autotrophs differ from heterotrophs in obtaining energy?

6. **CRITICAL THINKING** Why do scientists say that the environment "selects" the traits that allow an organism to survive and reproduce?

THE WORLD OF BIOLOGY

*O*ur *world abounds with a great variety of life. Giant tube worms thrive at the bottom of the oceans near bubbling volcanic vents. Red algae spread to cover the surface of arctic glaciers like a carpet. Bacteria grow in every part of the world, even in the pores of your skin.*

CHARACTERISTICS OF LIFE

All organisms, no matter how different from each other they may be, share certain features characteristic of all living things.

Cells

All living things are composed of cells. In multicellular organisms, some cells are specialized to play a specific role. The plant stem shown in Figure 1-8 contains many different cells, each separate from the surrounding cells, like many rooms in a large building. Cells are always very small. Large multicellular organisms contain many cells, while smaller organisms contain fewer cells.

Organization

All living things are highly organized at both the molecular and cellular levels. They take in substances from the environment and organize them in complex ways. In cells, specific cell structures carry out particular functions. In most kinds of multicellular organisms, cells and groups of cells are organized by their function. Several different cell types grouped together in the section of the plant stem are easily distinguished in Figure 1-8.

SECTION

OBJECTIVES

▲

List six characteristics of life.

●

Describe how a living thing is organized.

■

Explain why all living things on Earth are not yet well understood.

internetconnect

SCiLINKS NSTA

TOPIC: Characteristics of life
GO TO: www.scilinks.org
KEYWORD: HM011

FIGURE 1-8

The different types of cells in this plant stem are organized into structures that perform specific functions. The circular conducting tubes, shown in cross section (LM 19×), transport water and other substances up and down the plant stem.

FIGURE 1-9

All living things, even single cells, work to maintain a steady internal environment. Animals may have more than one mechanism that allows them to maintain a stable body temperature. This pine grosbeak, *Pinicola enucleator*, fluffs its feathers in cold weather to stay warm.

Word Roots and Origins

metabolism

from the Greek *metabole*, meaning "to change"

Energy Use

All living things use energy in a process called **metabolism** (muh-TAB-uh-LIZ-uhm), which is the sum of all of the chemical processes that occur in the organism. Organisms require energy to maintain their molecular and cellular organization as well as to grow and reproduce. Autotrophic organisms, such as green plants, use the food that they generate from photosynthesis for growth, maintenance, and reproduction.

Homeostasis

All living things maintain stable internal conditions. Even single cells work to keep their internal environment stable. A cell closely controls its water content by taking in or releasing water. A cell that takes in too much water will rupture and die. Multicellular organisms usually have more than one system for maintaining important aspects of their internal environment, like temperature. The feathers of the bird shown in Figure 1-9 become more erect in cold weather. This traps an insulating layer of air next to the bird's body.

Growth

All living things grow, as do many nonliving things. Nonliving things, like crystals or icicles, grow by accumulating more of the material they are made of. Living things grow as a result of cell division and cell enlargement. In unicellular organisms, cell division results in more organisms. **Cell division** is the formation of two cells from an existing cell, as shown in Figure 1-10. Newly divided cells enlarge until they are the size of a mature cell. In multicellular organisms, cell division and cell enlargement together result in growth.

The process by which an adult organism arises is called **development.** Development is produced by repeated cell divisions and cell differentiation. As a result of development, an adult organism is composed of many cells. Your body, for example, is composed of about 50 trillion cells, all of which derived from a fertilized egg.

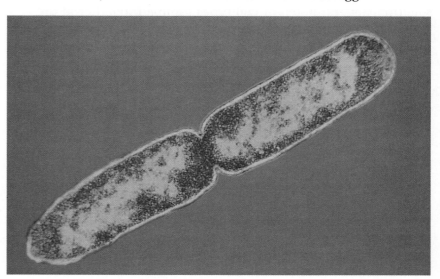

FIGURE 1-10

Cell division in this unicellular organism, *Escherichia coli* (TEM 98,000×), produces two identical offspring cells.

Reproduction

All species of organisms have the ability to reproduce. Reproduction is not essential to the survival of an individual organism. Because no organism lives forever, however, reproduction is essential for the continuation of a species. Glass frogs, such as the one shown in Figure 1-11, will lay many eggs in its lifetime. Of these, only a few offspring will reach adulthood and successfully reproduce.

During reproduction, many species have ways to combine the genetic information of individual members to produce offspring that are not identical to their parents. The frog shown in Figure 1-11 reproduces sexually. The eggs are fertilized by a male glass frog after they are laid. The resulting offspring carry traits of both parents.

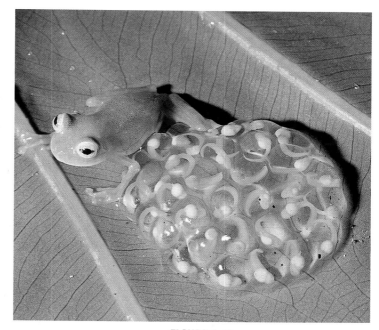

FIGURE 1-11

Many species of animals that lay eggs produce large numbers of eggs. Many of the eggs laid by the glass frog, *Centrolenella* sp., will not survive. In contrast, the offspring of animals that give birth to live offspring typically have a high rate of survival.

THE LIVING WORLD

The world of biology is so diverse and so rich that scientists have yet to explore all of it. Many organisms that have not been identified live in regions of the world that are difficult to explore, like dense tropical rain forests and deep ocean waters. Some organisms are so small that they easily escape detection. A single gram of fertile soil, for example, may contain as many as 2.5 billion unicellular organisms. In the dense forests of Vietnam, scientists recently discovered a new species of deer. It weighs between 40 and 50 kg (90 and 110 lb). It is one and a half times as large as any other known Asian deer species.

The wide variety of unstudied organisms shows us how much is still to be learned about life. Wherever you live, the world around you teems with life. This book will help you appreciate the living world and understand how scientists go about exploring and studying it.

SECTION 1-2 REVIEW

1. Name six characteristics that all living things share.

2. What are two levels of organization found in living things?

3. How does growth of a nonliving thing differ from growth of a living thing?

4. Why is reproduction an important characteristic of life?

5. Why are so many organisms yet to be discovered, identified, and described?

6. **CRITICAL THINKING** What would happen if all autotrophic organisms died, leaving only heterotrophic organisms?

OBJECTIVES

▲

Define and give examples of *observing, measuring, organizing and analyzing data, inferring,* and *modeling.*

●

Explain the relationship between hypothesizing, predicting, and experimenting.

■

Explain why good communication is so important in science.

◆

Describe the methods that scientists use in their work.

SCIENTIFIC METHODS

*O*ne of the best ways to begin studying science is to examine how scientists try to solve a problem or answer a question. Whatever they study, all scientists use certain methods to obtain knowledge. Understanding scientific methods will help you formulate strategies to answer questions you will encounter in your own scientific study or in your daily life. Consider how scientists searched for the cause of one of the deadliest infectious diseases in humans—Ebola hemorrhagic fever.

OBSERVING

In 1976, a deadly and contagious human disease appeared in several villages in the central African nation of the Democratic Republic of Congo, then known as Zaire. Local doctors observed a rapidly progressing and consistent sequence of symptoms in disease victims. Most had severe headaches, fever, bloody diarrhea, and vomiting. In the final stages of the disease, victims' internal organs bled uncontrollably and blood leaked through the nose, ears, and even the skin. Death from shock—collapse of the cardiovascular system due to loss of blood—followed rapidly. Teams of scientists from the the Centers for Disease Control and Prevention (CDC), the agency of the United States government responsible for monitoring diseases, and the World Health Organization (WHO) were sent to Zaire. Their job was to investigate the circumstances of this severe outbreak of what seemed to be a new disease.

internet**connect**

SC*LINKS* **TOPIC:** Scientific method
GO TO: www.scilinks.org
NSTA **KEYWORD:** HM014

ASKING A QUESTION

All scientific investigations begin with one or more questions. Think of the many questions that a scientist sent to investigate an outbreak of a disease would have. How is the disease transmitted among people? What caused the disease to appear suddenly in humans? How long after exposure to the agent of infection do the first symptoms of the disease occur? Do all victims die? The most fundamental question to be answered about the outbreak of a new disease is *What is the disease-causing agent?*

COLLECTING DATA

The longest phase of a scientific investigation is usually data collection. **Data** include any and all information that scientists gather in trying to answer their questions. Four important aspects of collecting data are described in the following paragraphs.

Observing

All scientific understanding of the natural world is based on observation. It is the observation of something unusual or unexplained that raises the first questions in a scientific investigation. Observation continues to be essential throughout all stages of scientific investigation. **Observation** typically employs one or more of the five senses to perceive objects or events. A scientist may observe the sound of the call of an animal in the wild. He or she may observe the appearance of an organism under a microscope, as the scientist is doing in Figure 1-12. Most observations in a scientific investigation are direct, although some things, like electricity, must be observed indirectly.

Measuring

Many kinds of observations involve quantitative data—data that can be measured in numbers. Scientists may measure the dimensions of an object, the number of objects in a group, the duration of an event, or other characteristics in precise units.

For example, in Zaire, the scientists recorded several types of quantitative data from their work in the field. These data included the number of people who displayed symptoms of the disease, the number of days that elapsed from the time symptoms first appeared until a victim died, and the number of people who died from the disease after they were infected. These data gave scientists a picture of the outbreak—an indication of how serious the disease was. The numbers they recorded revealed a grim picture. The outbreak had caused nearly 300 deaths. Death usually followed within a week after the first symptoms appeared, and the disease was extremely deadly. From 80 to 90 percent of the people who became infected died from the disease.

Word Roots and Origins

data

the plural of datum; remains unchanged from the Latin *datum*, meaning "a thing given"

FIGURE 1-12

Scientists make many of their observations within the confines of a laboratory.

Sampling

Scientific **sampling** is the technique of using a sample, that is, a small part, to represent an entire population. To be useful, samples must be large and random. That is, they should include as many subjects as possible, and scientists must be sure to sample a cross section of the population so that an accurate representation is obtained. The scientists working in Zaire took hundreds of blood samples, both from people stricken with the disease and from people who were apparently healthy.

These blood samples taken from the disease victims provided the first important clue to the nature of the disease. The samples were sent from Zaire to laboratories in Europe and to the CDC in Atlanta, Georgia. Scientists at the CDC and at the University of Anvers, in Belgium, isolated a strange, threadlike virus from the blood samples. Using a powerful electron microscope, the scientists at the CDC photographed the virus, shown in Figure 1-13.

FIGURE 1-13

Because of its threadlike structure, the Ebola virus (TEM 23,000×) is classified as a filovirus. *Filo-* is a prefix meaning "threadlike" and is derived from the Latin word *filum,* which means "thread."

Organizing Data

Data are of little use unless they are organized. Organizing data involves placing observations and measurements in some kind of logical order, such as in a graph, chart, table, or map. The scientists tracking Ebola fever organized many kinds of data. They organized quantitative data into tables and charts. Remember that these quantitative data gave them an initial picture of how deadly the disease was.

Another important goal of the scientists was to trace the identity of the first person who had become infected with the disease. This information would be an important clue for identifying where the virus came from and how it was transmitted to humans. To do this, scientists who track the spread of a disease may organize information on all reported cases of the disease into a flowchart. The scientists can then trace the thread of contagious spread backward in hopes of identifying the first infected person. A flowchart, similar to the one shown in Figure 1-14, serves as a "family history" of the disease.

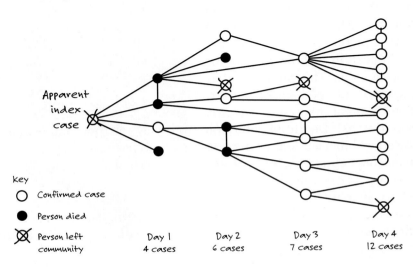

FIGURE 1-14

Scientists who trace the transmission of disease develop flowcharts much like this one so they can track the disease back to its source.

HYPOTHESIZING

When scientists have made many observations and collected sufficient data, they can suggest an explanation for what they have seen and recorded. This explanation, called a **hypothesis,** is a statement that explains their observations *and* can be tested.

Forming a Hypothesis

The central hypothesis in this complicated investigation was that the virus photographed by the CDC scientists caused the hemorrhagic fever. Although it may seem obvious that this is true, cause-and-effect relationships never can be assumed in a scientific investigation. Rather, evidence must be accumulated in every step.

Hypothesizing is a very important step in scientific investigation. A statement is testable if evidence can be collected that either does or does not support it. Recall the scientists' hypothesis about the identity of the infectious agent. It would not be supported if the infection with the virus did not cause symptoms of the disease.

Although a hypothesis may be supported by evidence, it can never be proved true beyond all doubt. At any time, new data might indicate that a previously accepted hypothesis does not hold true in all instances. Scientists often must refine and revise their original hypotheses—or even discard them—as they uncover new evidence.

Predicting

To test a hypothesis, scientists make a prediction that logically follows from the hypothesis. A **prediction** is a statement made in advance that states the results that will be obtained from testing a hypothesis, if the hypothesis is supported. A prediction most often takes the form of an "if-then" statement. In the case of Ebola fever, scientists made a prediction. If the virus were the true disease-causing agent, then introducing the virus into healthy tissue would cause cell death like that found in victims of the disease.

EXPERIMENTING

A hypothesis is often tested by carrying out an **experiment.** Experimenting is the process of testing a hypothesis or prediction by gathering data under controlled conditions.

Conducting a Controlled Experiment

Most experiments in biology are controlled experiments. A **controlled experiment** is based on a comparison of a **control group** with an **experimental group.** The control group and the experimental group are designed to be identical except for one factor. This factor is

Predicting Results

Materials 2 Petri dishes with agar, cellophane tape, wax pen

Procedure

1. Open one of the Petri dishes, and streak your finger across the surface of the agar.

2. Replace the lid, and seal it with cellophane tape. Label this Petri dish with your name and the number 1.

3. Seal the second Petri dish without removing the lid. Label this Petri dish with your name and the number 2.

4. Record a description of your actions for each Petri dish. Then write your prediction about what will happen in each dish.

5. Store your dishes as your teacher directs.

6. Record your observations.

Analysis

1. Was your prediction accurate? What evidence can you cite to support your prediction?

2. If you did not obtain the results you predicted, would you change your testing method or your prediction? Explain why and how you would make changes.

3. Evaluate the importance of obtaining a result that does not support your prediction.

called the **independent variable.** During the course of a controlled experiment, a scientist observes or measures another factor in both the control group and the experimental group. This factor is called the **dependent variable**—dependent because it is driven by or results from the independent variable.

A controlled experiment supported the hypothesis that Ebola fever was caused by the previously unknown virus that was isolated by scientists in Belgium and the United States. Scientists at the University of Anvers tried to confirm the link between the virus and the cell death that caused the symptoms of the disease. Because monkeys are genetically similar to humans, kidney cells from a species of African monkey were used in an animal model of human infection. Test tubes containing the monkey kidney cells were divided into an experimental group and a control group. Drops of blood that contained the virus, taken from a victim of Ebola fever in Zaire, were added to each test tube in the experimental group. No blood was added to the test tubes in the control group. In the experiment, the independent variable was the addition of blood to the monkey kidney cells. The dependent variable was the health of the cells.

Analyzing Data

After a scientist has collected and organized data from a field study or an experiment, the data must be analyzed. Analyzing data is the process of determining whether data are reliable and whether they support or do not support a hypothesis or prediction. Scientists analyze data in many ways. For example, they may use statistics to determine relationships between variables, compare the data with those obtained in other studies, and determine possible sources of experimental error.

Eleven days after the virus-containing blood was mixed with the monkey kidney cells, the cells in the experimental test tube were dead. Moreover, addition of liquid from the experimental test tubes to new test tubes containing healthy monkey kidney cells caused the death of those cells also, again after a period of 10 to 11 days.

DRAWING CONCLUSIONS

The goal of scientific investigation is to shed light on something previously not understood. The final step of most investigations is to produce a model.

Modeling

Modeling involves constructing a representation of an object, a system, or a process that helps show relationships among data. A **model** is essentially an *explanation* supported by data. It can be visual, verbal, or mathematical. Scientists sometimes use models to help generate new hypotheses or predictions. For example, scientists have examined the case histories of people who have died from Ebola fever to develop a model of how the virus is transmitted among humans. Close contact with an infected person is necessary. Direct contact with the blood of an infected person seems to be the likeliest way to become infected. Many people who had Ebola fever were infected in crowded hospitals, like the one shown in Figure 1-15, by contaminated needles and instruments. Scientists are not sure whether the virus can penetrate skin or enter through the nose or mouth. Perhaps a break must first be present in the skin or lining of the nose or mouth.

The model of Ebola virus transmission is far from complete. The first human case in the 1976 outbreak in Zaire was never identified. Scientists still do not know the identity of the animal species that harbors the virus in the wild or how the virus is spread to humans. Once scientists have developed a complete model of where the virus originates and how it is transmitted to humans, they can specify the precautions to take to avoid infection.

FIGURE 1-15

The Ebola virus spread in hospitals and clinics in Zaire because of overcrowded and unsanitary conditions.

Inferring

An **inference** (IN-fuhr-uhns) is a conclusion made on the basis of facts or premises rather than on direct observations. If you see smoke, you will probably infer that its source is a fire, even if you can't see the fire. In science, inferences are often drawn from data gathered from a field study or experiment, considered together with previous knowledge. Unlike a hypothesis, an inference is not directly testable. The scientists on the trail of the source of the Ebola virus made several important inferences from their work.

For example, based on the observations they made and the data they collected and analyzed, scientists inferred that the Ebola virus is carried by a small, forest-dwelling animal, possibly a bat. The virus may not cause the disease-carrying animals, or hosts, to become ill, as it does to humans. Scientists suspect that the host animals periodically move in search of food into regions inhabited or used by humans. When they do, they come in contact with people, some of whom contract the virus from the animals.

Forming a Theory

In science, a theory may be formed after many related hypotheses have been tested and supported with much experimental evidence. The word *theory* does not mean "wild guess"; it does not even mean "hypothesis." Rather, a **theory** is a broad and comprehensive statement of what is thought to be true. A theory is supported by considerable evidence and may tie together several related hypotheses. Few true theories are produced in science, relative to the volume of work performed and the number of hypotheses tested.

IMPLEMENTING SCIENTIFIC METHODS

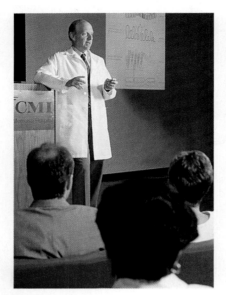

FIGURE 1-16

Throughout the world, scientists often gather to share what they have discovered. Each gathering is usually devoted to a specific subject or topic.

In real-life situations, scientists do not follow one single method of asking questions and seeking answers. Instead, scientists combine some of the processes of the scientific methods in a way that is best suited to answer the questions they ask.

Problem Solving

A field biologist might wish to investigate the animal source of Ebola fever in the rain forest. He or she might use scientific methods that combine observing, hypothesizing, sampling, organizing data, and analyzing data. Consider a laboratory biologist working to understand how the Ebola virus attacks body cells. He or she might use scientific methods that combine observing, measuring, organizing data, hypothesizing, predicting, experimenting, analyzing data, and constructing a model. A public health official would likely be concerned about the spread of Ebola fever in a population. He or she might use scientific methods that combine organizing data, analyzing data, predicting, and inferring.

Communicating

As you have seen in the case of Ebola fever, scientists do not work alone. They share the results of their studies with other scientists. They publish their findings in scientific journals or present them at scientific meetings, like the one shown in Figure 1-16. Sharing information is essential to progress in science. The work of every scientist is subject to examination and verification by other scientists. Communication allows scientists to build on the work of others. Recall that communication among scientists throughout the world enabled them to isolate the Ebola virus. The same kind of communication enabled scientists to recognize the outbreaks of Ebola fever that occurred in Zaire in 1995 and Gabon in 1996. Health-care workers responded much sooner than they had in the earlier outbreaks. Though many people died, a far worse epidemic was avoided thanks to good communication and cooperation among scientists and health-care workers.

SECTION 1-3 REVIEW

1. How are the processes of inferring and modeling useful to scientists?

2. What is the relationship between hypothesizing and experimenting in science?

3. What role does communication play in science?

4. Explain why there is no single scientific method.

5. How does a theory differ from a hypothesis?

6. **CRITICAL THINKING** "Science rarely develops absolute truths that apply to all living things." Based on what you have read about scientific processes, do you think this statement is true?

MICROSCOPY AND MEASUREMENT

To study the living world, biologists need to observe cells and their parts. The development of new tools and new techniques enables biologists to probe even deeper into life's secrets.

SECTION

1-4

OBJECTIVES

▲

Compare light microscopes with electron microscopes in terms of magnification and resolution.

●

Explain the advantage of the Système International d'Unités.

MICROSCOPES

Among the most widely used tools in biology are microscopes. A **microscope** is an instrument that produces an enlarged image of an object. Biologists use microscopes to study organisms, cells, and cell parts that are too small to otherwise be seen. Microscopes both enlarge the image made by an object and show its details. The increase of an object's apparent size is **magnification.** The power to show details clearly refers to **resolution** (REZ-uh-LU-shuhn). Microscopes vary in powers of magnification and resolution.

Light Microscopes

To see small organisms and cells, biologists typically use a **compound light microscope (LM),** as shown in Figure 1-17. To be viewed with a compound light microscope, a specimen is mounted on a glass slide. The specimen must be sliced thin enough to be transparent, or it must be very small. The slide holding the specimen is placed over the opening in the **stage** of the microscope. A light source, a light bulb or mirror in the base, directs light upward. Light passes through the specimen and through the **objective lens,** which is positioned directly above the specimen. The objective lens enlarges the image of the specimen. This magnified image is projected up through the body tube to the **ocular** (AHK-yoo-luhr) **lens** in the eyepiece, where it is magnified further.

FIGURE 1-17

In a compound light microscope, the image of a transparent specimen is enlarged as it passes through the objective and ocular lenses.

Ocular lens — Eyepiece

Body tube

Nosepiece

Objective lenses

Stage clip

Slide with specimen

Condenser

Light source

Stage

Coarse focus

Fine focus

Most light microscopes have a set of objective lenses with different powers of magnification. These lenses can be rotated into place by revolving the **nosepiece.** In a typical compound light microscope, the most powerful objective lens produces an image 40 times the actual size of the specimen. This factor of enlargement is called the **power of magnification** of the lens, and it is represented, in this case, as 40×. The standard ocular lens magnifies a specimen 10 times (10×). To compute the power of magnification of a microscope, the power of magnification of the strongest objective lens (in this case 40×) is multiplied by the power of magnification of the ocular lens (10×). This results in a total power of magnification of 400×.

Electron Microscopes

The resolution power of light microscopes is limited by the physical characteristics of light. At powers of magnification beyond about 2,000×, the image of the specimen becomes blurry. To examine specimens even smaller than cells, such as cell parts or viruses, scientists may choose from several types of electron microscopes. In an **electron microscope,** a beam of electrons—rather than a beam of light—produces an enlarged image of the specimen. Electron microscopes are much more powerful than light microscopes. Some electron microscopes can even show the contours of individual atoms in a specimen.

The **transmission electron microscope,** called a TEM, transmits a beam of electrons through a very thinly sliced specimen. Magnetic lenses enlarge the image and focus it on a screen or photographic plate. This produces an image like the one shown in Figure 1-18a. Transmission electron microscopes can magnify objects up to 200,000 times. But TEMs do have an important limitation—they cannot be used to view living specimens.

The **scanning electron microscope,** called an SEM, provides striking three-dimensional images, as you can see in Figure 1-18b. Specimens are not sliced for viewing. Rather, the surface of the specimen is sprayed with a fine metal coating. A beam of electrons is passed over the specimen's surface. This causes the metal coating to emit a shower of electrons. These electrons are projected onto a fluorescent screen or photographic plate, producing an image of the surface of the object. Scanning electron microscopes can magnify objects up to 100,000 times, and like the TEM, they cannot be used to view living specimens.

FIGURE 1-18

This unicellular organism, *Giardia lamblia,* looks very different when viewed by (a) transmission electron microscopy and (b) scanning electron microscopy.

(a)

(b)

MEASUREMENT

Scientists use a single, standard system of measurement. The official name of the measurement system is Système International d'Unités (International System of Measurements), or simply **SI**. You will use the same units when you make measurements in the laboratory.

Base Units

There are seven fundamental **base units** in SI that describe length, mass, time, and other quantities, as shown in Table 1-1. Multiples of a base unit (in powers of 10) are designated by prefixes, as shown in Table 1-2. For example, the base unit for length is the meter. One *kilo*meter is equal in length to 1,000 meters.

TABLE 1-1 *SI Base Units*

Base quantity	Name	Abbreviation
Length	meter	m
Mass	kilogram	kg
Time	second	s
Electric current	ampere	A
Thermodynamic temperature	kelvin	K
Amount of substance	mole	mol
Luminous intensity	candela	cd

TABLE 1-2 *Some SI Prefixes*

Prefix	Abbreviation	Factor of base unit
giga	G	1,000,000,000
mega	M	1,000,000
kilo	k	1,000
hecto	h	100
deka	da	10
deci	d	0.1
centi	c	0.01
milli	m	0.001
micro	μ	0.000001
nano	n	0.000000001
pico	p	0.000000000001

TABLE 1-3 SI Derived Units Often Used in Biology

Derived quantity	Name	Abbreviation
Area	square meter	m^2
Volume	cubic meter	m^3
Mass density	kilogram per cubic meter	kg/m^3
Specific volume	cubic meter per kilogram	m^3/kg
Celsius temperature	degree Celsius	°C

TABLE 1-4 Other Units Acceptable for Use with SI

Name	Abbreviation	Value in SI units
Minute	min	1 min = 60 s
Hour	h	1 h = 60 min = 3,600 s
Day	d	1 d = 24 h = 86,400 s
Liter	L	1 L = 1 dm^3 = 0.001 m^3
Metric ton	t	1 t = 1,000 kg

Derived Units

The base units in Table 1-1 cannot be used to measure surface area or velocity, among other things. Therefore, other important units, derived units, are used. **Derived units** are produced by the mathematical relationship between two base units or between two derived units. Table 1-3 shows some common derived units.

Other Units

Some units of measurement that are not part of the SI are accepted for use with SI units. They are units of time, volume, and mass, as shown in Table 1-4.

SECTION 1-4 REVIEW

1. How do microscopes differ in magnification and resolution?

2. How is the maximum power of magnification computed for a compound light microscope?

3. How does a scanning electron microscope work?

4. How does a transmission electron microscope work?

5. If SI measurement is no more accurate than the English system, why do scientists throughout the world use it?

6. CRITICAL THINKING Why might a scientist prefer to use the lower powers of a light microscope to observe aspects of unicellular organisms?

CHAPTER 1 REVIEW

SUMMARY/VOCABULARY

1-1
- Biology is the study of life, ranging from the study of unicellular organisms to the study of the global interactions among millions of organisms.
- Six themes serve to unify the study of biology: (1) cell structure and function; (2) stability and homeostasis; (3) reproduction and inheritance; (4) evolution; (5) interdependence of organisms; and (6) matter, energy, and organization.
- The cell is the basic unit of life. Organisms may be unicellular or multicellular.
- Living things maintain a stable level of internal conditions, called homeostasis.

- Reproduction involves the transmission of hereditary information from organisms to their offspring.
- Populations of organisms evolve over generations primarily by a process called natural selection.
- Organisms interact in important ways with each other and with their environments.
- Living things have highly organized structures that are maintained by a constant input of energy.
- Autotrophs obtain energy by making their own nutrients.
- Heterotrophs obtain energy from the nutrients they obtain from their environment.

Vocabulary

asexual reproduction (7)
autotroph (10)
biology (5)
differentiation (6)
DNA (7)

ecology (9)
ecosystem (9)
evolution (8)
evolve (8)
gene (7)

heterotroph (10)
homeostasis (6)
multicellular organism (6)
natural selection (8)
organism (5)

photosynthesis (10)
reproduction (7)
sexual reproduction (7)
unicellular organism (6)

1-2
- Living things are composed of cells.
- Living things are more highly organized than nonliving structures.
- Living things use energy in a process called metabolism.
- Living things have several mechanisms that help them maintain stable internal conditions.

- When living things grow, their cells enlarge and divide.
- Living things reproduce, producing offspring similar to themselves.
- There is a great deal yet to be learned about the living world.

Vocabulary

cell division (12)

development (12)

metabolism (12)

1-3
- Scientific investigations generally begin with observation.
- Methods scientists use in their work include (1) observing, (2) asking a question, (3) collecting data, (4) hypothesizing, (5) experimenting, and (6) drawing conclusions.
- A hypothesis is a statement that explains observations *and* that can be tested.

- In a controlled experiment, the experimental group is identical to the control group except for one factor called the independent variable.
- Communication is very important in science because scientists build on the work of others.

Vocabulary

control group (17)
controlled experiment (17)
data (15)
dependent variable (18)

experiment (17)
experimental group (17)
hypothesis (17)
independent variable (18)

inference (19)
model (18)
observation (15)
prediction (17)

sampling (16)
theory (19)

1-4 ■ Biologists often use a compound light microscope to see small things, like cells.
■ Electron microscopes provide higher magnification and better resolution than do light microscopes.

■ Système international d'unités (SI) is a standard system of measurement that uses seven fundamental base units.
■ All measurements scientists make are done using SI units, derived units, and other acceptable units.

Vocabulary

base unit (23)
compound light microscope (21)
derived unit (24)
electron microscope (22)

magnification (21)
microscope (21)
nosepiece (22)
objective lens (21)
ocular lens (21)

power of magnification (22)
resolution (21)
scanning electron microscope (SEM) (22)

SI (23)
stage (21)
transmission electron microscope (22)

REVIEW

Vocabulary

1. What is the difference between asexual reproduction and sexual reproduction?
2. Compare heterotrophs with autotrophs.
3. How do cell division and enlargement contribute to growth?
4. Explain the difference between formulating a model and inferring.
5. Describe the similarities and differences between a transmission electron microscope and a scanning electron microscope.

Multiple Choice

6. Reproduction involves the transfer of genetic information from (a) autotroph to heterotroph (b) parents to offspring (c) offspring to parents (d) unicellular organism to multicellular organism.
7. The theory of evolution by natural selection helps explain how complex organisms came into existence, why organisms of the past differ from those alive today, and how various groups of living organisms (a) develop (b) reproduce (c) obtain energy (d) are related to each other.
8. The hereditary material in living things is (a) CDC (b) thyroid hormone (c) carbon dioxide (d) DNA.
9. Organisms that obtain energy by taking in food are called (a) autotrophs (b) heterotrophs (c) homeostatic (d) reproducers.
10. Growth occurs by (a) organization and reproduction (b) adaptation and evolution (c) inferring and adapting (d) cell division and cell enlargement.
11. The combination of genetic information from two individuals occurs during (a) homeostasis (b) development (c) reproduction (d) differentiation.
12. The most important driving force in evolution is (a) cellular organization (b) differentiation (c) natural selection (d) development.
13. Data that are quantitative are always (a) described in words (b) represented by numbers (c) recorded on a tape recorder (d) seen through a microscope.
14. A hypothesis is a statement that (a) is identical to a theory (b) can be tested (c) is usually true (d) is always true.
15. The resolution of a microscope refers to (a) its power to increase an object's apparent size (b) its ability to show detail clearly (c) its series of interchangeable objective lenses (d) its power to scan the surface of an object.

Short Answer

16. Name the part of the compound light microscope denoted by each letter.

17. Why do biologists say that living things are organized?

18. What are the different results produced by cellular division in a unicellular organism and in a multicellular organism?

19. Explain how the process of natural selection can change traits over time.

20. What is an ecosystem?

21. Why have some animals only recently been discovered?

22. What is the relationship between a hypothesis and a prediction?

23. Describe a controlled experiment that was conducted to confirm the cause of Ebola fever.

24. What is a model?

25. What is an important limitation of SEMs and TEMs in observing organisms?

CRITICAL THINKING

1. One of the first branches of biology to be developed was taxonomy, the naming of organisms. Why is taxonomy important to communication about biology?

2. Rock crystals grow and become larger. How does this process differ from the way living things grow?

3. One of the most important parts of any scientific publication is the part called "Methods and Materials," in which the scientist describes the procedure used in the experiment. Why do you think such details are so important?

4. Scientists know that a disease-causing organism can cause overwhelming illness or death very quickly. Why would it not be adaptive for a disease-causing organism to kill its victims too quickly?

5. Look at the photographs below. The SEM, top, is of *Staphylococcus aureus*. The TEM, bottom, is also of *S. aureus*. Compare and contrast what each electron micrograph tells you about this organism.

EXTENSION

1. Read the chapter titled "Project Ebola" in Richard Preston's book *The Hot Zone*. The chapter describes the outbreak of the Ebola virus in the Reston, Virginia, primate research facility in 1989. Answer the following questions: Why was the research on Ebola virus done in a Level 4 area? Why was negative air pressure used in the lab? What special precautions did the scientists have to take before entering the Level 4 area?

2. Using a compound light microscope, observe prepared slides of unicellular organisms such as *Euglena* under three different powers of magnification. Draw a picture of each organism as it appears at each power of magnification, and write a brief description of the level of detail that you see.

Using SI Units

OBJECTIVES

- Express measurements in SI units.
- Read a thermometer.
- Measure liquid volume using a graduated cylinder.
- Measure mass using a balance.
- Determine the density (mass-to-volume ratio) of two different liquids.

PROCESS SKILLS

- measuring
- calculating

MATERIALS

- 75 mL light-colored sand
- 75 mL dark-colored sand
- 1100 mL graduated cylinder
- Celsius thermometers, alcohol filled (2)
- 5 oz plastic cups (4)
- graph paper
- heat-protective gloves
- light source
- stopwatch or clock
- ring stand or lamp support
- 25 mL corn oil
- 25 mL water
- clear-plastic cup
- balance

Background

1. What does the abbreviation *SI* stand for?
2. List the seven SI base units.

PART A Measuring Temperature

1. In your lab report, prepare a data table similar to Table A, above right.
2. Using a graduated cylinder, measure 75 mL of light-colored sand and pour it into one of the small plastic cups. Repeat this procedure with the dark-colored sand and another plastic cup.
3. Level the sand by placing the cup on your desk and sliding the cup back and forth.

TABLE A *SAND TEMPERATURE*

Time (min)	Temperature (°C)	
	Dark-colored sand	Light-colored sand
Start		
1		
2		
3		
4		
5		
6		
7		
8		
9		
10		

4. Insert one thermometer into each cup. The zero line on the thermometer should be level with the sand, as shown in the figure below. Re-level the sand if necessary.

5. ⚠️ CAUTION **Wear heat-protective gloves when handling the lamp. The lamp will become very hot and may burn you.** Using a ring stand or lamp support, position the lamp approximately 9 cm from the top of the sand, as shown in the figure below left. Make sure the lamp is evenly positioned between the two containers.

6. Before turning on the lamp, record the initial temperature of each cup of sand in your data table.

7. Note the time or start the stopwatch when you turn on the lamp. The lamp will become hot and warm the sand. Check the temperature of the sand in each container at one-minute intervals for 10 minutes. Record the temperature of the sand after each minute in your data table.

PART B Comparing the Density of Oil and Water

8. In your lab report, prepare a data table similar to Table B below.

TABLE B *DENSITY OF TWO LIQUIDS*		
a. Mass of empty oil cup	_____	g
b. Mass of empty water cup	_____	g
c. Mass of cup and oil	_____	g
d. Mass of cup and water	_____	g
e. Volume of oil	25 mL	
f. Volume of water	25 mL	
Calculating Actual Mass		
Oil Item c − Item a =	_____	g
Water Item d − Item b =	_____	g

9. Label one clean plastic cup "oil," and label another "water." Using a balance, measure the mass of each plastic cup, and record the value in your data table.

10. Using a clean graduated cylinder, measure 25 mL of corn oil and pour it into the plastic cup labeled "oil." Using a balance, measure the mass of the plastic cup containing the corn oil, and record the mass in your data table.

11. Using a clean graduated cylinder, measure 25 mL of water and pour it into the plastic cup labeled "water." Using a balance, measure the mass of the plastic cup containing the water, and record the mass in your data table.

12. To find the actual mass of the oil, subtract the mass of the empty cup from the mass of the cup and the oil together.

13. To find the density of the oil, divide the mass of the oil by the volume of the oil, as shown in the equation below:

Density of oil $= \dfrac{\text{mass of oil}}{\text{volume of oil}} =$ _____ g/mL

14. To find the mass of the water, subtract the mass of the empty cup from the mass of the cup and the water together.

15. To find the density of the water, divide the mass of the water by the volume of the water, as shown in the equation below:

Density of water $= \dfrac{\text{mass of water}}{\text{volume of water}} =$ _____ g/mL

16. Combine the oil and water in the clear cup and record your observations in your lab report.

17. ⚠️ Clean up your materials and wash your hands before leaving the lab.

Analysis and Conclusions

1. Graph the data you collected in Part A. Plot time on the *x*-axis and temperature on the *y*-axis.

2. Based on your data from Part A, what is the relationship between color and heat absorption?

3. How might the color of the clothes you wear affect how warm you are on a sunny 90° day?

4. In Part B, what did you observe when you combined the oil and water in the clear cup? Relate your observation to the densities that you calculated for the two liquids.

5. What could you infer about the value for the density of ice if you observe it to float in water?

6. How would your calculated values for density be affected if you misread the volume measurement on the graduated cylinder?

Further Inquiry

Pumice is a volcanic rock that has a density less than 1.00 g/cm³. How would you prove this if you did not have a balance to weigh the pumice? (Hint: the density of water is 1.00 g/cm³.)

CHEMISTRY

Living things are composed of the same materials and are made by the same processes as nonliving things are. These crystals of a substance called urate (LM 90×) are formed in the human kidney.

FOCUS CONCEPT: *Matter, Energy, and Organization*

As you read, become aware of how a basic knowledge of chemistry will help you understand and explain biological processes.

COMPOSITION OF MATTER

Earth supports an enormous variety of organisms. You have learned that all organisms share certain characteristics and life processes. The structure and function of all living things are governed by the laws of chemistry. An understanding of the fundamental principles of chemistry will give you a better understanding of living things and how they function.

OBJECTIVES

▲

Define *element, atom, compound,* and *molecule.*

●

Draw a model of the structure of an atom.

■

Explain what determines an atom's stability.

◆

Contrast ionic and covalent bonds.

MATTER

Everything in the universe is made of matter. **Matter** is anything that occupies space and has mass. **Mass** is the quantity of matter an object has. Mass and weight are not the same; the pull of gravity on an object is what gives an object the property of weight. The same mass would have less weight on the moon than it would on Earth because the moon has less gravitational pull.

Chemical changes in matter are essential to all life processes. Biologists study chemistry because all living things are made of the same kinds of matter that make up nonliving things. By learning how changes in matter occur, you will gain an understanding of the life processes of the organisms you will study.

ELEMENTS

Elements are pure substances that cannot be broken down chemically into simpler kinds of matter. More than 100 elements have been identified, though fewer than 30 are important to living things. In fact, more than 90 percent of the mass of all kinds of living things is composed of combinations of just four elements: oxygen, O, carbon, C, hydrogen, H, and nitrogen, N.

Each element has a different chemical symbol. A chemical symbol consists of one or two letters, as shown in Figure 2-1. In most cases, the symbol derives from the first letter or other letters in the name of the element, like C for carbon or Cl for chlorine. The Latin word *natrium* provides the symbol for sodium, Na. The symbol K, for potassium, comes from the Latin word *kalium.*

FIGURE 2-1

All of the elements are arranged on a chart known as the periodic table. Here you see information for three elements from the periodic table. Among the information provided in the periodic table are the atomic number, the chemical symbol, and the atomic mass for each element.

Atomic number ——— 2
Chemical symbol ——— **He**
                    Helium
Atomic mass ——— 4

9	10
F	**Ne**
Fluorine	Neon
19.00	20.18

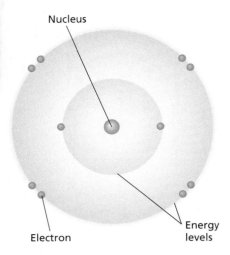

Nucleus

Electron

Energy levels

FIGURE 2-2

The electrons in this model of an atom are distributed in two energy levels. The innermost level holds a maximum of two electrons. The second level holds a maximum of eight electrons.

internet**connect**

SCI**LINKS**
NSTA

TOPIC: Atomic structures
GO TO: www.scilinks.org
KEYWORD: HM032

FIGURE 2-3

Below are shown some examples of the number of electrons found in the outermost energy level of elements.

ATOMS

The simplest particle of an element that retains all of the properties of that element is an **atom.** The properties of different kinds of atoms determine the structure and properties of the matter they compose. Atoms are so small that their true structure cannot be observed. However, scientists have developed models that describe the structure and properties of the atom, as shown in Figure 2-2.

Models of the atom are not meant to show exactly what atoms look like. Rather, they help us understand the structure of atoms and predict how they will act in nature.

The Nucleus

The central core, or **nucleus,** of an atom consists of two kinds of particles. One, the **proton,** has a positive electrical charge. The other, the **neutron,** has no electrical charge. Most of the mass of an atom is concentrated in its nucleus.

All atoms of a given element have the same number of protons. The number of protons in an atom is called the **atomic number** of the element. In the periodic table of elements, the atomic number generally appears directly above the chemical symbol, as shown in Figure 2-1. The atomic number of fluorine is 9, which indicates that each atom of the element fluorine has nine protons.

In an atom, the number of positively charged protons is balanced by an equal number of small, negatively charged particles called **electrons.** The electrical charges of the electrons offset those of the protons, making the net electrical charge of an atom zero.

Electrons

Electrons are high-energy particles with very little mass. They move about the nucleus at very high speeds in one of several different **energy levels,** like those shown in Figure 2-2.

Electrons in outer energy levels have more energy than those in inner energy levels. Each energy level can hold only a certain number of electrons. For example, the first energy level, nearest the nucleus, can hold up to two electrons. This is the outermost energy level for the elements hydrogen and helium. The second energy level can hold up to eight electrons. As shown in Figure 2-3, in most elements, the outer energy level is not filled.

| LITHIUM Li | BERYLLIUM Be | BORON B | CARBON C | NITROGEN N | OXYGEN O | FLUORINE F | NEON Ne |

COMPOUNDS

Under natural conditions, most elements do not exist by themselves; most elements readily combine with other elements. A pure substance that is made up of atoms of two or more elements is called a **compound.** In a compound, the proportions of each kind of atom are fixed. A chemical formula shows the kind and proportion of atoms of each element that forms a particular compound. For example, the chemical formula for water, H_2O, indicates that the atoms always combine in a proportion of two hydrogen atoms to one oxygen atom.

The physical and chemical properties of a compound differ from the physical and chemical properties of the individual elements that compose it. In nature, the elements oxygen and hydrogen are usually found as gases with the formulas O_2 and H_2. However, when oxygen gas and hydrogen gas combine to form H_2O, the result is a liquid at room temperature. The tendency of elements to combine and form compounds depends on the number and arrangement of electrons in their atoms. An atom is chemically stable when its outermost energy level is filled. Most atoms are not stable in their natural state. Thus, they tend to react, or combine with other atoms, in ways that make the atoms more stable.

Some elements, such as helium and neon, consist of atoms whose energy levels are filled with electrons. As shown in Figure 2-3, the second energy level of neon is its outermost energy level, and it is filled. Thus, neon tends not to react with other elements. By contrast, carbon, nitrogen, and oxygen consist of atoms with unfilled energy levels. Hence, most elements tend to undergo **chemical reactions,** combining in ways that cause their atoms to become stable. In chemical reactions, chemical bonds are broken, atoms are rearranged, and new chemical **bonds,** or attachments, are formed.

Covalent Bonds

A **covalent bond** forms when two atoms share one or more pairs of electrons. Water is made up of one oxygen atom and two hydrogen atoms held together by covalent bonds. Figure 2-4a shows that an atom of hydrogen needs a second electron to achieve stability, giving it two electrons in its outermost energy level. Oxygen needs two more electrons to give it a stable arrangement of eight electrons. Thus, in the presence of one another, hydrogen atoms and oxygen atoms can achieve stability by sharing pairs of electrons in a ratio of two atoms of hydrogen to one atom of oxygen, as shown in Figure 2-4b. The resulting compound, H_2O (water), is essential to the functioning of all living things.

A **molecule** is the simplest part of a substance that retains all of the properties of the substance and that can exist in a free state. For example, each molecule in hydrogen gas consists of two hydrogen atoms bonded to each other. Figure 2-4c shows a model of a water molecule. Some molecules—particularly many of the molecules that biologists study—are large and complex.

Word Roots and Origins

compound

from the Latin *componere*, meaning "to put together"

FIGURE 2-4

Two atoms of hydrogen and one atom of oxygen share electrons in covalent bonds to become stable. Covalent bonding results in the formation of molecules.

(a)

(b)

(c)

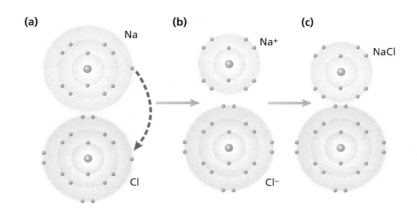

FIGURE 2-5

By losing its outermost electron, a sodium atom becomes an Na⁺ ion. By gaining one electron, a chlorine atom becomes a Cl⁻ ion. Because of their opposite charges, the Na⁺ and Cl⁻ ions are attracted to each other and form an ionic bond.

(a) Na / Cl   (b) Na⁺ / Cl⁻   (c) NaCl

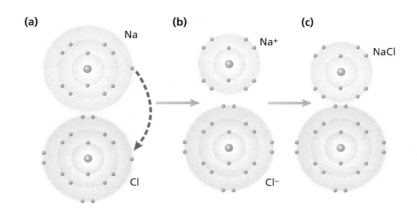

internet**connect**

SC*LINKS*

NSTA

TOPIC: Covalent and ionic bonds
GO TO: www.scilinks.org
KEYWORD: HM034

Ionic Bonds

As shown in Figure 2-5a, both sodium and chlorine atoms have unfilled outermost energy levels and are therefore reactive. Figure 2-5b shows how both atoms achieve stability in the presence of one another. The one outer electron of a sodium atom is transferred to a chlorine atom. This makes the sodium atom more stable than it was—its new outermost energy level is filled with eight electrons. But it also results in a sodium atom with a net positive electrical charge. The sodium atom has 11 protons (11 positive charges) balanced by only 10 electrons (10 negative charges). An atom or molecule with an electrical charge is called an **ion.** The sodium ion is written as Na^+.

As you can see in Figure 2-5b, by gaining an electron from a sodium atom, a chlorine atom has eight electrons in its outermost energy level, making it more stable. But with this additional electron, chlorine becomes a negatively charged ion called chloride, which is abbreviated as Cl^-.

Because positive and negative electrical charges attract each other, the sodium ion and the chloride ion attract each other. This attraction is called an **ionic bond.** The resulting compound, sodium chloride, NaCl, is an ionic compound and is familiar to you as common table salt.

SECTION 2-1 REVIEW

1. Define *element, atom, compound,* and *molecule.*

2. How are particles arranged in the atom?

3. How can we predict which elements are stable under natural conditions and which elements tend to undergo chemical reactions?

4. How does an ionic bond differ from a covalent bond?

5. Neon seldom, if ever, combines with other elements to form compounds. Why is this so?

6. **CRITICAL THINKING** In the early 1900s, hydrogen gas was used to inflate airships. After one large airship crashed and caught on fire, helium gas began to be used to inflate airships. Why was helium preferred over hydrogen?

ENERGY

One important characteristic of all living things is that they use energy. The amount of energy in the universe remains the same over time, but energy can change in form constantly. It is the flow of energy—from the sun to and through almost every organism on Earth—that biologists seek to understand when they study the chemistry of living things.

ENERGY AND MATTER

Scientists define **energy** as the ability to do work or cause change. Energy can occur in various forms, and one form of energy can be converted to another form. In a light bulb's filament, electrical energy is converted to radiant energy (light) and thermal energy (heat).

Energy in Living Things

Some forms of energy important to biological systems include chemical energy, thermal energy, electrical energy, and mechanical energy. Biologists often refer to free energy with respect to living systems. **Free energy** is the energy in a system that is available for work. For example, in a cell, it is the energy that is available to fuel cell processes. As energy flows through a single organism, it may be converted from one form to another. For example, if you ate breakfast this morning, your body is at work now changing the chemical energy found in food into thermal and mechanical energy, among other things.

States of Matter

Although it is not apparent when we observe matter, all the atoms and molecules in any substance are in constant motion. The rate at which atoms or molecules of a substance move determines its **state:** solid, liquid, or gas, as shown in Figure 2-6. Particles of a solid are tightly linked together in a definite shape, where they

SECTION

2-2

OBJECTIVES

▲

List the three states of matter, and explain how matter can change state.

●

Describe how energy changes are involved in chemical reactions.

■

Explain how enzymes affect chemical reactions in organisms.

◆

Explain what a redox reaction is.

SOLID   **LIQUID**   **GAS**

FIGURE 2-6

Matter exists as solids, liquids, and gases. You are familiar with all three states of water.

$$CO_2 + H_2O \rightleftharpoons H_2CO_3$$

FIGURE 2-7

The reaction illustrated in this figure is reversible. Because the products of the reaction remain in the blood, the reaction can proceed either from left to right or from right to left.

vibrate in place. A solid maintains a fixed volume and shape. Particles of a liquid are not as tightly linked as those in a solid. While a liquid maintains a fixed volume, its particles move more freely than those of a solid, giving a liquid its ability to flow and to conform to the shape of any container. Particles of a gas move the most rapidly. Gas particles have little or no attraction to each other, and they fill the volume of the container they occupy. To cause a substance to change from a solid to a liquid and from a liquid to a gas, thermal energy must be added to the substance.

ENERGY AND CHEMICAL REACTIONS

Living things undergo many thousands of chemical reactions as part of their life processes. Many reactions are very complex and are interrelated, involving a multistep sequence. Other reactions are rather simple. The one described in Figure 2-7 takes place in your blood.

The **reactants** are shown on the left side of the equation. In this reaction, the reactants are CO_2 and H_2O. The **products** of the reaction are shown on the right side. In this reaction, the product is H_2CO_3. Notice that the number of each kind of atom must be the same on either side of the arrow. In a chemical reaction, bonds present in the reactants are broken, the elements are rearranged, and new compounds are formed as the products. The two-direction arrow indicates that this chemical reaction can proceed either way. Carbon dioxide and water can combine to form carbonic acid, H_2CO_3, *or* carbonic acid can break down to carbon dioxide and water.

Energy Transfer

Much of the energy your body needs is provided by sugars from foods. Your body continuously undergoes a series of chemical reactions in which sugar and other substances are broken down to carbon dioxide and water. In this process, energy is released for use by your body. Chemical reactions that involve a net release of free energy are called **exergonic** (EKS-uhr-GAHN-ik) **reactions.** Reactions that involve a net absorption of free energy are called **endergonic** (EN-duhr-GAHN-ik) **reactions.**

Activation Energy

For most chemical reactions—both exergonic and endergonic—to begin, energy must be added to the reactants. In many chemical reactions, the amount of energy needed to start the reaction, called **activation energy,** is high. Figure 2-8 shows the activation energy for a hypothetical chemical reaction.

Certain chemical substances, known as **catalysts** (KAT-uh-LISTS), reduce the amount of activation energy that is needed for a reaction,

Activation Energy With and Without a Catalyst

Energy needed

Energy given off

Reactants

Energy needed without a catalyst

Energy needed with a catalyst

Products

Reaction progress

FIGURE 2-8

The blue curve shows the activation energy that must be supplied before this reaction can begin. The activation energy can be reduced, as shown by the pink curve, by adding a catalyst.

Quick Lab

Modeling Ionic Bonds

Materials toothpicks, mini marshmallows, peas

Procedure

Use marshmallows to represent chlorine. Use peas to represent sodium. Use toothpicks to create bonds. Make several models of NaCl (sodium chloride).

Analysis Use your models to identify each of the following: a sodium atom, a sodium ion, a chlorine atom, a chloride ion, an ionic bond, and a molecule of sodium chloride.

as shown in Figure 2-8. A reaction in the presence of the correct catalyst will proceed spontaneously or with the addition of a small amount of energy. **Enzymes** are an important class of catalysts in living things. A single organism may have thousands of different enzymes, each one tailor-made for a different chemical reaction.

Reduction-Oxidation Reactions

You know that there is a constant flow of energy into and throughout living things. Many of the chemical reactions that help transfer *energy* in living things involve the transfer of *electrons*. These reactions in which electrons are transferred between atoms are known as reduction-oxidation reactions, or **redox reactions.** In an **oxidation** (AHKS-uh-DAY-shuhn) **reaction,** a reactant loses one or more electrons, thus becoming more *positive* in charge. For example, remember that a sodium atom loses an electron to achieve stability when it forms an ionic bond, as shown in Figure 2-5. Thus, the sodium atom undergoes oxidation to form an Na$^+$ ion. In a **reduction reaction,** a reactant gains one or more electrons, thus becoming more *negative* in charge. When a chlorine atom gains an electron to form a Cl$^-$ ion, the atom undergoes reduction. Redox reactions always occur together. An oxidation reaction occurs, and the electron given up by one substance is then accepted by another substance in a reduction reaction.

SECTION 2-2 REVIEW

1. What are the three states of matter?

2. How can a substance be changed from a liquid to a gas?

3. State the difference between endergonic and exergonic reactions.

4. Explain how a catalyst affects a reaction.

5. Why does a reduction reaction always accompany an oxidation reaction?

6. **CRITICAL THINKING** Living things need a constant supply of energy, even though many of the chemical reactions they undergo release energy. Why is this true?

Blood Plasma Meets a Need

HISTORICAL PERSPECTIVE

Throughout history, people have understood the importance of blood, seeing it as the river of life that it is. Prior to the 1900s, severe bleeding often resulted in death. But today blood is stored at blood banks, where people "deposit" blood so that they or others can "withdraw" it when needed. Charles Drew was a pioneer in the work of blood transfusions, especially in the use of plasma and the development of blood banks.

Charles Drew

The Need

In the early 1930s, Charles Drew, a medical student at McGill University Medical School in Montreal, Quebec, faced a dilemma. Before him lay a man who needed a blood transfusion so that his leg could be amputated. Compatible blood donors could not be found; even the man's sister had a different blood type. So Drew gave his own blood, a perfect match, and the operation proceeded. After that experience, Drew understood more than ever the importance of finding a way to store blood.

Historical Highlights

Before the twentieth century, successful transfusions like Drew's were almost unknown. Of the few attempts made, some succeeded, but most did not. No one was sure why so many transfusions failed.

The early 1900s marked a breakthrough. The Austrian-born American physiologist Karl Landsteiner determined that there are four blood types—A, B, AB, and O—based on the compatibility of markers on the outer surface of red blood cells. Landsteiner's discovery explained why the outcome of transfusions had been so unpredictable. For his work, Landsteiner received the Nobel Prize in medicine or physiology in 1930.

Determining a person's blood type—called blood typing—became a vital component of transfusions. Blood types that are not compatible form clumps when mixed together. These clumps can block small blood vessels, causing serious complications and often resulting in the death of the patient.

In 1914, sodium citrate was first added to blood to prevent clotting. This made the storage of blood possible for the first time. Refrigerated blood could be stored for five to seven days. (Today whole blood can be safely stored for 21 to 49 days.) Nevertheless, in the early 1930s, blood banks were still uncommon. Most patients received blood directly from a donor.

In 1937, Bernard Fantus, a physician, collected and distributed blood for transfusions, establishing the first nonprofit blood bank at Cook County Hospital in Chicago. It was Fantus who coined the term *blood bank.* Charles Drew, however, was the one who recognized that a liquid solution in blood called *plasma* could help solve problems associated with storage, making transfusions available on a large scale.

The Composition of Blood

In 1938, Drew and physician John Scudder studied blood chemistry and transfusion, with a focus toward finding a safe way to preserve blood. Blood has two main components: cells and plasma. Three types of cells—red blood cells, white blood cells, and platelets—make up about 45 percent of blood. The other approximately 55 percent of blood is made up of plasma, an amber-colored solution containing more than 100 different solutes, including nutrients, antibodies, hormones, and proteins. Almost 90 percent of plasma is water.

Although plasma contains antibodies that may cause clumping when mixed with incompatible blood types, in most cases transfused plasma dilutes rapidly in the patient's blood, minimizing the risk of clumping. Because red blood cells carry the markers that determine ABO blood types, by removing the red blood cells from blood, the remaining plasma can usually be used safely without type testing. In addition, plasma can be dehydrated and easily stored.

Through his research, Drew concluded that although plasma lacks important components of whole blood, it might be a viable substitute for blood in emergency situations. For example, plasma could save lives on the battlefield.

Response to Wartime Needs

In 1940, Germany's attack on France created a need for a huge blood supply. As experts in transfusion met to decide how to respond, Drew presented his findings on plasma. Although his research was incomplete, the United States began to provide liquid plasma and whole blood for France. However, before any deliveries could be made, France fell to the German army. Soon the "Blood for Britain" program was under way, with Drew as its medical supervisor.

Drew coordinated the American effort. Working with the National Research Council and the American Red Cross, he set up collection cen-

Charles R. Drew, far left, appears in 1940 with the first mobile blood-collection unit.

ters and was in charge of coordinating the medical aspects of the program, including the establishment of uniform records, standard equipment, and criteria to ensure the safety of the final product. Americans gave blood generously. Drew wanted the blood banks to be well stocked when the United States entered the war—as it soon did.

The nation's blood supply was ready. Stored blood and plasma has subsequently saved thousands of lives—in both wartime and peacetime. Today blood banks are found in medical facilities worldwide.

Transfusion Update

Early in the 1980s, the practice of blood transfusion had to be reexamined. Some transfused blood was found to carry HIV, causing AIDS in a number of people. Hemophiliacs, whose blood does not clot, were especially vulnerable. It is estimated that half of the hemophiliacs in the United States contracted HIV before adequate testing of donated blood began.

Since 1985, careful screening for HIV, hepatitis, and other diseases has almost entirely removed the risk of receiving contaminated blood. Even so, the level of fear remains

high, accounting for a sharp decline in the amount of blood donated. Many people now bank their own blood for later use in surgery. Blood can also be collected during surgery and returned to the patient later.

The AIDS epidemic has triggered a race to create artificial blood. However, blood chemistry is extremely complex, and the process has proven more difficult than expected. Several companies have begun testing potential artificial-blood products. Some of these substitutes make use of chemically treated animal blood and outdated human blood. As a new century begins, the use of artificial blood may be, as one headline put it, "a heartbeat away."

Bags of blood ready for transfusion are kept in cold storage.

OBJECTIVES

▲

Define *solution, solute, solvent,* and *concentration.*

●

Explain the dissociation of water.

■

Contrast properties of acids and bases.

◆

Describe the use of the pH scale.

◆

Explain the action of buffers.

Word Roots and Origins

solvent

from the Latin *solvere,* meaning "to loosen"

SOLUTIONS

The chemistry of living things involves the study of solutions. A large proportion of the mass of living things is water, and the chemical reactions of life occur for the most part in water solutions. The electricity that courses through your nerves is transmitted through watery pathways of dissolved ions. Chemical messengers that regulate your body's metabolism move through the watery medium of your blood.

DESCRIBING SOLUTIONS

A **solution** is a mixture in which one or more substances are uniformly distributed in another substance. Solutions can be mixtures of liquids, solids, or gases. For example, plasma, the liquid part of blood, is a very complex solution. It is composed of many types of ions and large molecules, as well as gases, that are dissolved in water. The **solute** (SAHL-YOOT) is the substance dissolved in the solution. The particles that compose a solute may be ions, atoms, or molecules. The **solvent** is the substance in which the solute is dissolved. For example, when sugar, a solute, and water, a solvent, are mixed, a solution of sugar water results. Though the sugar dissolves in the water, neither the sugar molecules nor the water molecules are altered chemically. If the water is boiled away, the sugar molecules remain and are unchanged.

Solutions can be composed of various proportions of a given solute in a given solvent. Thus, solutions can vary in concentration. The **concentration** of a solution is the measurement of the amount of solute dissolved in a fixed amount of the solution. For example, a 2 percent saltwater solution contains 2 g of salt dissolved in enough water to make 100 mL of solution. The more solute dissolved, the greater the concentration of the solution. A **saturated solution** is one in which no more solute can dissolve.

Aqueous (AY-kwee-uhs) **solutions**—solutions in which water is the solvent—are universally important to living things. You should be able to think of many different aqueous solutions important to living things. Marine microorganisms spend their lives immersed in the sea, an aqueous solution. Most nutrients that plants need are in aqueous solutions in moist soil. Body cells exist in an aqueous solution of intercellular fluid and are themselves filled with fluid.

ACIDS AND BASES

One of the most important aspects of a living system is the degree of its acidity or alkalinity. What do we mean when we say *acid* and *alkaline*?

Dissociation of Water

In water, the force of attraction between molecules is so strong that the oxygen atom of one water molecule can actually remove the hydrogen atom from the other water molecule. This breaking apart of the water molecule into two ions of opposite charge is called **dissociation** and is shown by the chemical equation below.

$$H_2O \rightleftharpoons H^+ + OH^-$$

One water molecule, H_2O, dissociates to form two ions, H^+ and OH^-. The OH^- ion is known as the **hydroxide ion.** The free H^+ ion can react with another water molecule, as shown in the following equation.

$$H^+ + H_2O \rightleftharpoons H_3O^+$$

The H_3O^+ ion is known as the **hydronium ion.** Acidity or alkalinity is a measure of the relative amounts of hydronium ions and hydroxide ions dissolved in a solution. If the number of hydronium ions in a solution equals the number of hydroxide ions, the solution is said to be neutral. Pure water contains equal numbers of hydronium ions and hydroxide ions and is therefore a neutral solution.

Acids

If the number of hydronium ions in a solution is greater than the number of hydroxide ions, the solution is an **acid.** Consider what happens when hydrogen chloride, HCl, a gas, is dissolved in water. Some of its molecules dissociate to form hydrogen ions, H^+, and chloride ions, Cl^-.

$$HCl \rightleftharpoons H^+ + Cl^-$$

These free hydrogen ions combine with water molecules to form hydronium ions, H_3O^+. This aqueous solution contains many more hydronium ions than it does hydroxide ions, making it an acidic solution. Acids tend to have a sour taste. In concentrated forms, they are highly corrosive to some materials, as you can see in Figure 2-9.

─┤ Eco ▲ Connection ├─

Acid Precipitation

Acid precipitation, more commonly called *acid rain,* describes rain, snow, sleet, or fog that contains high levels of sulfuric and nitric acids. These acids form when sulfur dioxide gas, SO_2, and nitrogen oxide gas, NO, react with water in the atmosphere to produce sulfuric acid, H_2SO_4, and nitric acid, HNO_3.

Acid precipitation makes soil and bodies of water, such as lakes, more acidic than normal. These high acid levels can harm plant and animal life directly. A high level of acid in a lake may kill mollusks, fish, and amphibians. Even in a lake that does not have a very elevated level of acid, acid precipitation may leach aluminum and magnesium from soils, poisoning water-dwelling species.

Reducing fossil-fuel consumption, such as occurs in gasoline engines and coal-burning power plants, should reduce high acid levels in precipitation. You can help by learning about alternative fuel sources and legislation proposed to encourage or mandate use of non-fossil-fuel sources of energy.

FIGURE 2-9

Acids can have a significant impact on our environment. Sulfur dioxide, SO_2, which is produced when fossil fuels are burned, reacts with water in the atmosphere to produce acid precipitation. Acid precipitation can make lakes and rivers too acidic to support life and can even corrode stone, such as this marble carving.

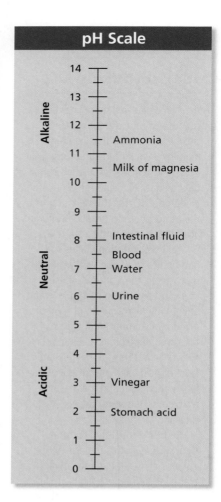

pH Scale

14 —
13 —
12 —
   Ammonia
11 —
   Milk of magnesia
10 —
9 —
8 — Intestinal fluid
   Blood
7 — Water
6 — Urine
5 —
4 —
3 — Vinegar
2 — Stomach acid
1 —
0 —

Alkaline — Neutral — Acidic

FIGURE 2-10

Some of your body fluids are acidic, while others are alkaline. A solution with a pH above 7 is alkaline, while a solution with a pH below 7 is acidic. Each unit on the pH scale reflects a tenfold change in acidity or alkalinity.

Bases

If sodium hydroxide, NaOH, a solid, is dissolved in water, some of it dissociates to form sodium ions, Na^+, and hydroxide ions, OH^-, as shown in the equation below.

$$NaOH \rightleftharpoons Na^+ + OH^-$$

This solution then contains more hydroxide ions than hydronium ions and is therefore defined as a **base.** The adjective *alkaline* refers to bases. Bases have a bitter taste. They tend to feel slippery because the OH^- ions react with the oil on our skin to form a soap. In fact, commercial soap is made by reacting a base with a fat.

pH

Scientists have developed a scale for comparing the relative concentrations of hydronium ions and hydroxide ions in a solution. It is called the **pH scale,** and it ranges from 0 to 14, as shown in Figure 2-10. A solution with a pH of 0 is very acidic, a solution with a pH of 7 is neutral, and a solution with a pH of 14 is very basic. A solution's pH is measured on a logarithmic scale. That is, the change of one pH unit reflects a tenfold change in the acidity or alkalinity. For example, a solution with a pH of 4 has 10 times more H_3O^+ ions than a solution with a pH of 5 and 100 times more H_3O^+ ions than a solution with a pH of 6. The pH of a solution can be measured with litmus paper or with some other chemical indicator that changes color at various pH levels.

Buffers

The control of pH is important for living systems. Enzymes such as those you read about in Section 2-2 can function only within a very narrow pH range. The control of pH in organisms is often accomplished with buffers. **Buffers** are chemical substances that neutralize small amounts of either an acid or a base added to a solution. As Figure 2-10 shows, the composition of your internal environment—in terms of acidity and alkalinity—varies greatly. Some of your body fluids, such as stomach acid and urine, are acidic. Others, such as intestinal fluid and blood, are basic or alkaline. Complex buffering systems maintain the pH values of your body's many fluids at normal and safe levels.

SECTION 2-3 REVIEW

1. What is a solution?
2. Describe the dissociation of water.
3. What pH value is neutral?
4. Define *acid* and *base*.
5. What is a buffer?

6. **CRITICAL THINKING** The active ingredient in aspirin is acetylsalicylic acid. Why would doctors recommend buffered aspirin for some people, especially those who have a "sensitive" stomach?

2-1
- Elements are substances that cannot be broken down by chemical means into simpler substances.
- Atoms are composed of protons, neutrons, and electrons. Protons and neutrons compose the nucleus of the atom. Electrons travel around the nucleus.
- Compounds consist of atoms of two or more elements that are joined by chemical bonds in a fixed proportion.
- Most elements react to form chemical bonds so that their atoms become stable.

- Atoms achieve stability when their outermost energy level is filled.
- A chemical reaction is the process of breaking chemical bonds, rearranging the atoms, and forming new bonds.
- A covalent bond is formed when two atoms share electrons.
- A molecule consists of two or more atoms held together by covalent bonds.
- An ionic bond is formed when one atom gives up an electron to another. The positive ion is then attracted to a negative ion to form the ionic bond.

Vocabulary

atom (32)	covalent bond (33)	ionic bond (34)	nucleus (32)
atomic number (32)	electron (32)	mass (31)	proton (32)
bond (33)	element (31)	matter (31)	
chemical reaction (33)	energy level (32)	molecule (33)	
compound (33)	ion (34)	neutron (32)	

2-2
- Addition of thermal energy to a substance can cause its state to change from a solid to a liquid and from a liquid to a gas.
- Chemical reactions that involve a net release of energy are called exergonic reactions. Chemical reactions that involve a net absorption of energy are called endergonic reactions.

- The activation energy is the amount of energy required for a chemical reaction to begin.
- Catalysts lower the amount of activation energy necessary for a reaction to begin.
- A chemical reaction in which electrons are exchanged between atoms is called a reduction-oxidation, or redox, reaction.

Vocabulary

activation energy (36)	enzyme (37)	product (36)	state (35)
catalyst (36)	exergonic reaction (36)	reactant (36)	
endergonic reaction (36)	free energy (35)	redox reaction (37)	
energy (35)	oxidation reaction (37)	reduction reaction (37)	

2-3
- A solution consists of a solute dissolved in a solvent, which is often water. A solution with water as the solvent is known as an aqueous solution.
- An acidic solution contains more hydronium ions than it does hydroxide ions. A basic or alkaline solution contains more hydroxide ions than it does hydronium ions.

- The pH scale indicates the relative concentration of hydronium ions and hydroxide ions in solution. The pH scale ranges from 0 to 14, with 0 being the most acidic, 7 being neutral, and 14 being the most alkaline.
- Buffers are chemicals that neutralize the effects of adding small amounts of either an acid or a base to a solution.

Vocabulary

acid (41)	buffer (42)	hydroxide ion (41)	solution (40)
alkaline (42)	concentration (40)	pH scale (42)	solvent (40)
aqueous solution (40)	dissociation (41)	saturated solution (40)	
base (42)	hydronium ion (41)	solute (40)	

REVIEW

Vocabulary

1. Explain the relationship between electrons, neutrons, and protons.
2. What is the difference between an element and a compound?
3. Distinguish the differences in composition between an acid and a base.
4. Identify the type of reaction that releases free energy.
5. How are the processes of oxidation and reduction related?

Multiple Choice

6. The nucleus of an atom is made up of (a) protons and neutrons (b) protons and electrons (c) elements and compounds (d) negatively charged particles.
7. High-energy particles that circle the nucleus of an atom are (a) ions (b) protons (c) electrons (d) neutrons.
8. The way in which elements bond to form compounds depends on the (a) structural formula of the compound (b) dissociation of the ions in the compound (c) number and arrangement of electrons in the atoms of the elements (d) model of the atom.
9. If an atom is made up of 6 protons, 7 neutrons, and 6 electrons, then its atomic number is (a) 19 (b) 13 (c) 7 (d) 6.
10. Atoms in a solid (a) are fixed in space and show no movement (b) are fixed in space but vibrate in place (c) move rapidly through space (d) repel each other.
11. The amount of energy required for a chemical reaction to begin is called (a) chemical energy (b) mechanical energy (c) electrical energy (d) activation energy.
12. The process in which a chemical reactant loses an electron, becoming more positively charged, is called (a) oxidation (b) reduction (c) metabolism (d) stabilization.
13. In a reduction reaction, an atom gains a(n) (a) proton (b) neutron (c) electron (d) nucleus.
14. An aqueous solution that contains more hydroxide ions than hydronium ions is a(n) (a) acid (b) base (c) gas (d) solid.

15. Acid formed from sulfur dioxide in the atmosphere is present in (a) rocks (b) acid precipitation (c) weak bases (d) pure water.

Short Answer

16. Use the pH scale shown below to answer the following questions:
    a. What is the most acidic body fluid represented?
    b. What is the most alkaline body fluid represented?
    c. What body fluid is closest to being a neutral solution?
    d. Which body fluid is most extremely acidic or basic; that is, which body fluid deviates the most from neutral pH?

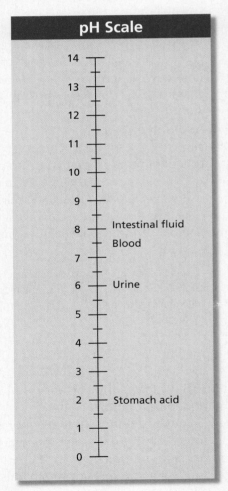

pH Scale

14
13
12
11
10
9
8 — Intestinal fluid
— Blood
7
6 — Urine
5
4
3
2 — Stomach acid
1
0

17. An oxygen atom has six electrons in its outermost energy level. Explain why two oxygen atoms must share four electrons when they form a covalent bond.

18. What is an ion?

19. How are electrons distributed in a covalent bond?

20. Name the physical states that matter can exist in.

21. In a chemical equation, what does a two-direction arrow mean?

22. Many reactions in the cell are exergonic. Why, then, do cells need a continuous supply of energy?

23. What happens when water dissociates?

24. What does the word *alkaline* mean?

25. What does a buffer do?

CRITICAL THINKING

1. Hydrogen gas exists as H_2 rather than H. Why is this so?

2. How can a substance be changed from a solid to a liquid? from a liquid to a gas?

3. A magnesium atom has two electrons in its outermost energy level. A sulfur atom has six electrons in its outermost level. How will the two atoms react to form a bond? Explain why this is considered a redox reaction.

4. A dam located on a fast-flowing mountain stream generates electricity. What kind of energy is transformed to create electricity?

5. The table shows melting and boiling points at normal pressure for five different elements or compounds. Above the boiling point, a compound or element exists as a gas. Below the freezing point, a compound or element exists as a solid. Use the table to answer the following questions:

a. Under normal temperature and pressure conditions, which substances exist as solids? as liquids? as gases?

b. Which substance exists as a liquid over the broadest range of temperature?

c. Which substance exists as a liquid over the narrowest range of temperature?

d. Which one of the substances are you least likely to encounter as a gas?

Melting and Boiling Points at Normal Pressure

Substance	Melting point (°C)	Boiling point (°C)
Aluminum	658	2330
Argon	−190	−186
Chlorine	−104	−34
Mercury	−39	357
Water	0	100

EXTENSION

1. Read "The Femtosecond Camera Shutter" in *Scientific American,* January 2000, on page 15, and answer the following questions: What is the main obstacle scientists encounter in observing chemical reactions step by step? What was the key process Dr. Zewail used to observe chemical reactions? What was the chemical reaction observed using this new technique? What goals may ultimately be achieved using this technique?

2. Dissolve table salt or sugar by stirring it into water at room temperature until it is saturated. (The solution is saturated when excess salt or sugar stays at the bottom of the container.) Remove the clear solution at the top with a spoon, and place the remaining saturated solution in the refrigerator. After two hours, observe the cooled solution. What do your observations tell you about the effect of temperature on molecules in solution?

INTERACTIVE EXPLORATION

Exploring the Activity of Biological Catalysts

OBJECTIVES

- Simulate the effect of pH, temperature, and enzyme concentration on the activity of two enzymes.
- Determine the optimal conditions for each enzyme.

MATERIALS

- computer with CD-ROM drive
- CD-ROM *Interactive Explorations in Biology: Cell Biology and Genetics*
- graph paper

Background

All organisms rely on enzymes to catalyze chemical reactions. Recall that an enzyme is a biological catalyst that increases the rate of a chemical reaction by lowering the level of activation energy necessary to start the reaction. Without enzymes, many of the chemical reactions that occur within living things would proceed too slowly to be useful. Enzymes speed up these reactions by bringing the reactants into close proximity and facilitating their interaction. Enzyme effectiveness depends on several factors. This interactive investigation

allows you to explore how three of these factors—enzyme concentration, temperature, and pH—affect the activity of two enzymes present in the human body, carbonic anhydrase and lysozyme. Carbonic anhydrase helps regulate carbon dioxide levels in red blood cells. Lysozyme breaks large sugar molecules into smaller ones during metabolism.

Prelab Preparation

1. Load and start the program Thermodynamics. You will see an animated diagram like the one below. Click the Navigation button, and then click the Topic Information button with the "key" icon on it. Read the focus questions, and review the following concepts: Reaction Rate, Enzyme Catalysis, Temperature and Reaction Rates, and pH Can Influence Enzyme Shape.
2. Click the word *Help* at the top left of the screen, and select How to Use This Exploration. Listen to the instructions for conducting the exploration. Click the Interactive Exploration button on the Navigation Palette to begin the exploration.

FEEDBACK METERS

Reaction Rate: *displays reaction rate as a percentage of the maximal reaction rate (V_{max})*

VARIABLES

Relative Enzyme Concentration: *varies the concentration of the enzyme*

Temperature: *varies the temperature*

pH: *varies the pH*

Procedure
PART A Carbonic Anhydrase Activity

1. Click the New Enzyme button until "Carbonic Anhydrase" appears at the top of the screen.
2. Click and drag the indicator so that the Relative Enzyme Concentration is 0.2.
3. Click the Plot Point button. The point that appears on the graph indicates the rate of reaction for this enzyme concentration, expressed as a percentage of V_{max}, the highest possible reaction rate. What is the reaction rate indicated by the Reaction Rate meter?
4. Repeat steps 2 and 3 until you have tested the following relative enzyme concentrations: 0.4, 0.6, 0.8, and 1.0.
5. Click the Plot Graph button. How does increasing the enzyme concentration affect the rate of reaction?
6. Make a table similar to Table A shown below.

TABLE A EFFECTS OF TEMPERATURE ON REACTION RATE

Temperature	Carbonic anhydrase % of V_{max}	Lysozyme % of V_{max}
0°C		
10°C		
20°C		
30°C		
40°C		
50°C		

7. Click and drag the indicator so that the Temperature meter indicates 0°C. Click the Plot Point button, and observe the result. In your table, record the reaction rate.
8. Repeat step 7 until you have tested the effects of the following temperatures: 10°C, 20°C, 30°C, 40°C, and 50°C.
9. Use graph paper to make a graph of temperature versus reaction rate. Draw a curve that connects your six points. What can you conclude about the effect of temperature on the activity of carbonic anhydrase?
10. Click the Plot Graph button. Compare your graph with the one shown on the screen. Explain any differences.

TABLE B EFFECTS OF pH ON REACTION RATE

pH	Carbonic anhydrase % of V_{max}	Lysozyme % of V_{max}
3		
4		
5		
6		
7		
8		

11. Make a table similar to Table B shown above.
12. Click and drag the indicator so that the pH meter indicates a pH of 3. Click the Plot Point button, and observe the result. In your table, record the reaction rate.
13. Repeat step 12 until you have tested the following pH values: 4, 5, 6, 7, and 8.
14. After testing all the values above, make a graph of pH versus reaction rate. Draw a curve that connects your points. What can you conclude about the effect of pH on the activity of carbonic anhydrase?
15. Click the Plot Graph button. Compare your graph with the graph on the screen. Explain any differences.

PART B Lysozyme Activity

16. Click the New Enzyme button until "Lysozyme" appears at the top of the screen.
17. Repeat steps 2–15 for the enzyme lysozyme, completing Table A and Table B.

Analysis and Conclusions

1. What is the optimal temperature for each enzyme? What is the optimal pH for each enzyme?
2. The optimal pH of pepsin, a stomach enzyme, is about 2, while the optimal pH of trypsin, an enzyme of the small intestine, is about 8. What must occur in your digestive tract between the stomach and the small intestine?

CHAPTER 3

BIOCHEMISTRY

The body of this jellyfish, Pseudorhiza haeckeli, *is almost 99 percent water.*

FOCUS CONCEPT: *Matter, Energy, and Organization*

As you read this chapter, notice how function depends on structure in each of the compounds you examine.

WATER

Compare the body of the jellyfish shown on the opposite page with your own body. The jellyfish will die if it is removed from its water environment. You can live in the driest parts of Earth. Jellyfish and humans seem utterly unlike each other, yet the bodies of both are made of cells filled with water. The chemical reactions of all living things take place in an aqueous environment. Water has several unique properties that make it one of the most important compounds found in living things.

POLARITY

Many of water's biological functions stem from its chemical structure. Recall that in the water molecule, H_2O, the hydrogen and oxygen atoms share electrons to form covalent bonds. However, these atoms do not share the electrons equally. An oxygen atom has eight protons in its nucleus and therefore eight positive charges to attract electrons, whereas a hydrogen atom has only one proton and therefore one positive charge. With its greater positive charge, the nucleus of the oxygen atom pulls the shared electrons toward its nucleus and away from the nucleus of the hydrogen atom. As a result, the electrical charge is unevenly distributed, as shown in the models of a water molecule shown in Figure 3-1.

Notice too in Figure 3-1 that the three atoms in a water molecule are not arranged in a straight line as you might expect. Rather, the two hydrogen atoms bond with the single oxygen atom at an angle. Although the total electrical charge on a water molecule is neutral, the region of the molecule where the oxygen atom is located has a

SECTION

3-1

OBJECTIVES

▲

Describe the structure of a water molecule.

●

Explain how water's polar nature affects its ability to dissolve substances.

■

List two of water's properties that result from hydrogen bonding.

FIGURE 3-1

The oxygen region of the water molecule is weakly negative, and the hydrogen regions are weakly positive. Notice the three very different ways to represent water, H_2O. You are familiar with the electron-energy-level model (a) from Chapter 2. The structural formula (b) is compact and easy to understand. The space-filling model (c) shows the three-dimensional structure of a molecule.

(a) Electron-energy-level model

(b) Structural formula

(c) Space-filling model

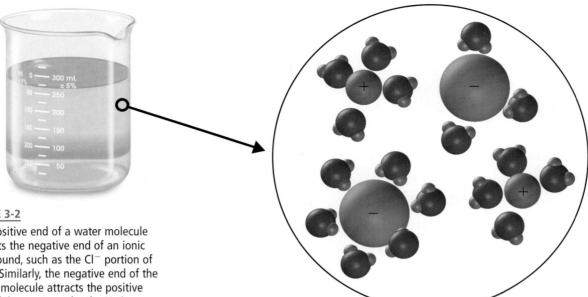

FIGURE 3-2

The positive end of a water molecule attracts the negative end of an ionic compound, such as the Cl^- portion of NaCl. Similarly, the negative end of the water molecule attracts the positive end of the compound—the Na^+ portion of NaCl. As a result, NaCl breaks apart, or dissociates, in water.

slightly negative charge, while the regions of the molecule where each of the two hydrogen atoms are located have a slightly positive charge. Because of this uneven pattern of charge, water is called a **polar** compound.

It is this polar nature that makes water very effective in dissolving many other substances. Water dissolves other polar substances, including sugars and some proteins, as well as ionic compounds, such as sodium chloride, NaCl. An ionic compound mixed with water tends to dissociate into ions. This is illustrated in Figure 3-2. This breaking up of an ionic compound frees ions to participate in many biological reactions. In your body, both sodium ions and chloride ions are essential to functions like muscle contraction and transmission of impulses in the nervous system. In fact, dissolved, dissociated ions are present in all of the aqueous solutions found in living things. Their concentration is critical to the normal operation of the many systems of your body.

FIGURE 3-3

The dotted lines in this figure represent hydrogen bonds. A hydrogen bond is a weak force of attraction between a hydrogen atom in one molecule and a negatively charged atom in a second molecule.

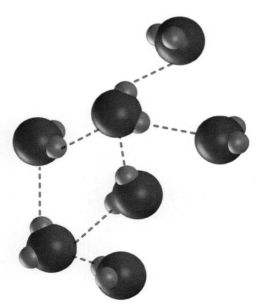

HYDROGEN BONDING

The polar nature of water also causes water molecules to be attracted to one another. The type of attraction that holds two water molecules together is called a **hydrogen bond.** As shown in Figure 3-3, a positive region of one water molecule is attracted to the negative region of another water molecule. Thus, a hydrogen bond tends to form between a hydrogen atom in one molecule and the region of negative charge on another molecule. A hydrogen bond is a weak bond that can be easily broken. Even so, the hydrogen bonds in water exert a significant attractive force, causing water to cling to itself and to other substances.

Cohesion and Adhesion

An attractive force between particles of the same kind is known as **cohesion.** You can see cohesion at work when you observe the surface tension of water. Cohesive forces resulting from water's hydrogen bonding are strong enough to cause water to act as if it has a thin "skin" on its surface. This is why water appears to bulge from the sides of a glass filled to the brim.

Adhesion is the attractive force between unlike sustances. Together, adhesion and cohesion enable water molecules to move upward through narrow tubes against the force of gravity. This property of water is known as **capillarity** (KAP-uh-LER-it-ee). You have seen capillarity at work if you have observed the flow of water into a flower through its stem, such as is shown in Figure 3-4.

Temperature Moderation

Water must gain or lose a relatively large amount of energy for its temperature to change. When water is heated, most of the thermal energy that the water initially absorbs breaks the hydrogen bonds between the molecules. Only after these bonds have been broken does the thermal energy increase the motion of the molecules and raise the temperature of the water. You read in Chapter 1 that all organisms must maintain homeostasis to live. In organisms, water's ability to absorb large amounts of energy helps keep cells at an even temperature despite temperature changes in the environment.

WATER   DYE

Liquid movement up a stem

FIGURE 3-4

Because of strong cohesive and adhesive forces, water can travel upward from the roots of flowers. In the flower on the right, the water, which has been dyed blue, has moved up through the stem to the flower's petals.

internetconnect

SC*LINKS*

NSTA

TOPIC: Hydrogen bonding
GO TO: www.scilinks.org
KEYWORD: HM051

SECTION 3-1 REVIEW

1. Describe the structure of a water molecule.

2. How do molecules of a polar compound differ from those of a nonpolar compound?

3. What happens when ionic compounds are mixed with water?

4. What are two properties of water that result from water's tendency to form hydrogen bonds?

5. What is capillarity?

6. **CRITICAL THINKING** Most automobiles have water-cooled engines. What must be true about a solution that can replace water in the cooling system, such as antifreeze?

OBJECTIVES

▲

Define *organic compound* and name three elements often found in organic compounds.

●

Explain why carbon forms so many different compounds.

■

Define *functional group* and explain its significance.

◆

Compare a condensation reaction with hydrolysis.

CARBON COMPOUNDS

*A*ll of the many compounds discovered can be classified in two broad categories: organic compounds and inorganic compounds. **Organic compounds** contain carbon atoms that are covalently bonded to other carbon atoms and to other elements as well—typically hydrogen, oxygen, and nitrogen. The chemistry of carbon is the chemistry of life.

CARBON BONDING

A carbon atom has four electrons in its outermost energy level. Remember from Chapter 2 that most atoms become stable when their outermost energy level contains eight electrons. A carbon atom therefore readily forms four covalent bonds with other elements. Unlike other elements, however, carbon also readily bonds with other carbon atoms, forming straight chains, branched chains, or rings, as shown in Figure 3-5. This tendency of carbon to bond with itself results in an enormous variety of organic compounds.

In the symbolic shorthand of chemistry, each line shown in Figure 3-5 represents a covalent bond formed when two atoms share a pair of electrons. A bond formed when two atoms share a pair of electrons is called a single bond. Carbon can also share two or even three pairs of electrons with another atom. Figure 3-6a shows a model for an organic compound in which six carbon atoms have formed a ring. Notice that each carbon atom forms four covalent bonds: a single bond with another carbon atom, a single bond with a hydrogen atom, and a double bond with a second carbon atom. In a double bond—represented by two parallel lines—atoms share two pairs of electrons. A triple bond, the sharing of three pairs of electrons, is shown in Figure 3-6b.

FIGURE 3-5

Carbon can bond in a number of ways to produce molecules of very different shapes, including straight chains, branched chains, and rings. These structures form the backbone of many different kinds of organic molecules.

Straight chain

Branched chain

Ring

(a) Benzene   **(b)** Acetylene   **(c)** Ethanol

FIGURE 3-6

Carbon can form (a) double or even (b) triple bonds to satisfy its need for eight electrons in its outermost energy level. Organic molecules can have many different shapes and patterns of bonding. Organic molecules can also have many different functional groups, which influence the properties of the molecule they are attached to. Notice the hydroxyl, —OH, group on this model of the alcohol ethanol (c).

FUNCTIONAL GROUPS

In most organic compounds, clusters of atoms, called **functional groups,** influence the properties of the molecules they compose. The functional group is the structural building block that determines the characteristics of the compound. One functional group important to living things, the hydroxyl group, —OH, is shown in Figure 3-6c.

An **alcohol** is an organic compound with a hydroxyl group attached to one of its carbon atoms. Locate the hydroxyl group in the alcohol shown in Figure 3-6c. The hydroxyl group makes an alcohol a polar molecule. Thus, alcohols have some properties similar to water, including the ability to form hydrogen bonds. The alcohol illustrated in Figure 3-6c is ethanol, which is found in alcoholic beverages. Ethanol causes cell death in the liver and brain of humans. The alcohol methanol, also called wood alcohol, can cause blindness or even death when consumed. Some alcohols, however, are needed by organisms to carry out their life processes. Humans, for example, need the alcohol glycerol to assemble certain molecules necessary for life.

LARGE CARBON MOLECULES

In many carbon compounds, the molecules are built up from smaller, simpler molecules known as **monomers,** such as the ones shown in Figure 3-7. As you can also see in Figure 3-7, monomers can bond to one another to form complex molecules known as polymers. A **polymer** consists of repeated, linked units. The units may be identical or structurally related to each other. Large polymers are called **macromolecules.**

Monomers link to form polymers through a chemical reaction called a **condensation reaction.** In the condensation reaction shown

Quick Lab

Demonstrating Polarity

Materials disposable gloves; lab apron; safety goggles; 3 test tubes; test-tube rack; 6 mL each of cooking oil, ethanol, and water

Procedure

1. Put on your disposable gloves, lab apron, and safety goggles.

2. Label the test tubes "A," "B," and "C."

3. In test tube A, put 3 mL of water and 3 mL of oil.

4. In test tube B, put 3 mL of oil and 3 mL of ethanol.

5. In test tube C, put 3 mL of ethanol and 3 mL of water.

6. With your thumb and middle finger, flick each test tube to mix the contents, and allow to set for 10–15 minutes.

7. Record your observations.

Analysis How does this activity demonstrate polarity of molecules that contain the –OH group?

FIGURE 3-7

A polymer is the result of bonding between monomers. The six-sided shape is an organic structural model of a molecule with a central carbon ring. The organic structure of a molecule shows the arrangement of carbon atoms in organic molecules.

FIGURE 3-8

The condensation reaction of one glucose molecule with one fructose molecule yields sucrose and water. One water molecule is produced each time two monomers form a covalent bond.

in Figure 3-8, two sugar molecules, glucose and fructose, combine to form the sugar sucrose, which is common table sugar. The two sugar monomers become linked by a C–O–C bridge. In the formation of that bridge, the glucose molecule releases a hydroxide ion, OH^-, and the fructose molecule releases a hydrogen ion, H^+. The OH^- and H^+ ions that are released in turn combine to produce a water molecule, H_2O.

The breakdown of some complex molecules, such as polymers, occurs through a process known as **hydrolysis** (HIE-DRAH-luh-sis). Hydrolysis is a reversal of a condensation reaction. The addition of water to some complex molecules, including polymers, under certain conditions can break the bonds that hold them together. As you can see in Figure 3-9, in hydrolysis a large molecule breaks apart.

Energy Currency

Life processes require a constant supply of energy. This energy is available to cells in the form of certain compounds that contain a large amount of energy in their overall structure. One of these compounds is **adenosine** (uh-DEN-uh-SEEN) **triphosphate,** more commonly referred to by its abbreviation, **ATP.**

Figure 3-9 shows the structure of an ATP molecule. Notice the three linked phosphate groups, $—PO_4^-$, that are attached to one another by covalent bonds. The covalent bond that holds the last phosphate group to the rest of the molecule is easily broken. When this bond is broken, much more energy is released than was required to break the bond. This conversion of energy is used by the cell to drive the chemical reactions that enable an organism to function.

FIGURE 3-9

The hydrolysis of ATP yields adenosine diphosphate and inorganic phosphate. In hydrolysis, a hydrogen ion from a water molecule bonds to one of the new molecules, and a hydroxide ion bonds to the other new molecule. Most hydrolysis reactions are exergonic.

Adenosine triphosphate (ATP)   Adenosine diphosphate (ADP) and inorganic phosphate

---

SECTION 3-2 REVIEW

1. What is an organic compound?

2. What property allows carbon compounds to exist in a number of forms?

3. Define *functional group* and give an example.

4. How does a polymer form?

5. How does a polymer break down?

6. **CRITICAL THINKING** Scientists can determine the age of a substance using a method that compares the amounts of different forms of carbon atoms present in the substance. Is this method more useful for organic substances or inorganic substances?

MOLECULES OF LIFE

Four main classes of organic compounds are essential to the life processes of all living things: carbohydrates, lipids, proteins, and nucleic acids. You will see that although these compounds are built from carbon, hydrogen, and oxygen, the atoms occur in different ratios in each class of compound. Despite their similarities, the different classes of compounds have different properties.

SECTION

3-3

OBJECTIVES

▲

Define *monosaccharide,* *disaccharide,* and *polysaccharide,* and discuss their significance to organisms.

●

Relate the sequence of amino acids to the structure of proteins.

■

Relate the structure of lipids to their functions.

◆

List two essential functions of nucleic acids.

CARBOHYDRATES

Carbohydrates are organic compounds composed of carbon, hydrogen, and oxygen in a ratio of about two hydrogen atoms to one oxygen atom. The number of carbon atoms in a carbohydrate varies. Carbohydrates exist as monosaccharides, disaccharides, or polysaccharides.

Monosaccharides

A monomer of a carbohydrate is called a **monosaccharide** (MAHN-oh-SAK-uh-RIED). A monosaccharide—or simple sugar—contains carbon, hydrogen, and oxygen in a ratio of 1:2:1. The general formula for a monosaccharide is written as $(CH_2O)_n$, where n is any whole number from 3 to 8. For example, a six-carbon monosaccharide $(CH_2O)_6$ would have the formula $C_6H_{12}O_6$. The most common monosaccharides are glucose, fructose, and galactose, as shown in Figure 3-10. Glucose is a main source of energy for cells. Fructose is found in fruits and is the sweetest of the monosaccharides. Galactose is found in milk and is usually combined with glucose or fructose. Notice in Figure 3-10 that glucose, fructose, and galactose have the same molecular formula, $C_6H_{12}O_6$, but their differing structures determine the slightly different properties of the three compounds. Compounds like these sugars, with a single chemical formula but different forms, are called **isomers** (IE-soh-muhrz).

internet connect

SC*L*INKS NSTA

TOPIC: Carbohydrates
GO TO: www.scilinks.org
KEYWORD: HM055

Glucose　　　　　Fructose　　　　　Galactose

FIGURE 3-10

Although glucose, fructose, and galactose have the same chemical formula, their structural differences result in different properties among the three compounds.

Disaccharides and Polysaccharides

In living things, two monosaccharides can combine in a condensation reaction to form a double sugar, or **disaccharide.** As you saw in Figure 3-8, sucrose, which is common table sugar, is composed of fructose and glucose. A **polysaccharide** is a complex molecule composed of three or more monosaccharides.

Animals store glucose in the form of the polysaccharide glycogen. Glycogen consists of hundreds of glucose molecules strung together in a highly branched chain. Much of the glucose that comes from food is ultimately stored in your liver and muscles as glycogen and is ready to be used for quick energy.

In plants, glucose molecules are linked in the polysaccharide starch. Starch molecules have two basic forms—highly branched chains that are similar to glycogen and long, unbranched chains that coil like a telephone cord. The large polysaccharide cellulose is also made by plants. Cellulose, which gives strength and rigidity to plant cells, makes up about 50 percent of wood. In a single cellulose molecule, thousands of glucose monomers are linked in long, straight chains. These chains tend to form hydrogen bonds with each other. The resulting structure is strong and can be broken down by hydrolysis only under certain conditions.

PROTEINS

Proteins are organic compounds composed mainly of carbon, hydrogen, oxygen, and nitrogen. Like the other macromolecules, proteins are formed from the linkage of monomers. The skin and muscles of animals are made mostly of proteins, as are many of the catalysts found in both plants and animals.

Amino Acids

The 20 different **amino acids,** the monomer building blocks of proteins, share a basic structure. As Figure 3-11 shows, each amino acid contains a central carbon atom covalently bonded to four other atoms or functional groups. A single hydrogen atom, highlighted in blue on the illustration, bonds at one site. A carboxyl group, —COOH, highlighted in green, bonds at a second site. An amino group, —NH_2, highlighted in yellow, bonds at a third site. And a functional group call the R group, highlighted in red, bonds at the fourth site.

The main difference among the different amino acids is found in their R groups. The R group can be as simple as the single hydrogen atom of glycine, shown in Figure 3-11a, or it can be more complex, such as the R group shown in the model of alanine, shown in Figure 3-11b. The differences among the amino acid R groups gives different proteins very different shapes. The different shapes allow proteins to perform many different roles in the chemistry of living things.

FIGURE 3-11

Amino acids differ only in the type of R group (shown in red) they carry. Glycine (a) has a simpler R group than alanine (b). The R group may be either polar or nonpolar. Amino acids with polar R groups can dissolve in water, while those with nonpolar R groups cannot.

(a) Glycine

(b) Alanine

Dipeptides and Polypeptides

Figure 3-12 shows how two amino acids bond to form a **dipeptide** (die-PEP-tied). In a condensation reaction, two amino acids form a covalent bond, called a **peptide bond.**

Amino acids can bond to each other one at a time, forming a very long chain called a **polypeptide** (PAH-lee-PEP-tied). Proteins are composed of one or more polypeptides. Some proteins are very large molecules, containing hundreds of amino acids. Often these long proteins are bent and folded upon themselves as a result of interactions—such as hydrogen bonding—among individual amino acids. Protein shape can also be influenced by conditions such as temperature or the type of solvent in which a protein is dissolved. When you cook an egg, heat changes the shape of proteins in the egg white. The firm, opaque result is very different from the clear, runny material you began with.

FIGURE 3-12

The peptide bond that binds amino acids together results from a condensation reaction that produces water.

Enzymes

Remember from Chapter 2 that enzymes—organic molecules that act as catalysts—are essential for the functioning of any cell. Most enzymes are proteins.

Figure 3-13 shows a model of enzyme action. Enzyme reactions depend on a physical fit between the enzyme molecule and its **substrate,** the reactant being catalyzed. Notice in Figure 13-3a that the enzyme and substrate have shapes that allow them to fit together like a lock and key. The linkage of the enzyme and substrate causes a slight change in the enzyme's shape, shown in Figure 13-3b. This shape change allows the enzyme to conform to the shape of the substrate and probably weakens some chemical bonds in the substrate, which is one way that enzymes reduce activation energy. After the reaction, the enzyme releases the products, as shown in Figure 13-3c. Like any catalyst, the enzyme itself is unchanged, so it can be used many times.

An enzyme may fail to work if its environment is changed in some way. For example, change in temperature or pH can cause a change in the shape of the enzyme or the substrate. If this happens, the reaction that the enzyme would have catalyzed cannot occur.

FIGURE 3-13

(a) In the lock-and-key model of enzyme action, the enzyme can attach only to a reactant with a specific shape. (b) The enzyme then flexes to conform to the reactant's shape. (c) The enzyme is unchanged by the reaction it participates in and is released to be used again.

Palmitic acid   Linoleic acid

FIGURE 3-14

Fatty acids have a polar carboxyl head, purple, and a nonpolar hydrocarbon tail, green.

FIGURE 3-15

The lipid bilayer of a cell membrane is made from a double row of phospholipids, arranged with their hydrophobic "tails" facing each other. In this illustration of phospholipid structure, the head represents polar carboxyl heads of two fatty acids.

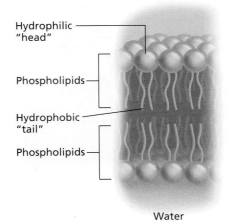

Hydrophilic "head"

Phospholipids

Hydrophobic "tail"

Phospholipids

Water

LIPIDS

Lipids are large, nonpolar organic molecules that do not dissolve in water. Lipid molecules have a higher ratio of carbon and hydrogen atoms to oxygen atoms than carbohydrates have. Lipids store energy efficiently. Lipid molecules have large numbers of carbon-hydrogen bonds, which store more energy than the carbon-oxygen bonds common in other organic compounds.

Fatty Acids

Fatty acids are unbranched carbon chains that make up most lipids. The model in Figure 3-14 shows that a fatty acid contains a long, straight carbon chain (from 12 to 28 carbons) with a carboxyl group, —COOH, attached at one end.

The two ends of the fatty-acid molecule have very different properties. The carboxyl end of the fatty-acid molecule is polar and is thus attracted to water molecules. Because of this attraction, the carboxyl end of the fatty-acid molecule is said to be **hydrophilic** (HIE-droh-FIL-ik), which means "water loving." In contrast, the hydrocarbon end of the fatty-acid molecule is nonpolar. This end tends not to interact with water molecules and is said to be **hydrophobic** (HIE-droh-FOH-bik), or "water fearing."

In saturated fatty acids, like palmitic acid, which is pictured in Figure 3-14, each carbon atom is covalently bonded to four atoms. The carbon atoms are in effect full, or "saturated." In contrast, you can see from the structural formula of a molecule of linoleic acid, shown in Figure 3-14, that the carbon atoms are not bonded to the maximum number of atoms that they can bond to. Instead, they have formed double bonds within the carbon chain. This type of fatty acid is said to be unsaturated.

Complex Lipids

Lipids are divided into categories according to their structure. Three classes of lipids important to living things contain fatty acids: triglycerides, phospholipids, and waxes. A **triglyceride** (trie-GLIS-uh-RIED) is composed of three molecules of fatty acid joined to one molecule of the alcohol glycerol. Saturated triglycerides are composed of saturated fatty acids. They typically have high melting points and tend to be solid at room temperature. Common dietary saturated triglycerides include shortening and animal fats. In contrast, unsaturated triglycerides are composed of unsaturated fatty acids and are usually liquid at room temperature. Unsaturated triglycerides are found primarily in plant seeds and fruits, where they serve as an energy and carbon source for sprouting plants.

Phospholipids have two, rather than three, fatty acids joined by a molecule of glycerol. As shown in Figure 3-15, the cell membrane is composed of two layers of phospholipids, which are referred to as the lipid bilayer. The inability of lipids to dissolve in water allows the membrane to form a barrier between the inside and outside of the cell. This bilayer arrangement of molecules produces a stable and effective barrier for a cell.

A **wax** is a type of structural lipid. A wax molecule consists of a long fatty-acid chain joined to a long alcohol chain. Waxes are highly waterproof, and in plants, wax forms a protective coating on the outer surfaces. Wax also forms protective layers in animals. For example, earwax helps prevent microorganisms from entering the middle ear.

Steroids

Unlike most other lipids, which are composed of fatty acids, **steroid** molecules are composed of four fused carbon rings with various functional groups attached to them. Many animal hormones, such as the male hormone testosterone, are steroid compounds. One of the most familiar steroids in humans is cholesterol. Cholesterol is needed by the body for nerve cells and other cells to function normally.

internetconnect

SCI**LINKS** NSTA

TOPIC: Steroids
GO TO: www.scilinks.org
KEYWORD: HM059

NUCLEIC ACIDS

Nucleic acids are very large and complex organic molecules that store important information in the cell. Just as computers use a binary system of zeros and ones to store information, nucleic acids use a system of four compounds to store hereditary information. A sequence of the four compounds arranged in a certain order acts as a code for the genetic instructions of the cell.

Deoxyribonucleic acid, or DNA, contains information that is essential for almost all cell activities, including cell division. **Ribonucleic** (RIE-boh-noo-KLEE-ik) **acid,** or **RNA,** stores and transfers information that is essential for the manufacturing of proteins. Both DNA and RNA are polymers, composed of thousands of linked monomers called **nucleotides** (NOO-klee-uh-TIEDS). As shown in Figure 3-16, each nucleotide is made of three main components: a phosphate group, a five-carbon sugar, and a ring-shaped nitrogen base. You will learn more about these important compounds in Chapter 10.

FIGURE 3-16

A nucleotide consists of a phosphate group, a five-carbon sugar, and a ring-shaped nitrogen base. DNA and RNA are very large molecules formed from thousands of nucleotides strung together in a chain.

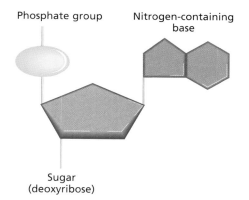

Phosphate group

Nitrogen-containing base

Sugar (deoxyribose)

SECTION 3-3 REVIEW

1. Define *monosaccharide, disaccharide,* and *polysaccharide.*

2. Describe the structure of amino acids and proteins.

3. Explain the relationship between an enzyme and its substrate.

4. How do the two ends of a fatty acid differ?

5. Name the two types of nucleic acids, and describe their functions.

6. **CRITICAL THINKING** High temperatures can weaken bonds between different parts of a protein molecule, thus changing its shape. How might this change alter the effectiveness of an enzyme?

The Structure of Insulin

Insulin is a hormone secreted by cells within the pancreas. It is essential in regulating the metabolism of carbohydrates and fats in the body. People with the disorder diabetes mellitus do not produce enough insulin. Some diabetes patients must take insulin injections to maintain normal metabolism.

In 1943, the British biochemist Frederick Sanger set out to analyze the insulin molecule. He was interested in proteins, and he chose insulin as the subject of his research mainly because, as he put it, "It was the only protein you could buy in pure form over the counter." He knew that an understanding of the structure of insulin could have important implications for medical practice. He spent the next 12 years studying the structure of insulin.

Biochemists already knew that proteins consist of combinations of 20 different amino acids linked together in chains. They also knew how to calculate the proportion of each amino acid in a given protein. What they did not know was the order in which the amino acids are linked in a specific protein. They correctly believed that the sequence of amino acids in a protein is crucial to the protein's function. Sanger's goal was to determine the amino acid sequence of insulin, and to do so, he had to develop new laboratory techniques.

Sanger began with a strategy familiar to chemists. He broke the insulin molecule into pieces. After splitting the chains of amino acids into short fragments, Sanger came to understand how they fit together. In his quest to determine the structure of insulin, he devised a new way to label the ends of a protein fragment.

Sanger learned that insulin is made up of two linked chains, one containing 30 amino acids and the other containing 21. He looked for fragments with overlapping sequences, which helped him discover how each chain was put together. By 1952, he had learned the amino acid sequences of both chains, but he still needed to understand how the two chains were linked to make up one insulin molecule. Three years later, Sanger reached his goal of identifying the molecular structure of insulin.

Sanger's work with insulin established him as the leader in his field, and in 1958 he received a Nobel Prize in chemistry. By demonstrating that each protein has a unique structure and likewise a unique sequence of amino acids, Sanger paved the way for the development of a technique that enabled the synthesis of insulin in the laboratory. In 1980, he received a second Nobel Prize in chemistry for his work in developing techniques for determining the sequence of nucleotides in molecules of DNA and RNA. Sanger is one of only four people to ever be awarded two Nobel Prizes.

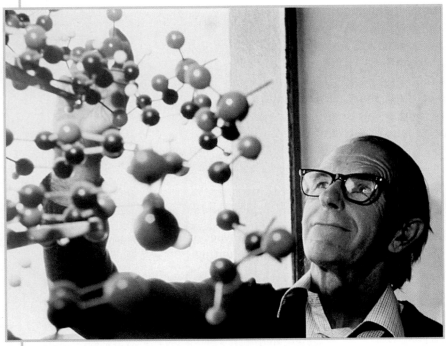

Frederick Sanger was the first scientist to determine the sequence of amino acids in a protein.

SUMMARY/VOCABULARY

3-1
- Water is a polar molecule in which the electrons are unevenly shared between the hydrogen and oxygen atoms.
- Because of its polar nature, water is effective in dissolving other substances to form solutions.

- Hydrogen bonding is responsible for the cohesion and capillarity that water molecules display.
- Water can absorb a large amount of thermal energy before its own temperature begins to rise.

Vocabulary

adhesion (51) cohesion (51) hydrogen bond (50) polar (50)
capillarity (51)

3-2
- An organic compound contains carbon that is covalently bonded both to other carbon atoms and often to atoms of other elements, including oxygen, hydrogen, and nitrogen.
- A carbon atom forms four covalent bonds with other atoms. Carbon atoms can bond with one another to form straight chains, branched chains, or rings.
- Simple molecules, known as monomers,

bond to one another to form complex molecules called polymers. Monomers are joined to form polymers in a condensation reaction. Polymers are broken down into monomers during hydrolysis.
- An alcohol is an organic compound that contains a hydroxyl group, OH^-, attached to one of its carbon atoms.
- Adenosine triphosphate (ATP) makes energy available to a cell.

Vocabulary

adenosine triphosphate (ATP) (54) condensation reaction (53) macromolecule (53) organic compound (52)
alcohol (53) functional group (53) monomer (53) polymer (53)
hydrolysis (54)

3-3
- A carbohydrate is an organic compound composed of carbon, hydrogen, and oxygen atoms in a ratio of about two hydrogen atoms to one oxygen atom. A monomer of a carbohydrate is called a monosaccharide.
- A double sugar is called a disaccharide. A complex sugar made of many monosaccharides is called a polysaccharide.
- A protein is an organic molecule that is formed from amino acids. An amino acid consists of a central carbon atom to which four functional groups are attached.
- Amino acids are joined by peptide bonds. A long chain of amino acids is called a polypeptide.
- Enzymes are catalysts that act in living

things. Enzyme action can be explained by the lock-and-key model. Most enzymes are proteins.
- Most lipids contain fatty acids, organic molecules that have a hydrophilic end and a hydrophobic end.
- Unsaturated lipids have one or more pairs of carbon atoms joined by double bonds. Saturated lipids have no double bonds between their carbon atoms.
- Lipids store more energy than the other types of organic molecules.
- Nucleic acids are organic molecules that store genetic information in the cell.

Vocabulary

amino acid (56) hydrophobic (58) peptide bond (57) steroid (59)
carbohydrate (55) isomer (55) phospholipid (58) substrate (57)
dipeptide (57) lipid (58) polypeptide (57) triglyceride (58)
disaccharide (56) monosaccharide (55) polysaccharide (56) wax (59)
fatty acid (58) nucleic acid (59) protein (56)
hydrophilic (58) nucleotide (59) ribonucleic acid (RNA) (59)

REVIEW

Vocabulary

1. Explain the relationship between amino acids, peptide bonds, and proteins.
2. How are the structures of monosaccharides, disaccharides, and polysaccharides related to each other?
3. Explain the relationship between a polypeptide and a peptide bond.
4. What is the difference between a hydrophilic substance and a hydrophobic substance?
5. Why is the structure of the cell membrane referred to as a bilayer?

Multiple Choice

6. Water helps keep the temperature of living things (a) high (b) low (c) below the freezing point (d) stable.
7. The distinguishing feature of a molecule of a polar compound is its (a) even distribution of electrical charge (b) uneven distribution of electrical charge (c) even temperature (d) uneven temperature.
8. The element that readily bonds to itself, forming long chains and rings, is (a) hydrogen (b) nitrogen (c) carbon (d) oxygen.
9. Plants store glucose in (a) a polysaccharide called starch (b) long proteins (c) complex lipid molecules called triglycerides (d) simple sugar molecules.
10. A very strong structural molecule in plants that is formed by hydrogen bonding between chains of glucose molecules is (a) starch (b) wax (c) cellulose (d) glycogen.
11. When two amino acids bond, (a) water is taken in by the product (b) hydrolysis occurs (c) a dipeptide is formed through a condensation reaction (d) a triglyceride is formed.
12. Lipids are distinguished from other organic molecules because they (a) contain carbon, hydrogen, and oxygen in a ratio of 1:2:1 (b) do not dissolve in water (c) dissolve easily in water (d) form large protein molecules.

13. Steroids differ from other lipid polymers in that steroids (a) do not occur in varied substances (b) are not hydrophilic (c) are not hydrophobic (d) are not composed of fatty-acid monomers.
14. Most enzymes are (a) lipids (b) phospholipids (c) proteins (d) carbohydrates.
15. A compound that stores hereditary information is (a) ATP (b) alcohol (c) DNA (d) protein.

Short Answer

16. Label the parts of the nucleotide below.

17. What are isomers?
18. What properties do alcohols and water share?
19. Compare and contrast a condensation reaction with a hydrolysis reaction.
20. Use a diagram to show how enzymes work.
21. How does the carboxyl end of the fatty-acid molecule differ from the hydrocarbon end of the molecule?
22. Compare and contrast the structures of triglycerides, phospholipids, and steroids. Which type of lipid is structurally unlike the other two?
23. What role does the compound ATP play in cellular activities?
24. What is an important characteristic of waxes, and why is this valuable to living things?
25. What structural role do phospholipids play in cells?

CRITICAL THINKING

1. Cells contain mostly water. What would happen to the stability of an organism's internal temperature with respect to environmental temperature changes if cells contained mostly oil, which does not have extensive hydrogen bonding?

2. The surface tension of water at room temperature is so great that you can actually "float" a small needle on the surface of water. (The needle doesn't truly float—it is denser than water. It is held in place by the force of hydrogen bonding between water molecules lying below and around the needle.) If the water were heated, what would happen to the needle and why?

3. Starch easily dissolves in water. Cellulose does not. Both substances, however, consist of chains of glucose molecules. What structural difference between starch and cellulose accounts for this different behavior in water?

4. Triglycerides in animals' bodies are usually solid fats, and those in plants are usually oils. However, many animals living in the Arctic and Antarctic have a greater number of triglycerides that are oils than do other animals. What advantage would the storage of body fat as oil instead of solid fat be to animals that live in freezing climates?

5. The specific heat of a substance is the amount of heat that must be added to 1 g of the substance to raise its temperature 1°C. Specific heat is measured in calories. Use the table to answer the following questions.
    a. What substance can absorb the greatest amount of heat before its own temperature rises?
    b. What do the two substances with the lowest specific heat values have in common?
    c. What property of ethanol might account for its relatively high specific heat?
    d. Which would be a better conductor of heat: iron or glass?
    e. What practical use would a substance with a very high specific heat have?

Specific Heats of Common Substances

Substance	Specific heat (cal)
Lead	0.03
Iron	0.10
Glass	0.20
Ethanol	0.60
Water	1.00
Liquid ammonia	1.23

EXTENSION

1. Read "Alien Haven" in *New Scientist*, September 18, 1999, on page 32, and answer the following questions: What are the "Goldilocks criteria" for a planet to be ideal for life? What is the "habitable zone," where a planet that can support life is most likely to be found?

2. Cut fibrous meat into four 1 in. cubes. Sprinkle three of the cubes with equal amounts of meat tenderizer, which contains a protein-splitting enzyme called papain. Place one cube in the refrigerator, leave one at room temperature, and place the other in an incubator at 32°C. For the fourth cube, place the same amount of meat tenderizer and a few tablespoons of water in a container, and boil the mixture for three minutes. (Do not allow the mixture to boil dry. Add water, tablespoon by tablespoon, as needed.) Pour the boiled mixture on the meat. After three hours, observe the texture of all four meat cubes. What do you conclude about the effect of temperature on the enzyme in meat tenderizer? Express your results as a graph showing temperature and the apparent level of activity of the enzyme.

Identifying Organic Compounds in Foods

OBJECTIVES

- Determine whether specific nutrients are present in a solution of unknown composition.
- Perform chemical tests using substances called *indicators.*

PROCESS SKILLS

- experimenting
- observing
- measuring

MATERIALS

- lab apron
- safety goggles
- disposable gloves
- 1 L beaker
- hot plate
- 9 test tubes
- labeling tape
- marker
- 10 mL graduated cylinder
- Benedict's solution
- 9 dropping pipets
- glucose solution
- unknown solution
- distilled water
- 9 glass stirring rods
- tongs or test-tube holder
- test-tube rack
- albumin solution
- sodium hydroxide solution
- copper sulfate solution
- vegetable oil
- Sudan III solution

Background

1. Carbohydrates, proteins, and lipids are nutrients that are essential to all living things. Some foods, such as table sugar, contain only one of these nutrients. Most foods, however, contain mixtures of proteins, carbohydrates, and lipids. You can confirm this by reading the information in the "Nutrition Facts" box found on any food label.

2. In this investigation, you will use chemical substances, called indicators, to identify the presence of specific nutrients in an unknown solution. By comparing the color change an indicator produces in the unknown food sample with the change it produces in a sample of known composition, you can determine whether specific organic compounds are present in the unknown sample.

3. Benedict's solution is used to determine the presence of monosaccharides, such as glucose. A mixture of sodium hydroxide and copper sulfate determine the presence of some proteins (this procedure is called the biuret test). Sudan III is used to determine the presence of lipids.

Procedure

   CAUTION Put on a lab apron, safety goggles, and gloves. In this lab, you will be working with chemicals that can harm your skin and eyes or stain your skin and clothing. If you get a chemical on your skin or clothing, wash it off at the sink while calling to your teacher. If you get a chemical in your eyes, immediately flush it out at the eyewash station while calling to your teacher. As you perform each test, record your data in your lab report, organized in a table like the one on the next page.

Test 1

1. **CAUTION Do not touch the hot plate. Use tongs to move heated objects. Turn off the hot plate when not in use. Do not plug in or unplug the hot plate with wet hands.** Make a water bath by filling a 1 L beaker half full with water. Then put the beaker on a hot plate and bring the water to a boil.

2. While you wait for the water to boil, label one test tube "1-glucose," label the second test tube "1-unknown," and label the third test tube "1-water." Using the graduated cylinder, measure 5 mL of Benedict's solution and add it to the "1-glucose" test tube. Repeat the procedure, adding 5 mL of Benedict's solution each to the "1-unknown" test tube and "1-water" test tube.

3. Using a dropping pipet or eyedropper, add 10 drops of glucose solution to the "1-glucose" test tube. Using a second dropping pipet, add 10 drops of the unknown solution to the "1-unknown" test tube. Using a third dropping pipet, add 10 drops of distilled water to the

TABLE A *IDENTIFICATION OF SPECIFIC NUTRIENTS BY CHEMICAL INDICATORS*

Test	Nutrient in test solution	Nutrient category (protein, lipid, etc.)	Result for known sample	Result for unknown sample	Result for distilled water
1					
2					
3					

"1-water" test tube. Mix the contents of each test tube with a clean stirring rod. **(It is important not to contaminate test solutions by using the same dropping pipet or stirring rod in more than one solution. Use a different dropping pipet and stirring rod for each of the test solutions.)**

4. When the water boils, use tongs to place the test tubes in the water bath. Boil the test tubes for 1 to 2 minutes.

5. **CAUTION Do not touch the test tubes with your hands. They will be very hot.** Use tongs to remove the test tubes from the water bath and place them in the test-tube rack. As the test tubes cool, an orange or red precipitate will form if large amounts of glucose are present. If small amounts of glucose are present, a yellow or green precipitate will form. Record your results in your data table.

Test 2

6. Label one clean test tube "2-albumin," label a second test tube "2-unknown," and label a third test tube "2-water." Using a dropping pipet, add 40 drops of albumin solution to the "2-albumin" test tube. Using a second dropping pipet, add 40 drops of unknown solution to the "2-unknown" test tube. Using a third dropping pipet, add 40 drops of water to the "2-water" test tube.

7. Add 40 drops of sodium hydroxide solution to each of the three test tubes. Mix the contents of each test tube with a clean stirring rod.

8. Add a few drops of copper sulfate solution, one drop at a time, to the "2-albumin" test tube. Stir the solution with a clean stirring rod after each drop. Note the number of drops required to cause the color of the solution in the test tube to change. Then add the same number of drops of copper sulfate solution to the "2-unknown" and "2-water" test tubes.

9. Record your results in your data table.

Test 3

10. Label one clean test tube "3-vegetable oil," label a second test tube "3-unknown," and label a third test tube "3-water." Using a dropping pipet, add 5 drops of vegetable oil to the "3-vegetable oil" test tube. Using a second dropping pipet, add 5 drops of the unknown solution to the "3-unknown" test tube. Using a third dropping pipet, add 5 drops of water to the "3-water" test tube.

11. **CAUTION Sudan III solution will stain your skin and clothing. Promptly wash off spills to minimize staining. Do not use Sudan III solution in the same room with an open flame.** Using a clean dropping pipet, add 3 drops of Sudan III solution to each test tube. Mix the contents of each test tube with a clean stirring rod.

12. Record you results in your data table.

13. Clean up your materials and wash your hands before leaving the lab.

Analysis and Conclusions

1. Based on the results you recorded in your data table, identify the nutrient or nutrients in the unknown solution.

2. What are the experimental controls in this investigation?

3. Explain how you were able to use the color changes of different indicators to determine the presence of specific nutrients in the unknown substance.

4. List four potential sources of error in this investigation.

Further Inquiry

Is there a kind of macromolecule that the tests in this lab did not test for? If so, list the kind of macromolecules not tested for, and give one reason why they were not tested for.

CELLS

66 *The cell is the natural granule of life in the same way as the atom is the natural granule of simple, elemental matter. If we are to take the measure of the transit to life and determine its precise nature, we must try to understand the cell.* 99

From "The Advent of Life" from *The Phenomenon of Man* by Pierre Teilhard de Chardin. Copyright © 1955 by Editions de Seuil. English translation copyright © 1959 by William Collins Sons & Co. Ltd., London and Harper & Row Publishers, Inc., New York. Reprinted by permission of *HarperCollins Publishers, Inc.*

Eukaryotic cells contain a number of complex internal structures.

Most cells are very small, but these frog eggs can be seen with the unaided eye.

White blood cells

The orange-stained immune-system cell shown above is attacking and ingesting the red-stained tumor cell. Mitochondria, below left, provide cells with the energy necessary for life.

CHAPTER 4

STRUCTURE AND FUNCTION OF THE CELL

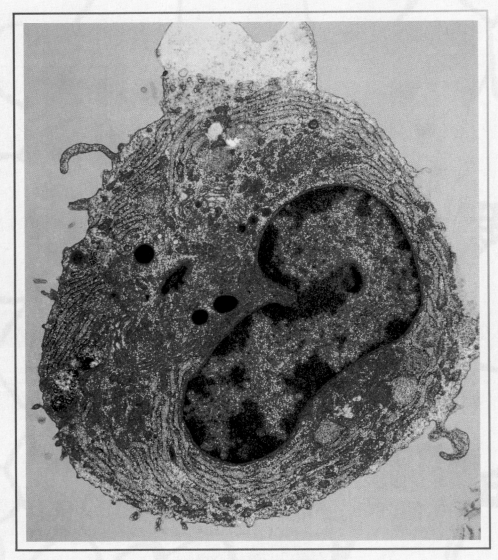

This human bone cell has a complex internal structure. (TEM 17,938×)

FOCUS CONCEPT: *Cell Structure and Function*

As you read, find examples of how cell structures vary with their functions.

Unit 1—*Cell Transport and Homeostasis*
Topics 1–2

4-1 *Introduction to the Cell*

4-2 *Parts of the Eukaryotic Cell*

4-3 *Multicellular Organization*

INTRODUCTION TO THE CELL

*Both living and nonliving things are composed of molecules made from chemical elements such as carbon, hydrogen, oxygen, and nitrogen. The organization of these molecules into cells is one feature that distinguishes living things from all other matter. A **cell** is the smallest unit of matter that can carry on all of the processes of life.*

OBJECTIVES

▲

Outline the discoveries that led to the development of the cell theory.

●

State the cell theory.

■

Identify a limiting factor on the size of cells.

◆

Describe the relationship between cell shape and cell function.

▲

Distinguish between prokaryotes and eukaryotes.

DISCOVERY OF THE CELL

Every living thing—from the tiniest bacterium floating in a drop of water to the largest whale—is made of one or more cells. How did scientists come to this conclusion? The discovery of cells was made possible by the development of the microscope in the early seventeenth century.

In 1665, the English scientist Robert Hooke (1635–1703) used a microscope to examine a thin slice of cork. Hooke wrote, "I could exceedingly plainly perceive it to be all perforated and porous," and he further described it as consisting of "a great many little boxes." When he turned his microscope to the stems of elder trees, carrots, and ferns, Hooke found that each showed a similar formation. These "little boxes" reminded him of the small rooms in which monks lived, so he called them cells.

What Hooke had observed were actually the remains of dead plant cells. The first person to observe living cells was a Dutch microscope maker, Anton van Leeuwenhoek (1632–1723). Although van Leeuwenhoek's microscope was rather simple, in 1673 it was powerful enough to enable him to open up a whole new world—the world of microscopic organisms, which had never before been seen.

The Cell Theory

About 150 years passed before scientists began to organize the observations begun by Hooke and van Leeuwenhoek into a unified theory known as the **cell theory.** This theory has three parts:

- All living things are composed of one or more cells.
- Cells are the basic units of structure and function in an organism.
- Cells come only from the reproduction of existing cells.

FIGURE 4-1

Although most cells are extremely small, some are large enough to be seen without a microscope. These frog egg cells, for instance, measure about 1.5 mm (0.1 in.) in diameter. Even larger are chicken eggs, which are several centimeters across. The egg cells of both frogs and chickens consist mainly of yolk, which serves as a stored nutrient for the developing embryo.

Early evidence for the cell theory was provided by a trio of German scientists. In 1838, the botanist Matthias Schleiden (1804–1881) concluded that all plants are composed of cells. A year later, the zoologist Theodor Schwann (1810–1882) came to the same conclusion about animals. In 1855, Rudolf Virchow (1821–1902), a physician who had been studying how disease affects living things, reasoned that cells come only from other cells. Over the years, modern scientists have gathered much additional evidence that strongly supports the cell theory.

CELL DIVERSITY

Not all cells are alike. Even cells within the same organism may show enormous diversity in size, shape, and internal organization. Your body, for example, contains at least 200 different cell types.

Size

A few types of cells, such as those shown in Figure 4-1, are large enough to be seen by the unaided eye. The nerve cells that extend down a giraffe's leg, for instance, can be up to 2 m (about $6\frac{1}{2}$ ft) long. However, most plant and animal cells are only about 10 to 50 μm (0.002 in.) in diameter, and some bacterial cells are only 0.2 μm (0.000008 in.) in diameter. Therefore, most cells are visible only with a microscope.

Cells are limited in size by the ratio between their outer surface area and their volume. Table 4-1 shows how growth affects this ratio. For a cuboidal cell, volume increases with the *cube* of the side length, but surface area increases with the *square* of the side length. This means that if a cell keeps the same shape as it grows, its volume will increase more rapidly than its surface area. This trend is important because the nutrients, oxygen, and other materials a cell requires must enter through its surface. Thus, as a cell grows larger, at some point its surface area becomes too small to allow these materials to enter the cell quickly enough to meet the cell's needs.

TABLE 4-1	*Surface Areas and Volumes of Cubes*			
	Side Length	Surface Area	Volume	Surface Area/Volume Ratio
	1 mm	6 mm^2	1 mm^3	6:1
	2 mm	24 mm^2	8 mm^3	3:1
	3 mm	54 mm^2	27 mm^3	2:1

NERVE CELL

SKIN CELLS

WHITE BLOOD CELL

Shape

Cells come in a variety of shapes. This diversity of form reflects a diversity of function. Examine the three human cells shown in Figure 4-2. The long extensions that reach out in various directions from the nerve cell enable the cell to receive and transmit nerve impulses. In contrast, the flat shape of dead skin cells is well suited to their function of covering the body surface. Some white blood cells can change shape, leave the blood, and enter the areas surrounding blood vessels. This allows them to move through narrow openings and to isolate, engulf, and destroy bacteria that invade the body.

Internal Organization

The micrographs in Figures 4-3 and 4-4 show that cells contain a variety of internal structures called **organelles.** An organelle is a cell component that performs specific functions for the cell. Just as the organs of a multicellular organism carry out the organism's life functions, the organelles of a cell maintain the life of the cell.

FIGURE 4-2

These photographs taken with a scanning electron microscope show three different types of cells that are found in the human body. Each cell type has a structure that enables it to perform its function effectively. (left 17,385×, middle 330×, right 23,250×)

Cell membrane

Nucleus

TEM

FIGURE 4-3

This plant cell, like other eukaryotic cells, is filled with membrane-bound organelles. The most prominent organelle is the nucleus. The entire cell is surrounded by a membrane. (TEM 105,661×)

In Figure 4-3, notice that the entire cell is surrounded by a thin membrane, called the **cell membrane.** Inside the cell are a variety of organelles, most of which are surrounded by their own membranes. The large organelle near the center of the cell is the **nucleus.** It contains the majority of the cell's genetic information and directs most of the activities of the cell. Organisms whose cells contain a membrane-bound nucleus and other organelles are called **eukaryotes** (yoo-KAR-ee-OHTS).

The cell shown in Figure 4-4 is a bacterium. It, too, has a cell membrane, but none of the organelles inside a bacterium are surrounded by a membrane. Although the genetic information of a bacterium may be concentrated in one part of the cell, a bacterium has no membrane-bound nucleus like that of a eukaryotic cell. Unicellular organisms that lack a membrane-bound nucleus and other organelles are called **prokaryotes** (proh-KAR-ee-OHTS). The difference between prokaryotes and eukaryotes is such an important distinction that prokaryotes are placed in two kingdoms, separate from eukaryotes.

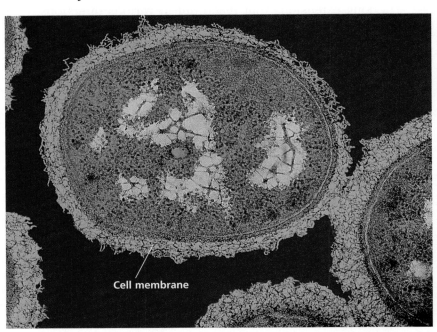

Cell membrane

FIGURE 4-4

This bacterial cell is surrounded by a membrane, but it has no nucleus or other membrane-bound organelles. (TEM 84,721×)

SECTION 4-1 REVIEW

1. What is the cell theory?

2. What single factor limits the size that most cells are able to attain?

3. Give two examples of how cells' shapes are suited to their functions.

4. What is an organelle?

5. How can you determine whether a unicellular organism is a prokaryote or a eukaryote?

6. **CRITICAL THINKING** The observations that led to the formation of the cell theory occurred within a 17-year period. Why do you think that more than one scientist made critical observations about cells within this period?

PARTS OF THE EUKARYOTIC CELL

The structures that make up a eukaryotic cell are determined by the specific functions carried out by the cell. Thus, there is no typical eukaryotic cell. Nevertheless, eukaryotic cells generally have three main components: a cell membrane, a nucleus, and other organelles.

OBJECTIVES

Describe the structure, composition, and function of the cell membrane.

Name the major organelles found in a eukaryotic cell, and describe their functions.

Describe the structure and function of the nucleus.

Describe three structures characteristic of plant cells.

CELL MEMBRANE

A cell cannot survive if it is totally isolated from its environment. All cells must take in nutrients and other materials, and they must also dispose of the wastes they produce. Therefore, both nutrients and wastes must pass through the cell membrane. The cell membrane controls the ease with which substances pass into and out of the cell—some substances easily cross the membrane, while others cannot cross at all. For this reason, the cell membrane is said to be **selectively permeable.**

The structure of the cell membrane depends on the functions the cell performs. In a multicellular organism, for example, some cells secrete materials into their environment for use elsewhere in the organism. Other cells recognize potentially harmful "invaders" and destroy them before they cause any damage. In each case, the cells are surrounded by membranes specialized for that task. No matter what the task, however, all cell membranes are made primarily of lipids and proteins.

Membrane Lipids

One of the major types of lipids in the cell membrane is phospholipid. Recall from Chapter 3 that each phospholipid molecule has a polar "head" and two nonpolar "tails." Because of its hydrophilic nature, the head of a phospholipid will orient itself so that it is as close as possible to water molecules. In contrast, the hydrophobic tails will tend to orient themselves away from water.

Cells are bathed in an aqueous, or watery, environment. Since the inside of a cell is also an aqueous environment, both sides of the cell membrane are surrounded by water molecules. These water molecules cause the phospholipids of the cell membrane to form two layers—a lipid bilayer. As you can see in Figure 4-5,

OUTSIDE OF CELL

Carbohydrate

Peripheral protein

Phospholipid heads

Phospholipid tails

Steroid

Lipid bilayer

Integral protein

Peripheral protein

Integral protein

INSIDE OF CELL

FIGURE 4-5

Cell membranes are composed mostly of a lipid bilayer and two types of proteins. Integral proteins are embedded within the membrane. Peripheral proteins are attached to both surfaces of the membrane.

the phospholipids are arranged so that their heads point outward, while their tails are confined to the interior of the membrane.

Figure 4-5 indicates that eukaryotic cell membranes also contain steroids, another type of lipid you encountered in Chapter 3. In membranes, the steroid molecules fit between the tails of the phospholipids. The major membrane steroid in animal cells is cholesterol. Other steroids are found in the cell membranes of plants.

Membrane Proteins

Some proteins are attached to the surfaces of the cell membrane. As shown in Figure 4-5, these **peripheral proteins** are located on both the interior surface and the exterior surface of the cell membrane. Weak bonds link peripheral proteins to membrane lipids or to other proteins that are embedded in the lipid bilayer. The proteins that are embedded in the bilayer are called **integral proteins.** Figure 4-5 shows that some integral proteins extend across the entire cell membrane and are exposed to both the inside of the cell and the exterior environment. Others extend either only to the inside or only to the exterior surface.

Notice in Figure 4-5 that the integral proteins exposed to the cell's external environment often have carbohydrates attached to them. These carbohydrates may hold adjoining cells together, or they may act as sites where viruses or chemical messengers such as hormones can attach.

Because the cell membrane is selectively permeable, cells must have mechanisms for transporting molecules through the lipid bilayer. Membrane proteins play an important role in this process. For example, some integral proteins form channels or pores through which certain substances can pass. Other proteins bind to a substance on one side of the membrane and carry it to the other side of the membrane. You will learn more about how substances cross the cell membrane in Chapter 5.

Fluid Mosaic Model of Cell Membranes

For many years, scientists thought that the molecular arrangement of lipids and proteins in the cell membrane was relatively static. But with the development of new techniques and instruments, including the scanning electron microscope, scientists have discovered that cell membranes are actually very dynamic. Today scientists use the **fluid mosaic model** to describe the cell membrane. According to this model, the lipid bilayer behaves more like a fluid than a solid. Because of this fluidity, the membrane's lipids and proteins can move laterally within the lipid bilayer, as indicated in Figure 4-6. As a result of such lateral movement, the pattern, or "mosaic," of lipids and proteins in the cell membrane is constantly changing.

FIGURE 4-6

The cell membrane is a dynamic structure, with both lipids and proteins moving laterally within the lipid bilayer. Scientists therefore describe the structure of the cell membrane in terms of a fluid mosaic model.

ORGANELLES

Between the cell membrane and the nucleus lies the **cytoplasm** (SIET-oh-PLAZ-uhm), which contains the various organelles of the cell. The organelles are bathed in a gelatin-like aqueous fluid called the **cytosol** (SIET-oh-SAWL). Dissolved in the cytosol are salts, minerals, and organic molecules. The major organelles are summarized in Table 4-2, and those that are found in animal cells are illustrated in Figure 4-7.

TABLE 4-2 *Organelles*

Organelle	Function
Mitochondrion	transfers energy from organic compounds to ATP
Ribosome	organizes the synthesis of proteins
Endoplasmic reticulum (ER)	prepares proteins for export (rough ER); synthesizes steroids, regulates calcium levels, breaks down toxic substances (smooth ER)
Golgi apparatus	processes and packages substances produced by the cell
Lysosome	digests molecules, old organelles, and foreign substances
Microfilaments and microtubules	contribute to the support, movement, and division of cells
Cilia and flagella	propel cells through the environment; move materials over the cell surface
Nucleus	stores hereditary information in DNA; synthesizes RNA and ribosomes
Cell wall*	supports and protects the cell
Vacuole*	stores enzymes and waste products
Plastid*	stores food or pigments; one type (chloroplast) transfers energy from light to organic compounds

*Cell walls, large vacuoles, and plastids are found in the cells of plants and some other eukaryotes, but not in the cells of animals.

Flagellum

Nucleus:
Nuclear pore
Nuclear envelope
Nucleolus
Chromatin

Mitochondrion

Ribosomes

Microfilaments

Lysosome

Cell membrane

Golgi
apparatus

Microtubules

Rough endoplasmic
reticulum

Smooth endoplasmic
reticulum

FIGURE 4-7

Most animal cells have a cell membrane, a nucleus, and a variety of other organelles.

Word Roots and Origins

mitochondrion

from the Greek *mitos*, meaning "thread," and *chondrion*, meaning "grain"

Mitochondria

Scattered throughout the cytosol are relatively large organelles called **mitochondria** (MIET-oh-KAHN-dree-uh), illustrated in Figure 4-8. Mitochondria are the sites of chemical reactions that transfer energy from organic compounds to ATP. Remember from Chapter 3 that ATP is the molecule that most cells use as their main energy currency. The energy of ATP ultimately drives most of the chemical reactions that occur in a cell. Therefore, mitochondria are usually more numerous in cells that have a high energy requirement. Liver cells, for instance, carry out a host of biochemical activities, and each cell may contain as many as 2,500 mitochondria. Muscle cells also contain many mitochondria.

If you look closely at Figure 4-8, you will notice that a mitochondrion is surrounded by two membranes. The smooth *outer* membrane serves as a boundary between the mitochondrion and

FIGURE 4-8

Mitochondria are surrounded by a double membrane. The inner membrane is composed of many folds called cristae. (TEM 232,000×)

the cytosol. The *inner* membrane has many long folds, known as **cristae** (KRIS-tee). The cristae greatly enlarge the surface area of the inner membrane, providing more space for the chemical reactions that occur in the mitochondrion.

Mitochondria have their own DNA, and new mitochondria arise only when existing ones grow and divide. These observations have led to a theory, discussed further in Chapter 15, that mitochondria developed from prokaryotic cells that lived inside eukaryotic cells. According to this theory, the prokaryotes may have gained protection by living inside the eukaryotes and, in turn, produced energy for the eukaryotes.

Ribosomes

The most numerous organelles in many cells are the **ribosomes** (RIE-buh-SOHMZ). Unlike most other organelles, ribosomes are not surrounded by a membrane. Each ribosome is an assemblage of two organic compounds—proteins and RNA. Inside the cell's nucleus, proteins and RNAs are packaged into ribosomes, which are then transported to the cytosol. Some ribosomes remain free within the cytosol, while others become attached to an organelle called the endoplasmic reticulum. You can see both free and attached ribosomes if you examine Figure 4-9 closely.

Ribosomes play important roles in the synthesis of proteins. Proteins to be used within the cytosol are produced on the ribosomes that are free in the cytosol. Proteins to be inserted into membranes or exported from the cell are produced on the ribosomes that are attached to the endoplasmic reticulum.

internet connect

SCI**LINKS**
NSTA

TOPIC: Eukaryotic cells
GO TO: www.scilinks.org
KEYWORD: HM076

Smooth ER

Rough ER

FIGURE 4-9

The small dark dots in this cell are ribosomes. Some are free in the cytosol, while others are attached to the rough ER. The smooth ER lacks attached ribosomes. (TEM 240,000×)

Endoplasmic Reticulum

The **endoplasmic reticulum** (EN-doh-PLAZ-mik ri-TIK-yuh-luhm), abbreviated ER, is a system of membranous tubules and sacs. The dark lines that you see in Figure 4-9 represent the membranes of the ER, while the lighter areas are the channels inside it. The ER functions primarily as an intracellular highway, a path along which molecules move from one part of the cell to another. The amount of ER inside a cell fluctuates, depending on the cell's activity.

A cell usually contains two types of ER, both of which are shown in Figure 4-9. One type appears to be covered with dark dots when viewed with an electron microscope. These dots are ribosomes, and they give the ER a rough appearance. Consequently, this type is known as **rough endoplasmic reticulum,** or rough ER. Rough ER is prominent in cells that make large amounts of proteins to be exported from the cell or inserted into the cell membrane.

The second type of ER is not covered with ribosomes. Because of their absence, this type of ER appears smooth and is therefore called **smooth endoplasmic reticulum,** or smooth ER. Smooth ER is involved in the synthesis of steroids in gland cells, the regulation of calcium levels in muscle cells, and the breakdown of toxic substances by liver cells. As you can see in Figure 4-9, rough ER and smooth ER may be continuous with each other.

Golgi Apparatus

The **Golgi** (GOHL-jee) **apparatus** is the processing, packaging, and secreting organelle of the cell. Like the endoplasmic reticulum, the Golgi apparatus is a system of membranes. Figure 4-10 shows that the Golgi apparatus appears as a series of flattened sacs with a characteristic convex shape in the cytosol. Working in close association with the endoplasmic reticulum, the Golgi apparatus modifies proteins for export by the cell. The role of the Golgi apparatus in protein synthesis will be discussed in Chapter 11.

Lysosomes

Lysosomes (LIE-suh-sohmz) are small, spherical organelles that enclose hydrolytic enzymes within single membranes. These enzymes can digest proteins, carbohydrates, lipids, DNA, and RNA. They may also digest old organelles as well as viruses and bacteria that have been ingested by a cell. Lysosomes are common in the cells of animals, fungi, and protists, but they are rare in plant cells. In some multicellular organisms, lysosomes play a role during early development. For example, the human hand begins as a solid structure in the embryo. As the embryo develops, lysosomal enzymes selectively destroy tissue to form the spaces between the fingers.

Cytoskeleton

Just as your body depends on your skeleton to maintain its shape and size, so a cell needs a structure to maintain its shape and size. In many cells, that structure is the **cytoskeleton,** a network of long protein strands located in the cytosol. Like ribosomes, these strands are not surrounded by membranes. In addition to providing support, the cytoskeleton participates in the movement of organelles within the cytosol. Two major components of the cytoskeleton are **microfilaments** and **microtubules.**

Microfilaments are threads made of a protein called **actin.** Each microfilament consists of many actin molecules that are linked together to form a polymer chain. Microfilaments constitute the smallest strands that make up the cytoskeleton. They contribute to cell movement and play a role in the contraction of muscle cells.

The largest strands of the cytoskeleton are hollow tubes known as microtubules. In many cells, microtubules extend outward from a central point near the nucleus to various sites near the cell membrane. When a cell is about to divide, bundles of microtubules come together and extend across the cell. These bundles, known as **spindle fibers,** are thick enough to be visible with a light microscope, as you can see in Figure 4-11. Spindle fibers assist in the movement of chromosomes during cell division. When cell division is complete, the spindle fibers are disassembled, and the microtubules resume their task of providing support to the cell.

FIGURE 4-10

A collection of smooth, membrane-bound sacs isolated from the endoplasmic reticulum is known as the Golgi apparatus. Although separated from each other, the endoplasmic reticulum and Golgi apparatus work closely together in preparing materials for release by the cell. (TEM 237,250×)

FIGURE 4-11

This cell is dividing in two. Its chromosomes, stained orange by a fluorescent dye, are moving to opposite ends of the cell. They are being pulled by the spindle fibers, which are stained green. (LM 3,696×)

FIGURE 4-12

Sperm cells propel themselves by moving a long flagellum back and forth. (LM 3,350×)

Cilia and Flagella

Cilia (SIL-ee-uh) and **flagella** (fluh-JEL-uh) are hairlike organelles that extend from the surface of the cell, where they assist in movement. Because of the variety of roles they play, cilia and flagella can be found in many eukaryotic cells.

When these organelles are short and present in large numbers on a cell, they are called cilia. The external surfaces of many unicellular organisms are covered with cilia. The movements of the cilia propel these tiny organisms through the water as they search for food or escape from predators. Cilia are also found on the surfaces of cells in multicellular organisms. The cells lining your respiratory tract, for example, bear numerous cilia that trap particles and debris from the air you inhale. As these cilia move, they sweep the trapped materials back up to your throat, where they are removed from your respiratory tract when you swallow.

When the hairlike organelles are long and less numerous on a cell, they are called flagella. On many cells, including the sperm cells illustrated in Figure 4-12, only one flagellum is present. By whipping back and forth, flagella can swiftly propel unicellular organisms or specialized cells in multicellular organisms, such as sperm cells.

Cilia and flagella have a similar internal structure. Notice in Figure 4-13 that both organelles are composed of nine pairs of microtubules arranged around a central pair.

FIGURE 4-13

Microtubules are important components of cilia and flagella. A cross section of a cilium shows that it consists of nine pairs of microtubules that surround a central pair. A flagellum has a similar structure. (TEM 38,000× left, 396,000× right)

Microtubules

Cilium

Cell membrane

FIGURE 4-14

The most prominent organelle in most eukaryotic cells is the nucleus, which is surrounded by a double membrane perforated with pores. These pores allow materials to be exchanged between the nucleus and the cytosol. Inside the nucleus is the nucleolus, where ribosomes are made before they are transported to the cytosol. (TEM 360,734×)

Nuclear pores

Nucleolus

Nuclear envelope

NUCLEUS

The nucleus is often the most prominent structure within a eukaryotic cell. It maintains its shape with the help of a protein skeleton known as the **nuclear matrix.** As indicated in Figure 4-14, the nucleus is surrounded by a double membrane called the **nuclear envelope.** Inside the nuclear envelope are fine strands of **chromatin,** a combination of DNA and protein. When a cell is about to divide, the chromatin strands coil up and become densely packed, forming **chromosomes.**

The nucleus stores hereditary information in its DNA. The nucleus is also the site where RNA is copied from DNA. In turn, RNA directs the synthesis of proteins, a process that occurs in the cytosol, as you have read. This means that RNA must travel from the nucleus to the cytosol before it can direct protein synthesis. RNA makes this journey by passing through **nuclear pores,** small holes in the nuclear envelope. Most nuclei also contain at least one spherical area called the **nucleolus** (noo-KLEE-uh-luhs). The nucleolus is the site where ribosomes are synthesized and partially assembled before they pass through the nuclear pores to the cytosol. Both the nuclear pores and the nucleolus are visible in Figure 4-14.

Word Roots and Origins

chromosome

from the Greek *chroma*, meaning "color," and *soma*, meaning "body"

internet connect

*SCi*LINKS.
NSTA

TOPIC: Plant cells
GO TO: www.scilinks.org
KEYWORD: HM081

PLANT CELLS

Most of the organelles and other parts of the cell just described are common to all eukaryotic cells. However, plant cells may have three additional kinds of structures—cell walls, vacuoles, and plastids—that are extremely important to plant function.

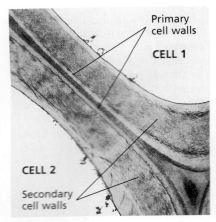

FIGURE 4-15

The two plant cells in this photograph each have their own primary and secondary cell walls. The primary walls are constructed first. Later, the secondary walls are formed inside the primary walls. (TEM 12,750×)

Cell Wall

Plant cells are covered by a rigid **cell wall that lies outside the cell** membrane. The rigidity of cell walls h~~~ of support and protect the plant. Cell walls contain long chai~~~ of support and protect the plex carbohydrates you read about n Ch~~ose, one of the complex embedded in proteins and other carbohy~~ The cellulose is entire structure. Pores in the cell wall allow io~~ harden the enter and exit the cell.

Figure 4-15 shows that cell walls are of two type~~ecules to secondary. While a plant cell is being formed, a prim~~ develops just outside the cell membrane. As the cell ~~ length, cellulose and other molecules are added, enlarging~~ wall. When the cell reaches its full size, a secondary cell wa~~ develop. As you can see in Figure 4-15, the secondary cell ~~ develops between the primary cell wall and the cell membrane. The secondary cell wall is tough and woody. Therefore, once it is completed, a plant cell can grow no further. When you pick up a piece of wood, you are holding secondary cell walls. The cells inside the walls have died and disintegrated.

Vacuoles

Vacuoles are a second common characteristic of plant cells. These fluid-filled organelles store enzymes and metabolic wastes. Often, as Figure 4-16 shows, they are quite large. In fact, some vacuoles may occupy 90 percent of a plant cell's volume, pushing all of the other organelles up against the cell membrane. Some of the wastes stored by vacuoles are toxic and must be kept away from the rest of the cell. The storage of these materials may be beneficial to a plant in other ways. For instance, the poisons that certain acacia trees have in their vacuoles provide a defense against plant-eating animals.

FIGURE 4-16

Much of the volume of these plant cells is occupied by a large vacuole in the center of the cell. The rest of the organelles are confined to a rim of cytosol around the periphery of the cell. (TEM 4,180×)

Thylakoid

Inner membrane   Outer membrane

FIGURE 4-17

Chloroplasts, like mitochondria and the nucleus, are surrounded by a double membrane. The thylakoids inside each chloroplast contain pigments involved in photosynthesis. (TEM 14,648×)

Plastids

A third distinguishing feature of plant cells is the presence of **plastids.** Plastids are organelles that, like mitochondria and the nucleus, are surrounded by two membranes and contain DNA. Some plastids store starch or fats, while others contain compounds called pigments, which absorb visible light.

The most familiar type of plastid is the **chloroplast,** illustrated in Figure 4-17. Each chloroplast encloses a system of flattened, membranous sacs called **thylakoids.** Chloroplasts are the organelles in a plant cell in which the energy of sunlight is converted into chemical energy in organic compounds. This conversion occurs in the thylakoids during the process of photosynthesis, which you will study in Chapter 6. Chloroplasts contain large amounts of a green pigment that gives leaves their green color. Different pigments in other types of plastids are responsible for the colors of fruits and flowers.

SECTION 4-2 REVIEW

1. Name the three main components of a eukaryotic cell.

2. Summarize the fluid mosaic model of the cell membrane.

3. Distinguish between the nucleus and the nucleolus.

4. Which organelles are surrounded by two membranes?

5. What structural feature do cilia and flagella have in common?

6. **CRITICAL THINKING** Plant cells have cell walls, but animal cells do not. Why do you think that is so?

Discovering a New World

HISTORICAL PERSPECTIVE

The first microscopes, made around 1600, had a single lens and were much like a powerful magnifying glass. Compound microscopes, those with two or more lenses, produced greater enlargement but caused blurred images. This problem, known as chromatic aberration, was not solved until more than a century later. Meanwhile, Anton van Leeuwenhoek, who lived in Holland from 1632 to 1723, made hundreds of simple, high-quality microscopes. He was the first person to view and describe the amazing miniature world of protozoa and bacteria.

Toy or Tool?

About 25 years after van Leeuwenhoek began his work with microscopes, Robert Hooke, a fellow scientist, noted that few scientists besides van Leeuwenhoek considered the microscope an essential tool. "I hear of none that make any other use of that instrument, but for diversion and pastime," Hooke wrote. *Diversion* and *pastime* are not words we usually connect with the microscope, a tool so basic to scientific work today that we can hardly imagine scientists, or students of science, being without one.

Why weren't more scientists using microscopes? The main reason is that early microscopes were of poor quality, and only an unusually diligent and persistent person could find them useful. Van Leeuwenhoek was such a person.

A linendraper by trade, van Leeuwenhoek spent most of his time on his hobby—science—and for him the microscope was a valuable

Anton van Leeuwenhoek

instrument. He ground his own high-quality lenses, more than 400 in his lifetime, and mounted them between thin brass plates. They magnified objects by 50 to 300 times, and van Leeuwenhoek never tired of peering through the lenses and making discoveries about animals, plants, and microorganisms.

Over a 50-year period beginning in 1673, van Leeuwenhoek sent letters to the British Royal Society describing his microscopic observations. Most of his letters were published in the society's journal, *Philosophical Transactions.*

Van Leeuwenhoek's first letter described what he called *animalcules,* or "tiny animals," which we now know as protozoa. He explained that he had found them

> *"in rain, which had stood but a few days in a new tub. . . . I saw, after divers observations, that the bodies consisted of 5, 6, 7, or 8 very clear globules."*

He said his animalcules sometimes "stuck out two little horns, which were continually moved, after the fashion of a horse's ears." Later, scientists would name them *Vorticella* and identify their "little horns" as *cilia,* or tiny hairs.

Father of Microbiology

Van Leeuwenhoek examined hundreds of objects, including the lenses of eyes, the striations of muscles, the mouthparts of insects, the detailed structures of plants, and many protozoa and bacteria found in rainwater, pond water, well water, saliva, and other liquids. He was the first person to accurately describe red blood cells.

Van Leeuwenhoek also examined human and animal spermatozoa and made correct guesses about the reproductive process of animals, even though fertilization would not be observed under the microscope until the 1800s. His observations disproved the long-held theory of spontaneous generation—the idea that life could grow out of nonliving substances. Some believed, for example, that fleas grew out of sand or dust, but van Leeuwenhoek refuted that idea in his letter to the Royal Society by describing the flea's development with great precision.

Van Leeuwenhoek's remarkable powers of observation enabled him to make accurate judgments not only of an object's structure but also of its size. For example, he thought 100 human red blood cells in a row would be nearly the width of a grain of coarse sand. That made each red cell about 8.5µm (0.0003 in.) in diameter, close to its actual measurement.

In addition to writing about his observations, van Leeuwenhoek drew sketches of what he saw. In fact, he was the first person to draw an image of bacteria; the drawing was published in *Philosophical Transactions* in 1683. Because of his studies of microorganisms, van Leeuwenhoek is often called the father of microbiology.

In 1674, van Leeuwenhoek sent a piece of cork, along with other samples, to the British Royal Society. This photograph shows what the piece of cork would have looked like through van Leeuwenhoek's most powerful microscope.

After van Leeuwenhoek

Even though van Leeuwenhoek had published reports about his many discoveries, the scientific community failed to recognize the microscope's significance for many years. In 1733, an amateur optician named Chester Moor Hall found a way to solve the persistent problem of chromatic aberration in compound lenses, and in 1774, the technique was applied to microscopes. By the 1820s, new types of microscopes were available, and the 1800s and 1900s brought frequent improvements. In 1931, the first electron microscope was invented, and in 1981, the scanning tunneling microscope began to reveal objects atom by atom. Today's work in microbiology, protozoology, bacteriology, and other fields depends on advanced microscopes, descendants of those simple lenses through which van Leeuwenhoek first saw his "animalcules."

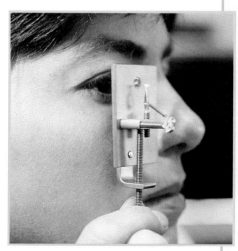

Van Leeuwenhoek's microscope consisted of a single lens. He placed a small drop of liquid on the tip of a fine point and peered through the lens to observe the miniature world hidden in the liquid. By turning a screw, van Leeuwenhoek could move the point closer to the lens, bringing objects in the liquid into focus.

SECTION

4-3

OBJECTIVES

▲

Distinguish between tissues, organs, and organ systems.

●

Describe the features of a colonial organism.

MULTICELLULAR ORGANIZATION

In a unicellular organism, one cell carries out all of the functions of life. In contrast, most cells in a multicellular organism are specialized to perform one or a few functions. Because of cell specialization, the cells of multicellular organisms depend on other cells in the organism for their survival.

TISSUES, ORGANS, AND ORGAN SYSTEMS

In most multicellular organisms, cells are organized into **tissues,** or groups of cells that carry out a specific function. In animals, epithelial tissue consists of sheets of closely packed cells that form surface coverings, such as the outermost living layer of the skin and the inside lining of the nose. The loosely scattered cells of connective tissue serve mainly to support and link together other tissues. Cells that pull against one another by contracting make up muscle tissue. Cells that are specialized for transmitting messages rapidly make up nervous tissue.

Several types of tissues that interact to perform a specific function form an **organ.** The stomach is one example of an organ. In the

FIGURE 4-18

Spongy tissue makes up the air sacs that in turn make up the lung, which is an organ. The lungs are part of the respiratory system.

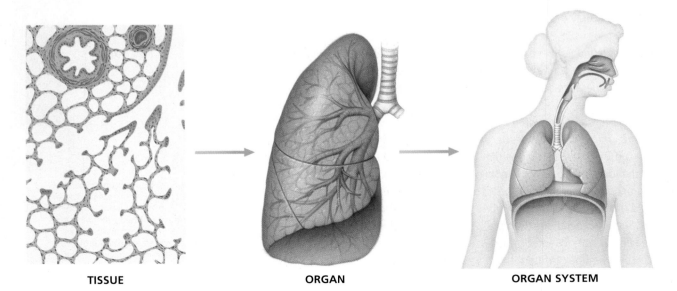

TISSUE   **ORGAN**   **ORGAN SYSTEM**

stomach, muscle tissue causes movement, epithelial tissue secretes enzymes, connective tissue holds the stomach together, and nervous tissue transmits messages back and forth between the stomach and the brain. All but the simplest animals have organs.

An **organ system** is made up of a group of organs that work together to perform a set of related tasks. For instance, the mouth, esophagus, stomach, intestines, and several other organs make up the digestive system. Each of these organs performs a specific function in the complex process of digesting food. Figure 4-18 illustrates the relationship between tissues and organs in another organ system, the respiratory system.

The different organ systems in a multicellular organism interact to carry out the processes of life. The digestive system, for example, extracts nutrients from food, while the respiratory system obtains oxygen from the environment and eliminates waste carbon dioxide. None of the body's organ systems could survive without the others.

Plants also have tissues and organs, although they are arranged somewhat differently from those in animals. A dermal tissue system forms the outer layer of a plant. A ground tissue system makes up the bulk of roots and stems. A vascular tissue system transports water throughout the plant. The four plant organs are roots, stems, leaves, and flowers.

EVOLUTION OF MULTI-CELLULAR ORGANIZATION

Fossil evidence suggests that the earliest cells on Earth were simple prokaryotes similar to some present-day bacteria. Like most bacteria, they lacked the internal structures required to synthesize their own nutrients. Instead, they depended on organic nutrients in the environment. As they reproduced and their numbers increased, however, they began to compete for limited environmental resources. Because of the increasing competition, cells with adaptations evolved. Some of these cells were eukaryotic. You will learn more about the evolution of prokaryotes and eukaryotes in Chapter 15.

Colonial Organizations

Eventually, some of the early unicellular eukaryotes may have begun to live in temporary groups, or colonies, with other cells of the same kind. Some of the cells in these colonies may have specialized in performing certain functions, such as converting energy. Biologists refer to such associations of cells as **colonial organisms.** A colonial organism is a collection of genetically identical cells that live together in a closely connected group.

An example of a colonial organism that exists today is the green alga *Volvox,* shown in Figure 4-19. A hollow *Volvox* sphere contains

Eco Connection

The Impact of Single Cells

Most people are familiar with the kinds of effects humans and other multicellular organisms can have on their environment. But single-celled organisms can also produce major environmental changes through their activities. One of the most important examples of such a change occurred about 2.8 billion years ago, when certain types of bacteria began producing oxygen as a byproduct of photosynthesis. As oxygen entered the Earth's atmosphere, the composition of the atmosphere changed dramatically. That set the stage for the evolution of animals and other organisms that require oxygen to live.

Even today, unicellular organisms continue to have a profound ecological impact. For example, about half the organic material produced through photosynthesis is made by single-celled eukaryotes known as algae. These simple but important organisms provide food for countless other organisms in marine and freshwater environments.

FIGURE 4-19

New *Volvox* colonies are formed in the interior of older ones and are released when the old colony ruptures. (LM 105×)

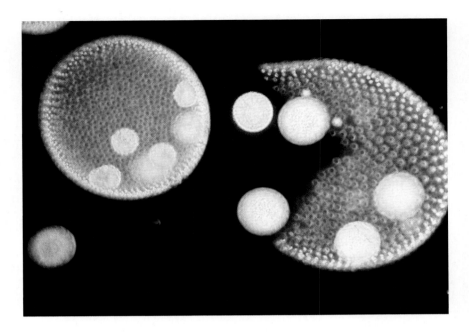

500 to 60,000 cells, each of which maintains its own individual existence. Many of the cells, though, carry out specific functions that benefit the whole colony. The outer cells use their flagella to propel the colony through the water. A few of the other cells are specialized for reproduction. They produce offspring colonies, which you can see in Figure 4-19 as the large green spheres contained within the main sphere.

Colonial organisms, such as *Volvox,* appear to straddle the border between a collection of unicellular organisms and a true multicellular organism. Although they lack tissues and organs, they exhibit the principle of cell specialization, which is found in all multicellular organisms. Biologists may be able to learn how multicellular organisms evolved by studying *Volvox* and other colonial organisms.

Many biologists believe that animals, plants, and fungi probably evolved from different varieties of colonial organisms hundreds of millions of years ago. Initially, all of the cells in each type of colony may have been very similar. As these primitive colonial organisms evolved, however, their cells became more specialized and less capable of living independently.

SECTION 4-3 REVIEW

1. What is a tissue?

2. What is an organ?

3. Give an example of an organ system, and name some of the parts that form it.

4. Name the plant tissue systems and organs.

5. To what extent are the individual cells within a *Volvox* colony independent of one another?

6. **CRITICAL THINKING** Green algae, such as *Codium,* enlarge by dividing the nucleus but do not form cell walls between the parent and offspring cells. Would you call *Codium* a unicellular or a multicellular organism? Explain your answer.

SUMMARY/VOCABULARY

4-1
- A cell is the smallest unit that can carry on all of the processes of life. The development of the microscope enabled scientists to take their first close look at cells.
- The cell theory states that (1) all living things are composed of one or more cells, (2) cells are the units of structure and function in an organism, and (3) cells come only from preexisting cells.

- The ratio of surface area to volume determines how large a cell can get. Most plant and animal cells are only about 10 to 50 μm in diameter.
- A cell's shape reflects its function.
- Eukaryotic cells contain a nucleus and membrane-bound organelles, but prokaryotic cells have neither.

Vocabulary

cell (69)	cell theory (69)	nucleus (72)	prokaryote (72)
cell membrane (72)	eukaryote (72)	organelle (71)	

4-2
- The cell membrane is selectively permeable and consists mostly of lipids and proteins. Both move constantly within the membrane, as described by the fluid mosaic model.
- Mitochondria are organelles in which the energy in organic compounds is transferred to ATP. Mitochondria are surrounded by a double membrane.
- Ribosomes are involved in the synthesis of proteins. Some ribosomes are free in the cytosol. Others are attached to the rough endoplasmic reticulum, which prepares proteins for export from the cell or insertion into the cell membrane. The smooth endoplasmic reticulum lacks ribosomes.
- The Golgi apparatus is the cell's processing, packaging, and secreting organelle.
- Lysosomes contain hydrolytic enzymes that digest organic compounds, old cell parts, and other materials.
- The cytoskeleton includes microfilaments and microtubules, strands of protein that help cells move and maintain their shape.

- Cilia and flagella assist in cell movement. Both are made of nine pairs of microtubules arranged around a central pair.
- The nucleus is surrounded by a double membrane and contains chromatin, a combination of DNA and protein. DNA stores hereditary information and directs the synthesis of RNA. RNA directs the synthesis of proteins in the cytosol.
- Plant cells contain three structures not found in animal cells: cell walls, vacuoles, and plastids.
- A rigid cell wall covers the cell membrane in plant cells and provides support and protection.
- Large fluid-filled vacuoles store enzymes and waste products within plant cells.
- Plastids store starch, fats, and pigments in plant cells. One type of plastid, the chloroplast, is the site where light energy is converted into chemical energy during photosynthesis.

Vocabulary

actin (79)	cytosol (75)	mitochondrion (76)	rough endoplasmic
cell wall (82)	endoplasmic reticulum (78)	nuclear envelope (81)	reticulum (78)
chloroplast (83)	flagellum (80)	nuclear matrix (81)	selectively permeable
chromatin (81)	fluid mosaic model (75)	nuclear pore (81)	membrane (73)
chromosome (81)	Golgi apparatus (78)	nucleolus (81)	smooth endoplasmic
cilium (80)	integral protein (74)	peripheral protein (74)	reticulum (78)
crista (77)	lysosome (79)	plastid (83)	spindle fiber (79)
cytoplasm (75)	microfilament (79)	ribosome (77)	thylakoid (83)
cytoskeleton (79)	microtubule (79)		vacuole (82)

4-3
- The cells in most multicellular organisms are organized into tissues, organs, and organ systems.
- The earliest cells on Earth were probably single-celled prokaryotes. Unicellular eukaryotes evolved later, followed by multicellular organisms.

- A colonial organism is a group of genetically identical cells that live together in closely connected groups. Some of the cells that make up a colonial organism are specialized to perform certain tasks, like movement or reproduction.

Vocabulary

colonial organism (87)   organ (86)   organ system (87)   tissue (86)

REVIEW

Vocabulary

1. The word part *eu-* means "true," *pro-* means "before," and *kary-* means "nucleus." With this information, explain why the words *prokaryote* and *eukaryote* are good terms for the organisms they describe. What do the terms suggest about the evolution of these organisms?
2. Compare cell membranes with cell walls in terms of their structure and function.
3. Explain the meaning of the terms *cytoplasm, cytosol,* and *cytoskeleton.*
4. Explain the relationship between microtubules, cilia, and flagella.
5. Choose the term that does not belong in the following group, and explain why it does not belong: Golgi apparatus, endoplasmic reticulum, chromatin, and mitochondria.

Multiple Choice

6. A prokaryote has (a) a nucleus (b) a cell membrane (c) membrane-bound organelles (d) all of the above.
7. The growth of cells is limited by the ratio between (a) volume and surface area (b) organelles and surface area (c) organelles and cytoplasm (d) nucleus and cytoplasm.
8. The major components of cell membranes are (a) lipids (b) proteins (c) nucleic acids (d) lipids and proteins.
9. The function of the Golgi apparatus is to (a) synthesize proteins (b) release energy (c) modify proteins for export (d) synthesize lipids.

10. Mitochondria (a) transport materials (b) release energy (c) make proteins (d) control cell division.
11. Ribosomes are (a) surrounded by a double membrane (b) manufactured in the cytosol (c) composed of proteins and RNA (d) attached to the smooth endoplasmic reticulum.
12. Lysosomes function in cells to (a) recycle cell parts (b) destroy viruses and bacteria (c) shape developing body parts (d) all of the above.
13. The nucleolus is (a) the control center of the cell (b) the storehouse of genetic information (c) the site where ribosomes are synthesized (d) none of the above.
14. Plastids (a) store pigments (b) store membranes (c) synthesize proteins (d) secrete proteins.
15. The stomach is an example of (a) a tissue (b) an organ (c) an organ system (d) none of the above.

Short Answer

16. Explain how microscopes have been helpful in the study of cells.
17. Identify the organelle illustrated in the micrograph below, and name the structures labeled *A* inside the organelle. Explain the significance of the shape of these structures.

A

18. What limits the maximum size of cells? Explain your answer.
19. How is the structure of cell membranes influenced by the reaction of phospholipids to water?
20. Why is the cell membrane said to be selectively permeable?
21. If a cell has a high energy requirement, would you expect it to have many or few mitochondria? Explain your answer.
22. Explain how the ribosomes, endoplasmic reticulum, and Golgi apparatus function together in protein synthesis.
23. **Unit 1—Cell Transport and Homeostasis**
 Write a report summarizing the roles of different types of cell-membrane proteins in the preservation of body organs donated for transplant.

CRITICAL THINKING

1. A mature human red blood cell has no nucleus or mitochondria. It consists primarily of a membrane surrounding hemoglobin, the protein molecule that carries oxygen. Suggest an advantage of the simple organization of human red blood cells.
2. The coils of a radiator provide a large surface area from which heat is radiated into a room. Which cell organelles have a structure similar to that of a radiator? How is their structure related to their function?
3. What characteristic of eukaryotic cells gives them a greater capacity for specialization than prokaryotic cells have? Explain your answer.
4. Livestock in the western United States often die after eating a locoweed, such as *Astragalus toanus.* The chemical that the plant contains is also poisonous to plants. How does locoweed keep from poisoning itself?
5. The graph below illustrates how the ratio between surface area and volume changes as a spherical cell's diameter increases. By what percentage does this ratio change when a cell grows from 1 μm to 2 μm in diameter? What is the maximum diameter the cell could

Area / Volume Ratio Versus Cell Size

EXTENSION

1. Read "The Nobel Prizes for 1999" in *Scientific American,* January 2000, on page 16. Prepare an oral report on how Günter Blobel, a scientist at Rockefeller University, won the Nobel Prize for Physiology or Medicine.
2. Use the resources in your school or public library to learn more about the work of Schleiden, Schwann, or Virchow. Write a brief report summarizing the processes that the researcher used to arrive at his conclusions about cells.
3. Place a sprig of the aquarium plant *Elodea* in water, and shine a bright light on it for an hour. Then examine a leaf under a light microscope, and make a drawing that indicates the direction of chloroplast movement. How do you think the movement of these organelles in response to light helps the cell to function?

Comparing Animal and Plant Cells

OBJECTIVE

- Examine the similarities and differences between the structure of cells in animals and the structure of cells in plants.

PROCESS SKILLS

- hypothesizing
- classifying
- observing

MATERIALS

- lab apron
- safety goggles
- compound light microscope
- forceps
- microscope slides and coverslips
- dropper bottle of Lugol's iodine solution
- prepared slides of human epithelial cells
- sprigs of *Elodea*
- prepared slides of three unknowns

Background

1. In this investigation, you will use a compound light microscope to observe cells from animals and plants. First you will view a prepared slide of human epithelial cells taken from the skin lining the mouth. Then you will make your own slide of a leaf from *Elodea,* a pond weed shown in the photograph on the next page.

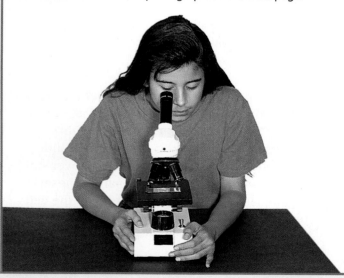

2. Based on your observations of human epithelial cells and *Elodea* leaf cells, you will be asked to classify three slides of unknown cells as either animal or plant cells.

3. Before you examine any cells, list the structural characteristics that distinguish animal cells from plant cells.

PART A   Animal Cells

1. **CAUTION   Handle glass microscope slides carefully. Dispose of broken glass separately in a container designated by your teacher.**

2. **CAUTION   Do not use electrical equipment with wet hands or near water.**

3. Examine a prepared slide of epithelial cells under low power. Locate cells that are separate from each other and place them in the center of the field of view. Examine the cells under high power. Adjust the diaphragm to reduce the light intensity and achieve greater clarity.

4. In your lab report, make a drawing of two or three cells as they appear under high power. Identify and label the cell membrane, the cytoplasm, the nuclear envelope, and the nucleus of one of the cells in your drawing.

PART B   Plant Cells

5. Carefully tear off a small leaf near the top of an *Elodea* sprig. Using forceps, place the whole leaf in a drop of water on a slide. Place a coverslip on top of the leaf.

6. Observe the leaf under low power. The outermost part of the cell is the cell wall. The many small, green organelles in the cells are chloroplasts.

7. Locate a cell that you can see clearly, and move the slide so that the cell is in the center of the field of view. Examine this cell under high power, and use the fine adjustment to bring the cell into focus.

8. Find an *Elodea* cell that is large enough to allow you to see the cell wall and the chloroplasts clearly. In your lab report, make a drawing of this cell. Label the cell wall and at least one chloroplast in your drawing.

9. The chloroplasts may be moving in some of the cells. If you observe no movement, warm the slide in your hand or shine a bright lamp on it for a minute or two. Then reexamine the slide under high power, and look for the movement of the cell's contents. This movement is called cytoplasmic streaming.

10. Because the cell membrane is pressed against the cell wall, you may not see it. Also, the abundance of chloroplasts may hide other organelles in the cells. You can make the cell membrane, vacuole, nucleus, and nucleolus more visible by making a stained wet-mount slide of *Elodea*.

11. ◆ ◆ ◆ Put on a lab apron and safety goggles. Prepare a wet-mount slide of *Elodea* as you did in step 4, but substitute Lugol's iodine solution for the water. Allow the iodine solution to diffuse throughout the leaf.

12. Observe the stained cells under low and high power. Make a drawing of a stained *Elodea* cell in your lab report. Label the central vacuole, nucleus, nucleolus, chloroplasts, cell wall, and cell membrane if they are visible.

PART C Identifying Unknown Cells

13. Make a data table like the one below to record your observations of the unknown specimens.

14. Obtain prepared slides of three unknown specimens from your teacher.

15. Observe each specimen under low and high power. In your data table, record the code number assigned to each unknown, each specimen's classification as plant or animal, and your reasons for classifying each specimen.

16. ◆ ◆ Clean up your materials and wash your hands before leaving the lab.

Analysis and Conclusions

1. According to your observations in this investigation, list several ways that plant and animal cells are structurally similar and several ways that they are different.

2. What do you think might be the function of cytoplasmic streaming in a plant cell? Lugol's iodine solution causes cytoplasmic streaming to stop. Why do you think this happens?

3. Which organelles that you read about in Chapter 4 did you not see in this investigation? Why do you think you were unable to see these organelles in your slides?

Further Inquiry

Use library resources to locate electron micrographs of cell structures that you were unable to see with the compound light microscope.

CLASSIFICATION OF UNKNOWN SPECIMENS		
Unknown (code number)	Classification (plant or animal)	Reasons for classification

HOMEOSTASIS AND TRANSPORT

A macrophage engulfs a human tumor cell. (SEM 3,520×)

FOCUS CONCEPT: *Stability and Homeostasis*

As you read, look for the ways that cells regulate the movement of materials across their membranes and thereby maintain internal balance despite changes in their environment.

Unit 1—*Cell Transport and Homeostasis*
Topics 3–6

5-1 *Passive Transport*

5-2 *Active Transport*

PASSIVE TRANSPORT

*Cell membranes help organisms maintain homeostasis by controlling what substances may enter or leave cells. Some substances can cross the cell membrane without any input of energy by the cell. The movement of such substances across the membrane is known as **passive transport.***

OBJECTIVES

▲

Explain how an equilibrium is established as a result of diffusion.

●

Distinguish between diffusion and osmosis.

■

Explain how substances cross the cell membrane through facilitated diffusion.

◆

Explain how ion channels assist the diffusion of ions across the cell membrane.

DIFFUSION

The simplest type of passive transport is diffusion. **Diffusion** is the movement of molecules from an area of higher concentration to an area of lower concentration. This difference in the concentration of molecules across a space is called a **concentration gradient.**

Consider what happens when you add a sugar cube to a beaker of water. As shown in Figure 5-1, the sugar cube sinks to the bottom of the beaker. That makes the concentration of sugar molecules much greater at the bottom of the beaker than at the top. As the cube dissolves, the sugar molecules begin to diffuse slowly through the water, moving from the bottom of the beaker to the top.

Diffusion is driven entirely by the kinetic energy the molecules possess. Because of their kinetic energy, molecules are in constant motion. They move randomly, traveling in a straight line until they hit an object, such as another molecule. When they hit something, they rebound and move off in a new direction, traveling in another straight line. If no object blocks their movement, they continue on their path. Thus, molecules tend to move "down" their concentration gradient, from areas where they are more concentrated to areas where they are less concentrated.

Equilibrium

In the absence of other influences, diffusion will eventually cause the concentration of molecules to be the same throughout the space the molecules occupy. When the concentration of the molecules of a substance is the same throughout a space, a state of **equilibrium** exists. Returning to the example in Figure 5-1, if the beaker of water is left undisturbed, at some point the concentration of sugar molecules will be the same throughout the beaker. The sugar concentration will then be at equilibrium.

FIGURE 5-1

Sugar molecules, initially in a high concentration at the bottom of a beaker, will move about randomly through diffusion. At equilibrium, the sugar concentration will be the same throughout the beaker. Diffusion occurs naturally because of the kinetic energy the molecules possess.

Sugar   Water

Observing Diffusion

Materials disposable gloves, lab apron, safety goggles, 600 mL beaker, 25 cm dialysis tubing, 15 mL starch solution (10 percent), 20 drops IKI, 300 mL water, 100 mL graduated cylinder, 20 cm piece of string (2)

Procedure

1. Put on your disposable gloves, lab apron, and safety goggles.
2. Pour 300 mL of water in the 600 mL beaker.
3. Add 20 drops of IKI to the water.
4. Open the dialysis tubing, and tie one end tightly with a piece of string.
5. Using the funnel, pour 15 mL of 10 percent starch solution into the dialysis tubing.
6. Tie the other end of the dialysis tubing tightly with the second piece of string, forming a sealed bag around the starch solution.
7. Place the bag into the solution in the beaker, and observe the setup for a color change.

Analysis What happened to the color in the bag? What happened to the color of the water around the bag? Explain your observations.

It is important to understand that even at equilibrium the random movement of molecules continues. But because there is no concentration gradient, molecules are just as likely to move in one direction as in any other. The random movements of many molecules in many directions balance one another, and equilibrium is maintained.

Diffusion Across Membranes

You learned in Chapter 4 that cell membranes allow some molecules to pass through, but not others. If a molecule can pass through a cell membrane, it will diffuse from an area of higher concentration on one side of the membrane to an area of lower concentration on the other side.

The ability of a molecule to diffuse across a cell membrane depends on the size and type of the molecule and on the chemical nature of the membrane. Remember from Chapter 4 that a membrane is made, in part, of a lipid bilayer and that certain proteins can form pores in the membrane. Molecules that can dissolve in lipids may pass through the membrane by diffusion. For example, because of their nonpolar nature, both carbon dioxide and oxygen dissolve in lipids. Molecules that are very small but not soluble in lipids may diffuse across the membrane by moving through the pores in the membrane.

OSMOSIS

Recall from Chapter 2 that a solution is composed of a solute dissolved in a solvent. In the sugar water described earlier, the solute was sugar and the solvent was water, and the solute molecules diffused through the solvent. It is also possible for solvent molecules to diffuse. In the case of cells, the solutes are organic and inorganic compounds, and the solvent is water. The process by which water molecules diffuse across a cell membrane from an area of higher concentration to an area of lower concentration is called **osmosis** (ahz-MOH-suhs). Because water moves down its concentration gradient, osmosis does not require cells to expend energy. Osmosis, therefore, is a type of passive transport.

Direction of Osmosis

The net direction of osmosis depends on the relative concentration of solutes on the two sides of the membrane. Examine Table 5-1. When the concentration of solute molecules outside the cell is *lower* than the concentration in the cytosol, the solution outside is **hypotonic** to the cytosol. In this situation, water diffuses *into* the cell until equilibrium is established. When the concentration of solute molecules outside the cell is *higher* than the concentration in the cytosol, the solution outside is **hypertonic** to the cytosol. In this situation, water diffuses *out of* the cell until equilibrium is established. When the concentrations of solutes outside and inside

TABLE 5-1   *Direction of Osmosis*

Condition	Net movement of water	
External solution is hypotonic to cytosol	into the cell	$H_2O \longrightarrow \quad \longleftarrow H_2O$
External solution is hypertonic to cytosol	out of the cell	$H_2O \longleftarrow \quad \longrightarrow H_2O$
External solution is isotonic to cytosol	none	$H_2O \rightleftarrows \quad \rightleftarrows H_2O$

the cell are equal, the outside solution is said to be **isotonic** to the cytosol. Under these conditions, water diffuses into and out of the cell at equal rates, so there is no net movement of water.

Notice that the prefixes *hypo-, hyper-,* and *iso-* refer to the relative solute concentrations of two solutions. Thus, if the solution outside the cell is *hypo*tonic to the cytosol, then the cytosol must be *hyper*tonic to that solution. Conversely, if the solution outside is *hyper*tonic to the cytosol, then the cytosol must be *hypo*tonic to the solution. Water tends to diffuse from hypotonic solutions to hypertonic solutions.

How Cells Deal with Osmosis

Cells that are exposed to an isotonic external environment usually have no difficulty keeping the movement of water across the cell membrane in balance. This is the case with the cells of vertebrate animals on land and of most other organisms living in the sea.

In contrast, many cells function in a hypotonic environment. Such is the case for unicellular freshwater organisms. Water constantly diffuses into these organisms. Because they require a relatively lower concentration of water in the cytosol to function normally, unicellular organisms must rid themselves of the excess water that enters by osmosis. Some of them, such as the paramecia shown in Figure 5-2, do this with **contractile vacuoles,** which are organelles that remove water. Contractile vacuoles collect the excess water and then contract, pumping the water out of the cell. Unlike diffusion and osmosis, this pumping action requires the cell to expend energy.

Other cells, including many of those in multicellular organisms, respond to hypotonic environments by pumping solutes out of the cytosol. This

FIGURE 5-2

The paramecia shown below live in fresh water, which is hypotonic to their cytosol. (a) Contractile vacuoles collect excess water that moves by osmosis into the cytosol. (b) The vacuoles then contract, returning the water to the outside of the cell. (LM 315×)

(a)

Vacuole filling with water

(b)

Vacuole contracting

(a) Hypotonic

(b) Hypertonic

Cell walls

FIGURE 5-3

These two photographs show cells in the skin of a red onion. (a) In a hypotonic environment, the cells are pressed against the cell walls (LM 90×). (b) In a hypertonic environment, the cells contract and pull away from the cell walls (LM 98×).

lowers the solute concentration in the cytosol, bringing it closer to the solute concentration in the environment. As a result, water molecules are less likely to diffuse into the cell.

Most of the time, plant cells also live in a hypotonic environment. In fact, the cells that make up plant roots may be surrounded by water. Water, therefore, moves by osmosis into plant cells, which swell as they fill with water. The swelling stops when the cell membrane is pressed against the inside of the cell wall, as Figure 5-3a shows. The cell wall is strong enough to resist the pressure exerted by the water inside the expanding cell. The pressure that water molecules exert against the cell wall is called **turgor pressure.**

In a hypertonic environment, water leaves the cells through osmosis. As shown in Figure 5-3b, the cells shrink away from the cell walls, and turgor pressure is lost. This condition is called **plasmolysis** (plaz-MAHL-uh-suhs). Plasmolysis is the reason that plants wilt if they don't receive enough water.

Some cells cannot compensate for changes in the solute concentration of their environment. Red blood cells in humans, for instance, lack contractile vacuoles, solute pumps, and cell walls. As you can see in Figure 5-4, these cells lose their normal shape when they are placed in an environment that is not isotonic to their

FIGURE 5-4

(a) In an environment that is isotonic to the cytosol, a human red blood cell keeps its normal shape—round and dimpled (SEM 37,125×). (b) In a hypertonic environment, the cell loses water and becomes shriveled (SEM 39,762×). (c) In a hypotonic environment, the cell gains water and swells (SEM 37,125×).

(a) Isotonic

(b) Hypertonic

(c) Hypotonic

cytosol. In a hypertonic environment, water leaves the cells, making them shrink and shrivel. In a hypotonic environment, water diffuses into the cells, causing them to swell and eventually burst. The bursting of cells is called **cytolysis** (sie-TAHL-uh-suhs).

FACILITATED DIFFUSION

Another type of passive transport is called **facilitated diffusion.** This process is used for molecules that cannot diffuse rapidly through cell membranes, even when there is a concentration gradient across the membrane. Such molecules may not be soluble in lipids, or they may be too large to pass through the pores in the membrane. In facilitated diffusion, the movement of these kinds of molecules across the cell membrane is assisted by specific proteins in the membrane. These proteins are known as **carrier proteins.**

The carrier proteins that serve in facilitated diffusion transport molecules from an area of higher concentration on one side of the membrane to an area of lower concentration on the other side. Because the molecules are moving down their concentration gradient, facilitated diffusion is passive transport. The cell does not have to supply additional energy to make it happen.

Figure 5-5 shows a model of how facilitated diffusion is thought to work. According to the model, a carrier protein binds to the molecule it transports. As soon as the carrier protein binds to the molecule, the carrier protein changes shape. This altered shape may shield the molecule from the hydrophobic interior of the lipid bilayer. Once shielded, the molecule can be transported across the cell membrane. On the other side of the membrane, the molecule is released from the carrier protein, which then returns to its original shape.

Word Roots and Origins

cytolysis

from the Greek *kytos,* meaning "hollow vessel," and *lysis,* meaning "loosening"

FIGURE 5-5

Facilitated diffusion occurs in three steps. (a) A carrier protein binds to a molecule on one side of the cell membrane. (b) The carrier protein changes shape, shielding the molecule from the interior of the membrane. (c) The molecule is released on the other side of the membrane.

(a)   **(b)**   **(c)**

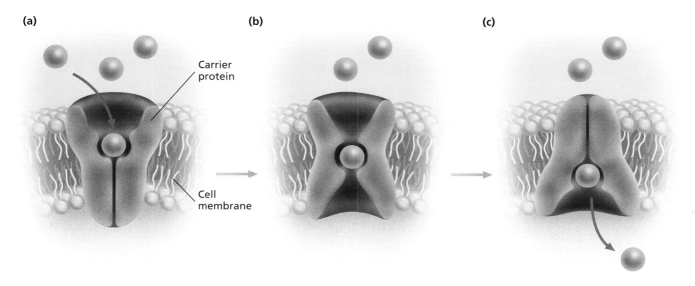

Carrier protein

Cell membrane

Purifying Water with Membranes

The tendency for water molecules to diffuse across membranes can be used to extract pure water from a mixture of water and solutes. If a dilute solution is separated from a more concentrated solution by a selectively permeable membrane, osmosis will occur, as water molecules diffuse from the dilute solution to the concentrated solution. However, if enough external pressure is applied to the concentrated solution, the opposite will happen: water molecules will diffuse from the concentrated solution to the dilute solution. This process, called reverse osmosis, effectively moves most of the water to one side of the membrane and leaves most of the solutes on the other side.

Reverse osmosis was initially developed for desalination plants, which produce fresh water from sea water. It is now also used to purify polluted water from a variety of sources, including manufacturing facilities and sanitary landfills. After the polluted water from these sources is purified through reverse osmosis, it is clean enough to be returned safely to the environment.

A good example of facilitated diffusion is the transport of glucose. As you learned in Chapter 3, many cells depend on glucose for much of their energy needs. But glucose molecules are too large to diffuse quickly across cell membranes. When the level of glucose within a cell is lower than the level of glucose outside the cell, carrier proteins accelerate the movement of glucose into the cell.

The transport of glucose illustrates two important properties of facilitated diffusion. First, facilitated diffusion can help substances move either into or out of a cell, depending on the concentration gradient. Thus, when the level of glucose is higher inside a cell than it is outside the cell, facilitated diffusion speeds the diffusion of glucose out of the cell. Second, the carrier proteins involved in facilitated diffusion are each specific for one type of molecule. For example, the carrier protein that helps with the diffusion of glucose and other simple sugars does not assist with the diffusion of amino acids.

DIFFUSION THROUGH ION CHANNELS

Another type of passive transport involves membrane proteins known as **ion channels.** Ions such as sodium (Na^+), potassium (K^+), calcium (Ca^{2+}), and chloride (Cl^-) are important for a variety of cell functions. Because they are not soluble in lipids, however, ions cannot diffuse across the lipid bilayer without assistance. Ion channels provide small passageways across the cell membrane through which ions can diffuse. Each type of ion channel is usually specific for one type of ion. Thus, most Na^+ ion channels will allow Na^+ ions to pass through them, but they will not accept Ca^{2+} or Cl^- ions.

Some ion channels are always open. Others have "gates" that open to allow ions to pass or close to stop their passage. The gates may open or close in response to three kinds of stimuli: stretching of the cell membrane, electrical signals, or chemicals in the cytosol or external environment. These stimuli therefore control the ability of specific ions to cross the cell membrane.

SECTION 5-1 REVIEW

1. Toward what condition does diffusion eventually lead, in the absence of other influences?

2. How is osmosis related to diffusion?

3. If the concentration of solute molecules outside a cell is lower than the concentration in the cytosol, is the external solution hypotonic, hypertonic, or isotonic to the cytosol?

4. What role do carrier proteins play in facilitated diffusion?

5. How is facilitated diffusion similar to diffusion through ion channels?

6. CRITICAL THINKING Sea water has a higher concentration of solutes than do human body cells. Why might drinking large amounts of sea water be dangerous for humans?

ACTIVE TRANSPORT

*I*n many cases, cells must move materials up their concentration gradient, from an area of lower concentration to an area of higher concentration. Such movement of materials is known as **active transport.** Unlike passive transport, active transport requires a cell to expend energy.

CELL MEMBRANE PUMPS

Carrier proteins not only assist in passive transport but also help with some types of active transport. The carrier proteins that serve in active transport are often called cell membrane "pumps" because they move substances up their concentration gradients. In other respects, the carrier proteins involved in facilitated diffusion and those involved in active transport are very similar. In both, the protein first binds to a specific kind of molecule on one side of the cell membrane. Once it is bound to the molecule, the protein changes shape, shielding the molecule from the hydrophobic interior of the lipid bilayer. The protein then transports the molecule across the membrane and releases it on the other side.

Sodium-Potassium Pump

One example of active transport in animal cells involves a carrier protein known as the **sodium-potassium pump.** As its name suggests, this protein transports Na^+ ions and K^+ ions up their concentration gradients. To function normally, many types of animal cells must have a higher concentration of Na^+ ions outside the cell and a higher concentration of K^+ ions inside the cell. The sodium-potassium pump works to maintain these concentration differences.

Follow the steps in Figure 5-6 to see how the sodium-potassium pump operates. First, three Na^+ ions bind to the carrier protein on the cytosol side of the membrane, as shown in Figure 5-6a. At the same time, the carrier protein splits a phosphate group from a molecule of ATP. As you can see in Figure 5-6b, the phosphate group also binds to the carrier protein. Figure 5-6c shows how the splitting of ATP supplies the energy needed to change the shape of the carrier protein. With its new shape, the protein carries the three Na^+ ions across the membrane and then releases them outside the cell.

At this point, the carrier protein has the shape it needs to bind two K^+ ions outside the cell, as Figure 5-6d shows. When the K^+ ions bind, the phosphate group is released, as indicated in Figure 5-6e, and the carrier protein changes shape again. This time, the change

SECTION

5-2

OBJECTIVES

▲

Distinguish between passive transport and active transport.

●

Explain how the sodium-potassium pump operates.

■

Compare and contrast endocytosis and exocytosis.

internetconnect

SC*i*LINKS
NSTA

TOPIC: Active transport
GO TO: www.scilinks.org
KEYWORD: HM101

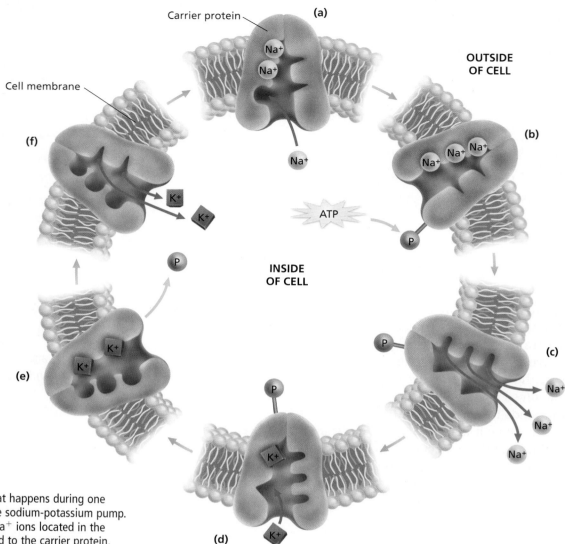

Carrier protein

(a)

OUTSIDE OF CELL

Na+
Na+

Na+

(b)

Na+ Na+ Na+
Na+

ATP

P

INSIDE OF CELL

P

(c)

Na+

Na+

Na+

Cell membrane

(f)

K+

K+

P

K+

K+

(e)

P

K+

(d)

K+

FIGURE 5-6

Follow what happens during one cycle of the sodium-potassium pump. (a) Three Na+ ions located in the cytosol bind to the carrier protein. (b) A phosphate group, represented by the letter P in the diagram, is removed from ATP and bound to the carrier protein. (c) The binding of the phosphate group changes the shape of the carrier protein, allowing the three Na+ ions to be released into the cell's environment. (d) Two K+ ions located outside the cell bind to the carrier protein. (e) The phosphate group is released, changing the shape of the carrier protein again. (f) The two K+ ions are released into the cytosol, and the cycle is ready to repeat.

in shape causes the carrier protein to release the two K+ ions inside the cell. As you can see in Figure 5-6f, at this point the carrier protein is ready to begin the process again. Thus, a complete cycle of the sodium-potassium pump transports three Na+ ions outside the cell and two K+ ions inside the cell. At top speed, the sodium-potassium pump can transport about 450 Na+ ions and 300 K+ ions per second.

The exchange of three Na+ ions for two K+ ions creates an electrical gradient across the cell membrane. That is, the outside of the membrane becomes positively charged and the inside of the membrane becomes negatively charged. In this way, the two sides of the cell membrane are like the positive and negative terminals of a battery. This difference in charge is important for the conduction of electrical impulses along nerve cells, as you will learn in Chapter 50. The sodium-potassium pump is only one example of a cell membrane pump. Other pumps work in similar ways to transport important metabolic materials across cell membranes.

ENDOCYTOSIS AND EXOCYTOSIS

Some substances, such as macromolecules and food particles, are too large to pass through the cell membrane by the transport processes you have studied so far. Cells employ two other transport mechanisms—endocytosis and exocytosis—to move such substances across their membranes. Endocytosis and exocytosis are also used to transport large quantities of small molecules into or out of cells at a single time. Both endocytosis and exocytosis require cells to expend energy. Therefore, they are types of active transport.

internet connect

SCi LINKS
NSTA

TOPIC: Endocytosis
GO TO: www.scilinks.org
KEYWORD: HM103

Endocytosis

Endocytosis (EN-doh-sie-TOH-suhs) is the process by which cells ingest external fluid, macromolecules, and large particles, including other cells. As you can see in Figure 5-7, these external materials are enclosed by a portion of the cell, which folds into itself and forms a pouch. The pouch then pinches off from the cell membrane and becomes a membrane-bound organelle called a **vesicle.** Some of the vesicles fuse with lysosomes, and their contents are digested by lysosomal enzymes. Other vesicles that form during endocytosis fuse with other membrane-bound organelles.

Biologists distinguish two types of endocytosis, based on the kind of material that is taken into the cell: **pinocytosis** (PIN-oh-sie-TOH-suhs) involves the transport of solutes or fluids, while **phagocytosis** (FAG-oh-sie-TOH-suhs) is the movement of large particles or whole cells. Many unicellular organisms feed by phagocytosis. In addition, certain cells in animals use phagocytosis to ingest bacteria and viruses that

FIGURE 5-7

During endocytosis, the cell membrane folds in and forms a small pouch. The pouch then pinches off from the cell membrane to become a vesicle.

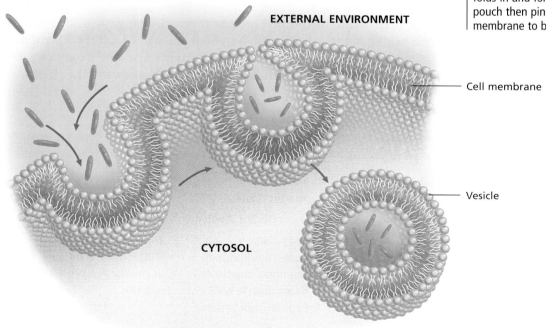

EXTERNAL ENVIRONMENT

Cell membrane

Vesicle

CYTOSOL

FIGURE 5-8

During exocytosis, a vesicle moves to the cell membrane, fuses with it, and then releases its contents to the outside of the cell.

Cell membrane

Vesicle

CYTOSOL

FIGURE 5-9

The vesicle shown here has just fused with the cell membrane, and the vesicle's contents are entering the external environment of the cell. (TEM, 71,250)

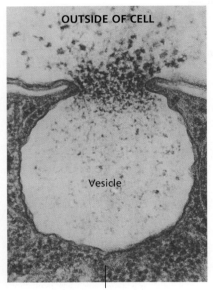

OUTSIDE OF CELL

Vesicle

INSIDE OF CELL

invade the body. These cells, known as **phagocytes,** allow lysosomes to fuse with the vesicles that contain the ingested bacteria and viruses. Lysosomal enzymes then destroy the bacteria and viruses before they can harm the animal.

Exocytosis

Exocytosis (EK-soh-sie-TOH-suhs), illustrated in Figure 5-8, is essentially the reverse of endocytosis. During exocytosis, vesicles in the cytoplasm fuse with the cell membrane, releasing their contents into the cell's external environment. Figure 5-9 shows a vesicle in the process of exocytosis. Cells may use exocytosis to release large molecules such as proteins. Recall that proteins are made on ribosomes and packaged into vesicles by the Golgi apparatus. The vesicles then move to the cell membrane and fuse with it, delivering the proteins outside the cell. As you'll learn in Chapters 50 and 51, cells in the nervous and endocrine systems also use exocytosis to release small molecules that control the activities of other cells.

SECTION 5-2 REVIEW

1. Explain the difference between passive transport and active transport.

2. What function do carrier proteins perform in active transport?

3. What provides the energy that drives the sodium-potassium pump?

4. Explain the difference between pinocytosis and phagocytosis.

5. Describe the steps involved in exocytosis.

6. **CRITICAL THINKING** During intense exercise, potassium tends to accumulate in the fluid surrounding muscle cells. What membrane protein helps muscle cells counteract this tendency? Explain your answer.

5-1
- Passive transport involves the movement of molecules across the cell membrane without an input of energy by the cell.
- Diffusion is the movement of molecules from an area of higher concentration to an area of lower concentration, driven by the molecules' kinetic energy. It eventually leads to equilibrium, a condition in which the concentration of the molecules is the same throughout a space or on both sides of a membrane.
- Molecules can diffuse across a cell membrane by dissolving in the lipid bilayer or by passing through pores in the membrane.
- Osmosis is the diffusion of water across a membrane. The net direction of osmosis is determined by the relative solute concentrations on the two sides of the membrane.
- When the solute concentration outside the cell is lower than that in the cytosol, the solution outside is hypotonic to the cytosol, and water will diffuse into the cell.

- When the solute concentration outside the cell is higher than that in the cytosol, the solution outside is hypertonic to the cytosol, and water will diffuse out of the cell.
- When the solute concentrations outside and inside the cell are equal, the solution outside is isotonic, and there will be no net movement of water.
- To remain alive, cells must compensate for the water that enters the cell in hypotonic environments and leaves the cell in hypertonic environments.
- In facilitated diffusion, a carrier protein binds to a molecule on one side of the cell membrane. The protein then changes its shape and transports the molecule down its concentration gradient to the other side of the membrane.
- Ion channels are proteins that provide small passageways across the cell membrane through which specific ions can diffuse.

Vocabulary

carrier protein (99)	diffusion (95)	hypotonic (96)	passive transport (95)
concentration gradient (95)	equilibrium (95)	ion channel (100)	plasmolysis (98)
contractile vacuole (97)	facilitated diffusion (99)	isotonic (97)	turgor pressure (98)
cytolysis (99)	hypertonic (96)	osmosis (96)	

5-2
- Active transport moves molecules across the cell membrane from an area of lower concentration to an area of higher concentration. It requires cells to expend energy.
- Some types of active transport are performed by carrier proteins called cell membrane pumps.
- One example of a cell membrane pump is the sodium-potassium pump. It moves three Na^+ ions into the cell's external environment for every two K^+ ions it moves into the cytosol. ATP supplies the energy that drives the pump.
- Endocytosis and exocytosis are active trans-

port mechanisms in which large substances cross the membrane inside vesicles.
- In endocytosis, the cell membrane folds around something in the external environment and forms a pouch. The pouch then pinches off and becomes a vesicle in the cytoplasm. Endocytosis includes pinocytosis, in which the vesicle contains solutes or fluids, and phagocytosis, in which the vesicle contains large particles or cells.
- In exocytosis, vesicles made by the cell fuse with the cell membrane, releasing their contents into the external environment.

Vocabulary

active transport (101)	phagocyte (104)	sodium-potassium
endocytosis (103)	phagocytosis (103)	pump (101)
exocytosis (104)	pinocytosis (103)	vesicle (103)

REVIEW

Vocabulary

1. Distinguish between diffusion and facilitated diffusion.
2. What does it mean to say that two solutions are isotonic?
3. How is plasmolysis related to turgor pressure in plant cells?
4. What is a contractile vacuole, and how does it function?
5. The word part *pino-* means "to drink," *phago-* means "to eat," and *cyto-* means "cell." With this information, explain why the words *pinocytosis* and *phagocytosis* are good names for the processes they describe.

Multiple Choice

6. During diffusion, molecules tend to move (a) up their concentration gradient (b) down their concentration gradient (c) in a direction that doesn't depend on the concentration gradient (d) from an area of lower concentration to an area of higher concentration.
7. The part of a cell that functions to maintain homeostasis relative to the cell's environment is the (a) cytosol (b) Golgi apparatus (c) nucleus (d) cell membrane.
8. Ion channels aid the movement of (a) molecules up a concentration gradient (b) carrier proteins within the lipid bilayer (c) ions across a cell membrane (d) water across a cell membrane.
9. Glucose enters a cell most rapidly by (a) facilitated diffusion (b) diffusion (c) osmosis (d) phagocytosis.
10. When the cells in a plant have low turgor pressure, the plant (a) is rigid (b) dies (c) wilts (d) explodes.
11. The sodium-potassium pump transports (a) Na^+ into the cell and K^+ out of the cell (b) Na^+ out of the cell and K^+ into the cell (c) both Na^+ and K^+ into the cell (d) both Na^+ and K^+ out of the cell.
12. A cell must expend energy to transport substances using (a) cell membrane pumps (b) facilitated diffusion (c) ion channels (d) osmosis.
13. Some animal cells engulf, digest, and destroy invading bacteria through the process of (a) exocytosis (b) phagocytosis (c) pinocytosis (d) all of the above.
14. Carrier proteins are important in (a) osmosis (b) endocytosis (c) diffusion (d) facilitated diffusion.
15. The drawing below shows a plant cell after the solute concentration of its environment has been changed. The new external environment is most likely (a) isotonic (b) hypertonic (c) hypotonic (d) none of the above.

Short Answer

16. What does it mean to say that diffusion eventually results in equilibrium?
17. Can all molecules diffuse through all cell membranes? Explain your answer.
18. Describe three structures characteristic of plant cells. Explain the function of each.
19. What determines the direction of net movement of water across a cell membrane?
20. How does the lipid bilayer of a membrane form a barrier to molecules?
21. How can a cell that consumes glucose speed up its intake of glucose from the environment?
22. How is ATP involved in maintaining the sodium and potassium gradients across a cell membrane?
23. Distinguish between endocytosis and exocytosis.
24. Write a report summarizing the roles of osmosis and diffusion in the preservation of body organs donated for transplants. Why must organs be preserved in special solutions prior to a transplant? Find out what kinds of substances these solutions contain.

CRITICAL THINKING

1. There is a higher concentration of air molecules inside an inflated balloon than there is outside the balloon. Because of their constant random motion, the molecules inside press against the balloon and keep it taut. How is the pressure exerted by these air molecules similar to turgor pressure? How is it different?

2. Sometimes water seeps through the concrete wall of a basement after a heavy rain, and the homeowner must remove it with a sump pump. How can this situation be compared to the action of a unicellular organism that lives in a pond?

3. When a cell takes in substances through endocytosis, the cell membrane forms an inside-out vesicle. That is, the outside of the cell membrane becomes the inside of the vesicle. What might this suggest about the structure of the cell membrane?

4. If a cell were exposed to a poison that blocked the cell's ability to manufacture ATP, what effect would that have on the cell membrane's transport processes?

5. Some plant cells have carrier proteins that transport sugar molecules and hydrogen ions (H^+) into the cytosol at the same time. These carrier proteins move sugar molecules up their gradient as hydrogen ions move down their gradient. How would the transport of sugar into these cells affect the pH of the cells' external environment? What would happen to the transport of sugar if hydrogen ions were removed from the external environment?

6. A gelatin block is prepared with a chemical indicator that turns pink in the presence of a base. The block is enclosed in a membrane and placed in a beaker of ammonium hydroxide solution. After half an hour, the block begins to turn pink. Account for the gelatin's pink color.

7. The two curves below show the rate at which glucose is transported across a cell membrane versus the concentration gradient of glucose. One curve represents the diffusion of glucose through the lipid bilayer, and the other curve represents the transport of glucose by facilitated diffusion. Which curve corresponds to facilitated diffusion? Explain your reasoning.

Glucose Transport

Rate of transport of glucose

X

Y

Glucose concentration gradient

EXTENSION

1. Read "Coming to Grips with the Golgi" in *Science*, December 18, 1999, on page 2169. Describe how the cisternal maturation model of the Golgi system differs from the vesicular transport model.

2. Kidney dialysis is the artificial filtering of blood to remove wastes in patients whose kidneys can no longer function well. Selectively permeable membranes are used in kidney dialysis and in other areas of medicine. Consult your local hospital, and obtain information on how kidney dialysis is performed and on the medical condition of the people who receive dialysis treatment.

3. Examine a number of food items at a grocery store. Find at least four foods for which salt is listed as a preservative. Keeping in mind what you have learned about osmosis, explain why salt is often used to preserve food.

INTERACTIVE EXPLORATION

Exploring the Role of Osmosis in Cystic Fibrosis

◄ ►

OBJECTIVES

- Simulate the effects of three different genotypes on the movement of water molecules and chloride ions through the cell membrane.
- Relate the symptoms of cystic fibrosis to the ability of water molecules and chloride ions to pass through the cell membrane.

MATERIALS

- computer with CD-ROM drive
- CD-ROM *Interactive Explorations in Biology: Human Biology*

Background

Cystic fibrosis is a fatal genetic disease that results from the failure of chloride ions (Cl^-) to pass through the cell membrane. As a result, chloride ions accumulate inside the cells of the body, drawing water into the cells. When this happens in the lungs, pancreas, and liver, a thick mucus builds up on the lining of these organs. The severe congestion that gradually develops usually causes death by the age of 30 in afflicted individuals.

In this interactive exploration, you will examine the three possible pairs of genes that an individual can have: two normal genes, represented by $+/+$; one cystic fibrosis gene and one normal gene, represented by cf/$+$; and two cystic fibrosis genes, represented by cf/cf. Then you will explore how these genetic combinations affect the membrane proteins involved in transporting Cl^- ions through the cell membrane.

Prelab Preparation

1. Load and start the program Cystic Fibrosis. Click the Topic Information button on the Navigation palette. Read the focus questions, and review the following concepts: Transport Channels, Osmosis, Mutation, and Cystic Fibrosis.

2. Click the word *File* at the top left of the screen, and select Interactive Exploration Help. Listen to the instructions for operating the exploration. Click the Exploration button at the bottom right of the screen to begin the exploration. You will see an animated drawing like the one below.

FEEDBACK METERS

Cl^- Ion Transfer: *the rate at which chloride ions move across the membrane*

Mucus Buildup: *how much mucus has accumulated on the cell*

Exterior/Interior Cl^- Concentration: *ratio of chloride ion concentration outside the cell to concentration inside the cell*

Exterior/Interior Water Concentration: *ratio of number of water molecules outside the cell to number inside the cell*

VARIABLE

Type of Mutation: *allows you to select one of three genotypes: +/+, cf/+, or cf/cf*

CHLORIDE ION AND WATER CONCENTRATION INSIDE CELLS

Genetic makeup	Exterior/interior Cl^- concentration	Exterior/interior water concentration	Mucus buildup
+/+	100%	normal	normal
cf/+	50%	normal	normal
cf/cf	20%	low	low

Procedure

Create a table like the one above for recording your data.

PART A Two Normal Genes (+/+)

1. Move the pointer to the Type of Mutation box, and click the +/+ button. The transport of Cl^- ions and water molecules in a person with this gene combination is normal. Note that water molecules and Cl^- ions are located both outside the cell (the portion of the screen above the cell membrane) and inside the cell (the portion of the screen below the cell membrane). Also note the position of the two CF proteins in the cell membrane.

2. Click the Start button to begin the simulation. Allow the simulation to run for two to three minutes. Describe how water molecules pass through the cell membrane. How does this differ from the passage of Cl^- ions through the membrane? What appears to be the function of the two CF proteins?

3. Click the Stop button. In your table, record the Exterior/Interior Cl^- Concentration, the Exterior/Interior Water Concentration, and the amount of mucus buildup outside the cell membrane.

PART B One Cystic Fibrosis Gene and One Normal Gene (cf/+)

4. Move the pointer to the Type of Mutation box, and click the cf/+ button. Describe what happens to the CF protein shown on the left and how this affects the Cl^- ion channel.

5. Click the Start button, and allow the simulation to run for two to three minutes. Describe the changes in the way water molecules and Cl^- ions move through the membrane. How will the change in the movement of water molecules and Cl^- ions affect the external surface of the cell?

6. Click the Stop button. In your table, record the same three variables that you recorded in step 3. On which side of the membrane are chloride ions at the higher concentration? On which side is water at the higher concentration? Compare the results with those you obtained in Part A, and explain any differences.

PART C Two Cystic Fibrosis Genes (cf/cf)

7. Move the pointer to the Type of Mutation box, and click the cf/cf button. An individual with this gene combination will be afflicted with cystic fibrosis. Describe what happens to both CF membrane proteins and how this affects the Cl^- ion channels.

8. Click the Start button, and allow the simulation to run for two to three minutes. Describe the changes in the movement of water molecules and Cl^- ions through the membrane. How will the external surface of the cell be affected?

9. Click the Stop button. Describe the difference between the cell's external environment and its internal environment. In your table, record the same variables that you recorded in steps 3 and 6. On which side of the membrane are chloride ions at the higher concentration? Compare the results with those you obtained in Parts A and B, and explain any differences.

Analysis and Conclusions

1. Why are the Cl^- ion channels, but not the water channels, said to have gates?

2. Use the term *hypotonic, hypertonic,* or *isotonic* to describe the cells that line the organs of individuals with cystic fibrosis.

3. How does an accumulation of chloride ions inside a cell result in a thickening of the mucus outside the cell?

PHOTOSYNTHESIS

Through photosynthesis, these corn plants obtain energy from the sun and store it in organic compounds.

FOCUS CONCEPT: *Matter, Energy, and Organization*

As you read about photosynthesis, notice the mechanisms in cells that keep the process operating.

Unit 2—*Photosynthesis*
Topics 1–6

CAPTURING THE ENERGY IN LIGHT

*All organisms use energy to carry out the functions of life. Some organisms obtain this energy directly from sunlight. They capture part of the energy in light and store it within organic compounds. The process by which this energy transfer takes place is called **photosynthesis.***

OBJECTIVES

▲

Explain how the structure of the chloroplast relates to its function.

●

Describe the role of chlorophylls and other pigments in photosynthesis.

■

Summarize the main events of electron transport.

◆

Describe what happens to a water molecule in photosynthesis.

▲

Explain how ATP is synthesized during the light reactions.

ENERGY FOR LIFE PROCESSES

You learned in Chapter 1 that organisms can be classified according to how they obtain energy. Organisms that manufacture their own food from inorganic substances and energy are autotrophs. Most autotrophs use photosynthesis to convert light energy from the sun into chemical energy, which they then store in various organic compounds, primarily carbohydrates. Plants are the most common example of photosynthetic organisms, but algae and some bacteria can also make their own organic compounds through photosynthesis.

Recall that animals and other organisms that cannot manufacture their own organic compounds from inorganic substances are called heterotrophs. Heterotrophs obtain food by eating autotrophs or by eating other heterotrophs that feed on autotrophs. For example, a caterpillar is a heterotroph that feeds directly on an autotroph, grass. A bird that eats caterpillars is also a heterotroph. The food that fuels the bird originates with autotrophs, but it passes *indirectly* to the bird through the caterpillars. In a similar way, all life ultimately depends on autotrophs.

Photosynthesis involves a complex series of chemical reactions, in which the product of one reaction is consumed in the next reaction. A series of reactions linked in this way is referred to as a **biochemical pathway.**

As you can see in Figure 6-1, autotrophs use the biochemical pathways of photosynthesis to manufacture organic compounds from carbon dioxide (CO_2) and water. During this conversion, molecular oxygen (O_2) is released.

Some of the energy stored in organic compounds is released by cells in another set of biochemical pathways, known as cellular

FIGURE 6-1

Many autotrophs produce organic compounds and oxygen through photosynthesis. Both autotrophs and heterotrophs produce carbon dioxide and water through cellular respiration.

respiration. As Figure 6-1 indicates, both autotrophs and heterotrophs perform cellular respiration. During cellular respiration in most organisms, organic compounds are combined with O_2 to produce ATP, yielding CO_2 and water as waste products. Thus, the products of photosynthesis, organic compounds and O_2, are reactants used in cellular respiration. The waste products of cellular respiration, CO_2 and water, are reactants used in photosynthesis. You will learn more about cellular respiration in Chapter 7. The rest of this chapter will focus on photosynthesis in plants.

LIGHT ABSORPTION IN CHLOROPLASTS

In plants, the initial reactions in photosynthesis are known collectively as the **light reactions.** They begin with the absorption of light in chloroplasts. Remember from Chapter 4 that a chloroplast is an organelle found in the cells of plants and in unicellular eukaryotes known as algae. While some algae may contain a single large chloroplast, a cell in the leaf of a plant may have 50 or more chloroplasts.

Most chloroplasts are similar in structure, regardless of the organism in which they are found. As you learned in Chapter 4, each chloroplast is surrounded by a pair of membranes. Inside the inner membrane is another system of membranes, arranged as flattened sacs called thylakoids. Figure 6-2 shows that the thylakoids are interconnected and that some are layered on top of one another to form stacks called **grana** (GRAY-nuh). Surrounding the thylakoids is a solution called the **stroma** (STROH-muh).

Light and Pigments

To explain how chloroplasts absorb light in photosynthesis, it is important to understand some of the properties of light. Light from the sun appears white, but it is actually composed of a variety of colors. As Figure 6-3 demonstrates, you can separate white light into its component colors by passing the light through a prism. The resulting array of colors, ranging from red at one end to violet at the other, is called the **visible spectrum.**

Light travels through space as waves of energy. These waves are analogous to the waves that travel

FIGURE 6-2

Photosynthesis in eukaryotes occurs inside the chloroplasts. The light reactions of photosynthesis take place in the thylakoids, which are stacked to form grana.

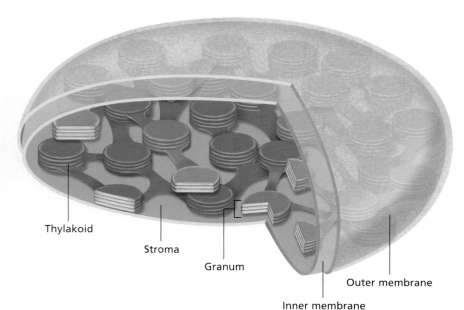

Thylakoid

Stroma

Granum

Inner membrane

Outer membrane

across a body of water when an object hits the surface. Like water waves, light waves can be measured in terms of their **wavelength,** the distance between crests in a wave. You can see in Figure 6-3 that the different colors in the visible spectrum have different wavelengths.

When white light strikes an object, its component colors can be reflected, transmitted, or absorbed by the object. However, the various colors will react differently if the object contains a **pigment,** which is a compound that absorbs light. Most pigments absorb certain colors more strongly than others. By absorbing certain colors, a pigment subtracts those colors from the visible spectrum. Therefore, the light that is reflected or transmitted by the pigment no longer appears white. For example, the lenses in green-tinted sunglasses contain a pigment that reflects and transmits green light and absorbs the other colors. As a result, the lenses look green.

Chloroplast Pigments

Located in the membrane of the thylakoids are a variety of pigments, the most important of which are called **chlorophylls** (KLOHR-uh-FILZ). There are several different types of chlorophylls. The two most common types are designated chlorophyll *a* and chlorophyll *b*.

A slight difference in molecular structure between chlorophyll *a* and chlorophyll *b* causes the two molecules to absorb different colors of light. As Figure 6-4 shows, chlorophyll *a* absorbs less blue light but more red light than chlorophyll *b* absorbs. Neither chlorophyll *a* nor chlorophyll *b* absorbs much green light. Instead, they allow green light to be reflected or transmitted. That is why young leaves and other plant structures that contain large amounts of chlorophyll look green.

Only chlorophyll *a* is directly involved in the light reactions of photosynthesis. Chlorophyll *b* assists chlorophyll *a* in capturing light energy, and therefore chlorophyll *b* is called an **accessory pigment.** Other compounds found in the thylakoid membrane, including the yellow, orange, and brown **carotenoids** (kuh-RAHT-uhn-OYDZ), also function as accessory pigments. Looking again at Figure 6-4, notice that the pattern of light absorption of one of the carotenoids differs from the pattern of either type of chlorophyll. By absorbing colors that chlorophyll *a* cannot absorb, the accessory pigments enable plants to capture more of the energy in light.

In the leaves of a plant, the chlorophylls are much more abundant and therefore mask the colors of the other pigments. But in the nonphotosynthetic parts of a plant, such as fruits and flowers, the colors of the other pigments may be quite visible. During the fall, many plants lose their chlorophylls, and their leaves take on the rich hues of the carotenoids.

400 nm   700 nm
Increasing wavelength

FIGURE 6-3

White light contains a variety of colors called the visible spectrum. Each color has a different wavelength, measured in nanometers.

FIGURE 6-4

The three curves on this graph show how three pigments involved in photosynthesis differ in the colors of light they absorb. Where a curve has a peak, much of the light at that wavelength is absorbed. Where a curve has a trough, much of the light at that wavelength is reflected or transmitted.

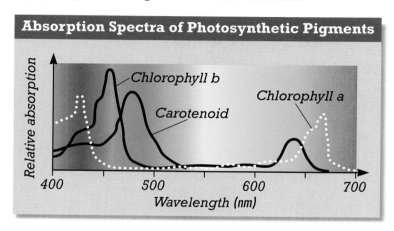

Absorption Spectra of Photosynthetic Pigments

Chlorophyll *b*

Chlorophyll *a*

Carotenoid

Relative absorption

400   500   600   700
Wavelength (nm)

ELECTRON TRANSPORT

The chlorophylls and carotenoids are grouped in clusters of a few hundred pigment molecules in the thylakoid membrane. Each cluster of pigment molecules is referred to as a **photosystem.** Two types of photosystems are known: **photosystem I** and **photosystem II.** They are similar in terms of the kinds of pigments they contain, but they have different roles in the light reactions, as you'll soon see.

The light reactions begin when accessory pigment molecules in both photosystems absorb light. By absorbing light, those molecules acquire some of the energy that was carried by the light waves. In each photosystem, the acquired energy is passed quickly to other pigment molecules until it reaches a specific pair of chlorophyll *a* molecules. The events that occur from this point on can be divided into five steps. Refer to Figure 6-5 as you follow these steps.

Step 1.   Light energy forces electrons to enter a higher energy level in the two chlorophyll *a* molecules of photosystem II. These energized electrons are said to be "excited."

Step 2.   The excited electrons have enough energy to leave the chlorophyll *a* molecules. Because they have lost electrons, the chlorophyll *a* molecules have undergone an oxidation reaction.

[handwritten note: Cytochrome complex: protein that pumps H+ inside against [gradient] from energy released from e⁻ during transport chain]

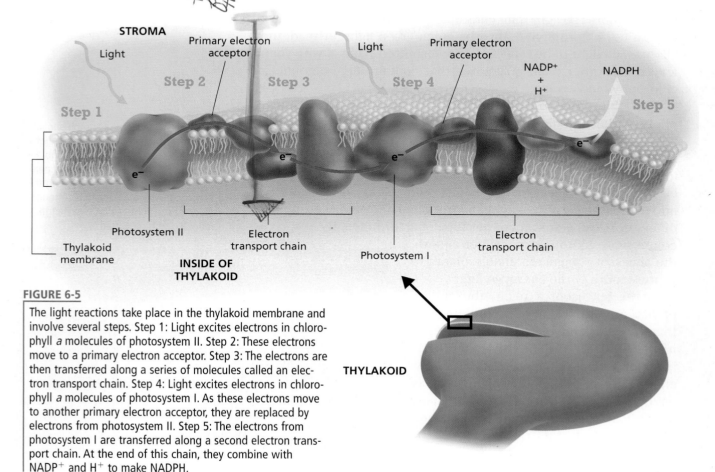

FIGURE 6-5

The light reactions take place in the thylakoid membrane and involve several steps. Step 1: Light excites electrons in chlorophyll *a* molecules of photosystem II. Step 2: These electrons move to a primary electron acceptor. Step 3: The electrons are then transferred along a series of molecules called an electron transport chain. Step 4: Light excites electrons in chlorophyll *a* molecules of photosystem I. As these electrons move to another primary electron acceptor, they are replaced by electrons from photosystem II. Step 5: The electrons from photosystem I are transferred along a second electron transport chain. At the end of this chain, they combine with NADP⁺ and H⁺ to make NADPH.

Remember from Chapter 2 that each oxidation reaction must be accompanied by a reduction reaction. This means that some substance must accept the electrons that the chlorophyll *a* molecules have lost. That substance is a molecule in the thylakoid membrane known as the **primary electron acceptor.**

Step 3. The primary electron acceptor then donates the electrons to the first of a series of molecules located in the thylakoid membrane. This series of molecules is called an **electron transport chain,** because it transfers electrons from one molecule to the next in series. As the electrons pass from molecule to molecule in the electron transport chain, they lose most of the energy that they acquired when they were excited. The energy they lose is harnessed to move protons into the thylakoid.

Step 4. At the same time light is absorbed by photosystem II, light is also absorbed by photosystem I. Electrons move from a pair of chlorophyll *a* molecules in photosystem I to another primary electron acceptor. The electrons that are lost by these chlorophyll *a* molecules are replaced by the electrons that have passed through the electron transport chain from photosystem II.

Step 5. The primary electron acceptor of photosystem I donates electrons to a different electron transport chain. This chain brings the electrons to the side of the thylakoid membrane that faces the stroma. There the electrons combine with a proton and **NADP$^+$**. NADP$^+$ is an organic molecule that accepts electrons during redox reactions. As you can see in Figure 6-5, this reaction causes NADP$^+$ to be reduced to NADPH.

Restoring Photosystem II

You read in Step 4 that electrons from chlorophyll molecules in photosystem II replace the electrons that leave chlorophyll molecules in photosystem I. If the electrons from photosystem II were not replaced, both electron transport chains would stop, and photosynthesis would not occur. The replacement electrons are provided by water molecules. As Figure 6-6 shows, an enzyme inside the thylakoid splits water molecules into protons, electrons, and oxygen. The following equation summarizes the reaction:

$$2H_2O \rightarrow 4H^+ + 4e^- + O_2$$

For every two molecules of water that are split, four electrons become available to replace those lost by chlorophyll molecules in photosystem II. The protons that are produced are left inside the thylakoid, while the oxygen diffuses out of the chloroplast and can then leave the plant. Thus, oxygen can be regarded as a byproduct of the light reactions—it is not needed for photosynthesis to occur. However, as you will learn in Chapter 7, the oxygen that results from photosynthesis is essential for cellular respiration in most organisms, including plants themselves.

FIGURE 6-6

The splitting of water inside the thylakoid releases electrons, which replace the electrons that leave photosystem II when it is illuminated.

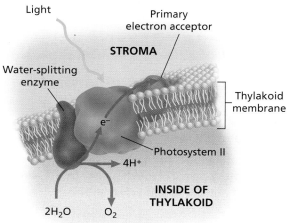

CHEMIOSMOSIS

An important part of the light reactions is the synthesis of ATP through a process called **chemiosmosis** (KEM-ee-ahz-MOH-suhs). Chemiosmosis relies on a concentration gradient of protons across the thylakoid membrane. Recall that some protons are produced from the breakdown of water molecules inside the thylakoid. Other protons are pumped from the stroma to the interior of the thylakoid. The energy required to pump these protons is supplied by the excited electrons as they pass along the electron transport chain of photosystem II. Both of these mechanisms act to build up a concentration gradient of protons. That is, the concentration of protons is higher inside the thylakoid than in the stroma.

The concentration gradient of protons represents potential energy. That energy is harnessed by a protein called **ATP synthase,** which is located in the thylakoid membrane, as Figure 6-7 shows. ATP synthase makes ATP by adding a phosphate group to **adenosine diphosphate,** or **ADP.** The energy that drives this reaction is provided by the movement of protons from the inside of the thylakoid to the stroma. Thus, ATP synthase converts the potential energy of the proton concentration gradient into chemical energy stored in ATP. Remember from Chapter 3 that ATP is the main energy currency of cells.

As you learned earlier, some of the protons in the stroma are used to make NADPH from $NADP^+$. Together, NADPH and ATP provide energy for the second set of reactions in photosynthesis, which are described in the next section.

ATP synthase is a multifunctional protein. By allowing protons to cross the thylakoid membrane, ATP synthase functions as a carrier protein. By catalyzing the synthesis of ATP from ADP, ATP synthase functions as an enzyme. You will encounter other examples of multifunctional proteins in later chapters.

FIGURE 6-7

During chemiosmosis, the movement of protons into the stroma of the chloroplast releases energy, which is used to manufacture ATP.

H+ (low concentration)

ATP   ADP + phosphate

ATP synthase

STROMA

Thylakoid membrane

INSIDE OF THYLAKOID

H+ (high concentration)

SECTION 6-1 REVIEW

1. Describe the structure and function of the thylakoids of a chloroplast.

2. What role do the accessory pigments play in photosynthesis?

3. What happens to the electrons that are lost by photosystem II? What happens to the electrons that are lost by photosystem I?

4. Name the three substances that are produced when water molecules are broken down during the light reactions.

5. How is ATP made in the light reactions?

6. **CRITICAL THINKING**   Explain how the light reactions would be affected if there were no concentration gradient of protons across the thylakoid membrane.

THE CALVIN CYCLE

*The second set of reactions in photosynthesis involves a biochemical pathway known as the **Calvin cycle**. This pathway produces organic compounds, using the energy stored in ATP and NADPH during the light reactions. The Calvin cycle is named after Melvin Calvin (1911–1997), the American scientist who worked out the details of the pathway.*

OBJECTIVES

▲

Summarize the main events of the Calvin cycle.

●

Describe what happens to the compounds made in the Calvin cycle.

■

Distinguish between C$_3$, C$_4$, and CAM plants.

◆

Explain how environmental factors influence photosynthesis.

CARBON FIXATION BY THE CALVIN CYCLE

In the Calvin cycle, carbon atoms from CO$_2$ are bonded, or "fixed," into organic compounds. This incorporation of CO$_2$ into organic compounds is referred to as **carbon fixation.** The Calvin cycle has three major steps, which occur within the stroma of the chloroplast. Refer to Figure 6-8 as you read the following summary of the steps in the Calvin cycle.

Step 1. CO$_2$ diffuses into the stroma from the surrounding cytosol. An enzyme combines a CO$_2$ molecule with a five-carbon carbohydrate called **RuBP.** The product is a six-carbon molecule that splits immediately into a pair of three-carbon molecules known as **PGA.** *(G3P)*

internet**connect**

TOPIC: Calvin cycle
GO TO: www.scilinks.org
KEYWORD: HM117

FIGURE 6-8

The Calvin cycle takes place in the stroma of the thylakoid and involves three major steps. Step 1: CO$_2$ combines with RuBP to form two molecules of PGA. Step 2: Each molecule of PGA is converted into a molecule of PGAL. Step 3: Most of the PGAL is converted back into RuBP, but some PGAL can be used to make a variety of organic compounds.

Step 2. PGA is converted into another three-carbon molecule, **PGAL,** in a two-part process. First, each PGA molecule receives a phosphate group from a molecule of ATP. The resulting compound then receives a proton from NADPH and releases a phosphate group, producing PGAL. In addition to PGAL, these reactions produce ADP, NADP$^+$, and phosphate. These three products can be used again in the light reactions to synthesize additional molecules of ATP and NADPH.

Step 3. Most of the PGAL is converted back into RuBP in a complicated series of reactions. These reactions require a phosphate group from another molecule of ATP, which is changed into ADP. By regenerating the RuBP that was consumed in Step 1, the reactions of Step 3 allow the Calvin cycle to continue operating. However, some PGAL molecules are not converted into RuBP. Instead, they leave the Calvin cycle and can be used by the plant cell to make other organic compounds, as explained in the next section.

The Balance Sheet for Photosynthesis

How much ATP and NADPH are required to make one molecule of PGAL from CO_2? Each turn of the Calvin cycle fixes one CO_2 molecule. Since PGAL is a three-carbon compound, it takes three turns of the cycle to produce each molecule of PGAL. For each turn of the cycle, two ATP molecules and two NADPH molecules are used in Step 2—one for each molecule of PGAL produced—and one more ATP molecule is used in Step 3. Therefore, three turns of the Calvin cycle use nine molecules of ATP and six molecules of NADPH.

Some of the PGAL and other molecules made in the Calvin cycle are built up into a variety of organic compounds, including amino acids, lipids, and carbohydrates. Among the carbohydrates are the monosaccharides glucose and fructose, the disaccharide sucrose, and the polysaccharides glycogen, starch, and cellulose. Most heterotrophs depend on the chemical energy that is stored in the organic compounds made by plants and other photosynthetic organisms.

Recall that water is split during the light reactions, yielding electrons, protons, and oxygen as a byproduct. Thus, the simplest overall equation for photosynthesis, including both the light reactions and the Calvin cycle, can be written as follows:

$$CO_2 + H_2O + \text{light energy} \rightarrow (CH_2O) + O_2$$

In the equation above, (CH_2O) represents the general formula for a carbohydrate. It is often replaced in this equation by the carbohydrate glucose, $C_6H_{12}O_6$, giving the following equation:

$$6CO_2 + 6H_2O + \text{light energy} \rightarrow C_6H_{12}O_6 + 6O_2$$

Keep in mind, however, that glucose is not actually produced by the pathways of photosynthesis. Glucose is included in the equation mainly to emphasize the relationship between photosynthesis and cellular respiration, which will be discussed in Chapter 7.

ALTERNATIVE PATHWAYS

The Calvin cycle is the most common pathway for carbon fixation. Plant species that fix carbon exclusively through the Calvin cycle are known as **C_3 plants** because of the three-carbon compound, PGA, that is initially formed. Other plant species fix carbon through alternative pathways and then release it to enter the Calvin cycle.

These alternative pathways are generally found in plants that evolved in hot, dry climates. Under such conditions, plants can rapidly lose water to the air. Most of the water loss from a plant occurs through small pores called **stomata** (STOH-muh-tuh), which are usually located on the undersurface of the leaves. As Figure 6-9 shows, plants can partially close their stomata when the air is hot and dry, thereby reducing water loss.

Stomata are also the major passageways through which CO_2 enters and O_2 leaves a plant. Thus, when a plant's stomata are partly closed, the level of CO_2 in the plant falls as CO_2 is consumed in the Calvin cycle. At the same time, the level of O_2 in the plant rises as the light reactions split water and generate O_2. Both of these conditions—a low CO_2 level and a high O_2 level—inhibit carbon fixation by the Calvin cycle. Plants with alternative pathways for carbon fixation have evolved ways of dealing with this problem.

The C_4 Pathway

One alternative pathway enables certain plants to fix CO_2 into four-carbon compounds. This pathway is therefore called the **C_4 pathway,** and plants that use it are known as C_4 plants. During the hottest part of the day, C_4 plants have their stomata partially closed. However, certain cells in C_4 plants have an enzyme that can fix CO_2 into four-carbon compounds even when the CO_2 level is low and the O_2 level is high. These compounds are then transported to other cells, where CO_2 is released and enters the Calvin cycle.

C_4 plants include corn, sugar cane, and crabgrass. Such plants lose only about half as much water as C_3 plants when producing the same amount of carbohydrate.

The CAM Pathway

Cactuses, pineapples, and certain other plants have a different adaptation to hot, dry climates. Such plants fix carbon through a pathway called **CAM.** Plants that use the CAM pathway open their stomata at night and close them during the day—just the opposite of what other plants do. At night, CAM plants take in CO_2 and fix it into a variety of organic compounds. During the day, CO_2 is released from these compounds and enters the Calvin cycle. Because CAM plants have their stomata open at night, when the temperature is lower, they grow fairly slowly. However, they lose less water than either C_3 or C_4 plants.

Word Roots and Origins

stoma

from the Greek *stoma*, meaning "mouth"

FIGURE 6-9

These SEMs show stomata in the leaf of a tobacco plant, *Nicotiana tabacum.* (a) When a stoma is open, water, carbon dioxide, and other gases can pass through it to enter or leave a plant (814×). (b) When a stoma is closed, passage through it is greatly restricted (878×).

(a) OPEN STOMA

(b) CLOSED STOMA

RATE OF PHOTOSYNTHESIS

The rate at which a plant can carry out photosynthesis is affected by the plant's environment. One of the most important environmental influences is light intensity. Figure 6-10a shows that as light intensity increases, the rate of photosynthesis initially increases and then levels off to a plateau. This plateau represents the maximum rate of photosynthesis. Higher light intensity causes more electrons in the chlorophyll molecules of both photosystems to become excited. As more electrons are excited, the light reactions occur more rapidly. At some light intensity, however, all of the available electrons are excited, and any further increase in light intensity will not increase the rate of photosynthesis.

CO_2 is another important influence on photosynthesis. Like increasing light intensity, increasing levels of CO_2 around a plant stimulate photosynthesis until the rate of photosynthesis reaches a plateau. Thus, a graph of the rate of photosynthesis versus CO_2 concentration would resemble Figure 6-10a.

A third environmental factor affecting photosynthesis is temperature. Raising the temperature accelerates the various chemical reactions involved in photosynthesis. As a result, the rate of photosynthesis increases as temperature increases, over a certain range. This effect is illustrated by the left half of the curve in Figure 6-10b. The rate of photosynthesis generally peaks at a certain temperature. At that temperature, many of the enzymes that catalyze the reactions in photosynthesis start to become unstable and ineffective. Also, the stomata begin to close, limiting water loss and CO_2 entry into the leaves. These conditions cause the rate of photosynthesis to decrease when the temperature is further increased, as shown by the right half of the curve in Figure 6-10b.

FIGURE 6-10

Environmental factors affect the rate of photosynthesis in plants. (a) As light intensity increases, the rate of photosynthesis increases and then levels off at a maximum. (b) As temperature increases, the rate of photosynthesis increases to a maximum and then decreases with further rises in temperature.

Environmental Influences on Photosynthesis

(a) Light intensity

(b) Temperature

SECTION 6-2 REVIEW

1. In what part of a chloroplast does the Calvin cycle take place?

2. Describe what can happen to PGAL molecules made in the Calvin cycle.

3. How many turns of the Calvin cycle are needed to produce a molecule of PGAL? How many molecules of ATP and NADPH are used in the process?

4. What plant structures control the passage of water out of a plant and carbon dioxide into a plant?

5. What is a C$_4$ plant?

6. **CRITICAL THINKING** Why does the rate of photosynthesis increase and then reach a plateau as the concentration of CO_2 around a plant increases?

SUMMARY/VOCABULARY

6-1

- Photosynthesis converts light energy into chemical energy through complex series of reactions known as biochemical pathways. Autotrophs use photosynthesis to make organic compounds from carbon dioxide and water.
- In plants and algae, photosynthesis occurs inside the chloroplasts.
- White light from the sun is composed of an array of colors called the visible spectrum. Different colors in the visible spectrum have different wavelengths.
- Pigments absorb certain colors of light and reflect or transmit the other colors.
- The light reactions of photosynthesis begin with the absorption of light by chlorophyll a and accessory pigments in the thylakoids.

- Accessory pigments absorb colors of light that aren't absorbed by chlorophyll a, and they transfer some of the energy in this light to chlorophyll a.
- Excited electrons that leave chlorophyll a travel along two electron transport chains, resulting in the production of NADPH. The electrons are replaced when water is split into electrons, protons, and oxygen in the thylakoid. Oxygen is released as a byproduct of photosynthesis.
- As electrons travel along the electron transport chains, a concentration gradient of protons builds up across the thylakoid membrane. The movement of protons down this gradient results in the synthesis of ATP through chemiosmosis.

Vocabulary

accessory pigment (113)
adenosine diphosphate (ADP) (116)
ATP synthase (116)
biochemical pathway (111)
carotenoid (113)

chemiosmosis (116)
chlorophyll (113)
electron transport chain (115)
granum (112)
light reactions (112)

$NADP^+$ (115)
photosynthesis (111)
photosystem (114)
photosystem I (114)
photosystem II (114)
pigment (113)

primary electron acceptor (115)
stroma (112)
visible spectrum (112)
wavelength (113)

6-2

- The ATP and NADPH produced in the light reactions drive the second part of photosynthesis, the Calvin cycle. In the Calvin cycle, CO_2 is incorporated into organic compounds, a process referred to as carbon fixation.
- The Calvin cycle produces a compound called PGAL. Three turns of the Calvin cycle are needed to produce one PGAL molecule.
- Most PGAL molecules are converted into another molecule that keeps the Calvin cycle operating. However, some PGAL molecules are used to make other organic compounds, including amino acids, lipids, and carbohydrates.

- In the overall equation for photosynthesis, CO_2 and water are the reactants, and carbohydrate and O_2 are the products.
- Some plants living in hot, dry climates supplement the Calvin cycle with the C_4 or CAM pathways. These plants carry out carbon fixation and the Calvin cycle either in different cells or at different times.
- The rate of photosynthesis increases and then reaches a plateau as light intensity or CO_2 concentration increases. Below a certain temperature, the rate of photosynthesis increases as temperature increases. Above that temperature, the rate of photosynthesis decreases as temperature increases.

Vocabulary

C_3 plant (119)
C_4 pathway (119)
Calvin cycle (117)

CAM (119)
carbon fixation (117)
PGA (117)

PGAL (118)
RuBP (117)
stoma (119)

REVIEW

Vocabulary

1. The prefix *chloro-* means "green." With this information, explain why the chlorophylls are well named.
2. What is the difference between *stroma* and *stomata*?
3. Explain what is meant by the term *carbon fixation*.
4. What is a biochemical pathway?
5. Choose the term that does not belong in the following group, and explain why it does not belong: electron transport chain, chemiosmosis, Calvin cycle, and photosystem II.

Multiple Choice

6. A product in the overall equation for photosynthesis is (a) O_2 (b) CO_2 (c) H_2O (d) RuBP.
7. A reactant used in the Calvin cycle is (a) H_2O (b) glucose (c) CO_2 (d) O_2.
8. Accessory pigments (a) add color to plants but do not absorb light energy (b) absorb colors of light that chlorophyll *a* cannot absorb (c) receive electrons from the electron transport chain of photosystem I (d) are not involved in photosynthesis.
9. C_4 plants (a) are usually found in cool, moist environments (b) lose more water than C_3 plants during photosynthesis (c) have no stomata (d) fix CO_2 into four-carbon compounds.
10. During photosynthesis, oxygen is produced when (a) PGA is converted into PGAL (b) CO_2 is fixed (c) water is split (d) ATP is converted into ADP.
11. The light reactions take place (a) on the outer membrane of the chloroplast (b) in the stroma (c) in the cytosol (d) on the thylakoid membrane.
12. During chemiosmosis, (a) ATP is synthesized from ADP (b) NADPH is synthesized from $NADP^+$ (c) water is broken down (d) electrons are removed from chlorophyll molecules.
13. Which of the following is NOT part of the light reactions? (a) splitting of water (b) electron transport (c) carbon fixation (d) absorption of light energy

14. Most of the PGAL made in the Calvin cycle is used to (a) synthesize carbohydrates (b) keep the cycle operating (c) convert light energy into chemical energy (d) drive the light reactions.
15. The reactions of the Calvin cycle take place (a) on the outer membrane of the chloroplast (b) in the stroma (c) in the cytosol (d) on the thylakoid membrane.

Short Answer

16. What is the difference between the roles of photosystems I and II in photosynthesis?
17. Explain how the Calvin cycle is an example of a biochemical pathway.
18. In what type of environment are most CAM plants found? How is the CAM pathway advantageous for that type of environment?
19. How is ATP made during photosynthesis?
20. Why do the leaves of some plants look green during the summer and then turn yellow, orange, or brown during the fall?
21. The diagram below shows a portion of a chloroplast. Identify the structure labeled X in the diagram. During photosynthesis, is the concentration of protons higher inside this structure or in the space surrounding it?

X

22. *Unit 2—Photosynthesis*

    Many plants have stomata that take in CO_2 at night and release it during the day. Why is this form of photosynthesis an advantage for plants living in a hot, dry climate?

CRITICAL THINKING

1. A famous scientist once said that wherever in the universe life exists, some of those life-forms must be colored. Why would the scientist make such a statement?

2. One of the accessory pigments used in photosynthesis is beta-carotene, a carotenoid found in high concentration in carrots. When one molecule of beta-carotene is split by an enzyme, two molecules of vitamin A are produced. Removal of a hydrogen atom from vitamin A produces retinal, the pigment involved in vision. Explain why eating carrots is important for good vision.

3. When the CO_2 concentration in the cells of a C_3 plant is low compared with the O_2 concentration, an enzyme combines RuBP with O_2 rather than with CO_2. What effect would this enzymatic change have on photosynthesis? Under what environmental conditions would it be most likely to occur?

4. All of the major components of the light reactions, including the pigment molecules clustered in photosystems I and II, are located in the thylakoid membrane. What is the advantage of having these components confined to the same membrane rather than dissolved in the stroma or the cytosol?

5. Cactuses and other CAM plants are very efficient at carrying out photosynthesis while conserving water. Why aren't they more common in environments where water is plentiful?

6. Some bacteria conduct a type of photosynthesis that makes ATP but does not produce NADPH or split water. How might the evolution of cellular respiration have been different if this had been the only type of photosynthesis to evolve?

7. The graph below shows how the percentage of stomata that are open varies over time for two different kinds of plants. One curve represents the stomata of a geranium, and the other curve represents the stomata of a pineapple. Which curve corresponds to the pineapple stomata? Explain your reasoning.

Daily Cycle of Stomatal Opening

EXTENSION

1. Read "Lake of Dreams" in *New Scientist,* December 4, 1999, on page 35. Write a report describing Lake Vostok and the characteristics that make it so unusual. Explain why some scientists think the lake may be similar to the geothermal vents near the Galápagos Islands.

2. When the sun's rays are blocked by a thick forest, clouds, dust from a volcanic eruption, or smoke from a large fire, what effect do you think this has on photosynthesis? How might it affect the levels of atmospheric carbon dioxide and oxygen? What experiments could scientists conduct in the laboratory to test your predictions?

3. Collect a sample of algae from a local pond. Divide the sample into two covered bowls, and keep one bowl in the dark and the other in the light. Keep both bowls at the same temperature. Every other day for 10 days, observe the algae with a dissecting microscope. Draw and record the organisms and debris that you see. What do your observations tell you about the role of light in pond life?

INTERACTIVE EXPLORATION

Examining the Rate of Photosynthesis

OBJECTIVES

- Simulate how the rate of photosynthesis is affected by variations in the intensity and wavelength of light.
- Relate the rate of photosynthesis to the production of ATP in a chloroplast.

MATERIALS

- computer with CD-ROM drive
- CD-ROM *Interactive Explorations in Biology: Cell Biology and Genetics*
- graph paper

Background

Photosynthesis is the process by which plants, algae, and some bacteria use the energy contained in light to make organic compounds, including carbohydrates. In the light reactions of photosynthesis, chlorophyll and other pigments absorb light, and electrons in these molecules are raised to higher energy levels. These excited electrons are passed through electron transport chains, resulting in the production of ATP and NADPH. In the Calvin cycle, ATP and NADPH are used in the synthesis of carbohydrates from carbon dioxide. Because the Calvin cycle cannot occur without ATP, the overall rate of photosynthesis depends on the rate of ATP production in the light reactions. This interactive exploration allows you to see how varying the intensity and wavelength of light affects the rate of ATP production in photosynthesis.

Prelab Preparation

1. Load and start the program Photosynthesis. You will see an animated cross section of a thylakoid membrane like the one below. Click the Navigation button, and then click the Topic Information button. Read the focus questions and review these concepts: Photons, Pigments, and The Action Spectrum of Photosynthesis.
2. Click the word *Help* at the top left of the screen, and select How to Use This Exploration. Listen to the instructions that explain the operation of the exploration. Click the Interactive Exploration button on the Navigation Palette to begin the exploration.

FEEDBACK METERS

% Maximal ATP: *ratio of number of ATP molecules produced to the maximum number that can be produced*

Number of ATP: *the number of ATP molecules that have been synthesized*

Relative Time: *how long the investigation has been running*

VARIABLES

Light Intensity: *the amount of light*

Wavelength of Light: *the wavelength of the light*

Procedure

PART A Effect of Light Intensity on the Rate of Photosynthesis

1. You will first investigate how varying light intensity affects the rate of photosynthesis. Create a data table like Table A shown below for recording your data.

TABLE A VARYING LIGHT INTENSITY AT A WAVELENGTH OF 650 NM

Light intensity (lux)	% Maximal ATP	Number of ATP
0		
40		
80		
120		
160		
200		

2. Click the word *Speed* at the top of the screen. Select Slow.
3. Click and slide the wavelength indicator to 650. Click and slide the light intensity indicator to 120 lux. A lux is a measure of light intensity.
4. Click the Start button. Observe the diagram of the protein at the bottom of the screen. What molecule is synthesized near this protein?
5. Allow the simulation to run for 30 seconds, as indicated on the relative time meter, and then click the Stop button. In your table, record the % Maximal ATP and the Number of ATP molecules that were produced.
6. Click the Reset button, and then click and slide the light intensity indicator to 160 lux.
7. Click the Start button and allow the simulation to run for 30 seconds, as indicated on the relative time meter.
8. Click the Stop button and record the % Maximal ATP and Number of ATP in your table.
9. Continue testing until you have evaluated all of the light intensities listed on your table.
10. Explain why the wavelength of light is kept constant in this series of steps.

PART B Effect of Wavelength on the Rate of Photosynthesis

11. Click the Reset button. Prepare a data table like Table B shown below.

TABLE B VARYING WAVELENGTH AT A LIGHT INTENSITY OF 200 LUX

Wavelength (nm)	% Maximal ATP	Number of ATP
400		
450		
500		
550		
600		
650		
700		
750		

12. Click and slide the light intensity indicator to 200 lux. Click and slide the wavelength of light indicator to 400 nanometers.
13. Click the Start button and allow the simulation to run for 30 seconds, as indicated on the relative time meter.
14. Click the Stop button and record the % Maximal ATP and Number of ATP in your data table.
15. Continue testing until you have evaluated all of the wavelengths of light listed on your table.
16. Explain why you did not vary the intensity of light in this part of the investigation.

Analysis and Conclusions

1. Prepare a bar graph that shows the % Maximal ATP on the *y*-axis and the intensity of light on the *x*-axis. Above each bar, indicate the number of ATP molecules produced.
2. What can you conclude about the effect of light intensity on the rate of photosynthesis?
3. Prepare another bar graph, plotting the % Maximal ATP versus the wavelength of light.
4. Refer to your second graph. What wavelengths of light are most effective for photosynthesis?
5. Which combination of wavelength and intensity of light would produce the highest rate of photosynthesis?

CELLULAR RESPIRATION

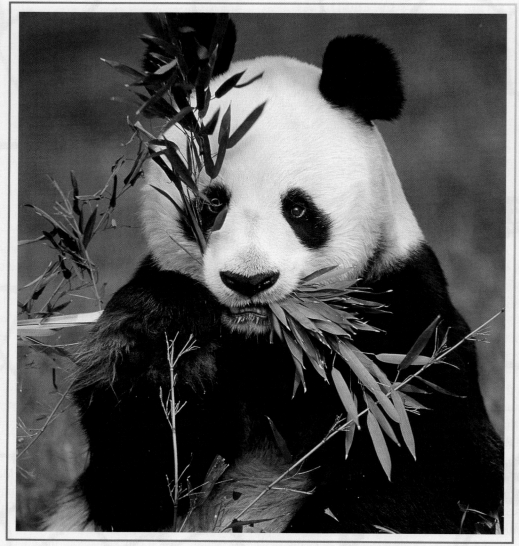

Like other heterotrophs, the giant panda, *Ailuropoda melanoleuca*, obtains organic compounds by consuming other organisms. Biochemical pathways within the panda's cells transfer energy from those compounds to ATP.

FOCUS CONCEPT: *Matter, Energy, and Organization*

As you read, compare the biochemical pathways described in this chapter with those you studied in the chapter on photosynthesis.

 Unit 3—*Cellular Respiration*
Topics 1–6

7-1 Glycolysis and Fermentation

7-2 Aerobic Respiration

GLYCOLYSIS AND FERMENTATION

All cells break down complex organic compounds into simpler molecules. Cells use some of the energy that is released in this process to make ATP.

SECTION

7-1

OBJECTIVES

▲

Define *cellular respiration.*

●

Describe the major events in glycolysis.

■

Compare and contrast lactic acid fermentation and alcoholic fermentation.

◆

Calculate the efficiency of glycolysis.

HARVESTING CHEMICAL ENERGY

You learned in Chapter 6 that autotrophs, such as plants, use photosynthesis to convert light energy from the sun into chemical energy, which is stored in carbohydrates and other organic compounds. Both autotrophs and heterotrophs depend on these organic compounds for the energy to power cellular activities. By breaking down these compounds into simpler molecules, cells release energy. Some of the energy is used to make ATP from ADP and phosphate. Remember from Chapter 3 that ATP is the main energy currency of cells. The complex process in which cells make ATP by breaking down organic compounds is known as **cellular respiration.**

As you can see in Figure 7-1, cellular respiration begins with a biochemical pathway called **glycolysis** (GLIE-KAHL-uh-suhs), which yields a relatively small amount of ATP. The other products of glycolysis can follow either of two main pathways, depending on whether there is oxygen in the cell. If oxygen is absent, the products of glycolysis may enter fermentation pathways that yield no

FIGURE 7-1

Cellular respiration harnesses the energy in organic compounds to produce ATP. The initial pathway in cellular respiration, called glycolysis, produces a small amount of ATP. Glycolysis can lead to fermentation if oxygen is absent or to aerobic respiration if oxygen is present. Most of the ATP produced in cellular respiration results from aerobic respiration.

additional ATP. Because they operate in the absence of oxygen, the fermentation pathways are said to be **anaerobic** (AN-uh-ROH-bik) **pathways.** If oxygen is present, the products of glycolysis enter the pathways of aerobic respiration. Aerobic respiration produces a much larger amount of ATP than does glycolysis alone.

Many of the reactions in cellular respiration are redox reactions. Recall from Chapter 2 that in a redox reaction, one reactant is oxidized while another is reduced. Although many kinds of organic compounds can be oxidized in cellular respiration, it is customary to focus on the simple sugar glucose, whose oxidation begins with glycolysis.

GLYCOLYSIS

Glycolysis is a pathway in which one six-carbon molecule of glucose is oxidized to produce two three-carbon molecules of **pyruvic** (pie-ROO-vik) **acid.** Like other biochemical pathways, glycolysis consists of a series of chemical reactions catalyzed by specific enzymes. All of the reactions of glycolysis take place in the cytosol of the cell. These reactions can be condensed into four main steps. Refer to Figure 7-2 as you read about each of these four steps.

Step 1.   Two phosphate groups are attached to glucose, forming a new six-carbon compound. The phosphate groups are supplied by two molecules of ATP, which are converted into two molecules of ADP in the process.

Step 2.   The six-carbon compound formed in Step 1 is split into two three-carbon molecules of PGAL. Recall from Chapter 6 that PGAL is also produced by the Calvin cycle in photosynthesis.

Step 3.   The two PGAL molecules are oxidized, and each receives a phosphate group. The product of this step is two molecules of a new three-carbon compound. As you can see in Figure 7-2, the oxidation of PGAL is accompanied by the reduction of two molecules of **NAD$^+$** to NADH. NAD$^+$, or nicotinamide adenine dinucleotide, is very similar to NADP$^+$, a compound you encountered in the light reactions of photosynthesis. Like NADP$^+$, NAD$^+$ is an organic molecule that accepts electrons during redox reactions.

Step 4.   The phosphate groups added in Step 1 and Step 3 are removed from the three-carbon compounds formed in Step 3. This reaction produces two molecules of pyruvic acid. Each phosphate group is combined with a molecule of ADP to make a molecule of ATP. Because a total of four phosphate groups were added in Step 1 and Step 3, four molecules of ATP are produced.

Notice that two ATP molecules were used in Step 1, but four were produced in Step 4. Therefore, glycolysis has a net yield of two ATP molecules for every molecule of glucose that is converted into pyruvic acid. What happens to the pyruvic acid depends on the type of cell and on whether oxygen is present.

FIGURE 7-2

Glycolysis takes place in the cytosol of cells and involves four main steps. Step 1: A molecule of glucose is converted into a new six-carbon compound. Step 2: The new six-carbon compound is split into two molecules of PGAL. Step 3: The two PGAL molecules are oxidized to produce two new three-carbon compounds. Step 4: The new three-carbon compounds are converted into two molecules of pyruvic acid. Note that two ATP molecules are used in Step 1, but four more are produced in Step 4. Thus, glycolysis results in a net production of two ATP molecules.

FERMENTATION

In the absence of oxygen, some cells can convert pyruvic acid into other compounds through additional biochemical pathways that occur in the cytosol. The combination of glycolysis plus these additional pathways is known as **fermentation.** The additional fermentation pathways do not produce ATP. However, they do regenerate NAD^+, which can be used to keep glycolysis going to make more ATP. There are many fermentation pathways, and they differ in terms of the enzymes that are used and the compounds that are made from pyruvic acid. Two common fermentation pathways result in the production of lactic acid and ethyl alcohol.

Lactic Acid Fermentation

In **lactic acid fermentation,** an enzyme converts pyruvic acid into another three-carbon compound, called lactic acid. As Figure 7-3a shows, lactic acid fermentation involves the transfer of two hydrogen atoms from NADH and H^+ to pyruvic acid. In the process, NADH is oxidized to form NAD^+. The resulting NAD^+ is used in glycolysis, where it is again reduced to NADH. Thus, the regeneration of NAD^+ in lactic acid fermentation helps to keep glycolysis operating.

Word Roots and Origins

fermentation

from the Latin *fermentum,* meaning "yeast"

TOPIC: Fermentation
GO TO: www.scilinks.org
KEYWORD: HM129

(a) LACTIC ACID FERMENTATION

(b) ALCOHOLIC FERMENTATION

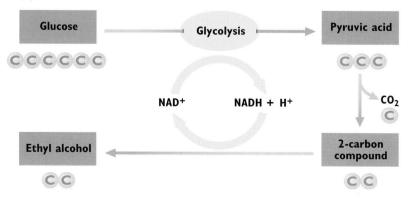

FIGURE 7-3

(a) Some cells engage in lactic acid fermentation when oxygen is absent. In this process, pyruvic acid is reduced to lactic acid and NADH is oxidized to NAD^+. (b) Other cells engage in alcoholic fermentation, converting pyruvic acid into ethyl alcohol. Again, NADH is oxidized to NAD^+.

FIGURE 7-4

In cheese making, fungi or bacteria are added to large vats of milk. The microorganisms carry out lactic acid fermentation, converting some of the sugar in the milk to lactic acid.

Lactic acid fermentation by microorganisms plays an essential role in the manufacture of food products such as yogurt and cheese, as illustrated in Figure 7-4. Lactic acid fermentation also occurs in your muscle cells during very strenuous exercise, such as sprinting at top speed. During this kind of exercise, muscle cells use up oxygen more rapidly than it can be delivered to them. As oxygen becomes depleted, the muscle cells begin to switch from aerobic respiration to lactic acid fermentation. Lactic acid accumulates in the muscle cells, making the cells' cytosol more acidic. The increased acidity may reduce the capacity of the cells to contract, resulting in muscle fatigue, pain, and even cramps. Eventually, the lactic acid diffuses into the blood and is transported to the liver, where it is converted back into pyruvic acid when oxygen becomes available.

Alcoholic Fermentation

Some plant cells and unicellular organisms, such as yeast, use a process called **alcoholic fermentation** to convert pyruvic acid into ethyl alcohol. This pathway requires two steps, which are shown in Figure 7-3b. In the first step, a CO_2 molecule is removed from pyruvic acid, leaving a two-carbon compound. In the second step, two hydrogen atoms are added to the two-carbon compound to form ethyl alcohol. As in lactic acid fermentation, these hydrogen atoms come from NADH and H^+, regenerating NAD^+ for use in glycolysis.

Alcoholic fermentation is the basis of the wine and beer industries. Yeast cells are added to the fermentation mixture to provide the enzymes needed for alcoholic fermentation. As fermentation proceeds, ethyl alcohol accumulates in the mixture until it reaches a concentration that inhibits fermentation. For wine, that concentration is around 12 percent. To make table wines, the CO_2 that is generated in the first step of fermentation is allowed to escape from the mixture through a one-way gas valve. To make sparkling wines, such as champagne, CO_2 is retained within the mixture, "carbonating" the beverage.

Bread making also depends on alcoholic fermentation performed by yeast cells. In this case, the CO_2 that is produced by fermentation makes the bread rise by forming bubbles inside the dough, and the ethyl alcohol evaporates during baking.

ENERGY YIELD

How efficient are the anaerobic pathways at obtaining energy from glucose and using it to make ATP from ADP? To answer this question, one must compare the amount of energy available in glucose with the amount of energy contained in the ATP that is produced by the anaerobic pathways. In such comparisons, energy is often measured in units of **kilocalories** (kcal). One kilocalorie equals 1,000 calories (cal).

Word Roots and Origins

kilocalorie

from the Greek *chilioi,* meaning "thousand," and the Latin *calor,* meaning "heat"

Scientists have calculated that the complete oxidation of a standard amount of glucose releases 686 kcal. Under the conditions that exist inside most cells, the production of a standard amount of ATP from ADP absorbs about 12 kcal. Recall that two ATP molecules are produced from every glucose molecule that is broken down by glycolysis.

$$\text{Efficiency of glycolysis} = \frac{\text{Energy required to make ATP}}{\text{Energy released by oxidation of glucose}}$$

$$= \frac{2 \times 12 \text{ kcal}}{686 \text{ kcal}} \times 100\% = 3.5\%$$

You can see that the two ATP molecules produced during glycolysis receive only a small percentage of the energy that could be released by the complete oxidation of each molecule of glucose. Much of the energy originally contained in glucose is still held in pyruvic acid. Even if pyruvic acid is converted into lactic acid or ethyl alcohol, no additional ATP is synthesized. It's clear that the anaerobic pathways are not very efficient in transferring energy from glucose to ATP.

The anaerobic pathways probably evolved very early in the history of life on Earth. The first organisms were bacteria, and they produced all of their ATP through glycolysis. It took more than a billion years for the first photosynthetic organisms to appear. The oxygen they released as a byproduct of photosynthesis stimulated the evolution of organisms that make most of their ATP through aerobic respiration.

By themselves, the anaerobic pathways provide enough energy for many present-day organisms. However, most of these organisms are unicellular, and those that are multicellular are very small. All of them have limited energy requirements. Larger organisms have much greater energy requirements that cannot be satisfied by the anaerobic pathways alone. These larger organisms meet their energy requirements with the more efficient pathways of aerobic respiration.

SECTION 7-1 REVIEW

1. Define *cellular respiration.*

2. What six-carbon molecule begins glycolysis, and what three-carbon molecules are produced at the end of glycolysis?

3. For each six-carbon molecule that begins glycolysis, how many ATP molecules are used and how many ATP molecules are produced?

4. What condition must exist in a cell for the cell to engage in fermentation?

5. How efficient is glycolysis?

6. CRITICAL THINKING A large amount of ATP in a cell inhibits the enzymes that catalyze the first few steps of glycolysis. How will this inhibition eventually affect the amount of ATP in the cell? Explain your answer.

Organelles as Organisms

This excerpt is from *The Lives of a Cell: Notes of a Biology Watcher*, by Lewis Thomas.

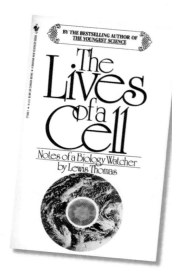

We seem to be living through the biologic revolution, so far anyway, without being upheaved or even much disturbed by it. . . .

It is not too early to begin looking for trouble. I can sense some, for myself anyway, in what is being learned about organelles. I was raised in the belief that these were obscure little engines inside my cells, owned and operated by me or my cellular delegates, private, submicroscopic bits of my intelligent flesh. Now, it appears, some of them, and the most important ones at that, are total strangers.

The evidence is strong, and direct. The membranes lining the inner compartment of mitochondria are unlike other animal cell membranes, and resemble most closely the membranes of bacteria. . . .

The chloroplasts in all plants are, similarly, independent and self-replicating lodgers. . . .

Actually, the suggestion that chloroplasts and mitochondria might be endosymbionts was made as long ago as 1885. . . . There is careful, restrained speculation on how they got there in the first place, with a consensus that they were probably engulfed by larger cells more than a billion years ago and have simply stayed there ever since.

The usual way of looking at them is as enslaved creatures, captured to supply ATP for cells unable to respire on their own, or to provide carbohydrate and oxygen for cells unequipped for photosynthesis. This master-slave arrangement is the common view of full-grown biologists, eukaryotes all. But there is the other side. From their own standpoint, the organelles might be viewed as having learned early how to have the best of possible worlds, with least effort and risk to themselves and their

progeny. Instead of evolving as we have done, manufacturing longer and elaborately longer strands of DNA, and running ever-increasing risks of mutating into evolutionary cul-de-sacs, they elected to stay small and stick to one line of work. To accomplish this, and to assure themselves the longest possible run, they got themselves inside all the rest of us.

It is a good thing for the entire enterprise that mitochondria and chloroplasts have remained small, conservative, and stable, since these two organelles are, in a fundamental sense, the most important living things on earth. Between them they produce the oxygen and arrange for its use. In effect, they run the place.

Reading for Meaning

What do you think Thomas means when he says that the organelles "run the place"? What makes them so important?

Read Further

The Lives of a Cell: Notes of a Biology Watcher is a collection of essays by Lewis Thomas. Thomas goes on in this essay to describe things about organelles that trouble him. Some are fairly serious concerns, such as Could my organelles catch a virus? Others are more whimsical, such as Who am I really if I'm mostly organelles? What actual problems might organelles cause?

AEROBIC RESPIRATION

*In most cells, the pyruvic acid that is produced in glycolysis does not undergo fermentation. Instead, if oxygen is available, pyruvic acid enters the pathways of **aerobic** (UHR-OH-bik) **respiration,** or cellular respiration that requires oxygen. Aerobic respiration produces nearly 20 times as much ATP as is produced by glycolysis alone.*

SECTION

7-2

OBJECTIVES

▲

Summarize the events of the Krebs cycle.

●

Summarize the events of the electron transport chain.

■

Relate aerobic respiration to the structure of a mitochondrion.

◆

Calculate the efficiency of aerobic respiration.

OVERVIEW OF AEROBIC RESPIRATION

Aerobic respiration has two major stages: the Krebs cycle and the electron transport chain. In the Krebs cycle, the oxidation of glucose that began with glycolysis is completed. As glucose is oxidized, NAD^+ is reduced to NADH. In the electron transport chain, NADH is used to make ATP. Although the Krebs cycle also produces a small amount of ATP, most of the ATP produced during aerobic respiration is made by the electron transport chain. The reactions of the Krebs cycle and the electron transport chain occur only if oxygen is present in the cell.

In prokaryotes, the reactions of the Krebs cycle and the electron transport chain take place in the cytosol of the cell. In eukaryotic cells, however, these reactions take place inside mitochondria rather than in the cytosol. The pyruvic acid that is produced in glycolysis diffuses across the double membrane of a mitochondrion and enters the **mitochondrial matrix.** The mitochondrial matrix is the space inside the inner membrane of a mitochondrion. Figure 7-5 illustrates the relationships between these mitochondrial parts. The mitochondrial matrix contains the enzymes needed to catalyze the reactions of the Krebs cycle.

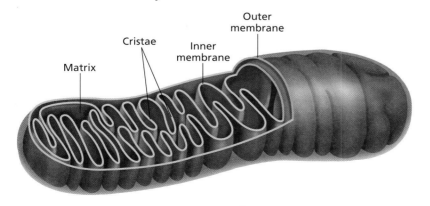

Outer membrane

Cristae

Inner membrane

Matrix

FIGURE 7-5

In eukaryotic cells, the reactions of aerobic respiration occur inside mitochondria. The Krebs cycle takes place in the mitochondrial matrix, and the electron transport chain is located in the inner membrane.

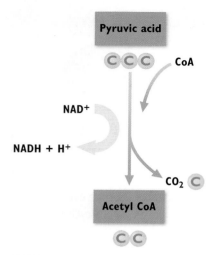

Pyruvic acid

C C C CoA

NAD⁺

NADH + H⁺

CO₂ C

Acetyl CoA

C C

FIGURE 7-6

In aerobic respiration, pyruvic acid combines with coenzyme A to form acetyl CoA. Notice that CO_2, NADH, and H⁺ are also produced in this reaction.

 Quick Lab

Comparing CO₂ Production

Materials disposable gloves, lab apron, safety goggles, 250 mL flask, 100 mL graduated cylinder, phenolphthalein solution, pipet, drinking straw, water, clock, sodium hydroxide solution

Procedure

1. Put on your disposable gloves, lab apron, and safety goggles.

2. Add 50 mL of water and four drops of phenolphthalein to the flask.

3. Use the straw to gently blow into the solution for 1 minute. Add the sodium hydroxide one drop at a time, and gently swirl the flask.

4. When the liquid turns pink, stop adding drops. Record the number of drops you used.

5. Empty and rinse your flask as your teacher directs, and repeat step 2. Walk vigorously for 2 minutes, and repeat steps 3 and 4.

Analysis Which trial produced the most carbon dioxide? Which trial used the most energy?

When pyruvic acid enters the mitochondrial matrix, it reacts with a molecule called coenzyme A to form **acetyl** (uh-SEET-uhl) **coenzyme A,** abbreviated **acetyl CoA** (uh-SEET-uhl KOH-AY). This reaction is illustrated in Figure 7-6. The acetyl part of acetyl CoA contains two carbon atoms, but as you learned earlier, pyruvic acid is a three-carbon compound. The carbon atom that is lost in the conversion of pyruvic acid to acetyl CoA is released in a molecule of CO_2. Figure 7-6 also indicates that this reaction reduces a molecule of NAD⁺ to NADH.

THE KREBS CYCLE

The **Krebs cycle** is a biochemical pathway that breaks down acetyl CoA, producing CO_2, hydrogen atoms, and ATP. The reactions that make up the cycle were identified by Hans Krebs (1900–1981), a German-British biochemist. The Krebs cycle has five main steps. In eukaryotic cells, all five steps occur in the mitochondrial matrix. Examine Figure 7-7 as you read about the steps in the Krebs cycle.

Step 1. A two-carbon molecule of acetyl CoA combines with a four-carbon compound, **oxaloacetic** (AHKS-uh-loh-uh-SEET-ik) **acid,** to produce a six-carbon compound, **citric** (SI-trik) **acid.** Notice that this reaction regenerates coenzyme A.

Step 2. Citric acid releases a CO_2 molecule and a hydrogen atom to form a five-carbon compound. By losing a hydrogen atom with its electron, citric acid is oxidized. The hydrogen atom is transferred to NAD⁺, reducing it to NADH.

Step 3. The five-carbon compound formed in Step 2 also releases a CO_2 molecule and a hydrogen atom, forming a four-carbon compound. Again, NAD⁺ is reduced to NADH. Notice that in this step a molecule of ATP is also synthesized from ADP.

Step 4. The four-carbon compound formed in Step 3 releases a hydrogen atom to form another four-carbon compound. This time, the hydrogen atom is used to reduce FAD to $FADH_2$. **FAD,** or flavin adenine dinucleotide, is a molecule very similar to NAD⁺. Like NAD⁺, FAD accepts electrons during redox reactions.

Step 5. The four-carbon compound formed in Step 4 releases a hydrogen atom to regenerate oxaloacetic acid, which keeps the Krebs cycle operating. The hydrogen atom reduces NAD⁺ to NADH.

Recall that in glycolysis one glucose molecule produces two pyruvic acid molecules, which can then form two molecules of acetyl CoA. Thus, one glucose molecule causes two turns of the Krebs cycle. These two turns produce six NADH, two $FADH_2$, two ATP, and four CO_2 molecules. The CO_2 is a waste product that diffuses out of the cells and is given off by the organism. The ATP can be used for energy. But note that each glucose molecule yields only two molecules of ATP through the Krebs cycle—the same number as in glycolysis.

FIGURE 7-7

The Krebs cycle takes place in the mitochondrial matrix and involves five main steps. Step 1: Acetyl CoA combines with oxaloacetic acid to produce citric acid. Step 2: Citric acid releases a CO_2 molecule to form a five-carbon compound. Step 3: The five-carbon compound releases a CO_2 molecule to form a four-carbon compound. Step 4: The four-carbon compound is converted into a new four-carbon compound. Step 5: The new four-carbon compound is converted back into oxaloacetic acid. In addition to CO_2, each turn of the Krebs cycle produces ATP, NADH, and $FADH_2$.

The bulk of the energy released by the oxidation of glucose still has not been transferred to ATP. That transfer requires the NADH and $FADH_2$ made in the pathways you have learned about so far. Recall that glycolysis produces two NADH molecules and that the conversion of pyruvic acid to acetyl CoA produces two more. Adding the six NADH molecules from the Krebs cycle gives a total of 10 NADH molecules for every glucose molecule that is oxidized. These 10 NADH molecules and the two $FADH_2$ molecules from the Krebs cycle drive the next stage of aerobic respiration. That is where most of the energy transfer from glucose to ATP actually occurs.

ELECTRON TRANSPORT CHAIN

The **electron transport chain** constitutes the second stage of aerobic respiration. In eukaryotic cells, the electron transport chain lines the inner membrane of the mitochondrion. Remember from Chapter 4 that the inner membrane has many long folds called cristae. In prokaryotes, the electron transport chain lines the cell membrane. ATP is produced by the electron transport chain when NADH and $FADH_2$ release hydrogen atoms, regenerating NAD^+ and FAD. To understand how ATP is produced, you must follow what happens to the electrons and protons that make up these hydrogen atoms.

internet **connect**

SCILINKS
NSTA

TOPIC: Krebs cycle
GO TO: www.scilinks.org
KEYWORD: HM135

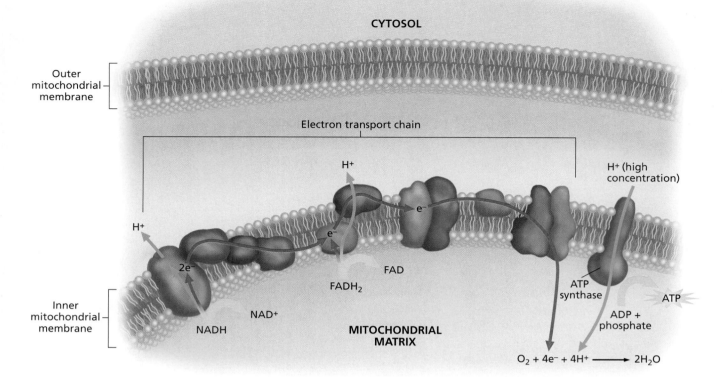

CYTOSOL

Outer mitochondrial membrane

Electron transport chain

H+

H+ (high concentration)

e-

H+

e-

2e-

FAD

FADH₂

ATP synthase

ATP

Inner mitochondrial membrane

NAD+

NADH

MITOCHONDRIAL MATRIX

ADP + phosphate

$O_2 + 4e^- + 4H^+ \longrightarrow 2H_2O$

FIGURE 7-8

NADH and FADH₂ supply electrons and protons to the electron transport chain. The electrons are passed along the chain from molecule to molecule in a series of redox reactions. The protons are pumped out of the mitochondrial matrix. As the protons return to the mitochondrial matrix through ATP synthase, they release energy, driving the synthesis of ATP. The final acceptor of electrons is oxygen, which also accepts protons in a reaction that forms water.

The electrons in the hydrogen atoms from NADH and FADH₂ are at a high energy level. In the electron transport chain, these high-energy electrons are passed along a series of molecules, as shown in Figure 7-8. As they move from molecule to molecule, the electrons lose some of their energy. The energy they lose is used to pump the protons of the hydrogen atoms from the mitochondrial matrix to the other side of the inner mitochondrial membrane. This pumping builds up a high concentration of protons in the space between the inner and outer mitochondrial membranes. In other words, a concentration gradient of protons is created across the inner mitochondrial membrane.

The concentration gradient of protons drives the synthesis of ATP by chemiosmosis, the same process that generates ATP in photosynthesis. As you can see in Figure 7-8, ATP synthase molecules are located in the inner mitochondrial membrane. ATP synthase makes ATP from ADP as protons move down their concentration gradient into the mitochondrial matrix.

The Role of Oxygen

ATP can be synthesized by chemiosmosis only if electrons continue to move from molecule to molecule in the electron transport chain. Obviously, the last molecule in the electron transport chain cannot keep all of the electrons it accepts. If it did, the electron transport chain would come to a halt. Consider what would happen if cars kept entering a dead-end, one-way street. At some point, no more cars could enter the street. Similarly, if the last molecule could not "unload" the electrons it accepts, then no more electrons could enter the electron transport chain and ATP synthesis would stop.

Here is where oxygen comes into play in aerobic respiration. Figure 7-8 shows that oxygen serves as the final acceptor of electrons. By accepting electrons from the last molecule in the electron transport chain, oxygen allows additional electrons to pass along the chain. As a result, ATP can continue to be synthesized by chemiosmosis. Oxygen also accepts the protons that were once part of the hydrogen atoms supplied by NADH and $FADH_2$. By combining with both electrons and protons, oxygen forms water, as shown in the following equation:

$$O_2 + 4e^- + 4H^+ \rightarrow 2H_2O$$

ENERGY YIELD

How many ATP molecules are made in aerobic respiration? Refer to Figure 7-9 as you calculate the total. Recall that glycolysis and the Krebs cycle each produce two ATP molecules for every glucose molecule that is oxidized. Furthermore, each NADH molecule that supplies the electron transport chain can generate three ATP molecules, and each $FADH_2$ molecule can generate two ATP molecules. Thus, the 10 NADH and two $FADH_2$ molecules made through aerobic respiration can produce up to 34 ATP molecules by the electron transport chain. Adding the four ATP molecules from glycolysis and the Krebs cycle gives a maximum yield of 38 ATP molecules per molecule of glucose.

The actual number of ATP molecules generated through aerobic respiration varies from cell to cell. In most eukaryotic cells, the NADH that is made in the cytosol during glycolysis cannot diffuse through the inner membrane of the mitochondrion. Instead, it must be actively transported into the mitochondrial matrix. The active transport of NADH consumes ATP. As a result, most eukaryotic cells produce only about 36 ATP molecules per glucose molecule.

How efficient is aerobic respiration in providing a cell with energy for cellular activities? Consider the efficiency when a cell generates 38 ATP molecules:

$$\frac{\text{Efficiency of}}{\text{aerobic respiration}} = \frac{\text{Energy required to make ATP}}{\text{Energy released by oxidation of glucose}}$$

$$= \frac{38 \times 12 \text{ kcal}}{686 \text{ kcal}} \times 100\% = 66\%$$

This means that aerobic respiration is nearly 20 times more efficient than glycolysis alone. In fact, the efficiency of aerobic respiration is quite impressive compared with the efficiency of

FIGURE 7-9

Follow each pathway to see how one glucose molecule can generate up to 38 ATP molecules in aerobic respiration.

machines that humans have designed and built. An automobile engine, for example, is only about 25 percent efficient in extracting energy from gasoline to move a car. Most of the remaining energy released from gasoline is lost as heat.

SUMMARIZING CELLULAR RESPIRATION

The complete oxidation of glucose in aerobic respiration is summarized by the following equation:

$$C_6H_{12}O_6 + 6O_2 \rightarrow 6CO_2 + 6H_2O + energy$$

Recall the equations for photosynthesis that you learned in Chapter 6. Notice that the equation above is the opposite of the overall equation for photosynthesis, if glucose is considered to be a product of photosynthesis. That is, the products of photosynthesis are reactants in aerobic respiration, and the products of aerobic respiration are reactants in photosynthesis. However, it is important to remember that aerobic respiration is not the reverse of photosynthesis. As you have seen, these two processes involve different biochemical pathways and occur at different sites inside cells.

Cellular respiration provides the ATP that all cells need to support the activities of life. But providing cells with ATP is not the only important function of cellular respiration. Cells also need specific organic compounds from which to build the macromolecules that compose their own structure. Some of these specific compounds may not be contained in the food a heterotroph consumes. However, the molecules formed at different steps in glycolysis and the Krebs cycle are often used by cells to make the compounds that are missing in food. Thus, another important function of cellular respiration is to provide carbon skeletons that can be built up into larger molecules needed by cells.

SECTION 7-2 REVIEW

1. What four-carbon compound is regenerated at the end of the Krebs cycle? With what two-carbon compound does it combine at the start of the Krebs cycle?

2. How is the synthesis of ATP in the electron transport chain of mitochondria similar to the synthesis of ATP in chloroplasts?

3. What role does oxygen play in aerobic respiration? What molecule does oxygen become a part of as a result of aerobic respiration?

4. In what part of a mitochondrion does the Krebs cycle occur? In what part of a mitochondrion is the electron transport chain located?

5. Calculate the efficiency of aerobic respiration if a cell generates 32 ATP molecules per molecule of glucose.

6. **CRITICAL THINKING** Sometimes protons leak out of a cell or are used for other purposes besides ATP production. How would this affect the production of ATP in aerobic respiration?

CHAPTER 7 REVIEW

SUMMARY/VOCABULARY

7-1 ■ Cellular respiration is the process by which cells break down organic compounds to release energy and make ATP. It includes anaerobic pathways, which operate in the absence of oxygen, and aerobic respiration, which occurs when oxygen is present.

■ Cellular respiration begins with glycolysis, which takes place in the cytosol of cells. During glycolysis, one glucose molecule is oxidized to form two pyruvic acid molecules. Glycolysis results in a net production of two ATP molecules and four NADH molecules.

■ Fermentation is a set of anaerobic pathways in which pyruvic acid is converted into other organic molecules in the cytosol.

Fermentation does not produce ATP, but it does regenerate NAD^+, which helps keep glycolysis operating.

■ In lactic acid fermentation, an enzyme converts pyruvic acid into lactic acid.

■ In alcoholic fermentation, other enzymes convert pyruvic acid into ethyl alcohol and CO_2.

■ Through glycolysis, only about 3.5 percent of the energy available from the oxidation of glucose is transferred to ATP.

■ The anaerobic pathways probably evolved very early in the history of life on Earth. For more than a billion years, they were the only pathways available for harvesting chemical energy.

Vocabulary

alcoholic fermentation (130)	fermentation (129)	kilocalorie (130)	NAD^+ (128)
anaerobic pathway (128)	glycolysis (127)	lactic acid fermentation (129)	pyruvic acid (128)
cellular respiration (127)			

7-2 ■ In the presence of oxygen, pyruvic acid is converted into acetyl CoA. In eukaryotic cells, this reaction occurs inside the mitochondrial matrix.

■ Acetyl CoA enters the Krebs cycle, a biochemical pathway that also takes place in the mitochondrial matrix. Each turn of the Krebs cycle generates three NADH, one $FADH_2$, one ATP, and two CO_2 molecules.

■ NADH and $FADH_2$ donate electrons to the electron transport chain, which lines the inner mitochondrial membrane. Electrons are passed from molecule to molecule in the transport chain in a series of redox reactions.

■ As electrons pass along the electron transport chain, protons donated by NADH and $FADH_2$ are pumped into the space between the inner and outer mitochondrial membranes. This pumping creates a concentration gradient of protons across

the inner mitochondrial membrane. As protons move down their gradient and back into the mitochondrial matrix, ATP synthase uses the energy released by their movement to make ATP.

■ During aerobic respiration, oxygen accepts both protons and electrons from the electron transport chain. As a result, oxygen is converted to water.

■ Aerobic respiration can produce up to 38 ATP molecules from the oxidation of a single molecule of glucose. This means that up to 66 percent of the energy released by the oxidation of glucose can be transferred to ATP. However, most eukaryotic cells produce only about 36 ATP molecules per molecule of glucose.

■ Besides transferring energy to ATP, cellular respiration also provides carbon skeletons that can be built up into larger molecules by cells.

Vocabulary

acetyl coenzyme A (134)	citric acid (134)	FAD (134)	mitochondrial matrix (133)
aerobic respiration (133)	electron transport chain (135)	Krebs cycle (134)	oxaloacetic acid (134)

REVIEW

Vocabulary

1. What molecule made during glycolysis is used in the later steps in fermentation?
2. What molecule made during the later steps in fermentation is used in glycolysis?
3. What molecules does the Krebs cycle make that the electron transport chain uses?
4. What molecule determines whether pyruvic acid will undergo fermentation or be converted for entry into the Krebs cycle?
5. What determines whether pyruvic acid will undergo lactic acid fermentation or alcoholic fermentation?

Multiple Choice

6. Before the Krebs cycle can proceed, pyruvic acid must be converted into (a) citric acid (b) glucose (c) acetyl CoA (d) NADH.
7. The net number of ATP molecules made directly by glycolysis is (a) 2 (b) 6 (c) 32 (d) 38.
8. In lactic acid fermentation, (a) NAD^+ is regenerated for use in glycolysis (b) lactic acid is converted into pyruvic acid (c) oxygen is consumed (d) electrons pass through the electron transport chain.
9. Which of the following is not a product of the Krebs cycle? (a) ATP (b) ethyl alcohol (c) CO_2 (d) $FADH_2$
10. Cellular respiration is similar to photosynthesis in that they both (a) produce ATP (b) involve chemiosmosis (c) make PGAL (d) all of the above.
11. ATP is synthesized in the electron transport chain when which of the following moves across the inner mitochondrial membrane? (a) NADH (b) protons (c) citric acid (d) oxygen
12. By accepting electrons and protons, the oxygen used in aerobic respiration turns into (a) CO_2 (b) H_2O (c) $C_6H_{12}O_6$ (d) ATP.
13. The Krebs cycle occurs in the (a) cytosol (b) outer mitochondrial membrane (c) mitochondrial matrix (d) space between the inner and outer mitochondrial membranes.
14. During each turn of the Krebs cycle, (a) two CO_2 molecules are produced (b) two ATP molecules are consumed (c) pyruvic acid combines with oxaloacetic acid (d) glucose combines with a four-carbon molecule.
15. Most of the ATP synthesized in aerobic respiration is made (a) during glycolysis (b) through fermentation (c) in the cytosol (d) through chemiosmosis.

Short Answer

16. Summarize the events that occur from the end of glycolysis through the first reaction of the Krebs cycle.
17. Why do most eukaryotic cells produce fewer than 38 ATP molecules for every glucose molecule that is oxidized by aerobic respiration?
18. How do the anaerobic pathways differ from the pathways of aerobic respiration, at the sites they occur in eukaryotic cells?
19. What causes your muscles to become fatigued and sometimes develop cramps when you exercise too strenuously?
20. How does aerobic respiration ultimately depend on photosynthesis?
21. What role does chemiosmosis play in aerobic respiration?
22. What role does oxygen play in aerobic respiration?
23. Refer to the diagram of the Krebs cycle shown below. How many carbon atoms are in each of the compounds represented by the letters A–E?

24. **Unit 3—*Cellular Respiration***

Write a report summarizing how exercise physiologists regulate the diet and training of athletes. Find out how diet varies according to the needs of each athlete. Research the relationship between exercise and metabolism.

CRITICAL THINKING

1. The enzyme that converts pyruvic acid into acetyl CoA requires vitamin B_1, also called thiamine. Like many other vitamins, thiamine cannot be made in the human body. What can you infer about the nutritional requirements of humans?

2. How does the folding of the inner mitochondrial membrane benefit aerobic respiration?

3. Yeast can produce ATP through either fermentation or aerobic respiration, depending on whether oxygen is present. If oxygen is present, yeast cells consume glucose much more slowly than if oxygen is absent. How can you explain this observation?

4. A person will breathe deeply and rapidly for some time after a period of very strenuous exercise. The longer and more intense the exercise was, the longer the deep breathing will continue after the exercise stops. Using your understanding of cellular respiration, explain why strenuous exercise stimulates deep breathing that continues after the end of exercise.

5. Some eukaryotic cells must use ATP to move NADH into the mitochondrial matrix. Knowing this, would you expect aerobic respiration to be more efficient or less efficient in prokaryotic cells than it is in eukaryotic cells? Explain your answer.

6. The graph below shows the rate of ATP production by a culture of yeast cells over time. At the time indicated by the dashed line, cyanide was added to the culture. Cyanide blocks the flow of electrons to O_2 from the electron transport chain in mitochondria. Explain why adding cyanide has the effect on ATP production that is indicated by the graph.

ATP Production

Cyanide added

Rate of ATP production

Time

EXTENSION

1. Read "First With a Flower" in *Natural History*, March 2000, on page 12. Explain how some plants are able to obtain energy to grow and bloom under a pack of snow before they are exposed to sunlight and before photosynthesis is able to begin. What adaptation does the skunk cabbage have that enables it to extend its flowering stalk from the snow while the air temperature is still below freezing?

2. Read "Mitochondria Make a Comeback" in *Science,* March 5, 1999, on page 1475. What does the author mean when she says that mitochondria are making a comeback? Describe four more areas of research in which mitochondria play a key role.

3. As you have learned, aerobic respiration is significantly more efficient than glycolysis alone in supplying cells with ATP. Develop a hypothesis to explain why anaerobic organisms have not become extinct but instead have continued to thrive in many regions of the world. Check library and on-line references to locate information about one anaerobic species that relates to your hypothesis.

4. Find a recipe for making leavened, or raised, bread and a recipe for making unleavened bread. What ingredient that is present in the recipe for leavened bread is missing from the recipe for unleavened bread? Explain why that ingredient is omitted from the recipe.

Observing Cellular Respiration

OBJECTIVES

- Measure the rate of cellular respiration in germinating seeds.
- Compare cellular respiration rates in germinating and nongerminating seeds.

PROCESS SKILLS

- experimenting
- collecting data
- analyzing data

MATERIALS

- volumeter jar and screw-on lid
- tap water at room temperature
- ring stand with support ring
- 8.5 in. × 11 in. piece of cardboard
- 8.5 in. × 11 in. sheet of white paper
- cellophane tape
- 40 germinating corn or pea seeds
- 40 nongerminating corn or pea seeds
- 100 mL graduated cylinder
- glass or plastic beads
- 3 plastic or paper cups
- 3 volumeters
- cotton
- 3 soda-lime packets
- forceps
- Pasteur pipet
- colored water
- ruler with millimeter markings

Background

1. When glucose is oxidized in aerobic respiration, what other substance is consumed and what substances are produced?
2. Write the balanced equation for the complete oxidation of glucose in aerobic respiration.

PART A   Setting Up the Apparatus

1. Pour room-temperature water into the volumeter jar until the jar is about two-thirds full. Screw on the lid.
2. Place the cardboard on top of the ring stand support ring, and tape a sheet of white paper to the cardboard. Adjust the support ring so that the cardboard is level, as shown in the illustration below.
3. **CAUTION   Keep the seeds, which may have been treated with a fungicide, away from your skin.** Place 40 germinating seeds in a graduated cylinder and measure their volume. Do the same for 40 nongerminating seeds.
4. Add beads to the seeds that have the smaller volume until the combined volume is the same as the volume of the other group of seeds. Then transfer both groups (one containing added beads) to separate plastic or paper cups. To a third cup, add a volume of beads equal to the volume of each of the other two cups.
5. Remove the stopper assemblies from three volumeter tubes and transfer the contents of the three cups to separate tubes. Place a 2 cm plug of dry cotton into each tube, leaving a gap of about 1 cm between the cotton and the seeds or beads.
6. **CAUTION   Soda lime is corrosive. Do not touch it. If it gets on your skin or clothing, wash it off at the sink. If it gets in your eyes, immediately flush it out at the eyewash station while calling to your teacher.** Using forceps, place a packet of soda lime wrapped in gauze on top of the cotton plug in each tube. Soda lime absorbs the CO_2 that is produced as a result of respiration.
7. Gently but firmly press the stopper assembly into each volumeter tube. Insert the tubes into the volumeter jar through the large holes in the lid.

8. Use a Pasteur pipet to place a small drop of colored water into the three capillary tubes. Tilt two of the tubes slightly until the drops are lined up with the outermost calibration mark. Carefully attach these tubes to the latex tubing on the two volumeter tubes containing seeds. Position the drop in the third capillary tube near the middle of the tube. Attach this tube to the volumeter tube that contains only beads. This volumeter is the control volumeter. Tape all three capillary tubes to the paper on the ring stand.

9. Wait 5 min for the temperature to become uniform throughout the volumeter jar. While you wait, make a data table like the one shown below. Then return the drops in the capillary tubes to their original positions by using the syringes to inject air into or withdraw air from the volumeter tubes, if necessary.

PART B Measuring Respiration Rates

10. On the paper beneath the capillary tubes, mark the position of one end of each drop of colored water. Note the time. Repeat this procedure every 5 min for 20 min. If respiration is rapid, you may have to reposition the drops as you did in Step 9. In which direction would you expect a drop to move if respiration in the volumeter tube were causing it to move?

11. Remove the paper from the ring stand and use a ruler to measure the distance moved by the drops during each time interval. If you repositioned any drops in Step 10, be sure to add this adjustment when you measure the distances. Enter the measurements in the "Uncorrected" columns in your data table.

12. 🗑 🧼 Clean up your materials and wash your hands before leaving the lab.

Analysis and Conclusions

1. No respiration should have occurred in the control volumeter, which contained only beads. Therefore, any movement of the drop in the control volumeter must have been caused by changes in the temperature of the volumeter jar or the air pressure in the classroom. Since these changes would have affected all three volumeters to the same extent, you must subtract the distance you measured for the control volumeter from the distances you measured for the other two volumeters. Do this calculation for each time interval, and enter the results in the "Corrected" columns in your data table.

2. Each capillary tube has a capacity of 0.063 mL between each 1 cm mark on the tube. Use this information to calculate the volume of O_2 consumed by the germinating and nongerminating seeds during each time interval. Enter these results in your data table.

3. Prepare a graph to show the volume of O_2 consumed versus time; use different symbols or colors to distinguish the points for the germinating seeds from those for the nongerminating seeds. Make sure each point represents the cumulative volume of O_2 consumed. For example, the point plotted for the 15–20 min interval should represent the volume consumed during that interval plus the volume consumed during all of the preceding intervals. Draw the best-fit line through the points for each group of seeds. From the slope of this line, calculate the average rate of respiration in milliliters of O_2 per minute for both groups of seeds.

4. Which group of seeds had the higher average rate of respiration? What is the significance of this difference in terms of a seed's ability to survive for long periods?

MEASUREMENTS OF CELLULAR RESPIRATION

Time interval (min)	Control	Germinating seeds		Nongerminating seeds		Volume of O_2 consumed (mL)	
		Uncorrected	Corrected	Uncorrected	Corrected	Germinating	Nongerminating
0–5							
5–10							
10–15							
15–20							

CELL REPRODUCTION

This human lymphocyte cell is dividing into two new cells. (17,687×)

FOCUS CONCEPT: *Reproduction and Inheritance*

In this chapter you will learn how cells reproduce by cell division. Pay attention to the steps of cell division in different kinds of cells.

Unit 4—Cell Reproduction
Topics 1–6

CHROMOSOMES

Recall from Chapter 3 that DNA is a long thin molecule that stores genetic information. The DNA in a human cell is estimated to consist of six billion pairs of nucleotides. To visualize the enormity of six billion pairs of nucleotides, imagine increasing a cell nucleus to the size of a basketball. Then imagine taking the DNA out of the basketball-sized nucleus and stretching it into a straight line. That line of DNA would stretch for 64 km (40 mi).

CHROMOSOME STRUCTURE

During cell division, the DNA in a eukaryotic cell's nucleus is coiled into very compact structures called chromosomes. Chromosomes are rod-shaped structures made of DNA and proteins. In Figure 8-1, you can see the many levels of DNA coiling required to form a chromosome.

The chromosomes of stained eukaryotic cells undergoing cell division are visible as darkened structures inside the nuclear membrane. Each chromosome is a single DNA molecule associated with proteins. The DNA in eukaryotic cells wraps tightly around proteins called **histones.** Histones help maintain the shape of the chromosome and aid in the tight packing of DNA. **Nonhistone** proteins are generally involved in controlling the activity of specific regions of the DNA.

OBJECTIVES

▲
Describe the structure of a chromosome.

●
Compare prokaryotic chromosomes with eukaryotic chromosomes.

■
Explain the differences between sex chromosomes and autosomes.

◆
Give examples of diploid and haploid cells.

FIGURE 8-1

As a cell prepares to divide, its DNA coils around proteins and twists into rod-shaped chromosomes.

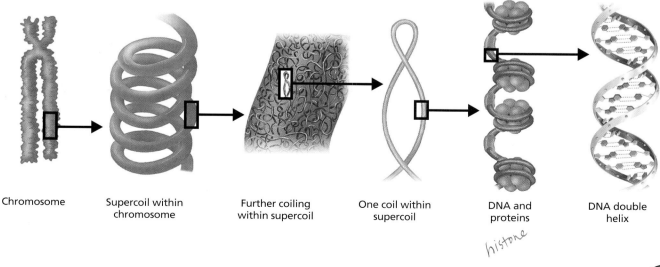

| Chromosome | Supercoil within chromosome | Further coiling within supercoil | One coil within supercoil | DNA and proteins | DNA double helix |

histone

FIGURE 8-2

Chromosomes, like this one isolated from a dividing human cell, consist of two identical chromatids. (TEM 12,542×)

Figure 8-2 shows a chromosome that was isolated from a dividing cell. Notice that the chromosome consists of two identical halves. Each half of the chromosome is called a **chromatid.** Chromatids form as the DNA makes a copy of itself before cell division. When the cell divides, each of the two new cells will receive one chromatid from each chromosome. The constricted area of each chromatid is called a **centromere.** The centromere holds the two chromatids together until they separate during cell division. As you will learn in the next section, centromeres are especially important for the movement of chromosomes during cell division.

Between cell divisions, DNA is not so tightly coiled into chromosomes. Regions of DNA uncoil in between cell divisions so they can be read and so the information can be used to direct the activities of the cell. The less tightly coiled DNA-protein complex is called chromatin.

As you might expect, chromosomes are simpler in prokaryotes than in eukaryotes. The DNA of most prokaryotes comprises only one chromosome, which is attached to the inside of the cell membrane. Prokaryotic chromosomes consist of a circular DNA molecule and associated proteins. As with eukaryotic chromosomes, prokaryotic chromosomes must be very compact to fit into the cell.

CHROMOSOME NUMBERS

Each species has a characteristic number of chromosomes in each cell. Table 8-1 lists the number of chromosomes found in some organisms. Fruit flies, for example, have only eight chromosomes in each cell. Some species of organisms have the same number of chromosomes. For example, potatoes, plums, and chimpanzees all have 48 chromosomes in each cell.

Sex Chromosomes and Autosomes

Human and animal chromosomes are categorized as either sex chromosomes or autosomes. **Sex chromosomes** are chromosomes that determine the sex of an organism, and they may also carry genes for other characteristics. In humans, sex chromosomes are either X or Y. Normal females have two X chromosomes, and normal males have an X and a Y chromosome. All of the other chromosomes in an organism are called **autosomes.** Two of the 46 human chromosomes are sex chromosomes, while the remaining 44 chromosomes are autosomes.

Every cell of an organism produced by sexual reproduction has two copies of each autosome. The organism receives one copy of each autosome from each parent. The two copies of each autosome are called **homologous chromosomes,** or homologues. Homologous chromosomes are the same size and shape and carry genes for the same traits. For example, if one chromosome in a pair of homologous chromosomes contains a gene for eye color, so will

TABLE 8-1 *Chromosome Numbers of Various Species*	
Organism	Number of chromosomes
Adder's tongue fern	1,262
Carrot	18
Cat	32
Chimpanzee	48
Dog	78
Orangutan	48
Earthworm	36
Fruit fly	8
Garden pea	20
Gorilla	48
Horse	64
Human	46
Lettuce	18
Sand dollar	52

the other chromosome in the homologous pair. Figure 8-3 shows a **karyotype,** which is a photomicrograph of the chromosomes in a dividing cell found in a normal human. Notice that the 46 human chromosomes exist as 22 homologous pairs of autosomes and two sex chromosomes (XY in males and XX in females). What is the sex of the person whose chromosomes are shown in Figure 8-3?

Diploid and Haploid Cells

Cells having two sets of chromosomes are said to be **diploid.** Diploid cells have both chromosomes for each homologous pair. Diploid cells also have two sex chromosomes in animals, including humans, and many other organisms that have sex chromosomes. All normal human cells, except reproductive cells (sperm cells and egg cells), are diploid cells. Diploid is commonly abbreviated as $2n$. In humans, the diploid, or $2n$, number of chromosomes is 46—22 pairs of homologous chromosomes and 2 sex chromosomes. If you count the number of chromosomes in the karyotype in Figure 8-3, you should find 46 chromosomes.

Human sperm cells and egg cells are **haploid** cells. These cells contain only one set of chromosomes. Haploid cells have half the number of chromosomes that are present in diploid cells. Thus, human haploid cells have only one chromosome of each homologous pair and only one sex chromosome. Haploid is abbreviated as $1n$. When a sperm cell ($1n$) and an egg cell ($1n$) combine to create the first cell of a new organism, the new cell will be diploid ($2n$). If the reproductive cells were diploid, the new cell would have too many chromosomes and would not be functional.

FIGURE 8-3

Karyotypes, like this one, are used to examine an individual's chromosomes. Karyotypes are made from a sample of a person's blood. White blood cells from the sample are treated chemically to stimulate mitosis and to arrest mitosis in metaphase. The chromosomes are then photographed, cut out, and arranged by size and shape into pairs.

SECTION 8-1 REVIEW

1. What are homologous chromosomes?

2. Describe the differences between a chromosome and a DNA molecule.

3. Compare the structure of prokaryotic chromosomes with that of eukaryotic chromosomes.

4. Contrast sex chromosomes with autosomes.

5. Using Table 8-1, list the haploid and diploid number of chromosomes for each organism.

6. **CRITICAL THINKING** Is there a correlation between the number of chromosomes and the complexity of an organism? Give support for your answer.

8-2

OBJECTIVES

▲

Describe the events
of binary fission.

●

Describe each phase
of the cell cycle.

■

Summarize the phases
of mitosis.

◆

Compare cytokinesis in
animal cells with cytokinesis
in plant cells.

Prokaryotic cell

DNA is copied

Cell begins to divide

Two identical haploid cells

FIGURE 8-4

Most prokaryotes reproduce by binary fission, in which two identical cells are produced from one cell.

CELL DIVISION

All cells are derived from the division of preexisting cells. Cell division is the process by which cells produce offspring cells. As you will see, cell division differs in prokaryotes and eukaryotes. In eukaryotes, cell division differs in different stages of an organism's life cycle.

CELL DIVISION IN PROKARYOTES

Binary fission is the division of a prokaryotic cell into two offspring cells. Binary fission consists of three general stages, which are outlined in Figure 8-4.

First the chromosome, which is attached to the inside of the cell membrane, makes a copy of itself, resulting in two identical chromosomes attached to the inside of the prokaryote's inner cell membrane. After the chromosome is copied, the cell continues to grow until it reaches approximately twice the cell's original size. Then a cell wall forms between the two chromosomes and the cell splits into two new cells. Each new cell contains one of the identical chromosomes that resulted from the copying of the original cell's chromosome.

CELL DIVISION IN EUKARYOTES

In eukaryotic cell division, both the cytoplasm and the nucleus divide. There are two kinds of cell division in eukaryotes. The first type of cell division that you will learn about is called mitosis. **Mitosis** results in new cells with genetic material that is identical to that of the original cell. Mitosis occurs in the reproduction of unicellular organisms as well as in the addition of cells to a tissue or organ in a multicellular organism.

The type of cell division that you will learn about in Section 8-3 is called meiosis. **Meiosis** reduces the chromosome number by half in new cells. The new cells join together later in the organism's life cycle to produce cells with a complete set of chromosomes.

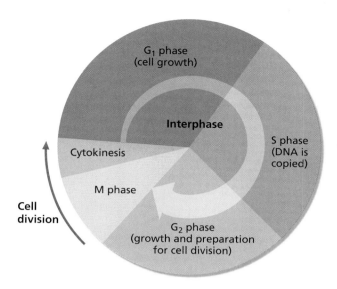

G₁ phase
(cell growth)

Interphase

Cytokinesis

S phase
(DNA is
copied)

M phase

Cell
division

G₂ phase
(growth and preparation
for cell division)

FIGURE 8-5

The life cycle of a cell—called the cell cycle—consists of interphase and cell division. Phases of growth, DNA replication, and preparation for cell division make up interphase. Cell division is divided into mitosis (division of the nucleus) and cytokinesis (division of the cytoplasm).

The Cell Cycle

The **cell cycle** is the repeating set of events that make up the life of a cell. Cell division is one phase of the cell cycle. The time between cell divisions is called **interphase.** Interphase is divided into three phases and cell division is divided into two phases, as illustrated in Figure 8-5.

During cell division, the chromosomes and cytoplasm are equally divided between two offspring cells. Cell division consists of mitosis and cytokinesis. During mitosis, or the **M phase,** the nucleus of a cell divides. **Cytokinesis** is the division of the cytoplasm of the cell.

Interphase

Notice in Figure 8-5 that cells spend most of their lifetime in interphase. Following cell division, offspring cells are approximately half the size of the original cell. During the first stage of interphase—called the **G_1 phase**—offspring cells grow to mature size. G_1 stands for the time gap following cell division and preceding DNA replication. After cells have reached a mature size, they typically proceed into the next phase of interphase, called the **S phase.** During the S phase, the cell's DNA is copied. The **G_2 phase** represents the time gap following DNA synthesis (S phase) and preceding cell division. The G_2 phase is a time during which the cell prepares for cell division.

Cells can also exit the cell cycle (usually from the G_1 phase) and enter into a state called the **G_0 phase.** During the G_0 phase, cells do not copy their DNA and do not prepare for cell division. Many cells in the human body are in the G_0 phase. For example, fully developed cells in the central nervous system stop dividing at maturity and normally never divide again.

Mitosis

Mitosis is the division of the nucleus, which occurs during cell division. Mitosis is a continuous process that is divided into four phases: prophase, metaphase, anaphase, and telophase.

Quick Lab

Identifying Prefixes and Suffixes

Materials dictionary, 3×5 in. index cards (18), pencil

Procedure

1. Write each of the following prefixes and suffixes on separate cards: *pro-, meta-, ana-, telo-, cyto-, oo-, inter-, -kinesis,* and *-genesis.*

2. Use a dictionary to find the definition of each prefix and suffix. Write the definitions on separate cards.

3. Play "Memory" with a partner. Mix the cards and place each one face down on the table. Turn over two cards. If the two cards consist of a prefix or suffix and its definition, pick up the cards and take another turn. If the two cards do not match, turn them face down again and leave them in the same place.

4. Repeat step 3 until no cards remain on the table. The player with the most pairs wins.

Analysis How does knowing the meaning of a prefix or suffix help you to understand the meaning of a word?

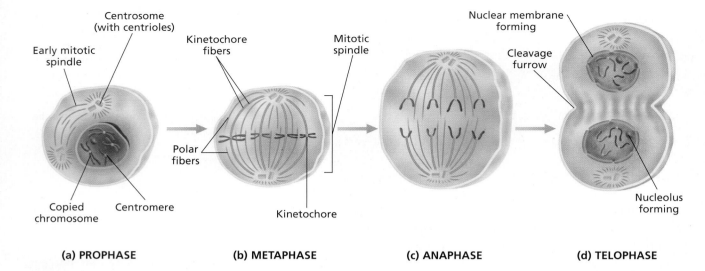

| (a) PROPHASE | (b) METAPHASE | (c) ANAPHASE | (d) TELOPHASE |

FIGURE 8-6

(a) During prophase, the copied DNA coils into chromosomes. (b) During metaphase, the chromosomes line up along the midline of the dividing cell. (c) During anaphase, the chromatids of each chromosome begin moving toward opposite poles of the cell. (d) During telophase, the chromosomes reach opposite poles of the cell, and the cytoplasm begins to divide.

Prophase is the first phase of mitosis. Prophase, shown in Figure 8-6, begins with the shortening and tight coiling of DNA into rod-shaped chromosomes that can be seen with a light microscope. Recall that during the S phase, each chromosome is copied. The two copies of each chromosome—called chromatids—stay connected to one another by the centromere. At this time, the nucleolus and the nuclear membrane break down and disappear.

Two pairs of dark spots called **centrosomes** appear next to the disappearing nucleus. In animal cells, each centrosome contains a pair of small, cylindrical bodies called **centrioles.** The centrosomes of plant cells lack centrioles. In both animal and plant cells, the centrosomes move toward opposite poles of the cell. As the centrosomes separate, **spindle fibers** made of microtubules radiate from the centrosomes in preparation for mitosis. This array of spindle fibers is called the **mitotic spindle,** which serves to equally divide the chromatids between the two offspring cells during cell division. Two types of spindle fibers make up the mitotic spindle: kinetochore fibers and polar fibers. **Kinetochore fibers** attach to a disk-shaped protein—called a **kinetochore**—that is found in the centromere region of each chromosome. Kinetochore fibers extend from the kinetochore of each chromatid to one of the centrosomes. **Polar fibers** extend across the dividing cell from centrosome to centrosome.

Metaphase is the second phase of mitosis. During metaphase, chromosomes are easier to identify using a microscope than during other phases; thus, karyotypes are typically made from photomicrographs of chromosomes in metaphase. During metaphase, the kinetochore fibers move the chromosomes to the center of the dividing cell. Once in the center of the cell, each chromosome is held in place by the kinetochore fibers.

During **anaphase,** the chromatids of each chromosome separate at the centromere and slowly move, centromere first, toward opposite poles of the dividing cell. When the chromatids separate, they are considered to be individual chromosomes.

Telophase is the fourth phase of mitosis. After the chromosomes reach opposite ends of the cell, the spindle fibers disassemble and the chromosomes return to a less tightly coiled chromatin state. A nuclear envelope forms around each set of chromosomes, and a nucleolus forms in each of the newly forming cells.

Cytokinesis

During telophase, the cytoplasm of the cell divides by a process called cytokinesis. In animal cells, cytokinesis begins with a pinching inward of the cell membrane midway between the dividing cell's two poles, as shown in Figure 8-7. The area of the cell membrane that pinches in and eventually separates the dividing cell into two cells is called the **cleavage furrow.** The cleavage furrow pinches the cell into two cells through the action of microfilaments.

Figure 8-8 shows cytokinesis in plant cells. In plant cells, vesicles formed by the Golgi apparatus fuse at the midline of the dividing cell, forming a membrane-bound cell wall called the **cell plate.** When complete, the cell plate separates the cell into two cells. In both animal cells and plant cells, offspring cells are approximately equal in size. Each offspring cell receives an identical copy of the original cell's chromosomes and approximately one-half of the original cell's cytoplasm and organelles.

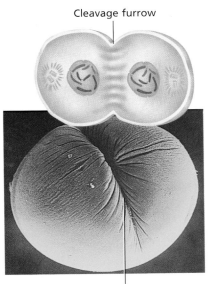

Cleavage furrow

Cleavage furrow

FIGURE 8-7

In animal cells, such as this frog cell, the cell membrane pinches in at the center of the dividing cell, eventually dividing the cell into two offspring cells. (SEM 78×)

Nuclei of new cells

Forming cell plate

Cell wall of original cell

Forming cell plate

Cell wall

FIGURE 8-8

In plant cells, such as this onion cell, a cell plate forms along the midline of the dividing cell, eventually dividing the cell into two offspring cells. (LM 4,104×)

SECTION 8-2 REVIEW

1. Describe the events of binary fission.

2. During which phase of the cell cycle are chromosomes copied?

3. Which phase of the cell cycle could you identify most readily with a light microscope? Explain your answer.

4. Describe the structure and function of the mitotic spindle.

5. Explain the main differences between cytokinesis in animal cells and cytokinesis in plant cells.

6. **CRITICAL THINKING** What would happen if cytokinesis took place before mitosis?

Research Notes

To View the Invisible

What controls the movement of chromosomes when the cell nucleus divides? This basic question has been studied by biologists for over 100 years. The answer will have great significance for society. Understanding what controls cell division in normal cells will help us understand what happens in cell anomalies, such as cancer.

In 1897, a German anatomist named Walther Flemming began to stain cells with a red dye in order to observe their internal contents during cell division. Because staining kills cells, Flemming had to view mitosis as a series of still images in the various stages of cell division. For many years after Flemming's work, it was not clear whether the spindle fibers, which emerge each time a cell reproduces, were permanent cellular structures. The debate over whether these fibers actively separate the chromosomes during cell division continued among cell biologists for more than 50 years.

During the early 1950s, a Japanese student named Shinya Inoue helped invent the techniques necessary to observe the dynamics of living cells. Inoue worked in the marine biology lab of his professor, Katsuma Dan, who was studying cell division in sea urchins. The electron microscopes they used produced the necessary high-resolution image but required killing and slicing the specimens. Sometimes, part of a cell was altered during the preparation. At the time, there were various light microscopes available that enabled observation of the dynamics of the living system. However, the resolution of those microscopes was not high enough to resolve fine details in the smallest areas of the cells. Dan challenged Inoue to develop a microscope that would allow biologists to study the movement of spindle fibers in dividing cells.

Inoue subsequently developed an improved microscope that enabled him to confirm the existence of spindle fibers in live sea urchin cells and to develop a model for the role the spindle fibers play in cell division. The very instability of the molecules that make up the spindle fibers suggested to Inoue a possible mechanism for chromosome movement. His experiments indicated that these fibers might move the chromosomes that are attached to them by assembling and disassembling. As the subunits of the molecules lengthened or shortened, the chromosomes that were attached to them moved. The bundle of spindle fibers that Inoue observed has since been identified as specialized microtubules. Not until the mid-1970s, however, were these fibers isolated from living cells.

At Woods Hole Oceanographic Institute, Inoue continued to be a pioneer in microscopy techniques for more than 40 years. He developed techniques to bring out the fine structural details of cellular organization, such as showing three-dimensional views of spindle fibers. According to Inoue, this opens up new opportunities for studies of developing embryos and cells undergoing mitosis without destroying the living cells. Such technological advances have brought science one step closer to understanding the complex dynamics of cell division.

Spindle microtubules

This micrograph (LM 1,080×) of the spindle apparatus during metaphase shows the spindle microtubules studied by Shinya Inoue. The wormlike structures in the center are the chromosomes.

MEIOSIS

Meiosis is a process of nuclear division that reduces the number of chromosomes in new cells to half the number in the original cell. The halving of the chromosome number counteracts a fusion of cells later in the life cycle of the organism. For example, in humans, meiosis produces haploid reproductive cells called **gametes.** *Human gametes are sperm cells and egg cells, each of which contains 23 (1n) chromosomes. The fusion of a sperm and an egg results in a zygote that contains 46 (2n) chromosomes.*

SECTION

8-3

OBJECTIVES

▲

List and describe the phases of meiosis.

●

Compare the end products of mitosis with those of meiosis.

■

Explain crossing-over and how it contributes to the production of unique individuals.

◆

Summarize the major characteristics of spermatogenesis and oogenesis.

STAGES OF MEIOSIS

Cells preparing to divide by meiosis undergo the G_1, S, and G_2 phases of interphase. Recall that during interphase, the cell grows to a mature size and copies its DNA. Thus, cells begin meiosis with a duplicate set of chromosomes, just as cells beginning mitosis do. Because cells undergoing meiosis divide twice, diploid (2n) cells that divide meiotically result in four haploid (1n) cells rather than two diploid (2n) cells. The stages of the first cell division are called meiosis I, and the stages of the second cell division are called meiosis II.

Meiosis I

The four phases of meiosis I are illustrated in Figure 8-9 on the next page. Notice how these phases compare with the corresponding phases of mitosis.

During prophase I, DNA coils tightly into chromosomes. As in the prophase of mitosis, spindle fibers appear. Then the nucleus and nucleolus disassemble. Notice how every chromosome lines up next to its homologue. The pairing of homologous chromosomes, which does not occur in mitosis, is called **synapsis.**

Each pair of homologous chromosomes is called a **tetrad.** In each tetrad, chromatids of the homologous chromosomes are aligned lengthwise so that the genes on one chromosome are adjacent to the corresponding genes on the other chromosome. During synapsis, the chromatids within a homologous pair twist around one another, as shown in Figure 8-10. Portions of chromatids may break off and attach to adjacent chromatids on the homologous chromosome—a process called **crossing-over.** This process permits the exchange of genetic material between maternal and paternal

internet**connect**

SC*LINKS*
NSTA

TOPIC: Meiosis
GO TO: www.scilinks.org
KEYWORD: HM153

Word Roots and Origins

tetrad

from the Greek *tetras,* meaning "four"

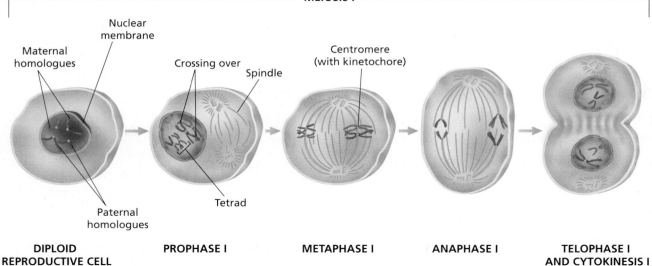

Maternal homologues

Nuclear membrane

Crossing over

Spindle

Centromere (with kinetochore)

Paternal homologues

Tetrad

DIPLOID REPRODUCTIVE CELL

PROPHASE I

METAPHASE I

ANAPHASE I

TELOPHASE I AND CYTOKINESIS I

FIGURE 8-9

Meiosis occurs in diploid reproductive cells. Before meiosis begins, the DNA of the diploid reproductive cells is copied. Meiosis I results in two haploid cells.

FIGURE 8-10

Crossing-over occurs when chromosomes that make up a tetrad exchange portions of their chromatids. Crossing-over results in an exchange of genes and in new combinations of genes.

chromosomes. Thus, crossing-over results in **genetic recombination** by producing a new mixture of genetic material.

During metaphase I, the tetrads line up randomly along the midline of the dividing cell. The orientation of the homologous pair of chromosomes is random with respect to the poles of the dividing cell. Spindle fibers from one pole attach to the centromere of one homologous chromosome. Spindle fibers from the opposite pole attach to the other homologous chromosome of the pair.

During anaphase I, each homologous chromosome (consisting of two chromatids attached by a centromere) moves to an opposite pole of the dividing cell, as shown in Figure 8-9. The random separation of the homologous chromosomes is called **independent assortment.** Independent assortment of the chromosomes results in a random separation of the maternal and paternal chromosomes, which results in genetic variation.

Telophase I is the final phase of meiosis I. During telophase I, the chromosomes reach the opposite ends of the cell, and cytokinesis begins. Notice that the new cells contain a haploid number of chromosomes.

During meiosis I, the original cell produces two new cells. Each new cell contains one chromosome from each homologous pair. The new cells contain half the number of chromosomes of the original cell. However, each new cell contains two copies of the chromosome because the original cell copied its DNA before meiosis I.

Meiosis II

Meiosis II occurs in each cell formed during meiosis I and is not preceded by the copying of DNA. The events of meiosis II are shown in Figure 8-11. In some species, meiosis II begins after the nuclear membrane re-forms in the new cells. In other species, meiosis II begins immediately following meiosis I.

Chromatids separate

Haploid offspring cells

PROPHASE II

METAPHASE II

ANAPHASE II

**TELOPHASE II
AND CYTOKINESIS II**

During prophase II, spindle fibers form and begin to move the chromosomes toward the midline of the dividing cell. In metaphase II, the chromosomes move to the midline of the dividing cell, facing opposite poles of the dividing cell. In anaphase II, the chromatids separate and move toward opposite poles of the cell.

In telophase II, a nuclear membrane forms around the chromosomes in each of the four new cells. Cytokinesis II occurs during telophase II, resulting in four new cells, each of which contains half of the original cell's number of chromosomes.

FIGURE 8-11

Meiosis II consists of prophase II, metaphase II, anaphase II, and telophase II. These events closely resemble those of mitosis. Meiosis II results in four haploid offspring cells.

Formation of Gametes

In animals, meiosis produces haploid reproductive cells called gametes, as shown in Figure 8-12. Because only those cells involved in the production of gametes divide by meiosis in animals, meiosis occurs only within their reproductive organs. In humans, meiosis occurs in the testes and in the ovaries.

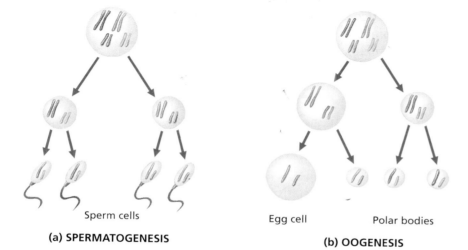

Sperm cells

(a) SPERMATOGENESIS

Egg cell

Polar bodies

(b) OOGENESIS

FIGURE 8-12

(a) In the formation of male gametes, the original cell produces four sperm cells by meiosis. (b) In the formation of egg cells, the original cell produces one egg and three polar bodies by meiosis. The egg cell receives most of the original cell's cytoplasm.

In the testes, meiosis is involved in the production of male gametes known as sperm cells or spermatozoa. In the development of sperm cells, a diploid reproductive cell divides meiotically to form four haploid cells called **spermatids.** Each spermatid then develops into a mature sperm cell. The production of sperm cells is called **spermatogenesis.**

Oogenesis (OH-oh-JEN-uh-sis) is the production of mature egg cells, or ova. During oogenesis, a diploid reproductive cell divides meiotically to produce one mature egg cell (ovum). During cytokinesis I and cytokinesis II of oogenesis, the cytoplasm of the original cell is divided unequally between new cells. As Figure 8-12 shows, one cell, which develops into a mature egg cell, receives most of the cytoplasm of the original cell. As a result, one egg cell is produced by meiosis. The other three products of meiosis, called **polar bodies,** degenerate.

Asexual and Sexual Reproduction

Asexual reproduction is the production of offspring from one parent. Asexual reproduction does not usually involve meiosis or the union of gametes. In unicellular organisms, such as bacteria, new organisms are created by either binary fission or mitosis. Asexual reproduction in multicellular organisms results from the budding off of portions of their bodies, as Figure 8-13 shows. The offspring from asexual reproduction are genetically identical to the parent.

Sexual reproduction is the production of offspring through meiosis and the union of a sperm and an egg. Offspring produced by sexual reproduction are genetically different from the parents because genes are combined in new ways in meiosis. In fact, except in the case of identical twins, sexually produced offspring contain unique combinations of their parents' genes. The evolutionary advantage of sexual reproduction is that it enables species to adapt rapidly to new conditions. For example, if disease strikes a crop of grain, a few plants may have genetic variations that make them resistant to the disease. While many individuals may die, these few resistant plants survive and reproduce.

FIGURE 8-13

Many plants, like this kalanchoe, produce offspring plantlets by asexual reproduction. Each plantlet, produced by mitotic cell divisions, is genetically identical to the parent plant.

SECTION 8-3 REVIEW

1. List two ways that meiosis differs from mitosis.

2. During which stage of meiosis is the diploid number of chromosomes reduced to the haploid number of chromosomes?

3. How many chromosomes do human gametes normally contain?

4. Explain the role of crossing-over in ensuring genetic variation.

5. Describe the primary differences between spermatogenesis and oogenesis.

6. **CRITICAL THINKING** Explain why the chromosomes in the haploid cells that are produced by meiosis I look different from those produced by meiosis II.

SUMMARY/VOCABULARY

8-1
- Chromosomes are tightly coiled DNA molecules and associated proteins.
- In eukaryotes, histone proteins help maintain the compact structure of chromosomes.
- In dividing cells, chromosomes are composed of two identical chromatids constricted together at a centromere.
- Chromosomes are categorized as either sex chromosomes or autosomes.
- Homologous chromosomes consist of one autosomal chromosome from each parent.
- Diploid (2n) is the number of chromosomes in cells that have homologous pairs of autosomes and two sex chromosomes.
- Haploid cells (1n) have half the number of chromosomes that are present in diploid cells.

Vocabulary

autosome (146)	diploid (147)	homologous chromosome (146)	nonhistone (145)
centromere (146)	haploid (147)	karyotype (147)	sex chromosome (146)
chromatid (146)	histone (145)		

8-2
- Cell division is the process by which cells reproduce themselves.
- Binary fission is the process of cell division in prokaryotes.
- The cell cycle is the repeating of events that make up the life of a cell. The cell cycle consists of cell division and interphase.
- Cell division in eukaryotes includes the division of the nucleus (mitosis) and the division of the cytoplasm (cytokinesis).
- Interphase consists of a phase of growth (G_1), a phase of DNA replication (S), and a phase of preparation for cell division (G_2).
- Mitosis is divided into prophase, metaphase, anaphase, and telophase. Mitosis results in two offspring cells that are genetically identical to the original cell.

Vocabulary

anaphase (150)	cleavage furrow (151)	kinetochore (150)	M phase (149)
binary fission (148)	cytokinesis (149)	kinetochore fiber (150)	polar fiber (150)
cell cycle (149)	G_0 phase (149)	meiosis (148)	prophase (150)
cell plate (151)	G_1 phase (149)	metaphase (150)	S phase (149)
centriole (150)	G_2 phase (149)	mitosis (148)	spindle fiber (150)
centrosome (150)	interphase (149)	mitotic spindle (150)	telophase (151)

8-3
- During meiosis, a cell divides twice.
- Crossing-over during meiosis results in genetic recombination.
- Spermatogenesis is the process by which sperm cells are produced. Oogenesis is the process that produces egg cells (ova).
- Asexual reproduction is the formation of offspring from one parent. Offspring produced by asexual reproduction are genetically identical to the parent.
- Sexual reproduction is the formation of offspring through the union of a sperm and an egg. Offspring produced by sexual reproduction are genetically different from the parents.

Vocabulary

asexual reproduction (156)	independent assortment (154)	polar body (156)	spermatogenesis (156)
crossing-over (153)	oogenesis (156)	sexual reproduction (156)	synapsis (153)
gamete (153)		spermatid (156)	tetrad (153)
genetic recombination (154)			

REVIEW

Vocabulary

1. Differentiate between a chromosome and a homologous chromosome pair.
2. Distinguish between mitosis, meiosis, and cytokinesis.
3. Distinguish between autosomes and sex chromosomes.
4. Distinguish between kinetochore fibers and polar fibers.
5. Explain the difference in meaning of the terms *haploid* and *diploid*.

Multiple Choice

6. Prokaryotic chromosomes (a) comprise at least two chromosomes (b) are made of DNA wrapped tightly around histone proteins (c) include histone and nonhistone proteins (d) consist of a circular DNA molecule.
7. A chromatid is (a) a dark stain (b) a dense substance within the nuclear membrane of a nondividing cell (c) one of two identical parts that make up a chromosome (d) the point at which each pair of chromatids is joined.
8. Every species has (a) haploid gametes (b) a distinctive number of chromosomes per cell (c) at least eight chromosomes per cell (d) a number of chromosomes that varies with the complexity of the organism.
9. Binary fission is (a) nuclear division of cells (b) eukaryotic cell division (c) sexual reproduction of prokaryotes (d) prokaryotic cell division.
10. Mitosis (a) can increase the number of body cells without changing the information contained in the DNA of those cells (b) is a means of reproducing sexually (c) is never triggered by cell size (d) results in offspring cells that are genetically different from the original cell.
11. Interphase is (a) composed of G_1, G_2, and G_3 (b) the time between meiosis I and meiosis II (c) a small part of the life cycle of a cell (d) a time of cell growth and development.
12. Cytokinesis (a) differs in animal and plant cells (b) does not occur in plant cells (c) immediately precedes mitosis (d) is a process of nuclear division.

13. Spermatogenesis produces (a) four haploid cells (b) four diploid cells (c) one haploid cell and three polar bodies (d) two haploid cells.
14. Oogenesis (a) produces diploid cells (b) requires meiotic cell divisions (c) produces four egg cells (d) produces one diploid cell and three polar bodies.
15. Crossing-over occurs during (a) mitosis (b) interphase (c) meiosis II (d) meiosis I.

Short Answer

16. What does the term *binary fission* refer to? In what type of organism does this type of cell division occur?
17. Discuss the events that occur in G_0, G_1, and G_2 phases.
18. Discuss the role of haploid cells in sexual reproduction.
19. What is the primary functional difference between mitotic anaphase and meiotic anaphase II?
20. Do asexual organisms have homologous chromosomes? Explain your answer.
21. Is there any functional difference between meiosis II and mitosis? Explain your answer.
22. Distinguish between sexual reproduction and asexual reproduction.
23. The photograph below shows cell division in a grasshopper testis. The offspring cells are gametes. Do you think the photograph shows mitosis or meiosis? Explain your answer.

24. **Unit 4—Cell Reproduction**

 Write a report summarizing how different cancer-fighting drugs kill cancer cells by interrupting the life cycle of the cells.

CRITICAL THINKING

1. Can mitosis occur in a cell in the absence of cytokinesis? Support your answer. If your answer is yes, provide a description of how the new cell would appear in the G_1 phase of the cell cycle.

2. If you consider the mass of DNA in a sperm (a haploid cell) to be 1, what would the relative value be for the DNA mass of a cell in the G_2 phase of the cell cycle?

3. Does a cell in metaphase II have the same mass of DNA as a diploid cell in the G_1 phase of the cell cycle? Assume that both cells are from the same animal. Explain your answer.

4. Would a human cell with *any* 23 chromosomes be haploid? Explain your answer.

5. For a cell to function efficiently, the magnitude of its surface area must greatly exceed that of its volume. Explain how cell division functions to maintain this relationship between surface area and volume and in doing so maintains cell homeostasis.

6. The events of mitosis in plants and animals are very similar with the exception of the absence of centrioles in plants. How has the absence of centrioles in plant cells influenced scientists' thinking about the function of centrioles in mitosis?

7. The graph below demonstrates the mass of DNA and chromosome number in each phase of mitosis. Based on the information presented in this graph, at which phase of mitosis are chromatids considered chromosomes? Explain your answer.

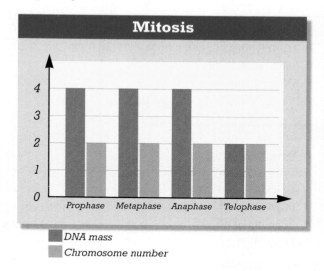

8. Develop graphs to illustrate the mass of DNA and chromosome number in each phase of meiosis I and meiosis II. Your graphs should be similar in format to the one shown for mitosis. For telophase, consider the DNA in only one of the offspring cells at the end of telophase. Let the number 1 represent the mass of DNA that is found in a human ovum. Let the number 1 equal the number of chromosomes found in a human ovum.

EXTENSION

1. Read "Cell Division Gatekeepers Identified" in *Science,* January 23, 2000, on page 477. Identify the cell structures that have been found to regulate the timing of cell division during mitosis. Describe the function of these structures. What conditions in reproductive cells might occur if these structures fail to function during cell division?

2. Read "Dolly's Mixture" in *New Scientist,* September 4, 1999, on page 5. Explain how

Dolly might not be the perfect clone she was once thought to be. What problems might this pose for researchers hoping to clone human tissue for transplants?

3. Do library or on-line research to find out how cancer cells differ from normal cells in relation to the cell cycle. Share the results of your research with your classmates.

Observing Mitosis in Plant Cells

OBJECTIVES

- Examine the dividing root-tip cells of an onion.
- Identify the phase of mitosis that different cells in an onion root tip are undergoing.
- Determine the relative length of time each phase of mitosis takes in onion root-tip cells.

PROCESS SKILLS

- observing
- classifying
- collecting
- organizing
- analyzing data
- calculating

MATERIALS

- compound light microscope
- prepared microscope slide of a longitudinal section of *Allium* (onion) root tip

Background

1. Mitosis is divided into four phases: prophase, metaphase, anaphase, and telophase.
2. Interphase is not considered a part of mitosis.
3. List the visible characteristics of each phase of mitosis.
4. In many plants, there are growth regions called meristems where mitosis is ongoing. Meristems are found in the tips of plant roots and shoots.

PART A   Identifying the Phases of Mitosis

1. Look at the photograph below of a longitudinal section of an onion root tip. Find the meristem on the photograph. As you can see, the meristem is located just behind the root cap.

ONION ROOT TIP

Apical meristem

Root cap

2. **CAUTION   Slides break easily. Use caution when handling them.** Using low power on your microscope, bring the meristem region on your slide into focus.

TABLE A RELATIVE DURATION OF EACH PHASE OF MITOSIS				
Phase of mitosis	Tally marks	Count	Percentage	Time (in minutes)
Prophase				
Metaphase				
Anaphase				
Telophase				

TABLE B DATA COLLECTED BY THE ENTIRE CLASS

Phase of mitosis	Count	Percentage	Time (in minutes)
Prophase			
Metaphase			
Anaphase			
Telophase			

3. Examine the meristem carefully. Choose a sample of about 50 cells. Look for a group of cells that appear to have been actively dividing at the time that the slide was made. The cells will appear in rows, so it should be easy to keep track of them. The dark-staining bodies are the nuclei.

4. In your lab report, prepare a data table like Table A.

5. For each of the cells in your sample, identify the stage of mitosis and place a mark in the "Tally marks" column beside the appropriate phase.

PART B Calculating the Relative Length of Each Phase

6. When you have classified each cell in your sample, count the tally marks for each phase and fill in the "Count" column. In which phase of mitosis were the greatest number of cells? In which phase were the fewest number of cells?

7. Calculate the percentage of cells found in each phase. Divide the number of cells in a phase by the total number of cells in your sample, and multiply by 100 percent. Enter the figures under "Percentage."

8. The percentage of cells found in each phase is a measure of how long each phase lasts. For example, if 25 percent of the cells are in prophase, then prophase takes 25 percent of the total time it takes for a cell to undergo mitosis. Mitosis in onion cells takes about 80 minutes. Calculate the actual time for each phase using this information and the percentage you have just determined.

$$\text{Duration of phase (in minutes)} =$$

$$\frac{\text{percentage}}{100} \times 80 \text{ minutes}$$

9. Record the actual time for each phase in your data table.

10. Make another data table, similar to Table B, shown above. Collect and record the count for each phase of mitosis for the entire class. Fill in the percentage and time information using the data collected by the entire class.

11. Clean up your materials before leaving the lab.

Analysis and Conclusions

1. What color are the chromosomes stained?

2. How can you distinguish between early and late anaphase?

3. According to your data table, which phase of mitosis lasts the longest? Why might this phase require more time than other phases of mitosis?

4. According to your data table, which phase takes the least amount of time?

5. How do your results compare with those of the entire class?

6. In this investigation, you assumed that the percentage of the total time that any given phase takes is equal to the percentage of cells in that phase at any moment. Why might this not be true for very small samples of cells?

Further Inquiry

1. Given the rate of mitosis in a type of animal cells, how could you determine how long each phase of mitosis takes in those cells?

2. Cancerous tissue is composed of cells undergoing uncontrolled, rapid cell division. How could you develop a procedure to identify cancerous tissue by counting the number of cells undergoing mitosis?

GENETICS

66 *. . . [G]enetics has come to occupy an important position at the center of the sciences of life . . . genetics became allied with biochemistry; it revolutionized bacteriology, played a major role in the emergence of the molecular biology of the fifties, resisted the challenge of ecology, took hold of cancer research and is even now reaching out to revolutionize taxonomy and its old rival embryology.* 99

From "Mendel, Mendelism and Genetics" by Robert C. Olby. Online, World Wide Web, July 2 1997. Copyright © 1997 by Robert C. Olby. Available http://www.netspace.org/MendelWeb/MWolby.html. Reprinted by permission of the author.

These tiger cub siblings look very similar to one another because they have inherited characteristics from their parents.

This researcher, above, is analyzing fragments of DNA that have been sorted into DNA fingerprints. The fruit fly at right is missing its right eye due to a genetic mutation.

Deoxyribonucleic acid (DNA)

This white-skinned, blue-eyed alligator has a genetic condition called leucism. The fruit fly, right, is often studied in genetics because it multiplies quickly and has only eight chromosomes.

FUNDAMENTALS OF GENETICS

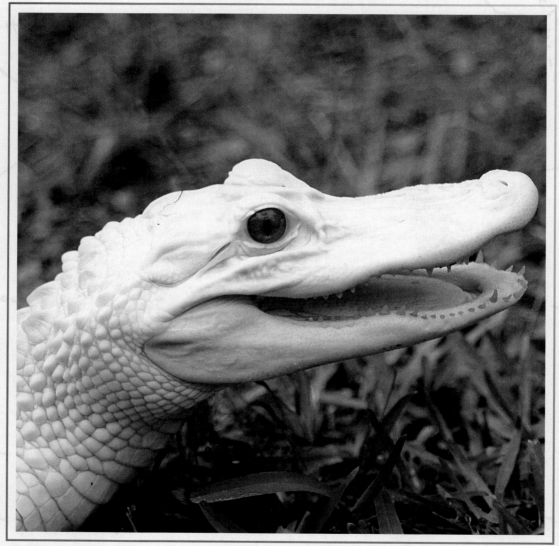

The unique appearance of this white-skinned, blue-eyed alligator is the result of a genetic condition.

FOCUS CONCEPT: *Reproduction and Inheritance*

As you read, notice how Mendel developed hypotheses to help predict the outcome of different genetic crosses.

Unit 5—Heredity
Topics 1–6

9-1 *Mendel's Legacy*

9-2 *Genetic Crosses*

MENDEL'S LEGACY

Genetics *is the field of biology devoted to understanding how characteristics are transmitted from parents to offspring. Genetics was founded with the work of Gregor Johann Mendel, an Austrian monk who experimented with garden peas. This section describes Mendel's experiments and the principles of genetics that resulted from them.*

OBJECTIVES

▲

Describe the steps involved in Mendel's experiments on garden peas.

●

Distinguish between dominant and recessive traits.

■

State two laws of heredity that were developed from Mendel's work.

◆

Explain the difference between an allele and a gene.

▲

Describe how Mendel's results can be explained by scientific knowledge of genes and chromosomes.

GREGOR MENDEL

In 1842, at the age of 21, Gregor Mendel entered a monastery in Brunn, Austria. His task of tending the garden gave him time to think and to observe the growth of many plants. In 1851 he entered the University of Vienna to study science and mathematics. His mathematics courses included training in the then-new field of statistics. Mendel's knowledge of statistics later proved valuable in his research on **heredity**—the transmission of characteristics from parents to offspring. When Mendel returned to the monastery, he taught in a high school and also kept a garden plot. Although he studied many plants, he is probably remembered most for his experiments with garden peas, *Pisum sativum.*

Mendel's Garden Peas

Mendel observed seven characteristics of pea plants. Each characteristic occurred in two contrasting **traits:** *plant height* (long or short stems), *flower position along stem* (axial or terminal), *pod color* (green or yellow), *pod appearance* (inflated or constricted), *seed texture* (smooth or wrinkled), *seed color* (yellow or green), and *flower color* (purple or white). Mendel used his knowledge of statistics to analyze his observations of these seven characteristics.

Mendel collected seeds from his pea plants, carefully recording the characteristics of the plant from which each seed was collected. The next year he planted the seeds. He observed that purple-flowering plants grew from the seeds obtained from purple-flowering plants, but he noticed that some white-flowering plants also grew from the seeds of purple-flowering plants. And when experimenting with the characteristic of plant height, he observed that while some tall plants grew from seeds obtained from tall plants, some short plants also grew from seeds obtained from tall plants. Mendel wanted to find an explanation for such variations.

Word Roots and Origins

heredity

from the Latin *hereditas,* meaning "heirship"

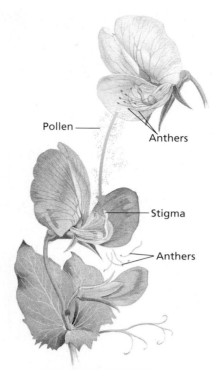

Pollen

Anthers

Stigma

Anthers

CROSS-POLLINATION

FIGURE 9-1

Mendel controlled the breeding of his pea plants and tracked the inheritance of traits by transferring pollen from the anthers of flowers on one plant to the stigma of flowers on a different plant.

SC**LINKS**
NSTA

TOPIC: Gregor Mendel
GO TO: www.scilinks.org
KEYWORD: HM166

Mendel's Methods

Mendel was able to document the traits of each generation's parents by carefully controlling how the pea plants were pollinated. **Pollination** occurs when pollen grains produced in the male reproductive parts of a flower, called the **anthers,** are transferred to the female reproductive part of a flower, called the **stigma.**

Self-pollination occurs when pollen is transferred from the anthers of a flower to the stigma of either the same flower or a flower on the same plant. **Cross-pollination** involves flowers of two separate plants. Pea plants normally reproduce through self-pollination.

Self-pollination can be interrupted—and cross-pollination performed—by removing the anthers from a flower and manually transferring the anther of a flower on one plant to the stigma of a flower on another plant, as shown in Figure 9-1. By doing this, Mendel was able to protect his flowers from receiving any other pollen that might be transferred by wind or insects, giving him more control over the pollination of his pea plants.

MENDEL'S EXPERIMENTS

Mendel studied each characteristic and its contrasting traits individually. He began by growing plants that were pure for each trait. Plants that are **pure** for a trait always produce offspring with that trait. For example, pea plants pure for the trait of yellow pods self-pollinate to produce offspring with yellow pods. The term **strain** denotes plants that are pure for a specific trait. Mendel produced strains by allowing the plants to self-pollinate for several generations. He eventually obtained 14 strains, one for each of the 14 traits he observed. He called each strain a parental generation, or **P$_1$ generation.**

Mendel then cross-pollinated these strains by transferring pollen from the anthers of a plant pure for one trait to the stigma of another plant pure for the contrasting trait. For example, if he wanted to cross a plant pure for the trait of yellow pods with one pure for the trait of green pods, he first removed the anthers from the plant that produced green pods. Then he dusted the pollen from a yellow-podded plant onto the stigma of a green-podded plant and allowed the seeds to develop.

When the plants matured, he recorded the number of each type of offspring produced by each P$_1$ plant. Mendel called the offspring of the P$_1$ generation the first filial generation, or **F$_1$ generation.** He then allowed the flowers from the F$_1$ generation to self-pollinate and collected the seeds. Mendel called the plants in this generation the second filial generation, or **F$_2$ generation.** Following this process, Mendel performed hundreds of crosses and documented the results of each by counting and recording the observed traits of every cross. Table 9-1 summarizes the results of many of Mendel's crosses.

TABLE 9-1 Mendel's Crosses and Results

Characteristic	P cross	F₁ generation	F₂ generation	Actual ratio	Probability ratio
Position of flowers along stem	axial × terminal	axial	651 axial 207 terminal	3.14:1	3:1
Height of plant	tall × short	tall	787 tall 277 short	2.84:1	3:1
Pod appearance	inflated × constricted	inflated	882 inflated 299 constricted	2.95:1	3:1
Pod color	green × yellow	green	428 green 152 yellow	2.82:1	3:1
Seed texture	smooth × wrinkled	smooth	5,474 smooth 1,850 wrinkled	2.96:1	3:1
Seed color	yellow × green	yellow	6,022 yellow 2,001 green	3.01:1	3:1
Flower color	purple × white	purple	705 purple 224 white	3.15:1	3:1

P₁

Green-podded plant   Yellow-podded plant

F₁

All green-podded plants

F₂

$\frac{3}{4}$ green-podded plants $\frac{1}{4}$ yellow-podded plant

FIGURE 9-2

Pure green-podded pea plants crossed with pure yellow-podded pea plants produce only green-podded plants. Yet when the F₁ generation is permitted to self-pollinate, some yellow-podded plants appear in the F₂ generation.

MENDEL'S RESULTS AND CONCLUSIONS

In one of his experiments, Mendel crossed a plant pure for green pods with one pure for yellow pods, as shown in Figure 9-2. The resulting seeds produced an F₁ generation with only green-podded plants. No yellow pods developed, even though one parent had been pure for yellow pods. Only one of the two traits found in the P₁ generation appeared in the F₁ generation.

Next Mendel allowed the F₁ plants to self-pollinate and planted the resulting seeds. When the F₂ generation plants grew, he observed that about three-fourths of the F₂ plants had green pods and about one-fourth had yellow pods.

Mendel's observations and his careful records led him to hypothesize that something within the pea plants controlled the characteristics he observed. He called these controls *factors*. Mendel hypothesized that each trait was inherited by means of a separate factor. Because the characteristics he studied had two alternative forms, he reasoned that there must be a *pair* of factors controlling each trait.

Recessive and Dominant Traits

Whenever Mendel crossed strains, one of the P₁ traits failed to appear in the F₁ plants. In every case, that trait reappeared in a ratio of about 3:1 in the F₂ generation. This pattern emerged in thousands of crosses and led Mendel to conclude that one factor in a pair may prevent the other from having an effect. Mendel hypothesized that the trait appearing in the F₁ generation was controlled by a **dominant** factor because it masked, or dominated, the other factor for a specific characteristic. The trait that did not appear in the F₁ generation but reappeared in the F₂ generation was thought to be controlled by a **recessive** factor.

Thus, a trait controlled by a recessive factor had no observable effect on an organism's appearance when it was paired with a trait controlled by a dominant factor.

The Law of Segregation

Mendel concluded that the paired factors separate during the formation of reproductive cells. This means that each reproductive cell, or gamete, receives only one factor of each pair. When two gametes combine during fertilization, the offspring have two factors controlling a specific trait. The **law of segregation** states that *a pair of factors is segregated, or separated, during the formation of gametes.*

The Law of Independent Assortment

Mendel also crossed plants that differed in two characteristics, such as in flower color and seed color. The data from these more-complex crosses showed that traits produced by dominant factors do not necessarily appear together. A green seed pod produced by a dominant factor could appear in a white-flowering pea plant, as Figure 9-3 shows. Mendel concluded that the factors for different characteristics are not connected. The **law of independent assortment** states that *factors for different characteristics are distributed to gametes independently.*

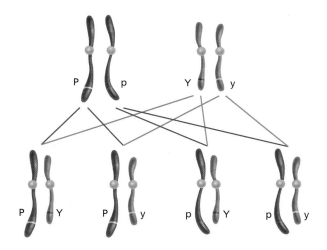

FIGURE 9-3

Independent assortment of these two pairs of homologous chromosomes would give the following allele combinations in gametes. *P* denotes flower color. *Y* denotes seed color.

CHROMOSOMES AND GENES

Most of Mendel's findings agree with what biologists now know about molecular genetics. **Molecular genetics** is the study of the structure and function of chromosomes and genes. Recall from Chapter 8 that a chromosome is a threadlike structure made up of DNA. A gene is the segment of DNA on a chromosome that controls a particular hereditary trait. Because chromosomes occur in pairs, genes also occur in pairs. Each of several alternative forms of a gene is called an **allele.** Mendel's *factors* are now called *alleles.*

Letters are used to represent alleles. Capital letters refer to dominant alleles, and lowercase letters refer to recessive alleles. For example, the dominant allele for the trait of green pod color may be represented by *G,* and the recessive allele for the trait of yellow pod color may be represented by *g.* Whether a letter is capitalized or lowercased is important. The actual letter selected to represent an allele is arbitrary.

Recall from Chapter 8 that during meiosis, gametes receive one chromosome from each homologous pair of chromosomes. This means that when the gametes combine in fertilization the offspring receives one allele for a given trait from each parent.

Mendel's law of independent assortment is supported by the fact that chromosomes segregate independently to gametes during meiosis. Therefore, the law of independent assortment is observed only for genes located on separate chromosomes or located far apart on the same chromosome.

SECTION 9-1 REVIEW

1. List the steps involved in Mendel's experiments on garden peas.

2. Define the terms *dominant* and *recessive.*

3. Differentiate genes from alleles.

4. State in modern terminology the two laws of heredity that resulted from Mendel's work.

5. How might Mendel's conclusions have differed if he had studied two traits determined by alleles carried on the same chromosome?

6. **CRITICAL THINKING** What happens during meiosis that would allow genes located on the same chromosome to separate independently of one another?

Jumping Genes

HISTORICAL PERSPECTIVE

The scientific study of heredity began with the work of Gregor Mendel. The rediscovery of Mendel's work in 1900 is said to mark the birth of the science of genetics. Geneticist Barbara McClintock, born in 1902, devoted her life to this new science. Ironically, certain assumptions about genetics, strongly believed but wrong, prevented early acceptance of McClintock's exciting conclusions.

Early Discoveries

Have you ever looked closely at ornamental corn, also called maize? Today it is planted and marketed for decorative use. In the fall, when the corn ripens, its red, brown, and purple ears are harvested and artistically arranged in centerpieces and door hangings.

In the late 1920s and early 1930s, at Cornell University, geneticists harvested the colorful plant for another purpose. They hoped to trace variations among maize plants to specific genes in an effort to discover how chromosomes carry specific traits to new generations.

As a graduate student at Cornell, Barbara McClintock began work on identifying and labeling the 10 chromosomes of maize. She developed new microscopic techniques and was able to visualize the parts of the maize chromosomes. Scientists were thrilled with her discovery because they could identify the chromosome that carried the gene for a particular trait.

After receiving her doctorate in botany in 1927, McClintock stayed at Cornell. Mostly she worked alone,

Barbara McClintock

wanting to observe everything for herself. She once said:

> No two plants are exactly alike. They're all different, and as a consequence, you have to know that difference.... I don't feel I really know the story if I don't watch the plant all the way along.

Discovering "Jumping Genes"

McClintock taught for several years at Cornell before taking a position as a research scientist at Cold Spring Harbor Laboratory, a scientific community on Long Island about 40 miles east of New York City. She stayed there for the rest of her life, working in maize genetics. There, during the 1940s and 1950s, she did the research and made the discovery for which she won the 1983 Nobel Prize in physiology or medicine.

The prevailing opinion among most geneticists in McClintock's time was that genes were lined up on chromosomes in unchanging places, much like beads on a string. McClintock's observations told her otherwise. The changes she saw in corn kernels and chromosomes led her to conclude that some genes, which she called transposons, are able to move to a new place on a chromosome or to a new chromosome entirely. These "jumping genes," she believed, cause differences to appear in a plant's offspring by either activating or inactivating the genes responsible for kernel color. Unlike with genetic recombination, which occurs during meiosis, transposons change the location of genes on chromosomes in the somatic cells of organisms.

McClintock observed two kinds of transposons: dissociators and activators. The dissociators could jump to a new place when signaled by others called activators. The dissociators would then cause changes in nearby genes on the chromosome and in the color of the kernels in maize. McClintock verified her conclusions through repeated experiments.

She Was Right
In the summer of 1951, at Cold Spring Harbor, McClintock presented her discovery at a meeting of scientists from around the world. Her presentation was not well received. McClintock summarized it best when she stated that her discovery went against "the dogma of the constancy of the genome." Although saddened

Ears of maize similar to these demonstrated to McClintock that certain genetic elements transpose.

by the lack of interest in her work, she was not discouraged. She knew that she was right and that the evidence would ultimately convince the world that transposons existed.

Why did most geneticists ignore McClintock's conclusions for so long? One reason was that their attention was directed to the work of the new molecular geneticists. Compared with their work, McClintock's seemed traditional, almost old-fashioned. Her fellow scientists were using electron microscopes capable of seeing molecules. Her methods—an ordinary microscope, crossbreeding, and observation—belonged to an earlier era. In working with maize genetics, she was "paddling upstream against the current of scientific opinion."

In the end, McClintock proved to be not behind her time but ahead of it. Biologist Allan Campbell once said of her discoveries, "The time was not ripe."

By the 1970s, the time was ripe. Molecular biologists, using electron microscopes and other technology, saw bits of DNA "jumping around" in bacteria. Transposons are thought to help bacteria better adapt to new environments. For example, transposons probably play a role in spreading genes for antibiotic resistance among bacteria. Scientists later found transposons in eukaryotes other than maize. Today all organisms, including humans, seem to have transposons.

Like McClintock, many geneticists now expect their understanding of transposons to help solve certain mysteries about evolution: how larger organisms developed from single cells and, in general, where new species come from. Transposons may also have medical applications, such as helping scientists discover how white blood cells make antibodies and what causes cells to sometimes multiply wildly, as in cancer.

OBJECTIVES

▲

Explain how probability
is used to predict the results
of genetic crosses.

●

Use a Punnett square to predict
the results of monohybrid and
dihybrid genetic crosses.

■

Explain how a testcross is
used to show the genotype of
an individual whose phenotype
is dominant.

◆

Differentiate a monohybrid cross
from a dihybrid cross.

GENETIC CROSSES

Today geneticists rely on Mendel's work to predict the likely outcome of genetic crosses. In this section, you will learn how to predict the probable genetic makeup and appearance of offspring resulting from specified crosses.

GENOTYPE AND PHENOTYPE

The genetic makeup of an organism is its **genotype** (JEN-uh-TIEP). The genotype consists of the alleles that the organism inherits from its parents. For example, the genotype of the white-flowering pea plant in Figure 9-4 consists of two recessive alleles for white flower color, represented as *pp*. The genotype of a purple-flowering pea plant may be either *PP* or *Pp*. Either of these two genotypes would result in a pea plant with purple flowers because the *P* allele is dominant.

The appearance of an organism as a result of its genotype is called its **phenotype** (FEE-noh-TIEP). The phenotype of a *PP* or a *Pp* pea plant is purple flowers, whereas the phenotype of a *pp* pea plant is white flowers. Human phenotypes can appear to be altered by behavior. Hair dye, contact lenses of varying colors, and plastic surgery can all change an individual's appearance, but they do not alter the individual's true phenotype or genotype.

FIGURE 9-4

The genotype of the pea plant on the left is *pp*. Its phenotype is white flowers. The phenotype of the pea plant on the right is purple flowers. Its genotype is either *Pp* or *PP*.

When both alleles of a pair are alike, the organism is said to be **homozygous** (HOH-moh-ZIE-guhs) for that characteristic. An organism may be homozygous dominant or homozygous recessive. For example, a pea plant that is homozygous dominant for flower color would have the genotype *PP*. A pea plant that is homozygous recessive for flower color would have the genotype *pp*. When the two alleles in the pair are different, the organism is **heterozygous** (HET-uhr-OH-ZIE-guhs) for that characteristic. A pea plant that is heterozygous for flower color would have the genotype *Pp*.

PROBABILITY

Probability is the likelihood that a specific event will occur. A probability may be expressed as a decimal, a percentage, or a fraction. Probability is determined by the following equation:

$$\text{Probability} = \frac{\text{number of times an event is expected to happen}}{\text{number of opportunities for an event to happen}}$$

For example, in Mendel's experiments the dominant trait of yellow seed color appeared in the F_2 generation 6,022 times. The recessive trait of green seed color appeared 2,001 times. The total number of individuals was 8,023 (6,022 + 2,001). Using the probability equation above, the probability that the dominant trait will appear in a similar cross is

$$\frac{6,022}{8,023} = 0.75$$

Expressed as a percentage, the probability is 75 percent. Expressed as a fraction, the probability is 3/4.

The probability that the recessive trait will appear in an F_2 generation is

$$\frac{2,001}{8,023} = 0.25$$

Expressed as a percentage, the probability is 25 percent. Expressed as a fraction, the probability is 1/4. Fractions can also be expressed as ratios. For example, the ratio 1:4 represents the same probability as 1/4. Probability tells us that there are three chances in four that an offspring of two heterozygous individuals will have the dominant trait and one chance in four that it will have the recessive trait.

The results predicted by probability are more likely to occur when there are many trials. For example, many coin tosses should yield a result of heads 50 percent of the time and tails 50 percent of the time. However, if you toss a coin only a few times, you might not get this result. But *each* time a coin is tossed, the probability of landing tails is 50 percent. Only after many, many tries would you be *likely* to get the percentage of heads predicted on the basis of probability, that is, 50 percent heads and 50 percent tails.

Quick Lab

Calculating Probability

Materials paper sack containing 20 jelly beans in an unknown number of color combinations

Procedure

1. Obtain a sack of 20 jelly beans from your teacher. Do not look into the sack. Do not eat the jelly beans. There are three possible colors of jelly beans that can be pulled from the sack. Pull one jelly bean out, and record the color. Return the jelly bean to the sack, and shake the bag to mix them.

2. Repeat step 1 until you have examined 20 jelly beans.

3. Determine the probability of each color of jelly bean that you pulled from the sack. Compare your results with those of the rest of the class.

Analysis Does anyone have the same probabilities as you? Are there some probabilities that are very close to yours? Are there some probabilities that are very different from yours? Based on these observations, determine the number of jelly beans of each color that are in your sack.

(pp)

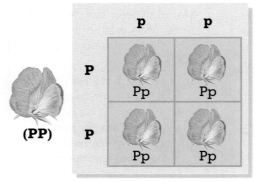

(PP)

FIGURE 9-5

A pea plant homozygous for purple flowers crossed with a pea plant homozygous for white flowers will produce only purple-flowering offspring. Note that all of the offspring will be heterozygous for flower color.

PREDICTING RESULTS OF MONOHYBRID CROSSES

A cross between individuals that involves one pair of contrasting traits is called a **monohybrid** (MAWN-oh-HIE-brid) **cross.** A cross between a pea plant that is pure for producing purple flowers and one that is pure for producing white flowers is an example of a monohybrid cross. Biologists use a diagram called a **Punnett** (PUHN-uht) **square,** like the one shown in Figure 9-5, to aid them in predicting the probability that certain traits will be inherited by offspring. The following examples show how a Punnett square can be used to predict the outcome of different types of crosses.

Example 1: Homozygous × Homozygous

The cross represented in Figure 9-5 is a monohybrid cross between a pea plant homozygous for purple flower color (*PP*) and a pea plant homozygous for white flower color (*pp*). The alleles contributed by the homozygous dominant parent are represented by *P*s on the left side of the Punnett square. The alleles contributed by the homozygous recessive parent are represented by *p*s across the top of the Punnett square. Each box within the Punnett square is filled in with the letters that are above it and beside it outside the square. The combinations of alleles in the four boxes indicate the possible genotypes that can result from the cross. The predicted genotype is *Pp* in every case. Thus, there is a 100 percent probability that the offspring will have the genotype *Pp* and thus the phenotype purple flower color.

Example 2: Homozygous × Heterozygous

Figure 9-6 shows a cross between a guinea pig that is homozygous dominant for the trait of black coat color (*BB*) and a guinea pig that is heterozygous for this trait (*Bb*). The letter *b* stands for the recessive allele. Genotype *bb* results in a brown coat. Notice that there are two possible genotypes that can result from this cross, *BB* or *Bb*. The probability of an offspring with the genotype *BB* is 2/4, or 50 percent. The probability of an offspring with the genotype *Bb* is also 2/4, or 50 percent. In other words, you could expect about 50 percent of the offspring resulting from this cross to be homozygous dominant for the black coat and about 50 percent to be heterozygous dominant for a black coat. The probable phenotype is black coat color in every case; thus, 4/4, or 100 percent, of the offspring are expected to have a black coat. What if the homozygous guinea pig had been homozygous recessive for coat color? In this case, the homozygote would have the genotype *bb*. Crossing a *bb* guinea pig with a *Bb* guinea pig is likely to produce about 50 percent *Bb* offspring and about 50 percent *bb* offspring.

FIGURE 9-6

Crossing a guinea pig homozygous for black coat color with one heterozygous for black coat color produces all black-coated offspring. Note that half of the offspring are predicted to be homozygous for coat color.

(Bb)

(BB)

(Bb)

(Bb)

FIGURE 9-7

Crossing two rabbits that are both heterozygous for black coat color tends to produce 50 percent heterozygous black individuals, 25 percent homozygous black individuals, and 25 percent homozygous brown individuals.

Example 3: Heterozygous × Heterozygous

In rabbits, the allele for black coat color (*B*) is dominant over the allele for brown coat color (*b*). The Punnett square in Figure 9-7 shows the predicted results of crossing two rabbits that are both heterozygous (*Bb*) for coat color. As you can see, 1/4 (25 percent) of the offspring are predicted to have the genotype *BB*, 1/2 (50 percent) are predicted to have the genotype *Bb*, and 1/4 (25 percent) are predicted to have the genotype *bb*. Thus, 3/4 (75 percent) of the offspring resulting from this cross are predicted to have a black coat. One-fourth (25 percent) of the offspring are predicted to have a brown coat.

The ratio of the genotypes that appear in offspring is called the **genotypic ratio.** The probable genotypic ratio of the monohybrid cross represented in Figure 9-7 is 1 *BB*:2 *Bb*:1 *bb*. The ratio of the offsprings' phenotypes is called the **phenotypic ratio.** The probable phenotypic ratio of the cross represented in Figure 9-7 is 3 black:1 brown.

Example 4: Testcross

Recall that in guinea pigs, both *BB* and *Bb* result in a black coat. How might you determine whether a black guinea pig is homozygous (*BB*) or heterozygous (*Bb*)? You could perform a **testcross,** in which an individual of unknown genotype is crossed with a homozygous recessive individual. A testcross can determine the genotype of any individual whose phenotype is dominant. You can see from Figure 9-8 that if the unknown genotype is homozygous black, all offspring will be black. If the individual with the unknown genotype is heterozygous black, about half of the offspring will be black. In reality, if the cross produced one brown offspring in a litter of eight, the genotype of the black-coated parent is likely to be heterozygous.

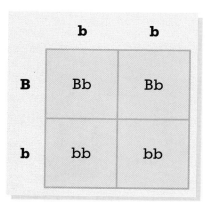

FIGURE 9-8

If a black guinea pig is crossed with a brown guinea pig and even one of the offspring is brown, chances are that the black guinea pig is heterozygous for coat color.

FIGURE 9-9

When red-flowering four o'clocks are crossed with white-flowering four o'clocks, all of the F₁ offspring produce pink flowers, an intermediate between the two phenotypes. When the F₁ generation is interbred, red-flowering, pink-flowering, and white-flowering plants are produced because the trait for red flower color has incomplete dominance over the trait for white flower color.

SCI LINKS
NSTA

TOPIC: Dominance
GO TO: www.scilinks.org
KEYWORD: HM176

FIGURE 9-10

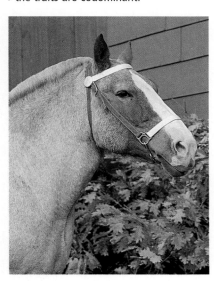

The roan coat of this horse consists of both white hairs and red hairs. Both phenotypes are expressed in individuals heterozygous for coat color when the traits are codominant.

Example 5: Incomplete Dominance

Recall that in Mendel's pea-plant crosses, one allele was completely dominant over another, a relationship called **complete dominance.** In complete dominance, heterozygous plants and dominant homozygous plants are indistinguishable in phenotype. For example, both pea plants *PP* and *Pp* for flower color have purple flowers.

Sometimes, however, the F₁ offspring will have a phenotype in between that of the parents, a relationship called **incomplete dominance.** Incomplete dominance occurs when two or more alleles influence the phenotype, resulting in a phenotype intermediate between the dominant trait and the recessive trait. In four o'clocks, for example, both the allele for red flowers (*R*) and the allele for white flowers (*r*) influence the phenotype. Neither allele is completely dominant over the other allele. When four o'clocks self-pollinate, red-flowering plants produce only red-flowering offspring, and white-flowering plants produce only white-flowering offspring. However, when red four o'clocks are crossed with white four o'clocks, the F₁ offspring all have *pink* flowers. One hundred percent of the offspring of this cross have the (*Rr*) genotype, which results in a pink phenotype.

What would be the result of crossing two pink-flowering (*Rr*) four o'clocks? As the Punnett square in Figure 9-9 shows, the probable genotypic ratio is 1 *RR*:2 *Rr*:1 *rr*. Given that neither the allele for red flowers (*R*) nor the allele for white flowers (*r*) is completely dominant, the probable phenotypic ratio is 1 red:2 pink:1 white.

Example 6: Codominance

Codominance occurs when both alleles for a gene are expressed in a heterozygous offspring. In codominance, neither allele is dominant or recessive, nor do the alleles blend in the phenotype. For example, the genes for both white coat color and red coat color are expressed in the horse shown in Figure 9-10. The capital letter *R* is used to indicate red coat color, and *R′* is used to indicate white coat color. Thus, the *RR′* symbol would represent the coat color of the roan horse in Figure 9-10.

PREDICTING RESULTS OF DIHYBRID CROSSES

A **dihybrid** (die-HIE-brid) **cross** is a cross between individuals that involves two pairs of contrasting traits. Predicting the results of a dihybrid cross is more complicated than predicting the results of a monohybrid cross because there are more possible combinations of alleles to work out. For example, to predict the results of a cross involving both seed texture and seed color, you have to consider how the four alleles from each parent can combine.

Homozygous × Homozygous

Suppose that you want to predict the results of a cross between a pea plant that is homozygous for round, yellow seeds and one that is homozygous for wrinkled, green seeds. In pea plants, the allele for round seeds (*R*) is dominant over the allele for wrinkled seeds (*r*), and the allele for yellow seeds (*Y*) is dominant over the allele for green seeds (*y*).

As Figure 9-11 shows, the Punnett square used to predict the results of a cross between a parent of the genotype *RRYY* and a parent of the genotype *rryy* will contain 16 boxes. The independently sorted alleles from one parent—*RY, RY, RY,* and *RY*—are listed along the left side of the Punnett square. The independently sorted alleles from the other parent—*ry, ry, ry,* and *ry*—are listed along the top of the Punnett square. Each box is filled with the letters that are above it and to the left of it outside the square. Notice that the genotype of all the offspring of this cross will be heterozygous for both traits, *RrYy;* therefore, the phenotype of all the offspring will have round, yellow seeds.

Quick Lab

Determining Genotypes

Materials pencil and paper

Procedure The ability to roll the tongue upward from the sides is a dominant, inherited trait. In one family, both parents and three children are all tongue rollers, while one child is not. Determine the genotype and phenotype of each parent.

Analysis Are the parents homozygous or heterozygous? Are the children homozygous or heterozygous?

rryy

RRYY

	ry	**ry**	**ry**	**ry**
RY	RrYy	RrYy	RrYy	RrYy
RY	RrYy	RrYy	RrYy	RrYy
RY	RrYy	RrYy	RrYy	RrYy
RY	RrYy	RrYy	RrYy	RrYy

FIGURE 9-11

This Punnett square shows a dihybrid cross between a pea plant that is homozygous recessive for wrinkled, green seeds *(rryy)* and a pea plant that is homozygous dominant for smooth, yellow seeds *(RRYY)*.

Heterozygous × Heterozygous

To determine the results of crossing two pea plants heterozygous for round, yellow seeds, the procedure is the same. As Figure 9-12 shows, the offspring of this dihybrid cross are likely to have nine different genotypes. These nine genotypes will result in pea plants with the following four phenotypes:

- 9/16 with round, yellow seeds (genotypes *RRYY, RRYy, RrYY,* and *RrYy*)
- 3/16 with round, green seeds (genotypes *RRyy* and *Rryy*)
- 3/16 with wrinkled, yellow seeds (genotypes *rrYY* and *rrYy*)
- 1/16 with wrinkled, green seeds (genotype *rryy*)

FIGURE 9-12

A dihybrid cross of two individuals heterozygous for both traits is likely to result in nine different genotypes and four different phenotypes.

RrYy

RrYy

	RY	**Ry**	**rY**	**ry**
RY	RRYY	RRYy	RrYY	RrYy
Ry	RRYy	RRyy	RrYy	Rryy
rY	RrYY	RrYy	rrYY	rrYy
ry	RrYy	Rryy	rrYy	rryy

SECTION 9-2 REVIEW

1. **Explain how you might go about determining the genotype of a purple-flowering pea plant.**

2. **What is the equation used to determine probability? In what ways can probability be expressed?**

3. **If you were to cross pink-flowering four o'clocks with white-flowering four o'clocks, what results would you expect? Provide a Punnett square to support your answer.**

4. **Explain how you would use a Punnett square to predict the probable outcome of a monohybrid cross.**

5. **Explain the difference between a monohybrid cross and a dihybrid cross. Give an example of each.**

6. **CRITICAL THINKING** The offspring of two short-tailed cats have a 25 percent chance of having no tail, a 25 percent chance of having a long tail, and a 50 percent chance of having a short tail. Based on this information, what can you hypothesize about the genotypes of the parents?

CHAPTER 9 REVIEW

SUMMARY/VOCABULARY

9-1
- The study of how characteristics are transmitted from parents to offspring is called genetics.
- Self-pollination, in which pollen is transferred from the anthers of a flower to either the stigma of the same flower or the stigma of another flower on the same plant, normally occurs in pea plants. Cross-pollination occurs when pollen is transferred between flowers of two different plants.
- Mendel concluded that inherited characteristics are controlled by factors that occur in pairs. In his experiments on pea plants, one factor in a pair masked the other. The trait that masked the other was called the dominant trait. The trait that was masked was called a recessive trait.

- We now know that the factors that Mendel studied are alleles, or alternative forms of a gene.
- The law of segregation states that a pair of factors is segregated, or separated, during the formation of gametes. The law of independent assortment is observed only for genes that are located on separate chromosomes or far apart on the same chromosome.
- The law of independent assortment states that factors for different characteristics are distributed to gametes independently. You know this to be true from your study of meiosis: during prophase I of meiosis, homologous chromosomes randomly migrate to opposite sides of the dividing cell.

Vocabulary

allele (169)	F_2 generation (166)	law of segregation (168)	recessive (168)
anther (166)	genetics (165)	molecular genetics (169)	self-pollination (166)
cross-pollination (166)	heredity (165)	P_1 generation (166)	stigma (166)
dominant (168)	law of independent	pollination (166)	strain (166)
F_1 generation (166)	assortment (169)	pure (166)	trait (165)

9-2
- The genotype is the genetic makeup of an organism. An organism's phenotype is its appearance as a result of its genotype.
- Probability is the likelihood that a specific event will occur. A probability may be expressed as a decimal, a percentage, or a fraction.
- A Punnett square can be used to predict the outcome of genetic crosses.
- A cross between individuals involving one pair of contrasting traits is a monohybrid cross.
- A testcross, in which an individual of unknown genotype is crossed with a homozygous recessive individual, can be used to determine the genotype of an individual whose phenotype is dominant.

- Complete dominance occurs when heterozygous individuals and dominant homozygous individuals are indistinguishable in phenotype.
- Incomplete dominance occurs when two or more alleles influence the phenotype, resulting in a phenotype intermediate between the dominant trait and the recessive trait.
- Codominance occurs when both alleles for a gene are expressed in a heterozygous offspring. Neither allele is dominant or recessive, nor do the alleles blend in the phenotype as they do in incomplete dominance.
- A cross between individuals involving two pairs of contrasting traits is called a dihybrid cross.

Vocabulary

codominance (176)	genotypic ratio (175)	monohybrid cross (174)	Punnett square (174)
complete dominance (176)	heterozygous (173)	phenotype (172)	testcross (175)
dihybrid cross (177)	homozygous (173)	phenotypic ratio (175)	
genotype (172)	incomplete dominance (176)	probability (173)	

REVIEW

Vocabulary

1. State and define the two laws of heredity.
2. Differentiate self-pollination from cross-pollination.
3. What is the difference between a dominant trait and a recessive trait?
4. Differentiate genotype from phenotype.
5. What is the difference between *homozygous* and *heterozygous*?

Multiple Choice

6. A procedure in which an individual of unknown genotype is crossed with a homozygous recessive individual to determine the genotype of the unknown individual is called a (a) monohybrid cross (b) dihybrid cross (c) hybrid cross (d) testcross.
7. A gene is a (a) segment of DNA (b) chromosome (c) segment of RNA (d) protein.
8. An example of a genotype of a heterozygous individual is (a) *pp* (b) *YY* (c) *Zz* (d) none of the above.
9. In a monohybrid cross of two heterozygous parents (*Pp*), one would expect the offspring to be (a) 1 *pp*:3 *PP* (b) 3 *Pp*:1 *pp* (c) 1 *PP*:2 *Pp*:1 *pp* (d) all *Pp*.
10. In a monohybrid cross between a homozygous dominant parent and a homozygous recessive parent, one would predict the offspring to be (a) 3:4 homozygous recessive (b) 2:4 homozygous recessive (c) 1:4 homozygous recessive (d) all heterozygous.
11. In guinea pigs, black fur is dominant. If a black guinea pig is crossed with a white guinea pig and the litter contains a white offspring, the genotype of the black-haired parent is probably (a) homozygous dominant (b) homozygous recessive (c) pure for the trait (d) heterozygous dominant.
12. Segregation of alleles occurs during (a) mitosis (b) meiosis (c) fertilization (d) pollination.
13. In a dihybrid cross between two heterozygous parents, the probability of obtaining an offspring that is homozygous recessive for both traits would be (a) none (b) 9/16 (c) 3/16 (d) 1/16.

14. If two parents with dominant phenotypes produce an offspring with a recessive phenotype, then (a) both parents are heterozygous (b) one parent is heterozygous (c) both parents are homozygous (d) one parent is homozygous.
15. Suppose that you have found a new species of plant. Some of the plants have red flowers and some have yellow flowers. You cross a red-flowering plant with a yellow-flowering plant, and all the offspring have orange flowers. You might assume that the alleles for flower color (a) have complete codominance (b) have incomplete dominance (c) are either dominant or recessive (d) have mutated.

Short Answer

16. Why did Mendel begin his experiments by allowing pea plants to self-pollinate for several generations?
17. Answer the following questions based on the Punnett square shown below:
    a. Does the Punnett square demonstrate a monohybrid cross or a dihybrid cross?
    b. List the genotypes of the parents.
    c. Give the genotypic ratio predicted by the Punnett square for the cross.

	QT	Qt	qT	qt
QT	QQTT	QQTt	QqTT	QqTt
Qt	QQTt	QQtt	QqTt	Qqtt
qT	QqTT	QqTt	qqTT	qqTt
qt	QqTt	Qqtt	qqTt	qqtt

18. Unit 5—*Heredity*

     Write a report summarizing how an understanding of heredity allows animal breeders to develop animals with desirable traits. Find out what kinds of animals are bred for special purposes.

19. Explain the difference between the P generation, F_1 generation, and F_2 generation.

20. When the dominant and recessive traits are known, why is it not necessary to use the term *homozygous* when referring to the genotype of an individual with a recessive phenotype?

21. Explain the difference between a monohybrid cross and a dihybrid cross.

22. How might crossing-over during meiosis affect the segregation of genes on the same chromosome?

23. Relate the events of meiosis to the law of segregation.

24. In pea plants, smooth seed texture is dominant over wrinkled seed texture. A gardener has a pea plant that produces smooth seeds. How can the gardener determine whether the plant is homozygous or heterozygous for the allele that determines seed texture?

25. In rabbits, the allele for black coat color (*B*) is dominant over the allele for brown coat color (*b*). Predict the results of a cross between a rabbit homozygous for black coat color (*BB*) and a rabbit homozygous for brown coat color (*bb*).

CRITICAL THINKING

1. One rule of probability can be expressed as the following: The probability of two independent events occurring simultaneously is the product of the probability of their occurring separately. If, for example, you had a pair of dice and rolled each die one at a time, what would be the probability that you would get two 4s? On the first roll, you would have a 1/6 chance. On the second roll, you would have a 1/6 chance. The probability of obtaining two 4s would be $1/6 \times 1/6 = 1/36$. Suppose you were playing a game with five dice. What is the chance of rolling a 6 on all five dice?

2. A cross between two pea plants with axial flowers and inflated pods gives the following offspring: 20 with axial flowers and inflated pods, 7 with axial flowers and constricted pods, and 5 with terminal flowers and inflated pods. What is the most probable genotype for the two parents? Explain the results and show the Punnett square. How can the explanation be checked?

3. Two black female mice are crossed with the same brown male mouse. Based on the information shown in the table below, answer the following questions:
   a. What are the genotypes of each parent?
   b. Which trait is dominant?
   c. Is the dominance of the trait in (b) completely dominant, incompletely dominant, or codominant? Explain your answer.

Results of Crossing Two Black Female Mice with One Brown Male Mouse	
P_1 generation	F_1 generation
female A × male A	9 black, 7 brown
female B × male A	14 black, 0 brown

EXTENSION

1. Read "The Genes of 1998" in *Discover*, January 1999, on page 33. Describe how a mutation on chromosome 8 causes a rare form of baldness. What might be one explanation for why humans no longer have a sharp sense of smell? Explain how a genetic disorder can actually cause a person to display symptoms of psychiatric illness.

2. Toss a penny and a nickel together 32 times, and record the results as they fall: number of times heads comes up for both the penny and the nickel, number of times tails comes up for both the penny and the nickel, number of times the penny is heads and the nickel is tails, and the number of times the penny is tails and the nickel is heads. Explain how this task illustrates independent assortment.

Modeling Monohybrid Crosses

OBJECTIVES

- Predict the genotypic and phenotypic ratios of offspring resulting from the random pairing of gametes.
- Calculate the genotypic ratio and phenotypic ratio among the offspring of a monohybrid cross.

PROCESS SKILLS

- predicting
- organizing
- analyzing data
- calculating

MATERIALS

- lentils
- green peas
- 2 Petri dishes

Background

1. How many traits are involved in a monohybrid cross? How many alleles are involved?
2. What prevents the expression of a recessive allele?
3. When gametes form, what happens to the alleles for each trait?

PART A Simulating a Monohybrid Cross

1. You will model the random pairing of alleles by choosing lentils and peas from Petri dishes. These dried seeds will represent the alleles for seed color. A green pea will represent *G*, the dominant allele for green seeds, and a lentil will represent *g*, the recessive allele for yellow seeds.
2. Each Petri dish will represent a parent. Label one Petri dish "female gametes" and the other Petri dish "male gametes." Place one green pea and one lentil in the Petri dish labeled "female gametes" and place one green pea and one lentil in the Petri dish labeled "male gametes."

3. Each parent contributes one allele to each offspring. Model a cross between these two parents by choosing a random pairing of the dried seeds from the two containers. Do this by simultaneously picking one seed from each container *without looking*. Place the pair of seeds together on the lab table. The pair of seeds represents the genotype of one offspring.
4. Record the genotype of the first offspring in your lab report in a table like Table A shown below.

TABLE A *GAMETE PAIRINGS*

Trial	Offspring genotype	Offspring phenotype
1		
2		
3		
4		
5		
6		
7		
8		
9		
10		

5. Return the seeds to their original dishes and repeat step 3 nine more times. Record the genotype of each offspring in your data table.
6. Based on each offspring's genotype, determine and record each offspring's phenotype. Assume that the allele for green seeds, *G*, is completely dominant over the allele for yellow seeds, *g*.

PART B Calculating Genotypic and Phenotypic Ratios

7. In your lab report, prepare a data table similar to Table B shown below.
8. Determine the genotypic and phenotypic ratios among the offspring. First count and record the number of homozygous dominant, heterozygous, and homozygous recessive individuals you recorded in Table A. Then record the number of offspring that produce green seeds and the number that produce yellow seeds under "Phenotypes" in your data table.
9. Calculate the genotypic ratio for each genotype using the following equation:

$$\text{Genotypic ratio} = \frac{\text{number of offspring with a given genotype}}{\text{total number of offspring}}$$

10. Calculate the phenotypic ratio for each phenotype using the following equation:

$$\text{Phenotypic ratio} = \frac{\text{number of offspring with a given phenotype}}{\text{total number of offspring}}$$

11. Now pool the data for the whole class, and record the data in your lab report in a table like Table C.
12. Compare your class's sample with your small sample of 10. Calculate the genotypic and phenotypic ratios for the class data, and record them in your data table.
13. Construct a Punnett square showing the parents and their offspring in your lab report.
14. Clean up your materials before leaving the lab.

Analysis and Conclusions

1. What trait is being studied in this investigation?
2. What are the genotypes of the parents? Describe the genotypes of both parents using the terms *homozygous* or *heterozygous,* or both.
3. What does each seed in the Petri dish represent?
4. When the seeds were selected and paired, what did the pairs represent?
5. Did tables B and C reflect a classic monohybrid-cross phenotypic ratio of 3:1?
6. When the class data were tabulated, did a classic monohybrid-cross ratio of a phenotype of 3:1 result?
7. If a genotypic ratio of 1:2:1 is observed, what must the genotypes of both parents be?
8. Show what the genotypes of the parents would be if 50 percent of the offspring were green and 50 percent of the offspring were yellow.
9. Construct a Punnett square for the cross of a heterozygous black guinea pig and an unknown guinea pig whose offspring include a recessive white-furred individual. What are the possible genotypes of the unknown parent?

Further Inquiry

Design a model to demonstrate a dihybrid cross of two parents that are heterozygous for two traits. Construct and complete a Punnett square for this cross.

TABLE B *OFFSPRING RATIOS*

Genotypes	Total	Genotypic ratio
Homozygous dominant (*GG*)		
Heterozygous (*Gg*)		
Homozygous recessive (*gg*)		____ : ____ : ____
Phenotypes		**Phenotypic ratio**
Green seeds		
Yellow seeds		____ : ____ : ____

TABLE C *OFFSPRING RATIOS (Entire Class)*

Genotypes	Total	Genotypic ratio
Homozygous dominant (*GG*)		
Heterozygous (*Gg*)		
Homozygous recessive (*gg*)		____ : ____ : ____
Phenotypes		**Phenotypic ratio**
Green seeds		
Yellow seeds		____ : ____ : ____

NUCLEIC ACIDS AND PROTEIN SYNTHESIS

The most common form of DNA found in living organisms has a spiral-staircase shape, as shown in this computer model of the molecule's structure.

FOCUS CONCEPT: *Cell Structure and Function*

As you read, pay attention to the roles that DNA and RNA play in storing information and making proteins.

Unit 6—Gene Expression
Topics 1–6

DNA

What hat enables cells to have different forms and to perform different functions? Ultimately the genetic source of this amazing diversity is deoxyribonucleic acid (DNA). The primary function of DNA in organisms is to store and transmit the genetic information that tells cells which proteins to make and when to make them. Proteins in turn form the structural units of cells and help control chemical processes within cells.

SECTION

10-1

OBJECTIVES

▲

Explain the principal function of DNA.

●

Describe the structure of DNA.

■

Define the term *complementary base pairing.*

◆

Explain the role of complementary base pairing in the replication of DNA.

▲

Summarize the main features of DNA replication.

STRUCTURE OF DNA

Recall from Chapter 3 that the nucleic acid DNA is an organic compound. DNA is made up of repeating subunits called nucleotides. Each DNA molecule consists of two long chains of nucleotides.

A DNA nucleotide has three parts: a sugar molecule called **deoxyribose;** a phosphate group, which consists of a phosphorus, P, atom surrounded by oxygen, O, atoms; and a molecule that is referred to as a **nitrogen-containing base** because it contains a nitrogen, N, atom. The three parts of a DNA nucleotide are illustrated in Figure 10-1. The deoxyribose sugar and the phosphate group are identical in all DNA nucleotides. However, the nitrogen-containing base may be any one of four different kinds.

The four nitrogen-containing bases found in DNA nucleotides are **adenine, guanine, cytosine,** and **thymine.** It is customary to represent nucleotides by the abbreviations for their nitrogen-containing bases. A nucleotide containing adenine is represented by an *A.* Likewise, C = cytosine, G = guanine, and T = thymine.

internet**connect**

SCiLINKS
NSTA

TOPIC: DNA
GO TO: www.scilinks.org
KEYWORD: HM185

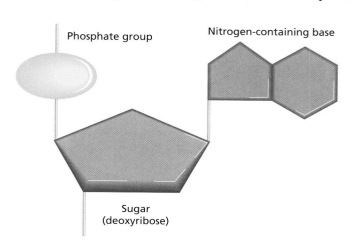

Phosphate group

Nitrogen-containing base

Sugar
(deoxyribose)

FIGURE 10-1

A DNA molecule is composed of a deoxyribose sugar molecule, a phosphate group, and one of four nitrogen-containing bases.

PURINES

Adenine

Guanine

PYRIMIDINES

Thymine

Cytosine

FIGURE 10-2

The four nitrogen-containing bases found in DNA are divided into two groups: purines and pyrimidines. Two-ringed bases are called purines. One-ringed bases are called pyrimidines.

Figure 10-2 shows the structure of these four nucleotides. Notice that adenine and guanine have two rings of carbon, C, and nitrogen, N, atoms. In contrast, cytosine and thymine have only one ring of carbon and nitrogen atoms. Bases that have two rings of carbon and nitrogen atoms, such as adenine and guanine, are called **purines. Pyrimidines** are bases that have one ring of carbon and nitrogen atoms, such as cytosine and thymine.

The Double Helix

In 1953, James Watson and Francis Crick suggested a model for the structure of DNA. The model proposed that DNA is composed of two nucleotide chains that wrap around each other to form a double spiral—similar to a spiral staircase. This shape is called a **double helix.** The double helix structure of DNA is illustrated in Figure 10-3.

FIGURE 10-3

The structure of DNA, which resembles a spiral staircase, is called a double helix.

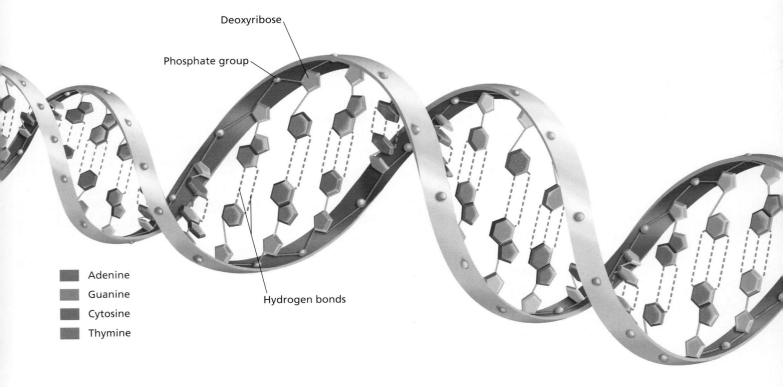

Deoxyribose

Phosphate group

Hydrogen bonds

Adenine
Guanine
Cytosine
Thymine

Watson and Crick relied heavily on scientific evidence reported by other scientists to construct the model. The model was inspired in part by X-ray photographs of DNA crystals, like the one shown in Figure 10-4, that had been studied by Rosalind Franklin and Maurice Wilkins. In addition, the model provided an explanation for how copies of DNA could be made and how genetic information might be stored and used within cells. In 1962, Watson, Crick, and Maurice Wilkins received the Nobel Prize in Medicine for their work on DNA. Rosalind Franklin had died in 1958 and thus was not recognized.

Note in Figure 10-3 that individual nucleotides are connected by covalent bonds between the deoxyribose sugar and phosphate molecules. The alternating deoxyribose sugar and phosphate molecules form a "backbone" to which the nitrogen-containing bases attach. Note also that the nitrogen-containing bases face toward the center of the helix and that they are perpendicular to the sugar-phosphate backbone.

By facing toward the center, the bases on one chain of DNA face the bases on the other chain of DNA, with which they form bonds called hydrogen bonds. The locations of the hydrogen bonds are indicated in Figure 10-3 by dotted lines. The hydrogen bonds help hold the two chains together. Hydrogen bonds are different from the covalent bonds and ionic bonds you read about in Chapter 2. A hydrogen bond is a relatively weak bond that usually forms between molecules. Hydrogen bonds form when two atoms share a hydrogen nucleus—one proton. The hydrogen bonds that form between the bases in DNA form between a hydrogen atom and either an oxygen or a nitrogen atom.

Notice that the base pairs are of uniform length because in each case one base is a double-ringed purine and the other is a single-ringed pyrimidine. The form of DNA that is most commonly found in living organisms has a right-hand twist, with each full turn consisting of ten base pairs.

Complementary Base Pairing

As Figure 10-3 shows, cytosine pairs with guanine, and adenine pairs with thymine. The DNA nucleotides normally pair in these combinations. These pairs of bases are called **complementary base pairs.** Two rules—called **base-pairing rules**—describe the pairing behavior of the bases. These rules simply state that cytosine bonds with guanine and adenine bonds with thymine.

Complementary base pairs are connected to each other by hydrogen bonds. Note that cytosine and guanine form three hydrogen bonds and adenine and thymine form two hydrogen bonds. As Figure 10-3 shows, the nucleotide sequence in one nucleotide chain of the DNA molecule is an exact complement of the nucleotide sequence in the other chain.

The complementary nucleotide chains in the DNA model led to suggestions of how DNA might copy itself. The ability of DNA to make exact copies of itself is important because, in most cases, cells that divide must pass exact copies of their DNA to offspring cells.

FIGURE 10-4

Rosalind Franklin's X-ray photographs of DNA indicated that DNA is a helix with a sugar-phosphate backbone on the outside and that the helix consists of more than one chain of nucleotides.

internet**connect**

SC*L*INKS
NSTA

TOPIC: Watson and Crick
GO TO: www.scilinks.org
KEYWORD: HM187

REPLICATION OF DNA

The process of copying DNA in a cell is called **replication.** During replication, the two nucleotide chains separate by unwinding, and each chain serves as a template for a new nucleotide chain.

DNA replication is illustrated in Figure 10-5. The first step is the separation of the two nucleotide chains. The point at which the two chains separate is called the **replication fork.** The chains are separated by enzymes called **helicases.** As the helicase enzymes move along the DNA molecule, they break hydrogen bonds between the complementary bases, and the chains separate.

As Figure 10-5 shows, enzymes called **DNA polymerases** bind to the separated chains of DNA. As DNA polymerases move along the separated chains, new chains of DNA are assembled using nucleotides in the surrounding medium that are complementary to the existing DNA chains. Nucleotides are joined to the new chains by covalent bonds between deoxyribose sugars and phosphate groups. They are joined to the original nucleotide chain by hydrogen bonds.

FIGURE 10-5

(a) During DNA replication, helicase enzymes separate DNA's two chains of nucleotides. (b) DNA polymerases bind to the separated chains of nucleotides. One nucleotide at a time, the enzyme constructs a new complementary chain of nucleotides. (c) At the end of replication, there are two identical copies of the original DNA molecule. Each DNA molecule is made of one chain of nucleotides from the original DNA molecule and one new chain of nucleotides.

Direction of unwinding

(a)

Helicase

Replication fork

DNA MOLECULE

(b)

Helicase

DNA Polymerase

Old DNA

New DNA

(c)

Old DNA

New DNA

Old DNA

IDENTICAL DNA MOLECULES

The complementary nature of the two chains of DNA is the foundation for accurate DNA replication. Suppose that the sequence of nucleotides in one chain of the original DNA molecule is A-T-T-C-C-G. DNA polymerases would produce a new nucleotide chain with the sequence of T-A-A-G-G-C.

DNA replication does not begin at one end of the molecule and proceed to the other. Rather, DNA polymerases begin replication simultaneously at many points along the separated nucleotide chains. Replication occurring simultaneously at different sites permits faster DNA replication. For example, replication is initiated simultaneously at about 6,000 sites in fruit fly DNA.

When replication is completed, two new exact copies of the original DNA molecule are produced and the cell is ready to undergo cell division. Each new DNA molecule consists of one new nucleotide chain joined by hydrogen bonds to a nucleotide chain from the original DNA molecule.

Accuracy and Repair

The process of DNA replication occurs with a high degree of accuracy—about one error in every 10,000 paired nucleotides. However, a change in the nucleotide sequence at even one location, called a **mutation,** may have serious effects in new cells. A combination of DNA proofreading and repair processes helps keep the error rate to one error per 1 billion nucleotides.

The number of errors and mutations in DNA replication is reduced as enzymes proofread DNA and repair errors. Most repair enzymes detect errors in the complementary base-paired structure of DNA. If noncomplementary bases are paired, the abnormal DNA structure can be recognized and repaired by specific enzymes.

Although DNA replication and proofreading prevent many replication errors, some errors do occur. In addition, DNA can be damaged by a variety of agents, including chemicals and ultraviolet radiation from the sun. Because cells are continuously proofreading and repairing their DNA, the number of mutations is reduced.

Eco ▲ Connection

DNA Repair Enzymes in Frogs

Around the world, frog and toad populations are in decline. Research on two declining species inhabiting the Oregon Cascade Range—Cascade frogs and western toads—suggests that these species' DNA repair enzymes are unable to keep up with mutations caused by increased exposure to ultraviolet radiation. Laboratory experiments showed that the DNA repair enzymes of Pacific tree frogs, whose populations do not appear to be decreasing, were better able to repair mutations than those of Cascade frogs and western toads.

SECTION 10-1 REVIEW

1. What are the main functions of DNA?

2. Identify the types and locations of covalent bonds and hydrogen bonds in a DNA molecule.

3. List the base-pairing rules.

4. What roles do enzymes play in DNA replication?

5. How would the deoxyribose sugar-phosphate backbone of nucleotide chains look if purines paired only with purines and pyrimidines paired only with pyrimidines?

6. **CRITICAL THINKING** A DNA molecule (labeled as A) replicates to produce two new DNA molecules (labeled as B). Both of the B DNA molecules then replicate to form four new DNA molecules (labeled as C). Are any nucleotide chains from A present in the C DNA molecules? Explain your answer. If you believe the answer is yes, how many of the A DNA nucleotide chains are present in the C DNA molecules?

OBJECTIVES

▲

Explain the
primary functions of RNA.

●

Compare the structure of RNA
with that of DNA.

■

Describe the
structure and function
of each type of RNA.

◆

Summarize the process
of transcription.

RNA

*R*ecall that the nucleotides in DNA molecules are grouped into genes that contain the information needed to make specific proteins. In eukaryotes, the genes directing protein production are in the nucleus, and the enzymes and amino-acid building blocks for protein production are in the cytosol. The nucleic acid called ribonucleic acid (RNA) is responsible for the movement of genetic information from the DNA in the nucleus to the site of protein synthesis in the cytosol.

STRUCTURE OF RNA

Like DNA, RNA is a nucleic acid made up of repeating nucleotides. However, as Figure 10-6 shows, RNA differs from DNA in its structure. The sugar molecule of every RNA nucleotide is **ribose,** whereas DNA nucleotides contain deoxyribose sugar. The name *ribonucleic acid* is derived from the name of its sugar, just as the name *deoxyribonucleic acid* is derived from the name of its sugar.

A second difference between RNA and DNA nucleotides is that thymine is rarely a part of RNA molecules. **Uracil,** a nitrogen-containing pyrimidine base, usually replaces thymine in RNA. As a result, uracil—not thymine—pairs with adenine in RNA.

RNA   DNA

■ Adenine
■ Guanine
■ Cytosine
■ Thymine
■ Uracil

FIGURE 10-6

Like DNA, RNA is a nucleic acid made up of repeating nucleotides. Some forms of RNA involved in protein synthesis are made up of a single chain of nucleotides. Notice also that the nucleotide uracil is found in RNA in place of the DNA nucleotide thymine.

Types of RNA

RNA exists in three different types. Each type of RNA has a different function. The three types of RNA and their common abbreviations are as follows:

Messenger RNA (mRNA) consists of RNA nucleotides in the form of a single uncoiled chain. mRNA carries genetic information from the DNA in the nucleus to the cytosol of a eukaryotic cell.

Transfer RNA (tRNA) consists of a single chain of about 80 RNA nucleotides folded into a hairpin shape that binds to specific amino acids. There are about 45 varieties of tRNA.

Ribosomal RNA (rRNA) is the most abundant form of RNA. rRNA consists of RNA nucleotides in a globular form. Joined by proteins, rRNA makes up the ribosomes where proteins are made.

TRANSCRIPTION

One function of RNA is to carry genetic information from DNA in the nucleus to the cytosol, where it can be used to produce proteins. The process by which genetic information is copied from DNA to RNA is called **transcription.** The process of transcription is shown in Figure 10-7.

FIGURE 10-7

During transcription, RNA polymerase binds to the promoter of a specific gene. Then a complementary copy of that gene's DNA base sequence is made using RNA nucleotides, thus forming the mRNA strand.

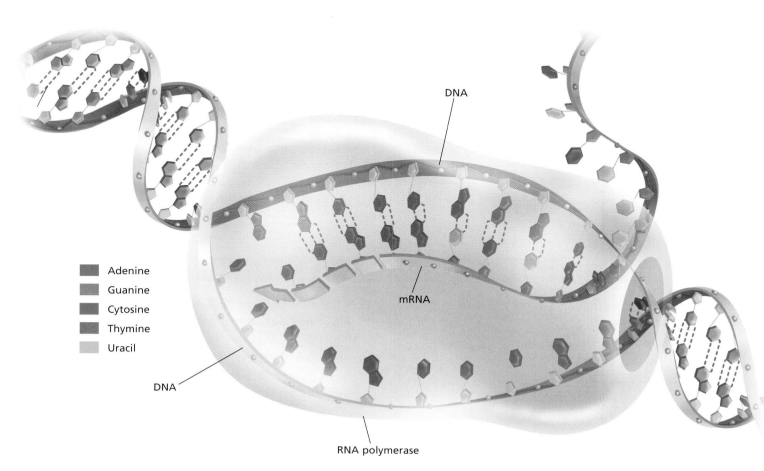

DNA

mRNA

- Adenine
- Guanine
- Cytosine
- Thymine
- Uracil

DNA

RNA polymerase

Steps of Transcription

Word Roots and Origins

transcription

from the Latin *scribere,* meaning "to write," and *trans,* meaning "across"

RNA polymerase, the primary transcription enzyme, synthesizes RNA copies of specific sequences of DNA. RNA polymerase initiates RNA transcription by binding to specific regions of DNA called **promoters.** The promoter marks the beginning of the DNA chain that will be transcribed. In eukaryotes, promoters mark the beginning of a single gene, but in prokaryotes a promoter may mark the beginning of several functionally related genes. When RNA polymerase binds to a promoter, the DNA molecule in that region separates. Only one of the separated DNA chains, called the template, is used for transcription.

RNA polymerase attaches to the first DNA nucleotide of the template chain. Then it begins adding complementary RNA nucleotides to the newly forming RNA molecule. In Figure 10-7, notice that complementary base pairing determines the nucleotide sequence of the RNA chain in transcription, just as it does in DNA replication. The base-pairing rules are identical to those in DNA replication, except that uracil pairs with adenine.

Transcription continues one nucleotide at a time until the RNA polymerase reaches a DNA region called the **termination signal.** The termination signal is a specific sequence of nucleotides that marks the end of a gene in eukaryotes and may mark the end of several functionally related genes in prokaryotes. At the termination signal, RNA polymerase releases both the DNA molecule and the newly formed RNA molecule. All three types of RNA molecules are transcribed in this process.

Products of Transcription

The products of transcription, called transcripts, are the different types of RNA molecules, including mRNA, tRNA, and rRNA. Although the instructions for making a protein are copied from DNA into mRNA, all three types of RNA are involved in the synthesis of proteins. Following transcription, mRNA moves through the pores of the nuclear membrane into the cytosol of the cell, where it will direct the synthesis of proteins.

SECTION 10-2 REVIEW

1. Define transcription. List the main steps involved in this process.

2. In what ways does the structure of RNA differ from that of DNA?

3. Describe the structure and function of each of the three types of RNA.

4. List three roles of RNA polymerase in transcription.

5. What basic principle ensures that the transcribed RNA molecule is carrying the right genetic message?

6. **CRITICAL THINKING** Does it matter which of the separated DNA chains is used for transcription? Discuss your answer.

PROTEIN SYNTHESIS

Now that you know how RNA is transcribed from DNA, you are ready to learn how the three types of RNA work together to produce proteins. The production of proteins is also called **protein synthesis.** The amount and kind of proteins that are produced in a cell determine the structure and function of the cell. In this way, proteins carry out the genetic instructions encoded in an organism's DNA.

PROTEIN STRUCTURE AND COMPOSITION

Like DNA and RNA, proteins are polymers. Proteins are made up of one or more polypeptides, each of which consists of a specific sequence of amino acids linked together by peptide bonds. Recall from Chapter 3 that there are 20 different amino acids that make up proteins. The polypeptides that make up one protein may consist of hundreds or thousands of the 20 different amino acids arranged in a particular sequence. The sequence of the amino acids determines how the polypeptides will twist and fold into the three-dimensional structure of the protein. The function of a protein depends on its ability to bind with other molecules within a cell; that is, the function depends on the protein's three-dimensional structure, which is determined by its amino-acid sequence.

THE GENETIC CODE

During protein synthesis, the sequence of nucleotides in an mRNA transcript is translated into a sequence of amino acids. A correlation between a nucleotide sequence and an amino-acid sequence—called the **genetic code**—is used by most organisms to translate mRNA transcripts into proteins.

The genetic information necessary for making proteins is encoded in series of three mRNA nucleotides. Each combination of three mRNA nucleotides is called a **codon.** Each codon codes for a specific amino acid. Table 10-1 on the next page lists the 64 codons and the amino acids and instructions they code for in almost all organisms. The near-universality of the genetic code supports the idea that all organisms are evolutionarily related.

▲

Describe the genetic code.

●

Distinguish between a codon and an anticodon, and state where each is found.

■

Explain the roles of the start codon and stop codons.

◆

Summarize the process of translation.

internet**connect**

SCi*LINKS*
NSTA

TOPIC: Genetic code
GO TO: www.scilinks.org
KEYWORD: HM193

Word Roots and Origins

synthesis

from the Greek *tithenai,* meaning "to put," and *syn,* meaning "together"

TABLE 10-1 Codons in mRNA

First base	Second base				Third base
	U	C	A	G	
U	UUU } Phenylalanine UUC UUA } Leucine UUG	UCU UCC Serine UCA UCG	UAU } Tyrosine UAC UAA } Stop UAG	UGU } Cysteine UGC UGA } Stop UGG } Tryptophan	U C A G
C	CUU CUC Leucine CUA CUG	CCU CCC Proline CCA CCG	CAU } Histidine CAC CAA } Glutamine CAG	CGU CGC Arginine CGA CGG	U C A G
A	AUU ⎫ AUC } Isolecine AUA ⎭ AUG } Start	ACU ACC Threonine ACA ACG	AAU } Asparagine AAC AAA } Lysine AAG	AGU } Serine AGC AGA } Arginine AGG	U C A G
G	GUU GUC Valine GUA GUG	GCU GCC Alanine GCA GCG	GAU } Aspartic GAC } acid GAA } Glutamic GAG } acid	GGU GGC Glycine GGA GGG	U C A G

Notice that several codons code for each amino acid listed in Table 10-1. Codons often differ from one another by the nucleotide in the third position. A few codons do not code for amino acids at all. Instead, these codons signal for translation of an mRNA to start or stop. The **start codon** (AUG), which also codes for the amino acid methionine, engages a ribosome to start translating an mRNA molecule. **Stop codons** (UAA, UAG, UGA) cause the ribosome to stop translating an mRNA.

TRANSLATION

The process of assembling polypeptides from information encoded in mRNA is called **translation.** The process of translation begins when mRNA leaves the nucleus through pores in the nuclear membrane. The mRNA then migrates to a ribosome in the cytosol, the site of protein synthesis.

tRNA and Anticodons

Amino acids floating freely in the cytosol are transported to the ribosomes by tRNA molecules. Notice in Figure 10-8 that a tRNA

FIGURE 10-8

Each tRNA transports a specific amino acid to the ribosomes during translation.

Site of amino acid attachment

Hydrogen bonds

Anticodon

Transfer RNA

Amino acid

Anticodon

Polypeptide chain

Peptide bond

Nuclear pore

Nucleus

Codon

Ribosome

Messenger RNA

Adenine

Guanine

Cytosine

Uracil

A U G G A C A C A U U U A U U C U G U G U C C C C U U G A G U G G A G A U U G G A C C G A U

FIGURE 10-9

During translation, amino acids are assembled from information encoded in mRNA. As each codon is sequentially paired with its anticodon, tRNA adds a specific amino acid to the growing polypeptide chain.

molecule has a region that bonds to a specific amino acid. Notice also that the loop opposite the site of amino-acid attachment bears a sequence of three nucleotides called an **anticodon.** The tRNA anticodon is complementary to and pairs with its corresponding mRNA codon.

Notice in Figure 10-9 that the same base-pairing rules followed during transcription are followed during translation. For example, a tRNA with an anticodon sequence of AAA would bind to the mRNA codon sequence of UUU and would be specific for the amino acid phenylalanine. Thus, the pairing of an anticodon with a codon ensures that the amino acids are added to the growing polypeptide in the order prescribed by the mRNA transcript.

Ribosomes

Ribosomes are composed of rRNA and proteins and are usually both free in the cytosol and attached to the endoplasmic reticulum. Ribosomes that are free in the cytosol, as shown in Figure 10-9, produce proteins that will be used within the cell. Membrane proteins and proteins that will be exported for use outside the cell are produced by ribosomes attached to the endoplasmic reticulum.

Ribosomes have three binding sites that are key to translation. One binding site holds an mRNA transcript so that its codons are accessible to rRNA molecules. The other two binding sites hold tRNAs whose anticodons pair with the mRNA codons.

Protein Assembly

The assembly of a polypeptide begins when a ribosome attaches to the start codon (AUG) on an mRNA transcript. Find the start codon on the mRNA transcript shown in Figure 10-9. The start codon pairs with the anticodon UAC on a tRNA. Because the tRNA that bears the UAC anticodon also carries the amino acid methionine, the first amino acid in every polypeptide is initially methionine. However, this first amino acid may be removed later; thus, all polypeptides do not actually begin with methionine.

As a ribosome moves along an mRNA transcript, each mRNA codon is sequentially paired with its tRNA anticodon, as Figure 10-9 shows. The pairing of an anticodon with a codon causes the specified amino acid to attach to the previously translated amino acid with a covalent bond called a peptide bond. In this way, amino acids are joined to a growing polypeptide chain in the order specified by an mRNA transcript. As each amino acid is added to the polypeptide chain, the ribosome moves three nucleotides—one codon—ahead on the mRNA transcript, where the next amino acid will be translated. Eventually, the ribosome reaches a stop codon, bringing translation to an end. At this point the mRNA is released from the ribosome and the polypeptide is complete.

As you can see in Figure 10-9, several ribosomes may simultaneously translate the same mRNA transcript. A new ribosome begins translating an mRNA transcript almost as soon as the preceding ribosome has moved out of the way. These ribosomes are often spaced as close as 80 nucleotides apart on an mRNA.

The polypeptide chain represents the protein's primary structure. As the polypeptide folds and associates with other polypeptides that make up the protein, it assumes the functional structure of the completed protein.

SECTION 10-3 REVIEW

1. Compare transcription with translation.

2. Distinguish a codon from an anticodon, and explain the significance of each.

3. How does the structure of tRNA relate to its function in translation?

4. Using the information in Table 10-1, list the amino acids that are coded for by the codons AGU, GGG, CCU, and GUG.

5. Explain the significance of the start codon and the stop codons. Do all polypeptides begin with the amino acid coded for by the start codon?

6. **CRITICAL THINKING** What would translation of the mRNA transcript UAACAAGGAGCAUCC produce?

SUMMARY/VOCABULARY

10-1
- DNA stores the information that tells cells which proteins to make and when to make them.
- DNA is made up of two chains of nucleotides.
- A DNA nucleotide is composed of a deoxyribose sugar molecule, a phosphate group, and a nitrogen-containing base. The four nitrogen-containing bases found in DNA nucleotides are adenine (A), guanine (G), cytosine (C), and thymine (T).
- Adenine and guanine are called purines. Cytosine and thymine are pyrimidines.
- Cytosine pairs with guanine, and adenine pairs with thymine. Complementary base pairs are connected to each other by hydrogen bonds.
- Before a cell divides, it copies its DNA by a process called replication. Replication results in two exact copies of the cell's DNA.
- Replication begins with the separation of the DNA chains by helicase enzymes. Then as DNA polymerases move along the separated chains, new chains of DNA are assembled using nucleotides in the surrounding medium.

Vocabulary

adenine (185)	deoxyribose (185)	mutation (189)	pyrimidine (186)
base-pairing rule (187)	DNA polymerase (188)	nitrogen-containing base	replication (188)
complementary base pair	double helix (186)	(185)	replication fork (188)
(187)	guanine (185)	purine (186)	thymine (185)
cytosine (185)	helicase (188)		

10-2
- Nucleotides in DNA are grouped into genes, which contain the information required for the production of specific proteins.
- Three forms of RNA are involved in protein synthesis: mRNA, tRNA, and rRNA.
- mRNA carries genetic information from the DNA in the nucleus to the cytosol of a eukaryotic cell. The process of copying genetic information from DNA to mRNA is called transcription.
- tRNA binds to specific amino acids, helping to form polypeptide chains.
- rRNA makes up the ribosomes where proteins are made.

Vocabulary

messenger RNA (mRNA)	ribose (190)	termination signal (192)	transfer RNA (tRNA) (191)
(191)	ribosomal RNA (rRNA) (191)	transcription (191)	uracil (190)
promoter (192)	RNA polymerase (192)		

10-3
- The production of proteins is also called protein synthesis.
- The genetic code shown in Table 10-1 is used by most organisms to translate mRNA transcripts into proteins.
- The genetic information necessary for making proteins is encoded in mRNA codons. Each codon codes for a specific amino acid.
- The process of assembling polypeptides from information encoded in mRNA is called translation. During translation, tRNA anticodons pair with corresponding mRNA codons, and amino acids are joined together to form a polypeptide.
- As a polypeptide folds and associates with other polypeptides, it assumes the functional structure of a completed protein.

Vocabulary

anticodon (195)	genetic code (193)	start codon (194)	translation (194)
codon (193)	protein synthesis (193)	stop codon (194)	

REVIEW

Vocabulary

1. Distinguish between a ribosome and ribosomal RNA.
2. Describe the difference between a termination signal and a stop codon.
3. Distinguish between mRNA, tRNA, and rRNA.
4. Describe the difference between a purine and a pyrimidine.
5. Define the term *protein synthesis*.

Multiple Choice Questions

6. DNA
   (a) encodes the information needed for making proteins within the cell
   (b) directs RNA to make lipids that are needed by the cell
   (c) directs RNA to produce glucose
   (d) produces carbohydrates.
7. The physical structure of the genetic code is DNA's sequence of (a) sugars (b) nucleotides (c) phosphates (d) hydrogen bonds.
8. Covalent bonds are found (a) between purines and pyrimidines (b) between nucleotide chains (c) in the sugar-phosphate backbones (d) between RNA and DNA molecules.
9. Complementary base pairing is important for (a) DNA replication (b) RNA transcription (c) RNA translation (d) all of the above.
10. Unlike DNA, RNA
    (a) is a polymer made up of nucleotides
    (b) contains the nitrogen-containing base thymine
    (c) contains the sugar ribose
    (d) does not contain the nitrogen-containing base uracil.
11. Codons are (a) sequences of proteins (b) a site on a tRNA (c) three-nucleotide sequences of mRNA (d) sequences of polypeptides.
12. The pattern of base pairing in DNA can be summarized as follows:
    (a) purines pair with purines
    (b) any purine can pair with any pyrimidine
    (c) adenine pairs with guanine
    (d) adenine pairs with thymine, and cytosine pairs with guanine.
13. The formation of peptide bonds occurs (a) in the nucleus (b) between amino acids (c) during DNA proofreading (d) during transcription.
14. Transcription occurs (a) at ribosomes in both prokaryotes and eukaryotes (b) in the cytosol of eukaryotes (c) in the nucleus of eukaryotes (d) as the last step of protein synthesis.
15. Transporting amino acids to ribosomes for assembly into needed proteins is the function of (a) DNA (b) mRNA (c) rRNA (d) tRNA.

Short Answer

16. What are some ways that the structure of a DNA molecule is related to its function?
17. Is there an advantage to multiple sites of DNA replication? Explain your answer.
18. Would hydrogen bonds or covalent bonds be more important for the identification of mismatches during DNA replication? Explain your answer.
19. What functions are carried out by those few codons that do not code for amino acids?
20. What is the role of ribosomes in protein synthesis?
21. What is the evolutionary significance of a near-universal genetic code?
22. The photograph below shows the DNA of a mammalian cell. What process is the DNA undergoing? What is the structure shown called? Explain your answer.

23. Unit 6—*Gene Expression*

 Write a report summarizing how antibiotics inhibit protein synthesis in bacteria. How do some antibiotics interfere with translation?

CRITICAL THINKING

1. Use Table 10-1 to find the codons that code for the amino acid alanine. How many codons code for alanine? How do they differ from one another? What significance might the differences have?

2. Refer again to Table 10-1. Using the table, determine the sequence of amino acids that is specified by the following list of codons: AUG UCU AAC AAA CAG GCU UAA.

3. A segment of DNA has the following sequence: AACTACGGTCTCAGCACTCCC. Write the mRNA transcript of this sequence of DNA. Next, write the tRNA anticodons that would pair with the mRNA transcript. Using Table 10-1, write the names of the amino acids coded for by the mRNA transcript.

4. What would happen to the translation process if one nucleotide were not transcribed correctly? Present a minimum of three possibilities.

5. How is a system composed of three bases per codon better suited to code for 20 amino acids than a system composed of two bases per codon?

6. Genetic engineering involves inserting segments of DNA taken from one organism into the DNA of another organism. What would be the likely result of an experiment in which a scientist replaces a faulty stop codon in the DNA of mouse cells with the codon UAG taken from the DNA of a frog, a pine tree, or a clam? What do the results of this experiment suggest about the evolutionary ancestry of these organisms?

7. The diagram below shows a model of the chemical structure of uracil. Compare this diagram with Figure 10-2. How does the chemical structure of uracil differ from the chemical structure of thymine? How is it possible for both thymine and uracil to bond with adenine? (You may wish to look again at the patterns of hydrogen bonding illustrated in Figure 10-3 to help you answer this question.)

URACIL

EXTENSION

1. Prepare a report on the contributions of one of the following scientists to the discovery of the structure of DNA: Erwin Chargaff, Francis Crick, Rosalind Franklin, Linus Pauling, James Watson, or Maurice Wilkins. The book *The Double Helix,* by James Watson, provides information about Watson and Crick's discovery. *The Eight Days of Creation,* by Horace Freeland, provides information about the work of all of these scientists on DNA.

2. Read "Genetics: Repairing the Genome's Spelling Mistakes" in *Science,* July 16, 1999, on page 316. What new gene-therapy technique is being used to correct genetic disorders in rats? What is the goal of this research if it is found to be safe?

3. Read "Gene Cloned for Stretchiest Spider Silk" in *Science News,* February 21, 1998, on page 119. Describe the protein structure that contributes to the extreme elasticity of spider silk.

Modeling Replication and Transcription of DNA

OBJECTIVES

- Construct and analyze a model of DNA.
- Simulate the process of replication using a model.
- Simulate the process of transcription using a model.

PROCESS SKILLS

- demonstrating
- identifying
- manipulating a model

MATERIALS

- plastic soda straws, cut into 3 cm sections (54)
- metric ruler
- scissors
- permanent marker
- 54 pushpins (12 red, 12 blue, 12 yellow, 12 green, and 6 white)
- 54 paper clips

Background

1. Describe the structure of DNA.
2. State the base-pairing rules.
3. List the steps involved in the copying of DNA before cell division.

4. What is mRNA, and what is its function in protein synthesis?
5. Describe the process of transcription.

PART A Making a Model of DNA

1. ◆ CAUTION **Always cut in a direction away from your face and body.** Cut the soda straws into 3 cm pieces to make 54 segments.

2. Insert a pushpin midway along the length of each straw segment as shown in the figure below. Push a paper clip into one end of each straw segment until it touches the pin.

3. Keeping the pins in a straight line, insert the paper clip from a blue-pushpin segment into the open end of a red-pushpin segment. Add additional straw segments to the red-segment end in the following order: green, yellow, blue, yellow, blue, yellow, green, red, red, and green. Use the permanent marker to label the blue-segment end "top." This chain of segments is one-half of your first model.

4. Assign nucleotides to the corresponding pushpin colors as follows: red = adenine, blue = guanine, yellow = cytosine, and green = thymine.

5. Construct the other half of your first model beginning with a yellow segment across from the blue pushpin at the top of your first model. Keep the pins in a straight line. Link segments together according to the base-pairing rules.

6. When you have completed your model of one DNA segment, make a sketch of the model in your lab report. Use colored pencils or pens to designate the pushpin colors. Include a key that indicates which nucleotide each color represents in your sketch.

PART B   Modeling DNA Replication

7. Place the chains parallel to each other on the table with the "top" blue pin of the first chain facing the "top" yellow pin of the second chain.

8. Demonstrate replication by simulating a replication fork at the top pair of pins. Add the remaining straw segments to complete a new DNA model. Be sure to follow the base-pairing rules.

9. Sketch the process of DNA replication in your lab report. Label the replication fork, the segments of original DNA, and the segments of new DNA in your sketch.

PART C   Modeling Transcription

10. Place the chains of one of the DNA models parallel to each other on the table. Take the other DNA model apart so that you can use the segments to construct a model of mRNA.

11. Assign the uracil nucleotide to the white pushpins. Using the available pushpins, construct a model of an mRNA transcript of the DNA segment. Begin by separating the two chains of DNA and pairing the mRNA nucleotides with the left strand of DNA as you transcribe from the top of the segment to the bottom of the segment.

12. In your lab report, sketch the mRNA model that you transcribed from the DNA segment.

13. Refer to Table 10-1 on page 194 to determine the sequence of amino acids you transcribed.

14. Clean up your materials before leaving the lab.

Analysis and Conclusions

1. How many nucleotides did the original DNA model contain?

2. Write the base-pair order for the DNA molecule you created, using the following code: red = adenine, blue = guanine, yellow = cytosine, and green = thymine.

3. What is the name given to the point where replication starts on a DNA molecule?

4. How does the replicated model of DNA compare to the original model of DNA?

5. What would the complementary bases be if one side of a DNA molecule had the bases adenine, cytosine, cytosine, thymine, thymine, and adenine?

6. Speculate about what would happen if the nucleotide pairs in the replicated model were not in the same sequence as the original model.

7. Write the mRNA transcription of the DNA sequence presented below.

        CTG TTC ATA ATT

   Next, write the tRNA anticodons that would pair with the mRNA transcription. Finally, write the amino acids coded for by the mRNA transcription using Table 10-1.

8. If you transcribed the "wrong" side of the DNA molecule, what would the result be? How might this affect the proteins that the organism produced?

9. What are the advantages of having DNA remain in the nucleus of eukaryotic cells?

Further Inquiry

Design models for some of the other molecules that are involved in protein synthesis. Use these models along with the DNA model you constructed in this investigation to demonstrate the steps of protein synthesis.

CHAPTER 11

GENE EXPRESSION

This fruit fly has only one eye due to a mutation in a gene that regulates development.

FOCUS CONCEPT: *Cell Structure and Function*

As you read this chapter, note how gene structure enables prokaryotic and eukaryotic cells to control how and when proteins are produced.

11-1 *Control of Gene Expression*

11-2 *Gene Expression and Development*

Unit 6—Gene Expression
Topics 1–6

CONTROL OF GENE EXPRESSION

Cells use information in genes to build hundreds of different proteins, each with a unique function. But not all proteins are required by the cell at any one time. By regulating gene expression, cells are able to control when each protein is made.

ROLE OF GENE EXPRESSION

Gene expression is the activation of a gene that results in the formation of a protein. A gene is said to be "expressed," or turned "on," when transcription occurs. But cells do not always need to produce all of the proteins for which their genes contain instructions. Recall from Chapter 3 that proteins have many different functions. Some proteins play a structural role. Others are enzymes that act as catalysts in chemical reactions. Mechanisms to control gene expression have evolved to ensure that each protein is produced only when it is needed.

The complete genetic material contained in an individual is called the **genome** (JEE-nohm). By regulating gene expression, cells are able to control which portion of the genome will be expressed and when. Gene expression occurs in two steps, transcription and translation. Gene expression begins when the enzyme RNA polymerase transcribes the DNA nucleotide sequence of a gene into a specific mRNA. During translation, this mRNA then migrates to a ribosome, where it is translated into a specific protein.

GENE EXPRESSION IN PROKARYOTES

Scientists first studied gene expression in prokaryotes. Much of our initial knowledge of gene expression comes from the work of French scientists Francois Jacob (1920–) and Jacques Monod (1910–1976). Jacob and Monod discovered how genes control the metabolism of the sugar lactose in *Escherichia coli*, a bacterium that lives in the human intestine.

OBJECTIVES

▲

Define the term *gene expression*.

●

Describe the regulation of the *lac* operon in prokaryotes.

■

Distinguish between introns and exons.

◆

Describe the role of enhancers in the control of gene expression.

Word Roots and Origins

genome

from the words *gene* and *chromosome*

Repressor protein

RNA polymerase

Repressor protein

Structural genes

Codes for

Regulator gene

Promoter

Operator

1

2

3

FIGURE 11-1

In the *lac* operon of *E. coli,* three structural genes code for the enzymes needed to utilize lactose. When lactose is absent, a repressor protein attaches to the operator. The presence of the repressor protein prevents RNA polymerase from binding to the structural genes, blocking transcription.

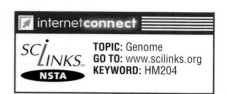

Found naturally in cow's milk, lactose is a disaccharide that is composed of the monosaccharides glucose and galactose. When you drink cow's milk, the presence of lactose stimulates *E. coli* to produce three enzymes. These three enzymes control metabolism of lactose and are adjacent on the chromosome. The production of these enzymes is controlled by three regulatory elements found within the DNA of *E. coli*. These three regulatory elements are as follows:

- **Structural genes** Genes that code for particular polypeptides are called *structural genes.* The structural genes studied by Jacob and Monod coded for the enzymes that allow *E. coli* to break down and utilize lactose.
- **Promoter** As you learned in Chapter 10, a promoter is a DNA segment that recognizes the enzyme RNA polymerase and thus promotes transcription.
- **Operator** An **operator** is a DNA segment that serves as a binding site for an inhibitory protein that blocks transcription and prevents protein synthesis from occurring.

The structural genes, the promoter, and the operator collectively form an operon. An **operon** (AHP-uhr-AHN) is a series of genes that code for specific products and the regulatory elements that control these genes. Researchers have found that the clustered arrangement of genes that forms an operon is a pattern that occurs commonly among bacteria. Jacob and Monod named the operon they studied the *lac* **operon** because its structural genes coded for the enzymes that regulate lactose metabolism. The *lac* operon includes the entire segment of DNA required to produce the enzymes involved in lactose metabolism.

In their work with the *lac* operon, Jacob and Monod found that the genes for the enzymes for lactose utilization were expressed *only* when lactose was present. How were the bacteria able to shut off these genes when lactose was absent? Their research showed that gene expression in the *lac* operon exhibits two forms: repression and activation.

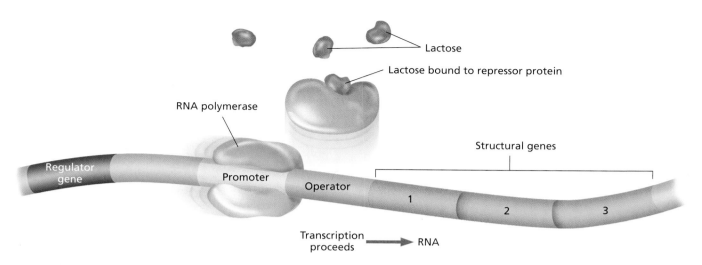

Labels in figure:
- Lactose
- Lactose bound to repressor protein
- RNA polymerase
- Regulator gene
- Promoter
- Operator
- Structural genes
- 1, 2, 3
- Transcription proceeds → RNA

FIGURE 11-2

When lactose is present, it acts as an inducer by binding to the repressor protein and removing it. The removal of the repressor protein allows the transcription of the three structural genes to proceed, producing mRNA.

Repression

In the absence of lactose, a protein called a repressor attaches to the operator. A **repressor protein** is a protein that inhibits a specific gene from being expressed. The attachment of the repressor protein to the operator prohibits RNA polymerase from binding to the structural genes and thus stops transcription from occurring. The blockage of transcription by the action of a repressor protein is called **repression.** Transcription of the structural genes is ultimately controlled by a **regulator gene,** which codes for the production of the repressor protein. The events of repression are summarized in Figure 11-1.

Activation

When lactose is present in the *E. coli* cell, it temporarily binds to the repressor protein on the operator and removes it. The removal of the repressor protein allows RNA polymerase to transcribe the structural genes of the *lac* operon. Since all three structural genes are turned on, all three enzymes required for lactose metabolism are produced. Because it activates, or induces, transcription, lactose acts as an inducer. An **inducer** is a molecule that initiates gene expression. The initiation of transcription by the removal of a repressor protein is called **activation.** Figure 11-2 shows the events that take place when lactose is present in the *E. coli* cell.

The *lac* operon illustrates in simple terms the great advantage of regulating gene expression. Cells of *E. coli* are able to shift between repression and activation, depending on whether lactose is present. Because lactose acts as an inducer, the *lac* operon is transcribed only in the presence of lactose. As a result, lactose induces its own metabolism. When the level of lactose drops, the repressor protein again binds to the operator, shutting off the *lac* operon. The three enzymes used in lactose metabolism are therefore not produced when lactose is not present. By controlling gene expression, *E. coli* conserves resources and produces only those proteins that are needed.

GENE EXPRESSION IN EUKARYOTES

Eukaryotes are vastly different from prokaryotes. Their genomes are much larger than those of prokaryotes. In addition, the DNA of eukaryotic cells is located in several individual chromosomes instead of in the single circular chromosome that occurs in prokaryotes. Finally, most eukaryotes are multicellular organisms made of specialized cells. Although each cell type contains a complete set of the organism's genes, only some of these genes are expressed at a given time. Different cell types produce different proteins. Not surprisingly, the control of gene expression in eukaryotes is far more complex than it is in prokaryotes. Although operons are common in prokaryotes, they have not been found in eukaryotes.

Structure of a Eukaryotic Gene

Much of the control of gene expression in eukaryotes occurs at the level of the individual chromosome. In eukaryotes, gene expression is partly related to the coiling and uncoiling of DNA within each chromosome. Recall from Chapter 8 that eukaryotic DNA is organized as fibers of chromatin wrapped around small specialized proteins called histones. Prior to mitosis or meiosis, the DNA and histones coil tightly, forming the structures we recognize as chromosomes. After mitosis or meiosis, certain regions of the DNA coils relax, thus making transcription possible. This uncoiled form, known as **euchromatin** (yoo-KROH-muh-tin), is the site of active transcription of DNA into RNA. However, some portions of the chromatin remain permanently coiled so that their genes can never be transcribed. Thus, the degree to which DNA is uncoiled indicates the degree of gene expression. Figure 11-3 shows transcription as it occurs in a cell.

As in the prokaryotes, the promoter is the binding site of RNA polymerase. In the eukaryotic gene, there are two kinds of segments beyond the promoter: introns and exons. **Introns** are the sections of a structural gene that do not code for amino acids and therefore are not translated into proteins. **Exons** are the sections of a structural gene that, when expressed, are translated into proteins.

The benefits of the intron-exon pattern of gene organization are not yet fully understood. However, scientists have noted that the pattern of actively coding portions of DNA interspersed among other noncoding portions of DNA may provide many options for producing different proteins. Perhaps the intron-exon pattern could facilitate the exchange of exons among homologous chromosomes during crossing-over in meiosis. This would result in new combinations of genes, enabling organisms to modify protein structures by replacing one exon with another. If this is the case, the intron-exon pattern of gene organization could serve as an additional source of the genetic diversity that is essential for evolution.

FIGURE 11-3

Multiple copies of mRNA are made as transcription occurs at several points along this DNA molecule. (11,055×)

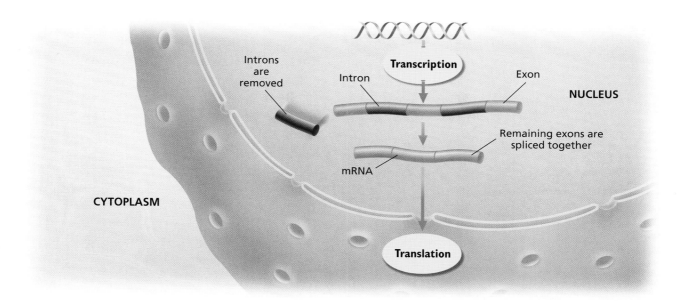

Introns are removed

Transcription

Intron

Exon

NUCLEUS

Remaining exons are spliced together

mRNA

CYTOPLASM

Translation

Control After Transcription

In prokaryotes, transcription and translation occur within the cytoplasm. In eukaryotes, however, transcription occurs in the nucleus, and then mRNA passes through the nuclear envelope and into the cytoplasm, where translation occurs. The physical separation of transcription and translation by the nuclear envelope gives eukaryotes more opportunities to regulate gene expression.

Unlike prokaryotes, eukaryotes can control gene expression by modifying RNA after transcription. When transcription occurs, both introns and exons are transcribed. The result is a large molecule known as pre-mRNA. **Pre-mRNA** is a form of messenger RNA (mRNA) that contains both introns and exons. A molecule of mRNA is formed when introns are removed from pre-mRNA and the remaining exons are spliced (joined) to one another, as shown in Figure 11-4. This occurs when an enzyme splits the pre-mRNA at each end of an intron and joins the exons. The end result is an mRNA containing the exons. The mRNA strand leaves the nucleus and enters the cytoplasm to begin the manufacture of a protein on the ribosomes. When needed, the nucleotides in the removed introns can be used again during the transcription of additional pre-mRNA. Similar RNA splicing occurs following the transcription of transfer RNA and ribosomal RNA.

The removal of introns and splicing of an mRNA molecule has also been found to occur in another way. In the early 1980s, Thomas Cech and his co-workers at the University of Colorado discovered that RNA molecules can act as biological catalysts. The work of Cech and others showed that RNA itself can act as a catalyst to splice introns out of mRNA molecules as they form in the nucleus. Until Cech's discovery, it was thought that all enzymes were proteins.

FIGURE 11-4

Both introns and exons are transcribed to form pre-mRNA. Enzymes cut out the introns and join the remaining exons together, forming mRNA.

Quick Lab

Modeling After-Transcription Control

Materials felt-tip markers, paper, scissors, tape

Procedure

1. Write a sentence that contains only three-letter words and makes sense.

2. Hide the words in random places in a long sequence of letters. This sequence should contain random letters and other three-letter words that make no sense in the sentence you are hiding. Print the sequence of letters all the same size, equally spaced, and with no breaks between them.

3. Trade papers with another team. Use scissors to cut out the "introns." Find the message, and reassemble it with tape.

Analysis What represents pre-mRNA in this activity? What represents mRNA?

FIGURE 11-5

Many enhancers are located far away from the genes they activate. Transcription factors facilitate transcription by binding to the enhancer and to the RNA polymerase. Bending of the DNA strand brings the enhancer close to the RNA polymerase and the transcription factors associated with it, enabling transcription to begin.

Enhancer Control

Eukaryotic genes on a DNA strand also have noncoding control sequences that facilitate transcription. Such a noncoding control sequence in a eukaryotic gene is called an **enhancer.** An enhancer must be activated for its associated gene to be expressed. Additional proteins, called **transcription factors,** bind to enhancers and RNA polymerase and regulate transcription. Figure 11-5 shows how an enhancer can facilitate transcription, even when it is far away from the gene that it affects.

Activation of enhancers has been studied in the expression of the gene controlling the production of estrogen, a female sex hormone. When estrogen is present in the cell, it binds to a receptor protein in the cytoplasm. The resulting estrogen-receptor protein complex then travels through the pores of the nuclear envelope, entering the nucleus. Once inside the nucleus, the estrogen-receptor protein complex attaches to the enhancer. This activates the enhancer, enabling transcription of specific genes and the synthesis of specific protein molecules to occur.

SECTION 11-1 REVIEW

1. How is it beneficial for organisms to be able to control gene expression?

2. What is the *lac* operon?

3. How does lactose affect the functioning of the *lac* operon?

4. Describe how the intron-exon pattern of gene organization can serve as a source of genetic diversity.

5. Distinguish between mRNA and pre-mRNA.

6. **CRITICAL THINKING**   What region of a prokaryotic gene is analogous to the enhancer region of a eukaryotic gene?

GENE EXPRESSION AND DEVELOPMENT

In Section 11-1 you learned how genes are turned on and off in prokaryotes and eukaryotes. Eukaryotes are far more complex than prokaryotes, and most eukaryotes are multicellular. The control of gene expression plays an important role in the growth of eukaryotes as different cells become specialized to perform different tasks.

SECTION

OBJECTIVES

▲

Recognize the relationship between gene expression and morphogenesis.

●

Describe the influence of homeotic genes on *Drosophila* development.

■

Summarize the role of the homeobox in eukaryotic development.

◆

List the key characteristics of cancer cells.

▲

Compare and contrast the roles of oncogenes and tumor-suppression genes.

CELL DIFFERENTIATION

All multicellular sexually reproducing organisms begin life as a fertilized egg, or zygote. Although every cell in the developing zygote contains the same genes, only a fraction of the genes are expressed. Certain genes are turned on and off as various proteins are needed at different times during the organism's life. For example, as eukaryotes grow, cells become specialized to perform different tasks. Muscle cells specialize in movement, while liver cells specialize in making enzymes that break down fat. The development of cells having specialized function is called **cell differentiation** (DIF-uhr-EN-shee-AY-shun). As organisms grow and develop, organs and tissues develop to produce a characteristic form. This development of form in an organism is called **morphogenesis** (MOR-foh-JEN-uh-sis).

Homeotic Genes

Homeotic (HOH-mee-AHT-ik) **genes** are regulatory genes that determine where certain anatomical structures, such as appendages, will develop in an organism during morphogenesis. Homeotic genes seem to be master genes of development that determine the overall body organization of multicellular organisms. One of the best-known examples of homeotic genes is found in *Drosophila*, the fruit fly. Each homeotic gene of *Drosophila* shares a common DNA sequence of approximately 180 nucleotide pairs. This specific DNA sequence within a homeotic gene regulates patterns of development and is called the **homeobox.** As the *Drosophila* embryo becomes an elongated larva, specific homeoboxes control the morphogenesis of specific regions in the larva. Each of these homeoboxes will also control a specific part of the adult *Drosophila*. As Figure 11-6 shows, a mutation in a homeotic gene can have devastating consequences.

Word Roots and Origins

homeobox

from the Greek *homoio*, meaning "the same"

FIGURE 11-6

(a) The fruit fly shown here is normal.
(b) This fruit fly has legs growing out of its head due to a homeotic mutation.

(a)

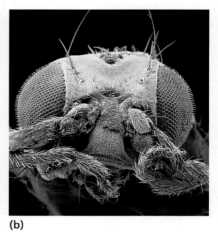
(b)

When a homeotic gene is translated, regulatory proteins are formed. It is thought that these proteins regulate development by switching groups of developmental genes on or off. Switching these genes on or off increases or decreases the rates of cell division in various areas of the developing organism. The resultant variation in growth rates in specific areas of the organism produces specific patterns of structural development.

The same or very similar homeobox sequences have been found in homeotic genes of many eukaryotic organisms. It is thought that all organisms may have similar homeoboxes that code for their anatomy. Figure 11-7 shows examples of homologous homeotic genes in *Drosophila* and mice.

internet**connect**

SC*LINKS*
NSTA

TOPIC: Chromosome
GO TO: www.scilinks.org
KEYWORD: HM210

CHROMOSOME

MOUSE   FRUIT FLY (*DROSOPHILA*)

FIGURE 11-7

In many eukaryotes, homeobox sequences govern the development of similar body regions. The gene sequence shown on this chromosome is found in both *Drosophila* and mice. A different color is used to represent each homeobox and the corresponding body region that it controls.

CANCER

A **tumor** is an abnormal proliferation of cells that results from uncontrolled, abnormal cell division. The cells of a **benign** (bi-NIEN) **tumor** remain within a mass. Benign tumors generally pose no threat to life unless they are allowed to grow until they compress vital organs. Examples of benign tumors are the fibroid cysts that occur in a woman's breasts or uterus. Warts are also benign tumors. Most benign tumors can be removed by surgery.

In a **malignant tumor,** the uncontrolled dividing cells invade and destroy healthy tissues elsewhere in the body. Malignant tumors are more commonly known as **cancer. Metastasis** (muh-TAS-tuh-sis) is the spread of cancer cells beyond their original site. When metastasis occurs, the cancer cells break away from the malignant tumor and travel to other parts of the body, where they invade healthy tissue and begin forming new tumors.

Kinds of Cancer

Malignant tumors can be categorized according to the types of tissues they affect. **Carcinomas** (KAR-si-NOH-muhs) grow in the skin and the tissues that line the organs of the body. Lung cancer, shown in Figure 11-8, and breast cancer are examples of carcinomas. **Sarcomas** (sahr-KOH-muhs) grow in bone and muscle tissue. **Lymphomas** (lim-FOH-muhs) are solid tumors that grow in the tissues that form blood cells. Tumors in blood-forming tissues may cause **leukemia** (loo-KEE-mee-uh), the uncontrolled production of white blood cells. Usually it takes several years for cancer to develop. However, when a vital organ, such as the liver or pancreas, is involved, the symptoms caused by organ dysfunction due to cancer may develop more rapidly.

FIGURE 11-8

(a) Tobacco smoke contains more than 15 known carcinogens. (b) The cancers in this diseased lung are examples of carcinomas. One-third of the cancer deaths in the United States are due to lung cancer. Lung cancer is one of the deadliest forms of cancer; 93 percent of lung cancer patients die within five years after diagnosis. More than 90 percent of lung cancer patients are smokers.

(a)

(b)

FIGURE 11-9

The hazardous-chemical workers shown in this photograph are removing asbestos from a refinery. Because it is heat resistant and flexible, asbestos has been used to insulate buildings. When inhaled in large amounts over long periods of time, asbestos particles have been shown to cause lung cancer.

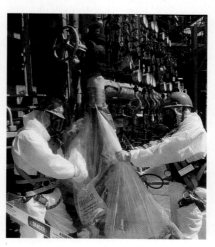

Cancer and the Cell Cycle

In normal cells, the frequency of cell division is governed by several factors. A cell must receive adequate nutrition before it can divide. Also, a cell must be attached to other cells, to a membrane, or to fibers between cells in order to divide. (Not all cells, of course, are destined to divide. Recall that cells of certain tissues, such as nervous tissue, cease dividing once they are formed.) Normal cells will stop dividing when they become too crowded, usually after 20 to 50 cell divisions. Cancer cells, however, continue to divide even when they are very densely packed, seemingly ignoring the normal cellular message to stop dividing. They also continue dividing after they are no longer attached to other cells, a trait that facilitates the spread of cancer cells throughout the body.

Causes of Cancer

What triggers the uncontrolled cell division that characterizes cancer? In normal cells, cell division is governed primarily by genes that regulate cell growth and division. Such genes code for **growth factors,** regulatory proteins that ensure that the events of cell division occur in the proper sequence and at the correct rate. Mutations that alter the expression of genes coding for growth factor proteins can lead to cancer. Such mutations can occur spontaneously but are more likely to occur as a result of the organism's exposure to carcinogens. A **carcinogen** (kahr-SIN-oh-jen) is any substance that increases the risk of cancer. Well-known carcinogens include tobacco, asbestos, and ionizing radiation, such as X rays or ultraviolet light from the sun. For example, cigarette tobacco has been found to be the cause of 90 percent of all lung cancers. Most carcinogens are **mutagens** (MYUT-uh-jens), agents that cause mutations to occur within a cell. Figure 11-9 shows hazardous-chemical workers removing the carcinogen asbestos from a refinery.

Whether a person actually develops cancer seems to depend on many factors. Some families exhibit higher-than-average rates of certain cancers, leading researchers to suspect a genetic predisposition to these types of cancer. With regard to cancers caused by mutagens, the number of exposures to the carcinogen and the amount of carcinogen in each exposure are significant factors. Mutations in gametes (egg or sperm cells) are especially important because these mutations are passed along to offspring.

Usually, more than one mutation is needed to produce a cancer cell. Perhaps this helps to explain why the cancer risk increases with the number of exposures to carcinogens and with the age of the individual. The longer an individual lives, the more mutations he or she will accumulate. Heightened awareness of the causes of cancer, combined with improved detection and treatment of the disease, has resulted in a decline in the number of deaths caused by cancer. In the United States, the cancer death rate fell by about 3 percent between the years 1991 and 1995, according to the National Cancer Institute.

The War on Cancer

Cancer, the leading cause of death in the United States, is a genetic disease caused by mutations in the genes that control cell division. Two kinds of genes that control cell division are proto-oncogenes and tumor-suppressor genes. Proto-oncogenes stimulate cell division, while tumor-suppressor genes inhibit cell division.

Under normal circumstances, these genes work together, enabling the body to replace and repair cells. However, a mutation in either a proto-oncogene or a tumor-suppressor gene can cause a cell to begin dividing uncontrollably. Such a cell may quickly become 2 cells, then 4, then 8, then 16, eventually forming a malignant tumor. The malignant tumor invades healthy tissues, often by spreading into the lymph tissues and blood vessels, which can transport cancer cells to distant sites in the body. A malignant tumor that is not destroyed quickly may become established in vital organs and interfere with their functions.

This woman joins other researchers around the world in the search for new cancer treatments.

One strategy for combating cancer is to stop the cell cycle of cancer cells so that they do not continue to divide. Most anticancer drugs interfere with the process of cell division at some step in the cell cycle. Anticancer drugs known as topoisomerase-1 inhibitors prevent the uncoiling of DNA that is necessary for replication. Another class of drugs works by damaging the cell's DNA so that it cannot be copied. Enzymes that monitor DNA replication will activate a series of steps that cause the cell to self-destruct if the DNA is too damaged for enzyme repair. However, these traditional anticancer drugs prevent cell division in all dividing cells, not just in cancer cells; thus, they damage healthy tissues too. A new class of anticancer drugs called farnesyltransferase inhibitors have been shown to target tumor cells but not normal cells.

Treating cancer cells based on their genetic makeup may also be helpful. For example, many cancer cells lack both normal copies of the tumor-suppressor gene p53. Cancer cells that have normal p53 genes tend to be very sensitive to chemotherapy, while those with mutant p53 genes often do not respond to chemotherapy treatment. Using a computer database that contains information about 350,000 potential anticancer compounds, oncologists have identified 112 possible compounds that may be effective against cancers associated with mutant p53 genes.

Simply keeping existing tumors under control is another way that cancer can be treated effectively. Malignant tumors typically stimulate their own growth by constructing a nourishing supply of blood vessels—a process called angiogenesis. Scientists know of more than 20 compounds that prevent angiogenesis. Currently, several of these compounds are being tested on human patients. Perhaps these compounds will be useful in slowing down or even stopping the growth of small clusters of cancer cells that are missed by other cancer treatments.

Combinations of several cancer therapies seem to be the best approach to fighting the war against cancer for now. By combining therapies, physicians may be able to eliminate tiny clusters of cancer cells that could rebound and kill patients. For example, combining chemotherapy and radiation has been shown to improve the condition of patients with advanced cancer of the nose and throat. Three years after treatment, 65 percent of patients who received both therapies were still alive, compared with a 24 percent survival rate among patients who received only radiation. In the coming years, cancer is likely to be considered a serious chronic disease. Like the chronic diseases diabetes and hypertension, perhaps cancers will be controlled with treatment for many years.

FIGURE 11-10

Mutations in proto-oncogenes or tumor-suppressor genes can destroy normal gene functioning, possibly resulting in cancer. A mutation in a proto-oncogene can cause it to become an oncogene, a gene that triggers cancer.

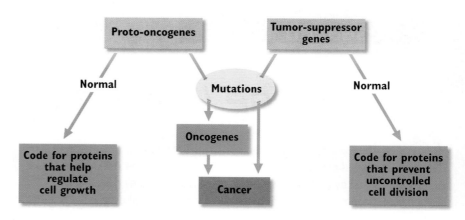

Oncogenes

An **oncogene** (AHN-koh-jeen) is a gene that causes cancer or other uncontrolled cell proliferation. Oncogenes begin as normal genes called **proto-oncogenes** that control a cell's growth and differentiation. Normally, proto-oncogenes code for proteins that regulate the rate of the cell cycle by controlling cell growth, cell division, and the ability of cells to adhere to one another. A mutation in a proto-oncogene may cause it to produce more protein or a protein that seems to be unusually active in triggering cell division. The rate of the cell cycle then increases, and cancer occurs as a result.

Other human genes suppress tumor formation. **Tumor-suppressor genes** code for proteins that prevent the uncontrolled rate of cell division. When tumor-suppressor genes mutate, the proteins for which they code are either defectively expressed or not expressed at all, causing a predisposition to cancer. Figure 11-10 summarizes the actions of oncogenes and tumor-suppressor genes.

Viruses and Cancer

Certain viruses can cause cancer in plants and animals. Many viral genes are actually oncogenes. Viruses can also stimulate uncontrolled growth in host cells by causing mutations in proto-oncogenes or tumor-suppressor genes, thus accelerating the rate of cell division in the host cell. Or they may activate the cell's own oncogenes. Viruses have been found to cause various kinds of leukemia.

internet**connect**

SC*LINKS*

NSTA

TOPIC: Oncogene
GO TO: www.scilinks.org
KEYWORD: HM214

SECTION 11-2 REVIEW

1. How can morphogenesis be affected by the control of gene expression?

2. What is the role of homeotic genes in *Drosophila*?

3. What does the presence of the homeobox among eukaryotes suggest about evolution?

4. List three ways in which cancer cells differ from normal cells.

5. Describe how mutations in proto-oncogenes or tumor-suppressor genes could cause cancer.

6. **CRITICAL THINKING** Why might X rays be more dangerous to an ovary or a testis than to muscle tissue?

SUMMARY/VOCABULARY

11-1
- Gene expression is the activation of a gene that results in the formation of a protein. Only a fraction of any cell's genes are expressed at any one time.
- Structural genes code for a particular product. Regulatory elements (a promoter and an operator) regulate the transcription of structural genes. In prokaryotes, the structural genes, the promoter, and the operator collectively form an operon.
- A promoter is the segment of DNA that recognizes the enzyme RNA polymerase and thus promotes transcription. An operator is the segment of DNA that can block transcription and thus prevent protein synthesis from occurring.
- In the bacterium *E. coli,* the *lac* operon codes for the three enzymes required for lactose metabolism.

- A repressor protein can inhibit a specific gene from being expressed. The blockage of transcription by the action of a repressor protein is called repression. A regulator gene controls the expression of a particular gene by coding for a repressor protein.
- An inducer is a molecule that initiates gene expression. In *E. coli,* lactose serves as an inducer.
- Eukaryotes do not have operons. The genomes of eukaryotes are larger and more complex than those of prokaryotes.
- Eukaryotic genes are organized into noncoding sections called introns and coding sections called exons.
- An enhancer must be activated for a eukaryotic gene to be expressed. Transcription factors initiate transcription by binding to enhancers and RNA polymerases.

Vocabulary

activation (205)	genome (203)	operon (204)	structural gene (204)
enhancer (208)	inducer (205)	pre-mRNA (207)	transcription factor (208)
euchromatin (206)	intron (206)	regulator gene (205)	
exon (206)	*lac* operon (204)	repression (205)	
gene expression (203)	operator (204)	repressor protein (205)	

11-2
- The development of specialized cells is called cell differentiation. The development of form in an organism is called morphogenesis. Both cell differentiation and morphogenesis are governed by gene expression.
- Homeotic genes are regulatory genes that determine where anatomical structures will be placed during development. Within each homeotic gene, a specific DNA sequence known as the homeobox regulates patterns of development. The homeoboxes of many

eukaryotic organisms appear to be very similar.
- Cancer is the uncontrolled growth of abnormal cells. Cancerous cells may form a tumor. Tumors may be benign or malignant.
- A carcinogen is any substance that increases the risk of cancer. Mutagens are substances that cause mutations.
- Mutations of proto-oncogenes or tumor-suppressor genes may lead to cancer.
- Some viruses can cause cancer.

Vocabulary

benign tumor (211)	growth factor (212)	malignant tumor (211)	proto-oncogene (214)
cancer (211)	homeobox (209)	metastasis (211)	sarcoma (211)
carcinogen (212)	homeotic gene (209)	morphogenesis (209)	tumor (211)
carcinoma (211)	leukemia (211)	mutagen (212)	tumor-suppressor gene
cell differentiation (209)	lymphoma (211)	oncogene (214)	(214)

REVIEW

Vocabulary

Explain the difference between the terms in each of the following sets:

1. operator, promoter
2. gene, genome
3. intron, exon
4. gene, homeotic gene
5. carcinogen, mutagen, oncogene

Multiple Choice

6. A repressor protein is coded for by a(n)
   (a) structural gene (b) regulator gene
   (c) promoter (d) enhancer.
7. Active DNA transcription in eukaryotes occurs within (a) an operon (b) an operator (c) an intron (d) euchromatin.
8. When present in an *E. coli* cell, lactose
   (a) binds with a repressor (b) stops transcription from occurring (c) binds with mRNA (d) acts as a regulator.
9. In eukaryotes, introns and exons are interspersed regions of a(n) (a) protein (b) DNA molecule (c) RNA molecule (d) transcription factor.
10. Enhancers (a) initiate transcription (b) join amino acids (c) unwind DNA (d) transport proteins into the nucleus.
11. The control of gene expression enables organisms to (a) reproduce more quickly (b) remove mutations from their DNA (c) produce proteins only when needed (d) form new combinations of genes.
12. Unlike eukaryotes, prokaryotes (a) have introns and exons (b) lack nuclei (c) have chromosomes of RNA (d) have enhancer sequences.
13. In eukaryotic cells, pre-mRNA contains (a) introns only (b) exons only (c) neither introns nor exons (d) both introns and exons.
14. A malignant tumor found in bone or muscle tissue is an example of (a) a sarcoma (b) leukemia (c) a carcinoma (d) a lymphoma.
15. The transformation of a normal gene into an oncogene may result in (a) a loss of cell division (b) the release of new viruses (c) cancer (d) the transcription of introns.

Short Answer

16. In which organism did Jacob and Monod study the *lac* operon? Where is this organism commonly found?
17. What causes the *lac* operon to shut off? Why can this mechanism be considered a feedback mechanism?
18. How does *E. coli* benefit by making enzymes to utilize lactose only when lactose is in the cellular environment?
19. Describe the events that take place after estrogen binds to a receptor protein in the cytoplasm.
20. How does cell differentiation differ from morphogenesis?
21. What happens when a malignant tumor undergoes metastasis?
22. Name three commonly known carcinogens.
23. What does it mean for a person to be "genetically predisposed" to cancer?
24. What does the study of homeoboxes suggest regarding the evolutionary relationships among eukaryotes?
25. Study the diagram of the *lac* operon shown below.
    a. Describe the role of the following elements shown in the diagram: promoter, operator, structural genes.
    b. What does it mean to say that a gene is turned "on"?
    c. Are the structural genes turned "on" in the diagram of the *lac* operon shown below?

Regulator gene Promoter Operator Structural genes 1 2 3

CRITICAL THINKING

1. A molecular biologist isolates mRNA from the brain and liver of a mouse and finds that the two types of mRNA are different. Can these results be correct, or has the biologist made an error? Explain your answer.

2. Kwashiorkor is a disease in children caused by a diet high in carbohydrates but lacking in complete protein. When children with kwashiorkor are suddenly put on a diet rich in protein, they may become very ill with ammonia poisoning, and some even die. The high level of ammonia in their blood is due to the inadequate metabolism of protein. What does this tell you about the enzymes that metabolize protein?

3. Mutations may occur in gametes or in body cells. In which cell type is a mutation likely to be a source of genetic variation for evolution? Why?

4. *Drosophila* feed on fermenting fruit, which often contains a large amount of alcohol. If *Drosophila* are fed a diet that has a high alcohol content, there is an increase in the amount of dehydrogenase, an enzyme that metabolizes alcohol, in the digestive tract. What does this increase tell you about the enzyme?

5. The graphs at right show the number of cigarettes smoked per capita per year since 1900 and the annual incidence of lung cancer among men and women. What is the relationship between the number of cigarettes smoked and the incidence of lung cancer? Why do you think the incidence of lung cancer among women has increased sharply in the last 30 years while the incidence of lung cancer among men has remained relatively stable during this period?

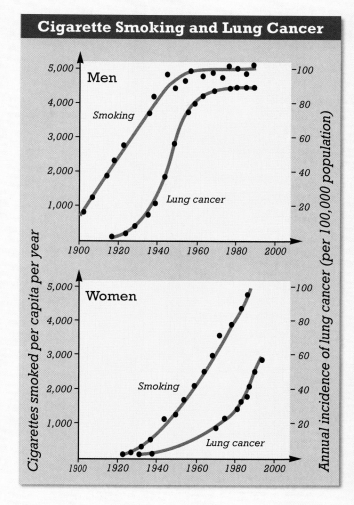

Cigarette Smoking and Lung Cancer

EXTENSION

1. Using your library, research forms of human cancer associated with viruses, such as leukemia (human T lymphotrophic virus), liver cancer (hepatitis B virus), Burkitt's lymphoma (Epstein-Barr virus), and cervical cancer (human Papillomavirus). Write a report on the symptoms, possible treatments, and prognoses of patients with these forms of cancer.

2. Construct a chart in which you compare and contrast the qualities in bacteria and fruit flies that make them ideal experimental tools for the scientist. Make sure to include similarities as well as differences between the two species.

3. Read "Got Cancer Killers?" in *Discover*, June 1999, on page 68. Write a short report about the potential cancer cure being researched at Lund University, in Sweden. Explain how the cancer-killing protein alpha-lactalbumin protects nursing infants. Describe the next step toward making a treatment available to cancer victims.

Modeling Gene Expression in the *Lac* Operon

OBJECTIVES

- Make a model of the *lac* operon.
- Demonstrate the mechanisms that regulate gene expression in the *lac* operon of *Escherichia coli*.
- Simulate the transcription of the structural genes in the *lac* operon.

PROCESS SKILLS

- comparing and contrasting
- identifying
- demonstrating
- manipulating a model

MATERIALS

- pipe cleaner
- large colored beads, 6
- colored modeling clay in three colors
- labeling tape
- marking pen
- pencil
- paper

Background

1. Define *gene*.
2. What is the role of RNA polymerase in protein synthesis?
3. Where does protein synthesis occur? What is the function of mRNA in protein synthesis?
4. What is the role of ribosomes during protein synthesis?
5. What are the roles of the operator, promoter, and structural genes within the *lac* operon?
6. How does the presence or absence of lactose affect the *lac* operon?
7. What is a regulator gene?

PART A Making a Model of the *Lac* Operon

1. In this investigation, you will use the materials provided to make a model of a *lac* operon. Allow the pipe cleaner to represent the portion of DNA that constitutes the *lac* operon.
2. Thread the pipe cleaner through three beads of similar size, shape, and color. These three beads represent the structural genes of the *lac* operon.
3. Add one bead to represent the operator portion of the *lac* operon. Also add beads to represent the promoter and the regulatory gene, respectively.
4. Using labeling tape and a marking pen, label each of the beads you have placed on the pipe cleaner. This represents a model of the *lac* operon.
5. Compare the sequence of the labeled beads on the pipe cleaner with the sequence of segments in the diagram of the *lac* operon in Figure 11-1. When your model of the *lac* operon correctly reflects the parts of the *lac* operon in the figure, proceed to Part B.

PART B The *Lac* Operon When It Is Turned Off

6. Choose one color of modeling clay to represent the enzyme RNA polymerase and choose another color to represent the repressor molecule. Use the modeling clay to mold an RNA polymerase molecule and a repressor molecule.
7. Using the molecules you made out of clay in step 6, modify your model of the *lac* operon so that it shows the *lac* operon when it is turned off.
8. In your lab report, draw your model of the *lac* operon when it is turned off. Label all parts of your drawing. How does the presence of the repressor molecule prevent transcription of the structural genes?

PART C The *Lac* Operon When It Is Turned On

9. Choose a third color of modeling clay to represent the inducer molecule. Use the modeling clay to form an inducer molecule.

10. Using the inducer molecule you made out of clay, modify your model of the *lac* operon so that it shows the *lac* operon when it is turned on.

11. Simulate the activation of the *lac* operon and the transcription of the structural genes.

12. In your lab report, prepare a diagram of your model that shows the expression of the structural genes in the *lac* operon. Include ribosomes and mRNA in your diagram. Label all parts of your diagram.

13. The graphic organizer below shows the sequence of steps that occurs after lactose enters *E. coli* cells. Copy this graphic organizer in your lab report. Complete the graphic organizer by describing what takes place during step 2 and step 3. Explain how the end product affects the events shown in the graphic organizer.

14. Clean up your materials before leaving the lab.

Step 1
Lactose enters cell

Step 2

Step 3

End products
Enzymes that break down lactose

Analysis and Conclusions

1. Compare the processes of repression and activation.

2. What substance serves as an inducer in the *lac* operon?

3. How might a mutation in the regulator gene affect the *lac* operon?

4. Look at the diagram you made in step 12. Refer to your diagram, and predict what will happen when the inducer is no longer present.

5. How would the loss of the promoter site from the operon affect the production of the enzymes needed to utilize lactose?

6. In homes and apartments, a consistent temperature is maintained by means of a thermostat, which regulates when heating (or air conditioning) is turned on or off. In what way does the *lac* operon function like a thermostat?

7. Biological processes often take place in a series of sequential steps called a biochemical pathway. Many biochemical pathways are controlled by feedback inhibition. In feedback inhibition, a pathway's end product affects an earlier step in the pathway and causes the pathway to stop. Explain why the *lac* operon in *E. coli* is considered an example of feedback inhibition.

Further Inquiry

1. Use classroom or library references to find additional examples of feedback inhibition in biology. Describe why models of feedback inhibition are sometimes called feedback loops.

2. The products of the *lac* operon are produced when lactose is present. In this way, the presence of a specific molecule stimulates transcription of the structural genes. In contrast, some operons are repressed when a specific molecule is present. Use classroom or library references to find out how the *trp* operon functions in *E. coli.* Then compare activation and repression in the *trp* operon with activation and repression in the *lac* operon.

INHERITANCE PATTERNS AND HUMAN GENETICS

These rod-shaped structures are human chromosomes as seen through a scanning electron microscope. (SEM, 5,148×)

FOCUS CONCEPT: *Reproduction and Inheritance*

As you read this chapter, note how Mendel's theories of inheritance (Chapter 9) and our knowledge of chromosome structure and protein synthesis (Chapters 10 and 11) have helped shape the study of genetics.

12-1 *Chromosomes and Inheritance*

12-2 *Human Genetics*

Unit 6—*Gene Expression*
Topics 1–6

CHROMOSOMES AND INHERITANCE

You have learned how DNA in chromosomes contains instructions for protein synthesis and how chromosomes are transmitted from one generation to the next. In this chapter you will learn how biologists use their knowledge of DNA and chromosome behavior to study how traits are inherited and expressed.

OBJECTIVES

▲

Explain the role of sex chromosomes in sex determination.

●

Describe how sex linkage affects the inheritance of traits.

■

Explain the effect of crossing-over on the inheritance of genes in linkage groups.

◆

Summarize the procedure involved in constructing a chromosome map.

▲

Distinguish between chromosome mutations and gene mutations.

SEX DETERMINATION

In the early 1900s, geneticist Thomas Hunt Morgan, of Columbia University, began breeding experiments with *Drosophila*, the fruit fly. *Drosophila* has four pairs of homologous chromosomes. Morgan observed that one chromosome pair was different in males than it was in females. In females, the two chromosomes in the pair were identical. In males, however, while one chromosome looked like those of the corresponding female pair, the other chromosome was shorter and hook-shaped. Morgan called the chromosome that appeared to be the same in males and females the X chromosome. He called the shorter, hook-shaped chromosome the Y chromosome. Morgan correctly hypothesized that the X and Y chromosomes are sex chromosomes. Recall from Chapter 8 that sex chromosomes determine an individual's sex. All of the other chromosomes, those not involved in sex determination, are called autosomes.

Like other chromosomes, the sex chromosomes form pairs and segregate into separate cells during meiosis I. As a result, the gametes that form during meiosis II each have *either* an X chromosome or a Y chromosome. In mammals and most insects, males have one X chromosome and one Y chromosome, which are symbolized XY, and females have two X chromosomes, which are symbolized XX. Gametes produced by males can contain either an X chromosome or a Y chromosome, whereas gametes produced by females contain only an X chromosome.

In humans and fruit flies, an egg that is fertilized by a sperm with an X chromosome will be a female zygote (XX), and an egg that is fertilized by a sperm with a Y chromosome will be a male zygote (XY). As shown in Figure 12-1, this system of sex determination means that 50 percent of the offspring of any mating will be male and 50 percent will be female.

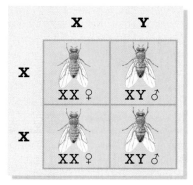

FIGURE 12-1

As this Punnett square shows, approximately half of all *Drosophila* offspring are likely to be female (♀), and half are likely to be male (♂).

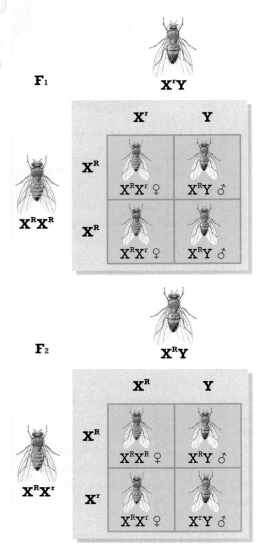

Sex Linkage

The discovery of the different sizes and shapes of the X and Y chromosomes led Morgan to hypothesize that more genes could be carried by the X chromosome than by the smaller Y chromosome. Genes found on the X chromosome are said to be **X-linked genes.** Genes found on the Y chromosome are **Y-linked genes.** The presence of a gene on a sex chromosome is called **sex linkage.**

Morgan's *Drosophila* experiments confirmed the existence of X-linked traits. Although most fruit flies have red eyes, a few males have white eyes. When Morgan crossed a white-eyed male with a red-eyed female, the results of the cross followed Mendel's predictions: the F_1 generation all had red eyes. Morgan next crossed members of the F_1 generation. The F_2 generation that resulted exhibited the expected ratio of three red-eyed flies to one white-eyed fly. However, all of the white-eyed flies were male.

Why were there no white-eyed females? Morgan hypothesized that the gene for eye color is carried on the X chromosome. Figure 12-2 shows his reasoning. Assume that the X chromosome carries the gene for eye color, either X^R (red eyes) or X^r (white eyes). If an $X^R X^R$ female (red-eyed) is crossed with an $X^r Y$ male (white-eyed), all of the F_1 females will be $X^R X^r$ (red-eyed) and all of the F_1 males will be $X^R Y$ (red-eyed). Note that the Y chromosome does not carry a gene for eye color. In the F_2 generation, half the females will be $X^R X^R$, and the other half will be $X^R X^r$; therefore, all of the females will be red-eyed. Half of the F_2 males will be $X^R Y$ (red-eyed), but the other half will be $X^r Y$ (white-eyed). Morgan correctly concluded that eye color in *Drosophila* is an X-linked trait.

FIGURE 12-2

Eye color is an X-linked trait in fruit flies. Alleles for eye color are carried on the X chromosome—*R* for red and *r* for white.

internet connect

SCiLINKS
NSTA

TOPIC: X-linked traits
GO TO: www.scilinks.org
KEYWORD: HM222

LINKAGE GROUPS

Because there are thousands more genes than there are chromosomes, each chromosome carries many genes. The genes located on one chromosome form a **linkage group.** Two or more genes that are found on the same chromosome are thus said to be linked. Because they are on the same chromosome, linked genes tend to be inherited together.

Morgan demonstrated the existence of linkage groups in his work with *Drosophila*. In *Drosophila* the allele *G* for gray body is dominant to the allele *g* for black body. The allele *L* for long wings is dominant to the allele *l* for short wings. Morgan crossed homozygous gray, long-winged (*GGLL*) flies with homozygous black, short-winged (*ggll*) flies to produce an F_1 generation of heterozygous gray, long-winged (*GgLl*) flies. Then he crossed members of this F_1 generation with one another (*GgLl* × *GgLl*) to produce an F_2 generation. Morgan knew that if the alleles for body color and wing length were on

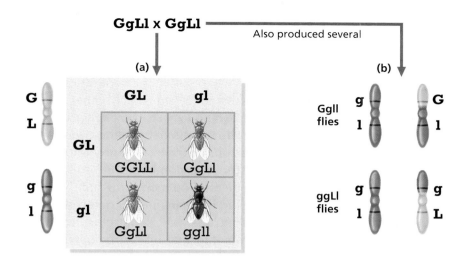

GgLl x GgLl ———— Also produced several ————→

(a)

	GL	**gl**
GL	GGLL	GgLl
gl	GgLl	ggll

(b)

Ggll flies
g l | G l

ggLl flies
g l | g L

FIGURE 12-3

(a) Because the genes for body color and wing length are linked, the cross *GgLl* × *GgLl* produces a 3:1 phenotypic ratio. (b) Crossing-over produces gametes with new combinations of alleles, leading to unexpected phenotypes among the offspring.

different chromosomes, they should assort independently and produce an F_2 generation with a phenotypic ratio of 9:3:3:1. Morgan predicted that if the alleles were on the same chromosome, however, an F_2 generation with a phenotypic ratio of 3 gray, long-winged flies: 1 black, short-winged fly would result. The results of the cross closely approximated this 3:1 ratio. Morgan hypothesized that the genes for body color and wing length are linked, as shown in Figure 12-3a.

Unexpectedly, the cross also produced several gray, short-winged (*Ggll*) flies and several black, long-winged flies (*ggLl*). If the genes for body color and wing length were indeed on the same chromosome, how could they be separated? Morgan realized that these results could have occurred only if the alleles had somehow changed or become rearranged. Mutations could have caused the changes, but mutations usually only occur in one individual out of tens of thousands. The alleles must therefore have become rearranged. Morgan inferred that this rearrangement had taken place through crossing-over. Recall from Chapter 8 that crossing-over is the exchange of pieces of DNA between homologous chromosomes. Figure 12-3b shows how crossing-over accounts for the unexpected phenotypes in the F_2 generation of Morgan's experiment.

Crossing-over does not create new genes or delete old ones. Instead, it changes the locations of genes among the chromosomes that carry them, thus producing new gene combinations, as shown in Figure 12-4.

FIGURE 12-4

When traits do not appear according to the expected ratio in offspring, crossing-over may have occurred. Parental gametes contain alleles on the same chromosome that have been inherited together. Crossover gametes contain new combinations of alleles that are not found in the parental gametes.

Homologous chromosomes

Crossover gametes

CROSSING-OVER DURING MEIOSIS

Parental gametes

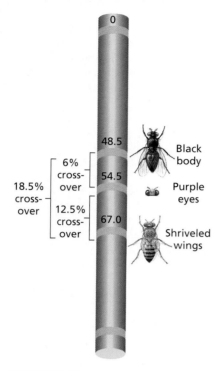

FIGURE 12-5

The genes for black body and purple eyes are separated by crossing-over 6 percent of the time, while the genes for purple eyes and shriveled wings are separated by crossing-over 12.5 percent of the time. The genes for black body and shriveled wings are separated by crossing-over 18.5 percent of the time.

Word Roots and Origins

somatic

from the Greek *sōmatikos,*
meaning "body"

CHROMOSOME MAPPING

The likelihood that crossing-over will result in the separation of two genes depends on the genes' distance from each other on the chromosome. The farther apart two genes are, the likelier they are to be separated by crossovers. The results of crossing-over appear in the offspring as new combinations of traits. The greater the percentage of offspring that show the new combination of traits, the farther apart the two genes are located on a chromosome.

Scientists can conduct breeding experiments to determine how frequently genes for particular traits are separated from one another among the offspring. This information can be used to prepare chromosome maps. A **chromosome map** is a diagram that shows the linear sequence of genes on a chromosome. Alfred H. Sturtevant, one of Morgan's students, used crossing-over data to construct a chromosome map of *Drosophila*.

To construct his chromosome map, Sturtevant compared the frequency of crossing-over for several genes. The percentage of crossing-over between the genes for two traits is proportional to the distance between them on a chromosome. For example, two genes that are separated by crossing-over 1 percent of the time are considered to be one **map unit** apart. Figure 12-5 illustrates how crossover percentages can be used to determine the positions of the genes for black body, purple eyes, and shriveled wings in *Drosophila*.

In recent years, new techniques of gene mapping have been developed. These techniques have helped to map the chromosomes of many species, even those with many chromosomes and tens of thousands of genes.

MUTATION

As you learned in Chapter 10, a change in the DNA of an organism is called a mutation. Mutations can involve an entire chromosome or a single DNA nucleotide, and they may take place in any cell. **Germ-cell mutations** occur in an organism's germ cells (gametes). Germ-cell mutations do not affect the organism itself, but they may be passed on to offspring if the affected gamete is fertilized. **Somatic** (soh-MAT-ik) **mutations** take place in an organism's body cells and can therefore affect the organism. Certain types of human skin cancer and leukemia result from somatic mutations. Somatic mutations are not passed on to offspring.

Lethal mutations cause death, often before birth. However, some mutations result in phenotypes that are beneficial. Organisms with beneficial mutations have a better chance of reproducing and therefore have an evolutionary advantage. Such mutations provide the variation upon which natural selection acts.

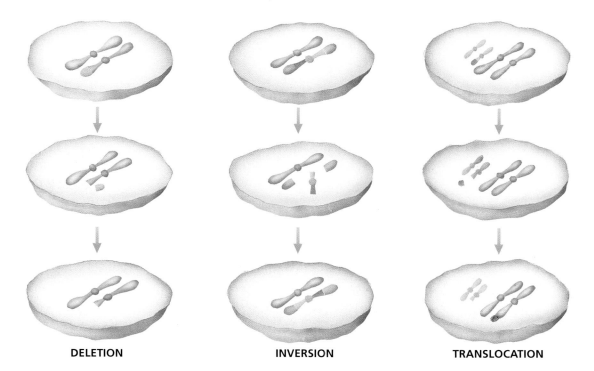

DELETION   INVERSION   TRANSLOCATION

Chromosome Mutations

Chromosome mutations are either changes in the structure of a chromosome or the loss of an entire chromosome. A **deletion** is the loss of a piece of a chromosome due to chromosomal breakage. As a consequence, all of the information carried by the missing piece may be lost. An **inversion** is a chromosome mutation in which a chromosomal segment breaks off and then reattaches in reverse orientation to the same chromosome. A chromosome mutation in which a chromosome piece breaks off and reattaches to another, nonhomologous chromosome is a **translocation.** Figure 12-6 shows these mutations.

Some types of chromosomal mutations alter the number of chromosomes found in the cell. **Nondisjunction** (NON-dis-JUHNK-shuhn) is the failure of a chromosome to separate from its homologue during meiosis. When nondisjunction occurs, one gamete receives an extra copy of a chromosome and the other gamete lacks the chromosome entirely. Human disorders resulting from nondisjunction are discussed in Section 12-2.

Gene Mutations

Gene mutation may involve large segments of DNA or a single nucleotide within a codon. As you will recall from Chapter 10, a codon consists of three nucleotides that cause a specific amino acid to be inserted into a polypeptide during protein synthesis. The substitution, addition, or removal of a single nucleotide is called a **point mutation.**

In point mutations called **substitutions,** one nucleotide in a codon is replaced with a different nucleotide, resulting in a new codon. An example of a substitution mutation is shown in Figure 12-7. If the new codon codes for the same amino acid as the original codon, the

FIGURE 12-6

In many chromosome mutations, a piece of chromosome breaks off. The piece may be lost or may reattach in a reversed position. In translocations, a broken piece attaches to a nonhomologous chromosome.

FIGURE 12-7

In a substitution, one nucleotide replaces another, forming a new codon that may signal the insertion of the wrong amino acid.

DNA → mRNA → Amino acid

NORMAL

DNA	mRNA	Amino acid
A C G	U G C	Cysteine
C T C	G A G	Glutamic acid
G T C	C A G	Glutamine
G T C		
T	A	

FRAME SHIFT MUTATION

	DNA	mRNA	Amino acid
G	A C C	U G G	Tryptophan
	T C G	A G C	Serine
	T C T	A G A	Arginine

FIGURE 12-8

Deleting a nucleotide causes all subsequent codons to be incorrectly read, resulting in a frame shift mutation. Adding a nucleotide will have the same effect.

substitution will have no effect. However, if the new codon is a "stop" codon or if it codes for a different amino acid, the resulting protein will be affected.

The genetic disorder **sickle cell anemia** (also called sickle cell disease) is caused by a point mutation that substitutes adenine for thymine in a single DNA codon, as shown in Figure 12-7. This substitution results in a defective form of the protein hemoglobin. Hemoglobin is found within red blood cells, where it binds with oxygen and transports it throughout the body. The red blood cells of people with two copies of the mutant allele for sickle cell anemia have a distorted, sickle shape, causing anemia (loss of red blood cells) and circulatory problems. Because of this, children with sickle cell anemia may suffer damage to the brain, heart, lungs, and many other organs and tissues. The sickle cell allele is especially widespread among African Americans. In the United States, approximately 1 out every 500 African Americans has sickle cell anemia.

Individuals who are heterozygous for the sickle cell allele make both normal and altered forms of hemoglobin and are generally healthy. In the United States, approximately 1 out of 10 African Americans is heterozygous for the sickle-cell allele and is therefore a carrier for sickle cell anemia. A simple blood test can reveal the presence of the allele.

Two forms of point mutations are nucleotide insertions and nucleotide deletions. In nucleotide deletion mutations, one or more nucleotides in a gene are lost. In insertion mutations, one or more nucleotides are added to a gene. Deletion and insertion mutations tend to have more serious effects than substitution mutations. Because each codon consists of a group of three sequential nucleotides, the addition or deletion of a single nucleotide causes the remaining codons to be incorrectly grouped, resulting in a **frame shift mutation,** as shown in Figure 12-8. In fact, frame shift mutations occur anytime the number of nucleotides inserted or deleted is not a multiple of three. Figure 12-8 shows a frame shift mutation that results from the deletion of one nucleotide. Thus, a frame shift mutation occurring near the beginning of a gene will prevent a number of codons from coding for the proper amino acids.

SECTION 12-1 REVIEW

1. How does the inheritance of sex chromosomes result in approximately equal numbers of males and females among the offspring of fruit flies?

2. Offer an explanation for why Morgan did not find white-eyed female *Drosophila* in the F₂ generation when he crossed white-eyed males with red-eyed females.

3. How does crossing-over show that genes are found on chromosomes?

4. How can crossing-over between two alleles be used to map their locations on chromosomes?

5. What are point mutations?

6. **CRITICAL THINKING** Biologists have observed that chromosome mutations often occur during nuclear division. Why do you think this is so? Explain your answer.

HUMAN GENETICS

*B*iologists have studied many different organisms in their search to discover the fundamental principles of genetics. These fundamental principles also apply to humans. Much of what we have discovered about the inheritance of traits has been learned in the study of human genetics.

SECTION

12-2

OBJECTIVES

▲

Show how pedigree analysis can be used to illustrate the inheritance of traits.

●

Explain the inheritance of ABO blood groups.

■

Give examples of traits or disorders transmitted by autosomal dominant, autosomal recessive, polygenic, and X-linked recessive inheritance.

◆

Compare sex-linked traits with sex-influenced traits.

▲

Explain how nondisjunction can cause human genetic disorders.

STUDYING HUMAN INHERITANCE

Patterns of inheritance are significantly more complicated to study among humans than among *Drosophila.* Humans have up to 20 times as many genes as *Drosophila,* and our 23 pairs of chromosomes are made up of about 100,000 genes. Geneticists have often focused on studying disease-causing genes because such genes are easily traced from one generation to the next and because they are of great concern to the human population.

Pedigree Analysis

Biologists discover how traits are inherited by studying phenotypes among members of the same species from one generation to the next. In particular, they often study members of the same family. In such studies, geneticists often prepare a **pedigree,** a family record that shows how a trait is inherited over several generations. Figure 12-9 shows a pedigree illustrating a trait that is inherited as

GENERATION   **INHERITANCE OF AN AUTOSOMAL RECESSIVE TRAIT**

MALE	FEMALE	
		Normal
		Carrier
		Displays trait

FIGURE 12-9

This pedigree shows the inheritance of an autosomal recessive trait. Pedigrees are particularly important if the trait is a genetic disorder and family members wish to know if they are carriers or if their children will have the disorder.

a recessive autosomal trait. When analyzing pedigrees, biologists find that certain phenotypes are usually repeated in predictable patterns from one generation to the next. These patterns are called **patterns of inheritance.** Individuals who have one copy of a recessive autosomal allele are called **carriers.** Carriers usually do not express the recessive allele, but they can pass it along to their offspring.

GENETIC TRAITS AND DISORDERS

Genes controlling human traits exhibit several patterns of inheritance. Some of these genes have been subjects of intense scientific interest because they cause genetic disorders. **Genetic disorders** are diseases or debilitating conditions that have a genetic basis. Table 12-1 lists several patterns of inheritance and examples of traits or disorders for each.

Traits Controlled by a Single Allele

Single-allele traits are controlled by a single allele of a gene. Geneticists have discovered that more than 200 human traits are governed by a single dominant allele. **Huntington's disease (HD)** is caused by a dominant allele located on an autosome and is therefore said to show an autosomal-dominant pattern of inheritance. The first symptoms of HD—mild forgetfulness and irritability—appear in victims in their thirties or forties. In time, HD causes loss of muscle control, uncontrollable physical spasms, severe mental illness, and eventually death. Unfortunately, most people who have the HD allele do not know they have the disease until after they have had children. Thus, the disease is unknowingly passed on from one generation to the next.

Recently, however, scientists have discovered a genetic marker for the HD allele. A **genetic marker** is a short section of DNA that is known to have a close association with a particular gene located nearby. Thus, the presence of a genetic marker in a DNA sample is a strong indicator that a particular allele (in this case, the allele for HD) is also present. People who have the genetic marker for the HD allele have a 96 percent chance of developing HD. By conducting a test on sample cells, geneticists are now able to inform a person of the presence of the marker before he or she becomes a parent.

More than 250 other single-allele traits are controlled by homozygous recessive alleles. Cystic fibrosis (CF) and sickle cell anemia are examples of single-allele recessive traits. Single-allele recessive traits are fully expressed only when the individual has two copies of the recessive allele and is thus homozygous recessive. Because cystic fibrosis and sickle cell anemia are caused by recessive alleles located on autosomes, they are said to show an autosomal-recessive pattern of inheritance.

TABLE 12-1
Patterns of Inheritance for Several Human Traits

Single Allele (Dominant)

Huntington's disease (HD)

Achondroplasia (dwarfism)

Cataracts

Polydactyly (extra fingers or toes)

Single Allele (Recessive)

Albinism

Cystic fibrosis

Phenylketonuria (PKU)

Hereditary deafness

X-Linked

Colorblindness

Hemophilia

Muscular dystrophy

Icthyosis simplex (scaly skin)

Polygenic

Skin, hair, and eye color

Foot size

Nose length

Height

Multiple Alleles

ABO blood groups

Traits Controlled by Multiple Alleles

Multiple-allele traits are controlled by three or more alleles of the same gene that code for a single trait. In humans, the ABO blood groups are controlled by the three alleles I^A, I^B, and i. Each individual's ABO blood group genotype consists of two of these alleles, which determine his or her ABO blood type. The alleles I^A and I^B are codominant (both are expressed when together), and both are dominant to the i allele. Table 12-2 shows the possible ABO blood group genotypes and the ABO blood types they produce.

Polygenic Traits

Although some human traits are governed by a single gene, most human characteristics are controlled by several genes. A trait that is controlled by two or more genes is called a **polygenic** (PAHL-ee-JEHN-ik) **trait.** Skin color, for example, is influenced by the additive effects of three to six genes. Each gene results in a certain amount of a brownish black pigment called melanin. The more melanin produced, the darker the skin; the less melanin produced, the lighter the skin. Eye color is also a polygenic trait. Light-blue eyes have very little melanin. Very dark brown eyes have a great deal of melanin. Polygenic traits show many degrees of variation.

It is important to note that the expression of many traits, particularly those that are governed by many genes, is influenced by the environment. For example, human height is a polygenic trait controlled by an unknown number of genes that play a role in determining the growth of the skeleton. However, height is also influenced by environmental factors, such as nutrition and disease.

X-Linked Traits

Colorblindness is a recessive X-linked disorder in which an individual cannot distinguish between certain colors. Recall that genes for X-linked traits are found only on the X chromosome. Although many forms of colorblindness exist, the most common is the inability to distinguish red from green. About 8 percent of males are colorblind.

Hemophilia (HEE-moh-FIL-ee-uh) is another recessive X-linked disease that occurs almost exclusively in males. This disorder impairs the ability of the blood to clot following a cut, bruise, or other injury. Another recessive X-linked trait in humans is **Duchenne muscular dystrophy** (DIS-troh-fee), a form of muscular dystrophy that weakens and progressively destroys muscle tissue. These and several other important genetic disorders are described in Table 12-3 on the following page.

Not all or even most X-linked traits are diseases. There are hundreds of genes on the X chromosome, but only a few are associated with diseases. The others code for proteins that perform many normally needed functions in the body.

Sex-Influenced Traits

The presence of male or female sex hormones influences the expression of certain human traits, called **sex-influenced traits.** In

TABLE 12-2
ABO Blood Types

Genotype	Blood type
$I^A I^A$	A
$I^A i$	A
$I^B I^B$	B
$I^B i$	B
$I^A I^B$	AB
ii	O

Quick Lab

Modeling Linkage

Materials two kinds of candy, toothpicks, pencil, paper

Procedure Use two kinds of candy to represent genes for two traits. Long noses are dominant over short noses. Large ears are dominant over small ears. One color of candy will represent the dominant allele, and a different color candy will represent the recessive allele. Use these materials to determine the outcome of a cross between two individuals, each heterozygous for both traits. Your teacher will tell you if the genes are linked or not linked.

1. Draw a large Punnett square on your paper. Use the appropriate alleles to make gametes for each individual. Then place the allele combinations in each square representing the possible zygotes from that cross.

2. If your team is working with genes that are linked, you must first use toothpicks to link the genes together before you arrange the gametes on your Punnett square.

Analysis What is the offspring's phenotypic ratio when the genes are not linked? What is the phenotypic ratio when the genes are linked? Explain the difference.

TABLE 12-3 Some Important Genetic Disorders

Disorder	Symptom	Defect	Pattern of inheritance	Frequency among human births
Huntington's disease	gradual deterioration of brain tissue in middle age; shortened life expectancy	production of an inhibitor of brain cell metabolism	autosomal dominant	1/10,000
Cystic fibrosis	mucus clogs lungs, liver, and pancreas; victims usually don't survive to adulthood	failure of chloride ion transport mechanism	autosomal recessive	1/2,080 (whites)
Sickle cell anemia	impaired blood circulation, organ damage	abnormal hemoglobin molecules	autosomal recessive	1/500 (African Americans)
Tay-Sachs disease	deterioration of central nervous system in infancy; death occurs in early childhood	defective form of enzyme hexosaminidase A	autosomal recessive	1/1,600 (Jews of European descent)
Phenylketonuria	failure of brain to develop in infancy; if untreated, causes death in childhood	defective form of enzyme phenylalanine hydroxylase	autosomal recessive	1/18,000
Hemophilia	failure of blood to clot	defective form of blood-clotting factor	X-linked recessive	1/7,000
Muscular dystrophy	wasting away of muscles; shortened life expectancy	muscle fibers degenerate	X-linked recessive	1/10,000

a sex-influenced trait, males and females have different phenotypes, even when they share the same genotype. For example, pattern baldness is controlled by the allele *B,* which is dominant in males but recessive in females. Both men and women who are homozygous (*BB*) will eventually lose their hair. The allele *B´* codes for the normal, nonbald phenotype. A heterozygous (*BB´*) woman will not lose her hair, but a heterozygous (*BB´*) man will. These differences in gene expression are due to higher levels of the male sex hormone testosterone in men, which interacts with the genotype *BB´* to produce baldness in men. The alleles that code for most sex-influenced traits are located on the autosomes. Therefore, males and females can have the same genotype, but the sex-influenced trait will be expressed in only one sex.

Disorders Due to Nondisjunction

Nondisjunction occurring during meiosis can cause gametes to lack a chromosome or to have an extra chromosome, as shown in Figure 12-10. If nondisjunction occurs during egg formation in humans, one egg will have 22 chromosomes instead of the normal 23 ($1n$) chromosomes. Another egg will have 24 chromosomes. If one of these eggs combines with a normal sperm, the resulting zygote will have either 45 or 47 chromosomes instead of the normal 46 ($2n$) chromosomes. A zygote with 45 chromosomes has only one copy of a particular chromosome, a condition called **monosomy** (MAHN-uh-SOH-mee). A zygote with 47 chromosomes has three copies of a particular chromosome, a condition called **trisomy** (trie-SOH-mee).

Such abnormalities in chromosomal number are often lethal. However, some instances of monosomy or trisomy allow development to proceed. An extra chromosome 21 results in **Down syndrome** (also called **trisomy-21**), which includes mild to severe mental retardation, characteristic facial features, muscle weakness, heart defects, and short stature.

Nondisjunction can also affect the sex chromosomes. Males with an extra X chromosome have Klinefelter's syndrome (XXY). These persons have some feminine characteristics and are sometimes mentally retarded and infertile. Individuals who have a single X chromosome instead of a pair of sex chromosomes have Turner's syndrome (XO, the O meaning that there is only one sex chromosome). People with Turner's syndrome have a female appearance, but they do not mature sexually and they remain infertile. Zygotes that receive only a single Y chromosome do not survive because the X chromosome contains information that is essential for development.

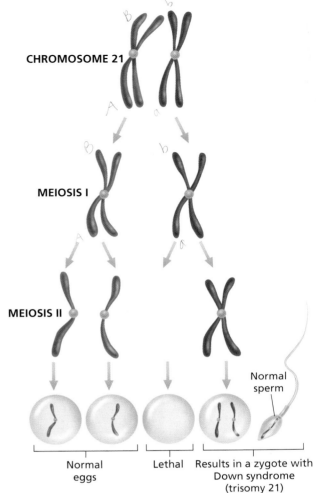

CHROMOSOME 21

MEIOSIS I

MEIOSIS II

Normal sperm

Normal eggs

Lethal

Results in a zygote with Down syndrome (trisomy 21)

FIGURE 12-10

Nondisjunction can cause abnormalities in chromosome number. Normal gametes have one copy of each chromosome. Down syndrome can result when a gamete (an egg, in the example shown here) containing two copies of chromosome 21 is fertilized by a normal sperm.

DETECTING HUMAN GENETIC DISORDERS

A person with a family history of genetic disorders may wish to undergo **genetic screening** before becoming a parent. Genetic screening is an examination of a person's genetic makeup. It may involve constructing a karyotype, a picture of an individual's chromosomes grouped in pairs and arranged in sequence. Other techniques test an individual's blood for the presence or absence of certain proteins. These procedures can detect potential genetic disorders that might be passed on to children. Couples at risk may wish to undergo **genetic counseling,** a form of medical guidance that informs them about problems that could affect their offspring.

Word Roots and Origins

monosomy

from the Greek *mono*, meaning "one," and *soma*, meaning "body" or "chromosome"

FIGURE 12-11

Fetal cells obtained by amniocentesis or chorionic villi sampling can be used to prepare fetal karyotypes, enabling physicians to diagnose chromosomal abnormalities before a child's birth.

Physicians can also diagnose more than 200 genetic disorders in the fetus using a variety of tools and techniques. Figure 12-11 shows amniocentesis and chorionic villi sampling, two forms of prenatal (before birth) testing that can reveal fetal abnormalities. During **amniocentesis** (AM-nee-OH-sen-TEE-sis) the physician removes a small amount of amniotic fluid from the amnion, the sac that surrounds the fetus, between the fourteenth and sixteenth weeks of pregnancy. Fetal cells and proteins from the fluid then can be analyzed and a karyotype can also be prepared. During **chorionic** (KOR-ee-ON-ik) **villi** (VIL-IE) **sampling** the physician obtains a sample of the chorionic villi, a tissue that grows between the mother's uterus and the placenta, between the eighth and tenth week of pregnancy. The villi have the same genetic makeup as the fetus because they were both coded for by fetal DNA. Tissue samples from the villi can be used to produce a karyotype.

In some cases, genetic screening is performed immediately after birth. In the United States, approximately 1 out of every 10,000 babies is afflicted with **phenylketonuria** (FEN-uhl-KEET-oh-NUHR-ee-uh), or **PKU,** a genetic disorder in which the body cannot metabolize the amino acid phenylalanine. The accumulation of excess phenylalanine causes severe brain damage. PKU can be detected by means of a blood test administered to infants during the first few days of life. The dangers of PKU can be eliminated by placing these infants on a special diet that lacks phenylalanine.

SECTION 12-2 REVIEW

1. A husband and wife are heterozygous for cystic fibrosis. Their son has cystic fibrosis. Their second child, a daughter, does not. Prepare a pedigree for this family.

2. A husband and wife have the ABO blood group genotypes $I^A I^B$ and ii. What ABO blood types can their children have?

3. Compare the inheritance of Huntington's disease with the inheritance of sickle cell anemia.

4. Is pattern baldness a sex-linked trait or a sex-influenced trait? Explain your answer.

5. How can nondisjunction change chromosome number?

6. **CRITICAL THINKING** Colorblindness is rare among females. Why? Explain your answer.

SUMMARY/VOCABULARY

12-1
- Sex chromosomes determine the sex of an organism.
- A sex-linked gene is found on one sex chromosome but not on the other. Genes found on the X chromosome are X-linked genes. Genes found on the Y chromosome are Y-linked genes.
- The genes found on one chromosome make up a linkage group. The genes found on a chromosome are said to be linked.
- Linked genes can be separated by crossing-over. The percentage of crossing-over between two genes is directly proportional to the distance between them.
- The frequency of crossing-over between

genes can be used to construct a chromosome map.
- Crossing-over creates new combinations of genes and therefore serves as a source of genetic variation.
- Germ-cell mutations occur in gametes and can be passed on to offspring. Somatic mutations occur in body cells and affect only the individual organism.
- Chromosome mutations are changes in the structure of a chromosome or the loss of an entire chromosome. Gene mutations are changes in one or more of the nucleotides in a gene.

Vocabulary

chromosome map (224)
deletion (225)
frame shift
 mutation (226)
germ-cell mutation (224)

inversion (225)
lethal mutation (224)
linkage group (222)
map unit (224)
nondisjunction (225)

point mutation (225)
sex linkage (222)
sickle cell anemia (226)
somatic mutation (224)
substitution (225)

translocation (225)
X-linked gene (222)
Y-linked gene (222)

12-2
- A pedigree is a family record that shows how a trait is inherited over several generations.
- Single-allele traits are controlled by a single allele of a gene. Multiple-allele traits are controlled by three or more alleles of a gene.
- Polygenic traits are controlled by two or more different genes.
- The genes for X-linked human traits, such as colorblindness, Duchenne muscular dystrophy, and hemophilia, are found on the X chromosome.
- A sex-influenced trait is expressed differently in men than it is in women, even when individuals have the same genotype.
- Nondisjunction during meiosis can cause

gametes to have one too few or one too many chromosomes. If such a gamete is fertilized, a genetic disorder such as monosomy ($2n=45$) or trisomy ($2n=47$) can occur.
- Genetic screening examines a person's genetic makeup and can identify people at risk of passing on genetic disorders to their children. Genetic counseling informs these individuals about problems that could affect their prospective offspring.
- A karyotype can be used to reveal chromosomal abnormalities.
- Amniocentesis and chorionic villi sampling enable physicians to test a fetus for the presence of genetic disorders.

Vocabulary

amniocentesis (232)
carrier (228)
chorionic villi
 sampling (232)
colorblindness (229)
Down syndrome (231)
Duchenne muscular
 dystrophy (229)

genetic counseling (231)
genetic disorder (228)
genetic marker (228)
genetic screening (231)
hemophilia (229)
Huntington's disease
 (HD) (228)

monosomy (231)
multiple-allele trait (229)
pattern of inheritance
 (228)
pedigree (227)
phenylketonuria
 (PKU) (232)

polygenic trait (229)
sex-influenced trait (229)
single-allele trait (228)
trisomy (231)
trisomy-21 (231)

REVIEW

Vocabulary

1. Distinguish between germ-cell mutations and somatic mutations.
2. Define the term *nondisjunction*.
3. Distinguish between multiple-allele traits and polygenic traits.
4. Describe the difference between a sex-linked trait and a sex-influenced trait.
5. Distinguish between amniocentesis and chorionic villi sampling.

Multiple Choice

6. If a heterozygous red-eyed female *Drosophila* is crossed with a red-eyed male *Drosophila,* (a) half the male offspring will be red-eyed and half will be white-eyed (b) three-fourths of the male offspring will be red-eyed and one-fourth will be white-eyed (c) all the offspring will be red-eyed (d) one-fourth of the male offspring will be red-eyed and three-fourths will be white-eyed.
7. A chromosomal map shows (a) whether a gene is autosomal or recessive (b) the positions of genes along a chromosome (c) the presence of mutant alleles (d) the sex of the individual.
8. The deletion of a single nucleotide results in (a) nondisjunction (b) monosomy (c) a frame shift mutation (d) a translocation.
9. Geneticists can use pedigrees to determine (a) environmental effects on trait expression (b) whether someone could be a carrier for a genetic disorder (c) the frequency of a gene in a population (d) the position of a gene on a chromosome.
10. A geneticist working with *Drosophila* discovers a mutant phenotype that appears only in males who are offspring of males showing the same phenotype. This information suggests that the mutant phenotype is (a) autosomal dominant (b) autosomal recessive (c) X-linked (d) Y-linked.
11. A man and a woman have the same genotype for a particular trait, yet only one of them expresses that trait. This evidence suggests that the trait is (a) sex-linked (b) polygenic (c) sex-influenced (d) multiple-allele.
12. Klinefelter's syndrome is an example of (a) monosomy (b) trisomy (c) a point mutation (d) translocation.
13. A karyotype can reveal (a) chromosomal abnormalities (b) blood type (c) point mutations (d) carriers for recessive traits.
14. Testing for phenylketonuria (PKU) enables physicians to (a) recognize abnormalities in chromosome number (b) prescribe a special diet (c) correct fetal defects before birth (d) determine the sex of a fetus.
15. The greatest amount of phenotypic variation is seen in (a) polygenic traits (b) single-allele traits (c) multiple-allele traits (d) sex-linked traits.

Short Answer

16. What evidence led Morgan to hypothesize that the gene for eye color in *Drosophila* is carried on the X chromosome?
17. Why is hemophilia carried by females but expressed in males and rarely in females?
18. What is a linkage group? How many linkage groups do humans have?
19. How does a chromosome mutation differ from a point mutation?
20. What is the pattern of inheritance of Huntington's disease?
21. What is a genetic marker?
22. List the possible genotypes for a person whose ABO blood group is type A.
23. The photograph below shows red blood cells taken from an individual. Notice that one of the red blood cells is bent, while the other one is normal. Does this person have sickle-cell anemia? What is this person's genotype with respect to sickle cell anemia?

24. Explain how you would distinguish the karyotype of a normal human male from that of a human male with Down syndrome.

25. Describe how the karyotype of an XXY human would differ from that of an XO human.

CRITICAL THINKING

1. In *Drosophila* the genes for body color and wing length are on the same chromosome. Gray body (*G*) is dominant to black body (*g*), and long wings (*L*) are dominant to short wings (*l*). Assume that both dominant alleles are on the same chromosome. Draw a Punnett square representing the cross *GgLl* × *GgLl*. Write the phenotypic and genotypic ratios that would be expected among the offspring, assuming that crossing-over does not occur.

2. Individuals who are heterozygous for sickle cell anemia generally have no symptoms of the disease. However, they should avoid extreme conditions that severely reduce the amount of oxygen available to the body, such as playing vigorous sports at high elevations. Explain why this would be advisable.

3. The karyotypes of some Down syndrome individuals show that they have 46 chromosomes. However, close examination of these karyotypes reveals that three copies of chromosome 21 are indeed present in these individuals. Explain how a translocation can account for this rare form of Down syndrome.

4. A 20-year-old man diagnosed with muscular dystrophy has a sister who is soon to be married. If you were the man, what would you tell your sister?

5. The individual shown in green in the pedigree below is afflicted with a genetic disorder. State the pattern of inheritance for the disorder and whether the disorder is autosomal or sex-linked. Explain your answer.

6. What advice might a genetic counselor give to the unaffected brother and sisters shown in the pedigree in question 5?

EXTENSION

1. Read "Chromosomes Show Plants' Secret Complexity" in *Science News,* December 18, 1999, on page 389. Explain why the mustard plant *Arabidopsis thaliana* is a favorite laboratory plant of geneticists.

2. Read "High Risk Defenses" in *Natural History,* February 1999, on page 40. Explain what Pythagoras meant when he said, "Do not eat broad beans!" Describe how the mutant gene for cystic fibrosis is a protection against typhoid fever.

3. Biologists have long been interested in studying the inheritance of traits in twins, particularly identical twins who have been raised apart. Do library or on-line research, and prepare a report on the study of twins in genetics.

4. Do library or on-line research, and prepare a report on the history of the use of *Drosophila* in genetic studies. Conclude your report with a list of the advantages of using *Drosophila.*

INTERACTIVE EXPLORATION

Meiosis: Down Syndrome

OBJECTIVES

- Compare the events of a normal meiotic division with those resulting in Down syndrome.
- Determine the relationship between parental age and the likelihood that an offspring will have Down syndrome.

MATERIALS

- computer with CD-ROM drive
- CD-ROM *Interactive Explorations in Biology: Cell Biology and Genetics*
- graph paper

Background

This interactive exploration allows you to learn about the cause of Down syndrome, an inherited condition that results in mental retardation, short stature, stubby hands and feet, and a characteristic heavy eyefold. This condition is a consequence of nondisjunction, or the failure of chromosomes to separate normally during meiosis. In this exploration, you will have the opportunity to examine how the age of each parent affects the events of meiosis.

Prelab Preparation

1. Load and start the program "Meiosis: Down Syndrome." You will see an animated diagram like the one below. Click the Navigation button, and then click the Topic Information button. Read the focus questions, and review the concepts of ploidy, meiosis, aneuploidy, and nondisjunction.
2. Now click the word *Help* at the top left of the screen, and select How to Use This Exploration. Listen to the instructions for operating the exploration. Click the Interactive Exploration button on the Navigation Palette to begin the exploration.

FEEDBACK METERS

Incidence of Down Syndrome: *displays the frequency of Down syndrome births for the combination of parents chosen*

VARIABLES

Age of Mother: *allows you to set the mother's age*

Age of Father: *allows you to set the father's age*

Procedure
PART A Normal Meiosis

1. Click the Normal button to observe a simulation of normal meiosis. For simplicity, this animation shows only two pairs of chromosomes.
2. Click the Detail button. Then click the Forward button (the one with the right-facing arrow) to progress through the eight steps of a normal meiotic division. As you view each step, read the caption and study the illustration.
3. Click the Close button.
4. Click the Start button to observe the same meiotic events in continuous motion. How many gametes formed after meiosis was completed?

PART B Nondisjunction

5. Click the Nondisjunction button.
6. Click the Detail button. Then click the Forward button to observe nondisjunction. As you view each step, read the caption and study the illustration. What differences between normal meiosis and nondisjunction do you observe in frame 4?
7. Click the Close button.
8. Click the Start button to observe nondisjunction in continuous motion.

PART C Effect of the Father's Age
Make a table like Table A shown below.

TABLE A EFFECT OF THE FATHER'S AGE	
Age of father	Incidence of Down syndrome
25	
30	
35	
40	
45	
50	

9. Click and slide the left-hand indicator so that the age of the mother is 25.
10. Click and slide the other indicator so that the age of the father is 25.
11. Click the Plot Point button. In your table, record the

probability that these parents will have a child with Down syndrome, shown by the meter labeled "Incidence of Down Syndrome per 1000 Live Births."

12. Repeat steps 10–11 five times, each time increasing the age of the father by five years. Make a graph of the age of the father versus the incidence of Down syndrome. What can you conclude about the effect of the father's age on the likelihood of having a child with Down syndrome?

PART D Effect of the Mother's Age
Make a table like Table B shown below.

TABLE B EFFECT OF THE MOTHER'S AGE	
Age of mother	Incidence of Down syndrome
25	
30	
35	
40	
45	
50	

13. Click the Reset Graph button.
14. Click and slide the indicator so that the age of the father is 25.
15. Click and slide the indicator so that the age of the mother is 25.
16. Click the Plot Point button. In your table, record the incidence of Down syndrome per 1,000 live births.
17. Repeat steps 15–16 five times, each time increasing the age of the mother by five years. Be sure to record the incidence of Down syndrome for each age. Make a graph of the mother's age versus the incidence of Down syndrome. What can you conclude about the effect of the mother's age on the likelihood of having a child with Down syndrome?

Analysis and Conclusions

1. In step 12, why did you hold the mother's age constant while varying the father's age?
2. In the United States, the age at which women have their first child has been increasing. How might this affect the incidence of Down syndrome?

DNA TECHNOLOGY

The alteration of a gene that controls ripening gives these genetically engineered tomatoes a better taste and a longer shelf life than other commercially grown tomatoes.

FOCUS CONCEPT: *Reproduction and Inheritance*

As you read, notice the ways that scientists are endowing organisms with traits that they did not inherit naturally by changing the organisms' genes.

Unit 6—*Gene Expression*
Topics 1–6

THE NEW GENETICS

An understanding of the molecular basis of inheritance has led to a new form of applied genetics called genetic engineering. **Genetic engineering** *is the application of molecular genetics for practical purposes. Genetic engineering can be used to identify genes for specific traits or to transfer genes for a specific trait from one organism to another organism.*

SECTION

13-1

OBJECTIVES

▲

Define *genetic engineering.*

●

Explain how restriction enzymes can be used to make recombinant DNA.

■

Explain how cloning vectors can be used to clone and transfer genes.

◆

List the steps in a gene-transfer experiment.

MANIPULATING GENES

The technology involved in genetic engineering is called **DNA technology.** DNA technology can be used to cure diseases, to treat genetic disorders, to improve food crops, and to do many other things that may improve the lives of humans. Before you can understand DNA technology, you should understand restriction enzymes and cloning vectors, which genetic engineers use to manipulate genes.

Restriction Enzymes

Recall that a DNA molecule is a long sequence of nucleotides. Genetic engineers use certain bacterial enzymes—called **restriction enzymes**—to cut DNA molecules into more manageable pieces. As Figure 13-1 shows, restriction enzymes recognize

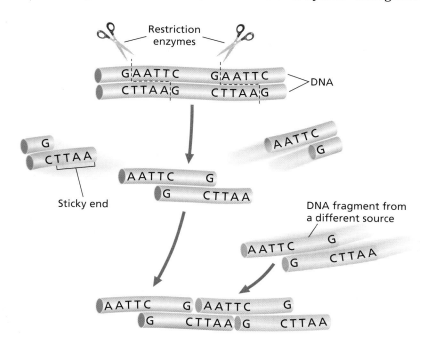

FIGURE 13-1

The restriction enzyme represented by the scissors in this figure recognizes the sequence CTTAAG on each chain of DNA. Then it cuts each chain between the A nucleotide and the G nucleotide, producing DNA fragments with sticky ends.

Bacterium
Plasmid
Main chromosome
Restriction enzyme cuts plasmid
Donor gene
Donor gene inserted into plasmid
Plasmid inserted into bacterium
Cloning of donor gene

FIGURE 13-2

A donor gene from another organism can be spliced into a plasmid. The plasmid containing the donor gene is then placed inside a bacterium. As the bacterium divides, the donor gene is cloned.

FIGURE 13-3

The tumor-causing gene in this plasmid can be replaced with a donor gene. When the harmless plasmid containing the donor gene is placed in bacteria, it can be used to transfer new genes into plants.

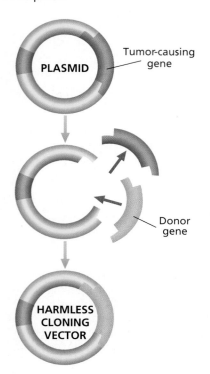

PLASMID
Tumor-causing gene
Donor gene
HARMLESS CLONING VECTOR

specific sequences of nucleotides. Then they cut the DNA at a specific site within the sequence.

The restriction enzyme shown in Figure 13-1 recognizes the nucleotide sequence CTTAAG on both chains of DNA. In one chain, the sequence runs from left to right; on the complementary chain, the sequence runs from right to left. The restriction enzyme cuts each chain separately between the G nucleotides and the A nucleotides. In this way, single-chain "tails" of DNA, called **sticky ends,** are created on each DNA segment cut by the restriction enzyme. Sticky ends readily bind to complementary chains of DNA. Thus, pieces of DNA that have been cut with the same restriction enzyme can bind together to form a new sequence of nucleotides.

Cloning Vectors

Restriction enzymes can be used to isolate a specific gene. Once a gene has been isolated, it can be transferred by a cloning vector to an organism. A **cloning vector** is a carrier that is used to clone a gene and transfer it from one organism to another. Many bacteria contain a cloning vector called a plasmid. A **plasmid** is a ring of DNA found in a bacterium in addition to its main chromosome.

To be used as a cloning vector in gene-transfer experiments, a plasmid is removed from a bacterium, as shown in Figure 13-2. Using restriction enzymes, the plasmid is then cut and a **donor gene**—a specific gene isolated from another organism—is spliced into it. Then the plasmid is returned to the bacterium, where it replicates as the bacterium divides, cloning the donor gene. A **gene clone** is an exact copy of a gene. The bacteria containing clones of the donor gene can then be used to infect other organisms and transfer the gene to them. For example, the cloning vector shown in Figure 13-3 was found in a bacterium that causes tumors in some plants, such as oak trees. The tumor-inducing bacterium contains a plasmid that can be modified to no longer cause tumors. This bacterium, once the plasmid is modified, can be used to transfer genes into plants by infecting the plants with the non-tumor-inducing bacterium.

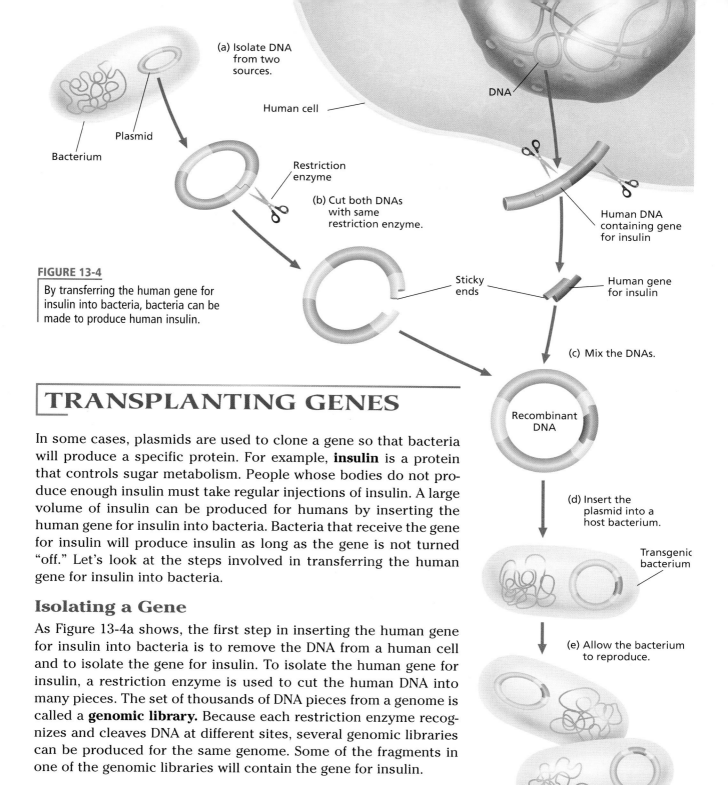

(a) Isolate DNA from two sources.

Human cell

Plasmid

Bacterium

DNA

Restriction enzyme

(b) Cut both DNAs with same restriction enzyme.

Human DNA containing gene for insulin

FIGURE 13-4

By transferring the human gene for insulin into bacteria, bacteria can be made to produce human insulin.

Sticky ends

Human gene for insulin

(c) Mix the DNAs.

Recombinant DNA

(d) Insert the plasmid into a host bacterium.

Transgenic bacterium

(e) Allow the bacterium to reproduce.

Bacteria able to produce insulin

TRANSPLANTING GENES

In some cases, plasmids are used to clone a gene so that bacteria will produce a specific protein. For example, **insulin** is a protein that controls sugar metabolism. People whose bodies do not produce enough insulin must take regular injections of insulin. A large volume of insulin can be produced for humans by inserting the human gene for insulin into bacteria. Bacteria that receive the gene for insulin will produce insulin as long as the gene is not turned "off." Let's look at the steps involved in transferring the human gene for insulin into bacteria.

Isolating a Gene

As Figure 13-4a shows, the first step in inserting the human gene for insulin into bacteria is to remove the DNA from a human cell and to isolate the gene for insulin. To isolate the human gene for insulin, a restriction enzyme is used to cut the human DNA into many pieces. The set of thousands of DNA pieces from a genome is called a **genomic library.** Because each restriction enzyme recognizes and cleaves DNA at different sites, several genomic libraries can be produced for the same genome. Some of the fragments in one of the genomic libraries will contain the gene for insulin.

Producing Recombinant DNA

The combination of DNA from two or more sources is called **recombinant DNA.** Inserting a donor gene, such as the human gene for insulin, into a cloning vector, such as a bacterial plasmid, results in a recombinant DNA molecule. As Figure 13-4c shows, recombinant DNA is produced when a plasmid is removed from a bacterial cell and a donor gene is inserted into the plasmid.

Cloning DNA

The plasmid containing recombinant DNA is inserted into a host bacterium. A host organism receiving recombinant DNA is called a **transgenic organism.** In this case, the transgenic organism is a bacterium containing both bacterial DNA and human DNA.

The transgenic bacterium is placed in a nutrient medium where it can grow and reproduce, as illustrated in Figure 13-4e. Within each bacterium, the plasmid is copied many times, and the donor gene for insulin is cloned. Thousands of bacteria are produced very quickly through cell division, resulting in thousands of bacteria that carry the gene for insulin. The transgenic bacteria can then be used to produce large amounts of insulin.

EXPRESSION OF CLONED GENES

Once a donor gene, such as the human gene for insulin, is transferred to a host cell, it is transcribed and translated as though it were in its own cell. However, not all of the genes in a cell's genome are expressed. Genes are often turned off until the proteins they code for are needed. As you can imagine, it can be difficult to induce host cells to express foreign genes. One way to induce a prokaryotic host cell to express a foreign gene is to also transfer the sequences (promoters) that turn on the foreign gene. In another method, genetic engineers insert a donor gene into prokaryotes beside a gene that is normally produced in large quantities within a cell. That way, the donor gene is expressed along with the host cell's frequently expressed gene.

An obstacle in the expression of eukaryotic genes in prokaryotic hosts is the difference in gene processing. As you know, eukaryotic DNA contains noncoding sequences that are not found in prokaryotic DNA. In order for a prokaryotic cell to receive a functional donor gene, only the coding sequences should be inserted into the host prokaryotic cell. Otherwise, the prokaryotic cell will not remove the noncoding sequences of the gene and the protein will not be produced. Thus, successful gene-transfer experiments require extensive knowledge of the processes required to express genes in different types of cells.

SECTION 13-1 REVIEW

1. Define *genetic engineering.*

2. What role do restriction enzymes play in genetic engineering?

3. How do sticky ends function?

4. Explain the role of cloning vectors in genetic engineering.

5. What steps are used to produce insulin using recombinant DNA and bacteria?

6. CRITICAL THINKING List three ways that genetic engineering could be used to improve the lives of humans.

DNA Technology Techniques

In Section 13-1, you learned about some of the tools and procedures genetic engineers use to manipulate genes and transplant them into other organisms. In this section, you will learn about some of the techniques used to analyze the nucleotide sequence of an individual's DNA.

DNA FINGERPRINTS

A **DNA fingerprint** is a pattern of bands made up of specific fragments from an individual's DNA. The banding patterns of DNA fragments from two different individuals may be compared to establish whether they are related. The DNA fingerprints of members of two different species can also be compared to determine how closely the species are related. Using DNA fingerprints to compare samples of blood or tissue found at a crime scene with a suspect's blood sample may even help solve a crime. The fragments of DNA in a DNA fingerprint appear as fuzzy bands of stain arranged in columns, like those shown in Figure 13-5.

OBJECTIVES

▲

Explain what a DNA fingerprint is and how it is prepared.

●

Distinguish between the following laboratory techniques: RFLP analysis, gel electrophoresis, and polymerase chain reaction.

■

Describe the purpose of the Human Genome Project and the potential uses of the information collected in the project.

◆

Explain how gene therapy may be used in humans.

FIGURE 13-5

If you look carefully at the DNA fingerprints that this researcher is examining, you will see many columns of bands. The pattern of bands in each column can be analyzed to establish whether two individuals are related.

Restriction
fragments

DNA +
restriction
enzyme

I   II   III

(a) RFLP analysis

(b) Gel electrophoresis

Longer
fragments

Shorter
fragments

Probes complementary
to the DNA fragments
being compared

(c) Radioactive probes
bind to DNA fragments

Photographic
film

(d) Completed DNA
fingerprint

FIGURE 13-6

(a) To make a DNA fingerprint, the DNA sample is first cut into many fragments by restriction enzymes. (b) The DNA fragments are then separated according to their size by gel electrophoresis. (c) Radioactive probes then bind to DNA fragments that have been selected for comparison. (d) Photographic film allows visualization of the radioactive probes that are bound to the DNA fragments, producing a DNA fingerprint.

Word Roots and Origins

electrophoresis

from the Latin *electrocus,* meaning "electricity," and the Greek *phoresis,* meaning "to carry"

Making a DNA Fingerprint

The method for preparing a DNA fingerprint is called restriction fragment length polymorphism (RFLP) analysis. **RFLP analysis** involves extracting DNA from a specimen of blood or other tissue and cutting it into fragments using restriction enzymes, as shown in 13-6a. The number of fragments and the length of each fragment vary from person to person.

The fragments of DNA are then separated using a technique called **gel electrophoresis.** Gel electrophoresis separates nucleic acids or proteins, primarily according to their size and charge. To make a DNA fingerprint, samples of the DNA being compared are placed in wells made on the gel, as shown in Figure 13-6b. An electric current is then run through the gel for a given period of time. The DNA fragments, which are negatively charged, migrate toward the positively charged end of the gel, but not all at the same rate. The pores in the gel allow smaller DNA fragments to migrate faster—and thus farther across the gel—than longer fragments, separating the fragments by size.

The final step in preparing a DNA fingerprint is making visible only the bands that are being compared. The DNA fragments that have been separated on the gel are split into single chains and blotted onto filter paper. Then **probes**—radioactive segments of DNA that are complementary to the segments being compared—are added to the filter paper. The probes bind to complementary fragments of DNA in the samples, forming visible bands when they are exposed to photographic film, as shown in Figure 13-6c. The exposed film is developed to reveal a DNA fingerprint. The bands can then be analyzed visually or by a computer.

Accuracy of DNA Fingerprints

The accuracy of DNA fingerprints depends on how unique the prints are. The complete nucleotide sequence of each individual is certainly unique for each person, except in the case of identical twins, who share identical DNA. However, complete sets of DNA are not compared in DNA fingerprints. The DNA technology in use today deals only with a small portion of a person's DNA. Nevertheless, DNA fingerprints are very accurate because they compare segments of DNA that tend to vary the most from person to person. The segments of DNA that vary the most are noncoding segments where the DNA repeats over and over. These repeated patterns are found throughout the genome.

A repeating pattern might consist of the bases GGAT on one chain, matched by the complementary sequence CCTA on the other chain. DNA fingerprinting typically compares the repeat patterns at five different sites. It is highly unlikely—less than one chance in a million—that all five sites compared in DNA fingerprints will match exactly between two people who are not identical twins. The odds against a match occurring through sheer chance multiply as more sites are compared.

Polymerase Chain Reaction

To make a DNA fingerprint, a certain amount of DNA is needed. If only a very tiny amount of DNA is available, the **polymerase chain reaction (PCR)** can be used to quickly make many copies of selected segments of the available DNA.

Notice in Figure 13-7 that PCR requires a DNA molecule or a fragment of DNA, a supply of the four DNA nucleotides, DNA polymerase (the enzyme involved in DNA replication), and primers. A **primer** is an artificially made single-stranded sequence of DNA required for the initiation of replication. When these ingredients are combined and incubated, the selected regions of DNA quickly

internet**connect**

SC*LINKS*
NSTA

TOPIC: DNA fingerprinting
GO TO: www.scilinks.org
KEYWORD: HM245

FIGURE 13-7

The polymerase chain reaction (PCR) can be used to multiply selected regions of DNA in a sample. Notice that the number of copies of the selected regions of DNA doubles with each cycle of the reaction.

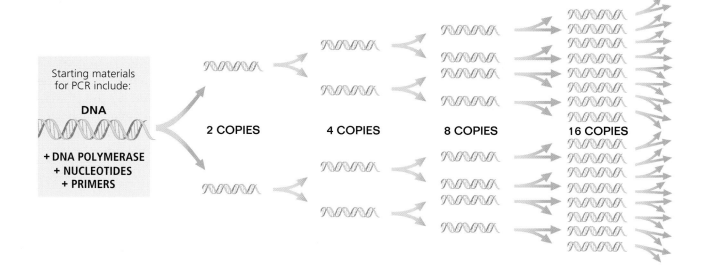

Starting materials for PCR include:

DNA

+ DNA POLYMERASE
+ NUCLEOTIDES
+ PRIMERS

2 COPIES   4 COPIES   8 COPIES   16 COPIES

Comparing Unique Characteristics

Materials ink pad, paper, pencil, scissors

Procedure

1. Cut four 3 in. squares of plain paper.

2. Draw lines on a full-sized sheet of paper that will divide that sheet into four equal squares.

3. Each team member will press his or her right thumb on the ink pad and then will quickly press the inked thumb in a square on the large sheet of paper and again on one of the small squares of paper.

4. Examine each of the thumbprints, and make a list of characteristics that the prints have in common. Describe how each thumbprint is different from the others. Then shuffle the four individual thumbprints, and try to match each one with its duplicate on the large sheet of paper.

Analysis What characteristics are common to all thumbprints? What characteristics made each thumbprint unique? How do a person's fingerprints relate to his or her DNA fingerprints?

double. Every five minutes, the sample of DNA doubles again, resulting in many copies of the sample in a short amount of time, as shown in Figure 13-7.

The new copies of the DNA sample can then be used to make a DNA fingerprint. PCR can use minuscule amounts of a specimen, as few as 50 white blood cells that might be found in a nearly invisible speck of blood, rather than the 5,000 to 50,000 cells needed for RFLP analysis. PCR is important not only for solving violent crimes but also for diagnosing genetic disorders from a few embryonic cells and for studying ancient fragments of DNA found in minute amounts.

HUMAN GENOME PROJECT

Using DNA technology, scientists all over the world are collaborating on one of the most ambitious research efforts in the history of genetics, the **Human Genome Project.** Two of the goals of the Human Genome Project are to determine the nucleotide sequence of the entire human genome—approximately 3 billion nucleotide pairs, or about 100,000 genes—and to map the location of every gene on each chromosome. In addition, the human genome is being compared with the genomes of other organisms in an effort to provide insight into fundamental questions about how genomes are organized, how gene expression is controlled, how cellular growth and differentiation are under genetic control, and how evolution occurs.

This project began in 1990. In 1996, the project had analyzed 1 percent of the 3 billion nucleotide pairs of DNA in the human genome. By knowing even 1 percent of the sequence, it is possible for scientists to establish the identity of and determine the function of about 16,000 genes. Genome research continues internationally at universities, laboratories, scientific institutions, and private companies.

It is hoped that the knowledge gained from the Human Genome Project will improve diagnoses, treatments, and even cures for the approximately 4,000 human genetic disorders. Scientists have already discovered specific genes responsible for several genetic disorders, including cystic fibrosis, Duchenne muscular dystrophy, and colon cancer. As many as 5 percent of the babies born in the United States each year are afflicted with a genetic disorder that could one day be treated or prevented using the information provided by the Human Genome Project. Identifying these genes and the defective proteins for which they code may make it possible to design therapies aimed at correcting the gene defects responsible for genetic disorders.

Gene Therapy

Treating a genetic disorder by introducing a gene into a cell or by correcting a gene defect in a cell's genome is called **gene therapy.** In 1990, doctors first began to develop and test gene therapies on

Recombinant-DNA Technology

This excerpt is from *Genethics: The Clash Between the New Genetics and Human Values,* by David Suzuki and Peter Knudtson.

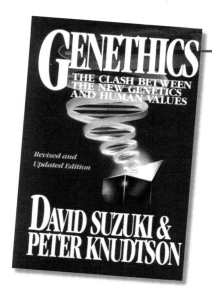

Already recombinant DNA technology, along with rapid DNA sequencing and other related laboratory techniques, has begun to offer profound new insights into the workings of genes. First, it has helped to establish the virtual universality of both the genetic code and the graceful molecular dances of genes in nature. Second, it has revolutionized the study of genes of multicellular organisms, including humans, that have long been inaccessible. In so doing, it has led to dramatic discoveries concerning the structure and function of genes in complex plants and animals. One such discovery is that their coded instructions for assembling amino acids into proteins—called *exons*—are often interspersed with long intervening segments of DNA—called *introns*—of largely unknown function. Introns are neatly removed from nuclear RNA molecules prior to protein synthesis. A second discovery is that the comparison of DNA sequences in different species can often serve as a faint chronological record of otherwise hidden evolutionary relationships. Third, recombinant DNA technology has already led to the complete chemical characterization of a number of relatively small viral genomes and has initiated that process in more complex species,

including our own. Finally, by facilitating the exchange of genetic components between cells of different species, it has exploded the boundaries of comparative genetics. We are now just beginning to grasp the evolutionary ingenuity with which the genes of different species—however interchangeable their codes—are variously packaged, punctuated and controlled.

But the rewards from recombinant DNA technology will be practical as well as intellectual. Genetic engineering holds great promise in agriculture—for modifying the productivity, growth requirements and nutrition of food crops. In medicine, it is opening up new vistas in the design of vaccines, in the diagnosis of disease and in genetic counseling, and even the possibility of new genetic therapies for ancient hereditary diseases. In the biotechnology industry, it already has established its value in the manufacture of antibiotics, hormones and an assortment of other biologically active substances.

For the first time, we find that we can command individual genes to do our bidding. In the future, we will forever be faced with the temptation to harness our knowledge of hereditary processes long before we have resolved the possible long-term consequences of

our applications. If history is any guide, we can expect no shortage of ingenious schemes to reap rewards from our genetic engineering skills. But each of us has a responsibility to ensure that equal imagination is devoted to the search for ways to apply this knowledge wisely and to share its fruits with all humankind.

Reading for Meaning

Suzuki and Knudtson point out some general applications for genetic engineering. List possible uses that you think would benefit humankind. What might be advantages and disadvantages of each item on your list?

Read Further

Suzuki and Knudtson's book, *Genethics,* raises concerns about modern technology's amazing techniques for manipulating genes and how those techniques will be used. When and for what purposes do you think we should perform such genetic engineering?

This patient is receiving gene therapy for cystic fibrosis. Dr. Terrence Flotte (left), of the University of Florida College of Medicine, administers healthy copies of the gene responsible for cystic fibrosis through the patient's nose.

humans. Gene therapy is well suited for treating genetic disorders that result from a deficiency of a single enzyme or protein. As you learned in Chapter 11, the genetic disorder cystic fibrosis is caused by one defective gene, resulting in the malfunction of a single protein. Some success has been reported with nasal sprays that carry a normal cystic fibrosis gene to the cells in the nose and lungs—cells that are particularly affected by a defective cystic fibrosis protein. Figure 13-8 shows the gene-therapy procedure that has been used with some cystic fibrosis patients. The treatment has to be repeated periodically because the cystic fibrosis gene is not inserted on a chromosome but rather in the nucleus of cells; thus, it is not passed on to future generations. Gene-therapy possibilities for hemophilia B, lung cancer, AIDS, ovarian cancer, brain tumors, malignant melanoma, and several other terminal diseases are also under way. Until the obstacles regarding how and where to insert genes safely and directly into eukaryotic chromosomes are overcome, gene therapy may offer only limited and temporary success as a treatment. But researchers hope to overcome these obstacles and to one day provide permanent cures for genetic disorders using gene therapy.

Ethical Issues

The Human Genome Project is producing much information about human susceptibility to disease. However, a genetic susceptibility to a disease does not ensure that the person will get the disease. Nor does such a gene indicate the severity of the disease, should it occur, or how the person would respond to treatment. Many people worry about how personal genetic information will be used. Some think this type of information could be used by insurance companies and employers to discriminate against individuals who are genetically susceptible to a disease. For example, an insurance company may decide to deny insurance to people who are predisposed to diseases that are expensive to treat. The information provided by the Human Genome Project will undoubtedly involve ethical decisions about how society should use the information.

SECTION 13-2 REVIEW

1. Define *DNA fingerprint,* and discuss the accuracy of using DNA fingerprints to establish relatedness.

2. Describe the major steps and techniques involved in preparing a DNA fingerprint.

3. Compare the polymerase chain reaction and DNA replication.

4. Describe the purpose of the Human Genome Project, and name the potential uses of the information collected in the project.

5. What is gene therapy, and how does it differ from traditional treatments for diseases?

6. **CRITICAL THINKING** What genetic disorders not discussed in this chapter might be treated using DNA technology?

PRACTICAL USES OF DNA TECHNOLOGY

The production of insulin by inserting the human gene for insulin into bacteria is one commercial use of DNA technology. DNA technology can also be used to produce prescription drugs and vaccines and to improve food crops.

OBJECTIVES

▲

Explain how DNA technology can be used to produce medical products.

●

Describe some ways that DNA technology can be used to improve crop yields and the food supply.

■

Discuss some environmental and ethical issues in genetic engineering.

PRODUCING PHARMA- CEUTICAL PRODUCTS

Many medicines are proteins. In the past, these proteins were derived from animal tissues or plants. Today, some proteins can be produced far more inexpensively using DNA technology. Insulin is one of the many products now produced through DNA technology. Table 13-1 lists several other pharmaceutical products produced in this way. As in the production of insulin, these pharmaceutical products can be produced in bulk by bacteria. Just as yeast are fermented in large vats in the production of beer, bacteria can be grown in large vats to produce specific proteins.

TABLE 13-1 *Medicines Produced by DNA Technology*

Product	Medical uses
Colony-stimulating factors	used to treat immune-system deficiencies by stimulating the production of white blood cells
Erythropoietin	used to treat anemia by stimulating the production of red blood cells
Growth factors	used to promote the healing of wounds by stimulating growth and differentiation of different types of cells
Human growth hormone	used as a treatment for dwarfism
Interferons	used to treat viral infections and some cancers by preventing the replication of viruses
Interleukins	used to treat a variety of conditions, including HIV infections, cancer, and immune deficiencies, by activating and stimulating different kinds of white blood cells
Tissue plasminogen activator	used to prevent heart attacks and strokes by dissolving blood clots
Atrial peptides	used to treat high blood pressure and kidney failure

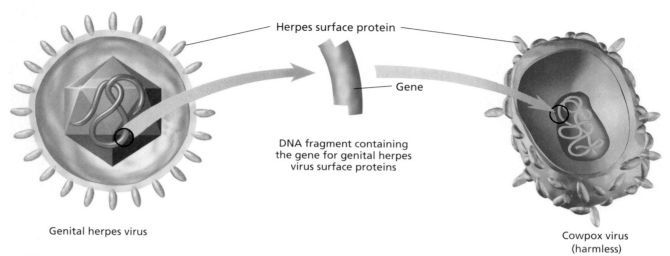

Herpes surface protein

Gene

DNA fragment containing
the gene for genital herpes
virus surface proteins

Genital herpes virus

Cowpox virus
(harmless)

FIGURE 13-9

The gene that codes for the surface
proteins of the genital herpes virus can
be transferred to a cowpox virus—a
virus that is harmless to humans—to
produce a vaccine against genital herpes. The cowpox virus then produces
the surface proteins characteristic of
the genital herpes virus. A person
receiving the vaccine will be protected
against genital herpes virus infections
in the future.

Word Roots and Origins

pathogen

from the Greek *pathos,*
meaning "suffering"

GENETICALLY ENGINEERED VACCINES

Many viral diseases, such as AIDS, smallpox, and polio, cannot be treated effectively by existing drugs. Instead, many viral diseases are combated by prevention, using vaccines. A **vaccine** is a solution that contains a harmless version of a virus or a bacterium. Traditionally, vaccines have been made of disease-causing agents— also called **pathogens**—that have been treated (chemically or phys- ically) so that they can no longer cause disease. Vaccines can also be produced using active pathogens that carry surface proteins that are the same as or very similar to a more-harmful virus. When a person receives a vaccine, his or her body recognizes the pathogen's surface proteins and mobilizes against the pathogen. In the future, if the same pathogen enters the body, the body is prepared to combat it quickly and to prevent or weaken the pathogen's effects.

Usually, a person who receives a vaccine does not become ill. However, on rare occasions a vaccine may cause the disease it is intended to protect people against. DNA technology can be used to produce effective vaccines, which may be safer than some tradi- tionally prepared vaccines. As Figure 13-9 shows, the genes for a disease-causing virus's surface proteins can be inserted into a harmless virus. The transplanted genes cause the harmless virus to produce the surface proteins that alert the body to the presence of the disease-causing virus. DNA technology can also be used to alter the genome of a pathogen so that it no longer causes a dis- ease. The altered pathogens can then be used as a vaccine against unaltered forms of the pathogen.

INCREASING AGRICULTURAL YIELDS

DNA technology has been used to develop new strains of plants, which in turn can be used to improve food crop yields. By transferring genes for enzymes that are harmful to hornworms into tomato plants, scientists can make tomato plants toxic to hornworms and effectively protect the plants from these pests, which otherwise could seriously damage them. Figure 13-10 shows a hornworm on a tomato plant that is not toxic to hornworms.

The crop cassava, used to make tapioca pudding and other food products, is highly susceptible to pests and diseases, which often cost farmers up to 80 percent of a cassava crop. Using DNA technology, scientists have made cassava plants resistant to some diseases. In addition, strains of wheat, cotton, and soybeans that are resistant to weed-controlling chemicals—called **herbicides**—have been developed. Such herbicide-resistant crops can be protected from weeds more easily and less expensively than crops that are susceptible to the herbicides.

Crops That Do Not Need Fertilizer

To make proteins and nucleic acids, all plants require the element nitrogen, N. Although nitrogen is the most abundant element found in the atmosphere, it is in a form that plants are unable to use. Some plants, such as soybeans and peanuts, have bacteria living in their roots that convert, or "fix," nitrogen in the atmosphere into forms of nitrogen that plants can use. Other types of plants take up nitrogen directly from the soil.

To help crops grow, farmers apply expensive nitrogen fertilizers to the soil. Currently, researchers are working to isolate and clone genes from nitrogen-fixing bacteria and transplant the genes into plants. It is hoped that transgenic food crops containing genes for nitrogen fixation will be able to grow in nitrogen-poor soil, where crops often are grown only after the soil has been treated with nitrogen fertilizers.

FIGURE 13-10

Tomato hornworms, like the member of *Manduca quinque maculata* shown here, feed on the leaves and fruits of tomatoes and other related plants. A large hornworm is capable of stripping a tomato plant of its foilage.

internetconnect

SCI*LINKS*
NSTA

TOPIC: Herbicides
GO TO: www.scilinks.org
KEYWORD: HM251

SAFETY AND ENVIRONMENTAL ISSUES

Many people are concerned about procedures of genetic engineering and the safety of genetically engineered products. In the United States, genetic engineering is regulated by the Food and Drug Administration (FDA), the National Institutes of Health Recombinant DNA Advisory Committee, the Department of Agriculture (USDA), and the Environmental Protection Agency (EPA). These organizations set standards for safety procedures and products and require special permits and labels for the sale and use of certain products.

Word Roots and Origins

herbicide

from the Latin *herba*, meaning "plant," and *cida*, meaning "to kill"

Genetically Engineered Foods

Some people are concerned that foods produced by genetic engineering could contain toxic proteins or substances that cause allergies in people who consume them. One precaution required by the FDA requires manufacturers of genetically engineered foods to provide scientific evidence that allergy-inducing properties have not been transferred to new foods when the new foods contain a gene transplanted from a food known to cause allergic reactions, such as peanuts. In general, however, foods produced by transgenic crops can be sold without special permits or labels if the product is identical to products produced by nontransgenic crops. However, if a genetically engineered food contains a new protein, carbohydrate, or fat, the FDA generally requires additional approval before the product can be introduced to the food supply.

Notice that the genetically-engineered tomatoes in Figure 13-11 look just like other tomatoes. Scientists isolated and cloned the gene that codes for an enzyme necessary for ripening in tomatoes. By changing this one gene in the genetically-engineered tomatoes, they were able to make a tomato that ripens without becoming soft. Typically, supermarket tomatoes are picked before they are ripe because ripe tomatoes are soft and bruise easily.

Genetically Engineered Crops

Some people are concerned that genetically engineered crops could spread into the wild and wipe out native plant species. In addition, they worry that transgenic crop plants could transmit their new genes to other species in neighboring areas. Rice and lawn grasses, for example, exchange genes in their pollen with native plants that are related to them. Exchanging these types of genes with wild plant species could cause powerful new "superweeds" that could take over large areas of land because they would have advantages over native plant species. Regulatory agencies sometimes require labels on the packages of transgenic plants to indicate their proper use and the risks of using transgenic plants that may pose hazards to the environment.

FIGURE 13-11

Plant physiologist Athanasios Theologis, shown here, genetically engineered tomatoes to ripen without becoming soft. His genetically engineered tomatoes are comparable to greenhouse-grown tomatoes, which taste better than commercially grown tomatoes that are picked while they are still green.

SECTION 13-3 REVIEW

1. List two types of medical products that can be produced using DNA technology.

2. What is a vaccine, and what are the benefits of producing vaccines using DNA technology?

3. List three traits for which genes are being transplanted into crop plants.

4. What benefit are plants that contain a nitrogen-fixing gene transplanted from bacteria?

5. Describe two potential safety and environmental problems that could result from genetic engineering.

6. **CRITICAL THINKING** The FDA does not require special labels for genetically engineered food products that are identical to similar products produced by traditional breeding techniques. Do you think that genetically engineered food products should be labeled as such? Why or why not?

SUMMARY/VOCABULARY

13-1
- Genetic engineering brings DNA technology and molecular genetics together for practical purposes.
- Restriction enzymes, which are used to isolate and transfer genes, are specific in the nucleotide sequences they recognize and cut. When a restriction enzyme cuts a piece of DNA, it creates single chains—called sticky ends—on the ends of each piece of DNA.

- Sticky ends bind to complementary sticky ends, forming recombinant DNA molecules out of DNA fragments from two or more organisms.
- Cloning vectors, such as plasmids and viruses, are used to clone and transplant genes from one organism to another one.
- Transgenic organisms contain a donor gene and express it just as they do their own DNA as long as the donor gene is turned on.

Vocabulary

cloning vector (240)	gene clone (240)
DNA technology (239)	genetic engineering (239)
donor gene (240)	genomic library (241)

insulin (241)	restriction enzyme (239)
plasmid (240)	sticky end (240)
recombinant DNA (241)	transgenic organism (242)

13-2
- A DNA fingerprint is a pattern of bands that represent certain fragments from an individual's DNA. These fragments are typically noncoding repeating sequences that vary from person to person.
- DNA fingerprints of individuals can be compared to establish relatedness. Chances are less than one in one million that five sites of DNA fingerprints from two people will match, unless the two people are identical twins. As the number of sites that are compared in a DNA fingerprint increases, so does validity of the DNA fingerprint.
- Gel electrophoresis is a technique used to separate DNA or protein fragments by their length and charge.

- Polymerase chain reaction (PCR) can be used to quickly make additional copies of segments of DNA when the original sample is small. The results of PCR can then be used to make a DNA fingerprint.
- The goal of the Human Genome Project is to determine the nucleotide sequence of the entire human genome and to map the location of all genes. This information might then be used to diagnose, treat, cure, and prevent human genetic disorders.
- Gene therapy refers to treating genetic disorders by correcting a defect in a gene or by providing a normal form of a gene. It is hoped that gene therapy can be used to cure genetic disorders in the future.

Vocabulary

DNA fingerprint (243)	gene therapy (246)
gel electrophoresis (244)	Human Genome Project (246)

polymerase chain reaction (PCR) (245)	primer (245)
	probe (244)
	RFLP analysis (244)

13-3
- DNA technology is used to produce medical products that are often safer and less expensive than those produced by conventional means.
- DNA technology is used to produce disease-resistant, pest-resistant, and herbicide-resistant crops. Perhaps these crops will improve the quality and quantity of the human food supply.

- Current research involves efforts to isolate genes from nitrogen-fixing bacteria and to transplant them into plants. Such transgenic plants may be able to grow in nitrogen-poor soil without the addition of fertilizers.
- Many safety, environmental, and ethical issues involved in the new DNA technology have not been resolved.

Vocabulary

herbicide (251)	pathogen (250)

vaccine (250)

REVIEW

Vocabulary

1. Define *recombinant DNA*.
2. Relate restriction enzymes to genomic libraries.
3. Relate a host organism, a donor gene, and a transgenic organism.
4. Distinguish between PCR and RFLP.
5. Distinguish between a primer and a probe.

Multiple Choice

6. A plasmid is (a) a cell (b) a nucleus (c) a bacterium (d) an extra ring of DNA.
7. A molecule containing DNA from two sources is called (a) recombinant DNA (b) RFLP DNA (c) a DNA clone (d) a plasmid.
8. Enzymes that cut DNA molecules in specific locations are called (a) sticky ends (b) restriction enzymes (c) cloning vectors (d) cloning enzymes.
9. Carriers used for transferring DNA from one organism to another are called (a) sticky ends (b) restriction enzymes (c) cloning vectors (d) cloning enzymes.
10. The host organism into which a cloning vector is placed is called a (a) plasmid (b) virus (c) donor (d) transgenic organism.
11. A eukaryotic donor gene is likely to be expressed in a prokaryotic host organism if (a) the donor gene is a promoter gene (b) the donor gene is transferred along with the genes that turn it on (c) the donor gene is placed beside a gene that is not expressed (d) all of these.
12. DNA technology has been used to (a) produce pharmaceutical products (b) produce herbicide-resistant crops (c) treat genetic diseases (d) all of these.
13. Gel electrophoresis is used to (a) separate DNA fragments (b) produce DNA fragments with sticky ends (c) cut DNA into fragments (d) quickly make copies of DNA.
14. PCR is used to (a) separate DNA fragments (b) produce DNA fragments with sticky ends (c) cut DNA into fragments (d) quickly make copies of DNA.
15. Genetic engineering has been used to make plants (a) toxic to insects (b) immune to vaccines (c) able to produce insulin (d) all of these.

Short Answer

16. Explain what happens when a restriction enzyme is used on DNA.
17. How is a DNA fingerprint prepared?
18. List three practical uses of PCR.
19. Explain how gel electrophoresis can be used to separate fragments of DNA.
20. What is a cloning vector?
21. The photograph below shows 8 columns on a gel. Several of these columns contain DNA fingerprints of samples taken from a crime scene, a victim, and four suspects. Indicate which suspect's DNA fingerprint matches the blood found at the crime scene. How likely is it that blood found at the crime scene belongs to the suspect?

KEY

1 Control	5 Suspect 1
2 Blood	6 Suspect 2
3 Victim	7 Suspect 3
4 Ladder	8 Suspect 4

22. Discuss the accuracy of DNA fingerprints.

23. State two possible benefits of the work being completed by the Human Genome Project.

24. Explain how gene therapy has been used to treat cystic fibrosis. Explain why gene therapy has not been used to cure cystic fibrosis.

25. Describe how genetic engineering can be used to produce vaccines.

26. List two ways that genetic engineering may increase crop yields.

CRITICAL THINKING

1. In the past, breeders developed new plant and animal varieties by selecting an organism with desirable traits, breeding it with another organism with similar traits, and then breeding the offspring so that the desirable traits would be passed on to the strain. Name an advantage and a disadvantage of genetic engineering techniques over traditional breeding techniques.

2. The United States government has stringent regulations requiring researchers to confine genetically engineered organisms to the laboratory. What concerns do you think might have led to the enactment of these regulations?

3. Natural selection is a mechanism of evolution whereby the members of a population who are best adapted to their environment survive and produce offspring. How is natural selection affected by genetic engineering?

4. How might an insect-resistant crop that is the product of genetic engineering affect a population of insects that depends on the crop for food?

5. Why do you think the United States authorized limited gene therapy trials?

6. Examine the restriction map of the bacterial plasmid pBR 322, shown below. This is a commonly used plasmid composed of 4,363 base pairs. The map shows sites at which certain restriction enzymes cut the DNA of the plasmid. For example, the restriction enzyme called *Sph*I cuts the plasmid at base pair 566. Suppose you want to isolate from the plasmid the gene that codes for resistance to the antibiotic tetracycline, which is indicated as Tc^R. What restriction enzymes would you use? How many base pairs make up the Tc^R gene? How might you check to be certain that your procedure was successful?

Restriction Map of pBR 322 DNA

EXTENSION

1. Read "DNA Detectives" in *Popular Science,* August 1999, on page 48. What is an advantage of providing hand-held gene readers to police investigators? What is a disadvantage?

2. Read "Genetic-Code Breaker" in *Discover,* March 2000, on page 22. According to Francis Collins, one of the Human Genome Project's chief researchers, what is the main reason that we should know the sequences of our 46 chromosomes?

3. Read "Who Owns Our Genes?" in *Time,* January 11, 1999, on page 51. Briefly explain the controversy in economics and ethics over the patenting of human genes as they are sequenced by laboratories.

Gel Electrophoresis

OBJECTIVES

- Use restriction enzymes to cut DNA.
- Separate DNA fragments of different sizes.

PROCESS SKILLS

- conducting agarose gel electrophoresis

MATERIALS

- protective clothing
- crushed ice
- ice bucket
- microtube rack
- microtube A—Uncut DNA
- microtube B—*Hind*III
- microtube C—*Bam*HI
- microtube D—*Eco*RI
- microtube E—Unknown
- permanent marker
- 0.5–10 µL micropipetter
- micropipetter tips
- 10× restriction buffer for each restriction enzyme
- 34 µL Lambda virus DNA
- 37°C water bath

- gel-casting tray
- 6-well gel comb
- 65°C hot-water bath
- 0.8% agarose
- hot mitt
- zipper-lock plastic bag
- 10 mL graduated cylinder
- 1× TBE buffer
- freezer
- 5 µL loading dye
- gel chamber and power supply
- WARD'S DNA stain
- staining trays
- distilled water
- metric ruler

Background

1. DNA has a negative charge and flows toward the positive end of a gel during electrophoresis. Small DNA fragments move faster than larger fragments.
2. The distance that each DNA fragment moves is used to calculate the R_f, or relative mobility, of a fragment. The R_f is used to calculate the number of base pairs in the fragment.

PART A   Cutting DNA

1. Wear safety goggles, gloves, and a lab apron at all times.
2. Fill an ice bucket with ice. Obtain one each of the following microtubes: A—Uncut DNA, B—*Hind*III,

C—*Bam*HI, D—*Eco*RI, and E—Unknown. Microtubes B–D contain 1 µL of the indicated restriction enzyme. Place all microtubes in the ice. *Restriction enzymes MUST be kept on ice until step 6.*

3. With a permanent marker, write the initials for everyone in your group *on the top* of microtubes A–E.
4. **CAUTION If you get a chemical on your skin or clothing, wash it off at the sink while calling to your teacher.** Set a micropipetter to 1 µL, and put a tip on the end of the micropipetter, as shown in (a) below. Using a new tip for each microtube, add 1 µL of the corresponding 10× restriction buffer to each of microtubes B–D. Place the buffer on the side of the tube. *Do not touch the micropipetter tips to the solutions in the microtubes.*

(a) MICROPIPETTER   **(b) CASTING TRAY**

5. Reset the micropipetter to 8 µL. Using the micropipetter and a new tip for each microtube, add 8 µL of the Lambda virus DNA to the side of each of microtubes B–D. Gently tap each microtube on your lab table until the solutions are thoroughly mixed. *Do not shake the microtubes!* Reset the micropipetter to 10 µL, and add 10 µL of Lambda DNA to microtube A.
6. Place all of the microtubes into a 37°C water bath. After 50–60 minutes, remove the microtubes from the water bath, and immediately put them into a freezer. If the class period ends before 50 minutes has passed, your teacher will give you further directions. While the restriction enzymes are working, go to Part B.

PART B   Preparing an Agarose Gel

7. Set up a gel-casting tray, as shown in (b). Place a gel comb in the grooves of the gel-casting tray. Make sure

that the comb does not touch the bottom of the tray. If it does, get another comb from your teacher.

8. Write the names of the members of your group on a paper towel. Carry your tray to the table with the melted agarose, and place your tray on the paper towel.

9. ⚠ Using a hot mitt, pour melted 0.8% agarose into your gel-casting tray until the agarose reaches a depth of 3 mm. Make sure that the agarose spreads evenly throughout the tray. *Do not move your gel tray before the agarose solidifies.*

10. Let the gel cool (about 20–30 minutes) until the agarose solidifies.

11. While the gel is cooling, write your name, the date, and your class period on a zipper-lock plastic bag. Pour 5 mL of $1\times$ TBE buffer into the bag.

12. When the gel has solidified, carefully remove the gel comb by pulling it straight up. If the comb does not come up easily, pour a little $1\times$ TBE buffer on the comb area. After removing the gel comb, open the plastic bag and carefully slide the gel tray into the bag. *Do not remove the gel from the gel-casting tray.* Store the gel according to your teacher's instructions.

PART C Running a Gel

13. Retrieve your microtubes (A–E) and your gel. If the materials in the microtubes are frozen, hold each tube in your hand until the solutions thaw.

14. Set a micropipetter to 1 μL, and place a tip on the end. Add 1μL of loading dye to each microtube. *Use a new tip for each microtube.* Gently tap each micro-tube on your lab table to thoroughly mix the solutions. *Do not shake the microtubes.*

15. Remove your gel (still in the gel-casting tray) from the plastic bag, and place it in a gel chamber. Orient the gel so that the wells are closest to the black wire, or anode.

16. Set a micropipetter to 10 μL, and place a new tip on the end. Open microtube A, and remove 10 μL of solution. Carefully place the solution into the well in lane 1, the left-most lane. To do this, place both elbows on the lab table, lean over the gel, and slowly lower the micropipetter tip into the opening of the well before depressing the plunger. *Do not jab the micropipetter tip through the bottom of the well.*

17. *Using a new micropipetter tip for each tube,* repeat step 16 for each of the remaining microtubes. Use lane 2 for microtube B, lane 3 for microtube C, lane 4 for microtube D, and lane 5 for microtube E.

18. Very slowly fill the gel chamber with $1\times$ TBE buffer until the level of the buffer is approximately 1–2 mm above the surface of the gel.

19. ⚠ **CAUTION Follow all of the manufacturer's precautions regarding the use of this equipment.** Close the gel chamber and connect it to a power supply according to your teacher's instructions.

20. Allow an electric current to flow through the gel. You will see a blue line moving away from the wells. When the blue line is approximately 5 mm from the end of the gel, disconnect the power supply and remove the gel. Store the gel overnight in the plastic bag.

PART D Analyzing a Gel

21. To stain a gel, carefully place the gel (wells up) into a staining tray. Pour WARD'S DNA stain into the staining tray until the gel is completely covered. Cover the staining tray, and label it with your initials. Allow the stain to sit for at least 2 hours. Next, carefully pour the stain into the sink drain, and flush it down the drain with water. *Do not let the stained gel slip out of the staining tray.*

22. To destain a gel, cover the gel with distilled water by pouring water to one side of the gel. Let the gel sit overnight (or at least 8–12 hours). The bands of DNA will appear as purple lines against a light background.

23. Calculate the R_f for each fragment using the following equation:

$$R_f = \frac{\text{distance in mm that DNA fragment migrated}}{\text{distance in mm from well to the dye}}$$

24. ⚠ Dispose of your materials according to your teacher's directions, and wash your hands before leaving the lab.

Analysis and Conclusions

1. Which two samples appear to have the same pattern of DNA bands?

2. Which restriction enzyme cut the DNA in the unknown sample? Justify your answer.

3. What are some measures that you took to prevent contamination of your DNA samples during this lab?

> 66 *The past, the finite greatness of the past! For what is the present, after all, but a growth out of the past.* 99

Walt Whitman

internetconnect

SCiLINKS
NSTA

National Science Teachers Association *sci*LINKS Internet resources are located throughout this unit.

Charles Darwin studied the giant tortoises, above, on the Galápagos Islands. Observations Darwin made during his voyage on the H.M.S. Beagle, right, led him to look for a mechanism by which evolution occurs.

Archaeologists scrutinize fossilized remains of human ancestors for clues to human evolution. Darwin observed a number of finches, right, on the Galápagos Islands and found that each species was adapted to a different food source.

Australopithecus robustus

ORIGIN OF LIFE

Molten rock breaks through Earth's crust in the form of a volcano. Conditions in a volcano are similar to those thought to have been present on early Earth.

FOCUS CONCEPT: *Matter, Energy, and Organization*

As you read, look for examples of the many scientific processes that help answer questions about how life began.

BIOGENESIS

*The principle of **biogenesis** (BIE-oh-JEN-uh-sis), which states that all living things come from other living things, seems very reasonable to us today. Before the seventeenth century, however, it was widely thought that living things could also arise from nonliving things in a process called **spontaneous generation**. This seemed to explain why maggots appeared on rotting meat and why fish appeared in ponds that had been dry the previous season—people thought mud might have given rise to the fish. In attempting to learn more about the process of spontaneous generation, scientists performed controlled experiments. As you read about these experiments, refer to the figures that show the experimental design.*

SECTION 14-1

OBJECTIVES

▲

Define *spontaneous generation*, and list some of the observations that led people to think that life could arise from nonliving things.

●

Summarize the results of experiments by Redi and by Spallanzani that tested the hypothesis of spontaneous generation.

■

Describe how Pasteur's experiment disproved the hypothesis of spontaneous generation.

REDI'S EXPERIMENT

Flies have often been viewed as pesky creatures. Most people are too busy trying to get rid of them to even think about studying them. In the middle of the seventeenth century, however, the Italian scientist Francesco Redi (1626–1697) noticed and described the different developmental forms of flies. Redi observed that tiny wormlike maggots turned into sturdy oval cases, from which flies eventually emerge. He also observed that maggots seemed to appear where adult flies had previously landed. These observations led him to question the commonly held belief that flies were generated spontaneously from rotting meat.

Figure 14-1 shows an experiment that Redi conducted in 1668 to test his hypothesis that meat kept away from adult flies would

FIGURE 14-1

In Redi's experiment, maggots were found only in the control jars because that was the only place where adult flies could reach the meat to lay eggs.

CONTROL GROUP

Maggots

EXPERIMENTAL GROUP

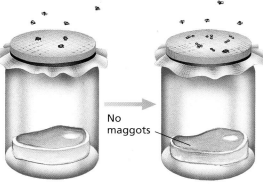

No maggots

remain free of maggots. The experimental group consisted of netting-covered jars that contained meat. The control group consisted of uncovered jars that also contained meat. The netting allowed air to enter and prevented flies from landing on the meat. After a few days, maggots swarmed over the meat in the open jars, while the net-covered jars remained free of maggots. Redi's experiment showed convincingly that flies come only from eggs laid by other flies. Redi's hypothesis was confirmed, and a major blow was struck against the hypothesis of spontaneous generation.

SPALLANZANI'S EXPERIMENT

FIGURE 14-2

In Spallanzani's experiment, he boiled meat broth in open flasks. Then he sealed the flasks of the experimental group by melting the glass necks of the flasks closed. The broth inside remained uncontaminated by microorganisms.

CONTROL GROUP

Broth is boiled.

Flask is open.

Days pass.

Broth becomes cloudy.

EXPERIMENTAL GROUP

Broth is boiled.

Seal of melted glass

Flask is sealed immediately.

Days pass.

Broth remains clear.

At about the same time that Redi carried out his experiment, other scientists began using a new tool—the microscope. Their observations with the microscope revealed that the world is teeming with tiny creatures. They discovered that microorganisms are simple in structure and amazingly numerous and widespread. Many investigators at the time thus concluded that microorganisms arise spontaneously from a "vital force" in the air.

In the 1700s, another Italian scientist, Lazzaro Spallanzani (1729–1799), designed an experiment to test the hypothesis of spontaneous generation of microorganisms, as shown in Figure 14-2. Spallanzani hypothesized that microorganisms formed not from air but from other microorganisms. He knew that microorganisms grew easily in food. Therefore, he decided to test their growth in meat broth. Spallanzani reasoned that boiling broth in a flask would kill all the microorganisms in the broth, on the inside of the glass, and in the air in the flask. For his experimental group, Spallanzani boiled clear, fresh broth until the flasks filled with steam. He then sealed the flasks by melting their glass necks closed while the broth was hot. The control-group flasks of broth were left open. The broth in the sealed flasks remained clear and free of microorganisms, while that in the open flasks became cloudy due to contamination with microorganisms.

Spallanzani concluded that the boiled broth became contaminated only when microorganisms from the air entered the flask. Spallanzani's opponents, however, objected to his method and disagreed with his conclusions. They claimed that Spallanzani had heated the experimental flasks too long, destroying the "vital force" in the air inside them. Air lacking this "vital force," they claimed, could not generate life. Thus, those who believed in spontaneous generation of microorganisms kept the idea alive for another century.

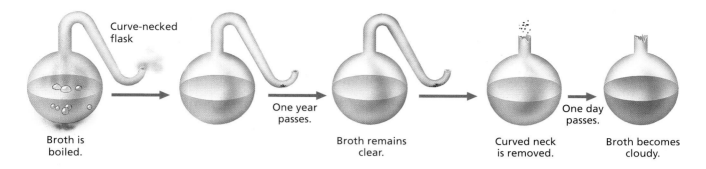

Curve-necked flask

Broth is boiled.

One year passes.

Broth remains clear.

Curved neck is removed.

One day passes.

Broth becomes cloudy.

FIGURE 14-3

In Pasteur's experiment, a flask with a curved but open neck prevented microorganisms from entering. Broth boiled in the flasks became contaminated by microorganisms only when the curved necks were removed from the flasks.

PASTEUR'S EXPERIMENT

By the mid-1800s the controversy over spontaneous generation had grown fierce. The Paris Academy of Science offered a prize to anyone who could clear up the issue once and for all. The winner of the prize was the French scientist Louis Pasteur (1822–1895).

Figure 14-3 shows how Pasteur set up his prize-winning experiment. To answer objections to Spallanzani's experiment, Pasteur made a curve-necked flask that allowed the air inside the flask to mix with air outside the flask. The curve in the neck of the flask prevented solid particles, such as microorganisms, from entering the body of the flask. Broth boiled inside the experimental curve-necked flasks remained clear for up to a year. But when Pasteur broke off the curved necks, the broth became cloudy and contaminated with microorganisms within a day. Pasteur reasoned that the contamination was due to microorganisms in the air.

Those who had believed in the spontaneous generation of microorganisms gave up their fight. With Pasteur's experiment, the principle of biogenesis became a cornerstone of biology.

Word Roots and Origins

biogenesis

from the Greek *bioun,* meaning "to live," and *gignesthai,* meaning "to be born"

SECTION 14-1 REVIEW

1. What does the term *spontaneous generation* mean?

2. Explain how Redi's experiment disproved the hypothesis of spontaneous generation in flies.

3. What caused people to think there was a "vital force" in the air that produced living organisms?

4. Did Spallanzani's experiment disprove the hypothesis that microorganisms could arise spontaneously from a "vital force" contained in the air? Explain why Spallanzani's procedure did or did not disprove such a possibility.

5. In conducting his experiment, Spallanzani demonstrated a technique that would become universally used in the preservation of food. What was this technique?

6. CRITICAL THINKING What would have happened if Pasteur had tipped one of his flasks so that the broth in the flask came into contact with the curve of the neck? Explain how this result would or would not have supported his conclusion.

OBJECTIVES

▲

Outline the modern scientific understanding of the formation of Earth.

●

Summarize the concept of *half-life*.

■

Describe the production of organic compounds in the Miller-Urey apparatus.

◆

Summarize the possible importance of cell-like structures produced in the laboratory.

EARTH'S HISTORY

The phylogenetic tree of all living things is a history of cell-based life. Cells may evolve and change, but new cells always arise from existing cells. How, then, did the first cells originate? Using models thought to approximate the conditions found on early Earth, scientists attempt to reconstruct the processes that gave rise to the first cellular life.

THE FORMATION OF EARTH

Evidence from computer models of the sun suggests that about 5 billion years ago, our solar system was a swirling mass of gas and dust, as shown in Figure 14-4. Over time, most of this material collapsed inward, forming the sun. The remaining gas, dust, and debris circled the young sun. The planets are thought to have been formed from repeated violent collisions of this space debris. During its 400-million-year-long period of formation, Earth grew increasingly large as it was bombarded by debris. These collisions not only added to Earth's mass but also released a great deal of thermal energy. Each collision between the young and growing Earth and a large piece of space debris, for example, would have released enough energy to melt the entire surface of Earth.

Earth's Age

The estimated age of Earth, more than 4 billion years, is about 700,000 times as long as the period of recorded history. It is about 50 million times as long as an average human life span. How can we determine what happened so long ago? Scientists have drilled deep into Earth and examined its many layers to establish a fairly complete picture of its geologic history. Early estimates of Earth's age were made from studying layers of sediment in Earth's crust. The age of Earth could not be estimated accurately, however, until the middle of the twentieth century, when modern methods of establishing the age of materials were developed.

Radioactive Dating

Methods of establishing the age of materials include the techniques known as **radioactive dating.** Recall from Chapter 2 that the atomic number of an element is the number of protons in the nucleus. All atoms of an element have the same atomic number, but their number of neutrons can vary. Atoms of the same element that differ in the number of neutrons they contain are called **isotopes**

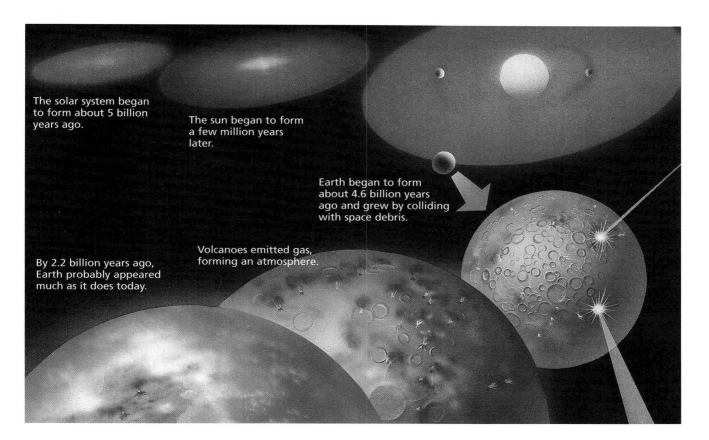

The solar system began to form about 5 billion years ago.

The sun began to form a few million years later.

Earth began to form about 4.6 billion years ago and grew by colliding with space debris.

Volcanoes emitted gas, forming an atmosphere.

By 2.2 billion years ago, Earth probably appeared much as it does today.

FIGURE 14-4

It took about one-half of a billion years for modern Earth to form from a swirling mass of gases.

(IE-suh-TOHPS). Most elements have several isotopes. The **mass number** of an isotope is the total number of protons and neutrons in the nucleus. The mass number of the most common carbon isotope is 12. If you recall that the atomic number of carbon is 6, you can calculate that this carbon isotope has six protons and six neutrons. Isotopes are designated by their chemical name followed by their mass number; for example, carbon exists as both *carbon-12* and *carbon-14*.

Some isotopes have unstable nuclei, which tend to undergo **radioactive decay;** that is, their nuclei tend to release particles or radiant energy, or both. Such isotopes are called **radioactive isotopes.** Rates of decay of radioactive isotopes have been determined for many isotopes. The length of time it takes for one-half of any size sample of an isotope to decay is called its **half-life.** Depending on the isotope, half-lives vary from a fraction of a second to billions of years.

The age of a material can be determined by measuring the amount of a particular radioactive isotope it contains. This quantity is compared with the amount of some other substance in the fossil that remains constant over time. For example, relatively young fossils can be dated by measuring the ratio of the amount of carbon-14, a radioactive isotope, to the amount of a stable isotope, carbon-12. Living things take carbon into their bodies constantly. Most of the carbon is in the form of carbon-12. A very small proportion of it, however, is in the form of carbon-14, which undergoes decay. This ratio of carbon-14 to carbon-12 is a known quantity for

Word Roots and Origins

isotope

from the Greek *iso,* meaning "equal," and *topos,* meaning "place"

TABLE 14-1	Some Isotopes Used in Radioactive Dating
Isotope	**Half-life**
Carbon-14	5,730 y
Thorium-230	75,000 y
Potassium-40	1,300,000,000 y
Uranium-238	4,500,000,000 y

living organisms. When an organism dies, its uptake of carbon stops, and decay of the existing carbon-14 continues. Thus, over time, the amount of carbon-14 declines with respect to the amount of the stable carbon-12. After 5,730 years, half of the carbon-14 in a sample will have decayed. After another 5,730 years, half of the remaining carbon-14 in the sample likewise will have decayed. Use of carbon-14 dating is limited to organic remains less than about 60,000 years old, like the leather quiver and wooden bow and arrows shown in Figure 14-5. Isotopes with longer half-lives are used to date older fossils and rocks. Some of the isotopes commonly used in radioactive dating procedures appear in Table 14-1.

Scientists have estimated Earth's age by using a dating method that is based on the decay of uranium and thorium isotopes in rock crystals. Collisions between Earth and large pieces of space debris probably caused the surface of Earth to melt many times as the planet was formed. Therefore, the age of the oldest unmelted surface rock should tell us when these collisions stopped and the cooling of Earth's surface began. Scientists have found zircon crystals that are 4.2 billion years old. We can infer that organic molecules could have survived and begun to accumulate sometime after this.

FIGURE 14-5

This deerskin quiver, with a wooden bow and arrows, is about 3,000 years old. Carbon-14 dating methods can be used for organic materials less than 60,000 years old.

THE FIRST ORGANIC COMPOUNDS

All of the elements found in organic compounds are thought to have existed on Earth and in the rest of the solar system when the Earth formed. But how and where were these elements assembled into the organic compounds found in life? One of the most popular hypotheses proposed to solve this puzzle was developed by the Soviet scientist Alexander I. Oparin in 1923. Oparin (1894–1980) suggested that the atmosphere of the primitive Earth was very different from that of today. Oparin thought the early atmosphere contained ammonia, NH_3; hydrogen gas, H_2; water vapor, H_2O; and compounds made of hydrogen and carbon, such as methane, CH_4. At temperatures well above the boiling point of water, these gases might have formed simple organic compounds, such as amino acids. According to Oparin, when Earth cooled and water vapor condensed to form lakes and seas, these simple organic compounds would have collected in the water. Over time these compounds could have entered complex chemical reactions, fueled by energy from lightning and ultraviolet radiation. These reactions, Oparin reasoned, ultimately would have resulted in the macromolecules essential to life, such as proteins.

The Experimental Synthesis of Organic Compounds

Oparin carefully developed his hypotheses, but he did not perform experiments to test them. So in 1953, an American graduate student, Stanley L. Miller (1930–), and his professor, Harold C. Urey (1893–1981), set up an experiment using Oparin's hypotheses as a starting point. Their apparatus, illustrated in Figure 14-6, included a chamber containing the gases Oparin assumed were present in the young Earth's atmosphere. As the gases circulated in the chamber, electric sparks, substituting for lightning, supplied energy to drive chemical reactions. The Miller-Urey experiment, and other variations that have followed, produced a variety of organic compounds, including amino acids.

Since the 1950s, scientists have continued to explore the origin of simple organic compounds. Their experiments have produced a variety of compounds, including various amino acids, ATP, and the nucleotides in DNA. Such results suggest many ways that vital organic compounds might have formed on the young Earth.

In recent years, new hypotheses regarding early Earth's atmosphere have been proposed by investigators who study planet formation. In contrast to Oparin's hypotheses, it has been suggested that the atmosphere of early Earth was composed largely of carbon dioxide, CO_2; nitrogen, N_2; and water vapor, H_2O. Laboratory simulations of these atmospheric conditions have shown that both carbon dioxide and oxygen gas interfere with the production of organic compounds. Therefore, it is thought that conditions in areas protected from the atmosphere, such as those that exist in undersea hot springs, might have favored the production of organic compounds.

Organic Compounds from Beyond Earth

Recently, a broad mixture of organic compounds was found in a newly fallen meteorite that was recovered before it was contaminated with organic compounds from Earth. These compounds, which had not been destroyed by heat as the meteoroid entered Earth's atmosphere, must have formed in space. Some scientists hypothesize that after the period of Earth's formation, some organic compounds may have accumulated on the surface of Earth in this way, carried by space debris rather than originating here.

Electrode

Water vapor, H_2, CH_4, and NH_3

Condenser

Water vapor forms.

H_2O

Organic compounds

FIGURE 14-6

Miller and Urey's apparatus was a model for the atmospheric and temperature conditions of early Earth.

 Quick Lab

Inferring Probability

Materials 3 × 5 in. cards (12) labeled with organic compounds

Procedure

1. Deal three cards, and try to make one of the following combinations: NH_2–CH_2–COOH, CH_3–COOH, or CH_3–CH_2–COOH. Each of these combinations represents an organic molecule.

2. Record your results. Replace the dealt cards in the set and shuffle the cards. Repeat the procedure 19 times.

3. Count the number of molecules you were able to form. Then calculate the probability of forming a molecule with each deal.

Analysis How can you compare a simple game of chance to the synthesis of organic compounds?

FROM MOLECULES TO CELL-LIKE STRUCTURES

FIGURE 14-7

Membrane-bound structures, such as these, have been formed in the laboratory under conditions that may have existed on early Earth. Structures such as these may have enclosed replicating molecules of RNA and may have been the forerunners of the first cells.

Sidney Fox (1912–) and others have done extensive research on the physical structures that may have given rise to the first cells. These cell-like structures, like the ones shown in Figure 14-7, form spontaneously in the laboratory from solutions of simple organic chemicals. The structures include **microspheres,** which are spherical in shape and are composed of many protein molecules that are organized as a membrane, and **coacervates** (coh-AS-uhr-vayts), which are collections of droplets that are composed of molecules of different types, including linked amino acids and sugars.

For many years, it had been assumed that all cell structures and the chemical reactions of life required enzymes that were specified by the genetic information of the cell. Both coacervates and microspheres, however, can form spontaneously under certain conditions. For example, the polymers that form microspheres can arise when solutions of simple organic chemicals are dripped onto the surface of hot clay. The heat vaporizes the water, encouraging polymerization. Coacervates and microspheres have a number of lifelike properties, including the ability to take up certain substances from their surroundings. Coacervates can grow, and microspheres can bud to form smaller microspheres. These properties of coacervates and microspheres show that some important aspects of cellular life can arise without direction from genes. Thus, these studies suggest that the gap between the nonliving chemical compounds and cellular life may not be quite as wide as previously thought.

When considering the evolution of cells from simpler structures, it is important to remember that microspheres and coacervates could not have responded to natural selection. Recall from Chapter 1 that natural selection is an important driving force of evolution—which is descent with modification, or change over generations. The laboratory-produced cell-like structures do not have hereditary characteristics. Thus, although these cell-like structures have some of the properties of life, they are not alive because they do not have heredity.

SECTION 14-2 REVIEW

1. The oldest rocks on Earth date from about 4.2 billion years ago. What does this suggest about the interval between 4.6 billion years ago, when the Earth started to form, and 4.2 billion years ago?

2. If a radioactive isotope had a half-life of 1 billion years, how much of it would be left after each of the following intervals of time: 1 billion years, 2 billion years, 3 billion years, and 4 billion years.

3. What are two possible sources of simple organic compounds on the early Earth?

4. What was Oparin's hypothesis, and how was it tested?

5. What properties do microspheres and coacervates share with cells?

6. **CRITICAL THINKING** Some radioactive isotopes that are used in medicine as tracers in the bloodstream have very short half-lives, often only a few years or less, rather than thousands of years. Would these isotopes also be useful in dating fossils? Why or why not?

THE FIRST LIFE-FORMS

A remote and desolate corner of Australia was nicknamed the North Pole by disappointed gold prospectors in the 1800s. But this region has been a "gold mine" after all for twentieth-century scientists. It was there that the oldest known cellular fossils—3.5-billion-year-old traces of early unicellular organisms—were found.

OBJECTIVES

▲

Explain the importance of the chemistry of RNA in relation to the origin of life.

●

List three inferred characteristics that describe the first forms of cellular life on Earth.

■

Name two types of autotrophy and explain the difference between them.

◆

Explain how photosynthesis and aerobic respiration are thought to be related.

▲

Define *endosymbiosis,* and explain why it is important in the history of eukaryotes.

THE ORIGIN OF HEREDITY

Chapter 10 provides a detailed explanation of how hereditary information affects the phenotype of cells. Recall that the hereditary information contained in a DNA molecule is first transcribed into an RNA message, and then the RNA message is translated into a protein, as shown in Figure 14-8. Thus, DNA serves as the template for RNA, which in turn serves as the template for specific proteins.

In recent years, scientists have taken a closer look at the DNA-RNA-protein sequence. Why is RNA necessary for this process? Why doesn't DNA, which is a template itself, carry out protein synthesis directly? The clues to a more complete understanding of RNA function may be found in its shape. Unlike DNA, RNA molecules can take on a great variety of shapes, for example, the t shape of transfer RNA, shown in Figure 14-8. These shapes are dictated by hydrogen bonds between particular nucleotides in an RNA molecule, much as the shapes of proteins depend on hydrogen bonds between particular amino acids. These questions and observations led to the speculation that some RNA molecules might actually behave like proteins and catalyze chemical reactions.

Amino acid

Protein chain

Transfer RNA

Messenger RNA

FIGURE 14-8

Messenger RNA is transcribed from a DNA template. Transfer RNA translates the three-base codons in the mRNA, assembling a protein from the specified amino acids.

Some species of archaebacteria, such as *Methanosarcina barkeri* pictured in Figure 14-9, are referred to as methanogens. Within these bacteria, hydrogen gas reacts with carbon dioxide to produce methane, a simple carbon compound. Methanogens are poisoned by oxygen, but they can live in watery environments where other bacteria have consumed all free oxygen, such as in swamps and even the intestines of animals.

Methanogens may prove useful to humans in two significant ways: they are currently used in the cleanup of organic waste, such as sewage, and they may eventually be harnessed for large-scale production of methane for use as a fuel source.

Other species of archaebacteria are being used in the cleanup of petroleum spills into soil, such as occur when underground gasoline tanks develop leaks. This technique, called bioremediation, often relies on bacteria already present in the soil. These bacteria are activated by application of nutrient-rich solutions formulated to their taste. As the bacteria multiply, they metabolize petroleum, releasing harmless byproducts.

Word Roots and Origins

archaebacteria

from the Greek *arche*, meaning "the beginning," and *bactron*, meaning "a staff"

THE ROLES OF RNA

In the early 1980s, researcher Thomas Cech (1947–) found that a type of RNA found in some unicellular eukaryotes is able to act as an enzyme. Cech used the term **ribozyme** (RIE-boh-ziem) for an RNA molecule that can act as an enzyme and promote a specific chemical reaction. Hypothetically, a ribozyme could act as an enzyme *and* have the ability to replicate itself.

Recent studies based on Cech's discovery have indicated that life may have started with self-replicating molecules of RNA. RNA molecules would have heredity and would be able to respond to natural selection and thus evolve. How could a single molecule respond to natural selection? Replication—or reproduction of the RNA molecule—might involve competing with other similar, but not identical, RNA molecules for a fixed number of available nucleotides. An RNA molecule that is more successful in getting nucleotides from its environment has an advantage over other RNA molecules. This advantage would then be passed on to the "offspring" of the RNA molecules, the new RNA molecules created by replication.

Since Cech's discovery, other ribozymal activities have been discovered, and it is clear that RNA plays a vital role in DNA replication, protein synthesis, RNA processing, and other basic biochemistry. Perhaps most or all of the chemistry and genetics of early cells were based on RNA.

As exciting as these discoveries have been, there are several questions left unanswered. For one thing, investigators still have not made or found a ribozyme capable of producing other ribozymes. Moreover, it is unclear how such RNA molecules could have evolved into cellular life. Perhaps self-replicating molecules of RNA started to evolve inside cell-like structures similar to microspheres or coacervates. If these RNA molecules were able to alter the phenotype of the cell-like structure that carried them, cellular life could have begun. The self-replicating RNA would have provided the hereditary information that the cell-like structures lack.

THE FIRST PROKARYOTES

What clues do we have about the nature of the first cellular life? When the first organisms arose, there was little or no oxygen gas in existence. Thus, the first cells must have been anaerobic. The small size of the oldest of the microfossils indicates that these early cells were prokaryotes. These cells probably were heterotrophs taking in organic molecules from their environment.

We can reason that a growing population of heterotrophs that depended on spontaneously formed organic molecules for food eventually would have removed most of these molecules from the environment. At this point, there would have been strong environmental pressure for autotrophs to evolve. These first autotrophs, however, probably did not depend on photosynthesis the way that most autotrophs do today.

Chemosynthesis

If we look for living organisms that may be similar to these early organisms, we find the **archaebacteria** (AR-kuh-bak-TIR-ee-uh). The archaebacteria constitute a kingdom of unicellular organisms, many of which thrive under extremely harsh environmental conditions. *Methanosarcina barkeri,* the archaebacterium shown in Figure 14-9, lives in anaerobic marine sediments. Many species of archaebacteria are autotrophs that obtain energy by chemosynthesis (KEE-moh-SIN-thuh-sis) instead of photosynthesis. In the process of **chemosynthesis,** CO_2 serves as a carbon source for the assembly of organic molecules. Energy is obtained from the oxidation of various inorganic substances, such as sulfur.

Photosynthesis and Aerobic Respiration

Oxygen, a byproduct of photosynthesis, was damaging to many early unicellular organisms. Oxygen could destroy some coenzymes essential to cell function. Within some organisms, however, oxygen bonded to other compounds, thereby preventing the oxygen from doing damage. This bonding was one of the first steps in aerobic respiration. Thus, an early function of aerobic respiration may have been to prevent the destruction of essential organic compounds by oxygen.

Some forms of life had become photosynthetic by 3 billion years ago. In the mid-1990s, scientists discovered traces of carbon in geological formations off the coast of Greenland. These traces were likely left by some type of photosynthetic organism more than 3.8 billion years ago. The 3.5-billion-year-old microfossils found in Australia, shown in figure 14-10, are probably of photosynthetic unicellular organisms that are related to modern **cyanobacteria** (SIE-uh-no-bak-TIR-ee-uh), a group of photosynthetic unicellular prokaryotes.

It took a billion years or more for oxygen gas levels to reach today's levels. The oxygen, O_2, eventually reached the upper part of the atmosphere, where it was bombarded with sunlight. Some wavelengths of sunlight can split O_2 to form highly reactive single oxygen atoms, O. These react with O_2 and form **ozone,** O_3. Ozone is poisonous to both plant and animal life, but in the upper atmosphere, a layer of ozone absorbs intense ultraviolet radiation from the sun. Ultraviolet radiation damages DNA, and without the protection of the ozone layer, life could not have come to exist on land.

FIGURE 14-9

This archaebacterium species, *Methanosarcina barkeri,* produces methane during metabolism. Archaebacteria are thought to be similar to the types of cellular life that first populated Earth about 4 billion years ago.

FIGURE 14-10

These filament-shaped microfossils from the Fig Tree Chert formation in northern Australia represent the oldest-known cellular life. These organisms lived 3.5 billion years ago.

Small aerobic prokaryote

Mitochondrion

Small photosynthetic prokaryote

Chloroplasts

Mitochondria

Mitochondria

LARGE PROKARYOTE **PRE-EUKARYOTE** **PRE-EUKARYOTE** **PRIMITIVE EUKARYOTE**

FIGURE 14-11

According to the hypothesis of endosymbiosis, large prokaryotic, unicellular organisms were invaded by smaller prokaryotic, unicellular organisms. These smaller organisms eventually gave rise to modern mitochondria and chloroplasts, which carry their own DNA and replicate independently from the rest of the cell that contains them.

THE FIRST EUKARYOTES

Recall from Chapter 4 that eukaryotic cells differ from prokaryotic cells in several ways. Eukaryotic cells are larger, their DNA is organized into chromosomes in a cell nucleus, and they contain membrane-bound organelles. How did such a complex type of cell evolve from the simple prokaryotes? A large body of evidence now suggests that between about 2.0 and 1.5 billion years ago, a type of small aerobic prokaryote entered and began to live and reproduce *inside* larger, anaerobic prokaryotes. Researcher Lynn Margulis (1938–) has proposed that what may have started as an invasion became a successful, mutually beneficial relationship—called **endosymbiosis** (EN-doh-sim-bee-OH-sis), shown in Figure 14-11. It is thought that the aerobic prokaryote eventually gave rise to modern mitochondria, which are the site of aerobic respiration in eukaryotic cells.

Sometime later, there was a second successful invasion of pre-eukaryotic cells. This time, the invader was a relative of modern photosynthetic cyanobacteria. These invaders eventually gave rise to chloroplasts, the sites of photosynthesis. There is compelling evidence to support this hypothesis of eukaryotic evolution. Both chloroplasts and mitochondria replicate independently from the replication cycle of the cell that contains them. Moreover, chloroplasts and mitochondria contain some of their own genes, which are different from those of the rest of the cell. These genes are found in the organelles themselves, in a circular piece of DNA, an arrangement characteristic of prokaryotic, though not eukaryotic, DNA.

SECTION 14-3 REVIEW

1. Why do different molecules of RNA assume many different shapes?

2. Why do scientists think the first forms of life on Earth were anaerobic?

3. How might aerobic respiration have protected early cells from damage?

4. What evidence supports the hypothesis that mitochondria were once free-living prokaryotic cells?

5. Explain how the first eukaryotes may have evolved.

6. **CRITICAL THINKING** Some forms of air pollution damage Earth's ozone layer. How might such damage affect life?

SUMMARY/VOCABULARY

14-1
- Before the 1600s, it was generally thought that organisms could arise from nonliving material by spontaneous generation.
- Redi showed in 1668 that rotting meat kept away from flies would not produce new flies. Maggots appeared only on meat that had been exposed to flies.
- Spallanzani showed in the 1700s that microorganisms would not grow in broth when its container was heated and then sealed. This seemed to indicate that microorganisms that cause food spoilage do not arise from spontaneous generation but, rather, are carried in the air.
- Pasteur used a variation of Spallanzani's design to prove that microorganisms are carried in the air and do not arise by spontaneous generation.

Vocabulary

biogenesis (261)   spontaneous generation (261)

14-2
- Earth is thought to have been formed by repeated collisions of debris moving through space.
- The mass number of an element is the total number of protons and neutrons in the nucleus. The number of neutrons in atoms of an element can vary. Atoms with varying numbers of neutrons are called isotopes.
- An isotope's half-life is the time it takes for one-half of a sample of the isotope to decay.
- The ages of objects like fossils and rocks can be determined by measuring the amount of radioactive decay that has occurred in radioactive isotopes found in the sample.
- The first simple organic compounds may have been formed at high temperatures on early Earth in an atmosphere of ammonia, hydrogen gas, and water vapor.
- Macromolecules important to life may have been assembled from simple organic compounds. Lightning may have supplied the energy for these chemical reactions.
- Some organic compounds may have been deposited on Earth by meteorites.
- Cell-like structures, including microspheres and coacervates, form spontaneously in certain kinds of solutions. These structures do not show heredity.

Vocabulary

coacervate (268)   isotope (264)   microsphere (268)   radioactive decay (265)
half-life (265)   mass number (265)   radioactive dating (264) radioactive isotope (265)

14-3
- In addition to its role as a template for protein assembly, some RNA molecules can act as enzymes.
- The first molecule that held hereditary information may have been RNA rather than DNA.
- RNA can assume different shapes, much as proteins do. These shapes depend on areas of attraction between the RNA nucleotides.
- The first cells that formed on Earth were probably heterotrophic prokaryotes.
- The first autotrophic cells probably used chemosynthesis to make food.
- An important initial function of aerobic respiration may have been to bind oxygen and prevent it from doing damage to early organisms.
- Eukaryotic cells may have evolved from large prokaryotic cells that were invaded by smaller prokaryotic cells. These small prokaryotic invaders may have been the ancestors of organelles, including mitochondria and chloroplasts.

Vocabulary

archaebacteria (271)   cyanobacteria (271)   ozone (271)   ribozyme (270)
chemosynthesis (271)   endosymbiosis (272)

REVIEW

Vocabulary

1. Explain the difference between biogenesis and spontaneous generation.
2. What is the relationship between radioactive decay and the half-life of an isotope?
3. Name two nonliving, cell-like structures that can form in certain solutions.
4. How is a ribozyme like an enzyme?
5. What is photosynthesis. What is chemosynthesis?

Multiple Choice

6. In the seventeenth and eighteenth centuries, the hypothesis of spontaneous generation was used to explain (a) how new life started (b) how simple organic compounds formed (c) how coacervates and microspheres formed (d) how eukaryotes evolved.
7. Redi's experiment was important because it showed that (a) maggots give rise to microorganisms (b) flies swarm on rotting meat (c) flies do not form from rotting meat (d) air contains a "vital force."
8. People objected to Spallanzani's experiment because he (a) used an open jar of meat as a control (b) boiled his flasks of broth for a long time (c) drew the necks of his flasks into a curved shape (d) did not have a control group.
9. The neck of Pasteur's flasks (a) allowed both air and particles to enter the flask (b) allowed air to enter the flask but kept particles out (c) allowed particles to enter but kept air out (d) kept both air and particles out.
10. During the first half-billion years of its existence, Earth and the other planets of the solar system grew by a process involving (a) the synthesis of organic molecules (b) collisions with space debris (c) flames from the sun (d) tidal forces generated on the moon.
11. The oldest fossil of cellular life found on Earth is (a) about 4.6 billion years old (b) about 4.2 billion years old (c) about 3.5 billion years old (d) less than 2 billion years old.
12. Coacervates and microspheres cannot evolve because they have no (a) genetic information (b) cell membrane (c) complex organic molecules (d) fluid in their interior.
13. Miller and Urey's experiment (a) proved Oparin's hypothesis about the origin of life (b) disproved Oparin's hypothesis about the origin of organic molecules (c) provided support for Oparin's hypothesis about the origin of organic molecules (d) is irrelevant to any hypothesis regarding the origin of life.
14. Coacervates and microspheres are (a) collections of organic molecules enclosed within a boundary (b) identical to the first forms of life (c) the oldest microfossils (d) new forms of bacteria.
15. The generation of organisms from nonliving material does not occur today mostly because (a) the presence of oxygen in the atmosphere prevents organic compounds from forming spontaneously (b) coacervates and microspheres take up all the extra nutrients on Earth (c) coacervates and microspheres cannot form today (d) there is not enough energy to drive the chemical reactions needed to form the complex organic compounds necessary for life.

Short Answer

16. Explain the role of the gases CH_4, H_2, and NH_3 and the role of the electric spark in the apparatus shown.

17. Why did the theory of biogenesis pose a dilemma regarding the origin of life?

18. What modern organisms are thought to be most like the first life-forms on Earth?

19. What environmental factors probably favored the evolution of autotrophs?

20. Organic compounds will not form in the Miller-Urey apparatus if O_2 is present. Why is this not a serious problem for scientists who study the origin of life?

21. How might the bonding of oxygen gas have served evolving organisms?

22. How did the formation of the ozone layer permit organisms to colonize land?

23. What energy sources do some nonphotosynthetic autotrophs use?

24. Why have many scientists who investigate the origin of life focused on RNA chemistry?

25. What problems remain with the hypothesis that ribozymes or similar molecules may have been the first self-replicating structures?

CRITICAL THINKING

1. People once believed fish could form from the mud in a pond that sometimes dried up. How could you demonstrate that this conclusion is false?

2. According to a recent hypothesis, lightning may not have existed on early Earth. How could you modify the Miller-Urey experiment to reflect this new idea? What sources of energy could you use to replace lightning?

3. RNA is copied the same way that DNA is copied—by base pairing. RNA, unlike double-stranded DNA, exists as a single strand. If a ribozyme is copied, would the copy be another identical ribozyme or something else? If the copy is not identical to the original, how could the original be replicated?

4. The term *chemical evolution* is sometimes applied to the series of events that might have resulted in the spontaneous origin of life. How do the events that are thought to have produced living organic matter from nonliving inorganic matter represent a process of evolution?

5. The graph below represents radioactive decay of an isotope. If the half-life of carbon-14 is 5,730 years, how many years would it take for $\frac{7}{8}$ of the original amount of carbon-14 in a sample to decay?

Amount Remaining of Radioactive Sample

EXTENSION

1. Read "To Hell and Back" in *Discover,* July 1999, on page 76, and answer the following questions: What were some of the extreme conditions in the environment where the microbes lived? What substances besides oxygen do some deep-Earth-dwelling bacteria use for respiration? What precautions were taken to protect the organisms in the rock samples from being poisoned by the surface atmosphere?

2. Investigators studying the atmosphere have observed a large, thin area in the ozone layer above the continent of Antarctica. Use current science magazines to find out about this phenomenon. Present a report to your class summarizing different hypotheses about the causes of this thinning of the ozone layer.

Making Microspheres

OBJECTIVES

- Make microspheres from amino acids by simulating the conditions found on early Earth.
- Compare the structure of microspheres with the structure of living cells.

PROCESS SKILLS

- observing
- comparing and contrasting
- modeling
- relating

MATERIALS

- safety goggles
- lab apron
- heat-protective gloves
- 500 mL beaker
- hot plate
- 125 mL Erlenmeyer flasks, 2
- ring stand with clamp
- balance
- amino acid mixture (of at least six different amino acids)
- glass stirring rod
- tongs
- clock or timer
- 1% sodium chloride (NaCl) solution
- 50 mL graduated cylinder
- dropper
- microscope slide
- coverslip
- compound light microscope
- 1% sodium hydroxide (NaOH) solution

Background

1. Microspheres are very small, spherical vessels that are bounded by a membranelike layer of amino acids. Microspheres can be created in the laboratory under controlled conditions.
2. How do microspheres differ from living cells?
3. How do microspheres resemble living cells?

4. What role might have been played by microspheres or similar structures before life began on Earth?

Procedure

1. Put on safety goggles, a lab apron, and heat-protective gloves before beginning this investigation.
2. **CAUTION Do not plug in or unplug the hot plate with wet hands. Use care to avoid burns when working with the hot plate. Do not touch the hot plate. Use tongs to move heated objects. Turn off the hot plate when not in use.** Fill a 500 mL beaker half full with water, and heat it on a hot plate. You will use the beaker as a hot-water bath. Leave space on the hot plate for a 125 mL Erlenmeyer flask, to be added later.
3. While waiting for the water to boil, clamp a 125 mL Erlenmeyer flask to a ring stand. Add 6 g of the amino acid mixture to the flask.
4. When the water in the beaker begins to boil, move the ring stand carefully so that the flask of amino acids sits in the hot-water bath.
5. When the amino acids have heated for 20 minutes, measure 10 mL of NaCl solution in a graduated cylinder and pour the solution into a second Erlenmeyer flask. Place the second flask on the hot plate beside the hot-water bath.

6. When the NaCl solution begins to boil, use tongs to remove the flask containing the NaCl solution from the hot plate. Then, while holding the flask with tongs, slowly add the NaCl solution to the hot amino acids while stirring.

7. Let this NaCl–amino acid solution boil for 30 seconds.

8. Remove the solution from the water bath, and allow it to cool for 10 minutes.

9. ◆ CAUTION **Slides break easily. Use caution when handling them.** Use a dropper to place a drop of the solution on a microscope slide, and cover the drop with a coverslip.

10. Place the slide on the microscope stage. Examine the slide under low power for tiny spherical structures. Then examine the structures under high power. These tiny sphere-shaped objects are microspheres.

11. ◆ CAUTION **If you get the sodium hydroxide (NaOH) solution on your skin or clothing, wash it off at the sink while calling to your teacher. If you get the sodium hydroxide solution in your eyes, immediately flush your eyes at the eyewash station while calling to your teacher.** Place a drop of 1% NaOH solution at the edge of the coverslip to raise the pH as you observe the microspheres. What happens?

12. In your lab report, make a table similar to the one shown below. Based on your observations of microspheres and cells, complete your table. Consider the appearance of microspheres and cells, their method of reproduction, their interaction with their environment, and any other characteristics that you observe.

13. ◆ ◆ Clean up your lab materials and wash your hands before leaving the lab.

Analysis and Conclusions

1. Suggest how the microspheres formed.

2. What did you observe when the pH was raised in step 11?

3. What does this suggest about the relationship of pH to microsphere formation?

4. Compare and contrast microspheres with living cells.

5. What characteristics would microspheres have to exhibit in order to be considered living?

6. How might the conditions you created in the lab be similar to those that are thought to have existed when life first evolved on Earth?

7. Predict what would happen to microspheres if they were placed in hypotonic and hypertonic solutions.

Further Inquiry

1. What do you think would happen if you added too much or too little heat? What happens to proteins at high temperatures? How can you test for the right amount of heat to use?

2. Do you think your microsphere experiment would have worked if you had substituted other amino acids? How can you test your hypothesis?

TABLE A *COMPARING MICROSPHERES WITH CELLS*

Cell-like characteristics	Characteristics that are not cell-like

CHAPTER 15

EVOLUTION: EVIDENCE AND THEORY

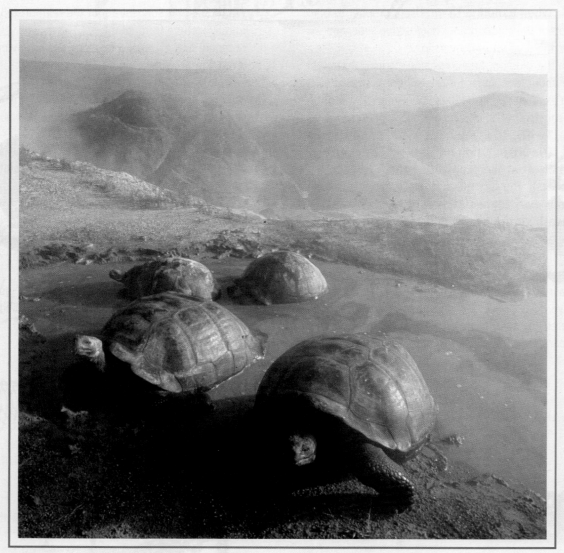

Giant tortoises, Geochelone elephantopus, *crowd a puddle on the Galápagos Islands.*

FOCUS CONCEPT: *Evolution*

As you read, note the many lines of evidence that support evolutionary theory.

THE FOSSIL RECORD

*F*ossil evidence shows a long history of life on Earth. The fossil record shows that forms of organisms appeared, lasted for long periods of time, and then disappeared, only to be followed by newer forms of life that also eventually disappeared. The history of life is one of constant change and a tremendous diversity of life-forms.

SECTION

15-1

OBJECTIVES

▲

Define *fossil,* and tell how the examination of fossils led to the development of evolutionary theories.

●

Explain the law of superposition and its significance to evolutionary theory.

■

Describe how early scientists inferred a succession of life-forms from the fossil record.

◆

Tell how biogeographic observations suggest descent with modification.

NATURE OF FOSSILS

A **fossil** is a trace of a long-dead organism. Fossils are often found in layers of sedimentary rock, which is formed when **sediment,** such as dust, sand, or mud, is deposited by wind or water. Sedimentary fossils usually develop from the hard body parts of an organism, such as the shell, bones, teeth, or, in the case of plants, the woody stem. Over long periods of time, hard minerals replace the tissue of the organism, leaving rocklike structures.

A type of fossil called a **mold** is essentially an imprint in rock in the shape of an organism. Limestone owes its spongelike texture to the many molds scattered throughout its structure. Some molds eventually are filled with hard minerals, forming a **cast,** a rocklike model of the organism.

As you can see in Figure 15-1, many different kinds of fossils have been found. Some fossils are in the form of lacy carbon tracings of a fern, captured for all time on a flat plate of slate. Others, such as the tracks of animals or the fossilized marks on the bones of some human ancestors, are evidence of behavior.

How did people in the past regard these natural curiosities? Perhaps the most widely held view was that fossils were simply a naturally occurring part of rocks. Beginning in the late seventeenth century, however, a flurry of scientific investigation occurred. In

(a)

(b)

FIGURE 15-1

There are several different types of fossils. (a) Amber, the fossilized sap of trees, holds well-preserved insects. (b) This fossilized shell is that of a trilobite, *Modocia typicalus,* a dominant life-form in early seas.

1668, Robert Hooke (1635–1703) published his conclusion that fossils are the remains of plants and animals. Hooke was one of the first scientists to study fossils, principally petrified wood, with the aid of a microscope. Hooke thought the detail he saw with the microscope was too fine and precise to have been formed by the rock itself. He hypothesized that living organisms had somehow been turned to rock.

DISTRIBUTION OF FOSSILS

Hooke's view was shared by another scientist of his time, Nicolaus Steno (1638–1686). Steno made an important contribution toward a modern understanding of Earth's geological and biological history. In 1669, he proposed the **law of superposition** (soo-puhr-puh- ZISH-uhn)**,** which states that successive layers of rock or soil were deposited on top of one another by wind or water. The lowest **stratum,** or layer, in a cross section of Earth is the oldest, while the top stratum

TABLE 15-1	*Geological History of Earth*			
Millions of years ago	**Era**	**Period**	**Epoch**	**Organisms**
0.01	Cenozoic	Quaternary	Recent	modern humans arise
1.8			Pleistocene	humans arise
5.3		Tertiary	Pliocene	large carnivores arise
23.8			Miocene	mammals diversify
33.7			Oligocene	diverse grazing animals arise
54.8			Eocene	early horses arise
65			Paleocene	more modern mammals arise
144	Mesozoic	Cretaceous		dinosaurs go extinct; mass extinction
208		Jurassic		dinosaurs diversify; birds arise
245		Triassic		primitive mammals arise; mass extinction; dinosaurs arise
290	Paleozoic	Permian		seed plants arise; reptiles diversify; mass extinction
354		Carboniferous		reptiles arise
417		Devonian		amphibians arise; mass extinction
443		Silurian		land plants arise
490		Ordovician		fishes arise; mass extinction
540		Cambrian		marine invertebrates arise
4,600	Precambrian			prokaryotes, then eukaryotes arise
	Formation of the Earth			

is the most recent. Thus, fossils within a single stratum are of the same approximate age. Using Steno's law, observers could establish the **relative age** of a fossil; that is, they could say that a given fossil was younger or older than another fossil. The fossil's **absolute age** (its age in years) could be estimated from radiological evidence.

Eventually the application of these geologic principles, coupled with modern technological methods, told a compelling story. The history of Earth, as shown in Table 15-1, is more than 100,000 times longer than recorded human history.

Succession of Forms

Fossil-bearing strata show that species of organisms appeared, existed for a while, and then disappeared, or became **extinct.** In turn, newer species continued to arise. In Table 15-1, notice the order in which different types of organisms arose, beginning with prokaryotes in the Precambrian era. The fossil record indicates that there were several **mass extinctions,** brief periods during which large numbers of species disappeared. Some of these life-forms were unlike any organisms alive today. Look back at Figure 15-1 to see the fossil of a trilobite, which lived during the Paleozoic era. Most trilobite species disappeared during the Permian extinction, 245 million years ago. Mass extinctions probably resulted from drastic changes in the environment, perhaps following periods of volcanic activity or collisions with asteroids. Ash and dust in the atmosphere may have blocked sunlight for long periods of time and caused a decrease in temperatures around the world.

Biogeography

The study of the geographical distribution of fossils and of living organisms is called **biogeography** (BIE-oh-jee-AH-gruh-fee). A comparison of recently formed fossil types with types of living organisms in the same geographic area shows that new organisms arise in areas where similar forms already lived. Thus, armadillos appeared in North and South America, where glyptodonts, shown in Figure 15-2, lived in the past. Modern kangaroos appeared only in Australia, where the now-extinct giant kangaroo had lived.

FIGURE 15-2

The modern armadillo (top) resembles the extinct glyptodont (bottom), although the glyptodont was much larger. Life-forms arise in the same areas where similar, older forms once existed.

SECTION 15-1 REVIEW

1. Define the term *fossil,* and name three different kinds of fossils.

2. What was Robert Hooke's contribution to the understanding of fossils?

3. How does the law of superposition allow paleontologists to assign relative ages to fossils?

4. In what geological era did the first organisms arise?

5. How do biogeographic observations suggest that a modification process caused new species to arise?

6. CRITICAL THINKING What can you conclude if you find identical examples of a fossilized organism in two adjacent geologic strata?

Solving the Burgess Puzzle

Were the animals that lived in the seas 550 million years ago, during the Cambrian period, more diverse than those that inhabit modern seas? A small limestone quarry tucked away 800 m above sea level in the Canadian Rocky Mountains is slowly yielding answers to this and other evolutionary puzzles. These rocks, which contain the fossil remains of organisms from a Cambrian sea buried by an ancient mudslide, are known collectively as the Burgess Shale (named for the Burgess Pass, where the quarry was found).

Discovered in 1909 by Charles Doolittle Walcott, head of the Smithsonian Institution at the time, the Burgess fossils remained in museum drawers until 1971, when Cambridge University professor Harry Whittington and two graduate students reexamined them.

Attaching a device known as a *camera lucida* to a microscope, the scientists used mirrors to project enlarged images of the fossils onto a flat surface. Then they carefully made illustrations of the ancient animal forms. In the process, they discovered that they could learn more from the large-scale drawings than they could from the actual tiny specimens.

The very fine-grained silt that surrounded the organisms helped preserve soft tissues in addition to bony structures. Thus, the remains of organisms that might have otherwise remained unknown were preserved. The variety of organisms found in the Burgess Shale is evidence of the explosion of life-forms that took place during the Cambrian period.

The Burgess organisms lived much as organisms do today. They lived in an ecosystem that included a wide range of animals, each with specialized organs for movement and feeding. Many of the organisms were ancestors of common sea creatures such as mollusks, segmented worms, and crustaceans. Whittington's team also discovered fossils of animals that were completely different from any inhabiting modern oceans.

What does this mean? The shale fossils reveal that the earliest multicellular animals included a much broader range of body plans than expected—some so different that they cannot be classified into any group of modern animals.

These conclusions about Cambrian life-forms are supported by recent discoveries in China, Australia, and Greenland. Scientists have unearthed similarly diverse and complex fossils dating back to the beginning of the Cambrian period, 550 million years ago. Thus, it appears that a high level of diversity and complexity developed in animals in a relatively short span of geologic time.

One of the most exciting Burgess finds was the discovery of the 5 cm (2 in.) long Pikaia gracilens. *It is a very early representative of phylum Chordata. Organizationally, it resembles the simple living chordate* Amphioxus.

THEORIES OF EVOLUTION

The word evolution *refers to an orderly succession of changes. Biological evolution is the change of populations of organisms over generations. Early scientists noticed that new life-forms appeared to be modifications of fossil forms found in the same geographical area. This strongly implied that a natural modification process was at work.*

SECTION

15-2

OBJECTIVES

▲

Define *evolution*.

●

Explain Lamarck's theory of evolution, and describe how it was flawed.

■

List some of the evidence that led Darwin to his idea of how species might change over time.

◆

Explain Darwin's two major theories.

LAMARCK'S EXPLANATION

The French scientist Jean Baptiste de Lamarck (1744–1829) was one of the first to propose a unifying hypothesis of species modification. Lamarck proposed that similar species descended from a common (the same) ancestor—thus, living species were descended from similar extinct species evident in the fossil record. Lamarck cataloged an extensive collection of invertebrates (animals without a backbone), and he related fossil forms to living animals based on their similar appearance.

To explain how species change, he hypothesized that acquired traits were passed on to offspring. An **acquired trait** is one that is not determined by genes. Instead, it arises during an organism's lifetime as a result of the organism's experience or behavior.

Lamarck made a study of the habits and physiology of shore birds, and he believed that the webbed foot of water birds resulted from repeated stretching of the membrane between the toes. Over time, Lamarck said, this produced a broad webbed foot, a trait that would be preserved by reproduction. In other words, offspring of parents who had acquired webbed feet would have webbed feet as well. In the same way, an organism that did not use some part of its anatomy, such as a tail, would produce offspring with a smaller version of that body part.

Lamarck's hypotheses were fiercely attacked, primarily by scientists who rejected the idea of evolution itself. Although Lamarck's hypothesis of the passage of acquired traits was easily disproved, his work was an important forerunner of modern evolutionary theory. Lamarck was the first to clearly state that types of organisms change over time and that new types of organisms are modified descendants of older types. This idea was presented more convincingly more than 50 years later by Charles Darwin.

FIGURE 15-3

Charles Darwin began the work that would lead to his theory of evolution when he was a young man.

Quick Lab

Analyzing Relationships

Materials set of hardware items, paper, pencil

Procedure

1. Find one object that has characteristics common to all the objects, and place it at the middle of the paper near the bottom. This is the "common ancestor" of all the hardware.

2. Separate the remaining objects into two groups that have a single, basic difference.

3. Form two branches from the common ancestor by arranging the members of each group on the paper. Each of the two branches may then form smaller branches in ascending order of complexity.

4. Draw lines connecting each object to the one above and below it, forming a tree.

Analysis What characteristic did the common ancestor have that made it similar to both groups? What criteria did you use to separate the two groups? What was the trend in the evolution of each group?

THE BEGINNING OF MODERN EVOLUTIONARY THOUGHT

In the mid-1800s, both Charles Darwin (1809–1882) and Alfred Wallace (1823–1913) independently proposed the hypothesis that species were modified by natural selection. In the process of **natural selection,** organisms best suited to their environment reproduce more successfully than other organisms. Thus, over generations, the proportion of organisms with favorable traits increases in a **population,** or interbreeding single-species group. While Darwin and Wallace announced their hypotheses at the same time, Darwin's name became more associated with evolutionary theory after his book *The Origin of Species* was published in 1859.

Charles Darwin

Darwin, shown as a young man in Figure 15-3, was born in 1809, the son of wealthy British physician. Darwin attended medical school at the University of Edinburgh and then enrolled at Cambridge University to study for the clergy. He had little enthusiasm for either course of study. At Cambridge University, a friendship with a professor of botany, John Henslow, awakened Darwin's interest in natural history. In 1831, Darwin sailed on the ship H.M.S. *Beagle.* The *Beagle* was chartered for a five-year mapping and collecting expedition to South America and the South Pacific. Darwin assumed the post of ship naturalist, which required that he collect specimens and keep careful records of his observations.

Voyage of the Beagle

Soon after leaving England, Darwin read a geology book that had been given to him by Henslow. This book, *Principles of Geology,* by Charles Lyell, emphasized the great age of Earth and the principles of **uniformitarianism** (YOON-uh-FORM-uh-TER-ee-uhn-IZ-uhm). The principles of uniformitarianism hold that the geological structure of Earth resulted from cycles of observable processes and that these same processes operate continuously through time. For example, silt is deposited by modern rivers in the same way it was deposited by ancient rivers. Modern volcanoes spew forth lava and ash in the same way those on early Earth did. Lyell's book spurred Darwin's interest in the study of geology, and it allowed him to consider the possibility that the modification of environments might be a very slow process requiring long periods of time. In Chile, Darwin observed the results of an earthquake. The land around a harbor had been lifted more than a meter (3.3 ft). In the nearby Andes Mountains, Darwin observed fossil shells of marine organisms in rock beds about 4,300 m (14,100 ft) above sea level. These observations convinced Darwin that Lyell was correct in saying that geologic changes, such as the elevation of the Andes, required many millions of years. Darwin reasoned that the formation of mountain ranges would slowly change habitats, requiring organisms that

North America

Europe

Asia

Atlantic
Ocean

Pacific
Ocean

Africa

Indian
Ocean

South
America

Galápagos
Islands

Australia

H.M.S. *Beagle*

lived there to adapt to these changes. Furthermore, he reasoned that the pace of those adaptations would be so slow with respect to a human life span that they would be difficult to detect.

During the *Beagle*'s five-year trip, as shown in Figure 15-4, Darwin often left the ship at one port and was picked up months later at another port. During his time on land, Darwin trekked hundreds of kilometers through unmapped regions. He collected many different types of fossils and observed thousands of species of organisms.

Analysis of Darwin's Data

When Darwin returned to England, in October 1836, his collections from the voyage were praised by experts from the scientific community. A bird specialist who studied Darwin's collection of finches from the Galápagos Islands reported that Darwin had collected 13 similar but separate species of finches. Each finch species has a distinctive bill that is specialized for a particular food source. Despite the bill differences, the overwhelming similarities of the Galápagos finches implied that the finches shared a recent common ancestor, meaning they descended from a single species. Over a period of years after returning to England, Darwin analyzed his data. Darwin considered the possibility that all of the islands' finches had descended from a few birds or even a single female that had been blown off course from South America, 1,000 km (620 mi) to the east. Because the Galápagos are geologically young islands (they are about 5 million years old), Darwin assumed that the offspring of the original finches had been adapting to different environments and food sources for a relatively short time. Darwin reasoned, therefore, that over many millions of years, many large differences could accumulate between species.

FIGURE 15-4

Darwin spent five years as the ship naturalist on the H.M.S. *Beagle* as the ship sailed around the world.

Publication of *The Origin of Species*

Darwin was forced to abandon his leisurely approach to the review and testing of his hypothesis on natural selection in 1858, when he was approached by a young naturalist, Alfred Wallace. Wallace had been collecting specimens in South America and the Malay Archipelago. Wallace asked Darwin to review his paper outlining the process of evolution by natural selection. This prompted Darwin to finally publish his own work on evolution by natural selection, which he had spent 21 years refining. Darwin's and Wallace's hypotheses were presented side by side to the Linnaean Society of London in 1858. The following year, Darwin published his now-famous book on the subject, *On the Origin of Species by Means of Natural Selection*, commonly known as *The Origin of Species*.

DARWIN'S THEORIES

Darwin's ideas about evolution and natural selection are summed up in two theories. In his first theory, Darwin stated that evolution, which is defined as descent with modification, occurs. In his second theory, Darwin proposed that a process he called natural selection causes evolution.

Descent with Modification

Darwin's first theory—*descent with modification*—states that the newer forms appearing in the fossil record are actually the modified descendants of older species. Recall that Lamarck had made the same argument. But Darwin's theory goes further. Darwin inferred that *all* species had descended from one or a few original types of life. Darwin thought that the different species of finches on the Galápagos Islands, shown in Figure 15-5, had descended from a recent common ancestor. He then reasoned that all living things probably had

FIGURE 15-5

The beaks of the Galápagos finches are adapted to different food sources. The beak of the large ground finch, *Geospiza magnirostris,* center, is suited to cracking the seeds that compose the bird's diet. The narrower beaks of the woodpecker finch, *Camarynchus pallidus,* top left, and the warbler finch, *Certhidea olivacea,* bottom right, are specialized for capturing insects.

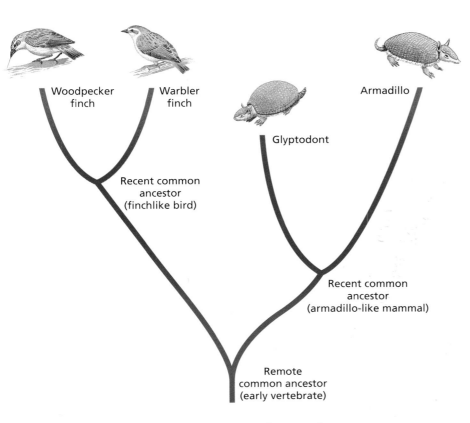

Woodpecker finch

Warbler finch

Glyptodont

Armadillo

Recent common ancestor (finchlike bird)

Recent common ancestor (armadillo-like mammal)

Remote common ancestor (early vertebrate)

FIGURE 15-6

Darwin reasoned that if the Galápagos finches were similar to each other because of recent common ancestry, then organisms that are more dissimilar, such as finches and armadillos, share a more remote ancestor.

likewise descended from one, or perhaps a few, remote common ancestors that lived a very long time ago. For example, all vertebrates, such as the birds and mammals shown in Figure 15-6, probably descended from a vertebrate that lived in the distant past. Bear in mind that the terms *recent ancestor* and *remote ancestor* are used in the context of geologic history—the span of time represented in Table 15-1—rather than in the context of a single human lifetime.

Darwin's first theory accounted for the fact that similar organisms arise in the same geographic location. Darwin's theory of evolution explained the observation that organisms give rise to others similar to themselves. Thus, it would be natural for modern kangaroos to evolve from a now-extinct ancestor very much like them.

Modification by Natural Selection

Darwin's second theory—*modification by natural selection*—states how evolution occurs. Darwin was heavily influenced by the English clergyman Thomas Malthus (1766–1834), who had published a thesis pointing out that populations (Malthus was referring to humans) have the potential of doubling and redoubling their numbers. Malthus proposed that the growth of human populations was limited by adverse conditions, such as war, disease, or a limited supply of resources.

Agreeing with Malthus's views, Darwin noted that although populations of all organisms have the potential to grow unchecked, most do not. He reasoned that the environment limits the growth of populations by increasing the rate of death or decreasing the rate of reproduction, or both.

Eco 🌲 **Connection**

Galápagos Islands

The exotic and fragile ecosystem of the Galápagos that fascinated Charles Darwin in the mid-1830s has been in danger since the discovery of the Galápagos in 1535. For 400 years, the islands were a favorite stopping place for pirates and whalers. Herman Melville, the author of *Moby Dick,* saw and wrote of the giants of the islands, the Galápagos tortoises, while on a whaling expedition in 1841. The tortoises, pictured in the opening photograph of this chapter, were a frequent target of sailors. The animals were valued as a meat source because they could live for long periods aboard ship with little or no food or water. Over the years, the tortoise population has been reduced from about 250,000 animals to about 15,000 animals.

Over the past 40 years, the government of Ecuador has taken steps to preserve and restore the Galápagos and their wildlife. The Charles Darwin Research Station conducts breeding programs for endangered animals and has bred and released several thousand tortoises, representing most of the 14 tortoise species found on the islands.

Darwin proposed that the environment may affect individual organisms in a population in different ways because individuals of a species are not identical. Some organisms have traits that make them better able to cope with their environment. Organisms that have a greater number of these favorable traits tend to leave more offspring than organisms with fewer beneficial traits. Darwin called the different degrees of successful reproduction among organisms in a population natural selection.

If a trait both increases the reproductive success of an organism *and* is inherited, then that trait will tend to be passed on to many offspring. A population of organisms **adapt** to their environment as their proportion of genes for favorable traits increases. The resulting change in the genetic makeup of a population is evolution. In an evolving population, a single organism's genetic contribution to the next generation is termed **fitness.** Thus, an individual with high fitness is well adapted to its environment and reproduces more successfully than an individual with low fitness.

Bear in mind that natural selection is not an active process. Organisms do not purposefully acquire traits that they need, although it may seem that this is true. The environment "selects" the traits that will increase in a population. The kinds of traits that are favorable depend on the demands of the environment. An organism may be able to run fast, or it may be strong or have coloring that acts as camouflage from predators. Traits that are favorable for some organisms in some environments are not necessarily favorable for all organisms or all environments. For example, the large body size of large mammals such as the elephant would not be beneficial to a species of flying birds if size prevented flight. A favorable trait is said to give the organism that has it an **adaptive advantage.**

Selection conditions change as the demands of the environment change. For example, a significant change in climate or available food can cause rapid evolutionary change as populations adapt to the change. If the environmental change is too extreme, however, populations cannot adapt quickly enough and they become extinct.

SECTION 15-2 REVIEW

1. What is an acquired characteristic? Do acquired characteristics change the genotype of an organism?

2. How did Lyell's book *Principles of Geology* help Darwin see that natural selection over many generations could explain species modification?

3. How many years have passed since the publication of *The Origin of Species*? Why is its publication still considered so important?

4. Do Darwin's theories of evolution by natural selection contradict the principles of biogeography? Why or why not?

5. What did Darwin think limits the growth of populations?

6. CRITICAL THINKING   If a favorable trait increases the life span of an organism without affecting reproductive success, does it contribute to evolution?

EVOLUTION IN PROCESS

Evolution is a continuous process. By examining genotypic and phenotypic evidence in modern organisms, we can see evidence that evolution has occurred. By considering species in relation to one another, we can also detect definite patterns of evolution.

EVIDENCE OF EVOLUTION

If organisms change through a process of gradual modifications, we should be able to see evidence of this process. Living things, in fact, display many different clues to their evolutionary history.

Homologous and Analogous Structures

It seems obvious that the beaks of the finches shown in Figure 15-5 derive from the same embryonic structure of each different species. Moreover, they are modifications of a feature found in an ancestor common to all birds. Similar features that originated in a shared ancestor are described as **homologous** (hoh-MAHL-uh-guhs) features.

Some examples of homologous features are not as obvious as the beaks of birds. Compare the forelimbs shown in Figure 15-7. Although the limbs look strikingly different and vary greatly in function, they are very similar in skeletal structure, and they derive from the same structures in the embryo. Homologous features can result from modifications that change an original feature

OBJECTIVES

▲

Describe the difference between homologous, analogous, and vestigial structures.

●

Tell how similarities in macromolecules and embryos of different species suggest a relationship between them.

■

Explain the difference between coevolution, and divergent and convergent evolution.

FIGURE 15-7

The forelimbs of the penguin, alligator, bat, and human all derive from the same embryological structures.

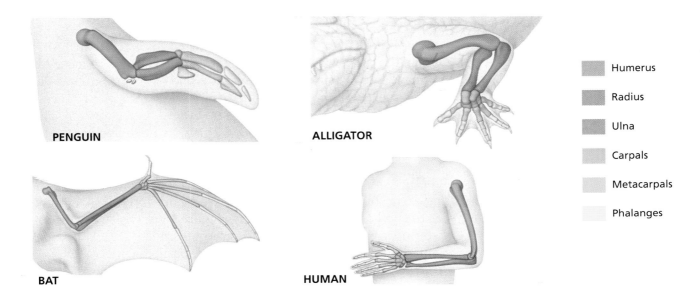

PENGUIN

ALLIGATOR

BAT

HUMAN

Humerus

Radius

Ulna

Carpals

Metacarpals

Phalanges

FIGURE 15-8

The wings of the hummingbird, *Selasphorus rufus*, top, and the humming moth, *Hemaris thysbe,* bottom, serve similar functions, but they differ in structure and derive from different embryological structures.

to two extremely different types, such as a wing and an arm. The presence of homologous features in different species indicates that the species shared a fairly recent common ancestor.

Analogous (uh-NAL-uh-guhs) features serve identical functions, and they look somewhat alike. They have very different embryological development, however, and may be very different in internal anatomy. Figure 15-8 shows a hummingbird and a humming moth. Both organisms can hover to feed on the sugar-rich nectar from flowers. There is no anatomical or embryological similarity, however, between their wings. Birds and insects differ greatly in anatomy and in embryological development. Although birds and insects do share a very remote ancestor, we can infer that their wings evolved independently and differently in more-recent ancestors of each animal.

Vestigial Structures

Many organisms have features that seem to serve no useful function. For example, humans have a tailbone at the end of the spine that is of no apparent use. The human appendix, a small, fingerlike projection from the intestine, also has no known function. Some snakes have tiny pelvic bones and limb bones. Whales also have pelvic bones, along with a four-chambered stomach like that of a cow.

These apparently useless features are said to be vestigial. **Vestigial** (ves-TIJ-ee-uhl) features were useful to an ancestor, but they are not useful to the modern organism that has them. The vestigial tailbone in humans is homologous to the functional tails of other vertebrate species. A vestigial feature in a modern organism is evidence that the structure *was* functional in some ancestor of the modern organism. Moreover, an organism with a vestigial feature probably shares common ancestry with an organism that has a functional version of the same feature.

So what sort of evolutionary clues can vestigial features provide? Consider that normal sperm whales, like all whales, have small pelvic bones but no hind legs. A very small percentage of sperm whales, however, have vestigial leg bones, and some sperm whales even have bone-supported bumps protruding from their body.

Whales probably are descended from an ancestor that lived on land. In the whales' genome, many of the genes needed to make hind legs have been **conserved,** or have remained unchanged. In normal whales, the genes for hind legs are turned off. In rare cases, however, the genes are partially turned on, and vestigial hind legs form. Thus, whales and other living things may display their evolutionary history in the usually unexpressed genes they carry.

Similarities in Embryology

The early stages of different vertebrate embryos are strikingly similar to each other, as you can see in Figure 15-9. The German zoologist Ernst Haeckel (1834–1919), who was also struck by these similarities, declared that "ontogeny recapitulates phylogeny." This statement can be translated to "embryological development repeats evolutionary history." We now know that this is a bit of an exaggeration. For example, during no stage of development does a gorilla look like an adult fish. In the early stages of development, all vertebrate embryos are similar, but those similarities fade as development proceeds. Nevertheless, the similarities in early embryonic stages of vertebrates can be taken as yet another indication that vertebrates share a common ancestry.

FISH   RABBIT   GORILLA

FIGURE 15-9

This is a modernized version of Haeckel's drawings of embryological stages in different species. Although modern embryologists have discovered that Haeckel exaggerated some features in his drawings, it is true that early embryos of many different vertebrate species look remarkably similar.

Similarities in Macromolecules

Darwin hypothesized that more-similar forms of organisms have a more recent common ancestor than do less-similar forms. He arrived at this hypothesis by observing anatomical features only. He could not have known how true this rule would prove at the molecular level—for homologous proteins, as well as RNA and DNA molecules. For example, many species have the red-blood-cell protein, hemoglobin. The amino acid sequences in the hemoglobin molecules of different species are similar, but not identical. The amino acid sequences in human hemoglobin and gorilla hemoglobin differ by one amino acid, while the hemoglobin molecules of humans and frogs differ by 67 amino acids. The number of amino acid differences in homologous proteins of two species is proportional to the length of time that has passed since the two species shared a common ancestor. Thus, the more-similar the homologous proteins are in different species, the more closely related the species are thought to be. Information provided by molecular biology can confirm the evolutionary histories suggested by fossils and anatomy.

PATTERNS OF EVOLUTION

There are several ways that species can change to adapt to their habitats. The pattern and speed of evolutionary change result from the changing requirements of the environment.

Coevolution

The change of two or more species in close association with each other is called **coevolution.** Predators and their prey sometimes co-evolve, parasites and their hosts often coevolve, and plant-eating animals and the plants they feed on also coevolve. One example of coevolution is plants and the animals that pollinate them.

In tropical regions, some species of bats feed on the nectar of flowers, as shown in Figure 15-10. These bats have a slender muzzle and a long tongue with a brushlike tip, which aid them in feeding. The fur on the bat's face and neck picks up pollen, which the bat takes to the next flower. Flowers that have coevolved with these bats are light in color, enabling the bats, which are active at night, to easily locate them. The flowers also have a fruity odor that is attractive to bats.

FIGURE 15-10

Some species of bats, such as this long-nosed fruit bat, have coevolved with the flowers they feed on.

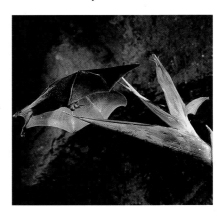

Convergent Evolution

Sometimes organisms that appear to be very similar, such as a shark and a porpoise, are not closely related at all. This kind of similarity is the result of **convergent evolution.** Convergent evolution occurs when the environment selects similar phenotypes, even though the ancestral types were quite different from each other. Sharks and porpoises have very different origins. Sharks are fishes, and porpoises are mammals. Many features of these animals are similar, however, and have been selected by the environment they share. Their large, streamlined bodies and even their fins resemble each other. Analogous structures, such as similar fins in very different animals, are associated with convergent evolution.

Divergent Evolution

In **divergent evolution,** two or more related populations or species become more and more dissimilar. Divergence is nearly always a response to differing habitats, and it can ultimately result in new species.

One important type of divergent evolution is adaptive radiation. In **adaptive radiation,** many related species evolve from a single ancestral species. The Galápagos finches are an example of adaptive radiation. They diverged in response to the availability of different types of food in their different habitats.

Sometimes the process of divergence can be sped up artificially, through **artificial selection.** All domestic dogs are the same species, *Canis familiaris.* Dogs have been bred by humans for certain phenotypic characteristics, resulting in different breeds with different traits, as you can see in Figure 15-11. Thus, the process of divergent evolution in this species has sped up many times beyond what could have occurred in nature. Divergent evolution operating over very long periods of time has produced the seemingly endless variety of species alive today.

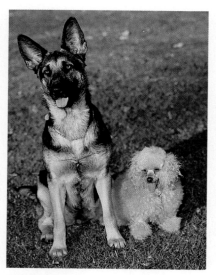

FIGURE 15-11

The rate of divergent evolution among dogs has been increased by artificial selection by humans.

SECTION 15-3 REVIEW

1. The mouthparts of an adult horsefly are modified for biting. The mouthparts of a mosquito are modified for piercing skin and sucking blood. Are the mouthparts of the two species homologous or analogous? Explain your answer.

2. Birds and bees have wings. Are their wings homologous features or analogous features? Explain your answer.

3. The hemoglobin of humans is nearly identical to that of a gorilla. What does this suggest about the length of time that has passed since the last common ancestor of humans and gorillas lived?

4. Fruit fly embryos and frog embryos differ from each other more than frog embryos and human embryos do. What does this tell us about how the three species are related?

5. Are vestigial structures acted on by natural selection?

6. **CRITICAL THINKING** Some monarch butterflies contain chemicals that are toxic to birds. Another species of butterfly, the viceroy, has some protection from predation because it closely resembles the monarch. What pattern of evolution is illustrated by this example?

CHAPTER 15 REVIEW

SUMMARY/VOCABULARY

 15-1
- A fossil is a trace of a long-dead organism.
- The law of superposition states that new geologic strata are deposited on top of older strata.
- The history of Earth and its life-forms can be inferred by examining the fossil record.

- The fossil record shows that new life-forms have arisen continually during the history of life on Earth.
- The study of biogeography shows that organisms arise in areas where similar, now-extinct organisms once lived.

Vocabulary

absolute age (281)	extinct (281)	mass extinction (281)	sediment (279)
biogeography (281)	fossil (279)	mold (279)	stratum (280)
cast (279)	law of superposition (280)	relative age (281)	

 15-2
- Lamarck proposed that species evolve over time. He incorrectly hypothesized that species modification is the result of acquired characteristics and that these characteristics can be passed on to offspring.
- Charles Darwin began his work on evolution when he was employed as a naturalist for a voyage of the H.M.S. *Beagle*.
- Darwin was influenced by Charles Lyell, who proposed the principles of uniformitarianism, which hold that the structure of Earth results from cycles of observable processes.

- Darwin found evidence of species modification in both modern and extinct species.
- Darwin hypothesized that related species, such as the Galápagos finches, descended from a common ancestor.
- Darwin wrote *The Origin of Species,* in which he proposed that natural selection is the principal driving force behind evolution.
- A population of organisms adapt to their environment as their proportion of genes for favorable traits increases.
- Evolution is the change in the genetic makeup of a population over generations.

Vocabulary

acquired trait (283)	adaptive advantage (288)	natural selection (284)	uniformitarianism (284)
adapt (288)	fitness (288)	population (284)	

 15-3
- Evidence supporting evolution is found in the body structures of living organisms. Homologous structures have a common evolutionary origin. Analogous structures are similar in function but have different evolutionary origins.
- A species with a vestigial structure probably shares evolutionary origins with a species that has a functional form of the structure.
- Similar embryological development among species indicates a common evolutionary history.

- Similarity in macromolecules such as RNA, DNA, and proteins indicates a common evolutionary history.
- In coevolution, two or more closely associated species, such as a predator and its prey, change in response to each other.
- In convergent evolution, organisms that are not closely related resemble each other because they have responded to similar environments.
- In divergent evolution, related populations become less similar as they respond to different environments. Adaptive radiation is a type of divergent evolution.

Vocabulary

adaptive radiation (292)	coevolution (291)	convergent evolution (292)	homologous (289)
analogous (290)	conserve (290)	divergent evolution (292)	vestigial (290)
artificial selection (292)			

EVOLUTION: EVIDENCE AND THEORY **293**

REVIEW

Vocabulary

1. What is the difference between a mold and a cast?
2. Explain the relationship between geologic strata and relative age.
3. What is the difference between an acquired trait and a genetic trait?
4. Distinguish between homologous structures and analogous structures.
5. How are divergent evolution and adaptive radiation related?

Multiple Choice

6. Lamarck's explanation for the modification of species depended on (a) inheritance of acquired characteristics (b) convergent evolution (c) the law of superposition (d) natural selection.
7. The idea that processes occurring now on Earth are much the same as those that occurred long ago is called (a) uniformitarianism (b) relativism (c) evolutionism (d) convergent evolution.
8. The observation that organisms arise in locations where similar, extinct organisms lived is referred to as (a) superposition (b) biogeography (c) uniformitarianism (d) evolution.
9. The similarities in the Galápagos finches implied (a) coevolution (b) convergent evolution (c) adaptive radiation (d) descent from different remote ancestors.
10. Difference in reproductive success is (a) an acquired trait (b) adaptive radiation (c) natural selection (d) coevolution.
11. Great similarity between species implies (a) recent common ancestry (b) remote common ancestry (c) successful reproduction (d) extinction.
12. Features that were useful in ancestors but are no longer useful are called (a) analogous features (b) vestigial features (c) homologous features (d) favorable traits.
13. Similar features in different species that originated in a shared ancestor are called (a) vestigial features (b) analogous features (c) homologous features (d) unexpressed genes.

14. A hummingbird and a humming moth have a number of superficial features in common with each other. This is an example of (a) divergent evolution (b) coevolution (c) convergent evolution (d) superposition.
15. The phylogenetic tree below implies that modern finches and armadillos (a) are unrelated (b) share a remote common ancestor (c) share a recent common ancestor (d) did not evolve from older forms of life.

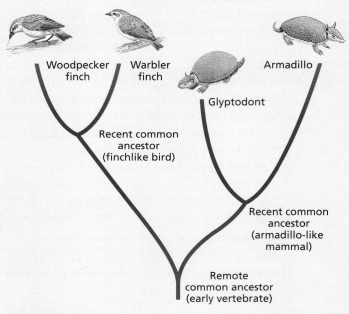

Woodpecker finch   Warbler finch   Glyptodont   Armadillo

Recent common ancestor (finchlike bird)

Recent common ancestor (armadillo-like mammal)

Remote common ancestor (early vertebrate)

Short Answer

16. What led Hooke to argue that fossils had once been living organisms?
17. What did Malthus observe about the potential for growth in populations?
18. How was Darwin's theory of evolution different from Lamarck's theory?
19. What does the existence of very similar embryological forms among species imply?
20. Why are some traits favorable for some species and not for others?
21. What pattern of evolution is demonstrated by the Galápagos finches?
22. What is an example of a vestigial structure in humans?
23. How does the structure of macromolecules, such as proteins, act as an index of relatedness between species?
24. What kind of evolution is demonstrated by nectar-feeding bats and the flowers they feed on?

25. Could a characteristic that is not controlled by genetics be selected by the environment? Would this characteristic contribute to the evolution of the organism that has it?

CRITICAL THINKING

1. In recent years, paleontologists have claimed that in some cases the evolution of a new species occurs quite suddenly—in less than a thousand years. Darwin stated that evolution was a gradual process. What effect does generation time have on evolution rate?

2. The process of natural selection throughout the history of life on Earth has resulted in the success of some species and the extinction of other species. Why has natural selection not resulted in the existence of a single best-adapted species?

3. Many vestigial traits, such as the human tailbone, seem to be largely neutral, that is, neither beneficial nor harmful. The appendix is an example of a vestigial structure in humans. How might having an appendix be harmful to humans?

4. The graph below shows the diversity of different groups of animals over time. The width of the colored-in areas is proportional to the number of different types of bivalves, mammals, roundworms, and trilobites that were alive during different eras. Use the graph to answer the following questions:
a. Which group was the last to evolve?
b. Which group is or was the most diverse? The least diverse?
c. Which group diversified rapidly soon after evolving?
d. Which group(s) became extinct?
e. Which groups did not live at the same time?

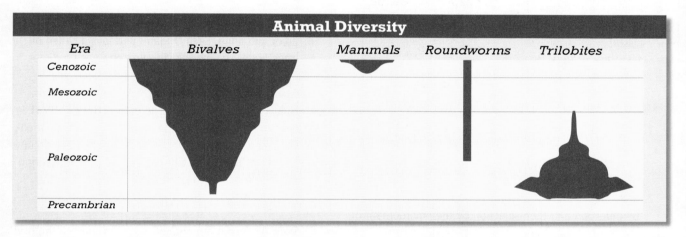

Animal Diversity

Era	Bivalves	Mammals	Roundworms	Trilobites
Cenozoic				
Mesozoic				
Paleozoic				
Precambrian				

EXTENSION

1. Read "A Dinosaur Named Sue" in *National Geographic,* June 1999, on page 47, and answer the following questions: What technique was used to examine the inside of the skull of the 67-million-year-old *Tyrannosaurus rex* fossil? How many *T. rex* fossils have ever been discovered, and what makes Sue unique? When and where was Sue discovered, and what was the principal reason Sue's ownership was in question?

2. Though he never became as famous as Charles Darwin, Alfred Wallace made many important contributions to the field of biology in the late nineteenth and early twentieth centuries. Use biographies, autobiographies, and an encyclopedia to find information on the life of Alfred Wallace. Write a short report highlighting Wallace's contributions to biology.

Modeling Selection

OBJECTIVES

- Simulate the generation of variation.
- Model the selection of favorable traits in new generations.

PROCESS SKILLS

- observing
- testing
- measuring

MATERIALS

- construction paper
- cellophane tape
- soda straws
- penny, or other coin
- six-sided die
- scissors
- meterstick or tape measure
- metric ruler

Background

1. The Egyptian Origami Bird *(Avis papyrus)* lives in arid regions of North Africa. Only the birds that can fly the long distances between oases live long enough to breed successfully.
2. Successful evolution requires the generation of variety by mutation and then selection by the environment of the most-fit individuals.

PART A Parental Generation

1. First cut two strips of paper, 2 cm × 20 cm each. Make a loop with one strip of paper, overlapping the paper 1 cm, and tape the loop closed. Repeat for the other strip. Tape one loop 3 cm from each end of the straw, as shown in the figure at the top of the next column. Mark the front end of the bird with a felt-tip marker. This bird will represent the parental generation.
2. In your lab report, prepare a data table like the one shown on the facing page.
3. Test how far your bird can fly by releasing it with a gentle overhand pitch. Test the bird twice. Then record the bird's average flight distance in your data table.

PART B F₁ Generation

4. Breed offspring. Each Origami Bird lays a clutch of three eggs. Assume that the first egg has no mutations. It is a clone of the parent.
5. Assume that the other two chicks have mutations. Follow the steps below to determine the effects of each mutation. Record the mutations and the dimensions of each offspring in your data table. The circumference of the wings can be calculated by measuring the length of the strips of paper used to form the wings and subtracting 1 cm for the overlap.

Step A A coin flip determines which part of the bird is affected by the mutation.
Heads = anterior (front)
Tails = posterior (back)

Step B A die throw determines how the mutation affects the wing.

 (1) = The wing position changes 1 cm toward the end of the straw.

 (2) = The wing position changes 1 cm toward the middle of the straw.

 (3) = The circumference of the wing increases 2 cm.

(4) = The circumference of the wing decreases 2 cm.

 (5) = The width of the wing increases 1 cm.

 (6) = The width of the wing decreases 1 cm.

Step C A mutation that results in a wing falling off or a wing with a circumference smaller than that of the straw is lethal. If you get a lethal mutation, disregard it and breed another chick.

6. Test the birds. Release each bird with a gentle overhand pitch. It is important to release the birds as uniformly as possible. Test each bird at least twice.

7. The most successful bird is the one that flies the farthest. Record the flight distance of each offspring bird in your data table.

PART C F₂ Generation

8. Assume that the most successful bird in the F₁ generation is the sole parent of the next (F₂) generation. Continue to breed, test, and record data for 10 generations.

9. Clean up your materials before leaving the lab.

Analysis and Conclusions

1. Did your selection process result in birds that fly better?
2. Describe two aspects of this investigation that model evolution of biological organisms.
3. Your most successful bird has a different lineage from the most successful bird of your neighboring groups. Compare your winning bird with those of your neighbors. How does it differ?
4. What might happen to your last bird if the environmental conditions change?
5. How might this lab help explain the observations Darwin made about finches on the Galápagos Islands?

Further Inquiry

A flock of Origami Birds is blown off the mainland and onto a very small island. These birds face little danger on the ground, but they experience significant risk when flying because they can be blown off the island. Birds that cannot fly at all are most likely to survive and reproduce. Continue the experiment for several generations, selecting birds that can't fly.

Generation	Coin flip (heads or tails)	Die throw (1–6)	Measurements of most successful offspring			Distance flown
Parental	not applicable	not applicable	anterior wing	width ___2___ cm circumference ___19___ cm		_____ m
			posterior wing	width ___2___ cm circumference ___19___ cm		
			anterior wing position posterior wing position	from front ___3___ cm from back ___3___ cm		
F₁			anterior wing	width _____ cm circumference _____ cm		_____ m
			posterior wing	width _____ cm circumference _____ cm		
			anterior wing position posterior wing position	from front _____ cm from back _____ cm		
F₂			anterior wing	width _____ cm circumference _____ cm		_____ m
			posterior wing	width _____ cm circumference _____ cm		
			anterior wing position posterior wing position	from front _____ cm from back _____ cm		

TABLE A *MUTATIONS AMONG OFFSPRING*

THE EVOLUTION OF POPULATIONS AND SPECIATION

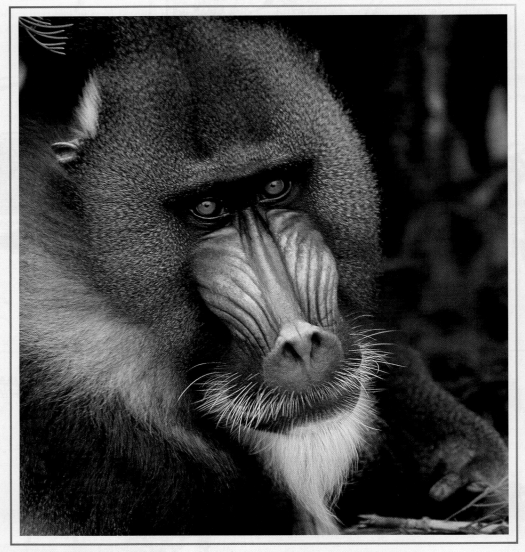

Sexual selection, which is one variation of natural selection, influences the development of extreme phenotypic traits, particularly in males. The vibrant red stripe on the blue muzzle of this male mandrill baboon, Mandrillus sphinx, *does not appear in females.*

FOCUS CONCEPT: *Reproduction and Inheritance*

As you read, pay attention to the steps that lead to the formation of new species.

16-1 *Genetic Equilibrium*

16-2 *Disruption of Genetic Equilibrium*

16-3 *Formation of Species*

GENETIC EQUILIBRIUM

By the time of Darwin's death, in 1882, the idea of evolution by natural selection had gained wide acceptance among scientists. But with the birth of the field of genetics in the early 1900s, spurred by the rediscovery of Mendel's work on the mechanics of inheritance, many questions about evolution and natural selection resurfaced.

SECTION

16-1

OBJECTIVES

▲

Explain the importance of the bell curve to population genetics.

●

Describe two causes of genotypic variation in a population.

■

Explain how to compute allele frequency and phenotype frequency.

◆

Explain Hardy-Weinberg genetic equilibrium.

VARIATION OF TRAITS IN A POPULATION

Population genetics is the study of evolution from a genetic point of view. Evolution is a gradual change in the genetic material of a population. Recall from Chapter 15 that a population consists of a collection of individuals of the same species that routinely interbreed. Populations are important to the study of evolution because a population is the smallest unit in which evolution occurs.

Within a population, individuals may vary in observable traits. For example, fish of a single species in a pond may vary in size. Biologists often study variation in a trait by measuring that trait in a large sample. Figure 16-1 shows a common result of such measurements. It is a graph of the frequency of lengths in a population of mature fish. Because the shape of the curve looks like a bell, it is called a **bell curve.** The bell curve shows that while a few fish in this population are extremely short and a few are extremely long, most are of average length. In nature, many quantitative traits in a population—such as height and weight—tend to show variation that follows a bell curve pattern.

🖅 internet**connect**

SC*L*INKS
NSTA

TOPIC: Population genetics
GO TO: www.scilinks.org
KEYWORD: HM299

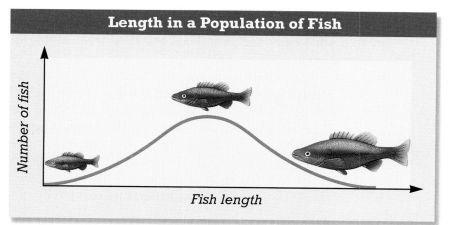

Length in a Population of Fish

Number of fish

Fish length

FIGURE 16-1

A bell curve illustrates that most members of a population have similar values for a given, measurable trait. Only a few individuals display extreme variations of the trait.

FIGURE 16-2

Many varied but similar phenotypes occur within families because members of a family share some alleles but not others.

Causes of Variation

What causes variation in traits? Some variations are influenced by environmental factors, such as the amount or quality of food available to an organism. Variation is often influenced by heredity. Usually, both factors play a role.

To consider variability, think about phenotypes within a single human family. Two parents, each with a distinct genotype, may produce several children. In the picture of the family in Figure 16-2, the two young-adult brothers are not identical to each other, even though their genotypes are combinations of the genotypes of the same two parents. Both young men resemble their father, though in different traits. The baby resembles his young father, his grandfather, and his uncle. Thus, these males representing three generations look similar but not identical. What causes the genes to vary? The answer lies in the way gametes are produced and in the way gametes fuse with each other.

Variations in genotype arise in three main ways. (1) *Mutation* results from flawed copies of individual genes. (2) *Recombination* is the reassociation of genes in a diploid individual. Recombination occurs during meiosis by the independent assortment of genes on nonhomologous, or different, chromosomes and by crossing-over between genes located on homologous chromosomes. (3) The *random fusion of gametes* is essentially a game of chance played by individual gametes. Often there are hundreds of millions of sperm involved in a mating. The one that actually fertilizes an egg is largely a matter of chance. These processes ensure that offspring are not carbon copies of their parents.

ALLELE FREQUENCIES AND THE GENE POOL

Population geneticists use the term **gene pool** to describe the total genetic information available in a population. It is easy to imagine genes for the next generation as existing in an imaginary pool. If you could inventory this pool and know the alleles that are present, then you could apply a simple set of rules based on probability theory to predict expected genotypes and their frequencies for the next generation.

Suppose, for example, that there are two forms of a hypothetical allele, *A* and *a*, in a set of 10 gametes. If half the gametes in the set (5 gametes) carry the allele *A*, we would say that the allele frequency of the *A* allele is 0.5, or 50 percent. **Allele frequency** is determined by dividing the number of a certain allele (five instances of the *A* allele) by the total number of alleles of all types in the population (10 gametes, each with either an *A* or an *a* allele). Remember that gametes are haploid and therefore carry only one form of the allele.

Predicting Phenotype

The population of four o'clock flowers, shown in Figure 16-3, illustrates how phenotype can change from generation to generation. Homozygous *RR* flowers are red. Homozygous *rr* flowers are white. Heterozygous *Rr* flowers are pink rather than red, as you might expect. These flowers show incomplete dominance for color, meaning heterozygotes show a trait that falls between the dominant trait and the recessive trait. Thus, homozygotes and heterozygotes can be easily identified by observing the phenotype.

Compare the parent generation with the offspring generation of the four o'clock flowers shown in Figure 16-3. There are equal numbers of plants with the *RR* genotype and the *Rr* genotype in the first generation. You can compute the phenotype frequencies from the figure. A **phenotype frequency** is equal to the number of individuals with a particular phenotype divided by the total number of individuals in the population. Phenotype frequencies in the first generation are 0.5 pink (4 pink plants out of a total of 8 plants), 0.5 red (4 red plants out of a total of 8 plants), and 0.0 white. Recall that allele frequencies are computed using the same principle: the allele frequencies in the first generation plants are 0.75 *R* (12 *R* alleles out of a total of 16 alleles) and 0.25 *r* (4 *r* alleles out of a total of 16 alleles).

We now can predict the genotypes and phenotypes of the second generation. If a male gamete encounters a female gamete, they will produce a new four o'clock plant whose genotype is the combination of both parental gametes. Thus, an *R* male gamete combined with an *R* female gamete will produce a plant with the *RR* genotype, which has red flowers. According to the laws of probability, the chance of an *R* gamete (a single allele) meeting with another *R* gamete is the arithmetic product of their allele frequencies in the gene pool:

frequency of *R* × frequency of *R* = frequency of *RR* pair
$$0.75 \times 0.75 = 0.5625$$

The expected frequency of the *rr* genotype is then

frequency of *r* × frequency of *r* = frequency of *rr* pair
$$0.25 \times 0.25 = 0.0625$$

FIGURE 16-3

Although the four o'clock flowers differ phenotypically from generation to generation, the allele frequencies remain the same.

FIRST GENERATION								PHENOTYPE FREQUENCY		ALLELE FREQUENCY
RR	*RR*	*Rr*	*Rr*	*RR*	*Rr*	*Rr*	*RR*	White 0 Pink 0.5 Red 0.5		*R* = 0.75 *r* = 0.25
SECOND GENERATION										
RR	*Rr*	*rr*	*RR*	*RR*	*Rr*	*RR*	*RR*	White 0.125 Pink 0.25 Red 0.625		*R* = 0.75 *r* = 0.25

The frequencies of all types expected in the second generation must add up to 1.0, just as fractions of a whole must add up to 1. Having established the probabilities of getting an *RR* and an *rr* plant, we can compute the expected frequency of the *Rr* plants. All those plants that are neither *RR* nor *rr* will be *Rr,* so

$$1.0 - \text{frequency of } RR - \text{frequency of } rr = \text{frequency of } Rr$$
$$1.0 - 0.5625 - 0.0625 = 0.375$$

FIGURE 16-4

This flock of mallards, *Anas platyrhynchos,* likely violates some or all of the conditions necessary for Hardy-Weinberg genetic equilibrium.

HARDY–WEINBERG GENETIC EQUILIBRIUM

It is clear from the example of the four o'clock flowers that phenotype frequencies can change dramatically from generation to generation. But what happens to allele frequencies over generations? A German physician, Wilhelm Weinberg (1862–1937), and a British mathematician, Godfrey Hardy (1877–1947), independently showed that allele frequencies in a population tend to remain the same from generation to generation unless acted on by outside influences. This is referred to as **Hardy-Weinberg genetic equilibrium,** and it is based on a set of assumptions about an ideal hypothetical population that is not evolving:

1. No net mutations occur; that is, allele frequencies do not change overall because of mutation.
2. Individuals neither enter nor leave the population.
3. The population is large (ideally, infinitely large).
4. Individuals mate randomly.
5. Selection does not occur.

Bear in mind that true genetic equilibrium is a theoretical state. Real populations, such as the flock of mallards in Figure 16-4, may violate conditions necessary for genetic equilibrium. By providing a model of how genetic equilibrium is maintained, Hardy-Weinberg genetic equilibrium allows us to consider what forces disrupt equilibrium.

Word Roots and Origins

equilibrium

from the Latin *aequilibris,* meaning "evenly balanced"

SECTION 16-1 REVIEW

1. How does the distribution of traits in a population look when displayed as a graph?

2. What is meant by the term *human gene pool*?

3. Fifty percent of an experimental population of four o'clock flowers are red-flowered plants, and 50 percent are white-flowered plants. What is the frequency of the *r* allele?

4. How is phenotype frequency computed?

5. What is genetic equilibrium?

6. **CRITICAL THINKING** Is it easier to analyze genotype by observing phenotype in organisms with complete dominance or in organisms with incomplete dominance?

THE FLAMINGO'S SMILE
REFLECTIONS IN NATURAL HISTORY
STEPHEN JAY GOULD

Opus 100

This excerpt is from the 100th in a regular series of columns by Stephen Jay Gould published in *Natural History* magazine. It was reprinted in a collection of Gould's columns called *The Flamingo's Smile.*

This passage describes some of the discoveries of Gould and fellow biologist David Woodruff as they began to study various species of Cerion, *a land snail of the West Indian islands.*

About fifteen names had been proposed for the *Cerions* of Grand Bahama and neighboring Abaco Island. After a week, Woodruff and I recognized that only two distinct populations inhabited these islands, each restricted to a definite and different environment. . . .

As Woodruff and I moved from island to island on Great Bahama Bank, we found the same pattern of two different populations, always in the same distinctive environments. On Little Bahama Bank, a dozen invalid names had fallen into this pattern. On Great Bahama Bank, they collapsed, literally by the hundred. About one-third of all *Cerion* "species" (close to 200 in all) turned out to be invalid names based on minor variants within this single pattern. We had reduced a chaos of improper names to a single, ecologically based order. . . .

Bahamian islands have two different kinds of coastlines. Major islands lie at the edge of their banks. The banks themselves are very shallow across their tops but plunge precipitously into deep ocean at their edges. Thus, bank-edge coasts abut the open ocean

and tend to be raw and windy. Dunes build along windy coasts and solidify eventually into rock (often mistakenly called "coral" by tourists). Bank-edge coasts are, therefore, usually rocky as well. By contrast, coastlines that border the interior parts of banks—I will call

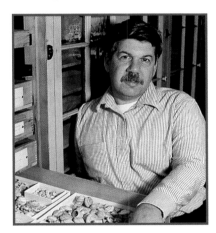

them bank-interior coasts—are surrounded by calm, shallow waters that extend for miles and do not promote the building of dunes. Bank-interior coasts, therefore, tend to be vegetated, low, and calm.

Woodruff and I found that bank-edge coasts in the northern Bahamas are invariably inhabited by thick-shelled, strongly ribbed, uniformly colored (white to darkish brown), relatively wide, and parallel-sided *Cerions.* To avoid writing most of the rest of this column in Latin, I will skip the formal names and refer to these forms as the

"ribby populations." Bank-interior coasts are the home of thin-shelled, ribless or weakly ribbed, variegated (usually with alternating blotches of white and brown), narrow, and barrel-shaped *Cerions*—the "mottled populations." (Mottled *Cerions* also live away from coasts in the centers of islands, while ribby *Cerions* are confined exclusively to bank-edge coasts.)

This pattern is so consistent and invariable that we can "map" hybrid zones even before we visit an island, simply by looking at a chart of bathymetry. Hybrid zones occur where bank-edge coasts meet bank-interior coasts. . . .

The distinction of mottled and ribby resolved nearly all the two hundred names previously given to *Cerions* from the northern Bahamas. . . .

Reading for Meaning
Make a chart comparing snails of the two snail populations Gould and Woodruff identified.

Read Further
Think about what you have learned about adaptations. What factors might have caused the differences between the two species of *Cerion* that Gould wrote about in this passage?

▲

List five conditions that can cause evolution to take place.

●

Give an example of how migration can affect evolution.

■

Define *genetic drift,* and tell how it affects endangered species.

◆

Contrast the effects of stabilizing, directional, and disruptive selection on variations in a trait over time.

▲

Give an example of sexual selection.

Word Roots and Origins

immigration

from the Latin *immigrare,* meaning "to go into"

DISRUPTION OF GENETIC EQUILIBRIUM

*E*volution is the change in a population's genetic material over generations, that is, a change of the population's allele frequencies or genotype frequencies. Any violation of the five conditions necessary for Hardy-Weinberg equilibrium can result in evolution.

MUTATION

The first requirement of genetic equilibrium is that allele frequencies not change overall because of mutations. Spontaneous mutations occur constantly, at a very low rate and under normal conditions. But if an organism is exposed to mutagens—mutation-causing agents such as radiation and certain chemicals—mutation rates can increase significantly. Mutations can affect genetic equilibrium by producing totally new alleles for a trait. Many, if not most, mutations are harmful. Because natural selection operates only on genes that are expressed, it is very slow to eliminate harmful recessive mutations. In the long run, however, beneficial mutations are a vital part of evolution.

MIGRATION

The second requirement of genetic equilibrium is that the population remain constant. **Immigration,** the movement of individuals into a population, and **emigration,** the movement of individuals out of a population, can change gene frequencies.

The behavioral ecology of some animal species encourages immigration and emigration. Common baboons live on the savannas of central Africa in social and breeding groups called troops. A troop is dominated by a few adult males, and it may have from 10 to 200 members. Females tend to remain with the troop they are born into, however, younger or less dominant males leave their birth troop, eventually joining another troop. This constant movement of male animals ensures gene flow. **Gene flow** is the process of genes moving from one population to another.

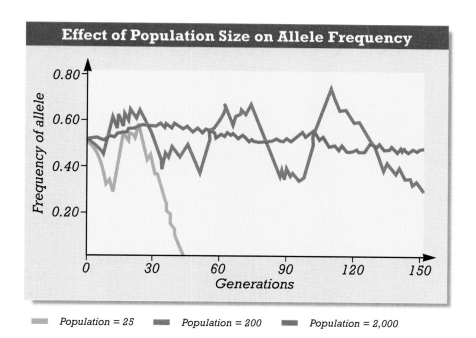

Effect of Population Size on Allele Frequency

Frequency of allele

0.80

0.60

0.40

0.20

0   30   60   90   120   150

Generations

Population = 25   Population = 200   Population = 2,000

FIGURE 16-5

Genetic drift is significant only in small and medium-sized populations. In a small population, a particular allele may disappear completely over a few generations. In a larger population, a particular allele may vary widely in frequency due to chance but still be present in enough individuals to be maintained in the population. In a much larger population, the frequency of a particular allele may vary slightly due to chance but remain relatively stable over generations.

GENETIC DRIFT

The third requirement of genetic equilibrium is the presence of a large population. The Hardy-Weinberg principle is based on the laws of probability, which do not necessarily hold for small and medium-sized populations. **Genetic drift** is the phenomenon by which allele frequencies in a population change as a result of random events, or chance. In small populations, the failure of even a single organism to reproduce can significantly disrupt the allele frequency of the population, as can greater-than-normal reproduction by an individual, resulting in genetic drift.

Figure 16-5 shows a graph of genetic drift in populations of three differing sizes. Small populations can undergo abrupt changes in allele frequencies, exhibiting a large degree of genetic drift, while large populations retain fairly stable allele frequencies, maintaining a small degree of genetic drift. In the smallest population shown in Figure 16-5, the frequency of the example allele reaches zero at about the 45th generation. If we assume that we started with two alleles for a trait, then only one allele is left and every individual is homozygous for the remaining allele. Once this happens, the population is in danger of becoming extinct because there is no variation for natural selection to act on. For example, a new disease could wipe out the entire population. This is why endangered species, like the northern elephant seal, *Mirounga angustirostris,* shown in Figure 16-6, remain in peril of extinction even if their numbers increase significantly from near-extinction.

FIGURE 16-6

Individuals of the once nearly extinct northern elephant seal, *Mirounga angustirostris,* have lost genetic variability—they are homozygous for all of their genes that have been tested. This result of genetic drift could cause extinction because it limits the species' ability to further evolve.

NONRANDOM MATING

The fourth requirement of genetic equilibrium is random matings, without regard to genetic makeup. Many species do not mate randomly. Mate selection is often influenced by geographic proximity, and this can result in mates with some degree of kinship. Matings of related individuals can amplify certain traits and can result in offspring with disorders caused by recessive genes, which, although rare, may be present in the genomes of related individuals.

In another example of nonrandom mating, individuals often select a mate that has similar physical characteristics and therefore probably has some similar genes. The selection of a mate based on similarity of characteristics is called **assortative mating.** While nonrandom mating can profoundly affect genotypes, that is, the *combinations* of alleles of a population, it does not affect overall allele frequencies.

NATURAL SELECTION

The fifth requirement of genetic equilibrium is the absence of natural selection. Natural selection is an ongoing process in nature, and it is the single most significant factor that disrupts genetic equilibrium. As you learned in Chapter 15, as a result of natural selection, some members of a population are more likely to contribute their genes to the next generation than are other members. Any of several broad types of natural selection—including stabilizing, directional, disruptive, and sexual—can cause evolution.

Stabilizing Selection

In **stabilizing selection,** individuals with the average form of a trait have the highest fitness. The average represents the optimum for most traits; extreme forms of most traits confer lower fitness on the individuals that have them. Consider a hypothetical species of lizard in which larger-than-average individuals might be more easily spotted, captured, and eaten by predators. On the other hand, lizards that are smaller than average might not be able to run fast enough to escape.

Figure 16-7a shows the effect of stabilizing selection on body size in these lizards. The red curve shows the initial variation in lizard size as a standard bell curve. The blue curve represents the variation in body size several generations after a new predator was introduced. This predator easily captured the large, visible lizards and the small, slower lizards. Thus, selection against these extreme body types reduced the size range of the lizards. Stabilizing selection is the most common kind of selection. It operates on most traits and results in very similar morphology between most members of a species.

(a)

Stabilizing Selection

Number of animals

Body size

(b)

Directional Selection

Number of animals

Tongue length

(c)

Disruptive Selection

Number of animals

Shell color

FIGURE 16-7

Stabilizing (a), directional (b), and disruptive (c) selection can all be illustrated as changes (shown in blue) of the normal bell curve (shown in red).

Directional Selection

In **directional selection,** individuals that display a more extreme form of a trait have greater fitness than individuals with an average form of the trait. Figure 16-7b shows the effects of directional selection on tongue length in anteaters. Anteaters feed by breaking open termite nests, extending their sticky tongue into the nest, and lapping up termites. Suppose that an area was invaded by a new species of termite that built very deep nests. Anteaters with long tongues could more effectively prey on these termites than could anteaters with short or average tongues. Thus, directional selection would act to direct the trait of tongue length away from the average and toward one extreme.

Disruptive Selection

In **disruptive selection,** individuals with either extreme variation of a trait have greater fitness than individuals with the average form of the trait. Figure 16-7c shows the effect of disruptive selection on shell color in marine animals called limpets. The shell color of limpets varies from pure white to dark tan. White-shelled limpets that are on rocks covered with goose barnacles, which are also white, are at an advantage. Birds that prey on limpets have a hard time distinguishing the white-shelled limpets from the goose barnacles. On bare, dark-colored rocks, dark-shelled limpets are at an advantage. Again, the limpet-eating birds have a hard time locating

FIGURE 16-8

Males sometimes display extreme traits, like the large tail of this peacock, *Pavo cristatus.* This trait is favorable if it attracts females and increases the reproductive fitness of the male.

the dark shells against the dark background. However, the birds easily spot limpets with shells of intermediate color, which are visible against both the white and dark backgrounds.

Sexual Selection

In many species of birds, the males are brightly colored and often heavily plumed, like the peacock shown in Figure 16-8. These elaborately decorated males are easy for predators to see. Why would natural selection work in favor of an organism being conspicuous to a predator? Females tend to choose the males they mate with based on certain traits. This is referred to as **sexual selection.** In order to leave offspring, a male must be selected by the female, and the peacock's gaudy plumage increases his chances of being selected. Extreme traits, such as heavy, brightly colored plumage, may give the female an indication of the quality of the male's genes. While survival to reproductive maturity is necessary, survival alone is not enough to further evolution. The genes of successful *reproducers,* rather than those of merely successful *survivors,* are amplified through natural selection.

SECTION 16-2 REVIEW

1. What is genetic drift?

2. Explain how mutation and immigration disrupt genetic equilibrium.

3. Compare and contrast stabilizing, directional, and disruptive selection.

4. What is sexual selection?

5. Name the five violations of the conditions necessary for Hardy-Weinberg genetic equilibrium that can cause evolution to occur.

6. CRITICAL THINKING Human newborns with either a very high or a very low birth weight are more likely to die in infancy. What type of selection does this seem to be?

FORMATION OF SPECIES

How many species of organisms exist on Earth today? Undiscovered species are so numerous that we have no accurate answer. For example, even small areas of tropical rain forests can contain thousands of species of plants, animals, and microorganisms. New species are discovered and others become extinct at an incredible rate. In this section, you will learn how one species can become two through a process called speciation.

OBJECTIVES

▲

Explain the difference between the morphological concept of species and the biological species concept.

●

Define *geographic isolation,* and explain how it can lead to speciation.

■

Name three kinds of reproductive isolation.

◆

Summarize the punctuated equilibrium hypothesis, and contrast it with the hypothesis of gradual change.

THE CONCEPT OF SPECIES

You have learned that existing species are essentially changed versions of older species. The process of species formation, **speciation** (SPEE-shee-AY-shun), results in many related populations of organisms. Some are very similar to their shared ancestral species, while other populations become quite different.

Morphological Concept of Species

For many years, scientists used the internal and external structure and appearance of an organism—its **morphology** (mor-FAHL-uh-jee)—as the chief criterion for classifying it as a species. Using the morphological concept of species, a species is defined primarily according to its structure and appearance. Because morphological characteristics are easy to observe, making species designations based on morphology proved convenient.

The morphological concept of species has limitations, however. There can be phenotypic differences among individuals in a single population. Notice, for example, the variation between the two red-tailed monkeys shown in Figure 16-9. To further complicate the matter, some organisms that appear different enough to belong to different species interbreed in the wild and produce fertile offspring. In response to the capacity of dissimilar organisms to reproduce, the biological species concept arose.

FIGURE 16-9

Individual red-tailed monkeys, *Cercopithecus ascanius,* can have different facial features.

(a)

(b)

FIGURE 16-10

Two types of pupfish that have limited ranges in the western United States are (a) *Cyprinodon macularius* and (b) *Cyprinodon nevadensis.*

The Biological Species Concept

According to the **biological species concept,** as proposed by German-born, American biologist Ernst Mayr (1904–), a species is a population of organisms that can successfully interbreed but cannot breed with other groups. While this definition is useful for living animals, the biological species concept does not provide a satisfactory definition for species of extinct organisms, whose reproductive compatibility cannot be tested. Nor is it useful for organisms that do not reproduce sexually. Thus, our modern definition of species includes components of both the morphological and biological species concepts. A species is a single type of organism. Members of a species are morphologically similar and can interbreed to produce fully fertile offspring. The many species alive today diverged from a smaller number of earlier species.

ISOLATING MECHANISMS

How do species give rise to other, different species? Speciation begins with isolation. In isolation, two parts of a formerly interbreeding population stop interbreeding. Two important types of isolation frequently drive speciation.

Geographic Isolation

Geographic isolation is the physical separation of members of a population. Populations may be physically separated when their original habitat becomes divided. A deep canyon could develop, a river could change course, or a drying climate in a valley could force surviving fragments of an original population into separate mountain ranges. Once the subpopulations become isolated, gene flow between them stops. Natural selection and genetic drift cause the two subpopulations to diverge, eventually making them incompatible for mating.

In pupfish, small freshwater fish shown in Figure 16-10, speciation following geographic isolation apparently took place in parts of the western United States, including the desert of Death Valley. Death Valley has a number of isolated ponds formed by springs. Each pond contains a species of fish that lives only in that one pond, but the fish species of various ponds in the area are quite similar.

How did these different populations of fish become isolated in Death Valley? Geologic evidence indicates that most of Death Valley was covered by a lake during the last ice age. When the ice age ended, the region became dry, and only small, spring-fed ponds remained. Members of a fish species that previously formed a single population in the lake may have become isolated in different ponds. The environments of the isolated ponds differ enough that the separate populations of fish diverged. Eventually, the fishes in the different ponds diverged enough to be considered separate species.

Reproductive Isolation

Sometimes groups of organisms within a population become genetically isolated without being geographically isolated. **Reproductive isolation** results from barriers to successful breeding between population groups in the same area. Reproductive isolation and the species formation that follows it may sometimes arise through disruptive selection. Remember that in disruptive selection, the two extremes of a trait in a given population are selected for and the organisms begin to diverge. Once successful mating is prevented between members of the two subpopulations, the effect is the same as what would have occurred if the two subpopulations had been geographically isolated. There are two broad types of reproductive isolation: **prezygotic** (pree-zie-GAHT-ik) **isolation,** which occurs *before* fertilization, and **postzygotic isolation,** which occurs *after* fertilization.

If two potentially interbreeding species mate and fertilization occurs, success is measured by the production of healthy, fully fertile offspring. But this may be prevented by one of several types of postzygotic isolation. The offspring of interbreeding species may not develop completely and may die early, or, if healthy, they may not be fertile. From an evolutionary standpoint, if death or sterility of offspring occurs, the parent organisms have wasted their gametes producing offspring that cannot, in turn, reproduce.

This situation favors prezygotic mechanisms, such as incompatible behavior, that reduce the chance of hybrid formation. For example, a mating call that is not recognized as such by a potential mate can contribute to isolation. Differences in mating times are another type of prezygotic isolation. Both mechanisms are in effect for the frogs shown in Figure 16-11. Their mating calls and peak mating times, as shown in the graph, differ, reducing the chance of interbreeding. As a result, the wood frog and the leopard frog are reproductively isolated. Though these two frogs interbreed in captivity, they do not interbreed where their ranges overlap in the wild. As you can see in Figure 16-11, the wood frog usually breeds in late March and the leopard frog usually breeds in mid-April.

Word Roots and Origins

prezygotic

from the Latin *prae,* meaning "before," and the Greek *zygotos,* meaning "yoked"

FIGURE 16-11

As the graph shows, peak mating activity in frog species can vary widely. Such variance, coupled with different calls, has led to reproductive isolation in the wood frog, *Rana sylvatica,* top, and the leopard frog, *Rana pipiens,* bottom.

Breeding Times in Frog Species

Wood frog
Peeper frog
Leopard frog
Pickerel frog
Tree frog
Green frog
Bull frog

Mating activity

March   April   May   June   July

GRADUAL   PUNCTUATED

FIGURE 16-12

In the model of speciation presented on the left, species evolve gradually, at a stable rate. In the punctuated equilibrium model of speciation, illustrated on the right, species arise abruptly and are quite different from the root species. These species then change little over time.

RATES OF SPECIATION

Speciation sometimes requires millions of years. But apparently some species can form more rapidly. For example, Polynesians introduced banana trees to the Hawaiian Islands about a thousand years ago. Today, there are several species of moths that are unique to the Hawaiian Islands and that feed only on bananas. Because these species are closely related to other plant-eating moths in Hawaii, it seems likely that they have descended from ancestral moths during the past thousand years, since bananas were introduced to Hawaii.

Divergence of organisms and thus speciation may not occur smoothly and gradually. Indeed, the fossil record suggests that rapid speciation may be the norm rather than the exception. The fossil record seems to indicate that many species existed without change for long periods of time. The periods of stability were separated by an "instant" change in terms of geologic time. That is, a change occurred in a few thousand, rather than a few million, years. Scientists call this pattern of species formation **punctuated equilibrium.** The *punctuated* part of this term refers to the sudden shift in form that is often seen in the fossil record. Figure 16-12 shows two contrasting models, punctuated and gradual, of the evolution of two hypothetical species of snakes.

SECTION 16-3 REVIEW

1. What are two shortcomings of the biological species concept?

2. How can geographic isolation lead to speciation? What is the principal cause of such speciation?

3. Give two examples of postzygotic isolation mechanisms.

4. What is less metabolically costly to an animal, prezygotic or postzygotic isolation? Why?

5. What is the hypothesis of punctuated equilibrium?

6. **CRITICAL THINKING** What effect would a very short generation time, such as that of bacteria, have on speciation?

SUMMARY/VOCABULARY

- Biologists study many different traits in populations, such as size and color.
- Traits vary and can be mapped along a bell curve, which shows that most individuals have average traits, while a few individuals have extreme traits.
- Variations in genotype arise by mutation, recombination, and the random fusion of gametes.

- The total genetic formation available in a population is called the gene pool.
- Allele frequencies in the gene pool do not change unless acted upon by certain forces.
- The Hardy-Weinberg genetic equilibrium, a theoretical model of a population in which no evolution occurs, tends to maintain the population as it is.

Vocabulary

allele frequency (300) gene pool (300) phenotype frequency (301) population genetics (299)
bell curve (299) Hardy-Weinberg genetic equilibrium (302)

- Evolution can take place if the genetic equilibrium of a population is disrupted.
- Immigration can bring new genes into a population, causing evolution.
- Nonrandom mating can alter the genotypes of a population, but it does not affect allele frequencies.
- Genetic drift operates in small populations; the contribution or lack of contribution of the genes of one or a few organisms can change the population's gene pool significantly.

- Stabilizing selection encourages the formation of average traits.
- Directional selection encourages the formation of more-extreme traits, such as a very long tongue in anteaters.
- Disruptive selection selects for extreme traits rather than average traits.
- In sexual selection, the development of traits that may seem harmful can actually enhance reproductive fitness if they encourage mating.

Vocabulary

assortative mating (306) emigration (304) genetic drift (305) sexual selection (308)
directional selection (307) gene flow (304) immigration (304) stabilizing selection (306)
disruptive selection (307)

- According to the biological species concept, a species is a population of organisms that can successfully interbreed and cannot breed with other groups.
- *Speciation* means species formation, and it always begins with a population that has become isolated.
- Geographic isolation results from the division of an original population.

- Reproductive isolation results from barriers to successful breeding. Prezygotic isolation occurs before fertilization. Postzygotic isolation occurs after fertilization and results in wasted gametes.
- Some scientists think that enormous phenotypic changes in species occur in sharp (punctuated) steps, rather than along a gradual curve, as Darwin proposed.

Vocabulary

biological species concept (310) morphology (309) punctuated equilibrium (312) reproductive isolation (311)
geographic isolation (310) postzygotic isolation (311) speciation (309)
prezygotic isolation (311)

REVIEW

Vocabulary

1. Explain why the term *bell curve* is appropriate for a graph of a normal distribution of traits.
2. Explain the relationship between allele frequency and phenotype frequency.
3. Distinguish between the terms *directional selection* and *disruptive selection*.
4. Name the two broad types of reproductive isolation.
5. Explain the difference between punctuated equilibrium and gradual evolution.

Multiple Choice

6. Phenotypic traits often vary between two extremes, with most individuals having an average version of the trait. This can be graphed as a (a) Punnet square (b) bell curve (c) straight line (d) genotype frequency table.
7. Variations in genotype arise by random fusion of gametes, mutation, and (a) recombination (b) translation (c) transcription (d) sorting by phenotype.
8. The total genetic information in a population is called the (a) allele frequency (b) phenotype frequency (c) gene pool (d) distribution of traits.
9. Saint Bernards and Chihuahuas (two breeds of domestic dogs) cannot mate normally owing to great differences in size. Thus, they are reproductively isolated to some extent. What type of isolating mechanism is operating here? (a) developmental (b) prezygotic (c) postzygotic (d) geographic.
10. If a population is in genetic equilibrium,
    (a) evolution is occurring
    (b) speciation is occurring
    (c) allele frequencies change from one generation to the next
    (d) allele frequencies remain the same from one generation to the next.
11. Mutations affect genetic equilibrium by
    (a) maintaining it (b) introducing new alleles (c) causing immigration (d) causing emigration.
12. Directional selection, disruptive selection, and stabilizing selection are all examples of (a) genetic equilibrium (b) natural selection (c) mutation (d) speciation.

13. The most common way for new species to form is through (a) mutation (b) stabilizing selection (c) geographic and reproductive isolation (d) genetic equilibrium.
14. The tendency for males to develop extreme versions of traits that appeal to females is a result of (a) random mating (b) speciation (c) reproductive isolation (d) sexual selection.
15. In the population of four o'clock flowers shown below, what is the allele frequency of the *R* allele? (a) 33% (b) 25% (c) 50% (d) 67%

Short Answer

16. What causes variations in the traits of organisms?
17. What conditions are necessary for Hardy-Weinberg equilibrium?
18. What is gene flow?
19. How can immigration alter allele frequencies in a population?
20. What results can be expected from nonrandom mating?
21. What type of selection is shown when the bell curve narrows over time?
22. What kind of selection can result in speciation?
23. What is the relationship between natural selection and sexual selection?
24. Why do prezygotic isolating mechanisms have an advantage over postzygotic isolating mechanisms?
25. What is the relationship between evolution and natural selection?

CRITICAL THINKING

1. Where populations of two related species of frogs overlap geographically, their mating calls are different. Where the species don't overlap, their calls are identical. What type of isolating mechanism is in operation?

2. Freeways may provide an effective geographic isolating mechanism for some slow-moving animals. Why are such artificial barriers not likely to result in complete speciation?

3. The most common definition of *species* states that a species is a group of organisms that can interbreed and produce fertile offspring in nature. A mule is a sterile offspring of a horse and a donkey. By the definition above, do a horse and a donkey belong to the same species? Explain your answer.

4. In the late nineteenth century, hunting reduced the population of the northern elephant seal to about 20 individuals. How might such a reduction in population have disrupted genetic equilibrium?

5. The graph below shows change in phenotype of two hypothetical species, A and B, over time. Use the graph to answer the following:
   a. What kind of evolution, punctuated or gradual, does the curve for species A represent?
   b. What kind of evolution does the curve for species B represent?
   c. Are the overall rates of change different for species A and B?
   d. What might have caused the vertical parts of the curve for species B?
   e. What do the horizontal parts of the curve for species B represent?

Phenotypic Change over Time in Two Species

A ■
B ■

Degree of phenotype change

0   1   2   3   4   5

Time (in millions of years)

EXTENSION

1. Read "Evolving Backward" in *Discover*, September 1998, on page 64. Describe the two hypotheses that Dr. Diamond has developed to explain why humans have lost evolutionary traits, such as tails and body hair. Describe the eyes of a blind mole rat, and explain how the mole rat uses them.

2. Visit an area where plants or animals are bred. Possible places include farms, zoos, arboretums, seed companies, and nurseries.

Find out how the breeders manipulate the genetic makeup of the plants or animals, and prepare an oral report on how this manipulation speeds up or slows down evolution. If you cannot visit one of the suggested locations, look in the *Readers' Guide to Periodical Literature* or use a CD-ROM-based index of periodic literature for articles on plant and animal breeding.

Predicting Allele Frequency

OBJECTIVES

- Demonstrate the effect of natural selection on genotype frequencies.

PROCESS SKILLS

- modeling
- predicting
- calculating
- analyzing

MATERIALS

- 200 black beads
- 200 white beads
- 3 containers
- labeling tape
- marking pen

Background

1. What is natural selection?
2. What is the result of natural selection?

PART A Random Mating

1. Obtain three containers, and label them "Parental," "Offspring," and "Dead."
2. Place 200 black beads and 200 white beads in the "Parental" container. Assume that each black bead represents a dominant allele for black coat *(B)* and that each white bead represents a recessive allele for white coat *(b)* in a hypothetical animal. Assume that the container holds gametes from a population of 200 of these hypothetical animals: 50 *BB*, 100 *Bb*, and 50 *bb*.
3. Without looking, remove two beads from the "Parental" container. What does this simulate?
4. In your lab report, make a data table like Table A below. Record the genotype and phenotype of the resulting offspring in your data table. Then put the alleles into the "Offspring" container.
5. Repeat steps 3 and 4 forty-nine times. Record the genotype and phenotype of each offspring in your data table.
6. Calculate the frequencies of alleles in the offspring. First make a table in your lab report like Table B shown on the next page. Then count and record the number of black beads in the "Offspring" container. This number divided by the total number of beads (100) and multiplied by 100% is the frequency of *B* alleles. Then count and record the number of white beads in the "Offspring" container. Determine the frequency of *b* alleles as you did with the *B* alleles.
7. Calculate the frequencies of phenotypes in the offspring. First make a table in your lab report like Table C, shown on the next page. Then count and record the number of offspring with black coat color. Divide this number by the total number of offspring (50) and

TABLE A *MATING*

Trial	Random mating		Nonrandom mating	
	Offspring genotype	Offspring phenotype	Offspring genotype	Offspring phenotype
1				
2				
3				
4				
5				

TABLE B ALLELE FREQUENCIES

Generation	Number of B alleles	B alleles/ total alleles	B allele frequency	Number of b alleles	b alleles/ total alleles	b allele frequency
Parental	200	200/400	50%	200	200/400	50%
Offspring						

TABLE C PHENOTYPE FREQUENCIES

Generation	Number of black animals	Black animals/ total animals	Frequency of black animals	Number of white animals	White animals/ total animals	Frequency of white animals
Parental	100	150/200	75%	50	50/200	25%
Offspring						

multiply by 100% to determine the frequency of black phenotype. Repeat this calculation to determine the frequency of white coat color among the offspring.

PART B Nonrandom Mating

8. Return the beads in the "Offspring" container to the container labeled "Parental."

9. Assume that animals with white-coat phenotype are incapable of reproducing. What is the genotype of animals with a white coat? To simulate this situation, remove 100 white beads from the container labeled "Parental," and set them aside.

10. Start by removing two beads from the container labeled "Parental," and record the results in your Table A. If the offspring has a white-coat phenotype, put its alleles in the container labeled "Dead." If the offspring has a black-coat phenotype, put its alleles in the container labeled "Offspring."

11. If animals with a white-coat phenotype cannot reproduce, predict what would happen to allele frequency if step 10 were repeated until the parental gene pool was empty. Write your prediction in your lab report.

12. Repeat step 10 until the parental gene pool is empty. Record the results of each pairing in your lab report in Table A. Compare your results with your prediction.

13. Transfer the beads from the "Offspring" container to the "Parental" container. Leave the beads that you

have placed in the "Dead" container in that container. Do not return those beads to the parental container.

14. Repeat step 10 again until the parental pool is empty. Record your results in your data table.

15. Repeat steps 13 and 14 two more times.

16. Calculate the frequencies of the final genotypes produced, as you did in Part A. Compare the results with your prediction from step 11.

17. Clean up your materials before leaving the lab.

Analysis and Conclusions

1. Compare the frequency of recessive alleles produced in Part A with that produced in Part B. Did you correctly predict the frequencies?

2. Did the frequency of the b allele change uniformly through all generations? If not, what happened?

3. Why did you remove 100 white beads from the "Parental" container in Step 9?

4. How did this change the phenotype frequency of white animals in the parental generation from the original ratio of 50/200?

Further Inquiry

If you continued Part B, would you eventually eliminate the b allele? Form a hypothesis and test it.

HUMAN EVOLUTION

Scientists Yoel Rak (seated at left), Donald Johanson (center), and William Kimbel (right), together with a group of Afar tribesmen, examine an early hominid jawbone at a field laboratory at Hadar, Ethiopia.

FOCUS CONCEPT: *Evolution*

As you read, pay attention to how scientific methods are used to formulate conclusions about human origins.

Louis and Mary Leakey were first drawn to Tanzania's Olduvai Gorge by the abundance of primitive stone tools that had been found in the vicinity.

measures the ratio of potassium to argon in volcanic rocks. This method determines age by measuring the radioactive decay of isotopes of potassium with sophisticated equipment. With this technique, the skull revealed that the origin of humans dated back at least 1.75 million years.

In 1960, the Leakeys discovered fossils of a hominid species that dated as far back as 2 million years. Details of the hominid's anatomy, such as tooth characteristics and size and shape of the skull, jaw, and leg bones, were quite different from those of the earlier fossils—they were much more like those of modern humans. The species was relatively large-brained and was probably a tool user. The species was therefore named *Homo habilis,* or "handy human."

Because some of the *Homo habilis* fossils came from the same rock layers as earlier finds, it appeared that this new species may have been a contemporary of *Australopithecus*. This was an important discovery because it implies that the course of human evolution was not necessarily an orderly progression, with one species giving rise to the next. Rather, the family tree of modern humans probably has many branches. Several species may have lived at once. Most early species probably died out without leaving descendants. Modern humans probably arose from a single ancestral line that successfully adapted and evolved while its cousins perished. *Homo habilis* was accepted as an early ancestor of modern humans.

In 1978, Mary Leakey made the dramatic discovery of several sets of bipedal footprints in volcanic ash at Laetoli, a site located south of Olduvai Gorge. When the ash was analyzed, the footprints were dated at 3.6 million years old, clearly demonstrating that human ancestors became bipedal very early.

The Research Continues

The Leakeys' early work formed the basis for much of the research into human origins that continues today. In addition to paleoanthropology, Louis Leakey had a lively interest in modern primates. He directly influenced Jane Goodall's research on chimpanzee behavior, Birute Galdikas Brindamour's research on orangutan behavior, and Dian Fossey's research on mountain gorilla behavior.

Louis and Mary Leakey's son Richard Leakey and his wife, Meave Leakey, are still actively excavating sites in eastern Africa. In 1984, at Lake Turkana, near Kenya's border with Ethiopia, Richard unearthed a skull and later an entire skeleton that at the time were the earliest known specimens of *Homo erectus,* the species that directly preceded *Homo sapiens.* In 1996, Meave Leakey and her team announced the discovery of the oldest known hominid species—*Australopithecus anamensis*. These discoveries underscore the elder Leakeys' contention that Africa is the ancestral home of the human family, the place where humans first became tool users, and ultimately is the cradle of humanity.

Years of painstaking work by the Leakeys produced a great variety of hominid fossils from several different periods.

17-2

OBJECTIVES

▲

Explain how the discovery of Lucy changed hypotheses about the evolution of bipedalism.

●

Explain the significance of finding fossils of hominids that are not ancestral to modern humans.

■

List the fossil finds of 1995, and discuss their significance regarding the evolution of bipedalism in hominids.

Word Roots and Origins

quadrupedal

from the Latin *quattour,* meaning "four," and *pes,* meaning "foot"

---

internetconnect

SCLINKS
NSTA

TOPIC: Fossil evidence of hominid evolution
GO TO: www.scilinks.org
KEYWORD: HM324

FOSSIL EVIDENCE OF HOMINID EVOLUTION

Scientists who study the fossil remains of early hominids have inferred the evolutionary trends toward a larger brain and bipedalism. The fossils of hominids, unlike those of apes and their ancestors, show a whole spectrum of unique adaptations for upright walking.

THE FIRST HOMINIDS

Bipedalism is the principal trait that defines the hominid line. Modern nonhuman anthropoid primates are **quadrupedal** (kwah-DROO-pi-duhl); that is, they walk on four limbs. The apelike ancestors of the first hominids likely were quadrupedal as well. How long ago did the first bipedal primate, that is, the first hominid, evolve? This question has not yet been answered conclusively.

In 1974, a 3.2-million-year-old fossil of a primate was found in the Afar Valley region of eastern Africa by Donald Johanson, shown in the photograph on the first page of this chapter, and his colleagues. The fossil, shown in Figure 17-4, is unusually well preserved. The cranial capacity, which is used as an approximation of brain size, is about equal to that of a chimpanzee (475 cm^3), or about one-third that of a modern human (1,400 cm^3). The fossil primate's height ranged from 1 to 1.5 m, probably varying according to gender. The pelvis and leg bones, however, clearly indicated that the fossil organism was an upright-walking hominid.

This find changed many ideas about the evolution of humans. It was generally thought that the hallmarks of hominids—bipedalism and a large brain with areas dedicated to higher reasoning and the production of speech—had all evolved at the same time. But the new fossil showed that upright walking had apparently come before many of these other adaptations that make the hominids unique among the anthropoid primates.

AUSTRALOPITHECUS

The new fossil find was given the species name *Australopithecus afarensis* (abbreviated *A. afarensis*), which means "southern ape of the Afar Valley." Unofficially this female fossil is called **Lucy.** Since 1974, other specimens of the same species have been discovered. They date from about 3 million to 3.9 million years ago.

Other Australopithecines

A number of other fossils that are similar to *A. afarensis* (Lucy) have been discovered from time to time. All of these finds have now been designated **australopithecines** (aw-STRAY-loh-PITH-uh-seenz)—organisms from the genus *Australopithecus*. *Australopithecus africanus,* which dates from about 2.3 to 3 million years ago, probably descended from *A. afarensis*. *A. africanus* was taller and heavier than Lucy and had a slightly larger cranial capacity, between 430 and 550 cm^3.

Two more-recent species, *Australopithecus robustus,* shown in Figure 17-5, and *Australopithecus boisei,* date from about 1 to 2.6 million years ago. These species had heavier skulls and larger teeth than *A. afarensis*. The cranial capacity in *A. robustus* and *A. boisei* ranged from 450 to 600 cm^3. The general appearance of these other australopithecines suggests that while they may have descended from *A. afarensis* (Lucy's species), they were probably not ancestral to modern humans.

In the past two decades, fossil finds of hominids have increased dramatically due to increased research on human origins. In 1995, Meave Leakey and her colleagues at the National Museums of Kenya announced the discovery of a new fossil representing a species distinct from and older than *A. afarensis*. This species, named *Australopithecus anamensis,* is 300,000 years older than any hominid fossil previously found. While the head and neck of *A. anamensis* share several features with modern chimpanzees, a shinbone found at the site indicates that *A. anamensis* was bipedal. Fossil evidence of very early bipedal primates is not limited to fossilized bones. Fossilized footprints dating back 3.6 million years further confirm that bipedalism occurred very early, before—and not as a result of—the rapid enlargement of the hominid brain.

FIGURE 17-4

The original fossil find of *Australopithecus afarensis* consisted of a partial skeleton. The fossil was given the nickname Lucy by the team of investigators who discovered it.

FIGURE 17-5

This well-preserved *Australopithecus robustus* skull shows the heavy bone structure and large teeth characteristic of the species.

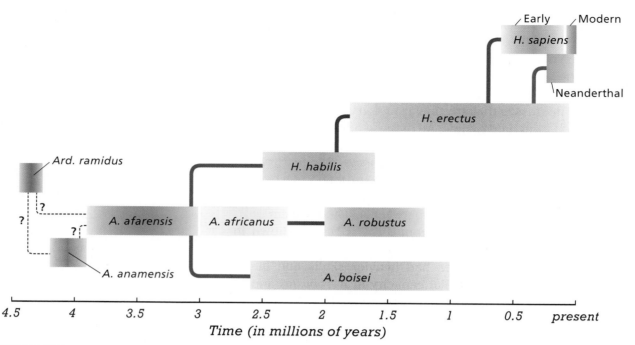

FIGURE 17-6

Physical anthropologists sometimes offer conflicting models of the progression of forms in human evolution. This phylogenetic tree represents one popular view.

An Older Hominid?

In 1995, Tim White (1950–), of the University of California–Berkeley, and his colleagues announced the discovery of fossils representing a new genus that predates the earliest known australopithecines by 200,000 years. Examination of these fossils may ultimately indicate whether the newly discovered primate, *Ardipithecus ramidus,* was bipedal and thus a hominid. It remains to be determined whether this species was ancestral to the australopithecines or whether it was one of several that died out during the course of human evolution.

It is important to understand that human evolution did not occur in a single, uninterrupted parade of increasingly humanlike forms. Rather, there is fossil evidence of several hominid forms that arose and died out, leaving no descendants. Moreover, as Figure 17-6 shows, it is clear that different species of hominids lived at the same time and, in some cases, in the same area. Thus, the human phylogenetic tree has many branches.

SECTION 17-2 REVIEW

1. Lucy was a small-brained hominid. What assumption did her discovery change?

2. What were the probable fates of *Australopithecus robustus* and *A. boisei*?

3. What does the existence of hominid species that were not ancestral to modern humans imply?

4. How do the ages of the fossil finds of 1995 compare with the ages of previous hominid finds?

5. *Ardipithecus* may be a hominid or a prehominid. What characteristic distinguishes hominids?

6. **CRITICAL THINKING** When analyzing fossils, scientists examine the foramen magnum, the opening for the spinal cord in the base of the skull. What does location of the foramen magnum on a skull tell about the posture of an animal?

HYPOTHESES OF HOMINID EVOLUTION

Starting in the early part of the twentieth century, scientists have worked continually to establish a robust fossil record of human evolution. This work has been rewarded by the discovery of many hominid life-forms, some of which are clearly identifiable as a known type, while others appear to be transitions between known types. As scientists fill in the puzzle of human evolution, they have been surprised by some of their discoveries: dead-end branches of the family tree, as well as evidence that two or more quite different hominid forms may have coexisted.

OBJECTIVES

▲

Name two behavioral advances made by *Homo* species.

●

Describe where Neanderthals are placed on the hominid phylogenetic tree.

■

Contrast the multiregional hypothesis of the evolution of modern humans with the hypothesis of recent African origin.

EARLY MEMBERS OF *HOMO,* THE HUMAN GENUS

In the early 1960s, paleoanthropologists working in East Africa found a hominid skull with a much larger brain case than that of the australopithecines. This fossil was the first evidence of an early hominid species that had a cranial capacity as large as 600 to 800 cm^3 but was only slightly taller than *A. afarensis.* The human-like morphology apparent in these fossils resulted in the grouping of this species in the human genus, *Homo.*

Homo habilis

Unlike australopithecine fossils, these newly discovered remains were found along with stone tools. This finding led to the naming of the new species as *Homo habilis,* meaning "handy human." Additional remains of *H. habilis* were later found in southern and eastern Africa, where the first fossils were found. These fossils are between 1.6 million and 2.5 million years old. Some studies of *H. habilis* skulls indicate that a region of the brain essential to speech may have existed in this species. Tool marks on animal bones found near the hominid fossils suggest that *H. habilis* ate meat.

Homo erectus

Fossils of *Homo erectus* (meaning "upright human") were found as early as 1891. They were originally found on the Pacific island of Java and have since been found in China, Europe, and Africa. Thus,

internetconnect

*SC*LINKS
NSTA

TOPIC: *Homo erectus*
GO TO: www.scilinks.org
KEYWORD: HM327

FIGURE 17-7

This reconstruction of a *Homo erectus* skull (a) shows a prominent brow, low forehead, and large, protruding teeth. Contrast these traits with those of the skull of a modern *Homo sapiens* (b).

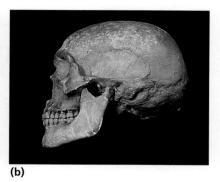

(a)   **(b)**

H. erectus was apparently the first hominid to travel out of Africa. *H. erectus* fossils range from 1.8 million to less than 50,000 years old.

Compared with modern humans, *H. erectus* had a thick skull, large brow ridges, a low forehead, and large, protruding teeth, as shown in Figure 17-7. Their cranial capacity ranged from 700 to 1,250 cm³, so the average brain size was about two-thirds that of modern humans. The fossil of an almost complete *H. erectus* skeleton, called the Turkana boy, is the remains of a 12-year-old male who stood about 1.7 m (5 ft 7 in.) tall. This means that *H. erectus* adults could easily have been as tall as modern humans.

Traces of charred bones indicate that *H. erectus* were hunters who used fires for cooking and probably for warmth. To survive in the colder climates of Europe and northern Asia, many *H. erectus* groups lived in caves.

FIGURE 17-8

Neanderthals had larger brains than modern humans, but they were shorter and stockier. They lived and hunted in groups. They disappeared about 35,000 years ago.

HOMO SAPIENS

An early, now-extinct form of our species, *Homo sapiens,* probably arose from *Homo erectus* about 800,000 years ago. Over the years, evidence of hominid forms that were transitional between *H. erectus* and *H. sapiens* has been found. Some skulls have the large brow ridges of *H. erectus* and the large cranial capacity of *H. sapiens.* When *H. sapiens* arose, they did not completely replace *H. erectus* right away. Recent finds of *H. erectus* fossils indicate that this species existed until as recently as 50,000 to 35,000 years ago. Thus, *H. sapiens* and *H. erectus* may have coexisted for more than 700,000 years.

Neanderthals

Many examples of a distinctive type of hominid fossil skeleton dating from 230,000 to 30,000 years ago have been found in Europe and Asia. They belong to a group of early *H. sapiens* called Neanderthals (nee-AND-uhr-TAHLZ). Neanderthals, shown in Figure 17-8, had heavy bones, thick brow ridges, and protruding teeth. However, the cranial capacity of Neanderthals averaged 1,450 cm³. This is slightly larger than the cranial capacity of modern humans. Neanderthals stood about 1.5 m (5 ft) tall but were heavily built. They lived in caves and stone shelters during the last ice age. Their carefully shaped stone tools, probably used to scrape animal hides, have led scientists to speculate that they wore clothing made of skins. Many paleoanthropologists think that Neanderthals were not ancestral to modern humans. In Europe, Neanderthals disappeared at approximately the same time that modern *H. sapiens* arrived in large numbers, leading some scientists to hypothesize that the Neanderthals were killed off violently or by disease and replaced by modern humans.

Modern *Homo sapiens*

The first fossil skeletons bearing a distinct resemblance to modern humans were discovered in caves in southwestern France. The fossils are about 35,000 years old. Older fossils of the same type have been found elsewhere in Europe, as well as in Africa, Asia, and even Australia. These early modern humans are referred to as Cro-Magnons, named for the cave where they were originally discovered. Cro-Magnons had a cranial capacity equal to that of modern humans, 1400 cm³. They are distinguished from Neanderthals by their high forehead and lack of protruding brow ridge and teeth. Taller than Neanderthals, they stood about 1.8 m (6 ft) tall.

The oldest truly modern *H. sapiens* fossils yet found are about 100,000 years old and were found in Africa. Modern *H. sapiens* probably coexisted with the Neanderthals for about 70,000 years and with *H. erectus* for more than 50,000 years. As the Neanderthals declined, modern humans became more advanced and prevalent. About 50,000 years ago, they became more efficient hunters and home builders, and their tools became distinctly more sophisticated.

SPREAD OF MODERN HUMANS

All modern humans belong to a single species, *Homo sapiens.* There are phenotypic differences, such as skin color, associated with people living in different regions. However, all *H. sapiens* are genetically similar enough to produce offspring together. How did these different phenotypes arise?

Multiregional Evolution

Some anthropologists propose that modern humans evolved in parallel all over Earth from different populations of *Homo erectus*. For this process to result in a single species of modern human, as actually exists, constant gene flow between the different populations would be necessary. Without exchanges of genes during the transition from *H. erectus* to *H. sapiens,* the different populations would tend to speciate into separate groups, in response to local environmental pressures.

If the **multiregional hypothesis,** outlined in Figure 17-9a, is correct, it would suggest that regional differences in phenotype have been developing for well over a million years. Some investigators

Quick Lab

Comparing Cranial Capacities

Materials calculator, 2 L plastic soda bottles (4), graduated cylinder, water, paper, pencil, wax marking pencil

Procedure

1. Using the data provided on pp. 327–329, calculate the average cranial capacity for *Homo habilis, Homo erectus,* and both groups of *Homo sapiens* (Neanderthals and modern humans).

2. Convert your averages to milliliters. (1 cm³ = 1 mL)

3. Label one of the plastic soda bottles *"Homo habilis."* Label another bottle *"Homo erectus."* Label the third bottle *"Homo sapiens (Neanderthal)"* and the fourth bottle "Modern *Homo sapiens."*

4. Fill a graduated cylinder with an amount of water equal to the average cranial capacity of *Homo habilis.* Pour the water in the appropriately labeled bottle.

5. Repeat step 4 for each of the remaining three species, and record your observations.

6. Calculate in cubic centimeters the change in average cranial capacity between each species over time.

Analysis Based on your calculations and observations of cranial capacities, which species had the smallest brain? How small was it? Which species had the largest brain? How large was it? Between which two species did you find the greatest change in cranial capacity? What trend can you observe in the change in cranial capacity over time? What might explain such a trend?

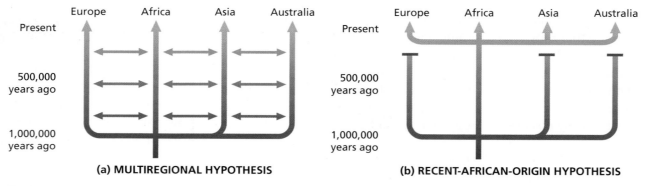

FIGURE 17-9

According to the multiregional hypothesis of human evolution (a), parallel populations of *H. sapiens* evolved from different *H. erectus* populations around the world. The hypothesis of recent African origin (b) states that modern *H. sapiens* evolved in Africa and spread throughout the world, replacing populations of *H. erectus* and early *H. sapiens*.

claim that Asian fossils of *Homo erectus* show the high cheek bones seen in modern *Homo sapiens* living in Asia.

Out of Africa

The more widely supported hypothesis, the **recent-African-origin hypothesis,** states that modern *Homo sapiens* originated in Africa only about 100,000 to 200,000 years ago and then, like *Homo erectus* before them, left Africa. They colonized the world, displacing and causing the extinction of *Homo erectus* and early *Homo sapiens,* such as the Neanderthals.

The recent-African-origin hypothesis gets much of its support from studies of the genes found in mitochondria. Because mitochondria reproduce asexually, their genes are not subject to the mixing caused by gene flow and meiosis. If humans were one large population dating back to over a million years ago, we should find human mitochondria that show a million years of accumulated mutational differences. Instead, most human mitochondria have very similar genes. The period of time needed for mitochondria to accumulate the differences actually seen is only 100,000 to 200,000 years—far short of a million years. Because all human mitochondria are so similar, supporters of this hypothesis infer that all modern humans came from one small group in Africa a fairly short time ago—100,000 or 200,000 years ago.

SECTION 17-3 REVIEW

1. What clues do paleoanthropologists look for when they try to determine the habits and capabilities of early hominids?

2. What are two behavioral advances that distinguished *Homo erectus* from *H. habilis*?

3. How did the body types of Neanderthals and modern humans differ?

4. What observations of mitochondrial DNA are used to support the hypothesis of recent African origins of modern *Homo sapiens*?

5. Which hypothesis of human evolution attempts to explain the origin of regional phenotypic differences?

6. **CRITICAL THINKING** According to the existing fossil evidence, Neanderthals died out about 30,000 years ago. Some anthropologists hypothesize that the Neanderthals were killed off by Cro-Magnons. Others hypothesize that the two groups interbred. What evidence would you look for to evaluate these two hypotheses?

SUMMARY/VOCABULARY

17-1 ■ Paleoanthropologists gather data from the fossilized remains of early hominids and their ancestors. The shapes of the bones may indicate whether the organism was bipedal. Other clues may indicate diet or habits.

■ Humans belong to the order of mammals known as primates. There are two divisions of primates: anthropoid primates and prosimian primates.

■ Most primates have nails, instead of claws, and prehensile hands and feet. Primates have color vision and depth perception.

■ Anthropoid primates include marmosets, monkeys, apes, and humans. Prosimian primates include lemurs, lorises, and tarsiers.

■ Anthropoid primates have large brains relative to their body size.

■ Bipedalism and language are two important traits found only in humans.

Vocabulary

anthropoid primate (320)
bipedalism (321)
dental formula (320)

great ape (320)
hominid (319)
opposable thumb (320)

paleoanthropologist (319)
pelvis (319)
prehensile (320)

primate (320)
prosimian primate (320)

17-2 ■ Bipedalism is the defining characteristic for the hominids—human ancestors.

■ The oldest known genus of hominids is *Australopithecus*. Its members are called australopithecines.

■ The earliest known hominid, *Australopithecus anamensis,* lived more than 4 million years ago.

■ At least two australopithecine lines, *A. africanus* and *A. boisei,* probably were not ancestral to modern humans. They became extinct more than 1 million years ago.

■ The discovery of Lucy, a nearly half-complete fossil of an early hominid, *Australopithecus*

afarensis, implies that hominids became bipedal before their brains began to dramatically enlarge.

■ *Ardipithecus ramidus* is a recent discovery. It is not clear whether it was bipedal. *Ard. ramidus* is 4.4 million years old.

■ The existence of hominid species not ancestral to modern humans implies that the hominid phylogenetic tree is bushy in appearance, with many branches representing species that died out, leaving no descendants.

Vocabulary

australopithecine (325)   Lucy (325)   quadrupedal (324)

17-3 ■ Early members of the genus *Homo, H. habilis* and *H. erectus,* probably were ancestral to modern humans. They had larger brains than the australopithecines and may have had speech.

■ Our species, *Homo sapiens,* probably evolved about 800,000 years ago.

■ The brains of members of the genus *Homo* were much larger than those of the australopithecines.

■ Neanderthals were early *Homo sapiens.* They may be ancestral to modern humans, or they may have died out and been replaced by modern humans.

■ Some anthropologists think that *H. sapiens* evolved in parallel from populations of *H. erectus* all over the world.

■ Some anthropologists propose that *H. sapiens* descended from *H. erectus* in Africa and then dispersed across Earth.

Vocabulary

multiregional hypothesis (329)

recent-African-origin hypothesis (330)

REVIEW

Vocabulary

1. What is the difference between a bipedal animal and a quadrupedal animal?
2. What does the term *dental formula* mean?
3. Why is a primate thumb described as "opposable"?
4. What is the relationship between cranial capacity and brain size?
5. What does the genus name *Australopithecus* mean?

Multiple Choice

6. The earliest primates probably lived in (a) grasslands (b) forests (c) deserts (d) tundra.
7. An important difference between anthropoids and prosimians is that anthropoids have (a) larger eyes (b) a larger brain (c) a longer tail (d) no depth perception.
8. The dental formula found in humans is found (a) in all animals (b) only in hominids (c) in apes and African and Asian monkeys. (d) only in marmosets.
9. Humans are better adapted to upright walking than chimpanzees are because humans have (a) a large brain (b) a cup-shaped pelvis (c) a big toe that is opposable to the other toes (d) the ability to use language.
10. The similarity of human and chimpanzee DNA suggests that the two species (a) are identical (b) shared a relatively recent ancestor (c) are not related (d) have stopped evolving.
11. Paleoanthropologists determine the manner of walking and the physical features of human ancestors on the basis of (a) fingerprint patterns (b) comparisons of living species (c) written descriptions in ancient sources (d) shapes of fossilized bones.
12. The earliest known bipedal human ancestor was (a) *A. anamensis* (b) *A. afarensis* (c) *A. africanus* (d) *A. boisei*.
13. The species *A. afarensis* probably (a) died out (b) gave rise to the genus *Ardipithecus* (c) was ancestral to later australopithicenes (d) lived after *A. africanus*.
14. *H. habilis* was so named because evidence indicates that this species (a) was bipedal (b) used language (c) made tools (d) ate meat.
15. Cro-Magnons are regarded as (a) a type of *Homo erectus* (b) a transitional species between *Ardipithecus* and the australopithecines (c) ancestors of Neanderthals (d) modern humans.

Short Answer

16. Study the figure below of the ape skull, top, and the human skull, bottom, and name three major differences between the two skulls.

17. Why is depth perception handy for climbing in trees?
18. How is upright walking a beneficial trait for humans?
19. What are two behavioral traits unique to humans?
20. How does the jaw of humans differ from that of apes?
21. How do paleoanthropologists use fossil evidence to draw conclusions about the brain size of hominids?
22. On what continent have most fossil remains of hominids been found?
23. How did Neanderthals accommodate the cold climate of northern Europe?

24. How does the brain size of *A. afarensis* (Lucy) compare with that of chimpanzees and that of modern humans?

25. How is the human spine adapted for standing erect, compared with the spine of a chimpanzee?

CRITICAL THINKING

1. From *H. habilis* to modern *H. sapiens,* there has been a trend for brain size to increase. Is it inevitable that any future descendant species of *H. sapiens* will have larger brains than we have? Explain your answer in terms of some form of natural selection, such as directional selection.

2. Compared with humans, apes do not have a well-developed voice box or well-developed facial muscles. How might the ape's anatomy affect its ability to use spoken language?

3. According to fossil evidence, *H. habilis* made stone tools. They traveled long distances to collect specific types of rock and minerals, and then they shaped the rocks by chipping them at the edges. What does this reveal about *H. habilis*'s ability to use foresight?

4. Cro-Magnon remains have been found with reindeer bones in certain areas of southern Europe. What does this fact suggest about the diet of Cro-Magnons and the environment in which they lived?

5. The two phylogenetic trees shown below express two different views of the relationship of Neanderthals to modern humans. If Neanderthals were very genetically different from modern humans, which tree would more likely be the correct one and why?

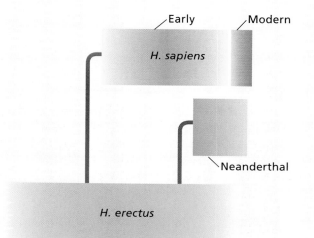

EXTENSION

1. Read "No, After You, Afarensis" in *Discover,* January 1999, on page 81. What physical characteristics of *Australopithecus africanus* cause Berger and McHenry to disagree about the human ancestry of *A. africanus*? What reasons are given to defend the current theory that *A. afarensis* is ancestral to *A. africanus*? How long ago did each of the three species of *Australopithecus* live?

2. Visit a local zoo to observe the behavior of monkeys, apes, or other primates. Pay close attention to the facial expressions of the animals. Notice the ways in which the animals interact. Take notes on what you observe. What similarities and differences do you see between the behavior of the primates you observed and that of humans? If it is not possible to visit a zoo, study pictures or videotapes of primates. What inferences can you make about primate behavior from the pictures?

Relating Amino Acid Sequences to Evolutionary Relationships

OBJECTIVES

- Observe the amino acid sequence of hemoglobin and cytochrome *c* in several species.
- Compare the amino acid sequences of the same protein in different species.
- Deduce evolutionary relationships among species.

PROCESS SKILLS

- comparing and contrasting
- classifying
- analyzing
- inferring

MATERIALS

- pencil
- paper

Background

1. Hemoglobin and cytochrome *c* are two proteins commonly studied by scientists attempting to deduce evolutionary relationships from differences in amino acid sequences.
2. Researchers believe that the greater the similarity that exists between the amino acid sequences of two species, the more closely related the two species are evolutionarily.
3. The greater the differences that exist in the amino acid sequences of two species, the more distantly related the two species are.
4. The longer two species have been diverging from a common ancestor, the greater the difference that can be expected in their amino acid sequences. This principle is based on the assumption that the rate of

Cytochrome *c* Amino Acid Sequences

	Horse	Chicken	Tuna	Frog	Human	Shark	Turtle	Monkey	Rabbit
42	Gln	Gln	Gln	Gln	Gln	Gln	Gln	Gln	Gln
43	Ala	Ala	Ala	Ala	Ala	Ala	Ala	Ala	Ala
44	Pro	Glu	Glu	Ala	Pro	Gln	Glu	Pro	Tyr
46	Phe	Phe	Tyr	Phe	Tyr	Phe	Phe	Tyr	Pro
47	Thr	Ser	Ser	Ser	Ser	Ser	Ser	Ser	Ser
49	Thr	Thr	Thr	Thr	Thr	Thr	Thr	Thr	Thr
50	Asp	Asp	Asp	Asp	Ala	Asp	Asp	Ala	Asp
53	Lys	Lys	Lys	Lys	Lys	Lys	Lys	Lys	Lys
54	Asn	Asn	Ser	Asn	Asn	Ser	Asn	Asn	Asn
55	Lys	Lys	Lys	Lys	Lys	Lys	Lys	Lys	Lys
56	Gly	Gly	Gly	Gly	Gly	Gly	Gly	Gly	Gly
57	Ile	Ile	Ile	Ile	Ile	Ile	Ile	Ile	Ile
58	Thr	Thr	Val	Thr	Ile	Thr	Thr	Ile	Thr
60	Lys	Gly	Asn	Gly	Gly	Gln	Gly	Gly	Gly
61	Glu	Glu	Asn	Glu	Glu	Gln	Glu	Glu	Glu
62	Glu	Asp	Asp	Asp	Asp	Glu	Glu	Asp	Asp
63	Thr	Thr	Thr	Thr	Thr	Thr	Thr	Thr	Thr
64	Leu	Leu	Leu	Leu	Leu	Leu	Leu	Leu	Leu
65	Met	Met	Met	Met	Met	Arg	Met	Met	Met
66	Glu	Glu	Glu	Glu	Glu	Ile	Glu	Glu	Glu
100	Lys	Asp	Ser	Ser	Lys	Lys	Asp	Lys	Lys
101	Ala	Ala	Ala	Ala	Ala	Thr	Ala	Ala	Ala
102	Thr	Thr	Thr	Gly	Thr	Ala	Thr	Ala	Thr
103	Asn	Ser	Ser	Ser	Asn	Ala	Ser	Asn	Asn
104	Glu	Lys	—	Lys	Glu	Ser	Lys	Glu	Glu

change of a specific amino acid sequence is the same in all species. Think of other methods used to determine evolutionary relationships. How is this method different?

PART A Cytochrome *c*

1. Cytochrome *c,* a protein found in the mitochondria of many species, consists of a chain of 104 amino acids. The figure on page 334 shows the corresponding parts of noncontinuous parts of the cytochrome *c* amino acid sequences of nine vertebrate species. The numbers along the left side of the figure refer to the position of these sequences in the chain. The letters identify the specific amino acids in the chain.

2. Make a table to record your data in your lab report. Label the columns of your data table "Species" and "Number of Differences from Human Cytochrome *c.*"

Hemoglobin Amino Acid Sequences

	Human	Chimpanzee	Gorilla	Monkey	Horse
87	Thr	Thr	Thr	Gln	Thr
88	Leu	Leu	Leu	Leu	Leu
89	Ser	Ser	Ser	Ser	Ser
90	Glu	Glu	Glu	Glu	Glu
91	Leu	Leu	Leu	Leu	Leu
92	His	His	His	His	His
93	Cys	Cys	Cys	Cys	Cys
94	Asp	Asp	Asp	Asp	Asp
95	Lys	Lys	Lys	Lys	Lys
96	Leu	Leu	Leu	Leu	Leu
97	His	His	His	His	His
98	Val	Val	Val	Val	Val
99	Asp	Asp	Asp	Asp	Asp
100	Pro	Pro	Pro	Pro	Pro
101	Glu	Glu	Glu	Glu	Glu
102	Asn	Asn	Asn	Asn	Asn
103	Phe	Phe	Phe	Phe	Phe
104	Arg	Arg	Lys	Lys	Arg
105	Leu	Leu	Leu	Leu	Leu
106	Leu	Leu	Leu	Leu	Leu
107	Gly	Gly	Gly	Gly	Gly
108	Asn	Asn	Asn	Asn	Asn
109	Val	Val	Val	Val	Val
110	Leu	Leu	Leu	Leu	Leu
111	Val	Val	Val	Val	Ala
112	Csy	Cys	Cys	Cys	Leu
113	Val	Val	Val	Val	Val
114	Leu	Leu	Leu	Leu	Val
115	Ala	Ala	Ala	Ala	Ala
116	His	His	His	His	Arg

For each vertebrate species, count the amino acids in the sequence that differ from the human sequence. List these in your data table.

3. In your lab report, list the eight vertebrate sequences in descending order according to the degree of similarity of their cytochrome *c* with that of humans. According to your analysis of the amino acid sequences, which species listed is most closely related to humans? Which species is least closely related to humans?

PART B Hemoglobin

4. Look at the hemoglobin sequences for the five species shown in the figure at left. Hemoglobin is the oxygen-carrying molecule of red blood cells. Only the portion of the chain between amino acid numbers 87 and 116 is shown in the figure.

5. In your lab report, make a table to record your data. Label the columns of your data table "Species" and "Number of Differences from Human Hemoglobin." In each species' sequence, count the number of amino acids that differ from the human sequence and list them in your data table, as you did in Part A.

6. In your lab report, list the four vertebrate sequences in descending order according to the degree of similarity of their hemoglobin with that of humans. According to your analysis of the amino acid sequences, which species listed is most closely related to humans? Which species is least closely related to humans?

Analysis and Conclusions

1. Why can it be said that proteins behave like molecular clocks?

2. There is a difference of only one amino acid in one portion of hemoglobin of gorillas and humans. What could have been responsible for this change?

3. If the amino acid sequences are similar in gorillas and humans, why would you expect the DNA of these two organisms to also be similar?

Further Inquiry

Would you expect to find the same number of differences in the cytochrome *c* and hemoglobin amino acid chains when comparing organisms? Or might one of these proteins have changed at a faster rate than the other? Why might the rates of change differ among proteins?

CLASSIFICATION

The pangolin, Manis temmincki, *is a species of scaly anteater found in eastern and southern Africa. Pangolins move slowly and, when threatened, curl into a ball, as this one has done.*

FOCUS CONCEPT: *Interdependence of Organisms*
As you read, consider how the classification of a species reflects its relationships with many related species.

18-1 *History of Taxonomy*

18-2 *Modern Phylogenetic Taxonomy*

18-3 *Two Modern Systems of Classification*

HISTORY OF TAXONOMY

Every year, thousands of new species are discovered. Biologists use the characteristics of each newly discovered species to classify it with organisms having similar characteristics. The ways we group organisms continue to change, and today these methods reflect the evolutionary history of organisms.

OBJECTIVES

▲

Describe Aristotle's classification system, and explain why it was replaced.

●

Explain Linnaeus's system of classification, and identify the main criterion he used to classify organisms.

■

List Linnaeus's levels of classification from the most general to the most specific.

◆

Name the primary criterion that modern taxonomists consider when they classify an organism.

EARLY SYSTEMS OF CLASSIFICATION

Taxonomy (taks-AHN-uh-mee) is the branch of biology that names and groups organisms according to their characteristics and evolutionary history. Organisms were first classified more than 2,000 years ago by the Greek philosopher Aristotle. Aristotle classified living things as either plants or animals. He grouped animals into land dwellers, water dwellers, and air dwellers. He also grouped plants into three categories, based on differences in their stems.

As modern science developed in the fifteenth and sixteenth centuries, Aristotle's system at first seemed adequate. Then, in a period of rapid scientific exploration, many new organisms were discovered. Biologists realized that Aristotle's categories were not adequate. They also found that using a common name, such as *robin* or *fir tree,* for an organism presented its own problems; common names varied from one locale to the next, just as they do today. Moreover, common names may not describe species accurately. For example, a jellyfish is not a fish at all. Some early scientists devised scientific names that consisted of long descriptions in Latin, but these names were difficult to remember and suggested nothing about how organisms were related to other organisms.

LINNAEUS'S SYSTEM

In response to the need for organization, the Swedish naturalist Carolus Linnaeus (1707–1778) devised a system of grouping organisms into hierarchical categories. For the most part, Linnaeus used an organism's morphology, that is, its form and structure, to categorize it.

Word Roots and Origins

morphology

from the Greek *morphe,* meaning "form," and *logos,* meaning "word"

FIGURE 18-1

Linnaeus's categorization scheme used a nested hierarchy. Seven levels of organization, each more specific than the last, allowed organisms to be grouped with similar organisms.

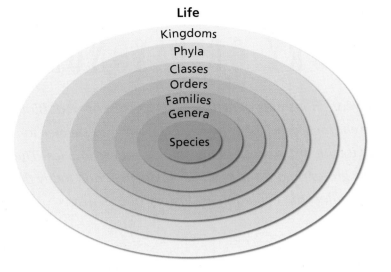

Life

Kingdoms
Phyla
Classes
Orders
Families
Genera

Species

Quick Lab

Practicing Classification

Materials paper, pencil

Procedure Using Table 18-1 as a model, classify a fruit or vegetable you would find in a grocery store. Use all seven levels of classification.

Analysis At which level did you assign the least specific name? At which level did you assign the most specific name? Would Aristotle have classified your item differently? Explain your answer.

Levels of Classification

Linnaeus devised a nested hierarchy of seven different levels of organization, as is shown in Figure 18-1. Linnaeus's largest category is called a **kingdom.** There are two kingdoms, plant and animal, which are the same as Aristotle's main categories. Each subset within a kingdom is known as a **phylum** (FIE-luhm), in the animal kingdom, or a **division,** in the plant kingdom. Within a phylum or division, each subset is called a **class,** and each subset within a class is called an **order.** Still smaller groupings are the **family** and then **genus** (JEE-nuhs). The smallest grouping of all, which contains only a single organism type, is known as the **species** (SPEE-sheez). Table 18-1 shows an example of how two similar organisms and one very different one fit into this classification system.

TABLE 18-1	*Classification Hierarchy of Organisms*		
	Bobcat	**Lion**	**Shaggy mane mushroom**
Kingdom	Animalia	Animalia	Fungi
Phylum/division	Chordata	Chordata	Basidiomycota
Class	Mammalia	Mammalia	Homobasidiomycetae
Order	Carnivora	Carnivora	Agaricales
Family	Felidae	Felidae	Copricaceae
Genus	*Lynx*	*Panthera*	*Coprinus*
Species	*Lynx rufus*	*Panthera leo*	*Coprinus comatus*

Binomial Nomenclature

In Linnaeus's system, the **species name** (also called the scientific name) of an organism has two parts. The first part of the name is the genus, and the second part is the **species identifier,** usually a descriptive word. Thus, we humans are known by our genus, *Homo,* and by our species identifier, *sapiens,* which means "wise." This system of two-part names is known as **binomial nomenclature** (bi-NOH-mee-uhl NOH-muhn-KLAY-chuhr). By custom, the genus name is capitalized and both names are underlined or written in italics. Linnaeus classified thousands of organisms, and a version of Linnaeus's system of classification and binomial nomenclature is still used today. Because species names are Latinized, they are the same in every language. This enables scientists around the world to identify organisms by the same name.

A species name may describe the organism. The microscopic amoeba *Chaos chaos,* shown in Figure 18-2, might never look the same way twice. Sometimes a scientific name is chosen to honor a person, or it may suggest the geographic range of the organism. *Linnaea borealis,* a species of flower that grows in northern regions, was Linnaeus's favorite. *Borealis* means "northern."

Linnaeus's choice of seven levels of classification was arbitrary. Significant variation in some species has led taxonomists to establish additional levels of organization. Botanists sometimes split species into subsets known as **varieties.** Peaches and nectarines are fruits of two slightly different varieties of the peach tree, *Prunus persica.* Zoologists refer to variations of a species that occur in different geographic areas as **subspecies.** The variety or subspecies name follows the species identifier. *Terrapene carolina triungui* is a subspecies of the common eastern box turtle, *Terrapene carolina,* and gets its name from having three, rather than four, toes on its hind feet.

To classify organisms, modern taxonomists consider the **phylogeny** (fie-LAHJ-uh-nee), or evolutionary history, of the organism. Much of Linnaeus's work in classification is relevant today, even in this phylogenetic context. By concentrating on morphology, Linnaeus focused on features that are largely influenced by genes and that are clues of common ancestry.

FIGURE 18-2

Names selected for some organisms reflect traits of the organism. The amoeba *Chaos chaos* (LM 56×) changes its shape constantly.

internet connect

SC*LINKS*
NSTA

TOPIC: Taxonomy
GO TO: www.scilinks.org
KEYWORD: HM339

SECTION 18–1 REVIEW

1. How did Aristotle classify organisms, and why did his method prove inadequate?

2. What criterion did Linnaeus use to classify organisms?

3. What are the seven levels of organization that Linnaeus used to categorize organisms?

4. What are two reasons that species names are more precise than common names?

5. What criterion do modern taxonomists use to classify organisms?

6. **CRITICAL THINKING** Linnaeus's work was done many years before that of Darwin and Mendel. Explain why many of Linnaeus's categories are still relevant in light of genetic and evolutionary relationships among organisms.

Creating Order Out of Chaos

HISTORICAL PERSPECTIVE

During the fifteenth and sixteenth centuries, the exploration of new lands brought large numbers of unknown animals and plants to the attention of naturalists. European explorers returned from other parts of the world with so many unidentified organisms that it became difficult to keep track of them all. Before the introduction of Carolus Linnaeus's binomial system, there was no accepted method for naming and classifying animals and plants. Linnaeus provided a system for grouping organisms in a manner that reflected the relationships between the organisms.

A Rose by Any Other Name . . .

People all over the world use familiar or common names for plants. Sometimes they use different names for the same plant or similar names for different plants. Imagine how difficult it must have been for people from different countries to share their knowledge about the natural world before there was a standard naming system for plants and other organisms.

These early naturalists needed a system for naming living things and placing them into groups of related organisms. The names needed to be short and descriptive—and they needed to be written in a language that was widely understood and accepted. Although there had been some earlier attempts at devising classification systems, Carolus Linnaeus was the first to develop a system that was widely used and accepted.

Carolus Linnaeus

Seeds of Change

Born in Sweden in 1707, Carolus Linnaeus had a great love of plants and nature, instilled in him by a father who educated him about the natural world and taught him the names of many plants. In 1732, while a lecturer at the University of Uppsala, Linnaeus undertook a trip to the then largely unexplored region of northern Scandinavia known as Lapland.

The Lapland journey helped to focus Linnaeus's attention on the need for a standard system of classification, a task that became his lifework. Using earlier research by the German botanist Rudolph Camerius, Linnaeus divided all flowering plants into 23 classes. These classes were based on the number, length, and arrangement of the stamens and pistils. His 24th class included the nonflowering plants, such as mosses.

Taking Root

The prominent Dutch botanist Jan Fredrick Gronovius was greatly impressed with Linnaeus's early botanical work. Gronovius paid for the publication of Linnaeus's *Systema Naturae* (1735), which contained the beginnings of Linnaeus's system for classifying animals and plants.

Linnaeus's greatest contribution to biology was the introduction of the binomial system, in which the

An illustration made to accompany Linnaeus's Systema Naturae *shows the division of flowering plants into 23 classes, based on the number, relative length, and arrangement of the stamens and pistil.*

species name of an organism consists of two parts based on Latin word roots. The concept of the genus name came from the French naturalist Joseph Tournefort. The concept of the second word, the species identifier, came from Linnaeus. Prior to the introduction of this two-part naming system, each type of plant was characterized by a 12-word description. Linnaeus was the first to apply the uniform use of binomials to all organisms. The advantage of this method is that it provides a standardized label for each kind of organism in place of the common name.

Linnaeus's classification system did not escape criticism by his contemporaries, however. He was denounced for imposing an artificial system on nature. Critics claimed his method of classification was based on a single, and perhaps the least important, characteristic of flowers—the arrangement of flower parts. Linnaeus acknowledged that he had sacrificed natural principles to some extent in order to devise a useful sorting principle. But his organizational system had brought together related groups.

Linnaeus first introduced his binomial system in the work *Species Planterum* (1753). This two-volume work contained every plant that Linnaeus was familiar with, and it demonstrated the utility of his system. After publication of *Species Planterum,* the binomial system became the most widely used system in botanical works. As Linnaeus commented in a letter to a friend:

Now the whole world is obsessed with writing in the field of botany, now they can go ahead without difficulty, thanks to my method.

Fruits of His Labor

Since Linnaeus first devised the binomial classification, the most dramatic change has been the systematic effort to make modern taxonomic schemes reflect evolutionary relationships. As Linnaeus himself did, modern scientists have proposed revisions of the traditional classification system. In light of recent research, they have proposed creating new kingdom designations for unicellular organisms. The names of these organisms, however, are still based on the Latin binomial system devised by Linnaeus.

Mertensia virginica, *known in the United States as the bluebell, illustrates the problem with using common names. In Europe and Asia, plants of the genus* Endymion *are called bluebells. Elsewhere, certain species of the genera* Campanula, Clematis, *and* Polemonium *are also commonly known as bluebells.*

▲

Define *phylogenetic tree,* and explain what information a phylogenetic tree shows.

●

List four types of evidence used to organize organisms in systematic taxonomy.

■

Name two differences found in the embryos of vertebrates and arthropods that suggest a very different phylogenetic history.

◆

Explain cladistic taxonomy, and identify one conclusion that is in conflict with classical, systematic taxonomy.

Word Roots and Origins

phylogenetic

from the Greek *phylon,* meaning "tribe," and *gignesthai,* meaning "to be born"

MODERN PHYLOGENETIC TAXONOMY

*M*ore than 200 years ago, Linnaeus based his classification system on the most evident characteristics of organisms—their morphology. Today, the young field of molecular biology can provide a wealth of information about an organism's molecular nature. When placing an organism into a taxonomic category, modern taxonomists may consider its morphology, chromosomal characteristics, nucleotide and amino acid sequences, and embryological development. These features are almost entirely inherited. Thus, consideration of all of them, together with information from the fossil record, is likely to yield reliable information about the phylogeny of an organism.

SYSTEMATICS

Most modern taxonomists agree that the classification of organisms should reflect their phylogeny. This phylogenetic approach is a cornerstone of a branch of biology called systematic taxonomy, or, more commonly, systematics. **Systematics** organizes the tremendous diversity of living things in the context of evolution. Systematic taxonomists use several lines of evidence to construct a phylogenetic tree.

A **phylogenetic tree** is a family tree that shows the evolutionary relationships thought to exist among groups of organisms. A phylogenetic tree represents a hypothesis, and it is generally based on several lines of evidence. Systematic taxonomists may evaluate an organism's morphology with respect to the morphology of similar and possibly ancestral organisms in the fossil record. Likewise, they may compare its morphology with that of living organisms. Patterns of embryological development, along with the degree of similarity of an organism's chromosomes and certain macromolecules to those of other organisms, provide further clues to phylogenetic relationships. A phylogenetic tree is subject to change, as is any hypothesis, as new information arises. A phylogenetic tree that shows possible relationships among phyla in the kingdom Animalia appears in Figure 18-3.

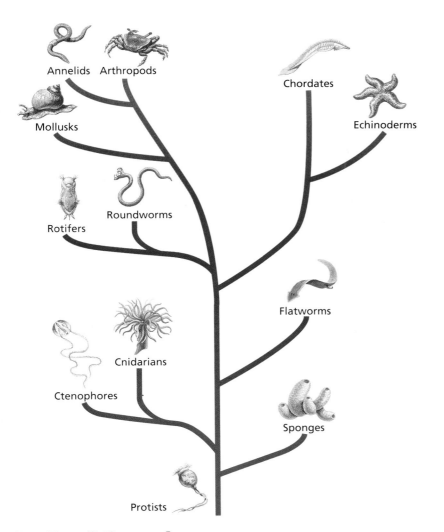

Annelids Arthropods

Mollusks

Chordates

Echinoderms

Rotifers

Roundworms

Flatworms

Ctenophores

Cnidarians

Sponges

Protists

FIGURE 18-3

The branches of this phylogenetic tree show that chordates and echinoderms shared a common ancestor more recently than did echinoderms and other animals, including mollusks and arthropods. Phylogenetic trees are generally derived from several lines of evidence, including morphological, embryological, and macromolecular similarities among organisms.

The Fossil Record

The fossil record often provides clues to evolutionary relationships, but it is important to understand that the fossil record cannot be read like a history book. Some organisms, such as some ocean-living invertebrates, have fairly complete fossil records. Other organisms have incomplete fossil records; there may be series of strata in which no fossils of the organism appear. The fossil record may provide the framework of a phylogenetic tree, but a systematic taxonomist would seek to confirm the information it provided with other lines of evidence.

Morphology

Taxonomists study an organism's morphology and compare it with the morphology of other living organisms. Recall from Chapter 15 that homologous features suggest descent from a common ancestor. Naturally, it is essential to separate those features that are *truly* homologous from those that *seem* homologous but are actually analogous. For example, insects, which are arthropods, and mammals, which are vertebrates, both have legs. But it is clear from the fossil record that legs evolved independently in the two groups. The greater the number of homologous morphological features two organisms share, the more closely related they are thought to be.

internet**connect**

SC*LINKS*
NSTA

TOPIC: Phylogenetic tree
GO TO: www.scilinks.org
KEYWORD: HM343

BLASTULA

**BLASTULA
CROSS SECTION**

**BLASTULA
CROSS SECTION**

Blastopore

**BLASTULA
CROSS SECTION**

FIGURE 18-4

The blastopore, an indentation of the blastula, forms in early embryological development. The blastopore becomes the posterior end of the digestive system in chordates (which include the vertebrates) and echinoderms. In other animal phyla, the blastopore becomes the anterior end of the digestive system.

Embryological Patterns of Development

Early patterns in embryological development provide evidence of phylogenetic relationships. They also provide a means of testing hypotheses about relationships that have been developed from other lines of evidence. Refer to Figure 15-12 in Chapter 15, which shows the great similarity among embryos of three species of vertebrates.

Differences among animal phyla may appear very early in embryological development. As development begins, the zygote starts to divide by mitosis. Within a matter of hours, a ball of cells called a **blastula** (BLAS-tyoo-luh), shown in Figure 18-4, forms. Soon after that, a small indentation, the **blastopore** (BLAS-toh-POR), develops on the outside of the blastula. Eventually this indentation will develop into the digestive system. In most animal phyla, the blastopore becomes the anterior end of the digestive system (the mouth). But in **echinoderms** (e-KIE-noh-DURHMZ), such as starfish and sand dollars, the blastopore becomes the posterior end of the digestive system, as it does in chordates, which include vertebrates. This pattern of development suggests that echinoderms are more closely related to vertebrates than they are to other invertebrates, such as mollusks, as shown in Figure 18-3.

Echinoderms and vertebrates share other important characteristics as well. In both phyla, each cell of the early embryo is potentially capable of forming the entire organism. For example, identical twins are formed when the early embryo splits in two. Each half becomes a complete individual, and the two individuals share the same genetic information. In contrast, when early embryos of fruit flies (phylum Arthropoda) are experimentally split, each part is already committed to becoming a certain part of the organism, such as the head. Thus, splitting an arthropod embryo will cause the two halves to die.

Chromosomes and Macromolecules

Taxonomists use comparisons of macromolecules such as DNA, RNA, and proteins as a kind of "molecular clock." Recall from Section 15-3 that scientists compare amino acid sequences for homologous protein molecules of different species. The number of amino acid differences is a clue to how long ago two species diverged from a shared evolutionary ancestor. This molecular-clock model is not a perfect one. It assumes that all changes in amino acid sequence are random and are not affected by natural selection. This is probably not true. Moreover, sequences of amino acids can change at different rates in different organisms. But the molecular-clock model is used, together with other kinds of data, to estimate degrees of relatedness between different species.

In a similar kind of analysis, biologists compare the karyotypes, or patterns of chromosomes, of two related species. Regions of chromosomes that have the same pattern of banding are clues to the degree of relatedness of organisms. The chromosomes of humans and chimpanzees show a surprising degree of similarity, as

(a)

(b)

FIGURE 18-5

Chimpanzees are genetically very similar to humans. (a) A karyotype of a chimpanzee's 24 chromosome pairs is remarkably similar to (b) a karyotype of a human's 23 chromosome pairs.

shown in Figure 18-5. One of the chromosomes in humans is homologous to two smaller chimpanzee chromosomes. This fused human chromosome and six inverted chromosome segments are the only observed chromosomal differences between the two species. In fruit flies, nearly that much chromosomal variation can be found within one species.

The comparison of chimpanzee and human chromosomes prompted several biologists to reevaluate the accepted estimate of how long ago chimpanzees and humans last shared an ancestor. Before chromosomal analysis, it was widely thought that the ancestors of humans and chimpanzees diverged from a common ancestor about 25 million years ago. After the comparisons of karyotypes and amino acid sequences in proteins, molecular biologists decreased the estimate from 25 million years to as little as 5 million years.

CLADISTICS

One relatively new system of phylogenetic classification is called **cladistics** (kluh-DIS-tiks). Cladistics uses certain features of organisms, called shared derived characters, to establish evolutionary relationships. A **derived character** is a feature that apparently evolved only within the group under consideration. For example, if the group being considered is birds, one example of a derived character is feathers. Most animals do not have feathers; birds are the only animals that do. Therefore, it is safe to assume that feathers evolved within the bird group and were not inherited from some distant ancestor of the birds.

Cladistic taxonomists agree that organisms that share a derived character—like feathers—probably share it because they inherited

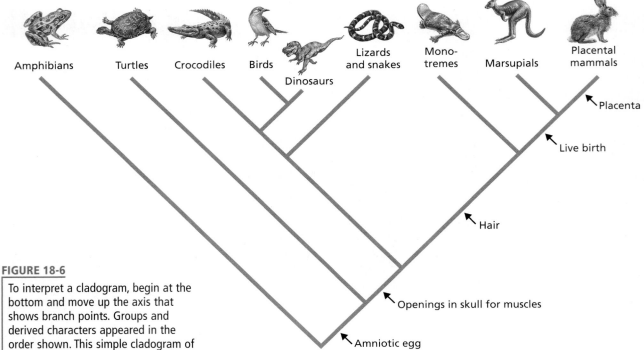

FIGURE 18-6

To interpret a cladogram, begin at the bottom and move up the axis that shows branch points. Groups and derived characters appeared in the order shown. This simple cladogram of terrestrial vertebrates indicates that amphibians arose first, turtles arose next, and placental mammals arose last. Only groups branching *above* a listing of a derived character share that character. Thus, amphibians do not have amniotic eggs, but all other groups do. Likewise, monotremes, marsupials, and placental mammals have hair, though no other groups do.

it from a common ancestor. So shared derived characters, particularly a *group* of several shared derived characters, are strong evidence of common ancestry between organisms that share them. Ancestry diagrams made by means of cladistic analysis, such as the one shown in Figure 18-6, are called **cladograms** (KLAD-uh-GRAMZ).

The application of cladistic taxonomy leads to a number of nontraditional conclusions. One of the most notable is that birds, crocodiles, and dinosaurs are more closely related to each other than any one of them is to a snake or lizard. In the more-classical systematic scheme used in this textbook, snakes, lizards, and crocodiles are classified in the reptile class, while birds are in a class by themselves. A related cladistic conclusion, which differs from that of classical taxonomy, is that the reptiles did not all spring from one common ancestor. Rather, reptiles are a composite of several branches that have occurred during the evolution of the vertebrates, as you can see in the cladogram of vertebrates shown in Figure 18-6.

SECTION 18-2 REVIEW

1. Define the term *phylogenetic tree.*

2. What is systematic taxonomy, and what kinds of data are used by a systematic taxonomist?

3. How can embryological evidence be used to show phylogenetic relationships that are not evident from either the study of morphology or the study of the fossil record?

4. What are two flaws of the molecular clock model in determining relatedness between species?

5. What is a shared derived character?

6. **CRITICAL THINKING** Why does the cladistic approach to classification suggest that the class Reptilia (reptiles) is not a phylogenetic classification?

TWO MODERN SYSTEMS OF CLASSIFICATION

*A*ristotle classified organisms as either plants or animals, but today we recognize that many forms of life are neither. In this section, you will read about two alternative classification systems that are in current use. But remember, organizational systems are imposed by humans and therefore may be flawed. As is true of everything in science, they are subject to change as new information arises.

SIX-KINGDOM SYSTEM

A classification system based on five kingdoms of organisms was preferred by taxonomists for many years. But further studies of bacteria have shown that there are two important subtypes with very different morphologies and properties. Recognition of these two broad types of bacteria has driven the acceptance of a newer, six-kingdom system, illustrated in Table 18-2, which is used in this textbook.

TABLE 18-2 *Six Kingdoms of Life*

Kingdom	Cell type	Number of cells	Nutrition
Archaebacteria	prokaryotic	unicellular	autotrophy and heterotrophy
Eubacteria	prokaryotic	unicellular	autotrophy and heterotrophy
Protista	eukaryotic	unicellular and multicellular	autotrophy and heterotrophy
Fungi	eukaryotic	unicellular and multicellular	heterotrophy
Plantae	eukaryotic	multicellular	autotrophy and (rarely) heterotrophy
Animalia	eukaryotic	multicellular	heterotrophy

OBJECTIVES

▲

Describe the six-kingdom system of classification.

●

List the characteristics that distinguish archaebacteria from eubacteria.

■

Explain why the protists are grouped together in the six-kingdom system in spite of having differences that are greater than those between plants and animals.

◆

Describe the evidence that prompted the creation of the three-domain system of classification.

▲

Explain the principal difference between the six-kingdom system and the three-domain system of classification.

FIGURE 18-7

Archaebacteria often live in very hostile environments that cannot support other forms of life, such as this hot spring, Morning Glory Pool, in Yellowstone National Park.

Kingdom Archaebacteria

The members of the **kingdom Archaebacteria** (AHR-kee-bak-TIR-ee-uh) are unicellular prokaryotes with distinctive cell membranes as well as biochemical and genetic properties that differ from all other kinds of life. Some species of archaebacteria are autotrophic, producing food by chemosynthesis. Their waste products may include flammable gases, such as methane. Many archaebacteria live in harsh environments such as sulfurous hot springs, as shown in Figure 18-7, and very salty lakes, and in anaerobic environments, such as in the intestines of mammals.

The prefix *archae-* comes from the Greek word for "ancient." Modern archaebacteria may be directly descended from and very similar to the first organisms on Earth, which flourished before the evolution of photosynthesis. These early archaebacterial ancestors evolved before the release of large amounts of oxygen gas into the environment.

Kingdom Eubacteria

The *eu* part of **eubacteria** (YOO-bak-TEER-ee-uh) means "true." Eubacteria are unicellular prokaryotes. Most of the bacteria that affect your life—those that cause tooth decay, turn milk into yogurt, and cause food poisoning—are members of the **kingdom Eubacteria.** Most species of eubacteria use oxygen, but a few species cannot live in the presence of oxygen.

At first glance, both eubacteria and archaebacteria may seem unimportant. But remember that they include the greatest number of living things on Earth. Moreover, their ancestors, which may have been quite similar to modern bacteria, were probably the first living things on Earth.

Both archaebacteria and eubacteria reproduce by binary fission, but they do have some ways to recombine genes, allowing evolution to occur. The very short generation times of bacteria (as little as 30 minutes) allow rapid evolutionary response to environmental change. If you have ever had an antibiotic-resistant bacterial infection, you have had experience with the remarkably fast evolution of bacteria.

FIGURE 18-8

Some protists are multicellular. This ocean-living giant kelp resembles a plant, but it lacks the organization of tissues found in true plants.

Kingdom Protista

The **kingdom Protista** (proh-TIS-tuh) is made up of a variety of eukaryotic, mostly single-celled organisms. Some species of **protists** (PROH-tists) exist as multicellular organisms, like the giant kelp shown in Figure 18-8. Although they look much like plants, multicellular protists lack specialized tissues. Being eukaryotes, they have a membrane-bound true nucleus with linear chromosomes, and they have membrane-bound organelles.

It is difficult to make generalizations about the protists because many protist species are more distantly related to each other than plants are to animals. The kingdom Protista contains all eukaryotes that are not plants, animals, or fungi, more than 50,000 species in all. The sexual cycles of many protists are unknown, but most are thought to have some process of genetic recombination.

Euglena and the amoebas are common types of unicellular protists. *Euglena,* shown in Figure 18-9, can feed on other organisms in the manner of an animal, but it also has chloroplasts and can perform photosynthesis if light is available. Amoebas, such as the one shown in Figure 18-2, feed on other organisms and respond to touch and light. Yet *Euglena* is not a plant, and amoebas are not animals—both are protists.

FIGURE 18-9

Euglena gracilis (LM 580×), like all species of *Euglena,* is a unicellular protist that can be autotrophic or heterotrophic, depending on its environmental conditions.

Kingdom Fungi

The **kingdom Fungi** (FUHN-jee) is made up of heterotrophic unicellular and multicellular eukaryotic organisms. Fungi absorb nutrients rather than ingesting them the way some protists, such as amoebas, do. While sexual cycles are not known for many fungi, it is likely that all species have some way of promoting gene recombination. The well-studied mold *Neurospora* has a standard sexual cycle and has been used extensively in the study of meiosis and in the genetic control of physiological functions. There are over 100,000 species of fungi, including mushrooms, puffballs, rusts, smuts, mildews, and molds.

FIGURE 18-10

Orchids, like this *Paphiapedilum rothschildionum,* are found in tropical climates. Flowers contain the plant's gametes, or reproductive cells.

Kingdom Plantae

As you might have expected, the **kingdom Plantae** (PLAN-tee) consists of multicellular plants. All except for a few parasitic forms are autotrophic and use photosynthesis as a source of energy. Most plants live on land, and most have a sexual cycle based on meiosis. More than 350,000 species of plants have been identified. They include mosses, ferns, conifers, and flowering plants, like the orchid shown in Figure 18-10.

Kingdom Animalia

The **kingdom Animalia** (AN-uh-MAH-lee-uh) is made up of eukaryotic, multicellular heterotrophic organisms. Most animals have symmetrical body organization and move about their environment. Almost all animals have a standard sexual cycle that employs meiosis for the recombination of genes.

A six-kingdom system

| Eubacteria | Archaebacteria | Protista | Plantae | Fungi | Animalia |

A three-domain system

| Bacteria (eubacteria) | Archaea (archaebacteria) | Eukarya (eukaryotes) |

FIGURE 18-11

The three-domain system highlights the importance of archaebacteria as a life-form. This system is often used by molecular biologists. Notice that the domain Eukarya includes members of the kingdoms Protista, Plantae, Fungi, and Animalia, which are all made up of eukaryotic organisms.

Word Roots and Origins

domain

from the Latin *dominium,* meaning "right of ownership"

THREE-DOMAIN SYSTEM

The young science of molecular biology has led to an alternative to the six-kingdom system. By comparing sequences of ribosomal RNA in different organisms, molecular biologist Carl Woese (1928–), of the University of Illinois, has estimated how long ago pairs of different organisms shared a common ancestor. Because all organisms, even prokaryotes, have ribosomes, the ribosomal RNA molecule can be used to study the degree of relationship between any two living things. The phylogenetic tree drawn from these data shows that living things seem to fall naturally into three broad groups, or **domains.** Plants, animals, and fungi are one small twig of a large branch—a domain—that includes all the eukaryotes. These domains are shown in comparison with the six kingdoms in Figure 18-11.

Domain Archaea (ahr-KEE-uh) is known in the six-kingdom system as kingdom Archaebacteria. **Domain Bacteria** is known in the six-kingdom system as the kingdom Eubacteria.

Domain Eukarya (yoo-KAR-ee-uh) consists of the protists, the fungi, and the plants and animals. All eukaryotes have true nuclei with linear chromosomes and membrane-bound organelles. Most of the variation in this domain is among the protists. Surprisingly, when considered from the perspective of the complete diversity of life on Earth, the fungi, plants, and animals are quite similar to each other.

SECTION 18-3 REVIEW

1. What are the six kingdoms in the six-kingdom system of classification?

2. What are two things that make archaebacteria difficult to study?

3. What is the most heterogeneous kingdom in terms of morphology?

4. What kind of evidence indicates that organisms fall naturally into three broad domains?

5. Why do protists, fungi, plants, and animals share a domain in the six-kingdom system?

6. CRITICAL THINKING In the five-kingdom system, which is still used by some scientists, all species of bacteria are grouped in the kingdom Monera. Why might there have been only one bacteria kingdom recognized in the past?

SUMMARY/VOCABULARY

18-1
- Taxonomy is the science of grouping organisms according to their morphology and evolutionary history.
- Carolus Linnaeus originated a seven-level hierarchy system for classifying organisms according to their morphology. Moving from the most general to the most specific, the levels are called kingdom, phylum, class, order, family, genus, and species. A version of this system is still in use.
- A species name consists of the genus name together with a species identifier. A species denotes a single organism type.

Vocabulary

binomial nomenclature (339)	family (338)
class (338)	genus (338)
division (338)	kingdom (338)
	order (338)

phylogeny (339)	species name (339)
phylum (338)	subspecies (339)
species (338)	taxonomy (337)
species identifier (339)	variety (339)

18-2
- A modern approach to taxonomy is systematics, which analyzes the diversity of organisms in the context of their evolutionary history.
- Scientists consider several lines of evidence when classifying organisms according to their evolutionary history.
- An organism's relationship to organisms in the fossil record as well as to living organisms is taken into account in the formulation of a phylogenetic tree.
- Similarities in patterns of embryological development provide clues to the degree of relatedness of different organisms.
- Molecular similarities, such as those found in homologous proteins of different organisms, also indicate how closely organisms are related.
- Shared derived characters, those traits that developed within a certain group, are clues to the degree of relatedness among organisms. The system that uses shared derived characters to deduce evolutionary history is called *cladistics*.

Vocabulary

blastopore (344)	cladistics (345)
blastula (344)	cladogram (346)

derived character (345)	phylogenetic tree (342)
echinoderm (344)	systematics (342)

18-3
- Many modern taxonomists use the six-kingdom system of classification, which recognizes the unique nature of the archaebacteria.
- Archaebacteria, some of which live in extremely harsh environments, have been largely ignored until recently. Scientists now think archaebacteria closely resemble the first kinds of organisms to live on Earth.
- An alternative classification system that employs three broad domains groups all eukaryotic organisms under the domain Eukarya. Eubacteria (domain Bacteria) and archaebacteria (domain Archaea) form each of the other two domains.

Vocabulary

domain (350)	eubacteria (348)
domain Archaea (350)	kingdom Animalia (349)
domain Bacteria (350)	kingdom Archaebacteria (348)
domain Eukarya (350)	

kingdom Eubacteria (348)	protist (348)
kingdom Fungi (349)	
kingdom Plantae (349)	
kingdom Protista (348)	

REVIEW

Vocabulary

1. Distinguish between a species name and a common name.
2. What is the difference between a phylum and a division?
3. Using a dictionary, find the meaning of the word parts *phylo-* and *-geny* in *phylogeny.* Explain why this term is appropriate for discussing common ancestry of organisms.
4. What is the difference between a subspecies and a variety?
5. Look up the roots of the word *echinoderm.* How does what you found relate to the properties of a group that includes starfish, sand dollars, and sea urchins?

Multiple Choice

6. A species name includes information about (a) species and phylum (b) division and genus (c) genus and order (d) genus and species.
7. Aristotle classified plants on the basis of differences in their (a) stems (b) flowers (c) leaves (d) roots.
8. Linnaeus classified organisms based on similarities of their (a) genes (b) homologous proteins (c) morphology (d) embryology.
9. A group of related classes of organisms make up a (a) genus (b) order (c) phylum (d) kingdom.
10. The kingdom Animalia is divided into phyla. At the same level of organization, the kingdom Plantae is divided into (a) classes (b) divisions (c) species (d) genera.
11. Some animal species are divided into (a) identical species (b) varieties (c) subspecies (d) twin species.
12. Classifying organisms according to their presumed evolutionary history is called a (a) six-kingdom approach (b) morphological approach (c) phylogenetic approach (d) three-domain approach.
13. The kingdom Protista includes (a) bacteria (b) plants (c) algae (d) mushrooms.
14. Some protists are similar to plants in that they (a) carry on photosynthesis (b) have plantlike organization of tissues (c) ingest nutrients (d) are unicellular.
15. Taxonomists can use data from RNA-sequencing techniques to (a) predict future changes in species (b) estimate when two species diverged from a common ancestor (c) determine species name (d) explain the origin of life.

Short Answer

16. List the seven levels of Linnaeus's classification hierarchy from most general, *A*, to most specific, *G*.

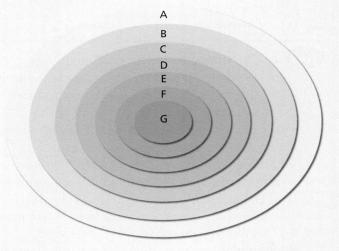

17. How were Aristotle's and Linnaeus's classification systems for organisms similar?
18. Why are species names important in scientific work?
19. What are the differences between plants and fungi?
20. How do amino acid sequences function as a "biological clock"?
21. What do we call the system of classification that is based on an analysis of shared derived characters?
22. Name three things you might learn about an organism by investigating the meaning of its scientific name.
23. How might a taxonomist use embryological evidence in classifying an organism?
24. How do some archaebacteria produce food?
25. What do plants and fungi have in common with animals?

CRITICAL THINKING

1. Scientists agree that evolution has occurred and continues to occur, and that all of the organisms on Earth are related to each other to varying degrees. It is also obvious that the course of evolution proceeded in one way only, yet scientists often disagree about phylogenetic histories of organisms. Cladistic taxonomists regard reptiles in a different light than do more classical taxonomists. Why might scientists disagree with each other about the course of evolution?

2. The evolutionary history of reptiles can be studied using comparisons of their sequences of macromolecules. The degree of difference can be related to the time that has passed since any two species descended from a common ancestor. Would the phylogenetic tree derived from macromolecular comparisons probably more closely resemble the results of cladistic analysis or the standard classification of all reptiles as a single class of vertebrates?

3. Biologists think that there are probably millions of undescribed and unclassified species on Earth. Why might so many species still be undescribed or unclassified today?

4. Legs are an example of a shared derived character in vertebrates. Arthropods, such as lobsters and crickets, also have legs, but they are not accepted as a character shared with vertebrates. Why?

5. A number of years ago scientists found a living fish, called a coelacanth and pictured below, that was thought to have become extinct about 65 million years ago. The earliest fossils of coelacanths are about 350 million years old. Thus, the appearance of the coelacanth has remained unchanged for 350 million years. Although it is impossible to compare macromolecules such as proteins of a 350-million-year-old fossil coelacanth with that of a freshly caught coelacanth, what would you expect to find if you could?

EXTENSION

1. Read "Robust About Face" in *Science News,* April 24, 1999, on page 267. Describe the features of the head of *Australopithecus robustus.* Where do some researchers place *A. robustus* in the human lineage? According to Melanie McCollum, why is this cladistic reasoning misleading?

2. Visit the zoo, and list the scientific names of all the animals you see, or use your library to research 10 organisms. Record the scientific and common names of these organisms. For each animal, list a trait that led taxonomists to classify the organism in its particular genus or family.

3. Collect half a cup of water from a shallow pond. Using a microscope, study several samples from the water. Draw the organisms you find, and classify them as best you can into kingdom and phylum.

Using and Formulating Dichotomous Keys

OBJECTIVES

- Use a dichotomous key to identify leaves.
- Construct a dichotomous identification key.

PROCESS SKILLS

- identifying
- classifying
- designing
- interpreting
- organizing data
- comparing and contrasting

MATERIALS

- pencil
- paper
- shoes
- masking tape
- marker

Background

1. Who developed the classification system that scientists use today to classify and group organisms according to their inherited traits?
2. Taxonomy is the science of naming and classifying organisms according to their characteristics and evolutionary history.
3. Why is classification essential to biology?
4. A dichotomous key uses pairs of contrasting, descriptive statements to lead to the identification of an organism (or other object).
5. The principle behind dichotomous keys—the forced choice—is used in many different situations to narrow the path toward an answer. If you have ever had your eyes examined for corrective lenses, you are familiar with the series of forced choices that end with the choice of the correct lenses for your eyes.

PART A   Using a Dichotomous Key

1. Field guides often use dichotomous keys to identify organisms. Use the dichotomous key shown here to identify the tree leaves below. Begin with the paired descriptions 1a and 1b, and follow the directions. Proceed through the list of paired descriptions until you identify the leaf in question. In your lab report, write the names of the leaves as you identify them.

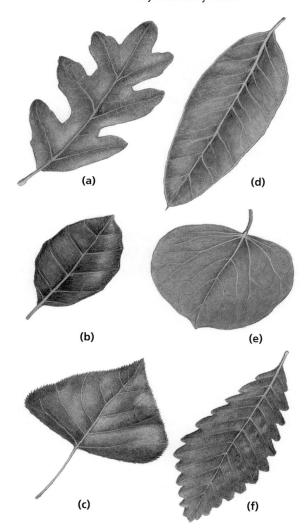

(a)

(d)

(b)

(e)

(c)

(f)

Dichotomous Key for Identifying Common Leaves

1a. If the edge of the leaf has no teeth, or lobes, go to 2 in the key.

1b. If the edge of the leaf has teeth, or lobes, go to 3 in the key.

2a. If the leaf has slightly wavy edges, it is a shingle oak.

2b. If the leaf has smooth edges, go to 4 in the key.

3a. If the leaf edge is toothed, it is a Lombardy poplar.

3b. If the leaf edge has lobes, go to 5 in the key.

4a. If the leaf is heart-shaped with veins branching from the base, it is a redbud.

4b. If the leaf is not heart-shaped, it is a live oak.

5a. If the leaf edge has a few large lobes, it is an English oak.

5b. If the leaf edge has many small lobes, it is a chestnut oak.

PART B Making a Dichotomous Key

2. Gather 10 different single shoes, and use masking tape and a marker to label the soles of the shoes with the owner's name. The labeled shoes should then be placed on a single table in the classroom.

3. Form small groups. Discuss the appearance of the shoes. In your lab report, make a table like the one below that lists some general characteristics of the shoes, such as the type and size. Also list the names of the students who own the shoes. Complete the chart by describing the characteristics of each person's shoe.

4. Use the information in your table to make a dichotomous key that can be used to identify the owner of each shoe. Remember that a dichotomous key includes pairs of opposing descriptions. At the end of each description, the key should either identify an object or give directions to go to another specific pair of descriptions. Write your dichotomous key in your lab report.

5. After all groups have completed their key, exchange keys with a member of another group. Use the key to identify the owner of each shoe, and then verify the accuracy of your identification by reading the label on the shoe. If the key has led you to an inaccurate identification, return the key so that corrections can be made.

6. Clean up your materials before leaving the lab.

Analysis and Conclusions

1. What other characteristics might be used to identify leaves with a dichotomous key?

2. Were you able to identify the shoes using another group's key? If not, describe the problems you encountered.

3. How was it helpful to list the characteristics of the shoes before making the key?

4. Does a dichotomous key begin with general descriptions and then proceed to more specific descriptions, or vice versa? Explain your answer, giving an example from the key you made.

5. Are dichotomous keys based on a phylogenetic or morphological approach to classification? Explain your answer.

Further Inquiry

List characteristics that might be used to identify birds or other animals using a dichotomous key. Compare your list of characteristics with those used in a dichotomous key in a field guide for identifying birds or other animals.

TABLE A *DISTINGUISHING FEATURES OF A SAMPLE OF SHOES*

	Left/right	Men's/women's	Laced/slip-on	Color	Size	Owner
1						
2						
3						
4						
5						

Unit 5

ECOLOGY

❝ *We and our fellow vertebrates are largely along for the ride on this planet. If we want to perpetuate the dream that we are in charge of our destiny and that of our planet, it can only be by maintaining biological diversity—not by destroying it. In the end, we impoverish ourselves if we impoverish the biota.* ❞

From "Diverse Considerations," by Thomas E. Lovejoy, from *Biodiversity*, edited by E. O. Wilson. Copyright © 1988 by the National Academy of Sciences. Reprinted by permission of **National Academy Press.**

internet connect

SCiLINKS NSTA
National Science Teachers Association *sci*LINKS Internet resources are located throughout this unit.

Coral reef communities are second only to rain forests in diversity.

Bears are among the largest terrestrial predators.

The biosphere

Mimicry helps this mantid hide from both predators and potential prey.

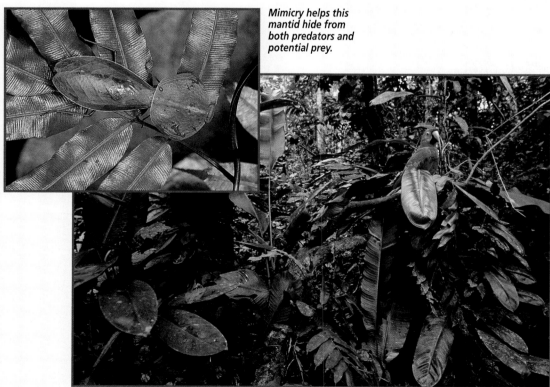

Tropical rain forests are richer in species than other areas of Earth.

INTRODUCTION TO ECOLOGY

This is a view of the biosphere as seen from space.

FOCUS CONCEPT: *Interdependence of Organisms*

As you read, notice that all organisms affect and are affected by the living and nonliving components of their environment.

ECOLOGY

Ecology is the study of the interactions between organisms and the living and nonliving components of their environment. The Earth includes a tremendous variety of living things. Each organism depends in some way on other living and nonliving things in its environment. Ecology involves collecting information about organisms and their environments, looking for patterns, and seeking to explain these patterns.

TODAY'S ENVIRONMENT

Although the field of ecology was not named until 1866, ecological information and understanding have always been crucial to humans. Before the development of agriculture, about 10,000–12,000 years ago, our ancestors obtained all of their food by hunting animals and gathering grains, seeds, berries, nuts, and plants. For them, survival depended on practical knowledge about the environment. While our understanding of the environment has grown much more sophisticated, our need for information has grown more urgent. Over the past few decades, humans have changed the environment on a greater scale than ever before in history. Learning how to improve our effect on the environment is critical to the survival of our species.

The Exploding Human Population

The most significant environmental change is probably the rapid increase in the number of people on Earth. The world's human population has tripled from 2 billion in 1930 to 6 billion people in 1999. This increase in population is unprecedented in the history of our species. According to recent projections by the United Nations, in the year 2050 the world's population will be between 7.8 billion and 12.5 billion. Figure 19-1 on the following page shows that our present numbers are already causing severe crowding in some areas. An increasing population requires increasing amounts of energy, food, and space for the disposal of waste. Providing for the needs of this growing population will take an increasingly greater share of Earth's resources.

The Sixth Mass Extinction

As the human population has increased, many other species have declined in number or become extinct. For example, on the

▲

Define the term *ecology*, and explain why ecology is important.

●

List and describe three human-caused environmental problems.

■

Identify the five different levels of organization in ecology.

◆

Explain the theme of interconnectedness.

▲

Identify the importance of models to ecology.

Word Roots and Origins

ecology

from the Greek words *oikos*, meaning "house," and *logos*, meaning "study of"

FIGURE 19-1

Most of our planet is already very crowded, as this photograph of people in New York City shows. Scientists are concerned about how our quality of life will be affected if our population doubles within the next 50 years. If our population continues to grow at its present rate, the environment that supports us may collapse.

FIGURE 19-2

The impact of humans has destroyed the habitats of many of the bird species native to the Hawaiian Islands. This destruction has caused the extinction of about 60 species of birds, including the birds shown below.

Hawaiian Islands, where isolation fostered the evolution of a diverse and unique set of species, 60 of the 100 species of native birds have disappeared since the first human colonists arrived. They were eliminated by habitat destruction, overhunting, and introduced diseases and predators. Two of these extinct birds are shown in Figure 19-2. Worldwide, about 20 percent of the species of birds have become extinct in the last 2,000 years. Today extinction is occurring most rapidly in the tropics.

Paleontologists have found evidence in the fossil record of five major mass extinctions, episodes in which a large percentage of Earth's species became extinct in a relatively short time. The sixth mass extinction is happening now. Currently, species are disappearing faster than at any time since the last mass extinction—the disappearance of the dinosaurs 65 million years ago. Scientists estimate that about one-fifth of the species in the world may disappear in just the next century.

(a) Nukupu'u, *Heterorhynchus lucidus*

(b) Greater Koa, *Telespiza palmeri*

The Thinning Ozone Layer

The ozone layer in the upper atmosphere protects the living organisms on Earth by absorbing ultraviolet (UV) radiation from the sun. Industrial chemicals called chlorofluorocarbons (CFCs) and some related chemicals react with ozone and are destroying the ozone layer. In 1985, British scientists discovered an ozone "hole," a region of an abnormally low ozone level, over Antarctica, as shown in Figure 19-3. This discovery led to a treaty in 1992 to ban CFCs and other ozone-destroying chemicals.

Although ozone depletion is occurring to some degree over most of the planet, the reduction in the ozone level over Antarctica by 1996 was about 50 percent of its maximum density. About 1 percent of the UV radiation from the sun gets through the ozone shield to reach Earth's surface. That 1 percent is responsible for all sunburns and for more than a half-million skin cancers each year.

Climatic Changes

Although carbon dioxide and water vapor are transparent to visible light, they intercept much of the reflected heat and direct it back toward Earth. This natural phenomenon, known as the **greenhouse effect,** is the mechanism that insulates Earth from the deep freeze of space. However, human activities are changing the composition of the atmosphere and thereby influencing climate. One prediction of possible future changes in climate is shown in Figure 19-4. When fossil fuels, such as coal, oil, and natural gas, are burned to provide energy, carbon dioxide is released. The burning of large amounts of fossil fuels has caused the concentration of carbon dioxide in the atmosphere to increase by about 25 percent in the last 100 years. A

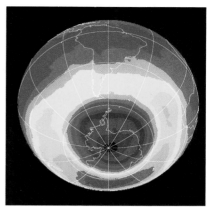

FIGURE 19-3

The ozone shield over Antarctica fluctuates in density seasonally, sometimes to a low of half the original density. The ozone shield is diminishing all over the planet as well.

FIGURE 19-4

The regions of the world that are likely to become wetter or drier as a result of global warming are shown below. Global warming and changes in rainfall are likely to be variable and unpredictable, so predictions cannot be entirely accurate. Predictions for the darker colored areas have a higher probability of being correct.

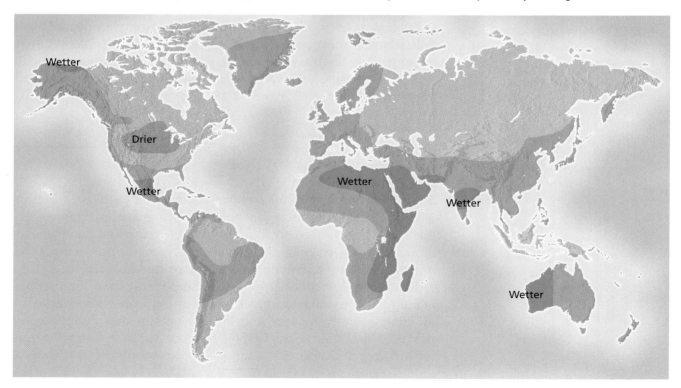

FIGURE 19-5

Ecology has been organized into several levels because of the complexity of the science.

Modeling the Greenhouse Effect

Materials 1 qt jars (2), graduated cylinder, aluminum foil, transparent tape, thermometer, water

Procedure

1. Put 750 mL of cold tap water in each jar.
2. Measure and record the initial water temperature in each jar, and record the time it was measured.
3. Cover one jar with a single layer of aluminum foil, and secure the foil with tape. Leave the top of the other jar uncovered.
4. Place both jars in the same sunny window or under a plant light.
5. Before the end of the class period, record the temperature of the water in each jar and the time it was measured.

Analysis Did you discover a temperature difference between the jars when you measured the temperatures the second time? If so, which jar of water was warmer? How does this activity model the greenhouse effect?

global warming of the atmosphere is now occurring because of heat trapped by excess "greenhouse" gases, such as carbon dioxide.

Since 1860, the average global temperature has risen about 0.6°C (1°F), and most scientists agree that this increase was caused by higher levels of carbon dioxide in the atmosphere. Furthermore, scientists project that the average global temperature will increase 1.5°C to 4.5°C (3°F to 8°F) by the year 2100. This increase in average temperature may change global weather patterns and cause rising sea levels due to melting polar icecaps.

Ecological knowledge is essential for solving environmental problems. However, any proposed solution to an environmental problem must draw on knowledge from a variety of fields, including ecology, chemistry, physics, and geology, and it must take into account economic and political realities.

LEVELS OF ORGANIZATION

Scientists recognize a hierarchy of different levels of organization within organisms. Each organism is composed of one or more cells. Each cell is composed of molecules, which in turn are composed of atoms, and so on. Likewise, ecologists recognize a hierarchy of organization in the environment, as illustrated in Figure 19-5.

Each level has unique properties that result from interactions among its components, and these unique properties cannot be identified simply by studying lower levels in the hierarchy. For practical reasons, ecologists often focus their research on one level of organization. But they also recognize that each level is influenced by processes at other levels.

The Biosphere

The broadest, most inclusive level of organization is the **biosphere** (BIE-oh-SFEER), the thin volume of Earth and its atmosphere that supports life. All organisms are found within the biosphere. It is about 20 km (13 mi) thick and extends from about 8 to 10 km (5 to 6 mi) above the Earth's surface to the deepest parts of the oceans. In comparison, the Earth's diameter is about 12,700 km (7,900 mi), or more than 600 times the thickness of the biosphere. If Earth were the size of an apple, the biosphere would only be as thick as the apple's skin. Ecologists often describe the biosphere as a thin film of life covering an otherwise lifeless planet. Living things are not distributed evenly throughout the biosphere. Most organisms are found within a few meters of the surface of the land or oceans.

Ecosystems

The biosphere is composed of smaller units called ecosystems. An **ecosystem** (EK-oh-SIS-tuhm) includes all of the organisms and the nonliving environment found in a particular place. Consider a pond ecosystem. It contains a variety of living things, such as fish, turtles, aquatic plants, algae, insects, and bacteria. These organisms interact in ways that affect their survival. For instance, insects and fish eat aquatic plants, and turtles eat fish. The pond ecosystem also includes all the nonliving (physical and chemical) aspects of the pond that influence its inhabitants. The chemical composition of the pond—how much dissolved oxygen and carbon dioxide it contains, its supply of nitrogen, its pH—helps to determine what kinds of organisms live in the pond and how abundant they are. A very important physical factor is the amount of sunlight the pond receives, because sunlight is the ultimate source of energy for the pond's inhabitants.

Communities, Populations, and Organisms

While an ecosystem contains both the living and nonliving components, a community includes only organisms. A **community** is all the interacting organisms living in an area. For instance, all the fish, turtles, plants, algae, and bacteria in the pond described above make up a community. Although it is less inclusive than an ecosystem, a community is still very complex, and it may contain thousands of species. Ecologists studying a community often focus on how species interact and how these interactions influence the nature of the community. Remember that the word *community* has a specific meaning in biology that differs from its meaning in everyday speech.

Below the community level of organization is the population level, where the focus is on the members of a single species. A **population** includes all the members of a species that live in one place at one time.

The simplest level of organization in ecology is that of the organism. Research at this level concentrates on the adaptations that allow organisms to overcome the challenges of their environment.

A KEY THEME IN ECOLOGY

An important fact to keep in mind as you study ecology is that no organism is isolated. The theme of the interconnectedness of all organisms is central to the study of ecology. All organisms interact with other organisms in their surroundings and with the nonliving portion of their environment. Their survival depends on these interactions. Thus, each ecosystem is a network in which organisms are linked to other organisms and to the nonliving environment. Ecologists refer to this quality as interconnectedness or interdependence. For example, you could not survive without the plants and other photosynthetic organisms that produce oxygen. Your cells need oxygen to release the energy in food, and cells will die if deprived of oxygen for even a few minutes. Conversely, photosynthetic organisms depend on the release of carbon dioxide gas by the cellular respiration of other organisms, such as humans, and geochemical processes, such as volcanic eruptions. Carbon dioxide gas is an essential raw material for making carbohydrates.

Disturbances in Ecosystems

An important consequence of interconnectedness is that any disturbance or change in an ecosystem can spread through the network of interactions and affect the ecosystem in widespread and often unexpected ways. To see one example, look at Figure 19-6, which shows some of the interrelationships among species in an oak forest. The number of people who get sick with Lyme disease,

FIGURE 19-6

All of the very different species shown are ecologically connected in the forest. An unusually plentiful crop of acorns helps support a large population of deer and mice, which help support a large population of ticks. Ticks carry the bacterium that causes Lyme disease. They pass on the disease to humans who visit the forest.

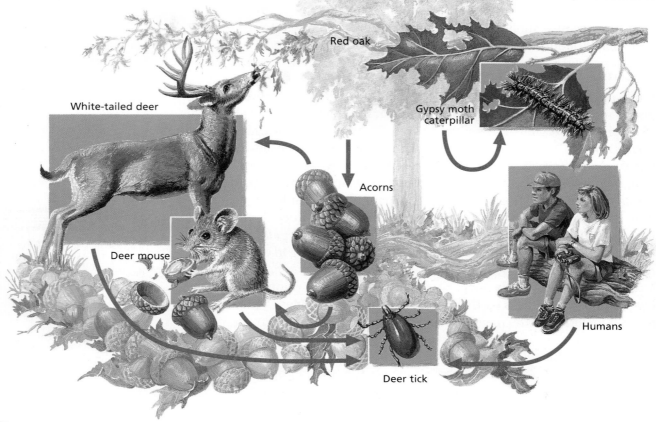

Red oak

White-tailed deer

Gypsy moth caterpillar

Acorns

Deer mouse

Humans

Deer tick

a bacterial infection that can damage the nervous system, is related to acorn production in forests in the eastern United States.

Oak trees typically produce few acorns (or none at all) in most years. Every few years, however, they produce a huge crop of acorns, setting off a chain of events within the ecosystem. The abundance of acorns enables deer and mice, which feed on acorns, to have more offspring that survive, and their populations grow. More deer and mice can support more ticks, so the tick population also increases. Lyme disease is spread by the bite of the deer tick. The number of people bitten by ticks (and potentially exposed to Lyme disease) depends on the number of ticks and the number of people in the forest. In general, as the population of ticks increases, the number of Lyme disease cases increases.

internet**connect**

SCI**LINKS**
NSTA

TOPIC: Threats to ecosystems
GO TO: www.scilinks.org
KEYWORD: HM365

ECOLOGICAL MODELS

Ecological knowledge is vital, but ecosystems are extremely complex and difficult to study. One way that ecologists deal with this complexity is to use models. A model may be visual, verbal, or mathematical. An ecologist might use a graphical model to show how sunlight, rainfall, and temperature affect the growth of plants. Ecologists construct models to help them understand the environment and to make predictions about how the environment might change. Figure 19-4 is a model based on scientific predictions about how climates may change. In ecology, models are typically expressed as graphs, diagrams, or mathematical equations. Figure 19-5 is a model in the form of a diagram.

A model can be used to test a hypothesis about an ecosystem. Scientists use models to make predictions about the future behavior of the ecosystem, and these predictions can be tested by comparing them with observations from the natural world. Models are widely used to help plan and evaluate solutions to environmental problems. It is important to keep in mind, however, that models are simplified systems designed only to mimic the behavior of the natural world. A model is limited in its application, therefore, because it cannot account for the influence of every variable in a real environment.

SECTION 19-1 REVIEW

1. Why was knowledge about the environment important to the earliest members of our species? Why is such knowledge important now?

2. What is causing the thinning of the ozone layer?

3. How does a population differ from a community?

4. Describe one example of interdependence.

5. Why are models so useful in ecology?

6. CRITICAL THINKING Why is it important to understand challenges in a species' environment in order to understand the species' evolution? Relate your answer to what Darwin referred to as "the struggle for survival."

The Rise and Fall of Island Species

HISTORICAL PERSPECTIVE

In the mid-1800s, Charles Darwin observed and collected organisms in the Galápagos Islands. His fieldwork led to the theory of natural selection as a mechanism for evolution. About a century later, mathematician and ecologist Robert H. MacArthur also studied species found on islands. With taxonomist and zoogeographer Edward O. Wilson, MacArthur developed the theory that provided the title to their book, The Theory of Island Biogeography. *Biogeography is the study of the geographical distribution of plants and animals. Today this field has increasing relevance for ecologists and for all who care about the survival of species.*

Robert H. MacArthur and Edward O. Wilson

A Project in Biogeography

By the mid-1950s, Edward O. Wilson had studied insect species he had found on a number of islands. His specialty was myrmecology, the biology of ants. After many years of study and fieldwork, Wilson wanted to go beyond the simple collection and description of organisms, a desire that meshed well with the thinking of Robert H. MacArthur.

MacArthur began his career as a mathematician, but he later moved to mathematical ecology. He was interested in patterns and ideas and in a bigger picture of nature. He wanted to understand the fundamental principles in the science of ecology.

MacArthur and Wilson each brought specific strengths to the field of biogeography. Soon after the two

men met, in 1959, they began the project that led to their book. In their book, MacArthur and Wilson explain why they chose to concentrate on the study of species on islands: "In the science of biogeography, the island is the first unit that the mind can pick out and begin to comprehend."

Seeing the Patterns

Wilson noticed that the number of ant species on an island tends to correlate with the size of the island. He also

noticed that when a new ant species arrives on an island, one of the species already on the island becomes extinct, which, in this context, means that they cease to exist on the island. However, the total number of ant species remains constant. Wilson and MacArthur called that constant number of species an equilibrium.

When they examined the data closely, MacArthur and Wilson found that the same pattern exists among bird species in the Philippines, Indonesia, and New Guinea. In each case, when one species of animal disappeared from an island, a new one moved in, but the total number of species remained constant.

MacArthur and Wilson graphed their data, as shown on the facing page. The downward slope of the immigration (colonization) line shows that the number of species

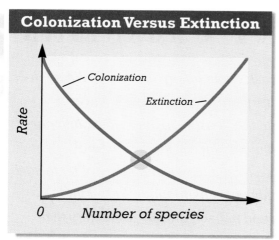

Colonization Versus Extinction

Rate / *0* / *Number of species*

Colonization

Extinction

This simple model represents the equilibrium of numbers of island species. Note that the rate of colonization is highest when the number of species is lowest, as shown on the model at the y-axis. The rate of extinction is highest and the rate of colonization is lowest when the number of species is at a maximum. At what point are the rates of colonization and extinction equal?

that moved in decreased as the island became crowded. That is, the rate of colonization slowed with an increase in the number of species. The upward slope of the extinction line shows that as the island grew more crowded, more species became extinct. In other words, the rate of extinction increased with an increase in the number of species. The crossing point is an equilibrium, the constant number of species for that island.

Constructing a Model

MacArthur and Wilson developed a mathematical model to explain their observations. The mathematics of the theory is complex, but the broad outlines center on two observable patterns:

1. Large islands have more species than small islands have.
2. Remote islands—those located far from the mainland or from a larger island—have fewer species than less-remote ones.

Earlier biogeographers had explained these phenomena from a historical perspective. They reasoned, for example, that a remote island took eons to fill up with species, so an island with few species probably has a relatively short history. In MacArthur and Wilson's model, size and isolation—not the age of the island—regulate the number of immigrations and extinctions.

Testing and Predicting

Could their model be used to predict the number of species on an island? MacArthur and Wilson decided to test their model on Krakatau, an island in Indonesia on which a volcano had erupted in 1883, killing every living thing on the island. The eruption left Krakatau much like a newborn island. Equally important, the return of plant and animal life to the island had been carefully recorded since Krakatau was first revisited, in 1886.

Using their model, MacArthur and Wilson predicted that at the point of equilibrium, the number of bird species would be about 30. After examining the records of bird life at Krakatau, they learned that their prediction had come close. The number of species had climbed to 27 before leveling off. Five species were new to the island,

but an equal number had become extinct, maintaining the equilibrium number of 27.

New Ways of Thinking

The response from other scientists to *The Theory of Island Biogeography*, published in 1967, was mixed. At the very least, the theory introduced in the book has stimulated further research in the field of biogeography. This in turn has led to increased knowledge about how an environment's geography affects its ecology. MacArthur and Wilson looked beyond isolated facts and events to investigate similarities, patterns, and ongoing processes. By reflecting on the larger picture, perhaps biogeographers can help increase awareness of the importance of biodiversity.

This model shows effects that the size and remoteness of an island have on species equilibrium. Note that far (remote), small islands reach an equilibrium (shown at 1) with fewer species than near, large islands (shown at 4).

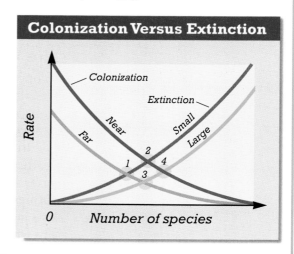

Colonization Versus Extinction

Rate / *0* / *Number of species*

Colonization

Extinction

Far / *Near* / *Small* / *Large*

1 / *2* / *3* / *4*

OBJECTIVES

▲

Contrast abiotic factors with biotic factors, and list two examples of each.

●

Explain the importance of tolerance curves.

■

Describe some adaptations that allow organisms to avoid unfavorable conditions.

◆

Explain the concept of the niche.

▲

Contrast the fundamental niche with the realized niche.

ECOLOGY OF ORGANISMS

Some basic questions to ask about an organism are, Where does it live? and Why does it live there? The answers to these questions are complex and involve the organism's evolutionary history, its tolerances and requirements, the history and conditions of its **habitat** *(where it lives), and many other factors. In this section you will study how environments affect the distribution of organisms and how organisms respond to their environments.*

BIOTIC AND ABIOTIC FACTORS

Ecologists separate the environmental factors that influence an organism into two classes. The living components of the environment are called **biotic** (bie-AHT-ik) **factors.** Biotic factors include all of the living things that affect the organism. The nonliving factors, called **abiotic** (AY-bie-AHT-ik) **factors,** are the physical and chemical characteristics of the environment. Important abiotic factors include temperature, humidity, pH, salinity, oxygen concentration, amount of sunlight, availability of nitrogen, and precipitation. The importance of each factor varies from environment to environment.

Abiotic and biotic factors are not independent; organisms change their environment and are influenced by those changes. For example, the availability of nitrogen in the soil affects how fast plants can grow, and plants affect nitrogen availability by absorbing nitrogen compounds from the soil.

The Changing Environment

Abiotic factors are not constant. They vary from place to place and over time, as shown in Figure 19-7. Consider temperature, which is probably the most important abiotic factor. Temperature changes on several different scales. It varies from hour to hour, from day to day, from season to season, and from year to year. A glance at a weather map in the newspaper will confirm that temperature also varies from place to place in a predictable way. Phoenix is usually warmer than Los Angeles and nearly always warmer than Seattle. Also important to organisms are the small differences in temperature within a habitat, such as the difference between an area in the shade of a tree and an area exposed to direct sunlight.

Responses to a Changing Environment

Organisms are able to survive within a wide range of environmental conditions. Some heat-tolerant bacteria live far below Earth's surface at temperatures as high as 110°C (230°F), while some plants can withstand temperatures as low as −70°C (−94°F). However, no single organism can survive both of these extremes. Rather, organisms are adapted to function within a specific range of temperatures. It is possible to determine this range for an organism by measuring how efficiently it performs at different temperatures. A graph of performance versus values of an environmental variable, such as temperature, is called a **tolerance curve.** Figure 19-8 shows a tolerance curve for a species of fish. Here, performance was measured by the fish's maximum possible swimming speed. Notice that the fish's swimming speed is highest at intermediate temperatures, within what is called its optimal range. The fish can survive and function at temperatures outside its optimal range, but its performance is greatly reduced. The fish cannot survive outside its tolerance limits.

An organism cannot live in areas where it is exposed to conditions that fall outside its tolerance limits. In some cases, an organism's range may be determined by its tolerance to just one factor, such as temperature. In most cases, however, the levels of several factors, such as pH, temperature, and salinity, must fall within the organism's tolerance range.

Temperature Tolerance Curve

Zones of physiological intolerance (no performance)
Zones of physiological stress (reduced performance)

Swimming speed

Low · Temperature · High

Acclimation to Temperature

Fish raised at 5°C
Fish raised at 25°C

FIGURE 19-9

Fish raised at 25°C are acclimated to higher temperatures and are able to tolerate much warmer temperatures than the fish raised at 5°C.

FIGURE 19-10

An organism can be a regulator or a conformer, or both. The lizard, represented by the blue line, is a conformer with regard to body temperature, whereas humans, represented by the red line, regulate internal temperature.

Body Temperature Maintenance

Human Lizard

Acclimation

Some organisms can adjust their tolerance to abiotic factors through the process of **acclimation** (AK-luh-MAY-shuhn). For instance, goldfish raised at different temperatures have somewhat different tolerance curves, as shown in Figure 19-9. If you spend a few weeks at a high elevation, you will acclimate to reduced oxygen levels, or "thin air." Over time, the number of red blood cells in your body will increase, thereby increasing the amount of oxygen your blood can carry. Be sure not to confuse acclimation with adaptation. Acclimation occurs within the lifetime of an individual organism. Adaptation is genetic change in a species or population that occurs over many generations.

Control of Internal Conditions

Environments fluctuate in temperature, light, moisture, salinity, and other chemical factors. There are two ways for organisms to deal with some of these changes in their environment. **Conformers** are organisms that do not regulate their internal conditions; they change as their external environment changes. For example, the body temperature of desert lizards rises and falls with the temperature of the lizards' environment, as shown in Figure 19-10. The internal conditions of a conformer remain within the optimal range only as long as environmental conditions remain within that range.

In contrast, **regulators** are organisms that use energy to control some of their internal conditions. Regulators can keep an internal condition within the optimal range over a wide variety of environmental conditions. Your body temperature, for instance, remains within a few degrees of 37°C (99°F) throughout the day. Pacific salmon, which spend part of their lives in salt water and part in fresh water, are conformers to environmental temperatures but are regulators of their internal salt concentration.

Escape from Unsuitable Conditions

Some species can survive unfavorable environmental conditions by escaping from them temporarily. For example, desert animals usually hide underground or in the shade during the hottest part of the day. Many desert species are active at night, when temperatures are much lower. A longer-term strategy is to enter a state of reduced activity, called **dormancy**, during periods of unfavorable environmental conditions. Throughout most of the United States, winter temperatures are too cold for reptiles and amphibians to tolerate, but these animals survive by hiding underground and becoming dormant until spring. Another strategy is to move to another, more favorable habitat. This is called **migration**. A familiar example of migration is the seasonal movements of birds, which spend spring and summer in cooler climates

Sunlight

Carbon dioxide

Water

Nutrients

Oxygen

Water

Food containing energy and nutrients

and then migrate to warmer climates in the fall. They remain in the warmer climate until spring, when they return to the cooler climate. Birds thus avoid the low temperatures and food scarcity of winter.

Resources

Whether a species can survive in a particular habitat depends on the suitability of environmental conditions and also on the availability of **resources,** the energy and materials the species needs. Food, energy, nesting sites, water, and sunlight are examples of resources that are often required by animals or plants. The resources essential for survival differ from species to species. As you can see in Figure 19-11, plants require a very different set of resources than animals do.

THE NICHE

A species' **niche** (NICH) is its way of life, or the role the species plays in its environment. The niche includes the range of conditions that the species can tolerate, the methods by which it obtains needed resources, the number of offspring it has, its time of reproduction, and all of its other interactions with its environment. When studying the niche of a species, scientists usually concentrate on a few features that can be readily measured, such as where the species lives, what time of day it is active, and what it eats. Figure 19-12 shows an aspect of the feeding behavior of a common species of songbird.

The **fundamental niche** is the range of conditions that a species can potentially tolerate and the range of resources it can potentially use. In reality,

FIGURE 19-11

Plants and animals are able to share the same spaces because they each have different requirements for survival.

FIGURE 19-12

The graph below illustrates the blue-gray gnatcatcher's feeding behavior. The darkest shade in the center of the contour lines indicates that most prey are captured between 3 m and 5 m above ground. The prey most frequently captured averaged about 4 mm in length.

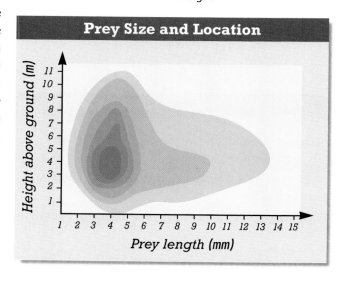

Prey Size and Location

Height above ground (m)

Prey length (mm)

FIGURE 19-13

Each of these circles represents the fundamental and realized niche of a species. The center of each circle represents optimal conditions. Farther from the center, conditions are less ideal. Note that the fundamental niches can overlap but the realized niches cannot. Ecologically similar species do not occupy the same realized niche.

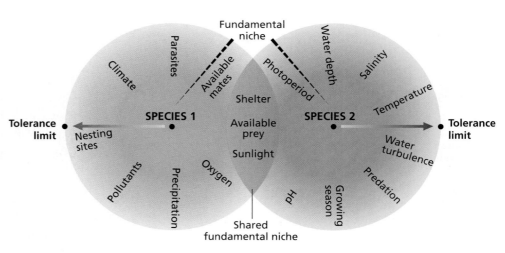

a species may have to restrict its activity to avoid predators, or competition with other species may prevent it from using a resource. The **realized niche** of a species is the range of resources it actually uses. The fundamental niche will usually include a much broader set of conditions than the realized niche. The darkest blue area in Figure 19-12 indicates a realized niche. The progressively lighter shades indicate increasing intolerance to environmental conditions as the birds' niche changes from realized to fundamental.

Niche Differences

A species' niche can change within a single generation. For example, caterpillars eat the leaves of plants. After feeding for some time, they transform into butterflies, which feed on nectar.

Generalists are species with broad niches; they can tolerate a range of conditions and use a variety of resources. An example of an extreme generalist is the Virginia opossum, which is found across much of the United States. The opossum feeds on almost anything, from eggs and dead animals to fruits and plants. In contrast to the opossum is the koala of Australia, which feeds only on leaves from a few species of eucalyptus trees. Species that have narrow niches, such as the koala, are called **specialists.**

Word Roots and Origins

niche

from the Old French *nichier,* meaning "to nest"

SECTION 19-2 REVIEW

1. List three abiotic factors that can affect an organism.

2. What does a tolerance curve indicate about an organism?

3. What is migration? Give an example of migration.

4. How is an organism's niche different from its habitat?

5. List two factors that might cause an organism to restrict its use of a resource.

6. **CRITICAL THINKING** Explain why two different species do not occupy exactly the same niche.

SUMMARY/VOCABULARY

19-1
- Ecology is the study of the relationships between organisms and their environment, including both the living and nonliving components.
- Ecological knowledge was crucial to the survival of our early human ancestors. Ecology is essential today because humans are changing the world rapidly and on a global scale.
- The human population is growing extremely rapidly. It has tripled in size in about 70 years.
- Rapid growth of the human population has caused the extinction of many other species of organisms. The rate of extinction today is higher than at any time since the extinction of the dinosaurs.
- Industrial chemicals released into the atmosphere are destroying the ozone layer, the protective shield around Earth that absorbs harmful ultraviolet radiation from the sun.
- Burning of fossil fuels has increased atmospheric levels of carbon dioxide. Most scientists think this is causing global warming, or a rise in global temperatures.
- The science of ecology is usually organized into five levels, each of which has unique properties: organism, population, community, ecosystem, and biosphere.
- Species in ecosystems interact with other species and with their nonliving environment. As a result, a disturbance that affects one species can spread to other species in the ecosystem.
- Because ecosystems are so complex, ecologists rely on models, simplified systems that mimic the behavior of the natural world.

Vocabulary

biosphere (363)
community (363)
ecology (359)
ecosystem (363)
greenhouse effect (361)
population (363)

19-2
- An organism's habitat is where it lives.
- Two kinds of factors influence organisms: biotic factors, which are living things, and abiotic factors, which are nonliving things or processes, such as climate, sunlight, and pH.
- The environment changes over time and from place to place.
- Each organism can tolerate a range of environmental conditions. A graph showing this range is called a tolerance curve.
- Over a short period of time, organisms can adjust their tolerance curves through the process of acclimation.
- Species follow two strategies in dealing with environmental change. Regulators control their internal conditions, while conformers' internal conditions vary with the environment.
- Species often escape unfavorable environmental conditions by migrating to a new habitat or by becoming dormant and waiting out the unfavorable conditions.
- A species' niche is its way of life, or its role in an ecosystem.
- A species' fundamental niche is the range of conditions that it can potentially tolerate and the resources that it can potentially use. In the face of competition or predation, a species may use a smaller range of resources or live in a reduced range of conditions. These actual resources used and conditions best tolerated make up a species' realized niche.
- Species with broad niches are called generalists, while species with narrow niches are called specialists.

Vocabulary

abiotic factor (368)
acclimation (370)
biotic factor (368)
conformer (370)
dormancy (370)
fundamental niche (371)
generalist (372)
habitat (368)
migration (370)
niche (371)
realized niche (372)
regulator (370)
resource (371)
specialist (372)
tolerance curve (369)

REVIEW

Vocabulary

1. Define the term *ecology*.
2. How is a community different from an ecosystem?
3. List two abiotic factors that influence you.
4. In what way is migration similar to dormancy?
5. Distinguish between regulators and conformers.

Multiple Choice

6. The number of species on Earth (a) is exactly 1.5 million (b) has increased over the last 2,000 years (c) is smaller than the number that occurred during the time of the dinosaurs (d) is decreasing rapidly.
7. The thinning of the ozone layer is caused by (a) CFCs (b) carbon dioxide (c) oxygen gas (d) carbon monoxide.
8. Which of the following is not one of the five main levels of organization within ecology? (a) biosphere (b) ecosystem (c) atom (d) community (e) population
9. An ecosystem includes (a) all the members of one species (b) all the living and nonliving factors in an environment (c) all parts of Earth where life exists (d) all members of a species in the same area.
10. Which of the following is not true of models? (a) They are simplified systems that mimic the natural world. (b) They can be tested by comparison with real situations. (c) They help scientists make predictions. (d) They exactly duplicate reality.
11. Abiotic factors in an ecosystem can include (a) plants (b) animals (c) sunlight (d) micro-organisms.
12. An animal could migrate to avoid (a) a hurricane (b) cold temperatures in winter (c) an extreme cold snap (d) a volcanic eruption.
13. A species' fundamental niche (a) cannot be larger than its realized niche (b) changes in response to predators or competitors (c) can be larger or smaller than its realized niche (d) is always as large as or larger than its realized niche.

14. Which of the following is not a resource needed by animals? (a) water (b) food (c) carbon dioxide (d) oxygen
15. Which of the following is not true of an organism's tolerance for an environmental variable?
    (a) Its performance is usually best at inter-mediate values.
    (b) Its performance can be illustrated with a tolerance curve.
    (c) Its tolerance levels cannot vary over the organism's lifetime.
    (d) Tolerance levels can change through acclimation.

Short Answer

16. Explain how an understanding of intercon-nectedness in ecosystems might help a health official determine how much money to allocate for the treatment of people with Lyme disease.
17. Why are models so valuable to ecologists? What are some limitations of models?
18. The biotic and abiotic factors in an ecosys-tem can interact. Give two examples of such interactions.
19. What is a tolerance curve? What application does it have to ecology?
20. Give two examples of environmental condi-tions that bears avoid by hibernating in winter.
21. Examine the diagram below of a tolerance curve. Briefly describe the conditions in each zone of tolerance and the reactions a species may have to them.
22. What is acclimation? How is acclimation dif-ferent from adaptation by natural selection?

Salinity Tolerance Curve

Intolerance Stress Optimal Stress Intolerance

Oxygen Consumption

Tolerance limit

Tolerance limit

Low salinity   High salinity

23. Describe two methods, not including acclimation, that organisms use to respond to unfavorable conditions in their environment.

24. Ecologically speaking, humans are considered generalists rather than specialists. Explain why.

25. What abiotic factors might account for differences in net primary productivity in ecosystems?

CRITICAL THINKING

1. In the fall, many kinds of songbirds migrate from the United States to Central America or South America. Explain the benefits of migration for songbirds. What are some consequences of this behavior?

2. The gypsy moth is a destructive insect pest. In the ecosystem illustrated in Figure 19-6, the caterpillars of the gypsy moth negatively affect oak trees by consuming their leaves. The number of caterpillars in the forest fluctuates, and every few years the caterpillar population increases dramatically. Trace the effects that a large increase in the caterpillar population might have on the other members of this ecosystem. How might an increase in caterpillars affect the incidence of Lyme disease? Explain your answer.

3. Ecologists have identified several characteristics that increase the likelihood that a species will become extinct. Specialization is one such characteristic. Explain why a very specialized species is likely to be more vulnerable to extinction.

4. Evaluate the following statement: Though the field of ecology had not been defined in Charles Darwin's day, Darwin was an ecologist.

5. Explain why scientists believe that ecology and evolution are tightly linked.

6. Study the diagram of the niche of a species of songbird below. Where does the bird capture most of its food? Which sizes of insects does it prefer?

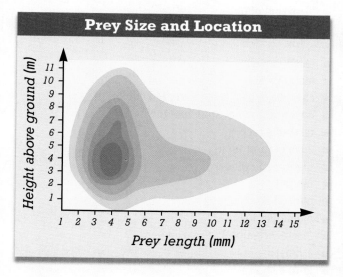

Prey Size and Location

Height above ground (m) / Prey length (mm)

EXTENSION

1. Read "The Final Countdown" in *Audubon*, November–December 1999, on page 65. According to E. O. Wilson, how does biodiversity measure the value of an ecosystem? How will the loss of biodiversity affect human life?

2. Pick a small outdoor area—a lawn, or window box. With a string, mark off a 1,000 cm² area and carefully count the plants and animals found there. Note the number of species found, and identify as many as you can. Compare your findings with those of your classmates.

3. Using library resources or an on-line database, research the Biosphere 2 project. What is Biosphere 2, and where is it located? What were the goals and outcomes of the first two-year experiment in Biosphere 2? What scientific criticisms were leveled at the project?

Observing Habitat Selection

OBJECTIVES

- Assess the effect of light on habitat selection by brine shrimp.

PROCESS SKILLS

- observing
- measuring
- collecting data
- organizing data
- analyzing data

MATERIALS

- safety goggles
- marking pen
- clear, flexible plastic tubing (44 cm long)
- 4 test tubes with stoppers
- test-tube rack
- 2 corks to fit tubing
- graduated cylinder
- funnel
- brine shrimp culture
- aluminum foil
- 3 screw clamps
- 1 pipet
- Petri dish
- methyl cellulose
- fluorescent lamp or grow light
- 14 pieces of screening
- calculator

Background

1. Recall that a species' habitat is a specific area where it lives.
2. A species habitat selection depends on how well the location fits within the species' tolerance range. The more optimal all limiting factors are within a portion of an organism's range, the more likely the organism is to select that area for its habitat.
3. What limiting factors might be involved in habitat selection?
4. What is a niche?

PART A   Setting Up

1. Mark the plastic tubing at 12 cm, 22 cm, and 32 cm from one end so that you will have the tube divided into four sections. Starting at one end, label the sections 1, 2, 3, and 4. Label four test tubes 1, 2, 3, and 4.
2. Place a cork in one end of the tubing. Use a graduated cylinder and a funnel to transfer about 50 mL of brine shrimp into the tubing. Cork the open end, and lay the tubing on the desktop.
3. You and your partner will complete either Part B or Part C and then share your results with the other students on your team. **CAUTION You will be working with live animals. Be sure to treat them gently and to follow directions carefully.**

PART B   Control Group

1. Cover the tubing with aluminum foil, and let it remain undisturbed for 30 minutes. While you are waiting, create a data table like Table A, below, in your lab report to record the numbers of shrimp in each section of the tubing.

TABLE A CONTROL GROUP

Test tube number	Count 1	Count 2	Count 3	Count 4	Count 5	Average number of shrimp in test tube
1						
2						
3						
4						

2. After 30 minutes have passed, attach screw clamps to each spot that you marked on the tubing. While your partner holds the corks firmly in place, tighten the middle clamp first, and then tighten the outer clamps.
3. Immediately pour the contents of each section of tubing into the test tube labeled with the corresponding number.

4. CAUTION **Put on safety goggles before handling methyl cellulose. If you get methyl cellulose in your eyes, immediately flush it out at the eyewash station while calling to your teacher.** Stopper test tube 1 and invert it gently to distribute the shrimp. Use a pipet to draw a 1 mL sample of shrimp culture and transfer the culture to a Petri dish. Add a few drops of methyl cellulose to the Petri dish to slow down the shrimp. Count the live shrimp, and record the count in your lab report.

5. Dispose of the shrimp as your teacher directs. Repeat step 4 four more times for a total of five counts from test tube 1.

6. Calculate the average number of shrimp in test tube 1, and record the result in the data table you made in your lab report.

7. Repeat steps 4–6 for the contents of each of the remaining test tubes.

8. Clean up your materials and wash your hands before leaving the lab.

9. In your lab report, make a histogram showing the total number of shrimp you counted in each section of tubing.

PART C Experimental Group

1. Set a fluorescent lamp 20 cm away from the tubing.

2. Cover section 1 of the tubing with eight layers of screening. Place four layers of screening on section 2 and two layers of screening on section 3. Leave section 4 uncovered. Leave this setup in place for 30 minutes. While you are waiting, create a data table in your lab report like Table B, below, to record the numbers of shrimp in each section of the tubing.

TABLE B EFFECTS OF LIGHT ON BRINE SHRIMP

Test tube number	Count 1	Count 2	Count 3	Count 4	Count 5	Average number of shrimp in test tube
1						
2						
3						
4						

3. After 30 minutes have passed, attach screw clamps to each spot that you marked on the tubing. While your partner holds the corks firmly in place, tighten the middle clamp first, and then tighten the outer clamps.

4. Immediately pour the contents of each section of tubing into the test tube labeled with the corresponding number.

5. CAUTION **Put on safety goggles before handling methyl cellulose. If you get methyl cellulose in your eyes, immediately flush it out at the eyewash station while calling to your teacher.** Stopper test tube 1 and invert it gently to distribute the shrimp. Use a pipet to draw a 1 mL sample of shrimp culture and transfer the culture to a Petri dish. Add a few drops of methyl cellulose to the Petri dish to slow down the shrimp. Count the live shrimp, and record the count in your lab report.

6. Dispose of the shrimp as your teacher directs. Repeat Step 5 four more times for a total of five counts from test tube 1.

7. Calculate the average number of shrimp in test tube 1 and record the result in the data table you made in your lab report.

8. Repeat steps 5–7 for the contents of each of the remaining test tubes.

9. Clean up your materials and wash your hands before leaving the lab.

10. In your lab report, make a histogram showing the number of shrimp in each section of tubing. Identify each section with the amount of screening.

Analysis and Conclusions

1. How did the brine shrimp react to the changes in light?

2. Why was a control (Part B) necessary?

3. How do the histograms made by different groups compare?

Further Inquiry

Design an experiment to test the reaction of brine shrimp to a gradient of heat.

CHAPTER 20

POPULATIONS

This is part of a population of bottlenose dolphins, Tursiops truncatus.

FOCUS CONCEPT: *Interdependence of Organisms*

As you read the chapter, notice how even very simple models can help you understand population processes.

20-1 *Understanding Populations*

20-2 *Measuring Populations*

20-3 *Human Population Growth*

UNDERSTANDING POPULATIONS

The human population of the world was about 6 billion in 1996, three times its size in 1900. During this period of rapid human population growth, populations of many other species have decreased dramatically. Will the human population continue to grow? Will populations of other species continue to get smaller? Will other species continue to become extinct? An understanding of populations is crucial to answering these questions.

▲
Explain the differences between population size, density, and dispersion.

●
Describe the three main patterns of population dispersion.

■
Explain the importance of a population's age structure.

◆
Contrast the three main types of survivorship curves.

PROPERTIES OF POPULATIONS

A population is a group of organisms that belong to the same species and live in a particular place at the same time. All of the bass living in a pond during a certain period of time constitute a population because they are isolated in the pond and do not interact with bass living in other ponds. The boundaries of a population may be imposed by a feature of the environment, such as a lake shore, or they can be arbitrarily chosen to simplify a study of the population.

The properties of populations differ from those of individuals. An individual may be born, it may reproduce, or it may die. A population study focuses on a population as a whole—how many individuals are born, how many die, and so on.

Population Size

A population's size is the number of individuals it contains. Size is a fundamental and important population property, but it can be difficult to measure directly. If a population is small and composed of immobile organisms, such as plants, its size can be determined simply by counting individuals. More often, though, individuals are too abundant, too widespread, or too mobile to be easily counted, and scientists must estimate the number of individuals in the population. Suppose that a scientist wants to know how many oak trees live in a 10 km² patch of forest. Instead of searching the entire patch and counting all the oak trees, the scientist could count the trees in a smaller section of the forest, such as a 1 km² area, and use this

FIGURE 20-1

These migrating wildebeests in East Africa are too numerous and mobile to be counted. Scientists must use sampling methods at several locations to monitor changes in the population size of the animals.

value to estimate the population of the larger area. If the small patch contains 25 oaks, an area 10 times larger likely would contain 10 times as many oak trees, so a reasonable estimate for the population's size is 250 oak trees. A similar kind of sampling technique must be used to estimate the size of the population shown in Figure 20-1.

This kind of estimate assumes that the distribution of trees in the forest is the same as that of the sampled patch. If this assumption is not accurate, the estimate will be inaccurate. Estimates of population size are based on certain key assumptions, so they all have the potential for error.

Population Density

Population density measures how crowded a population is. Population density is always expressed as the number of individuals per unit of area or volume. For example, the population density of humans in the United States is about 30 people per square kilometer. Table 20-1 shows the population densities for several countries. These estimates are calculated for the total land area. Some areas of a country may be sparsely populated, while other areas are very densely populated.

Dispersion

A third population property is dispersion. **Dispersion** (di-SPUHR-zhuhn) is the spatial distribution of individuals within the population. In a clumped distribution, individuals are clustered together. In an even distribution, individuals are separated by a fairly consistent distance. In a random distribution, each individual's location is independent of the locations of other individuals in the population. The three possible patterns of dispersion are illustrated in Figure 20-2a. Clumped distributions often occur when resources such as food or living space are clumped. Clumped distributions may also occur because of a species' social behavior, such as when zebras gather into herds or birds form flocks. Even distributions usually result from social interactions, but the interactions result in individuals getting as far away from each other as possible. For example, each gannet, which are the birds shown in Figure 20-2c, stakes out a small area on the coast and defends it from other gannets. Each gannet tries to maximize its distance from all of its neighbors, resulting in an even distribution of individuals. A random distribution usually results from seed dispersal by the wind or by birds, as in the third illustration in Figure 20-2a. Forests or a field of wildflowers result from random seed dispersal.

TABLE 20-1 *Population Densities*	
Country	**Population density (individuals/ km²)**
Japan	330
United Kingdom	240
Kenya	50
Mexico	50
United States	30
Russia	10

(a)   CLUMPED

EVEN

RANDOM

(b) CLUMPED DISPERSION

(c) EVEN DISPERSION

The dispersion pattern of a population sometimes depends on the scale at which the population is observed. The gannets shown in Figure 20-2c are evenly distributed on a scale of a few meters. If the scale of observation is the entire island on which the gannets live, however, the distribution appears clumped because the birds live only near the shore.

FIGURE 20-2

Illustrated in (a) are the three dispersion patterns—clumped, even, and random. Turtles commonly clump together to bask in the sun. Birds often are observed in even dispersions as a result of social interactions. A forest is an example of random dispersion. Close up, the fishes in (b) may appear to be in an even distribution, but further away, they can be seen to be clumped. The birds in (c) are evenly distributed, but at a great distance they appear to be clumped.

POPULATION DYNAMICS

All populations are dynamic—they change in size and composition over time. To understand these changes, more knowledge is needed about the population than its size, density, and dispersion. One important measure is the **birth rate,** the number of births occurring in a period of time. In the United States, for example, there are about 4 million births per year. A second important measure is the **death rate,** or **mortality rate,** which is the number of deaths in a period of time. The death rate for the United States is about 2.4 million deaths per year. Another important statistic is **life expectancy,** or how long on average an individual is expected to live. In the United States in 1996, the life expectancy for a man was 72 years, and for a woman it was 79 years.

FIGURE 20-3

These two diagrams show the age structure by gender of two countries. A comparison indicates that Country A has a higher percentage of young people and a lower percentage of elderly people than Country B does.

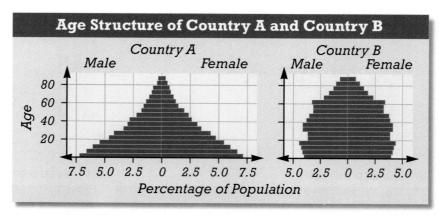

Age Structure of Country A and Country B

Age Structure

The distribution of individuals among different ages in a population is called **age structure.** Age structures are often presented in graphs, as in Figure 20-3. Many important population processes vary with age. In many species, including humans, very old individuals do not reproduce. Populations with a high percentage of young individuals have a greater potential for rapid growth.

Patterns of Mortality

The mortality rate data of different species tend to conform to one of three curves on a graph, as shown in Figure 20-4. These curves are called **survivorship curves** because they show the likelihood of survival at different ages throughout the lifetime of the organism. In humans or elephants, for instance, the likelihood of dying is small until late in life, when mortality increases rapidly. This pattern of mortality produces the Type I survivorship curve. For other organisms, such as some species of birds, the probability of dying does not change throughout life, giving a linear, or Type II, survivorship curve. Many organisms are very likely to die when young. If an individual survives this early period, however, it has a good chance of surviving to old age. This type of survivorship curve, called Type III, is characteristic of animals such as oysters, salmon, and many insects.

FIGURE 20-4

Humans have a Type I survivorship curve. Some species of birds have a Type II survivorship curve. Some species of fish are examples of a Type III survivorship.

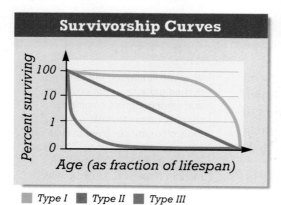

Survivorship Curves

■ Type I ■ Type II ■ Type III

SECTION 20-1 REVIEW

1. Explain how two populations can be the same size but have different densities.

2. Explain why even distributions usually result from social interactions between individuals.

3. Explain how it is possible to conclude from Figure 20-3 that the life expectancy of individuals in Country B is greater than that of individuals in Country A.

4. How does Figure 20-3 indicate which country's population has the greatest potential for rapid growth?

5. Explain why natural selection might favor a high reproduction rate in organisms with Type III survivorship curves.

6. **CRITICAL THINKING** Explain two difficulties an ecologist might have in counting a population of migratory birds. Develop and explain a method for estimating the size of such a population.

MEASURING POPULATIONS

Charles Darwin calculated that a single pair of elephants could increase to a population of 19 million individuals within 750 years. The fact that the world is not overrun with elephants is evidence that some factor or factors restrain the population growth of elephants. In this section you will study how populations grow and what factors limit their growth.

POPULATION GROWTH RATE

Demographers, scientists who study population dynamics, define the **growth rate** of a population as the amount by which a population's size changes in a given time.

Whether a population grows, shrinks, or remains the same size depends on four processes: birth, death, emigration, and immigration. **Immigration** (im-uh-GRAY-shuhn) is the movement of individuals into a population, and **emigration** (em-i-GRAY-shuhn) is the movement of individuals out of the population. Two of these processes—birth and immigration—add individuals to a population, while the other two processes—death and emigration—subtract individuals from the population. For simplicity's sake, demographers usually assume that immigration and emigration are zero when calculating a population's growth rate. By making this simple assumption, a population's growth rate can be described mathematically and can be graphed.

It is customary for demographers to divide large populations into groups of 1,000 and to present data per capita, meaning per individual. Birth rates, death rates, and growth rates for a large population are usually expressed per capita. For example, if there are 52 births and 14 deaths per 1,000 individuals in a large population in one year, the per capita birth rate would be $^{52}/_{1,000}$, or 0.052 births per individual per year. The per capita death rate would be $^{14}/_{1,000}$, or 0.014 deaths per individual per year. The per capita growth rate can be found by the following simple equation:

$$\text{birth rate} - \text{death rate} = \text{growth rate}$$

FIGURE 20-5

The graph of exponential population growth has a characteristic J shape. The exponential model indicates infinite, constantly increasing population growth.

Using the same example, we can calculate the per capita growth rate as follows:

$$0.052 \text{ (births per capita)} - 0.014 \text{ (deaths per capita)}$$
$$= 0.038 \text{ (growth per capita)}$$

To find the number of new individuals that will be added to the population in a year, simply multiply the per capita growth rate by the number of individuals in the population. If the population in our example numbers 50,000, the population will increase by 1,900 individuals in one year.

$$0.038 \times 50,000 = 1,900$$

If the growth rate is a positive number, the population is increasing. If it is a negative number, the population is shrinking.

THE EXPONENTIAL MODEL

The **exponential** (EKS-poh-NEN-shuhl) **model** of population growth describes a population that increases rapidly after only a few generations; the larger the population gets, the faster it grows. This is called **exponential growth.** In constructing an exponential model of population growth, it is assumed that birth rates and death rates remain constant, however large the population becomes.

Predictions Based on the Exponential Model

One way to understand predictions based on the exponential model is to look at a graph of population size over time. Population growth, according to the exponential model, follows the characteristic J-shaped curve shown in Figure 20-5. As you can see on the graph, the population grows slowly when it is small, but its growth speeds up as more and more individuals are added to the population. We can predict that the population will grow indefinitely and at an increasingly rapid rate based on the exponential model. Figure 20-6 shows the exponential growth of bacteria in a laboratory culture.

FIGURE 20-6

The population increase of bacteria in the laboratory produces a characteristic graph of exponential growth. With this kind of graph, the size of the population of bacteria at any future time can be predicted if the culture is provided with unlimited resources, such as food.

Limitations of the Exponential Model

The ultimate test of an exponential model is how well it matches the growth pattern of a real population. Do populations grow exponentially? The answer is yes, but only under rare conditions and for short periods of time. For example, populations of bacteria and other microorganisms can grow exponentially in the laboratory

Data Table					
Time	0	1	2	3	4
Bacteria count	1,000	2,000	4,000	8,000	16,000

if they are provided with an abundance of food and space and if their waste is removed.

In reality, populations cannot grow indefinitely because the resources they depend on become scarce and wastes accumulate. All populations are limited by their environment. A factor that restrains the growth of a population is called a **limiting factor.**

As a population grows, competition among individuals for the shrinking supply of resources intensifies, and each individual, on average, obtains a smaller share. This reduces each individual's ability to fight off disease, to grow, and to reproduce. The results for the population are a declining birth rate and an increasing mortality rate. Figure 20-7 shows how increasing population size affected the growth of a species of plant.

FIGURE 20-7

The graph displays the results of an experiment that tests how the growth of a plant is affected under three conditions of crowding. Under the condition of least crowding, the plants were observed to grow larger.

THE LOGISTIC MODEL

The **logistic** (loh-JIS-tik) **model** of population growth builds on the exponential model but accounts for the influence of limiting factors. Birth rates and death rates are not constant, but vary with population size: birth rates decline and death rates rise as the population grows. The logistic model includes a new term, **carrying capacity** (symbolized by K), the number of individuals the environment can support over a long period of time.

A graph of logistic growth looks like a stretched-out letter S. Examine Figure 20-8. When the population size is small, birth rates are high and death rates are low, and the population grows at very near the exponential rate, as shown in region A. As the population size approaches the carrying capacity, however, the population growth rate falls due to the falling birth rate and the increasing death rate, as shown in region B. When a population size is at its carrying capacity, the birth rate equals the death rate and growth stops, as shown in region C. This type of growth is known as **logistic growth.**

The logistic model, like the exponential model, contains some assumptions. One such assumption is that the carrying capacity is constant and does not fluctuate with environmental changes. In reality, carrying capacity does fluctuate. It is greater when prey is abundant, for instance, and smaller when prey is scarce. The logistic and exponential models are not accurate representations of real populations, but they are an important tool that scientists use to study population growth and regulation.

FIGURE 20-8

The graph of logistic population growth describes a population stabilizing around K, the carrying capacity. The logistic graph is similar to the exponential graph in region A. In region B, the graph begins to indicate a slowing rate of increase. In region C, the graph indicates that the population has become stable, neither growing nor getting smaller.

POPULATION REGULATION

Two kinds of limiting factors, which control population size, have been identified. **Density-independent factors,** such as weather, floods, and fires, reduce the population by the same proportion, regardless of the population's size. For example, if a forest fire destroys a population of chipmunks, it does not matter if the population of chipmunks is 1 or 100. An unseasonable cold snap is a density-independent factor because its severity and duration are completely independent of population size. **Density-dependent factors** include resource limitations, such as shortages of food or nesting sites, and are triggered by increasing population density.

Population Fluctuations

All populations fluctuate in size. Some population fluctuations are clearly linked to environmental changes. For example, a drought may reduce a population of deer living in a forest. Some population fluctuations are not obviously connected to environmental fluctuations, and explaining their occurrence is much more difficult. The famous population cycles of the snowshoe hare, first described by Charles Elton, one of the pioneers of ecology, is shown in Figure 20-9. Elton obtained more than 70 years of records showing the number of snowshoe hare pelts the Hudson's Bay Company of Canada purchased from trappers. He assumed that the number of pelts purchased in a year indicated the size of the snowshoe hare population. The records showed that the hare population underwent a very regular cycle, with about 10 years between peaks in population size. When Elton examined the records for the number of lynx pelts purchased, he found that the lynx, a medium-sized species of cat that preys on snowshoe hares, also followed a population cycle. The peaks in the lynx population usually occurred one or two years after peaks in the hare population.

Elton thought that each species was the cause of the other's cycle. Thus, when the population of snowshoe hares increased, providing more food for the lynxes, the lynx population also increased. The increased lynx population then ate more hares, so the hare population decreased. With less food, more lynxes starved and the lynx population declined, allowing the hare population to increase and start the cycle over again. However, the observation that the same cycles occur in snowshoe hare populations living on islands without lynxes indicates that this explanation is inaccurate. Another possible explanation is that the lynx cycle is dependent on the hare population but the hare cycle is dependent on some other factor.

FIGURE 20-9

The hare and the lynx (a) were observed by Elton to have parallel changes in their population cycles. The graph below (b) shows the data recorded by Elton supporting his idea that each animal controlled the other animal's cycle. You can see that the cycles fluctuate together. Because hares show the same population cycles when there are no lynxes present, it is now known that lynxes are not controlling factors in the hares' cycles.

(a)

Snowshoe hare Lynx

(b)

Perils of Small Populations

The rapidly growing human population has caused extreme reductions in the populations of some other species and subspecies. For instance, fewer than 200 Siberian tigers remain in the wild due to overhunting and habitat destruction. Even greater reductions have been experienced by the California condor, which was once found throughout the southwestern United States. By the 1980s, the condor's wild population was down to nine individuals.

Small populations, such as the cheetahs shown in Figure 20-10, are particularly vulnerable to extinction. Environmental disturbances, such as storms, fires, floods, or disease outbreaks, can kill off the entire population or leave too few individuals to maintain the population. Also, the members of a small population may be descended from only a few individuals, increasing the likelihood of **inbreeding,** or mating with relatives. Offspring of related parents often have fewer offspring, are more susceptible to diseases, and have a shorter life span. Inbreeding in small populations often leads to decreased genetic variability, and, over evolutionary time, may reduce the population's ability to adapt to changing environmental conditions.

FIGURE 20-10

Biologists estimate that there are fewer than 15,000 cheetahs remaining in the wild. Inbreeding in small populations, such as the one shown, leads to a loss of genetic diversity or variability. Cheetahs are bred in captivity in an effort to maintain their remaining genetic variability. Some of these cheetahs may eventually be released into the wild.

SECTION 20-2 REVIEW

1. Explain what is described by the exponential model.

2. According to the exponential model, how do birth and death rates change with population size?

3. Describe two differences between the exponential model and the logistic model.

4. List two density-independent factors.

5. Explain how inbreeding can threaten the survival of a small population.

6. **CRITICAL THINKING** Write a brief paragraph supporting the assumption that immigration and emigration are insignificant factors when studying global human population growth.

20-3

OBJECTIVES

▲

Explain how the development of agriculture changed the pattern of human population growth.

●

Describe the change in human population growth that began around 1650.

■

Describe how growth rates have changed since World War II.

◆

Compare the general standard of living in developed countries with that in developing countries.

internetconnect

TOPIC: History of population growth
GO TO: www.scilinks.org
KEYWORD: HM388

HUMAN POPULATION GROWTH

In the time it takes you to read this chapter, the human population will grow by about 10,000 people. The rapid growth of the human population over the last several centuries is unprecedented in history. What caused this rapid growth? How long can it continue? This section examines these and other questions about the human population explosion.

HISTORY OF HUMAN POPULATION GROWTH

From the origin of *Homo sapiens,* more than 500,000 years ago, until about 10,000–12,000 years ago, the human population grew very slowly. During this time, humans lived in small nomadic groups and obtained food by hunting animals and gathering roots, berries, nuts, shellfish, and fruits. This way of life is called the **hunter-gatherer lifestyle.** By studying the few hunter-gatherer societies that exist today, scientists have learned that the low rate of population growth results from small populations and high mortality rates, especially among infants and young children, who never reach reproductive maturity.

The Development of Agriculture

The hunter-gatherer lifestyle began to change about 10,000 to 12,000 years ago, when humans discovered how to domesticate animals and cultivate certain plants for food. This dramatic change in lifestyle is called the **agricultural revolution,** and it led to profound changes in every aspect of life. Most important, agriculture greatly stabilized and increased the available food supply. As a result, the human population began to grow faster. About 10,000 years ago, there were between 2 million and 20 million people on Earth. By about 2,000 years ago, the population had increased to between 170 million and 330 million.

The Population Explosion

As you can see in Figure 20-11, human population growth continued through the Middle Ages, despite some short-term reversals. The outbreak of bubonic plague in 1347–1352 is thought to have killed about 25 percent of the population of Europe. Human population growth began to accelerate after 1650, primarily because of a sharp decline in death rates. There are many reasons for the decline in death rates, including better sanitation and hygiene, control of disease, increased availability of food, and improved economic conditions. While death rates fell, birth rates remained high, resulting in rapid population growth. The human population was about 500 million in 1650 and had risen to about 1 billion by 1800 and 2 billion by 1930.

Mortality rates fell sharply again in the decades immediately following World War II because of improvements in health and hygiene in the world's poorer countries. Birth rates in these countries remained high, pushing the per capita growth rate to its highest values. It took most of human history for the human population to reach 1 billion, but the population grew from 3 billion to 5 billion in just the 27 years between 1960 and 1987.

Human Population Growth

FIGURE 20-11

The J shape of the graph is characteristic of exponential growth. Many ecologists agree that the current human population growth rate is not sustainable.

Population Growth Today

The global growth rate peaked in the late 1960s at about 0.021 per capita. Because birth rates have decreased in many countries, the growth rate has gradually declined slowly to its current level of about 0.014 per capita. This decline has led some people to mistakenly conclude that the population is not increasing. In fact, the number of people that will be added to the world population this year is larger than it was when the growth rate was at its peak. This is simply a function of today's greater population size. For example, in 1970 there were about 3.7 billion people, and the growth rate was about 0.0196. In 1970, therefore, about 3,700,000,000 × 0.0196, or about 73 million people, were added to the world's population. In 1999 there were 6 billion people and the growth rate was 0.014 per capita, so the number of people added to the population was 6,000,000,000 × 0.014, or 84 million.

Today about 20 percent of the world's population live in **developed countries.** This category includes all of the world's modern, industrialized countries, such as the United States, Japan, Germany, France, the United Kingdom, Australia, Canada, and Russia. On average, people in developed countries are better educated, healthier, and live longer than the rest of the world's population. Population growth rates in developed countries are very low —less than 0.01 per capita. The populations of some of these countries, such as Russia, Germany, and Hungary, are shrinking because death rates exceed birth rates.

Most people (about 80 percent of the world's population) live in **developing countries,** a category that includes most countries in Asia and all of the countries in Central America, South America, and Africa. In general, these countries are poorer than the more-

Quick Lab

Demonstrating Population Doubling

Materials pencil, paper, sheet of newspaper

Procedure

1. Make a data table. Label the columns "Fold number," "Number of layers," and "Power of 2." Write the numbers 1-10 in the first column.

2. Fold a sheet of newspaper repeatedly in half, as your teacher demonstrates. Fill in your data table after each fold.

Analysis What can you conclude about the speed at which populations grow by doubling?

TABLE 20-2 Population Statistics for Selected Countries

Country	Population (millions)	Growth rate (per capita)	Projected population in 2025 (millions)	Estimated doubling time (years)
China	1,200	0.011	1,500	64
India	950	0.019	1,400	37
United States	265	0.006	335	117
Brazil	161	0.017	202	41
Russia	148	−0.005	153*	N/A
Japan	126	0.002	126	350
Nigeria	104	0.031	246	23
Mexico	95	0.022	142	32
Germany	82	−0.001	79*	N/A
United Kingdom	59	0.002	63	350
France	58	0.003	64	233
South Africa	45	0.023	70	30
Kenya	28.2	0.027	49	26
Australia	18	0.008	23	88
Haiti	7.3	0.023	11	30

* projection assumes per capita growth rate will increase to a positive value
N/A = Not applicable

developed countries, and their populations are growing much faster—at a growth rate of more than 0.02 per capita. Table 20-2 shows some population statistics for several countries.

The human population explosion will eventually stop. The only questions still to be answered are How large will the population be? and Will the planet be able to support the population over the long term? The answers to both questions depend on whether we use our resources wisely so that the future productivity of Earth's ecosystems is not compromised.

SECTION 20-3 REVIEW

1. What effect did the agricultural revolution have on the growth of the human population?

2. Explain why mortality rates began to decline rapidly around 1650.

3. Why did population growth rates increase rapidly after World War II?

4. How do population growth rates in the developing countries compare with those of the developed countries?

5. How do living standards in the developing countries compare with those in the developed countries?

6. CRITICAL THINKING   In five or six sentences, differentiate between growth rate and birth rate, and evaluate the statement that a decreasing birth rate may lead to a decreasing growth rate.

SUMMARY/VOCABULARY

20-1
- A population is a group of individuals of the same species living in the same place in the same time period.
- A population's size is the number of individuals it contains. Population density is a measure of how crowded the population is. The dispersion pattern—random, even, or clumped—indicates the distribution of individuals within the population.

- A population's age structure indicates the percentage of individuals at each age.
- Populations show three patterns of mortality: Type I (low mortality until late in life), Type II (constant mortality throughout life), and Type III (devastating mortality early in life followed by low mortality for the remainder of the life span).

Vocabulary

age structure (382)　　　death/mortality rate (381)　　　life expectancy (381)　　　survivorship curve (382)
birth rate (381)　　　dispersion (380)　　　population density (380)

20-2
- Four processes determine whether a population will shrink or grow: birth, death, immigration, and emigration.
- The exponential model describes perpetual growth at an increasing rate in a population. The model assumes constant birth and death rates and no immigration or emigration.
- In the logistic model, birth rates fall and death rates climb as the population grows.
- The carrying capacity is the number of individuals the environment can support for an indefinite period of time. At the carrying capacity, birth and death rates are equal, and the population size is stable.

- Density-independent factors kill the same percentage of a population regardless of its size. Density-dependent factors kill more individuals in large populations than in small ones.
- Populations fluctuate over time due to environmental changes.
- Small populations are less able to rebound from environmental changes, they are more likely to experience inbreeding, and their genetic diversity is often low.

Vocabulary

carrying capacity (385)　　　emigration (383)　　　immigration (383)　　　logistic growth (385)
density-dependent factor (386)　　　exponential growth (384)　　　inbreeding (387)　　　logistic model (385)
　　　exponential model (384)　　　limiting factor (385)
density-independent factor (386)　　　growth rate (383)

20-3
- About 10,000–12,000 years ago, human population growth was slow.
- The development of agriculture increased the growth rate of the population. Improvements in hygiene, diet, and economic conditions around 1650 further accelerated population growth.

- The population grew at its fastest rate in the decades immediately after World War II, largely because of better sanitation and medical care in the poorer countries.
- Today, population growth is faster in the less-developed countries and slower in the more-developed countries.

Vocabulary

agricultural revolution (388)　　　developed countries (389)　　　developing countries (389)　　　hunter-gatherer lifestyle (388)

REVIEW

Vocabulary

Explain the difference between the terms in each of the following pairs:

1. density-dependent factor, density-independent factor
2. density, dispersion
3. exponential growth, logistic growth
4. carrying capacity, density
5. developing countries, developed countries

Multiple Choice

6. A clumped distribution (a) occurs when individuals are evenly spaced (b) may occur when resources are concentrated (c) occurs only because of social interactions between individuals (d) occurs only among plants.

7. Life expectancy (a) refers to the maximum life span of an individual (b) is the average life span (c) depends only on birth rates (d) is the same for all species.

8. Population growth (a) is a group of individuals of the same species living in the same place (b) is the spatial distribution of organisms in a population (c) is the change in the number of individuals in a population over a period of time (d) occurs only if all individuals in the population survive and reproduce.

9. In the exponential model, the growth rate (a) is the same as the birth rate (b) is the change in population size after birth and death rates have been accounted for (c) changes with population size (d) is zero at the carrying capacity.

10. According to the exponential model, (a) population growth stops at the carrying capacity (b) population growth increases and then decreases (c) the immigration rate falls with increasing population size (d) population growth continues indefinitely.

11. Which of the following is not true of the carrying capacity in the logistic model? (a) varies with population size (b) remains constant (c) represents the maximum sustainable population (d) is the population size at which the birth rate equals the death rate.

12. Which of the following is not a density-independent factor for a population of deer in a forest? (a) a period of freezing weather (b) the number of cougars in the forest (c) a drought (d) a landslide

13. Inbreeding can be harmful to a population because it (a) increases the genetic variability of the population (b) increases the rate of evolution in the population (c) can increase mortality rate of offspring (d) decreases the carrying capacity.

14. During the hunter-gatherer period of human history, (a) death rates were high (b) crops were cultivated to provide food (c) the population grew to 1 billion individuals (d) population growth rates were high.

15. The cause of the decline in death rates following World War II was (a) introduction of genetically engineered crops (b) a decrease in life expectancy (c) improved hygiene and medical care (d) declining birth rates.

Short Answer

16. A scientist observes that the population of turtles in a pond shows a clumped distribution. Explain two reasons why turtles might show this kind of distribution.

17. Describe how an even distribution differs from a random distribution. Draw an example of each type of distribution.

18. What is a survivorship curve? What are the three types of survivorship curves? Name an organism that shows each kind of curve.

19. Explain one key assumption of the exponential model of population growth. What does the model help scientists predict about changes in population size over time?

20. Explain three reasons why small populations are particularly vulnerable to extinction.

21. Examine the graph below. Explain how the logistic model describes population changes in region A, region B, and region C.

Logistic Population Growth

Region A | Region B | Region C

Carrying capacity (K)

Number of individuals

Time

22. What was the agricultural revolution? What effect did it have on population growth? Before the agricultural revolution occurred, how did people obtain food?

23. The human population began to grow very rapidly about 1650. Describe three factors that caused this change in the rate of population growth.

24. Unit 7–Ecosystem Dynamics

 Write a report summarizing how the availability of resources on a ranch determine the carrying capacity of the ranch. What are the risks of maintaining a population of livestock that exceeds the carrying capacity of the ranch?

CRITICAL THINKING

1. Because we humans have more power to alter our environment than other animals do, we can affect the carrying capacity of our environment. How do we increase or decrease the carrying capacity of our local area?

2. The cause of the population cycle of the snowshoe hare is still a mystery. Suggest two possible explanations for why this cycle occurs. Describe how you would test each possibility.

3. Explain how disease could be a density-dependent factor in a population.

4. Describe an imaginary population, and name at least two density-dependent factors that

affect the population when it has reached carrying capacity. Draw a graph of what you think logistic population growth would look like for the population. Include the effects that a density-independent event might have on the graph.

5. The population of country X is projected to grow rapidly in the next few decades, while slow growth is projected for country Y. Using only the age structures in the figure below, explain why these projections are plausible.

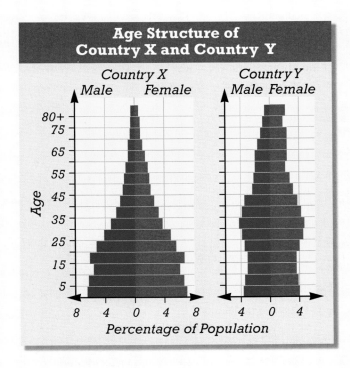

Age Structure of Country X and Country Y

EXTENSION

1. Read "Japan's Harsh Reality Check" in *Newsweek,* January 10, 2000, on page 57. According to the article, how does Japan's aging society and low birthrate influence how Japan will rank as a world power in the twenty-first century? Why is the slowed birthrate in Japan unlikely to change?

2. Using library resources or an on-line database, obtain information about how the United States population census is conducted. Examine the results of the 1990

census, and answer these questions. What was the population of the United States in 1990? How much larger was the 1990 population than the 1980 population? Which state grew by the greatest percentage? Which states showed reductions in population?

3. Obtain population records for your town, city, or county. Try to get data that cover as long a period of time as possible. Make a graph that shows changes in population size. Describe any patterns you see in the data.

Studying a Yeast Population

OBJECTIVES

- Observe the growth and decline in a population of yeast cells.
- Apply the underlying principles to changes in human populations.

PROCESS SKILLS

- calculating
- measuring
- collecting data
- organizing data
- analyzing data

MATERIALS

- yeast culture
- 1 mL pipet
- test tube
- iodine in dropper bottle
- microscope slide ruled in 2 mm squares
- safety goggles
- coverslip
- compound microscope

Background

1. What is a population?
2. List three properties of populations.
3. What is carrying capacity?
4. What are some common limiting factors that prevent populations from exceeding their carrying capacity?
5. How can populations be sampled to achieve an accurate count?

PART A Day 1

1. CAUTION **Put on a lab apron, goggles, and disposable gloves.**
2. Your teacher will transfer approximately 1 mL of the yeast culture to a test tube and then add 2 drops of iodine to the test tube. **CAUTION Work with care—iodine is a poison and an eye irritant. If you get iodine on your skin or clothing, wash it off at the sink while calling to your teacher. If you get iodine in your eyes, immediately flush**

your eyes with water at the eyewash station while calling to your teacher.

3. Use the 1 mL pipet to transfer 0.1 mL (one drop) from the test tube to a ruled microscope slide. Carefully lower a coverslip over the drop. **CAUTION Slides break easily. Use caution when handling them.**

4. Using the compound light microscope, view your slide under low power. Perform the following steps to estimate the total number of yeast cells in 0.1 mL. Note the appearance of your yeast culture. Your culture should look similar to the one shown in the photograph labeled (a) below.

(a)   (b)

5. Each slide is ruled in 2 mm squares. The figure below shows only 3 of these 2 mm squares. You will be counting the cells in six 2 mm squares. Focus on the yeast cells and notice the black grid lines on the slide. Switch to the 400× objective, and align the slide so that you can just see the top left corner of one 2 mm square, area 1, shown in the figure below.

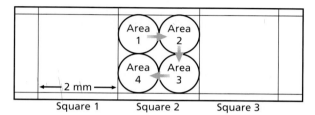

6. Count all the yeast cells in area 1, and record the number in a data table similar to the one on the facing page.

ESTIMATED NUMBER OF YEAST CELLS IN 0.1 mL OF CULTURE

Time (hours)	Number of cells per 2 mm square						Average	Population size (cells/0.1 mL)
	1	2	3	4	5	6		
0								
24								
48								
72								
96								

7. Move the slide to area 2. Continue counting cells and recording data in your lab report until you have counted the cells in each of the four areas that make up one 2 mm square. Add the total number of cells in the square, and record this number in your lab report.

8. Switch the microscope to low power, and move the slide one square to the left. Under high power, count the cells and record the number in your lab report.

9. Repeat steps 5–8 until you have counted the cells in a total of six squares. Add the total number of cells you counted in the six squares. Calculate the average number of yeast cells in a 2 mm square by dividing the total by 6. Record this number in your data table under "Average."

10. Clean up your materials and wash your hands before leaving the lab.

PART B Days 2–5

11. Repeat steps 1–10 each day for four more days. Record your data for 24, 48, 72, and 96 hours. Note any changes in the appearance of your yeast culture in your lab report. If possible, repeat steps 1–10 again after the weekend. The yeast culture may have changed in appearance to resemble the photograph labeled (b) on the facing page.

12. To find the total population of yeast cells in 1 mL of yeast culture (the amount in the test tube), multiply the average number of cells counted in a 2 mm square by 2,500.

13. Graph your data using the values you calculated for the entire test-tube population over the five-day period.

14. Clean up your materials and wash your hands before leaving the lab.

Analysis and Conclusions

1. What effect does iodine have on yeast cells?
2. Why were several areas counted and then averaged each day?
3. When was the most rapid growth? the slowest growth?
4. When was the growth peak reached?
5. How did the yeast population change over time?
6. What limiting factors probably caused the yeast population to decline?
7. If you kept counting for several more days, what do you think would happen to the yeast population?
8. What limiting factors that affect yeast also affect human populations?
9. Did the growth rate of the yeast population more closely follow the predictions of the exponential model or the logistic model? Defend your answer.
10. In what ways do population growth and decline in a yeast population resemble growth and decline in a human population? In what ways do they differ?
11. To find the total number of cells in 1 mL, you multiplied the number of cells you counted in a 2 mm square by 2,500. To see why this works, calculate the volume of fluid in one of the small squares. The fluid forms a layer about 0.1 mm thick on the microscope slide. So the volume is 2 mm $\times$ 2 mm $\times$ 0.1 mm = 0.4 mm^3. Now convert to milliliters, remembering that 1 mL = 1 cm^3 and 1 cm^3 = 1,000 mm^3. Finally, divide your answer into 1 mL to find what multiplier you need to use to go from the number of cells per square to the number of cells per milliliter.

Further Inquiry

Is it possible to set up a population of yeast that continues to grow for a week without declining? Would it be possible to keep the population size growing indefinitely?

CHAPTER 21

COMMUNITY ECOLOGY

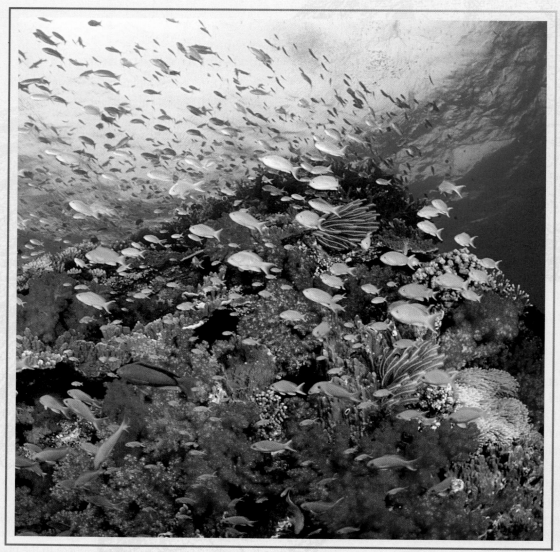

This coral-reef community rivals a tropical rain forest in number of species.

FOCUS CONCEPT: *Interdependence of Organisms*

As you read, note how evolution shapes the interactions among species in a community.

Unit 7—Ecosystem Dynamics
Units 1–6

21-1 *Species Interactions*

21-2 *Properties of Communities*

21-3 *Succession*

SPECIES INTERACTIONS

*J*ust as populations contain interacting members of a single species, communities contain interacting populations of many species. This chapter introduces the five major types of close interactions, or **symbioses**, among species—predation, parasitism, competition, mutualism, and commensalism. These symbiotic relationships help determine the nature of communities.

PREDATION

Predation is a powerful force in a community. In predation, one individual, the **predator,** captures, kills, and consumes another individual, the **prey.** Predation influences where and how species live by determining the relationships in the food web. Predation is also an effective regulator of population size.

Predators, Prey, and Natural Selection

Natural selection, the major mechanism of evolution, favors adaptations that improve the efficiency of predators at finding, capturing, and consuming prey. For example, rattlesnakes have adaptations for locating their prey with an acute sense of smell and with specialized heat-sensitive pits located below each nostril, as shown in Figure 21-1. These pits enable a rattlesnake to aim its strike at warm-bodied prey with great accuracy, even in the dark. Other predator adaptations include the webs of spiders; the sharp, flesh-cutting teeth of wolves and coyotes; and the striped pattern of a tiger's coat, which provides camouflage in the tiger's grassland habitat.

OBJECTIVES

▲

Distinguish predation from parasitism.

●

Evaluate the importance of mimicry as a defense mechanism.

■

Describe two ways plants defend themselves against herbivores.

◆

Explain how competition can affect community structure.

▲

Contrast mutualism with commensalism, and give one example of each type of relationship.

FIGURE 21-1

A rattlesnake is able to detect a variation in temperature of as little as 0.1°C, which helps it locate prey. To disable its prey, the snake injects a strong, fast-acting poison through sharp, hollow fangs.

(a)

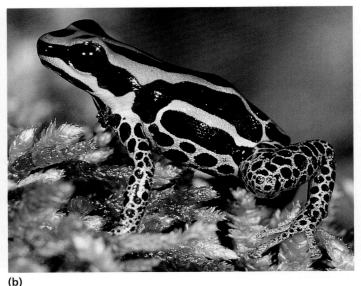

(b)

FIGURE 21-2

Favorable coloration helps many organisms escape predation. The mantis in (a), *Chaenadodus rhombicollis,* cannot readily be detected among the leaves. The frog in (b), *Dendrobates matrimaculatus,* is brightly colored to warn other organisms that it is extremely poisonous.

A predator's survival depends on its ability to capture food, but a prey's survival depends on its ability to avoid being captured. Therefore, natural selection has favored ways for the prey to avoid, escape, or otherwise ward off predators. Some organisms flee when a predator approaches. Others escape detection by hiding or by resembling an inedible object. Can you find the mantis shown in Figure 21-2a, for example? Some organisms, like the frog shown in Figure 21-2b, are poisonous and use bright colors to warn other organisms of their toxicity.

Mimicry

Deception is important in antipredator defenses. In a defense called **mimicry,** a harmless species resembles a poisonous or distasteful species. The harmless mimic is protected because it is often mistaken to be its dangerous look-alike. The king snake shown in Figure 21-3b is a mimic of the poisonous coral snake shown in Figure 21-3a.

Another form of mimicry is when two or more dangerous or distasteful species look similar. Many kinds of bees and wasps have similar patterns of alternating yellow and black stripes, for example. This kind of mimicry benefits each species involved because a predator that encounters an individual of one species will avoid similar individuals.

Plant-Herbivore Interactions

Animals that eat plants are known as **herbivores.** Ecologists usually classify the relationship between plants and herbivores as a form of predation.

Through natural selection, plants have evolved adaptations that protect them from being eaten. Physical defenses, such as sharp thorns, spines, sticky hairs, and tough leaves, can make the plant more difficult to eat. Plants have also evolved a range of chemical defenses. They synthesize chemicals from products of their metabolism, called **secondary compounds,** that are poisonous, irritating,

Word Roots and Origins

parasite

from the Latin word *parasitus,* meaning "one who eats at the table of another"

(a) Eastern coral snake, *Micrurus fulvius fulvius*

(b) Scarlet king snake, *Lampropeltis triangulum elapsoides*

FIGURE 21-3

The scarlet king snake is easy to differentiate from the coral snake. In the coral snake, the red and yellow rings are together. In the king snake, they are separated by a black ring. Also, the coral snake has a black snout, while the king snake has a red snout.

or bad-tasting. Some examples of secondary compounds that provide a defensive function include strychnine (found in the leaves of plants of the genus *Strychnos*) and nicotine (which is toxic to insects and is found in tobacco leaves). Poison ivy and poison oak produce an irritating chemical that causes a rash on most people. Although secondary compounds are usually toxic, many also have medicinal uses. A large number of drugs, including morphine, atropine, codeine, taxol, and quinine, are derived from the secondary compounds of plants.

PARASITISM

Parasitism is a species interaction that resembles predation in that one individual is harmed while the other individual benefits. In parasitism, one individual, known as the **parasite,** feeds on another individual, known as the **host.** But while most forms of predation immediately remove an individual of the prey species from the population, parasitism usually does not result in the immediate death of the host. Often, the parasite feeds on the host for a long time instead of killing it.

Parasites can be grouped into two general categories, based on how they interact with their host. **Ectoparasites** (EK-toh-PER-uh-siets) are external parasites; they live on their host but do not enter the host's body. Examples of ectoparasites are ticks, fleas, lice, leeches, lampreys, and mosquitoes. **Endoparasites** (EN-doh-PER-uh-siets) are internal parasites, and they live inside the host's body. Familiar endoparasites are disease-causing bacteria, protists such as malaria parasites, and tapeworms.

Evolution of Parasites and Their Hosts

Parasites can have a strong negative impact on their host, affecting both the health and reproduction of the host. Consequently, parasitism has stimulated the evolution of a variety of defenses in hosts. Skin is an important defense that prevents most parasites from entering the body. Openings through which parasites could pass,

Quick Lab

Analyzing Predation

Materials 4.1 m white string, 4 stakes, 40 toothpicks, stopwatch or kitchen timer, meterstick

Procedure

1. Mark off a 1 m square in a grassy area using the stakes and string.

2. One partner will scatter the toothpicks randomly throughout the square. The other partner will have 1 minute to pick up as many toothpicks as possible, one at a time. Repeat this procedure until each team has performed five trials.

3. Record your team's results on a data table.

Analysis Which colors of toothpicks were picked up most often? Which were picked up least often? How do you account for this difference?

(a)

(b)

FIGURE 21-4

The ticks in (a) are ectoparasites that can sicken and occasionally kill their host by infection or disease. A tapeworm, the endoparasite shown in (b), can grow to 20 m or more in length and can cause illness and death by intestinal blockage and by robbing its host of nutrition.

FIGURE 21-5

The graph shows the negative effect of competition on populations. When *Paramecium aurelia* and *Paramecium caudatum* were grown separately, they each grew to twice the density that they reached when they were grown together, as shown. When grown together, *Paramecium aurelia* proved to be the better competitor for the available food resource. Eventually, *Paramecium caudatum* died out because it could not compete for food.

such as the eyes, mouth, and nose, are defended chemically by tears, saliva, and mucus. Parasites that get past these defenses still may be attacked by the cells of the immune system. Figure 21-4 shows two examples of parasites.

Adaptations of Parasites

Natural selection favors adaptations that allow a parasite to efficiently exploit its host. Parasites are usually specialized anatomically and physiologically. Tapeworms are so specialized for a parasitic lifestyle that they do not even have a digestive system. They live in the small intestine of their host and absorb nutrients directly through their skin.

COMPETITION

Competition results from fundamental niche overlap—the use of the same limited resource by two or more species. Some species of plants release toxins into the soil that prevent individuals of other species from growing nearby, restricting the living space of the other species. More often, one organism will be able to use a resource more efficiently, leaving less of the resource available to the other species.

Research Studies on Competition

Soviet ecologist G. F. Gause was one of the first to study competition in the laboratory. In test tubes stocked with a food supply of bacteria, Gause raised some species of paramecia, separately and in various combinations. *Paramecium caudatum* and *Paramecium aurelia* thrived when grown separately. As you can see in Figure 21-5, when the two species were combined, *Paramecium caudatum* always died out because *Paramecium aurelia* was a more efficient predator of bacteria. Ecologists use the principle of **competitive exclusion** to describe situations in which one species is eliminated from a community because of competition for the same limited resource. In competitive exclusion, one species uses the resource

Competitive Exclusion in Paramecia

P. aurelia

P. caudatum

Population density by volume

200

150

100

50

0

4   8   12   16   20   24

Days

more efficiently and has a reproductive advantage that eventually eliminates the other species.

Joseph Connell's study of barnacles along the Scottish coast in the 1960s demonstrates competition in the wild. Connell studied two species of barnacles, *Semibalanus balanoides* and *Chthamalus stellatus,* that live in the inter-tidal zone, the portion of the shore that is exposed during low tide. Each species formed a distinct band within the intertidal zone, as shown in Figure 21-6, with *Chthamalus* living higher on the rocks than *Semibalanus* did. Connell demonstrated that this difference was partly due to competition. When a rock covered with *Chthamalus* was transplanted to the lower zone, *Chthamalus* was clearly able to tolerate the conditions in the lower zone. However, *Semibalanus* settled on the rock and eventually crowded out *Chthamalus.* Connell concluded that competition restricted the range of *Chthamalus.* Although it could survive lower on the rocks, competition from *Semibalanus* prevented it from doing so. Intolerance to long periods of drying when the tide was out probably restricted the range of *Semibalanus* to the lower zone.

Competition and Community Structure

Competition has the potential to be an important influence on the nature of a community. The composition of a community may change through competitive exclusion. Competitors may also evolve niche differences or anatomical differences that lessen the intensity of competition. Natural selection favors differences between potential competitors. These differences are often greatest where the ranges of potential competitors overlap. This phenomenon is called **character displacement.**

An example of character displacement is provided by Darwin's finches. These finches feed on seeds. Birds with larger beaks can crack open and eat larger seeds, so beak size is a good indicator of diet. Two species of Darwin's finches are very similar to each other. On islands where only one of two similar species is found, birds of the two species have the same size beak. But on an island where both birds are found, their beak sizes are different. They have evolved a character displacement that enables them to feed on different-sized seeds and reduce competition.

As Darwin noted, competition is likely to be most intense between closely related species that require the same resources. When similar species coexist, each species uses only part of the available resources. This pattern of resource use is called **resource partitioning.** For example, consider three species of warblers that live in spruce and fir trees and feed on insects. The late Princeton ecologist Robert MacArthur discovered that the warblers differ in where they forage. Each kind of warbler hunts for insects only in a particular section of the tree. As a result, competition among the species is reduced.

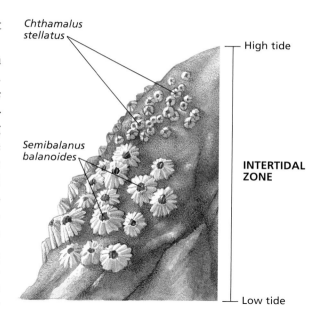

Chthamalus stellatus

Semibalanus balanoides

High tide

INTERTIDAL ZONE

Low tide

FIGURE 21-6

Although *Chthamalus* is capable of surviving in the lower intertidal zones, it is crowded out by *Semibalanus*. *Semibalanus* is unable to survive in the upper zone, which is frequently above the tidal level for extended periods. *Semibalanus* is the most efficient competitor in the areas that are usually under water.

internetconnect

SC*LINKS*
NSTA

TOPIC: Competition
GO TO: www.scilinks.org
KEYWORD: HM401

MUTUALISM AND COMMENSALISM

Mutualism is a cooperative relationship in which both species derive some benefit. Some mutualistic relationships are so close that neither species can survive without the other. An example of such mutualism involves ants and a shrub called bull's horn acacia. The ants nest inside the acacia's large thorns and receive food from the plant. The ants protect the acacia from predation by herbivores and trim back vegetation that shades the shrub.

Pollination is one of the most important mutualistic relationships on Earth. Animals such as bees, butterflies, flies, beetles, bats, and birds pollinate many flowering plants. Animals that carry pollen are called **pollinators.** A flower is a lure for pollinators, which are attracted by the flower's color, pattern, shape, or scent. The plant usually provides food for its pollinators. As the animal feeds in the flower, it picks up a load of pollen, which it will carry to the next flower of the same species it visits, as shown in Figure 21-7.

Commensalism is an interaction in which one species benefits and the other is not affected. Some cases of commensalism may be mutualisms in which the benefit to the second organism hasn't yet been identified. One example of commensalism is the relationship between cattle egrets and Cape buffalo in Tanzania. The birds feed on small animals such as insects and lizards that are forced out of their hiding places by the buffalo's movement through the grass.

FIGURE 21-7

Some bats are active at night and locate their food by sound or smell instead of by sight. Flowers pollinated by nectar-feeding bats do not need to be brightly colored, but they usually do have a strong fragrance. As the bat feeds on the flower's nectar, it becomes smeared with pollen, as shown. The bat then carries the pollen to the next flower it feeds on.

SECTION 21-1 REVIEW

1. Explain how predators differ from parasites. Give an example of each kind of organism.

2. Some harmless flies resemble bees and wasps. What is this mechanism called? Evaluate its importance as a defense mechanism.

3. Describe two chemical defenses of plants.

4. Explain the advantage of character displacement and give an example.

5. If cattle egrets removed ticks from Cape buffalo, would their relationship still be considered commensalism? Explain your answer.

6. **CRITICAL THINKING** Explain how two similar species of birds are able to inhabit the same area and even nest in the same tree without occupying the same niche.

PROPERTIES OF COMMUNITIES

The investigation of community properties and interactions is an active area of ecology. What properties are most significant in structuring a community? What determines species richness and abundance? These questions are central to a study of communities.

SPECIES RICHNESS AND DIVERSITY

One characteristic of a community is its **species richness,** the number of species it contains. A related measure is **species diversity,** which relates the number of species in the community to the relative abundance of each species. These two measures provide slightly different information. Species richness is a simple count of the species in the community. Each species contributes one count to the total, regardless of whether the species' population size is one or 1 million. In contrast, species diversity suggests each species' importance because it takes into account how common each species is in the community. To calculate the species diversity of a community, an ecologist must measure or estimate the population size of all the species in the community.

Patterns of Species Richness

Species richness varies with latitude (distance from the equator). As a general rule, the closer a community is to the equator, the more species it will contain. Species richness is greatest in the tropical rain forests. For example, entomologists E. O. Wilson and Terry Erwin identified nearly as many species of ants in a single tree in Peru as can be found in the entire British Isles.

Why are there more species in the tropics than there are in the temperate zones? One hypothesis is that temperate habitats are younger, having formed since the last ice age. Therefore, tropical habitats were not disturbed by the ice ages, while habitats at latitudes farther north were. Also, the climate is more stable in the tropics. This stability allowed species to specialize to a greater degree than they could in temperate regions, where the climate is more variable. Another hypothesis suggests that because plants

OBJECTIVES

▲

Explain the difference between species richness and species diversity.

●

Describe how species richness varies with latitude, and explain a hypothesis for this pattern.

■

Explain the cause and consequences of the species-area effect.

◆

Explain the two main views of the relationship between species richness and stability.

FIGURE 21-8

This species-richness map of North American and Central American birds shows that fewer than 100 species of birds inhabit arctic regions, whereas more than 600 species occupy some tropical regions. This is evidence that species richness increases nearer the equator. Equatorial rain forests are biologically the richest habitats on Earth.

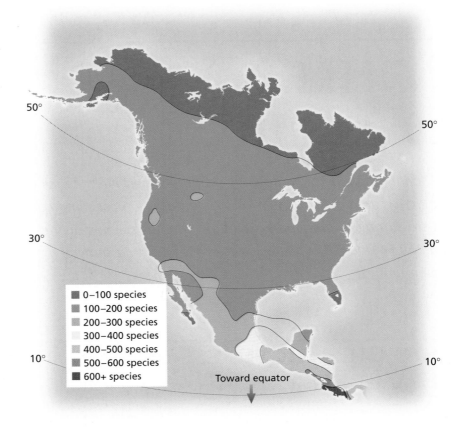

■	0–100 species
■	100–200 species
■	200–300 species
□	300–400 species
□	400–500 species
■	500–600 species
■	600+ species

Toward equator

can photosynthesize year-round in the tropics, there is more energy available to support more organisms. It is likely that the high diversity of species in the tropics, as indicated in Figure 21-8, is the result of several factors acting together.

The Species-Area Effect

Another pattern of species richness is that larger areas usually contain more species than smaller areas do. This relationship is called the **species-area effect.** The species-area effect is most often applied to islands, where area is clearly limited by geography. In the Caribbean, for example, more species of reptiles and amphibians live on large islands, such as Cuba, than on small islands, such as Redonda, as shown in Figure 21-9. Because all of these islands are close together, differences in species richness cannot be due to differences in latitude. Why does species richness increase with increasing area? Larger areas usually contain a greater diversity of habitats and thus can support more species.

The species-area effect has one very important practical consequence—reducing the size of a habitat reduces the number of species it can support. Today, natural habitats are shrinking rapidly under pressure from the ever-growing human population. About 2 percent of the world's tropical rain forests is destroyed each year, for example. The inevitable result of the destruction of habitats is the extinction of species.

FIGURE 21-9

As shown in the graph, the large islands of Cuba and Hispaniola have about 100 species (of reptiles and amphibians). The small island of Redonda has only about five species of reptiles and amphibians. In general, species diversity increases as available habitat area increases. This principle is true whether the boundaries of the area are created by shoreline, as on an island, or by encroaching human population, as in the construction of housing in a natural area.

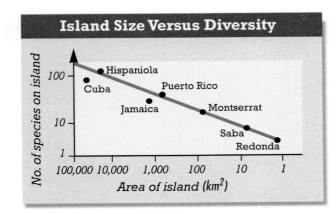

Island Size Versus Diversity

No. of species on island

Hispaniola
Cuba
Puerto Rico
Jamaica
Montserrat
Saba
Redonda

Area of island (km²)

Species Interactions and Species Richness

Interactions among species sometimes promote species richness. Several studies have demonstrated that predators can prevent competitive exclusion from occurring among their prey. In the 1960s, Robert Paine of the University of Washington showed the importance of the sea star *Pisaster*, shown in Figure 21-10, in maintaining the species richness of communities on the Washington coast. Paine removed all *Pisaster* individuals from one site and for several years prevented any new *Pisaster* individuals from settling there. This change caused a dramatic shift in the community. The mussel *Mytilus*, which had previously coexisted with several other species, became much more abundant and spread over the habitat, crowding out other species. The species richness of the community fell from 15 to 8 during the course of the study. Evidently, *Mytilus* was the superior competitor for space on the rocks, but its population was normally held in check by predation from *Pisaster*.

Community Stability

One of the most important characteristics of a community is how it responds to disturbance. The **stability** of a community indicates its resistance to change. For many years, most ecologists agreed that stability was directly related to species richness. Communities with more species, they presumed, would contain more links between species. These links would, in a sense, disperse the effects of the disturbance and prevent disruption of the community. One line of evidence cited in support of this view was the vulnerability of agricultural fields, which usually contain one species of crop plant, to outbreaks of insect pests.

David Tilman of the University of Minnesota and John Dowling of the University of Montreal investigated how the response to drought in a small plot of grasses was affected by species richness. They grew varying numbers of species in many small plots of land and subjected each to drought. They found that plots with more species present lost a smaller percentage of plant mass than plots with fewer species. The plots with more species also took less time to recover from the drought. They concluded that species richness improves a community's stability.

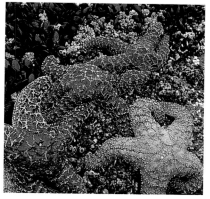

FIGURE 21-10

When the sea star *Pisaster* was removed from an area where the sea stars had preyed on the mussel *Mytilus*, the mussels crowded out many of the other competing species in the area. Predation by the sea star on the mussel promoted diversity by controlling the superior competitor—the mussel.

internet**connect**

SC**LINKS**
NSTA

TOPIC: Species interaction
and richness
GO TO: www.scilinks.org
KEYWORD: HM405

SECTION 21-2 REVIEW

1. What is the difference between species richness and species diversity?

2. Explain the relationship between species richness and latitude.

3. Why is the species-area effect important in efforts to conserve species?

4. Describe how predation can affect species diversity.

5. Explain how species richness contributes to community stability.

6. **CRITICAL THINKING** Explain how the example of agricultural fields supports the idea that species richness promotes stability.

Distinguish between primary and secondary succession.

●

Identify some of the characteristics of pioneer species.

Describe the sequence of changes occurring at Glacier Bay.

◆

Explain the successional changes that can occur when an existing community is disrupted.

SUCCESSION

Disturbances such as fires, landslides, hurricanes, and floods trigger a sequence of changes in the composition of a community. Certain species flourish immediately after the disturbance, then are replaced by other species, which are replaced by still others. Over time, the composition of the community changes.

SUCCESSIONAL CHANGES IN COMMUNITIES

During the summer and early fall of 1988, fires burned large areas of Yellowstone National Park, affecting nearly 300,000 hectares (720,000 acres). If you visit Yellowstone today, you will find that regrowth is well under way in the burned areas. In time, if there are no further disturbances, the burned areas of Yellowstone National Park will undergo a series of regrowth stages. The gradual, sequential regrowth of species in an area is called **succession** (SUHK-SE-shuhn). You can see early stages of succession in abandoned fields, in vacant lots, along roads, and even in sidewalks or parking lots where weeds are pushing up through cracks in the concrete.

Ecologists recognize two types of succession. **Primary succession** is the development of a community in an area that has not supported life previously, such as bare rock, a sand dune, or an island formed by a volcanic eruption. **Secondary succession** is the sequential replacement of species that follows disruption of an existing community. The disruption may stem from a natural disaster, such as a forest fire or a strong storm, or from human activity, such as farming, logging, or mining.

Any new habitat, whether it is a pond left by heavy rain, a freshly plowed field, or newly exposed bedrock, is an invitation to many species that are adapted to be good pioneers. The species that predominate early in succession—called the **pioneer species**—tend to be small, fast-growing, and fast-reproducing. Pioneer species are well suited for invading and occupying a disturbed habitat. For example, they are often very good at dispersing their seeds, which enables them to quickly reach disrupted areas. Some of the pioneers that might be found in a vacant lot or abandoned field in the eastern United States include horseweed, crabgrass, and ragweed.

(a)

(b)

(c)

FIGURE 21-11

Ecologists study the process of primary succession by examining a variety of areas at different successional stages. These photos were taken at different locations at Glacier Bay, Alaska; the changes they illustrate take about 200 years. Shown in (a) is lifeless glacial "till" (pulverized bare rocks) left in the wake of the retreating glacier. Shown in (b) is an early stage of succession in which small plants and shrubs are growing on the site. A mature forest is shown in (c), an end stage of succession.

Primary Succession

Primary succession often proceeds very slowly because the minerals necessary for plant growth are unavailable. For example, when glaciers last retreated from eastern Canada, about 12,000 years ago, they left a huge stretch of barren bedrock from which all the soil had been scraped. This geologic formation, called the Canadian Shield, was a place where plants and most animals could not live. Repeated freezing and thawing broke this rock into smaller pieces. In time, lichens—mutualistic associations between fungi and either algae or cyanobacteria—colonized the barren rock. Acids in the lichens and mildly acidic rain washed nutrient minerals from the rock. Eventually, the dead organic matter from decayed lichens along with minerals from the rock began to form a thin layer of soil in which a few grasslike plants could grow. These plants then died, and their decomposition added more organic material to the soil. Soon shrubs began to grow, and then trees appeared. Today much of the Canadian Shield is densely populated with pine, balsam, and spruce trees, whose roots cling to soil that in some areas is still only a few centimeters deep. A similar series of changes has been documented at Glacier Bay, Alaska, shown in Figure 21-11.

(a)

(b)

(c)

FIGURE 21-12

In (a), a recently abandoned agricultural field is being pioneered by weeds. Eventually, taller plants and shrubs will shade out the pioneers, as shown in (b). Next, a forest of pine or cottonwood may be succeeded by a hardwood forest. The whole process, if there are no further disturbances, takes about 100 years.

Secondary Succession

Secondary succession occurs where an existing community has been cleared by a disturbance, such as agriculture, but the soil has been left intact. In secondary succession, it commonly takes about 100 years for the original ecosystem to return through a series of well-defined stages. In eastern temperate regions, secondary succession typically begins with annual grasses, mustards, and dandelions. Succession proceeds with perennial grasses and shrubs, continues with trees like dogwoods, and often continues to a deciduous forest, as shown in Figure 21-12.

THE COMPLEXITY OF SUCCESSION

The traditional description of succession is that the community proceeds through a predictable series of stages until it reaches a stable end point, called the **climax community.** The organisms in each stage alter the physical environment in ways that make it less favorable for their own survival but more favorable for the organisms that eventually succeed them. In a sense, each stage paves the way for the next, leading ultimately to the climax community, which remains constant for a long period of time.

When ecologists began to study and document many instances of succession, they found a complex picture. Some so-called climax communities, for example, are not stable and continue to change. Instead of proceeding inevitably toward the climax community, succession may be regularly "reset" by disturbances. For example, many grasslands give way to forests, but periodic fires prevent the forests from developing. There may be many possible successional pathways in a particular area. The actual path followed may depend on the identities of the species present, the order in which they arrive, the climate, and many other factors. Ecologists agree that the idea of a single successional pathway ending in a stable climax community is too simple to describe what actually occurs in nature.

SECTION 21-3 REVIEW

1. What is the difference between primary succession and secondary succession?

2. How are plants we think of as weeds, such as ragweed, well adapted to be pioneer species?

3. Identify one of the initial colonists in succession at Glacier Bay.

4. Describe secondary succession, and distinguish between pioneer species and a climax community.

5. How do frequent fires alter succession in a community?

6. **CRITICAL THINKING** Describe the geological process of soil formation. Explain its importance to succession.

CHAPTER 21 REVIEW

SUMMARY/VOCABULARY

21-1
- Ecologists recognize five major kinds of species interactions in communities: predation, parasitism, competition, mutualism, and commensalism.
- The interaction in which one organism kills and eats another is predation. Predators have evolved many ways to efficiently find and capture prey. Prey have evolved many ways to defend themselves against predators.
- Mimicry is a defense mechanism in which a harmless species gains protection by its resemblance to a poisonous or distasteful species, or in which two or more poisonous or distasteful species resemble each other.
- Parasitism involves one organism feeding on, but not always killing, another.

- Parasites are grouped into two general categories—external parasites (ectoparasites) and internal parasites (endoparasites).
- Competition occurs when two or more species use the same scarce resource.
- Competition may cause competitive exclusion, the extinction of one competitor from the community. It may also be a strong selective force in the evolution of niche differences among competitors.
- In mutualism, both interacting species benefit. The relationship between flowering plants and their pollinators is an example of mutualism.
- In commensalism, one species benefits and the other is not affected.

Vocabulary

character displacement (401)	ectoparasite (399)	mutualism (402)	prey (397)
commensalism (402)	endoparasite (399)	parasite (399)	resource partitioning (401)
competition (400)	herbivore (398)	parasitism (399)	secondary compound (398)
competitive exclusion (400)	host (399)	pollinator (402)	symbiosis (397)
	mimicry (398)	predator (397)	

21-2
- Species richness is the number of species in a community.
- Species diversity incorporates both species richness and the abundance of each species.
- As a general rule, species richness is greatest near the equator.

- Larger areas generally support more species. This is called the species-area effect.
- Species interactions such as predation can promote species richness.
- Species richness improves a community's stability.

Vocabulary

species-area effect (404)	species diversity (403)	species richness (403)	stability (405)

21-3
- Succession is a change in the species composition of a community. Primary succession is the assembly of a community on newly created habitat. Secondary succession is the change in an existing community following a disturbance.
- Pioneer species are the initial colonists of a disturbed area. They are usually small organisms that grow fast, reproduce quickly, and disperse their seeds well.

- Succession at Glacier Bay proceeded from bare debris left behind by a retreating glacier to small plants such as mosses, to alders, to spruce and hemlocks.
- Secondary succession occurs in areas where the original ecosystem has been cleared by a disturbance, such as clearing for agriculture. It proceeds from plants commonly thought of as weeds to a stable end point called a climax community.

Vocabulary

climax community (408)	primary succession (406)	secondary succession (406)	succession (406)
pioneer species (406)			

REVIEW

Vocabulary

1. Explain the difference between mutualism and commensalism.
2. Describe resource partitioning and competition, and explain how they are related.
3. What is the difference between ectoparasites and endoparasites?
4. How do competitive exclusion and character displacement differ?
5. Distinguish between species richness and the species-area effect.

Multiple Choice

6. In which of the following interactions do both species benefit? (a) competition (b) predation (c) mutualism (d) commensalism
7. An example of a parasite is (a) a lion (b) a tick (c) a deer (d) a snake.
8. Which of the following is not a plant defense against herbivores? (a) thorns (b) tough leaves (c) secondary compounds (d) lysozyme
9. The evolution of anatomical differences in response to competition is called (a) competitive exclusion (b) character displacement (c) niche release (d) convergence.
10. Which of the following is true of a mimic?
    (a) It is poisonous or distasteful.
    (b) It is identical to a poisonous species.
    (c) It closely resembles a poisonous species.
    (d) An example is the coral snake.
11. Species richness (a) is greater on large islands than it is on small islands (b) is lowest in the tropics (c) is increasing worldwide (d) is greater on small islands than on large islands.
12. In the experiment with the sea star *Pisaster* and the mussel *Mytilus,* (a) elimination of the mussel *Mytilus* increased the number of sea stars (b) species richness of the community increased over time (c) removal of the sea star led to a decrease in species richness (d) removal of the sea star led to an increase in species diversity.
13. Primary succession occurs (a) on bare rock (b) in a disrupted habitat (c) after a forest fire (d) only on dry land.
14. The feeding behavior of warblers is an example of (a) niche overlap (b) resource partitioning (c) mutualism (d) character displacement.
15. Which is not true of secondary compounds?
    (a) They are part of a defense mechanism.
    (b) They can be poisonous and taste bad.
    (c) They are metabolized as food by plants.
    (d) They compose the irritant produced by poison ivy.

Short Answer

16. Describe two evolutionary adaptations that enable organisms to be efficient predators.
17. What are secondary compounds, and what is their function? List two examples of secondary compounds.
18. Explain some of the ways your body defends itself against parasites.
19. Describe the experiments G. F. Gause conducted on competition in *Paramecium.* What were the results of these experiments?
20. In the study of competition between two species of barnacles, *Semibalanus* was clearly the superior competitor, yet *Chthamalus* was not excluded from the community. Explain why.
21. What benefits do ants derive from their relationship with the bull's horn acacia? What benefits does the acacia receive from the ants?
22. Examine the island map below. Which island will probably have more species of plants and animals, Island A or Island B? Explain your answer.

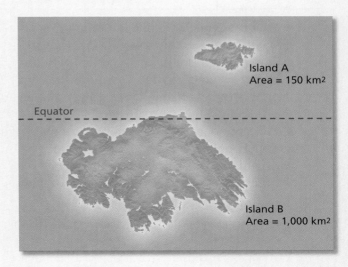

Island A
Area = 150 km2

Equator

Island B
Area = 1,000 km2

23. *Unit 7—Ecosystem Dynamics*

Write a report summarizing how artificial ecosystems, used in the management and treatment of wastewater and pollutants, can demonstrate succession.

c. Suppose the birds are seed-eating finches and the tree produces large and small seeds. Each of the birds has either a small beak or a large beak. Explain the evolutionary phenomenon demonstrated in this case. Would a bird with a medium-sized beak be able to coexist in the tree? Explain why or why not.

CRITICAL THINKING

1. A scientist studies a community and finds no evidence of competition. The scientist concludes that competition has never had an effect on the structure of the community. Is this a valid conclusion? Explain your answer.

2. Some plants are pollinated by only one pollinator. Explain why this might be advantageous to the plant. Explain why this specificity could also lead to the extinction of the plant species.

3. Explain why it is usually harder to measure the species diversity of a community than it is to measure its species richness.

4. Examine the figure of the warblers on the right.
   a. Each bird is shown in the part of the tree where it usually nests. Explain how three closely related species of warbler are able to coexist in the same tree. What phenomenon is demonstrated by their coexistence?
   b. What might happen if only a single species of insect inhabited the spruce tree? Explain the phenomenon that might be demonstrated in this case.

Blackburnian warbler

Bay-breasted warbler

Myrtle warbler

EXTENSION

1. Ants have mutualistic relationships with a variety of different organisms. Use an on-line database or conduct library research to identify two mutualisms (besides those mentioned in the text) between ants and other species. Write a report that summarizes what you have learned. Be sure to explain the nature of each interaction and the benefits each species receives.

2. Read "Hidden Existence" in *Audubon*, March–April 1999, on page 56. Describe two

ways some animals are able to hide in plain view. Explain how an animal might combine camouflage coloration with specialized behavior to avoid predators. Camouflage is important to prey animals, but how does it help predators?

3. Choose two flowering plants that live in your area. Find out what pollinators visit the flowers. Make drawings that show the flowers and their pollinators.

Nitrogen Fixation in Root Nodules

OBJECTIVES

- Examine root nodules in legumes.
- Investigate the differences between legume (bean) and a nonlegume (radish).
- View active cultures of *Rhizobium*.

PROCESS SKILLS

- recognizing relationships
- hypothesizing
- comparing and contrasting

MATERIALS

- protective gloves
- 2 three-inch flowerpots
- 2 cups of soil
- 2 mixing sticks
- 1.2 mL (1/4 tsp) of *Rhizobium* bacteria per pot
- 2 bean seeds
- 2 radish seeds
- 2 microscope slides
- 2 coverslips
- 1 prepared reference slide of a legume root-nodule cross-section infected with *Rhizobium*
- compound light microscope
- stereoscope or magnifying glass
- scalpel

Background

1. Define *symbiosis,* and give an example of three types of symbiotic associations.
2. Nitrogen-fixing bacteria and leguminous plants have a symbiotic relationship.
3. Root nodules are swellings in the roots of leguminous plants that are infected with nitrogen-fixing bacteria.
4. *Rhizobium* is a genus of nitrogen-fixing bacteria. *Rhizobium* exists in soil and infects the root nodules of leguminous plants.
5. Green root nodules indicate actively reproducing bacteria that are not fixing nitrogen. Pink nodules indicate bacteria that are actively fixing nitrogen but not reproducing.

PART A   Growing the Test Plants

1. Fill two flowerpots with soil. Using a mixing stick, stir approximately 1/4 teaspoon of the *Rhizobium* mixture into each pot.
2. Plant two bean seeds in one pot and label it "bean," and two radish seeds in the other and label it "radish." Water each pot so that the soil is moist but not saturated. Label the two pots.
3. Place the plants where they will receive direct sunlight. Water the soil when necessary to keep the soil moist but not saturated. Do not fertilize these plants.
4. After approximately one week, check to see if both seeds germinated in each pot. If they did, remove the smaller seedling. The plants will be ready to be examined after six to eight weeks. Monitor the plants each day. Give them enough water to keep the soil slightly moist, and keep them in direct sunlight. Note: The radish seeds will germinate faster than the bean seeds.
5. Clean up your materials and wash your hands before leaving the lab.

PART B   Observing the Roots of Beans

6. Prepare a data table similar to the one below. As you work, record your observations in your data table.
7. CAUTION **Wear disposable gloves while handling plants. Do not rub any plant part or plant juice on your eyes or skin.** Remove the bean plant from the pot by grasping the bottom of the stem and gently pulling the plant out. Be careful not to injure the plant. Carefully remove all dirt from the roots.
8. View the roots of the bean plant under a stereoscope. Compare the appearance of the bean root system

OBSERVATIONS OF RHIZOBIUM	
Appearance of nodule	
Color of nodule	
Number of nodules	
Number of pink nodules	
Number of green nodules	

with the photograph above. Note the formation of any nodules on your bean plant's roots. Draw a root with a nodule in your lab report, and label each structure.

9. ⬦ **CAUTION** **Use the scalpel with care. A scalpel is a very sharp instrument. Always make cuts with the blade facing away from your body. If you cut yourself, quickly apply direct pressure to the wound and call for your teacher.** Remove a large nodule from the bean root and carefully cut it in half with a scalpel. The pink nodules contain active nitrogen-fixing bacteria. The green nodules contain bacteria but cannot fix nitrogen because they are actively reproducing. *Rhizobium* will begin fixing nitrogen only after it stops reproducing. View the cross section under a stereoscope. Note the arrangement of bacteria within the cell. Draw a cell infected with bacteria in your lab report. Label the nodule, cell, and bacteria.

PART C   Observing the Roots of Radishes

10. ⬦ **CAUTION** **Wear disposable gloves while handling plants. Do not rub any plant part or plant juice on your eyes or skin.** Remove the radish plant from the pot by grasping the bottom of the stem and gently pulling the plant out. Be careful not to injure the plant. Carefully remove all dirt from the roots.

11. Examine the roots of the radish plant under a stereoscope. Compare the radish roots with the roots of the bean plant that you have already examined. Are there any nodules on the roots of the radish plant? Draw

the root of the radish plant in your lab report. Label the drawing "Radish."

PART D   Preparing a Wet Mount of *Rhizobium*

12. ⬦ **CAUTION** **Handle the slide and coverslip carefully. Glass slides break easily and the sharp edges can cut you.** Prepare a wet mount by placing part of a nodule from the root of a bean plant on a microscope slide, adding a drop of water, and covering with a coverslip.

13. Place the slide on a flat surface. Gently press down on the slide with your thumb; use enough pressure to squash the nodule. Make sure the coverslip does not slide.

14. Examine the slide under a microscope. Draw and label a cell and the arrangement of bacteria in the cell in your lab report. Note what power of magnification you used.

15. Compare your wet mount preparation with the prepared reference slide of *Rhizobium* and the photograph on the right. A cell infected with *Rhizobium* should have a similar appearance to the photograph at right.

16. ⬦ ⬦ Clean up your materials and wash your hands before leaving the lab.

Analysis and Conclusions

1. Which plant had the most nodules?
2. How many nodules were found on the radish plants?
3. How do legumes become infected with bacteria in nature?
4. What kind of relationship exists between the legume plant and *Rhizobium*? How does this relationship benefit the legume plant? How does this relationship benefit the bacteria?
5. If you were to grow legumes without root nodules to use as experimental controls, why should you plant the seeds in sterile soil?

Further Inquiry

Perform the experiment using beans with and without *Rhizobium*. Count the number of leaves on each plant, and measure the mass of each whole plant as well as the masses of roots, stems, and leaves separately. Predict which part of the plant will have the greatest difference in mass.

CHAPTER 22

ECOSYSTEMS AND THE BIOSPHERE

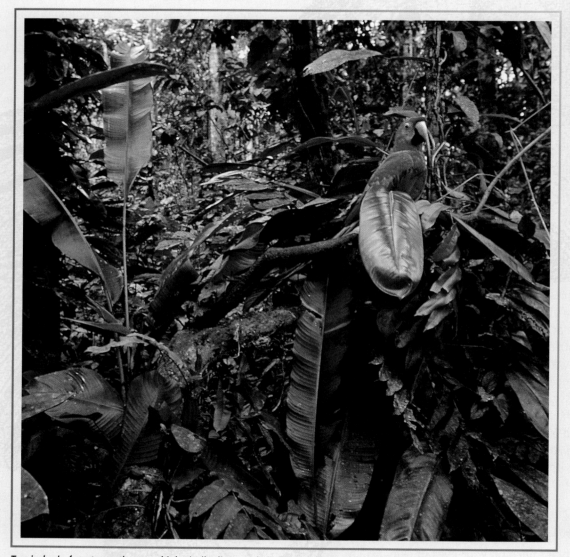

Tropical rain forests are the most biologically diverse of all the biomes on Earth. Shown is the scarlet macaw, Ara macao.

FOCUS CONCEPT: *Interdependence of Organisms*

As you read, note how organisms interact with each other and with their environment to survive in the different kinds of ecosystems on Earth.

Unit 7—*Ecosytem Dynamics*
Topics 1, 3– 6

22-1 *Energy Transfer*

22-2 *Ecosystem Recycling*

22-3 *Terrestrial Ecosystems*

22-4 *Aquatic Ecosystems*

ENERGY TRANSFER

All organisms need energy to carry out essential functions, such as growth, movement, maintenance and repair, and reproduction. In an ecosystem, energy flows from the sun to autotrophs, then to organisms that eat the autotrophs, then to organisms that feed on other organisms. The amount of energy an ecosystem receives and the amount that is transferred from organism to organism have an important effect on the ecosystem's structure.

SECTION

22-1

OBJECTIVES

▲

Contrast producers with consumers.

●

Explain the important role of decomposers in an ecosystem.

■

Contrast a food web with a food chain.

◆

Explain why ecosystems usually contain only a few trophic levels.

PRODUCERS

Autotrophs, which include plants and some kinds of protists and bacteria, manufacture their own food. Because autotrophs capture energy and use it to make organic molecules, they are called **producers.** Most producers are photosynthetic, so they use solar energy to power the production of food. However, some autotrophic bacteria do not use sunlight as an energy source. These bacteria carry out **chemosynthesis** (KEE-mo-SIN-thuh-sis), which means they produce carbohydrates by using energy from inorganic molecules. In terrestrial ecosystems, plants are usually the major producers. In aquatic ecosystems, photosynthetic protists and bacteria are usually the major producers.

Measuring Productivity

Gross primary productivity is the rate at which producers in an ecosystem capture energy. Photosynthetic producers use the energy they capture to make sugar. Some of the sugar is used for cellular respiration, some for maintenance and repair, and some to make new organic material through either growth or reproduction. Ecologists refer to the organic material in an ecosystem as **biomass.** Producers add biomass to an ecosystem by making organic molecules.

Only energy stored as biomass is available to other organisms in the ecosystem. Ecologists often measure the rate at which biomass accumulates, and this rate is called **net primary productivity.** Net primary productivity is typically expressed in units of energy per unit area per year ($kcal/m^2/y$) or in units of mass per unit area per year ($g/m^2/y$). Net primary productivity equals gross primary productivity minus the rate of respiration in producers.

Figure 22-1 shows that net primary productivity can vary greatly from one ecosystem to another. For example, the average rate of net

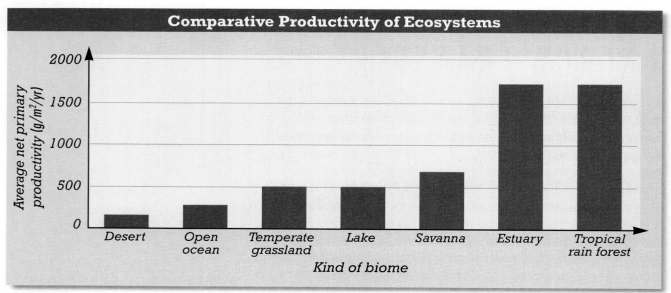

Comparative Productivity of Ecosystems

Average net primary productivity (g/m²/yr) vs *Kind of biome*

Biomes (left to right): Desert, Open ocean, Temperate grassland, Lake, Savanna, Estuary, Tropical rain forest

FIGURE 22-1

As the histogram shows, the net primary productivity in a tropical rain forest is very similar to the net primary productivity in an estuary. Temperate grasslands and freshwater lakes are also very similar in productivity.

primary productivity in a tropical rain forest is 25 times greater than the rate in a desert of the same size. Although rain forests occupy only 5 percent of Earth's surface, they account for almost 30 percent of the world's net primary productivity. Variations in three factors—light, temperature, and precipitation—account for most of the variation in productivity among terrestrial ecosystems. An increase in any of these three variables usually leads to an increase in productivity. In aquatic ecosystems, productivity is usually determined by only two factors: light and the availability of nutrients.

CONSUMERS

All animals, most protists, all fungi, and many bacteria are heterotrophs. Unlike autotrophs, heterotrophs cannot manufacture their own food. Instead they get energy by eating other organisms or organic wastes. Ecologically speaking, heterotrophs are **consumers.** They obtain energy by consuming organic molecules made by other organisms. Consumers can be grouped according to the type of food they eat. **Herbivores** eat producers. An antelope that eats grass is a herbivore. So are the minute zooplankton that feed on phytoplankton floating in oceans and lakes. **Carnivores** eat other consumers. Lions, bald eagles, cobras, and praying mantises are examples of carnivores. **Omnivores** eat both producers and consumers. The grizzly bear, whose diet ranges from berries to salmon, is an omnivore.

Detritivores (dee-TRIE-ti-vorz) are consumers that feed on the "garbage" of an ecosystem, such as organisms that have recently died, fallen leaves and branches, and animal wastes. A vulture is an example of a detritivore. Bacteria and fungi belong to a class of detritivores called decomposers. **Decomposers** cause decay by breaking down the complex molecules in dead tissues and wastes into simpler

3

2

1

FIGURE 22-2

In an ecosystem, all organisms that feed on the same kind of food are in the same trophic level. In this figure, the autotrophs (grass and tree) are on the first trophic level, herbivores (zebra and giraffe) are on the second trophic level, and carnivores (lion and leopard) are on the third trophic level.

molecules. Some of the molecules released during decay are absorbed by the decomposers, and some of them are returned to the soil or water. The action of the decomposers makes the nutrients contained in the dead bodies and wastes of organisms available to autotrophs. Thus, the process of decomposition recycles chemical nutrients.

ENERGY FLOW

Whenever one organism eats another, molecules are metabolized and energy is transferred. As a result, energy flows through an ecosystem, moving from producers to consumers. One way to follow the pattern of energy flow is to group organisms in an ecosystem based on how they obtain energy. An organism's **trophic** (TROH-fik) **level** indicates the organism's position in the sequence of energy transfers, as shown in Figure 22-2. For example, all producers belong to the first trophic level. Herbivores belong to the second trophic level, and the predators of herbivores belong to the third level. Most ecosystems contain only three or four trophic levels.

Food Chains and Food Webs

A **food chain** is a single pathway of feeding relationships among organisms in an ecosystem that results in energy transfer. A food chain may begin with grass, which is a primary producer. The chain may continue with a consumer of grass seeds—a meadow mouse. Next on the chain may be a carnivorous snake, which kills and eats the mouse. A hawk then may eat the snake.

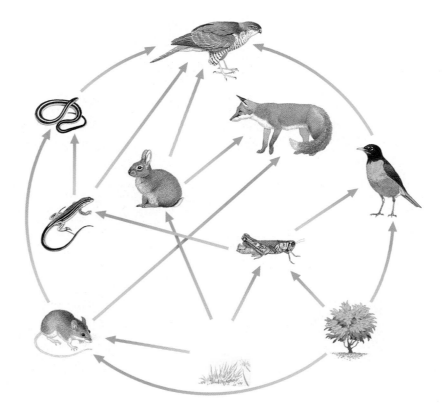

The feeding relationships in an ecosystem are usually too complex to be represented by a single food chain. Many consumers eat more than one type of food. In addition, more than one species of consumer may feed on the same organism. Many food chains interlink, and a diagram of the feeding relationships among all the organisms in an ecosystem would resemble a web. For this reason, the interrelated food chains in an ecosystem are called a **food web.** Figure 22-3 shows a simplified food web.

Quantity of Energy Transfers

Roughly 10 percent of the total energy consumed in one trophic level is incorporated into the organisms in the next level. The ability to maintain a constant body temperature, the ability to move, and a high reproductive rate are functions that require a lot of energy. The kinds of organisms that have those characteristics will transfer less energy to the next trophic level than organisms that do not. For example, grass transfers more energy to a moose than the moose transfers to a wolf. The measured values for energy transfer from one trophic level to the next can range from 20 percent to less than 1 percent. In a recent study of wolves and moose on Isle Royale, Michigan, ecologists found that only 1.3 percent of the total energy consumed by the moose on the island was transferred to the wolves through the wolves' predation on the moose. Figure 22-4 represents the rate at which each trophic level in an ecosystem stores energy as

FIGURE 22-4

This diagram represents energy transfer through four trophic levels. The amount of energy transferred from one level to another can vary, so the structure shown can vary. What is always true, however, is that the top level is much smaller than the lowest level. Hence, energy-transfer diagrams are always roughly pyramidal in shape.

TROPHIC LEVELS

4 — Large carnivores

3 — Small carnivores

2 — Herbivores

1 — Producers

organic material. The pyramid shape of the diagram represents the low percentage of energy transfer from one trophic level to another.

Why is the percentage of energy transfer so low? One reason is that some of the organisms in a trophic level escape being eaten. They eventually die and become food for decomposers, but the energy contained in their bodies does not pass to a higher trophic level. Even when an organism is eaten, some of the molecules in its body will be in a form that the consumer cannot break down and use. For example, a cougar cannot extract energy from the antlers, hooves, and hair of a deer. Also, the energy used by prey for cellular respiration cannot be used by predators to synthesize new biomass. Finally, no transformation or transfer of energy is 100 percent efficient. Every time energy is transformed, such as during the reactions of metabolism, some energy is lost as heat.

To understand this idea better, consider what happens when a deer eats 1,000 kcal of leaves. About 350 kcal are eliminated as urine, dung, and other wastes. Another 480 kcal are lost as heat. Only about 170 kcal are actually stored as organic matter, mostly as fat. Producers use and transfer energy in a similar way. A plant stores only about 1–5 percent of the solar energy that it converts to sugar as organic material. The rest is reflected off the plant, used in its life processes, or lost in the form of heat.

Short Food Chains

The low rate of energy transfer between trophic levels explains why ecosystems rarely contain more than a few trophic levels. Because only about 10 percent of the energy available at one trophic level is transferred to the next trophic level, there is not enough energy in all the organisms at the highest trophic level to support additional levels.

Organisms belonging to the lowest trophic level are usually much more abundant than organisms belonging to the highest level. If you go on a safari in Kenya or Tanzania, for example, you will see about 1,000 zebras, gazelles, wildebeest, and other herbivores for every lion or leopard you see, and there are far more grasses, trees, and shrubs than there are herbivores. Higher trophic levels contain less energy, and, as a consequence, they can support fewer individuals.

SECTION 22-1 REVIEW

1. Why are autotrophs essential components of an ecosystem?

2. What role do decomposers play in an ecosystem? Why is this role important?

3. How does a food chain differ from a food web?

4. Give two reasons for the low rate of energy transfer within ecosystems.

5. Explain why the same area of land can support more herbivores than carnivores.

6. CRITICAL THINKING   Suppose you remove the rabbits, grasshoppers, birds, and mice (the herbivores) from a food web that also includes grass, mushrooms, lizards, and hawks. Which organisms would be affected and how?

22-2

OBJECTIVES

▲

Define *biogeochemical cycle.*

●

Trace the steps of the water cycle.

■

Summarize the major steps
in the nitrogen cycle.

◆

Describe the steps
of the carbon cycle.

ECOSYSTEM RECYCLING

*W*hile energy flows through an ecosystem, water and
minerals, such as carbon, nitrogen, calcium, and phosphorus,
are recycled and reused. Each substance travels through a
biogeochemical *(BIE-oh-GEE-oh-KEM-i-kuhl)* **cycle,** moving
from the abiotic portion of the environment, such as the
atmosphere, into living things, and back again.

THE WATER CYCLE

Water is crucial to life. Cells contain 70 percent to 90 percent water,
and water provides the aqueous environment in which most of life's
chemical reactions occur. The availability of water is one of the key
factors that regulate the productivity of terrestrial ecosystems.
However, very little of the available water on Earth is trapped within
living things at any given time. Bodies of water such as lakes, rivers,
streams, and the oceans contain a substantial percentage of the
Earth's water. The atmosphere also contains water—in the form of
water vapor. In addition, some water is found below ground. Water
in the soil or in underground formations of porous rock is known as

FIGURE 22-5

In the water cycle, water falls to Earth's
surface as precipitation. Some water
reenters the atmosphere by evaporation
and transpiration. Some water runs into
streams, lakes, rivers, and oceans. Other
water seeps through the soil and into
the ground water. Follow the pathways
of the water cycle in the figure.

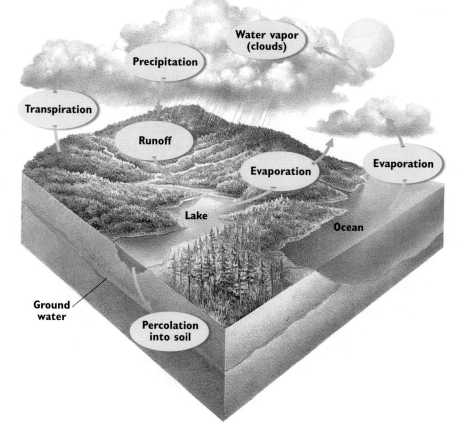

ground water. The movement of water between these various reservoirs, known as the **water cycle,** is illustrated in Figure 22-5.

Three important processes in the water cycle are evaporation, transpiration, and precipitation. Evaporation adds water as vapor to the atmosphere. Heat causes water to evaporate from the oceans and other bodies of water, from the soil, and from the bodies of living things. At least 90 percent of the water that evaporates from terrestrial ecosystems passes through plants in a process called **transpiration.** In transpiration, plants take in water through their roots, and they release water and take in carbon dioxide through the stomata in their leaves. Animals also participate in the water cycle, but their impact is less significant than that of plants. Animals drink water or obtain it from their food. They release this water when they breathe, sweat, or excrete.

Water leaves the atmosphere through precipitation. The amount of water the atmosphere can hold depends on abiotic factors, such as temperature and air pressure. Once the atmosphere becomes saturated with water vapor, precipitation occurs in the form of rain, snow, sleet, hail, or fog.

THE CARBON CYCLE

Together, photosynthesis and cellular respiration form the basis of the **carbon cycle,** which is illustrated in Figure 22-6. During photosynthesis, plants and other autotrophs use carbon dioxide (CO_2), along with water and solar energy, to make carbohydrates. Both autotrophs and heterotrophs use oxygen to break down carbohydrates during

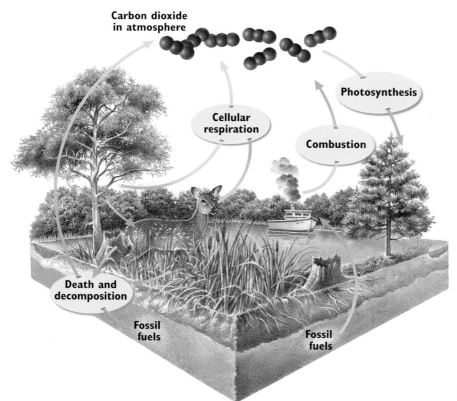

Carbon dioxide in atmosphere

Cellular respiration

Photosynthesis

Combustion

Death and decomposition

Fossil fuels

Fossil fuels

Quick Lab

Modeling Ground Water

Materials disposable gloves, lab apron, 3 L plastic bottle (cut in half), small stones (250 mL), dry sod with grass, water, graduated cylinder, 500 mL beaker

Procedure

1. Put on your lab apron and disposable gloves.

2. Invert the top half of the plastic bottle and place it inside the bottom half of the bottle to form a column.

3. Place the stones in the bottom of the inverted top half of the bottle. Place a chunk of dry sod with grass on top of the stones.

4. Pour 250 mL of water over the sod, and observe how the water penetrates the soil and moves through the column.

5. When the water is no longer draining, remove the top half of the column and pour the water from the bottom of the column into a beaker. Measure the volume of liquid in the beaker.

Analysis What is the volume of the water that drained through the sod? How much of the water remained in the soil? Where does the water go when applied to a real lawn or crop? What might the fate of fertilizer or pesticides be that are applied to a lawn or crop?

FIGURE 22-6

Carbon exists in the atmosphere in the form of carbon dioxide. Cellular respiration, combustion, and decomposition of organic matter are the three major sources of carbon dioxide. By burning large amounts of fossil fuels, humans are increasing the amount of carbon dioxide in the atmosphere.

cellular respiration. The byproducts of cellular respiration are carbon dioxide and water. Decomposers release carbon dioxide into the atmosphere when they break down organic compounds.

Human Influence on the Carbon Cycle

In the last 150 years, the concentration of carbon dioxide in the atmosphere has risen nearly 30 percent. Almost half of this increase has occurred in the last 40 years. Human activities are responsible for the increase. Our industrial society depends on the energy released by the burning of fossil fuels—coal, oil, and natural gas. Fossil fuels are the remains of organisms that have been transformed by decay, heat, and pressure into energy-rich organic molecules. Burning releases the energy in these molecules, but it also releases carbon dioxide. Carbon dioxide is also added to the atmosphere by the burning of vegetation. Today large areas of tropical rain forest are being burned to create farmland and pasture for cattle. The burning of vegetation adds carbon dioxide to the atmosphere, and the destruction of vegetation removes plants that could have absorbed carbon dioxide from the atmosphere through photosynthesis.

FIGURE 22-7

This figure shows the cycling of nitrogen within an ecosystem. Bacteria are responsible for many of the steps in the nitrogen cycle, including the conversion of atmospheric nitrogen into ammonia. Nitrogen-fixing bacteria live in the soil or in the roots of plants. Plants take up the ammonia produced by the bacteria. Animals get nitrogen by eating plants or other animals.

THE NITROGEN CYCLE

All organisms need nitrogen to make proteins and nucleic acids. The complex pathway that nitrogen follows within an ecosystem is called the **nitrogen cycle.** Consider how nitrogen cycles within the terrestrial ecosystem shown in Figure 22-7. Nitrogen gas, N_2, makes up about 78 percent of the atmosphere, so it might seem that nitrogen would be readily available for living things. However, shortages

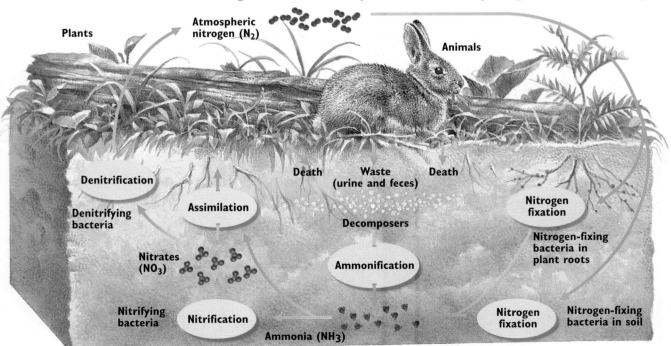

of nitrogen often limit the productivity of plants—and therefore the productivity of ecosystems. Most plants can use nitrogen only in the form of nitrate. The process of converting nitrogen gas to nitrate is called **nitrogen fixation.** Organisms rely on the actions of bacteria that are able to transform nitrogen gas into a usable form. Separate groups of **nitrogen-fixing bacteria** convert nitrogen gas into ammonia, then nitrite, and then nitrate, which plants can use.

Nitrogen-fixing bacteria live in the soil and in the roots of some kinds of plants, such as beans, peas, clover, and alfalfa. These plants have evolved a complex mutualistic relationship with nitrogen-fixing bacteria. The plant provides the bacteria with a home—airtight swellings on its roots—and supplies them with carbohydrates. In exchange, the bacteria produce usable nitrogen for the plant. Excess nitrogen produced by the bacteria is released into the soil.

Recycling Nitrogen

The bodies of dead organisms contain nitrogen, mainly in proteins and nucleic acids. Urine and dung also contain nitrogen. Decomposers break down the corpses and wastes of organisms and release the nitrogen they contain as ammonia. This process is known as **ammonification** (ah-MAHN-i-fi-KAY-shuhn). Through ammonification, nitrogen that would otherwise be lost is reintroduced into the ecosystem.

Bacteria in the soil take up ammonia and oxidize it into nitrites, NO_2^-, and nitrates, NO_3^-. This process, called **nitrification** (NIE-tri-fi-KAY-shuhn), is carried out by bacteria. The erosion of nitrate-rich rocks also releases nitrates into an ecosystem. Plants use nitrates to form amino acids. Nitrogen is returned to the atmosphere through **denitrification.** Denitrification occurs when anaerobic bacteria break down nitrates and release nitrogen gas back into the atmosphere.

Plants can absorb nitrates from the soil, but animals cannot. Animals obtain nitrogen in the same way they obtain energy—by eating plants and other organisms and then digesting the proteins and nucleic acids.

SECTION 22-2 REVIEW

1. Describe the biogeochemical cycle.

2. Where do nitrogen-fixing bacteria live? What crucial function do they perform?

3. Describe the role of decomposers in the nitrogen cycle.

4. How has the burning of fossil fuels affected the carbon cycle?

5. Through what process does most water vapor enter the atmosphere? Explain the process.

6. **CRITICAL THINKING** Explain two ways that the burning of vegetation affects carbon dioxide levels in the atmosphere. How do you think the removal of vegetation affects oxygen levels in the atmosphere?

OBJECTIVES

▲

Describe the differences between tundra and taiga biomes.

●

Contrast temperate grassland with savanna.

■

Describe three water-conservation adaptations of desert organisms.

◆

Compare tropical rain forests with temperate deciduous forests.

TERRESTRIAL ECOSYSTEMS

Biomes (BIE-ohmz) are very large terrestrial ecosystems that contain a number of smaller but related ecosystems within them. A certain biome may exist in more than one location on Earth, but similar biomes have similar climates and tend to have inhabitants with similar adaptations.

THE SEVEN MAJOR BIOMES

Biomes are distinguished by the presence of characteristic plants and animals, but they are commonly identified by their dominant plant life. For example, hardwood trees, such as beeches and maples, are the dominant form of plant life in the deciduous forest biome. Most ecologists recognize seven major biomes, shown on the map in Figure 22-8, and several minor biomes. In this section, you will learn about the characteristics of the seven major biomes: tundra, taiga, temperate deciduous forest, temperate grassland, desert, savanna, and tropical rain forest.

Because abiotic factors change gradually over a landscape, biomes seldom have distinct boundaries. As climate varies over the Earth's surface, for example, deserts tend to gradually change into grasslands, tundra into taiga, and so on. Figure 22-8 shows how the

FIGURE 22-8

The seven biomes cover most of the Earth's land surface. Antarctica is not shown because it has no biomes.

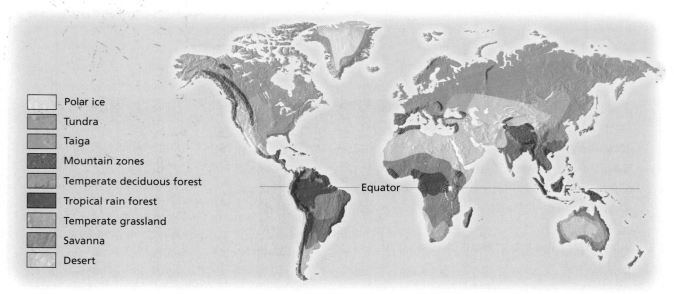

- Polar ice
- Tundra
- Taiga
- Mountain zones
- Temperate deciduous forest
- Tropical rain forest
- Temperate grassland
- Savanna
- Desert

Equator

TABLE 22-1 Characteristics of the Major Biomes

Biome	Average yearly temperature range	Average yearly precipitation	Soil	Vegetation
Tundra	−26°C to 12°C	<25 cm	moist, thin topsoil over permafrost; nutrient-poor; slightly acidic	mosses, lichens, dwarf woody plants
Taiga	−10°C to 14°C	35–75 cm	low in nutrients; highly acidic	needle-leaved evergreen trees
Temperate deciduous forest	6°C to 28°C	75–125 cm	moist; moderate nutrient levels	broad-leaved trees and shrubs
Temperate grassland	0°C to 25°C	25–75 cm	deep layer of topsoil; very rich in nutrients	dense, tall grasses in moist areas; short clumped grasses in drier areas
Desert	7°C to 38°C	<25 cm	dry, often sandy; nutrient-poor	succulent plants and scattered grasses
Savanna	16°C to 34°C	75–150 cm	dry, thin topsoil; porous, low in nutrients	tall grasses, scattered trees
Tropical rain forest	20°C to 34°C	200–400 cm	moist, thin topsoil; low in nutrients	broad-leaved ever-green trees and shrubs

seven major biomes are distributed over the Earth. The figure also shows the areas that cannot be classified into one of the seven major biomes. Because climate varies with elevation, mountains contain a variety of communities and do not belong to any one biome. Table 22-1 describes the major biomes and lists their average annual temperature and rainfall.

TUNDRA

The **tundra** (TUHN-druh) is a cold and largely treeless biome that forms a continuous belt across northern North America, Europe, and Asia. It is the largest and northernmost biome, covering about one-fifth of the world's land surface. **Permafrost,** a permanently frozen layer of soil under the surface, characterizes the tundra. Even the surface soil above the permafrost remains frozen for all but about eight weeks of the year. Figure 22-9 shows some of the plants of the tundra.

Trees do not usually grow in the tundra because the winters are long and bitterly cold and because permafrost prevents their roots from penetrating far into the soil. The

FIGURE 22-9

This photograph shows that the tundra is usually bleak and uniform in appearance, although there may be bright patches of color in the summer season.

tundra receives little precipitation and has a very short growing season of about two months. Cold temperatures retard decay, so the soil is often low in nutrients. For these reasons, tundra plants are usually small and grow slowly. Grasses, sedges, and mosses are common.

Animals that inhabit the tundra include caribou, musk oxen, snowy owls, arctic foxes, lemmings, and snowshoe hares. In the brief summer, the frozen soil thaws, creating a patchwork of ponds and bogs. Swarms of mosquitoes and black flies appear, and ducks, geese, and predatory birds arrive in great numbers to feed.

FIGURE 22-10

Organisms of the taiga are adapted for dry, cold conditions and a reduced availability of food in the winter season. The conifers have needles, which are leaf adaptations to conserve water.

TAIGA

South of the tundra is the **taiga** (TIE-guh), a forested biome dominated by cone-bearing evergreen trees, such as pines, firs, hemlock, and spruce. Taiga stretches across large areas of northern Europe, Asia, and North America. During the long winter, snow covers and insulates the ground, protecting tree roots against freezing.

Plants living in the taiga are adapted for long and cold winters, short summers, and nutrient-poor soil. On the cone-bearing evergreen trees, called conifers, the waxy needles remain all winter long. The shape of the needle is a leaf adaptation that reduces water loss. The stomata of conifers are partially enclosed in the needle, which helps the tree conserve water. Typical mammals of this biome include moose, bears, wolves, and lynx. Some animals stay in the forest year-round, while others migrate to warmer climates in the fall and return in the spring. Many species hibernate six to eight months of the year. Figure 22-10 shows a representative area of taiga.

Word Roots and Origins

taiga

from the Russian word *taiga,* meaning "a transitional plant community"

TOPIC: Temperate forests
GO TO: www.scilinks.org
KEYWORD: HM426

TEMPERATE DECIDUOUS FORESTS

Temperate deciduous forests are characterized by trees that lose all of their leaves in the fall. Deciduous forests stretch across eastern North America, much of Europe, and parts of Asia and the Southern Hemisphere. These regions have pronounced seasons, with precipitation evenly distributed throughout the year. Compared with taiga, temperate deciduous forests have warmer winters and longer summers, and they receive more precipitation. Deciduous trees have broad, thin leaves with a large surface area that permits maximum

FIGURE 22-11

A temperate deciduous forest is characterized by trees that lose their leaves in the winter. This adaptation to conserve water also creates an energy loss for the tree. The tree will never recover the energy that went into its leaf formation, but the decaying leaves on the forest floor will add nutrients to the soil. Temperate deciduous forests are inhabited by a variety of animals, such as cardinals and white-tailed deer.

light absorption. Familiar deciduous trees include the birch, beech, maple, oak, hickory, sycamore, elm, willow, and cottonwood. White-tailed deer, foxes, raccoons, and squirrels are typical mammals of the temperate deciduous forests. Large areas of temperate deciduous forest in the United States, Europe, and Asia have been cut for timber or cleared to make way for farms, towns, and cities. Figure 22-11 shows a stand of trees in a temperate deciduous forest.

TEMPERATE GRASSLANDS

Temperate grasslands are, as the name suggests, dominated by grasses. Temperate grasslands usually form in the interior of continents, at about the same latitude as temperate deciduous forests. However, rainfall patterns make these areas too dry to support trees. This biome once covered large areas of North America, Asia, Europe, Australia, and South America. Grasslands are known by different names in different parts of the world: *prairie* in North America, *steppes* in Asia, *pampas* in South America, and *veldt* in southern Africa.

Temperate grasslands have rich, fertile soil. In areas that have remained relatively undisturbed by humans, grasslands support large herds of grazing mammals, such as the bison shown in Figure 22-12. Grass can survive continuous grazing by animals and occasional fires that sweep across the area because the actively growing part of the plant is at or below the ground, rather than at the tip of the stem. Because grasslands have such rich soil, much of the world's temperate grassland has been transformed into farmland for growing crops such as wheat and corn. Only fragments of undisturbed prairie remain in the United States.

FIGURE 22-12

Temperate grasslands once covered a large portion of the United States and supported huge herds of herbivores, such as the bison shown below. Today, several conservation organizations are actively attempting to preserve this valuable, endangered biome.

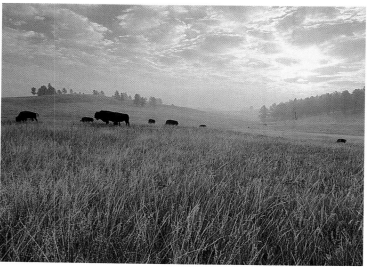

DESERTS

Deserts are areas that receive an average of less than 25 cm (9.9 in.) of rainfall per year. Large parts of North Africa, central Australia, southwestern North America, and eastern Asia are desert. Contrary to popular belief, deserts are not hot all the time. So-called cold deserts, such as the Great Basin in the western United States and the Gobi in eastern Asia, are hot in summer but cold in winter. Even in hot deserts, temperatures may fall by as much as 30°C (54°F) at night because the dry air is a poor insulator, allowing the heat that builds up during the day to escape.

Desert vegetation is often sparse and consists mainly of plants that have adapted to the dry climate. The leaves of the creosote bush of the United States and Mexico, for example, have a waxy coating that reduces evaporation. To limit water loss through transpiration, some desert plants open their stomata only at night. The saguaro cactus, which is found in southern Arizona and southeastern California, as well as in northern Mexico, has an expandable body, an adaptation that allows it to store water. A single saguaro can hold about 1,000 kg (2,200 lb) of water. The saguaro, as seen in Figure 22-13, has evolved sharp protective spines, a leaf adaptation that protects the plant from thirsty herbivores.

Desert animals must conserve water just as the plants do. Many animals avoid the heat of the day by hiding in small spots of shade or by burrowing into the ground. Others, such as kit foxes and some kinds of lizards and snakes, are active only at night, when loss of water to evaporation is low.

FIGURE 22-13

A desert biome may appear lifeless at first glance. But on closer inspection, the desert reveals many living things. All of the organisms of the desert biome are adapted to dry, often hot conditions and are adapted for conserving energy. The saguaro cactus shown stores water from the infrequent rains of the desert.

FIGURE 22-14

The savanna biome is an area rich in wildlife, where great herds of large herbivores exist. Because of the large number of herbivores, this area also supports many large carnivores. The climate of a savanna experiences only two seasons—wet and dry.

SAVANNAS

Savannas (suh-VAN-uhz) are tropical or subtropical grasslands with scattered trees and shrubs. The savannas of Africa are the best known, but this biome also occurs in South America and Australia. Savannas receive more rainfall than deserts, but less than tropical rain forests. Alternating wet and dry seasons characterize savannas. Like temperate grasslands, savannas support large numbers of herbivores, such as zebras, wildebeest, giraffes, and gazelles, as shown in Figure 22-14. Large carnivores, such as lions, leopards, and cheetahs, feed on these herbivores.

Because most of the rain falls during the wet season, the plants and animals of the savanna must be able to deal with prolonged periods of drought. Some trees of the savanna shed their leaves during the dry season to conserve water, and the above-ground parts of grasses often die during the dry season and regenerate after a period of rain.

TROPICAL RAIN FORESTS

Tropical rain forests are characterized by tall trees like those shown in Figure 22-15. Tropical rain forests are found near the equator in Asia, Africa, South America, and Central America. The stable, year-round growing season and abundant rainfall combine to make the tropical rain forest the most productive biome.

Competition for light is intense in the tropical rain forest. Most of the plants are trees, and some have evolved to grow as tall as 50 to 60 m (164 to 197 ft). The treetops form a continuous layer, called the **canopy,** that shades the forest floor. Though you may think of the tropical rain forest as an impenetrable jungle, much of the forest floor is relatively free of vegetation because so little sunlight reaches the ground. The very dense growth known as jungle is found along riverbanks and in disrupted areas where sunlight can reach the forest floor. Small plants called **epiphytes,** as shown in Figure 22-15a, which would not get enough light on the forest floor, often live on the branches of tall trees. These plants, which include mosses and orchids, use other organisms as support, but they are not parasitic because they make their own food.

Tropical rain forests have the highest species richness of all the biomes. One hectare of tropical rain forest (about the size of two football fields) may contain as many as 300 species of trees. An area of temperate deciduous forest of the same size, by contrast, would probably contain fewer than 10 species of trees. Animal life is also very diverse in the tropical rain forest. The sloth, pictured in Figure 22-15b, is a rain forest mammal. Colorful birds, such as parrots and toucans, many kinds of monkeys, and a variety of snakes and lizards are among the vertebrate inhabitants of this biome. The variety of insects is particularly diverse in tropical rain forests. There may be more than 8 million species of tree-dwelling beetles in the tropical rain forest biome alone. Overall, tropical rain forests probably contain about one-fifth of the world's known species.

FIGURE 22-15

Animal life is as diverse as plant life in the rain forest, as reflected by the epiphyte, shown in (a), and the three-toed sloth, a tree dweller of the rain forest, shown in (b).

(a)

(b)

SECTION 22-3 REVIEW

1. Why would it be unusual to find a tree in the tundra?

2. What two similarities are shared by temperate grassland and savanna?

3. Describe two adaptations of the saguaro cactus for water conservation.

4. List at least one animal that lives in each of these biomes: desert, temperate grassland, and tundra.

5. Why do many animals in the tropical rain forest live in trees?

6. **CRITICAL THINKING** Explain the benefits deciduous trees gain from shedding their leaves in the fall. Describe some possible disadvantages of shedding leaves.

The Forest and the Sea

The following account is from *The Forest and the Sea*, by Marston Bates.

When a botanist visited the South American forest station where Marston Bates was working, Bates and the visitor climbed up onto a platform high in the forest canopy. Mosquitoes began buzzing about them.

In the course of our mosquito studies we had found that each different species had its characteristic flight habits. Some kinds were found only near the ground, others only high in the trees; some that were most common high in the trees in the morning or afternoon would come down near the ground during the midday hours, showing a sort of daily vertical migration.

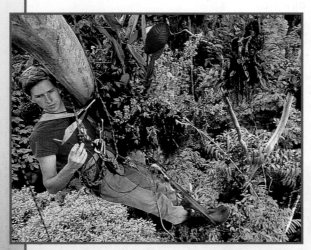

While I was explaining this to my friend, it struck me, that this is just the way animals act in the sea. Most life is near the top, because that is where the sunlight strikes and everything below depends on this surface. Life in both the forest and the sea is distributed in horizontal layers.

The analogy, once thought of, was easily developed. The vocabulary for life in the sea could be transferred to the forest. In the treetops we were in what marine students call the pelagic zone—the zone of active photosynthesis, where sunlight provides the energy to keep the whole complicated biological community going. Below, we had been in the benthos, the bottom zone, where organisms live entirely on second-hand materials that drift down from above—on fallen leaves, on fallen fruits, on roots and logs. Only a few special kinds of green plants were able to grow in the rather dim light that reached the forest floor.

My mosquitoes acted in some ways like the microscopic floating life of the sea, the plankton. Each species among the plankton organisms has a characteristic vertical distribution: some living only near the surface, others only at considerable depths, and so forth. The plankton organisms in general show a daily vertical migration, coming to the surface at night and sinking during the day: a migration to which my mosquitoes were only a feeble counter part. But insects on land are only partially analogous with the plankton of the sea. A major portion of the plankton consists of microscopic plants, busy using the energy of the sun and the dissolved carbon dioxide of the water to build up starch and thus provide the basis for all the rest of the life of the sea. These microscopic plants would correspond not to the insects of the forest, but to the leaves of the trees.

The forest insects would correspond only to the animal component of the plankton: to the copepods and tiny shrimp and larval fish which live directly on the plants or on each other at the very beginning of the endless chain of who eats whom in the biological community.

Reading for Meaning

Bates compared living forms of the forest with those of the sea. Why does he say that mosquitoes and plankton are "only partly analogous"?

Read Further

In *The Forest and the Sea*, Bates presents observations based on his field studies in two very different biomes. What advantages might be found in comparing seemingly dissimilar organisms?

AQUATIC ECOSYSTEMS

As terrestrial organisms, we tend to focus on the other land-dwelling organisms we see around us. But life may have arisen in the sea and only recently (in geological terms) colonized the land. Water covers about three-fourths of Earth and is home to a variety of organisms. In this section we will look at some of the inhabitants of aquatic ecosystems.

OCEAN ZONES

The ocean covers about 70 percent of Earth's surface and has an average depth of 3.7 km (2.3 mi). The deepest parts of the ocean are about 11 km (6.8 mi) deep. The water contains about 3 percent salt, mostly sodium chloride, a factor that profoundly affects the biology of the organisms that live there. Another important variable affecting marine organisms is the availability of light. Because water absorbs light, sunlight penetrates only the upper few hundred meters of the ocean. The **photic** (FOH-tik) **zone** is the part of the ocean that receives sunlight. The rest of the ocean falls within the **aphotic** (AY-FOH-tik) **zone,** the cold and dark depths where sunlight cannot penetrate. Photosynthesis cannot occur in the aphotic zone because of the lack of sunlight.

Ecologists recognize three zones extending out from land, as illustrated in Figure 22-16. Along ocean shores, the tides produce a rhythmic rise and fall of the water level in an area called the **intertidal zone.** Farther out is the **neritic** (nee-RI-tik) **zone,** which extends

SECTION
22-4

OBJECTIVES

▲

Contrast the aphotic and photic zones in the ocean.

●

Describe the differences between the neritic zone and the oceanic zone.

■

Explain how organisms near deep-sea vents obtain energy.

◆

Contrast eutrophic lakes with oligotrophic lakes.

FIGURE 22-16

This diagram shows the various zones of the ocean. The neritic zone generally extends from the intertidal zone to the point where water depth is about 180 m (590 ft). The photic zone varies in depth, depending on how far light penetrates into the water.

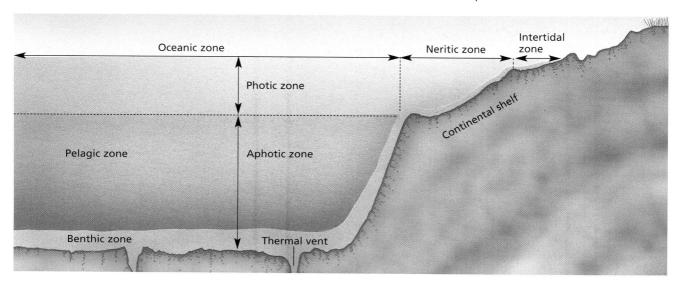

Oceanic zone · Neritic zone · Intertidal zone · Photic zone · Continental shelf · Pelagic zone · Aphotic zone · Benthic zone · Thermal vent

FIGURE 22-17

The intertidal zone shown here is similar to intertidal zones all over the planet. Some are artificially created by the construction of rocky protective bulkheads along former stretches of beach. An open beach is part of the intertidal zone, but it is usually distinguished from the rocky intertidal zones and not as rich in species as rocky intertidal zones.

internet connect

SCILINKS
NSTA

TOPIC: Aquatic ecosystems
GO TO: www.scilinks.org
KEYWORD: HM432

over the continental shelf. The water in the neritic zone is relatively shallow (no more than a few hundred feet deep). Beyond the continental shelf is the **oceanic zone,** which is the deep water of the open sea. The neritic and oceanic zones are further divided. The open ocean is known as the **pelagic** (pi-LA-jik) **zone,** while the ocean bottom is known as the **benthic zone.**

The Intertidal Zone

Organisms in this zone are adapted to periodic exposure to air during low tide. Crabs avoid dehydration by burrowing into the sand or mud. Clams, mussels, and oysters retreat into their shells at low tide. Organisms living in the intertidal zone must be able to withstand the force of crashing waves. Sea anemones cling to rocks with a muscular disk, and sea stars use tube feet to adhere to surfaces. Figure 22-17 shows some of the organisms living in the intertidal zone of the California coast.

The Neritic Zone

The neritic zone is the most productive zone in the ocean, supporting more species and numbers of organisms than any other zone. The water throughout most of the neritic zone is shallow enough for photosynthesis to occur. Strong currents called upwellings carry nutrients from the ocean bottom and mix them with nutrients contained in runoff from land. These waters are rich in **plankton,** communities of small organisms that drift with the ocean currents. Plankton is consumed by many larger organisms. Numerous fishes, squid, sea turtles, and other animals also live in these waters.

Coral reefs form in the neritic zone of tropical areas. Like tropical rain forests, coral reefs are very productive and rich in species. A coral reef is built over a long time by coral animals. They construct external skeletons of a hard chemical compound called calcium carbonate. As the animals grow and die, the skeletons accumulate over time to form a reef, as shown in Figure 22-18, that is home to many species of fishes, crustaceans, mollusks, and other animals. Some species of coral have a mutualistic relationship with photosynthetic protists, from which they receive food.

FIGURE 22-18

Coral reefs, such as the one pictured here, are among the most diverse ecosystems on Earth. Coral reefs are built from the skeletal remains of tiny marine animals and are continually growing just below the surface of warm sunlit seas.

The Oceanic Zone

The oceanic zone contains fewer species than the neritic zone. Even in photic areas, nutrient levels are too low to support as much life. Although the productivity per square meter of open ocean is very low because the ocean covers such a vast area, the total productivity of the oceanic zone is high. About half of the photosynthesis that occurs on Earth takes place in the oceanic zone. The producers of the upper parts of the oceanic zone are protists and bacteria in the plankton. Animals living in the oceanic zone include fishes, mammals such as whales, and many invertebrates.

In the aphotic zone, animals feed primarily on sinking plankton and dead organisms. Organisms living deep in the ocean must cope with near-freezing temperature and crushing pressure. Deep-sea organisms, like the squid shown in Figure 22-19, have slow metabolic rates and reduced skeletal systems. Fishes in these depths have large jaws and teeth and expandable stomachs that can accommodate the rare prey that they can catch.

In the 1970s, scientists found diverse communities living near volcanic vents 2,500 m (8,200 ft) below the surface. These vents release water that is rich in minerals and often exceeds 750°C. Chemosynthetic bacteria that use energy contained in hydrogen sulfide (H_2S) are the producers for this ecosystem. An assortment of unique clams, crabs, and worms feed on these bacteria. Clam-worms living near thermal vents have lost their digestive system over evolutionary time and receive all of their food directly from chemosynthetic bacteria living in their bodies.

Estuaries

An **estuary** (ES-tyoo-eree) occurs where freshwater rivers and streams flow into the sea. Examples of estuary communities include bays, mud flats, and salt marshes. The shallow water ensures plenty of light, and rivers deposit large amounts of mineral nutrients. However, the interaction between fresh water and salt water causes great variation in temperature and salinity. In addition, like the intertidal zone, much of the ground surface of an estuary is exposed during low tide. Inhabitants of estuaries are adapted for frequent change. For example, some kinds of mangrove trees have special glands on their leaves that eliminate excess salt water taken up by the roots. Soft-shell clams lie buried in mud with only their long siphons protruding above the surface. The siphon filters plankton from the salt water at high tide and detects predators at low tide, contracting whenever it senses danger. Figure 22-20 is an example of an estuary.

FIGURE 22-19

Organisms in the deep sea have many adaptations to their environment. The squid *Vampyroteuthis* sp., in the photograph is adapted to eating a large quantity of food at once because prey is hard to find.

FIGURE 22-20

Estuaries are almost as species rich as tropical rain forests. The plant life is often uniform, but the bird and aquatic diversity is enormous. Estuaries are the ocean's nurseries. Many marine organisms hatch and spend their juvenile life stages in the estuary. The dense vegetation protects them from pounding wave action and gives them cover from predators. Estuaries are vital to marine animals that are used as food by people all over the world. Examples of food animals that begin life in estuaries are shrimp, mullet, redfish, and anchovies.

FRESHWATER ZONES

Low levels of dissolved salts characterize freshwater ecosystems. The salt content of fresh water is about 0.005 percent. Examples of freshwater ecosystems include lakes, ponds, clear mountain streams, and slow sediment-rich rivers.

Lakes and Ponds

Ecologists divide lakes and ponds into two categories. **Eutrophic** (yoo-TRAH-fik) lakes are rich in organic matter and vegetation, making the waters relatively murky. The giant water lily pictured in Figure 22-21 is growing in a shallow eutrophic pond. **Oligotrophic** (AH-li-goh-TRAH-fik) **lakes** contain little organic matter. The water is much clearer, and the bottom is usually sandy or rocky. Fishes inhabit both eutrophic and oligotrophic lakes. Freshwater lakes and ponds also support mammals, such as the otter and muskrat, and birds, such as ducks and loons.

FIGURE 22-21

The Amazon water lily, *Victoria amazonica*, is adapted to life in shallow eutrophic ponds. As organic matter accumulates, the lake or pond will eventually fill in and disappear.

Rivers and Streams

A river is a body of water that flows down a gradient, or slope, toward its mouth. Water flows swiftly down steep gradients, and organisms are adapted to withstand powerful currents. For example, the larvae of caddis flies and the nymphs of mayflies cling to the rocky bottom, while brook trout and other fishes have evolved the strength to face upstream while feeding on drifting invertebrates. Slow-moving rivers and their backwaters are richer in nutrients and therefore support a greater diversity of life. Rooted plants and the fishes that feed on them are adapted to the weaker currents of slow-moving rivers.

SECTION 22-4 REVIEW

1. Distinguish between the photic and aphotic zones.

2. What are two sources of nutrients in the neritic zone?

3. What role do chemosynthetic bacteria play in deep-sea-vent ecosystems?

4. What is the main difference between oligotrophic and eutrophic lakes?

5. What might happen to organisms living in a fast-moving river if a dam is built on the river?

6. **CRITICAL THINKING** Estuaries serve as breeding sites and nurseries for thousands of species of marine animals. What characteristics of estuaries make them advantageous places for marine organisms to reproduce? What are some possible disadvantages?

SUMMARY/VOCABULARY

22-1
- Autotrophic organisms are the primary producers. They manufacture carbohydrates using energy from the sun. Consumers obtain energy by eating other organisms.
- Gross primary productivity is the rate at which autotrophs capture energy. Net primary productivity is the rate at which primary producers make new biomass.

- Decomposers feed on dead bodies and wastes and release the nutrients they contain.
- A single pathway of energy transfer is called a food chain. A network showing all paths of energy transfer is called a food web.
- Food chains are short because a large amount of energy is used at each trophic level. There are fewer individuals and less biomass at higher trophic levels.

Vocabulary

biomass (415)
carnivore (416)
chemosynthesis (415)
consumer (416)
decomposer (416)

detritivore (416)
food chain (417)
food web (418)
gross primary productivity (415)

herbivore (416)
net primary productivity (415)

omnivore (416)
producer (415)
trophic level (417)

22-2
- Materials such as carbon, nitrogen, and water are cycled within ecosystems.
- The three key processes in the water cycle are evaporation, transpiration, and precipitation.
- Few organisms can use nitrogen directly from the environment. Nitrogen-fixing bacteria in the soil and in plant roots transform nitrogen gas into ammonia, which plants can use.
- Photosynthesis and cellular respiration are

the two main processes of the carbon cycle. Cellular respiration adds carbon dioxide to the atmosphere, while photosynthesis removes it.
- By burning large amounts of fossil fuels and vegetation, humans are disrupting the carbon cycle. Many scientists think the rising level of carbon dioxide in the atmosphere will lead to global warming.

Vocabulary

ammonification (423)
biogeochemical cycle (420)
carbon cycle (421)

denitrification (423)
ground water (421)
nitrification (423)

nitrogen cycle (422)
nitrogen fixation (423)
nitrogen-fixing bacteria (423)

transpiration (421)
water cycle (421)

22-3
- On land, there are seven major types of ecosystems, known as biomes.
- Tundra is a cold biome characterized by permafrost under the surface.
- Taiga is warmer than tundra and receives more precipitation. It is dominated by conifer forests.
- The trees in temperate deciduous forests shed all of their leaves in the fall.
- Temperate grasslands occur in areas with cold winters and hot summers. They are

dominated by grasses and herds of grazing animals.
- Deserts receive less than 25 cm (9.9 in.) of precipitation per year. Their inhabitants have adaptations for water conservation.
- Savannas are tropical grasslands with alternating wet and dry seasons. They are dominated by herds of grazing animals.
- Tropical rain forests receive abundant rainfall and have a year-round growing season. They contain more species than any other biome.

Vocabulary

biome (424)
canopy (429)
desert (428)

epiphyte (429)
permafrost (425)
savanna (428)

taiga (426)
temperate deciduous forest (426)

temperate grassland (427)
tropical rain forest (429)
tundra (425)

22-4
- The photic zone in the ocean receives light, while the aphotic zone does not. There are three major zones in the ocean—the intertidal zone, the neritic zone, and the oceanic zone.
- In the intertidal zone, organisms must be able to tolerate drying and pounding by waves.
- The neritic zone receives nutrients from the bottom of the ocean and from land. It is the ocean's richest zone in terms of the number of species and individuals.

- Production in the oceanic zone is limited by a shortage of nutrients.
- Estuaries are very productive areas where rivers and streams flow into the sea.
- Oligotrophic lakes are clear and lacking in nutrients. Eutrophic lakes are rich in nutrients and are often murky.
- Rivers and streams are characterized by a gradient in elevation.

Vocabulary

aphotic zone (431)
benthic zone (432)
estuary (433)

eutrophic (434)
intertidal zone (431)
neritic zone (431)

oceanic zone (432)
oligotrophic lake (434)
pelagic zone (432)

photic zone (431)
plankton (432)

REVIEW

Vocabulary

Explain the difference between the terms in each of the following pairs.

1. producer, decomposer
2. gross primary productivity, net primary productivity
3. tundra, taiga
4. nitrogen fixation, ammonification
5. biomass, biome

Multiple Choice

6. The major producers found in aquatic ecosystems are (a) photosynthetic protists (b) chemosynthetic bacteria (c) aquatic plants (d) heterotrophic protists.
7. Decomposers benefit an ecosystem by (a) manufacturing energy (b) returning nutrients to the soil (c) controlling the population (d) removing toxic substances.
8. Which of the following organisms from the African savanna would you expect to be the least abundant? (a) grass (b) lion (c) zebra (d) grasshopper
9. Which of the following is not true of the nitrogen cycle?
   (a) Plants absorb nitrogen gas directly from the atmosphere.
   (b) Bacteria convert nitrogen gas into ammonia.

   (c) Plants absorb ammonia from the soil.
   (d) Animals obtain nitrogen by eating other organisms.
10. The combustion of fossil fuels has increased atmospheric levels of (a) ammonia (b) nitrogen (c) CFCs (d) carbon dioxide.
11. One reason trees are unusual in the tundra is that (a) large herbivores eat them (b) there is not enough rainfall to support them (c) permafrost prevents root growth (d) grass and shrubs crowd them out.
12. Which of the following is not true of tropical rain forests?
    (a) They are found near the equator.
    (b) They have the highest species richness of any biome.
    (c) They show wide seasonal changes in temperature.
    (d) They are rapidly disappearing.
13. The neritic zone (a) receives nutrients from land (b) receives little sunlight (c) is exposed to the air by low tide (d) supports very few species.
14. Estuaries are among the most productive areas on Earth because (a) they are home to vast coniferous forests (b) they support great herds of herbivores (c) they have shallow, nutrient-laden water (d) they support many large predators.
15. Eutrophic lakes are (a) clear (b) murky (c) swift (d) small.

Short Answer

16. Explain the difference between a herbivore, a carnivore, and an omnivore. Give an example of each type of organism.

17. Examine the diagram of the food web below. How do you think the food web would be affected if the grass and the shrub were both eliminated? Explain your answer.

18. Why is a food web a more complete picture of the feeding relationships in an ecosystem than a food chain is?

19. Explain the difference between the terms *decomposer* and *detritivore*.

20. How does the transfer of energy in an ecosystem differ from the transfer of nutrients?

21. Describe the benefits nitrogen-fixing bacteria gain from the plants they inhabit. What does the plant receive from the bacteria?

22. Transpiration accounts for most of the water loss in plants. Explain why plants cannot shut their stomata for long periods of time.

23. Give two reasons why the destruction of tropical rain forests contributes to an increase in carbon dioxide levels in the atmosphere.

24. Unit 7—*Ecosystem Dynamics*

Write a report summarizing how artifical ecosystems are used to eliminate pollutants from wastewater. Find out what kinds of factories or plants use artificial ecosystems.

CRITICAL THINKING

1. Explain why farmers often grow alfalfa, clover, or beans in a field after they have grown corn.

2. Nitrogen, water, and carbon are recycled and reused within an ecosystem, but energy is not. Explain why energy cannot be recycled.

3. Thinning of the ozone layer may lead to reduced populations of photosynthetic plankton in the ocean. Explain how this would affect the carbon cycle.

4. This rare species of squid has several adaptations for living in very deep water. Explain some of the selective pressures that exist at great depths.

EXTENSION

1. Study an area near your home or school. Make a list of all the consumers, producers, and decomposers you observe. Draw a food web using the organisms you have observed.

2. Read "When Nature Goes Nuts" in *National Wildlife,* October–November 1999, on page 48. Choose three different animals mentioned in the article, and explain how each

animal depends on the oak tree. What does the U.S. Forest Service blame for the decline of the oak?

3. Use library resources or an on-line database to research eutrophication of lakes. What is eutrophication? What causes eutrophication, and how does it affect the lake's inhabitants?

Constructing and Comparing Ecosystems

OBJECTIVES

- Observe the interaction of organisms in a closed ecosystem.
- Compare this ecosystem with others observed in nature.

PROCESS SKILLS

- observing
- recognizing relationships
- hypothesizing

MATERIALS

- large glass jar with lid for each ecosystem
- pond water or dechlorinated tap water
- gravel, rocks, and soil
- graph paper
- 8½ × 11 in. acetate sheets
- several colored pens for overhead transparencies

Ecosystem 1

- pinch of grass seeds
- pinch of clover seeds
- 10 mung-bean seeds
- 3 earthworms
- 4–6 isopods
- 6 mealworms
- 6 crickets

Ecosystem 2

- strands of *Anacharis, Fontinallis,* and foxtail
- duckweed
- *Chlamydomonas* culture
- black ram's horn snail
- 4 guppies or platys

Ecosystem 3

- small, clear glass container for water environment
- pinch of grass seeds
- pinch of clover seeds
- pond snails

- 2 *Anacharis* strands
- 10 *Daphnia*
- 3 *Fontinallis* strands
- *Chlamydomonas*
- 4 guppies or platys

Background

1. How are living things affected by nonliving things in the environment?
2. Relate the theme of interdependence among organisms to ecosystems.
3. How do different types of organisms interact?

Experiment Setup

1. In this investigation, you will observe organisms in one of three different ecosystems. Look at the organisms listed in the materials list and choose the ecosystem you would like to observe. Which organisms might be the most numerous? Which organisms might decrease in number? Hypothesize how the organisms will interact.
2. Form a group with classmates who have all chosen the same ecosystem. As a group, prepare the environment in a jar with a chosen substrate. Go to Part A, Part B, or Part C for set-up instructions for your ecosystem.
3. Put lids on the containers, and let the ecosystem remain undisturbed in indirect sunlight for a week. Go to Part D after one week.

PART A Setting Up Ecosystem 1

1. Place the soil in the bottom of the jar about 4 or 5 in. deep. Clean soil off the inside of the jar.
2. Place rocks in and on top of the soil in a natural-looking arrangement.
3. Moisten the soil carefully. Do not saturate the soil.
4. Plant the seeds according to the package instructions.
5. Clean up your materials and wash your hands before leaving the lab.

PART B   Setting Up Ecosystem 2

6. Place about 2 in. of clean gravel in the bottom of the jar.

7. Gently fill the jar with pond water or dechlorinated tap water until the jar is about three-fourths full.

8. Add the plants and algae to your ecosystem.

9. ⬥ ⬥ Clean up your materials and wash your hands before leaving the lab.

PART C   Setting Up Ecosystem 3

10. Place a small, clear glass container, such as a mayonnaise jar, inside the larger jar and against one side.

11. Carefully place soil in the larger jar, filling around the smaller jar so that you can see through both jars on one side. Do not place any soil on the side where the two jars touch. Clean any soil from the sides of the jar that may obstruct your view.

12. Place some rocks on the soil, and moisten the soil carefully.

13. Place 1 in. of gravel inside the smaller jar and gently fill with pond water or dechlorinated tap water to the level of the soil.

14. Place the algae and the aquatic plants in the water. Plant the grass seeds and clover seeds in the soil in separate areas of the jar.

15. ⬥ ⬥ Clean up your materials and wash your hands before leaving the lab.

PART D   Observing Your Ecosystem

16. Place the chosen animals in the jar and loosely replace the lid.

17. Observe the jar for a few minutes daily.

18. Make a chart in your lab report to record the original number of each species in your ecosystem. Record daily any changes you observe.

19. Make a graph for each species in your chart, and plot the number of organisms as a function of time. Place a clear acetate sheet over each graph. Using a pen used for overhead transparencies, trace each graph onto the acetate sheet. Use a different colored pen and a different acetate sheet for each organism.

20. Compare the acetate sheets of two organisms that you hypothesized would interact—a predator and its prey, for example. Hold one sheet on top of the other and analyze both graphs. Record the results in your lab report.

21. ⬥ ⬥ Clean up your materials and wash your hands before leaving the lab.

Analysis and Conclusions

1. What happened to the organisms in your ecosystem? How did their population sizes change?

2. What are some possible causes of the change in the populations you observed?

3. Construct a food chain for the ecosystem you observed. Which organisms were producers? Which organisms were consumers?

4. What could you learn if you set up more than one jar in an identical manner?

5. How does your ecosystem resemble a natural ecosystem? How does it differ?

6. How did your observation compare with your hypothesis? If the results differed from what you expected, explain what might have caused the difference.

7. Look at your graphs, and determine what kind of relationship exists between predator and prey populations.

8. How would you modify the ecosystem if you were to repeat this investigation?

Further Inquiry

Develop an experiment to study the effects of certain abiotic factors—including temperature, light, and moisture—on the organisms in the ecosystem you constructed.

ENVIRONMENTAL SCIENCE

Gorillas are one species whose survival is threatened by the growing human population.

FOCUS CONCEPT: *Interdependence of Organisms*

As you read, notice how a knowledge of biology helps us understand larger environmental processes.

Unit 7—*Ecosytem Dynamics*
Topics 1–6

HUMANS AND THE ENVIRONMENT

*In Chapter 22, you learned how environmental factors influence organisms within particular ecosystems. Large-scale environmental forces also have significant effects on human populations. A new field of study called **environmental science** uses biological principles to look at the relationships between humans and the Earth. Environmental science is becoming increasingly important because humans are rapidly changing the global environment.*

SECTION

23-1

OBJECTIVES

▲

Give an example of how global systems are linked together.

●

Identify several effects of El Niño on human populations.

■

Describe two ways that humans have modified the composition of the atmosphere, and identify the possible consequences of these changes.

◆

Explain how future human population growth could affect the environment.

A GLOBAL CONNECTION

You might not guess that wind patterns off the coast of Australia would have anything to do with fish harvests in South America or winter weather in the United States, but they do. What connects these events is a complex interaction between air and water currents that is first set in motion by solar energy. When the sun's rays strike air near the surface of the Earth, the molecules are heated and the air, which becomes less dense, starts to rise. As the air rises, it gets closer to outer space and eventually starts to cool. Cooling air becomes more dense and sinks. We can draw this pattern of rising and falling air using a loop called a **convection** (kuhn-VEK-shuhn) **cell.** Groups of convection cells form the system of global air circulation that helps determine climate, as shown in Figure 23-1.

In the southern Pacific Ocean, the usual pattern of convection cells creates a wind that blows from east to west and pushes warm surface water

North Pole

Tundra
60° Taiga
Deciduous forest and grassland

30° Desert

0° Tropical rain forest

30° Desert

Deciduous forest and grassland
60°

South Pole

FIGURE 23-1

Warming and cooling air form loops called convection cells in Earth's atmosphere. These air currents influence where different ecosystems are located and also create oceanic circulation patterns.

FIGURE 23-2

These two drawings show a comparison of water and atmospheric circulation in normal (left) and El Niño (right) years. The red arrows indicate the movement of warm oceanic currents, and the yellow arrows indicate the movement of air. In an El Niño year, the cold upwelling is blocked by warm water moving toward the coast of Peru.

from South America toward Australia, as shown in Figure 23-2. Along the South American coast, cold water rises from deeper in the ocean and replaces the warm water. This rising current is called an **upwelling,** and it brings with it organic material and nutrients that support an abundance of plankton. The plankton, in turn, support large populations of fish.

One kind of fish that is abundant in these conditions is the anchovy, a main export of the South American country of Peru and a popular pizza topping. Anchovies provide a livelihood not only to fishermen but also to packers, shippers, netmakers, boat builders, and other workers. Diving sea birds eat anchovies too. When these birds come back to shore to roost and digest their food, they excrete a white phosphorus-rich substance called guano. Some guano deposits are dug up and sold as high-quality fertilizer, another major Peruvian export.

El Niño

The Peruvian economy, along with sea birds, depends on normal atmospheric conditions. But sometimes, usually in December, the normal east-to-west winds do not form over the Pacific Ocean. Instead, winds push warm water eastward toward the coast of South America, as illustrated in Figure 23-2. When these conditions occur, the warm surface water cuts off the upwelling of nutrients. This event is called **El Niño** (meaning "the child") because it usually happens near Christmas.

With fewer nutrients, the fish populations decline and Peruvian anchovy exports decrease. Fewer anchovies mean fewer birds and reduced guano production. Because all convection cells are linked in the atmosphere, the effects of El Niño extend beyond Peru. Under a strong El Niño, northeastern Australia can suffer summer drought, leading to reduced grain production there. The southeastern United States gets higher rainfall in El Niño years, boosting agriculture while also decreasing forest fires.

internet connect

SC LINKS
NSTA

TOPIC: El Niño
GO TO: www.scilinks.org
KEYWORD: HM442

442   *CHAPTER 23*

HUMAN INFLUENCES ON GLOBAL SYSTEMS

Global systems, such as the interconnected system of convection cells, link people and economies from across the world. Examine the following examples of how humans have unintentionally changed the global systems on which we depend.

Declining Ozone

As you learned in Chapter 14, ozone, O_3, is a naturally occurring gas that is vital to life on Earth. Ozone in the upper atmosphere screens out most of the ultraviolet radiation from the sun that causes mutations. Humans, if exposed to ultraviolet radiation, suffer increased rates of skin cancer and cataracts (clouding of the lens of the eye). People are advised to wear sunscreen and sunglasses to protect against the ultraviolet radiation that is not blocked by ozone.

Several kinds of human-made chemicals are diminishing the ozone shield, allowing more ultraviolet radiation to reach the Earth's surface. The most important of these ozone-destroying chemicals are known as **chlorofluorocarbons,** or CFCs. Originally thought to be harmless, CFCs have been used as coolants in refrigerators and air conditioners and as the propellant in aerosol spray cans. They have also been used to make plastic-foam products and to clean electronic equipment. In the upper atmosphere, CFCs act as catalysts that break down ozone much faster than it is formed by natural processes. Scientists have estimated that a single CFC molecule can help destroy up to 100,000 ozone molecules.

Beginning in the 1980s, atmospheric measurements have indicated some alarming declines in ozone levels. Ozone destruction is most severe over the Earth's polar regions, and for a few weeks every year, an ozone "hole," a zone of very low ozone concentration, forms over Antarctica, as shown in Figure 23-3. In 1991 an international study estimated that even a 10 percent worldwide decrease in ozone levels would cause 300,000 new cases of skin cancer in humans. Other organisms, including plants and photosynthetic algae, are also harmed by high levels of ultraviolet radiation, so ozone depletion could modify entire ecosystems over time.

The evidence of widespread and worsening damage to the ozone layer led to international agreements to stop production of CFCs by the end of 1995. Because the substitutes for CFCs are initially more expensive, the developed countries are contributing to a fund to help the developing countries make the changeover. A global environmental success story, these agreements have already cut CFC production by more than 75 percent. Environmental scientists estimate that if the terms of the agreements continue to be followed, the ozone layer will start to build up again, perhaps recovering completely in 50 to 100 years. The effort to protect the ozone layer is a good example of how scientists and policy makers can work together to solve an environmental problem.

FIGURE 23-3

These computer-generated images are based on satellite measurements of ozone levels over Antarctica.

OCTOBER 1979

OCTOBER 1988

OCTOBER 1996

——INCREASING OZONE LEVEL——>

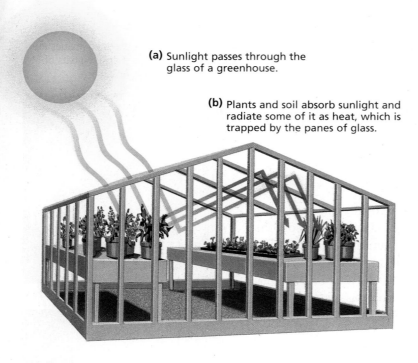

(a) Sunlight passes through the glass of a greenhouse.

(b) Plants and soil absorb sunlight and radiate some of it as heat, which is trapped by the panes of glass.

FIGURE 23-4

Solar energy in the form of light penetrates a greenhouse, but the reradiated heat does not immediately escape. In the atmosphere, gases such as carbon dioxide trap heat and warm the surface.

Quick Lab

Calculating CO_2 Production

Materials pencil, paper

Procedure A young tree can remove 11 kg of CO_2 from the atmosphere in a year. Each liter of gasoline burned by a car produces 3 kg of CO_2. Suppose you are taking a trip by car. Your round-trip mileage is 250 km, and you get 13 km/L of gas. Calculate how many young trees are needed in 1 year to remove the CO_2 that was produced from your single trip.

Analysis In 1 year, how many trees are required to remove the CO_2 produced by 100 cars taking the same trip and getting the same number of kilometers per liter? Discuss with your classmates whether your trip was ecologically efficient. What alternative transportation methods might be more ecologically efficient?

Increasing Carbon Dioxide

Carbon dioxide, CO_2, is a naturally occurring gas that is a raw material of photosynthesis and a byproduct of cellular respiration. It is also released when fossil fuels, such as natural gas, coal, and petroleum, are burned in homes, power plants, and motor vehicles. Around the middle of the nineteenth century, before humans began to substantially increase their use of fossil fuels, carbon dioxide levels in the atmosphere were fairly stable, at about 280 parts per million (ppm). Since 1850, carbon dioxide levels have risen nearly 30 percent, to 360 ppm, and they seem likely to increase as the world's use of fossil fuels grows. According to some projections, by the year 2100 the concentration of CO_2 in the atmosphere might be twice what it was in 1850.

The concentration of carbon dioxide in the atmosphere influences how much heat from the sun is trapped by the atmosphere. The atmosphere's ability to retain heat is called the greenhouse effect. As you can see in Figure 23-4, the glass in a greenhouse allows the sun's rays in but prevents heat from escaping. The same process happens in cars left in the sun with the windows rolled up.

Effects of Rising Carbon Dioxide Levels

If you look at climatic records derived from ice-core samples, shown in Figure 23-5, it is apparent that temperature changes over the last 160,000 years correspond to changes in atmospheric carbon dioxide concentration. Scientists call this type of matching relationship a **correlation.** Because temperature changes correlate with changes in carbon dioxide level, the long-term pattern suggests that a **cause-and-effect relationship** might exist between these two variables. In a cause-and-effect relationship, a change in one variable directly leads to a change in the other variable. Even a strong correlation does not prove the existence of a cause-and-effect relationship, but experiments enable scientists to establish a connection between two variables.

It is not possible to carry out a global experiment that would conclusively demonstrate a cause-and-effect relationship between carbon dioxide levels and rising temperatures. Instead, environmental scientists rely on computer models that simulate the Earth's climate. Because so many factors besides carbon dioxide levels have to be taken into account (wind patterns, ocean temperatures, and effects of ecosystems on CO_2 levels, to name a few), these models are very complicated. It is like predicting the weather hundreds of years in advance.

Change in Temperature

Carbon Dioxide Level

By varying carbon dioxide levels in these climate models, scientists can simulate the possible effects of CO_2 on temperature. The results of these simulations are consistent: doubling carbon dioxide concentration leads to higher average global temperatures—in the range of 1.0°C to 4.5°C (2°F to 8°F). The exact temperature change depends on the particular assumptions built into the model, but nearly all scientists studying this problem have concluded that increased carbon dioxide levels cause temperature increases in the atmosphere.

Measurements of temperatures from around the world support this conclusion. The recent rapid increase in atmospheric carbon dioxide has been accompanied by higher global temperatures, as shown in Figure 23-6. Today the average global temperature is about 0.6°C (1°F) higher than it was in 1860. An international panel of scientists notes that temperatures are expected to rise an additional 2°C (4°F) within the next century. Although this may not seem significant, this increase can have global effects on rainfall patterns, soil moisture, and sea level. These factors might shift agricultural regions of the world and disrupt natural ecosystems. Specific effects on a particular country or state cannot be predicted yet, but most models project that the effects will be felt most strongly in temperate and polar regions.

FIGURE 23-5

These graphs show data representing 150,000 years of Earth's climatic history. Although the correlation is not perfect, in general, high levels of carbon dioxide correlate with temperature increases and low levels correlate with temperature decreases. As of 1995, carbon dioxide levels had risen to 360 ppm, higher than any part of this record.

TOPIC: Global warming
GO TO: www.scilinks.org
KEYWORD: HM445

Change in Global Temperature

FIGURE 23-6

Although temperatures fluctuate from year to year, a general warming trend is evident over the last 140 years. During this same period, carbon dioxide levels have risen 30 percent, mainly due to the increased use of fossil fuels.

We do not fully understand all aspects of the relationship between carbon dioxide and temperature increases, but most environmental scientists see some potential difficulties for humans and other species if current trends continue. Some scientists have called for international agreements to reduce carbon dioxide emissions. Others think we need to get better information before taking any action, noting some evidence that "excess" carbon dioxide might be absorbed by the oceans and soil.

FUTURE POPULATION GROWTH

You learned in Chapter 20 that the Earth's human population is currently 6 billion and growing at the rate of about 90 million people per year. The United Nations estimates that by the year 2050 the world's population could more than double, to 12.5 billion. How would a doubling of the Earth's population affect ozone levels, carbon dioxide concentrations, and other environmental conditions, such as the availability of clean water, open space, and wildlife habitats?

Although ozone levels may increase and stabilize, doubling the number of people will likely mean more fossil-fuel use and more clearing and burning of forests, which in turn will increase carbon dioxide levels and hasten global warming. Fresh water constitutes less than 3 percent of the water on Earth, and two-thirds of the world's population already lacks a reliable source of drinking water. Doubling the population could also require twice as many homes, schools, hospitals, landfills, and roads, all of which decrease the amount of undeveloped land. Humans already are using 40 percent of the net primary productivity of the Earth; if we double our use, many other organisms will be unable to survive.

SECTION 23-1 REVIEW

1. What causes the upwelling off the coast of South America? How does this upwelling affect the economy of Peru?

2. Describe the consequences of El Niño.

3. How have CFCs affected the atmosphere? How might this change affect humans?

4. How have scientists used computer models to help understand the effects of rising carbon dioxide levels?

5. Describe some possible effects of a continued increase in the human population.

6. **CRITICAL THINKING** Some scientists have argued that rising carbon dioxide levels might lead to increased food production. Explain the logic behind this argument.

Environmental Eyes in the Skies

Governments, educational institutions, and even private corporations from around the world have sent satellites into orbit to monitor global environmental changes. The satellites use various devices to collect and measure information about Earth's surface and relay it back to Earth, often in "real time." That is, observers on Earth can view the images at the same time the satellite's instruments are observing them.

One system of polar-orbiting satellites, which circle Earth in a north-to-south orbit each day, sends information to the National Oceanic and Atmospheric Administration. These satellites carry equipment that measures clouds, provides temperature and moisture data from Earth's surface through the atmosphere, measures the energy emitted by the sun, and measures radiation striking and leaving the Earth. The satellites also receive emergency signals from people in distress. ARGOS, a French-provided satellite system, collects information from sensors placed in various locations, such as on ships, buoys, weather balloons, and even birds and other animals. The ARGOS satellites provide both short-term information, such as storm warnings, and ongoing information, such as global changes in pollution levels and vegetation cover.

Hans Tømmervik conducts research projects in Tromsø, Norway, a busy seaport located north of the Arctic Circle. Tømmervik's primary concern has been the effect of air pollution on the natural environment of the Norwegian-Russian border area, located hundreds of kilometers east of Tromsø. In one project, Tømmervik and fellow scientists used information from remote-sensing satellites to map changes in the area's vegetation cover from 1973 to 1988. They compared vegetation-cover maps with sulfur dioxide emission levels for the same years. A time sequence of satellite images showed that the area with lichen-dominated vegetation had decreased by 85 percent over 15 years, while desert-like conditions had increased by more than five times. During the same time, emission levels of sulfur dioxide had increased dramatically. The scientists developed a pollution-impact map on the basis of the vegetation maps. The map clearly shows how the impact of pollution varies with distance from the pollution source.

Satellite monitoring of the environment has made large gains since the end of the Cold War between the United States and the former Soviet Union. Satellites that these nations previously used for spying on each other are now being used to monitor environmental conditions. These satellites have much better resolution than satellites currently used for environmental-science information gathering. Some are capable of viewing objects that are less than 15 cm (6 in.) across. The scientific community stands to benefit not only from better equipment but also from international sharing of expertise in designing sensors and interpreting data.

1973

1988

Between 1973 and 1988, a satellite monitored the effects of pollution on a 10,000 km² area along the border between Russia and Norway. One of the main discoveries was that lichen-covered areas (light green on maps) decreased by 85 percent, while there was a fivefold increase in bare, eroded, and damaged areas (violet on maps).

23-2

OBJECTIVES

▲

Define *biodiversity,* and explain three ways to measure it.

●

Describe global patterns of biodiversity.

■

Identify two strategies for conserving biodiversity in developing countries.

◆

Distinguish between utilitarian and nonutilitarian reasons for conserving biodiversity.

FIGURE 23-7

This chart shows the number of individuals of four moth species captured at four sites.

THE BIODIVERSITY CRISIS

Although some extinctions of species are natural events that have been going on since life began, environmental scientists have noted that humans are now causing species to become extinct much faster than in the past. Because extinction is irreversible and stops the evolution of future species, biologists are urgently trying to learn more about how we can conserve species.

BIODIVERSITY

Biodiversity refers to the variety of organisms in a given area. Biodiversity can be measured in several ways. Looking at Figure 23-7, it seems easy to say that Site A has more biodiversity than Site B and less than Sites C and D. Recall from Chapter 21 that the number of species in an area is called species richness. In this example, species richness for Site A is 3, for Site B is 1, for Site C is 4, and for Site D is 4. For quick comparisons between sites, biologists often find that species richness is a very useful estimate of biodiversity.

Now compare Site C with Site D. Each site has four moth species, but the moth communities are not the same. Site C has three individuals of each species of moth, while Site D has one individual of

SITE A

SITE B

SITE C

SITE D

each of three species and nine individuals of the fourth species. Even though the species richness (4) and the total number of individuals (12) are the same, biologists would expect these two communities to behave differently. Thus, biologists often determine how many individual organisms belong to each species, a measure called **evenness.** In our example, Site C has greater evenness than Site D. For detailed comparisons between communities, biodiversity is sometimes expressed as a quantity called species diversity (a concept introduced in Chapter 21), which combines species richness and evenness.

Because evolution depends on the presence of genetic variation within a population, as you learned in Chapter 15, some biologists would want to know the genetic makeup of each moth. With this information, biologists can calculate the **genetic diversity,** or amount of genetic variation, for each site. In the long run, genetic diversity might be the most important measure of biodiversity, but it is the one we know the least about.

MEASURING EARTH'S BIODIVERSITY

If we use the species-richness measure of biodiversity, how much biodiversity is there on Earth? Estimates vary, but most biologists are confident that there are at least 10 million species on Earth—and possibly as many as 30 million. These are staggering numbers, especially because, in about 200 years of cataloging, scientists have named and described fewer than 3 million species.

When most people think of nature, they tend to focus on mammals. Humans seem to have a basic attraction to large mammals, especially to those that have big heads, big eyes, and a cuddly appearance like pandas. Yet mammals are a very small fraction of biodiversity. Insects and plants are far more representative of life on Earth, as illustrated in Figure 23-8.

FIGURE 23-8

This diagram shows the known species richness of the Earth, with representatives drawn to a size that is proportional to their abundance. Although people tend to think mainly of mammals, there are many more species of insects and plants. Data from tropical forests, which are still largely unexplored, suggest that insects may represent an even greater fraction of the Earth's biodiversity than is shown here.

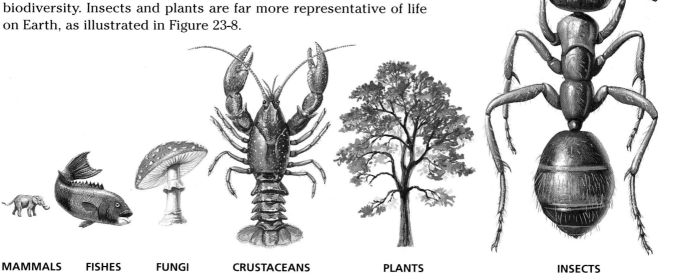

| MAMMALS | FISHES | FUNGI | CRUSTACEANS | PLANTS | INSECTS |

FIGURE 23-9

This graph illustrates the changes in biodiversity, measured as the number of families of marine organisms, over time. At present, biodiversity is at an all-time high. Arrows point to the five known mass extinctions. A sixth extinction is under way due to human activities.

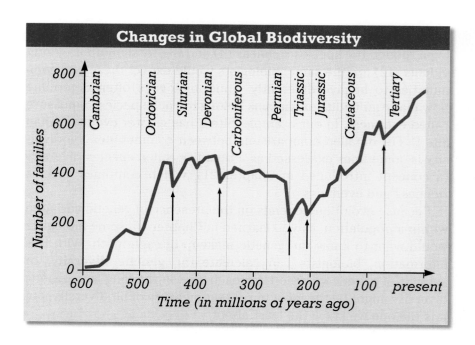

Reducing Biodiversity

You can see in Figure 23-9 that we are living in a time of very high biodiversity. But we are also living in a time of very rapid extinction. Biologists estimate that up to 20 percent of existing species may become extinct by the year 2030. As you learned in Chapter 15, five mass extinctions, large and relatively rapid declines in biodiversity, have occurred in the history of life. The mass extinction currently under way is different because humans are the cause. We do not know what the consequences of eliminating millions of species will be.

The greatest threat to biodiversity is the rapid destruction of natural habitats to provide for the needs and wants of the growing human population. In general, humans convert complex, self-sustaining natural ecosystems into simplified systems, such as farmland and urban areas, that cannot sustain as many species. For example, since the discovery of agriculture 10,000 years ago, more than half the world's tropical rain forests have been destroyed, and half of what remains is likely to be gone by the year 2020. Because tropical rain forests have the highest species richness of any biome, containing up to one-fifth of all species on Earth, their destruction is especially damaging to biodiversity.

Ways to Save Biodiversity

The United States became prosperous partly by converting forests and native prairies into farms. The tropics and other regions of high biodiversity often include some of the economically poorest countries on Earth. These countries are trying to use their natural resources to build their economies and raise the standard of living for their citizens, just as the United States did. Several conservation strategies offer ways for developing countries to benefit economically from preserving their biodiversity. For example, in a **debt-for-nature swap,** richer countries or private conservation organizations pay off some of the debts of a developing country. In exchange, the developing country agrees to take steps to protect its biodiversity, such as setting up a preserve or launching an education program for its citizens. Another idea to help local people make money from an intact ecosystem is to set up a national park to attract tourists. People who want to see the ecosystem and its unique organisms will pay money for nature guides, food, and lodging. This idea is called **ecotourism.**

Word Roots and Origins

utilitarian

from the Latin *utilitas,* meaning "useful"

THE IMPORTANCE OF BIODIVERSITY

One way to weigh the importance of biodiversity is called **utilitarian value;** it involves thinking of the economic benefits biodiversity provides to humans. For example, different plants and animals can be harvested for food, and trees can be cut to build homes and provide fuel. Some species are valuable as sources of medicines. Given that most of the world's species have not been named or described, it is reasonable to expect that some undiscovered species will also have medical benefits. Ecosystem functions crucial to our survival, such as the water cycle and nitrogen cycle, depend on living organisms. Harvard University biologist E. O. Wilson summed up the importance of biodiversity when he said, "Biological diversity is the key to the maintenance of the world as we know it."

Another way to weigh the importance of biodiversity is called **nonutilitarian value.** Basically, some people believe that life-forms have value simply because they exist, apart from any human uses of them. Intrinsic value is often associated with moral or religious beliefs that are beyond the scope of biology. Many people attach both utilitarian and nonutilitarian value to biodiversity.

Everyone is familiar with the Declaration of Independence, which led to the separation of the United States from England. Some biologists have called for a "Declaration of Interdependence," an acknowledgment of the connections between organisms, including humans, and their environments. Recognizing interdependence is what environmental science is all about.

SECTION 23-2 REVIEW

1. Explain how species richness and evenness differ.

2. What is genetic diversity?

3. How many species of organisms are there?

4. What is a debt-for-nature swap?

5. List three utilitarian uses of biodiversity.

6. **CRITICAL THINKING** Explain why the conservation of genetic diversity is necessary for the long-term conservation of biodiversity.

23-3

OBJECTIVES

▲

Contrast conservation biology with restoration biology.

●

Describe current efforts to conserve migratory birds.

■

Discuss the biological principles and social issues related to wolf reintroduction.

◆

Explain the plan to restore the Everglades.

TAKING ACTION

Although biologists have just begun to learn how nature works, they are now being called upon to help conserve threatened wildlife and restore ecosystems. Science, public involvement, and new partnerships have led to several environmental success stories. You too can contribute. Becoming aware of your local environment can link you to community action and global issues.

CONSERVATION AND RESTORATION BIOLOGY

As the human population has increased, the influence of humans on natural ecosystems has also increased. In the United States during the last 200 years, over 99 percent of native prairies have been replaced with farmland or urban development, and most of the old-growth forests have been cut. Loss of so much of these vegetation types has meant losses of biodiversity.

Biologists are being asked to develop plans to protect and manage the remaining areas that still have much of their biodiversity. A new discipline, called **conservation biology,** seeks to identify and maintain natural areas. In areas where human influence is greater—such as agricultural areas, former strip mines, and drained wetlands—biologists may have to reverse major changes and replace missing ecosystem components. For example, returning a strip-mined area to a grassland may involve contouring the land surface, introducing bacteria to the soil, planting grass and shrub seedlings, and even using periodic fires to manage the growth of vegetation. Dealing with a more extreme case like this is called **restoration biology.**

At present, even the best scientific efforts may not be enough to completely restore an area to its original condition. But by using their understanding of ecological principles such as energy flow, species interactions, and biogeochemical cycling, biologists can often make improvements. Let's look at three examples of conservation and restoration biology: the conservation of migratory birds, the reintroduction of the gray wolf to Yellowstone National Park, and new plans to restore the Everglades.

CONSERVING MIGRATORY BIRDS

Imagine weighing as little as 20 g (just a bit more than a floppy disk) and flying nonstop over open ocean for 100 hours before reaching land to rest and feed. This is exactly what blackpoll warblers like the one shown in Figure 23-10 do. The blackpoll warbler is one of the 200 species of **migratory birds** that travel twice each year between North America and Latin America. Migratory birds take advantage of long days and abundant prey in northern tundra and forest ecosystems, where they breed and raise their young. Then, as autumn approaches and the food supply decreases, they fly south to warmer ecosystems that can sustain them during nonbreeding months. Examples of migratory birds you may recognize include the Canada goose, sandhill crane, barn swallow, and scarlet tanager.

Most migratory birds tend to follow generally north-south routes along rivers, mountains, and coastlines. These routes are called **flyways.** Figure 23-11 shows the four major flyways in North America. As many as 5 billion individual birds depend on suitable habitat being available at each end of their migratory journey. Some birds fly along coastlines or over land and make several stopovers for food or rest along the way. If food or habitat is lacking along their way or at their destination, they may not breed and may even die.

FIGURE 23-10

Each fall, blackpoll warblers migrate more than 2,500 km (1,600 mi) over the ocean to reach their wintering grounds in South America.

FIGURE 23-11

This map shows the four flyways commonly used by North American migratory birds. Birds tend to follow landscape features such as rivers, mountains, and coastlines.

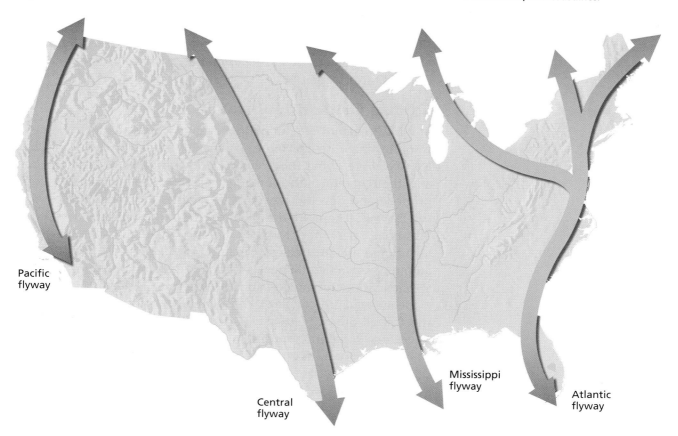

Pacific flyway

Central flyway

Mississippi flyway

Atlantic flyway

FIGURE 23-12

Nationwide surveys of breeding populations of ducks indicate long-term declines in some species.

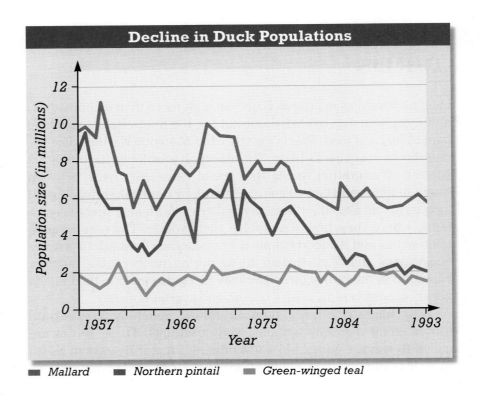

Decline in Duck Populations

Population size (in millions)

Year

■ Mallard   ■ Northern pintail   ■ Green-winged teal

In recent years, scientists, with the help of outdoor recreationists such as hunters and birdwatchers, have documented significant declines in the populations of some migratory birds, including ducks, shorebirds, and songbirds. The number of ducks recorded in the winter of 1993 was the lowest since the surveys began, in 1955, as shown in Figure 23-12. This period was marked by the loss of 60 to 90 percent of prairie wetlands and over 50 percent of all United States wetlands.

Saving Critical Habitat

In 1903, President Theodore Roosevelt established the first national wildlife refuge, to conserve wading birds in Florida. As we have learned more about the preferred travel routes of migratory birds and their habitat and food requirements, biologists have helped propose and develop new wildlife refuges at critical places along the flyways. There are now 500 refuges in the United States, covering about 4 percent of the total area of our country. The refuges are also home to 220 species of mammals, 250 species of reptiles and amphibians, and 200 species of fish, including one-third of all the species on the threatened and endangered species lists.

Because migratory birds also depend on winter habitats outside the United States, conservation efforts have to be international. Migratory songbirds are the focus of a new U.S. Fish and Wildlife Service program, called Partners in Flight–Aves de las Americas, covering the United States and Mexico. The Western Hemisphere Shorebird Reserve Network operates in Central America and South America. Deforestation and coastal development projects remain major threats to migratory birds in these areas.

REINTRODUCTION OF THE WOLF

Gray wolves, shown in Figure 23-13, formerly ranged over most of the United States. For nearly a century, wolves were shot, trapped, and poisoned by people who feared for their own safety or who wanted to protect their livestock. Today the gray wolf is an endangered species, protected by law. In the contiguous 48 states, it is found primarily in Montana and Minnesota. The 1995 total population of wolves in these states was about 2,500 animals. Alaska and Canada have approximately 62,000 wolves.

The current status of wolves in the United States has much to do with human attitudes. Many people fear wolves because of childhood stories. Although sick wolves and wolf-dog hybrids have attacked people, there is no documented case of a healthy wild wolf ever killing a person in North America. Some ranchers regard wolves as threats to their livelihood. As humans have reduced natural-prey populations, some wolves have occasionally attacked livestock to survive. However, only a tiny percentage of livestock in the United States is ever lost to wolf predation. Other people associate positive qualities with wolves. Some view the wolf as a symbol of wilderness, even though wolves are adaptable and do not require wilderness areas to survive.

To a biologist, the wolf is a top carnivore that is dynamically involved with prey species, such as elk and moose. Restoration ecologists became interested in reintroducing wolves to Yellowstone National Park, shown in Figure 23-14, because until about 60 years ago wolves were the top predators of deer, moose, and elk within the park. With the eradication of the wolf—and because no hunting is allowed in national parks—elk populations had grown so large that they may have exceeded the carrying capacity of the park. A proposal was made to reintroduce the wolf to help control elk numbers, to restore a well-known species to the park, and to increase enjoyment of the park for its 3 million annual visitors.

FIGURE 23-13

The gray wolf is an endangered species that is the ancestor of the domestic dog. Adult wolves weigh about 45 kg (100 lb) and are about 2 m (6 ft) long from the nose to the tip of the tail. Wolves are social and commonly form packs with two to eight members.

internet**connect**

SC*LINKS*
NSTA

TOPIC: Wolf
GO TO: www.scilinks.org
KEYWORD: HM455

FIGURE 23-14

Yellowstone National Park is the oldest national park in the United States. Wolves lived there until about 60 years ago, when they were exterminated by hunting.

FIGURE 23-15

Before being released in Yellowstone Park, the wolves were kept in pens for three months to allow them to become accustomed to their new surroundings. This strategy is called soft release.

The Wolf Reintroduction Plan

After many years of public hearings involving people with a wide range of opinions, the National Park Service agreed to reintroduce wolves to Yellowstone. Special precautions were taken to protect the interests of ranchers opposed to the effort. First, ranchers are permitted to kill wolves that are seen attacking their livestock. Second, individual wolves that become a nuisance to humans will be relocated. Third, a private conservation organization, Defenders of Wildlife, set up a $100,000 fund to reimburse ranchers for any economic losses caused by wolves. This group also offers $5,000 to private landowners who agree to let wolves breed on their property. These financial arrangements were key factors in the approval of the reintroduction program.

Before reintroduction, biological information about wolves and Yellowstone was gathered to give the wolves their best chance of survival. In 1995, 14 wolves from Canada were placed in pens at release sites within the park, as shown in Figure 23-15. Fifteen more were released in central Idaho. In 1996, 17 more wolves were released in Yellowstone, and though 11 wolves were killed (some illegally), about 20 pups from both years survived. As of January 1997, the total number of wolves in and around Yellowstone was 40, and their breeding success continues to be monitored.

RESTORING THE EVERGLADES ECOSYSTEM

An enormous amount of biological information must be gathered in order to reintroduce a single species into an ecosystem and monitor it over time. But imagine what is involved in restoring an entire ecosystem that has been severely damaged. A new federal, state, and local partnership has been formed to restore one of the largest and most species-rich national parks in the United States—the Everglades, shown in Figure 23-16.

FIGURE 23-16

Everglades National Park contains only about 20 percent of the Everglades ecosystem. The map below shows some of the key features related to the decline and restoration of Everglades National Park.

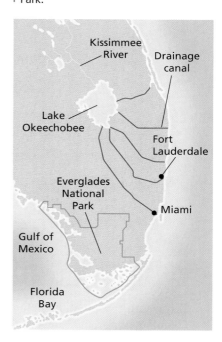

Early in this century, land developers were attracted to the large beaches and semitropical climates of southern Florida. They found extensive wetlands that were hard to build on and mosquito populations that discouraged new residents. Over time, a series of drainage canals was dug to intercept water moving south from Lake Okeechobee and divert it to the ocean, drying out the land. The non-native melaleuca tree was also planted to take large amounts of water out of the soil.

At that time, few people could foresee the ecological consequences of these actions, but Marjorie Stoneman Douglas did. She helped acquire land to create Everglades National Park and in 1947 wrote a book, *The Everglades: River of Grass,* that explained how the Everglades functioned. It is not stagnant water, but rather a unique, slow-moving river 80 km (50 mi) wide and 15 cm (6 in.) deep. The Everglades is nearly flat and is dominated by saw grass, yet it is home to over 100 species of water birds. Douglas led a lifetime crusade for the Everglades, which in just 50 years experienced a 50 percent reduction in the amount of wetlands, a doubling of salinity in Florida Bay that killed sea grass and shrimp nurseries, and a 90 percent reduction in populations of wading birds. The diversion of water also prevented the ground water from being replenished, creating water shortages for farmers and residents of Miami. Rain washed fertilizers from agricultural fields and polluted the water that did make it to the park. Heavy metals, such as mercury, poisoned park life.

The newly approved 20-year plan for the Everglades ecosystem includes eliminating some of the drainage canals, restoring the Kissimmee River to its original channel, cutting back stands of melaleuca trees, and purchasing more than 40,000 hectares (100,000 acres) for park protection. It is the most ambitious ecosystem-restoration project attempted in the United States.

GETTING INVOLVED

It is important for individuals to get involved in conservation, and the best place to start is at home. The first step is to learn about your local environment. For example, apply these questions to where you live.

1. *Name five native plants, and determine their seasons. Can they be used for landscaping homes or businesses?*

2. *Name five resident birds and five migratory birds. Are there any special laws that protect them?*

3. *Name two major agricultural crops. How do farmers or ranchers obtain water for crops or livestock?*

4. *Trace the path of water that you use from when it falls as precipitation to when it flows from your faucet. Where does the water go after you have used it, and how is it treated?*

5. *Name three endangered species in your area. If any species have become extinct, what was the cause?*

6. *Trace the path of garbage after it is collected. Does your sanitation department support recycling?*

7. *Describe the primary geological processes that helped form the land where you live. If the land was shaped by water, wind, glaciers, or volcanoes, are any of these still contributing to geologic change?*

8. *Find the names and addresses of two nongovernment conservation associations that are active in your region. Will they allow you to act as a volunteer?*

Exploring these questions may lead you to your own ideas about what you can do to maintain biodiversity or improve the ecological integrity in your area. A new environmental field, called **urban ecology,** involves people who are interested in the challenge of increasing biodiversity in the most heavily developed areas.

SECTION 23-3 REVIEW

1. How are conservation biology and restoration biology different? How are they similar?

2. Why are some populations of migratory birds declining?

3. Give three reasons why wolves are being restored to Yellowstone National Park.

4. What rules have been made to protect the interests of ranchers concerned about wolves?

5. How did the diversion of water from the Everglades lead to environmental problems?

6. CRITICAL THINKING What benefits might people living near Yellowstone National Park receive from the reintroduction of wolves?

SUMMARY/VOCABULARY

23-1
- Currents of air and water are linked into a global system that is responsible for climate.
- El Niño events occur when the normal east-to-west winds across the southern Pacific ocean reverse, causing a variety of effects on organisms worldwide, including humans.
- Over a short time period, humans have affected global systems, including altering the composition of the atmosphere by decreasing ozone levels and increasing carbon dioxide levels.

- Industrial chemicals called CFCs are destroying the ozone layer. A treaty to ban CFC production has been signed.
- From the results of computer models of the atmosphere, a large majority of scientists have concluded that increased carbon dioxide levels have resulted in warmer surface temperatures on the Earth. Scientists expect temperatures to continue to rise as fossil fuel use and carbon dioxide levels increase.

Vocabulary

cause-and-effect relationship (444)
chlorofluorocarbons (443)
convection cell (441)
correlation (444)
El Niño (442)
environmental science (441)
upwelling (442)

23-2
- *Biodiversity* refers to the variety of life found in a given area and can be measured in different ways, including by species richness, evenness, and genetic diversity.
- Scientists estimate that there are at least 10 million species on Earth and may be as many as 30 million. Scientists have described fewer than 3 million species so far.
- Insects and plants make up the majority of species on Earth, especially in tropical rain forests, which are rapidly being destroyed.

- Two new ideas for conserving tropical biodiversity are debt-for-nature swaps and ecotourism.
- People value biodiversity for utilitarian reasons, which emphasize economic benefits from species. Some of these benefits include medicines, foods, and other useful products, as well as ecosystem services. Non-utilitarian reasons for conserving biodiversity draw on the assertion that living things have intrinsic value. This assertion often derives from moral or religious beliefs.

Vocabulary

biodiversity (448)
debt-for-nature swap (450)
ecotourism (451)
evenness (449)
genetic diversity (449)
nonutilitarian value (451)
utilitarian value (451)

23-3
- Conservation biology and restoration biology are two new disciplines. Conservation biologists are concerned with identifying and maintaining areas that are still relatively undisturbed, whereas restoration biologists are usually involved with repairing badly damaged ecosystems.
- Populations of some migratory birds appear to be in decline due to habitat destruction by humans, but they are being

helped by new refuges and international partnerships.
- After a 60-year absence, the gray wolf has been successfully reintroduced in small numbers to Yellowstone National Park to help control elk populations and to increase public enjoyment.
- A new 20-year plan to restore the Everglades ecosystem has recently been approved.

Vocabulary

conservation biology (452)
flyway (453)
migratory bird (453)
restoration biology (452)
urban ecology (458)

REVIEW

Vocabulary

1. Define the term *environmental science.*
2. What are flyways?
3. What chemical elements would you expect to find in chlorofluorocarbons?
4. Describe ecotourism.
5. What is an upwelling, and what connection does it have to El Niño?

Multiple Choice

6. Which of the following is a consequence of El Niño? (a) decreased anchovy production (b) greater number of fires in the southern United States (c) increased guano production (d) ozone depletion
7. Ozone protects organisms from (a) meteor impacts (b) harmful radiation (c) salt depletion (d) cold temperatures.
8. Which of the following is not a use for CFCs? (a) fuel (b) coolant in refrigerators (c) propellant in aerosol cans (d) cleaning electronics.
9. Since 1850, carbon dioxide levels have (a) decreased by 30 percent (b) remained about the same (c) increased by 30 percent (d) not been measured accurately.
10. Which of the following is *not* true of biodiversity?
    (a) It is decreasing.
    (b) It consists mostly of mammals and reptiles.
    (c) It has declined sharply at least five times in the past.
    (d) It is higher in tropical rain forests than in any other biome.
11. Biologists estimate that most species on Earth are (a) insects (b) plants (c) mammals (d) fungi.
12. Benefits from biodiversity include (a) medicines (b) useful products (c) water purification (d) all of the above.
13. Stopovers are used by migratory birds to (a) breed (b) seek new habitat (c) avoid predators (d) feed and rest.
14. Wolves (a) are carnivores (b) need wilderness areas (c) are usually solitary (d) usually attack humans.

15. Which of the following is true about the Everglades ecosystem?
    (a) It is a stagnant swamp.
    (b) It has doubled in size over the last 50 years.
    (c) It supports very few species.
    (d) It has been damaged by pollution.

Short Answer

16. Explain how convection cells are associated with biomes.
17. What happens during El Niño? Describe two ways that El Niño affects the economy of countries other than Peru.
18. What do environmental scientists mean by *interdependence*? Give an example of interdependence from this chapter.
19. Explain the difference between a correlation and a cause-and-effect relationship. How can scientists distinguish between the two?
20. How could future human population growth affect the environment?
21. Describe some of the different attitudes toward wolves. How have these attitudes affected the status of wolves?
22. Which of the communities in the table below has the highest species richness? the greatest evenness? Explain your answers.

Species Richness and Evenness

Number of individuals of each species

Community	1	2	3	4
A	7	1	1	1
B	3	3	4	0
C	0	9	0	1

23. **Unit 7—*Ecosystem Dynamics***

Write a report summarizing ways that humans can work to reduce the depletion and pollution of ground water. How would more efficient use of ground water benefit ecosystems?

CRITICAL THINKING

1. You are aware of some of the connections between plankton, anchovies, humans, and birds. Suggest other species interactions that are likely to be influenced by El Niño.

2. The formation of the ozone layer depended on the presence of oxygen in the atmosphere. Drawing on what you have learned about the history of life, explain how organisms affected and were affected by the forming ozone layer.

3. There are no substitutes for clean, fresh water, which is in short supply worldwide. Environmental scientists think fresh water may become a limiting factor on human population growth. Explain how you could estimate Earth's carrying capacity for humans based just on the availability of fresh water. What information do you need in order to make this estimate? How might technological advances change your estimate?

4. What question would you add to the list shown on page 458? Explain your choice. Share your question with your classmates.

5. As part of the global treaty to eliminate CFCs, developed countries are contributing to a fund to help the developing countries buy CFC substitutes. What benefits do the developed countries receive from this investment?

6. It is a widely held belief that the birth rate declines when countries make progress toward industrialization. However, birth rate has declined in Sri Lanka and Costa Rica, countries with minimal industrial development. How might these data be explained?

7. Look at the graph below. Notice that although the long-term trend is toward higher carbon dioxide levels, the carbon dioxide concentration fluctuates during each year, falling in the spring and summer and rising in the fall. What do you think causes this fluctuation?

Increase in CO_2 Levels

Carbon dioxide concentration (ppm)

360

350

340

330

1974   1978   1982   1986   1990   1994

Year

EXTENSION

1. In 1995, three scientists—Paul Crutzen, Sherwood Rowland, and Mario Molina— were awarded the Nobel Prize in chemistry for their work on the ozone layer. Use library resources or an on-line database to research each scientist's contribution to our understanding of the ozone layer. Write a short report that summarizes what you have learned.

2. Form a cooperative team with another member of your class. Work with your partner to answer the questions listed on page 458. You may need to consult several sources of information, including the library, an on-line

database, local government agencies, and a nearby university, zoo, or botanical garden. When you have answered all of the questions, prepare a poster that displays what you have learned.

3. Read "In the Wake of the Spill" in *National Geographic,* March 1999, on page 96. Describe the ecological disaster that occurred in Alaska's Prince William Sound just after midnight on March 24, 1989. Which was more effective in the recovery of the ecosystem, nature or cleaning crews? Explain. What other unrelated ecological changes are happening in Alaska?

Testing the Effects of Thermal Pollution

OBJECTIVES

- Model the effects of thermal pollution on living organisms.
- Apply the underlying scientific principles to environmental issues.

PROCESS SKILLS

- hypothesizing
- experimenting
- observing
- organizing data
- analyzing data

MATERIALS

- 400 mL beakers, 2
- ice
- hot water
- thermometer
- U-shaped glass tubing, 30 cm long
- 2 corks to fit both ends of the tubing
- 125 mL beaker
- water
- *Paramecium* culture
- hand lens
- stopwatch or clock
- glass-marking pen or wax pencil

Background

1. Some power plants use water from rivers as a coolant. After the water is used, it is much hotter than the water in the river.
2. What is a pollutant?
3. How can heat be considered a pollutant?
4. How can power plants release nonharmful water?

Procedure

1. Discuss the objectives of this investigation with your partners. Develop a hypothesis concerning the effect of temperature on *Paramecium*.

2. Design an experiment using the given materials to test your hypothesis. In your experiment, *Paramecium* will be contained in the U-shaped tube. One large beaker will be filled with ice, and the other large beaker will be filled with hot water. Other materials that you can use in your experiment are listed in your materials list.

3. In designing your experiment, decide which factor will be an independent variable. Plan how you will vary your independent variable. In your lab report, list your independent variable and your method of varying it.

4. Decide which factor will be the dependent variable in your experiment. Plan how you will measure your dependent variable. In your lab report, list your dependent variable and your method of measuring it.

5. In most experiments, a control is necessary. Plan your control, and describe it in your lab report.

6. Discuss your planned experiment with your teacher. Proceed with your experiment only after you have received your teacher's permission to do so.

7. ⚠️ CAUTION **Water hotter than 60°C can scald. Be careful handling hot water, and alert your teacher if you burn yourself.** Fill a 400 mL beaker with ice and water. Make sure that ice remains in the beaker for the entire experiment. Fill another 400 mL beaker with 60°C tap water.

8. In a 125 mL beaker, gently swirl 20 mL of water and 20 mL of *Paramecium* culture. Your teacher will provide aged tap water or spring water for you to use during this step. (Chlorinated water would kill *Paramecium*.)

9. While your partner holds the test tube steady, carefully pour the *Paramecium*-and-water mixture into the U-shaped tube. Fill the tube completely, leaving just enough room for a cork at each end of the tube. Make sure there are no large air bubbles in the tube. Place a cork at each end of the tube.

10. Create a table similar to the one at right to record your data. For example, the table below is designed to

record the number of *Paramecia* in three parts of the U-shaped tube over time. Design your data table to fit your own experiment. Remember to allow plenty of space for recording your data.

11. Proceed with your experiment, using the tube, ice water, hot water, and hand lens to observe any response of *Paramecium* to the environment.

12. As you conduct your experiment, record your results, including the number of *Paramecium* and the time involved, in your data table. Organize your data so that others reading your lab report will be able to understand the results of your experiment.

13. Clean up your materials and wash your hands before leaving the lab.

Analysis and Conclusions

1. Did the results of your experiment support your hypothesis? Explain your answer.
2. What effect did heat and cold have on *Paramecium* in your experiment?
3. What evidence do you have that *Paramecium* preferred one temperature range to another?
4. What are some possible sources of error in your experiment?

5. How might a pollutant cause an increase in the number of organisms? Explain.
6. Judging from your experiment, how do you think other organisms might react to a change in water temperature?
7. How could a power plant change the type of organisms that live in the water where it releases its cooling water?

Further Inquiry

Develop a hypothesis about the effects of acid rain on *Paramecium,* and design an experiment to test your hypothesis.

OBSERVATIONS OF PARAMECIA

		Number of *Paramecia*		
		Cold end	Hot end	Middle
	0			
Elapsed	15			
time	30			
(seconds)	45			
	60			
	75			

Unit 6

MICROORGANISMS

" *In the leaves of every forest, in the flowers of every garden, in the waters of every rivulet, there are worlds teeming with life...* "

From *Thoughts on Animalcules,* or *A Glimpse of the Invisible World Revealed by the Microscope,* by G. A. Mantell, as quoted in Primo Levi's book *Other People's Trades.*

Mushrooms, members of the kingdom Fungi, are important decomposers in nature.

internetconnect

sci LINKS
NSTA

National Science Teachers Association *sci*LINKS Internet resources are located throughout this unit.

These rod-shaped bacteria are members of the kingdom Eubacteria and the species E. coli.

Diatoms, members of the phylum Protista, are unicellular, photosynthetic organisms that live in oceans and lakes.

Pelomyxa carolinensis

These Petri dishes contain bacterial cultures. Scientists often grow bacteria in the laboratory in order to study them more easily.

BACTERIA

These bacteria are called Clostridium perfringens. They are commonly found in soil and are the cause of the disease gas gangrene. (SEM 17,100×)

FOCUS CONCEPT: *Cell Structure and Function*

As you read, notice that bacteria have complex structural, nutritional, and genetic properties even though they are single-celled microorganisms.

BACTERIAL EVOLUTION AND CLASSIFICATION

Bacteria are the most numerous organisms on Earth as well as the most ancient—they were probably the first forms of life. It is likely that all other organisms evolved from bacteria. The earliest fossils show that bacteria existed long before other forms of life evolved.

OBJECTIVES

▲

Define *bacteria, eubacteria,* and *archaebacteria,* and note the relationships between them.

●

Describe the methods used to classify bacteria.

■

Name and describe three known types of archaebacteria.

◆

Distinguish Gram-positive bacteria from Gram-negative bacteria.

▲

Describe the significance of cyanobacteria in the formation of the Earth's present atmosphere.

EVOLUTION

Bacteria are microscopic prokaryotes. Rock deposits found in Australia contain fossils of bacteria that existed on Earth about 3.5 billion years ago. Evidence in the fossil record indicates that eukaryotes are about 2.5 billion years old and modern humans arose about 100,000 years ago.

Bacteria have evolved into many different forms, and they are now a part of nearly every environment on Earth. They have even been found at the bottom of oceanic trenches 9.6 km (6 mi) below the water's surface and in Arctic and Antarctic regions. Evolution has yielded hundreds of thousands of species of bacteria that are adapted to places where no other organisms can live.

Classification

Unlike most other organisms, bacteria have few morphological differences that can be used to classify them. For example, bacteria do not vary in size and shape to the extent that other types of organisms do. Traditionally, bacteria have been grouped based on their structure, physiology, molecular composition, and reaction to specific types of stains, rather than on their evolutionary relationships. By comparing ribosomal RNA sequences, scientists have found that there are two vastly different types of bacteria. The bacteria that we generally refer to as germs are classified in the kingdom Eubacteria. In this text, members of the kingdom Eubacteria are sometimes referred to as **eubacteria** (YOO-bak-TEER-ee-uh), but more frequently, members of this kingdom are simply called bacteria. The other type of bacteria are called **archaebacteria** (AHR-kee-bak-TEER-ee-uh). These bacteria, which are more ancient than the eubacteria, are classified in the kingdom Archaebacteria.

KINGDOM ARCHAEBACTERIA

Scientists treat archaebacteria as a separate kingdom because these organisms are so different from other bacteria. For example, archaebacteria have unusual lipids in their cell membranes and have introns in their DNA. Their cell walls are also characterized by the absence of **peptidoglycan** (PEP-tuh-doh-GLIE-KAHN), a protein-carbohydrate compound found in the cell walls of eubacteria. While archaebacteria have some genes that resemble eubacterial genes, they also have genes that closely resemble those found in eukaryotes. This suggests that archaebacteria probably evolved from an ancestral organism that gave rise to other forms of life on Earth.

Archaebacteria were first discovered in extreme environments, such as swamps, salt lakes, and hot springs. Until recently, scientists believed that archaebacteria lived only in these extreme environments. However, by testing samples of surface water in the North Pacific and Antarctic Oceans for the presence of archaebacterial genomic sequences, scientists have discovered that archaebacteria may be more common than once thought.

Methanogens (meth-AN-uh-jenz), a broad phylogenetic group of archaebacteria, are named for their unique method of harvesting energy by converting H_2 and CO_2 into methane gas. Because oxygen is a poison to them, methanogens can live only in anaerobic conditions, such as at the bottom of a swamp and in sewage, where they are the source of marsh gas, as shown in Figure 24-1. They can also be found thriving in the intestinal tracts of humans and other animals, such as cows.

Extreme halophiles (HAL-uh-FIELZ), which are salt-loving archaebacteria, live in environments with very high salt concentrations, such as the Great Salt Lake and the Dead Sea. High salt concentrations would kill most bacteria, but this high concentration is beneficial to the growth of extreme halophiles, and these organisms use salt to generate ATP.

Thermoacidophiles (THUHR-moh-uh-SID-oh-fielz), a third group of archaebacteria, live in extremely acidic environments that have extremely high temperatures, such as hot springs. Some thermoacidophiles thrive at temperatures up to 110°C (230°F) and at a pH of less than 2. Thermoacidophiles live near volcanic vents on land or near hydrothermal vents, cracks in the ocean floor miles below the surface that leak scalding acidic water.

FIGURE 24-1

Some archaebacteria, such as the methanogens that are found in the muddy bottom of this swamp, live in anaerobic conditions. Methanogens produce methane, which you can see bubbling up through the water.

A Geologic Hot Spot

In 1977, the submarine *Alvin* drifted slowly through the cold, dark waters off the coast of Ecuador, in the Galápagos Rift of the South Pacific. On board was a team of marine geologists from the Woods Hole Oceanographic Institution led by Robert D. Ballard. They were seeking hydrothermal vents—fissures in the Earth's crust that release heat and minerals into the surrounding water. At an ocean depth of 2550 m (8,366 ft), they found hydrothermal vents and underwater hot springs teeming with marine life.

At the time, scientists believed that no living organism could survive the harsh combination of extremely high temperatures, high pressure, and total darkness. To their surprise, when the geologists developed their film, they found ghostly images of huge clamshells and previously unknown giant tube worms thriving among the bare lava. At those depths, no sunlight penetrates to support photosynthesis. What were the vent organisms using for food?

When chemist John Edmond, who was aboard the *Alvin,* analyzed the water samples, he found that they contained a large amount of dissolved hydrogen sulfide. Later, researchers following up on Ballard's deep-sea find confirmed that bacteria from vent waters, when cultured under pressures and temperatures found in a deep-sea environment, metabolize hydrogen sulfide as an energy source in a process known as chemosynthesis. To test the idea that the larger organisms used these bacteria for food, marine biologists continued to observe the organisms living in vent communities.

These biologists discovered that the dominant vent animals—clams, mussels, and giant tube worms— have a symbiotic relationship with the vent bacteria. Using microscopes, they found that the tube worms, for example, have colonies of bacteria living in their tissues. Tube worms are red because they are filled with hemoglobin. In humans, hemoglobin transports oxygen to cells. In tube worms, hemoglobin binds with hydrogen sulfide and carries it to the bacteria. The bacteria then oxidize the hydrogen sulfide, producing carbon compounds that in turn nourish the worms.

Similar communities of organisms have since been found at hundreds of geologic hot spots around the world. In December 1993, an *Alvin* expedition to the East Pacific Rise, an underwater mountain range southwest of Acapulco, Mexico, was conducted to study a recently formed hydrothermal vent.

At the site, thickets of 1.2 m (4 ft) long tube worms were found planted on the ocean floor. Measurements indicated that these tube worms grew at a rate of 84 cm (33 in.) per year, making them the fastest-growing marine organisms known.

The 1993 expedition was only one in a series of dives to the East Pacific Rise. The first visit had taken place in 1989, when scientists first discovered the vent community. Then, in April 1991, the team of scientists was surprised to find another hydrothermal vent at the site. A recent volcanic eruption at the site produced the hottest hydrothermal vent ever recorded. Scientists named the site Tube Worm Barbecue after retrieving tube worms with charred flesh. One of the scientists reported that bacteria in the vent communities were so plentiful that there appeared to be a snow blizzard. After the eruption, the only living organisms that remained on the ocean floor were centimeters of bacterial mats. However, by March 1992 the bacterial mats had been replaced by new life.

With the discovery of hydrothermal vents, there are many questions to be asked concerning their significance. As research continues, scientists will study the light source that these vents give off and its effect on the organisms that reside there.

A vent-dwelling crab is spotted by the remote-operated sub Alvin.

(a) BACILLI

(b) COCCI

(c) SPIRILLA

FIGURE 24-2

The most common shapes among bacteria are represented here by (a) *Escherichia coli,* bacilli; (b) *Micrococcus luteus,* cocci (SEM 117,300×); and (c) *Spirillum volutans,* spirilla. (SEM 19,900×)

KINGDOM EUBACTERIA

Eubacteria account for most bacteria; they occur in many shapes and sizes and have distinct biochemical and genetic characteristics. Most eubacteria have one of three basic shapes, as shown in Figure 24-2. Eubacteria that are rod-shaped are called **bacilli** (buh-SIL-ie). Sphere-shaped eubacteria are called **cocci** (KAHK-sie), and spiral-shaped eubacteria are called **spirilla** (spie-RIL-uh). When cocci occur in chains, they are called **streptococci** (STREP-tuh-KAHK-sie); grapelike clusters of cocci are called **staphylococci** (STAF-uh-loh-KAHK-sie).

Eubacteria can be divided into as many as 12 different phyla according to their evolutionary relationships. Because bacteria diversified so long ago, scientists disagree on how they should be classified phylogenetically. Table 24-1 lists several generally recognized phyla of bacteria and their properties.

TABLE 24-1 *Some Phyla of Bacteria and Their Properties*

Phylum	Shape	Motility	Metabolism	Gram reaction
Cyanobacteria	bacilli, cocci	gliding; some nonmotile	aerobic, photosynthetic autotrophic	Gram-negative
Spirochetes	spirals	corkscrew motion	aerobic and anaerobic; heterotrophic	Gram-negative
Gram-positive bacteria	bacilli, cocci	flagella; some nonmotile	aerobic and anaerobic; heterotrophic, photosynthetic	mostly Gram-positive
Proteobacteria	bacilli, cocci, spiral	flagella; some nonmotile	aerobic and anaerobic; heterotrophic; unusual metabolism; and photosynthetic autotrophic	Gram-negative

Crystal violet

Iodine

Alcohol

Safranin

(a) Application of crystal violet

(b) Application of iodine

(c) Alcohol wash

(d) Application of safranin

Gram Stain

Most species of eubacteria can also be grouped into two categories based on their response to a laboratory technique called the **Gram stain,** which is shown in Figure 24-3. **Gram-positive** bacteria retain the Gram stain and appear purple under the microscope. **Gram-negative** bacteria do not retain the purple stain and take up a second pink stain instead. Because Gram-positive bacteria have a thicker layer of peptidoglycan in their cell wall than Gram-negative bacteria do, they are able to retain the Gram stain. Figure 24-4 compares the cell walls of these two groups of bacteria. Gram-positive and Gram-negative bacteria also differ in several other ways. For example, they have different susceptibilities to antibacterial drugs, they produce different toxic materials, and they react differently to disinfectants. For these reasons, the Gram stain is useful for identifying and grouping eubacteria.

FIGURE 24-3

In the Gram-stain procedure, bacteria that have been placed on a slide are stained with a purple dye solution called crystal violet (a). The purple dye is washed off with water, and then a solution of iodine is added to the slide (b). The bacteria are rinsed with alcohol (c) and then restained with a pink dye solution called safranin (d). Gram-positive bacteria will retain the purple dye and appear purple, while Gram-negative bacteria will appear pink from the pink dye solution.

internet**connect**

SC*LINKS*

NSTA

TOPIC: Eubacteria
GO TO: www.scilinks.org
KEYWORD: HM471

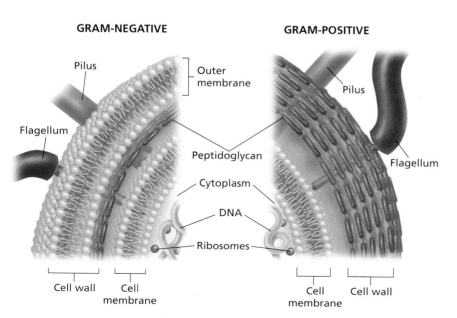

GRAM-NEGATIVE   GRAM-POSITIVE

Pilus

Outer membrane

Pilus

Flagellum

Peptidoglycan

Flagellum

Cytoplasm

DNA

Ribosomes

Cell wall   Cell membrane

Cell membrane   Cell wall

FIGURE 24-4

The drawing demonstrates the similarities and differences between Gram-negative bacteria and Gram-positive bacteria.

Quick Lab

Predicting the Spread of Disease

Materials disposable gloves, lab apron, and safety goggles; clear plastic cup with liquid

Procedure

1. Put on your disposable gloves, lab apron, and safety goggles.

2. Obtain a cup of liquid from your teacher.

3. Pour the contents of your cup into a classmate's cup. Have the classmate pour half the liquid back into your cup. Circulate around the room and repeat this step with two other classmates at random. Choose classmates you do not know well, and do not touch hands with anyone.

4. If one of your classmates had a highly contagious bacterial disease, predict how likely it is that you have "caught" the disease. Then your teacher will test the liquid in each student's cup to see who else has caught the disease. Count the number of students who are "infected."

Analysis How did the actual results compare with your prediction? How many students became infected? Was direct contact needed?

Phylum Cyanobacteria

The cyanobacteria are photosynthetic; that is, they use photosynthetic chemicals to capture sunlight, harvest the energy to produce carbohydrates, and give off oxygen as a waste product. Recall that the atmosphere of early Earth was filled with the oxygen produced by cyanobacteria, which allowed aerobic organisms to develop.

Cyanobacteria, once classified as blue-green algae, are now considered eubacteria because they lack a membrane-bound nucleus and chloroplasts. Unlike other eubacteria, however, the cyanobacteria are encased in a jellylike substance and often cling together in colonies.

Certain cyanobacteria grow in chains. Some of these cells form specialized cells called **heterocysts.** Heterocysts contain enzymes for fixing atmospheric nitrogen. Cyanobacteria that form heterocysts make nitrogen available to plants in a form that plants can use.

Cyanobacteria, such as *Anabaena,* thrive on phosphates and nitrates that accumulate in a body of water. The sudden increase in the number of cyanobacteria due to a high availability of nutrients is called **eutrophication** (YOO-troh-fuh-KAY-shuhn), or **population bloom.** Following eutrophication, many of the cyanobacteria die and are decomposed by heterotrophic bacteria. The increasing population of heterotrophic bacteria consume available oxygen in the water, causing other organisms in the water, such as fish, to die from lack of oxygen.

Phylum Spirochetes

Spirochetes (SPIE-roh-KEETS) are Gram-negative, spiral-shaped heterotrophic bacteria. Some spirochetes are aerobic, and some are anaerobic. They all move by means of a corkscrew-like rotation. Spirochetes live freely, symbiotically, or parasitically. One well-known spirochete is *Treponema pallidum,* which causes the sexually transmitted disease syphilis.

Phylum Gram-Positive Bacteria

Despite its name, not all members of this phylum are Gram-positive. A few species of Gram-negative bacteria are also grouped in this phylum because they share molecular similarities with Gram-positive bacteria. Members of this phylum include the species of streptococci that causes strep throat.

Milk becomes yogurt when certain Gram-positive bacilli grow in milk and produce lactic acid. Gram-positive bacilli are also found in the oral cavity and in the intestinal tract, where they retard the growth of disease-causing bacteria. Lactobacilli, Gram-positive bacilli found on the teeth, are known to cause tooth decay through the release of acid.

Actinomycetes (AK-tuh-noh-MIE-seets) are Gram-positive bacteria that form branching filaments. They grow in the soil and produce many **antibiotics,** chemicals that inhibit the growth of or kill other microscopic organisms.

Phylum Proteobacteria

The proteobacteria make up one of the largest and most diverse phylum among bacteria. This group is divided into several subdivisions, including enteric bacteria, chemoautotrophic bacteria, and nitrogen-fixing bacteria.

Enteric bacteria are Gram-negative heterotrophic bacteria that inhabit animal intestinal tracts and can live in either aerobic or anaerobic conditions. This group includes the well-known organism *Escherichia coli* (abbreviated *E. coli*). *E. coli* lives in the human intestine where it produces vitamin K and assists enzymes in the breakdown of foods. Other genera of enteric bacteria are responsible for many diseases. For example, bacteria in the genus *Salmonella* are responsible for many cases of food poisoning.

Chemoautotrophs (KEEM-oh-AW-toh-TROHFS) are Gram-negative bacteria that can extract energy from minerals by oxidizing the chemicals in these minerals. For example, iron-oxidizing bacteria, live in freshwater ponds that contain a high concentration of iron salts. The iron bacteria oxidize the iron in the salts to obtain energy.

As you learned in Chapter 22, nitrogen-fixing bacteria, which include some Gram-negative rods, live both freely and symbiotically with plants. *Rhizobium* is one example of nitrogen-fixing bacteria that live symbiotically with plants.

Nitrogen-fixing bacteria are vital to the success of many ecosystems. Although almost 80 percent of Earth's atmosphere is composed of nitrogen gas, N_2, plants and animals are unable to use it. *Rhizobium* is able to convert nitrogen gas to a form of nitrogen that plants can most easily use. Nitrogen-fixing bacteria colonize many plants, such as beans, soybeans, peas, alfalfa, and clover. By inducing plants to form nodules on their roots, nitrogen-fixing bacteria receive organic compounds that they need while providing the plants with nitrogen in a form they can use. *Rhizobium* is considered a major microbial source of soil nitrogen. *Rhizobium* can produce about 250 kg (114 lb) of fixed nitrogen per hectare (2.5 acres) of alfalfa in a single year, whereas the free-living nitrogen-fixing *Azotobacter* genus can produce only 2.5 kg (1.1 lb) of fixed nitrogen per hectare of alfalfa in a year.

SECTION 24-1 REVIEW

1. Explain how the terms *bacteria, eubacteria,* and *archaebacteria* relate to one another.

2. List the characteristics that are used to classify bacteria.

3. List the habitats of three types of archaebacteria.

4. Distinguish between Gram-positive bacteria and Gram-negative bacteria.

5. Describe the significance of cyanobacteria in the formation of the Earth's atmosphere.

6. **CRITICAL THINKING** Why are methanogens and cyanobacteria unable to live in the same environment?

OBJECTIVES

▲

Describe the structure
of a bacterial cell.

●

Describe three ways that
bacteria move.

■

Compare the heterotrophic modes
of nutrition in bacteria with
the autotrophic modes.

Discuss the various types of
environments that bacteria occupy.

List three types of genetic
recombination used by bacteria.

BIOLOGY OF BACTERIA

Viewed through a light microscope, bacteria appear to be relatively simple rods, spheres, and other forms. However, the electron microscope reveals a great amount of detailed structure within each form. These detailed structures are responsible for the activities carried out by bacteria.

STRUCTURE

Bacteria are typically composed of a cell wall, a cell membrane, and cytoplasm. Some bacteria have distinctive structures, such as endospores, capsules, and outer membranes. The variety of structures among bacteria is due to adaptations to individual niches. A summary of bacterial structures is presented in Table 24-2.

Cell Wall

With a few exceptions, both eubacteria and archaebacteria have a cell wall. Unlike plant cell walls, eubacterial cell walls are made of peptidoglycan. Peptidoglycan is composed of short chains of amino acids, or peptides, and carbohydrates. Archaebacterial cell walls are composed of a different compound. In Gram-negative eubacteria, the cell wall includes an outer membrane that is composed of a layer of lipids and sugars. The outer membrane protects these bacteria against some kinds of antibiotics by preventing their entry into the cell. Thus, many antibiotics have no effect on Gram-negative bacteria.

Cell Membrane and Cytoplasm

The bacterial cell membrane, which is composed of a lipid bilayer, is similar to the eukaryotic cell membrane. However, in bacteria, the cell membrane contains the enzymes that catalyze the reactions of cellular respiration. Because bacteria do not have mitochondria, they use their cell membranes to create proton gradients and to carry out cellular respiration.

The cell membranes of photosynthetic bacteria have internal foldings called thylakoids. These structures are homologous to the thylakoids found in plant chloroplasts. Like those in plant chloroplasts, bacterial thylakoids contain photosynthetic pigments and carry out the function of harvesting light energy.

Unlike eukaryotic cells, bacterial cells do not contain membrane-bound organelles. The cytoplasm of bacterial cells is made of a viscous solution of ribosomes and DNA. The bacterial DNA is arranged

TABLE 24-2 Structural Characteristics of a Bacterial Cell

Structure	Function
Cell wall	protects the cell and gives it shape
Outer membrane	protects the cell against some antibiotics (only present in Gram-negative cells)
Cell membrane	regulates movement of materials into and out of the cell; contains enzymes important to cellular respiration
Cytoplasm	contains DNA, ribosomes, and organic compounds required to carry out life processes
Chromosome	carries genetic information inherited from past generations
Plasmid	contains some genes obtained through genetic recombination
Capsule and slime layer	protect the cell and assist in attaching the cell to other surfaces
Endospore	protects the cell against harsh environmental conditions, such as heat and drought
Pilus	assists the cell in attaching to other surfaces, which is important for genetic recombination
Flagellum	moves the cell

in a single, closed loop. In addition to the main chromosome, some species of bacteria also have plasmids, self-replicating loops of DNA, in their cytoplasm.

Capsules and Pili

Many bacterial species produce an outer covering called a **capsule.** The capsule is made of polysaccharides that cling to the surface of the cell and protect it against drying or harsh chemicals. It also protects an invading bacterium from the host body's white blood cells, which could otherwise engulf it. When a capsule consists of a fuzzy coat of sticky sugars, it is called a **glycocalyx** (GLIE-koh-KAY-liks). The glycocalyx enables bacteria to attach to the surface of host cells and tissues.

Pili (PIL-ee) are short, hairlike protein structures found on the surface of some species of bacteria. Pili help bacteria adhere to host cells. Pili are also used to transfer genetic material from one bacterium to another.

Endospores

A bacterial **endospore** is a dormant structure that is produced by some Gram-positive bacterial species that are exposed to harsh environmental conditions. Endospores consist of a thick outer covering that surrounds the cell's DNA. Although the original cell may be destroyed by harsh conditions, its endospore will survive. Endospores are not reproductive cells. Instead, they help bacteria resist high temperatures, harsh chemicals, radiation, drying, and other environmental extremes. When conditions become favorable, the endospore will open, allowing the living bacterium to emerge and to begin multiplying. Endospores can be formed by species of the genera *Bacillus* and *Clostridium.*

Word Roots and Origins

pili

from the Latin *pilus,* meaning "hair"

Movement Structures

Many bacteria use flagella to move. Flagella, which are made of protein, turn and propel the bacterium in an erratic, "run-and-tumble" motion. Bacteria can have a single flagellum or a tuft of flagella. Some species of bacteria have flagella at both ends of the cell, and other species of bacteria are completely surrounded by flagella, as is the bacterium shown in Figure 24-5.

The bacteria that lack flagella have other methods of movement. For example, myxobacteria produce a layer of slime and then glide through it. Wavelike contractions of the outer membrane propel the organism through the slime. Some spiral-shaped bacteria move by a corkscrew-like rotation. These organisms have flexible cell walls and filaments within the cell walls that, when contracted, cause the bacterium to turn and move ahead.

FIGURE 24-5

Some bacteria, such as this Gram-negative *Salmonella,* move by means of flagella.

NUTRITION AND GROWTH

Depending on the species, bacteria may be heterotrophic or autotrophic. Heterotrophic bacteria use organic matter as a source of nutrition. Heterotrophic bacteria that feed on dead and decaying material are called **saprophytes** (SAP-ruh-FIETS). Autotrophic bacteria obtain their energy from sunlight or minerals.

Bacteria that use sunlight as an energy source, such as cyanobacteria, are called **photoautotrophs** (FOH-toh-AW-toh-trohfs). These autotrophs use light-trapping compounds similar to those used by plants to obtain energy. As you learned in the previous section, chemoautotrophs, another group of autotrophic organisms, oxidize inorganic compounds to obtain energy. For example, members of the genus *Nitrosomonas* oxidize ammonia, NH_3, to form nitrite, NO_2, and harvest the resulting energy.

Many bacteria are **obligate anaerobes** (AHB-luh-git AN-uhr-OHBZ), which means they cannot survive in the presence of oxygen. The obligate anaerobe *Clostridium tetani* causes tetanus. **Facultative anaerobes** (FAK-uhl-TAY-tiv AN-uh-ROHBZ) can live with or without oxygen. *Escherichia coli,* which is common in the human digestive tract, is a facultative anaerobe. Bacteria that cannot survive without oxygen are called **obligate aerobes.** The obligate aerobe *Mycobacterium tuberculosis* lives in the lungs and causes tuberculosis.

Bacteria have varying temperature requirements for growth. Some bacteria grow best in cold temperatures of 0–20°C (32–68°F). Other bacteria grow best in temperatures that range from 20°C (68°F) to 40°C (104°F). **Thermophilic** (THUHR-moh-FIL-ik) bacteria grow best in temperatures between 40°C (104°F) and 110°C (230°F). Most bacterial species grow best at a pH of 6.5 to 7.5 (7.0 is neutral). Certain species, such as those used to produce yogurt and sour cream, prefer acidic environments of a pH of 6.0 or lower.

TABLE 24-3   *A Comparison of Three Genetic Recombination Methods*

Characteristic	Transformation	Conjugation	Transduction
Method of DNA transfer	across cell wall and cell membrane of recipient	through a conjugation bridge between two cells	by a virus
Plasmid transfer	yes	yes	not likely
Chromosome transfer	no	sometimes	no
Antibiotic resistance acquired	yes	yes	sometimes

GENETIC RECOMBINATION

Table 24-3 summarizes three nonreproductive ways that bacteria can acquire and express new combinations of genetic material. **Transformation** occurs when a bacterial cell takes in DNA from its external environment. The new DNA is then substituted for a similar DNA fragment in the chromosome of the bacterial cell.

Bacterial **conjugation** is the process by which two living bacteria bind together and one bacterium transfers genetic information to the other. In order for conjugation to take place, the genetic donor must have a specialized plasmid and pilus. The specialized pilus binds to a recipient bacterium that does not have the specialized plasmid and forms a **conjugation bridge,** a passageway for the transfer of the genetic information. The plasmid replicates in the donor bacterium, and one copy of the plasmid passes through the conjugation bridge to the recipient bacterium. After the DNA transfer, the cells detach.

In **transduction,** a virus obtains a fragment of DNA from a host bacterium. As the viruses replicate inside the bacterium, they produce new copies of the bacterial DNA fragment. After the newly formed viruses have been released, they carry the bacterial gene to a new bacterium, where it can be expressed by the recipient bacterium.

SECTION 24-2 REVIEW

1. List the various structures of the bacterial cell, and describe their function.

2. Describe three types of movement among bacteria.

3. What specific terms are used to describe the oxygen requirements of bacteria?

4. In what key way do photoautotrophs and chemoautotrophs differ?

5. List and summarize three methods of genetic recombination in bacteria.

6. **CRITICAL THINKING** What eukaryotic structures are functionally similar to the bacterial cell membrane and its infoldings?

OBJECTIVES

▲

Describe the ways that bacteria can cause disease in humans.

●

Specify how antibiotic resistance has come about, and describe ways that bacteria resist antibiotics.

■

List three ways that bacteria are helpful to humans.

BACTERIA AND HUMANS

*M*uch of our knowledge about bacteria is a result of the study of the diseases they cause in humans. In addition to what we have learned about pathogenic bacteria and how they cause disease, we have also learned how bacteria benefit us. Bacteria are used in food preparation and in environmental, chemical, and mining processes.

BACTERIA AND DISEASE

The scientific study of disease is called **pathology** (path-AHL-uh-jee). Bacteria that cause disease are called pathogens. Some diseases caused by bacteria are listed in Table 24-4.

Some bacteria cause disease by producing poisons called **toxins** (TAHK-sins). **Exotoxins** (EKS-oh-TAHK-sins) are toxins that are made of protein. Exotoxins are produced by Gram-positive bacteria and are secreted into the surrounding environment. For example, tetanus is a disease caused by an exotoxin.

TABLE 24-4   *A Summary of Bacterial Diseases*

Disease	Pathogen	Areas affected	Mode of transmission
Botulism	*Clostridium botulinum*	nerves	improperly preserved foods
Cholera	*Vibrio cholerae*	intestine	contaminated water
Dental caries (tooth decay)	*Streptococcus mutans, sanguis,* and *salivarius*	teeth	bacteria enter the mouth from the environment
Gonorrhea	*Neisseria gonorrhoeae*	urethra, fallopian tubes, epididymis	person-to-person by sexual contact
Lyme disease	*Borrelia burgdorferi*	skin, joints, heart	tick bite
Rocky Mountain spotted fever	*Rickettsia ricketsii*	blood, skin	tick bite
Salmonella food poisoning	*Salmonella*	intestine	contaminated water and food
Strep throat	*Streptococcus pyogenes*	upper respiratory tract, blood, skin	person-to-person by sneezes, coughs, or direct contact
Tetanus	*Clostridium tetani*	nerves at synapses	contaminated wounds
Tuberculosis	*Mycobacterium tuberculosis*	lung, bones, other organs	person-to-person by coughs

Endotoxins, toxins made of lipids and carbohydrates, are associated with the outer membrane of Gram-negative bacteria, such as *E. coli*. While exotoxins are steadily released by living Gram-positive bacteria, endotoxins are not released by Gram-negative bacteria until the bacteria die. Once released, endotoxins cause fever, body aches, and weakness, and they damage the vessels of the circulatory system.

Bacteria also cause disease by destroying body tissues. As bacteria adhere to cells, they secrete digestive enzymes. These enzymes allow further tissue invasion. For example, some *Streptococci* bacteria produce a blood-clot-dissolving enzyme that allows infectious bacteria to spread to other tissues.

Word Roots and Origins

endotoxin

from the Greek *endon,* meaning "within," and *toxicon,* meaning "poison"

Antibiotics

Antibiotics are drugs that combat bacteria by interfering with various cellular functions. For example, **penicillin** interferes with cell-wall synthesis. **Tetracycline** (TE-truh-SIE-klin) interferes with bacterial protein synthesis. Many antibiotics are derived from chemicals that bacteria and fungi produce. Antibiotics protect bacteria and fungi from other microscopic invaders. Other antibiotics, such as **sulfa drugs,** are synthesized in laboratories. Many antibiotics are able to affect a wide variety of organisms; they are called **broad-spectrum antibiotics.** Some antibiotics, their mechanisms of action, and target bacteria are listed in Table 24-5.

Antibiotic Resistance

When a population of bacteria is exposed to an antibiotic, the bacteria that are most susceptible to the antibiotic die first. However, a few mutant bacteria that are resistant to the antibiotic may continue to grow. A resistant population then grows from these mutant bacteria through reproduction and genetic recombination. In this

TABLE 24-5   *A Summary of Common Antibiotics*

Antibiotic or synthetic drug	Mechanism of action	Target bacteria
Penicillin	inhibits cell-wall synthesis	Gram-positive bacteria
Ampicillin	inhibits cell-wall synthesis	broad spectrum
Bacitracin	inhibits cell-wall synthesis	Gram-positive bacteria; used as a skin-ointment
Cephalosporin	inhibits cell-wall synthesis	Gram-positive bacteria
Tetracycline	inhibits protein synthesis	broad spectrum
Streptomycin	inhibits protein synthesis	Gram-negative bacteria, tuberculosis
Sulfa drug	inhibits cell metabolism	bacterial meningitis, urinary-tract infections
Rifampin	inhibits RNA synthesis	Gram-positive bacteria and some Gram-negative bacteria
Quinolines	inhibit DNA synthesis	urinary-tract infections

FIGURE 24-6

Bacteria can be tested for their sensitivity to antibiotics by growing them in a Petri dish with paper disks containing different antibiotics. As the antibiotics diffuse into the agar, the bacteria's growth will be inhibited by the antibiotic if the bacteria are sensitive to that antibiotic.

way, antibiotics provide a selective advantage to antibiotic-resistant bacteria. Because antibiotics have been overused, many diseases that were once easy to treat are becoming more difficult to treat.

The mechanisms of antibiotic resistance vary. In some bacteria, cell walls prevent passage of the antibiotic. Still other bacteria secrete enzymes that destroy or alter the antibiotic, as penicillin-resistant bacteria do. Figure 24-6 shows a method of testing bacterial resistance and sensitivity toward antibiotics.

USEFUL BACTERIA

Bacteria affect our lives in many positive ways. In sewage treatment, for example, bacteria break down the remains of organic matter in dead plant and animal waste, recycling carbon and nitrogen. Bacteria also turn sewage into simpler organic compounds. Bacteria, along with other microorganisms, recycle compounds from dead organisms, making them available to other organisms through the process of decay. Many bacteria are also able to fix carbon dioxide and create organic compounds.

Bacteria are also useful in producing and processing food. For example, bacteria ferment the lactose in milk to produce sour-milk products such as buttermilk, sour cream, and yogurt. Other species of bacteria digest the protein in milk and produce unripened cheeses such as ricotta and cottage cheese. Fermented foods are also produced by bacteria. Sauerkraut is produced when bacteria digest the carbohydrates in cabbage, and pickles result from the fermentation of cucumbers.

Bacteria are also used in industrial chemical production. They produce organic chemicals and fuels. Some are useful in mining for minerals and in petroleum recovery, while other bacteria and their products are used as insecticides. Bacteria are also used to help clean up environmental disasters caused by humans, such as chemical and oil spills.

SECTION 24-3 REVIEW

1. Describe ways that bacteria cause human disease.

2. Describe the function of antibiotics in nature.

3. List three antibiotics used to treat disease and the mechanism of action of each.

4. List some of the positive uses of bacteria.

5. Explain how antibiotic resistance arises in bacteria and how bacteria resist antibiotics.

6. **CRITICAL THINKING** Why would a pickle processor carry out the preparation of pickles in anaerobic conditions?

SUMMARY/VOCABULARY

24-1 ■ Bacteria are prokaryotic single-celled organisms. They occur in several variations of three basic shapes: rods, spheres, and spirals.

■ Bacteria are the oldest and most populous organisms. They are believed to have existed on Earth for about 3.5 billion years.

■ Bacteria are classified in two kingdoms: Archaebacteria, which includes ancient forms of life, and Eubacteria, which includes most bacteria.

■ The archaebacteria include the methanogens, which produce methane gas; the extreme halophiles, which live in very salty environments; and the thermoacidophiles, which live in extremely acidic environments at extremely high temperatures.

■ The Gram stain is used to group bacteria into two groups; Gram-positive and Gram-negative bacteria.

■ The cyanobacteria are photosynthetic bacteria that probably produced much of the oxygen in the Earth's atmosphere.

Vocabulary

actinomycete (472)
antibiotic (472)
archaebacterium (467)
bacillus (470)
chemoautotroph (473)
coccus (470)

enteric bacterium (473)
eubacterium (467)
eutrophication (472)
extreme halophile (468)
Gram-negative (471)
Gram-positive (471)

Gram stain (471)
heterocyst (472)
methanogen (468)
peptidoglycan (468)
population bloom (472)
spirillum (470)

spirochete (472)
staphylococcus (470)
streptococcus (470)
thermoacidophile (468)

24-2 ■ The major structures of the bacterial cell include a cell wall, a cell membrane, cytoplasm, a capsule, pili, endospores, ribosomes, and movement structures.

■ Aerobic and anaerobic bacteria differ in whether they need an oxygen-rich environment or an oxygen-free environment.

Different species live under different temperature conditions, ranging from 0°C to 110°C. Most bacterial species grow best at a neutral pH.

■ Genetic recombination in bacteria can occur through transformation, conjugation, and transduction.

Vocabulary

capsule (475)
conjugation (477)
conjugation bridge (477)
endospore (475)

facultative anaerobe (476)
glycocalyx (475)
obligate aerobe (476)
obligate anaerobe (476)

photoautotroph (476)
pilus (475)
saprophyte (476)
thermophilic (476)

transduction (477)
transformation (477)

24-3 ■ Many bacteria are pathogens. Diseases may result from toxins produced by bacteria, from the destruction of body tissues, or from bacterial enzymes interfering with normal body processes.

■ Antibiotics inhibit the growth of bacteria. Antibiotic-resistant bacteria destroy antibiotics, or prevent entry of the antibiotic into the cytoplasm.

■ Helpful bacteria are used to convert sewage into simpler organic compounds, to produce and process food, to produce industrial chemicals, to mine for minerals, to produce insecticides, and to clean up chemical and oil spills.

Vocabulary

broad-spectrum
  antibiotic (479)
endotoxin (479)

exotoxin (478)
pathology (478)

penicillin (479)
sulfa drug (479)

tetracycline (479)
toxin (478)

REVIEW

Vocabulary

In each of the following sets, choose the term that does not belong, and explain why it does not belong.

1. heterotroph, saprophyte, chemoautotroph
2. methanogen, spirochetes, enteric bacteria
3. archaebacterium, exotoxin, pathogen
4. pilus, conjugation, endospore
5. cyanobacterium, anaerobe, enteric bacteria

Multiple Choice

6. Bacteria produce yogurt from milk by (a) conjugation (b) aerobic respiration (c) fermentation (d) fixing nitrogen.
7. Rod-shaped bacteria are called (a) cocci (b) bacilli (c) halophiles (d) spirilla.
8. Thermoacidophiles are (a) eubacteria (b) cyanobacteria (c) archaebacteria (d) spirochetes.
9. Gram-positive bacteria stain (a) blue (b) pink (c) red (d) purple.
10. Eutrophication is the result of (a) antibiotics (b) pathogens (c) bacterial conjugation (d) population explosions.
11. Bacterial DNA is (a) a closed loop (b) encased in a capsule (c) linear (d) found in the nucleus.
12. The glycocalyx helps bacteria (a) survive unfavorable environmental conditions (b) stick to surfaces (c) metabolize gaseous nitrogen (d) ingest food.
13. During nitrogen fixation, gaseous nitrogen is converted to (a) carbon (b) ammonia (c) nitrate (d) methane.
14. An organism that must have oxygen to survive is (a) an obligate aerobe (b) a facultative anaerobe (c) a facultative aerobe (d) an obligate anaerobe.
15. Genetic recombination in bacteria can occur during the process of (a) conjugation (b) heterocyst formation (c) binary fission (d) endospore production.

Short Answer

16. Which bacteria move about by rotation?
17. List one distinguishing characteristic of each of the three main groups of archaebacteria.
18. Why are cyanobacteria no longer classified as algae?
19. Describe the capsule of a bacterium and its function.
20. Explain how saprophytic bacteria contribute to the recycling of nutrients in the environment.
21. How do chemoautotrophs harvest energy from their environment?
22. Describe one way bacteria can exchange genetic information.
23. Identify the metabolic process that bacteria use to make food products such as pickles and sauerkraut.
24. List some diseases caused by bacteria, and list the organs they affect.
25. Label the parts of the bacterium below.

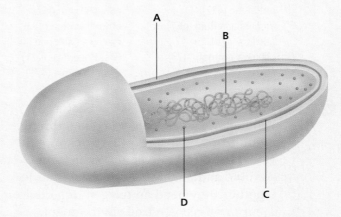

CRITICAL THINKING

1. Scientists have only recently discovered fossilized bacteria. Explain why this discovery may have taken so long.
2. *Clostridium tetani,* the bacterium that causes tetanus, is an obligate anaerobe. From this information, would you infer that a deep puncture wound or a surface cut would be more likely to become infected by tetanus bacteria? Explain the reason for your inference.
3. Penicillin works by interfering with the ability of bacteria to polymerize the peptidoglycan cell wall. Given this fact, explain why Gram-positive bacteria are more susceptible to the effects of penicillin than are Gram-negative bacteria.

4. Some of the bacteria that are normally found in the human intestinal tract are beneficial. For example, *E. coli* produces vitamin K. However, *E. coli* can also cause diarrhea under exceptional circumstances, and it can cause serious infections if it invades other parts of the body. Other bacteria found in the digestive tract do not produce substances the body can use, but they do not produce substances that are harmful either. What positive role might they play?

5. Thermal-vent communities, which are extremely hot regions of ocean in areas where the Earth's crust is open, have some of the densest and most productive populations known to exist. What might explain this?

6. Over the last 20 years, the number of antibiotic-resistant bacterial pathogens has steadily increased. This is thought to be a result of antibiotic abuse by patients and doctors. Doctors tend to overprescribe antibiotics for patients who demand a quick fix for their illness. Just recently, the World Health Organization has established a global computer database so that doctors can report outbreaks of antibiotic resistance. What are the potential benefits of this database?

7. The antibiotic-sensitivity report (above right) lists several antibiotics that a bacterium from a patient is susceptible to. Based on these data, what do you infer is the Gram reaction of the pathogen? A "−" sign indicates that the bacterium is not sensitive to

Antibiotic-Sensitivity Report

Antibiotic	Sensitivity
Penicillin	−
Cephalosporin	−
Streptomycin	+++
Tetracycline	++
Bacitracin	−
Rifampin	−
Ampicillin	+++

the antibiotic, and a "+" sign means that it is sensitive to the antibiotic. A "+++" sign means that it is very sensitive to the antibiotic.

8. Examine the photograph below of bacteria that have been treated with a Gram stain. Would you hypothesize that these bacteria produce endotoxins? Explain your answer.

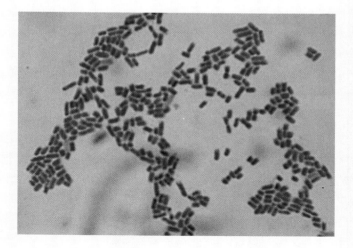

EXTENSION

1. Read "The Cholera Lesson" in *Discover*, February 1999, on page 71. According to microbiologist Rita Colwell, where does the cholera-causing organism *Vibrio cholerae* live between outbreaks? Describe the methods she is designing to predict and prevent widespread disease.

2. Research and write a report on the use of bacteria in either the processing of foods or

the treatment of sewage.

3. Visit or telephone your local public-health department, and ask for information on bacterial diseases that have been reported in your area in recent weeks. Report your findings to the class.

Culturing Bacteria

OBJECTIVES

- Test common surfaces for the presence of bacteria.
- Learn a simple procedure for culturing bacteria.

PROCESS SKILLS

- observing
- hypothesizing
- experimenting
- collecting data
- analyzing data

MATERIALS

- Petri dish with nutrient agar
- glass-marking pen
- 4 sterile cotton swabs
- distilled water
- tape
- protective gloves

Background

1. Culturing bacteria involves growing microorganisms in a nutrient medium that is favorable for growth.
2. What are favorable conditions for the growth of most bacteria?
3. List some places in your school where bacteria are likely growing.
4. If bacteria reproduce once an hour and you start with one bacterium, how many bacteria do you have after 24 hours?

PART A Setting Up the Experiment

1. Discuss with your laboratory partner(s) places in school that would be likely to contain bacteria or that have conditions under which bacteria grow best. Make a list of three places where you will test for the presence of bacteria. Do not choose places outside your laboratory without your teacher's permission.
2. Obtain a Petri dish with nutrient agar from your teacher. Divide your Petri dish into four equal quadrants by writing on the outer bottom surface of the dish with the marking pen. Label the quadrants 1, 2, 3, and 4, as shown in the photograph at left. Also label the bottom of the dish with your group name or number. Do not mark on the top of the Petri dish because it will rotate with respect to the agar.
3. Use quadrant 1 as a control. Take a sterile cotton swab, and moisten it with distilled water. Be careful not to touch the cotton swab to any other surfaces, including your fingers. Remove the cover to the Petri dish, and rub the cotton swab across the nutrient agar in quadrant 1. Be careful to not tear the surface of the agar. Replace the cover immediately.
4. Take another sterile cotton swab, and moisten it with distilled water. Swipe the moistened swab across a surface that you have decided to test for the presence of bacteria. Be careful not to touch the cotton swab to any other surface. Touching the swab to other surfaces could contaminate the swab with bacteria other than that from your selected surface.

5. Remove the cover to the Petri dish, and rub the cotton swab across the nutrient agar in quadrant 2. This process transfers bacteria from the surface you have sampled to the nutrient agar in the Petri dish. Replace the cover immediately.

6. Repeat steps 4–6 for quadrants 3 and 4, using a clean cotton swab each time. Be sure to note in your lab report the areas that you swipe for each quadrant.

7. After you have swiped a sample in each quadrant of the Petri dish, seal the Petri dish with tape.
CAUTION **Do not open the Petri dish again. Treat the contents of the Petri dish as you would any other pathogens.**

8. Place the Petri dish in a warm place with the cover side down for 24 hours.

9. Dispose of the cotton swabs according to your teacher's directions.

10. Clean up your lab materials and wash your hands before leaving the lab.

PART B   Collecting Data

11. In your lab report, create a data table similar to the model shown below. Allow plenty of space to record your observations for each quadrant swabbed.

12. Check the Petri dish daily for bacterial growth until you no longer find new bacterial colonies (about seven days). Check your Petri dish and record your observations in your data table. What is happening that enables you to see bacteria? What does each colony represent?

13. Discard your Petri dish as directed by your teacher.

Analysis and Conclusions

1. On which surfaces did you find the most bacteria? the fewest bacteria? Did your results conform to your expectations? Explain.

2. Compare the colonies of bacteria that grew in each quadrant. What can you tell about the bacteria from the kind of colonies they produced?

3. What are some possible sources of error in the procedure you followed?

4. Combine the data obtained by the entire class. Which surfaces yielded the most bacteria?

5. Which of the surfaces that you sampled would you prefer to use as a food-preparation area? Explain your choice.

6. Would the amount of surface area that you sampled with your swab affect the number of colonies that grew on your dish? Explain your answer.

7. Can you tell by looking at the colonies on the dish if they would cause disease? Why or why not?

8. What test described in this chapter could you use to partially identify your bacteria? What characteristics of the bacteria could you learn from this test?

Further Inquiry

Design an experiment to test the effects of one variable, such as temperature or the presence of anitbacterial soap, on the growth of bacteria. What would you use as a control in your experiment?

PRESENCE OF BACTERIA ON COMMON SURFACES

Surface swabbed	Day 1	Day 2	Day 3	Day 4	Day 5	Day 6	Day 7

VIRUSES

The human immunodeficiency virus (HIV), shown here stained pink, is the cause of acquired immune deficiency syndrome (AIDS). (TEM 29,640×)

FOCUS CONCEPT: *Interdependence of Organisms*

As you read, note how the structure and replication cycle of viruses distinguish them from living organisms.

25-1 **Structure**

25-2 **Viral Replication**

25-3 **Viruses and Human Disease**

STRUCTURE

*A **virus** is a nonliving particle composed of a nucleic acid and a protein coat. Although viruses are not living organisms, they are of interest to biologists because they cause many diseases in living organisms. Viruses are also quite useful in genetic research because they can change how a cell functions. The study of viruses is called **virology** (vie-RAH-luh-jee).*

OBJECTIVES

▲

Describe the structure and classification of viruses.

●

Describe the achievement of Wendell Stanley in the development of virology.

■

Identify the range of sizes and shapes among viruses.

◆

List the characteristics used to group viruses.

▲

Compare and contrast viroids and prions with viruses.

ADVENT OF VIROLOGY

By the late 1800s, scientists knew that some factor smaller than bacteria could transmit disease. But they lacked the technology to see these structures and to study them in depth. Scientists gained more awareness of the nature of viruses in 1935, when Wendell Stanley (1904–1971) crystallized the tobacco mosaic virus, an agent responsible for the mosaic mottling and withering of tobacco leaves. His work suggested that viruses might be chemicals rather than tiny cells. Until Stanley's crystallization of a virus, viruses were thought to be primitive cells that were perhaps ancestors of bacteria. Table 25-1 compares viruses with cells.

Virology now provides clues to the biochemistry of living organisms, including mutation, the combination of genetic material from different sources, and other essential processes of genetics. Also, pharmaceutical companies use viruses to develop new antiviral medications, and researchers continue to investigate the mechanisms of viral replication.

TABLE 25-1 *A Comparison of Viruses and Cells*

Characteristics of life	Virus	Cell
Growth	no	yes
Homeostasis	no	yes
Metabolism	no	yes
Mutation	yes	yes
Nucleic acid	DNA or RNA	DNA
Reproduction	only within host cell	independently by cell division
Structure	nucleic acid core, protein covering, and, in some cases, an envelope	cytoplasm, cell membrane, cytoskeleton, and, in the eukaryotic cell, organelles

FIGURE 25-1

This view of the human immuno-deficiency virus (HIV) displays some of the virus's structural features.

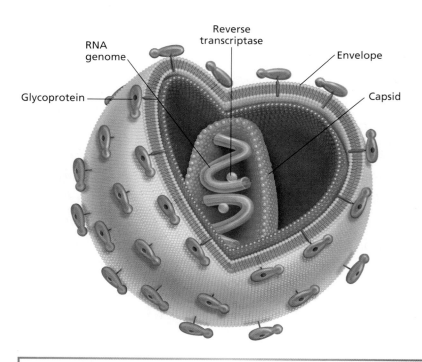

Reverse transcriptase

RNA genome

Envelope

Glycoprotein

Capsid

Word Roots and Origins

virus

from the Greek *ios*, meaning "poison"

Quick Lab

Calculating Nanometers

Materials meterstick with millimeter marks, paper, scissors, tape, pencil

Procedure Cut the paper into strips, and tape the strips together to form one strip that is 2 m long. On the paper, mark and label lines at 1 m, 20 cm, 2 cm, and 2 mm.

Analysis

1. Write an equation beside the 1 m line to show that 1 m contains 1 billion nanometers.

2. Write an equation at the end of the paper strip that shows the relationship between the length of the paper in meters and the length of the paper in nanometers.

3. How many nanometers are in 1 cm? How many nanometers are in 2 cm? in 20 cm? Write equations beside the 2 cm and the 20 cm marks to show the centimeter relationships to nanometers.

4. How many millimeters are in 1 m? How many nanometers are in 1 mm? How many nanometers are in 2 mm? Write an equation by the 2 mm mark to show its relationship to nanometers.

CHARACTERISTICS OF VIRUSES

Viruses are among the smallest biological particles capable of causing disease in living organisms. Viruses range in size from the extremely small poliovirus, which is 20 nm in diameter, to the large smallpox virus, which is about 250 nm in diameter—about the same size as the smallest bacterium. One nanometer is equal to 0.001 µm (0.00000004 in.).

Viruses are constructed of compounds usually associated with cells, but they are not considered living organisms. They have some, but not all, of the characteristics of life listed in Chapter 1. They have no nucleus, cytoplasm, organelles, or cell membrane, and they are not capable of carrying out cellular functions. Moreover, viruses are able to replicate only by infecting cells and using the organelles and enzymes within cells.

Viral Structure

All viruses have two essential features—a nucleic acid and a protein coat surrounding it. Viral nucleic acid may be either DNA or RNA, but not both. The shape of the nucleic acid may be helical, a closed loop, or a long strand, depending on the virus. The protein coat surrounding the nucleic acid is called a **capsid** (KAP-sid).

Some viruses have a membrane-like structure outside the capsid called an **envelope.** The envelope, which is made mostly of lipids, is taken from a host cell membrane during replication. The envelope allows new viruses to infect host cells during the first stage of viral replication. Enveloped viruses include influenza, chickenpox, herpes simplex, and **HIV** (human immunodeficiency virus). Refer to the model of HIV in Figure 25-1 to identify each of the viral structures.

On the surface of the envelope are projections made of glycoprotein. These **glycoprotein** (GLIE-koh-PROH-teen) projections are protein-containing sugar chains that the virus uses to attach to a host cell.

Viral Shape

A virus's shape may be determined by its capsid or its nucleic acid. Figure 25-2 shows two examples of virus shapes. Some viruses have the shape of an **icosahedron** (ie-KOH-suh-HEE-druhn), which is a geometric shape with 20 triangular faces. The viral capsid forms this shape. Icosahedral viruses include those that cause herpes simplex, chickenpox, and polio.

Other viruses are shaped like a **helix** (HEE-liks). A helix resembles a coiled spring. The viral nucleic acid is responsible for this shape. The rabies, measles, and tobacco mosaic viruses are helical viruses.

TOBACCO MOSAIC VIRUS
(helical)

POLIO VIRUS
(icosahedral)

FIGURE 25-2

Viruses occur in different shapes. Helical and icosahedral are two examples of virus shapes.

GROUPING VIRUSES

The grouping of viruses is based on the presence of a capsid structure and an envelope. Viruses are also grouped according to whether they contain RNA or DNA and whether the nucleic acid is single-stranded or double-stranded. Therefore, viruses are grouped based on their shape and structure. Some common viral groups are presented in Table 25-2.

Virus Types

DNA and RNA viruses differ in the way they use the host cell's machinery to produce new viruses. For example, upon entering the host cell, a DNA virus may act in one of two ways: the virus may directly produce RNA that then makes more viral proteins or it may join with the host cell's DNA to direct the synthesis of new viruses.

TABLE 25-2	*Some Common Viruses of Humans*		
Viral group	**Nucleic acid**	**Shape and structure**	**Examples of diseases they cause**
Papovaviruses	DNA	icosahedral, non-enveloped	warts, cancer
Adenoviruses	DNA	icosahedral, non-enveloped	respiratory and intestinal infections
Herpesviruses	DNA	icosahedral, enveloped	herpes simplex, chickenpox, shingles, infectious mononucleosis
Poxviruses	DNA	complex brick-shaped, enveloped	smallpox, cowpox
Picornaviruses	RNA	icosahedral, non-enveloped	poliomyelitis, hepatitis, cancer
Myxoviruses	RNA	helical, enveloped	influenza A, B, and C
Rhabdoviruses	RNA	helical, enveloped	rabies
Retroviruses	RNA	icosahedral, enveloped	AIDS, cancer

FIGURE 25-3

Viroids, which cause certain plant diseases, are infective RNA strands without capsids.

RNA viruses replicate differently from DNA viruses. Upon entering the host cell, viral RNA is released into the host cell's cytoplasm. There, it uses the host cell's ribosomes to produce new viral proteins.

Some RNA viruses, known as **retroviruses** (RE-troh-VIE-ruhs-uhz), contain an enzyme called reverse transcriptase in addition to RNA. **Reverse transcriptase** (tran-SKRIP-tays) uses RNA as a template to make DNA. The viral DNA is integrated into the host genome. The DNA then makes an RNA transcript of itself. This RNA is then translated into proteins that become part of new viruses. Reverse transcriptase is so named because it reverses the normal process of transcription, in which DNA serves as a template for producing RNA.

Viroids and Prions

Even simpler than viruses are the disease-causing agents called viroids and prions. **Viroids** (VIE-roidz) are the smallest known particles that are able to replicate. A viroid consists of a short, single strand of RNA and has no capsid, as shown in Figure 25-3. These simple RNA molecules are able to disrupt plant cell metabolism and damage entire crops. Economically important plants that have been affected by viroids include potatoes, cucumbers, avocados, and oranges.

Prions (PREE-ahnz) are abnormal forms of proteins that clump together inside a cell. This clumping activity eventually kills the cell, perhaps by blocking the cell's molecular traffic. Found on the surface of mammalian cells and in the brain of hosts, prions are composed of about 250 amino acids and have no associated nucleic acid.

Prions have been linked to certain diseases of the brain in humans and animals, such as scrapie. Scrapie is a disease in sheep that is characterized by slow degeneration of the nervous system. As the nervous system decays, the animals develop tremors and scrape their bodies against fence posts and tree trunks.

Bovine spongioform encephalopathy (BSE), or "mad cow disease," is a fatal brain disease of cattle that may be linked to prions. The prion that is thought to cause mad cow disease may be similar to one implicated in a human brain disease called Creutzfeld-Jakob (KROITZ-felt-YAK-ohb) disease (CJD).

SECTION 25-1 REVIEW

1. What are the two essential components of a virus?

2. What was the accomplishment of Wendell Stanley?

3. Explain how viruses are grouped.

4. What role do nucleic acids play in the grouping of viruses?

5. How do viroids and prions compare with viruses?

6. **CRITICAL THINKING** Are viruses considered to be living organisms? Justify your answer by referring to the characteristics of life presented in Chapter 1.

VIRAL REPLICATION

*Because viruses are not cells, they can replicate only by invading a host cell and using the enzymes and organelles of the host cell to make more viruses. Because they depend on host cells for replication, viruses are called **obligate intracellular parasites.** Outside the host cell, a virus is a lifeless particle with no control over its movements. It is spread by the wind, in water, in food, or via blood or other body secretions.*

OBJECTIVES

▲

Describe a bacteriophage.

●

Summarize the five phases of the lytic cycle.

■

Compare the lytic and lysogenic cycles of viral replication.

◆

Differentiate between a prophage and a provirus.

▲

Summarize how viruses may have evolved.

THE BACTERIOPHAGE

In the 1950s, scientists gained a better understanding of viral replication through their work with **bacteriophages** (bak-TEER-ee-uh-fay-juz), which are viruses that infect bacteria. Bacteriophage replication cycles have been found to be similar to those of the viruses that cause colds, measles, and acquired immune deficiency syndrome. The most commonly studied bacteriophages, T phages, are known to infect a bacterium found in the human digestive tract, *Escherichia coli.*

Examine the structure of the bacteriophage particle in Figure 25-4. Bacteriophages are composed of an icosahedral head that contains a nucleic acid. Beneath the head is a contractile tail that includes a collar and a sheath. The contractile tail helps inject the nucleic acid into the host cell. The tail rests on a base plate from which tail fibers emerge. These fibers assist the virus in attaching to a host cell. As you read about the replication cycles of bacteriophages, notice how the structure of the bacteriophage suits its function.

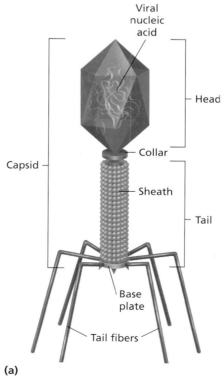

Viral nucleic acid

Head

Collar

Capsid

Sheath

Tail

Base plate

Tail fibers

(a)

FIGURE 25-4

(a) This diagram shows the structural complexity of a bacteriophage. (b) This transmission electron micrograph shows a cross section of an *E. coli* cell being attacked by several bacteriophages. Some of the bacteriophages can be seen developing within the cell's cytoplasm, and some can be seen outside the cell. (TEM 138,600×)

(b)

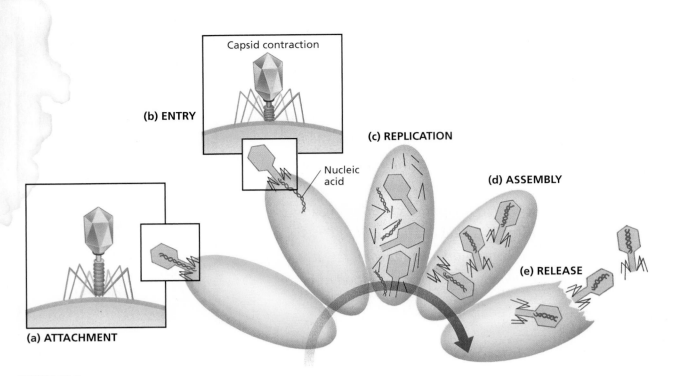

(b) ENTRY Capsid contraction

Nucleic acid

(c) REPLICATION

(d) ASSEMBLY

(e) RELEASE

(a) ATTACHMENT

FIGURE 25-5

The lytic cycle of a virulent bacterio-phage includes five steps: (a) attach-ment of the virus to a susceptible host cell, (b) entry of the viral DNA into the host cell, (c) replication of viral DNA, (d) assembly of new viruses, and (e) release of new viruses from a lysed host cell.

THE LYTIC CYCLE

During the **lytic cycle,** a virus invades a host cell, produces new viruses, destroys the host cell, and releases newly formed viruses. Viruses that undergo the lytic cycle are called **virulent** because they cause disease. The lytic cycle consists of five phases, as shown in Figure 25-5.

As Figure 25-5a shows, the bacteriophage first attaches to a sus-ceptible bacterium by attaching its tail fibers to a receptor site. **Receptor sites** are specific sites that viruses recognize and attach to on the host cell's surface. If the bacteriophage does not find a recep-tor site, it cannot infect the cell. This specificity is true for many other viruses. For example, hepatitis virus infects only liver cells, and the glycoproteins on the surface of HIV and influenza enable them to attach only to specific types of cells.

Next the bacteriophage releases an enzyme that weakens a spot in the cell wall of the host, as shown in Figure 25-5b. Then the phage presses its sheath against the cell and injects its DNA into the host cell through the weak spot in the cell wall. The bacterio-phage leaves its capsid outside the host cell.

As Figure 25-5c shows, the virus then takes control of the host's protein-synthesizing mechanisms, transcribing mRNA from the viral DNA. The resulting bacteriophage mRNA is translated by ribo-somes and enzymes in the host cell into viral proteins and enzymes that form bacteriophage capsids. The viral DNA in the host bacteria is also replicated during this phase.

The replicated viral genes are enclosed in the newly created virus capsids, as shown in Figure 25-5d. The assembly of new virus particles usually occurs in the cytoplasm, but it also may take place in a eukaryotic host cell's nucleus.

During the last phase of the lytic cycle, one of the enzymes that is produced by the bacteriophage genome causes the host cell to disintegrate, releasing the new bacteriophages. Cell disintegration, which is shown in Figure 25-5e, is called **lysis** (LIE-sis). In enveloped viruses, the newly formed viruses move to the cell surface and force their way through the cell membrane. As a result, the virus leaves the cell with a piece of the host cell membrane attached to the capsid. This "borrowed" cell membrane fragment becomes the viral envelope.

Word Roots and Origins

lysis

from the Greek *lysis,* meaning "loosening" or "dissolving"

THE LYSOGENIC CYCLE

Some viruses can infect a cell without causing its immediate destruction. Viruses that stay in their host cell for an extended period of time—days, months, or years—are in a **lysogenic** (lie-soh-JEN-ik) **cycle.** A virus that replicates through the lysogenic cycle and does not kill the host cell immediately is called a **temperate** virus. Examples of a DNA and an RNA virus replicating through the lysogenic cycle are discussed below.

Lysogeny in Bacteriophages

Temperate bacteriophages enter bacteria in the same way that a virulent bacteriophage does, as shown in Figures 25-6a and 25-6b. The tail fibers of the temperate bacteriophage attach to a specific receptor site on the bacterial cell wall. Then the bacteriophage injects its DNA into the host cell. Instead of immediately creating new RNA and viral proteins, however, the bacteriophage DNA integrates itself into the host cell's DNA, as shown in Figure 25-6c. The bacteriophage DNA molecule that integrates itself into a specific

FIGURE 25-6

The lysogenic cycle of a temperate bacteriophage involves (a) the attachment of the virus to the host cell, (b) injection of viral DNA, (c) integration of the viral DNA into the host genome, and (d) multiplication of the host cell with the viral DNA.

(a) ATTACHMENT — Bacteriophage

— Host cell

— Viral nucleic acid

Host cell genome

(b) INJECTION

(c) INTEGRATION

(d) CELL MULTIPLICATION

site of the host cell's genome is called a **prophage** (PROH-fahj). The prophage replicates whenever the host bacterium reproduces, as shown in Figure 25-6d. As the host DNA replicates, so does the viral DNA, and each bacterial offspring is infected with a prophage. During the lysogenic cycle, the prophage does not harm the host cell. However, radiation or certain chemicals can cause a prophage to become virulent. Figure 25-7 shows that when the prophage becomes virulent, it enters the lytic cycle, proceeding with replication and destroying the host cell.

Lysogeny in HIV

The normal lysogenic cycle usually involves DNA viruses, but it can also involve RNA viruses, such as HIV, the virus that causes AIDS. When HIV infects a susceptible white blood cell, it attaches to receptor sites on the host cell's surface and enters the cell by fusing with the cell membrane. Next, viral RNA and reverse transcriptase are released into the cell's cytoplasm. Reverse transcriptase then transcribes the viral RNA into DNA. Recall from Section 25-1 that reverse transcriptase uses RNA as a template to make DNA.

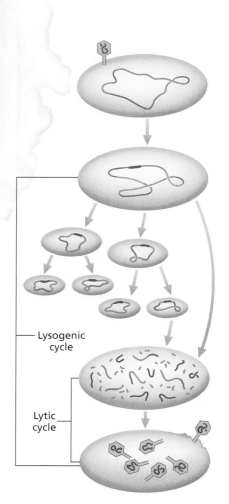

FIGURE 25-7

In the lysogenic cycle, a bacteriophage enters a cell and remains inactive in the host's genome until an external stimulus causes the virus to enter the lytic cycle.

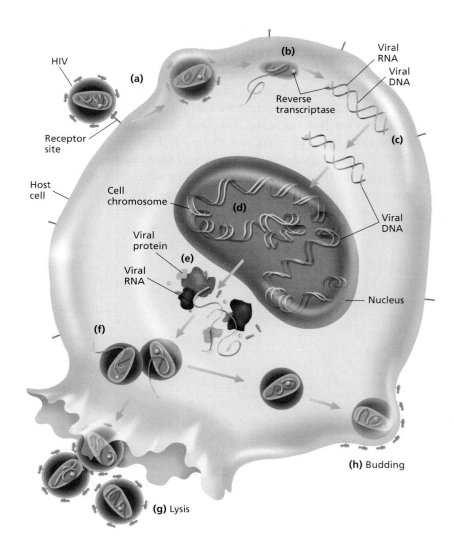

FIGURE 25-8

This figure traces the steps of HIV replication in a host cell. (a) HIV attaches to the receptor site. (b) The viral RNA is released from the capsid, and (c) reverse transcription takes place. (d) The viral DNA is integrated into the host genome. (e) Viral RNA and viral proteins are produced, and (f) viral assembly takes place. The assembled viral particles leave the cell through lysis (g) or budding (h).

As shown in Figure 25-8, the viral DNA molecule produced by reverse transcriptase inserts itself into the host cell's genome for an unspecified period of time. This viral DNA molecule is called a **provirus** (proh-VIE-rus). The lysogenic cycle ends when the provirus is transcribed into RNA and translated into viral proteins. These proteins are used in the assembly of new HIV particles containing capsids and enzymes. The new HIV particles are released after they lyse the cell or bud from the cell after taking a part of the cell's membrane for their viral envelope.

EVOLUTION

Because viruses depend on cells to replicate, most scientists reason that viruses evolved from early cells. The first viruses were probably naked pieces of nucleic acid that were able to travel from one cell to another, perhaps through damaged cell membranes. Over time, genes that allowed viruses to invade healthy cells evolved.

For example, when influenza viruses invade the human body, the immune system will destroy most of the viruses. However, a few of the viruses will escape destruction, enter cells, and begin producing thousands of copies of themselves within a few days.

How were a few viruses able to avoid destruction and begin replicating? These viruses are usually the result of mutations in the viral nucleic acid. Just as mutations in bacterial cells enable bacteria to become resistant to antibiotics, mutations in viruses can enable viruses to evade the immune system. Viruses that mutate quickly, such as the influenza virus and HIV, make it difficult for the immune system to immediately recognize and destroy them. The immune system will respond to the new strain of viruses eventually, but not until many new viruses are formed. Thus, it is difficult to develop vaccines that prevent these viral infections over long periods of time. To avoid this problem, the flu vaccine targets a different strain of influenza virus each year.

SECTION 25-2 REVIEW

1. Discuss the activities of a virus during the lytic cycle.

2. Compare and contrast the lytic and lysogenic cycles.

3. Describe the structure of a bacteriophage.

4. Explain the difference between a prophage and a provirus.

5. Discuss how the earliest viruses may have originated.

6. **CRITICAL THINKING**   During the lytic cycle, the assembly of new viral particles can sometimes take place in the host cell's nucleus. This assembly in the host cell's nucleus does not occur with bacteriophage particles. Why?

OBJECTIVES

▲

Name four viral diseases that result in serious illness in humans.

●

Compare the two types of viral vaccines, and discuss other forms of viral-disease prevention.

■

Discuss the relationship between viruses and cancer.

◆

Outline the onset of a virus outbreak.

VIRUSES AND HUMAN DISEASE

Viral diseases are among the most widespread illnesses in humans. These illnesses range from mild fevers to some forms of cancer and include several other severe and fatal diseases. Transmission of these illnesses varies; some are transmitted by human contact, while others are transmitted through water or an insect bite.

INFECTIOUS DISEASES

Many significant viral diseases are caused by viruses that use humans as their natural hosts. Some of the most common human viral diseases include the common cold, chickenpox, measles, mumps, polio, rabies, and hepatitis. Viral infections can affect various organs of the human body, including the brain, liver, heart, lungs, and the skin.

Rabies is transmitted from the bite of an infected animal, which carries the virus in its saliva. When a person is infected, the virus travels from the wound to the central nervous system. Symptoms of rabies include fever, headache, throat spasms, paralysis, and coma. Rabies is so lethal that few people have survived its effects.

Chickenpox is a highly contagious viral disease. The virus multiplies in the lungs and uses the network of blood vessels to reach the skin. Symptoms include fever and a skin rash. Transmission occurs from direct contact with the skin rash, which is the source of infectious virus particles, and through the air. Fortunately, the disease is usually mild, and recovery is usually followed by a lifelong resistance to reinfection. However, if all of the chickenpox virus is not destroyed, it can persist in the nerve cells as a provirus and cause a disease called shingles later during adulthood. Shingles results in a more severe case of chickenpox; the fever is higher, the immune system weakens, and pneumonia can occur. Like chickenpox, shingles is also defined by a skin rash. However, this painful rash is limited to an area of skin serviced by a particular neural pathway. For instance, the rash has been known to occur on only one side of the chest. The shingles rash can shed chickenpox viruses and infect susceptible children and adults. Note the characteristic skin rash of shingles in Figure 25-9.

FIGURE 25-9

The shingles rash, shown below, usually affects only one part of the body.

PREVENTION AND TREATMENT

The control of viral diseases is accomplished in two ways: vaccination to prevent disease and administration of **antiviral drugs**—drugs that interfere with viral nucleic acid synthesis—to infected patients. Unfortunately, there are few antiviral drugs compared with drugs used to treat bacterial, fungal, and parasitic infections. The most successful approach to controlling viral diseases has been prevention through vaccination. The Centers for Disease Control and Prevention in Atlanta, Georgia, is committed to the control and prevention of disease through research, as shown in Figure 25-10, and education.

Types of Virus Vaccines

As you will recall from Chapter 13, a vaccine is a preparation of pathogens or other materials that stimulates the body's immune system to provide protection against that pathogen. Some vaccines consist of inactivated or attenuated viruses. **Inactivated** viruses do not replicate in a host system. **Attenuated** viruses are viruses that have been genetically altered so that they are incapable of causing disease under normal circumstances. In general, vaccines made from attenuated viruses are preferred over those made from inactivated viruses because protection is greater and lasts longer. Additional doses of some vaccines, called booster shots, can extend a person's protection against some viruses.

By the 1960s, vaccines for measles, mumps, and rubella had been developed. The hepatitis B vaccine became available in the 1980s, and the chickenpox and hepatitis A vaccines were developed in the 1990s. Scientists continue to work on the development of an AIDS vaccine, but the genetic diversity and mutability of the virus create a problem for vaccine development. Educating people about HIV transmission is currently the best approach to slowing the spread of AIDS.

Smallpox Eradication Program

Smallpox once killed 40 percent of the people it infected, leaving the other 60 percent scarred and often blind. Smallpox is a DNA virus that is transmitted by nasal droplets emitted during sneezing and coughing. Symptoms include fever, headache, backache, and the development of a skin rash. This virus is hardy enough to be spread through infected blankets and clothing. Figure 25-11 shows a person infected with smallpox.

Vaccination played an important role in the eradication of smallpox. The World Health Organization began the smallpox eradication program in 1967. It ended in 1980, with the official declaration that smallpox had been eradicated. The program included vaccination and the quarantine of infected people. The last naturally acquired smallpox case occurred in Somalia in 1977.

FIGURE 25-10

This technician is working in a level-4 laboratory at the Centers for Disease Control and Prevention (CDC). Workers in a level-4 laboratory use the highest level of security procedures to protect themselves from the world's deadliest viruses, such as Lassa fever virus, Ebola virus, and smallpox virus.

Word Roots and Origins

vaccine

from the Latin *vaccinus*, which means "pertaining to cows"

FIGURE 25-11

Smallpox is characterized by lesions covering the face, shoulders, chest, and in a later stage, arms and legs.

FIGURE 25-12

This physician is administering two different antiviral drugs—DDI (didexoyinosine) and AZT (azidothymidine)—to this AIDS patient. Because of HIV's ability to rapidly adapt to antiviral drugs, it is often necessary to administer more than one drug at a time in order to reduce the amount of virus in a patient.

internet **connect**

SC**LINKS**
NSTA

TOPIC: AIDS virus
GO TO: www.scilinks.org
KEYWORD: HM498

Other Antiviral Approaches

One important part of viral disease prevention is the control of animals that spread viral disease. Yellow fever was completely eradicated in the United States through mosquito-control programs. Annual rabies vaccinations keep pets free of infection and protect humans too. Wildlife officials in the western part of the United States set out meat that contains an oral rabies vaccine to control the spread of rabies in coyotes and wolves.

Treatment of virally infected patients includes the use of antiviral agents. **Acyclovir** (ay-SIE-kloh-VEER) is used against herpes simplex and chickenpox, and **azidothymidine** (ay-ZIED-oh-THIE-mi-deen) **(AZT)** inhibits the reverse transcriptase of retroviruses, such as HIV. These drugs interfere with the synthesis of viral nucleic acids. Another class of drugs, called **protease inhibitors,** interferes with the synthesis of viral capsids during viral replication. Combinations of protease inhibitors and AZT have been shown to be helpful in slowing the progression from HIV infection (lysogenic phase) to AIDS (lytic phase). Figure 25-12 shows an AIDS patient undergoing treatment.

Antibiotics are not effective in the treatment of viral diseases. Antibiotics are used specifically to attack bacterial cells' metabolic machinery. Because viruses use only the host cell's machinery, antibiotics are of no use in destroying viruses.

EMERGING VIRUSES

As medical researchers work to find cures for existing viral diseases, newly discovered viruses are emerging in different parts of the world. Emerging viruses are viruses that exist in isolated habitats, but infect humans when these habitats are developed. For example, Figure 25-13 shows a tropical forest in the Democratic Republic of Congo (formerly Zaire), where the emerging Ebola virus has been known to exist. When these forests are cleared, humans may be exposed to virus-infected animals. If these viruses can infect humans, they may spread with deadly consequences.

FIGURE 25-13

The remote tropical forests of the Democratic Republic of Congo (formerly Zaire) are the hiding places of the deadly Ebola virus.

The AIDS Virus

The following is the introduction to Robert C. Gallo's article
"The AIDS Virus," from the January 1987 issue of *Scientific American.*

I
t is a modern plague: the first great pandemic of the second half of the 20th century. The flat, clinical-sounding name given to the disease by epidemiologists—acquired immune deficiency syndrome—has been shortened to the chilling acronym AIDS. First described in 1981, AIDS is probably the result of a new infection of human beings that began in central Africa, perhaps as recently as the 1950's. From there it probably spread to the Caribbean and then to the U.S. and Europe. By now as many as two million people in the U.S. may be infected. In the endemic areas of Africa and the Caribbean the situation is much worse. Indeed, in some areas it may be too late to prevent a disturbingly high number of people from dying.

In sharp contrast to the bleak epidemiological picture of AIDS, the accumulation of knowledge about its cause has been remarkably quick. Only three years after the disease was described its cause was conclusively shown to be the third human retrovirus: human *T*-lymphotropic virus III (HTLV-III), which is also called human immunodeficiency virus (HIV). Like other retroviruses, HTLV-III has RNA as its genetic material. When the virus enters its host cell, a viral enzyme called reverse transcriptase exploits the viral RNA as a template to assemble a corresponding molecule of DNA. The DNA travels to the cell nucleus and inserts itself among the host's chromosomes, where it provides the basis for viral replication.

In the case of HTLV-III the host cell is often a *T*4 lymphocyte, a white blood cell that has a central role in regulating the immune system. Once it is inside a *T*4 cell, the

virus may remain latent until the lymphocyte is immunologically stimulated by a secondary infection. Then the virus bursts into action, reproducing itself so furiously that the new virus particles escaping from the cell riddle the cellular membrane with holes and the lymphocyte dies. The resulting depletion of *T*4 cells—the hallmark of AIDS—leaves the patient vulnerable to "opportunistic" infections by agents that would not harm a healthy person.

How HTLV-III manages to replicate in a single burst after lying low, sometimes for years, is one of the most fundamental questions confronting AIDS researchers. Another important question is the full spectrum of diseases with which the virus is associated. Although most of the attention given to the virus has gone to AIDS, HTLV-III is also associated with brain disease and several types of cancer. In spite of such lingering questions, more is known about the AIDS virus than is known about any other retrovirus. The rapidity of that scientific advance was made possible partly by the discovery in 1978 of the first human retrovirus, HTLV-I, which causes leukemia. In its turn the new knowledge is making possible the measures that are desperately needed to treat AIDS and prevent its spread.

Reading for Meaning
What does Gallo mean by "opportunistic" infections? Use Gallo's description and the context of the article to figure it out.

Read Further
Gallo's article tells what was known about the AIDS virus in 1987. What new information might be included in a follow-up article about the AIDS virus today?

TABLE 25-3 *Viruses Linked to Human Cancers*

Type of virus	Mode of transmission	Type of cancer
Human T lymphotropic	mother-to-child transmission, body fluids, sexual contact	leukemia
Hepatitis B	body fluids, sexual contact, mother-to-child transmission	liver cancer
Epstein-Barr	physical contact	Burkitt's lymphoma
Human papillomavirus	sexual contact	cervical cancer

Examples of emerging viruses include hantavirus, which caused an outbreak of pneumonia in the southwestern United States in 1993; Machupo virus, which exists in South America; HIV, which originated in Africa; Ebola virus, which is found in Africa; and Lassa fever virus, which exists in West Africa. There are four known strains of the Ebola virus, all of which probably evolved from a common ancestor. One of these strains sickens only monkeys, but the other three strains are deadly to humans. Ebola's sudden emergence within the population of the Democratic Republic of Congo has left medical researchers puzzled over the identity of the animal host that carried the original Ebola virus strain.

VIRUSES AND CANCER

Recall that cancer is a condition that results from the uncontrolled reproduction of cells, which invade surrounding tissue. Scientists believe that cancers may be traced to genes within normal cells. When these genes are mutated by an outside agent, such as cigarette smoke, asbestos, sunlight, chemicals, or radiation, they may stimulate the cells to multiply uncontrollably. Cancer genes may also be triggered by certain lysogenic viruses. Some viruses associated with cancer are summarized in Table 25-3.

SECTION 25-3 REVIEW

1. List two diseases that are the result of a viral attack on the human nervous system.

2. Discuss the differences between attenuated and inactivated viruses.

3. Why are antibiotics not effective in the treatment of viral diseases?

4. Explain how human actions have contributed to the increase of emerging viral diseases.

5. Which replication cycle are viruses found in when they stimulate the activation of cancer genes?

6. CRITICAL THINKING Consider how emerging viruses develop. Would you consider emerging viruses to be new viruses? Why or why not?

CHAPTER 25 REVIEW

SUMMARY/VOCABULARY

25-1
- Viruses are biological particles composed of nucleic acid and a protein coat. Enveloped viruses also have a membrane enclosing them.
- Viruses are not usually considered living organisms because they lack most of the characteristics of living things.
- Wendell Stanley was the first scientist to report the crystallization of tobacco mosaic virus in 1935. This suggested that viruses might be chemicals rather than primitive cells.
- Viruses range in size from about 20 nm to about 250 nm in diameter.
- Many viruses have the shape of an icosahedron, which is a geometric figure contain-

ing 20 triangular faces. Other viruses take the shape of a helix, which resembles a coiled spring.
- Some viruses include a membrane-like envelope, with glycoprotein projections extending from the envelope.
- Viruses are grouped into families based on their nucleic acid type, their capsid structure, and the presence or absence of an envelope.
- Viruses probably originated from fragments of host-cell nucleic acid material.
- Viroids are viruslike particles composed of RNA only. Prions are pathogenic particles composed of protein only.

Vocabulary

capsid (488)　　helix (489)　　prion (490)　　viroid (490)
envelope (488)　　HIV (488)　　retrovirus (490)　　virology (487)
glycoprotein (489)　　icosahedron (489)　　reverse transcriptase (490)　　virus (487)

25-2
- Bacteriophages are viruses that infect bacteria. Their discovery has increased scientists' understanding of virus replication.
- Replication by viruses occurs by either the lytic cycle or the lysogenic cycle.
- During the lytic cycle, the viral genome is released into the host cell, and replication of the virus follows immediately. Cellular components are used to make new viruses. A viral enzyme then causes host cell lysis and death.

- HIV infects specific white blood cells and remains in them as proviruses. As the immune system begins to fail, opportunistic infections occur; this condition is called AIDS.
- In the lysogenic cycle, the nucleic acid of the virus becomes part of the host cell's chromosome and remains with the cell in this form for many generations. HIV follows this pattern.

Vocabulary

bacteriophage (491)　　lytic cycle (492)　　prophage (494)　　temperate (493)
lysis (493)　　obligate intracellular　　provirus (495)　　virulent (492)
lysogenic cycle (493)　　parasite (491)　　receptor site (492)

25-3
- Vaccination and antiviral drug therapy are two major approaches to controlling and preventing the spread of viral diseases.
- Emerging viruses do not usually infect humans, but they can when environmental

conditions favor their contact with and infection of human populations.
- Several viruses are implicated in the development of cancers such as leukemia, Burkitt's lymphoma, and liver cancer.

Vocabulary

acyclovir (498)　　attenuated (497)　　inactivated (497)
antiviral drug (497)　　azidothymidine (AZT) (498)　　protease inhibitor (498)

REVIEW

Vocabulary

1. In a dictionary, look up the words *obligate, intracellular,* and *parasite,* and relate virus activity to the meaning of these words.
2. Viral infection is usually very specific. Identify the structure of the cell surface that permits only specific viruses to infect it.
3. Distinguish a virus from a provirus.
4. Use what you know about the meaning of the word *lysis* to explain the meanings of *lytic* and *lysogenic* cycles. If necessary, use your dictionary to help you.
5. Explain the meaning of the term *reverse transcriptase.*

Multiple Choice

6. A virus is a biologically active particle composed of (a) enzymes and fats (b) mitochondria and lysosomes (c) protein and nucleic acid (d) carbohydrates and ATP.
7. Which of the following was a key event in the development of virology? (a) the discovery of ribosomes (b) the discovery of nutrient agar (c) the crystallization of a virus (d) the discovery of protein structure
8. The term *icosahedron* refers to the structure of the viral (a) nucleic acid (b) capsid (c) lipid layer (d) receptor site.
9. Certain viruses have reverse transcriptase, an enzyme that (a) synthesizes RNA using DNA as a template (b) unites viral DNA with host DNA (c) synthesizes DNA using RNA as a template (d) assists the release of viruses from the host cell.
10. An essential aspect of viral replication is the (a) release of the viral nucleic acid in the cytoplasm of the host cell (b) entry of the viral envelope to the cytoplasm of the host cell (c) union of the viral envelope with the nuclear membrane of the cell (d) release of the viral capsid into the host cell nucleus.
11. Viroids differ from viruses in their (a) larger size (b) absence of a capsid (c) absence of nucleic acids (d) ability to cause disease in plants.
12. The head region of a bacteriophage is used to (a) attach the phage to the bacterial wall (b) enclose the nucleic acid (c) transmit the nucleic acid to the bacterium (d) take over the genetic machinery of the cell.
13. Lysis refers to the disintegration of (a) the bacteriophage capsid on entering the cell (b) the DNA of the host cell (c) a bacteriophage enzyme (d) the host cell.
14. Temperate viruses are those that (a) take over the genetic machinery of the host cell (b) are composed solely of protein (c) attach themselves to the ribosomes of the host cell (d) integrate their viral genes into the DNA of the host cell.
15. One virus that participates in the lysogenic cycle is (a) the measles virus (b) the rabies virus (c) HIV (d) the polio virus.

Short Answer

16. Explain the activity of reverse transcriptase.
17. Describe the structure of HIV.
18. DNA and RNA viruses differ in the way that they utilize the host cell's machinery to produce new viruses. Explain these differences.
19. Name the animal diseases that result from prion activity.
20. Identify the lettered steps in the figure below and identify the cycle.

(a)

(b)

(c)

(d)

_____ CYCLE

21. What are some of the useful attributes of viruses?

22. Distinguish between a virulent virus and a temperate virus.

23. What causes a temperate bacteriophage to become virulent?

24. Explain the methods humans use to control viral diseases.

25. What agents can trigger cells to multiply uncontrollably?

CRITICAL THINKING

1. Some people suggest that the drug AZT (azidothymidine) can help patients infected with HIV. This drug blocks the enzyme reverse transcriptase. Explain how AZT might help HIV-infected patients.

2. People who have had a hepatitis B viral infection have a greater chance of developing liver cancer later in life, especially if they are exposed to aflatoxin. Aflatoxin is a mold toxin found in some foods, such as contaminated peanuts. What does this relationship suggest to you about the role of the hepatitis virus in causing cancer?

3. Lambda is a bacteriophage that attacks *E. coli* and may enter a lysogenic cycle. Once it enters the lysogenic cycle, the phage inhibits the entry of more phages. What is the evolutionary advantage to the phage of "immunizing" its host against further lambda infections?

4. Shingles is a disease caused by the same herpes virus that causes chickenpox. How do you account for the fact that shingles often appears years after the initial chickenpox attack?

5. Based on your knowledge of HIV structure and replication, describe one way to interrupt the replication of HIV.

6. Based on your understanding of virus replication, how might scientists cultivate or artificially reproduce viruses in the laboratory?

7. Look at the graph below. Discuss how the sharp jump in the number of viruses outside the cell corresponds to the phases of the lytic cycle.

Growth Curve of Viruses

Number of viruses outside the cell

Time

EXTENSION

1. Read "What New Things Are Going to Kill Me?" in *Time,* November 8, 1999, on page 86. Explain why Richard Preston thinks that new microbes are the ticking time bomb in the new century.

2. Call your local hospital or family doctor, and ask how viral diseases are diagnosed. If possible, visit the clinical laboratory of a hospital to see how the tests are done.

3. Research and write a report on a preventable viral disease, such as polio or smallpox. In your report, discuss the process scientists followed in identifying the cause of the disease, isolating the virus, formulating a vaccine, and testing the vaccine.

4. Read "Down but Not Out" in *New Scientist,* February 5, 2000, on page 20. The World Health Organization plans to eradicate polio by 2005 and stop vaccinating people. Explain why some polio experts believe that stopping vaccinations is unwise, even though the disease has been eradicated.

Tobacco Mosaic Virus

OBJECTIVES

- Study the effect of cigarette tobacco on leaves of tobacco plants.

PROCESS SKILLS

- observing
- comparing and contrasting
- experimenting

MATERIALS

- lab apron
- protective gloves
- safety goggles
- 2 tobacco or tomato plants
- glass-marking pencil
- tobacco from several brands of cigarettes
- mortar and pestle
- 10 mL 0.1 M dibasic potassium phosphate solution
- 100 mL beaker
- cotton swabs
- 400 grit carborundum powder

Background

1. The tobacco mosaic virus, TMV, infects tobacco as well as other plants.
2. Plants that are infected with TMV have lesions and yellow patches on their leaves.
3. In what form do viruses exist outside host cells?

4. The tobacco mosaic virus is an RNA virus with rod-shaped capsids and proteins arranged in a spiral.
5. Plants damaged by wind, low temperatures, injury, or insects are more susceptible to plant viruses than healthy plants are.
6. Plant viruses are transmitted by insects, gardening tools, inheritance from the parent, and sexual reproduction.
7. Most viral diseases in plants have no known cures, but scientists are breeding various genetic forms of plants that are resistant to certain viruses.
8. Describe how viruses spread among organisms.
9. In this investigation, you will test whether tobacco from cigarettes can infect tobacco plants with TMV.

PART A Setting Up the Experiment

1. Put on a lab apron, gloves, and goggles before beginning this investigation.
2. Obtain two tobacco plants that have not been infected with TMV. Label one of the plants "control plant." Label the other plant "experimental plant."
3. CAUTION **Use poisonous chemicals with extreme caution. Keep your hands away from your face when handling plants or chemical mixtures.** Place pinches of tobacco from different brands of cigarettes into a mortar. Add 5 mL of dibasic potassium phosphate solution, and grind the mixture with a pestle as shown in the figure at left.
4. Pour the mixture into a labeled beaker. This mixture can be used to test whether cigarette tobacco can infect plants with TMV.
5. Wash your hands and all laboratory equipment used in this step with soap and water to avoid the accidental spread of the virus.
6. Moisten a sterile cotton swab with the mixture, and sprinkle a small amount of carborundum powder onto the moistened swab. Apply the mixture to two leaves on the "experimental" plant by swabbing the surface of the leaves several times. Why do you think swabbing the leaves with carborundum powder might facilitate infection?

7. Moisten a clean swab with dibasic potassium phosphate solution, and sprinkle a small amount of carborundum powder onto the moistened swab. This swab should *not* come into contact with the mixture of cigarette tobacco. Swab over the surface of two leaves on the control plant several times.

8. Do not allow the control plants to touch the experimental plants. Keep both plants away from other plants that may be in your investigation area, such as houseplants or garden plants. Wash your hands after handling each plant to avoid the accidental spread of TMV.

9. Treat both plants in precisely the same manner. The only difference between the two plants should be the experimental factor—exposure to cigarette tobacco. Both plants should receive the same amount of light and water.

10. Clean up your materials according to your teacher's instructions and wash your hands before leaving the lab.

PART B   Collecting Data

11. In your lab report, create a data table similar to the model shown below. Allow plenty of space to record your observations of each plant.

12. Check the control and experimental plants each day for one week. Record your observations of each plant in your lab report. Wash your hands after handling each plant to prevent contaminating your results.

Analysis and Conclusions

1. What differences, if any, did you detect in the two plants after one week?

2. Did the plants exposed to cigarette tobacco become infected with the tobacco mosaic virus?

3. Why do you think it was necessary to use tobacco from different brands of cigarettes?

4. What are some of the possible sources of error in the experiment?

5. Greenhouse operators generally do not allow smoking in their greenhouses. Aside from health and safety issues, how might your results support this practice?

Further Inquiry

The tobacco mosaic virus is capable of infecting different species of plants. Design an experiment to determine which of several types of plants are susceptible to the virus.

	OBSERVATIONS OF TOBACCO PLANTS	
Day	**Control plants**	**Experimental plants**
1		
2		
3		
4		
5		
6		
7		

PROTOZOA

Stentor *displays two of the characteristics of protozoa, unicellularity and lack of tissue differentiation.*

FOCUS CONCEPT: *Structure and Function*

As you read this chapter, note the wide variations in the shape, size, structure, and adaptations of protozoa as well as the features they have in common.

26-1 *Overview of Protozoa*

26-2 *Protozoan Diversity*

OVERVIEW OF PROTOZOA

*The kingdom Protista contains a diverse collection of eukaryotic organisms—protozoa, algae, slime molds, and water molds. Collectively, these organisms are called **protists.** Protists are sometimes described as animal-like, plantlike, and funguslike. However, all protists are eukaryotic and lack tissue differentiation.*

SECTION

26-1

OBJECTIVES

▲

Describe the characteristics of protozoa.

●

Explain the role some protozoa play in aquatic ecosystems.

■

Discuss a classification scheme used to identify protozoa.

◆

Name an adaptation that enables some protozoa to survive harsh environmental conditions.

▲

Briefly explain the evolution of protozoa.

CHARACTERISTICS

Protozoa are single-celled microscopic organisms that are noted for their ability to move independently. Biologists have identified about 65,000 species of protozoa, almost half of which are extinct species identified from fossils. Protozoa live in many different environments; they can drift in the ocean, creep across vegetation in freshwater rivers and ponds, crawl in deep soil, and even reproduce in the bodies of other organisms. The protozoan shown in Figure 26-1 lives in the gut of termites.

Most protozoans are heterotrophic, obtaining their nutrients by ingesting small molecules or cells. These particles are usually broken down in **food vacuoles,** membrane-bound chambers that contain digestive enzymes.

Many species of protozoa are free-living, while others are parasitic. Free-living protozoa live in any habitat where water is available at some time during the year. Many species make up **zooplankton,** a population of organisms that constitutes one of the primary sources of energy in aquatic ecosystems. Other free-living protozoa live in the soil. Parasitic protozoa usually have complex life cycles that take place in the cells, tissues, and bloodstream of their hosts. Several species cause a variety of serious human diseases, including malaria, amebic dysentery, and giardiasis.

Reproduction

All protozoa are capable of asexual reproduction, usually by binary fission. During binary fission, a protozoan divides into two essentially identical individuals. Some species reproduce by **multiple fission,** a form of cell division that results in a number of identical individuals.

While all protozoa can reproduce asexually, a few species also reproduce sexually, through **conjugation.** During conjugation in protozoa, individuals from opposite mating strains pair and exchange genetic material. Conjugation in protozoa is a more complex process than conjugation in bacteria.

FIGURE 26-1

The phylum Zoomastigina includes *Trichonympha,* a protozoan that inhabits the gut of termites and helps the termite digest the cellulose in its diet.

(a) *Zoothamnium*, a ciliate

(b) *Plasmodium*, a sporozoan

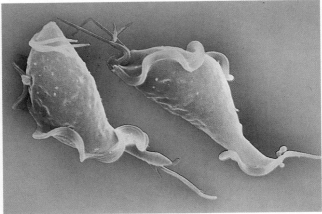

(c) *Trichomonas vaginalis*, a zooflagellate

(d) *Amoeba proteus*, a sarcodine

FIGURE 26-2

These organisms are representatives of the four phyla of protozoa.

Classification

Protozoa are members of the kingdom Protista, along with algae, slime molds, and water molds. Research into the evolutionary relationships among these organisms is constantly yielding new information and altering protistan classification. For this reason, biologists are always reevaluating the classification scheme. Protozoa are sometimes classified into four phyla: Sarcodina (SAHR-kuh-DIEN-uh), Ciliophora (sil-ee-AHF-uhr-uh), Zoomastigina (ZOH-uh-mas-tuh-JIEN-uh), and Sporozoa (spor-uh-ZOH-uh). A representative of each group is shown in Figure 26-2. The characteristics of these four phyla, along with representative genera, are summarized in Table 26-1.

Adaptations

Many species of protozoa have physiological mechanisms for monitoring conditions in their environment. For example, many free-living species have a localized region of pigment called an **eyespot.** Eyespots detect changes in the quantity and quality of light. Certain protozoan species also sense physical and chemical changes or obstacles in their environment. For instance, some protozoa will back up and bypass a noxious chemical.

Most protozoa are separated from their environment only by their delicate external cell membrane. These fragile organisms can survive in environments where extreme conditions often exist.

TABLE 26-1　A Summary of Protozoa

Phylum	Common name	Locomotion	Nutrition type	Representative genera
Sarcodina	sarcodines	pseudopodia	heterotrophic; some parasitic	*Amoeba* *Radiolaria* *Naegleria*
Ciliophora	ciliates	cilia	heterotrophic; some parasitic	*Paramecium* *Tetrahymena* *Balantidium*
Zoomastigina	zooflagellates	flagella	heterotrophic; some parasitic	*Trypanosoma* *Leishmania* *Giardia* *Trichonympha*
Sporozoa	sporozoans	(none in adult)	heterotrophic; some parasitic	*Plasmodium* *Toxoplasma*

Their hardiness is in part due to their ability to form cysts. A **cyst** is a dormant form characterized by a hardened external covering in which metabolic activity has ceased. Many species of protozoa form cysts in response to changes in the environment, such as nutrient deficiency, drought, decreased oxygen concentration, or pH or temperature changes. Cyst formation is extremely important to many protozoa that must survive such conditions between hosts. When favorable environmental conditions return, a protozoan emerges from the cyst and resumes metabolic activities.

Evolution

As you learned in Chapter 14, the first prokaryotes evolved more than 3.5 billion years ago. These organisms were the only life-forms on Earth for almost 2 billion years. About 1.5 billion years ago, the first eukaryotic organisms evolved. Protozoa are the descendants of these early eukaryotes. The first eukaryotes probably evolved through endosymbiosis, a process in which one prokaryote lives inside another and gradually both host and guest become dependent on one another.

Word Roots and Origins

cyst

from the Greek *kystis,* meaning "sac"

SECTION 26-1 REVIEW

1. What kind of organisms are found in the kingdom Protista? What characteristics do they share?

2. What are protozoa? How do they reproduce? What kinds of environments do they inhabit?

3. What role do some protozoa play in aquatic environments?

4. What is a cyst? Under what conditions might certain protozoa form cysts?

5. Why are protozoa considered some of the oldest existing life-forms?

6. **CRITICAL THINKING**　On what basis can protozoa be classified? Does this classification scheme reflect evolutionary relationships among protozoa?

The Origin of Eukaryotic Cells

HISTORICAL PERSPECTIVE

In the late nineteenth and early twentieth centuries, French, Russian, and American scientists speculated that mitochondria contained hereditary information similar to that found in the nucleus. They hypothesized that mitochondria evolved as a result of a symbiotic relationship between different types of bacteria. Attempts to culture mitochondria were unsuccessful, and given the popular view of bacteria as agents of disease, scientists generally disregarded the hypothesis that mitochondria evolved from symbiotic bacteria.

A "Dead" Hypothesis Reappears

In the 1950s, as an undergraduate at the University of Chicago, Lynn Margulis became interested in genetics and inheritance through her readings of the works of noted scientists. Although she had started college when she was only 15 years old, Margulis was not intimidated by the complexity of genetics. As a graduate student in genetics at the Universities of Wisconsin and California, she began to question well-established ideas about heredity and evolution. While at the University of Wisconsin, Margulis

became aware of patterns of inheritance in components of the cytoplasm in plants and algae that did not seem to result from genes in the nucleus. After discussing her observations with her advisor, cell biologist Hans Ris, she concluded that the cytoplasm contains genes that function separately from those in the nucleus.

Using an electron microscope, Margulis and Ris were able to study chloroplasts and mitochondria in detail. They observed that both of these organelles have properties in common with modern bacteria. Both chloroplasts and mitochondria con-

tain ribosomes and circular DNA, and they reproduce by binary fission.

These observations, along with the papers of biologists who had earlier suggested that hereditary information could be found in the cytoplasm, led Margulis to infer that the genes in chloroplasts and mitochondria may have had a different evolutionary origin than the genes in the nucleus. Margulis developed a hypothesis referred to as serial endosymbiosis. In this hypothesis, she proposed that eukaryotes evolved from symbiotic relationships established between anaerobic bacteria and intracellular aerobic bacteria.

| Small aerobic prokaryote | Mitochondrion | Small photosynthetic prokaryote | Chloroplasts |

LARGE PROKARYOTE   PRE-EUKARYOTE   PRE-EUKARYOTE   Mitochondria   PRIMITIVE EUKARYOTE

The Evolution of Mitochondria and Chloroplasts

To explain the selective pressure for endosymbiosis, Margulis hypothesized that there was an "oxygen holocaust" on Earth about two billion years ago. The amount of oxygen in the atmosphere increased sharply, probably as a result of bacterial photosynthesis. The rise in oxygen levels killed most bacteria—but not all bacteria. Some small, oxygen-utilizing bacteria invaded larger, anaerobic or nonoxygen-utilizing bacteria. Although many of the anaerobic bacteria were unable to adapt to their new "guests" and died, a few survived and became a living food source for the invaders. In effect, the larger bacteria became hosts to parasitic aerobic bacteria. In turn, the invading, aerobic bacteria supplied some of the energy derived from their aerobic respiration to the host cell. Margulis proposed that these aerobic invaders may have been the evolutionary forerunners of modern mitochondria.

Margulis further hypothesized that chloroplasts evolved from an ancient invasion—this time by small, photosynthetic bacteria similar to modern blue-green bacteria. Thus, in addition to energy-producing components (the primitive mitochondria), the large host cells now had components that could produce food using simple molecules and the energy from sunlight. These increasingly complex host cells were primitive eukaryotes, the ancestors of modern algae and plants. What began as a parasitic relationship evolved to the mutual benefit of both host and parasite, resulting in the emergence of eukaryotic cells.

An Unpopular Idea

Margulis's article presenting her hypothesis was rejected by 15 journals before it was published in 1966 in the *Journal of Theoretical Biology.* In 1970, when she published an expanded account of her hypothesis in a book called *Origin of Eukaryotic Cells,* most biologists still rejected her ideas because of the absence of fossil evidence to support it.

In defending her hypothesis, Margulis cited experiments performed by Kwang Jeon, of the University of Tennessee. Jeon had infected a species of amoeba with a bacterial parasite. By culturing those amoebas that survived the infection, Jeon eventually produced a line of amoebas that were actually dependent on the bacteria for survival. Essentially, symbiosis and the selection that followed produced a new kind of amoeba in five years. Other studies in the late 1960s supported Margulis's endosymbiosis hypothesis.

By 1981, when Margulis published a revised version of her book, titled *Symbiosis in Cell Evolution,* her hypothesis was supported by a wealth of evidence and had become widely accepted. Since then, many more reports of endosymbiotic relationships have been published.

In one recent study, scientists at the University of Pennsylvania found evidence of endosymbiosis between protozoa and green algae. DNA from a previously unknown organelle in protozoa was identified as being similar to DNA found in algae plastids.

A Fast-Changing Science

In her preface to the 1992 edition of *Symbiosis in Cell Evolution,* Margulis refers to significant changes in biology. She calls the difference between prokaryotes and eukaryotes the most fundamental division in the organization of the living world. This certainly is a big change from the time when biologists considered the division of plants and animals to be the most basic division. As Margulis and others continue to explore microorganisms, there will undoubtedly be other changes in our understanding of the evolution of life.

Kwang Jeon provided experimental evidence that supported Margulis's hypothesis of evolution through endosymbiosis.

SECTION

26-2

OBJECTIVES

▲

Explain how sarcodines
have contributed to
Earth's geological features.

●

Describe a type of
sexual reproduction
that occurs in ciliates.

■

Identify four human diseases
caused by zooflagellates.

◆

Discuss the life cycle
of *Plasmodium*.

PROTOZOAN DIVERSITY

The broad diversity of protozoa is evident in the four major phyla identified by biologists. The phyla are distinguished by their form of locomotion, and each group contains a number of parasites that cause serious human diseases. The complexity of protozoa sets them apart from the relatively simple structures of bacteria and viruses.

PHYLUM SARCODINA

Biologists have classified 40,000 species of protozoa in the phylum Sarcodina (SAHR-kuh-DIE-nuh). Sarcodines include hundreds of species of amoebas, which inhabit fresh water, salt water, and soil. One of the most unusual sarcodines is *Pelomyxa carolinensis,* shown in Figure 26-3. These protozoa are found living on mud, rocks, and other surfaces in shallow, slow-moving streams and ponds.

Most sarcodines have flexible cell membranes and are constantly thrusting out **pseudopodia** (SOO-duh-POH-dee-uh). Pseudopodia are large, rounded cytoplasmic extensions that function in movement. A pseudopodium forms when the **endoplasm,** the inner portion of the cytoplasm, pushes the **ectoplasm,** the outer layer, forward to create a blunt, armlike extension. Simultaneously, other pseudopodia retract, and the cytoplasm flows in the direction of the new pseudopodium. This form of movement, referred to as **ameboid movement,** is illustrated in Figure 26-4. Ameboid movement is a form of **cytoplasmic streaming,** the internal flowing of a cell's cytoplasm.

Sarcodines also use pseudopodia for feeding. Sarcodines live on other protists, which they engulf by phagocytosis. When a sarcodine feeds, it surrounds the food with its pseudopodia. A portion of the cell membrane then pinches together and surrounds the food in a food vacuole, in a process called endocytosis. Enzymes from the cytoplasm then enter the vacuole and digest the food. Undigested food leaves the cell in a reverse process called exocytosis.

Most freshwater sarcodines have an internal structure that is similar to that of the amoeba shown in Figure 26-4. Notice the **contractile vacuole,** an organelle that expels fluid from the cell. Freshwater organisms are usually hypertonic relative to their environment, so water diffuses into them. To maintain homeostasis, many freshwater protozoa have contractile vacuoles that rid the cell of excess water.

FIGURE 26-3

Sarcodines, such as this *Pelomyxa,* are characterized by cytoplasmic extensions called pseudopodia. By thrusting pseudopodia outward, a sarcodine can move across a surface or capture prey. (240×)

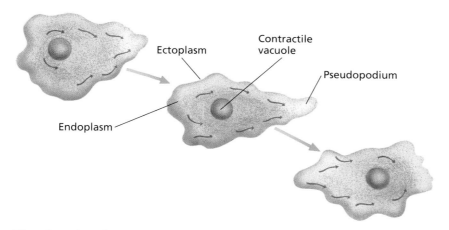

FIGURE 26-4

Ectoplasm

Contractile
vacuole

Pseudopodium

Endoplasm

Ameboid movement is powered by cytoplasmic streaming (indicated here with arrows). As the cytoplasm surges forward to form a new tubelike pseudopodium, other pseudopodia retract.

Ecological Role

Many sarcodines are "naked," that is, their cell membranes are exposed directly to the environment. Some have their delicate cell membranes covered with a protective **test,** or shell. For example, **foraminifera** (FOHR-a-MIN-i-fohr-uh) are an ancient group of shelled sarcodines found primarily in oceans. Their tests, shown in Figure 26-5, have many chambers and are made of calcium carbonate. Slender pseudopodia extend through tiny openings in the test. The group of sarcodines called **radiolarians** (RAY-dee-OH-LER-ee-uhnz) is among the oldest known. Most radiolarians live in shallow, open water. Their tests contain silicon dioxide and usually have a radial arrangement of spines that extend through the shell. One example of their intricate tests is shown in Figure 26-6.

Foraminifera and radiolarians have existed since Precambrian times (more than 600 million years ago) and have left excellent fossil records. For millions of years, the tests of dead foraminifera have been sinking to the bottom of the ocean, where they have built up a calcium-rich layer of sediment. These sedimentary layers can be seen as limestone and chalk deposits that formed in the sea and later emerged as dry land. The chalk deposits in many areas of England, including the White Cliffs of Dover, were formed in this way. The Great Pyramids of Egypt were built with stones quarried from limestone beds that are made of a type of large foraminiferan that flourished during the early Tertiary period (between 7 and 70 million years ago). The tests of dead radiolarians have contributed to the formation of a type of rock called chert.

Human Diseases

Although most amoebas are free-living, some species live in the intestines of humans or other animals. One such amoeba, *Entamoeba histolytica,* can cause serious illness in humans. This amoeba enters the body via contaminated food and water. It lives in the large intestine, where it secretes enzymes that attack the intestinal lining and cause deep ulcers. If this occurs, a sometimes fatal disease called **amebic dysentery** may result. Affected individuals feel intense pain, and complications arise when the amoebas are carried by the blood to the liver and other organs.

FIGURE 26-5

Foraminifera once inhabited these hard shells called tests.

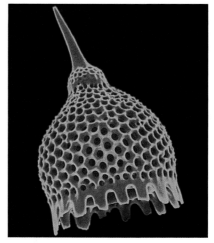

FIGURE 26-6

The phylum Sarcodina includes radiolarians, such as the one shown above, which are also covered by protective tests.

FIGURE 26-7

Like all ciliates, paramecia such as *Paramecium* above move by using short, hairlike projections called cilia.

FIGURE 26-8

Paramecia have two types of nuclei: a large macronucleus and one or more small micronuclei. Paramecia have an oral groove, mouth pore, and gullet, into which food particles are drawn by currents produced by the beating cilia. They also have an anal pore, through which undigested waste is expelled from food vacuoles.

PHYLUM CILIOPHORA

The 8,000 species that make up the phylum Ciliophora (SIL-EE-AWF-uh-ruh) swim by means of cilia, which are short, hairlike cytoplasmic projections that line the cell membrane. Members of the genus *Paramecium* are among the most thoroughly studied ciliates. Like all paramecia, *Paramecium,* shown in Figure 26-7, is abundant in ponds and slow-moving streams that contain plants and decaying organic matter. As you can see, a paramecium has cilia arranged in rows across its cell membrane. The cilia beat in synchronized strokes that pass in waves across the cell, causing the protozoan to rotate on its axis. Paramecia and other ciliates feed on bacteria, algae, and other small organisms that are found in all types of marine and freshwater habitats.

Internal Structure

Ciliates have the most elaborate organelles of any protozoa. Figure 26-8 illustrates the basic structure of a paramecium. A clear, elastic layer of protein, called a **pellicle,** surrounds the cell membrane. The pellicle has a funnel-like depression called an **oral groove,** which is lined with cilia. These beating cilia create water currents that sweep food down the groove to the **mouth pore.** The mouth pore opens into a **gullet,** which forms food vacuoles that circulate throughout the cytoplasm. Organic molecules in the vacuole are digested and absorbed. Molecules that are not digested move to the **anal pore,** where they are expelled.

Ciliates are multinucleate; that is, they have at least one macronucleus and one micronucleus. The large **macronucleus** contains

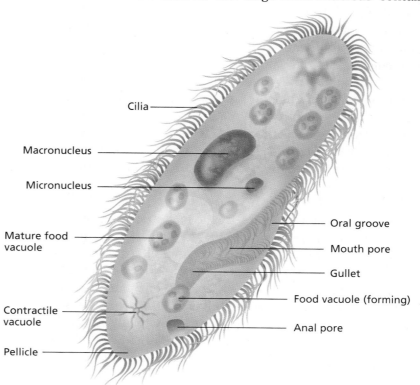

Cilia

Macronucleus

Micronucleus

Mature food vacuole

Contractile vacuole

Pellicle

Oral groove

Mouth pore

Gullet

Food vacuole (forming)

Anal pore

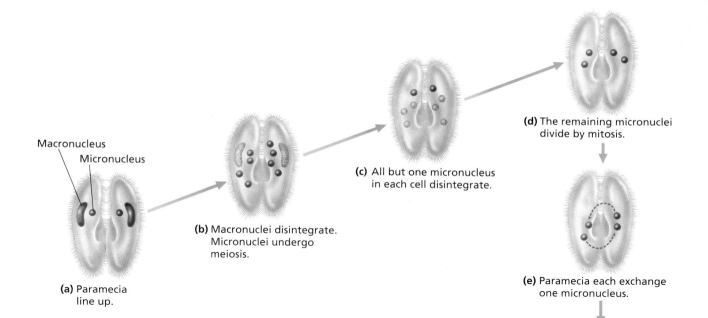

Macronucleus
Micronucleus

(a) Paramecia line up.

(b) Macronuclei disintegrate. Micronuclei undergo meiosis.

(c) All but one micronucleus in each cell disintegrate.

(d) The remaining micronuclei divide by mitosis.

(e) Paramecia each exchange one micronucleus.

(f) Micronuclei fuse.

(g) Paramecia separate and macronucleus re-forms.

(h) Each paramecium divides.

multiple copies of DNA and is responsible for metabolic and developmental functions. The macronucleus is also necessary for asexual reproduction. The smaller **micronucleus** participates in the exchange of genetic material between individuals during conjugation.

Reproduction

Asexual reproduction in ciliates occurs by binary fission. In this process, only the micronucleus divides by mitosis. The macronucleus, which has up to 500 times more DNA than the micronucleus, simply elongates and splits in half. One of the two halves goes to each new cell.

Sexual reproduction occurs in many ciliates by the process of conjugation. Conjugation in paramecia is illustrated in Figure 26-9. Conjugation begins when two organisms from opposite mating strains line up and join together. The macronucleus in each paramecium disintegrates. Each diploid micronucleus then undergoes meiosis, producing four haploid micronuclei. In each paramecium, all but one micronucleus disintegrate. The remaining micronucleus divides by mitosis, producing two identical haploid micronuclei. The two paramecia then exchange one micronucleus. The two micronuclei in each paramecium then fuse to form one diploid micronucleus. The two paramecia separate, and a macronucleus forms in each paramecium from products of mitotic divisions of the micronucleus. Although genetic material is exchanged during conjugation, no new cells are produced.

Following conjugation, each paramecium divides, producing a total of four genetically identical paramecia. Because genetic material is exchanged between the two original paramecia, the four offspring paramecia are genetically different from either original paramecium.

FIGURE 26-9

Paramecium reproduces by conjugation, a form of sexual reproduction in which genetic material is exchanged by two mating organisms.

FIGURE 26-10

PHYLUM ZOOMASTIGINA

The 2,500 species that make up the phylum Zoomastigina (ZOO-uh-MAST-uh-JIE-nuh) are characterized by the presence of one or more flagella, long hairlike structures that are made up of microtubules and are used for moving. The rapid whipping motion of the flagella pushes or pulls the protozoan through water. Many zooflagellates are free-living species that move through lakes and ponds, where they feed on small organisms. Some of the most primitive protozoa are found in this phylum. *Giardia lamblia* is shown in Figure 26-10.

internet**connect**

SC*i*LINKS₋
NSTA

TOPIC: Zoomastigina
GO TO: www.scilinks.org
KEYWORD: HM516

Human Disease

Some of the most important protozoan parasites are zooflagellates. Many of them belong to the genus *Trypanosoma*. They live in the blood of fish, amphibians, reptiles, birds, and mammals and are carried from host to host by bloodsucking insects, such as flies. Some species are nonpathogenic, but others produce severe diseases in humans and animals. For example, two species of *Trypanosoma* can cause African **trypanosomiasis** (TRIP-uh-NOH-soh-MIE-uh-sis), or sleeping sickness. Trypanosomiasis is transmitted by the tsetse fly, which lives only in Africa. The disease is characterized by increasing fever, lethargy, mental deterioration, and coma. Another species, called *Trypanosoma cruzi,* causes **Chagas' disease.** Chagas' disease is transmitted by an insect called the "kissing bug." Patients with Chagas' disease suffer from fever and severe heart damage.

A zooflagellate called *Leishmania donovani* is transmitted by sand flies. It causes leishmaniasis, a blood disease that afflicts millions of people in Africa, Asia, and Latin America. The disease is characterized by disfiguring skin sores, and it can be fatal. A leishmanial sore is shown in Figure 26-11.

Giardia lamblia causes **giardiasis** (JEE-ahr-DIE-uh-sis), an illness characterized by severe diarrhea and intestinal cramps. Several kinds of animals carry the parasite and contaminate water with their feces. Hikers and others who are likely to drink contaminated water are susceptible to giardiasis, and thousands of cases occur annually in the United States. The disease is usually not fatal, and drugs hasten recovery.

FIGURE 26-11

This person has leishmaniasis, which is caused by several species of *Leishmania*. *Leishmania* infects the skin, and some species infect major internal organs.

PHYLUM SPOROZOA

All 6,000 species in the phylum Sporozoa (SPOHR-uh-ZOH-uh) have adult forms with no means of locomotion. Most species are parasitic and have complex life cycles in which they develop a spore, an infective form protected by a resistant coat.

Sporozoans are carried in the blood and other tissues of their hosts, where they absorb nutrients and destroy host cell tissues. The sporozoan shown in Figure 26-12 is *Toxoplasma gondii,* a parasite found in birds, rodents, and domestic cats. In humans, it can cause **toxoplasmosis** (TAHKS-oh-plaz-MOH-sis), a disease that causes few or no symptoms in adults with healthy immune systems but that can be dangerous to a developing fetus or newborn. Some adults can become seriously ill with flu-like symptoms. One species of sporozoan closely related to *Toxoplasma* causes coccidiosis, a deadly disease that affects birds and young cattle.

FIGURE 26-12

The sporozoan *Toxoplasma gondii* is pictured above in a section of human liver.

Plasmodium

The best-known sporozoan is *Plasmodium,* the protozoan that causes malaria. **Malaria** is a very serious disease characterized by severe chills, fever, sweating, fatigue, and great thirst. Victims die of anemia, kidney failure, or brain damage. The genus *Plasmodium* has caused more human deaths than any other genus in history. According to the World Health Organization, malaria afflicts 500 million people annually, killing as many as 2.7 million.

Four species of *Plasmodium* infect humans, and all have life cycles that involve the female *Anopheles* mosquito. When an infected mosquito bites a person, *Plasmodium* **sporozoites** enter the bloodstream and travel to liver cells, where they divide repeatedly. New spores called **merozoites** emerge and infect red blood cells, where they reproduce asexually. At regular intervals, the merozoites burst out of the red blood cells and release toxins into the blood. The destruction of red blood cells and the release of toxin in the blood cause the fever, anemia, and other symptoms of malaria. The merozoites infect other red blood cells and again reproduce asexually. This asexual reproduction can happen many times over a long period of time. Merozoites of some species remain in the liver and do not come out for months or years. Thus, an infected person could take antimalarial drugs and cure the infection in the blood, only to become ill again when the merozoites leave the liver cells. There are, however, antimalarial drugs that prevent the reoccurrence of malaria by killing the liver-stage parasites.

Some of the merozoites in the blood develop into specialized cells called **gametocytes.** When a female *Anopheles* bites the infected person, it ingests these gametocytes. In the mosquito's digestive system, the sperm and eggs combine to form a zygote. The nucleus of the zygote divides repeatedly to form more sporozoites. When the zygote bursts, the sporozoites migrate to the

---

Eco Connection

Protozoan Biocontrol

Scientists from the United States Department of Agriculture are conducting field studies with the protozoan *Edhazardia aedis* to test its effectiveness as a control agent of disease-carrying mosquitoes. The chemical DDT was used previously, but it was banned in the 1970s after it was discovered to be harmful to bird populations. *E. aedis,* which was discovered in Argentina, infects mosquito larvae in the water and kills them. Scientists think that this protozoan will prevent disease while causing no environmental damage.

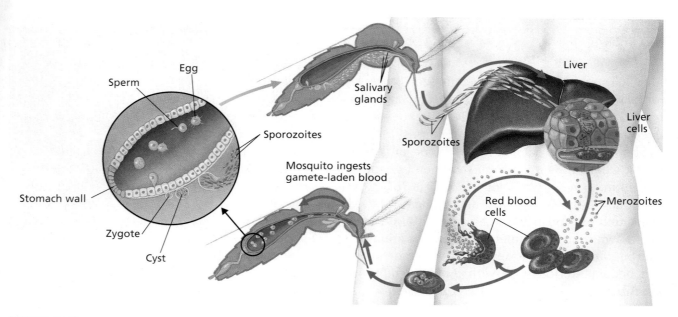

FIGURE 26-13

Malaria is caused by a sporozoan of the genus *Plasmodium. Plasmodium* is transmitted from host to host by female *Anopheles* mosquitoes. The host experiences attacks of chills and fever each time infected red blood cells burst and release the parasites that have multiplied within them. Some parasites develop into spores, which are picked up by uninfected *Anopheles* mosquitoes that bite the host.

body cavity and salivary glands of the mosquito. When the insect bites another person, the life cycle begins again. One effective way to reduce human deaths from malaria is to control mosquito populations. Without the mosquito hosts, the *Plasmodium* protozoans cannot complete their life cycle. The malaria life cycle is illustrated in Figure 26-13.

Malaria is usually cured with a drug derived from the cinchona tree, which is native to the Americas. This drug, quinine, has been used to treat malaria for over 500 years. As you learned in Chapter 24, bacteria can evolve resistance to antibiotics; similarly, sporozoans can evolve resistance to antimalarial drugs. Resistance to antimalarial drugs is a significant worldwide problem. Many more people will die from malaria despite the availability of drugs. Pharmaceutical companies have developed new drugs related to quinine, such as chloroquine and primaquine, but *Plasmodium* has evolved resistance to these newer quinine-related drugs. Although experimental malaria vaccines have not been successful, molecular techniques may offer new hope that a successful vaccine will be developed.

SECTION 26-2 REVIEW

1. What are pseudopodia? What function do they serve in sarcodines?

2. How have sarcodines built geological features of the environment?

3. What is conjugation? How is this process advantageous for ciliates, such as *Paramecium*?

4. What kinds of disease can zooflagellates cause in humans?

5. Describe the life cycle of *Plasmodium,* the sporozoan that causes malaria. What features typical of sporozoans does this life cycle exhibit?

6. **CRITICAL THINKING** How might health workers attempt to control diseases caused by protozoa?

CHAPTER 26 REVIEW

SUMMARY/VOCABULARY

26-1
- Protozoa are unicellular eukaryotic organisms classified in the kingdom Protista. They are found in moist habitats, and they include free-living and parasitic forms. Most species of protozoa are heterotrophic organisms that obtain nutrients by the process of phagocytosis.
- Many scientists believe that protozoa evolved from prokaryotes about 1.5 billion years ago.
- Many species of protozoa have adaptations for responding to changes in the environment. Such adaptations include eyespots and cyst formation.
- Protozoa are placed into four groups, according to the type of locomotion they display. The sarcodines move by means of pseudopodia, the ciliates move by means of cilia, the zooflagellates move by means of flagella, and the sporozoans are unable to move in the adult form.

Vocabulary

conjugation (507)	eyespot (508)	multiple fission (507)	protozoa (507)
cyst (509)	food vacuole (507)	protist (507)	zooplankton (507)

26-2
- The phylum Sarcodina consists of protozoa that move by means of pseudopodia. Sarcodines include amoebas, foraminifera, and radiolarians.
- Sarcodines move by means of cytoplasmic streaming. In this process, the endoplasm pushes the ectoplasm outward to form a pseudopodium. Pseudopodia are also used for phagocytosis.
- Most sarcodines are free-living, but the sarcodine *Entamoeba histolytica* is parasitic and causes the human disease amebic dysentery.
- The phylum Ciliophora consists of protozoa that move by means of cilia. Ciliates include the well-studied *Paramecium*. Paramecia have a complex array of organelles, including a macronucleus, a micronucleus, an oral groove, and an anal pore.
- Ciliates reproduce by binary fission as well as by sexual reproduction. Ciliates exchange genetic material by a process called conjugation.
- The phylum Zoomastigina consists of protozoa that move by means of flagella. Zooflagellates include *Trypanosoma,* a species that causes African sleeping sickness.
- Other important human diseases caused by zooflagellates are Chagas' disease, leishmaniasis, and giardiasis.
- The phylum Sporozoa is made up of protozoa that have complex life cycles in which they develop a spore. Virtually all species of sporozoans are parasites in humans and other animals.
- The sporozoan *Plasmodium* causes the disease malaria. Plasmodium has a complex life cycle. The *Anopheles* mosquito transmits the parasite, which causes extensive damage to the red blood cells in a victim.

Vocabulary

amebic dysentery (513)	endoplasm (512)	merozoite (517)	radiolarian (513)
ameboid movement (512)	foraminiferan (513)	micronucleus (515)	sporozoite (517)
anal pore (514)	gametocyte (517)	mouth pore (514)	test (513)
Chagas' disease (516)	giardiasis (516)	oral groove (514)	toxoplasmosis (517)
contractile vacuole (512)	gullet (514)	pellicle (514)	trypanosomiasis (516)
cytoplasmic streaming (512)	macronucleus (514)	pseudopodium (512)	
ectoplasm (512)	malaria (517)		

REVIEW

Vocabulary

1. Compare the following terms: protozoa, protozoan, and protist.
2. Research the meaning of the word *pseudopodium*. Why is this an appropriate term for the structure it defines?
3. Distinguish between the two regions of cytoplasm known as ectoplasm and endoplasm.
4. Research the meaning of the word *zooplankton*. Explain the relationship between the word's meaning and its roots.
5. Define the words *ciliate, zooflagellate,* and *sporozoan.*

Multiple Choice

6. Most scientists believe that protists evolved from (a) free-living worms (b) trypanosomes (c) prokaryotes (d) euglenoids.
7. Protozoan habitats are characterized by the presence of (a) algae (b) moisture (c) blood (d) soil.
8. Some protozoa monitor light quality with (a) pseudopodia (b) eyespots (c) cilia (d) contractile vacuoles.
9. Pseudopodia are extensions of a sarcodine's (a) pellicle (b) cytoplasm (c) cilia (d) test.
10. A pellicle is a characteristic of the (a) zooflagellates (b) sarcodines (c) ciliates (d) sporozoans.
11. Ciliates, such as *Paramecium,* have (a) hard outer tests (b) parasitic life cycles that involve *Anopheles* mosquitoes (c) a complex array of organelles (d) silicon dioxide in their cell membranes.
12. Flagella are characteristic of members of the phylum (a) Zoomastigina (b) Sarcodina (c) Sporozoa (d) Ciliophora.
13. African sleeping sickness is transmitted by (a) tsetse flies (b) *Anopheles* mosquitoes (c) kissing bugs (d) muskrats.
14. Members of the phylum Sporozoa do not cause (a) toxoplasmosis (b) malaria (c) giardiasis (d) coccidiosis.
15. Malaria is transmitted by (a) tsetse flies (b) *Anopheles* mosquitoes (c) kissing bugs (d) *Trypanosoma cruzi.*

Short Answer

16. Describe the process of ameboid movement and how it helps with the amoeba's nutrition.
17. What adaptive significance does the contractile vacuole have in the freshwater sarcodine?
18. Describe a potentially fatal human disease caused by an amoeba.
19. Explain the process of conjugation in *Paramecium.* How does it differ from the process of conjugation in bacteria?
20. How does a ciliate, such as *Paramecium,* capture and digest food?
21. Why are ciliates considered the most complex group of protozoa?
22. Explain how parasitic zooflagellates infect their hosts. Give two examples.
23. What characteristic of sporozoans distinguishes them from the three other protozoan groups?
24. Draw a simplified life cycle of *Plasmodium,* showing the protozoan activity in both the mosquito and the human hosts.
25. Identify the protozoa that once inhabited the shells shown in the figure below. How have they contributed to the geological formation of Earth?

CRITICAL THINKING

1. Many scientists suggest that paramecia are more complex than amoebas. What adaptations in paramecia would justify this claim?

2. Many protozoa feed by means of pseudopodia. What stimulus might cause these cytoplasmic extensions to form?

3. The process of conjugation is complex. It requires an expenditure of energy and other resources. Relate the high biological cost of conjugation to the adaptive advantage of exchanging genetic material.

4. Scientists are trying to develop a vaccine against malaria, but because malaria has several life stages, scientists must decide which life stage to develop a vaccine against. Some scientists are trying to develop a vaccine against gametocytes as a way of controlling malaria. If they are successful in developing this vaccine, how will it help people living in areas where malaria regularly occurs? Explain your answer.

5. Many parasitic protozoa, such as *Entamoeba histolytica,* are able to form cysts whenever they pass out of a host. Why is cyst formation an advantage to a parasitic protozoan?

6. Some protozoan parasites are very difficult to grow in test tubes because they lose the ability to produce certain key enzymes or growth factors when outside their host. How is this host-parasite relationship similar to that described in the hypothesis of endosymbiosis? How is it different?

7. Study the micrograph below showing the sporozoan *Plasmodium.* What evolutionary advantage does *Plasmodium* gain by forming gametocytes?

EXTENSION

1. Read "Intruder in the Heart" in *Discover,* December 1998, on page 38. Why is Chagas' disease so difficult to diagnose? Describe how humans become infected with Chagas' disease. What is the main reason heart transplantation is seldom an effective treatment for Chagas' disease?

2. Write a report on the types of protozoa found in zooplankton in the ocean. In your report, include information about the species of fish that depend on these protozoa as a food source.

3. Collect water from at least three sources— ponds, lakes, taps, or ditches—and examine the samples under a microscope. Count the different kinds of protozoa in each sample, and draw sketches of all the types you see.

4. Read "New Combination Vaccine May Fight Malaria" in *Science News,* February 20, 1999, on page 117. How many people die of malaria each year? Describe how the new vaccine works against malaria.

Observing *Paramecium*

- Observe protozoa under a compound light microscope.
- Compare *Paramecium* with *Euglena*.
- Test the effects of different solutions on the movement of a paramecium's contractile vacuoles.

- observing
- comparing and contrasting
- collecting data
- analyzing data

- safety goggles
- medicine droppers
- *Paramecium* culture
- *Euglena* culture
- microscope slides
- methyl cellulose
- coverslips
- compound light microscope
- stopwatch or clock with second hand
- distilled water
- paper towels
- salt water

Background

1. List some of the general characteristics of the kingdom Protista.
2. Distinguish between protists and protozoa.
3. Distinguish members of the phylum Ciliophora from other phyla of protozoa.
4. What foods do ciliates eat? How do they take in and digest food?
5. What function does the contractile vacuole serve in the *Paramecium*?

PART A   Comparing *Paramecium* with *Euglena*

1. **CAUTION   Put on safety goggles. If you get methyl cellulose in your eyes, immediately flush it out at the eyewash station while calling to your teacher. Slides break easily. Use caution when handling them.** Using a medicine dropper, place one drop of methyl cellulose on a microscope slide.
2. Place one drop of *Paramecium* culture on the methyl cellulose to slow the paramecia down, and cover them with a coverslip.
3. Use the low-power setting of your microscope to locate the paramecia and observe their movement. Then change to the high-power setting.
4. Examine one paramecium under the high-power setting of your microscope. Check for the structural details of the paramecium by changing the fine adjustment and altering the light conditions. If the organism moves out of view, move the slide to keep up with it. If you are unsuccessful, return to low power to scan a larger field, and begin again.
5. Make a sketch of a paramecium in your lab report. Label the cilia, oral groove, mouth pore, and gullet in your sketch. Note the color of the food vacuoles.
6. Remove the coverslip. Add one drop of *Euglena* culture to the slide. Cover and examine under high power. *Euglena* is a protist that you will study in Chapter 27. Its green color is due to chloroplasts.
7. As you view these two protists, note the relative sizes of the two kinds of organisms. Compare their means of locomotion.
8. Observe the food vacuoles in the paramecia. Did they change color after you added the *Euglena* culture to the slide?

PART B Observing the Contractile Vacuoles of *Paramecium*

9. In your lab report, prepare a data table similar to the one shown below.

10. Find a paramecium that is easy to observe, and identify its contractile vacuoles—the two roundish forms at each end of the organism. Count how many times the contractile vacuoles fill and empty in one minute. Record your data in your data table in the row labeled "Culture medium."

11. Repeat step 10, observing two different paramecia.

12. Use a clean medicine dropper to put some distilled water at one edge of the coverslip. Draw the distilled water to the other side of the slide by placing a paper towel at the opposite edge of the coverslip.

13. Count how many times the contractile vacuoles fill and empty in one minute when the paramecium is in distilled water. Record the number of pulses per minute in your data table in the row labeled "Distilled water." Repeat the process using two different paramecia.

14. Using a clean medicine dropper, put some salt water at one edge of the coverslip. Draw the salt water to the other side of the slide by placing a paper towel at the opposite edge of the coverslip as you did in step 12. Then count the number of times the contractile vacuoles fill and empty in one minute in the saltwater environment. Record the number of pulses per minute in your data table in the row labeled "Salt water." Repeat the process using two different paramecia.

15. Average the number of pulses per minute by adding the counts you obtained for each environment and dividing by 3. Record the average pulses per minute in the last column of your data table.

16. Clean up your lab materials and wash your hands before leaving the lab.

Analysis and Conclusions

1. Based on your observations in Part A, is *Paramecium* autotrophic or heterotrophic? Explain your answer.

2. Explain any changes in the color of the food vacuoles in Part A.

3. What effect did the distilled water have on the paramecium's contractile vacuoles in Part B?

4. What effect did the salt water have on the paramecium's contractile vacuoles?

5. Did you use a control in Part B? Explain your answer.

6. Return to the data table you completed in Part B. Using the terms *isotonic, hypotonic,* and *hypertonic,* describe the three different environments you observed the paramecium in.

7. Explain how the external environment affected the number of pulses of the contractile vacuoles. (Hint: Compare the effects of a hypotonic solution with those of a hypertonic solution.)

8. Explain how contractile vacuoles are important to the survival of paramecia living in freshwater environments.

9. *Paramecium* is among the protists called protozoa, which means "first animals." In what way is this description accurate or misleading?

Further Inquiry

Design an experiment to test the responses of protozoa to a range of temperatures or a range of pH.

CONTRACTILE VACUOLE PULSES

Environment	Number of pulses per minute			Average pulses per minute
	paramecium 1	paramecium 2	paramecium 3	
Culture medium				
Distilled water				
Salt water				

CHAPTER 27

ALGAE AND FUNGUSLIKE PROTISTS

Algae, such as these kelp, Macrocystis pyrifera, off the coast of California, are giants among protists. They grow in massive groves that support large numbers of aquatic organisms.

FOCUS CONCEPT: *Structure and Function*

As you read this chapter, note that algae and funguslike protists are extremely diverse groups of organisms that vary in structure, reproduction, and biochemistry.

OVERVIEW OF ALGAE

Algae are plantlike organisms that belong to the kingdom Protista. Although most species of algae are unicellular, some, such as the Macrocystis pyrifera *shown on the opposite page, are large, multicellular organisms. Algae differ from protozoa, which are also classified in the kingdom Protista, in that they manufacture their food through the process of photosynthesis. This section explores the basic characteristics of algae.*

OBJECTIVES

▲

Compare algae with other protists.

●

Explain how algae differ from plants.

■

Describe the various body structures of algae.

◆

Identify the characteristics used to classify algae into seven phyla.

▲

Summarize the events of asexual and sexual reproduction in representative genera of algae.

CHARACTERISTICS

Algae are a diverse group of protists. They range in size from microscopic single-celled organisms to large seaweeds that may be hundreds of feet long. Unlike protozoa, which are heterotrophic, **algae** are autotrophic protists—they have chloroplasts and produce their own carbohydrates by photosynthesis. In the past, some classification systems placed algae in the plant kingdom. However, algae lack tissue differentiation and thus have no true roots, stems, or leaves. The reproductive structures of algae also differ from those of plants; they form gametes in single-celled **gametangia** (GAM-uh-TAN-jee-uh), or gamete chambers. Plants, by contrast, form gametes in multicellular gametangia. For these reasons, algae are classified as protists.

Despite their diversity, different kinds of algae have several features in common. For example, most algae are aquatic and have flagella at some point in their life cycle. In addition, algal cells often contain **pyrenoids** (pie-REE-NOYDZ), organelles that synthesize and store starch.

STRUCTURE

The body portion of an alga is called a **thallus** (THAL-uhs). The thallus of an alga is usually haploid. A variety of thallus formats characterize algae. In some species, the thallus consists of a single cell. In other species, it is made up of many cells in varying arrangements. Four types of algae are recognized, based on the following body structures: unicellular, colonial, filamentous, and multicellular.

Unicellular algae have a structure that consists of a single cell. Most unicellular algae are aquatic organisms that compose the **phytoplankton,** a population of photosynthetic organisms that

Word Roots and Origins

algae

from the Latin *alga,* meaning "seaweed"

(a)

(b)

(c)

(d)

FIGURE 27-1

Algae are characterized by a variety of body structures. (a) *Chlamydomonas* is a flagellated unicellular organism (2,905×). (b) An example of a colonial green alga is *Volvox* (400×). (c) *Spirogyra* is a green alga with a filamentous body form (291×). (d) Some multicellular algae are sheetlike; *Ulva* has a thin, leaflike form.

forms the foundation of aquatic food chains. Through photosynthesis, phytoplankton produces almost half the world's carbohydrates, thereby providing important nutrients for numerous aquatic organisms. Such unicellular algae are also among the major producers of oxygen in the atmosphere. The *Chlamydomonas* in Figure 27-1a is an example of a unicellular alga.

Colonial algae, such as *Volvox,* shown in Figure 27-1b, have a structure that consists of groups of cells acting in a coordinated manner. Some of these cells become specialized. This division of labor allows colonial algae to move, feed, and reproduce efficiently.

Filamentous algae, such as *Spirogyra,* shown in Figure 27-1c, have a slender, rod-shaped thallus composed of rows of cells joined end to end. Other species of filamentous algae have specialized structures that anchor the thallus to the ocean bottom. This adaptation secures the alga in one place as it grows toward the sunlight at the water's surface.

Multicellular algae often have a large, complex thallus. For instance, *Ulva,* shown in Figure 27-1d, has a leaflike thallus that may be several centimeters wide but only two cells thick. The giant kelp, *Macrocystis,* is among the largest of the multicellular algae. It has rubbery leaflike portions, stemlike regions, and enlarged air bladders.

CLASSIFICATION

Algae are classified into seven phyla, based on their color, type of chlorophyll, form of food-storage substance, and cell wall composition. All known phyla contain the light-absorbing photosynthetic pigment chlorophyll *a.* However, different types of algae also contain other forms of chlorophylls—such as chlorophylls *b, c,* or *d*—that absorb slightly different wavelengths of light. Some phyla also have accessory pigments that give them their characteristic color. The seven phyla of algae are summarized in Table 27-1.

TABLE 27-1 Seven Phyla of Algae

Phylum	Thallus format	Photosynthetic pigments	Form of food storage	Cell wall composition
Chlorophyta (green algae, 7,000 species)	unicellular, colonial, filamentous, and multicellular	chlorophylls *a* and *b*, carotenoids	starch	polysaccharides, primarily cellulose
Phaeophyta (brown algae, 1,500 species)	multicellular	chlorophylls *a* and *c*, carotenoids, fucoxanthin	laminarin (an oily carbohydrate)	cellulose with alginic acid
Rhodophyta (red algae, 4,000 species)	multicellular	chlorophyll *a*, phycobilins, carotenoids	starch	cellulose or pectin, many with calcium carbonate
Bacillariophyta (diatoms, 11,500 species)	mostly unicellular; some colonial	chlorophylls *a* and *c*, carotenoids, xanthophyll	leucosin (an oily carbohydrate)	pectin, many with silicon dioxide
Dinoflagellata (dinoflagellates, 1,100 species)	unicellular	chlorophylls *a* and *c*, carotenoids	starch	cellulose
Chrysophyta (golden algae, 850 species)	mostly unicellular; some colonial	chlorophylls *a* and *c*, xanthophyll, carotenoids	laminarin (an oily carbohydrate)	cellulose
Euglenophyta (euglenoids, 1,000 species)	unicellular	chlorophylls *a* and *b*, carotenoids, xanthophyll	paramylon (a starch)	no cell wall, protein-rich pellicle

REPRODUCTION

Many species of algae reproduce both asexually and sexually. Sexual reproduction in algae is often triggered by environmental stress. Some species reproduce only asexually.

Both asexual and sexual reproduction have been studied extensively in the unicellular green alga *Chlamydomonas*. As a mature organism, *Chlamydomonas* exists as a flagellated haploid cell. During asexual reproduction, the alga first absorbs its flagellum. Then the haploid cell divides mitotically up to three times, and from two to eight haploid flagellated cells called **zoospores** (ZOH-oh-SPOHRZ) develop within the parent cell. These motile asexual reproductive cells break out of the parent cell, disperse, and eventually grow to full size.

Sexual reproduction in *Chlamydomonas* also begins by haploid cells dividing mitotically to produce either "plus" or "minus" gametes. (The *plus* and *minus* terminology describes gametes that look similar but differ in chemical composition.) A plus gamete and a minus gamete come into contact with one another and shed their cell walls. They fuse and form a diploid zygote, which develops a thick protective wall. A zygote in such a resting state is called a **zygospore** (ZIE-go-SPOHR). A zygospore can withstand unfavorable environmental conditions. When favorable conditions exist, the thick wall opens and

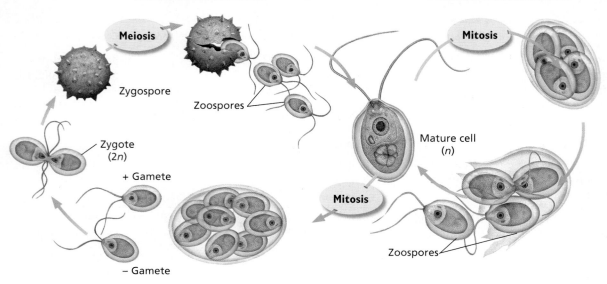

FIGURE 27-2

The unicellular green alga *Chlamydomonas* reproduces asexually by mitosis. It also reproduces sexually when gametes of opposite mating types fuse.

the living zoospore emerges. It then undergoes meiosis, forming numerous haploid *Chlamydomonas* cells that grow into mature organisms. The life cycle of *Chlamydomonas* is illustrated in Figure 27-2.

Reproduction in Multicellular Algae

Reproduction of multicellular algae varies widely among the phyla. Reproduction in red and brown algae is particularly complex, with that of the red algae often involving three states in a sexual life cycle. Examination of the following algal life cycles illustrates some of the reproductive variation in algae.

Oedogonium is a filamentous green alga. As shown in Figure 27-3, *Oedogonium* has cells specialized for producing gametes. Recall that the modified cells that produce and hold the gametes are called unicellular gametangia. The male unicellular gametangium, called an **antheridium** (AN-thuh-RID-ee-um), produces sperm. The female unicellular gametangium, called an **oogonium** (OH-uh-GOH-nee-um), produces

FIGURE 27-3

Oedogonium reproduces sexually by producing male and female gametes. The sperm, released into the surrounding water, swim to the egg.

an egg. The antheridium releases flagellated sperm into the surrounding water, where they swim to an oogonium and enter through small pores. After fertilization, the resulting zygote is released from the oogonium and forms a thick-walled, resting spore. The diploid spore then undergoes meiosis, forming four haploid zoospores that are released into the water. Each zoospore settles and divides. One of the new cells becomes a rootlike **holdfast,** and the other divides and forms a new filament.

The filamentous green alga *Spirogyra* reproduces sexually by a process called conjugation. During conjugation, two filaments align side by side. The walls of adjacent cells then dissolve and a conjugation tube forms between the cells. One cell contains a plus gamete. Its contents move through the conjugation tube, enter the adjacent cell, and fuse with the minus gamete. After fertilization, the resulting zygote develops a thick wall, falls from the parent filament, and becomes a resting spore. It later produces a new *Spirogyra* filament.

The leaflike alga *Ulva* has a sexual reproductive cycle that is characterized by a pattern called **alternation of generations.** As illustrated in Figure 27-4, a life cycle that exhibits alternation of generations has two distinct multicellular phases—a haploid, gamete-producing phase called a **gametophyte** (guh-MEE-tuh-FIET) and a diploid, spore-producing phase called a **sporophyte** (SPOHR-uh-FIET). The adult sporophyte has reproductive cells called **sporangia** (spoh-RAN-jee-uh), which produce haploid zoospores by meiosis. The zoospores divide mitotically and form motile spores, which settle on rocks and grow into multicellular, haploid gametophytes. Note that the gametophyte looks exactly like the sporophyte. The gametophyte produces gametangia and then produces plus and minus gametes that unite and form zygotes. As shown in Figure 27-4, the diploid zygote completes the cycle by dividing mitotically into a new diploid sporophyte.

The phenomenon of alternation of generations in green algae is important because it also occurs in more-complex land plants. However, in plants the gametophyte and sporophyte generations do not resemble each other as they do in *Ulva.* Also, the male and female gametes (sperm and egg) in plants are developed in multicellular reproductive structures, rather than in the unicellular gametangia seen in *Ulva.*

FIGURE 27-4

The multicellular green alga *Ulva* has a life cycle characterized by alternation of generations. Its haploid and diploid forms are equal in appearance and duration.

SECTION 27-1 REVIEW

1. In what ways do algae differ from protozoa?

2. How are algae similar to plants? How are they different?

3. How is body structure used to group algae?

4. What characteristics are used to classify algae into seven phyla?

5. Describe the general process of reproduction in the unicellular alga *Chlamydomonas*.

6. **CRITICAL THINKING** What adaptive advantage do you think different types of chlorophylls confer on algae?

OBJECTIVES

▲

Explain why the phylum Chlorophyta is considered the most diverse phylum of algae.

●

Describe the characteristics of the members of the phyla Phaeophyta and Rhodophyta.

■

Describe the essential characteristics of diatoms, and explain their industrial importance.

▲

List the important structural characteristics associated with dinoflagellates.

●

Discuss why *Euglena* is considered both a protozoan and an alga.

ALGAL DIVERSITY

The seven phyla of algae are a showcase of diversity. Microscopic forms, such as diatoms, dinoflagellates, and euglenoids, differ enough to be placed in separate phyla. Pigmentation distinguishes the green algae, red algae, brown algae, and golden algae, which are also placed in separate phyla.

PHYLUM CHLOROPHYTA

The phylum Chlorophyta (KLOH-rah-FIED-uh) contains more than 7,000 identified species of organisms called green algae. Members of this phylum have an amazing number of forms and reproductive methods. Their body structures range from single cells and colonial forms to multicellular filaments and sheets. Most species, such as the *Caulerpa racemosa* shown in Figure 27-5a, are aquatic. However, some species, such as the *Protococcus* shown in Figure 27-5b, inhabit moist terrestrial environments, such as the soil, rock surfaces, and tree trunks. Some species live as symbiotic partners in the cells of invertebrates or as part of organisms called lichens.

Biologists reason that green algae gave rise to land plants. Evidence supporting this idea includes the fact that both groups of organisms have chloroplasts that contain chlorophylls *a* and *b*. Both also have many carotenoids and store their food as starch. In addition, both green algae and plants have cell walls made of cellulose.

FIGURE 27-5

The bunch-of-grapes (a) is an example of a marine green algae. These Chlorophyta are found worldwide. Other Chlorophyta, such as the green *Protococcus* growing on this tree (b), are found in moist environments on land.

(a)

(b)

PHYLUM PHAEOPHYTA

The phylum Phaeophyta contains approximately 1,500 species of organisms called brown algae. Brown algae are mostly marine, and they include the plantlike organisms called seaweeds and kelps. They are most common along rocky coasts where ocean water is cool. A few species, such as *Sargassum,* are found far offshore, where they form dense floating mats.

The brown algae contain chlorophylls *a* and *c* and a large amount of pigment called **fucoxanthin** (FYOO-koh-ZAN-thin), which gives them their characteristic brown color. The food they produce is stored as **laminarin,** a carbohydrate with glucose units that are linked differently than those in starch.

All brown algae are multicellular, and most are large, often reaching lengths of more than 45 m (147 ft). Some of the largest algae known are classified in the phylum Phaeophyta. The large brown alga shown in Figure 27-6 is *Macrocystis,* a genus that thrives in intertidal zones. Individual alga can grow to a length of 100 m (328 ft). The thallus is anchored to the ocean bottom by a rootlike holdfast. The stemlike portion of the alga is called the **stipe.** And the leaflike region, modified to capture sunlight for photosynthesis, is called the **blade.** The cell walls of *Macrocystis* contain alginic acid, a source of a commercially important substance called **alginate.** Alginate is used in cosmetics and various drugs, as food, and as a stabilizer in most ice creams.

FIGURE 27-6

Macrocystis is an example of brown algae. Also known as giant kelp, this species is a member of the phylum Phaeophyta.

Word Roots and Origins

stipe

from the Latin *stipes,* meaning "log" or "trunk of a tree"

PHYLUM RHODOPHYTA

The phylum Rhodophyta contains 4,000 species of organisms called red algae. A few species of red algae live in fresh water or on land, but most are marine seaweeds. Red algae are usually smaller than brown algae and are found as deep as 200 m (657 ft). The red alga *Corallina* is shown in Figure 27-7.

Red algae contain chlorophyll *a* and pigments called **phycobilins.** Phycobilins play an important role in absorbing light for photosynthesis. These pigments can absorb the wavelengths of light that penetrate deep into the water. Thus, they may make it possible for red algae to live at depths where algae lacking these pigments cannot survive. Despite their common name, not all red algae are red. The depth at which they live in the ocean determines the amount of pigment they have. Because Rhodophyta live at varying depths, their color also varies.

Certain species of red algae have cell walls that are coated with a sticky substance called **carageenan** (KAR-uh-GEEN-uhn). Carageenan is a polysaccharide used in the production of cosmetics, gelatin capsules, and some types of cheese. **Agar,** which is used as a gel-forming base for culturing microbes, is also extracted from the cell walls of red algae.

FIGURE 27-7

Although not as large as the Phaeophyta, the Rhodophyta, such as this *Corallina,* are often referred to as seaweeds.

FIGURE 27-8

Diatoms, such as these, usually reproduce asexually. Sexual reproduction among diatoms is rare. (320×)

PHYLUM BACILLARIOPHYTA

The phylum Bacillariophyta contains 11,500 species of organisms called diatoms. **Diatoms** are abundant in both freshwater and marine environments. Their cell walls, commonly called shells, consist of two pieces that fit together like a box with a lid. Each half is called a **valve.** The shells contain silicon dioxide. Figure 27-8 shows two types of diatoms. **Centric diatoms** have circular or triangular shells and are most abundant in marine environments. **Pennate diatoms** have rectangular shells and are most abundant in freshwater ponds and lakes. Some pennate diatoms move by secreting threads that attach to the surface of the water. When these threads contract, they pull the diatom forward.

Diatoms are an abundant component of phytoplankton and are important producers in freshwater and marine food webs. They are an essential source of nutrients for microscopic heterotrophs. In addition, they release an abundance of oxygen.

When diatoms die, their shells sink and accumulate in large numbers, forming a layer of material called **diatomaceous** (DIE-uh-tuh-MAY-shuhs) **earth.** Diatomaceous earth is slightly abrasive and is a major component of many commercial products, such as detergents, paint removers, fertilizers, insulators, and some types of toothpaste.

FIGURE 27-9

Dinoflagellates, such as these, often harbor endosymbiotic cyanobacteria. Dinoflagellates can also be endosymbionts in sponges, jellyfish, corals, and some types of protozoa. (450×)

PHYLUM DINOFLAGELLATA

The phylum Dinoflagellata contains 1,100 species of organisms called dinoflagellates. Dinoflagellates are small, usually unicellular organisms. Most are photosynthetic, but a few species are colorless and heterotrophic. Along with diatoms, dinoflagellates are one of the major producers of organic matter in marine environments.

Photosynthetic dinoflagellates usually have a yellowish green to brown color due to a large amount of pigments called carotenoids as well as other pigments and chlorophylls *a* and *c*. Most dinoflagellates have two flagella of unequal length, as shown in Figure 27-9. Each flagellum fits into one of two grooves that run perpendicular to each other. Movement of the flagella causes the dinoflagellate to spin like a top through the water. Dinoflagellates' cell walls are made of cellulose plates that look like armor when seen under a microscope.

Some species of dinoflagellates, such as *Noctiluca,* can produce **bioluminescence,** a display of sparkling light often seen in ocean water at night. Other species produce toxins and red pigments. When their populations explode, they turn the water brownish red, resulting in a phenomenon known as **red tide.** Red tides are fairly common in the Gulf of Mexico off the coast of Florida. When shellfish, including oysters, feed on the dinoflagellates, they also consume the toxins, which are dangerous to humans who eat the shellfish.

PHYLUM CHRYSOPHYTA

The phylum Chrysophyta contains about 850 species of organisms called golden algae. Most of the golden algae live in fresh water, but a few are found in marine environments. The cells form highly resistant cysts that enable them to survive beneath frozen surfaces of lakes in winter and dry lake beds during summer. Two flagella of unequal length are located at one end of each cell.

Most of the species placed in this phylum are some shade of yellow or brown due to the presence of large amounts of carotenoids. They also have chlorophylls *a* and *c*. Golden algae store much of their surplus energy as oil and are important in the formation of petroleum deposits.

internet**connect**

SC/LINKS
NSTA

TOPIC: Bioluminescence
GO TO: www.scilinks.org
KEYWORD: HM533

FIGURE 27-10

Euglena gracilis, shown below, is a familiar type of euglenoid. It is propelled by a long flagellum. An eyespot guides it toward light.

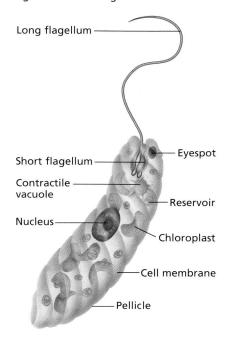

Long flagellum

Short flagellum

Contractile vacuole

Nucleus

Eyespot

Reservoir

Chloroplast

Cell membrane

Pellicle

PHYLUM EUGLENOPHYTA

The phylum Euglenophyta contains approximately 1,000 species of flagellated unicellular algae called **euglenoids.** Euglenoids show both plantlike and animal-like characteristics. They are plantlike in that many have chlorophyll and are photosynthetic; they are animal-like in that they lack a cell wall and are highly motile. Euglenoids contain chlorophylls *a* and *b* and the pigments known as carotenoids. Most species live in fresh water, but a few are found in moist environments, such as in soil or in the digestive tracts of certain animals.

A familiar genus of euglenoids is *Euglena,* shown in Figure 27-10. *Euglena* is abundant in fresh water, especially water polluted by excess nutrients. This protist has an elastic, transparent pellicle made of protein just beneath its cell membrane. It also has a contractile vacuole to rid the cell of excess water. Because *Euglena* lacks a cell wall, it is fairly flexible and can change its shape as it swims about. Although usually photosynthetic, if *Euglena* is raised in a dark environment, it will not form chloroplasts and will become heterotrophic.

SECTION 27-2 REVIEW

1. Why are green algae considered a diverse group of algae?

2. Which phylum contains the largest multicellular forms of algae? In what way are these algae commercially important?

3. What characteristics enable red algae to exist in deep marine environments?

4. What is a diatom? What useful commercial products do the shells of these algae yield?

5. Which phylum is composed of unicellular organisms that usually have two flagella and a cell wall made of cellulose plates?

6. **CRITICAL THINKING** If a *Euglena* that is raised in the dark loses its chloroplasts, will it grow new ones if it is returned to the light?

SECTION

27-3

OBJECTIVES

▲

Describe the two forms
that characterize the life cycle
of the slime mold.

●

Describe the environment
in which slime molds live.

■

Outline the basic life cycles
of the two groups of slime molds.

◆

Point out the unique
characteristics of water molds.

FUNGUSLIKE PROTISTS

The kingdom Protista contains a number of funguslike protists in addition to the algae. Among these are the slime molds and water molds. These organisms have unique life cycles that set them apart from the protozoa, algae, and fungi. However, like all of these groups, they are eukaryotic. They are multicellular or large multinucleate heterotrophic organisms with very little tissue specialization.

SLIME MOLDS

Slime molds are a curious group of organisms. They spend part of their lives in a mobile, amoeba-like feeding form, engulfing organic matter and bacteria much as protozoa do. However, they also produce funguslike reproductive structures, which is why they were once classified as fungi. Slime molds are typically found growing on damp soil, rotting logs, decaying leaves, or other decomposing organic matter in moist areas. These organisms appear as glistening, viscous masses of slime: some are white, but most are yellow or red.

Biologists recognize two groups of slime molds—the cellular slime molds (phylum Acrasiomycota) and the plasmodial slime molds (phylum Myxomycota). These groups are not closely related, but they share certain characteristics. For example, both types have life cycles with two phases: a mobile feeding stage and a stationary reproductive stage. During reproduction, slime molds produce a spore-bearing structure called a **fruiting body.**

Phylum Acrasiomycota

The phylum Acrasiomycota (ah-KRAYZH-ee-oh-mie-KOH-tuh) comprises about 65 species of cellular slime molds. **Cellular slime molds** live as individual haploid cells that move about like amoebas. Each cell moves as an independent organism, creeping over rotting logs and soil or swimming in fresh water, ingesting bacteria and other food.

When food or water becomes scarce, the cells release a chemical that attracts nearby cells and causes them to gather by the hundreds or thousands to form a dense structure called a pseudoplasmodium, as shown in Figure 27-11. A **pseudoplasmodium** is a coordinated colony of individual cells that resembles a slug, and it leaves a slimy trail as it crawls over decaying logs, leaves, and twigs. During this stage, the cells move as one unit, even though each cell retains its cell membrane and identity. Eventually, the

FIGURE 27-11

The well-known cellular slime mold *Dictyostelium discoideum* can be easily grown in the laboratory. Approximately 65 other species of cellular slime molds are known to exist. (80×)

FIGURE 27-12

The plasmodial slime mold *Physarum* has a bright yellow plasmodium. This naked mass of cytoplasm feeds on bacteria and other microorganisms. The reproductive structures are stalked fruiting bodies.

pseudoplasmodium settles and forms a fruiting body in which haploid spores develop. When the fruiting body breaks open, the wind disperses the spores to new locations. Each spore may grow into an individual amoeboid cell, thus completing the life cycle.

Phylum Myxomycota

Approximately 450 species of **plasmodial slime molds** compose the phylum Myxomycota (MIKS-oh-mie-KOH-tuh). During the feeding stage of its life cycle, a plasmodial slime mold is a mass of cytoplasm called a **plasmodium,** and it may be as large as several square meters. Each plasmodium is **multinucleate,** meaning it contains thousands of nuclei. As the plasmodium moves along the forest floor, it engulfs decaying leaves and other debris by the process of phagocytosis.

When food or water is scarce, the plasmodium crawls to an exposed surface and begins to reproduce, as shown in Figure 27-12. It forms stalked fruiting bodies in which haploid spores form by meiosis. The spores are very resistant to adverse conditions. Under favorable conditions, they crack open and give rise to haploid reproductive cells. Two such cells fuse, and their nuclei combine to form a diploid nucleus. Repeated divisions by mitosis follow, but the cells do not undergo cytokinesis, so the result is the multinucleated cytoplasm characteristic of the plasmodium.

Quick Lab

Observing Slime Mold

Materials slime mold culture, oatmeal, vinegar, cotton swab, dissecting microscope

Procedure

1. Observe the movement of the slime mold. Identify the plasmodium, the nuclei, and the food vacuoles. Draw and label the structures you have observed.

2. Drop a small bit of oatmeal near an outside edge of the slime mold.

3. Dip the swab in vinegar and touch it to the slime mold.

Analysis How does a slime mold move? How does it react to oatmeal? To vinegar?

WATER MOLDS

A **water mold** is a funguslike organism composed of branching filaments of cells. Most water molds are aquatic and are commonly found in bodies of fresh water. However, some live in the soil, and some are parasites. For example, water molds are familiar as the white fuzz on diseased aquarium fish or on organic matter floating on water.

Phylum Oomycota

The phylum Oomycota includes a number of organisms that are pathogenic to plants. For example, the water mold *Phytophthora infestans* causes late blight in potatoes and was responsible for the Irish potato famine in the mid-1800s. **Blight** is a disease of plants characterized by quickly developing decay and discoloring of leaves, stems, and flowers. Late blight is demonstrated in Figure 27-13.

FIGURE 27-13

Potato blight is caused by the water mold *Phytophthora infestans.* Between 1845 and 1849, the late blight of potatoes devastated farms in Ireland, forcing the mass emigration of Irish people to countries such as Australia and the United States.

FIGURE 27-14

Downy mildew on grapes is caused by *Plasmopara viticola,* which grows on the leaves and fruit of grapes. This protist can cause significant economic harm if it is not carefully controlled.

FIGURE 27-15

Chytrids, such as this *Allomyces,* are considered by many scientists to be more like fungi than like protists, but the presence of motile cells has caused them to be classified as protists. Although most are aquatic, some live in moist soil. (70×)

Another example of a plant pathogenic oomycete is *Plasmopara viticola.* This organism infects grape plants, attacking the leaves and the fruit. *Plasmopara* infection causes the grape leaves to wilt and die. Young grape plants are also attacked and may also wilt and die from *Plasmopara* infection. *Plasmopara* may also infect vegetables and other fruits. Figure 27-14 shows a grape plant infected with *Plasmopara viticola.*

Water molds reproduce asexually and sexually. During asexual reproduction, they produce motile, flagellated reproductive zoospores. Zoospores germinate into threadlike cells, which accumulate to form a matlike mass. Some zoospores form a reproductive structure called a sporangium, in which new zoospores are produced.

During sexual reproduction, the cells of the water mold develop egg-containing and sperm-containing structures. Fertilization tubes grow between the two types of structures, enabling haploid sperm cells to fertilize haploid egg cells and form diploid zygotes. A zygote develops into a new mass of filaments, from which asexual sporangia as well as sexual oogonia and antheridia form.

Phylum Chytridiomycota

Biologists place approximately 750 protist species in the phylum Chytridiomycota (kie-TRID-ee-oh-mie-KOH-tuh). The **chytrids** (KIE-tridz) are primarily aquatic protists characterized by gametes and zoospores with a single, posterior flagellum. Most chytrids are unicellular. Some chytrids have long filamentous bodies that anchor the organism. Many chytrids are parasites on algae, plants, and insects, while others are saprophytes.

Until recently, biologists classified this phylum with the protists, but many biologists now think that chytrids should be classified as fungi. Chytrids and fungi have similar characteristics; they have similar methods for absorbing nutrients through the cell wall, cell walls that are made of the same type of material, and long filamentous bodies. Fungi also share similar types of enzymes and biochemical pathways with chytrids. Because of all of these similarities, biologists think that chytrids are a link between protists and fungi. An example of a chytrid is shown in Figure 27-15.

SECTION 27-3 REVIEW

1. What two phases are found in the life cycle of slime molds?

2. In which phyla are the slime molds classified?

3. What are the distinctive features of the pseudoplasmodium, and which organisms form this structure?

4. When do the plasmodial slime molds form their fruiting body?

5. What are the characteristic features of water molds?

6. **CRITICAL THINKING** What evolutionary advantage do pseudoplasmodia gain by producing fruiting bodies?

SUMMARY/VOCABULARY

27-1 ■ The kingdom Protista includes algae, which are mostly aquatic organisms that contain chlorophyll. Algae include microscopic single cells and giant marine kelps.

■ Algae produce large amounts of organic matter, which serves as nutrients for other organisms. Algae also add an enormous amount of oxygen to the atmosphere.

■ The body portion of an alga is the thallus. It may consist of a single cell, a colony of cells, a filament, or a complex multicellular arrangement.

■ Algae can be classified into seven phyla, based on color, type of chlorophyll, and form of food-storage substances.

■ Algae reproduce asexually by mitosis and sexually by more-complex methods.

■ In the leaflike alga *Ulva,* an alternation of generations takes place, with a gametophyte and sporophyte phase.

Vocabulary

algae (525)	filamentous alga (526)	oogonium (528)	thallus (525)
alternation of generations (529)	gametangium (525)	phytoplankton (525)	unicellular alga (525)
	gametophyte (529)	pyrenoid (525)	zoospore (527)
antheridium (528)	holdfast (529)	sporangium (529)	zygospore (527)
colonial alga (526)	multicellular alga (526)	sporophyte (529)	

27-2 ■ The phylum Chlorophyta consists of green algae. Green algae contain chlorophylls *a* and *b,* carotenoids, and cell walls made of cellulose.

■ The phylum Phaeophyta is made up of brown algae. Brown algae contain chlorophylls *a* and *c* and carotenoids including fucoxanthin.

■ The phylum Rhodophyta consists of red algae. Red algae contain chlorophyll *a* and phycobilins.

■ The phylum Bacillariophyta is made up of diatoms. These unicellular algae have shells that contain silicon dioxide.

■ The phylum Dinoflagellata includes the dinoflagellates. Dinoflagellates contain chlorophylls *a* and *c* and carotenoids. Most species have two flagella.

■ The phylum Chrysophyta consists of the golden algae. Golden algae contain chlorophylls *a* and *c* and large amounts of carotenoids.

■ The phylum Euglenophyta is made up of euglenoids, such as *Euglena.* Euglenoids show both plantlike and animal-like characteristics.

Vocabulary

agar (531)	carageenan (531)	euglenoid (533)	phycobilin (531)
alginate (531)	centric diatom (532)	fucoxanthin (531)	red tide (532)
bioluminescence (532)	diatom (532)	laminarin (531)	stipe (531)
blade (531)	diatomaceous earth (532)	pennate diatom (532)	valve (532)

27-3 ■ Slime molds are eukaryotes. Their life cycles include a creeping amoeba-like form and a reproductive spore-bearing form.

■ Slime molds are classified into phylum Acrasiomycota and phylum Myxomycota.

■ The phylum Oomycota contains funguslike organisms called water molds. Water molds are composed of branching filaments.

Vocabulary

blight (535)	fruiting body (534)	plasmodial slime mold (535)	pseudoplasmodium (534)
cellular slime mold (534)	multinucleate (535)	plasmodium (535)	water mold (535)
chytrid (536)			

REVIEW

Vocabulary

In the following groups of terms, choose the term that does not belong, and explain why it does not belong.

1. gametophyte, sporophyte, fruiting body
2. chlorophyll *a,* carotenoids, phytoplankton
3. plasmodium, blade, holdfast
4. water mold, cellular slime mold, kelp
5. diatomaceous earth, red tide, bioluminescence

Multiple Choice

6. The green alga *Chlamydomonas* reproduces asexually by forming (a) a zygote (b) a gametophyte (c) zoospores (d) an opposite mating type.
7. The green alga *Ulva* forms a sporophyte that has structures called (a) sporangia (b) antheridia (c) gametangia (d) carageenan.
8. The green alga *Oedogonium* produces a unicellular female gametangium called (a) an antheridium (b) a zygospore (c) a conjugation tube (d) an oogonium.
9. Red algae contain an accessory pigment called (a) phycobilin (b) fucoxanthin (c) carotene (d) xanthophyll.
10. The phenomenon know as red tide is caused by a population explosion of (a) diatoms (b) red algae (c) water molds (d) dinoflagellates.
11. Many types of algae have flagellated reproductive cells called (a) sporangia (b) zoospores (c) zygospores (d) sporophytes.
12. A pyrenoid is an organelle that (a) lends golden algae their yellow color (b) anchors seaweeds to the ocean floor (c) makes and stores starch (d) enables some types of algae to produce light.
13. Biologists believe that the most likely ancestors of land plants are members of the phylum (a) Chrysophyta (b) Euglenophyta (c) Phaeophyta (d) Chlorophyta.
14. The feeding stage of a plasmodial slime mold is called (a) an amoeba (b) a fruiting body (c) a plasmodium (d) a zygospore.
15. In addition to protozoa and algae, the kingdom Protista contains organisms called (a) euglenoids (b) slime molds (c) dinoflagellates (d) diatoms.

Short Answer

16. How are algae similar to protozoa? How are they different? What characteristics do algae share with plants? What characteristics differ?
17. List the characteristics used to classify algae into seven phyla.
18. Compare the types of food-storage molecules found in the seven types of algae. What is the most common food-storage molecule used by algae?
19. List the types of pigments found in the seven phyla of algae. What is the most common photosynthetic pigment found in algae?
20. What is a thallus? What kinds of thallus formats are found in algae?
21. Summarize three types of sexual reproduction that occur in algae. Does sexual reproduction in algal protists occur in only multicellular algae?
22. Why are euglenoids described as both plantlike and animal-like organisms? Explain how euglenoids can be both heterotrophic and autotrophic.
23. What is a fruiting body? At what point of their life cycle do slime molds form fruiting bodies?
24. Define the term *multinucleate.* What kind of protists are characterized by this form of cell structure?
25. Identify the structures in the figure below. What is the name of this organism?

CRITICAL THINKING

1. Several years ago, many botanists classified algae as plants. They also classified flagellated *Euglena* as photosynthetic protozoa. Algae are now classified as protists, and *Euglena* is now considered an alga. What do these changes tell you about the classification systems of living things?

2. In the Pacific Northwest of the United States, people believe it is unsafe to collect and eat shellfish during the months that lack an *r* in their name. Name these months, and give a possible scientific explanation for the belief. Keep in mind that shellfish obtain their food by filtering water.

3. The horsetail plant, *Equisetum,* has silicon dioxide in the outer cells of its stem. Diatoms also contain silicon dioxide in their shells. Explain whether the presence of this compound in both organisms indicates a close relationship. (Hint: Consider the types of evolution described in Chapter 15.)

4. Scientists often use a pigment called phycoerythrin to label parts of cells so that they can be seen with a special type of microscope that uses ultraviolet light. Phycoerythrin fluoresces under ultraviolet light. Because ultraviolet light is a higher frequency of light, it can penetrate deeper into water than can visible light. Based on this information and what you read in this chapter, which phylum of algae do you think produces phycoerythrin? Justify your answer.

5. Explain how the absence of a cell wall in *Euglena* makes the function of the contractile vacuole critical.

6. Examine the drawing of lateral conjugation in *Spirogyra* in which adjacent cells of the same filament have conjugated. Explain whether this type of conjugation offers more or less genetic recombination than does sclariform conjugation, in which conjugation is between the cells of two different filaments.

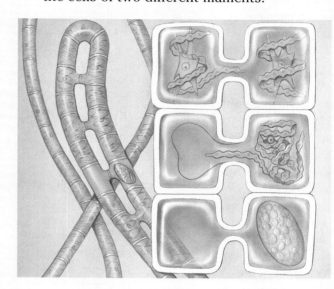

EXTENSION

1. Read "The Lurking Perils of *Pfiesteria*" in *Scientific American,* August 1999, on page 42. Prepare a report that discusses the role *Pfiesteria piscicida* has in fish kills in several major estuaries. Include in your report a description of the toxic and nontoxic forms *Pfiesteria* can assume. Describe the toxin's indirect effects on the survival of fish. Explain how *Pfiesteria* can be dangerous to people.

2. Visit your local grocery store or supermarket, and find at least three items that contain carageenan, a polysaccharide derived from red algae.

3. Gather samples of soil, dead leaves, old grass, and fresh leaves. Place each sample in a jar or test tube filled with clean water, and leave the samples near a light source. Examine the samples under a microscope once a week, and make drawings of the types of organisms you find. What do your observations reveal about the different habitats of algae?

Classifying Green Algae

OBJECTIVES

- Observe live specimens of green algae.
- Compare unicellular, colonial, thalloid, and filamentous green algae.
- Classify genera of colonial green algae.

PROCESS SKILLS

- observing
- comparing and contrasting
- classifying
- inferring

MATERIALS

- culture of *Chlamydomonas*
- colonial green algae culture (*Chlamydomonas, Eudorina, Gonium, Pandorina, Volvox,* and *Hydrodictyon*)
- culture of *Spirogyra*
- 3 depression slides
- 3 coverslips
- 3 medicine droppers
- compound light microscope

Background

1. Distinguish between the terms *protozoa* and *algae*.
2. Green algae are either unicellular, colonial, filamentous, or thalloid.
3. Explain why green plants are thought to have evolved from green algae.

Chlamydomonas

4. List characteristics of green algae. Include ways that algae differ from plants.
5. How do green algae differ from other algae?

PART A Observing Unicellular Green Algae

1. Make a table similar to the one below in your lab report. Allow substantial space in your data table for labeled sketches of the different kinds of green algae you will view in this investigation. Use your data table to record your observations of each kind of green algae that you view.

2. CAUTION **Slides break easily. Use caution when handling them.** Prepare a wet mount of the *Chlamydomonas* culture by placing a drop of the culture on a microscope slide with a medicine dropper and placing a coverslip on top of the specimen.

OBSERVATIONS OF GREEN ALGAE		
Genus	Sketch of organism	Type of green algae (unicellular, colonial, filamentous, or thalloid)

3. Examine the slide of *Chlamydomonas,* first under low power and then under high power.

4. In your lab report, make a sketch of *Chlamydomonas.* Label the cell wall, flagella, nucleus, and chloroplasts, if they are visible.

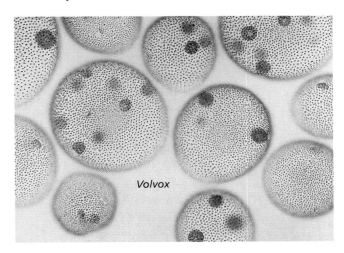

Volvox

PART B   Observing and Identifying Colonial Green Algae

5. ⚠ CAUTION **Slides break easily. Use caution when handling them.** Prepare a wet mount of the colonial green algae culture, using a clean medicine dropper, a clean microscope slide, and a clean coverslip.

6. Examine the slide of mixed colonial green algae under low power, switching to the high-power setting as needed for clarity. Your slide should resemble the photograph of *Volvox* above. How many different kinds of colonial green algae can you find?

7. In your data table, draw each type of colonial green algae you observe. How are these algae different in appearance from *Chlamydomonas*?

8. Use the dichotomous key, above right, to identify each type of colonial green algae. Choose an alga, and start at 1. Decide which choice describes the alga. If the alga is not identified, go to the next number and make the next decision. Continue until you identify the alga. Then label your drawing of the alga according to the identification you made.

PART C   Observing Filamentous Green Algae

9. ⚠ CAUTION **Slides break easily. Use caution when handling them.** Prepare a wet mount of the *Spirogyra* culture, using a clean medicine dropper, a clean microscope slide, and a clean coverslip.

DICHOTOMOUS KEY FOR COLONIAL GREEN ALGAE

1a	single cells	*Chlamydomonas*
1b	colony of cells	go to 2
2a	colony flattened or netlike	go to 3
2b	colony round	go to 4
3a	netlike colony	*Hydrodictyon*
3b	flattened colony	*Gonium*
4a	more than 100 cells in colony	*Volvox*
4b	fewer than 100 cells in colony	go to 5
5a	cells close together	*Pandorina*
5b	cells apart from each other	*Eudorina*

10. Examine *Spirogyra* under low power. Switch to the high-power setting if you need more magnification to see the specimen clearly. How does *Spirogyra* differ in appearance from the other kinds of algae you have observed in this investigation?

11. In your data table, make a sketch of *Spirogyra.* Label the filaments and the individual cells in your drawing. Also label the spiral-shaped chloroplasts if they are visible.

12. ⚠ ⚠ Clean up your lab materials and wash your hands before leaving the lab.

Analysis and Conclusions

1. What characteristics did all of the algae you viewed have in common?

2. Describe examples of specialization in the different kinds of algae you viewed. In which types of algae do some cells depend on others?

3. What differences did you observe between small and large colonies of algae?

4. Which specializations in algae are characteristic of green plants?

Further Inquiry

How might you search for evidence of evolutionary relationships among algae and between algae and green plants?

CHAPTER 28

FUNGI

Fungi, such as these mushrooms, are important decomposers in nature.

FOCUS CONCEPT: *Cell Structure and Function*

As you read, note how the distinctive traits of fungi, such as their structure and physiology, enable them to affect their environment and thus human health.

OVERVIEW OF FUNGI

In the six-kingdom classification of organisms, fungi are in their own kingdom. They differ from other organisms in several ways, including in structure, in method of reproduction, and in methods of obtaining nutrients.

CHARACTERISTICS

Fungi are eukaryotic, nonphotosynthetic organisms, and most are multicellular heterotrophs. Most fungi are microscopic molds or yeasts. **Molds,** such as the fungus that grows on bread and oranges, are tangled masses of filaments of cells. **Yeasts** are unicellular organisms whose colonies resemble those of bacteria. Yeasts are best known as the microorganisms that make bread rise.

Filaments of fungi are called **hyphae** (HIE-fee). The cell walls of hyphae contain **chitin** (KIE-tin), a complex polysaccharide not found in bacteria, protists, or other microorganisms but found in insects. The presence of chitin distinguishes cell walls of fungi from those of plants, which have cellulose but no chitin. Fungi range in size from the microscopic yeast to the largest organism in the world—the fungus *Armillaria,* which lives underground and occupies a space of up to eight hectares (861,000 ft^2). The study of fungi is called **mycology** (mie-KAHL-uh-jee).

While animals and many microorganisms ingest their nutrients before digesting them, fungi secrete enzymes and then absorb the digested nutrients through their cell wall. Like animals, fungi store energy in the form of glycogen. Most fungi are saprophytic, that is, they live on organic compounds that they absorb from dead organisms in the environment. This characteristic makes fungi a very important recycler of organic material in nature.

Structure of Fungi

A mat of hyphae visible to the unaided eye is a **mycelium** (mie-SEE-lee-uhm). The hyphae of fungi that commonly grow on old bread and fruit form mycelia. In some species, the cells that make up hyphae are divided by cross sections called **septa** (SEP-tuh). Hyphae whose cells are divided by septa are called septate hyphae. The hyphae of species that do not have septa are called **coenocytic** (SEE-noh-SIT-ik). The general structures of septate and nonseptate hyphae are shown in Figure 28-1. Hyphae increase in length by cellular growth and division at the tip. As the hyphae grow, the size of the mycelium increases. When hyphae encounter organic matter, such

(a) SEPTATE HYPHAE

(b) COENOCYTIC HYPHAE

FIGURE 28-1

The hyphae of some fungi have separating walls called septa (a). The hyphae of other fungi do not have septa and are called coenocytic (b).

Yeast

Mycelia

FIGURE 28-2

This light micrograph shows the dimorphic fungus *Paracoccidioides brasiliensis* as it changes from its unicellular yeast form to a mycelial form. Note how the hyphae grow out from the yeast.

FIGURE 28-3

Fungi reproduce asexually in many different ways. Yeasts (a) pinch off a piece of their cell to produce new cells. The common bread mold *Rhizopus stolonifer* (b) produces a hyphal stalk to disperse its spores. *Penicillium* produces unprotected conidia (c).

(a)

(b)

(c)

as a tree trunk or dead animal, they secrete digestive enzymes and then absorb the digested nutrients.

Several species of fungi are able to change their form in response to changes in their environment. For example, *Histoplasma capsulatum*, which causes a severe disease in humans that can resemble tuberculosis, normally grows as a mycelium on the ground. However, when it invades a human, the increased temperature and available nutrients cause the fungus to grow unicellularly as a yeast. This ability to change, demonstrated in Figure 28-2, is called **dimorphism** (die-MOR-FIZ-uhm).

Asexual Reproduction

Most fungi reproduce both sexually and asexually. Asexually, fungi produce thousands of genetically identical haploid spores, usually on modified cells of the hyphae. When these spores are placed in favorable environmental conditions, they germinate and grow new hyphae, which will form a mycelium and can produce thousands of new asexual spores.

A variety of asexual spores are formed by different fungi. For example, **sporangiophores** (spoh-RAN-jee-oh-FOHRZ) are specialized hyphae that look like upright stalks. On top of a sporangiophore is an enclosing sac called a **sporangium** (spoh-RAN-jee-UHM). Inside each sporangium, spores called **sporangiospores** (spoh-RAN-jee-oh-SPOHRZ) are made. *Rhizopus,* the black mycelial fungus that is commonly found growing on bread, is an example of a sporangiospore-forming fungus.

Other fungi form spores called **conidia** (koh-NID-ee-uh), which are formed without the protection of an enclosing sac. Conidia are formed on top of a stalklike structure called a **conidiophore** (koh-NID-ee-uh-FOHR). *Penicillium,* which produces penicillin and cheese, is a fungus that reproduces asexually by means of conidia.

Asexual reproduction may also occur by **fragmentation.** In this process, a septate hypha dries and shatters, releasing individual cells that act as spores. The fungus that causes athlete's foot reproduces this way.

Yeast reproduce by a process called budding. **Budding** is an asexual process in which part of a yeast cell pinches itself off to produce a small offspring cell. Budding may be repeated many times. Three types of asexual reproduction are shown in Figure 28-3.

TABLE 28-1 *The Three Phyla of Fungi*

Phylum and number of species	Structure	Asexual reproduction	Sexual reproduction (where identified)	Examples
Zygomycota 600 species	coenocytic hyphae	spores from sporangia	conjugation results in zygospores	*Mucor, Rhizopus, Penicillium* species
Basidiomycota 25,000 species	septate hyphae	rare	basidia produce basidiospores	*Puccinia, Ustilago* (mushrooms)
Ascomycota 60,000 species	septate or unicellular hyphae	conidia, budding	asci produce ascospores	bread yeast, morel

Sexual Reproduction

Many but not all species of fungi are also able to reproduce sexually. Fungi are neither male nor female. They occur in mating types that are sometimes called "minus" and "plus." When two different mating types of the same species encounter one another, the hyphae of one mating type fuse with the hyphae of the opposite mating type. These fused hyphae give rise to a specialized structure, which produces and scatters genetically diverse spores. Unlike most eukaryotes, most fungi are haploid throughout most of their life cycle.

The ability of some fungi to reproduce both sexually and asexually provides an adaptive advantage. When the environment is favorable, rapid asexual reproduction ensures an increased spread of the species. During environmental stress, sexual reproduction ensures genetic recombination, increasing the likelihood that offspring will be better adapted to the new environmental conditions.

Evolution

The first fungi were probably unicellular organisms that might have clung together after mitosis to form a long filament of cells. Biologists think fungi colonized dry land at about the same time that early plants did. They reason that fungi, like other eukaryotes, arose from prokaryotes, possibly by endosymbiosis. According to the fossil record, all modern phyla of fungi had evolved by about 300 million years ago. These phyla are listed in Table 28-1.

Eco Connection

Fungi in the Food Chain

The well-known northern spotted owl depends indirectly on a forest fungus for its survival. The owls prey on northern flying squirrels, and the squirrels depend on truffles for the bulk of their diet. Truffles are the sexual reproductive structure of some fungal species.

internet**connect**

SC*LINKS*
NSTA

TOPIC: Fungi
GO TO: www.scilinks.org
KEYWORD: HM545

SECTION 28-1 REVIEW

1. How do fungi obtain nutrients?

2. Why does a fungus that reproduces both sexually and asexually have an evolutionary advantage over an organism that reproduces only asexually?

3. Describe dimorphism.

4. What characteristic makes fungi an important resource recycler?

5. Compare how fungi obtain nutrients with how protists obtain nutrients.

6. CRITICAL THINKING Based on fossil evidence, scientists think that fungi adapted to land dwelling at about the same time plants did. Explain why fungi might have adapted to land dwelling before plants did.

▲

List the characteristics that distinguish the three phyla of fungi.

●

Identify the common sexual reproductive traits of the three phyla of fungi.

■

Define *mycorrhiza* and *lichens,* and distinguish between them.

◆

Explain the importance of mycorrhizae and lichens to the environment.

FIGURE 28-4

Zygomycetes can reproduce both sexually and asexually. Sexually, when two compatible mating types meet, they produce specialized cells called gametangia. After the gametangia fuse, the nuclei from both types fuse and eventually produce genetically diverse zygospores.

CLASSIFICATION

*T*he approximately 100,000 species of fungi are classified in three phyla. Traditionally, fungi have been classified according to their structure and form of sexual reproduction. While these are no longer the sole bases of classification, these characteristics are still useful in identifying fungi.

PHYLUM ZYGOMYCOTA

Most species in the phylum Zygomycota (ZIE-goh-MIE-koh-tuh) are terrestrial organisms found primarily in soil that is rich in organic matter. The hyphae of zygomycetes are coenocytic.

Rhizopus stolonifer, the common bread fungus, which is illustrated in Figure 28-4, is in phylum Zygomycota. The hyphae that anchor the mold to the surface of the bread and that penetrate the bread's surface are called **rhizoids** (RIE-zoydz). Digestive enzymes produced by rhizoids break down organic compounds to release nutrients in the bread. Other hyphae, called **stolons** (STOH-lahnz), grow across the surface of the bread.

Sexual reproduction in zygomycetes is called conjugation. Conjugation in fungi occurs when two compatible mating types meet and hyphae from each mating type line up next to each other. Short branches form on the hyphae of both strains and grow outward until they touch each other. A septum forms near the tip of each branch, and a cell called a gametangium develops. A **gametangium** (GAM-ee-TAN-jee-uhm) is a sexual reproductive structure that contains a nucleus of a mating type. The nucleus within each parent's gametangium divides several times. When the gametangia

ASEXUAL REPRODUCTION

Sporangium
Sporangiophore
Sporangiospores

Developing hypha

Meiosis

Rhizoid

Two (1*n*) mating types meet

Gametangia

Zygote

Zygosporangium

Zygospore (1*n*) germination

SEXUAL REPRODUCTION

fuse, the nuclei mix and fuse in pairs, each pair containing a nucleus from each mating type. The fused gametangia, called a **zygosporangium** (ZIE-goh-spohr-AN-jee-uhm), forms a thick wall and becomes dormant. Germination depends on environmental conditions. A sporangiophore grows from the diploid zygosporangium and produces a sporangium, which ruptures and releases haploid spores.

Word Roots and Origins

rhizoid

from the Greek *rhiza*, meaning "root"

PHYLUM BASIDIOMYCOTA

Basidiomycetes (bah-SID-ee-oh-MIE-seets) are often called club fungi because they produce small clublike reproductive structures called **basidia** (bah-SID-ee-uh) during sexual reproduction. Sexual reproduction in basidiomycetes is outlined in Figure 28-5.

The spore-bearing structure of basidiomycetes is an aboveground structure called the **basidiocarp** (bah-SID-ee-oh-KARP). Mushrooms are basidiocarps. The basidiocarp consists of a stem called a stalk and a flattened structure known as a cap. On the underside of the cap are rows of gills that radiate out from the center. Each gill is lined with thousands of dikaryotic basidia. Cells containing two nuclei are called **dikaryotic** (die-KAR-ee-OH-tik). In each basidium, two nuclei fuse to form a zygote (2*n*). The zygote undergoes meiosis to form four haploid nuclei. These develop into four **basidiospores** (bah-SID-ee-oh-SPOHRZ), which are then released into the air. Under favorable environmental conditions, basidiospores germinate to produce haploid mycelia that grow underground. When compatible mating types encounter one another, their hyphae fuse and form a basidiocarp, which emerges aboveground.

FIGURE 28-5

On the gills of the basidiocarp, thousands of dikaryotic basidia form (a). The haploid nuclei inside each basidium fuse to form a diploid nucleus (b). The diploid nucleus undergoes meiosis, producing basidiospores. The basidiocarp releases the basidiospores (c), which fall to the ground and germinate. Underground, the hyphae of compatible mating types fuse and form a mycelium (d). Secondary mycelia intertwine and grow to form a basidiocarp (e).

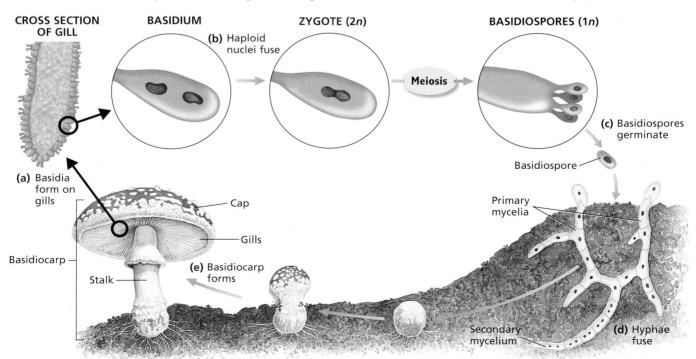

CROSS SECTION OF GILL   BASIDIUM   ZYGOTE (2*n*)   BASIDIOSPORES (1*n*)

(b) Haploid nuclei fuse

Meiosis

(c) Basidiospores germinate

Basidiospore

(a) Basidia form on gills

Cap

Gills

Basidiocarp

Stalk

(e) Basidiocarp forms

Primary mycelia

Secondary mycelium

(d) Hyphae fuse

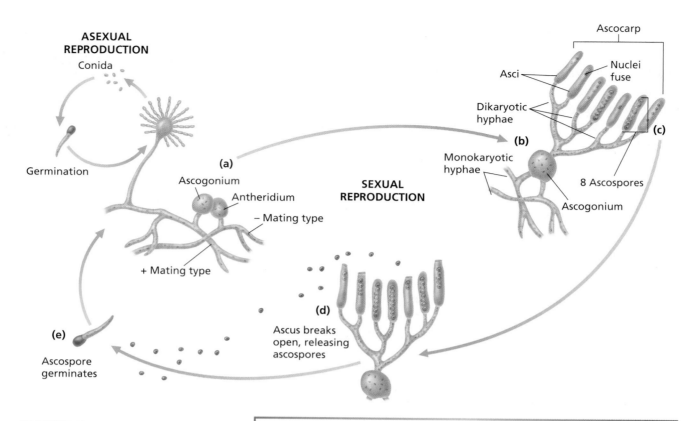

ASEXUAL REPRODUCTION

Conida

Germination

(a)

Ascogonium

Antheridium

– Mating type

+ Mating type

SEXUAL REPRODUCTION

Ascocarp

Asci

Nuclei fuse

Dikaryotic hyphae

(b)

(c)

Monokaryotic hyphae

8 Ascospores

Ascogonium

(d)

Ascus breaks open, releasing ascospores

(e)

Ascospore germinates

Compatible mating types form special structures (a) that fuse to form an ascogonium (b). From the ascogonium, dikaryotic hyphae grow and intertwine with monokaryotic hyphae to form an ascocarp. The tips of the dikaryotic hyphae form asci inside, and ascospores form (c). When the ascus ruptures (d), it releases the ascospores, which then germinate (e) to form new monokaryotic hyphae.

FIGURE 28-7

The ascocarp of this ascomycete, *Sarcoscypha coccinea,* is the sexual reproductive structure from which ascospores are released.

PHYLUM ASCOMYCOTA

Ascomycetes (ASK-oh-MIE-seets) are distinguished by the presence of saclike compartments where sexually produced spores form. Ascomycetes, also called sac fungi, live parasitically and in various habitats, including salt water, fresh water, and land.

Sexual reproduction in the ascomycetes begins when the hyphae of two compatible mating types form male and female haploid gametangia. The female gametangium is called an **ascogonium** (AS-koh-GOH-nee-uhm), and the male gametangium is called an **antheridium** (AN-thuhr-ID-ee-uhm), as shown in Figure 28-6. As the ascogonium and antheridium approach one another, a tube forms between them and the nuclei from the antheridium cross the tube and enter the ascogonium. Dikaryotic hyphae grow out of the ascogonium and intertwine with the monokaryotic hyphae of the original fungi (parents) to form a visible cuplike structure called the **ascocarp** (AS-koh-KAHRP). Cells that contain one nucleus are called **monokaryotic** (mah-noh-KAR-ee-OH-tik). An example of an ascocarp is shown in Figure 28-7.

Within the ascocarp, sacs called **asci** (AS-kee) develop at the tips of the dikaryotic hyphae. Within the asci, the haploid nuclei fuse. The zygotes undergo meiosis once and divide again by mitosis to form eight haploid nuclei. The eight nuclei form walls and become **ascospores** (AS-koh-SPOHRZ), which are released. When an ascospore germinates, a new haploid hypha emerges.

The traditional brewer's and baker's yeasts *(Saccharomyces cerevisiae)* are ascomycetes. *S. cerevisiae* makes bread rise and ferments grapes to make wine and grain to make beer.

Deuteromycota

Fungi that do not have a sexual stage are placed in a group called **fungi imperfecti,** or deuteromycota. Recent phylogenetic analyses have led some mycologists to place these fungi in the other three established phyla. Most species of fungi that were formerly classified as fungi imperfecti can now be classified in the phylum Ascomycota. However, some biologists disagree with this reclassification.

MYCORRHIZAE AND LICHENS

A **mycorrhiza** (MIE-koh-RIE-zah) is a symbiotic association between a fungus and plant roots, as shown in Figure 28-8. Over 90 percent of plants contain such fungi on their roots. The fungus absorbs and concentrates phosphate and other ions for delivery to the plant root and provides a secondary root system. In turn, the fungi receive sugars synthesized by the plant during photosynthesis. Many zygomycetes and basidiomycetes form mycorrhizae. These mycorrhizal relationships coevolved with plants.

Lichens (LIE-kenz) represent symbiotic relationships between a fungus and a photosynthetic partner (usually a cyanobacterium or green alga). Most fungi in lichens are ascomycetes. The photosynthesizer synthesizes sugars for the fungus, while the fungus provides moisture, shelter, and anchorage for the photosynthesizer. The fungus produces acids that decompose rocks making minerals available to the lichen. The chemical decomposition of rocks by lichens contributes to the production of soil.

Lichens are identified according to their distribution and structure. **Crustose** lichens grow as a layer on the surface of rocks and trees. **Fruticose** lichens are shrublike, and some grow up to 1.5 m (5 ft) in length. **Foliose** lichens live on flat surfaces, where they form matlike growths with tangled bodies. One example of a lichen is shown in Figure 28-9.

FIGURE 28-8

In this light micrograph, the stained hyphae of the mycorrhizae have infiltrated the plant root cells. (300×)

FIGURE 28-9

Lichens are grouped according to their type of body. For example, this red lichen is a crustose lichen that grows on rocks.

SECTION 28-2 REVIEW

1. Explain why some fungi are called club fungi, and identify their phylum.

2. Compare and contrast the basidiocarp with the ascocarp.

3. Explain why lichens are important to the environment.

4. Describe the Ascomycota life cycle.

5. Explain the benefits plants and fungi derive from a mycorrhizal relationship.

6. **CRITICAL THINKING** Morels are ascomycetes that resemble mushrooms. Even though they resemble Basidiomycota they are classified as Ascomycota. What evolutionary mechanism causes fungi of one phylum to resemble fungi of another phylum?

OBJECTIVES

▲

Describe three ways that fungi cause disease in humans.

●

Describe the types of food that fungi provide.

■

Provide examples of fungi's industrial importance.

FUNGI AND HUMANS

*F*ungi are important to humans. Some fungi cause devastating human and plant diseases, while others serve as important food sources for humans. Fungi are also used to produce chemicals, fuels, and pharmaceutical compounds.

FUNGI AND HUMAN DISEASE

Fungi can sometimes attack the tissues of living plants and animals and cause disease. Fungal disease is a major concern for humans because fungi attack not only us but also our food sources, making fungi competitors with humans for nutrients.

Mold spores can cause mild to serious allergies in some people. Billions of mold spores can become airborne and may then be inhaled, triggering an allergic reaction. Sniffling, sneezing, and respiratory distress are symptoms of an allergic reaction. Fungi can also infect and poison humans. Table 28-2 lists some infectious human fungal diseases.

Fungal Skin Infections

Fungi may infect the skin, hair, nails, and tissues of the body. For example, fungi on the skin can cause athlete's foot or ringworm, as shown in Figure 28-10. Ringworm, so named because people once thought they saw living worms in the rings on the skin, can occur almost anywhere on the skin. Athlete's foot occurs on the foot and between the toes.

Another fungal pathogen is *Candida albicans*. This yeast is commonly found in the mouth, intestine, and, in women, in the vaginal tract. It exists in balance with other microorganisms, such as bacteria. However, when conditions change, such as when some antibiotics are used or when pregnancy or illness occurs, then *Candida albicans* can flourish.

Other Fungal Illnesses

Serious fungal diseases that involve the internal organs are often caused by dimorphic fungi such as *Histoplasma capsulatum, Paracoccidiodes brasiliensis, Coccidioides immitis,* and *Blastomyces dermatitidis.* If their spores are inhaled, they can cause severe respiratory illness and spread to many other organs, sometimes resulting in death. They grow as a mold on the ground, but when they infect a human, they become unicellular. *H. capsulatum,* which often

FIGURE 28-10

Ringworm is a fungal infection of the skin. The dried skin that falls off a lesion is contaminated with fungal spores. These spores can infect other people and spread the infection.

TABLE 28-2   Summary of Human Fungal Diseases

Disease	Symptoms	Fungus	Route of transmission
Athlete's foot	fluid-filled blisters, scaly skin, itching	*Trichophyton* species (Ascomycete) or *Epidermophyton* species	contact with skin lesions or contaminated floors
Ringworm	ring-shaped skin lesions	*Microsporum, Trichophyton* (Ascomycetes)	contact with skin lesions, contaminated floors, or contaminated objects
Vaginal yeast infection	burning sensation, itching, discharge	*Candida*	contact with fecal material, diabetes; antibiotic treatments increase susceptibility
Tinea cruris (jock itch)	intense itching, ring-shaped lesions	*Microsporum, Trichophyton* (Ascomycetes)	contact with skin lesions, contaminated floors, or contaminated objects
Histoplasmosis	fever, chills, headache, body aches, chest pains, nonproductive cough	*Histoplasma capsulatum* (Ascomycete)	inhalation of airborne conidia

grows as a mold in the feces of birds, can become airborne when dried feces are disturbed and can then be inhaled.

Sometimes humans accidentally eat poisonous mushrooms. For example, *Amanita* species contain extremely dangerous toxins that can destroy a person's liver within one week. Figure 28-11 shows an example of an *Amanita* mushroom. The danger of *Amanita* mushrooms is reflected in their nicknames—"death angel" and "destroying angel."

Other fungal poisons include the **aflatoxins** (AF-luh-TAHKS-ins), poisons produced by some species of *Aspergillus.* Aflatoxins cause liver cancer. Fungi that make aflatoxin may be found as contaminants in peanuts and in grains such as corn and grain sorghum.

FUNGI IN INDUSTRY

Fungi produce many products used in nonfood industries. For example, *Penicillium* species produce penicillin, and *Cephalosporium* species produce cephalosporin antibiotics. *Rhizopus* causes chemical transformations of specific chemicals to make cortisone and similar drugs. Cortisone is used to reduce joint swelling.

The yeast *Saccharomyces cerevisiae* is an important tool in genetic engineering. For example, the vaccine for hepatitis B was developed by inserting hepatitis B genes into yeast plasmids. The yeast uses the inserted viral genes to produce viral proteins that are used as vaccines. Yeast is also used to produce ethanol, a main ingredient in the automobile fuel gasohol.

FIGURE 28-11

Poisonous mushrooms, such as this *Amanita virosa,* harm people when they are mistaken for edible mushrooms. Intense abdominal pain, vomiting, and diarrhea occur, followed by a short recovery period. Damage occurs in the liver, kidneys, and muscles. The symptoms persist for about six to eight days, and death occurs in about 50 to 90 percent of the cases.

FIGURE 28-12

Morels and truffles are prized by gourmets for their delicate flavor. Truffles (top) grow in association with oak trees. Truffle hunters often use specially trained pigs or dogs to help find truffles. Morels (bottom) grow wild in the Americas and are usually found in the spring.

TABLE 28-3 *Food Products and Fungi*	
Type of food	**Fungus**
Cheeses: blue, brie, Camembert, Gorgonzola, Limburger, Roquefort	*Penicillium* species
Beer, wine	*Saccharomyces carlsbergensis, Saccharomyces cerevisiae*
Soy products: miso (Japanese), soy sauce, tempeh (Indonesian), tofu (Japanese)	*Aspergillus oryzae, Rhizopus* species, *Mucor* species
Nutritional yeast	*Saccharomyces* species
Breads	*Saccharomyces cerevisiae*

Fungi and Food Industries

Many fungi are valuable food sources for humans. Yeast, such as *Saccharomyces,* is an important nutritional supplement because it contains vitamins, minerals, and other nutrients. Mushrooms are also an important food. *Agaricus* (white button), shiitake, and portabella mushrooms are often found in grocery stores in the United States. In other parts of the world, people prize the taste of other fungi, such as truffles and morels, which are pictured in Figure 28-12. Truffles and morels are ascocarps found near the roots of trees. Table 28-3 summarizes some of the uses of fungi in food.

Fungi not only can add value to food but also can take value away. Many fungi are important plant pathogens that attack grain or fruit. For example, wheat rust is a basidiomycete that attacks wheat grains. Other fungi can attack food crops such as corn, beans, onions, squashes, and tomatoes.

Fungi also produce several chemical compounds that are important to the food-processing industry, such as citric and gluconic acids. Citric acid is used in soft drinks and candies. Gluconic acid is fed to chickens to enhance the hardness of eggshells. *Ashbya gossypii* is a producer of vitamin B_2, an important nutritional supplement.

SECTION 28-3 REVIEW

1. Explain how fungi cause disease in humans.

2. Which fungi cause athlete's foot and vaginal yeast infection?

3. List the types of foods that are derived from fungi.

4. Name three nonfood products produced by fungi.

5. Explain how fungi compete with humans for nutrients.

6. **CRITICAL THINKING** Why would upsetting the balance of microorganisms in the body, such as occurs during antibiotic treatments, cause a yeast infection?

SUMMARY/VOCABULARY

28-1
- Fungi are eukaryotic, nonphotosynthetic organisms that can be unicellular or multicellular.
- Fungi are among the most important decomposers of organic matter in the soil. Fungi secrete extracellular enzymes that digest material and absorb simple organic molecules from the environment.
- All modern phyla of fungi had evolved by

300 million years ago. Fungi probably evolved from the prokaryotes and then adapted to various terrestrial environments.
- Hyphae are tangled masses of fungal filaments. Some species have partitions called septa in their hyphae that separate the individual cells.
- Most fungi reproduce asexually and sexually.

Vocabulary

budding (544)	conidiophore (544)	mold (543)	sporangiophore (544)
chitin (543)	dimorphism (544)	mycology (543)	sporangiospore (544)
coenocytic (543)	fragmentation (544)	mycelium (543)	sporangium (544)
conidium (544)	hypha (543)	septa (543)	yeast (543)

28-2
- The phylum Zygomycota is coenocytic. Asexual sporangiospores form within sacs called sporangia. Sexual reproduction results in zygospores.
- The phylum Basidiomycota includes mushrooms. Mushrooms, or basidiocarps, are sexual reproductive structures. Basidiocarps produce basidia, which produce basidiospores.
- Most fungi are found in the phylum Ascomycota, also called the sac fungi. The intertwining of the hyphae produces a visible ascocarp, which resembles a cup. Mating produces ascospores.

- Yeast are unicellular Ascomycota. They reproduce asexually by budding. Yeast are used for brewing, baking, and genetic engineering.
- Mycorrhizae are symbiotic relationships between plant roots and fungi. Fungi provide nutrients to the plant and derive nutrients from the plant.
- Lichens represent symbiotic relationships between fungi and cyanobacteria, or green algae. Fungi dissolve nutrients from rock. Algae and cyanobacteria provide fungi with carbohydrates. Lichens are highly sensitive to environmental changes.

Vocabulary

antheridium (548)	basidium (547)	foliose (549)	monokaryotic (548)
ascocarp (548)	basidiocarp (547)	fruticose (549)	mycorrhiza (549)
ascogonium (548)	basidiospore (547)	fungi imperfecti (549)	rhizoid (546)
ascospore (548)	crustose (549)	gametangium (546)	stolon (546)
ascus (548)	dikaryotic (547)	lichen (549)	zygosporangium (547)

28-3
- *Candida albicans* is an opportunistic pathogen that causes disease in the oral, intestinal, and vaginal tissues of humans.
- Fungi cause diseases such as athlete's foot, ringworm, and jock itch, and these diseases are easily spread.
- Pathogenic fungi that cause serious disease include *Histoplasma capsulatum, Blastomyces dermatitidis,* and *Coccidioides*

immitis. H. capsulatum is associated with bird droppings.
- Some fungi, such as portabella mushrooms and yeasts, are edible. *Amanita* mushrooms, among others, are poisonous.
- In industry, fungi produce antibiotics, fuels, and foods. Yeasts are also valuable genetic-engineering research tools.

Vocabulary

aflatoxin (551)

REVIEW

Vocabulary

1. Distinguish between a mycorrhiza and a rhizoid.
2. Differentiate between a sporangiophore, a sprangiospore, and a sporangium.
3. Differentiate between an ascocarp, an ascogonium, an ascospore, and an ascus.
4. Distinguish between *monokaryotic* and *dikaryotic.*
5. Differentiate between basidia, a basidiocarp, and a basidiospore.

Multiple Choice

6. Hyphae of the phylum Zygomycota are considered (a) coenocytic (b) monokaryotic (c) nonnuclear (d) plasmodial.
7. The common edible mushroom found in your grocery store is classified in the phylum (a) Basidiomycota (b) Ascomycota (c) Oomycota (d) Zygomycota.
8. The female gametangium in sac fungi is called an (a) oogonium (b) ascogonium (c) antheridium (d) oospore.
9. Fungi that feed on decaying organic matter are said to be (a) saprophytic (b) parasitic (c) mutualistic (d) symbiotic.
10. The fungus *Rhizopus* usually can be found growing on (a) soil (b) fruit (c) bread (d) decaying logs.
11. The walls that separate cells in fungal hyphae are known as (a) rhizoids (b) gills (c) asci (d) septa.
12. Lichens represent symbiotic associations of fungi and (a) roots (b) roundworms (c) water molds (d) green algae.
13. The gills of a mushroom are the sites of spore-bearing structures known as (a) basidia (b) conidiophores (c) basidiocarps (d) ascocarps.
14. In a mycorrhiza, a fungus lives in a symbiotic relationship with a (a) virus (b) slime mold (c) plant (d) bacterium.
15. All of the following human diseases are caused by a species of fungus, except (a) ringworm (b) athlete's foot (c) histoplasmosis (d) influenza.

Short Answer

16. How do the sexual reproductive structures in the three phyla of fungi resemble one another? How do they differ?
17. Explain why biologists think fungi colonized dry land at the same time as plants did.
18. How does a coenocytic hypha differ from a septate hypha? Name two examples of fungi that are coenocytic and two more that are septate.
19. Explain how fungi contribute to nutrient cycling in the environment.
20. Describe mutualism, and give an example of such a relationship involving fungi.
21. Explain what a rust is and how it affects humans.
22. What similarities are there between a mycorrhiza and a lichen?
23. Describe three ways that fungi cause disease in humans and three ways that fungi are useful or beneficial to humans.
24. Describe how a fungus growing in feces can infect a person's lungs. Name an example of a fungus that can do this.
25. Identify the lettered structures in the figure below. What phylum does this organism represent?

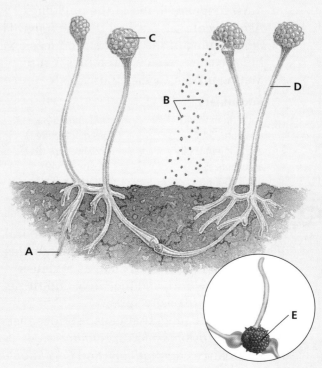

CRITICAL THINKING

1. The cell walls of fungi and the exoskeletons of insects and crustaceans contain chitin. Tell whether this is of phylogenetic significance, and explain why.

2. Many fungi are fatally poisonous to mammals. What adaptive advantage do toxins give to a fungus?

3. Long before antibiotics were discovered, it was common practice to place a piece of moldy bread on wounds. Explain why this practice might have helped the wounds heal.

4. Fungi such as *Penicillium* engage in a kind of chemical warfare against other microorganisms by producing chemicals that diffuse outward and kill nearby organisms. Explain how producing antibiotics is an adaptive advantage for fungi.

5. Most fungi grow best at temperatures of about 15°C to 21°C. *Aspergillus fumigatus,* however, can grow well at 37°C. Knowing this, where would you expect *A. fumigatus* to grow?

6. *Drosophila,* the common fruit fly, ingests juices from ripe fruit and yeast. How might the fruit fly help speed the natural decay of fruit?

7. When transplanting a wild plant to garden soil, it is very important to include some of the soil from the original habitat. Give a possible explanation, based on the information from this chapter.

8. A winemaker experimenting with three different strains of yeast charts the number of viable yeast as the grapes ferment. The three strains were grown in separate containers, at the same temperature, and with the same type of grape. Why does strain C survive longer than strains A or B?

Growth of Three Strains of Yeast

Numbers of live yeast cells

A   B   C

Time (in hours)

EXTENSION

1. Read "Joyous Mushrooms" in *Natural History,* September 1999, on page 48. Describe the work of natural historian, amateur mycologist, and artist Mary Elizabeth Banning.

2. Use the library to research the ways that medical science has been influenced by the study of fungi. Investigate the discovery of penicillin and other drugs derived from fungi. Investigate the role played by fungi in various diseases.

3. Prepare a yeast culture by adding a pinch of baker's yeast to a mixture of nine parts water and one part molasses. Allow the culture to ferment, and examine it under a microscope. Make a drawing of several yeast cells, and identify any visible cell parts.

4. Read "The Lichen Connection" in *Popular Science,* July 1998, on page 22. Describe how lichens are valuable to earthquake researchers.

Observing Fungi on Food

OBJECTIVES

- Recognize fungal growth on food.
- Identify environmental conditions that favor the growth of fungi on food and those that inhibit it.

PROCESS SKILLS

- designing an experiment
- collecting data
- organizing data
- analyzing results

MATERIALS

- safety goggles
- lab apron
- disposable gloves
- 2 sterile Petri dishes with nutrient medium (such as potato dextrose agar)
- 2 sterile Petri dishes with nutrient medium and propionic acid
- fungal samples
- stereomicroscope
- toothpicks
- wax pencil
- masking tape

Background

1. How do multicellular fungi, such as molds, obtain nutrients?
2. How do multicellular fungi reproduce and grow?
3. What ecological role do fungi fulfill?
4. How might fungi growing on food harm someone who eats it?

PART A Experimental Setup

1. CAUTION **Put on safety goggles, a lab apron, and disposable gloves.** Obtain four sterile Petri dishes, two with nutrient medium and two with nutrient medium plus propionic acid. Label the dishes for the presence or absence of propionic acid.

2. Examine the fungal samples through a dissecting microscope. Select a dense growth of a fungus from which you will take samples.

3. Use a toothpick to scoop up a small sample of the fungus you have selected. In the two Petri dishes without propionic acid, gently touch the sample to the medium in four places. Raise the lids of the dishes as little as possible while doing this. Do the same for the two Petri dishes with propionic acid, using a clean toothpick and another small sample of the same fungus. Dispose of the toothpicks according to the teacher's instructions.

4. Place a piece of masking tape on opposite sides of each dish to hold the lid and bottom together. Label each Petri dish with your name.

5. Design an experiment to determine which of two opposite environmental conditions is better for fungal growth. Some possible combinations are warm/cold, light/dark, and moist/dry. Label one of the two environmental conditions you selected on a dish with propionic acid. Label the other environmental condition on the other two Petri dishes (one with propionic acid and one without). Then incubate all four dishes under the appropriate conditions.

FUNGAL GROWTH IN DIFFERENT ENVIRONMENTS

Dish	Environmental condition	Propionic acid?	Source of fungus	Growth
1				
2				
3				
4				

6. Create a data table similar to the model above to record your experimental observations for your lab report. For example, the table above is designed to record any growth that may occur under two different environmental conditions (warm/cold, sunlight/dark, moist/dry), source of the fungus, and if propionic acid is present. Design your data table to fit your own experiment. Remember to allow plenty of space to record your observations. Be sure to label your Petri dishes with the appropriate environmental conditions and with the date on which the experiment was begun.

PART B   Comparing Amounts of Growth

7. After one week, examine each dish under the stereo-microscope without opening the dish.
8. Record your observations in your data table in your lab report.
9. Examine dishes belonging to other groups, especially those grown under different environmental conditions.

10. Add your observations of those dishes to your lab report.
11. Clean up your materials and wash your hands before leaving the lab. Dispose of all materials according to instructions provided by your teacher.

Analysis and Conclusions

1. Besides the environmental conditions you chose, what additional factor was tested in your experiment?
2. What steps were taken in your experiment to avoid contamination of the plates?
3. How would contamination of the plates affect the results of your experiment? What are the possible sources of contamination of your experiment?
4. What does extensive fungal growth on a plate indicate? What does lack of fungal growth on a plate indicate?
5. What effect does propionic acid have on fungal growth? How do you know?
6. Why do you think propionic acid is added to foods?
7. Which environmental conditions favor fungal growth? Which inhibit it?
8. Compare the results for the different kinds of fungi grown. Did fungi from certain food sources grow more rapidly than others?
9. Based on your conclusions, under what conditions would you keep a nonsterile food product if you wanted to prevent it from becoming moldy?
10. Has this lab changed your attitude toward food storage? If so, how?

Further Inquiry

Design an experiment that determines the kinds of food that best support fungal growth and whether the presence of chemicals inhibits fungal growth.

PLANTS

“ *The day passed delightfully. Delight itself, however, is a weak term to express the feelings of a naturalist who, for the first time, has wandered by himself in a Brazilian forest. The elegance of the grasses, the novelty of the parasitical plants, the beauty of the flowers, the glossy green of the foliage, but above all the general luxuriance of the vegetation, filled me with admiration.* ”

Charles Darwin, *Voyage of the Beagle*

These autumn leaves show bright colors because they have lost most of their chlorophyll.

Rafflesia arnoldii *has the largest known flowers. Although they are large and beautiful, these flowers emit the smell of rotting meat, which attracts flies as pollinators.*

Strawberry plants have aboveground stems that are able to form new plants.

This cotton boll developed from the ovary of a flower of a cotton plant.

Orchid cactus

THE IMPORTANCE OF PLANTS

Rice fields, often called paddies, thrive in regions with abundant rainfall. Rice is a prime food source for more than 60 percent of the world's population. About 90 percent of the world's rice is grown in Asia, primarily in China and India.

FOCUS CONCEPT: *Interdependence of Organisms*

As you read, pay attention to the relationship between plants and humans. Recognize how plants have changed over time. Describe how plants have been used to improve human existence.

29-1 *Plants and People*

29-2 *Plants and the Environment*

PLANTS AND PEOPLE

*P*lants are essential to our survival because they produce virtually all our food. We eat plants either directly, in the form of fruits, vegetables, and grains, or indirectly, by eating animals that consume plants. Plants also provide medicines, clothing, paper, cosmetics, and many other products. Plants play a major role in the continuous cycling of the Earth's water, oxygen, carbon dioxide, and mineral nutrients. The study of plants is called **botany** (BAHT-nee).

OBJECTIVES

▲

Describe ways that people use plants.

●

Distinguish between cereals, root crops, legumes, fruits, and vegetables.

■

Explain how humans have increased food production in the world.

◆

List three plants that are widely used as medicines.

PLANTS AS FOOD

Of the more than 350,000 plant species, people use at least 10,000 species for food. Incredibly, fewer than 20 plant species provide more than 90 percent of our food supply. The cultivation of plants for food probably began about 11,000 years ago in the Middle East. Wheat, barley, lentils, and peas were the first domesticated food crops. Growing plants and raising animals for human use is called **agriculture** (AG-ri-KUHL-chuhr). People propagated, or reproduced, individual plants that had valuable characteristics, such as plants that produced the largest or tastiest fruits.

In the 11,000 years that humans have been cultivating plants, we have changed many of the plants so much that they could not grow and survive without us. For example, the wild wheat stalk, as shown in Figure 29-1, breaks easily in the wind, an adaptation that increases the dispersal of its seeds. But early farmers used seeds from plants with stalks that did not break easily for replanting. When these plants were grown, the seeds could be harvested before they fell from the plant. This form of selection—with people acting as selecting agents—has resulted in high-quality food plants.

You have probably eaten Thompson Seedless grapes, McIntosh apples, or Valencia oranges. They are just three examples of the several hundred thousand different cultivars. The word *cultivar* is a contraction of the terms *cultivated* and *variety*. **Cultivars** (KUHL-ti-VAHRZ) are selected by people, and they have at least one distinguishing characteristic that sets them apart from other members of their species. The famous Japanese flowering cherry trees in Washington, D.C., Yoshino cherries, are another example of a cultivar.

FIGURE 29-1

Wheat is one of the world's most important food crops. It is used to make breads, crackers, macaroni, and spaghetti.

Word Roots and Origins

agriculture

from the Latin *ager*, meaning "field," and *cultura*, meaning "cultivation"

FOOD CROPS

Food crops are usually classified partly by use and partly by family. The classification system in Table 29-1 is not like the taxonomic classification used by scientists because most categories contain species that are not closely related. Also, many crops fit into more than one category. For example, corn is a cereal, but it can also be classified as an oil crop, a sweetener, a vegetable, and a beverage.

Cereals

Cereals are grasses that contain grains. Grains are the edible, dry fruits of a cereal. Over half of the world's cultivated land is devoted to cereal crops, such as rice, wheat, corn, oats, sorghum, rye, and millet. Worldwide, cereals provide about 50 percent of the calories in the average human diet. In addition, much of the harvested grain is used for animal feed, so it is indirectly consumed by people as meat, poultry, eggs, and dairy products.

Wheat and corn are produced in the largest amounts. Wheat grows well in moderate to cold climates, including parts of the United States, Russia, and Canada. The United States is the leading producer of corn, also called maize. Rice is different from other cereals because it grows best in shallow water, as shown on page 560. Rice thrives in areas with warm temperatures.

TABLE 29-1 *Food Crops*	
Category	**Example plants**
Cereals	rice, wheat, corn, oats, sorghum, rye, barley, millet
Root crops	potato, cassava, sweet potato, yam, taro
Legumes	soybean, peanut, bean, pea, alfalfa, lentils
Fruits	apple, peach, banana, grape, orange, blueberry, pineapple, cherry, mango, pear
Nuts	peanut, walnut, cashew, pecan, coconut, almond, macadamia, filbert, pistachio
Vegetables	spinach, cabbage, sweet corn, pea, turnip, asparagus, tomato, artichoke, zucchini
Forages	cereals, legumes, grasses
Oils	cottonseed, rapeseed, palm, sesame, soybean, corn, safflower, sunflower
Beverages	coffee, tea, cola, cacao, fruit juice, grape (wine), corn (whiskey), barley and hops (beer)
Sweeteners	sugar cane, sugar beet, sugar maple, corn
Spices	pepper, cinnamon, vanilla, paprika, cloves, saffron, nutmeg, ginger, allspice
Herbs	rosemary, thyme, sage, dill, basil, oregano, mint
Flavorings	cacao (chocolate), coconut, carob, licorice, quinine
Colorings	red beet, anatto, turmeric, saffron, carrot
Additives	guar, locust bean, citrus (pectin), gum arabic, chicle tree
Garnishes	sesame, caraway, and poppy seeds; parsley; pimento
Snacks	popcorn, sunflower seeds, pumpkin seeds

Root Crops

Root crops are roots or underground stems that are rich in carbo-hydrates. In many parts of the world, root crops substitute for cereals in providing the major part of the diet. However, diets of root crops or cereals alone are usually low in some important amino acids. To correct this deficiency, other foods, such as legumes or animal protein, must be eaten.

Root crops include potatoes, beets, carrots, radishes, rutabagas, and turnips. You may have eaten tapioca pudding, which comes from a plant grown in the tropics called cassava, shown in Figure 29-2.

Legumes

Legumes are members of the pea family and bear protein-rich seeds in pods. Soybean, shown in Figure 29-3, is the most impor-tant legume crop because it is produced in the largest amount and has many important uses. Soybean is used to make vegetable oil, soy milk, soy sauce, tofu, and margarine. Alfalfa and clover are legumes used mainly as feed for livestock. Legumes are important in agriculture because they improve the nitrogen content of soil. Recall from Chapter 24 that the bacteria *Rhizobium* form a symbi-otic relationship with many legumes.

Fruits, Vegetables, and Nuts

Many "vegetables" we know, such as tomatoes, green beans, and squash, are actually taxonomically classified as fruits. A **fruit** is the part of a flowering plant that usually contains seeds. Foods derived from the leaves, stems, seeds, and roots of nonwoody plants are often called **vegetables.** Vegetables are excellent sources of many important vitamins and minerals, making them an essential part of a healthy diet. Most **nuts** have a hard outer layer and contain a dry, one-seed fruit. Nuts include almonds, walnuts, pecans, and hazel-nuts. Peanuts are commonly considered to be nuts but are taxo-nomically classified as legumes.

Spices, Herbs, and Flavorings

Other food crops add variety and pleasure to our diet by flavoring our water, beverages, and food. More than half the population get daily stimulation from caffeine in coffee, tea, and cola drinks. Both **spices** and **herbs** are used to add taste to food. In general, spices come from plant parts other than the leaf and are tropical. Herbs usually come from leaves and usually can be grown in a home gar-den. Flavorings, such as chocolate and coconut, are not usually considered spices or herbs and are therefore placed in a separate category. Another flavor, quinine, is used to make tonic water. **Quinine** comes from the bark of the cinchona tree and is used to treat malaria.

Food Production

For decades, experts have been predicting widespread food short-ages due to the continuing increase in the world population.

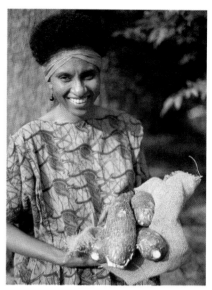

FIGURE 29-2

An important root crop in South America is cassava, which has thick roots that are eaten like potatoes. The starch-filled roots of cassava can be 30–120 cm (1–4 ft) long.

FIGURE 29-3

Soybean is an important legume crop grown in the midwestern and southern parts of the United States. The soybean plant is covered with short, fine hairs and is usually 60–120 cm (2–4 ft) tall. It is an inexpensive and useful source of protein.

Making Your Own Fertilizer—Composting

Many people are making their own fertilizer through a technique called composting. Compost is a type of organic fertilizer made from decayed plant matter. Compost improves the texture of soil and provides inorganic nutrients for plants.

It's easy to start your own compost pile. Collect dead plant matter, such as grass clippings, leaves, coffee grounds, or sawdust. Make a pile by alternating layers of plant matter with a thin layer of soil or manure. Sprinkle water on the pile to speed the process of decay. After the compost has been allowed to decay for about six months, it should be ready for use in your garden.

Word Roots and Origins

pesticide

contains the suffix -*cide*, from the Latin *cida*, meaning "cut down" or "kill"

However, massive food shortages have not occurred mainly because of increased use of irrigation, fertilizers, and pesticides. Improvements in cultivars; farm machinery; food preservation techniques; and methods of controlling diseases, weeds, and pests have also helped improve food production. **Fertilizers** supply plants with essential mineral nutrients like nitrogen and phosphorus. **Pesticides** are chemicals that kill undesirable organisms that eat crops, such as some insects.

People have made many trade-offs to support an adequate food supply. The negative consequences include massive soil erosion, depletion of fossil fuel and water supplies, pollution, and destruction of wild populations of plants and animals as more land is cultivated.

NONFOOD USES OF PLANTS

In addition to providing us with food, plants provide us with thousands of other essential products. It is hard to imagine how we could live without plants, given the variety of products that contain substances from plants.

Medicines

The ancient Greeks treated headaches with the bark of white willow, which contains the chemical salicin. This use gave scientists the idea to test a similar chemical, acetylsalicylic (uh-SEET-uhl-SAL-uh-SIL-ik) acid. The willow is in the genus *Salix,* hence the names *salicin* and *salicylic.* You know acetylsalicylic acid as **aspirin,** the world's most widely used medicine. Besides pain relief, aspirin is used to thin blood and thereby prevent heart attacks and strokes. Plants were our first medicines, and early plant biologists, like Linnaeus, were often medical doctors. Many modern medicines either still come from plants or were originally obtained from plants and are now synthesized in the laboratory. Table 29-2 lists examples of plants that

TABLE 29-2 *Plants in Medicine*

Plant	Genus name	Drug	Use
Cinchona	*Cinchona*	quinine	treat malaria and certain disorders of heart rhythm
Foxglove	*Digitalis*	digitalis	treat heart disease, help regulate heart rate
Yam	*Dioscorea*	cortisone	treat inflammation and allergies
White willow	*Salix*	acetylsalicylic acid (aspirin)	relieve pain, prevent heart attacks and strokes
Yew	*Taxus*	taxol	treat ovarian cancer, breast cancer, and some types of lung cancer

(a)

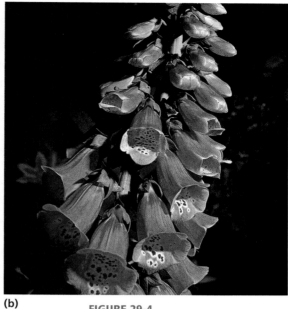

(b)

are used in medicine. Two of these plants, yew and foxglove, are shown in Figure 29-4. Scientists are currently evaluating thousands of plant species that may have medicinal properties. Scientists are very concerned about the destruction of rain forests because many rain-forest plant species have yet to be researched. In addition to medicines, plants provide many other products, which are summarized in Table 29-3 on page 566.

Your local health-food store carries a wide range of plant products that claim to prevent disease or improve health. These substances are not regulated by the Food and Drug Administration (FDA). For example, it is reported that garlic and *Echinacea* (purple coneflower) may improve immune response. Consumers should remember that the effectiveness and safety of herbal remedies have not been confirmed by the rigorous scientific testing that new medicines must undergo before receiving FDA approval. The FDA, pharmaceutical companies, and health-care providers are working together to investigate the claims of those who market these remedies.

Clothing and Fabric Dyes

Figure 29-5 shows cotton, which is used to make most of our clothing. The original jeans of Levi Strauss were made with sailcloth woven from hemp. Strauss later switched to cotton. Some expensive clothing is woven with linen, which is made from the flax plant. Artificial fabrics, like rayon, arnel, and cellulose acetate, are made from processed wood fibers. Leather is made from animal hides, but it is usually treated with tannin, a chemical obtained from many tree species. Tanning makes leather stronger and prevents it from rotting.

Prior to the mid-1800s, fabrics were dyed with natural plant dyes. Today most clothing is colored with dyes manufactured from coal, which consists of the remains of ancient plants.

TABLE 29-3 Nonfood Uses of Plants

Use	Example plants
Brooms/brushes	broomcorn, palms, coconut
Building materials	trees, bamboo, reeds, palms, grasses
Carpets/mats	jute, coconut (coir), cotton, trees
Clothing	cotton, flax (linen), ramie, pineapple, trees (rayon and arnel)
Cosmetics	corn, avocado, carrot, almond, cacao, soybean, macadamia, aloe
Fabric dyes	indigo (blue), madder (red), onion (yellow), black walnut (brown), peach (green), maple (pink)
Fuels	trees, bamboo, water hyacinth, grain alcohol, vegetable oils, gopher plant
Furniture	redwood, oak, rattan, teak, willow (wicker), rushes
Hair dyes	henna, rhubarb, chamomile, black walnut
Incense	frankincense, myrrh, cinnamon
Inks	soybean, flax (linseed oil), tung-oil tree
Leather	black wattle, quebracho, Spanish chestnut (tannin)
Lipstick	jojoba, castor bean, carnauba palm, soybean, coconut
Medicines	foxglove (digitalis), cinchona (quinine), yew (taxol), opium poppy (morphine, codeine), yam (cortisone), aloe, ipecac, ginseng, ginkgo, guarana, purple coneflower, kudzu, saw palmetto
Miscellaneous	cork oak (cork), incense cedar (pencil shafts), trees (disposable baby diapers and cellulose acetate plastic), kapok (life preserver stuffing), rosary pea (bead necklaces), water hyacinth (water purification), lignum vitae (submarine engine bearings)
Musical instruments	ebony (black piano keys), maple (violins), reed (woodwind reeds), African blackwood (woodwinds)
Ornamentals	shade trees, shrubs, lawns, cut flowers, Christmas trees, houseplants
Paints	flax (linseed oil), tung-oil tree, soybean, pine (turpentine)
Paper/cardboard	trees, cotton, flax, hemp, bamboo, papyrus
Perfumes	rose, orange, lavender, orchids, sandalwood, lilac, jasmine, lily of the valley, pine
Pesticides/repellents	tobacco (nicotine sulfate), derris (rotenone), chrysanthemum (pyrethrum), citronella grass, garlic, citrus
Rope	hemp, agave (sisal)
Rubber	rubber tree, guayule
Shampoo	palm oil, coconut, jojoba, aloe, trees, herbs, fruits
Soaps	coconut, palm oil, cacao, lavender, herbs, fruits
Sports equipment	balata (golf balls), persimmon (golf club heads), ash (baseball bats), ebony and ash (pool cues)
Toothpaste	mint, wheat, palm oil, coconut
Tourist attractions	redwoods, giant sequoias, saguaro cactuses, fall foliage, Holland flower bulbs
Waxes	carnauba palm, cauassu, candelilla, bayberry

Fuels

Most of the energy we use for heat, electricity, and machine fuel comes from fossil fuels—coal, oil, and natural gas. Fossil fuels are composed of stored photosynthetic energy from millions of years ago. In developing nations, much of the fuel comes from wood or other plant materials. For example, grains can be fermented into alcohol and mixed with gasoline to make **gasohol.** Gasohol, which is made of about 10 percent alcohol, is an alternative fuel for automobiles.

Other Uses of Plants

Ornamental trees, shrubs, and other plants outside our homes do much more than provide beauty. Besides their decorative function, they improve the environment by preventing soil erosion, reducing noise, providing habitats for wild animals, acting as windbreaks, providing shade, and moderating temperatures, which, in turn, reduces home heating and cooling costs. Scientists have also found that ornamental plants improve our mental well-being. Gardening has long been a popular hobby in the United States, and it is an important form of exercise for millions of people.

Many plants have become major tourist attractions, such as the California redwoods shown in Figure 29-6. Every fall, people visit the forests of the northeastern United States to view the spectacular leaf colors.

Plants are essential to our survival because they produce virtually all of our food, and they enhance our lives in many ways. Growing cut flowers is now a multibillion-dollar-a-year industry, and it is only a small part of the huge business of growing and using plants. Plants can also provide the inspiration to develop innovative products. The cocklebur plant provided the idea for hook and loop fasteners when the hooked fruit was caught in the inventor's clothing. Plants have made our lives better in numerous ways, and they undoubtedly will continue to do so in the future.

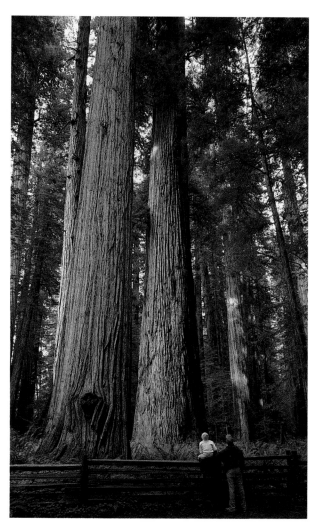

FIGURE 29-6

The redwood trees that grow along the West Coast of the United States are a majestic sight. Redwoods usually grow 60–84 m (200–275 ft) high. The bark is very thick, making the trees resistant to fires.

SECTION 29-1 REVIEW

1. Describe ways that people use plants.

2. Distinguish between cereals, root crops, legumes, fruits, and vegetables.

3. List three plants that are widely used as medicines.

4. List several personal grooming products that use ingredients from plants.

5. Explain three environmental benefits of having ornamental trees around a house.

6. **CRITICAL THINKING** How might transferring specific genes from legumes into rice plants help reduce malnutrition?

George Washington Carver: Healer of the Soil

HISTORICAL PERSPECTIVE

Throughout the 1800s, cotton was the main cash crop and was called king of the South. As the century drew to a close, few people saw any reason for change. One man who did, however, was George Washington Carver. In 1896, Carver came to Alabama to teach scientific agriculture and direct the research department at Tuskegee Institute. But he had greater goals—to free African Americans from the ignorance and poverty left by slavery and to free the South of its dependence on cotton.

Scientific Agriculture

After the Civil War, the South remained an agricultural economy, with its recovery dependent on its farmers. Former slaves and masters devoted themselves to raising cotton to sell to eager markets. But George Washington Carver spent his life teaching another, better way.

All his life, Carver was intrigued by plants. He collected them, carried them around, identified and studied them, and even drew them. Like his teachers at Iowa State College of Agriculture (now Iowa State University), Carver believed American agriculture could be transformed by applying scientific principles.

After Carver earned a master's degree in agriculture and botany in 1896, Booker T. Washington, the founder of Tuskegee Institute (now Tuskegee University), invited him to head the school's agriculture department. Carver knew he had found a place where he could carry on his research.

Better Soil, Bigger Crops

When Carver saw the desolate fields around Tuskegee, he understood the problem. Planting the same crop in the same soil year after year had taken its toll. Great forests had been felled to make room for cotton, and without tree roots to hold the soil, millions of tons had washed away, along with valuable plant nutrients.

George Washington Carver

Carver and his students started a 20-acre school "farm." Later Carver said,

> They told me it was the worst soil in Alabama, and I believed them. But it was the only soil I had. I could either sit down and cry over it or I could improve it.

The first year, the soil yielded five bales of cotton, 120 bushels of sweet potatoes, and a net loss of $16.50. Each year thereafter, the soil and the harvest improved as Carver and his students made compost, spread fertilizer, planted various crops, and rotated the crops from year to year. After a few growing seasons, some cotton bushes bore as many as 275 giant white bolls.

The farm demonstrated what Carver had told his students: each plant needs certain things, the soil carries certain things, and it's up to the farmer to make any necessary changes to the soil. The depleted soil lacked nitrogen because cotton is a voracious nitrogen consumer, but legumes, such as cowpeas, peanuts, and soybeans, extract nitrogen from air and return it to the soil. The roots of legumes make nitrogen in the air available in a form that plants can use, and thereby enrich the soil with nitrogen.

From Shampoo to Axle Grease

Carver's contributions to southern farming were many, but he is best known for the many new uses he found for the peanut. Peanuts, he said, restore the soil's nitrogen and are easy to plant, grow, and harvest.

Carver traveled throughout the Southern states, trying to promote the growing of peanuts.

At one point, Carver wondered if he had made a mistake. Farmers were growing a surplus of peanuts, but was there a market? Farmers would continue to plant peanuts only if they could sell them. Carver returned to his laboratory, where he created more than 300 peanut products. By 1950, the soil-enriching peanut was the second largest crop in the South. Carver experimented with other plants, including soybeans and sweet potatoes. Over 100 products were developed from the sweet potato plant by Carver. In fact, the Center for Sweet Potato Research is located on the Tuskegee University campus.

Presidential Praises

Carver answered hundreds of letters, wrote a series of farm bulletins, displayed his products at fairs, and met with agriculture secretaries of the United States—and even the president. President Theodore Roosevelt once told him, "There is no more-important work than what you are doing." In 1930, the Roosevelt Medal was given to Carver for his contributions to science. Carver spent his life leading African Americans forward. In the process, he paved the way for a better life for an entire region.

Working in his laboratory, George Washington Carver developed more than 300 products using peanuts. He also developed flour, molasses, rubber, and postage stamp glue from sweet potatoes.

Another reason to appreciate Carver's work is that he taught conservation long before that word became popular. He showed that certain "weeds" could make useful products, reminding us that seemingly useless plants may someday serve humanity as vital medicines and food products. Carver once said, "We can learn to synthesize materials for every human need from the things that grow."

In 1951, a national monument was established to honor George Washington Carver. This tribute to his extraordinary life in science is located on a Missouri farm—where he was born.

OBJECTIVES

▲

Define *plant ecology.*

●

Give two examples of how plants recycle elements in the environment, and explain why this recycling is essential to humans.

■

Explain how plants benefit from interactions with animals.

◆

Explain the beneficial interactions between plants, fungi, and bacteria.

▲

Describe how people have damaged wild plant populations.

PLANTS AND THE ENVIRONMENT

*B*ased solely on weight, algae and photosynthetic bacteria are dominant organisms in the oceans, and plants are dominant on land. Photosynthetic plants are called producers because they make food for other living things. Organisms that eat other organisms, like animals, are called consumers and depend on plants for a source of organic compounds.

PLANT ECOLOGY

The study of the interactions between plants and the environment is called **plant ecology.** The most important interaction involves the ability of plants to capture solar energy through photosynthesis. In photosynthesis, plants absorb carbon dioxide from the air, produce sugar and starch, and break apart water, releasing oxygen into the air. Consumers use sugar and oxygen in aerobic respiration and produce carbon dioxide and water. Organic compounds from plants provide consumers with energy, building blocks, and essential molecules like vitamins and fiber.

Plants also provide organisms with inorganic nutrients. Plant roots are very efficient at mining the soil for inorganic nutrients, such as nitrogen, phosphorus, potassium, iron, and magnesium. Plants use these inorganic nutrients in the organic compounds they make. Consumers ingest these organic compounds and incorporate the inorganic nutrients into their own bodies. Eventually, these same

FIGURE 29-7

About half of the world's species of plants and animals live in tropical rain forests. Scientists are very concerned about the destruction of rain forests because many plant species have yet to be researched, and some may have medicinal properties.

inorganic nutrients are returned to the soil when the consumer's waste material or dead body is decomposed by bacteria and fungi. Plants thus play a major role in the continuous cycling of the Earth's water, oxygen, carbon dioxide, and inorganic nutrients.

Plants are also responsible for the formation and maintenance of soil. Roots bind soil particles together, leaves reduce the soil-eroding impact of wind and rain, and dead plant parts add organic matter to the soil.

Plant-Animal Interactions

Plants interact with animals in many fascinating ways. Many flowering plants attract pollinators, animals that carry pollen from one plant to another. Usually the pollinator gets a reward for its efforts in the form of food from nectar. The size, shape, color, and odor of many flowers make them attractive to their pollinators. For example, Figure 29-8 shows that in some orchid species, the flowers have evolved to look and smell like the female of their wasp or bee pollinators. A male wasp or bee lands on a flower believing he has located a mate. The pollen he touches sticks to his body and is transferred to the next orchid he visits. In this case, the flower lures the pollinator with the promise of a mate, but fools the insect into picking up pollen without receiving a reward.

Plant-Microbe Interactions

Two important aspects of plant ecology are plant interactions with fungi and with bacteria. Plant-microbe interactions may be harmful to plants, as in the case of fungal and bacterial diseases. Diseases often cause major crop losses. However, bacteria and fungi also form important beneficial relationships with plants.

The majority of plant species form mycorrhizae, which are symbiotic relationships between fungi and the roots of a plant. A mycorrhizal fungus infects a root, often changing the root structure. However, the fungus does not harm the root. Instead, it greatly increases the root's ability to absorb water and other inorganic nutrients, such as phosphorus and potassium. In return, the root supplies the fungus with energy.

The roots of many plant species also form beneficial associations with bacteria. Some bacteria can take nitrogen gas from the air and "fix" it, or convert it to a form that plants can use. Plants of the legume family, such as peas, beans, and peanuts commonly host bacteria that fix nitrogen.

Protecting Native Plants

We protect and care for many plants that provide us with food, clothing, shelter, and other products. However, humans have drastically changed natural plant populations by introducing foreign plant species, diseases, and animals. Introduced plants, like the water hyacinth shown in Figure 29-9, kudzu, crabgrass, and dandelion have become widespread weeds. **Weeds** are undesirable plants that often crowd out crop plants or native plant species. For

FIGURE 29-8
Some orchid species have evolved to resemble their wasp or bee pollinators.

FIGURE 29-9
The water hyacinth has become a weed that clogs waterways in the southeastern United States.

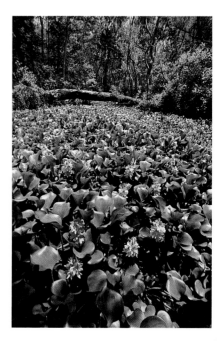

example, water hyacinths float on lakes and rivers, growing so fast and dense that they impede boats and shade underwater plants. The introduction of a fungal disease, chestnut blight, in 1904 virtually wiped out the American chestnut as a dominant forest tree in the eastern United States. Government inspectors now carefully screen plant materials entering the country to prevent the introduction of new plant pests.

FIGURE 29-10

Giant ragweed, which can grow to more than 4 m (13 ft.) tall, produces massive amounts of pollen that is a major cause of hay fever. The small, dull flowers indicate that it is wind-pollinated.

HARMFUL PLANTS

Despite the many benefits plants provide, some plants can also cause harm. Many deaths are caused by addictive plant products, such as tobacco, cocaine, opium, and alcohol. Some plant species are poisonous when eaten or touched. Poison ivy and poison oak give an itchy rash to millions of Americans each year. Children are often poisoned, though usually not fatally, when they eat the leaves or colorful berries of house or garden plants. Despite widespread reports to the contrary, the popular Christmas plant poinsettia is not deadly, but its sap may cause skin irritation. However, holly berries and all parts of American mistletoe are poisonous.

Tens of millions of people suffer from pollen allergies, one cause of hay fever. **Hay fever** is an allergic reaction that results in sneezing, a runny nose, and watering eyes. Pollen allergies occur at three seasons. In early spring, deciduous trees, such as oak, ash, birch, and sycamore release pollen. In late spring or early summer, it is mainly wild and pasture grasses that cause allergy problems. Of the cereal crops, only rye pollen seems to be an important cause of allergies. In late summer and fall, the highly allergenic pollen of ragweeds, shown in Figure 29-10, affects people. Contrary to popular belief, large, colorful flowers do not cause hay fever. Pollen that causes allergies comes from small, drab flowers that are wind-pollinated.

SECTION 29-2 REVIEW

1. What is plant ecology?

2. How do plants continuously recycle the Earth's inorganic nutrients?

3. How do plants benefit from their interactions with animals?

4. How do plants benefit from their interactions with fungi and bacteria?

5. How do plants harm people?

6. **CRITICAL THINKING**   Explain how people have damaged wild plant populations by introducing foreign organisms.

CHAPTER 29 REVIEW

SUMMARY/VOCABULARY

 ■ The branch of biology that studies plants is called botany. The practical applications of botany are evident in agriculture, which is the raising of crops and livestock for food or other uses.

■ Humans have cultivated plants for at least 11,000 years and have changed many plant species so much, via selection, that these plants can no longer survive in the wild.

■ There are several hundred thousand plant cultivars, or cultivated varieties, that are given names, such as McIntosh apple.

■ Food crops can be classified in many ways, including by their usage and by their taxonomic classification.

■ The major part of the human diet is provided by a few cereal crops in the grass family, especially corn, wheat, and rice.

■ The identification of fruits and vegetables is sometimes confusing because everyday definitions are different from botanical definitions. Many of our common vegetables, such as green beans, tomatoes, squash, and pumpkins, are actually fruits. Botanically speaking, a fruit is the part of a flowering plant that usually contains seeds.

■ Plants provide many important medicines, such as digitalis, quinine, morphine, and cancer drugs.

■ Several factors have increased food production, including the use of fertilizers and pesticides. As land is cultivated to produce an adequate food supply, the health of the environment is compromised by soil erosion, depleted water supplies, and pollution.

■ Plants provide thousands of nonfood products, including clothing, fabric dye, lumber, paper, cosmetics, fuel, cork, rubber, turpentine, and pesticides.

■ Ornamental plants improve the human environment in many important ways: they provide shade, minimize soil erosion, reduce noise, and lower home energy costs.

Vocabulary

agriculture (561)	cultivar (561)	herb (563)	quinine (563)
aspirin (564)	fertilizer (564)	legume (563)	root crop (563)
botany (561)	fruit (563)	nut (563)	spice (563)
cereal (562)	gasohol (567)	pesticide (564)	vegetable (563)

 ■ Based on weight, plants are the dominant organisms on land.

■ Photosynthetic plants are producers, and animals are consumers.

■ Plants play a major role in recycling the Earth's water, oxygen, carbon dioxide, and inorganic nutrients.

■ Plants provide animals with inorganic nutrients as well as organic nutrients.

■ Most plant roots are infected with beneficial mycorrhizal fungi, which greatly increase the roots' ability to absorb inorganic nutrients.

■ Most nitrogen in living organisms must first be fixed by bacteria, which may live in association with plant roots, especially the roots of legumes.

■ Plants associate with animals in many mutually beneficial ways, such as providing food to animals that protect them or carry their pollen.

■ People have negatively affected wild plant populations by introducing foreign species of plants, animals, and disease organisms.

■ Hay fever, or pollen allergies, is caused by the small flowers of certain wind-pollinated plants, not by ornamental flowers.

Vocabulary

hay fever (572)	plant ecology (570)	weed (571)

REVIEW

Vocabulary

1. Distinguish between botany and agriculture.
2. Define *cultivar,* and give two examples of popular cultivars.
3. List three cereals.
4. List three medicinal plants.
5. What are mycorrhizae, and how do they benefit a plant?

Multiple Choice

6. Plants provide us with (a) energy (b) oxygen (c) inorganic elements (d) all of the above.
7. Some plants attract pollinators by producing (a) spines (b) grains (c) toxic chemicals (d) modified flowers.
8. Organisms that use plants as food are referred to as (a) predators (b) consumers (c) producers (d) pollinators.
9. The cultivation of plants by humans probably began in (a) the Middle East (b) South America (c) North America (d) Northern Europe.
10. The foxglove plant aids in the treatment of heart disease because it is the source of a medication called (a) quinine (b) morphine (c) digitalis (d) taxol.
11. Edible underground structures that store nutrients are called (a) root crops (b) legumes (c) forage crops (d) grains.
12. Legumes can produce seeds that are protein-rich even in unfertilized soil because of their associations with bacteria that (a) break down carbohydrates (b) absorb oxygen (c) fix nitrogen (d) produce carbon.
13. Plants that are the major source of food for the world today are called (a) spices (b) root crops (c) legumes (d) cereals.
14. Pollen allergies most likely would be caused by pollen from (a) a bee-pollinated flower (b) a large colorful flower (c) a wind-pollinated flower (d) a fragrant flower.
15. During photosynthesis, plants produce (a) carbon dioxide (b) quinine (c) oxygen (d) water.

Short Answer

16. Distinguish between a fruit and a vegetable.
17. List three nonfood, nonmedicinal uses of plants.
18. Why can't people survive solely on a diet of cereals?
19. Why are pharmaceutical companies and health care providers sometimes skeptical of herbal remedies?
20. Explain how plants and microbes interact in mutually beneficial ways.
21. Describe how people act as selecting agents in the evolution of food plants.
22. List several grooming products that use ingredients from plants.
23. What adaptive advantage might colorful flowers have for plants?
24. Name three addictive plant products.
25. Describe how ornamental trees improve the environment.

CRITICAL THINKING

1. Native American farmers often grow corn, pole beans, and squash together. The drawing below shows how the pole beans climbed the corn while the squash carpeted the ground around the corn. What advantage might each plant gain from this arrangement? What advantage is this to the human diet?

2. One explanation for the sudden extinction of dinosaurs is that they starved after an asteroid hit the Earth. The impact created huge dust clouds that blocked out the sunlight and prevented photosynthesis. How would people obtain food and oxygen if the same thing were to happen today?

3. If all animals disappeared from the Earth, what effects, positive and negative, would this have on plants?

4. During the rainy season in the Brazilian rain forest, the rivers flood the land. Many fish from these rivers then swim among the land plants and eat their fruit. How might this intermingling of fish and plants help the plants?

5. Suppose a friend asks you why corn, which he or she considers to be a vegetable, is listed as a cereal crop in the encyclopedia. To answer this question, write a paragraph that explains why corn is a cereal crop, agriculturally, and why it is also a fruit, botanically. Include other examples of foods that are classified as vegetables or grains, but are also fruits.

6. How did artificial selection by humans play a role in the origin of agricultural crops? How is artificial selection similar to natural selection?

7. Many athletes consume carbohydrates before a competition to increase their endurance. The table below shows a variety of legumes and grains that can be purchased at a grocery store. Compare their prices and nutritional backgrounds. Determine which food is the least expensive source of carbohydrates.

Common Legumes and Grains					Per serving			
Food	Package size	Price	Serving (g)	Calories	Total fat (g)	Total carbo-hydrate (g)	Total protein (g)
Navy beans	454 g	.69	45	80	0	23	8
Rice	907 g	.79	45	150	0	35	3
Barley	454 g	.49	45	100	0	24	3
Soybeans	454 g	.89	45	170	8	14	15
Spaghetti	907 g	.79	45	200	1	34	6

EXTENSION

1. Examine the labels of some processed foods, such as ice cream, yogurt, crackers, and margarine. Determine the types of plants that were used in their preparation.

2. Read "The Bromeliads of the Atlantic Forest" in *Scientific American,* March 2000, on page 86. Describe at least one interaction between bromeliads and an animal of the forest. How are these plants endangered?

3. Read "Redwoods in the Mist" in *National Wildlife,* April/May 1999, on page 8. Discuss how Todd Dawson of Cornell University explains why tall redwood trees might not have to transport water all the way from their roots to their tops. What role does fog play in the process?

4. Using field guides from a library, determine which plants in your school grounds or in a nearby park are native and which are foreign. For foreign species, list the continent of origin.

Comparing Soil-Grown Plants with Hydroponic Plants

OBJECTIVES

- Compare hydroponic plant-cultivation techniques with conventional plant-cultivation techniques.
- Observe the germination of wheat seeds over a two-week period.

PROCESS SKILLS

- analyzing data
- measuring
- comparing and contrasting

MATERIALS

- 2 clear plastic cups
- plastic-foam floater with 6 holes in it
- 50 mL of potting soil
- cheesecloth (must be large enough to cover the plastic-foam floater)
- 12 wheat seeds
- 50 mL of complete nutrient solution
- plastic dropper
- labeling tape
- marking pen
- 50 mL graduated cylinder
- metric ruler

Background

1. Hydroponic cultivation is a technique for growing plants in a solution that contains all of the inorganic nutrients the plant needs. Plants that are grown hydroponically do not require soil.
2. The beginning of growth in a seed is called *germination.*

PART A Day 1

1. Using the marking pen and the labeling tape, label one clear plastic cup "Soil Cultivated," and label the other plastic cup "Hydroponically Cultivated."
2. Fill the cup labeled "Soil Cultivated" halfway with moist potting soil. Place six wheat seeds on the surface of the soil; use the distance between the holes in the foam floater as a guide to determine the spacing of the wheat seeds. (Do not place the floater on the soil.)
3. Press the seeds into the soil until they are approximately 0.5 cm below the surface. Cover the seeds with soil, and press down firmly.
4. Water the seeds with 10 mL of distilled water.
5. Add 50 mL of complete nutrient solution to the cup labeled "Hydroponically Cultivated," and place the plastic-foam floater on the surface of the solution, as shown in the figure below.
6. Place the cheesecloth on top of the floater, as illustrated in the figure. Press lightly at the location of the holes in the floater to moisten the cheesecloth.

7. Place the remaining six wheat seeds on top of the cheesecloth in the cup labeled "Hydroponically Cultivated." Position the seeds so that each one lies in an indentation formed by the cheesecloth in a hole in the floater. Press each seed lightly into the hole until the seed coat is moistened.

8. Place both cups in a warm, dry location. Water the soil-cultivated seeds as needed, monitoring the amount of water added. Aerate the roots of the hydroponic plants every day by using a clean plastic dropper to blow air into the nutrient solution.
9. In your lab report, prepare data tables similar to Table A and Table B. Write your observations of the seeds in your data tables.
10. Clean up your lab materials and wash your hands before leaving the lab.

TABLE A *OBSERVATIONS OF SOIL-GROWN PLANTS*		
Day	Appearance of seedlings	Average height (mm)
1		
2		
3		
4		
5		
6		
7		
8		
9		
10		
11		
12		
13		
14		

TABLE B *OBSERVATIONS OF HYDROPONICALLY GROWN SEEDS*		
Day	Appearance of seedlings	Average height (mm)
1		
2		
3		
4		
5		
6		
7		
8		
9		
10		
11		
12		
13		
14		

PART B Days 2–14

11. Compare the contents of each cup every day for two weeks, and record the appearance of the wheat seedlings in your data tables. If you are unable to observe your seedlings over the weekend, be sure to note in your data table that no observations were made on those days.

12. Each time that you observe the seedlings after they have begun to grow, measure their height and record the average height of the seedlings in each cup in your data tables. To find the average height for one cup, add the heights of each seedling in the cup together and divide by the number of seedlings (6).

13. After the seeds in the cup containing nutrient solution have germinated and formed roots, allow an air pocket to form between the floater and the surface of the nutrient solution. A portion of the roots should still be submerged in the nutrient solution. The air pocket allows the roots of the seeds to absorb the oxygen necessary for metabolic processes while continuing to absorb nutrients from the nutrient solution. Continue to observe and record the progress of the seedlings in each cup on a daily basis.

14. Clean up your lab materials and wash your hands before leaving the lab.

Analysis and Conclusions

1. Based on the data you recorded, which seeds germinated more quickly? Which seeds attained the greatest height?

2. Compare your results with those of your classmates. Were the results the same for each group of students?

3. You planted six seeds in each cup. Why do you think the lab had you do this instead of having you plant a single seed in each cup? Why is the use of more than one sample important?

4. How could hydroponic growing techniques be useful to countries that have either a growing season that is too short to grow a variety of crops or soil that does not support most agricultural crops?

Further Inquiry

The nutrient solution you used in this investigation should have provided all of the inorganic nutrients that the wheat seeds needed for proper growth. How could you determine exactly which inorganic nutrients a plant requires by using hydroponic cultivation?

CHAPTER 30

PLANT EVOLUTION AND CLASSIFICATION

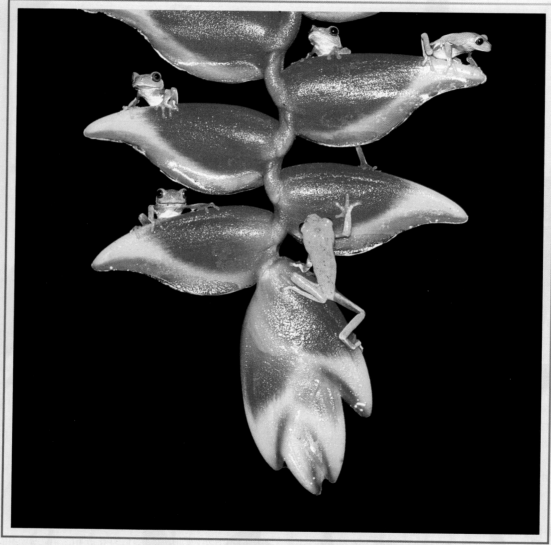

Red-eyed tree frogs are climbing on this colorful Heliconia flower. These organisms are from the tropical rain forest of Belize, a country in Central America. Worldwide, tropical rain forests are home to almost half the world's species of plants and animals.

FOCUS CONCEPT: *Evolution*

As you read, look for the characteristics that reveal how plants have adapted to conditions on land.

OVERVIEW OF PLANTS

Plants dominate the land and many bodies of water. Plants exhibit tremendous diversity. Some plants are less than 1 mm (0.04 in.) in width, and some plants grow to more than 100 m (328 ft) in height. The 12 phyla, or divisions, of kingdom Plantae include more than 270,000 species. Some plants complete their life cycle in a few weeks, while others may live nearly 5,000 years.

ADAPTING TO LAND

Although life had flourished in the oceans for more than 3 billion years, no organisms lived on land until about 430 million years ago, when a layer of ozone formed. The ozone protected organisms from the sun's ultraviolet radiation. Eventually, small club-shaped plants began to grow in the mud at the water's edge.

Preventing Water Loss

The move from water to land offered some organisms distinct advantages, including more exposure to sunlight for photosynthesis, increased carbon dioxide levels, and a greater supply of inorganic nutrients. However, the land environment also presented challenges. Plants on land are susceptible to drying out through evaporation.

One early adaptation to life on land was the **cuticle** (KYOOT-ih-kuhl), a waxy protective covering on plant surfaces that prevents water loss. Although the cuticle protects a plant by keeping water in the plant, it also keeps out carbon dioxide. Plants that had small openings in their surfaces, called stomata, were able to survive. Stomata allow the exchange of carbon dioxide and oxygen.

Reproducing by Spores and Seeds

Successful land plants also developed structures, such as spores and seeds, that helped protect reproductive cells from drying out. A **spore** is a haploid reproductive cell surrounded by a hard outer wall. Spores allowed the widespread dispersal of plant species. Eventually, most plants developed seeds. A **seed** is an embryo surrounded by a protective coat. Seeds also contain **endosperm,** a tissue that provides nourishment for the developing plant. Figure 30-1 shows the unusual seed adaptation of the sugar maple tree; the winged seeds get caught in the wind and twirl to the ground. Seeds are more effective at dispersal than spores are.

FIGURE 30-1

The leaves of a sugar maple tree are covered with a waxy cuticle that prevents water loss. The seeds are found inside a winged fruit. The wings help the seeds disperse away from the parent tree, usually twirling down to the ground.

Transporting Materials Throughout the Plant

Certain species of plants evolved **vascular** (VAS-kyu-luhr) **tissue,** a type of tissue that transports water and dissolved substances from one part of the plant to another. Two types of specialized tissue make up vascular tissue. **Xylem** (ZIE-luhm) carries water and inorganic nutrients in one direction, from the roots to the stems and leaves. **Phloem** (FLOH-uhm) carries organic compounds, such as carbohydrates, and some inorganic nutrients in any direction, depending on the plant's needs. Vascular tissue also helps support the plant, which is an important function for land plants. Aquatic plants are mainly supported by the water around them.

Some plants developed woody tissue and grew to great heights, giving them an advantage in gathering light. **Woody tissue** is formed from several layers of xylem, usually concentrated in the center of the stem. Woody stems are usually brown and rigid. Nonwoody plants are usually called **herbaceous** because they have soft, usually green stems. Because the vascular tissue is not surrounded by rigid sclerenchyma cells, the stems of herbaceous plants are flexible.

CLASSIFYING PLANTS

Study the classification of plants in Table 30-1. The 12 phyla of plants, formerly referred to as *divisions,* can be divided into two groups based on the presence of vascular tissue. The three phyla of

TABLE 30-1 *The 12 Phyla of the Plant Kingdom*

Type of plant	Phylum	Common name	Approximate number of species
Nonvascular	Bryophyta	mosses	10,000
	Hepatophyta	liverworts	6,500
	Anthocerophyta	hornworts	100
Vascular, seedless	Psilotophyta	whisk ferns	10–13
	Lycophyta	club mosses	1,000
	Sphenophyta	horsetails	15
	Pterophyta	ferns	12,000
Vascular, seed			
Gymnosperms	Cycadophyta	cycads	100
	Ginkgophyta	ginkgoes	1
	Coniferophyta	conifers	550
	Gnetophyta	gnetophytes	70
Angiosperms	Anthophyta	flowering plants	240,000
	class Monocotyledones	monocots	70,000
	class Dicotyledones	dicots	170,000

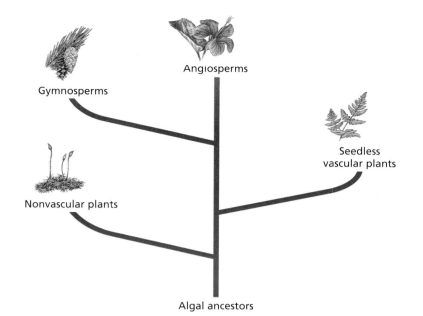

Gymnosperms

Angiosperms

Nonvascular plants

Seedless
vascular plants

Algal ancestors

FIGURE 30-2

This phylogenetic tree shows how plants evolved from green algae. The earliest plants were nonvascular and radiated into more-complex forms of vascular plants.

nonvascular plants have neither true vascular tissue nor true roots, stems, or leaves. Most members of the nine phyla of **vascular plants** have vascular tissue and true roots, stems, and leaves.

Notice in Table 30-1 that vascular plants can be further divided into two groups, seedless plants and seed plants. Seedless plants include the phylum of ferns and three phyla made up of plants closely associated with ferns. **Seed plants**—plants that produce seeds for reproduction—include four phyla of gymnosperms and one phylum of angiosperms. **Gymnosperms** (JIM-nuh-SPUHRMZ), which include pine trees, produce seeds that are not enclosed in fruits. **Angiosperms** (AN-jee-uh-SPUHRMZ), also known as flowering plants, produce seeds within a protective fruit. Examples are apple and orange trees.

The Fossil Record of Plants

Figure 30-2 shows the origins of major plant groups. Much of what we know about plant phylogeny has come from studying the fossil record. The fossil record is incomplete, but scientists think that plants evolved from an ancestor of green alga. The strongest evidence supporting this hypothesis lies in the similarities between modern green algae and plants. Both have the same photosynthetic pigments—chlorophylls *a* and *b*, both store energy as starch, and both have cell walls made of cellulose.

Alternating Life Cycles

All plants have a life cycle that involves two phases. The first phase consists of a diploid ($2n$) **sporophyte** (SPOR-uh-FIET) plant that produces spores. The second phase consists of a haploid ($1n$) **gametophyte** (guh-MEET-uh-FIET) plant that produces eggs and sperm. The two plant phases are named for the type of reproductive cells they produce. This type of life cycle, which alternates between the gametophyte phase and sporophyte phase, is called **alternation of generations.**

Eco Connection

Reforestation Efforts

The process of replacing trees that have died or been cut down is called reforestation. Natural reforestation occurs when seeds grow into new seedlings. Throughout the world, many governments and private landowners do not replace trees after land has been cleared to produce timber, build roads, and construct buildings.

Deforestation is occurring at a rate of several hundred thousand square miles per year. Although this rate seems overwhelming and daunting, people can help reforestation efforts by planting seeds or seedlings in their own community. Trees can be planted in yards, in pots on patios or balconies, and along streets. It's best to choose trees that are well adapted to your area.

Many neighborhoods and local organizations sponsor tree-planting programs. Besides providing beautification, these programs can help educate people about the importance of trees. For more information, call your local or state parks department, the U.S. Forest Service, a county extension agent, or a nearby college forestry department.

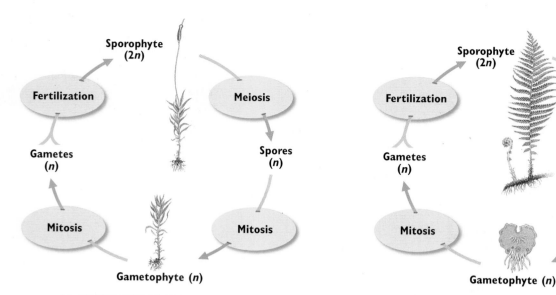

(a) NONVASCULAR PLANT LIFE CYCLE

(b) VASCULAR PLANT LIFE CYCLE

FIGURE 30-3

In the life cycle of a plant, there is an alternation of the haploid gametophyte generation and the diploid sporophyte generation. (a) The life cycle of a nonvascular plant, such as a moss, is characterized by a gametophyte that is larger than the sporophyte. (b) The life cycle of a vascular plant, such as a fern, is characterized by a large sporophyte and a very small gametophyte.

Figure 30-3 shows the life cycles of a nonvascular plant and a vascular plant. In alternation of generations, the gametophyte (1n) produces structures that form gametes—eggs and sperm—by mitosis. Once an egg is fertilized by a sperm and produces a zygote, the plant begins the diploid phase of its life cycle. The zygote divides by mitosis to form a sporophyte plant. The sporophyte (2n) produces structures that undergo meiosis to form haploid spores. These spores are released by most seedless plants but are retained by seed plants. The life cycle begins again when spores divide by mitosis to form new gametophytes.

In nonvascular plants, the gametophyte is the dominant phase. In contrast, the sporophyte is the dominant phase of vascular plants. Oak trees are large sporophytes that dominate some parts of our landscape. In seedless vascular plants, the gametophyte is usually a separate small organism quite different from the sporophyte. In seed plants, the gametophyte is a very small parasite of the sporophyte. For example, gametophytes of flowering plants are microscopic parts of their flowers.

SECTION 30-1 REVIEW

1. What are the similarities between today's plants and green algae?

2. How does the cuticle represent an adaptive advantage for early land plants?

3. How has the evolution of spores contributed to the chances of success for land plants?

4. What is the main difference between vascular plants and nonvascular plants?

5. Describe alternation of generations, and explain how it differs in vascular plants and nonvascular plants.

6. **CRITICAL THINKING** Why are vascular plants the most successful land plants?

NONVASCULAR PLANTS

The three phyla of nonvascular plants are collectively called **bryophytes.** *Botanists have identified 16,600 species of bryophytes. They lack vascular tissue and do not form true roots, stems, and leaves. These plants usually grow on land near streams and rivers.*

SECTION

30-2

OBJECTIVES

▲

Name three types of plants that make up the bryophytes.

●

List distinguishing characteristics shared by nonvascular plants.

■

Compare sporophytes in bryophytes with gametophytes in bryophytes.

◆

Describe the environmental importance of bryophytes.

▲

Name the main ways people use *Sphagnum* moss.

CLASSIFYING BRYOPHYTES

Bryophytes are the most primitive type of plants. Overall, their characteristics are more closely related to plants than to algae. Bryophytes are mostly terrestrial and have an alternation-of-generations life cycle. Bryophytes are seedless, and they produce spores. Because they do not have vascular tissue, they are very small, usually 1–2 cm (less than 1 in.) in height.

Bryophytes need water to reproduce sexually because the sperm must swim through water to an egg. In dry areas, bryophytes can reproduce sexually only when adequate moisture is available. The asexual production of haploid spores does not require water.

Phylum Bryophyta

Almost every land environment is home to at least one species of moss in the phylum Bryophyta (brie-AHF-uh-tuh). The thick green carpets of moss you see on shady forest floors actually consist of thousands of tiny moss gametophytes. Each gametophyte is attached to the soil by rootlike structures called **rhizoids** (RIE-zoidz). Unlike roots, rhizoids do not have vascular tissue. But rhizoids do function like roots by anchoring the moss and by absorbing water and inorganic nutrients.

Moss gametophytes are usually less than 3 cm (1 in.) tall, as shown in Figure 30-4. The moss sporophyte is attached to and dependent on the larger gametophyte. Gametophytes may be male, female, or contain both male and female reproductive parts.

Mosses are called *pioneer plants* because they are often the first species to inhabit a barren area. This is an important environmental function because mosses gradually accumulate inorganic and organic matter on the surface of rocks, creating a layer of soil in which other plants can grow. In areas devastated by fire, volcanic action, or human activity, pioneering mosses can help trigger the development of new biological communities. They also help prevent soil erosion by covering the soil surface and absorbing water.

FIGURE 30-4

The leafy carpet of moss gametophytes is topped by sporophytes. Mature sporophytes release their spores, which can then grow into a new generation of gametophytes.

FIGURE 30-5

(a) A leafy liverwort has two rows of leaves growing on a stem. (b) A thalloid liverwort has very flat, thin leaves.

(a)

(b)

Sphagnum (SFAG-nuhm), or peat moss, is a genus of moss that is a major component of peat bogs in northern parts of the world. Peat moss consists of partially decomposed plant matter. In many northern European and Asian countries, peat moss is mined and dried for use as fuel. Sphagnum produces an acid that slows down decomposition in the swamplike bogs. Sphagnum is widely used to enhance the water-retaining ability of potting and gardening soils. Sphagnum is also used by florists to pack bulbs and flowers for shipping.

Phyla Hepatophyta and Anthocerophyta

Phylum Hepatophyta (HEP-uh-TAHF-uh-tuh) includes the liverworts, unusual-looking plants that grow in moist, shady areas. Most liverworts have thin, transparent leaflike structures arranged along a stemlike axis, as shown in Figure 30-5a. Some liverworts have a **thalloid** (THAL-oid) form—that is, a flat body with distinguishable upper and lower surfaces, as shown in Figure 30-5b. All liverworts lie close to the ground. This is an adaptation that allows them to absorb water readily. In some species, the gametophyte is topped by an umbrella-shaped structure that holds the reproductive cells.

Phylum Anthocerophyta (AN-thoh-suh-RAHF-uh-tuh) includes the hornworts, which resemble liverworts, as shown in Figure 30-6. They grow in moist, shaded areas. They share an unusual characteristic with algae: each cell usually has a single large chloroplast rather than numerous small ones.

FIGURE 30-6

Hornworts grow in warm, moist, shaded habitats. Look for hornworts growing along roads or near streams.

SECTION 30-2 REVIEW

1. What advantage do bryophyte gametophytes that are either male or female have over bryophyte gametophytes that have both male and female structures?

2. List two characteristics shared by all bryophytes.

3. What role do mosses play in the early development of biological communities?

4. What are the main uses of sphagnum moss?

5. Why are bryophytes classified with plants instead of with algae?

6. **CRITICAL THINKING** Why can't sphagnum moss grow as large as maple or oak trees?

Earth's Green Mantle

This excerpt is from Rachel Carson's book *Silent Spring.*

The earth's vegetation is part of a web of life in which there are intimate and essential relations between plants and the earth, between plants and other plants, between plants and animals. Sometimes we have no choice but to disturb these relationships, but we should do so thoughtfully, with full awareness that what we do may have consequences remote in time and place. But no such humility marks the booming "weed killer" business of the present day, in which soaring sales and expanding uses mark the production of plant-killing chemicals.

One of the most tragic examples of our unthinking bludgeoning of the landscape is to be seen in the sagebrush lands of the West, where a vast campaign is on to destroy the sage and to substitute grasslands. If ever an enterprise needed to be illuminated with a sense of the history and meaning of the landscape, it is this. For here the natural landscape is eloquent of the interplay of forces that have created it. It is spread before us like the pages of an open book in which we can read why the land is what it is, and why we should preserve its integrity. But the pages lie unread.

The land of the sage is the land of the high western plains and the lower slopes of the mountains that rise above them, a land born of the great uplift of the Rocky Mountain system many millions of years ago. It is a place of harsh extremes of climate: of long winters when blizzards drive down from the mountains and snow lies deep on the plains, of summers whose heat is relieved by only scanty rains, with drought biting deep into the soil, and drying winds stealing moisture from leaf and stem.

As the landscape evolved, there must have been a long period of trial and error in which plants attempted the colonization of this high and windswept land. One after another must have failed. At last one group of plants evolved which combined all qualities needed to survive. The sage—low-growing and shrubby—could hold its place on the mountain slopes and on the plains, and within its small gray leaves it could hold moisture enough to defy the thieving winds. It was no accident, but rather the result of long ages of experimentation by nature, that the great plains of the West became the land of the sage. . . .

So in a land which nature found suited to grass growing mixed with and under the shelter of sage, it is now proposed to eliminate the sage and create unbroken grassland. Few seem to have asked whether grasslands are a stable and desirable goal in this region. Certainly nature's own answer was otherwise. The annual precipitation in this land where the rains seldom fall is not enough to support good sod-forming grass; it favors rather the perennial bunchgrass that grows in the shelter of the sage.

Reading for Meaning

In this passage, Carson asserts that altering the natural plant life of a region may be a change for the worse. What facts does she use to support her argument?

Read Further

Carson's book *Silent Spring* describes how human activities, including the use of pesticides, endanger our environment. What are some questions we should ask before we disturb the relationships between ourselves and the plants and animals with whom we share Earth?

OBJECTIVES

▲

List two main characteristics of vascular plants.

●

Distinguish between seedless plants and seed plants.

■

Distinguish between gymnosperms and angiosperms.

◆

Summarize the adaptive advantages of seeds.

▲

Distinguish between monocots and dicots.

VASCULAR PLANTS

Vascular plants contain specialized conducting tissues (xylem and phloem) that transport water and dissolved substances from one part of the plant to another. Vascular plants can grow larger and live in more environments than nonvascular plants. The strong stems of vascular plants allow the plants to grow tall, enabling them to rise above other plants and receive more sunlight than shorter plants do.

SEEDLESS VASCULAR PLANTS

Seedless vascular plants dominated the Earth until about 200 million years ago. Characteristics of the four phyla of seedless vascular plants are summarized in Table 30-2. The first three phyla are called fern allies, while members of the last phylum are ferns. Spores are the mobile sexual reproductive parts of all seedless plants.

Phylum Psilotophyta

The phylum Psilotophyta (sie-lah-TAHF-uh-tuh) is represented by whisk ferns, illustrated in Figure 30-7. Despite their name, whisk ferns are not ferns at all. They have no roots or leaves and produce spores on the ends of short branches. These features suggest that whisk ferns resemble early land plants. Whisk ferns are epiphytes, which means they grow on other plants, but they are not considered parasites.

FIGURE 30-7

The whisk fern has branched stem tips. These rare plants are found in tropical and subtropical regions.

TABLE 30-2	*Seedless Vascular Plants*			
Example plant	**Phylum**	**Features**	**Size**	**Location**
Whisk ferns	Psilotophyta	• produce reproductive structures on the ends of forked branches • no roots or leaves	• about 30 cm (1 ft) tall	• tropical and temperate regions, as far north as South Carolina
Club mosses	Lycophyta	• evergreens that produce spores in cones • have roots	• about 5 cm (2 in.) tall	• tropical and temperate regions, on forest floors, in swamps, or as epiphytes
Horsetails	Sphenophyta	• jointed stems • outer cells of stems contain silica, the major component of sand	• about 60–90 cm (2–3 ft) tall	• tropical and temperate regions, usually in moist soil
Ferns	Pterophyta	• leaves • most have an underground stem • most produce spores on the underside of their leaves	• range from less than 1 cm (0.4 in.) to 25 m (82 ft) tall	• all climates, on forest floors, as epiphytes, some in full sun, some aquatic

Phylum Lycophyta

The phylum Lycophyta (lie-KAHF-uh-tuh) contains the club mosses, shown in Figure 30-8. Because they look like miniature pine trees, club mosses are also called ground pines. They produce a **strobilus** (STROH-bi-luhs), or cone, which is a cluster of sporangia-bearing modified leaves. Club mosses were once widely collected as Christmas decorations.

Another member of phylum Lycophyta is a spike moss called *Selaginella lepidophylla,* native to the American Southwest. *Selaginella* turns brown and curls up in a ball during drought. However, when moistened, the plant uncurls and turns green again after a few hours.

internetconnect

SC*LINKS*
NSTA

TOPIC: Vascular plants
GO TO: www.scilinks.org
KEYWORD: HM587

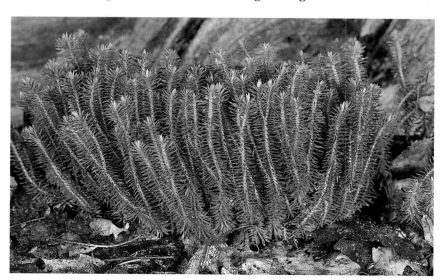

FIGURE 30-8

The club moss, sometimes known as a ground pine, is a member of the phylum Lycophyta. The tips of the aerial stems contain conelike structures.

Phylum Sphenophyta

The phylum Sphenophyta (sfee-NAHF-uh-tuh) includes horsetails, or *Equisetum*. Horsetails have jointed photosynthetic stems that contain silica, with scalelike leaves at each joint. American pioneers used horsetails to scrub pots and pans; hence, they are frequently called scouring rushes. As you can see in Figure 30-9, the shoots are often highly branched and remind some people of a horsetail.

Phylum Pterophyta

Ferns probably originated over 350 million years ago. Ferns belong to the phylum Pterophyta (tuhr-AHF-uh-tuh) and represent a diverse group. Some are floating plants that are less than 1 cm (0.4 in.) across. Ferns also grow above the Arctic Circle and in desert regions. The largest living ferns are tree ferns, shown in Figure 30-10. These ferns can reach 25 m (82 ft) in height, and some have leaves 5 m (16 ft) long.

Most ferns have an underground stem called a **rhizome** (RIE-zohm). The fibrous rhizomes of some ferns are commonly used as a growing medium for orchids. The tightly coiled new leaves of ferns are called **fiddleheads.** The young fiddleheads of some species are eaten by humans as a vegetable. Fiddleheads uncoil and develop into mature leaves called **fronds.**

FIGURE 30-9

The horsetail, *Equisetum,* has hollow, jointed stems that contain silica. About 300 million years ago, *Equisetum* was a large tree, growing with large club moss trees and ferns in steaming swamps. Over millions of years, the trees and other plant life in the swamps died, became buried, and turned into coal.

FIGURE 30-10

Tree ferns, such as the *Dicksonia antarctica* shown here, look like palm trees but are actually the largest living ferns. Sometimes epiphytic ferns grow on the trunk of tree ferns. Orchids are often cultivated on sections of trunk cut from tree ferns. Tree ferns live in the tropics and subtropics.

VASCULAR SEED PLANTS

The mobile sexual reproductive part of seed plants is the multicellular seed. Seeds are an evolutionary success story. Plants with seeds have a greater chance of reproductive success than seedless plants. Inside the tough, protective outer coat of a seed is an embryo and a nutrient supply. When conditions are too hot or too cold, or too wet or too dry, the seed remains inactive. When conditions favor growth, the seed sprouts, or **germinates**—that is, the embryo begins to grow into a young plant, called a **seedling.**

There are two main groups of seed-bearing vascular plants, gymnosperms and angiosperms. The four phyla of gymnosperms produce naked seeds, which means the seeds are not enclosed and protected in fruits. Most gymnosperms are evergreen and bear their seeds in cones. A **cone** is a reproductive structure composed of hard scales. The seeds of a conifer lie open on the surface of the scales. The one phylum of angiosperms produces seeds that are enclosed and protected in fruits. Angiosperms are commonly referred to as flowering plants. Cones serve some of the same functions for gymnosperms that flowers serve for angiosperms.

Phylum Cycadophyta

Cycads (SIE-KADZ) are gymnosperms of the phylum Cycadophyta. Although cycads flourished during the age of the dinosaurs, only about 100 species survive today. Most are native to the tropics and

FIGURE 30-11

The cycad is a gymnosperm that looks like a palm or fern. Cycads can sometimes grow to 18 m (60 ft) in height. Some cycads live for almost a thousand years.

Quick Lab

Examining Ferns

Materials disposable gloves, lab apron, potted fern, hand lens, water

Procedure

1. Put on your disposable gloves and lab apron.
2. Choose a frond of the fern, and examine its underside for the structures that contain spores.
3. Wash the soil from the underground structures. Examine the fern's horizontal stems and roots.

Analysis How do ferns differ from nonvascular plants? What enables ferns to surpass nonvascular plants in height and size? From what part of the fern do the fronds grow?

grow slowly. Many are endangered because of habitat loss, over-collection, and their slow growth. Most cycads have fernlike, leathery leaves at the top of a short, thick trunk. Cycad plants are either male or female, and they bear large cones like those shown in Figure 30-11. Cycads are mostly used as ornamental plants.

Phylum Ginkgophyta

Like cycads, ginkgoes (GINK-ohz) flourished during the time of the dinosaurs. The only species existing today is *Ginkgo biloba,* which is native to China. It is called a living fossil because it closely resembles fossil ginkgoes that are 125 million years old. The ginkgo tree has fan-shaped leaves that fall from the tree at the end of each growing season—an unusual characteristic for a gymnosperm. Trees that lose their leaves at the end of the growing season, like the ginkgo, are called **deciduous.** Most gymnosperms are ever-greens and retain their leaves year-round.

Ginkgoes are tolerant of air pollution, making them good plants for urban settings. Ginkgo seeds are considered a delicacy in China and Japan. Notice the plum-shaped, fleshy seeds on the ginkgo shown in Figure 30-12. They are often mistakenly called berries or fruits.

Phylum Coniferophyta

The conifers (KOHN-uh-fuhrz), which are gymnosperms of the phylum Coniferophyta, include pine, cedar, redwood, fir, spruce, juniper, cypress, and bald cypress trees. They are very important sources of wood, paper, turpentine, resin, ornamental plants, and Christmas trees. Gin is flavored with juniper seeds. Amber is yellow or brownish yellow fossilized resin that once flowed from ancient conifers. Prehistoric insects are often preserved in amber, a fact that figured prominently in the plot of the novel *Jurassic Park,* by Michael Crichton.

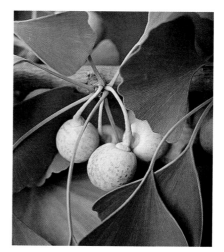

FIGURE 30-12

The ginkgo, *Ginkgo biloba,* has unusual fan-shaped leaves and large seeds. This gymnosperm tree can reach heights of 24 m (80 ft).

(a) Fir needles and cones

(b) Pine needles and cones

(c) Yew needles and seeds

FIGURE 30-13

The needles and cones of conifers come in many shapes and sizes. (a) The fir tree displays its female cones. Its needle-shaped leaves grow evenly all around the branch. (b) The pine tree shows its small male and larger female cones. Some pines reach heights of 60 m (200 ft). (c) The seed of the yew tree is surrounded by a red covering that looks like a berry. Its leaves are flat, pointed needles that are dark green on top and pale green underneath.

Conifers are woody plants, and most have needle or scalelike leaves, as shown in Figure 30-13. A conifer usually bears both male and female cones. Small male cones typically grow in clusters. Male cones release clouds of dustlike pollen, and then the cones fall from the branches. The pollen falls or blows into the larger female cones, where the egg cells are attached to the scales of the cone. After pollination, the female cone closes up tightly. This protects the developing seeds, which mature after one or two years. The mature seeds are released when the female cone opens.

Redwoods and giant sequoia trees provide a majestic forest setting along the West Coast of the United States. These conifers are the Earth's tallest and most massive living organisms. The tallest living coastal redwood, *Sequoia sempervirens,* is about 110 m (360 ft) tall, the height of a 30-story building. The most massive tree is a giant sequoia, *Sequoiadendron giganteum,* estimated to weigh 5,600 megagrams (6,200 tons).

Phylum Gnetophyta

An odd group of cone-bearing gymnosperms called gnetophytes (NEE-tuh-FIETS) have vascular systems that more closely resemble those of angiosperms. As Figure 30-14 shows, *Ephedra* (ih-FED-ruh) is a genus of desert shrubs with jointed stems that look like horsetails. It is the source of the drug **ephedrine,** which is used as a decongestant.

FIGURE 30-14

Ephedra viridis, called Mormon tea, grows on the rim of the Grand Canyon. This highly branched shrub has small, scale-like leaves. It is the source of the medicine ephedrine and is brewed to make a tea.

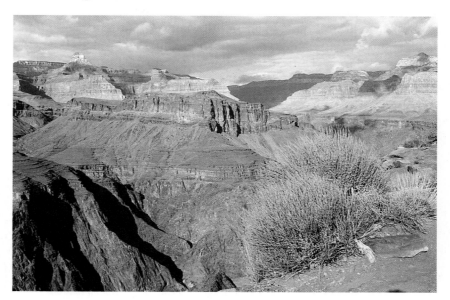

Figure 30-15 shows the unique *Welwitschia mirabilis* plant. The plant's stem is only a few centimeters tall but can grow to 1 m (3.3 ft) in diameter. Two leaves grow from the stem. The leaves elongate from their base and then become tattered and split lengthwise by the wind. A mature leaf may be nearly 1 m (3.3 ft) wide and 3 m (10 ft) long. *Welwitschia* grows in the Namib Desert of southwestern Africa. The Namib Desert lies near the Atlantic Ocean, so a thick night fog often rolls in over the desert. *Welwitschia* apparently gets most of its water from the dew that condenses from the fog.

FIGURE 30-15

Welwitschia mirabilis has a short, wide stem and twisting leaves. The female plants of this unusual gymnosperm bear large seed cones that are bright scarlet in color.

Phylum Anthophyta

The largest phylum of plants, Anthophyta (an-THAHF-uh-tuh), includes over 240,000 species of flowering plants. Angiosperms, or the flowering plants, are seed plants characterized by the presence of a flower and fruit. You may recall from Chapter 29 that botanists define a fruit as a ripened ovary that surrounds the seeds of angiosperms. The **ovary** is the female part of the flower that encloses the egg(s).

Angiosperms grow in many forms and occupy diverse habitats. Some are herbaceous plants with showy flowers, such as violets and impatiens. Others, such as rose bushes, are shrubs. Some angiosperms are vines, like grape and ivy plants. Oak, aspen, and birch trees are all flowering plants that have woody stems, although you may never have noticed their small flowers. Grasses are also angiosperms, but you must look closely to see their small, highly modified flowers. The world's largest flower, which can grow to 1 m (3.3 ft) in diameter, is produced by *Rafflesia,* shown in Figure 30-16.

The Evolution of Angiosperms

Angiosperms first appeared in the fossil record about 135 million years ago. By about 90 million years ago, angiosperms had probably begun to outnumber gymnosperms. What led to the success of this new kind of plant? Several factors were probably involved. In many angiosperms, seeds germinate and produce mature plants, which in turn produce new seeds, all in one growing season. This is a tremendous advantage over gymnosperms, which often take 10 or more years to reach maturity and produce seeds. Also, the fruits of flowering plants protect seeds and aid in their dispersal. Angiosperms also have a more efficient vascular system and are more likely to be associated with mycorrhizae than gymnosperms are. Angiosperms also may gain an advantage by using animal pollination rather than the less-efficient wind pollination method used by gymnosperms. However, wind pollination is used by many successful angiosperms, such as the grasses and many deciduous trees. Finally, angiosperms are more diverse than gymnospems, so they occupy more niches, such as in aquatic, epiphytic, and parasitic environments.

FIGURE 30-16

The stinking-corpse lily, *Rafflesia arnoldii,* has the world's largest flowers but no leaves or stems. The flowers can be male or female, and they are pollinated by flies. The plant lacks chlorophyll and is parasitic on a woody vine native to Southeast Asia.

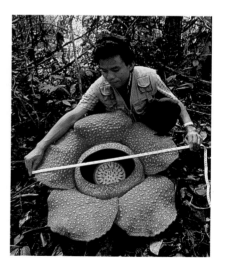

TABLE 30-3 *Comparing Monocots and Dicots*

Plant type	Embryos	Leaves	Stems	Flower parts	Examples
Monocots	One cotyledon	Parallel venation	Scattered vascular bundles	Usually occur in threes	lilies, irises, orchids, palms, tulips, bananas, pineapples, onions, bamboo, coconut, wheat, corn, rice, oats, barley, sugarcane
Dicots	Two cotyledons	Net venation	Radially arranged vascular bundles	Usually occur in fours or fives	beans, lettuce, oaks, maples, elms, roses, carnations, cactuses, most broad-leaved forest trees

Monocots and Dicots

The flowering plants classified under phylum Anthophyta are divided into two classes—Monocotyledones (monocots) and Dicotyledones (dicots). The primary feature that distinguishes these two groups is the number of **cotyledons** (KAHT-e-LEE-duhnz), or seed leaves, in a plant embryo. **Monocots** (MAHN-uh-KAHTS) usually have one cotyledon in their embryo, while **dicots** (DIE-KAHTS) typically have two. By comparison, gymnosperms usually have two or more cotyledons.

Characteristics used to identify monocots and dicots are shown in Table 30-3. Most mature monocot leaves have several main **veins,** or bundles of vascular tissue, running roughly parallel to each other. This is called **parallel venation.** Most dicots have one or more nonparallel main veins that branch repeatedly, forming an interconnected network. This is called **net venation.** When viewed in cross section under a microscope, most monocot stems have scattered vascular bundles, while the vascular bundles of dicot stems are arranged in a circle. It is best to use more than one characteristic to determine whether a species is a monocot or a dicot.

internetconnect

SCLINKS
NSTA

TOPIC: Monocots/dicots
GO TO: www.scilinks.org
KEYWORD: HM592

SECTION 30-3 REVIEW

1. **What are the two main tissues of all vascular plants?**

2. **What are the main differences between gymnosperms and angiosperms?**

3. **How do male cones differ from female cones?**

4. **What are three characteristics that distinguish monocots from dicots?**

5. **What reproductive advantages do seed plants have over seedless vascular plants and nonvascular plants?**

6. **CRITICAL THINKING** How do humans use seedless vascular plants and seed plants?

SUMMARY/VOCABULARY

30-1
- All plants are multicellular, most live on land, and almost all are photosynthetic.
- There are 12 phyla and over 270,000 species of living plants. Three phyla are nonvascular plants, and the rest are vascular plants.
- Plants originated about 430 million years ago, when a green algae adapted to land.
- The evolution of spores and seeds helped plants colonize land.
- The main function of xylem is to carry water and inorganic nutrients. Phloem carries organic compounds and some inorganic nutrients.
- All plants have a life cycle known as alternation of generations. In alternation of generations, a haploid gametophyte produces gametes, which unite and give rise to a diploid sporophyte. Through meiosis, the sporophyte produces haploid spores, which develop into gametophytes.
- The gametophyte is the dominant phase in nonvascular plants, while the sporophyte is dominant in vascular plants.

Vocabulary

alternation of generations (581)	gametophyte (581)	seed (579)	vascular plant (581)
angiosperm (581)	gymnosperm (581)	seed plant (581)	vascular tissue (580)
cuticle (579)	herbaceous (580)	spore (579)	woody tissue (580)
endosperm (579)	nonvascular plant (581)	sporophyte (581)	xylem (580)
	phloem (580)		

30-2
- The three phyla of nonvascular plants are called bryophytes. These plants do not have true roots, stems, or leaves. They are very small and often live in moist areas.
- Sphagnum moss, found in peat bogs, is an important bryophyte because of its acidity and moisture-holding capacity.

Vocabulary

bryophyte (583)	rhizoid (583)	sphagnum (584)	thalloid (584)

30-3
- All nine phyla of vascular plants contain vascular tissue, xylem, and phloem. The sporophyte generation is dominant in the life cycle of all vascular plants.
- Whisk ferns have no true roots or leaves.
- Ferns are the dominant phylum of seedless plants, and they have sporangia on their leaves.
- Seed plants are either gymnosperms, which are characterized by naked seeds and no flowers, or angiosperms, which have flowers and seeds enclosed by a fruit.
- Conifers, the dominant living gymnosperms, form vast forests in the Northern Hemisphere.
- Various species of flowering plants have numerous adaptations that give them an advantage over gymnosperms.
- Angiosperms, or flowering plants, are the dominant phylum today, with over 240,000 species.
- Dicots are distinguished from monocots on the basis of several characteristics: cotyledon number, leaf venation, arrangement of stem vascular tissue, and number of flower parts.

Vocabulary

cone (588)	ephedrine (590)	monocot (592)	rhizome (588)
cotyledon (592)	fiddlehead (588)	net venation (592)	seedling (588)
deciduous (589)	frond (588)	ovary (591)	strobilus (587)
dicot (592)	germinate (588)	parallel venation (592)	vein (592)

REVIEW

Vocabulary

1. Explain the difference between a gametophyte and a sporophyte.
2. Explain the difference between angiosperms and gymnosperms.
3. List two ways that monocots and dicots differ.
4. Describe the functions of xylem and phloem.
5. Compare and contrast spores and seeds.

Multiple Choice

6. The phylum Bryophyta includes (a) mosses and club mosses (b) hornworts and liverworts (c) liverworts and cycads (d) conifers and ginkgoes.
7. Mosses help start new biological communities by (a) detecting air pollution (b) forming new soil (c) producing spores (d) slowing decomposition.
8. Look at the diagram of the plant life cycle below. The process that occurs at *X* is (a) fertilization (b) meiosis (c) mitosis (d) meiosis and mitosis.

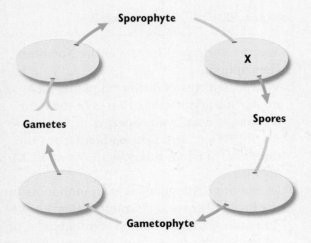

Sporophyte

X

Gametes

Spores

Gametophyte

9. The presence of silica in the outer cells of the plant is a characteristic of (a) ferns (b) mosses (c) horsetails (d) club mosses.

10. Flowering plants are in the phylum (a) Psilotophyta (b) Anthophyta (c) Gnetophyta (d) Sphenophyta.
11. Seedless vascular plants include all of the following *except* (a) ferns (b) horsetails (c) cycads (d) club mosses.
12. Gymnosperms include all of the following *except* (a) cycads (b) gnetophytes (c) ginkgoes (d) horsetails.
13. The great success of angiosperms is due in part to (a) a highly efficient vascular system (b) seeds protected by fruits (c) animal dispersion of pollen, fruits, and seeds (d) all of the above.
14. A monocot has (a) parallel leaf venation (b) two seed leaves (c) four-part flowers (d) five-part flowers.
15. The distinguishing feature of all plants is the presence of (a) vascular tissue (b) pollen grains (c) a cuticle (d) rhizoids.

Short Answer

16. When did the first land plants probably develop?
17. Why did it take about 3 billion years after life developed in the oceans for plants to first appear on land?
18. Which phylum of organisms is believed to represent the ancestors of land plants? Why?
19. What is the genetic difference between the gametophyte and the sporophyte?
20. How does alternation of generations in nonvascular plants differ from that in vascular plants?
21. What factor limits the size of nonvascular plants?
22. Why do nonvascular plants usually live in moist environments?
23. What is the principal distinguishing feature of vascular plants?
24. What are the structural features found in vascular plants that are lacking in nonvascular plants?
25. Why are ferns and flowering plants placed in different phyla?

CRITICAL THINKING

1. Steven Spielberg has hired you to landscape his new $110 million Jurassic Park theme ride with living plants similar to those that grew during the Jurassic period. What plant phyla could you use? Give examples of specific plants that you would use as shade trees, shrubs, and low-growing ground cover.

2. Fossil trees are easier to find than fossils of small plants. Give two possible explanations.

3. The water lily, shown below, is an aquatic vascular plant. Do you think its cuticle would be thicker on the upper surface of the leaf or on the lower surface? Explain.

4. Luminous moss, *Schistostega pennata*, has cells shaped like lenses, with chloroplasts spread out behind the curving cell membrane. In what sort of environment would you expect to find this moss?

5. Cactuses are vascular plants that are adapted to dry environments. What specific adaptations might have been selected for during evolution?

6. In the chart below, indicate which groups of plants have vascular tissue. Also indicate which groups of plants have a dominant sporophyte as part of their life cycle.

Plant Evolution

Phylum	Has vascular tissue	Has dominant sporophyte
Anthophyta		
Bryophyta		
Coniferophyta		
Hepatophyta		
Pterophyta		

EXTENSION

1. Read "Tasty Brazil Nuts Stun Harvesters and Scientists" in *Smithsonian,* April 1999, on page 38. Describe a Brazil nut pod, and compare it to the familiar Brazil nuts we find in the grocery store. How are the nuts harvested? Explain the role of the agouti in the survival of the Brazil nut.

2. Go to your local garden center and get a handful of sphagnum moss. Let it air-dry. Determine the mass of the moss to the nearest 0.1 g. Then submerge the moss in water, and let it sit overnight. Remove the moss, let the excess water drain off, and determine the mass of the moss again. Calculate the percentage of increase in mass.

3. Collect one or more fern fronds with mature but unopened sporangia, and place them in an envelope to dry. Soak a clean 7.5 cm diameter clay flowerpot in distilled water or rainwater overnight. Fill the pot with wet sphagnum moss, and place it upside down in a pan of distilled water. Sprinkle the fern spores from the envelope on the flowerpot's upturned surface, and cover the pot with a bell jar or clear 2 L plastic soda bottle with its base cut off. Place the setup in indirect light, and keep it watered. Watch for the development of fern gametophytes in a week or two.

Observing Plant Diversity

OBJECTIVES

- Compare similarities and differences among phyla of living plants.
- Relate structural adaptations to the evolution of plants.

PROCESS SKILLS

- observing
- comparing and contrasting
- classifying
- relating structure and function

MATERIALS

- live and preserved specimens representing four plant phyla
- stereomicroscope or hand lens
- compound light microscope
- prepared slides of male and female gametophytes of mosses and ferns

Background

1. How do plants you commonly see compare with their ancestors, the green algae?
2. What are the differences between nonvascular plants and vascular plants? How do these differences relate to the size of a plant?
3. What is alternation of generations? Is it found in all plants?
4. Do all plants produce spores? Do all plants produce seeds? What are the advantages of producing seeds?
5. What do you think was the evolutionary pressure that resulted in colorful flowers?

Procedure

1. ◆ CAUTION **Keep your hands away from your face while handling plants.** You will travel to four stations to observe plants that are representatives of four phyla of plants. Record the answers to the questions in your lab report.

STATION 1 Mosses

2. Use a stereomicroscope or a hand lens to examine the samples of mosses, which are bryophytes. Which part of the moss is the gametophyte? Which part of the moss is the sporophyte? Make a sketch of your observations in your lab report. In your drawing, label the gametophyte and sporophyte portions of the moss plant and indicate whether each is haploid or diploid.
3. Use a compound microscope to look at the prepared slides of male and female gametophytes. What kinds of reproductive cells are produced in each of these structures? Draw the cells in your lab report.
4. Do mosses have roots? How do mosses obtain water and nutrients from the soil?

STATION 2 Ferns

5. Look at the examples of ferns at this station. The fern leaf is called a frond. Use the hand lens to examine the fronds.
   a. How does water travel throughout a fern? List observations supporting your answer.
   b. Make a drawing of the fern plant in your lab report.

Indicate whether the leafy green frond in your drawing is haploid or diploid.

   c. Search the underside of the fern fronds for evidence of reproductive structures. Make a drawing of your findings in your lab report. What kind of reproductive cells are produced by these structures?

6. Examine the examples of fern gametophytes.

   a. Locate and identify the reproductive organs found on the gametophytes. In your lab report, sketch and label these organs and identify the reproductive cells produced by each.

   b. Are the gametophytes haploid or diploid?

7. In what ways are ferns like bryophytes? In what ways are they different?

STATION 3 Conifers

8. The gymnosperms most familiar to us are conifers. Look at the samples of conifers at this station.

   a. When you look at the limb of a pine tree, which portion (gametophyte or sporophyte) of the plant life cycle are you seeing?

   b. In what part of the conifer would you find reproductive structures?

9. Name an evolutionary advancement found in gymnosperms but lacking in ferns.

STATION 4 Angiosperms

10. Draw one of the representative angiosperms at this station in your lab report. Label the representative angiosperm as a monocot or a dicot, and list at least two characteristics you used to identify it.

11. Name an evolutionary development that is present in both gymnosperms and angiosperms but absent in bryophytes and ferns.

12. How do the seeds of angiosperms differ from those of gymnosperms?

13. Examine the fruits found at this station. How have fruits benefited angiosperms?

14. Clean up your materials and wash your hands before leaving the lab.

Analysis and Conclusions

1. In bryophytes, how do the sperm travel from the male gametophyte to the female gametophyte?

2. In angiosperms, how do the sperm get to the part of the flower containing the egg?

3. Which portion of the plant life cycle is dominant in bryophytes? Which portion is dominant in ferns, gymnosperms, and angiosperms?

4. What is a seed? Why is the seed a helpful adaptation for terrestrial plants?

5. Why are gymnosperms referred to as *naked* seed plants?

6. Which group of plants is the most successful and diverse today? What are some adaptations found among members of this group?

Further Inquiry

1. Find out how the geographic distribution of the phyla of living plants relates to their structures.

2. Research the deforestation of tropical rain forests. How are the different groups of plants affected by deforestation?

CHAPTER 31

PLANT STRUCTURE AND FUNCTION

This Dahlia "flower" is really a cluster of small, individual flowers. Dahlia is a member of the family of plants called the composites, which also includes sunflowers and daisies.

FOCUS CONCEPT: *Cell Structure and Function*

As you read, notice how the roots, stems, and leaves perform different functions for a plant. Plant tissues are organized for specialized functions.

PLANT CELLS AND TISSUES

Plants have adapted to a range of environments over the course of their evolution. As plants grow, their cells become specialized for particular functions. The patterns of specialized tissues vary in each of the plant organs—the root, the stem, and the leaf. They also vary depending on the plant's stage of growth and taxonomic group. This chapter examines the structure and function of roots, stems, and leaves.

OBJECTIVES

▲

Describe the three kinds of plant cells.

●

Explain the differences between the three plant tissue systems.

■

Describe the main types of meristems.

◆

Differentiate between monocot and dicot meristems.

▲

Differentiate between primary and secondary growth.

SPECIALIZED PLANT CELLS

All organisms are composed of cells. Recall from Chapter 4 that plant cells have unique structures, including a central vacuole, plastids, and a thick cell wall that surrounds the cell membrane. These common features are found in the three types of specialized plant cells—parenchyma, collenchyma, and sclerenchyma—which are shown in Figure 31-1. Small changes in the structure of these plant cells help make different functions possible. The three types of plant cells are arranged differently in roots, stems, and leaves.

Parenchyma (puh-REN-kuh-muh) cells are usually loosely packed cube-shaped or elongated cells that contain a large central vacuole and have thin, flexible cell walls. Parenchyma cells are involved in many metabolic functions, including photosynthesis, storage of water and nutrients, and healing. These cells usually form the bulk of nonwoody plants. For example, the fleshy part of an apple is made up mostly of parenchyma cells.

The cell walls of **collenchyma** (koh-LEN-kuh-muh) cells are thicker than those of parenchyma cells. Collenchyma cell walls are also irregular in shape. The thicker cell walls provide more support for

FIGURE 31-1

Plants are composed of three types of specialized cells. (a) Parenchyma cells are usually cube-shaped with thin walls. (b) Collenchyma cells are elongated with irregularly thickened cell walls. (c) Sclerenchyma cells are cube-shaped or elongated and have thick, rigid cell walls.

(a) PARENCHYMA

(b) COLLENCHYMA

(c) SCLERENCHYMA

the plant. Collenchyma cells are usually grouped in strands. They are specialized for supporting regions of the plant that are still lengthening. Celery stalks contain a great amount of collenchyma cells.

Sclerenchyma (skluh-REN-kuh-muh) cells have thick, even, rigid cell walls. They support and strengthen the plant in areas where growth is no longer occurring. This type of cell usually dies at maturity, providing a frame to support the plant. The gritty texture of a pear fruit is due to the presence of sclerenchyma cells.

TISSUE SYSTEMS

Cells that work together to perform a specific function form a tissue. Tissues are arranged into systems in plants, including the dermal system, ground system, and vascular system, which are summarized in Table 31-1. These systems are further organized into the three major plant organs—the roots, stems, and leaves. The organization of each organ reflects adaptations to the environment.

Dermal Tissue System

The **dermal tissue system** forms the outside covering of plants. In young plants, it consists of the **epidermis** (EP-uh-DUHR-muhs), the outer layer made of parenchyma cells. In some species, the epidermis is more than one cell layer thick. The outer epidermal wall is often covered by a waxy layer called the **cuticle,** which prevents water loss. Some epidermal cells of the roots develop hairlike extensions that increase water absorption. Openings in the leaf and stem epidermis are called stomata. Stomata regulate the passage of gases and moisture into and out of the plant. In woody stems and roots, the epidermis is replaced by dead cork cells.

TABLE 31-1	*Characteristics of Plant Tissue Systems*				
Tissue system	**Type of cells**	**Location**	**Function in roots**	**Function in stems**	**Function in leaves**
Dermal tissue system	flat, living parenchyma (epidermal cells) in nonwoody parts; flat, dead parenchyma (cork cells) in woody parts	outermost layer(s) of cells	absorption, protection	gas exchange, protection	gas exchange, protection
Ground tissue system	mostly parenchyma, usually with some collenchyma and fewer sclerenchyma	between dermal and vascular in nonwoody plant parts	support, storage	support, storage	photosynthesis
Vascular tissue system	elongated cells—dead xylem and living phloem, also parenchyma and sclerenchyma (fibers)	tubes throughout plant	transport, support	transport, support	transport, support

Ground Tissue System

Dermal tissue surrounds the **ground tissue system,** which consists of all three types of plant cells. Ground tissue functions in storage, metabolism, and support. Parenchyma cells are the most common type of cell found in ground tissue. Nonwoody roots, stems, and leaves are made up primarily of ground tissue. Cactus stems have large amounts of parenchyma cells for storing water in dry environments. Plants that grow in waterlogged soil often have parenchyma with large air spaces that allow air to reach the roots. Nonwoody plants that must be flexible to withstand wind have large amounts of collenchyma cells. Sclerenchyma cells are found where hardness is an advantage, such as in the seed coats of hard seeds and in the spines of cactuses.

Vascular Tissue System

Ground tissue surrounds the **vascular tissue system,** which functions in transport and support. Recall from Chapter 30 that the term *vascular tissue* refers to both xylem and phloem. Xylem tissue conducts water and mineral nutrients primarily from roots upward in the plant. Xylem tissue also provides structural support for the plant. Phloem tissue conducts organic compounds and some mineral nutrients throughout the plant. Unlike xylem, phloem is alive at maturity.

In angiosperms, xylem has two major components—tracheids and vessel elements. Both are dead cells at maturity. Look at Figure 31-2a. A **tracheid** (TRAY-kee-id) is a long, thick-walled sclerenchyma cell with tapering ends. Water moves from one tracheid to another through **pits,** which are thin, porous areas of the cell wall. A **vessel element**, shown in Figure 31-2b, is a sclerenchyma cell that has either large holes in the top and bottom walls or no end walls at all. Vessel elements are stacked to form long tubes called **vessels.** Water moves more easily in vessels than in tracheids. The xylem of most seedless vascular plants and most gymnosperms contains only tracheids, which are considered a primitive type of xylem cell. The vessel elements in angiosperms probably evolved from tracheids. Xylem also contains parenchyma cells and sclerenchyma cells.

The conducting parenchyma cell of angiosperm phloem is called a **sieve tube member.** Look at Figure 31-2c. Sieve tube members are stacked to form long **sieve tubes.** Compounds move from cell to cell through end walls called **sieve plates.** Each sieve tube member lies next to a specialized parenchyma cell, the **companion cell,** which assists in transport. Phloem also usually contains sclerenchyma cells called fibers. Commercially important hemp, flax, and jute fibers are phloem fibers.

Vascular tissue systems are also modified for environmental reasons. For example, xylem forms the wood of trees, providing the plants with strength while conducting water and mineral nutrients. In aquatic plants, such as duckweeds, xylem is not needed for support or water transport and may be nearly absent from the mature plant.

FIGURE 31-2

(a) Tracheids are long and thin, and they contain pits in their cell walls. (b) Vessel elements are shorter and wider than tracheids. Both tracheids and vessel elements transport water. (c) Sieve tube members are long and tubular, and they contain pores in their cell walls. Sugar is transported through sieve tube members and companion cells.

(a) TRACHEID

(b) VESSEL ELEMENT

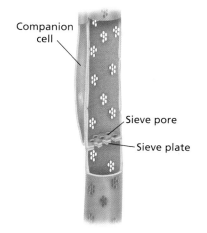

(c) SIEVE TUBE MEMBER

TABLE 31-2	Types of Meristems	
Type	**Location**	**Function**
Apical meristem	tips of stems and roots	growth; increase length at tips
Intercalary meristem	between the tip and base of stems and leaves	growth; increase length between nodes
Lateral meristem	sides of stems and roots	growth; increase diameter

GROWTH IN MERISTEMS

Plant growth originates mainly in **meristems** (MER-i-STEMZ), regions where cells continuously divide. Look at Table 31-2. Most plants grow in length through **apical** (AP-i-kuhl) **meristems** located at the tips of stems and roots. Some monocots have **intercalary** (in-TUHR-kah-ler-ee) **meristems** located above the bases of leaves and stems. Intercalary meristems allow grass leaves to quickly regrow after being grazed or mowed.

Gymnosperms and most dicots also have **lateral meristems,** which allow stems and roots to increase in diameter. Lateral meristems are located near the outside of stems and roots. There are two types of lateral meristems, the vascular cambium and the cork cambium. The **vascular cambium,** located between the xylem and phloem, produces additional vascular tissues. The **cork cambium,** located outside the phloem, produces cork. Cork cells replace the epidermis in woody stems and roots, protecting the plant. **Cork** cells are dead cells that provide protection and prevent water loss.

You have probably noticed how trees grow taller and wider over time. Growth in length is called **primary growth** and is produced by apical and intercalary meristems. Growth in diameter is called **secondary growth** and is produced by the lateral meristems—that is, by the vascular cambium and cork cambium.

SECTION 31-1 REVIEW

1. What are the differences between tracheids and vessel elements? How does water travel through each structure?

2. What kinds of meristems do monocots and dicots have in common? What kinds do they not share?

3. Would you expect to find sclerenchyma cells near meristems? Why or why not?

4. Would you expect to find sclerenchyma and collenchyma cells in roots?

5. Distinguish between the primary growth and secondary growth in a tree.

6. **CRITICAL THINKING** Describe the factors that influence the transport of water through xylem tissue.

ROOTS

Plants have three kinds of organs—roots, stems, and leaves. Roots are the structures that typically grow underground. Roots are important because they anchor the plant in the soil. They also absorb and transport water and mineral nutrients. The storage of water and organic compounds is provided by roots.

OBJECTIVES

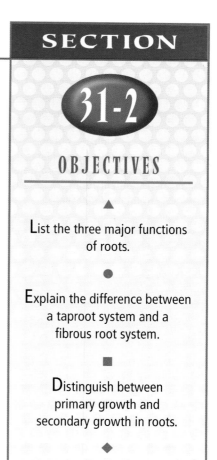

▲

List the three major functions of roots.

●

Explain the difference between a taproot system and a fibrous root system.

■

Distinguish between primary growth and secondary growth in roots.

◆

Describe primary root tissues.

TYPES OF ROOTS

When a seed sprouts, it produces a primary root. If this first root becomes the largest root, it is called a **taproot,** as illustrated in Figure 31-3a. Many plants, like carrots and certain trees, have taproots. Contrary to what you might think, even taproots rarely penetrate the ground more than a meter or two. A few species, such as cottonwoods, do have some roots that grow 50 m (164 ft) deep to tap into underground water supplies. However, tall trees rarely have roots as deep as their height aboveground.

In some plants, the primary root does not become large. Instead, numerous small roots develop and branch to produce a **fibrous root system,** like that shown in Figure 31-3b. Many monocots, such as grasses, have fibrous root systems. Fibrous roots of monocots often develop from the base of the stem rather than from other roots.

internet**connect**

SCILINKS
NSTA

TOPIC: Types of roots
GO TO: www.scilinks.org
KEYWORD: HM603

(a) TAPROOT SYSTEM

(b) FIBROUS ROOT SYSTEM

FIGURE 31-3

Plants can have either a taproot system or a fibrous root system. (a) Many dicots, including the radish, have a large central taproot with small lateral roots. (b) Most monocots, including grasses, have a highly branched fibrous root system.

FIGURE 31-4

Some plants grow adventitious roots from aboveground parts, including stems and leaves. (a) Corn plants grow prop roots at their base to provide additional stability. (b) This orchid displays another type of adventitious root, called an air root. These plants live on tree branches and absorb water and mineral nutrients from the surface of the tree and from the air.

(a) **(b)**

Specialized roots that grow from stems and leaves are called **adventitious roots.** Figure 31-4a shows the prop roots of corn, which help keep the plant's stems upright. The air roots of an epiphytic orchid, shown in Figure 31-4b, obtain water and mineral nutrients from the air. Air roots on the stems of ivy and other vines enable them to climb walls and trees.

ROOT STRUCTURES

Study Figure 31-5. Notice that the root tip is covered by a protective **root cap,** which covers the apical meristem. The root cap produces a slimy substance that functions like lubricating oil, allowing the root to move more easily through the soil as it grows. Cells that are crushed or knocked off the root cap as the root moves through the soil are replaced by new cells produced in the apical meristem, where cells are continuously dividing. Look at Figure 31-6 on the next page. **Root hairs,** which are extensions of epidermal cells, increase the surface area of the root and thus increase the plant's ability to absorb water and mineral nutrients.

Root structures are adapted for several functions. Root hairs on the epidermis greatly increase the surface area available for absorption. Most roots also form partnerships with mycorrhizal fungi, whose threadlike hyphae also increase the surface area for absorption. The spreading, usually highly branched root system increases the amount of soil that the plant can "mine" for water and mineral nutrients and aids in anchoring the plant. The large amount of root parenchyma usually functions in storage and general metabolism. Roots are dependent on the shoots for their energy, so they must store starch to use as an energy source during periods of little or no photosynthesis, such as winter.

FIGURE 31-5

The root cap protects the apical meristem of a root tip. The primary growth of a root is caused by cell division occurring in the apical meristem.

Apical meristem

Root cap

FIGURE 31-6

The root tip of this seedling has many root hairs, which help the plant absorb water and mineral nutrients from the soil. Root hairs grow from the outer layer of cells, called the epidermis.

Primary Growth in Roots

Roots increase in length through cell division, elongation, and maturation in the root tip. Dermal tissue matures to form the epidermis, the outermost cylinder of the root. Ground tissue in roots matures into two specialized regions: the cortex and the endodermis. The **cortex** is located just inside the epidermis, as you can see in Figure 31-7. This largest region of the primary root is made of loosely packed parenchyma cells.

The innermost cylinder of the cortex is the **endodermis** (EN-doh-DUHR-mis), also shown in Figure 31-7. Endodermal cell walls contain a narrow band of a waterproof substance that stops further movement of water through the cell walls. To enter farther into the root than the endodermis, water and dissolved substances must pass through the selectively permeable membrane of a root cell. Once inside the cell membrane, dissolved substances can move from cell to cell via small channels in cell walls that interconnect the cytoplasm of adjoining cells.

Vascular tissue in roots matures to form the innermost cylinder of the root. In most dicots and gymnosperms, xylem makes up the central core of the root, as shown in Figure 31-7b. Dicot root xylem

internet**connect**

TOPIC: Root structures
GO TO: www.scilinks.org
KEYWORD: HM605

FIGURE 31-7

(a) This cross section of a dicot root shows the arrangement of vascular tissue and ground tissue. Note how the xylem tissue forms an X in the center. The cortex and the endodermis, which are composed of ground tissue, surround the vascular tissue. (b) This cross section of a monocot root shows a prominent endodermis, the innermost layer of the cortex. The center of the root, called the pith, is made up of parenchyma cells.

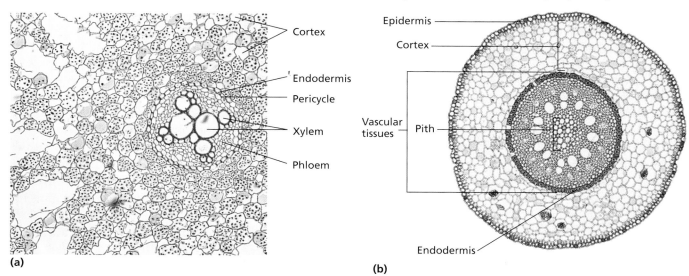

(a) Cortex, Endodermis, Pericycle, Xylem, Phloem

(b) Epidermis, Cortex, Vascular tissues, Pith, Endodermis

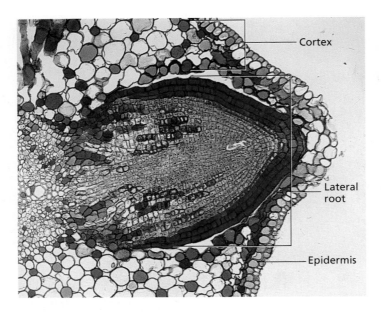

Cortex

Lateral
root

Epidermis

FIGURE 31-8

The vascular core of a primary root is surrounded by the pericycle, a tissue that produces lateral roots.

Quick Lab

Observing Roots

Materials wilted radish seedlings, hand lens, Petri dish, water, pipet

Procedure

1. Place the wilted radish seedlings in a Petri dish. Observe them with the hand lens. Record your observations.

2. Using a pipet, cover only the roots with water. Observe the seedlings with the hand lens every 5 minutes for 15 minutes. Record each of your observations.

3. Use the hand lens to observe the roots. Draw and label what you see.

Analysis What happened to the wilted seedlings when you put them in water? How can you explain what happened? Describe two functions of a root.

usually has a fluted structure with pockets of phloem between the xylem lobes. In monocots, the center of the root usually contains a pith of parenchyma cells, as Figure 31-7b shows. Monocot root xylem occurs in many patches that circle the pith. Small areas of phloem occur between the xylem patches.

The outermost layer or layers of the central vascular tissues is termed the **pericycle** (PER-i-SIE-kuhl). Lateral roots are formed by the division of pericycle cells. The developing lateral root connects its vascular tissues and endodermis to those of the parent root. Figure 31-8 shows how a lateral root grows out through the parent root's endodermis and cortex, finally emerging from the epidermis.

Secondary Growth in Roots

Dicot and gymnosperm roots often experience secondary growth. Secondary growth begins when a vascular cambium forms between primary xylem and primary phloem. Pericycle cells form the vascular cambium at the ends of the xylem lobes, where no phloem is located. The vascular cambium produces secondary xylem toward the inside of the root and secondary phloem toward the outside. The expansion of the vascular tissues in the center of the root crushes all the tissues external to the phloem, including the endodermis, cortex, and epidermis. A cork cambium develops in the pericycle to replace the crushed cells with cork.

ROOT FUNCTIONS

Besides anchoring a plant in the soil, roots serve two other primary functions. They absorb water and a variety of minerals or mineral nutrients that are dissolved in the soil. Roots are selective about which minerals they absorb. Roots absorb some minerals and exclude others. Table 31-2 lists the 13 minerals that are essential for all plants. They are absorbed mainly as ions. Carbon, hydrogen, and oxygen are not listed because they are absorbed as water and carbon dioxide.

Plant cells use some minerals, such as nitrogen and potassium, in large amounts. These elements are called **macronutrients** and are required in relatively large amounts (usually more than 1,000 mg/kg of dry matter). Plant cells use other minerals, such as manganese, in smaller amounts. These are called **micronutrients** and are required in relatively small amounts (usually less than 100 mg/kg of dry matter).

Adequate amounts of all 13 mineral nutrients in Table 31-3 are required for normal growth. Plants with deficiencies show

TABLE 31-3 Essential Mineral Nutrients in Plants

Macronutrients

Element	Absorbed as	Use in plants
Nitrogen	NO_3^-, NH_4^+	part of proteins, nucleic acids, chlorophyll, ATP
Phosphorus	$H_2PO_4^-$	part of nucleic acids, ATP, phospholipids, coenzymes
Potassium	K^+	required for stomatal opening and closing, enzyme cofactor
Calcium	Ca^{2+}	part of cell walls and cell membranes
Magnesium	Mg^{2+}	part of chlorophyll
Sulfur	SO_4^{2-}	part of proteins

Micronutrients

Element	Absorbed as	Use in plants
Iron	Fe^{2+}	part of cytochromes in electron transport
Manganese	Mn^{2+}	required by many enzymes
Boron	$B(OH)_3$	thought to be involved in carbohydrate transport
Chlorine	Cl^-	required to split water in photosynthesis
Zinc	Zn^{2+}	essential part of many enzymes
Copper	Cu^{2+}	essential part of many enzymes
Molybdenum	MoO_4^{2-}	required for nitrogen metabolism

characteristic symptoms and reduced growth. Severe mineral deficiencies can kill a plant. Excess amounts of some essential mineral nutrients also can be toxic to a plant.

Roots are often adapted to store carbohydrates or water. Phloem tissue carries carbohydrates made in leaves to roots. Carbohydrates that roots do not immediately use for energy or building blocks are stored. In roots, these excess carbohydrates are usually converted to starch and stored in parenchyma cells. You are probably familiar with the storage roots of carrots, turnips, and sweet potatoes. The roots of some species in the pumpkin family store large amounts of water, which helps the plants survive during dry periods.

SECTION 31-2 REVIEW

1. What are the major functions of the root system?

2. What are the differences between a taproot system and a fibrous root system?

3. What is the difference between primary growth and secondary growth? What types of tissues are involved in each type of growth?

4. Explain how root hairs increase the ability of a plant to absorb water from the soil.

5. Name two areas of the root where you would probably find parenchyma cells.

6. **CRITICAL THINKING** Why might a taproot system be an advantage to some plants, while a fibrous root system might be an advantage to others?

OBJECTIVES

▲

Describe the differences between monocot stems and dicot stems.

●

List five differences and five similarities between the structure of roots and the structure of stems.

■

Explain how annual rings are formed.

◆

Describe the pressure-flow model for organic-compound movement in the phloem.

▲

Describe the cohesion-tension theory for water movement in the xylem.

STEMS

In contrast to roots, which are mainly adapted for absorption and anchoring, stems are usually adapted to support leaves. Whatever their sizes and shapes, stems also function in transporting materials and providing storage.

TYPES OF STEMS

The various differences in stem shape and growth represent adaptations to the environment. Several types of stems are shown in Figure 31-9. Strawberry runners grow along the soil surface and produce new plants at their nodes. Stems such as the edible white potato tuber are modified for storing energy as starch. Cactuses have green fleshy stems that both store water and carry on all the plant's photosynthesis. Stems of the black locust and the honeylocust develop sharp thorns to protect the plant from animals. These stem modifications are related to environmental adaptations.

(a)

FIGURE 31-9

Stems provide a supporting framework for leaves. Some plants produce stems that are modified for other functions. (a) A strawberry plant has stolons, which are horizontal, aboveground stems that form new plants. (b) The potato plant has tubers, which are enlarged, short, underground stems used for storing starch. (c) A cactus is called a succulent because of its fleshy, water-storing stems.

(b)

(c)

STEM STRUCTURES

Stems have a more complex structure than roots, yet they are similar in many ways. Did you know that a sign nailed 2 m (7 ft) high on a tree will remain 2 m high, even though the tree may grow much taller? That is because most stems, like roots, grow in length only at their tips, where apical meristems produce new primary tissues. Stems, like roots, grow in circumference through lateral meristems.

The surfaces of stems have several features that roots lack, as Figure 31-10 shows. Stems are divided into segments called **internodes.** At each end of an internode is a **node.** Initially, one or more leaves are attached at each node. At the point of attachment of each leaf, the stem bears a lateral bud. A **bud** is capable of developing into a new shoot. A bud contains an apical meristem and is enclosed by specialized leaves called **bud scales.** The tip of each stem usually has a terminal bud. When growth resumes in the spring, the terminal bud opens, and the bud scales fall off. The bud

Quick Lab

Observing Stems

Materials winter twig, fresh stem with leaves, hand lens or dissecting microscope

Procedure

1. Observe the twig with the hand lens. Locate several buds, and identify the bud scales. Locate leaf scars. Identify a node and an internode. Draw and label the twig.

2. Observe the fresh stem with the hand lens. Locate and identify the stem, nodes, internodes, buds, and a leaf. Draw and label the fresh stem.

Analysis How are a node and an internode related? How are a bud and a node related? How are the two stems alike? How are they different?

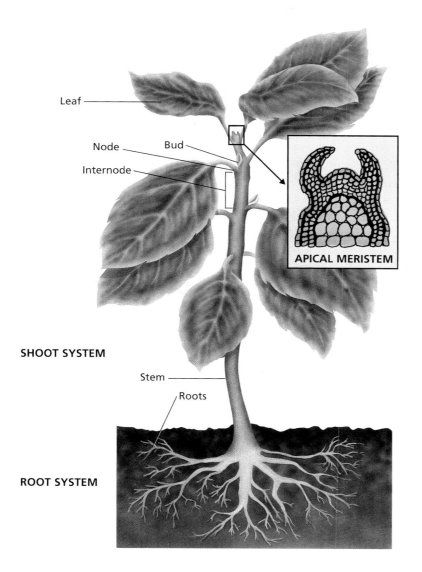

Leaf

Node

Bud

Internode

APICAL MERISTEM

SHOOT SYSTEM

Stem

Roots

ROOT SYSTEM

FIGURE 31-10

Apical meristems, responsible for the primary elongation of the plant body, are found in the shoot tips and root tips. Each leaf is attached to the stem at a node. The space between nodes, called the internode, is much larger in the older part of the stem. When the shoot tip is pinched off, the lateral buds begin to grow, resulting in a bushier plant.

(a) MONOCOT STEM

Epidermis

Vascular bundles

Ground tissue

(b) DICOT STEM

Vascular bundle

Phloem　Xylem

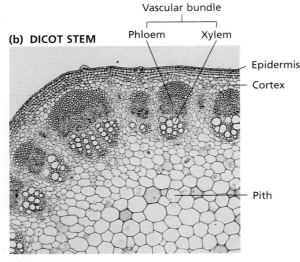

Epidermis

Cortex

Pith

FIGURE 31-11

Compare the two basic types of stems. (a) The cross section of a herbaceous stem of corn, a monocot, shows the vascular bundles scattered throughout the ground tissue. (b) In the sunflower, a dicot, the vascular tissues appear as a single ring of bundles between the cortex and the pith.

scales leave scars on the stem surface. Trees and shrubs often are identified in winter by these twig characteristics.

Root tips have a permanent protective layer, the root cap. The stem apical meristem is protected by bud scales only when the stem is not growing. A surface bud forms very close to the stem tip with one or more buds at each node. In contrast, lateral roots originate farther back from the root tip and form deep inside the root at no particular location along the root axis.

Primary Growth in Stems

As in roots, apical meristems of stems give rise to the dermal, ground, and vascular tissues. Locate each of these tissues in Figure 31-11. As you can see, the dermal tissue is represented by the epidermis, or the outer layer of the stem. Its main functions are to protect the plant and to reduce the loss of water to the atmosphere while still allowing gas exchange through stomata.

In gymnosperm and dicot stems, ground tissue usually forms a cortex and a pith. The cortex lies just inside the epidermis, as it does in the root. The cortex frequently contains flexible collenchyma cells. The **pith** is located in the center of the stem. The ground tissue of monocot stems is usually not clearly separated into pith and cortex.

Vascular tissue formed near the apical meristem occurs in bundles—long strands that are embedded in the cortex. Look at the vascular bundles in Figure 31-11. Each bundle contains xylem tissue and phloem tissue. Xylem is usually located toward the inside of the stem, while phloem is usually located toward the outside.

Compare the arrangement of vascular bundles in monocots and dicots. Monocot stem vascular bundles are usually scattered throughout the ground tissue. Stem vascular bundles of dicots and gymnosperms usually occur in a single ring. Most monocots have no secondary growth, and they retain the primary growth pattern their entire lives. However, in many dicots and gymnosperms, the primary tissues are eventually replaced by secondary tissues.

Secondary Growth in Stems

Stems increase in thickness due to the division of cells in the vascular cambium. The vascular cambium in dicot and gymnosperm stems first arises between the xylem and phloem in a vascular bundle. Eventually the vascular cambium forms a cylinder. The vascular cambium produces secondary xylem to the inside and secondary phloem to the outside. It usually produces much more secondary xylem than it does secondary phloem. Secondary xylem is called **wood.** Occasionally, the vascular cambium produces new cambium cells, which increase its diameter.

Older portions of the xylem eventually stop transporting water. They often become darker than the newer xylem due to the accumulation of resins and other organic compounds produced by the few live cells remaining in the xylem. This darker wood in the center of a tree is called **heartwood,** as shown in Figure 31-12a. The functional, often lighter-colored wood nearer the outside of the trunk is **sapwood.** In a large-diameter tree, the heartwood keeps getting wider while the sapwood remains about the same thickness.

The phloem produced near the outside of the stem is part of the bark. **Bark** is the protective outside covering of woody plants. It consists of cork, cork cambium, and phloem. The cork cambium produces cork near the outside. However, cork cells are dead at maturity and cannot elongate, so the cork ruptures as the stem continues to expand in diameter. This results in the bark of some trees, such as oaks and maples, appearing rough or irregular in texture.

During spring, when water is plentiful, the vascular cambium forms new xylem tissue with cells that are wide and thin walled. This wood is called **springwood.** In summer, when water is more limited, the vascular cambium produces **summerwood,** which has smaller cells with thicker walls. In a stem cross section, the abrupt change between small summerwood cells and the following year's large springwood cells produces an **annual ring.** The circles that look like rings on a target in Figure 31-12 are the annual rings of the stem. Because one ring is usually formed each year, you can estimate the age of the stem by counting its annual rings. Annual rings also form in dicot and gymnosperm roots, but they are often less pronounced because the root environment is more uniform. Annual rings often do not occur in tropical trees because of their uniform year-round environment.

FIGURE 31-12

(a) This cross section of a mature woody stem shows secondary growth, which results in a thicker stem. Wood consists of secondary xylem. The dark-colored wood is called heartwood and the light-colored wood is called sapwood. (b) You can see the annual rings produced by alternating springwood cells and summerwood cells. The abundant water of the spring season helps expand the cells walls of springwood cells.

Springwood

Summerwood

Rays

Heartwood

Sapwood

Annual ring

(a)

(b)

STEM FUNCTIONS

Stems function in the transportation and storage of nutrients and water, and they support the leaves. Carbohydrates, some plant hormones, and other organic compounds are transported in the phloem. The movement of carbohydrates occurs from where the carbohydrates are made or have been stored, called a **source,** to where they are stored or used, called a **sink.** Botanists use the term **translocation** to refer to the movement of carbohydrates through the plant. For example, in most plants, carbohydrates move from the leaves to the roots, to the shoot apical meristems, and to the developing flowers or fruits. Carbohydrates may be newly made in photosynthetic cells or may have been stored as starch in roots or stems.

Movement in the phloem is explained by the **pressure-flow hypothesis,** which states that carbohydrates are actively transported into sieve tubes. Look at Figure 31-13. As carbohydrates enter the sieve tubes, water is also transported in by osmosis. Thus, a positive pressure builds up at the source end of the sieve tube. This is the pressure part of the hypothesis.

At the sink end of the sieve tube, this process is reversed. Carbohydrates are actively transported out, water leaves the sieve tube by osmosis, and pressure is reduced at the sink. The difference

FIGURE 31-13

In the pressure-flow model, carbohydrates are pushed through the phloem by the pressure that results from the movement of water into the phloem by osmosis. The blue arrows indicate water movement, and the red arrows indicate carbohydrate movement.

Phloem   Xylem

(a) Sugar from source enters phloem.

SOURCE

(b) Water from xylem enters phloem.

(c) Pressure pushes sugar down.

Companion cell

SINK

(d) Sugar from phloem enters sink.

● Water

● Sugar

in pressure causes water to flow from source to sink—carrying dissolved substances with it. Transport in the phloem can occur in different directions at different times.

Transport of Water

The transport of water and mineral nutrients occurs in the xylem of all plant organs, but it occurs over the greatest distances in the stems of tall trees. During the day, water is constantly evaporating from the plant, mainly through leaf stomata. This water loss is called **transpiration** (TRAN-spuh-RAY-shuhn). The large amount of water lost from the plant is a result of the plant's need to obtain carbon dioxide from the air. Exactly how do huge trees, like redwoods, move water and mineral nutrients up their 100 m tall trunks?

According to the **cohesion-tension theory,** water is pulled up the stem xylem by the strong attraction of water molecules to each other, a property of water called cohesion. The movement also depends on the rigid xylem walls and the strong attraction of water molecules to the xylem wall, which is called adhesion. The thin, continuous columns of water extend from the leaves through the stems and into the roots. As water evaporates from the leaf, the water column is subject to great tension. However, the water column does not break because of cohesion and it does not pull away from the xylem walls because of adhesion. The only other possibility is for it to be pulled upward. The pull at the top of the tree extends all the way to the bottom of the column. As water is pulled up the xylem, more water enters the roots from the soil to replace the lost water.

Storing Water and Nutrients

With abundant parenchyma cells in the cortex, plant stems are adapted for storage in most species. In some species, storage is a major function. Cactus stems are specialized for storing water. The roots of a cactus are found close to the soil surface, enabling them to absorb rainwater quickly and transport it to the cactus's fleshy stem. Sugar-cane stems store large amounts of sucrose. The edible white potato is a stem that is specialized for storing starch. The "eyes" of white potatoes are buds that have the ability to develop into new shoots.

Word Roots and Origins

transpiration

from the Latin *trans*, meaning "across," and the Latin *spirare*, meaning "to breathe"

internet**connect**

SC*LINKS*
NSTA

TOPIC: Transpiration
GO TO: www.scilinks.org
KEYWORD: HM613

SECTION 31-3 REVIEW

1. How does the arrangement of vascular tissues in a stem differ between monocots and dicots?

2. Describe five differences and five similarities between the structure of roots and the structure of stems.

3. Explain the difference between summerwood and springwood and tell how they form annual rings.

4. Describe how water moves through xylem tissue.

5. Describe the movement of carbohydrates within phloem tissue.

6. **CRITICAL THINKING** Some squirrels damage trees by stripping off portions of the bark. Why would a squirrel eat bark?

Nature's Chemical Arsenal

Plants depend heavily on chemical compounds for their survival because they are unable to otherwise escape herbivores. Such defensive compounds are called secondary compounds because they have no known function in plant growth. Secondary compounds are the active ingredients in many familiar medicines, including aspirin and taxol.

Secondary compounds are unique not only to each plant species but often to specific parts of a plant. For example, the chemicals found in a plant's flowers are likely to attract pollinators, while the chemicals found in the same plant's leaves may be toxic. With so many plants and plant parts in existence, scientists have a multitude of chemical compounds to study in their search for new medicines.

Eloy Rodriguez, a plant chemist at Cornell University, has found a surprising way to track down secondary compounds that are likely to be helpful to humans—by studying how animals may medicate themselves in the wild with plants. He named this new discipline zoopharmacognosy.

Rodriguez and his colleagues found that non-human primates, which suffer from many of the same illnesses as humans, tend to eat only one kind of plant, or even one part of one kind of plant, when they have a particular illness. For example, Richard Wrangham, a Harvard University primatologist, observed that East African chimpanzees suffering from parasitic infections eat *Aspilia* leaves. When Rodriguez analyzed the chemistry of *Aspilia,* he identified one of the chemicals extracted from the plant's leaves as thiarubrine-A. Rodriguez's experiments on thiarubrine-A demonstrated that the chemical has antibiotic effects on bacteria, fungi, and intestinal parasites.

Another plant eaten by chimpanzees is *Rubia cordifolia.* Several chemicals collected from this plant, grouped together as cyclic hexapeptides, are being investigated by the National Institutes of Health as a possible therapeutic agent against cancer. Laboratory tests with mice have shown that at the dosages ingested by chimpanzees, these chemicals have low toxicity. So if further research documents the chemicals' effectiveness as a weapon against cancer, they may provide the benefits of chemotherapy with less serious side effects.

After Rodriguez's research team began presenting its results on zoopharmacognosy, animal behaviorists began reporting similar observations of other animals. In 1996, Andrew Dobson, a professor at Princeton University, suggested that the diet of the African green monkey should be studied by researchers looking for new compounds to combat AIDS because the virus is thought to have originated in green monkeys.

Meanwhile, Rodriguez is concerned that he and other plant researchers face a race against time. Potentially life-saving plants found in tropical areas of the world are becoming extinct as the rain forests rapidly disappear. Rodriguez urges other researchers to join him in investigating the animals and plants that have coexisted in this region, using the innovative approaches that he pioneered.

Plant researcher Eloy Rodriguez shows students in his lab some of the chemicals extracted from plant leaves.

LEAVES

Most leaves are thin and flat, an adaptation that helps them capture sunlight for photosynthesis. Although this structure may be typical, it is certainly not universal. Like roots and stems, leaves are extremely variable. This variability represents adaptations to environmental conditions.

TYPES OF LEAVES

Look at the leaves in Figure 31-14a. The coiled structure is a **tendril,** a specialized leaf found in many vines, such as peas and pumpkins. It wraps around objects to support the climbing vine. In some species, like grape, tendrils are specialized stems.

An unusual leaf modification occurs in carnivorous plants such as the pitcher plant, shown in Figure 31-14b. In carnivorous plants, leaves function as food traps. These plants grow in soil that is poor in several mineral nutrients, especially nitrogen. The plant receives substantial amounts of mineral nutrients when it traps and digests insects and other small animals.

Leaves, or parts of leaves, are often modified into spines that protect the plant from being eaten by animals, as shown in Figure 31-14c. Because spines are small and nonphotosynthetic, they greatly reduce transpiration in desert species such as cactuses.

SECTION

31-4

OBJECTIVES

▲

Identify the difference between a simple leaf and a compound leaf.

●

Describe the tissues that make up the internal structure of a leaf.

■

Describe adaptations of leaves for special purposes.

◆

Explain the importance of stomata.

FIGURE 31-14

Many plants have developed leaf adaptations. (a) The pea plant has tendrils that climb. (b) The pitcher plant has tubular leaves that trap insects. (c) The barberry has spines that protect against herbivores.

(a)

(b)

(c)

(a) SIMPLE LEAF

(b) COMPOUND LEAF

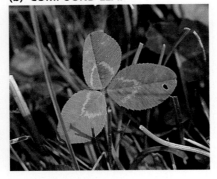

(c) DOUBLY COMPOUND LEAF

FIGURE 31-15

(a) A sugar-maple leaf is called a simple leaf because it has only one blade. (b) A white clover leaf is called a compound leaf because the leaf blade is divided into distinct leaflets. (c) The honeylocust has a doubly compound leaf because each leaflet is subdivided into smaller leaflets.

LEAF STRUCTURES

Leaves come in a wide variety of shapes and sizes and are an important feature used for plant identification. Leaves can be round, straplike, needlelike, or heart-shaped. The broad, flat portion of a leaf, called the **blade,** is the site of most photosynthesis. The blade is usually attached to the stem by a stalklike **petiole.** The maple leaf shown in Figure 31-15a is a **simple leaf;** it has a single blade. In **compound leaves,** such as the white clover in Figure 31-15b, the blade is divided into **leaflets.** In some species, the leaflets themselves are divided. The result is a doubly compound leaf, such as that of the honeylocust shown in Figure 31-15c.

Leaves consist of three tissue systems. The dermal tissue system is represented by the epidermis. In most leaves the epidermis is a single layer of cells coated with a nearly impermeable cuticle. Water, oxygen, and carbon dioxide enter and exit the leaf through stomata in the epidermis. Epidermal hairs are often present and usually function to protect the leaf from insects and intense light.

The number of stomata per unit area of leaf varies by species. For example, submerged leaves of aquatic plants have few or no stomata. Corn leaves have up to 10,000 stomata per square centimeter on both upper and lower surfaces. Scarlet oak has over 100,000 stomata per square centimeter on the lower leaf surface and none on the upper surface. Regardless of their exact distribution, stomata are needed to regulate gas exchange.

In most plants, photosynthesis occurs in the leaf **mesophyll** (MEZ-oh-FIL), a ground tissue composed of chloroplast-rich parenchyma cells. In most plants, the mesophyll is organized into two layers, which are shown in Figure 31-16. The **palisade mesophyll** layer occurs directly beneath the upper epidermis and is the site of most photosynthesis. Palisade cells are columnar and appear to be packed tightly together in one or two layers. However, there are air spaces between the long side walls of palisade cells. Beneath the palisade layer is the **spongy mesophyll.** It consists of irregularly shaped cells surrounded by large air spaces, which allow oxygen, carbon dioxide, and water to diffuse into and out of the leaf.

The vascular tissue system of leaves consists of vascular bundles called **veins.** Veins are continuous with the vascular tissue of the stem and the petiole, and they lie embedded in the mesophyll. Veins branch repeatedly so that each cell is usually less than 1 mm (0.04 in.) from a vein.

Venation is the arrangement of veins in a leaf. Leaves of most monocots, such as grasses, have **parallel venation,** meaning that several main veins are roughly parallel to each other. The main veins are connected by small, inconspicuous veins. Leaves of most dicots, such as sycamores, have **net venation,** meaning that the main vein or veins repeatedly branch to form a conspicuous network of smaller veins.

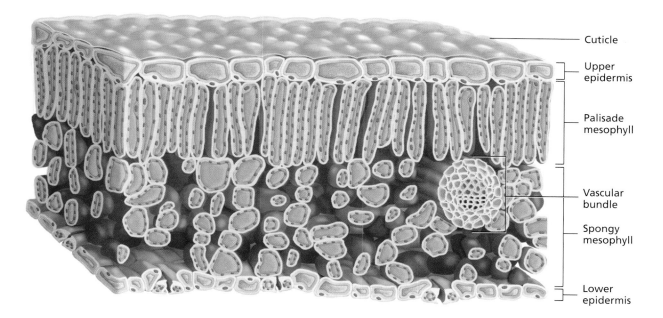

Cuticle

Upper
epidermis

Palisade
mesophyll

Vascular
bundle

Spongy
mesophyll

Lower
epidermis

LEAF FUNCTIONS

Leaves are the primary site of photosynthesis in most plants. Mesophyll cells in leaves use light energy, carbon dioxide, and water to make carbohydrates. Light energy also is used by mesophyll cells to synthesize amino acids, fats, and a variety of other organic molecules. Carbohydrates made in a leaf can be used by the leaf as an energy source or as building blocks. They also may be transported to other parts of the plant, where they are either stored or used for energy or building blocks.

A major limitation to plant photosynthesis is insufficient water due to transpiration. For example, about 98 percent of the water that is absorbed by a corn plant's roots is lost through transpiration. However, transpiration may benefit the plant by cooling it and by speeding the transport of mineral nutrients through the xylem.

Modifications for Capturing Light

Leaves absorb light, which, in turn, provides the energy for photosynthesis. Leaves often adapt to their environment to maximize light interception. On the same tree, leaves that develop in full sun are thicker, have a smaller area per leaf, and have more chloroplasts per unit area. Shade-leaf chloroplasts are arranged so that shading of one chloroplast by another is minimized, while sun-leaf chloroplasts are not.

In dry environments, plants often receive more light than they can use. These plants often have structures that reduce the amount of light absorbed. For example, many desert plants have evolved dense coatings of hairs that reduce light absorption. The window plant shown in Figure 31-17 protects itself from its dry environment by growing underground. Only its transparent leaf tips protrude above the soil to gather light for photosynthesis.

FIGURE 31-16

Cells from all three tissue systems are represented in the internal structure of a leaf. The epidermis is part of the dermal system, and the vascular bundle is part of the vascular system. The mesophyll is ground tissue made of parenchyma cells, and it generally contains chloroplasts. Note that the palisade mesophyll layer is more dense than the spongy mesophyll layer.

FIGURE 31-17

The unusual transparent leaf tips of this window plant channel light to the plant's buried leaves.

(a)

(b)

FIGURE 31-18

Scanning electron micrographs of monocot and dicot leaves show how the arrangement of stomata in each is different. (a) In the corn leaf, the stomata are in a parallel arrangement, which is typical of monocots. (b) In the potato leaf, the stomata are in a random arrangement, which is typical of dicots. For both monocots and dicots, the movement of water in the guard cells of each stoma is regulated by potassium ions (K^+).

TOPIC: Leaf functions
GO TO: www.scilinks.org
KEYWORD: HM618

Gas Exchange

Plants obtain carbon dioxide for photosynthesis from the air. Plants must balance their need to open their stomata to receive carbon dioxide and release oxygen with their need to close their stomata to prevent water loss through transpiration. A stoma is bordered by two kidney-shaped guard cells. **Guard cells** are modified cells found on the leaf epidermis that regulate gas and water exchange. Figure 31-18 shows how the stomata are arranged differently in monocots and dicots.

The stomata of most plants open during the day and close at night. The opening and closing of a stoma is regulated by the amount of water in its guard cells. When epidermal cells of leaves pump potassium ions (K^+) into guard cells, water moves into the guard cells by osmosis. This influx of water makes the guard cells swell, which causes them to bow apart to form a pore. During darkness, potassium ions are pumped out of the guard cells. Water then leaves the guard cells by osmosis. This causes the guard cells to shrink slightly and the pore to close.

Stomata also close if the plant experiences a shortage of water. The closing of stomata greatly reduces further water loss and may help the plant survive until the next rain. However, stomata closure virtually shuts down photosynthesis by cutting off the supply of carbon dioxide.

SECTION 31-4 REVIEW

1. What is the difference between a simple leaf and a compound leaf?

2. Describe the basic function of each of the three leaf tissues.

3. What are three types of specialized leaves?

4. Explain the function of the guard cells in regulating stomatal opening and closing.

5. Why do plants grown in greenhouses in winter rarely grow as fast as the same type of plant grown outside in the summer even if the temperatures are the same in both locations?

6. **CRITICAL THINKING** Why is it an advantage for a plant to have most of its stomata on the underside of a horizontal leaf?

SUMMARY/VOCABULARY

31-1 ■ Plants consist of three types of cells—parenchyma, sclerenchyma, and collenchyma.

■ The dermal system consists of the epidermis, or the outermost layer of cells; it functions in absorption and protection in the roots and in gas exchange and protection in stems and leaves.

■ The bulk of leaves, nonwoody stems, and nonwoody roots is ground tissue, which functions in storage, metabolism, and support.

■ Vascular tissue consists of xylem, which carries water and mineral nutrients, and phloem, which transports organic compounds and some mineral nutrients.

■ An increase in length, called primary growth, occurs mainly at the tips of stems and roots in the apical meristems.

■ In secondary growth, the stems and roots increase in diameter in the lateral meristems.

Vocabulary

apical meristem (602)	epidermis (600)	primary growth (602)	tracheid (601)
collenchyma (599)	ground tissue system (601)	sclerenchyma (600)	vascular cambium (602)
companion cell (601)	intercalary meristem (602)	secondary growth (602)	vascular tissue system (601)
cork (602)	lateral meristem (602)	sieve plate (601)	vessel (601)
cork cambium (602)	meristem (602)	sieve tube (601)	vessel element (601)
cuticle (600)	parenchyma (599)	sieve tube member (601)	
dermal tissue system (600)	pit (601)		

31-2 ■ Roots anchor the plant and store and absorb water and mineral nutrients from the soil.

■ A taproot system has a large primary root, and a fibrous root system has many small branching roots.

■ Young roots produce root hairs, which are extensions of epidermal cells that increase the surface area for absorption.

■ The root endodermis prevents substances from entering or leaving the root vascular tissue without passing through a cell membrane.

Vocabulary

adventitious root (604)	fibrous root system (603)	pericycle (606)	root hair (604)
cortex (605)	macronutrients (606)	root cap (604)	taproot (603)
endodermis (605)	micronutrients (606)		

31-3 ■ Stems function in the transportation and storage of nutrients and water.

■ The stems of monocots usually have scattered vascular bundles and usually lack secondary growth.

■ Dicot stems have vascular bundles arranged in a ring and often produce abundant secondary growth.

■ Secondary growth consists primarily of secondary xylem, called wood.

■ In nontropical areas, secondary xylem in stems forms one annual ring each year.

■ The outer bark of trees consists of cork produced by the cork cambium.

■ The cohesion-tension theory describes the process of how water is pulled up through the xylem tissue.

■ The pressure-flow hypothesis describes the process of how organic compounds are transported in the phloem tissue.

Vocabulary

annual ring (611)	heartwood (611)	sapwood (611)	summerwood (611)
bark (611)	internode (609)	sink (613)	translocation (612)
bud (609)	node (609)	source (613)	transpiration (613)
bud scale (609)	pith (610)	springwood (611)	wood (611)
cohesion-tension theory (612)	pressure-flow hypothesis (613)		

31-4 ■ The identification of plants is based on the shape, size, and arrangement of leaf blades. Plants with simple leaves or compound leaves are common.

■ Photosynthesis occurs mostly in the palisade mesophyll, which consists of rows of closely packed cells, and the loosely packed spongy mesophyll.

■ Gas exchange in leaves is controlled by stomata, or small openings in the leaf.

■ Most of the water absorbed by a plant evaporates from the stomata during transpiration.

■ Two guard cells surround each stoma. When the guard cells gain water, the stoma opens. When the guard cells lose water, the stoma closes.

Vocabulary

blade (616)
compound leaf (616)
guard cell (618)
leaflet (616)

mesophyll (616)
net venation (616)
palisade mesophyll (616)
parallel venation (616)

petiole (616)
simple leaf (616)
spongy mesophyll (616)

tendril (615)
vein (616)
venation (616)

REVIEW

Vocabulary

In each of the following sets, choose the term that does not belong and explain why.

1. wood, bark, epidermis, cork
2. sieve tube member, mesophyll, tracheid, vessel element
3. apical meristem, primary xylem, vascular cambium, endodermis
4. root hair, transpiration, vessel element, collenchyma
5. blade, cork, petiole, vein

Multiple Choice

6. Nonfunctional xylem in the center of a tree trunk is (a) summerwood (b) sapwood (c) heartwood (d) springwood.
7. Mesophyll is the site of (a) water absorption (b) storage (c) photosynthesis (d) secondary growth.
8. Water moves between tracheids through (a) end walls (b) stomata (c) vessel elements (d) pits.
9. Stomata open and close due to water pressure changes in the (a) guard cells (b) sieve tube member (c) root hairs (d) cortex.
10. The root apical meristem is protected by the (a) bud scales (b) cuticle (c) root cap (d) cortex.
11. Collenchyma and sclerenchyma function mainly in (a) storage (b) photosynthesis (c) support (d) transport.

12. Most monocots do not have (a) primary growth (b) secondary growth (c) xylem (d) phloem.
13. A waterproof substance occurs in cell walls of (a) cortex (b) endodermal cells (c) palisade mesophyll cells (d) vessel elements.
14. The main site of photosynthesis in cactuses is the (a) root (b) leaf (c) flower (d) stem.
15. A structure found in stems but not in roots is (a) epidermis (b) vascular tissue (c) node (d) cortex.

Short Answer

16. What causes a plant stem or root to grow in diameter?
17. Explain the difference between heartwood and sapwood.
18. Describe the different arrangements of vascular bundles in the stems and leaves of monocots and dicots.
19. What substances are transported through the tissue shown in the photograph below?
20.

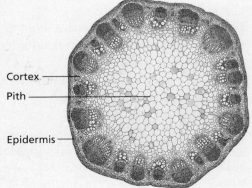

Cortex
Pith
Epidermis

Distinguish between woody plants and non-woody plants, and give an example of each.

21. Explain the difference between primary growth and secondary growth.

22. Briefly describe the cohesion-tension theory of water movement in the xylem.

23. List three modified types of leaves.

24. How are a sweet potato and a white potato different? How are they similar?

25. Explain how guard cells regulate the opening and closing of stomata.

CRITICAL THINKING

1. Copy the chart shown below on a sheet of paper. Fill in the plant structures corresponding to the human structures listed in the chart.

Common Structural Functions

Function	Human structure	Plant structure
Gas exchange	lungs	a.
Circulation	blood vessels	b.
Water intake	mouth	c.
Energy intake	mouth	d.
Protective covering	skin	e.
Internal support	skeleton	f.
Energy storage	fat cells	g.

2. When transplanting a plant, it is important that you not remove any more soil than necessary from around the roots. From your knowledge of the function of roots and root hairs, why do you think is this so important?

3. Suppose you examine a tree stump and notice that the annual rings are thinner and closer together 50 rings in from the edge. What would you conclude about the climate in the area 50 years ago?

4. Girdling is the removal of a narrow strip of bark all the way around a tree trunk. What effects might girdling have on a plant's shoots and roots?

5. What causes a knot in a board, like that shown in the photograph below?

EXTENSION

1. Read "Why Tulips Can't Dance" in *Science News,* February 5, 2000, on page 95. Describe how the stem structures of tulips and daffodils compare. How does the stem structure of daffodils contribute to the plants' ability to bend in gusty winds?

2. Measure transpiration in a common non-woody plant. Buy two small flowering plants or tomato plants from a local nursery. Get plants as identical in size as possible. Make sure the plants are well watered, and then cover the pots with a plastic bag. Tie the bag shut around the base of the plant's stem without injuring the stem. Weigh each pot to the nearest gram and record the mass. Place one plant in the dark and one plant in bright light. Weigh the pots again after two hours, and calculate the amount of transpiration in grams as follows: transpiration = initial mass − final mass. If there is no difference in transpiration, extend the length of the experiment. Which treatment resulted in the most transpiration? Why?

Observing Roots, Stems, and Leaves

OBJECTIVES

- Observe the tissues and structures that make up roots, stems, and leaves.
- Explain how roots, stems, and leaves are adapted for the functions they perform.

PROCESS SKILLS

- observing
- identifying
- relating structure and function

MATERIALS

- prepared slides of the following tissues:
  - *Allium* root tip longitudinal section
  - *Syringa* leaf cross section
  - *Ranunculus* root cross section
  - *Ranunculus* stem cross section
  - *Zea mays* stem cross section
- compound light microscope

Background

1. Which plant tissues are responsible for the absorption of water and mineral nutrients?
2. How is sugar, which is produced in the leaf, moved to other parts of the plant?
3. How are woody and herbaceous stems different, and how are they alike?
4. What tissues are continuous in the root, stem, and leaf?
5. How does the leaf conserve water?

PART A   Roots

1. ⚠ CAUTION **Glass slides may break and cut you.** Observe the prepared slide of the *Allium* root tip under low power. Locate the root cap and the root tip meristematic cells. You may look at the photograph on page 604 for help. Note the long root hairs in the area above the root tip.
2. In your lab report, draw the root tip that you observe, and label the root cap, meristem, and root hairs in your drawings.

Ranunculus *root (275×)—a dicot*

3. Change slides to the root cross section of the dicot *Ranunculus.* This slide should look similar to the photograph shown above. The inner core is the vascular tissue, which is surrounded by the endodermis. This area of the tissue is involved in the transport of water, mineral nutrients, and organic compounds. Look for the star-shaped xylem and the smaller phloem cells surrounding the xylem.
4. In your lab report, draw what you see, and identify the xylem tissue and the phloem tissue in your drawing.
5. Locate the cortex, where starch is stored, which surrounds the vascular cylinder. Outside the cortex, find the epidermal cells and their root hairs. Draw a one-quarter section of the root tissues. Label all the tissues in your lab report.

PART B   Stems

6. Observe a prepared slide of the stem of *Zea mays,* a monocot, and find the epidermis and the photosynthetic layer. It should look like the photograph on the next page. In the center, look for the vascular bundles made up of xylem and phloem. Draw a diagram showing the location of the vascular bundles and the epidermis layer as they appear when viewed under low power.
7. Switch to high power, and observe a vascular bundle. Draw the vascular bundle, and label the tissues.
8. Observe a cross section of *Ranunculus,* a herbaceous dicot stem. Compare your slide with the photograph of

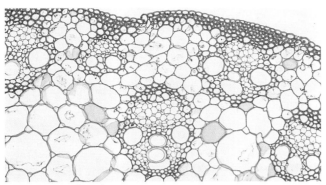

Zea mays *stem (130×)—a monocot*

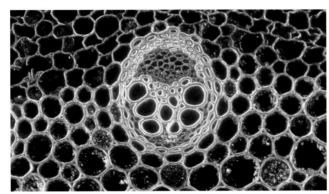

Ranunculus *stem (151×)—a dicot*

Ranunculus shown above. Look for the epidermis and cortex layers. Notice that in a dicot, the stem is more complex than the root. Note the arrangement of the vascular bundles. In your lab report, draw what you observe. Label the epidermis, cortex, and individual vascular bundles.

9. Focus on a vascular bundle under high power. Draw and label a diagram of a vascular bundle in your lab report.

PART C Leaves

10. Observe a prepared slide of a lilac leaf, *Syringa*, shown below, under low power, and find the lower epidermis.

Syringa *leaf (530×)*

11. Identify the stomata on the lower epidermis of the lilac leaf. Find the guard cells that open and close a particular stoma. Locate an open stoma and a closed stoma. Draw and label diagrams of the stomata and the guard cells in your lab report.

12. Look at the center part of the cross section. Note the spongy texture of the mesophyll layer. Locate a vein containing xylem and phloem. Now identify the palisade layer, the upper epidermis, and finally the clear, continuous, noncellular layer on top. This layer is called the cuticle. Draw and label a diagram of your observations in your lab report.

13. Clean up your materials before leaving the lab.

Analysis and Conclusions

1. In the dicot root that you observed, where are phloem and xylem located?
2. Where are the xylem and phloem found in the herbaceous stem that you observed?
3. How are the vascular bundles different in the monocot and dicot stems that you observed?
4. How are the root cap cells different from the root tip meristematic cells?
5. What is the function of the root hairs?
6. How do the arrangements of xylem and phloem differ in roots, stems, and leaves?
7. What is the function of a stoma?
8. What is the function of the air space in the mesophyll of the leaf?
9. Which leaf structures help to conserve water?
10. Which tissues of the leaf are continuous with the stem and root tissues? How is this functional?
11. Look at the various tissues found in your drawings of roots, stems, and leaves. Classify each tissue as either dermal tissue, ground tissue, or vascular tissue.

Further Inquiry

The parts of a flower are actually modified stems and leaves. Design—but do not carry out—a procedure for dissecting a flower. Include a diagram of the parts of the flower to be viewed. Use references from the library to determine which kinds of flowers are best for dissection.

PLANT REPRODUCTION

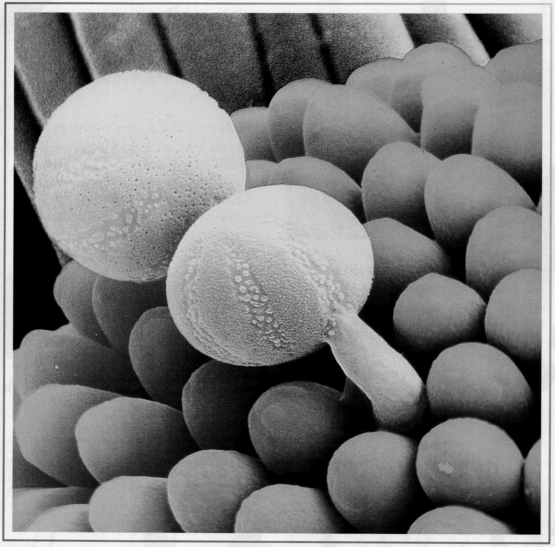

Two pollen grains are on the stigma of a flower of goose grass, Galium aparine. A pollen tube, seen growing out of one of these pollen grains, will travel toward the ovary.

FOCUS CONCEPT: *Evolution*

As you read, note the many plant adaptations that help ensure the successful reproduction, protection, and dispersal of offspring.

PLANT LIFE CYCLES

A life cycle includes all of the stages of an organism's growth and development. Recall from Chapter 30 that a plant's life cycle involves two alternating multicellular stages—a diploid (2n) sporophyte stage and a haploid (1n) gametophyte stage. This type of life cycle is called alternation of generations. Also recall that the size of gametophytes and sporophytes varies among the plant groups.

SECTION

32-1

OBJECTIVES

▲

Describe the life cycle of a moss.

●

Describe the life cycle of a typical fern.

■

Describe the life cycle of a gymnosperm.

◆

Compare and contrast homospory and heterospory.

THE LIFE CYCLE OF MOSSES

The dominant form of a moss is a clump of leafy green gametophytes. Look at the moss life cycle illustrated in Figure 32-1. Moss gametophytes produce gametes in two types of reproductive structures—antheridia and archegonia. An **antheridium** (AN-thuhr-ID-ee-uhm) is a male reproductive structure that produces hundreds of flagellated sperm by mitosis. An **archegonium** (AWR-kuh-GOH-nee-uhm) is a female reproductive structure that produces a single egg by mitosis. During moist periods, sperm break out of the antheridia and swim to the archegonia. One sperm fertilizes the egg at the base of an archegonium, forming a diploid zygote. Through repeated mitotic divisions, the zygote forms an embryo and develops into a sporophyte.

FIGURE 32-1

The life cycle of a moss includes a relatively large, leafy green gametophyte, which produces gametes, and a smaller sporophyte, which grows from the tip of the gametophyte and produces only one type of spore. The flagellated sperm must swim to the eggs.

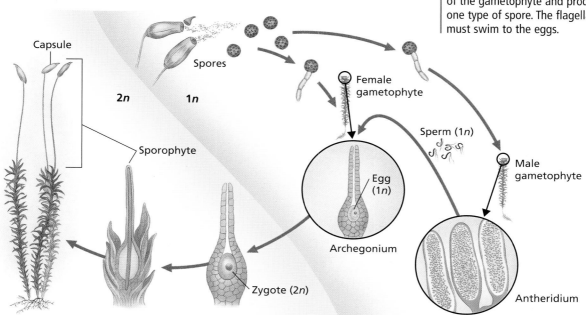

Capsule

Spores

2n   **1n**

Sporophyte

Female gametophyte

Sperm (1*n*)

Egg (1*n*)

Male gametophyte

Archegonium

Zygote (2*n*)

Antheridium

A moss sporophyte begins as a thin stalk that grows from the tip of a gametophyte. The sporophyte remains attached to the gametophyte and depends on it for nourishment. Soon, cells at the tip of a stalk form a sporangium, called the capsule. Cells in the capsule undergo meiosis to form haploid spores, which are all the same. The production of one type of spore is called **homospory** (hoh-MAHS-puh-ree). Therefore, the life cycle of mosses is called *homosporous* (hoh-MAHS-puh-ruhs) *alternation of generations.* When the spores are mature, the capsule splits open, and the spores are carried away by the wind. Spores that land in favorable environments grow into new gametophytes.

THE LIFE CYCLE OF FERNS

The life cycle of a fern, shown in Figure 32-2, is similar to the moss life cycle. Like mosses, most ferns are homosporous. And as in mosses, the fern sporophyte grows from the gametophyte. But in the fern life cycle, the sporophyte, not the gametophyte, is the dominant generation. Fern gametophytes are tiny (about 10 mm, or 0.5 in., in diameter), flat plants that are anchored to the soil by rhizoids. Both antheridia and archegonia form on the lower surface of a fern gametophyte. When water is present, sperm released by antheridia swim to archegonia. One sperm fuses with the egg in an archegonium, forming a zygote, which is the first cell of a new sporophyte.

The zygote grows into an embryo and then into a young fern sporophyte through mitotic cell division. The sporophyte crushes the gametophyte as it grows. A mature fern sporophyte usually has compound leaves called fronds, which grow from an underground

FIGURE 32-2

The life cycle of most ferns includes a large sporophyte, which produces only one type of spore, and a small gametophyte, which produces gametes. Both the eggs and sperm are produced on the same gametophyte. The flagellated sperm must swim to the eggs.

Sorus

Frond

Fiddlehead

Rhizome

Roots

ADULT SPOROPHYTE

2n   **1n**

Spores

Sporangium releasing spores

Zygote (2n)

Antheridium

Sperm (1n)

MATURE GAMETOPHYTE

Egg (1n)

Archegonium

stem, or rhizome. In most ferns, certain cells on the underside of the fronds develop into sporangia. In many ferns, the sporangia are grouped together in clusters called **sori** (SOH-ree). Cells inside a sporangium undergo meiosis, forming haploid spores. At maturity, the sporangium opens and the spores are catapulted 1 cm (0.4 in.) or more and are then carried away by air currents. When the spores land, and if conditions are right, they grow into new gametophytes.

THE LIFE CYCLE OF CONIFERS

Unlike mosses and most ferns, gymnosperms produce two types of spores—male **microspores** and female **megaspores.** Microspores grow into male gametophytes, while megaspores grow into female gametophytes. The production of different types of spores is called **heterospory** (HET-uhr-AHS-puh-ree). Thus, the gymnosperm life cycle is called *heterosporous* (HET-uhr-AHS-puh-ruhs) *alternation of generations.* All seed plants, spike mosses, quillworts, and a few fern species also have heterospory, which ensures that a sperm will fertilize an egg from a different gametophyte and increases the chance that new combinations of genes will occur among the offspring.

Figure 32-3 shows the life cycle of a pine, which is a conifer, the most common kind of gymnosperm. The conifer life cycle illustrates how seed plants reproduce without water for sperm to swim through. The familiar pine tree is a sporophyte. Like humans, pines cannot sexually reproduce until they are mature. Depending on the species, pines take from 3 to more than 30 years to reach adulthood.

In pines, sexual reproduction takes more than two years. During the first summer, a mature pine tree produces separate male and

FIGURE 32-3

The life cycle of a gymnosperm includes a large sporophyte, which produces two types of spores, and microscopic gametophytes, which produce gametes. Female gametophytes produce eggs, and male gametophytes produce sperm. The nonflagellated sperm reach the eggs through a pollen tube.

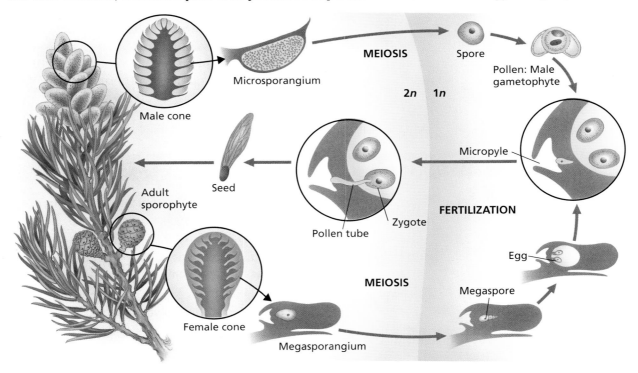

MEIOSIS   Spore

Microsporangium

Pollen: Male gametophyte

Male cone

2n   1n

Micropyle

Seed

Adult sporophyte

Zygote

FERTILIZATION

Pollen tube

Egg

MEIOSIS

Female cone

Megaspore

Megasporangium

female cones. The male cones produce microsporangia, while the female cones produce megasporangia. The following spring, cells in all sporangia undergo meiosis and divide to produce haploid spores. These spores never leave the parent to develop independently. **Megasporangia** produce megaspores, which develop into **megagametophytes,** or female gametophytes. A thick layer of cells called an **integument** (in-TEG-yoo-muhnt) surrounds each megasporangium. The integument has a small opening called the **micropyle** (MIE-kroh-PIEL). Together, a megasporangium and its integument form a structure called an **ovule** (AHV-yool). Two ovules develop on each scale of a female cone. **Microsporangia** produce microspores, which develop into **microgametophytes,** or male gametophytes. A **pollen grain** is a microgametophyte of a seed plant.

The male cones of a pine release huge numbers of pollen grains, as seen in Figure 32-4. Pine pollen travels on the wind, and only a few grains may land on a female cone. The pollen grains drift between the cone scales until they reach the ovules. The arrival of a pollen grain at the micropyle of a pine ovule is called pollination. A drop of fluid at the micropyle captures the pollen grain. As the fluid dries, the pollen grain is drawn into the micropyle. After pollination, the female gametophyte within the ovule produces archegonia and eggs.

After pollination, the pollen grain begins to grow a **pollen tube,** a slender extension of the pollen grain that enables sperm to reach an egg. Unlike the sperm of seedless plants, pine sperm do not have flagella and they do not swim to an egg. The pollen tube takes about a year to reach an egg only a few millimeters away. During this time, two sperm develop in the pollen tube. When the pollen tube reaches an archegonium, one sperm unites with an egg to form a zygote. The other sperm and the pollen tube die. Over the next few months, the zygote develops into an embryo as the ovule matures into a seed.

Seed plants benefit from having a life cycle with microscopic gametophytes. The microscopic gametophytes are enclosed in structures produced by the much larger sporophyte. These structures provide a way for the sperm to fertilize the eggs without water. Sexual reproduction in seed plants can therefore take place independent of seasonal rains or other periods of moisture.

FIGURE 32-4

The male cones (pollen cones) of pines produce millions of pollen grains. The male cones then die. Wind-pollinated species typically produce large amounts of pollen. Large numbers of pollen grains increase the odds that female cones (seed cones) will be pollinated.

SECTION 32-1 REVIEW

1. Distinguish between an antheridium and an archegonium, and state the function of each.

2. Draw a generalized diagram of alternation of generations showing the haploid and diploid phases of the moss life cycle.

3. List three differences between the life cycle of a fern and that of a pine.

4. How are the spores of seed plants different from the spores of bryophytes and most ferns?

5. In what way did the enclosure of the male gametophyte contribute to the great evolutionary success of seed plants?

6. **CRITICAL THINKING**   Many mosses and ferns live in the desert. Why do you think this is so?

SEXUAL REPRODUCTION IN FLOWERING PLANTS

You have probably admired flowers for their bright colors, attractive shapes, and pleasing aromas. These characteristics are adaptations that help ensure successful sexual reproduction by attracting animal pollinators. But some flowers are not colorful, large, or fragrant. Such flowers rely on wind or water for pollination.

PARTS OF A FLOWER

Recall from Chapter 30 that early land plants lacked leaves and roots and consisted only of stems. Leaves evolved from branches of stems. Botanists consider flowers to be highly specialized branches and the parts of a flower to be specialized leaves. All of these specialized leaves form on the swollen tip of a floral "branch," which is called the **receptacle.**

Flower parts are usually found in four concentric whorls, or rings. Figure 32-5 shows a classic flower with all of the flower parts. **Sepals** (SEE-puhlz) make up the outermost whorl of flower parts. They surround and protect the other parts of a developing flower before it opens. **Petals** make up the next whorl. Most animal-pollinated flowers have brightly colored petals. The petals and sepals of wind-pollinated plants are usually small or absent.

The two innermost whorls of flower parts contain the reproductive structures. The male reproductive structures are **stamens** (STAY-muhnz), each of which consists of an anther and a filament. An **anther** contains microsporangia, which produce microspores that develop into pollen grains. A stalklike **filament** supports an anther. The innermost whorl contains the female reproductive structures, which are called **carpels** (KAHR-puhlz). One or more carpels fused together make up the structure called a **pistil.** The enlarged base of a pistil is called the **ovary.** A **style,** which is usually stalklike, rises from the ovary. The tip of the style is called the **stigma.** Generally, a stigma is sticky or has hairs, enabling it to trap pollen grains. Most species of flowering plants have flowers with both stamens and pistils. However, some species have flowers with only stamens (male flowers) or pistils (female flowers).

OBJECTIVES

▲

Identify the four main flower parts, and state the function of each.

●

Describe ovule formation and pollen formation in angiosperms.

■

Relate flower structure to methods of pollination.

◆

Describe fertilization in flowering plants.

▲

Compare and contrast the gymnosperm and angiosperm life cycles.

FIGURE 32-5

This diagram shows a flower with all four whorls of flower parts— sepals, petals, stamens, and carpels. Many flowers lack one or more of these whorls.

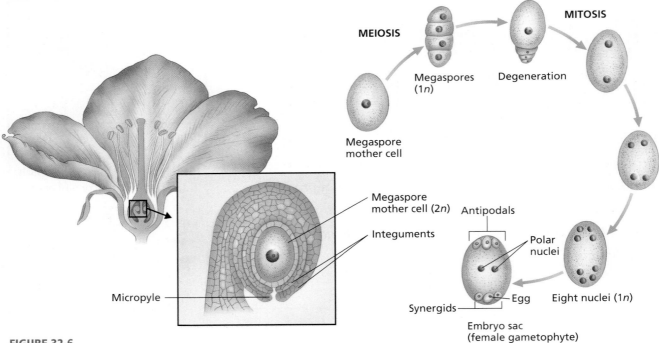

MEIOSIS

Megaspores (1n)

MITOSIS

Degeneration

Megaspore mother cell

Megaspore mother cell (2n)

Integuments

Micropyle

Antipodals

Polar nuclei

Synergids

Egg

Eight nuclei (1n)

Embryo sac (female gametophyte)

FIGURE 32-6

A cross section of an immature ovule from a flower reveals a single large cell, a megaspore mother cell. This cell undergoes meiosis and produces four megaspores. One of the megaspores undergoes a series of divisions that result in the formation of an embryo sac (a female gametophyte).

OVULE FORMATION

In flowering plants, ovules form in the ovary of a pistil. As Figure 32-6 shows, an angiosperm ovule consists of a megasporangium surrounded by two integuments. Like the integument of a pine ovule, these two integuments do not completely enclose the megasporangium. At one end of the ovule is the micropyle, through which a pollen tube can enter.

Initially, an ovule contains a large diploid cell called a megaspore mother cell. A **megaspore mother cell** undergoes meiosis and produces four haploid megaspores. Only one of the megaspores enlarges. The other three die and disappear. In most species, the remaining megaspore undergoes three consecutive mitotic divisions to produce eight haploid nuclei. These nuclei migrate to certain locations within the ovule. As you can see in Figure 32-6, the nuclei are initially arranged in two groups of four, with one group at each end of the cell. Here is what happens next:

- One nucleus from each group migrates to the center of the cell. These two nuclei are called **polar nuclei** because they came from the ends, or poles, of the cell.
- Cell walls form around each of the remaining six nuclei.
- One of the three cells nearest the micropyle enlarges and becomes the egg. The remaining five cells die after fertilization.

The resulting structure, which is microscopic and usually contains seven cells and eight nuclei, is called an **embryo sac.** The embryo sac is a mature female gametophyte, or megagametophyte. The embryo sac is another feature seen in angiosperms but not in gymnosperms.

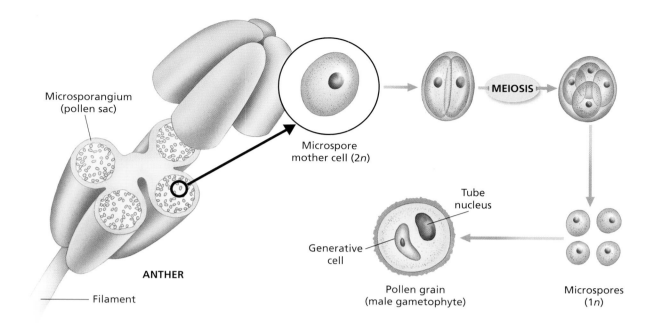

Microsporangium
(pollen sac)

Microspore
mother cell (2n)

MEIOSIS

Tube
nucleus

Generative
cell

ANTHER

Filament

Pollen grain
(male gametophyte)

Microspores
(1n)

FIGURE 32-7

A cross section of the anther of a flower reveals four pollen sacs (microsporangia). Microspore mother cells within the microsporangia undergo meiosis and produce microspores. Each microspore then develops into a two-celled pollen grain (a male gametophyte).

POLLEN GRAIN FORMATION

In flowering plants, pollen grains form in the anthers of stamens. Figure 32-7 shows how pollen forms in anthers. An anther contains four microsporangia, or pollen sacs. Initially, the pollen sacs contain many diploid cells called **microspore mother cells.** Each of these cells undergoes meiosis and produces four haploid microspores. A microspore undergoes mitosis and divides into two haploid cells. A thick wall then develops around the microspore. The resulting two-celled structure is a pollen grain, which is the male gametophyte, or microgametophyte. The larger of the two cells is the **tube cell,** which contains the tube nucleus. When a pollen grain germinates, the tube nucleus causes the tube cell to grow through the style, forming a pollen tube. The smaller of the two cells is the **generative cell,** which divides by mitosis to form two sperm.

internetconnect

SC*LINKS*
NSTA

TOPIC: Pollination
GO TO: www.scilinks.org
KEYWORD: HM631

POLLINATION

Before a sperm can fertilize the egg contained in an embryo sac, pollen must be transferred from an anther to a stigma. This process is called pollination. Recall from Chapter 9 that pollination involving the same flower, flowers on the same plant, or flowers from two genetically identical plants is called self-pollination. In contrast, pollination involving two genetically different plants is called cross-pollination. Plants produced by cross-pollination are called hybrids.

FIGURE 32-8

These long, tubular flowers are adapted for pollination by hummingbirds, which have long beaks adapted for reaching the nectar located deep in the flowers.

The type of pollination is of great concern to growers of many fruit crops. Some cultivars of fruit crops, such as apples and peaches, will produce fruit when they are self-pollinated. Others must be cross-pollinated in order to produce fruit. Date palms and kiwis produce male and female flowers on separate plants. Therefore, a few male plants must be grown to pollinate the mostly female crop.

The pollination of flowering plants occurs in several ways. Flower structure promotes self-pollination in some plants, such as peas and beans, which have flowers with petals that completely enclose both the male and female flower parts. Aquatic plants, such as sea grasses, often have pollen that is dispersed by water. Many plants, such as oaks and grasses, release their pollen into the air. The flowers of wind-pollinated angiosperms are small and lack showy petals and sepals. Successful wind pollination depends on four conditions: the release of large amounts of pollen, the ample circulation of air to carry pollen, the relative proximity of individuals to one another, and dry weather to ensure that pollen is not washed from the air by rain.

Most plants with colorful or fragrant flowers are pollinated by animals. Bright petals and distinctive odors attract animals that feed on pollen and **nectar,** which is a nourishing solution of sugars. When animals gather nectar, the pollen sticks to their bodies. The animals deposit some of the pollen on other flowers as they collect more nectar. Pollinators include bats, bees, beetles, moths, butterflies, hummingbirds, monkeys, mosquitoes, and people. Of course, people pollinate to obtain desirable seeds or fruits, not to obtain nectar. The long beak of a hummingbird, such as the one shown in Figure 32-8, is adapted to collect nectar from flowers. As the hummingbird collects the nectar, pollen from the flowers is deposited on the hummingbird's body.

FERTILIZATION

Fertilization, which is the union of gametes, follows pollination. In order for fertilization to occur, a pollen tube must grow to an egg, and sperm must form. Unlike a conifer's pollen tubes, which take about a year to reach an egg, an angiosperm's pollen tubes usually reach an egg a day or two after pollination. The sequence of events leading to angiosperm fertilization is shown on the next page in Figure 32-9.

When a pollen grain germinates, the nucleus of its tube cell forms a pollen tube that grows through the stigma and style toward the ovary. As the pollen tube grows, its generative cell divides mitotically to form two haploid sperm. The pollen tube grows to an ovule within the ovary and enters it through the micropyle. After the pollen tube penetrates the ovule's embryo sac, the sperm can reach the egg through the passageway that has been formed.

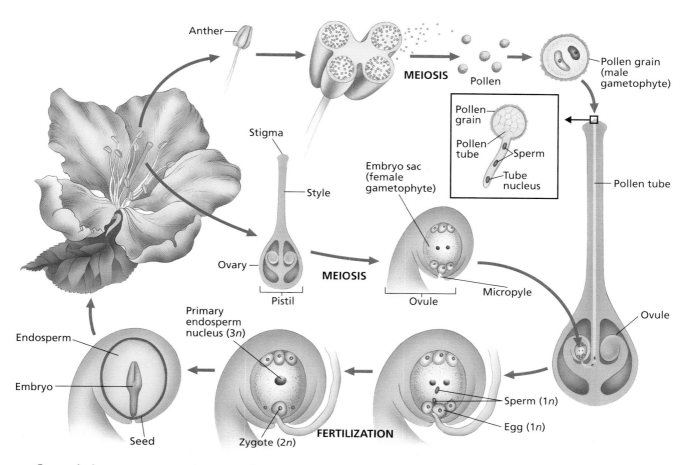

Anther

MEIOSIS
Pollen

Pollen grain (male gametophyte)

Stigma

Style

Pollen grain

Pollen tube — Sperm

Tube nucleus

Pollen tube

Embryo sac (female gametophyte)

Ovary

Pistil

MEIOSIS

Ovule

Micropyle

Ovule

Primary endosperm nucleus (3n)

Endosperm

Sperm (1n)

Embryo

FERTILIZATION

Egg (1n)

Seed

Zygote (2n)

One of the two sperm fuses with the egg, forming a diploid zygote. The zygote eventually develops into an embryo. The second sperm fuses with the two polar nuclei, producing a triploid (3n) nucleus. This nucleus then develops into a tissue called endosperm. The endosperm provides nourishment for the embryo. Kernels of corn are mostly endosperm. In many plants, however, the endosperm is absorbed by the embryos as the seeds mature. As you can see, two types of cell fusion occur in the embryo sac: one that produces the zygote and one that produces the endosperm. This process, which is called **double fertilization,** is unique to angiosperms.

FIGURE 32-9

Following pollination, a pollen grain germinates and forms a pollen tube, which grows through the style and enters an ovule through its micropyle. Two sperm travel down the pollen tube. One fertilizes the egg in the ovule's embryo sac, forming a zygote. The other sperm fertilizes the two polar nuclei, forming the endosperm. This process is called double fertilization.

SECTION 32-2 REVIEW

1. Draw a generalized flower and show the four types of flower parts in relation to each other. Be sure to label each structure.

2. Which process in angiosperms, ovule formation or pollen formation, is more similar to the process as it occurs in gymnosperms? Justify your answer.

3. How do the flowers of wind-pollinated plants differ from the flowers of animal-pollinated plants?

4. Why is fertilization in flowering plants called double fertilization?

5. How are the conifer and angiosperm life cycles similar? How are they different?

6. **CRITICAL THINKING** Why is cross-pollination considered to be an adaptive advantage over self-pollination?

▲

Name different types of fruits.

●

Describe several adaptations
for fruit and seed dispersal.

■

Compare and contrast the
structure and germination
of different types of seeds.

◆

Recognize the advantages and
disadvantages of asexual
reproduction.

▲

Describe methods of
vegetative propagation.

DISPERSAL AND PROPAGATION

*F*ruits and seeds normally result from sexual reproduction
in flowering plants. Fruits are adapted for dispersing seeds,
while seeds function in the dispersal and propagation of
plants. Many plants also propagate (produce new individuals)
through asexual reproduction.

DISPERSAL OF FRUITS AND SEEDS

Recall from Chapter 20 that one property of populations is dispersion, the spacial distribution of the individuals. If individual plants
are too close together, they must compete with each other for
available water, nutrients, and sunlight. One reason for the success
of the seed plants is the development of structures that are
adapted for dispersing offspring—fruits and seeds.

Fruits and seeds are dispersed by animals, wind, water, forcible
discharge, and gravity. You may have walked through a field and
unwittingly collected burrs, or stickers, on your shoes or socks.
These burrs are fruits, and you helped disperse them. The smell,
bright color, or flavor of many fruits attract animals. When animals
eat such fruits, the seeds often pass unharmed through their digestive system.

Fruits and seeds dispersed by wind or water are adapted to
those methods of dispersal. Orchids have tiny, dustlike seeds that
can easily be carried by a slight breeze. Figure 32-10 shows an
example of seeds adapted for wind dispersal. Many plants that
grow near water produce fruits and seeds that contain air chambers, which allow them to float. Coconuts, for example, may float
thousands of kilometers on ocean currents.

The most dramatic method of seed dispersal occurs in plants
that forcibly discharge their seeds from their fruits. The tropical
sandbox tree, which has fruits that hurl seeds up to 100 m (328 ft),
seems to hold the distance record.

Although gymnosperms do not produce fruits, their cones may
help protect seeds and aid in seed dispersal. Pine seeds are often
dispersed when gravity causes cones to drop and roll away from
the parent tree. Pine seeds have wings that aid in wind dispersal.

FIGURE 32-10

Milkweed seeds have "parachutes"
that help them drift with the wind.

TYPES OF FRUITS

Botanists define a fruit as a matured ovary. Many different types of fruits have evolved among the flowering plants. Figure 32-11 shows examples of some of these fruit types. Fertilization usually initiates the development of fruits. Fruits protect seeds, aid in their dispersal, and often delay their sprouting. Fruits are classified mainly on the basis of how many pistils or flowers form the fruit and whether it is dry or fleshy. Table 32-1 presents a classification system for fruits. Notice that fruits with common names that include "nut" or "berry" may not be nuts or berries. You may have heard the fleshy seeds of ginkgo, juniper, and yew referred to as berries. These names are misleading because ginkgo, juniper, and yew are gymnosperms, which do not form fruits.

FIGURE 32-11

A pea pod is a simple fruit. A raspberry is an aggregate fruit. A pineapple is a multiple fruit.

TABLE 32-1 *Fruit Classification*

Major categories and types of fruits	Examples
I. Simple fruit—formed from one pistil of a single flower	
A. Dry at maturity	
1. Usually splits open	
a. Legume—splits along two sides to form two halves	pea, peanut, black locust
b. Follicle—splits along one side	milkweed, columbine
c. Capsule—splits in a variety of other ways	poppy, tulip
2. Usually does not split open	
a. Grain—thin ovary wall fused to seed coat	corn, wheat
b. Nut—thick, woody ovary wall not fused to single seed	oak, chestnut
c. Achene—thin ovary wall not fused to single seed	sunflower, dandelion
d. Samara—like an achene but with a thin, flat wing	ash, elm, maple
B. Fleshy at maturity and usually not opening	
1. Usually contains only one seed	
a. Drupe—stony inner layer around the seed	cherry, coconut, pecan
2. Usually contains many seeds	
a. Pome—core with seeds surrounded by papery ovary walls; outer part formed from sepals	apple, pear
b. Typical berry—thin skin	grape, tomato, banana
c. Pepo—berry with a thick, hard rind	watermelon, cucumber
d. Hesperidium—berry with leathery, easily removed skin	orange, grapefruit, lemon
II. Aggregate fruit—formed from several pistils of a single flower	
A. Dry at maturity	tulip tree, magnolia
B. Fleshy at maturity	raspberry, strawberry
III. Multiple fruit—formed from several flowers growing together	
A. Dry at maturity	sweetgum, sycamore
B. Fleshy at maturity	pineapple, fig

Plumule
Hypocotyl
Radicle
Hilum
Cotyledons
Seed coat

(a) BEAN SEED

Endosperm (3n)
Seed coat fused to ovary wall
Cotyledon
Plumule
Epicotyl
Hypocotyl
Radicle

(b) CORN GRAIN

Wing
Seed coat
Cotyledons
Female gametophyte (1n)
Radicle

(c) PINE SEED

FIGURE 32-12

(a) A bean seed has two cotyledons and no endosperm. (b) A corn grain contains a single seed, which has one cotyledon and endosperm. (c) A pine seed has eight cotyledons and tissue from the female gametophyte.

Quick Lab

Predicting Seed Dispersal

Materials five different fruits, balance or scale

Procedure

1. Create a data table that has at least five rows. Your table should have six columns with the following headings: "Fruit name," "Fruit type" (from Table 32-1, p. 635), "Dry/fleshy," "Seed mass in grams," "Whole fruit mass in grams," and "Dispersal method."

2. Examine your fruits, and fill in your data table. Discuss with your group how characteristics of fruits and seeds might relate to dispersal methods.

Analysis Form a hypothesis about a dispersal method for one of the fruits you have examined. Describe how you might test your hypothesis.

STRUCTURE OF SEEDS

As you learned in Chapter 30, a seed is a plant embryo surrounded by a protective coat called the **seed coat.** The structure of seeds differs among the major groups of seed plants—angiosperms, which include monocots and dicots, and gymnosperms. To understand some of the differences, examine the seeds shown in Figure 32-12.

Look at the bean seed, which has been opened to reveal the structures inside. Most of the interior of a bean seed is filled by two large, fleshy cotyledons (seed leaves), which are part of the embryo. Recall that angiosperms are classified as either monocots or dicots, based on the number of cotyledons in their embryos. Therefore, beans are dicots. A mature bean seed has no endosperm. The endosperm was absorbed by the fleshy cotyledons.

Between the two cotyledons of a bean seed are the three parts that make up the rest of the embryo: the **radicle,** or embryonic root; the **hypocotyl** (HIE-poh-KAHT-uhl), which is the stem between the cotyledons and the radicle; and the **epicotyl** (EP-i-KAHT-uhl), which is the stem above the cotyledons. The epicotyl, along with any embryonic leaves, is called the **plumule** (PLOO-MYOOL). Along the concave edge of the seed is the **hilum** (HIE-luhm), which is a scar that marks where the seed was attached to the ovary wall.

Now examine the corn grain in Figure 32-12b. Technically, a corn grain is a fruit, but the seed occupies almost the entire grain. The wall of the fruit is very thin and is fused to the seed coat. A single umbrella-shaped cotyledon is pressed close to the endosperm. The cotyledon of a monocot seed does not store nutrients, as bean cotyledons do. Instead, it absorbs nutrients from the endosperm and transfers them to the embryo.

Finally, look at the pine seed in Figure 32-12c. A pine seed contains an embryo with an average of eight needle-like cotyledons. The embryo is surrounded by tissue of the female gametophyte. Like the triploid endosperm of angiosperm seeds, the haploid tissue of the female gametophyte functions as a source of nourishment for the embryo.

SEED GERMINATION

Many plants are easily grown from seeds. Although its embryo is alive, a seed will not germinate, or sprout, until it is exposed to certain environmental conditions. Delaying germination often assures the survival of a plant. For example, if seeds that mature in the fall were to sprout immediately, the young plants could be killed by cold weather. Similarly, if a plant's seeds were to sprout all at once and all of the new plants died before producing seeds, the species could become extinct. Many seeds will not germinate even when exposed to conditions ideal for germination. Such seeds exhibit **dormancy,** which is a state of reduced metabolism. The longevity of dormant seeds is often remarkable. Recently, a botanist germinated lotus seeds that were almost 1,000 years old.

Conditions Needed for Germination

Environmental factors, such as water, oxygen, and temperature, trigger seed germination. Most mature seeds are very dry and must absorb water to germinate. Water softens the seed coat and activates enzymes that convert starch in the cotyledons or endosperm into simple sugars, which provide energy for the embryo to grow. As the embryo begins to grow, the softened seed coat cracks open. This enables the oxygen needed for cellular respiration to reach the embryo. In addition, seeds germinate only if exposed to temperatures within a certain range. Many small seeds need light for germination. This adaptation prevents the seeds from sprouting if they are buried too deeply in the soil.

Some seeds germinate only after being exposed to extreme conditions, as illustrated in Figure 32-13. Some seeds, such as black locust seeds, germinate after passing through the digestive systems of animals. Acids in the digestive system wear away the hard seed coat,

Word Roots and Origins

dormancy

from the Latin *dormire,*
meaning "to sleep"

internet**connect**

SC*LINKS*
NSTA

TOPIC: Seeds
GO TO: www.scilinks.org
KEYWORD: HM637

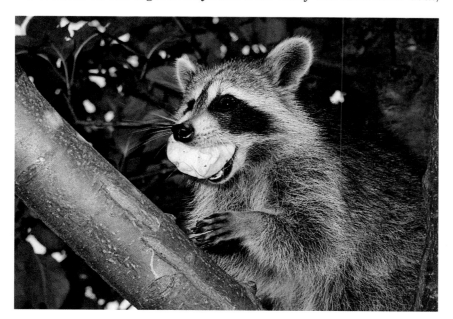

FIGURE 32-13

Many animals, including this raccoon, eat apples or other fruits. The seeds found in a fruit are swallowed by an animal and are exposed to acids as they pass through the animal's digestive system. The acids wear away the seed coat, allowing water and oxygen to enter and enabling the growing embryo to break out.

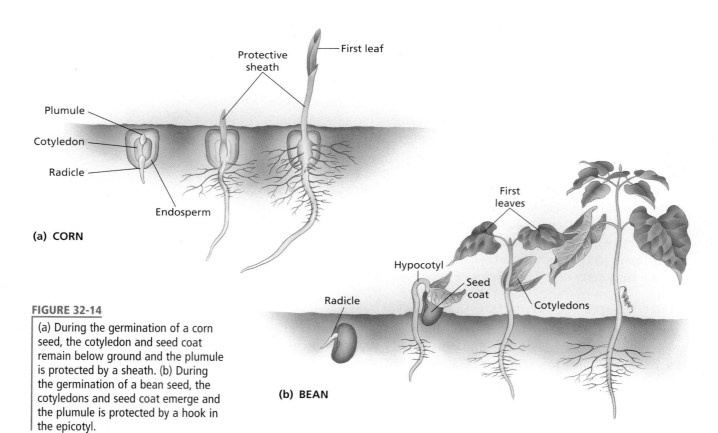

Protective sheath — **First leaf**

Plumule

Cotyledon

Radicle

Endosperm

(a) CORN

First leaves

Hypocotyl

Radicle

Seed coat

Cotyledons

(b) BEAN

FIGURE 32-14

(a) During the germination of a corn seed, the cotyledon and seed coat remain below ground and the plumule is protected by a sheath. (b) During the germination of a bean seed, the cotyledons and seed coat emerge and the plumule is protected by a hook in the epicotyl.

and as an added bonus, the seed is deposited with a bit of natural fertilizer. Other seeds, such as apple seeds, must be exposed to near-freezing temperatures for several weeks before they sprout. This temperature requirement prevents the seeds from germinating in the fall and thus ensures that the seedlings will not be killed by the cold temperatures of winter. The cold temperatures cause chemical changes within the seed. These changes enable the embryo to grow.

Process of Germination

Figure 32-14 compares seed germination in corn and beans. The first visible sign of seed germination is the emergence of the radicle. In beans, the entire root system develops from the radicle. In corn, most of the root system develops from the lower part of the stem. Soon after the radicle breaks the seed coat, the shoot begins to grow.

In some seeds, such as bean seeds, the hypocotyl curves and becomes hook-shaped. Once the hook breaks through the soil, the hypocotyl straightens. This straightening pulls the cotyledons and the plumule into the air. The plumule's embryonic leaves unfold, synthesize chlorophyll, and begin photosynthesis. After their stored nutrients are used up, the shrunken bean cotyledons fall off.

In contrast, the cotyledon of the corn seed remains underground and transfers nutrients from the endosperm to the growing embryo. Unlike the bean shoot, the corn hypocotyl does not hook or elongate, and the cotyledon remains below ground. Instead, the corn plumule is protected by a sheath as it pushes through the soil. When the shoot breaks through the soil surface, the leaves of the plumule unfold.

ASEXUAL REPRODUCTION

Recall that asexual reproduction is the production of an individual without the union of gametes. Elaborate technology has recently yielded some success in the asexual reproduction, or cloning, of mammals. Even so, movies and books that depict people who create **clones,** or exact duplicates of themselves, are still science fiction. However, asexual reproduction is common in the plant kingdom. Asexual reproduction can be an advantage to individuals that are well-adapted to their environment. Many new individuals can be produced in a short period of time, enabling the clones to spread rapidly and fill the available space. A disadvantage of asexual reproduction is the lack of genetic variation among the offspring. All of the offspring are genetically identical to the parent and to each other. Thus, the clones have the same tolerance to an environment and are attacked by the same diseases and pests. Many of our cultivars are clones.

In nature, plants reproduce asexually in a variety of ways. One type of asexual reproduction is shown in Figure 32-15. Reproduction with usually nonreproductive parts, such as leaves, stems, or roots, is termed **vegetative reproduction.** Many different types of structures specialized for vegetative reproduction have evolved among the plants. Table 32-2 lists some of these structures.

FIGURE 32-15

New plants are produced from the runners (or stolons) of an airplane plant. This plant is sometimes called a spider plant. Each new plant found on the runner can be put into a glass of water to grow roots. This is an example of vegetative propagation.

VEGETATIVE PROPAGATION

People often use vegetative structures to propagate plants. The use of vegetative structures to produce new plants is called **vegetative propagation.** Many species of plants are vegetatively propagated from specialized structures such as runners, rhizomes, bulbs, and tubers. People have also developed several methods of propagating plants from other vegetative parts. These methods include layering, grafting, and using cuttings and tissue cultures.

TABLE 32-2 *Plant Structures Adapted for Vegetative Reproduction*		
Name	**Description**	**Examples**
Runner (stolon)	horizontal, aboveground stem that produces leaves and roots at its nodes; a new plant can grow from each node	strawberry, spider plant, Boston fern
Rhizome	horizontal, belowground stem that produces leaves and roots at its nodes; a new plant can grow from each node	ferns, horsetails, iris, ginger, sugar cane
Bulb	very short, underground monocot stem with thick, fleshy leaves adapted for storage; bulbs divide naturally to produce new plants	tulip, daffodil, onion, garlic, hyacinth
Tuber	underground, swollen, fleshy stem specialized for storage; the buds on a tuber can grow into new plants	potato, caladium, Jerusalem artichoke

Cuttings

In some plants, roots will form on a cut piece of a stem, or shoots will form on a piece of a root. Pieces of stems and roots that are cut from a plant and used to grow new plants are called **cuttings.** Plants such as African violets can be grown from leaf cuttings, which will form both roots and shoots. Cuttings are widely used to propagate houseplants, ornamental trees and shrubs, and fruit crops such as grapes, figs, and olives.

Layering

In some species, such as raspberries, roots form on stems where they make contact with the soil. People often stake branch tips to the soil or cover the bases of stems with soil to propagate such plants. The process of causing roots to form on a stem is called **layering.** Air layering, which involves wounding a stem and placing moist sphagnum moss around the wound, is another common form of layering.

Grafting

Grafting is the joining of two or more plant parts to form a single plant. In grafting, a bud or small stem of one plant is attached to the roots or stems of a second plant. The vascular cambium of both parts must be aligned for a graft to be successful. Grafting enables the desirable characteristics of two cultivars to be combined. For example, an apple cultivar with excellent fruit can be grafted onto one with disease-resistant roots. Grafting is used to propagate virtually all commercial cultivars of fruit and nut trees and many ornamental trees and shrubs.

Tissue Culture

Figure 32-16 shows plants grown by **tissue culture,** the production of new plants from pieces of tissue placed on a sterile nutrient medium. Unlike most animal cells, plant cells contain functional copies of all the genes needed to produce a new plant. Thus, it is possible for a whole plant to regrow from a single cell. Millions of identical plants can be grown from a small amount of tissue. Tissue culture is used in the commercial production of orchids, houseplants, cut flowers, fruit plants, and ornamental trees, shrubs, and nonwoody plants.

FIGURE 32-16

Tissue culture can be used to grow round-leaved sundews, *Drosera rotundifolia.* The jelly in the Petri dish is a sterile soil substitute that contains needed nutrients.

SECTION 32-3 REVIEW

1. List 10 different types of fruits, and give an example of each type.

2. Name three common methods of fruit and seed dispersal, and give an example of each method.

3. How do the structure and germination of a bean seed differ from the structure and germination of a corn seed?

4. Compare asexual reproduction with sexual reproduction.

5. Make a table that compares structures and methods used for the vegetative propagation of plants.

6. CRITICAL THINKING Why is seed dormancy an evolutionary advantage?

SUMMARY/VOCABULARY

32-1 ■ Plants have a life cycle called alternation of generations, in which a multicellular haploid gametophyte stage alternates with a multicellular diploid sporophyte stage.

■ Mosses and most ferns are homosporous (produce only one type of spore).

■ In the moss life cycle, a spore develops into a leafy green gametophyte that produces eggs in archegonia and swimming sperm in antheridia. A moss sporophyte grows from a gametophyte and is dependent on it for nourishment.

■ In the fern life cycle, a spore develops into a small flat gametophyte that produces

eggs in archegonia and swimming sperm in antheridia. A sporophyte grows from a gametophyte but later crushes it and is not dependent on it for nourishment.

■ All seed plants, spike mosses, and quill-worts as well as a few fern species are het-erosporous (produce two types of spores, male microspores and female megaspores).

■ The conifer life cycle features a reduced male gametophyte (pollen grain) and sperm without flagella. A sperm reaches an egg through a pollen tube that grows into a female gametophyte.

Vocabulary

antheridium (625)	integument (628)	microgametophyte (628)	ovule (628)
archegonium (625)	megagametophyte (628)	micropyle (628)	pollen grain (628)
heterospory (627)	megasporangium (628)	microsporangium (628)	pollen tube (628)
homospory (626)	megaspore (627)	microspore (627)	sorus (627)

32-2 ■ Flowers are reproductive structures of angiosperms. Most familiar flowers consist of four whorls of parts—protective sepals, colorful petals, pollen-producing stamens, and egg-containing carpels.

■ Many flowering plants have flowers adapted for animal pollination or for wind pollination.

■ In angiosperms, the female gametophyte is

a microscopic embryo sac that usually has eight nuclei and is found within an ovule.

■ Double fertilization is a unique feature of angiosperms. Two sperm reach the embryo sac through a pollen tube. One sperm combines with the egg to form a zygote. A second sperm combines with two polar nuclei to form a triploid nutritive tissue, the endosperm.

Vocabulary

anther (629)	generative cell (631)	petal (629)	stamen (629)
carpel (629)	megaspore mother cell (630)	pistil (629)	stigma (629)
double fertilization (633)	microspore mother cell (631)	polar nuclei (630)	style (629)
embryo sac (630)	nectar (632)	receptacle (629)	tube cell (631)
filament (629)	ovary (629)	sepal (629)	

32-3 ■ Angiosperm seeds are enclosed by fruits, which protect seeds and aid in dispersal.

■ Seeds need water, oxygen, suitable tempera-tures, and sometimes light to germinate.

■ Asexual reproduction enables plants to spread rapidly in a favorable environment.

■ Plants naturally reproduce vegetatively with specialized structures such as bulbs, rhizomes, runners, and tubers.

■ People propagate plants asexually by using cuttings, layering, grafting, and tissue culture.

Vocabulary

clone (639)	grafting (640)	plumule (636)	vegetative propagation (639)
cutting (640)	hilum (636)	radicle (636)	vegetative reproduction (639)
dormancy (637)	hypocotyl (636)	seed coat (636)	
epicotyl (636)	layering (640)	tissue culture (640)	

REVIEW

Vocabulary

1. How is a megaspore related to a megasporangium?
2. Explain the differences between a gametophyte and a sporophyte.
3. List three similarities between an ovule and an ovary.
4. What do pomes, berries, and drupes have in common?
5. Using a dictionary, find the meaning of the word roots in *epicotyl* and *hypocotyl*. Explain why these terms are appropriate for the structures they describe.

Multiple Choice

6. Moss sperm are produced in (a) antheridia (b) anthers (c) archegonia (d) sori.
7. In pollen, the generative cell forms (a) polar nuclei (b) sperm (c) the epicotyl (d) endosperm.
8. The integuments of an ovule are interrupted by (a) a microspore (b) a micropyle (c) a hilum (d) a stamen.
9. The pistil of a flower is made up of (a) styles (b) ovaries (c) carpels (d) anthers.
10. The microspores in an anther become (a) megaspores (b) pollen grains (c) eggs (d) sperm.
11. Pollination occurs when (a) a sperm fuses with an egg (b) insects ingest nectar (c) a spore leaves a sporangium (d) pollen lands on a stigma.
12. Which of the following terms applies to angiosperms but not to gymnosperms? (a) integument (b) pollen (c) seed (d) double fertilization
13. The epicotyl in a dicot seed is part of the (a) hilum (b) hypocotyl (c) plumule (d) cotyledon.
14. Asexual reproduction in plants occurs in all but which of the following ways? (a) Sperm unite with eggs. (b) New plants form on runners. (c) Seed plants form bulbs. (d) New plants grow in tissue culture.

15. The process shown in the photograph below is termed (a) grafting (b) cutting (c) tissue culture (d) layering.

Short Answer

16. What are two important differences between the life cycle of a typical fern and that of a seed plant?
17. How is heterospory an advantage over homospory?
18. List four factors that promote successful wind pollination.
19. Draw a diagram showing the events and plant structures involved in pollination.
20. How does the process of fertilization occur in flowering plants?
21. How does the process of fertilization in conifers differ from the process of fertilization in flowering plants?
22. List three types of seed dispersal, and give an example of each.
23. In many seeds, the epicotyl forms a hook as the embryo emerges from the seed. What is the advantage of this hook?
24. Compare asexual reproduction with sexual reproduction in terms of their advantages and disadvantages.
25. Describe several methods of vegetative reproduction.

CRITICAL THINKING

1. How is the growth habit of mosses an advantage for their method of sexual reproduction?

2. Suppose that a type of fern normally has a 2*n* chromosome number of 12. Also suppose that meiosis does not occur in the formation of spores, which grow into new gametophytes. What will be the chromosome number of the gametes produced by these gametophytes? What will be the chromosome number of a zygote that results from the fusion of two of these gametes?

3. Why do you think there are more heterosporous plants than there are homosporous plants?

4. In many flowers with both stamens and pistils, the stigma is located well above the anthers. What is the value of such an arrangement?

5. Following the self-pollination of some plants, the pollen tubes die before reaching ovules. What is the significance of this event?

6. Why are fruits and seeds a nutritious source of food for humans and other animals? How is this an advantage for plants?

7. Why do plants with fleshy fruits usually have seeds with hard seed coats?

8. The acorns (nuts) of many oak trees often germinate on the surface of ground that is hard or covered with grass. The new root may grow several centimeters before it reaches a crack or soft spot where it can enter the ground. How is the germinating seed able to survive and grow in such conditions?

9. If you were to discover a new type of rose, would you use seeds or vegetative parts to propagate the rose and produce large numbers of identical plants? Justify your answer.

10. In the photograph below, the houseplant on the left shows a *Sansevieria trifasciata*, which has yellow-edged leaves. A section of the leaf, or a leaf cutting, can be used to produce new plants. However, as shown on the right side of the photograph, only shoots with all-green leaves and no yellow edges will form. How do you explain this?

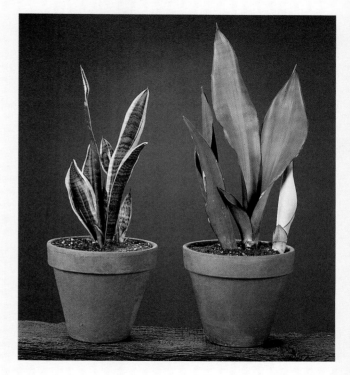

EXTENSION

1. Buy a 5 cm (2 in.) or longer piece of ginger root at a supermarket. Examine it closely and determine if it is really a root. Plant it about 1 cm (0.4 in.) below the surface in a container of potting soil, keep it watered, and place it in a lighted area. Describe what happens over a period of two months.

2. Visit a commercial fruit-tree orchard and find out how the trees are propagated and pollinated.

3. Read "Life in Bloom" in *Natural History,* May 1999, on page 66. What are three factors that contribute to the life span of a flower?

4. Read "She Loves Me, She Loves Me Not" in *National Wildlife*, January 1999, on page 10. Describe the mystery that plant geneticists have discovered about the instant and strong attraction flowers have for their own species' pollen.

5. Try air-layering an overly tall houseplant, such as a dieffenbachia or a dracena.

Comparing Seed Structure and Seedling Development

OBJECTIVES

- Observe the structures of dicot and monocot seeds.
- Compare the structure of dicot and monocot embryos.
- Compare the development of dicot and monocot seedlings.

PROCESS SKILLS

- relating structure to function
- comparing and contrasting
- identifying
- collecting data

MATERIALS

- 1 pea seed soaked overnight
- 6 bean seeds soaked overnight
- 6 corn kernels soaked overnight
- stereomicroscope
- scalpel
- Lugol's iodine solution in dropper bottle
- paper towels
- 2 rubber bands
- 2 150 mL beakers
- glass-marking pen
- metric ruler
- microscope slide
- medicine dropper
- compound light microscope

Background

1. What are the parts of a seed?
2. In what ways are seeds like their parent plant?
3. How do monocotyledons and dicotyledons differ?
4. What changes occur as a seed germinates?

PART A Seed Structure

1. Obtain one each of the following seeds—pea, bean, and corn.
2. Remove the seed coats of the pea and bean seeds. Open the seeds, and locate the two cotyledons in each seed.

3. Using the stereomicroscope, examine the embryos of the pea seed and the bean seed.
4. In your lab report, draw the pea and bean embryos and label all of the parts that you can identify.
5. ⬥ **CAUTION Use the scalpel carefully to avoid injury.** Examine a corn kernel, and find a small, oval, light-colored area that shows through the seed coat. Use the scalpel to cut the seed in half along the length of this area. Place a drop of iodine solution on the cut surface.
6. Use the stereomicroscope to examine the corn embryo. In your lab report, sketch the embryo and label all the parts that you can identify.

PART B Seedling Development

7. Set five corn kernels on a folded paper towel. Roll up the paper towel, and put a rubber band around the roll. Stand the roll in a beaker with 1 cm of water in the bottom. The paper towel will soak up water and moisten the corn. Keep water at the bottom of the beaker, but do not allow the corn kernels to be covered by the water.

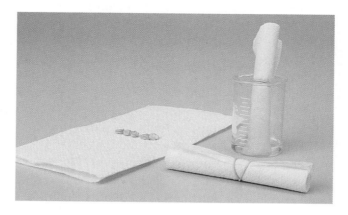

8. Repeat step 7 with five bean seeds.
9. After three days, unroll the paper towels and examine the corn and bean seedlings. Use a glass-marking pen to mark the roots and shoots of the developing

seedlings. Starting at the seed, make a mark every 0.5 cm along the root of each seedling. And again starting at the seed, make a mark every 0.5 cm along the stem of each seedling. Measure the distance from the last mark on the root to the root tip of each seedling. Also measure the distance from the last mark on the stem to the shoot tip of each seedling. Record these data in your lab report.

10. Draw a corn seedling and a bean seedling in your lab report. Using a fresh paper towel, roll up the seeds, place the rolls in the beakers, and add fresh water to the beakers.

11. Make a data table similar to the one shown below in your lab notebook. Expand your table by adding columns under each "Roots" and "Stems" head to account for every section of the roots and stems of your seedlings.

12. After two days, reexamine the seedlings. Measure the distance between the marks, and record the data in your data table.

13. ◆ CAUTION **Use the scalpel carefully to avoid injury.** Using the scalpel, make a cut about 2 cm from the tip of the root of a bean seedling. Place the root tip on a microscope slide and add a drop of water. Using a compound light microscope on low power, observe the root tip. In your lab report, draw the root tip.

14. ◆ ◆ Clean up your materials and wash your hands before leaving the lab.

Analysis and Conclusions

1. What protects the tips of corn shoots as they push through the soil? What protects the bean shoots?
2. What types of leaves first appear on the bean seedling?
3. What substance does the black color in the corn kernel indicate? Why might you expect to find this substance in the seed?
4. Examine the data you recorded for steps 9 and 12. Has the distance between the marks changed? If so, where has it changed?
5. What parts of the embryo were observed in all seeds on the third day?
6. How does the structure and development of the corn kernel differ from the structure and development of the pea and bean seeds?
7. What was the source of nutrients for each seed embryo? What is your evidence?
8. Describe the growth in the seedlings you observed.
9. Corn and beans are often cited as representative examples of monocots and dicots, respectively. Relate the seed structure of each to the terms *monocotyledon* and *dicotyledon*.

Further Inquiry

Design an experiment to find out how monocots and dicots compare in general plant growth and in the structure of their leaves and flowers.

CORN AND BEAN SEEDLING GROWTH AFTER TWO DAYS

| Seedling | Corn seedlings | | | | Bean seedlings | | | |
| | Roots | | Stems | | Roots | | Stems | |
	Seed to first mark	Root tip to last mark	Seed to first mark	Shoot tip to last mark	Seed to first mark	Root tip to last mark	Seed to first mark	Shoot tip to last mark
1								
2								
3								
4								
5								

PLANT RESPONSES

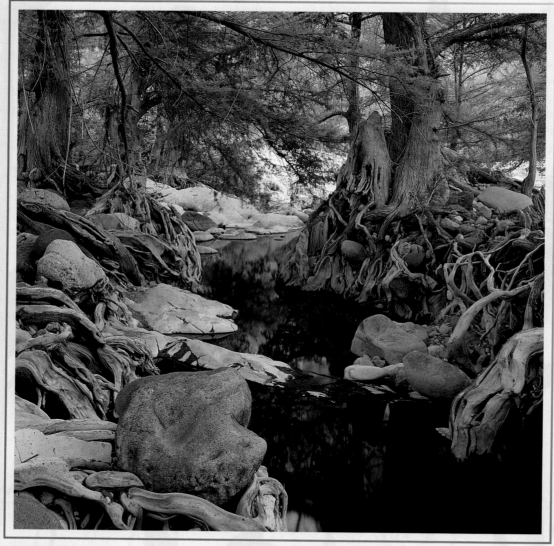

Montezuma baldcypress trees, Taxodium mucronatum, with their tangled roots, line the banks of the Rio Cuchujaqui in the southern region of the Mexican state of Sonora.

FOCUS CONCEPT: *Evolution*

As you read, notice how plants respond to their environment and to hormones. Plant responses to environmental conditions are adaptive advantages.

PLANT HORMONES

The growth and development of a plant are influenced by genetic factors, external environmental factors, and chemicals inside the plant. Plants respond to many environmental factors, such as light, gravity, water, inorganic nutrients, and temperature.

GROUPS OF HORMONES

Plant **hormones** are chemical messengers that affect a plant's ability to respond to its environment. Hormones are organic compounds that are effective at very low concentrations; they are usually synthesized in one part of the plant and transported to another location. They interact with specific target tissues to cause physiological responses, such as growth or fruit ripening. Each response is often the result of two or more hormones acting together.

Because hormones stimulate or inhibit plant growth, many botanists also refer to them as plant **growth regulators.** Many hormones can be synthesized in the laboratory, increasing the quantity of hormones available for commercial applications. Botanists recognize five major groups of hormones: auxins, gibberellins, ethylene, cytokinins, and abscisic acid. These groups of hormones are examined in Table 33-1 on the next page.

Auxins

Auxins (AWK-suhnz) are hormones involved in plant-cell elongation, apical dominance, and rooting. A well known natural auxin is **indoleacetic** (IN-DOHL-uh-SEET-ik) **acid,** or **IAA.** Developing seeds produce IAA, which stimulates the development of a fleshy fruit. Figure 33-1 shows how the removal of seeds from a strawberry prevents the fruit from enlarging. The application of IAA after removing the seeds causes the fruit to enlarge normally.

(a)　　　　　　　(b)　　　　　　　(c)

FIGURE 33-1

(a) Strawberry plants produce a fleshy, heart-shaped fruit that is covered with yellow seeds. (b) When the seeds are removed from the fruit, the growth of the fruit is retarded. (c) When the seeds are removed and the fruit is treated with an auxin, growth is normal.

TABLE 33-1 *Five Groups of Plant Hormones*

Plant hormone	Function	Features	Examples
Auxins	• promote cell growth • promote root formation on stem and leaf cuttings • promote apical dominance • increase number of fruits • prevent dropping of fruit • prevent sprouting of stored potatoes and onions	• produced in growing regions of plant (shoot tips, young leaves, developing fruit) • important role in tropisms	• indoleacetic acid, IAA (natural) • naphthalene acetic acid, NAA (synthetic) • herbicides 2,4-D and Agent Orange (synthetic)
Gibberellins (GA)	• promote elongation growth • promote germination, and seedling growth • increase size of fruit • overcome bud dormancy • substitute for long-day or vernalization requirements for flowering	• produced in all parts of plant, especially in immature seeds • more than 80 types	• GA_3 (natural)
Ethylene	• promotes ripening of fruit • promotes flowering in mangoes and pineapples • promotes abscission	• produced in fruits, flowers, leaves, and roots • colorless gas	• ethephon (synthetic) breaks down and releases ethylene (natural)
Cytokinins	• promote cell division • promote lateral bud growth in dicots	• produced in developing roots, fruits, and seeds • auxin-to-cytokinin ratio is important	• zeatin (natural) • kinetin (synthetic) • benzyladenine (synthetic)
Abscisic acid (ABA)	• promotes stomatal closure • promotes dormancy • inhibits other hormones • blocks growth	• produced in leaves • expensive to synthesize	• ABA (natural or synthetic)

IAA is produced in actively growing shoot tips and developing fruit, and it is involved in elongation. Before a cell can elongate, the cell wall must become less rigid so that it can expand. IAA triggers an increase in the plasticity, or stretchability, of cell walls, allowing elongation to occur.

Synthetic Auxins

Chemists have synthesized several inexpensive compounds similar in structure to IAA. Synthetic auxins, like **naphthalene** (NAF-thuh-LEEN) **acetic** (uh-SEET-ik) **acid,** or **NAA,** are used extensively to promote root formation on stem and leaf cuttings, as shown in Figure 33-2. Gardeners often spray auxins on tomato plants to increase the number of fruits on each plant.

(a) **(b)**

FIGURE 33-2

(a) This coleus plant, *Coleus hybridus,* is growing roots in pure water. (b) This coleus stem cutting has been treated with the auxin NAA. Roots form more rapidly when the stem is treated with NAA. Both cuttings were taken at the same time.

When NAA is sprayed on young fruits of apple and olive trees, some of the fruits drop off so that the remaining fruits grow larger. When NAA is sprayed directly on fruits—such as apples, pears, and citrus fruits—several weeks before they are ready to be picked, NAA prevents the fruits from dropping off the trees before they are mature. The fact that auxins can have opposite effects—causing fruit to drop or preventing fruit from dropping—illustrates an important point. The effects of a hormone on a plant often depend on the stage of the plant's development.

NAA is used to prevent the undesirable sprouting of stems from the base of ornamental trees. As discussed in Chapter 32, stems contain a lateral bud at the base of each leaf. In many stems, these buds fail to sprout as long as the plant's shoot tip is intact. The inhibition of lateral buds by the presence of a shoot tip is called **apical dominance.** If the shoot tip of a plant is removed, the lateral buds begin to grow. If IAA or NAA is applied to the cut tip of the stem, the lateral buds remain dormant. This adaptation is manipulated to cultivate beautiful ornamental trees. NAA is used commercially to prevent buds from sprouting on potato tubers during storage.

Another important synthetic auxin is **2,4-D,** which is a herbicide, or weedkiller. It selectively kills dicots, such as dandelions and pigweed, without injuring monocots, such as lawn grasses and cereal crops. Given our major dependence on cereals for food, 2,4-D has been of great value to agriculture. A mixture of 2,4-D and another auxin, called **Agent Orange,** was used to defoliate jungles in the Vietnam War. A nonauxin contaminant in Agent Orange has caused severe health problems in many people who were exposed to it.

Gibberellins

In the 1920s, scientists in Japan discovered that a substance produced by the fungus *Gibberella* caused fungus-infected plants to grow

FIGURE 33-3

The bird's nest ferns, *Asplendium nidus,* shown in (a) and (b) are the same age. The fern in (b), however, has been treated with gibberellin, which stimulates the leaves to grow larger.

abnormally tall. The substance, named **gibberellin** (JIB-uh-REL-uhn), was later found to be produced in small quantities by plants themselves. It has many effects on a plant, but it primarily stimulates elongation growth. Spraying a plant with gibberellins will usually cause the plant to grow to a larger than normal height, as shown in Figure 33-3.

Like auxins, gibberellins are a class of hormones that have important commercial applications. Almost all seedless grapes are sprayed with gibberellins to increase the size of the fruit, as Figure 33-4 shows. Beer makers use gibberellins to increase the alcohol content of beer by increasing the amount of sugar produced in the malting process. Gibberellins are also used to treat seeds of some food crops because they break seed dormancy and promote uniform germination.

Ethylene

The hormone **ethylene** (ETH-uh-LEEN) is responsible for the ripening of fruits. Unlike the other four classes of plant hormones, ethylene is a gas at room temperature. Ethylene gas diffuses easily through the air from one plant to another. The saying "One bad apple spoils the barrel" has its basis in ethylene gas. One rotting apple will produce ethylene gas, which stimulates nearby apples to ripen and eventually spoil.

Ethylene is usually applied in a solution of **ethephon** (ETH-uh-fohn), a synthetic chemical that breaks down to release ethylene gas. It is used to ripen bananas, honeydew melons, and tomatoes. Oranges, lemons, and grapefruits often remain green when they are ripe. Although the green fruit tastes good, consumers will not usually buy them. The application of ethylene to green citrus fruits causes the development of desirable citrus colors, such as yellow and orange.

In some plant species, ethylene promotes **abscission,** which is the detachment of leaves, flowers, or fruits from a plant. Cherries and walnuts are harvested with mechanical tree shakers. Ethylene treatment increases the number of fruits that fall to the ground

FIGURE 33-4

Almost all of the raisins produced in California are made from Thompson Seedless grapes. Normal Thompson Seedless grapes are smaller than those treated with a gibberellin hormone. The grapes on the left were treated with a gibberellin. As you can see, the addition of a gibberellin to grapes stimulates the grapes to grow larger.

when the trees are shaken. Leaf abscission is also an adaptive advantage for the plant. Dead, damaged, or infected leaves drop to the ground rather than shading healthy leaves or spreading disease. The plant can minimize water loss in the winter, when the water in a plant is often frozen.

Cytokinins

Cytokinins (sie-toh-KIE-nuhnz) promote cell division in plants. Produced in the developing shoots, roots, fruits, and seeds of a plant, cytokinins are very important in the culturing of plant tissues in the laboratory. A high ratio of auxins to cytokinins in a tissue-culture medium stimulates root formation. A low ratio promotes shoot formation. Cytokinins are also used to promote lateral bud growth of flower crops.

Abscisic Acid

Abscisic (ab-SIS-ik) **acid,** or **ABA,** generally inhibits other hormones, such as IAA. It was originally thought to promote abscission, hence its name. Botanists now know that ethylene is the main abscission hormone. ABA helps to bring about dormancy in a plant's buds and maintains dormancy in its seeds. ABA causes the closure of a plant's stomata in response to drought. Water-stressed leaves produce large amounts of ABA, which triggers potassium ions to be transported out of the guard cells. This causes the stomata to close. It is too costly to synthesize ABA for agricultural use.

Other Growth Regulators

Many growth regulators are widely used on ornamental plants. These substances do not fit into any of the five classes of hormones. For example, utility companies in California often apply **growth retardants,** chemicals that prevent plant growth, to trees to prevent them from interfering with overhead utility lines. It is less expensive to apply these chemicals than to prune the trees. Also, azalea growers sometimes apply a chemical to kill an azalea's terminal buds rather than hand-pruning them. Scientists are still searching for a hormone to slow the growth of lawn grass so that it does not have to be mowed so often.

Word Roots and Origins

abscisic

from the Latin *abscisus,* meaning "to cut off"

internet**connect**

SC*i*LINKS.
NSTA

TOPIC: Plant growth regulators
GO TO: www.scilinks.org
KEYWORD: HM651

SECTION 33-1 REVIEW

1. What are important commercial uses of auxins, gibberellins, and ethylene?

2. Explain one way ethylene differs from the other plant hormones.

3. How are a plant's shoot tip and lateral buds affected by apical dominance?

4. Why are growth retardants often sprayed on potted flowers?

5. Explain how auxins and cytokinins interact.

6. **CRITICAL THINKING** What factors influence the effect of a hormone on target cells?

OBJECTIVES

▲

Explain the difference between tropisms and nastic movements.

●

List the environmental stimuli to which plants respond and the tropism for each stimulus.

■

Explain the current hypotheses regarding auxins and their function in phototropism and gravitropism.

◆

Describe common nastic movements and explain how they help a plant survive.

PLANT MOVEMENTS

Plants appear immobile because they are rooted in place. However, time-lapse photography reveals that parts of plants frequently move. Most plants move too slowly for us to notice. Plants move in response to several environmental stimuli, such as light, gravity, and mechanical disturbances. These movements fall into two groups, tropisms and nastic movements.

TROPISMS

A **tropism** (TROH-piz-uhm) is a plant movement that is determined by the direction of an environmental stimulus. Movement toward an environmental stimulus is called a *positive* tropism, and movement away from a stimulus is called a *negative* tropism. Each kind of tropism is named for its stimulus. For example, a plant movement in response to light coming from one direction is called **phototropism.** Thus, in Figure 33-5, the shoot tips of a plant that grow toward the light source are positively phototropic. The various types of tropisms are summarized in Table 33-2.

Phototropism

Phototropism is illustrated by the movement of the sprouts in Figure 33-5. Light causes the hormone auxin to move to the shaded side of the shoot. The auxin causes the cells on the shaded side to elongate more than the cells on the lighted side. As a result, the shoot bends toward the light and exhibits positive phototropism. In some plant stems, phototropism is not caused by auxin movement.

FIGURE 33-5

The way these new sprouts of the flowering shamrock, *Oxalis rubra,* grow toward a light is an example of positive phototropism. The auxin hormone stimulates the cells on the shaded side of the plant stem to elongate.

TABLE 33-2	*Various Plant Tropisms*	
Tropism	Stimulus	Positive example
Phototropism	light	plant leans toward light
Thigmotropism	contact with object	vine twines around a tree
Gravitropism	gravity	roots grow downward
Chemotropism	chemical	pollen tube grows toward ovule

In these instances, light causes the production of a growth inhibitor on the lighted side. Negative phototropism is sometimes seen in vines that climb on flat walls where coiling tendrils have nothing to coil around. These vines have stem tips that grow away from light, toward the wall. This brings adventitious roots or adhesive discs in contact with the wall on which they can cling.

Solar tracking is the motion of leaves or flowers as they follow the sun's movement across the sky, as shown in Figure 33-6. By continuously facing toward a moving light source, the plant maximizes the light available for photosynthesis.

Thigmotropism

Thigmotropism is a plant's growth response to touching a solid object. Tendrils and stems of vines, such as morning glories, coil when they touch an object. Thigmotropism allows some vines to climb other plants or objects, increasing its chance of intercepting light for photosynthesis. It is thought that an auxin and ethylene are involved in this response.

Quick Lab

Visualizing Phototropism

Materials 2 in. pots (2) containing potting soil, 4 bean seeds, cardboard box

Procedure

1. Plant two bean seeds in each pot. Label each pot for your group. Place one pot in a window or under a plant light.

2. Cut a rectangular window in the box, and place the box over the second pot so that the window faces the light. Place the box in a different location from the open pot. Keep both pots moist for several days.

3. Remove the box 2–3 days after the seedlings have emerged from the soil. Compare the seedlings grown in the light with the ones grown in the box. Sketch your observations.

Analysis How are the seedlings different? How do you account for the difference? Describe or draw what you think the cells inside the curved part of the stem look like.

Word Roots and Origins

thigmotropism

from the Greek *thiga*, meaning "touch," and *tropos*, meaning "turning"

FIGURE 33-6

These sunflower plants face the sun as it sets in the evening. In the morning, they face the sun as it rises, then they follow it as it moves across the sky. This form of phototropism is called solar tracking.

FIGURE 33-7

This photograph was taken seven days after three cuttings of the inch plant, *Zebrina pendula,* were placed in growing tubes in different orientations. Notice that the two lower cuttings have started to grow upward, while the cutting on top, which was placed upright to begin with, has not changed its direction of growth. The growth movement of the lower cuttings is caused by the plants' response to gravity and is called negative gravitropism. When the roots turn and begin to grow in a downward direction, the movement is called positive gravitropism.

Gravitropism

Gravitropism is a plant's growth response to gravity. A root usually grows downward and a stem usually grows upward—that is, roots are positively gravitropic and stems are negatively gravitropic.

Like phototropism, gravitropism appears to be regulated by auxins. One hypothesis proposes that when a seedling is placed horizontally, auxins accumulate along the lower sides of both the root and the stem. This concentration of auxins stimulates cell elongation along the lower side of the stem, and the stem grows upward. A similar concentration of auxins inhibits cell elongation in the lower side of the root, and the root grows downward, as shown in Figure 33-7.

Chemotropism

A plant's growth in response to a chemical is called **chemotropism.** After a flower is pollinated, a pollen tube grows down through the stigma and style and enters the ovule through the micropyle. The growth of the pollen tube in response to chemicals produced by the ovule is an example of a chemotropism.

NASTIC MOVEMENTS

Plant movements that occur in response to environmental stimuli but that are independent of the direction of stimuli are called **nastic movements.** These movements are regulated by changes in the water pressure of certain plant cells.

Thigmonastic Movements

Thigmonastic (THIG-mah-NAS-tik) **movements** are a type of nastic movement that occurs in response to touching or shaking a plant. Many thigmonasties involve rapid plant movements, such as the closing of the leaf trap of a Venus' flytrap or the folding of a plant's leaves in response to being touched. Figure 33-8 shows how the leaves of a sensitive plant fold within a few seconds after being touched. This movement is caused by the rapid loss of turgor pressure in certain cells, a process similar to that which occurs in guard cells. Physical stimulation of the plant leaf causes potassium

FIGURE 33-8

(a) *Mimosa pudica,* also called the sensitive plant, is a small shrub that has leaflets. (b) When a leaflet is touched, it folds together. This rapid movement is a thigmonastic movement.

(a)

(b)

(a)

(b)

FIGURE 33-9

A common houseplant is the prayer plant, *Maranta leuconeura*. (a) During the day, the leaf blades of the prayer plant are oriented horizontally in response to light. (b) During the night, the leaf blades are oriented vertically. This movement is called nyctinastic movement.

ions to be pumped out of the cells at the base of leaflets and petioles. Water then moves out of the cells by osmosis. As the cells shrink, the plant's leaves move. It is believed that the folding of a plant's leaves in response to touch discourages insect feeding.

In addition, thigmonastic movements may help prevent water loss in plants. When the wind blows on a plant, the rate of transpiration is increased. So if the leaves of a plant fold in response to the "touch" of the wind, water loss is reduced. This could be an important adaptive advantage to a plant.

Nyctinastic Movements

Nyctinastic (NIK-tuh-NAS-tik) **movements** are plant movements in response to the daily cycle of light and dark. Nyctinastic movements involve the same type of osmotic mechanism as thigmonastic movements, but the changes in turgor pressure are more gradual. Nyctinastic movements occur in many plants, including bean plants, honeylocust trees, and silk trees. The prayer plant, shown in Figure 33-9, gets its name from the fact that its leaf blades are vertical at night, resembling praying hands. During the day, the leaf blades of the prayer plant are horizontal. The botanist Linnaeus planted many different species of plants with nyctinastic movements in a big circle to make a "flower clock." The nyctinastic movements of each species occurred at a specific time of day.

*internet***connect**

SC*i*LINKS℠
NSTA

TOPIC: Nastic movements
GO TO: www.scilinks.org
KEYWORD: HM655

SECTION 33-2 REVIEW

1. How do a tropism and a nastic movement differ?

2. Define the three major plant tropisms, and give an example of each.

3. How does auxin cause plant movements in response to light and gravity?

4. What adaptive advantage might nastic movements provide a plant?

5. How do nastic movements occur?

6. **CRITICAL THINKING** Why is it an advantage for plant growth and development to be regulated by stimuli received from the environment?

▲

Define *critical night length,* and explain its role in flowering.

●

Describe vernalization, and give an example of a human application of this phenomenon.

■

Describe what causes the spectacular fall leaf colors.

◆

What is the role of phytochrome in plant responses?

SEASONAL RESPONSES

In nontropical areas, plant responses are strongly influenced by seasonal changes. For example, many trees shed their leaves in the fall, and most plants flower only at certain times of the year. How do plants sense seasonal changes? Although temperature is involved in some cases, plants mark the seasons primarily by sensing changes in night length.

PHOTOPERIODISM

A plant's response to changes in the length of days and nights is called **photoperiodism.** Photoperiodism affects many plant processes, including the formation of storage organs and bud dormancy. However, the most-studied photoperiodic process is flowering. Some plants require a particular night length to flower. In other species, a particular night length merely makes the plant flower sooner than it otherwise would.

Critical Night Length

Researchers have found that the important factor in flowering is the amount of darkness, or night length, that a plant receives. Each plant species has its own specific requirement for darkness, called the **critical night length.** Although scientists now know that night length, and not day length, regulates flowering, the terms short-day plant, and long-day plant are still used. A **short-day plant** flowers when the days are short and the nights are longer than a certain length. Conversely, a **long-day plant** flowers when the days are long and the nights are shorter than a certain length.

Responding to Day Length and Night Length

Plants can be divided into three groups, depending on their response to the photoperiod, which acts as a season indicator. One group, called **day-neutral plants** (DNPs), are not affected by day length. DNPs for flowering include tomatoes, dandelions, roses,

TABLE 33-3 *Flowering Photoperiodism*		
Type of plant	**Conditions needed for flowering**	**Seasons of flowering**
Day-neutral plant (DNP)	not affected by day-night cycle	spring to fall
Short-day plant (SDP)	short days (long nights)	spring, fall
Long-day plant (LDP)	long days (short nights)	summer

corn, cotton, and beans. DNPs and the other two groups of plants are summarized in Table 33-3.

Short-day plants (SDPs) flower in the spring or fall, when the day length is short. For example, ragweed flowers when the days are shorter than 14 hours, and poinsettias flower when the days are shorter than 12 hours. Chrysanthemums, goldenrods, and soybeans are SDPs for flowering.

Long-day plants (LDPs) flower when days are long, usually in summer. For example, wheat flowers only when the days are longer than about 10 hours. Radishes, asters, petunias, and beets are LDPs for flowering.

Adjusting the Flowering Cycles of Plants

Examine Figure 33-10, which compares the flowering of an SDP with that of an LDP. With an 8-hour night, the LDP flowers but the SDP does not. With a 16-hour night, the SDP flowers and the LDP does not. However, if a 16-hour night is interrupted in the middle by one hour of light, the LDP flowers and the SDP does not. This response shows that the length of uninterrupted darkness is the important factor. Even though there is a daily total of 15 hours of darkness, the SDP does not flower because of that one hour of light. Flower growers who want to obtain winter flowering of LDPs simply expose them to a low level of incandescent light in the middle of the night. Summer flowering of SDPs is obtained by covering the plants in the late afternoon with an opaque cloth so that the SDPs receive enough darkness.

Regulation by Phytochrome

Plants monitor changes in day length with a bluish, light-sensitive pigment called **phytochrome** (FIET-uh-KROHM). Phytochrome exists in two forms, based on the wavelength of the light that it absorbs. The form that absorbs red rays is called P_r, and the form that absorbs far red (infrared) rays is called P_{fr}. Daylight converts P_r to P_{fr}. In the dark, P_{fr} is converted to P_r. Besides photoperiodism, phytochrome is involved in bud dormancy and seed germination.

FIGURE 33-10

The figure compares a short-day plant (SDP) with a long-day plant (LDP) in three variations of night length. The SDP has a critical night length of 14 hours. The LDP has a critical night length of 10 hours.

SDP   LDP

A   16 hours   8 hours

B   8 hours   16 hours

C   8 hours   7.5 hours   7.5 hours

☐ Light   ☐ Dark

VERNALIZATION

Vernalization is a low-temperature stimulation of flowering. Vernalization is important for fall-sown grain crops, such as winter wheat, barley, and rye. For example, wheat seeds are sown in the fall and survive the winter as small seedlings. Exposure to cold winter temperatures causes the plants to flower in early spring, and an early crop is produced. If the same wheat is sown in the spring, it will take about two months longer to produce a crop. Thus, cold temperatures are not absolutely required for most cultivars, but they do quicken flowering. Farmers often use vernalization to grow and harvest their crops before a summer drought sets in.

A **biennial** plant is a plant that lives for two years, usually producing flowers and seeds during the second year. Biennial plants, such as carrots, beets, celery, and foxglove, survive their first winter as short plants. In the spring, their flowering stem elongates rapidly, a process called **bolting.** Most biennials must receive vernalization before they flower during the second year. They then die after flowering. One botanist kept a biennial beet alive for over three years by protecting it from exposure to cold temperatures. Treating a biennial with gibberellin is sometimes a substitute for cold temperatures and can stimulate the plant to flower.

FIGURE 33-11

The colors of the carotenoids are visible in these autumn leaves, which have lost most of their chlorophyll.

Fall Colors

Some tree leaves are noted for their spectacular fall color. The changing **fall colors** are caused mainly by a photoperiodic response but also by a temperature response. As nights become longer in the fall, leaves stop producing chlorophyll. As the chlorophyll degrades, it is not replaced. Other leaf pigments, the carotenoids (kuh-RAHT-uhn-OYDZ), become visible as the green chlorophyll degrades. Carotenoids include the orange carotenes and the yellow xanthophylls (ZAN-thuh-filz). The carotenoids were always in the leaf; they were just hidden by the more abundant chlorophyll. Another group of pigments found in leaves, the anthocyanins (AN-thoh-SIE-uh-ninz), are produced in cool, sunny weather. Anthocyanins produce beautiful red and purplish-red colors.

SECTION 33-3 REVIEW

1. Distinguish between short-day and long-day plants.

2. How do flower growers get short-day plants, such as chrysanthemums, to flower at any time of year?

3. How does phytochrome enable plants to detect changes in seasons?

4. How do farmers use vernalization to their benefit?

5. Explain why tree leaves change color in the fall.

6. **CRITICAL THINKING** Why would the term *nyctoperiodism* be a better term for describing the process known as photoperiodism?

SUMMARY/VOCABULARY

33-1
- Small concentrations of plant hormones are formed in many plant parts and transported to other locations in the plant, where they regulate almost all aspects of growth and development.
- Hormones are natural chemicals. Many hormones can be synthesized in the laboratory.
- There are five major groups of plant hormones: auxins, gibberellins, ethylene, cytokinins, and abscisic acid.
- Synthetic auxins are used for many purposes, including to promote rooting of cuttings, to kill weeds, to prevent bud sprouting, and to stimulate or prevent fruit drop.

- Apical dominance is the inhibition of lateral bud growth by auxin produced by the terminal bud.
- Gibberellins are used to increase the size of seedless grapes, to stimulate seed germination, and to brew beer.
- Growth retardants interfere with gibberellins and are widely used to reduce plant height.
- Ethylene, the only gaseous hormone, promotes abscission, fruit ripening, and pineapple flowering.
- Cytokinins stimulate cell division and growth of lateral buds.
- Abscisic acid promotes dormancy and stomatal closing in response to water shortage.

Vocabulary

2,4-D (649)
abscisic acid (ABA) (651)
abscission (650)
Agent Orange (649)
apical dominance (649)

auxin (647)
cytokinin (651)
ethephon (650)
ethylene(650)
gibberellin (GA) (650)

growth regulator (647)
growth retardant (651)
hormone (647)

indoleacetic acid (IAA) (647)
naphthaleneacetic acid (NAA) (648)

33-2
- Tropisms are plant-growth movements in which the direction of growth is determined by the direction of the environmental stimulus.
- Most stems and leaves are positively phototropic, but some vine stems are positively thigmotropic or negatively phototropic, which

allows them to climb walls.
- Roots are usually positively gravitropic, and shoots are usually negatively gravitropic.
- Nastic plant movements result from an environmental stimulus and are independent of the direction of the stimuli.

Vocabulary

chemotropism (654)
gravitropism (654)
nastic movement (654)

nyctinastic movement (655)
phototropism (652)
solar tracking (653)

thigmonastic movement (654)
thigmotropism (653)

tropism (652)

33-3
- Photoperiodism is the triggering of a plant response, such as flowering or dormancy, by relative length of light and darkness.
- Plants fit in one of three photoperiodic classes for flowering: day-neutral, short-day, and long-day.
- Plants sense night and day lengths using the pigment phytochrome.

- Vernalization is the promotion of flowering by cold temperatures.
- Fall colors in tree leaves are caused by chlorophyll degradation, which reveals yellow pigments that have always been present, and by the synthesis of red pigments.

Vocabulary

biennial (658)
bolting (658)
critical night length (656)

day-neutral plant (DNP) (656)
fall color (658)

long-day plant (LDP) (657)
photoperiodism (656)
phytochrome (657)

short-day plant (SDP) (657)
vernalization (658)

REVIEW

Vocabulary

In the following sets of related words, explain the differences between the terms.

1. thigmotropism, gravitropism, chemotropism
2. hormone, plant growth regulator
3. vernalization, abscission, photoperiodism
4. positive phototropism, negative phototropism, nastic movement
5. critical night length, short-day plant, long-day plant

Multiple Choice

6. Exposure of some plants to cold promotes flowering, a process called (a) photoperiodism (b) vernalization (c) dormancy (d) thermotropism.
7. The growth of roots above the soil surface, where oxygen would be more available, is called (a) negative gravitropism (b) negative chemotropism (c) positive phototropism (d) positive chemotropism.
8. Nastic movements occur (a) without a stimulus (b) toward a stimulus (c) away from a stimulus (d) independent of the direction of the stimulus.
9. Cytokinins promote cell (a) aging (b) division (c) storage (d) transport.
10. Fall color changes in tree leaves are caused by the synthesis of (a) chlorophyll (b) carotenoids (c) xanthophylls (d) anthocyanins.
11. Seedless grapes are usually treated with (a) cytokinins (b) gibberellins (c) ethylene (d) abscisic acid.
12. A ripe avocado will cause nearby avocados to ripen through the release of (a) auxin (b) ethylene (c) abscisic acid (d) gibberellin.
13. Abscission layers are areas where (a) leaves fall off stems (b) plants sense night length (c) abscisic acid is produced (d) cuttings are produced.
14. The tropism that is a response to touch is (a) phototropism (b) thigmotropism (c) chemotropism (d) gravitropism.
15. A hormone that is a gas is (a) auxin (b) gibberellin (c) ethylene (d) abscisic acid.

Short Answer

16. Explain how shoot tips and lateral buds are influenced by apical dominance.
17. Define a biennial plant, and explain why vernalization is important in its life cycle.
18. Define critical night length, and explain how it applies to photoperiodism.
19. How might a fruit grower use ethylene on crops?
20. Describe three ways a home gardener could use auxin.
21. What is an adaptive advantage of leaf abscission?
22. Name two factors that affect the influence a hormone will have.
23. Why is 2,4-D effective as a weedkiller in cornfields?
24. Explain why tree leaves change color in autumn.
25. Look at the photograph below. Explain how negative phototropism could result in greater absorption of sunlight for photosynthesis.

CRITICAL THINKING

1. Suppose you placed a green banana in each of several plastic bags, placed a ripe pear in half of the bags, and then sealed all of the bags. Which group of bananas (with or without pears) do you think would ripen sooner? Justify your answer.

2. Suppose that a friend who lives in North Dakota gives you some seeds from a plant that you admired when you saw it growing in your friend's yard. You plant the seeds at your home in Georgia, but they fail to germinate. Based on your knowledge of seed germination, what might be preventing the germination of the seeds?

3. If abscisic acid were inexpensive, what would be some of its possible agricultural or gardening uses?

4. If a whole potato tuber is planted, only one or two buds at one end will sprout. However, if the potato is cut into pieces that each have a bud, all the buds will sprout. Explain why.

5. Potted poinsettias purchased for Christmas will often survive in people's homes for many years but will rarely bloom again. Explain why this happens.

6. The growth of most deciduous trees in the northern United States and Canada, where winters are severe, is regulated strictly by photoperiodism. That is, temperature plays no part in the regulation of their yearly growing cycle. Explain why this is significant.

7. The seasonal loss of leaves by trees and shrubs serves the adaptive advantage of conserving nutrients. What other adaptive advantages might loss of leaves provide?

8. Suppose you notice that your neighbor has a perfect lawn and that some of the trees in your yard have distorted leaves, like those in the photo shown below. What is the probable cause of the leaves' unusual appearance?

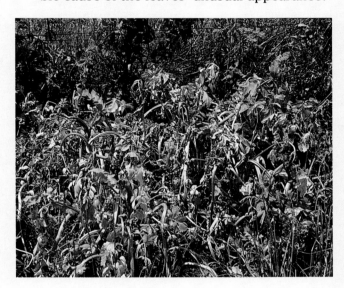

EXTENSION

1. Read the book *The Private Life of Plants: A Natural History of Plant Behaviour*, by David Attenborough (Princeton University Press). This book accompanies a six-hour television series that is available on videotape. Attenborough spent three years taking incredible time-lapse photography to show how plants respond to various stimuli.

2. Try taking time-lapse photos to capture plant movements using either a regular camera or a video camera with an automatic time-lapse feature.

3. Select several plant species, and plant six seeds of each species in separate pots of soil. Allow the seeds to sprout and grow until the plants are about 10 cm tall. Lay the pots on their sides and observe how long it takes the plants to point upward again. Do the species differ in their rate of bending?

4. Read about Charles Darwin's famous experiments on Venus' flytraps in his book *Insectivorous Plants*. If you can obtain a potted Venus' flytrap, repeat Darwin's experiments to determine how many touches are needed to make the leaf trap close.

Testing the Effect of Gibberellin on Plant Growth

OBJECTIVE

- Study the effect of gibberellin on the growth of bean seedlings.

PROCESS SKILLS

- observing
- hypothesizing
- measuring
- comparing and contrasting
- collecting data
- organizing data

MATERIALS

- safety goggles
- lab apron
- disposable gloves
- 2 flowerpots, 20 cm or larger
- marking pen
- labeling tape
- potting-soil mixture
- 10 bean seedlings, at least 3 cm tall
- centimeter ruler
- cotton swabs
- gibberellic acid solution (contains gibberellin)
- water

Background

1. Gibberellins are found in all parts of plants, but are most concentrated in immature seeds. Gibberellins are only one group of many hormones that affect plant functions.
2. What is the major effect of gibberellins on plant tissues?

PART A Setting Up

1. Discuss the objective of this investigation with your lab partners. You will apply gibberellic acid solution to the leaves and shoot tips of one group of bean seedlings, and you will apply only water to an identical group of bean seedlings. Develop a hypothesis about the effect of gibberellic acid solution on bean seedlings. Record your hypothesis in your lab report.

2. **CAUTION Wear safety goggles, a lab apron, and disposable gloves at all times during this investigation.**
3. Obtain two flowerpots, and label them A and B. Also write your initials on the flowerpots.
4. Fill each flowerpot with potting-soil mixture. The pots should be filled to the same level.
5. **CAUTION Keep the seeds, which may have been treated with a fungicide, away from your skin.** Plant five bean seedlings in each flowerpot, spacing them evenly around the edge. Each seedling's roots should be at least 1 cm below the soil surface.
6. Measure the height of each plant in pot A to the nearest millimeter. Measure from the soil surface to the shoot tip. In your lab report, record your measurements in a data table similar to the table on the facing page.
7. Average the height of the five seedlings. In your lab report, record your average measurement under "Initial height" in a data table like the one shown.
8. Repeat steps 6 and 7 using the plants in pot B.
9. Wet a cotton swab with water. Rub the water over the leaves and shoot tips of each seedling in pot A.
10. **CAUTION Gibberellic acid is an irritant. If you get gibberellic acid solution on your skin or clothing, rinse it off at the sink while calling to your teacher. If you get gibberellic acid solution in your eyes, flush it out immediately at an eyewash station while calling to your teacher.** Wet a clean cotton swab with gibberellic acid solution. Apply the solution to the seedlings in pot B by rubbing the cotton swab on the leaves and shoot tips.
11. Place both flowerpots in a window or other area where they are likely to get light. The seedlings should receive the same amount of water, sunlight, darkness, and air circulation.
12. Clean up your materials and wash your hands before leaving the lab.

PART B Observing the Results

13. Each day over the next 10 days, measure the height of each seedling. Average the height of the seedlings in each flowerpot, and record the average height in your data table.
14. Calculate the average change in height for each day. For example, the average change in height during the second day is equal to the average height on day 2 minus the average height on day 1.
15. If you are unable to make measurements over the weekend, simply record in your data table the number of days that elapsed since the last measurement was taken. To calculate the average change in height for the days when measurements were not taken, you will need to divide the amount of change by the number of days that have elapsed since your last measurement.
16. At the end of 10 days, clean up your materials according to your teacher's instructions.

Analysis and Conclusions

1. Use the data you have recorded to calculate the percentage increase—between your first measurement and your last measurement—in the average height of the two groups of plants.
2. Use your data to make a line graph of height as a function of time. Label the x-axis of your graph *Time,* and measure time in days. Label the y-axis *Height,* and measure height in millimeters.
3. Do your data support your hypothesis? Explain why or why not.
4. What differences, other than height, did you detect in the bean seedlings?
5. What were some of the possible sources of error in this experiment?
6. How might a knowledge of plant regulatory chemicals be of use to farmers and other plant growers?

Further Inquiry

Design an experiment to determine whether gibberellic acid accelerates the germination of bean seeds.

FLOWERPOT A: *EFFECTS OF WATER ON BEAN SEEDLINGS*

Day	Height (mm)	Total change in height (mm)
Initial		
1		
2		
3		
4		
5		
6		
7		
8		
9		
10		

FLOWERPOT B: *EFFECTS OF GIBBERELLIC ACID ON BEAN SEEDLINGS*

Day	Height (mm)	Total change in height (mm)
Initial		
1		
2		
3		
4		
5		
6		
7		
8		
9		
10		

unit
8

INVERTEBRATES

internet connect

SC_iLINKS
NSTA

National Science Teachers Association *sci*LINKS Internet resources are located throughout this unit.

> ❝ *It has taken biologists some 230 years to identify and describe three quarters of a million insects; if there are indeed at least thirty million, as Erwin (Terry Erwin, the Smithsonian Institute) estimates, then, working as they have in the past, insect taxonomists have ten thousand years of employment ahead of them.* ❞

From "Endless Forms Most Beautiful," from *The Sixth Extinction: Patterns of Life and the Future of Humankind,* by Richard Leakey and Roger Lewin. Copyright © 1995 by Sherma B. V. Reprinted by permission of *Doubleday, a division of Bantam Doubleday Dell Publishing Group, Inc.*

This Sally lightfoot crab lives on bare volcanic rock on the Galápagos Islands.

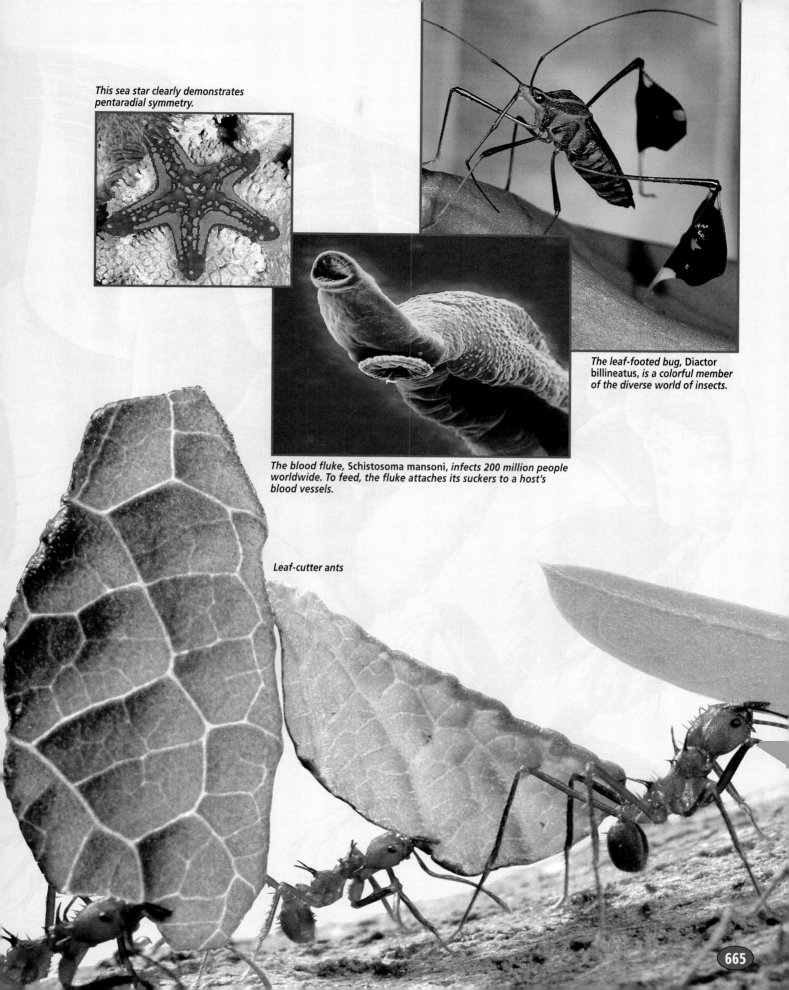

This sea star clearly demonstrates pentaradial symmetry.

The leaf-footed bug, *Diactor billineatus,* is a colorful member of the diverse world of insects.

The blood fluke, *Schistosoma mansoni, infects* 200 million people worldwide. To feed, the fluke attaches its suckers to a host's blood vessels.

Leaf-cutter ants

INTRODUCTION TO ANIMALS

The diversity of animal life is staggering. Animals have adapted to Earth's lushest environments and to its harshest environments. This Sally Lightfoot crab, Grapsus grapsus, lives on the bare volcanic rock of the geologically young Galápagos Islands.

FOCUS CONCEPT: *Matter, Energy, and Organization*

As you read about the characteristics of different animals, notice the relationship between structure and function in animals' bodies.

34-1 The Nature of Animals

34-2 Animal Bodies

34-3 Comparison of Invertebrates and Vertebrates

34-4 Fertilization and Development

ORIGIN AND CLASSIFICATION

The first animals probably arose in the sea. The structural characteristics of invertebrates suggest that they were the first multicellular animals and that they evolved from protists. Because protists are both heterotrophic and eukaryotic, scientists have inferred that multicellular invertebrates may have developed from colonies of loosely connected, flagellated protists, like the one shown in Figure 34-2.

What path did cell specialization take in these early organisms? Colonial protists may have lost their flagella over the course of evolution as individual cells in the colony grew more specialized. They may have been similar to modern colonial protists that do show some degree of cell specialization, such as some species of algae. In these species, the gametes are distinct from nonreproductive cells. A similar division of labor in early colonial protists may have been the first step toward multicellularity.

Taxonomists have grouped animals into several phyla, based on their evolutionary history, which is inferred from morphology and other factors. Recall from Chapter 18 that taxonomy is an ever-changing branch of science. Therefore, it should not be surprising that the actual number and names of animal phyla continue to be debated. Many taxonomists recognize 30 or more different animal phyla, though some phyla contain a very small number of species. Eleven animal phyla will be discussed in detail in this unit and in Unit 9. Ten of these phyla include only invertebrates. The eleventh phylum, Chordata, includes all vertebrate species as well as a small number of invertebrate marine chordates. Although vertebrates are particularly conspicuous to us, they make up a small segment of kingdom Animalia.

SECTION 34-1 REVIEW

1. Define the words *invertebrate* and *vertebrate.*

2. What are four important characteristics common to most animals?

3. How is cell specialization related to multicellularity?

4. How are nervous tissue and muscle tissue interrelated, and why are they important to animals?

5. What unicellular organisms are thought to have been the immediate ancestors of the first animals?

6. **CRITICAL THINKING** Why is colonialism, the grouping together of like organisms, thought to be one of the first steps in the evolution of multicellularity?

OBJECTIVES

▲

Define the terms *dorsal, ventral, anterior,* and *posterior.*

●

Describe two types of symmetry found in animals.

■

Name the trait that is strongly associated with bilateral symmetry.

◆

List two functions of the body cavity in animals.

▲

List three structural features that taxonomists use to classify animals.

●

List four features found only in chordates.

ANIMAL BODIES

*T*axonomic organization is based on phylogenetic relationships. Today, systematic taxonomists classify animals according to similarities in morphology and other criteria, including the similarity of embryological development and the similarity of certain macromolecules. Recall from Chapter 18 that taxonomists since Linnaeus's time have used an organism's morphology to classify it with similar organisms. Morphology, however, is not confined to external appearance. A survey of an animal's morphology also assesses the internal structure of the body and organization at the level of fundamental tissue types.

BODY STRUCTURE

The term **symmetry** refers to a consistent overall pattern of structure. The simplest animals, sponges, display no symmetry, as is shown in Figure 34-3a. Moreover, although sponges are multicellular, their cells are not organized into tissues. Animal bodies range from those that lack true tissues and an organized body shape, such as that of a sponge, to those that have very organized tissues and a consistent body shape, as is found in most other animal phyla.

Patterns of Symmetry

Some animals have a top side and a bottom side, but no front and back end or right and left end. These animals are said to display radial symmetry. In **radial symmetry,** similar parts branch out in all directions from a central line. Cnidarians, such as sea anemones, jellyfishes, and the hydra pictured in Figure 34-3b, are radially symmetrical.

Most animals have a **dorsal** (top) and **ventral** (bottom) side, an **anterior** (head) and **posterior** (tail) end, and a right and left side, as shown in the moth pictured in Figure 34-3c. Such animals have two similar halves on either side of a central plane and are said to display **bilateral symmetry.** Bilaterally symmetrical animals tend to exhibit cephalization. **Cephalization** (SEF-uh-li-ZAY-shun) is the concentration of sensory and brain structures in the anterior end of the animal; a cephalized animal has a head. As a cephalized animal swims, burrows, walks, or flies through its environment, the head precedes the rest of the body, sensing danger, prey, or a potential mate.

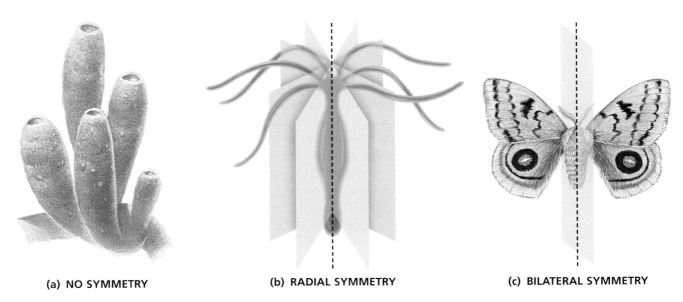

(a) NO SYMMETRY   **(b) RADIAL SYMMETRY**   **(c) BILATERAL SYMMETRY**

FIGURE 34-3

(a) The sponge lacks a consistent pattern of structure. (b) The hydra, an aquatic animal, displays radial symmetry. (c) The moth displays bilateral symmetry and cephalization.

Germ Layers

Germ layers are fundamental tissue types found in the embryos of all animals except sponges, which have no true tissues. The embryos of cnidarians and ctenophores have only two germ layers, but all other animals form three distinct germ layers very early in their development. Every body feature, organ, and tissue—from teeth to toenails—arises from one of these germ layers.

Body Cavities

Most animals have some type of body cavity, a fluid-filled space that forms between the digestive tract and the outer wall of the body during development. Some animals, such as flatworms, have three germ layers but have a solid body. These animals lack a body cavity.

In the roundworm shown in Figure 34-4, the body cavity aids in movement by providing a firm structure against which muscles can contract. The body cavity also allows some degree of movement of the exterior of the body with respect to the internal organs, resulting in more freedom of movement for the animal. Finally, the fluid in the body cavity acts as a reservoir and medium of transport for nutrients and wastes, which diffuse into and out of the animal's body cells.

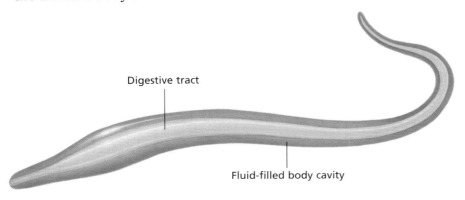

Digestive tract

Fluid-filled body cavity

FIGURE 34-4

The body of a roundworm is held erect by its fluid-filled body cavity, which is firm but flexible, like a balloon filled with water.

ANIMAL DIVERSITY

Similarities in body plans and patterns of development allow biologists to classify animals and hypothesize about their evolutionary history. Biologists use information from modern species and extinct species to develop cladograms and classical phylogenetic trees, such as the one shown in Figure 34-5, that show relationships between taxonomic groups. Animal phyla shown on the same branch of the phylogenetic tree, such as roundworms and rotifers, are thought to be related to each other more closely than they are to other animals and are characterized by important similarities in morphology. Conversely, animals shown in different parts of the tree are thought to be more distantly related.

- *Multicellularity and a limited degree of cell specialization* characterize the sponges. Sponges have no organized body shape and no true tissues.
- *True tissues in two layers* are found in the cnidarians and the ctenophores.
- *True tissues in three layers and bilateral symmetry* characterize all of the other animal phyla. Among these, phylogenetic categories are based on the absence or presence and type of body cavity and on fundamental patterns of development.

FIGURE 34-5

This phylogenetic tree of animals shows the evolutionary relationships thought to exist among 11 major animal phyla.

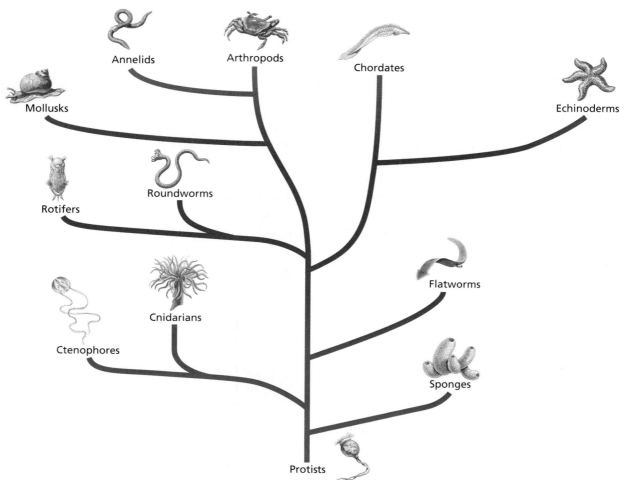

Invertebrates

The 10 invertebrate phyla pictured in Figure 34-5 are a remarkably heterogeneous group. Their body plans range from the complete absence of body symmetry and true tissues, as is found in sponges, to the bilateral symmetry and specialized body parts found in arthropods, such as the spider shown in Figure 34-6. In fact, the primary trait that links all invertebrates is the absence of a backbone. Invertebrates constitute the greatest number of animal species as well as most of the individual animals alive today.

Chordates

The eleventh phylum shown in Figure 34-5 is Chordata. The name **chordate** (KOHR-dayt) refers to the **notochord,** a firm, flexible rod of tissue located in the dorsal part of the body. At some stage of their development, all chordates have a notochord, as well as a dorsal nerve cord, pharyngeal pouches, and a postanal tail. The **dorsal nerve cord** is a hollow tube lying just above, or dorsal to, the notochord. **Pharyngeal** (fuh-RIN-jee-uhl) **pouches** are small outpockets of the anterior part of the digestive tract. The **postanal tail** consists of muscle tissue and lies behind the posterior opening of the digestive tract.

A few chordate species retain their early chordate characteristics all their lives. In most vertebrates, a subphylum of the chordates, the dorsal nerve cord develops into the brain and the spinal cord, which runs within the hollow backbone. In aquatic vertebrates, such as fishes and amphibians, the pharyngeal pouches have evolved into gills, which are used for breathing. In most vertebrates, the notochord appears only in the embryonic stage. It is replaced by the backbone early in development.

Vertebrates

Although vertebrates constitute only one subphylum of the phylogenetic tree of all animals, they merit extensive discussion from a human perspective. Humans are vertebrates, and the ecology of humans includes extensive interaction with other vertebrate species. For example, fishes, birds, and many species of mammals are primary food sources for humans.

FIGURE 34-6

The palm spider, *Nephila* sp., is an arthropod, with a segmented body and body parts specialized for trapping, killing, and eating its prey.

internet**connect**

SCI*LINKS*
NSTA

TOPIC: Vertebrates
GO TO: www.scilinks.org
KEYWORD: HM673

SECTION 34-2 REVIEW

1. Define the terms *anterior* and *posterior*. What type of body symmetry includes both an anterior end and a posterior end?

2. What common feature is not found in radially symmetric animals?

3. What are two functions of the body cavity?

4. In determining an animal's phylogenetic history, what are three body features that taxonomists consider?

5. What happens to the notochord and dorsal nerve cord as most vertebrates develop?

6. CRITICAL THINKING How does having a head help an animal?

OBJECTIVES

▲

Compare the body plans and development of invertebrates and vertebrates.

●

Define the term *segmentation,* and name a phylum of segmented animals.

■

Explain the difference between an open circulatory system and a closed circulatory system.

◆

Describe the digestive system found in most invertebrate phyla, and compare it with vertebrate digestive systems.

FIGURE 34-7

The sea hare, *Aplysia californica,* is a shell-less mollusk with a simple nervous system.

COMPARISON OF INVERTEBRATES AND VERTEBRATES

*C*omparative anatomy, the study of the structure of animal bodies, is one of the oldest disciplines in biology. Some modern scientists work to establish the relationships between different animals, while others try to establish the relationships between the form and function of morphological features of animals and the role of these features in animal ecology.

INVERTEBRATE CHARACTERISTICS

While it may be difficult for us to see many similarities between a clam and an octopus, they are classified in the same phylum. Adult invertebrates show a tremendous amount of morphological diversity.

Symmetry

Invertebrates display radial or bilateral symmetry. The radial symmetry of a jellyfish, which drifts rather than swims, allows the animal to receive stimuli from all directions. Most invertebrates have bilateral symmetry, which is an adaptation to a more motile lifestyle. Bilateral symmetry allows for cephalization, which is present in varying degrees in different animals. Some bilaterally symmetric invertebrates, like the sea hare shown in Figure 34-7, are not highly cephalized. *Aplysia* does not have a true, centralized brain and is capable of only simple responses to its environment. Other invertebrates, such as squids and octopuses, are highly cephalized, with a distinct head and a nervous system dominated by a well-organized brain.

Segmentation

Animals in some invertebrate phyla are segmented. **Segmentation** in animals refers to a body composed of a series of repeating similar units. Segmentation is seen in its simplest form in the earthworm, an annelid in which each unit of the body is very similar to the next one. Within the phylum Arthropoda, however, segments may look different and have different functions. In many arthropod species, two or more segments are fused into larger functional units. In the arthropod shown in Figure 34-8, fusion of the anterior segments has resulted in a large structure that includes the animal's head and chest regions.

Support of the Body

Invertebrate bodies have diverse means of support. Sponges have a simple skeleton that supports their soft tissue; the dried, brown, irregularly shaped "natural sponge" found in stores is this skeleton. The bodies of some other invertebrates, such as roundworms, are supported by the pressure of their fluid-filled body cavity.

An **exoskeleton** is a rigid outer covering that protects the soft tissues of many animals, including arthropods, such as lobsters, and mollusks, such as clams. An exoskeleton, however, limits the size and impedes the movement of the organism. Moreover, an exoskeleton does not grow, but must be shed and replaced as the animal grows.

Respiratory and Circulatory Systems

Animals produce carbon dioxide, CO_2, as a byproduct of metabolism. Therefore, carbon dioxide in the blood must be exchanged with oxygen, O_2, from the environment. This process is called **gas exchange,** and it occurs most efficiently across a moist membrane. In the simplest aquatic invertebrates, gas exchange occurs directly through the covering of the body. Aquatic arthropods and mollusks, however, have **gills,** organs specialized for gas exchange in water.

In most animals, the **circulatory system** moves blood or a similar fluid through the body to transport oxygen and nutrients to cells. At the same time, carbon dioxide and wastes are transported away from the cells. Sponges and cnidarians have no circulatory system, so nutrients and gases are exchanged directly with the environment by diffusion across cell membranes. Arthropods and some mollusks have an **open circulatory system,** in which blood-like circulatory fluid is pumped from vessels in the body into the body cavity, and then is returned to the vessels. Annelids and other mollusks have a closed circulatory system. In a **closed circulatory system,** blood circulates through the body in tubular vessels. The exchange of gases, nutrients, and wastes occurs between body cells and very small blood vessels that lie near each cell.

Digestive and Excretory Systems

In sponges, digestion occurs within individual cells. In cnidarians, a central chamber with one opening serves as the digestive system.

FIGURE 34-8

In animals such as this crayfish, *Procambarus* sp., segments are fused, producing larger structures. The head and chest structure in this animal results from the fusion of several segments. Segments may also give rise to other structures, such as limbs.

internet**connect**

SCI**LINKS**
NSTA

TOPIC: Invertebrates
GO TO: www.scilinks.org
KEYWORD: HM675

Most other invertebrates, however, have a digestive tract, or **gut,** running through their body. In these animals, food is broken down and nutrients are absorbed by specialized cells that line the gut.

In simple aquatic invertebrates, wastes are excreted as dissolved ammonia, NH_3. In terrestrial invertebrates, specialized excretory structures filter ammonia and other wastes from the body cavity. The ammonia is then converted to less toxic substances and water is reabsorbed by the animal before the waste is excreted.

Nervous System

The extraordinary degree of diversity among invertebrates is reflected in their nervous systems. Sponges have no neurons, although individual cells can react to environmental stimuli in much the same way protozoa can. Neurons evolved in cnidarians, which have a very simple, loosely connected nervous system. Within a single invertebrate phylum, Mollusca, we can trace a step-wise progression of cephalization and the evolution of the brain. The mollusks have very diverse nervous systems. Recall the sea hare, shown in Figure 34-7. Although its head is not well defined, and its nervous system can perform only simple information processing, the sea hare can learn to contract a part of its body in response to certain stimuli. Contrast this simple behavior with that of a highly cephalized mollusk, such as the octopus. The octopus shows very complex decision-making behavior, and it can build a shelter from debris it finds on the ocean floor.

Reproduction and Development

Invertebrates are capable of some form of sexual reproduction, and many can also reproduce asexually. Some invertebrates, such as earthworms, are hermaphrodites. A **hermaphrodite** (huhr-MAF-roh-DIET) is an organism that produces both male and female gametes, allowing a single individual to function as both a male and a female.

Invertebrates may undergo indirect or direct development. Animals that undergo **indirect development** have an intermediate larval stage, as is shown in Figure 34-9. A **larva** is a free-living, immature form of an organism. Many insects, which constitute a class of arthropods, have indirect development.

FIGURE 34-9

Animals with indirect development, such as this beetle, have an intermediate, larval stage. A larva is an immature form that exhibits physical traits different from the adult form.

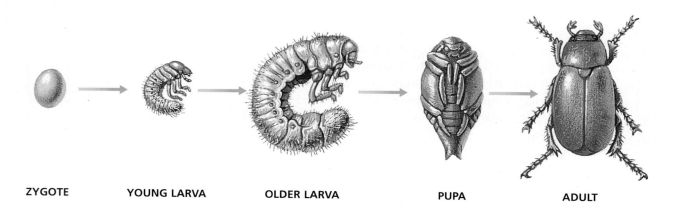

ZYGOTE   YOUNG LARVA   OLDER LARVA   PUPA   ADULT

In contrast, in **direct development,** the young animal is born or hatched with the same appearance and way of life it will have as an adult; no larval stage occurs. Although most invertebrates undergo indirect development, a few, such as grasshoppers, undergo direct development.

FIGURE 34-10

Vertebrates, such as birds, are segmented animals. Segmentation is evident in the repeating structures of the animal's backbone and ribs.

VERTEBRATE CHARACTERISTICS

Classes of vertebrates include fishes, amphibians, reptiles, birds, and mammals. All vertebrate classes except fishes spend part or all of their life on land. Many characteristics of terrestrial vertebrates are adaptations to life on land and fall into two broad categories: support of the body and conservation of water.

Support of the Body

In addition to a backbone, vertebrates have an **endoskeleton,** an internal skeleton that can support a large, heavy body. The endoskeleton grows as the animal grows.

Although it is not immediately apparent, vertebrates are segmented animals. Segmentation is evident in the ribs and the **vertebrae** (VUHR-tuh-BREE), the repeating bony units of the backbone, as shown in Figure 34-10. As terrestrial vertebrates evolved from aquatic vertebrates, their limbs and associated muscles evolved to give the animals better support and greater mobility. For example, the legs of amphibians, the first land vertebrates to evolve, are positioned away from the body, as shown in Figure 34-11a. However, the legs of mammals, such as the deer shown in Figure 34-11b, are positioned directly beneath the body, allowing the animal to move faster and with a longer stride. Humans show an extreme version of this trait: we are bipedal, and our head is positioned directly over our body.

FIGURE 34-11

(a) The legs of amphibians, such as this frog, *Agalychnis saltator,* are sharply bent and positioned away from the body. (b) The legs of terrestrial mammals, such as this deer, *Odocoileus virginianus,* are straighter than those of amphibians, providing greater mobility and speed.

(a)

(b)

Identifying Animal Characteristics

Materials 3×5 in. note cards (20), 5 pictures of vertebrates, 5 pictures of invertebrates

Procedure

1. Working in pairs, one partner will write one different vertebrate characteristic on each of 10 note cards. The other partner will write one different invertebrate characteristic on each of 10 note cards.

2. Designate one partner as the dealer. Place the animal pictures upside down in a stack. The dealer will shuffle and deal all the cards. Turn over one animal picture.

3. The nondealer plays first by laying down as many cards as possible that describe characteristics of the pictured animal. If no card matches, the play is passed to the other player. When neither partner can play, another picture is turned up and play continues.

4. Play ceases when neither student can play or when no pictures are left. The player who is holding the fewest number of cards wins.

Analysis Why are morphological characteristics used to identify organisms? What are the disadvantages of using only morphological characteristics to identify an organism?

Body Coverings

The outer covering of an animal is called the **integument** (in-TEG-yoo-muhnt). While the integuments of fishes and most amphibians are adapted only to moist environments, the integuments of most terrestrial vertebrates are adapted to hold water inside the body. All animal bodies are composed of water-filled cells, and if the water content of the cells is reduced appreciably, the animal will die. The outer covering of terrestrial vertebrates, such as reptiles, birds, and mammals, is largely watertight. Integuments also serve other purposes. The moist skin of an amphibian functions as a respiratory organ for the exchange of gases. The scales of a reptile help protect it from predators. The feathers of birds and the fur of mammals efficiently insulate the body.

Respiratory and Circulatory Systems

Gas exchange occurs in the gills of aquatic vertebrates, including fishes and larval amphibians, but these gills do not function out of water. **Lungs** are organs for gas exchange composed of moist, membranous surfaces deep inside the animal's body. Lungs evolved in terrestrial vertebrates.

Vertebrates have a closed circulatory system with a multichambered, pumping heart. In some vertebrates, the multichambered heart separates oxygenated and deoxygenated blood, improving the efficiency of the circulatory system over that found in other vertebrates and many invertebrates.

Digestive and Excretory Systems

Digestion in vertebrates occurs in the gut, which runs from the mouth, at the anterior end, to the anus, at the posterior end. In many vertebrates, the gut is very long with respect to the length of the body, increasing the surface area over which nutrients are absorbed. The human digestive tract is nearly 7 m (23 ft) long. It is folded to fit into a body one-fourth its length.

Vertebrates have the same waste-disposal problems as invertebrates. They must deal with the very toxic ammonia their bodies produce, and most vertebrates must expel wastes while conserving water. Like invertebrates, most vertebrates convert ammonia to less toxic substances. In most vertebrates, organs called **kidneys** filter wastes from the blood while regulating water levels in the body.

Nervous System

Vertebrates have highly organized brains and the control of specific functions occurs in specific centers in the brain. The structure and function of the nervous system varies among vertebrate orders. For example, within the brain of a fish, much of the tissue processes sensory information. In Figure 34-12, the elongated structure that projects in front of the fish's eye processes only information about smell. Fishes have limited neural circuitry devoted to decision making. A fish's responses to stimuli in its environment are rigid, that is, they vary little from situation to situation and from fish to fish.

Other animals, such as dogs, display complex and flexible behavior. Much of the tissue in the dog's brain is given over to neural circuitry that is involved in decision making, and its brain is large with respect to body size, as Figure 34-12 shows.

Reproduction and Development

In most fish and amphibian species, eggs and sperm are released directly into the water, where fertilization takes place. In reptiles, birds, and mammals, the egg and sperm unite within the body of the female, increasing the likelihood that the egg will be fertilized.

The fertilized egg—the zygote—of many fishes, amphibians, reptiles, and birds develops outside the body. The developing embryo is nourished by the yolk of the egg and protected by jelly-like layers or by a shell. The zygotes of some species of fishes, amphibians, and reptiles remain inside the body of the female, nourished by the yolk, until they hatch. In contrast, most mammals give birth to live offspring. Embryos of placental mammals develop in the female's body, nourished by the mother's blood supply, until the young are born.

With the exception of amphibians and some fishes, vertebrates undergo direct development. Over the course of direct development, the young and the adults can share the same resources—an advantage if those resources are plentiful.

FIGURE 34-12

A comparison of the brain of a fish with the brain of a mammal, such as a dog, shows that the size of the brain with respect to the body is larger in the dog. In the dog, the areas devoted to complex processing and decision making, such as the heavy, wrinkled structure that dominates its brain, are also larger.

SECTION 34-3 REVIEW

1. What is segmentation, and what trend is apparent in the segmented bodies of arthropods?

2. How does a closed circulatory system function, and how does it differ from an open circulatory system?

3. How are vertebrates related to chordates?

4. How is the digestive chamber of a cnidarian different from that of most other invertebrates and all vertebrates?

5. What is a primary function of the body covering of terrestrial animals?

6. **CRITICAL THINKING** How is the degree of an animal's cephalization related to its behavior?

The Cell Surface: Embryonic Development and Beyond

HISTORICAL PERSPECTIVE

The mysteries of embryonic growth and development have engaged scientists since ancient times. Until the last century, it was largely unknown how a large, multicellular animal was produced from a source too small to see. Early scientists debated whether the embryo is pre-formed as a miniature individual (a homunculus) or is entirely undifferentiated in form, becoming more specialized only as it grows and develops. The field of developmental biology, which advanced rapidly in the late 1800s and throughout the 1900s, owes much to the pioneering efforts of biologist Ernest Everett Just. Just demonstrated that the differentiation of the embryonic cells during early development is the result of the interaction between the cytoplasm and the nucleus of the egg. Just's later work helped establish that the cell membrane is more than a boundary layer. Rather it plays a critical role as a gatekeeper and conduit for information vital to the cell.

First Steps

In 1899, the German-born American scientist Jacques Loeb, who worked at the University of Chicago and at Woods Hole Marine Biological Laboratory in Cape Cod, Massachusetts, began a study of the early development of eggs. Loeb made the surprising discovery that certain environmental disturbances could initiate development of unfertilized sea urchin eggs. When Loeb pricked the eggs with a needle or changed the salt concentration of the solution surrounding them, the eggs began to divide as if they had been fertilized by sperm. This phenomenon is known as *parthenogenesis,* and it is now known that it occurs in

Ernest Everett Just

nature in every major group of invertebrates. To explain his findings of forced parthenogenesis in the laboratory, Loeb initially hypothesized that the physical and chemical agents he used in his experiments mimicked sperm function and that agents from outside the egg—such as sperm—are necessary for development to begin.

Challenging a Well-Established Model

A decade later, a young biologist named Ernest Just began conducting his own research in cell biology. In 1911, while working at the Woods Hole laboratories, Just made an important discovery about cell cleavage, the successive cell divisions leading to the formation of the embryo. Just conducted experiments in chemical-induced parthenogenesis in sea urchins, marine worms, and sand dollars, and he also observed normal fertilization of eggs by sperm cells. In contrast to Loeb's original hypothesis—that sperm or something like it is necessary to trigger development—Just proposed that the egg contains the necessary mechanism for development. Just's subsequent work confirmed the role of the egg cytoplasm in the initiation of cleavage. This new understanding of the importance of the cytoplasm to development prompted Just to take a closer look at the individual components of the egg cell. He studied the relationship between the nucleus and the cytoplasm as well as the arrangement of different cytoplasmic components throughout the egg. In his later work, he focused on the role of the cell surface.

Some animal eggs, such as these sea urchin eggs, can be induced to begin development without being fertilized by sperm.

More Than a Boundary

Just maintained that there is a membrane around animal cells and that this membrane is a fundamental part of the living system of the cell.

Initially, some scientists doubted that the cell membrane existed because its cellular structure could not be easily distinguished using the microscopes of the day. Just, however, was correct about the existence of the cell membrane and its extraordinary functions as a gateway for passage into and out of the cell and as an active participant in cell-to-cell communication.

In his 1939 book, *The Biology of the Cell Surface,* Just wrote:

> It [the cell surface] is keyed to the outside world as no other part of the cell. It stands guard over the peculiar form of the living substance, and is a buffer against the attacks of the surroundings and the means of communication with it.

Meeting Modern Challenges

Just's experiments, which highlighted the relationship between the nucleus and the cytoplasm and the significance of the cell membrane, have proved helpful in understanding how a cell carries out its basic functions. Today, we understand the role of the cytoplasm in tissue differentiation as that of controlling the transcription of genetic information from the nucleus. Modern researchers using electron microscopes have resolved the fine

structure of the cell membrane, revealing it to be an active cellular component. Despite the limited technology available to him, Just's pioneering research in cell biology has proved sound, and his techniques and discoveries are relevant to research in cell biology today.

In 1915, when he was 32 years old, Just was awarded the first Spingarn Medal by the National Association for the Advancement of Colored People for his work in cell biology. This medal, the organization's highest honor, continues to be presented in recognition of outstanding achievements by African Americans. From 1920 to 1931, Just held a National Research Rosenwald fellowship in biology. He served as vice-president of the American Zoological Society and as associate editor of the *Journal of Morphology,* of *The Biological Bulletin,* and of *Physiological Zoology.* Ernest Everett Just died in 1941.

OBJECTIVES

▲

List the steps of fertilization and development through gastrulation.

●

Identify the three primary germ layers, and list two body parts formed from each germ layer.

■

Define *protostome* and *deuterostome*.

◆

Contrast spiral cleavage with radial cleavage, and name the category of organisms that undergo each type of cleavage.

▲

Contrast schizocoely with enterocoely.

FERTILIZATION AND DEVELOPMENT

Development of a multicellular animal from an egg cell is a truly remarkable process. Each cell has the same set of genes that are used to build an animal, yet animals have many different kinds of cells. From the fertilized egg come large numbers of cells—many millions in humans—that consistently give rise to structural features of the animal body.

FERTILIZATION AND EARLY DEVELOPMENT

In most animals, fertilization is the union of female and male reproductive cells, the eggs and sperm. Fertilization results in the combination of haploid sets of chromosomes from two individuals into a single diploid cell, the zygote.

Gametes

In most animal species, the sperm cell, shown in Figure 34-13, is specialized for movement—it is very streamlined and small. The head of the sperm contains chromosomes, while the tail of the sperm is composed of a large flagellum.

The egg is typically large, owing to its large store of cytoplasm and yolk. The size of a species egg seems to depend on how long the food supply in the yolk must last. In aquatic animals, in which the embryo begins to feed itself early, eggs are small and there is little yolk. In sharp contrast, the embryos of birds must live on the yolk until they hatch. In these eggs, the yolk volume is very large.

Fertilization

At the start of fertilization, the sperm's cell membrane fuses with the egg's cell membrane, and the nucleus of the sperm enters the cytoplasm of the egg. The fusion of the cell membranes of the egg and sperm causes an electrical change that blocks entry to the egg by other sperm cells. The sperm nucleus merges with the egg nucleus to form the diploid nucleus of the zygote. Once a zygote is formed, replication of DNA begins, and the first cell division soon follows.

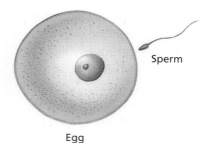

Sperm

Egg

FIGURE 34-13

The small, flagellated sperm is adapted for motility and speed. It must seek out and fertilize the much larger, yolk-filled egg.

Cleavage and Blastula Formation

The divisions of the zygote immediately following fertilization are termed **cleavage.** As Figures 34-14a–c show, as cleavage progresses, the number of cells increases, from 2 to 4, then to 8, and so on. During cleavage, mitotic divisions rapidly increase the number of cells, but the cells do not grow in size. Thus, the cell divisions of cleavage yield smaller and smaller individual cells. Cleavage increases the surface-area-to-volume ratio of each cell, which enhances gas exchange and other environmental interactions.

In most species, cleavage produces a raspberry-shaped mass of 16 to 64 cells. As the number of dividing cells further increases, the mass becomes a hollow ball of cells called a **blastula,** as shown in Figure 34-14d. The central cavity of a blastula is called the **blastocoel** (BLAS-toe-SEEL), shown in Figure 34-14e.

GASTRULATION

At the start of the next stage of development, shown in Figure 34-15a, an area of the blastula begins to collapse inward, much the way a partially inflated soccer ball would collapse if a fist were pressed into it. This infolded region of the blastula, called the **blastopore,** is shown in Figure 34-15b. A fundamental reorganization of the cells of the hollow blastula begins with the formation of the blastopore. This process, called **gastrulation,** transforms the blastula into a multilayered embryo, called the **gastrula.** Gastrulation is marked by changes in the shape of cells, together with changes in their adhesion to other cells.

As the inward folding, shown in Figure 34-15c, continues, the now cup-shaped embryo enlarges and a deep cavity, called the **archenteron,** develops. This cavity will function as the gut. Forming the outer layer of the gastrula is the outer germ layer, the **ectoderm,** shown in blue in Figure 34-15c. The inner germ layer, the **endoderm,** is shown in yellow. In most phyla, the gastrula does not remain a two-layer structure. As development progresses, a third layer, the **mesoderm,** forms between the endoderm and the ectoderm.

Recall that each of the three germ layers formed during gastrulation is a forerunner to certain parts of the fully formed body. The archenteron, which is surrounded by the endoderm, forms the throat passage, including gills or lungs, and the gut and its

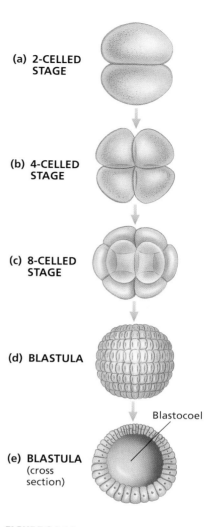

(a) 2-CELLED STAGE

(b) 4-CELLED STAGE

(c) 8-CELLED STAGE

(d) BLASTULA

Blastocoel

(e) BLASTULA (cross section)

FIGURE 34-14

During cleavage, the zygote divides repeatedly (a–c) without undergoing cell growth, producing a many-celled hollow blastula (d and e).

Blastocoel

(a) EARLY GASTRULATION

Blastocoel   Blastopore

(b) MID-GASTRULATION

Endoderm
Ectoderm
Archenteron
Blastocoel

(c) GASTRULA

FIGURE 34-15

Echinoderms undergo the gastrulation process shown here. The blastula is reorganized (a and b), forming the cup-shaped gastrula (c). Other phyla have somewhat different patterns of gastrulation.

associated organs, such as the pancreas and liver. The ectoderm forms the outer layer of the skin, the hair, nails, and the nervous system.

The versatile mesoderm forms a multitude of body parts, including the skeleton, muscles, inner layer of the skin, the circulatory system, and the lining of the body cavity.

PATTERNS OF DEVELOPMENT

A body cavity completely lined by mesoderm is called a **coelom.** Most phyla have a coelom, and, like patterns of symmetry and number of germ layers, the coelom is a feature which taxonomists use to classify animals with similar phylogenetic origins. The distinct patterns of cleavage and coelom formation found in different animal phyla are additional clues to their phylogenetic history.

Blastopore Fate and Cleavage

Recall from Figure 34-5 that echinoderms and chordates share a branch of the phylogenetic tree of animals, and mollusks, annelids, and arthropods share another branch. There are two distinct patterns of development in animals that have a coelom. In the embryos of mollusks, arthropods, and annelids, the blastopore develops into a mouth, and another opening eventually arises and develops into an anus. These organisms are called **protostomes** (PROHT-oh-STOHMZ), which means "first mouth." Many protostomes undergo **spiral cleavage,** in which the cells divide in a spiral arrangement. Each cell in the blastula nestles between two cells of the adjacent row, as is shown in the top left frame of Figure 34-16.

In contrast, in the embryos of echinoderms and chordates, the blastopore develops into an anus, and a second opening in the embryo becomes the mouth. These organisms are called **deuterostomes** (DOOT-uhr-oh-STOHMZ), which means "second mouth." Most deuterostomes undergo **radial cleavage,** in which the cell divisions are parallel to or at right angles to the axis from one pole of the blastula to the other, as shown in the top right frame of Figure 34-16.

Protostomes and deuterostomes also differ in how early the cells of the embryo specialize. If the cells of some protostome embryos are separated at the four-cell stage of development, each cell will develop into only one-fourth of a complete embryo and the developing organism will die. Thus, the path of each cell is determined early in the development of the protostome in a pattern called **determinate cleavage.** In contrast, if the cells of most four-celled deuterostome embryos are separated, each cell will embark on its own path to become a separate organism. This type of development is called **indeterminate cleavage.** Indeterminate cleavage very early in embryo development in humans can result in identical twins.

Protostome Development

SPIRAL CLEAVAGE
(determinate)

Top   Side

SCHIZOCOELY

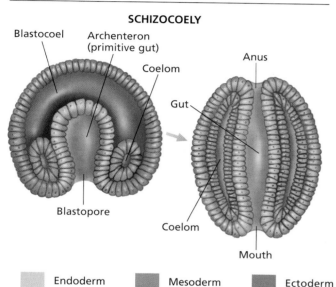

Blastocoel
Archenteron
(primitive gut)
Coelom
Anus
Gut
Blastopore
Coelom
Mouth

Deuterostome Development

RADIAL CLEAVAGE
(indeterminate)

Top   Side

ENTEROCOELY

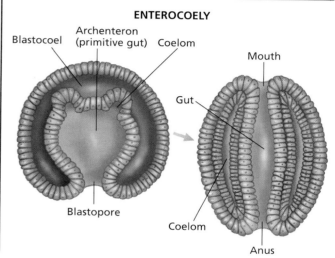

Blastocoel
Archenteron
(primitive gut)   Coelom
Mouth
Gut
Blastopore
Coelom
Anus

Endoderm   Mesoderm   Ectoderm

Coelom Formation

The way in which the coelom forms in many protostomes differs from the way it forms in many deuterostomes. The lower left frame of Figure 34-16 shows coelom formation in protostomes. Cells located at the junction of the endoderm and ectoderm (at the rim of the cup-shaped embryo) split away toward the interior of the gastrula. Rapid division of these cells (shown in pink) in the blastocoel forms the mesoderm. This process of mesoderm formation is called **schizocoely** (SKIZ-oh-SEEL-ee), or "split body cavity."

The lower right frame of Figure 34-16 shows coelom formation in deuterostomes. The mesoderm forms when the cells lining the dorsal, or top, part of the archenteron begin dividing rapidly. These rapidly dividing cells (shown in pink) roll outward into the blastocoel, forming the mesoderm. This process of mesoderm formation is called **enterocoely** (EN-tuhr-oh-SEEL-ee), meaning "gut body cavity." During both enterocoely and schizocoely, mesodermal cells spread out to completely line the coelom, and the blastocoel disappears. Thus, in both protostomes and deuterostomes, mesoderm lines the interior of the outer body wall and surrounds the gut.

FIGURE 34-16

Many protostomes undergo spiral cleavage during early development, while many deuterostomes undergo radial cleavage. In protostomes, the coelom arises by schizocoely, and the blastopore becomes the mouth. In deuterostomes, the coelom arises by enterocoely, and the blastopore becomes the anus.

Ectoderm

Mesoderm

Endoderm

(a) ACOELOMATE   (b) PSEUDOCOELOMATE   (c) COELOMATE

FIGURE 34-17

In three-layered acoelomates (a), the endodermic gut is surrounded by a solid layer of mesoderm. In pseudo-coelomates (b), the endodermic gut is suspended in a fluid-filled cavity which is surrounded by mesoderm. In coelo-mates (c), the endodermic gut is sur-rounded and suspended by mesoderm, which also surrounds the coelom.

Types of Body Cavities

Compare the cross sections of an acoelomate, a pseudocoelomate, and a coelomate shown in Figure 34-17. In **acoelomates** (UH-SEE-luh-mayts), such as flatworms, the body cavity is absent. The interior of the animal is solid, as shown in Figure 34-17a. The endodermic gut, shown in yellow, and the outer covering of the animal, shown in blue, are connected by the solid tissue of the mesoderm.

In some phyla, including rotifers and roundworms, the meso-derm lines the interior of the coelom but does not surround the exterior of the endodermic gut. This type of body cavity, shown in Figure 34-17b, is called a **pseudocoelom** (SOO-doh-SEE-luhm), which means "false body cavity." In **pseudocoelomates,** such as the one shown in Figure 34-17b, mesoderm lines the fluid-filled coelom, and the endodermic gut is suspended in the fluid of the coelom.

In **coelomates** (SEE-luh-MAYTS), animals with a true coelom, such as the one shown in Figure 34-17c, mesoderm lines the body cavity and surrounds and supports the endodermic gut. The mesoderm also forms the tissues of attachment for the organs located in the coelom, such as the liver and the lungs. Mollusks, annelids, arthro-pods, chordates, and echinoderms are coelomates.

Look back at the phylogenetic tree in Figure 34-5 and locate the acoelomate, pseudocoelomate, and coelomate phyla. How does their placement on the phylogenetic tree reflect their body type?

SECTION 34-4 REVIEW

1. Beginning with fertilization, list the steps of development through mesoderm formation.

2. What are the three germ layers formed in all embryos except those of sponges, cnidarians, and ctenophores? Name two body parts that arise from each germ layer.

3. What is a protostome? What is a deuterostome? How does cleavage in these groups differ?

4. Humans and other vertebrates sometimes pro-duce two or more identical offspring. What type of cleavage can result in the formation of identi-cal offspring?

5. How is the mesoderm formed in schizocoely, and how does this process differ from enterocoely?

6. **CRITICAL THINKING**   What adaptive advantage is associated with indeterminate cleavage?

CHAPTER 34 REVIEW

SUMMARY/VOCABULARY

34-1
- Animals are multicellular and heterotrophic, and their cells lack walls. Most animals reproduce sexually and can move.
- Animals have cells that are specialized for different functions.
- Most animals ingest their food and digest it within their bodies.

- Most animals reproduce sexually, though some also reproduce asexually.
- Movement and response to the environment are governed by an animal's nervous tissue and muscle tissue.
- The first animals may have evolved from colonial protists.

Vocabulary

cell junction (667)
differentiation (668)

ingestion (668)
invertebrate (667)

neuron (668)
specialization (667)

vertebrate (667)
zygote (668)

34-2
- Sponges, the simplest animals, have no true tissue and no body symmetry. All other animals have tissue.
- In the bodies of animals with radial symmetry, similar parts branch out in all directions from a central line. Animals with bilateral symmetry have similar halves. Bilateral symmetry is associated with cephalization, that is, having a head.

- Most animals have three germ layers. All body features arise from one of the germ layers.
- At some stage of their lives, all members of phylum Chordata have a notochord, a dorsal nerve cord, a postanal tail, and pharyngeal pouches.

Vocabulary

anterior (670)
bilateral symmetry (670)
cephalization (670)
chordate (673)

dorsal (670)
dorsal nerve cord (673)
germ layer (671)
notochord (673)

pharyngeal pouch (673)
postanal tail (673)
posterior (670)

radial symmetry (670)
symmetry (670)
ventral (670)

34-3
- Invertebrates have no body symmetry or are radially or bilaterally symmetrical; vertebrates are bilaterally symmetrical.
- A segmented body is composed of repeating similar units. Some invertebrates and all vertebrates are segmented.
- Some invertebrates have an exoskeleton. All vertebrates have an endoskeleton.
- The simplest invertebrates have no circulatory system. Arthropods and some mollusks have an open circulatory system. Other mollusks, annelids, and vertebrates have a closed circulatory system.

- Sponges digest food within individual cells. Cnidarians digest food in a central chamber. Other invertebrates and all vertebrates have a gut.
- Some invertebrates have loosely connected circuits of neurons. Some invertebrates and all vertebrates have a well-defined brain.
- Most invertebrates and vertebrates are capable of some form of sexual reproduction, and some invertebrates can also reproduce asexually.

Vocabulary

circulatory system (675)
closed circulatory system (675)
direct development (677)
endoskeleton (677)

exoskeleton (675)
gas exchange (675)
gill (675)
gut (676)
hermaphrodite (676)

indirect development (676)
integument (678)
kidney (678)
larva (676)
lung (678)

open circulatory system (675)
segmentation (674)
vertebra (677)

34-4 ■ During the first cell divisions in the zygote, called cleavage, cells divide repeatedly.
■ The mass of cells produced by cleavage continues to divide, producing the blastula.
■ During gastrula formation, the germ layers —the ectoderm, the endoderm, and in most phyla, the mesoderm—are defined.
■ The endoderm-lined central cavity of the embryo forms the throat passage, gills or lungs, and the gut and its accessory organs.
■ In most protostomes, each cell of the blastula nestles between two cells of adjacent rows; the blastopore develops into the mouth. Separation of cells of the early embryo cause it to die. The mesoderm forms from the division of cells at the junction of the endoderm and the ectoderm in a process called schizocoely.
■ In most deuterostomes, each cell in the blastula rests directly over the cell of the next row, and the blastopore develops into the anus. Separation of cells of the early embryo results in the development of multiple embryos. The mesoderm forms from cell divisions at the top of the archenteron in a process called enterocoely.
■ Acoelomates have no body cavity. Psuedocoelomates have a body cavity partially lined with mesoderm, and coelomates have a coelom.

Vocabulary

acoelomate (686)
archenteron (683)
blastocoel (683)
blastopore (683)
blastula (683)
cleavage (683)

coelom (684)
coelomate (686)
determinate cleavage (684)
deuterostome (684)
ectoderm (683)
endoderm (683)

enterocoely (685)
gastrula (683)
gastrulation (683)
indeterminate cleavage (684)
mesoderm (683)

protostome (684)
pseudocoelom (686)
pseudocoelomate (686)
radial cleavage (684)
schizocoely (685)
spiral cleavage (684)

REVIEW

Vocabulary

1. Distinguish between cell specialization and differentiation.
2. Identify the structures that allow the formation of tissue from many separate cells.
3. Distinguish between radial symmetry and bilateral symmetry.
4. What is the difference between a coelomate and an acoelomate?
5. Compare determinate cleavage with indeterminate cleavage.

Multiple Choice

6. The process that occurs during development in multicellular organisms and leads to cell specialization is (a) asexual reproduction (b) evolution (c) differentiation (d) fertilization
7. Animals must eat because they are (a) not autotrophic (b) not heterotrophic (c) neither autotrophic nor heterotrophic (d) both autotrophic and heterotrophic.
8. Animals that have no true tissues are the (a) chordates (b) ctenophores (c) cnidarians (d) sponges.
9. Fundamental tissue types in the embryo are called (a) notochords (b) germ layers (c) pharyngeal pouches (d) coeloms.
10. Gas exchange in many aquatic phyla takes place in the (a) lungs (b) gut (c) kidneys (d) gills.
11. The repeating units of the backbone are called the (a) integument (b) exoskeleton (c) notochord (d) vertebrae.
12. A feature in vertebrates that is an adaptation to life on land is (a) lungs (b) gills (c) kidneys (d) a gut.
13. The process that takes place as the zygote begins to divide immediately after fertilization is (a) gastrulation (b) cleavage (c) meiosis (d) organ formation.
14. Organisms in which the blastopore develops into the anus are called (a) protostomes (b) gastrulae (c) pseudocoelomates (d) deuterostomes.

15. The process of mesoderm formation by division of the cells at the top of the archenteron is called (a) indeterminate cleavage (b) determinate cleavage (c) schizocoely (d) enterocoely.

Short Answer

16. Explain how neural tissue and muscle tissue work together in an animal's body to allow the animal to respond to its environment.
17. What probable changes did early colonial flagellates undergo as they evolved into the first animals?
18. What can you infer if two phyla are represented on the same branch of a phylogenetic tree?
19. What are four features common to all chordates at some time in their life, and what has happened to two of these features in an adult human?
20. How does indirect development differ from direct development, and which type is found in vertebrates?
21. What happened to the position of the body with respect to the legs as vertebrates adapted to life on land?
22. How do the problems of disposal of body waste differ in terrestrial and aquatic animals?
23. How does the body cavity of a pseudocoelomate differ from that of a coelomate?
24. Name two body parts formed by each of the following: endoderm, mesoderm, and ectoderm.
25. What structure does the archenteron become in a developing animal?

CRITICAL THINKING

1. From the perspective of a single cell, what is one advantage of cell specialization and one disadvantage of cell specialization?
2. Considering that an endoskeleton can support more weight than an exoskeleton, would a large-bodied animal with an exoskeleton be more likely to live in the water or on land? Why?
3. On mammals and birds, the head is positioned higher with respect to the body than it is on amphibians and reptiles. Why might it be helpful to have a head positioned over the body?
4. Observe the body of the animal pictured below, and answer the following questions.
   a. What kind of symmetry does the animal display?
   b. Is it cephalized?
   c. How many germ layers does it have?
   d. How many openings does its digestive system have?
   e. Does it have neurons?

EXTENSION

1. Read "Early Learning" in *New Scientist,* January 29, 2000, on page 6, and answer the following questions: What is the focus of the study by Gilly and Preuss at Hopkins Marine Station in California? What reasons did scientists give for choosing to study squids to find out more about adult humans? How does the behavior of an adult squid differ from the behavior of a juvenile squid in reaction to a mild shock?

2. Some human disorders result from problems in very early stages of embryo development. Research two disorders related to embryonic development, and write a brief report outlining the probable cause of each disorder, the embryonic stage at which the problem occurs, and the physical manifestations of the disorder in the child or adult.

Sheep's Heart Dissection

OBJECTIVES

- Describe the appearance of the external and internal structures of a sheep's heart.
- Name the structures and functions of a sheep's heart.

PROCESS SKILLS

- observing structures
- identifying
- demonstrating

MATERIALS

- sheep's heart
- dissecting tray
- blunt metal probe
- scissors
- scalpel
- tweezers

Background

1. The heart has a left and a right side. It has two upper chambers, the left and right atria, and two lower chambers, the left and right ventricles. Why do multiple chambers result in a more efficient heart?

2. Blood enters the heart from the body through the superior or inferior vena cava. The blood then enters the right atrium and flows through valves into the right ventricle. Blood flows from the right ventricle through the pulmonary artery to the lungs. What process occurs in the lungs?

3. Oxygenated blood flows from the lungs through the pulmonary veins to the left atrium. Then it flows through valves into the thick-walled left ventricle. Blood flows from the left ventricle through the large aorta to the rest of the body.

Procedure

1. In this lab, you will observe the external structure of a sheep's four-chambered heart and dissect the heart to study its internal structure.

2. [icons] Put on safety goggles, gloves, and a lab apron.

3. Place a sheep heart in a dissecting tray. Turn the heart so that the ventral surface is facing you, as shown in the diagram below. Use the diagram of the ventral view to locate the left and right atria, the left and right ventricles, the aorta, the superior and inferior vena cava, and the pulmonary arteries. Turn the heart over. Use the diagram of the dorsal view to locate once again the structures just named, as well as the pulmonary veins.

4. Use a blunt metal probe to explore the blood vessels that lead into and out of the chambers of the heart.

5. Locate a diagonal deposit of fat along the lower two-thirds of the heart. This serves as a guideline to mark the wall between the two ventricles. Use this fatty deposit to guide your incision into the heart.

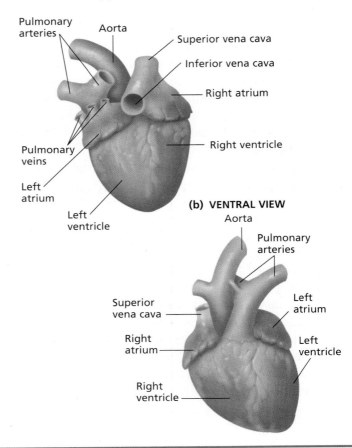

(a) DORSAL VIEW

Pulmonary arteries
Aorta
Superior vena cava
Inferior vena cava
Right atrium
Pulmonary veins
Right ventricle
Left atrium
Left ventricle

(b) VENTRAL VIEW

Aorta
Pulmonary arteries
Superior vena cava
Left atrium
Right atrium
Left ventricle
Right ventricle

6. Follow the cutting diagram below very carefully to study the anatomy of the *right* side of the heart.

7. ◆ Again turn the heart with the ventral surface facing you and the apex pointing downward. Use scissors to cut along line 1. **CAUTION** **Always cut in a direction away from your face and body.** Cut just deep enough to go through the atrial wall. Continue the cut into the right ventricle. With a probe, push open the heart at the cut, and examine the internal structure.

(a) VENTRAL VIEW   **(b) VENTRAL VIEW**

8. Cut along line 2, and extend the cut upward toward the pulmonary artery. Cut just deep enough to go through the ventricle wall. Complete the cut on line 3. Cut downward along the pulmonary artery, around through the wall of the right atrium, and upward along the right superior vena cava.

9. With tweezers, carefully lift the resulting flap to expose the structures underneath.

10. Follow the cutting diagram above very carefully to study the anatomy of the *left* side of the heart.

11. Start to cut on line 4 at the top of the left atrium, and continue into the left ventricle. Cut just deep enough to go through the ventricle wall.

12. Cut on line 5 across the middle of the left ventricle into the aorta. Leave a small margin between this cut and the cut previously made for line 2. Begin to cut on line 6 on the left atrium where cut 4 began. Extend this cut around and through the pulmonary artery upward on the aorta to the right of cut 5.

13. With tweezers, carefully lift up the resulting flap to expose the structure underneath.

14. Observe the thick septum dividing the left and right ventricles. Also note the greater thickness of the walls of the left ventricle.

15. Locate the tricuspid valve between the right atrium and ventricle. Locate the mitral valve between the left atrium and ventricles. Observe that the valves are connected by fibers to the inner surface of the ventricle. Use a probe to explore the openings in the valves.

16. ◆ With a scalpel, cut across a section of the aorta and a section of the vena cava. Compare the thickness of their walls.

17. ◆ Dispose of your materials according to the directions from your teacher.

18. ◆ Clean up your work area and wash your hands before leaving the lab.

Analysis and Conclusions

1. Trace the path of blood from the right atrium to the aorta.

2. Pulmonary circulation carries blood between the heart and the lungs. Systemic circulation carries blood to the rest of the body. In what chambers of the heart does pulmonary circulation begin and end? In what chamber does systemic circulation begin and end?

3. What is the function of the septum separating the left and right ventricles?

4. What is the function of the mitral and tricuspid valves?

5. Why are the walls of the left ventricle thicker than the walls of the right ventricle?

Further Inquiry

The heartbeat originates in a small bundle of tissue in the right atrium. This bundle is the sinoatrial, or S-A, node. Read about the S-A node. What does it do? Why is the S-A node known as the pacemaker?

SPONGES, CNIDARIANS, AND CTENOPHORES

Delicate polyps of Monet's tube coral, Dendrophyllia gracilis, extend from a hard skeleton.

FOCUS CONCEPT: *Stability and Homeostasis*

As you read, notice how specialized functions related to feeding, reproduction, and other activities are performed in animals with simple body plans and few or no organs.

35-1 *Porifera*

35-2 *Cnidaria and Ctenophora*

PORIFERA

Invertebrates are animals that do not have a backbone. Rather than being classified according to shared characteristics, invertebrates are an arbitrary classification of extremely diverse animals that share the absence of a characteristic. Invertebrates comprise more than a dozen phyla and more than a million species. About 97 percent of all animal species known are invertebrates, among the simplest of which are sponges.

SECTION

35-1

OBJECTIVES

▲

Define *invertebrates*, and explain why they are such a diverse group.

●

Describe the basic body plan of a sponge.

■

Describe the process of filter feeding in sponges.

◆

Contrast the processes of sexual and asexual reproduction in sponges.

STRUCTURE AND FUNCTION OF SPONGES

Sponges are aquatic animals that make up the phylum Porifera (pohr-IF-uhr-uh). These simple organisms clearly represent the transition from unicellular to multicellular life. Sponges have no gastrula stage, exhibit less cell specialization than most other animals, and have no true tissues or organs. There are about 10,000 species of sponges. About 150 species live in fresh water, while the rest are marine.

Early biologists thought sponges were plants, and most sponges do resemble plants in some ways. Adult sponges are **sessile,** which means they attach themselves firmly to a surface and do not move. Sponges grow in many shapes, sizes, and colors, and they often look like mossy mats, cactuses, or blobs of fungus. They can be as small as 1 cm (0.4 in.) in length or as large as 2 m (6.6 ft) in diameter.

Body Plan

The basic body plan of a sponge, as shown in Figure 35-1, suggests many relationships between structure and function. The body wall consists of two layers of cells separated by a jellylike substance. In simple sponges, the body wall surrounds a hollow cylinder that is closed at the bottom and open at the top. The interior of the cylinder is lined with **collar cells.** By beating their flagella, collar cells draw water into the sponge through numerous pores that penetrate the body wall. In fact, the name *Porifera* comes from a Latin word meaning "pore-bearer." The water that is pumped into the interior of the sponge leaves through the **osculum** (AHS-kyoo-luhm), the opening at the top of the sponge that you can see in Figure 35-1.

A sponge would collapse without some type of supporting structure. In some sponges, support is provided by a simple skeleton made of a network of protein fibers called **spongin** (SPUHN-jin). Other sponges have skeletons consisting of **spicules,** tiny, hard particles

internetconnect

*SCi*LINKS NSTA

TOPIC: Sponges
GO TO: www.scilinks.org
KEYWORD: HM693

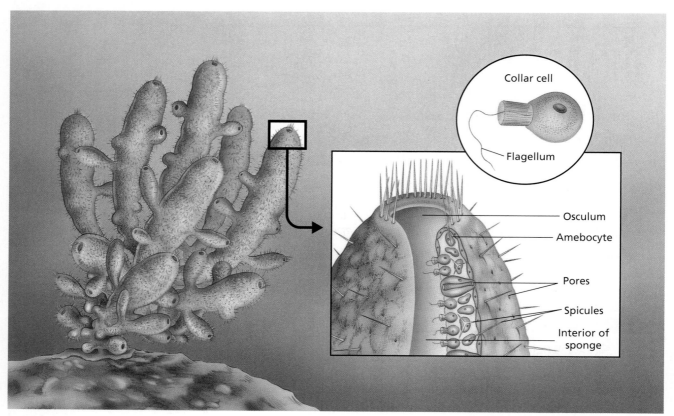

Collar cell

Flagellum

Osculum

Amebocyte

Pores

Spicules

Interior of sponge

FIGURE 35-1

The body of a sponge is a hollow cylinder. Water is drawn into the cylinder through many small pores and exits through the opening at the top of the sponge, called the osculum.

of calcium carbonate or silicon dioxide that are often shaped like spikes. Calcium carbonate is one of the compounds that give bones and teeth their hardness, and silicon dioxide is the major component of glass and quartz. Still other sponges have a combination of spongin and spicules. Differences in the composition of the skeleton have enabled biologists to divide sponges into three classes.

Feeding and Digestion

Because they are sessile, sponges cannot pursue their food. Instead, most sponges feed by screening food out of the water that the collar cells pump through their body. This feeding method is called **filter feeding.** The food of such sponges includes bacteria, protozoans, unicellular algae, and bits of organic matter. However, scientists have discovered one species of sponge that uses movable filaments covered with hooked spicules to snare small shrimp. The shrimp are then absorbed into the sponge's body.

The food that a sponge collects is engulfed and digested by collar cells. Nutrients then pass from the collar cells to other cells that crawl about within the body wall, bringing the nutrients to the rest of the body. Scientists call these crawling cells **amebocytes** (uh-MEE-buh-siets) because they resemble amoebas. Locate the amebocytes in Figure 35-1. This procedure for distributing food shows how sponges are related to their protozoan ancestors. Carbon dioxide and other wastes produced by the sponge's cells diffuse into the water passing through the sponge. The water carries these wastes away as it flows out through the osculum.

Word Roots and Origins

amebocyte

from the Greek *amoibe,* meaning "change," and *kytos,* meaning "hollow vessel"

Reproduction

Sponges can reproduce asexually by forming small buds that break off and live separately. The sponge illustrated in Figure 35-1 has many buds that are still attached. During droughts or cold weather, some freshwater sponges produce internal buds called **gemmules** (JEM-yoolz). Each gemmule is a food-filled ball of amebocytes surrounded by a protective coat made of organic material and spicules. Gemmules can survive harsh conditions that may kill the adult sponge that formed them. When conditions improve, the sponge cells emerge from the gemmules and grow into new sponges.

Sponges also have remarkable powers of **regeneration,** the ability to regrow missing parts. In fact, a small piece of a sponge can regenerate a complete new sponge. In some species, even particles small enough to pass through a cloth strainer can regenerate.

Sponges can also reproduce sexually. As you can see in Figure 35-2, sperm released into the water from one sponge enter the pores of another sponge. Collar cells in the second sponge engulf the sperm and transfer them to amebocytes, which carry the sperm to an egg. After the egg is fertilized, it develops into a larva. A larva is an immature stage of an animal that is usually very different in form from the adult. Flagella on the larva's surface enable the larva to leave the parent sponge and swim about as it is carried along by the current. Eventually, the larva settles and attaches to an object. Its cells then reorganize to form an adult sponge.

Some species of sponges have separate sexes, but in most species each individual produces both eggs and sperm. Any individual organism that produces both eggs and sperm is called a hermaphrodite (her-MAF-roh-diet). Self-fertilization rarely, if ever, occurs in hermaphroditic species. Instead, the sperm of one individual usually fertilize the eggs of another individual. Since all hermaphrodites produce eggs, the chances of successful fertilization are greater than they would be if only half of the population (females) produced eggs. Hermaphroditism is common in many invertebrates that are sessile, that move slowly, or that live in low-density populations.

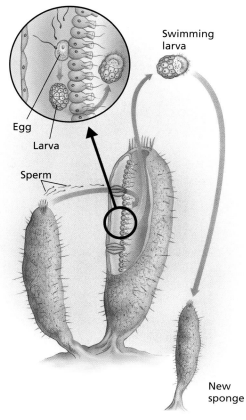

Swimming larva

Egg

Larva

Sperm

New sponge

FIGURE 35-2

The union of a sponge egg and sperm ultimately results in a swimming larva that escapes from the parent sponge and grows into a new individual.

SECTION 35-1 REVIEW

1. Define *invertebrate.* Why is it not surprising that a group defined in this way includes a wide diversity of species?

2. What is the difference between spongin and spicules? What function do they both perform?

3. Describe how most sponges feed.

4. How do gemmules help some freshwater sponges survive unfavorable conditions?

5. What role do amebocytes play in the sexual reproduction of sponges?

6. CRITICAL THINKING Since sponges are sessile animals, how is it possible for a population of sponges to spread out into a larger area?

SECTION

35-2

OBJECTIVES

▲

Name and describe the two
body forms of cnidarians.

●

Describe the common
characteristics of cnidarians.

■

Identify the three classes
of cnidarians, and give an
example of each.

◆

Describe the common
characteristics of ctenophores.

CNIDARIA AND CTENOPHORA

*Cnidaria (nie-DER-ee-uh) and Ctenophora (tee-NAHF-uhr-uh)
are two phyla of radially symmetrical invertebrates. The
animals in these phyla are somewhat more complex than the
sponges. Their cells are organized into tissues, and they have
a few simple organs. All members of the phyla Cnidaria and
Ctenophora are aquatic, and most live in the ocean.*

STRUCTURE AND FUNCTION OF CNIDARIANS

Tiny freshwater hydra, stinging jellyfish, and flowerlike coral all
belong to the phylum Cnidaria. Animals in this phylum are called
cnidarians. As you can see in Figure 35-3, the body of a cnidarian may
be either vase-shaped or bell-shaped. The vase-shaped form, called a
polyp (PAHL-ip), is specialized for a sessile existence. In contrast, the
bell-shaped **medusa** (me-DOO-suh) is specialized for swimming.

Figure 35-3 also shows that all cnidarians have bodies constructed of two cell layers—an outer **epidermis** and an inner **gastrodermis.** Between these layers is a jellylike material known as
mesoglea (mez-uh-GLEE-uh). In the center of the body is a hollow gut
called the **gastrovascular cavity,** which has a single opening, or
mouth. Surrounding the mouth are numerous flexible extensions
called **tentacles.**

FIGURE 35-3

The contrasting forms of medusae and
polyps result from different arrangements of the same body parts.

Tentacle

Mouth

Epidermis

Mesoglea

Gastrovascular
cavity

Gastrodermis

Tentacle

Mouth

MEDUSA

POLYP

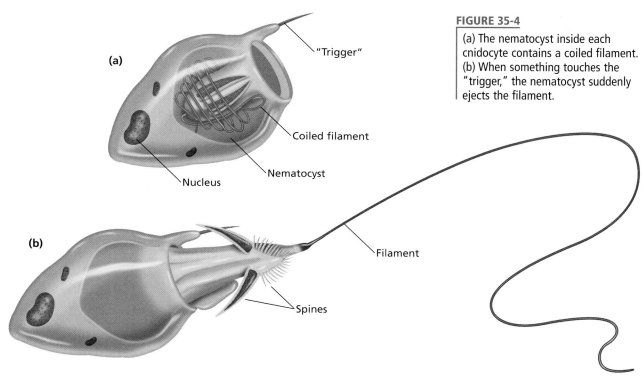

"Trigger"

(a)

Coiled filament

Nematocyst

Nucleus

(b)

Filament

Spines

FIGURE 35-4

(a) The nematocyst inside each cnidocyte contains a coiled filament. (b) When something touches the "trigger," the nematocyst suddenly ejects the filament.

Feeding and Defense

One of the distinguishing features of cnidarians is the presence of **cnidocytes** (NIE-duh-siets), which give the phylum its name. Cnidocytes are specialized cells used for defense and capturing prey. Figure 35-4 reveals that each cnidocyte contains an organelle called a **nematocyst** (nuh-MAT-uh-sist), which has a long filament coiled up inside it. In some cnidarians, the cnidocytes are concentrated in the epidermis, especially on the tentacles. When an object brushes against the "trigger" on a cnidocyte, the nematocyst inside it suddenly pushes the filament out of the cell with great force. Some nematocysts have filaments with sharp tips and spines that puncture the object and inject poison. Others have filaments that adhere to the object by wrapping around it.

The relationship between structure and function is clearly seen in the way cnidarians feed. The tentacles capture small animals with their nematocysts and paralyze them with the poison they inject. The tentacles then push the prey into the gastrovascular cavity through the mouth. After enzymes inside the gastrovascular cavity break up the prey, cells lining the cavity absorb the nutrients. Undigested food and waste are expelled through the mouth.

Nervous System

The nervous system in cnidarians is composed of a diffuse web of interconnected nerve cells called a **nerve net.** In many cnidarians, like the polyp shown in Figure 35-5, the nerve net is distributed uniformly throughout the entire body. There is no brain or similar structure that controls the rest of the nerve net. In the medusa form of some cnidarians, however, some of the nerve cells are clustered in rings around the edge of the bell-shaped body.

FIGURE 35-5

The interconnected nerve cells in the nerve net of this cnidarian coordinate the animal's responses to its environment.

Nerve cells

FIGURE 35-6

Obelia (a) and *Physalia,* the Portuguese man-of-war (b), are two examples of colonial hydrozoans. *Obelia* consists solely of polyps, while *Physalia* is made of both polyps and medusae. (*Obelia:* LM 13×)

The nerve net enables cnidarians to respond to specific stimuli in their environment. For example, when cells in the epidermis are touched, they relay a signal to nerve cells. The nerve cells, in turn, transmit a signal via the nerve net to contractile cells, which can cause the animal to withdraw from the stimulus. In cnidarians with the simplest nerve nets, a stimulus anywhere on the body causes signals to be sent through the nerve net in all directions. These signals bring about a contraction of the entire body.

The nerve net also coordinates the complex activities of the body that are necessary for feeding and traveling through the environment. The movements by which the tentacles bring prey to the mouth and push it into the gastrovascular cavity are controlled by the nerve net, as are the rhythmic contractions of the body that propel swimming medusae through the water.

Classification

Scientists divide cnidarians into three classes—Hydrozoa, Scyphozoa, and Anthozoa—and the members of these classes are known as hydrozoans, scyphozoans, and anthozoans, respectively. Some species of hydrozoans live only as polyps, some live only as medusae, some alternate between these two forms, and some live as mixed colonies of polyps and medusae. Scyphozoans spend most of their lives as medusae, while anthozoans live only as polyps.

CLASS HYDROZOA

The class Hydrozoa includes about 3,700 species, most of which live as colonial organisms in the oceans. One example of a colonial hydrozoan is *Obelia.* As Figure 35-6a illustrates, *Obelia* has many polyps attached to branched stalks. Some of the polyps function in gathering food, while others are responsible for reproduction.

Perhaps the most remarkable hydrozoan is the Portuguese man-of-war, *Physalia,* shown in Figure 35-6b. This hydrozoan exists as a colony of medusae and polyps. Its gas-filled float, which can

(a)

(b)

measure as much as 30 cm (1 ft) across, keeps the colony at the surface of the ocean. The polyps in the colony are specialized for feeding, digestion, or sexual reproduction. Tentacles up to 20 m (65 ft) long dangle from the feeding polyps and carry large numbers of cnidocytes. The Portuguese man-of-war preys mostly on small fish, but its cnidocytes contain a poison that can be painful and even fatal to humans.

Hydras

One hydrozoan that has been extensively studied is the hydra. Hydras are not typical hydrozoans because they exist only as polyps, they are not colonial, and they live in fresh water. Hydras range from 1 to 4 cm (0.4 to 1.6 in.) in length. Most hydras are white or brown, but some, like the one shown in Figure 35-7, appear green because of the algae that live symbiotically inside cells of their gastrodermis. Hydras can be found in quiet ponds, lakes, and streams. They attach themselves to rocks or water plants by means of a sticky secretion produced by cells at the hydra's base.

A hydra can leave one place of attachment and move to another. This can happen when the base secretes bubbles of gas, which cause the hydra to float upside down on the surface of the water. Hydras can also move by somersaulting. This peculiar movement occurs when the tentacles and the mouth end bend over and touch the bottom while the base pulls free.

During warm weather, hydras generally reproduce asexually. Small buds, like the one you can see in Figure 35-8, develop on the outside of the hydra's body. These buds grow their own tentacles and then separate from the body and begin living independently.

Sexual reproduction usually occurs in the fall, when low temperatures trigger the development of eggs and sperm. The eggs are produced by meiosis along the body wall in swellings called

FIGURE 35-7

The green color of this hydra, *Chlorohydra viridissima,* comes from the algae that live inside the hydra's cells. (LM 30×)

TOPIC: Hydra
GO TO: www.scilinks.org
KEYWORD: HM699

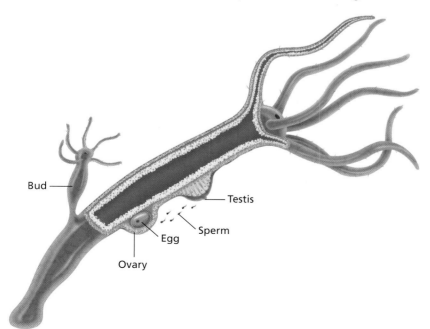

Bud

Testis

Egg

Sperm

Ovary

FIGURE 35-8

Hydras can reproduce either asexually, by forming buds, or sexually, by producing sperm that fertilize eggs.

ovaries. Motile sperm are formed by meiosis in similar swellings called **testes.** In some species, eggs and sperm are produced in the same hermaphroditic individual, as indicated in Figure 35-8. In other species, the individuals are either male or female. In either case, sperm are released into the water, and those that reach ovaries can fertilize egg cells. Each fertilized egg then divides and grows into an embryo. A hard covering protects the embryo through the winter, and in the spring the embryo hatches out and develops into a new hydra.

CLASS SCYPHOZOA

The name *Scyphozoa* (sie-foh-ZOH-uh) means "cup animals," which describes the medusa, the dominant form of the life cycle of this class. There are more than 200 species of scyphozoans, known commonly as jellyfish. The cups of the medusae range from 2 cm (0.8 in.) to 4 m (13 ft) across, and some species have tentacles that are several meters long. Pulsating motions of the cup propel the jellyfish through the water. Like the Portuguese man-of-war, some jellyfish carry poisonous nematocysts that can cause severe pain and even death in humans.

The common jellyfish *Aurelia* is a scyphozoan whose life cycle includes both medusa and polyp forms. As you can see in Figure 35-9, adult medusae release sperm and eggs into the water, where fertilization occurs. The resulting zygote divides many times to form a blastula. The blastula then develops into a ciliated larva called a **planula** (PLAN-yuh-luh), which attaches to the ocean bottom. The planula becomes a polyp by developing a mouth and tentacles at the unattached end. As the polyp grows, it forms a stack of medusae that detach and develop into free-swimming jellyfish.

FIGURE 35-9

The common jellyfish *Aurelia* reproduces when sperm from an adult male medusa fertilize eggs from an adult female medusa. Each fertilized egg produces a blastula, which develops into a larva known as a planula. The planula forms a polyp, which produces more medusae.

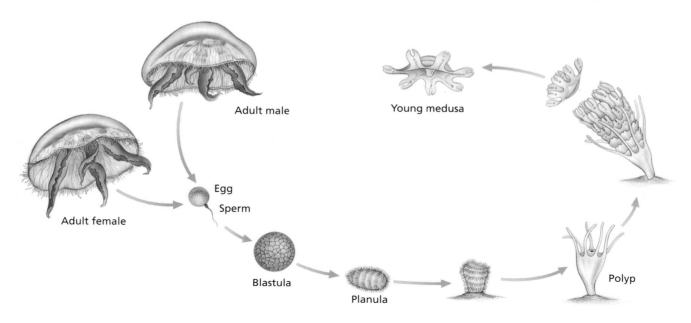

Adult male

Young medusa

Adult female

Egg
Sperm

Blastula

Planula

Polyp

CLASS ANTHOZOA

The name *Anthozoa* means "flower animals," which is a fitting description for the approximately 6,100 marine species in this class. Two examples of anthozoans are sea anemones and corals, which are shown in Figure 35-10.

Sea anemones are polyps commonly found in coastal areas, where they attach themselves to rocks and other submerged objects. Anemones feed on fishes and other animals that swim within reach of their tentacles. However, some anemones in the Pacific Ocean have a symbiotic relationship with the clownfish, as Figure 35-11 demonstrates. The two animals share food and protect each other from predators. The movements of the clownfish also help prevent sediments from burying the anemone. For reasons that are not entirely clear, the anemone does not fire its nematocysts when the clownfish touches its tentacles.

Corals are small polyps that usually live in colonies. Each polyp cements its calcium carbonate skeleton to the skeletons of adjoining polyps in the colony. When the polyps die, their hardened skeletons remain, serving as the foundation for new polyps. Over thousands of years, these polyps build up large, rocklike formations known as **coral reefs.** Only the top layer of the reef contains the living polyps. Coral reefs provide food and shelter for an enormous and colorful variety of fishes and invertebrates.

Coral reefs are restricted to a band of ocean within 30 degrees north or south of the equator. They form only at shallow depths in warm, clear waters. These conditions are necessary in order for photosynthesis to be carried out by algae that live symbiotically inside the coral cells. The corals depend on the algae to provide oxygen and to speed up the accumulation of calcium from the sea water. The algae in turn depend on the corals to supply vital nutrients.

(a)

(b)

FIGURE 35-10

Anthozoans, including this crimson anemone, *Cribrinopsis fernaldi* (a), and this golden cup coral, *Tubastraea* (b), live as polyps along ocean coasts.

FIGURE 35-11

The clownfish, *Amphiprion ocellaris*, lives symbiotically among the tentacles of sea anemones. The anemone's stinging tentacles protect the clownfish from predators. The clownfish, in turn, drives away other fish that try to feed on the anemone.

PHYLUM CTENOPHORA

The phylum Ctenophora includes about 100 species of marine animals known as ctenophores. A typical ctenophore is shown in Figure 35-12. The name *Ctenophora* means "comb holder" and refers to the eight comblike rows of cilia that run along the outside of the animal. Because ctenophores resemble jellyfish, they are often called comb jellies.

Ctenophores differ from jellyfish and other cnidarians in several ways. Rather than pulsating like jellyfish, they move through the water by beating their cilia. They are the largest organisms to move in this fashion. Also, most ctenophores do not have cnidocytes. Instead, they have cells called **colloblasts,** which secrete a sticky substance that binds to their prey. Colloblasts are usually located on two tentacles. Ctenophores also have a sensory structure called an **apical organ** at one end of their body. This organ enables a ctenophore to sense its orientation in the water. Nerves running from the apical organ coordinate the beating of the cilia. Most ctenophores are hermaphroditic.

One of the most striking features of ctenophores is their **bioluminescence** (BIE-oh-LOO-muh-NES-ens), or production of light. Bioluminescent ctenophores often occur in large swarms near the surface of the ocean, creating a spectacular display at night.

FIGURE 35-12

A ctenophore, *Pleurobrachia pileus,* moves through the water by beating its cilia, trailing its two long tentacles behind it.

SECTION 35-2 REVIEW

1. What are the two basic body forms a cnidarian may have?

2. What are three characteristics that all cnidarians have in common?

3. Name the three classes of cnidarians, and give an example of each.

4. Describe two examples of symbiosis found among cnidarians.

5. Describe three characteristics of ctenophores.

6. **CRITICAL THINKING** For a cnidarian, what might be the advantage of having a life cycle consisting of both medusae and polyps, instead of just polyps?

SUMMARY/VOCABULARY

35-1
- Invertebrates, animals without a backbone, are a diverse group of over a million species.
- The phylum Porifera is made up of sponges, sessile invertebrates that have no true tissues or organs. The simplest sponges are hollow cylinders.
- The body wall of a sponge is composed of two layers of cells. The body is supported by a skeleton made of spongin, spicules, or both.
- Collar cells lining the inside of a sponge beat their flagella, drawing a current of water into the sponge through pores in the body wall. Water leaves through the osculum, an opening at the top of the sponge.
- Sponges feed by filtering small organisms and organic matter out of the water that passes through their body. Nutrients are distributed through the body by amebocytes, which crawl about within the body wall.
- Sponges can reproduce asexually, through budding or regeneration, as well as sexually. Most sponges are hermaphroditic, meaning that a single animal can produce both eggs and sperm.

Vocabulary

amebocyte (694)	gemmule (695)	sessile (693)	spongin (693)
collar cell (693)	osculum (693)	spicule (693)	
filter feeding (694)	regeneration (695)	sponge (693)	

35-2
- Animals in the phylum Cnidaria can be either sessile polyps or swimming medusae. Some cnidarians alternate between polyp and medusa stages during their life cycles.
- The body of a cnidarian consists of two cell layers—an outer epidermis and an inner gastrodermis—separated by a jellylike mesoglea.
- Cnidarians have cells called cnidocytes, which contain organelles known as nematocysts. When a cnidocyte is stimulated, its nematocyst ejects a filament that can paralyze or ensnare prey.
- Cnidarians feed by capturing small animals with their nematocysts and pushing the animals into their gastrovascular cavity with their tentacles.
- The cnidarian nervous system is a diffuse web of interconnected nerve cells called a nerve net.
- The three classes of cnidarians are Hydrozoa (which includes animals such as the hydra), Scyphozoa (jellyfish), and Anthozoa (which includes sea anemones and corals).
- Hydrozoans may live as polyps, medusae, or mixed colonies of polyps and medusae. Scyphozoans spend most of their lives as medusae. Anthozoans live only as polyps.
- Animals in the phylum Ctenophora move through the water by beating the cilia that occur in eight rows on the outside of their body.
- Ctenophores capture prey with a sticky substance secreted by cells called colloblasts, which are usually located on a pair of tentacles.
- An apical organ at one end of the body enables ctenophores to sense their orientation in the water. Most ctenophores are hermaphroditic and bioluminescent.

Vocabulary

apical organ (702)	epidermis (696)	mesoglea (696)	planula (700)
bioluminescence (702)	gastrodermis (696)	nematocyst (697)	polyp (696)
cnidocyte (697)	gastrovascular cavity (696)	nerve net (697)	tentacle (696)
colloblast (702)	medusa (696)	ovary (700)	testis (700)
coral reef (701)			

REVIEW

Vocabulary

1. Explain why *Porifera* is a good name for the phylum of sponges.
2. Explain how sponges feed. What term describes this method of feeding?
3. Describe and name the two body forms of cnidarians. For each body form, give an example of a cnidarian that has that form.
4. What is the difference between a cnidocyte and a nematocyst?
5. What is the function of a ctenophore's apical organ?

Multiple Choice

6. All invertebrates (a) live in water (b) have tentacles (c) have no backbone (d) are hermaphrodites.
7. A hydra shows (a) asymmetry (b) spherical symmetry (c) radial symmetry (d) bilateral symmetry.
8. The structures that propel ctenophores through the water are (a) rows of cilia (b) colloblasts (c) apical organs (d) polyps.
9. Spongin and spicules are important to a sponge because they (a) trap food (b) provide support (c) remove wastes (d) produce offspring.
10. Both feeding and sexual reproduction in sponges involve (a) gemmules and collar cells (b) spicules and gemmules (c) amebocytes and spongin (d) collar cells and amebocytes.
11. The primary basis for classifying sponges is (a) their shape (b) their color (c) the composition of their skeleton (d) the method by which they reproduce.
12. Characteristics of cnidarians include all of the following *except* (a) nematocysts (b) collar cells (c) gastrovascular cavity (d) tentacles.
13. The cnidarian body form that is specialized for swimming is called a (a) medusa (b) polyp (c) planula (d) blastula.
14. The movements of cnidarians are coordinated by their (a) mesoglea (b) nematocysts (c) nerve net (d) gastrodermis.

15. Colloblasts are (a) cells that draw water through sponges (b) cells that secrete a sticky substance in ctenophores (c) stages in the life cycle of a jellyfish (d) medusae that live in colonies.

Short Answer

16. Describe three ways that sponges represent the transition from unicellular to multicellular life.
17. How does a cnidarian capture and ingest its prey?
18. Describe the path of water through a sponge, and explain what causes water to flow through a sponge.
19. How is a sponge's usual method of feeding suited to its sessile lifestyle?
20. Describe the specialization that is found among the individuals that make up a Portuguese man-of-war.
21. Describe the process of sexual reproduction in sponges.
22. What benefit does a sea anemone obtain from its symbiotic relationship with a clownfish? What benefit does the clownfish obtain from this relationship?
23. Why do coral reefs form only at shallow depths?
24. Describe two ways that ctenophores differ from cnidarians.
25. In the diagram of a hydra shown below, identify the cell layers labeled A and B, the material between them labeled C, and the cell labeled D.

CRITICAL THINKING

1. Radial symmetry is found only among animals that live in water. Why is radial symmetry better suited to animals that live in water than to animals that live on land?

2. A hermaphroditic sponge generally produces eggs and sperm at different times. Based on your knowledge of sexual reproduction, why do you think it is evolutionarily advantageous for a sponge not to produce eggs and sperm at the same time?

3. Compare and contrast the life cycle of *Aurelia* with alternation of generations in mosses, which you studied in Chapter 32. Be sure to list similarities and differences.

4. Hydras generally reproduce asexually during warm weather and sexually in the fall. Based on what you have learned about the hydra embryo, what do you think is the advantage to the hydra of reproducing sexually when the weather turns cool?

5. Sponge larvae have flagella on the outside of their body, whereas adult sponges have flagella in their internal cavity. How is this structural difference related to functional differences between the larval and adult stages in the life cycle of a sponge?

6. A single species of sponge may assume different appearances due to differences in substrate, availability of space, and the velocity and temperature of water currents. How might these factors make the classification of sponges confusing? What features besides outward appearance can biologists use to classify sponges and eliminate some of this confusion?

7. What would happen to a coral reef if pollution or sediment caused the water around the reef to become less clear? Explain your answer.

8. The pie chart below shows the relative numbers of species in each class of the phylum Cnidaria. Which segment of the chart represents scyphozoans? How do you know?

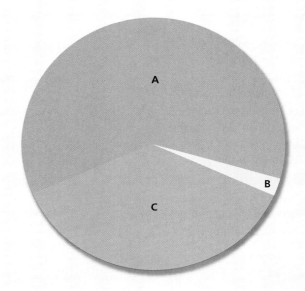

EXTENSION

1. Read "Transparent Animals" in *Scientific American,* February 2000, on pp. 80–89. Describe some of the survival benefits of having a body made of gelatinous material that is nearly transparent. What is the major drawback to having a transparent and gelatinous body? Why is scooping these organisms up from the depths of the ocean using large nets almost impossible?

2. Create a chart that summarizes information about all of the phyla you will study in this unit. Use headings such as Symmetry, Feeding and Digestion, Reproduction, and Habitats. Begin your chart by filling in the information for the phyla Porifera, Cnidaria, and Ctenophora. Continue your chart as you work through the unit.

3. Natural sponges are preferred to synthetic ones for some uses, such as in surgery. Find out what methods are used to gather and prepare sponges for use by surgeons and others. Write a report based on your findings, and present it to your class.

4. Research the most common ways to neutralize a jellyfish sting. Investigate why these treatments are effective, and present the information to the class.

Observing Hydra Behavior

OBJECTIVES

- Observe live specimens of hydra.
- Determine how hydras respond to different stimuli.
- Determine how hydras capture and feed on prey.

PROCESS SKILLS

- observing
- relating structure to function

MATERIALS

- silicone culture gum
- microscope slide
- hydra culture
- 2 medicine droppers
- compound microscope
- methylene blue solution
- vinegar
- stereomicroscope
- filter paper cut into pennant shapes
- forceps
- concentrated beef broth
- *Daphnia* culture

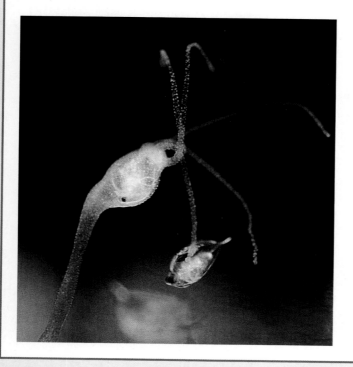

Background

1. How do animals respond to stimuli in their environment?
2. What is a hydra?
3. What characteristics do hydras share with other cnidarians?
4. How does a sessile animal, such as a hydra, obtain food?
5. What is a nematocyst?

PART A   Close-up Examination of a Hydra

1. **CAUTION Slides break easily. Use care when handling them.** Using a long piece of silicone culture gum, make a circular "well" on a microscope slide, as shown in the illustration below.

Silicone culture gum

2. **CAUTION You will be working with a live animal. Be sure to treat it gently and to follow directions carefully.** With a medicine dropper, gently transfer a hydra from the culture dish to the well on the slide, making sure the hydra is in water. The hydra should be transferred quickly; otherwise, it may attach itself to the medicine dropper. Allow the hydra to settle. As you go through the following steps, add water to the slide periodically to replace water that has evaporated, and keep the hydra wet.

3. Examine the hydra under the low-power setting of a compound microscope. Add a drop of methylene blue solution to the well containing the hydra to make the tentacles more visible. Identify and draw the hydra's body stalk, mouth, and tentacles in your lab report.

4. In your lab report, make a data table like the one shown on the next page. As you complete the following steps, record your observations in your data table.

5. As you continue to observe the hydra at low power, add a drop of vinegar to the well. What happens to

the bumps on the tentacles? These bumps are cnidocytes. Is vinegar a normal part of a hydra's diet? Why do you think vinegar is used in this step?

6. Transfer the hydra to the culture dish labeled "Used hydras." Rinse the well on your microscope slide with water to remove all traces of methylene blue and vinegar.

PART B   Feeding Behavior

7. Hydras eat small invertebrates, such as *Daphnia*. With a medicine dropper, gently transfer another hydra to the well on your slide. Then transfer live *Daphnia* to the well in the same manner.

8. Observe the hydra carefully with the high-power setting of the stereomicroscope. Watch for threadlike nematocysts shooting out from the hydra. Some nematocysts release a poison that paralyzes prey. If the hydra does not respond after a few minutes, obtain another hydra from the culture dish and repeat this procedure. Do you think the hydra's response is triggered by water vibrations, by chemicals that *Daphnia* releases, or by *Daphnia* touching the hydra?

9. Observe the way the hydra captures and ingests *Daphnia,* and record your observations in your data table. How long does it take for a hydra to ingest a *Daphnia*?

10. Transfer the hydra to the culture dish labeled "Used hydras." Rinse the well on your microscope slide with water to remove the *Daphnia*.

PART C   Response to Stimuli

11. Transfer another hydra to the well on your slide, and examine it with the high-power setting of the stereomicroscope. Using forceps, move the long tip of a pennant-shaped piece of filter paper near the hydra's tentacles. Be careful not to touch the hydra with the filter paper. Observe the hydra's response to the filter paper, and record your observations in your data table.

12. Now observe how the hydra responds to a chemical stimulus. Dip the same piece of filter paper in beef broth, and repeat the procedure in step 11. Again, be careful not to touch the hydra. Record the hydra's response to the beef broth in your data table.

13. Finally, investigate how the hydra responds to touch. Using the long tip of a clean pennant-shaped piece of filter paper, touch the hydra's tentacles, mouth, and body stalk. **CAUTION Touch the hydra gently.** Record your observations in your data table.

14. Transfer the hydra to the culture dish labeled "Used hydras." Clean up your materials and wash your hands before leaving the lab.

Analysis and Conclusions

1. Based on your observations, how do you think a hydra behaves when it is threatened in its natural habitat?
2. Describe a hydra's feeding behavior.
3. What happens to food that has not been digested by a hydra?
4. What was the purpose of using the clean filter paper in step 11?
5. Did the hydra show a feeding response or a defensive response to the beef broth? Explain.
6. How is a hydra adapted to a sessile lifestyle?
7. How is the feeding method of a hydra different from that of a sponge?

Further Inquiry

Design an experiment to determine how hydras respond to other stimuli, such as light.

OBSERVATIONS OF HYDRA BEHAVIOR	
Behavior	**Observations**
Response to vinegar	
Feeding behavior	
Response to filter paper	
Response to beef broth on filter paper	
Response to touch with filter paper	

CHAPTER 36

FLATWORMS, ROUNDWORMS, AND ROTIFERS

Many of the internal organs of this rotifer are visible through its transparent skin. (LM 675×)

FOCUS CONCEPT: *Matter, Energy, and Organization*

As you read, note the increased complexity of body plans in these phyla compared with those of sponges, cnidarians, and ctenophores. Also notice how organisms are modified for a free-living or parasitic way of life.

36-1 *Platyhelminthes*

36-2 *Nematoda and Rotifera*

PLATYHELMINTHES

*M*embers of the phylum Platyhelminthes (*PLAT-ee-hel-MINTH-eez*) are called **flatworms.** Their bodies develop from three germ layers and are more complex than those of sponges, cnidarians, and ctenophores. Flatworms have bilaterally symmetrical bodies, with dorsal and ventral surfaces, right and left sides, and anterior and posterior ends.

OBJECTIVES

▲

State the distinguishing characteristics of flatworms.

●

Describe the anatomy of a planarian.

■

Compare and contrast free-living and parasitic flatworms.

◆

Diagram the life cycle of a fluke.

▲

Describe the life cycle of a tapeworm.

STRUCTURE AND FUNCTION OF FLATWORMS

Flatworms are the simplest animals with bilateral symmetry. You learned in Chapter 34 that the tissues in bilaterally symmetrical animals develop from three germ layers: ectoderm, mesoderm, and endoderm. In flatworms, the three germ layers are pressed against one another to form a solid body. Since flatworms do not have a hollow cavity between the endoderm and the mesoderm, they belong to a group of animals known as acoelomates, a name that means "without a hollow."

The acoelomate body plan gives flatworms the thin, flat bodies for which they are named. This body shape ensures that no cell in a flatworm is very far from the animal's external environment. Thus, the cells can exchange oxygen and carbon dioxide directly with the environment through diffusion, allowing flatworms to survive without a circulatory system or respiratory system. Like cnidarians, most flatworms have a gastrovascular cavity, a gut with a single opening. Food is taken in and digested in the gastrovascular cavity, and any undigested material is eliminated through the same opening. Most of the sensory organs and nerve cells of flatworms, such as the marine species shown in Figure 36-1, are located at the anterior end of the body. As you learned in Chapter 34, this characteristic is known as cephalization.

The more than 18,000 species of flatworms are divided into three classes: Turbellaria, Trematoda, and Cestoda. Trematodes and cestodes (SES-tohdz) live as parasites on or inside other animals, whereas almost all turbellarians are nonparasitic, or free-living. Parasites probably evolved from free-living organisms. As they evolved, some organs that were advantageous to free living became modified for parasitism, while others were lost entirely. Thus, parasitic flatworms are structurally simpler than their free-living relatives.

FIGURE 36-1

Many of the sensory organs in this marine flatworm, *Euryletta,* are concentrated in the two tentacles at the anterior end of its body. This characteristic is an example of cephalization.

CLASS TURBELLARIA

The majority of the 4,500 species in the class Turbellaria live in the ocean. However, the most familiar turbellarian is the freshwater planarian *Dugesia,* which is shown in Figure 36-2. Planarians have a spade-shaped anterior end and a tapered posterior end. They move through the water by swimming with a wavelike motion of their body. Over solid surfaces, planarians glide on a layer of mucus that they secrete, propelled by the cilia that cover their body.

Digestion and Excretion in Planarians

Planarians feed by scavenging for bits of decaying plant or animal matter. They also prey on smaller organisms, such as protozoa. The food is ingested through a muscular tube, the **pharynx** (FAR-eenks), which the planarian extends from the middle of its body. As Figure 36-2a indicates, the pharynx leads to the highly branched gastrovascular cavity. Cells lining the cavity secrete digestive enzymes and absorb nutrients and small pieces of food. The nutrients then diffuse to other body cells.

Organisms that live in fresh water must deal with the water that constantly enters their bodies by osmosis. Planarians eliminate excess water through a network of excretory tubules that run the length of the body. Figure 36-2b shows that each tubule is connected to several **flame cells,** which are so named because they enclose tufts of beating cilia that resemble flickering candle flames. The flame cells collect the excess water, which is then transported through the tubules and excreted from numerous pores scattered over the body surface.

FIGURE 36-2

The organ systems of a planarian carry out the functions that allow it to maintain its free-living existence. (a) The digestive system consists of the pharynx and gastrovascular cavity, which has many branches. (b) In the excretory system, flame cells collect excess water, which travels through excretory tubules to pores on the surface of the body. (c) The nervous system is a ladderlike arrangement of nerves with two cerebral ganglia at the anterior end. (d) Since planarians are hermaphrodites, their reproductive system includes both testes and ovaries.

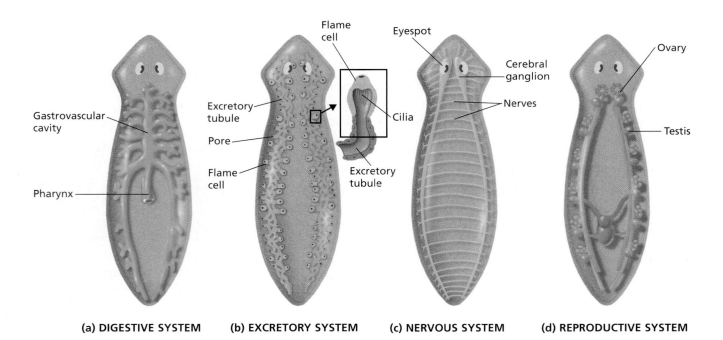

(a) DIGESTIVE SYSTEM   (b) EXCRETORY SYSTEM   (c) NERVOUS SYSTEM   (d) REPRODUCTIVE SYSTEM

Neural Control in Planarians

The planarian nervous system is more complex than the nerve net of cnidarians, as Figure 36-2c illustrates. Two clusters of nerve cells at the anterior end, the **cerebral ganglia** (suh-REE-bruhl GAN-glee-uh), serve as a simple brain. They receive information from sensory cells and transmit signals to the muscles along a ladderlike arrangement of nerves. A planarian's nervous system gives it the ability to learn. For example, a planarian normally moves away from light, but it can be trained to remain still when illuminated.

Planarians sense the intensity and direction of light with two cup-shaped **eyespots** located near the cerebral ganglia. You can see the eyespots in Figure 36-2c. Other sensory cells respond to touch, water currents, and chemicals in the environment. These cells are distributed over the body, but most are concentrated at the anterior end.

Reproduction in Planarians

Because planarians are free-living and motile, they can encounter and mate with other individuals of the same species. As Figure 36-2d shows, planarians are hermaphrodites—they have both male sex organs (testes) and female sex organs (ovaries). When two planarians reproduce sexually, they simultaneously fertilize each other. Their eggs are laid in protective capsules that stick to rocks or debris and hatch in two to three weeks.

Planarians also reproduce asexually, generally during the summer. During asexual reproduction, the body constricts just behind the pharynx. While the posterior part of the worm is attached to a solid surface, the anterior part moves forward until the worm splits in two. This type of asexual reproduction is known as **fission.** The two halves then regenerate their missing parts to produce two complete planaria. During regeneration, each part of the planarian retains information about its original orientation in the body. If a piece is cut from the middle of a planarian, the anterior end will always regenerate a head and the posterior end will regenerate a tail.

CLASS TREMATODA

The class Trematoda consists of about 9,000 species of **flukes,** leaf-shaped flatworms that parasitize many kinds of animals, including humans. Some flukes live inside their host, in the blood, intestines, lungs, liver, or other organs. Others live on the external surface of aquatic hosts such as fish and frogs.

Structure of Flukes

A fluke clings to the tissues of its host by means of an anterior sucker and a ventral sucker, which are shown in Figure 36-3. The anterior sucker surrounds the fluke's mouth, which draws the host's body fluids into the gastrovascular cavity. A fluke's nervous

FIGURE 36-3

Suckers on this blood fluke, *Schistosoma mansoni,* attach the fluke to the blood vessels of its host. (SEM 550×)

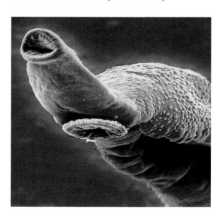

system is similar to a planarian's, but flukes have no eyespots, and their other sensory structures are very simple.

The entire external surface of a fluke is covered by a continuous sheet of fused cells called the **tegument.** The outer zone of the tegument consists of a layer of proteins and carbohydrates that make the fluke resistant to the defenses of the host's immune system. The tegument also protects the fluke against the enzymes secreted by the host's digestive tract.

Reproduction and Life Cycle of Flukes

Most flukes have highly developed reproductive systems and are hermaphroditic. The eggs are stored in a long, coiled tube called the **uterus** until they are ready to be released. Each fluke may produce tens of thousands of eggs at a time.

Flukes have complicated life cycles. A good example is provided by the blood flukes of the genus *Schistosoma.* Follow the steps in Figure 36-4 to see how the schistosome life cycle operates. Adult schistosomes live inside human blood vessels. Therefore, a human is the schistosome's **primary host,** the host from which the adult parasite derives its nourishment and in which sexual reproduction occurs. Unlike most flukes, schistosomes have separate sexes. Eggs produced by the female are fertilized by the male. Some of the fertilized eggs make their way to the host's intestine or bladder and are excreted with the feces or urine. Those that enter fresh water develop into ciliated larvae that swim about. If the larvae encounter a snail of a particular species within a few hours, they burrow into the snail's tissues and begin to reproduce asexually. The snail

FIGURE 36-4

Adult blood flukes of the genus *Schistosoma* live in the blood vessels of humans, their primary hosts. As the inset shows, fertilized *Schistosoma* eggs are released into the blood vessels. (a) The eggs pass out of the primary host in feces or urine. (b) In water, the eggs develop into ciliated larvae. (c) The larvae burrow into snails, which serve as intermediate hosts. (d) The larvae develop tails, escape from the snail, and swim about. (e) The tailed larvae bore through the exposed skin of a person and settle in the blood vessels. There they develop into adults, and the cycle repeats.

(e) Human (primary host)

Eggs

(a) Egg

(b) Ciliated larva

(c) Snail (intermediate host)

(d) Tailed larva

serves as the schistosome's **intermediate host,** the host from which the larvae derive their nourishment. Eventually, the larvae develop tails and escape from the snail. These tailed larvae swim through the water, and if they find the bare skin of a human, they penetrate the skin, enter a blood vessel, and develop into adults. At this point, the cycle begins again.

Not all schistosome eggs leave the human body, however. Many are carried by the blood to the lungs, intestines, bladder, and liver, where they may block blood vessels and cause irritation, bleeding, and tissue decay. The resulting disease, called **schistosomiasis** (SHIS-tuh-soh-MIE-uh-suhs), can be fatal. It affects 200 to 300 million people, mostly in Asia, Africa, and South America.

Other kinds of flukes cause less-serious diseases in humans. For example, a small brown fluke common in freshwater lakes of North America is responsible for **swimmer's itch,** a condition characterized by minor skin irritation and swelling.

internet connect

SCLINKS NSTA

TOPIC: Tapeworms
GO TO: www.scilinks.org
KEYWORD: HM713

CLASS CESTODA

About 5,000 species of **tapeworms** make up the class Cestoda. Tapeworms live in the intestines of almost all vertebrates. Humans may harbor any of seven different species. Tapeworms enter their host when the host eats raw or undercooked food containing eggs or larvae. A tapeworm infection may cause digestive problems, weight loss, lack of energy, and anemia, which is a decrease in the number of red cells in the blood.

FIGURE 36-5

A tapeworm grows by adding proglottids behind its scolex. Each proglottid contains both male and female reproductive organs.

Structure of Tapeworms

Like flukes, tapeworms are surrounded by a tegument that protects them from their host's defenses. As Figure 36-5 shows, at the anterior end of a tapeworm is a knob-shaped organ, the **scolex** (SKOH-leks), which is adorned with hooks and suckers that enable the worm to attach to its host. A short neck connects the scolex with a long series of body sections called **proglottids** (proh-GLAHT-idz). As a tapeworm grows, it adds proglottids just behind the neck, pushing the older proglottids toward the rear. A single tapeworm may have 2,000 proglottids and exceed 10 m (33 ft) in length.

The excretory system and nervous system of a tapeworm are similar to those of other flatworms. However, tapeworms lack eyespots and other light-sensitive structures, and they have no mouth, gastrovascular cavity, or other digestive organs. They absorb nutrients directly from the host's digestive tract through their tegument. The tegument is highly folded, which increases the surface area available for absorption.

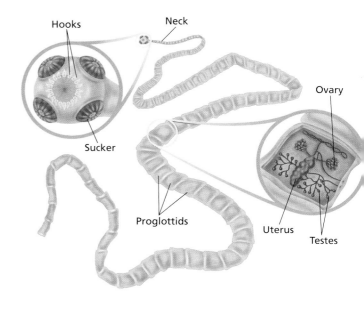

Hooks
Neck
Sucker
Proglottids
Ovary
Uterus
Testes

Reproduction and Life Cycle of Tapeworms

Nearly all tapeworms are hermaphrodites. You can see in Figure 36-5 that each proglottid contains both male and female reproductive organs, but little else. As the proglottids move to the rear of the tapeworm, they grow, mature, and begin producing eggs. The oldest proglottids are almost completely filled with 100,000 or more eggs. Eggs in one proglottid are usually fertilized by sperm from a different proglottid, either in the same individual or a different individual if the host has more than one tapeworm.

The life cycle of the beef tapeworm, *Taeniarhynchus,* is illustrated in Figure 36-6. Like the blood fluke, the beef tapeworm has two hosts. The primary host is a human. In the human intestine, mature proglottids break off from the adult and are eliminated with the host's feces. If the feces are deposited on the ground, the proglottids crawl out of the feces and onto nearby vegetation. The eggs they release may remain alive for several months before the vegetation is eaten by a cow, the intermediate host. Inside the cow, the eggs develop into larvae that burrow through the cow's intestine and enter the bloodstream. The larvae then make their way to muscle tissue and form **cysts,** or dormant larvae surrounded by protective coverings. Humans become infected when they eat beef that has not been cooked sufficiently to kill the worms inside the cysts. Once a cyst enters the human intestine, the cyst wall dissolves and releases the worm. The worm then attaches to the intestinal wall and develops into an adult, beginning the cycle again.

Another tapeworm that infects humans is the pork tapeworm, *Taenia solium.* Its life cycle is similar to that of the beef tapeworm, except that a pig serves as the intermediate host.

FIGURE 36-6

Adult beef tapeworms live in the intestines of humans, their primary hosts. (a) Proglottids pass out of the primary host in feces, crawl onto vegetation, and release their eggs. (b) A cow, the intermediate host, ingests the eggs when it eats the vegetation. The eggs hatch into larvae that form cysts in the cow's muscles. (c) When a person eats undercooked beef, the larvae develop into adult tapeworms in the person's intestine, and the cycle repeats.

Human (primary host)

(c)

Cysts in muscle

Proglottid

Cow (intermediate host)

(b)

Eggs

(a)

SECTION 36-1 REVIEW

1. Why are flatworms called acoelomates?

2. What is a flame cell?

3. Describe two ways in which a planarian shows cephalization.

4. How does the blood fluke *Schistosoma* affect the human body?

5. How do tapeworms obtain nutrients without a mouth or a digestive system?

6. **CRITICAL THINKING** Why is it an adaptive advantage that a parasite not kill its host?

NEMATODA AND ROTIFERA

Members of the phyla Nematoda (NEE-muh-TOHD-uh) and Rotifera (roh-TIF-uhr-uh) have bilaterally symmetrical bodies that contain a fluid-filled space. This space holds the internal organs and serves as a storage area for eggs and sperm. It also supports the body and provides a structure against which the muscles can contract.

PHYLUM NEMATODA

The phylum Nematoda is made up of **roundworms,** worms with long, slender bodies that taper at both ends. Roundworms are among several phyla of animals known as pseudocoelomates. As you learned in Chapter 34, pseudocoelomates are so named because they have a pseudocoelom, a hollow, fluid-filled cavity that is lined by mesoderm on the outside and endoderm on the inside.

Roundworms range in length from less than 1 mm to 120 cm (4 ft). In contrast to cnidarians, ctenophores, and flatworms, which have a gastrovascular cavity with a single opening, roundworms have a digestive tract with two openings. Food enters the digestive tract through the mouth at the anterior end, and undigested material is eliminated from the **anus** (AY-nuhs) at the posterior end. A digestive tract represents a significant advancement over a gastrovascular cavity because food moves through the tract in only one direction. This allows different parts of the tract to be specialized for carrying out different functions, such as enzymatic digestion and absorption of nutrients. Most roundworms have separate sexes and are covered by a protective, noncellular layer called the **cuticle** (KYOO-ti-kuhl).

About 80,000 species of roundworms are known, but biologists estimate that there may be 500,000 or more species. The vast majority of roundworm species are free-living on land, in salt water, and in fresh water. One free-living roundworm, *Caenorhabditis elegans,* is a favorite organism of scientists studying developmental biology. However, about 150 species of roundworms are parasites of plants and animals. Humans are host to about 50 roundworm species. As you read about these roundworms, notice their adaptations for parasitism.

OBJECTIVES

▲

Describe the body plan of a pseudocoelomate.

●

Explain the relationship between humans and three types of parasitic roundworms.

■

Describe the anatomy of a rotifer.

Eco 🌲 Connection

Roundworms for Your Garden—Just Add Water

Gardeners are always looking for ways to control the pests that attack their plants. One way to do this without using potentially dangerous chemicals is to introduce organisms that naturally attack the pests. Some garden supply companies now sell kits containing millions of microscopic roundworms. The roundworms that are released are guaranteed to seek out and kill hundreds of varieties of insects. Other types of soil-dwelling roundworms consume bacteria and fungi that attack plants.

However, not all roundworms are good for plants. Some species parasitize the roots of plants. Effective pest control with roundworms requires a knowledge of which species are harmful and which are beneficial.

Ascaris

Ascaris (AS-kuh-ris) is a genus of roundworm parasites that live in the intestines of pigs, horses, and humans. These roundworms feed on the food that passes through the intestines of their host. As Figure 36-7 shows, they can become so numerous that they completely block the host's intestines if left untreated. The adult female can reach lengths of up to 30 cm (1 ft). The much smaller male has a hooked posterior end that holds the female during mating.

One *Ascaris* female can produce up to 200,000 eggs every day. The fertilized eggs escape from the host's body in the feces. If they are not exposed to direct sunlight or high temperatures, they can remain alive in the soil for years. *Ascaris* eggs enter the body of another host when the host ingests contaminated food or water. The eggs develop into larvae in the intestines, and the larvae bore their way into the bloodstream and are carried to the lungs and throat. There they are coughed up, swallowed, and returned to the intestines, where they mature and mate, completing the life cycle. If the infection is severe, the larvae in the lungs can block air passages and cause bleeding from small blood vessels.

Hookworms

Hookworms are another group of intestinal parasites. As you can see in Figure 36-8, a hookworm's mouth has cutting plates that clamp onto the intestinal wall. Hookworms feed on their host's blood, and because they remove much more blood than they need for food, a heavy hookworm infection can cause anemia. Hookworm infections in children can result in slowed mental and physical development.

Like *Ascaris,* hookworms release their eggs in the host's feces. The eggs produce larvae in warm, damp soil, and the larvae enter new hosts by boring through the host's feet. They then travel through the blood to the lungs and throat. Swallowing takes them to the intestines, where they develop into adults. Hookworms infect more than 400 million people worldwide. Approximately 90 percent of all infections occur in tropical and semitropical regions.

FIGURE 36-7

This pig intestine is completely blocked by *Ascaris* roundworms.

Plates

Hookworm

Intestinal wall

FIGURE 36-8

The hookworm *Ancyclostoma caninum* uses its plates to cut into the host's intestine, releasing blood on which the hookworm feeds. (LM 40×)

FIGURE 36-9

Larvae of the *Trichinella* roundworm coil up inside cysts in their hosts' muscle tissue. The cysts are stained blue in this light micrograph (100×).

Trichinella

Roundworms of the genus *Trichinella* infect humans and a variety of other mammals, including pigs. Adult *Trichinella* worms live embedded in the walls of the host's intestine. They produce larvae that travel through the bloodstream to the muscles, where they form cysts. Figure 36-9 shows one such cyst. People become infected when they eat undercooked meat—usually pork—that is contaminated with cysts. After they are eaten, the cysts release the larvae, which burrow into the intestinal wall and mature into adults. *Trichinella* infections are responsible for the disease **trichinosis** (TRIK-i-NOH-sis), which causes muscle pain and stiffness. It can even cause death if large numbers of cysts form in the heart muscle. However, trichinosis is now rare in the United States. Farmers cook meat scraps before feeding them to hogs, government inspectors examine pork for cysts, and meatpackers generally freeze pork, killing the worms.

Other Parasitic Roundworms

The most common roundworm parasite of humans in the United States is the **pinworm,** *Enterobius,* which infects about 16 percent of adults and 30 percent of children. Despite their high rate of infection, pinworms do not cause any serious disease. Adult pinworms are 5–10 mm (0.2–0.4 in.) in length and resemble white threads. They live and mate in the lower portion of the intestine. At night, the females migrate out of the intestine and lay eggs on the skin around the anus. When an infected person scratches during sleep, the eggs are picked up by the person's hands and spread to anything the person touches. Eggs that are ingested hatch in the intestine, where the worms develop into adults.

Filarial (fuh-LAR-ee-uhl) **worms** are disease-causing roundworms that infect over 250 million people in tropical countries. The most dangerous filarial worms live in the lymphatic system, a part of the circulatory system that collects excess fluid around cells and returns it to the blood. The adult worms can be as long as 100 mm (4 in.). The larvae they produce enter the blood and are picked up by mosquitoes that draw blood from an infected person. The larvae develop into an infective stage inside the mosquitoes and are injected into the blood of another person when the mosquitoes

Quick Lab

Comparing Flatworms and Roundworms

Materials living planarian, preserved specimens of tapeworms, male and female *Ascaris*, hand lens

Procedure Examine specimens of tapeworms, *Ascaris*, and the living planarian. Try to locate the following structures on each worm: anterior end, posterior end, mouth, eyespot, hooks, suckers, auricles, and anus. Draw each worm and label each of the features you located.

Analysis

1. List the features found on the posterior and anterior end of each worm.

2. Which worm has a separate mouth and an anus?

3. Which worm "absorbs" digested nutrients?

4. Which worm has a digestive tract instead of a gastrovascular cavity?

feed again. Inside the new host, the larvae complete their development and settle in the lymphatic system. When they are present in large numbers, filarial worms can block the lymphatic vessels, causing fluid to accumulate in the limbs. In severe cases, the limbs become extremely swollen and filled with connective tissue, a condition known as **elephantiasis.** Another type of filarial worm infects dogs. It lives in the heart and large arteries of the lungs and is responsible for **heartworm disease.**

PHYLUM ROTIFERA

Another group of pseudocoelomates are the 1,750 species in the phylum Rotifera. Members of this phylum are called **rotifers.** Most rotifers are transparent, free-living animals that exist in fresh water. They typically range in length from 100 to 500 μm, with males being much smaller than females. Many rotifers can survive without water for long periods, during which they dry up and look like grains of sand. When wet conditions return, they absorb water and resume their activities.

As Figure 36-10 illustrates, rotifers have a crown of cilia surrounding their mouth. Under a microscope, the crown with its beating cilia looks like a pair of rotating wheels. Rotifers use their cilia to sweep food—algae, bacteria, and protozoans—into their digestive tract. You can follow the path of food through the tract by referring to Figure 36-10. Food moves from the mouth to the **mastax,** a muscular organ that breaks the food into smaller particles. The food is further digested in the stomach, and the nutrients are absorbed in the intestine. Indigestible material passes from the intestine to the **cloaca** (kloh-AY-kuh), a common chamber into which the digestive, reproductive, and excretory systems empty. Like planarians, rotifers use flame cells and excretory tubules to collect excess water in the body. The excess water, along with wastes from the intestine and eggs from the ovaries of females, leaves the cloaca through the anus. Rotifers exhibit cephalization, with a pair of cerebral ganglia and, in some species, two eyespots at the anterior end of the body.

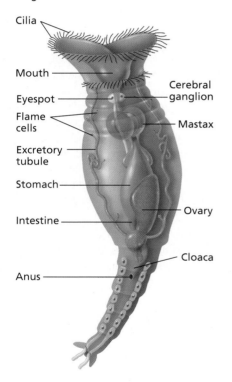

FIGURE 36-10

Cilia surrounding the mouth of a rotifer sweep food into the animal's digestive tract.

Cilia

Mouth

Eyespot

Flame cells

Excretory tubule

Stomach

Intestine

Anus

Cerebral ganglion

Mastax

Ovary

Cloaca

SECTION 36-2 REVIEW

1. What are two features of roundworms and rotifers that flatworms do not have?

2. How are *Ascaris* roundworms transmitted from one host to another?

3. How are hookworms transmitted from one host to another?

4. What is *trichinosis*?

5. What is the function of the cilia on the anterior end of a rotifer?

6. **CRITICAL THINKING** How is the body shape of a parasitic roundworm adapted to the worm's way of life?

36-1 ■ The phylum Platyhelminthes is made up of flatworms, the simplest animals with bilateral symmetry. Flatworms are acoelomates, animals that develop from three germ layers and that lack a hollow cavity between the endoderm and the mesoderm.

■ Most flatworms have a gastrovascular cavity, a gut with a single opening. These cephalized animals also have excretory, nervous, and reproductive systems.

■ The class Turbellaria consists mostly of nonparasitic flatworms, including the freshwater planarian. Planarians are sexually reproducing hermaphrodites that can also reproduce asexually, by splitting in two and regenerating the missing parts.

■ The class Trematoda consists of parasitic flukes. Flukes have complex life cycles in which they alternate between two types of hosts: a primary host, from which the adults derive their nourishment and in which sexual reproduction occurs, and an intermediate host, from which the larvae derive their nourishment. Some flukes live in the internal organs of their host, while others live on the external surface of their host.

■ The class Cestoda consists of parasitic tapeworms. Adult tapeworms live inside the intestines of vertebrates. Lacking a digestive system, tapeworms absorb nutrients through their body surface. Tapeworms have a long series of body sections called proglottids, each of which contains reproductive structures. Tapeworm life cycles also involve primary and intermediate hosts.

Vocabulary

cerebral ganglion (711)	flatworm (709)	proglottid (713)	tapeworm (713)
cyst (714)	fluke (711)	schistosomiasis (713)	tegument (712)
eyespot (711)	intermediate host (713)	scolex (713)	uterus (712)
fission (711)	pharynx (710)	swimmer's itch (713)	
flame cell (710)	primary host (712)		

36-2 ■ Members of the phyla Nematoda and Rotifera are pseudocoelomates. They have a hollow, fluid-filled cavity called a pseudocoelom between the mesoderm and the endoderm. They also have a digestive tract with a mouth at the anterior end and an anus at the posterior end.

■ The phylum Nematoda consists of roundworms. Most roundworms are free-living, but some are parasites of plants and animals.

■ *Ascaris* infects people who consume food or water containing *Ascaris* eggs. The eggs develop into larvae that migrate through the body and mature in the intestines.

■ Hookworm larvae in the soil burrow through a person's feet. The larvae migrate through the body and mature in the intestines.

■ *Trichinella* infects people who consume undercooked meat containing *Trichinella* cysts. The cysts release larvae, which burrow into the intestinal wall and develop into adults.

■ Pinworms live in the lower intestine and lay eggs on the skin around the anus. After being transmitted by the hands to other objects, the eggs may be ingested. They then hatch in the intestine, where the worms mature.

■ Filarial worms include species that live in the human lymphatic system. Their larvae are transmitted between hosts by mosquitoes.

■ Rotifers are small animals, and most of them live as nonparasites in fresh water. The cilia surrounding their mouth sweep food into their digestive tract.

Vocabulary

anus (715)	elephantiasis (718)	hookworm (716)	rotifer (718)
cloaca (718)	filarial worm (717)	mastax (718)	roundworm (715)
cuticle (715)	heartworm disease (718)	pinworm (717)	trichinosis (717)

REVIEW

Vocabulary

1. Distinguish between the terms *acoelomate* and *pseudocoelomate*.
2. Choose the term that does not belong in the following group, and explain why it does not belong: eyespot, flame cell, gastrovascular cavity, proglottid.
3. What is a tegument, and where is it found?
4. What is the function of the mastax in a rotifer?
5. The word part *roti-* means "wheel," and the suffix *-fera* means "bearer." With this information, explain why Rotifera is a good phylum name for the organisms it describes.

Multiple Choice

6. A pseudocoelom is located (a) in the endoderm (b) in the ectoderm (c) between the mesoderm and the ectoderm (d) between the endoderm and the mesoderm.
7. A planarian uses its pharynx to help it (a) move (b) reproduce (c) feed (d) respond to light.
8. Blood flukes of the genus *Schistosoma* reproduce sexually (a) in water (b) inside a snail (c) inside a cow's intestine (d) inside a human's blood vessels.
9. A tapeworm uses its scolex to (a) attach itself to its host (b) force food into its mouth (c) reproduce (d) eliminate excess water.
10. Most rotifers (a) are parasitic (b) live in the soil (c) feed with the help of cilia (d) have a gastrovascular cavity.
11. The animal shown in the photograph below is a (a) flatworm (b) roundworm (c) tapeworm (d) rotifer.

12. A characteristic that differentiates round-worms from flatworms is (a) the presence of a mesoderm (b) the presence of an anus (c) a bilaterally symmetrical body plan (d) cephalization.
13. Flame cells (a) collect excess water (b) respond to light (c) produce eggs (d) produce sperm.
14. In a fluke, the long, coiled tube that stores eggs until they are ready to be released is the (a) excretory tubule (b) mastax (c) tegument (d) uterus.
15. Humans become infected with tapeworms when they (a) eat undercooked meat containing tapeworm cysts (b) drink water containing tapeworm eggs (c) walk barefoot on contaminated soil (d) wade in contaminated water.

Short Answer

16. Explain how a flatworm can survive without a circulatory system or a respiratory system.
17. Describe the nervous system of a planarian.
18. How do planarians reproduce?
19. Arrange the following steps in the schistosome life cycle in the correct order, beginning with the first step after sexual reproduction.
    a. Tailed larvae swim through the water.
    b. Ciliated larvae swim through the water.
    c. Larvae penetrate the skin of a human.
    d. Larvae reproduce asexually in the intermediate host.
    e. Larvae burrow into a snail.
    f. Larvae enter a blood vessel and develop into adults.
    g. Fertilized eggs leave the primary host in the feces or urine.
20. What are some adaptations of flukes to a parasitic way of life?
21. How are tapeworms specialized for a parasitic way of life?
22. What are some features shared by round-worms and rotifers?
23. What is the difference between a primary host and an intermediate host?
24. Describe the life cycle of the roundworm *Ascaris*.
25. How can people avoid becoming infected with the beef tapeworm?

CRITICAL THINKING

1. When would asexual reproduction be advantageous to a free-living flatworm?

2. Parasites are host-specific. This means that they must find the correct host species in order to survive. Suggest a mechanism whereby a parasite could recognize its correct host species.

3. The Aswan High Dam across the Nile River in Egypt was completed in 1970. The dam was built to increase the supply of irrigation water, control major flooding, and provide a source of hydroelectric power. Since the dam was built, however, there has been an increase in the incidence of schistosomiasis in the region. Why do you think this has happened?

4. Why do biologists use the term *eyespot* instead of *eye* to refer to the light-sensitive structures at the anterior end of a planarian?

5. Look again at the diagram of a rotifer in Figure 36-10. Notice the two extensions, called spurs, at the rotifer's posterior end. Suggest a possible function for the spurs.

6. Hookworm infections are extremely common in China, where rice is grown in paddies that are periodically flooded. Considering what you know about how hookworms invade the body, why do you think hookworm infections are so common in this part of the world?

7. A person infected with a tapeworm may show symptoms such as tiredness, loss of weight, and anemia, which could indicate any number of diseases. How might a doctor be certain that the symptoms are caused by a tapeworm?

8. Some rotifers can survive being dried out for as long as four years. When they are placed in water again, they revive. For what kind of environment might this characteristic be adaptive?

9. The two curves below show the number of parasite eggs released each day by a person infected with both *Schistosoma* and *Ascaris* parasites. One curve represents *Schistosoma* eggs, and the other curve represents *Ascaris* eggs. At the time indicated by the arrow, the person was given a medicine that kills adult parasites in the digestive tract. Which curve corresponds to *Schistosoma* eggs? Explain your reasoning.

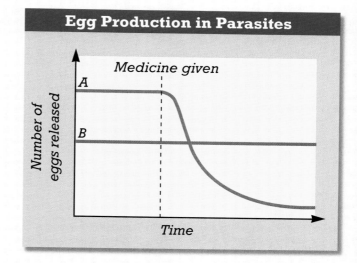

Egg Production in Parasites

Medicine given

A

B

Number of eggs released

Time

EXTENSION

1. Read "Wonderful Worms" in *New Scientist*, August 7, 1999, on page 4. Explain why people living in developed countries, who are free of intestinal parasites, are more likely to suffer from inflammatory bowel disease.

2. Collect a sample of moist soil, or soil and sand from the bottom of a pond. Using a dissecting microscope or a large magnifier, look for roundworms or rotifers, and observe their behavior.

3. Collect a sample of pond water, or place dried grass and other plants in a container of water for a few days. With the use of a microscope, examine the water for rotifers. (If you can't find any rotifers, your teacher may be able to obtain a culture of rotifers from a biological supply house.) Describe the feeding behavior of the rotifers you find.

Observing Flatworm Responses to Stimuli

OBJECTIVES

- Observe the feeding behavior of flatworms.
- Study the response of flatworms to different stimuli.

PROCESS SKILLS

- observing
- experimenting
- collecting data
- analyzing data

MATERIALS

- *Dugesia*
- culture dish
- stereomicroscope
- blunt probe
- test tube
- test-tube rack
- aluminum foil
- wax pencil
- medicine dropper
- cork stopper
- stopwatch or clock
- sheet of white paper
- raw liver
- small flashlight

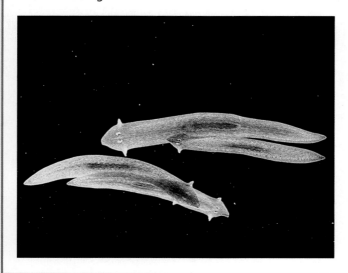

Background

1. *Dugesia,* a planarian, is a nonparasitic flatworm belonging to the class Turbellaria. What are some characteristics of this class?
2. What are some characteristics of the phylum Platyhelminthes?
3. What is meant by cephalization, and why is it an important evolutionary advance?
4. What structures does a planarian have that enable it to sense light, and where are these structures located?

PART A Observing a Flatworm

1. CAUTION **You will be working with a live animal. Be sure to treat it gently and to follow directions carefully.** Use a medicine dropper to transfer one flatworm to a small culture dish. Gently cover the flatworm with water from the culture jar. Why should you use water from the culture jar instead of tap water?
2. Examine the flatworm under the low-power setting of the stereomicroscope. Notice the shape of its body. What kind of symmetry does it have? What structural features demonstrate this symmetry? Does the flatworm appear to have a distinct head and tail? How can you tell?
3. Observe how the flatworm moves. Look carefully at the surface of the flatworm under high power. Can you see any structures that could account for its movement?

PART B Response to Touch

4. In your lab report, make a data table like the one shown. As you complete the following steps, record your observations of the flatworm in your data table.
5. CAUTION **Touch the flatworm gently.** Using a blunt probe, gently touch the posterior end of the flatworm. Notice its response. Now gently touch its anterior end. How does the response compare? What can you conclude from your observations?

PART C Feeding Behavior

6. Place a tiny piece of raw liver in the culture dish. Observe the flatworm for several minutes and describe its feeding response in your data table. Why is it important to use flatworms that have not been recently fed?

7. After several minutes, use the probe to gently turn the flatworm over. What do you observe? If you have time, watch as the flatworm eats the liver. Where do you think the undigested waste will come out?

PART D Response to Gravity

8. With a wax pencil, draw a line around the middle of a test tube.

9. Fill the test tube almost full with water from the culture jar. Then use a medicine dropper to transfer one flatworm to the test tube. Seal the test tube with a cork stopper.

10. Hold the test tube horizontally and move it slowly back and forth until the flatworm is centered on the line you drew.

11. To test whether the flatworm can sense gravity, place the test tube vertically in the test-tube rack. Which way should the flatworm move to show a positive response to gravity? Observe the flatworm for several minutes. Use a stopwatch to measure the amount of time the flatworm spends above the line and below the line. Record the times in your data table.

PART E Response to Light

12. Check the lighting in the room. The light must be low and even during this part of the investigation.

13. Using a piece of aluminum foil, make a cover that is big enough to fit over the bottom half of the test tube you used in Part D. Set the cover aside. Place the test tube horizontally on a white sheet of paper. Make sure the test tube is level. Why is it important for the test tube to be level in this experiment?

14. Position the flashlight so that it will shine directly on the test tube, but do not turn it on.

15. Wait for the flatworm to move to the center line. Then gently place the foil cover over the bottom half of the test tube and turn the flashlight on. Which way should the flatworm move to show a positive response to light? Observe the movements of the flatworm. Use the stopwatch to measure the amount of time the flatworm spends in each half of the test tube. Record the times in your data table.

16. Return the flatworm to the culture jar. Then clean up your materials and wash your hands before leaving the lab.

Analysis and Conclusions

1. What evidence does the flatworm show of cephalization?

2. The flatworm has an incomplete digestive system and no circulatory system. How do you think a flatworm's food gets to the cells after it is digested?

3. How does the flatworm respond to gravity? Is the response positive or negative?

4. How does the flatworm respond to light? Is the response positive or negative?

5. Are the flatworm's anterior and posterior ends equally sensitive to light?

Further Inquiry

Design an experiment to study the responses of flatworms to other stimuli, such as vibrations or sound.

OBSERVATIONS OF FLATWORM BEHAVIOR

Behavior	Observations
Response to touch with blunt probe	
Feeding behavior	
Response to gravity	
Response to light	

MOLLUSKS AND ANNELIDS

This Caribbean octopus, Octopus briareus, *is an active predator with a complex brain.*

FOCUS CONCEPT: *Evolution*

As you read, notice the diversity in these two phyla of animals, which share the coelomate body plan and usually develop from trochophore larvae.

37-1 *Mollusca*

37-2 *Annelida*

MOLLUSCA

Despite their very different appearances, invertebrates such as clams, snails, slugs, and octopuses belong to the same phylum, Mollusca. Members of this phylum are called **mollusks,** *a name that comes from the Latin* molluscus, *which means "soft." Although some mollusks have soft bodies, most have a hard shell that protects and conceals them.*

▲

Summarize the adaptive advantages of a true coelom.

●

Identify two features shared by mollusks and annelids.

■

Describe the structure and function of the radula.

◆

Name the characteristics of four major classes of mollusks.

CHARACTERISTICS OF MOLLUSKS

The phylum Mollusca is a diverse group of more than 112,000 species. Among animals, only the phylum Arthropoda has more species. Some mollusks are sedentary filter feeders, while others are fast-moving predators with complex nervous systems.

Mollusks are among several phyla of animals known as coelomates. As you learned in Chapter 34, coelomates are so named because they have a true coelom, a hollow, fluid-filled cavity that is completely surrounded by mesoderm. Coelomates differ from *pseudo*coelomates, such as roundworms, which have a body cavity lined by mesoderm on the outside and endoderm on the inside.

A coelom has several advantages over a pseudocoelom. With a coelom, the muscles of the body wall are separated from those of the gut. Therefore, the body wall muscles can contract without hindering the movement of food through the gut. A coelom also provides a space where the circulatory system can transport blood without interference from other internal organs. The coelomate body plan is shared by annelids, which are discussed in the second half of this chapter, and by three major phyla of animals covered in Chapters 38–40: arthropods, echinoderms, and chordates, including humans.

Another feature that is shared by most aquatic mollusks and annelids is a larval stage of development called a **trochophore** (TRAHK-uh-FOHR), illustrated in Figure 37-1. In some species, the trochophore hatches from the egg case and exists as a free-swimming larva. Cilia on the surface of a free-swimming trochophore propel the larva through the water and draw food into its mouth. As free-swimming trochophores are carried by ocean currents and tides, they contribute to the dispersal of their species. The presence of a trochophore in mollusks and annelids suggests that these two groups of animals may have evolved from a common ancestor.

FIGURE 37-1

A trochophore is a larva that develops from the fertilized egg of most mollusks and annelids. Cilia at both ends and in the middle propel free-swimming trochophores through the water.

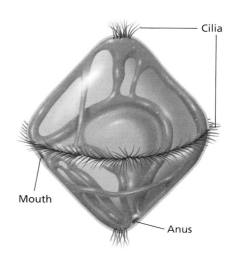

Cilia

Mouth

Anus

FIGURE 37-2

In the basic body plan of a mollusk, the body is divided into the head-foot and the visceral mass, which contains the internal organs. Covering the visceral mass is the mantle, which secretes the shell.

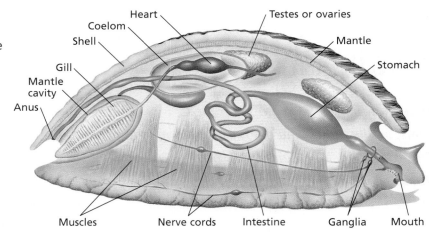

Heart
Coelom
Shell
Gill
Mantle cavity
Anus
Testes or ovaries
Mantle
Stomach
Muscles
Nerve cords
Intestine
Ganglia
Mouth

▨ Visceral mass
▨ Head-foot

FIGURE 37-3

Inside the mouth (a), many mollusks have a radula, a band of tissue covered with teeth that can scrape food from other surfaces. The SEM in (b) shows the sharp edges of these teeth. (600×)

Radula
Mouth
Teeth

(a)

(b)

BODY PLAN OF MOLLUSKS

Figure 37-2 shows that the body of a mollusk is generally divided into two main regions: the head-foot and the visceral mass. As its name suggests, the **head-foot** consists of the head, which contains the mouth and a variety of sensory structures, and the foot, a large, muscular organ usually used for locomotion. Above the head-foot is the **visceral** (VIS-uhr-uhl) **mass,** which contains the heart and the organs of digestion, excretion, and reproduction. As you can see in Figure 37-2, the coelom is limited to a space around the heart. Covering the visceral mass is a layer of epidermis called the **mantle.**

In most mollusks, the mantle secretes one or more hard shells containing calcium carbonate. Although shells protect the soft bodies of mollusks from predators, they also reduce the surface area available for gas exchange. This disadvantage was overcome by the evolution of another structural adaptation, gills. Providing a large surface area in contact with a rich supply of blood, gills are specialized for the exchange of gases with water. Figure 37-2 also shows that the delicate gills of mollusks are protected within the **mantle cavity,** a space between the mantle and the visceral mass.

Like the animals you studied in Chapter 36, most mollusks are bilaterally symmetrical. This symmetry is apparent in the nervous system, which consists of paired clusters of nerve cells called **ganglia.** The ganglia are situated in the head-foot and visceral mass and are connected by two pairs of long nerve cords. Nerve cells in the ganglia control the muscles involved in locomotion and feeding and process sensory information from specialized cells that respond to light, touch, and chemicals in the environment.

The main feeding adaptation of many mollusks is the **radula** (RAD-yuh-luh). As Figure 37-3 shows, in most species the radula is a flexible, tongue-like strip of tissue covered with tough, abrasive teeth that point backward. Through evolution, the radula has become adapted for a variety of functions in different mollusks. Terrestrial snails use the radula to cut through the leaves of garden plants, while aquatic snails use it to scrape up algae or to drill

TABLE 37-1 Features of Three Classes of Mollusks

Feature	Gastropoda	Bivalvia	Cephalopoda
External shell	one (most species); none (slugs and nudibranchs)	two	none (except chambered nautilus)
Head	yes	no	yes
Radula	yes	no	yes
Locomotion	crawling (most)	sessile (most)	rapid swimming

holes in the shells of other mollusks. The cone shell has a harpoon-shaped radula that it uses to capture fish and inject venom.

Most biologists use structural differences to divide mollusks into eight classes. Three of these classes are discussed below: Gastropoda (gas-TRAHP-uh-duh), Bivalvia (bie-VALV-ee-uh), and Cephalopoda (SEF-uh-LAHP-uh-duh). Table 37-1 summarizes the major features of these three classes.

Word Roots and Origins

gastropod

from the Greek *gaster,* meaning "belly," and *podion,* meaning "foot"

CLASS GASTROPODA

The largest and most diverse class of mollusks is Gastropoda, whose members are called **gastropods** (GAS-truh-PAHDZ). Most of the 90,000 species of gastropods, including snails, abalones, and conchs, have a single shell. Others, such as slugs and nudibranchs, have no shell at all.

Gastropods undergo a process called **torsion** during larval development. During torsion, the visceral mass twists around 180 degrees in relation to the head. This twisting brings the mantle cavity, gills, and anus to the front of the animal, as shown in Figure 37-4. Because of torsion, a gastropod can withdraw its head into its mantle cavity when threatened. Coiling of the shell is unrelated to torsion.

Wavelike muscular contractions of the foot move gastropods smoothly over surfaces. You can see these contractions if you look closely at the underside of a snail or slug as it crawls across a window pane or the side of an aquarium.

Gastropods have an open circulatory system, meaning that the circulatory fluid, called **hemolymph,** does not remain entirely within vessels. Instead, it is collected from the gills or lungs, pumped through the heart, and released directly into spaces in the tissues. These fluid-filled spaces compose what is known as a **hemocoel** (HEE-muh-SEEL), or blood cavity. From the hemocoel, the hemolymph returns via the gills or lungs to the heart.

Snails

Snails are gastropods that live on land, in fresh water, and in the ocean. Two eyes at the end of delicate

FIGURE 37-4

In a gastropod, such as this snail, the mantle cavity, anus, and gills are near the head as a result of torsion during development.

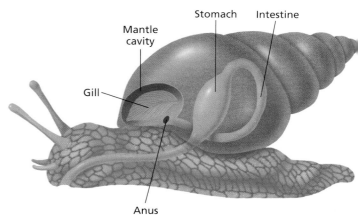

Mantle cavity

Stomach   Intestine

Gill

Anus

FIGURE 37-5

The extensions on the back of this horned nudibranch, *Hermissenda crassicornia*, provide a large surface area for gas exchange.

tentacles on the head help the snail locate food. If danger arises, the tentacles retract into the head. Aquatic snails respire through gills in the mantle cavity. In land snails, the mantle cavity acts as a modified lung that exchanges oxygen and carbon dioxide with the air. The thin membrane lining the mantle cavity must be kept moist to allow gases to diffuse through it. For this reason, land snails are most active when the air has a high moisture content. Snails survive dry periods by becoming inactive and retreating into their shells. They seal the opening to their shell with a mucous plug, which keeps them from drying out.

Land snails are hermaphrodites, but aquatic snails have separate sexes. In either case, the eggs are almost always fertilized internally when two individuals mate.

Other Gastropods

Slugs are terrestrial gastropods that look like snails without shells. Like land snails, slugs respire through the lining of their mantle cavity. They avoid desiccation by hiding in moist, shady places by day and feeding at night.

Nudibranchs, like the one shown in Figure 37-5, are marine gastropods that lack shells. *Nudibranch* means "naked gill," which refers to the fact that gas exchange occurs across the entire body surface of these animals. The surface of most nudibranchs is covered with numerous ruffles or delicate, fingerlike extensions that increase the total area available for gas exchange.

Some gastropods show unusual adaptations of the foot. In pteropods, or "sea butterflies," for example, the foot is modified into a winglike flap that is used for swimming rather than crawling.

FIGURE 37-6

The two valves that make up the hinged shell of a bivalve can separate, allowing water to circulate through the animal. Some bivalves, like this calico scallop, *Aequipecten viradians*, have a row of eyes near the outer margin of each valve.

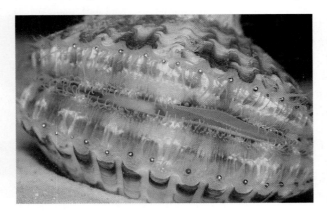

CLASS BIVALVIA

Members of the class Bivalvia include aquatic mollusks, such as clams, oysters, and scallops. These mollusks are called **bivalves** because, as Figure 37-6 shows, their shell is divided into two halves, or valves, connected by a hinge. A bivalve can close its shell by contracting the powerful **adductor muscles** that are attached to the inside surface of each valve. You can see the adductor muscles in Figure 37-7. When the adductor muscles relax, the valves open.

Each valve consists of three layers that are secreted by the mantle. The thin outer layer protects the shell against acidic conditions in the water. The thick middle layer of calcium carbonate strengthens the shell. The smooth, iridescent inner layer protects the animal's soft body. If a grain of sand or other irritant gets inside the shell of a bivalve, the mantle coats it with the same material that lines the inner layer. Multiple applications of this material form a pearl.

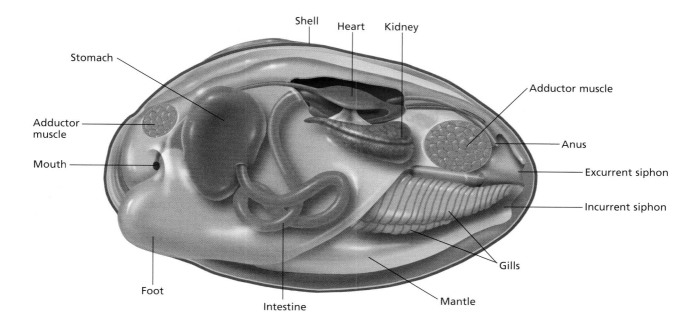

Shell Heart Kidney

Stomach

Adductor muscle

Adductor muscle

Anus

Mouth

Excurrent siphon

Incurrent siphon

Gills

Foot

Mantle

Intestine

FIGURE 37-7

In this illustration, one valve has been omitted to show a clam's anatomy. The internal structure of a clam is typical of most bivalves.

In contrast with gastropods, which move about in search of food, most bivalves are sessile. Some species extend their muscular foot into the sand and fill the foot with hemolymph to form a hatchet-shaped anchor. The muscles of the foot then contract, pulling the animal down into the sand. As an adaptation for a sessile existence, bivalves usually are filter feeders. They are the only mollusks without a radula.

Bivalves lack a distinct head. Their nervous system consists of three pairs of ganglia: one pair near the mouth, another pair in the digestive system, and the third pair in the foot. The ganglia are connected by nerve cords. Nerve cells in the ganglia receive information from sensory cells in the edge of the mantle that respond to touch or to chemicals in the water. Some bivalves also have a row of small eyes along each mantle edge. Stimuli detected by these sensory structures can trigger nerve impulses that cause the foot to withdraw and the shell to close.

Clams

Clams are bivalves that live buried in mud or sand. The mantle cavity of a clam is sealed except for a pair of hollow, fleshy tubes called **siphons,** which you can see in Figure 37-7. Cilia beating on the gills set up a current of water that enters through the **incurrent siphon** and leaves through the **excurrent siphon.** As the water circulates inside the clam, the gills filter small organisms and organic debris from the water. The filtered material becomes trapped on the gills in a sticky mucus that moves in a continuous stream toward the mouth. Water passing over the gills also exchanges oxygen and carbon dioxide with the hemolymph.

Most species of clams have separate sexes. Marine clams reproduce by shedding sperm and eggs into the water, and fertilization occurs externally. The fertilized egg becomes a trochophore that eventually settles to the bottom and develops into an adult. In some species, the adults may weigh 200 kg (440 lb) and be over 1 m (3.3 ft) across. In most freshwater clams, eggs are fertilized internally by sperm that enter through the incurrent siphon. The larvae that develop are discharged into the water through the excurrent siphon. If they contact a passing fish, they may live as parasites on its gills or skin for several weeks before settling to the bottom.

Other Bivalves

Oysters are bivalves that become permanently attached to a hard surface early in their development. Some are grown commercially as food or as sources of cultured pearls. Scallops can move through the water by repeatedly opening their valves and snapping them shut. This motion expels bursts of water, creating a form of jet propulsion. The teredo, or shipworm, is one of the few bivalves that does not filter-feed. Instead, it bores into driftwood or ship timbers and ingests the particles that are produced by the drilling. The wood cellulose is broken down by symbiotic bacteria that live in the shipworm's intestine.

CLASS CEPHALOPODA

Members of the class Cephalopoda include octopuses, squids, cuttlefishes, and chambered nautiluses. These marine mollusks are called **cephalopods** (SEF-uh-luh-PAHDZ), a term that means "head-foot." The name refers to the fact that a cephalopod's foot is concentrated in its head region. Cephalopods are specialized for a free-swimming, predatory existence. Extending from the head is a circle of tentacles, as you can see in Figure 37-8. The tentacles' powerful suction cups allow cephalopods to grasp objects and capture prey. Cephalopods kill and eat their prey with the help of a pair of jaws that resemble a parrot's beak.

The nervous system is more advanced in cephalopods than in any other group of mollusks. The cephalopod brain, which is the largest of any invertebrate brain, is divided into several lobes and contains millions of nerve cells. The large number of nerve cells enables cephalopods to process information in sophisticated ways. Octopuses, for example, can learn to solve simple problems, perform tasks, and discriminate between objects on the basis of their shape or texture. The sensory systems of cephalopods are also well developed. Most cephalopods have highly advanced eyes that are capable of forming images of objects. The tentacles contain numerous cells that sense chemicals in the water.

Cephalopods have a closed circulatory system, which means blood circulates entirely within a system of vessels. Closed circulatory systems transport fluid more rapidly than open circulatory systems do. Thus, nutrients, oxygen, and carbon dioxide are carried quickly through the body of these highly active animals. Cephalopods also have separate sexes. The male uses a special-

FIGURE 37-8

Cephalopods, like this cuttlefish, *Sepia latimanus,* have several long tentacles surrounding their mouth. The streamlined body of many cephalopods enables them to swim rapidly in pursuit of prey.

ized tentacle to transfer packets of sperm from his mantle cavity to the mantle cavity of the female, where fertilization occurs. The female lays a mass of fertilized eggs and guards the eggs until they hatch. Unlike other mollusks, cephalopods develop from an egg into a juvenile without becoming a trochophore.

Many cephalopods can release a cloud of ink into the water to temporarily distract predators. They also have pigment cells called **chromatophores** (kroh-MAT-uh-FOHRS), which are located in the outer layer of the mantle. Chromatophores can produce a sudden change in the color of a cephalopod, allowing the animal to blend in with its surroundings.

FIGURE 37-9

The chambered nautilus is the only cephalopod with an external shell.

Squids

Squids are cephalopods with ten tentacles. The longest two tentacles are used for capturing prey, and the other eight force the prey into the squid's mouth. The muscular mantle propels the squid swiftly through the water by pumping jets of water through an excurrent siphon. Most squids grow to about 30 cm (1 ft) in length, but a few species can be much longer. The giant squid, *Architeuthis,* may reach a length of 18 m (about 60 ft) and a weight of more than 3,300 kg (about 3.5 tons). It is the world's largest known invertebrate.

Octopuses and Chambered Nautiluses

Octopuses have eight tentacles and share many characteristics with squids, including their methods of escaping from predators. Instead of using jet propulsion to chase prey, however, octopuses are more likely to crawl along the bottom with their tentacles or lie in wait in caves and rock crevices. Octopuses seldom exceed 30 cm (1 ft) in diameter, although the giant Pacific octopus may grow to a diameter of 2.5 m (about 8 ft).

The chambered nautilus, shown in Figure 37-9, is the only existing cephalopod that has retained its external shell. The shell is coiled and divided into a series of gas-filled chambers separated by partitions. The soft body of the nautilus is confined to the outermost chamber. As the nautilus grows, it moves forward in its shell, makes a new partition, and fills the chamber behind the partition with gas. The gas makes the nautilus buoyant.

internet**connect**

SCiLINKS

NSTA

TOPIC: Squids
GO TO: www.scilinks.org
KEYWORD: HM731

SECTION 37–1 REVIEW

1. What is one advantage of a true coelom over a pseudocoelom?

2. What is a trochophore? In what phyla of animals is it found?

3. What is a radula, and what is it used for?

4. Why are land snails more active when the air around them is moist?

5. In what ways is a squid adapted for a predatory way of life?

6. **CRITICAL THINKING** Suggest why an open circulatory system is sufficient to meet the needs of a gastropod.

Leeches:
New Uses for an Old Remedy

Why are leeches called blood-suckers? Do they really suck blood? Yes, they do, and although it may sound disgusting, their role as bloodsuckers could help save your life.

For centuries, leeches were a common tool of medical practice. In the second century A.D., the Greek physician Galen described the usefulness of leeches in removing blood from patients, a procedure called bloodletting. An excess of blood in the body was believed to be responsible for a variety of illnesses, from headaches and fevers to heart disease. Physicians regarded the leech's habit of feeding on blood as a simple way to remove this "bad blood" from a patient's body. Bloodletting remained very common in Europe through the early nineteenth century, and leeches were grown in ponds and harvested in large numbers for use in medicine. In fact, bloodletting was prescribed so often that physicians themselves were sometimes referred to as leeches. During the late 1800s, however, medical science discredited the idea that excess blood causes disease, and bloodletting fell out of favor.

Surprisingly, leeches are making a comeback in medicine, although with new purposes. One of these purposes is to increase the success rate of operations to reattach severed limbs, fingers, or toes. Such operations involve microsurgery, a process in which surgeons reconnect tendons, blood vessels, and nerves using tiny instruments and powerful microscopes. Along with today's sophisticated technology, some surgeons have added an unlikely tool—the leech.

During microsurgery, physicians can reconnect arteries but not small veins, which are more delicate. As a result, circulation in the reattached limb, finger, or toe is impaired, and the tissues may become congested with blood. If this happens, the tissues of the reattached part die, and the part cannot heal and rejoin the body. One solution to this problem is to place leeches on the reattached body part. There, they begin to suck out the accumulated blood, relieving congestion and allowing the tissues to remain healthy until the veins can grow back. At a cost of about $7.00 apiece, leeches are an inexpensive treatment for a serious problem.

Leeches have medical uses that go beyond their ability to remove blood. Scientists have known since the 1800s that leech saliva contains a powerful anticoagulant, a substance that inhibits blood clotting. The leech's anticoagulant, called hirudin, can cause four hours or more of steady bleeding. The word *hirudin* derives from the scientific name of the medicinal leech, *Hirudo medicinalis.* Today hirudin is made through genetic engineering, without the aid of leeches. It has proven useful in the treatment of some heart patients, particularly those who have had heart attacks, who suffer from angina, or who have undergone angioplasty, a procedure to open blocked arteries. One research study even indicated that hirudin may be effective against the spread of cancer.

The amazing uses that have been found for a substance in leech saliva are encouraging to medical researchers, who continue to explore how knowledge of invertebrate organisms can be beneficially combined with medical technology.

Leeches have been applied to this patient's sutures across his upper back to reduce congestion of blood. Each leech can remove up to 5 mL of blood.

ANNELIDA

Colorful feather-duster worms, common earthworms, and bloodsucking leeches are all members of the phylum Annelida (uh-NEL-uh-duh). An animal in this phylum is called an **annelid** *(AN-uh-LID), a term that means "little rings." The name refers to the many body segments that make an annelid look like it is composed of a series of rings.*

SECTION

37-2

OBJECTIVES

▲

List the advantages of body segmentation.

●

Explain how earthworms move.

■

Describe the organ systems of earthworms.

◆

Distinguish between the three classes of annelids.

CHARACTERISTICS AND CLASSIFICATION OF ANNELIDS

The phylum Annelida consists of about 15,000 species of bilaterally symmetrical, segmented worms. Segmentation is the most distinctive feature of annelids. Like mollusks, annelids have a true coelom, but the coelom in annelids is divided into separate compartments by partitions. Division of the coelom represents an evolutionary advance over the earliest wormlike coelomates. In an undivided coelom, the force of muscle contraction in one part of the body is transmitted to other parts by the fluid in the coelom. A segmented coelom enables different parts of the body to contract or expand independently. In addition, duplication of some of the organ systems in each segment provides a form of insurance against injury. If one segment becomes disabled, the others can still function.

Most annelids have external bristles called **setae** (SEE-tee), and some have fleshy protrusions called **parapodia** (PAR-uh-POH-dee-uh). Both of these structures are visible in Figure 37-10. The number of setae and the presence or absence of parapodia provide the basis for dividing annelids into three classes: Oligochaeta (AHL-uh-goh-KEET-uh), Polychaeta (PAHL-ee-KEET-uh), and Hirudinea (HIR-yuh-DIN-ee-uh). All organ systems are well developed in most members of each class.

CLASS OLIGOCHAETA

Annelids of the class Oligochaeta generally live in the soil or in fresh water and have no parapodia. *Oligochaeta* means "few bristles," and as the name suggests, these annelids have a few setae on each segment. The most familiar member of the class Oligochaeta is the earthworm. As you read about the earthworm, look for adaptations that enable this animal to lead a burrowing life.

FIGURE 37-10

Numerous setae help this bristle worm move through its environment. The setae extend from fleshy flaps called parapodia. The bristle worm is a member of the class Polychaeta and genus *Hermodice*.

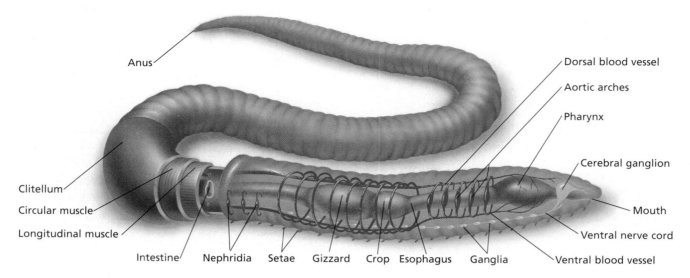

Anus

Dorsal blood vessel

Aortic arches

Pharynx

Cerebral ganglion

Clitellum

Circular muscle

Longitudinal muscle

Mouth

Ventral nerve cord

Intestine   Nephridia   Setae   Gizzard   Crop   Esophagus   Ganglia   Ventral blood vessel

FIGURE 37-11

The segmentation of annelids, such as this earthworm, is visible both externally and internally. Some of the internal structures, such as ganglia and nephridia, are repeated in each segment.

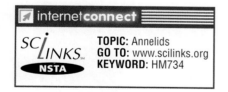

internet**connect**

SCI*LINKS*
NSTA

TOPIC: Annelids
GO TO: www.scilinks.org
KEYWORD: HM734

Structure and Movement

An earthworm's body is divided into more than 100 segments, most of which are virtually identical. Figure 37-11 shows that circular and longitudinal muscles line the interior body wall of an earthworm. To move, the worm anchors some of the middle segments by their setae and contracts the circular muscles in front of those segments. Contraction of the circular muscles increases the pressure of the coelomic fluid in those segments. This increased pressure elongates the animal and pushes the anterior end forward. Setae in the anterior segments then grip the ground as the longitudinal muscles contract, pulling the posterior segments forward. This method of locomotion in earthworms is an example of the kind of movement made possible by segmentation.

Feeding and Digestion

Earthworms ingest soil as they burrow through it. Soil is sucked into the mouth by the muscular pharynx. The soil then passes through a tube called the **esophagus** (ee-SAHF-uh-guhs) to a temporary storage area known as the **crop.** From the crop, the soil moves to a thick, muscular part of the gut called the **gizzard.** Find these parts of the digestive tract in Figure 37-11. The gizzard grinds the soil, releasing and breaking up organic matter. As the soil passes through the long intestine, digested organic compounds and nutrients in the soil are absorbed by the blood. An infolding of the intestinal wall called the **typhlosole** (TIF-luh-SOHL) increases the surface area available for digestion and absorption. Undigested material is eliminated from the earthworm's body through the anus.

Earthworms play an important role in maintaining the fertility of soil. By decomposing dead leaves and other organic materials, earthworms help release nutrients into the soil. The burrows made by earthworms allow air to penetrate into the soil, bringing oxygen to plant roots and soil microorganisms. Earthworms also loosen the soil, making it easier for roots to grow and for water to seep in.

Circulation

A closed circulatory system transports oxygen, carbon dioxide, nutrients, and wastes through the body of an earthworm. The blood travels toward the posterior end through a ventral blood vessel and then returns to the anterior end through a dorsal blood vessel. As you can see in Figure 37-11, five pairs of muscular tubes, the **aortic** (ay-OHR-tik) **arches,** link the dorsal and ventral blood vessels near the anterior end of the worm. Contractions of the ventral blood vessel and the aortic arches force blood through the circulatory system.

Respiration and Excretion

Earthworms have no specialized respiratory organs. Oxygen and carbon dioxide diffuse directly through the skin, which contains many small blood vessels. This exchange of gases can take place only if the skin is moist. Therefore, earthworms avoid dry ground and extreme heat. Secretions of mucus and the presence of a thin cuticle also help keep an earthworm's skin moist.

Earthworms eliminate cellular wastes and excess water through excretory tubules called **nephridia** (ne-FRID-ee-uh), some of which are shown in Figure 37-11. Each segment except the first three and the last one contains a pair of nephridia. As coelomic fluid passes through the nephridia, some of the water is reabsorbed by blood vessels. The remaining fluid and the wastes dissolved in it are released from the body through pores on the ventral surface.

Neural Control

The nervous system of an earthworm consists of a chain of ganglia connected by a ventral nerve cord. Most body segments contain a single ganglion. Nerves branching from each ganglion carry impulses to the muscles and from the sensory cells in that segment. In the most anterior segments, several ganglia are fused to form the cerebral ganglia, or brain, as you can see in Figure 37-11. One of the main functions of the cerebral ganglia is to process information from simple sensory structures that respond to light, touch, chemicals, moisture, temperature, and vibrations. Although these sensory structures are found in all segments, they are especially concentrated at the anterior end.

Reproduction

Earthworms are hermaphrodites, but an individual worm cannot fertilize its own eggs. Mating occurs when two earthworms press their ventral surfaces together with their anterior ends pointing in opposite directions. The two worms are held together by their setae and by a film of mucus secreted by each worm's **clitellum** (klie-TEL-uhm). The clitellum, also visible in Figure 37-11, is a thickened section of the body. Each earthworm injects sperm into the mucus. The sperm from each worm move through the mucus to the pouchlike **seminal receptacle** of the other, where they are stored. The worms then separate, and after several days the clitellum of each worm secretes a tube

Word Roots and Origins

nephridium

from the Greek *nephros,* meaning "kidney," and *idion,* meaning "small" made of mucus and a tough carbohydrate known as **chitin** (KIE-tin). As this tube slides forward, it picks up the worm's eggs and the stored sperm from the other worm. Fertilization occurs inside the tube, which closes up to form a protective case. The young worms develop inside the case for 2–3 weeks before hatching.

CLASSES POLYCHAETA AND HIRUDINEA

About two-thirds of all annelids are members of the class Polychaeta and are called polychaetes. *Polychaeta* means "many bristles," which refers to the numerous setae that help polychaetes move. The setae project from parapodia, some of which function in gas exchange. Polychaetes differ from other annelids in that they have antennae and specialized mouthparts. They are also the only annelids that have a trochophore stage in development. Most polychaetes, like the one shown in Figure 37-10, live in marine habitats. Some are free-swimming predators that use their strong jaws to feed on small animals. Others feed on sediment as they burrow through it or use their tentacles to scour the ocean bottom for food.

Hirudinea is the smallest class of annelids, consisting of about 300 species of leeches. Most leeches live in calm bodies of fresh water, but some species live among moist vegetation on land. Leeches have no setae or parapodia. At each end of a leech's body is a sucker that can attach to surfaces. By attaching the anterior sucker and then pulling the rest of the body forward, leeches can crawl along solid objects. Aquatic leeches can also swim with an undulating movement of their body. Many leeches are carnivores that prey on small invertebrates, but some species, including the one shown in Figure 37-12, are parasites that suck blood from other animals. After attaching themselves to the skin of their host, parasitic leeches secrete an anaesthetic that prevents the host from feeling their presence. They also secrete a substance that prevents blood from clotting. If undisturbed, a leech can ingest 10 times its own weight in blood.

FIGURE 37-12

The leech *Haemadipsa* sp. is a parasite that sucks blood from animals, including humans. Other leeches are free-living carnivores.

SECTION 37-2 REVIEW

1. What are the advantages of a segmented body?

2. How are an earthworm's circular and longitudinal muscles used in locomotion?

3. How does an earthworm exchange oxygen and carbon dioxide with its environment?

4. How do polychaetes differ from earthworms?

5. How are some leeches adapted to a parasitic lifestyle?

6. **CRITICAL THINKING** How is the form of parasitism that some leeches engage in different from that of a tapeworm or a liver fluke, which you read about in Chapter 36?

SUMMARY/VOCABULARY

37-1 ■ Mollusks have a true coelom and usually develop from a pear-shaped larva called a trochophore. Their body is divided into the head-foot and the visceral mass, which contains the internal organs.

■ Most mollusks have at least one shell, which is secreted by a layer of epidermis called the mantle. Aquatic mollusks have gills through which they exchange gases with water.

■ The main feeding adaptation of most mollusks is the radula, a tongue-like structure that is modified in different species for scraping, drilling, or harpooning.

■ Gastropods undergo a process called torsion, in which the visceral mass twists during larval development. Snails and most other gastropods have a single shell, while some gastropods, such as slugs and nudibranchs, lack shells. Gastropods move by means of wavelike, muscular contractions of the foot and have an open circulatory system.

■ Bivalves have a shell that is divided into two valves, which they can pull together by contracting powerful adductor muscles. Bivalves lack a distinct head and have no radula. Most are sessile and filter food from the water. In clams, water enters through an incurrent siphon and exits through an excurrent siphon. Food is strained from the water as it passes through the gills.

■ Cephalopods, including octopuses and squids, are free-swimming, predatory mollusks with numerous tentacles. They have an advanced nervous system with a large brain and well-developed sensory organs. Cephalopods have a closed circulatory system and do not pass through a trochophore stage during development.

Vocabulary

adductor muscle (728)	ganglion (726)	incurrent siphon (729)	siphon (729)
bivalve (728)	gastropod (727)	mantle (726)	torsion (727)
cephalopod (730)	head-foot (726)	mantle cavity (726)	trochophore (725)
chromatophore (731)	hemocoel (727)	mollusk (725)	visceral mass (726)
excurrent siphon (729)	hemolymph (727)	radula (726)	

37-2 ■ Annelids have a true coelom and a body that is divided into many segments. Most annelids have external bristles called setae, and some have fleshy protrusions called parapodia.

■ Members of the class Oligochaeta generally live in the soil or in fresh water. They have no parapodia and relatively few setae.

■ The most familiar member of the class Oligochaeta is the earthworm, which feeds on organic matter as it burrows through the soil. Earthworms have a closed circulatory system. They exchange gases through their skin and eliminate cellular wastes and excess water through excretory tubules called nephridia.

■ Polychaetes have numerous setae that project from parapodia. They also have antennae and specialized mouthparts, and they pass through a trochophore stage during their development. Most polychaetes live in the ocean.

■ Members of the class Hirudinea—leeches—live in fresh water or on land. They have no setae or parapodia. Many leeches are carnivores that prey on small invertebrates, but some are bloodsucking parasites.

Vocabulary

annelid (733)	clitellum (735)	gizzard (734)	seminal receptacle (735)
aortic arch (735)	crop (734)	nephridium (735)	seta (733)
chitin (736)	esophagus (734)	parapodium (733)	typhlosole (734)

REVIEW

Vocabulary

1. How does a coelom differ from a pseudo-coelom?
2. What is the difference between an open circulatory system and a closed circulatory system?
3. What are chromatophores, and of what value are they to a cephalopod?
4. What are the functions of the crop and the gizzard in an earthworm?
5. What is the function of the nephridia in an earthworm?

Multiple Choice

6. Mollusks and annelids share all of the following characteristics except (a) a coelom (b) a trochophore larva (c) segmentation (d) bilateral symmetry.
7. Gills are organs specialized for (a) gas exchange (b) movement (c) digestion (d) excretion.
8. Most bivalves are (a) predators (b) parasites (c) land dwellers (d) filter feeders.
9. The only mollusks with a closed circulatory system are (a) gastropods (b) bivalves (c) cephalopods (d) snails.
10. Terrestrial snails and slugs require an environment with a high moisture content in order to (a) reproduce (b) feed (c) respire (d) all of the above.
11. Slugs are members of the class (a) Gastropoda (b) Cephalopoda (c) Polychaeta (d) Oligochaeta.
12. Annelids are divided into three classes based partly on the number of their (a) segments (b) setae (c) nephridia (d) aortic arches.
13. Earthworms respire by means of (a) gills (b) lungs (c) diffusion across the skin (d) all of the above.
14. The movement of earthworms involves (a) pressure in the coelomic fluid (b) muscle contractions (c) traction provided by setae (d) all of the above.
15. Parapodia are a distinguishing characteristic of the class (a) Polychaeta (b) Oligochaeta (c) Hirudinea (d) Bivalvia.

Short Answer

16. What functions are performed by the cilia on a free-swimming trochophore?
17. What are the main parts in the basic body plan of a mollusk?
18. What is torsion? What effect does it have on the location of a snail's mantle cavity?
19. Describe how the radula is modified in different groups of mollusks.
20. How is the structure of a gill related to its function?
21. Why do earthworms require a moist environment?
22. Describe the organization of an earthworm's nervous system.
23. What characteristics distinguish polychaetes from other annelids?
24. Arrange the following steps in the locomotion of an earthworm in the correct order, beginning after the worm anchors some of its middle segments by their setae.
    a. The posterior segments are pulled forward.
    b. The anterior end moves forward as the worm elongates.
    c. Setae in the anterior segments grip the ground as the longitudinal muscles contract.
    d. The pressure of the coelomic fluid increases.
    e. The circular muscles contract.
25. Identify the structures labeled A through F in the diagram below.

CRITICAL THINKING

1. Clams and other aquatic mollusks reproduce by releasing sperm and eggs into the water. How might this process affect the reproductive success of these mollusks? Would you expect aquatic mollusks to release many sperm and eggs or only a few?

2. Clams are aquatic and earthworms are terrestrial. Nevertheless, the feeding methods of clams and earthworms are basically similar. Explain how they are similar.

3. Humans value pearls for their luster and color, features that are of no significance to an oyster. Furthermore, making a pearl consumes resources that an oyster could use for other purposes, such as strengthening its shell. Given these facts, of what advantage is it to an oyster to manufacture a pearl?

4. For quite a while after an earthworm is cut in half, both halves will continue to move about, and both will retract if they are touched. What do these observations suggest about the role the brain has in coordinating these movements?

5. Land snails are hermaphrodites. Of what advantage is this characteristic to the land snail?

6. Many clams have very long incurrent and excurrent siphons. For example, the siphons of a clam called the geoduck, *Panope generosa,* may exceed one meter in length. What is the adaptive advantage of such long siphons? Keep in mind the habitat of most clams.

7. A mutation results in the birth of an earthworm that lacks moisture-sensing cells in its skin. Explain why this earthworm is less likely to survive than one with such sensory cells.

8. The graph below plots the movement of the anterior end of an earthworm over an interval of several seconds, as the worm crawled along a flat surface. Was the anterior end of the worm moving or stationary during the periods represented by the horizontal sections of the graph? Which of the earthworm's sets of muscles were contracting during the periods represented by the horizontal sections? Explain your answers.

Earthworm Movement

EXTENSION

1. Read "Sponging Off Mussels" in *National Wildlife,* February/March 2000, on page 10. Explain why the zebra mussel is an ecological pest. How does the native sponge in the Great Lakes help solve the problem?

2. Many people collect the shells of mollusks as a hobby. You may be able to see some of these shells in your school, in the homes of friends or relatives, or at a local museum. Using a book such as the *National Audubon Society Field Guide to North American Seashore Creatures,* identify five shells or pictures of shells. Draw each one, and under each drawing give the common name, the scientific name, the part of the world where it is found, and the size.

3. Research an annelid or mollusk species that was not covered in this chapter. Gather information on the anatomy, feeding, habitat, and reproduction of that species. How does the species you chose illustrate an evolutionary adaptation to the environment in which it lives?

Observing Earthworm Behavior

OBJECTIVES

- Observe a live earthworm.
- Test how an earthworm responds to light, moisture, and ammonia.
- Test the effect of temperature on heart rate.

PROCESS SKILLS

- observing
- hypothesizing
- experimenting
- collecting data
- analyzing data

MATERIALS

- safety goggles
- live earthworm
- shallow pan
- paper towels
- medicine dropper
- hand lens
- black paper or piece of cardboard
- fluorescent lamp
- 2 cotton swabs
- 3% aqueous ammonia solution
- 15 cm Petri dish
- thermometer
- stopwatch or clock with second hand
- 2 plastic tubs for water baths
- warm tap water
- ice cubes

Background

1. How does an earthworm benefit from cephalization?
2. Describe how gases enter and exit an earthworm's body.

PART A   Observing an Earthworm

1. **CAUTION You will be working with a live animal. Be sure to treat it gently and to follow directions carefully.** Place a moist paper towel in a pan, and place an earthworm on the paper towel. **CAUTION Rinse the earthworm frequently with water from a medicine dropper to prevent the worm from drying out and becoming lethargic.**

2. Observe the behavior of the earthworm for a few minutes. Identify the earthworm's anterior and posterior ends by watching it move in the pan. As the worm crawls around in the pan, it will lead with its anterior end.

3. Locate the earthworm's clitellum. Is the clitellum closer to the anterior end or the posterior end? What is the function of the clitellum?

4. Identify the earthworm's dorsal and ventral surfaces by gently rolling the worm over. The dorsal surface will be on top after the worm rights itself.

5. Pick up the earthworm and feel its skin with your fingers. One surface of the earthworm should feel slightly rougher than the other. The roughness is due to the hairlike setae that project from the earthworm's skin. On which surface are the setae located? Use a hand lens to examine the setae up close.

6. Return the earthworm to the pan, and use the hand lens to find a thick purple line running along the dorsal surface of the worm. This line is the dorsal blood vessel. Does the earthworm have an open or a closed circulatory system?

7. Draw a picture of the earthworm, and label its anterior and posterior ends, dorsal and ventral surfaces, clitellum, setae, and dorsal blood vessel.

PART B   Earthworm Responses to Stimuli

8. In this part of the laboratory investigation, you will test the earthworm's responses to three different stimuli. With your lab partners, develop three separate hypotheses that describe an earthworm's responses to light, moisture, and a base. In your lab report, make a data table like the one on the next page.

9. To test the earthworm's response to light, cover half of the pan with black paper or cardboard. Check the lighting in the room. The light must be low and even during this test. Position the fluorescent lamp over the uncovered portion of the pan. Place the earthworm in the center of the pan and observe its movements. Record your observations in your data table.

OBSERVATIONS OF EARTHWORM BEHAVIOR

Behavior	Observations
Response to light	
Response to moisture	
Response to water on a swab	
Response to ammonia	

10. To test the earthworm's response to moisture, turn off the fluorescent lamp, move it away from the pan, and remove the paper covering half of the pan. Place a piece of dry paper towel on one side of the pan and a piece of wet paper towel on the other side of the pan. Lay the earthworm across the two paper towels. Observe the earthworm's response to the two environments, and record your observations in your data table.

11. To test the earthworm's response to ammonia, make sure the paper towels on both sides of the pan are wet. Moisten a cotton swab with water. Hold the cotton swab first near the earthworm's anterior end and then near its posterior end. Do not touch the earthworm with the swab. Record your observations in your data table.

12. **CAUTION Wear safety goggles at all times during the following procedure. If you get ammonia on your skin or clothing, wash it off at the sink while calling to your teacher. If you get ammonia in your eyes, immediately flush it out at the eyewash station while calling to your teacher.** Moisten a different cotton swab with ammonia solution and repeat step 11. Do not touch the earthworm with the swab or the ammonia solution. Record your observations in your data table.

PART C Effect of Temperature on Heart Rate

13. In this part of the laboratory investigation, you will examine how an earthworm's heart rate changes as its body temperature changes. Add enough tap water to a Petri dish to barely cover the bottom of the dish. Place an earthworm in the dish.

14. Using a hand lens, look for rhythmic contractions of the dorsal blood vessel. Each contraction represents a single heartbeat. Calculate the worm's heart rate by counting the number of contractions that occur in exactly one minute. This is easiest to do if one person counts contractions while another person watches a stopwatch or clock.

15. Place a thermometer next to the worm in the petri dish and measure the temperature. Record the worm's heart rate and the temperature in a table on the chalkboard.

16. Float the Petri dish containing the worm on top of either a warm-water bath or a cold-water bath. Place the thermometer next to the worm in the Petri dish, and watch the temperature until it reaches either 30°C (for the warm-water bath) or 10°C (for the cold-water bath).

17. Remove the Petri dish from the water bath and immediately begin counting heartbeats for exactly one minute. After one minute, measure the temperature in the dish again. Calculate the average temperature to the nearest degree. Record the worm's heart rate and the average temperature in the table on the chalkboard.

18. Using data from the whole class, graph heart rate as a function of temperature. Draw the best-fit curve through the points.

19. Return the earthworm to the container from which you obtained it. Clean up your materials and wash your hands before leaving the lab.

Analysis and Conclusions

1. State whether your hypotheses in Part B were supported by your observations. Explain.
2. What is the adaptive advantage of the earthworm's responses to light and moisture?
3. List variables that, if not controlled, might have affected the results in Part B.
4. Describe the relationship between the earthworm's heart rate and temperature as shown by your graph.

Further Inquiry

Design an experiment to determine which colors of light an earthworm is sensitive to or which areas on an earthworm are sensitive to light.

CHAPTER 38

ARTHROPODS

*The jointed appendages and hard exoskeleton of this flame lobster,
Enoplometopus occidentalis, are characteristic of arthropods.*

FOCUS CONCEPT: *Evolution*

As you read, note the ways in which the basic arthropod body plan has
become modified for life in diverse environments.

38-1 *Phylum Arthropoda*

38-2 *Subphylum Crustacea*

38-3 *Subphyla Chelicerata
and Uniramia*

PHYLUM ARTHROPODA

*T*hree-fourths of all animal species belong to the phylum Arthropoda (ahr-THRAHP-uh-duh). This phylum contains a diverse assortment of bilaterally symmetrical coelomates, including lobsters, crabs, spiders, millipedes, centipedes, and insects. The characteristics of these animals have enabled them to adapt to almost every environment on Earth.

SECTION

38-1

OBJECTIVES

▲

Describe the distinguishing characteristics of arthropods.

●

Relate the structure of the arthropod exoskeleton to its function.

■

Explain the process of molting in an arthropod.

◆

Name the four subphyla of the phylum Arthropoda, and describe the characteristics of each subphylum.

CHARACTERISTICS OF ARTHROPODS

Members of the phylum Arthropoda are called **arthropods** (AHR-thruh-PAHDS). Like the annelids you studied in Chapter 37, arthropods are segmented animals. In arthropods, however, the body segments bear jointed extensions called **appendages,** such as legs and antennae. In fact, *arthropod* means "jointed foot."

Another distinguishing feature of arthropods is their exoskeleton, which provides protection and support. As Figure 38-1 shows, the arthropod exoskeleton is made up of three layers that are secreted by the epidermis, which lies just beneath the layers. The waxy outer layer is composed of a mixture of protein and lipid. It repels water and helps prevent desiccation in terrestrial species. The middle layer, which provides the primary protection, is composed mainly of protein and chitin. In some arthropods, the middle layer is hardened by the addition of calcium carbonate. The inner layer also contains protein and chitin, but it is flexible at the joints, allowing arthropods to move freely. Muscles that attach to the inner layer on either side of the joints move the body segments relative to each other.

The arthropod body shows a high degree of cephalization. A variety of segmented appendages around the mouth serve as sensors and food handlers. Most arthropods have segmented antennae at the anterior end of the body that are specialized for sensing the environment and detecting chemicals. Most arthropods also have **compound eyes**—eyes composed of many individual light detectors, each with its own lens. In addition, many arthropods have simpler structures that sense light intensity. These sensory structures on the head send nerve impulses to the brain, which coordinates the animal's actions. As in annelids, impulses travel from the brain along a ventral nerve cord, which links ganglia in the other segments of the body. All arthropods have open circulatory systems.

FIGURE 38-1

The arthropod exoskeleton consists of three layers that cover the epidermis. Wax in the outer layer is secreted by wax glands. Sensory hairs projecting from the exoskeleton allow arthropods to respond to vibrations and chemicals in their environment.

Sensory hair

Outer layer
Middle layer
Inner layer
Epidermis

Wax gland

MOLTING

Because an arthropod's skeleton lies on the outside of its body, an arthropod cannot grow without periodically shedding its exoskeleton. This process is called **molting.** Figure 38-2 shows an insect in the process of molting. An arthropod molts many times during its life, and with each molt it becomes larger.

In between molts, the tissues of an arthropod swell until they put a good deal of pressure on the exoskeleton. A hormone is then produced that induces molting. In response to this hormone, the cells of the epidermis secrete enzymes that digest the flexible inner layer of the exoskeleton. At the same time, the epidermis begins to synthesize a new exoskeleton, using much of the digested material. Eventually the outer layer of the old exoskeleton loosens, breaks along specific lines, and is shed. The new exoskeleton, which is flexible at first, stretches to fit the enlarged animal.

It takes a few days for the new exoskeleton to become as hard as the one it replaced. During this time, the animal is extremely vulnerable to predators and, in the case of terrestrial arthropods, susceptible to desiccation. For these reasons, arthropods usually remain in hiding from the time they begin to molt until their new exoskeleton has hardened. The "soft-shelled crabs" sold in some restaurants are crabs that have been caught immediately after molting, while their new exoskeleton is still flexible.

EVOLUTION AND CLASSIFICATION

Animals with arthropod characteristics first appeared more than 600 million years ago. Because all arthropods have a true coelom, an exoskeleton, and jointed appendages, biologists have long inferred that they all evolved from a common ancestor.

The various groups of arthropods living today have undergone similar changes during evolution. For example, ancestral arthropods probably had one pair of appendages on every segment, but most living species have some segments that lack appendages. Ancestral arthropods also had bodies consisting of many segments that were nearly identical, but in most living species the segments are fused into a number of larger structures called **tagmata** (tag-MAHT-uh). The various tagmata are specialized to perform functions such as feeding, locomotion, and reproduction.

Arthropods are divided into four subphyla on the basis of differences in development and in the structure of mouthparts and other appendages. The possible evolutionary relationships among these subphyla are indicated in the phylogenetic tree shown in Figure 38-3.

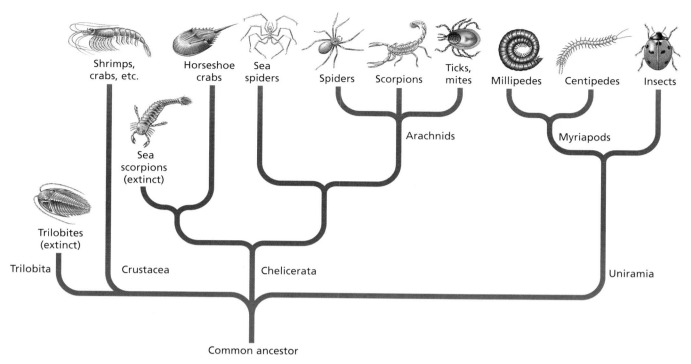

FIGURE 38-3

This phylogenetic tree shows the relationships between the four subphyla of arthropods: Trilobita, Crustacea, Chelicerata, and Uniramia.

- Trilobita (TRIE-luh-BIET-uh) includes extinct animals called trilobites, which had similar, paired appendages on each body segment.
- Crustacea (KRUHS-TAY-shuh) includes shrimps, lobsters, crabs, crayfish, barnacles, isopods, copepods, and water fleas. Members of this subphylum, known as **crustaceans,** have branched antennae and a pair of chewing mouthparts called **mandibles.**
- Chelicerata (kuh-LIS-uh-RAHT-uh) includes spiders, scorpions, mites, ticks, sea spiders, and horseshoe crabs. Members of this subphylum are distinguished from other arthropods by the absence of antennae and the presence of pincerlike mouthparts called **chelicerae** (kuh-LIS-uh-ree).
- Uniramia (YOO-nuh-RAY-mee-uh) includes centipedes, millipedes, and insects. The members of this subphylum also have antennae and mandibles, but their appendages are unbranched. *Uniramia* means "one branch." Uniramia is the only group that seems to have evolved on land.

Word Roots and Origins

chelicera

from the Greek *chele,* meaning "claw," and *keras,* meaning "horn"

SECTION 38-1 REVIEW

1. What characteristics are shared by all arthropods?

2. How many layers are there in an arthropod's exoskeleton? What is the main function of each layer?

3. What is a compound eye?

4. What is molting?

5. What is the major structural difference between members of the subphyla Crustacea and Uniramia?

6. CRITICAL THINKING   After its old exoskeleton has been shed but before the new one has hardened, an aquatic arthropod absorbs water and swells. What is the adaptive advantage of this behavior?

SECTION

38-2

OBJECTIVES

▲

Describe the characteristics of crustaceans.

●

Give examples of crustaceans that are adapted to marine, freshwater, and land environments.

■

Explain the functions of the appendages on a crayfish.

◆

Summarize digestion, respiration, circulation, and excretion in the crayfish.

SUBPHYLUM CRUSTACEA

The subphylum Crustacea contains approximately 40,000 species. Crustaceans are abundant in oceans, lakes, and rivers, and a few species are even found on land. Some crustaceans are sessile, while others move by walking on legs, swimming with paddle-like appendages, or drifting with the currents.

CHARACTERISTICS AND DIVERSITY OF CRUSTACEANS

Crustaceans are the only arthropods that have two pairs of appendages on their head that serve as feelers. Each of the other body segments generally has a pair of appendages, and at least some of those appendages are branched. Although some crustaceans have 60 or more body segments, most crustaceans have only 16–20 segments, which are fused into several tagmata. The exoskeletons of aquatic crustaceans, such as lobsters, often contain large amounts of calcium carbonate, making them extremely hard. Some small crustaceans exchange carbon dioxide and oxygen through the thin areas of their exoskeleton, but larger crustaceans respire with gills.

During the development of most crustaceans, the embryo becomes a free-swimming larva called a **nauplius** (NAH-plee-uhs), which looks quite different from the adults of its species. As you can see in Figure 38-4, a nauplius has three pairs of appendages and a single eye in the middle of its head. Through a series of molts, the nauplius eventually takes on the adult form.

Crustaceans exist in a range of sizes, but most are small. For example, copepods, like the one shown in Figure 38-5a, are no larger than the comma in this sentence. Copepods are extremely abundant in some marine environments. In fact, they may be the most abundant animals in the world. Copepods constitute an important part of the ocean's **plankton,** the collection of small organisms that drift or swim weakly near the surface of a body of water. In freshwater environments, on the other hand, much of the plankton is composed of crustaceans known as water fleas, which are about the size of copepods. A common type of water flea, *Daphnia,* is illustrated in Figure 38-5b. At the other end of the crustacean size spectrum is the Japanese spider crab, shown in Figure 38-5c. With a leg span of 4 m (13 ft), it is the largest living arthropod.

FIGURE 38-4

The free-swimming nauplius larva is an early stage in the development of most crustaceans. It has one eye and three pairs of appendages.

Eye

Appendages

(a)

(b)

(c)

FIGURE 38-5

Crustaceans include tiny species such as the copepod *Cyclops* (a) and the water flea *Daphnia* (b), as well as giants like the Japanese spider crab, *Macrocheira kaempferi* (c).

Barnacles, like the one shown in Figure 38-6, are marine crustaceans that are adapted to a sessile lifestyle as adults. Free-swimming barnacle larvae attach themselves to rocks, piers, boats, sea turtles, whales, and just about any other surface. They then develop a very hard shell of calcium carbonate that completely encloses the body in most species. Their swimming appendages are replaced by six pairs of long legs called **cirri** (SIR-ie), each of which is covered with hairlike setae. The cirri extend through openings in the shell, sweeping small organisms and food particles from the water and directing them to the mouth.

Sow bugs and pill bugs are terrestrial members of a group of crustaceans called **isopods.** *Isopod* means "equal legs," which refers to the seven pairs of identical legs on these crustaceans. Terrestrial isopods can lose water quickly through their exoskeletons. Therefore, they live only in moist environments, such as those found under leaves and rocks, in crevices around garden beds, and in the spaces between house foundations and sidewalks. In addition, pill bugs are capable of rolling into a ball when disturbed or threatened with desiccation. Sow bugs and pill bugs generally feed on decaying vegetation, but they may also eat garden bulbs, vegetables, and fruits that lie on or in the soil.

FIGURE 38-6

Barnacles, like *Lepas anatifera*, are sessile marine crustaceans that filter food from the water with the help of their modified legs.

THE CRAYFISH

The crayfish is a freshwater crustacean that has been well studied because of its relatively large size and abundance. Crayfish are structurally similar to lobsters, their marine relatives. Both are called **decapods** (DEK-uh-PAHDS), a name that means "ten feet," because they have five pairs of legs. Shrimps and crabs are also decapods. The remainder of this section explores some of the details of crayfish structure and function.

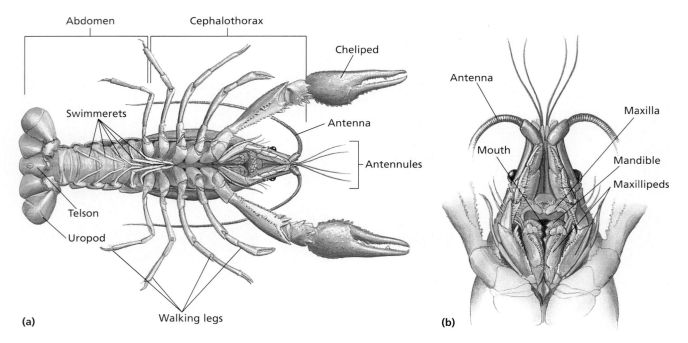

Abdomen   Cephalothorax

Cheliped

Antenna

Antennules

Swimmerets

Telson

Uropod

Walking legs

(a)

Antenna

Maxilla

Mouth

Mandible

Maxillipeds

(b)

FIGURE 38-7

(a) Each of the 20 body segments of a crayfish except the telson bears a pair of appendages, which can be seen in this ventral view. (b) The appendages of the anterior cephalothorax are visible in this closer ventral view.

Quick Lab

Observing Crayfish Behavior

Materials crayfish in container with water, tapping instrument

Procedure

Gently tap the anterior (head) end of the crayfish, and record your observations. Tap the posterior (tail) end of the crayfish, and record your observations.

Analysis Describe each behavioral response you observed when you tapped the crayfish. How does each behavior aid the animal in its survival?

External Structure

The body of a crayfish is divided into two major sections: the cephalothorax (SEF-uh-luh-THOHR-aks) and the abdomen. The **cephalothorax,** in turn, consists of two tagmata: the head, which has five segments, and the **thorax,** which has eight segments and lies posterior to the head. The dorsal exoskeleton of the segments in the cephalothorax is fused into a single, tough covering known as the **carapace** (KAR-uh-PAYS). The **abdomen,** the tagma that lies posterior to the cephalothorax, is divided into seven segments. The seventh abdominal segment, called the **telson,** forms a flat paddle at the posterior end of the crayfish. Powerful muscles can bend the abdomen suddenly, propelling the animal rapidly backward in a movement referred to as a tailflip.

A pair of appendages is attached to each segment of the crayfish except the telson, as you can see in Figure 38-7. The **antennules** serve as feelers sensitive to touch, taste, and equilibrium. The long **antennae** are also feelers; they respond to touch and taste. Crayfish chew food with their mandibles and manipulate it with their two pairs of **maxillae** and three pairs of **maxillipeds** (mak-SIL-uh-PEDS). The posterior pair of maxillae also function in respiration and the maxillipeds are sensitive to touch and taste. The most anterior pair of appendages on the thorax, the **chelipeds** (KEE-luh-PEDS), end in large pincers used for capturing food and for defense. The four pairs of walking legs carry the crayfish over solid surfaces; the first two pairs end in small pincers that can grasp small objects. The **swimmerets,** which are attached to the anterior five abdominal segments, create water currents and function in reproduction. The **uropods** (YUR-uh-PAHDS), on the sixth abdominal segment, help propel the crayfish during tailflips. Table 38-1 summarizes the crayfish appendages and their functions.

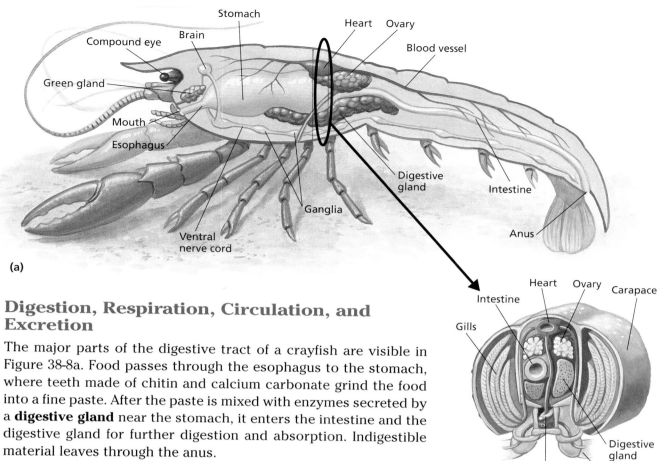

(a)

(b)

FIGURE 38-8

The major internal organs of a crayfish are seen in this cutaway side view (a) and cross section through the heart region (b).

Digestion, Respiration, Circulation, and Excretion

The major parts of the digestive tract of a crayfish are visible in Figure 38-8a. Food passes through the esophagus to the stomach, where teeth made of chitin and calcium carbonate grind the food into a fine paste. After the paste is mixed with enzymes secreted by a **digestive gland** near the stomach, it enters the intestine and the digestive gland for further digestion and absorption. Indigestible material leaves through the anus.

Like all but the smallest crustaceans, crayfish use gills for respiration. Figure 38-8b shows that the gills extend from the base of each walking leg into a chamber under the carapace. As a crayfish walks, its legs circulate water across its gills. Feathery branches on the posterior pair of maxillae also help direct water over the gills. Each gill is covered by an extension of the exoskeleton that is thin enough to permit gases to diffuse across the gill surface.

TABLE 38-1	*Crayfish Appendages*
Appendage	**Function**
Antennule	touch, taste, equilibrium
Antenna	touch, taste
Mandible	chew food
Maxilla	manipulate food, draw water currents over gills
Maxilliped	touch, taste, manipulate food
Cheliped	capture food, defense
Walking leg	locomotion over solid surfaces
Swimmeret	create water currents, transfer sperm (males), carry eggs and young (females)
Uropod	propulsion during tailflips

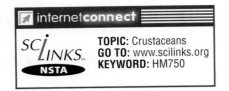
The main components of the crayfish's open circulatory system are shown in Figures 38-8a and 38-8b. The dorsal heart pumps hemolymph into several large vessels that carry it to different regions of the body. Hemolymph leaves the vessels and enters the hemocoel, bathing the various tissues. It then passes through the gills, where it exchanges carbon dioxide and oxygen with the water. From the gills, the hemolymph returns to the dorsal part of the crayfish and enters the heart.

As freshwater organisms, crayfish live in a hypotonic environment. Recall from Chapter 5 that a hypotonic environment is one in which the concentration of solute molecules is lower than that in the organism's cells. Therefore, water constantly enters the tissues of a crayfish by osmosis. This excess water is eliminated by excretory organs called **green glands,** which are visible in Figure 38-8a. The dilute fluid collected by the green glands leaves the body through a pore at the base of the antennae.

Neural Control

The nervous system of the crayfish is illustrated in Figure 38-8a. It is typical of arthropods and is similar to the nervous system of annelids. The crayfish brain consists of a pair of ganglia above the esophagus that receive nerve impulses from the eyes, antennules, and antennae. Two bundles of nerve fibers extend from the brain and pass around either side of the esophagus to a ganglion that controls the mandibles, maxillae, and maxillipeds. The ventral nerve cord runs posteriorly from this ganglion, connecting a series of ganglia that control the appendages and muscles in the segments of the thorax and abdomen.

Crayfish sense vibrations and chemicals in the water with thousands of small sensory hairs that project from the exoskeleton. Sensory hairs are visible in Figure 38-1. These sensory hairs are distributed over the entire body, but they are especially concentrated on the antennules, antennae, mouthparts, chelipeds, and telson. The compound eyes of a crayfish are set on two short, movable stalks. Each eye has more than 2,000 light-sensitive units with their own lenses. At the base of the antennules are organs that can detect the animal's orientation with respect to gravity.

SECTION 38-2 REVIEW

1. What characteristics are shared by most or all crustaceans?

2. Name one crustacean that lives in the ocean, one that lives in fresh water, and one that lives on land.

3. What are the functions of the mandibles and the chelipeds on a crayfish?

4. What structural adaptations of crayfish promote effective respiration in water?

5. What is the function of a crayfish's green glands?

6. **CRITICAL THINKING** In what year of its life would you expect a crayfish to grow most rapidly, given what you know about molting? Explain your reasoning.

SUBPHYLA CHELICERATA AND UNIRAMIA

*Unlike crustaceans, nearly all members of the subphyla Chelicerata and Uniramia are terrestrial. The major group in Chelicerata is the class Arachnida (uh-RAK-nuh-duh), which contains over 70,000 species. In Uniramia, members of the classes Diplopoda (di-PLAHP-uh-duh) and Chilopoda (ki-LAHP-uh-duh) have many body segments, and most segments have one or two pairs of legs. Thus, they are commonly called **myriapods** (MIR-ee-uh-PAHDZ), which means "many feet."*

SECTION

38-3

OBJECTIVES

▲

List the characteristics of the class Arachnida.

●

Explain the adaptations spiders have for predatory life on land.

■

List the distinguishing characteristics of scorpions and of mites and ticks.

◆

Describe similarities and differences between millipedes and centipedes.

CLASS ARACHNIDA

Members of the class Arachnida, called **arachnids,** include spiders, scorpions, mites, and ticks. Like crayfish and other decapod crustaceans, arachnids have a body that is divided into a cephalothorax and an abdomen. The cephalothorax in arachnids usually bears six pairs of jointed appendages: one pair of chelicerae; one pair of **pedipalps,** which aid in holding food and chewing; and four pairs of walking legs.

Anatomy of a Spider

Spiders range in length from less than 0.5 mm to as large as 9 cm (3.5 in.) in some tropical tarantula species. As you can see in Figure 38-9, the body of a spider is constricted between the cephalothorax

FIGURE 38-9

The major internal organs of a spider are seen in this cutaway side view. The inset shows a closer view of a book lung, one of the spider's adaptations to life on land.

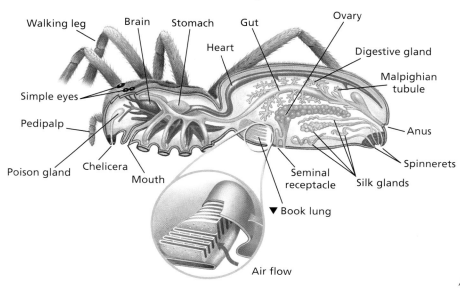

Walking leg · Brain · Stomach · Gut · Ovary · Heart · Digestive gland · Malpighian tubule · Simple eyes · Pedipalp · Anus · Poison gland · Chelicera · Mouth · Seminal receptacle · Silk glands · Spinnerets · ▼ Book lung · Air flow

TOPIC: Arachnida
GO TO: www.scilinks.org
KEYWORD: HM752

FIGURE 38-10

The black widow, *Latrodectus mactans* (a), and the brown recluse, *Loxosceles reclusa* (b), are the only two spiders in the United States whose venom is dangerous to humans. Note the red hourglass-shaped spot on the abdomen of the black widow and the dark violin-shaped marking on the cephalothorax of the brown recluse.

(a)

(b)

and the abdomen. The chelicerae are modified as fangs and are used to inject venom into prey. The venom is produced by poison glands in the cephalothorax and flows through ducts in the chelicerae to the tips of the fangs. Most spiders have eight simple eyes at the anterior end of the cephalothorax. Each simple eye has a single lens.

On the tip of the abdomen of many spiders are three pairs of organs called **spinnerets,** which are visible in Figure 38-9. Each spinneret is composed of hundreds of microscopic tubes that connect to silk glands in the abdomen. A protein-containing fluid produced in the silk glands hardens into threads as it is pulled from the spinnerets. Spiders use their silk threads to spin webs, build nests, and protect eggs. Some young spiders even move to new habitats when the wind pulls them through the air by their threads.

The nervous, digestive, and circulatory systems of spiders are similar to those of crustaceans. Because spiders are terrestrial, however, their respiratory system is quite different. In some spiders, respiration occurs in **book lungs,** paired sacs in the abdomen with many parallel folds that resemble the pages of a book. The folds in a book lung provide a large surface area for gas exchange. Other spiders have a system of tubes called **tracheae** (TRAY-kee-ee) that carry air directly to the tissues from openings in the exoskeleton known as **spiracles.** Some spiders have both book lungs and tracheae.

The excretory system of spiders is also modified for life on land. The main excretory organs, called **Malpighian** (MAL-PIG-ee-uhn) **tubules,** are hollow projections of the digestive tract that collect body fluids and wastes and carry them to the intestine. After most of the water is reabsorbed, the wastes leave the body in a nearly solid form with the feces. Thus, the Malpighian tubules help spiders conserve water in terrestrial environments. Some spiders also have **coxal glands,** organs that remove wastes and discharge them through openings at the base of some of the legs.

Life of a Spider

Spiders feed mainly on insects, although some can catch fish, frogs, and even birds. Different species of spiders are adapted to capture their prey in different ways. Some chase after prey, some hide beneath trapdoors waiting for prey to approach, and some snare prey in webs spun from silk. When an insect becomes trapped in the sticky web, the spider emerges from its hiding place near the edge of the web and paralyzes the insect with its venom. Many spiders also immobilize their prey by wrapping them in silk. They can then consume the body fluids of the prey at a later time.

Spider venom is usually harmless to humans, and most spiders bite only when they or their young are threatened. There are, however, two kinds of spiders in the United States whose bites can be serious and occasionally fatal to humans. They are the black widow and the brown recluse, shown in Figure 38-10. The black widow has a bright red or orange mark shaped like an hourglass on the ventral surface of its abdomen. Its venom attacks the nervous system. The brown recluse has a violin-shaped mark on the dorsal surface of its cephalothorax. Therefore, it is sometimes called the "violin spider." The venom of the brown recluse digests the tissues surrounding the bite.

A male spider is usually smaller than a female of the same species. When the male is mature, he transfers sperm to special sacs in the tips of his pedipalps. The sperm are then placed in the seminal receptacle of the female during mating. As soon as mating has occurred, the male darts away. If he is not quick enough, he may be eaten by the female. Eggs are fertilized as they pass out of the female into a silken case that she has spun. The female may carry the egg case with her or attach it to a web or plant. The young spiders hatch in about two weeks and undergo their first molt before leaving the case.

Scorpions

Scorpions, like the one shown in Figure 38-11, differ from spiders in two ways. Scorpions have large, pincerlike pedipalps, which they hold in a forward position. They also have a large stinger on the last segment of the abdomen, which is curled over the body. Scorpions usually hide during the day and hunt at night, mostly for insects and spiders. They seize prey with their pedipalps and inject venom into the prey with their stinger. Only a few species of scorpions have venom that can be fatal to humans. Most scorpions live in tropical or semitropical areas, but some are found in dry temperate or desert regions.

Mites and Ticks

Mites and ticks are the most abundant and most specialized arachnids. About 30,000 species have been identified, but the actual number of species may be much larger than that. Unlike spiders and scorpions, mites and ticks have a completely fused cephalothorax and abdomen, with no sign of separation between them.

Most mites are less than a millimeter in length, and some are small enough to live on particles of dust. They can be found in freshwater, marine, and terrestrial habitats. Many mites are entirely free living, while others are parasites during at least part of their life cycle. Spider mites parasitize fruit trees and many other agricultural crops by sucking the fluid from their leaves. The larvae of harvest mites— also known as chiggers—attach themselves to the skin of vertebrates, including humans. They break the skin with their chelicerae and feed on blood, causing swelling and itching. Other species of mites live on the bodies of chickens, dogs, cattle, humans, and other animals, where they feed on sloughing skin, hair, and feathers.

Ticks range in length from a few millimeters to 3 cm (a little over 1 in.). Many parasitic ticks, including the lone star tick shown in Figure 38-12, pierce their host's skin to feed on blood. In the process, they can transmit bacteria and other microorganisms that cause diseases such as Rocky Mountain spotted fever and Lyme disease.

FIGURE 38-11

Scorpions, like *Paruroctonus mesaensis*, have pincerlike pedipalps and a venomous stinger at the end of their abdomen.

FIGURE 38-12

The lone star tick, *Amblyomma americanum*, is an arachnid that parasitizes humans and other mammals.

(a)

(b)

FIGURE 38-13

(a) Millipedes, like *Narceus americanus*, have a rounded body and two pairs of legs on each body segment except the last two. (b) Centipedes, including *Scolopendra*, have a flattened body and one pair of legs on each body segment except the first and the last two.

MYRIAPODS

Myriapods—millipedes and centipedes—are members of the subphylum Uniramia. Early myriapods may have been the first animals to appear on land, and all present-day myriapods are terrestrial. Their bodies are highly segmented, and the segments bear appendages that show little variation. Like insects, myriapods have a single pair of unbranched antennae. However, myriapods do not have a waxy exoskeleton. They avoid desiccation by living in damp environments under leaves, rocks, and logs.

Class Diplopoda

The class Diplopoda consists of millipedes. Most millipedes have two pairs of legs on each body segment except the last two. The legs are well adapted for burrowing through humus and soil, but because they are short, millipedes move slowly. As you can see in Figure 38-13a, the bodies of millipedes are rounded.

Millipedes have short antennae and two groups of simple eyes on their head. They have poor vision, but a good sense of smell. Millipedes use their maxillae and mandibles to chew on plants or decaying plant matter in the soil. When threatened, they coil up and may secrete a noxious fluid that contains cyanide.

Class Chilopoda

Centipedes are members of the class Chilopoda. Centipedes may have as few as 15 or as many as 175 pairs of legs. In tropical regions centipedes reach lengths of 30 cm (12 in.). Their bodies are more flattened than those of millipedes, and their legs are longer relative to their body, as Figure 38-13b shows. Each body segment behind the head, except the first segment and the last two segments, has one pair of jointed legs. The appendages on the first segment are modified into a pair of poison claws. Long antennae and two clusters of simple eyes are located on the head.

Centipedes can move quickly in search of earthworms, insects, and other prey. They kill the prey with their poison claws and use their mandibles and maxillae to tear it apart. Most centipedes are not harmful to humans.

SECTION 38-3 REVIEW

1. What are the characteristics of arachnids?

2. Define *pedipalps,* and explain their function.

3. How is the excretory system of spiders adapted for life on land?

4. Name two ways in which scorpions differ from spiders.

5. How are millipedes and centipedes different?

6. **CRITICAL THINKING**   How might the feeding habits of spiders benefit humans?

SUMMARY/VOCABULARY

38-1 ■ Arthropods are segmented animals that have jointed appendages, an exoskeleton, a high degree of cephalization, a ventral nerve cord, and an open circulatory system.

■ To grow, an arthropod must shed its exoskeleton periodically in a process called molting.

■ The subphylum Trilobita includes extinct animals called trilobites.

■ Members of the subphylum Crustacea have branched antennae and a pair of chewing mouthparts called mandibles.

■ Members of the subphylum Chelicerata lack antennae and have pincerlike mouthparts called chelicerae.

■ Members of the subphylum Uniramia have antennae, mandibles, and unbranched appendages.

Vocabulary

appendage (743)	chelicera (745)	crustacean (745)	molting (744)
arthropod (743)	compound eye (743)	mandible (745)	tagma (744)

38-2 ■ Crustaceans include shrimps, lobsters, crabs, crayfish, barnacles, isopods, copepods, and water fleas.

■ Crustaceans have two pairs of feelers on their head and one pair of usually branched appendages on their other body segments. Their exoskeletons often contain large amounts of calcium carbonate.

■ Most crustaceans are aquatic, respire with gills, and go through a nauplius larval stage during development.

■ The body of a crayfish is divided into a cephalothorax and an abdomen. The appendages on each body segment are specialized for sensing, feeding, respiration, locomotion, or reproduction.

Vocabulary

abdomen (748)	cheliped (748)	isopod (747)	swimmeret (748)
antenna (748)	cirrus (747)	maxilla (748)	telson (748)
antennule (748)	decapod (747)	maxilliped (748)	thorax (748)
carapace (748)	digestive gland (749)	nauplius (746)	uropod (748)
cephalothorax (747)	green gland (750)	plankton (746)	

38-3 ■ Arachnids include spiders, scorpions, mites, and ticks. Their bodies are divided into a cephalothorax and an abdomen, and they usually have six pairs of jointed appendages: one pair of chelicerae, one pair of pedipalps, and four pairs of walking legs.

■ Spiders have eight simple eyes, and chelicerae modified as fangs that can inject venom. They produce silk threads that are used for prey capture and other functions. Spiders are terrestrial; they respire by means of book lungs, tracheae, or both, and they use Malpighian tubules to excrete wastes while conserving water.

■ Scorpions have large, pincerlike pedipalps and a stinger on the last segment of the abdomen.

■ Mites and ticks have a completely fused cephalothorax and abdomen. Many species are parasitic, and some spread diseases that affect humans.

■ Myriapods include millipedes and centipedes. Millipedes have rounded bodies and two pairs of jointed legs on each body segment except the last two. Centipedes have flattened bodies and one pair of jointed legs on each body segment except the first and the last two.

Vocabulary

arachnid (751)	Malpighian tubule (752)	pedipalp (751)	spiracle (752)
book lung (752)	myriapod (751)	spinneret (752)	trachea (752)
coxal gland (752)			

REVIEW

Vocabulary

1. Name the appendages on the cephalothorax of a crayfish.
2. Name the appendages on the abdomen of a crayfish.
3. Choose the term that does not belong in the following group, and explain why it does not belong: scorpion, centipede, mite, spider.
4. What are tagmata?
5. Distinguish between chelicerae and mandibles of arthropods.

Multiple Choice

6. All arthropods have (a) a cephalothorax (b) spiracles (c) jointed appendages (d) antennae.
7. The exoskeleton of an arthropod (a) provides protection and support (b) plays a role in movement (c) contains chitin (d) all of the above.
8. Myriapods are members of the subphylum (a) Arachnida (b) Chelicerata (c) Chilopoda (d) Uniramia.
9. The major respiratory organs of crayfish are the (a) gills (b) lungs (c) tracheae (d) book lungs.
10. Compound eyes (a) have a single lens (b) are composed of many individual light detectors (c) are found in all arthropods except the crayfish (d) are located on the abdomen of scorpions.
11. Spiders feed mainly on (a) plants (b) decayed matter (c) insects (d) other spiders.
12. Mites and ticks differ from spiders by having (a) mandibles (b) a unique respiratory system (c) two pairs of antennae (d) a fused cephalothorax and abdomen.
13. Book lungs help spiders respire on land by (a) providing a large surface area for the exchange of gases (b) carrying air directly to tissues (c) both a and b (d) neither a nor b.
14. Centipedes and millipedes differ in (a) the way their bodies are shaped (b) the number of legs they have on each segment (c) their feeding habits (d) all of the above.
15. The subphylum of modern arthropods that is primarily aquatic is (a) Crustacea (b) Chelicerata (c) Trilobita (d) Uniramia.

Short Answer

16. Arrange the following steps in the molting of an arthropod in the correct order:
    a. The old exoskeleton loosens, breaks along specific lines, and is shed.
    b. Enzymes digest the inner layer of the exoskeleton.
    c. A hormone is produced that induces molting.
    d. The epidermis begins to synthesize a new exoskeleton.
17. What criteria do biologists use to classify arthropods into four subphyla?
18. What evolutionary trends have all three subphyla of modern arthropods undergone?
19. Contrast the process of respiration in crayfish and spiders.
20. In what ways are spiders adapted for a predatory way of life?
21. Describe how a spider produces silk threads.
22. How do parasitic ticks spread diseases?
23. What defensive behaviors are common in millipedes?
24. How do myriapods avoid desiccation in terrestrial environments?
25. Identify the structures labeled *A* through *F* in the diagram below.

CRITICAL THINKING

1. The water flea *Daphnia* eats algae. It also has a prominent eyespot. How might the eyespot be connected with the ability of *Daphnia* to find food?
2. Barnacles are sessile crustaceans. What structural adaptation do barnacles have that enables them to compete with motile organisms for food? What structural adaptation do barnacles have that might protect them from predators?
3. The cephalothorax of a crayfish is covered by the carapace, a single, fused plate of exoskeleton. What are some possible advantages and disadvantages of this fused structure?
4. Like other arthropods, crayfish are cephalized, with a variety of specialized sensory structures on their head. However, crayfish also have a high concentration of sensory hairs on their telson. What might be the advantage of having so many sensory structures at the posterior end of the animal?
5. The American lobster, *Homarus americanus,* is a nocturnal organism. Marine biologists have discovered that the lobster's senses of taste and smell are over 1,000 times more powerful than those senses in humans. The lobster uses taste and smell both to search for food and to detect mates. What adaptive advantage would these highly developed senses provide for the lobster?
6. Aquatic arthropods, such as crabs and crayfish, typically have thicker, stronger exoskeletons than do terrestrial arthropods, such as spiders and insects. What advantage does a thick, strong exoskeleton provide in an aquatic environment?
7. Arthropods first invaded land about 400 million years ago. They have survived several mass extinctions in which many other kinds of organisms became extinct. What characteristics have enabled arthropods to thrive?
8. The graph below shows how the weight of a spider changed over the first 60 days of its life. What events occurred at the beginning of each sharp upward turn in the curve? Why did the spider's weight increase more gradually between these events?

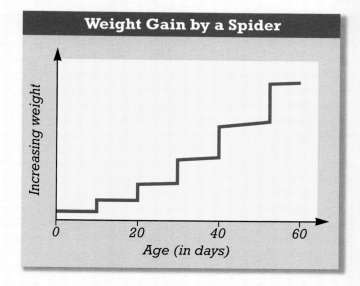

Weight Gain by a Spider

Increasing weight (y-axis)

Age (in days) — 0, 20, 40, 60

EXTENSION

1. Read "Having Mom for Dinner" in *Natural History,* April 1999, on page 21. What is the usual form of cannibalism in the animal world? What is the unusual form of cannibalism that is practiced by the spider *Amaurobius ferox*? How many eggs does the spider lay at one time? What does the mother spider do to protect herself from being eaten by her young?
2. Contact your local public health department and ask for information about arthropod-transmitted diseases that might be found in your area. If possible, find out how many cases of each disease have been reported in the last year. Report your findings to the class, or prepare a table summarizing your findings.
3. Do library research to discover the life history of a horseshoe crab, a sea spider, or a tick. Before beginning your research, examine Figure 38-3 for the phylogenetic relationships of these three types of arthropods.

Behavior of Pill Bugs

OBJECTIVES

- Review characteristics of the phylum Arthropoda and the subphylum Crustacea.
- Observe the external anatomy of a living terrestrial isopod.
- Investigate the behavior of terrestrial isopods.

PROCESS SKILLS

- observing
- hypothesizing
- experimenting

MATERIALS

- 5 live pill bugs or sow bugs for each pair of students
- 1 plastic medicine dropper
- water
- potato
- 3 sheets of filter paper cut to fit a Petri dish
- Petri dish with cover
- aluminum foil
- bright lamp or flashlight
- 4 fabrics of different texture
- cellophane tape
- scissors

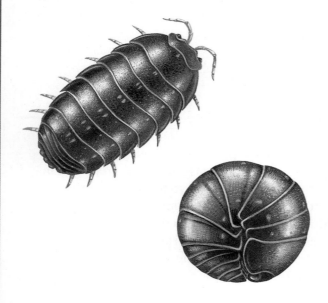

Background

1. What are the major characteristics of the members of the phylum Arthropoda and the subphylum Crustacea?
2. Why are pill bugs called isopods?
3. How are pill bugs different from most other crustaceans?

PART A Response to Light

1. Put several drops of water on a piece of filter paper until the paper becomes slightly moist. Place the filter paper in the bottom of a Petri dish. Cover half the bottom of the Petri dish with aluminum foil.
2. Check the lighting in the room. The light must be low and even during this part of the investigation.
3. ⚠ **CAUTION You will be working with live animals. Be sure to treat them gently and to follow directions carefully.** Place five pill bugs in the center of the filter paper. Shine a lamp directly over the Petri dish so that half the filter paper is brightly illuminated and the other half is in darkness, shaded by the foil.
4. Based on your knowledge of the natural habitat of pill bugs, can you predict where they will go? Make a data table like the one shown, and record your prediction as well as the actual responses of the pill bugs.

PART B Response to Moisture

5. Cut a piece of filter paper in half. Moisten one of the halves with water and place it in the bottom of a Petri dish. Make sure that drops of water do not leak onto the bottom of the dish.
6. Place the dry half of the filter paper in the bottom of the Petri dish, leaving a 2 mm gap between it and the damp filter paper.
7. Place five pill bugs along the boundary between the wet and dry areas. Place the top on the dish.
8. To which side do you predict the pill bugs will move? Write your prediction in your data table. Observe the pill bugs for 3 to 5 minutes, and record your observations in your data table. Do your observations agree with your predictions?

PART C Response to Food

9. Again dampen a piece of filter paper and place it in the bottom of a Petri dish. Next place a thin slice of potato near the edge of the dish.
10. Place five pill bugs in the Petri dish opposite the potato slice, and place the lid on the dish.
11. Where do you predict the pill bugs will go? Write your prediction in your data table. Observe the pill bugs for 3 to 5 minutes, and record your observations in your data table. Do your observations agree with your predictions?

PART D Response to Surface Texture

12. Trace the outline of the bottom of a Petri dish on one of the fabrics. Cut the circle out of the fabric and fold it in half. Then cut along the fold to produce two half-circles.
13. Repeat step 12 using the other three fabrics. You should now have eight half-circles.
14. Tape together two half-circles, each of a different fabric. Place the two-fabric circle in the bottom of a Petri dish, tape side down, as shown in the figure below.
15. On a sheet of paper, draw the fabric circle and label the two types of fabric that make up the circle.

16. Place a pill bug in the center of the circle and observe its movements. One student should keep track of the amount of time the animal spends on each fabric. On the drawing that was made in step 15, the other student should draw the path the pill bug travels in the circle. After 5 minutes, stop your observations and record the amount of time the pill bug spent on each fabric.
17. Repeat steps 14–16 for two other pairs of fabrics.
18. Return the pill bugs to their container. Clean up your materials and wash your hands before leaving the lab.

Analysis and Conclusions

1. In Part A, why was the entire filter paper moistened?
2. In Part B, why was there a slight separation between the wet and dry halves of the filter paper?
3. In Part C, why was the entire filter paper moistened?
4. In Part D, which fabric did the pill bugs prefer? Describe the texture of that fabric.
5. How do the responses of pill bugs to light, moisture, and food in these experiments reflect adaptations to their natural surroundings?
6. How is being able to detect surface texture a good adaptation for pill bugs in their natural habitat?

Further Inquiry

1. Design an experiment to investigate the response of pill bugs to temperature. Think carefully about how you will construct your apparatus. Seek approval from your teacher before you actually conduct this experiment. How do you think the pill bugs will respond?
2. Design an experiment to investigate whether pill bugs have preferences for certain types of food.

OBSERVATION OF PILL-BUG BEHAVIOR

Stimulus	Prediction	Observation
Light		
Moisture		
Food		

INSECTS

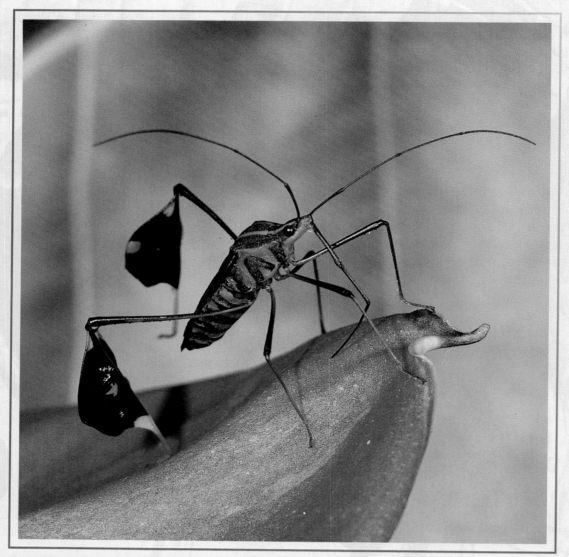

The leaf-footed bug, Diactor bilineatus, *is a colorful member of the extremely diverse world of insects.*

FOCUS CONCEPT: *Evolution*

As you read, look for the structural, developmental, and behavioral adaptations that have made insects such a successful group of animals.

39-1 *The Insect World*

39-2 *Insect Behavior*

THE INSECT WORLD

Insects have thrived for more than 300 million years, since long before the rise and fall of the dinosaurs. The story of insects is one of great biological success through evolution and adaptation. Today, insects account for about three-fourths of all animal species on Earth.

CHARACTERISTICS AND CLASSIFICATION OF INSECTS

Many of the adaptations that have made insects successful are characteristics they share with other arthropods, such as a segmented body, jointed appendages, and an exoskeleton. Insects belong to the class Insecta in the subphylum Uniramia, which, as you may recall from Chapter 38, also includes millipedes and centipedes. The body of an insect is divided into three tagmata: the head, thorax, and abdomen. Like other members of the subphylum Uniramia, insects have mandibles and one pair of antennae on their head, and the antennae and other appendages are unbranched. The thorax has three pairs of jointed legs and, in many species, one or two pairs of wings. The abdomen is composed of 9 to 11 segments, and in adults it has neither wings nor legs.

Most insects are small. Among the smallest is the fairyfly, which is only 0.2 mm (0.008 in.) in length. Some insects are much larger. For example, the African Goliath beetle exceeds 10 cm (4 in.) in length, and the atlas moth has a wingspan of more than 25 cm (10 in.). These two giants of the insect world are shown in Figure 39-1.

OBJECTIVES

▲

State the major characteristics of the class Insecta.

●

Explain why insects are so successful.

■

List both harmful and beneficial effects of insects on human society.

◆

Describe the external structure and organ systems of a grasshopper.

▲

Explain incomplete and complete metamorphosis in insects.

FIGURE 39-1

Two of the largest insects are the African Goliath beetle, *Goliathus meleagris* (a), and the atlas moth, *Attacus atlas* (b).

(a)

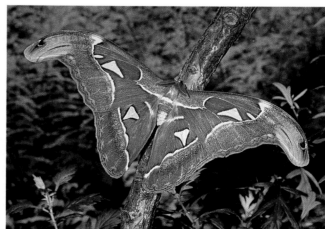

(b)

The study of insects is called **entomology** (ENT-uh-MAHL-uh-jee), and the scientists who engage in it are known as entomologists. Entomologists classify insects into more than 30 orders based on characteristics such as the structure of mouthparts, number of wings, and type of development. Several of the more common insect orders are listed in Table 39-1.

TABLE 39-1 *Common Insect Orders*

Order	Number of species	Examples	Type of metamorphosis	Characteristics	Significance to humans
Thysanura ("bristled tail")	2,400	bristletails silverfish firebrats	none	chewing mouthparts	feed on paste in wallpaper and starch in book bindings and labels
Anoplura ("unarmed tail")	2,400	sucking lice	incomplete	wingless; piercing, sucking mouthparts	parasitize humans, other mammals, and birds; transmit diseases
Dermaptera ("skin wing")	1,000	earwigs	incomplete	two pairs of wings; biting mouthparts; pincerlike appendages at tip of abdomen	damage plants; transmit diseases
Ephemeroptera ("for-a-day wing")	1,500	mayflies	incomplete	membranous wings (triangular forewings); nonfunctioning mouthparts in adults	nymphs serve as food for freshwater fish
Hemiptera ("half wing")	55,000	true bugs	incomplete	two pairs of wings during part of life; piercing, sucking mouthparts	damage crops and garden plants
Homoptera ("like wing")	20,000	aphids mealy bugs cicadas	incomplete	membranous wings held like roof over body (some species wingless); piercing, sucking mouthparts	damage crops and garden plants
Isoptera ("equal wing")	2,000	termites	incomplete	at times, two pairs of membranous wings; chewing mouthparts	decompose wood in buildings; recycle resources in forests
Odonata ("toothed")	5,000	dragonflies damselflies	incomplete	two pairs of long, narrow, membranous wings; chewing mouthparts	destroy harmful insects; nymphs serve as food for freshwater fish
Orthoptera ("straight wing")	30,000	grasshoppers crickets katydids cockroaches	incomplete	two pairs of straight wings; chewing mouthparts	damage crops, garden plants, and stored foods

The Success of Insects

Insects live almost everywhere in the world except in the deep ocean. Water striders glide on the surface of oceans and lakes, beetles inhabit the hottest deserts, and snow fleas survive on permanent glaciers. Entomologists have described and classified more than 700,000 insect species, or about three times as many species

Order	Number of species	Examples	Type of metamorphosis	Characteristics	Significance to humans
Coleoptera ("sheathed wing")	500,000	weevils ladybugs beetles	incomplete	hard forewings, membranous hind wings; chewing mouthparts	destroy crops; prey on other insects
Diptera ("two wing")	80,000	mosquitoes flies gnats	complete	one pair of wings (hind pair reduced to knobs); sucking, piercing, or lapping mouthparts	carry diseases; destroy crops; pollinate flowers; act as decomposers
Hymenoptera ("membrane wing")	90,000	bees wasps ants	complete	two pairs of membranous wings (some species wingless); biting, sucking or lapping mouthparts; many have constriction between thorax and abdomen; some species social	pollinate flowers; make honey; destroy harmful insects
Lepidoptera ("scaled wing")	140,000	butterflies moths	complete	large, scaled wings; chewing mouthparts in larvae, siphoning mouthparts in adults	pollinate flowers; larvae and pupae produce silk; larvae damage clothing and crops
Neuroptera ("nerve wing")	4,600	dobsonflies lacewings ant lions	complete	two pairs of membranous wings; sucking or chewing mouthparts in larvae, chewing mouthparts in adults	destroy harmful insects; larvae serve as food for freshwater fish
Siphonaptera ("tubed, wingless")	1,200	fleas	complete	wingless as adults; chewing mouthparts in larvae, sucking mouthparts in adults	parasitize birds and mammals; carry diseases

FIGURE 39-2

Some insects are harmful to humans, but most are beneficial. (a) Termites, such as *Reticulitermes flavipes,* can destroy a building by feeding on the wood. (b) The blister beetle, *Lutta fulvipennis,* cross-fertilizes plants by spreading pollen from flower to flower as it searches for nectar.

as exist in all other animal groups combined. Based on current knowledge, some entomologists believe that as many as 10 million insect species may exist. In terms of their widespread distribution and great abundance, insects are extremely successful.

One of the most important factors responsible for the remarkable success of insects is their ability to fly, which enables them to escape from predators and disperse rapidly into new environments. Like other arthropods, insects also benefit from having a light but sturdy exoskeleton and jointed appendages that perform a variety of functions. In addition, most insects are small, so several species can inhabit different local environments within an area without competing with one another for food or other resources. Finally, insects generally have very short life spans and produce large numbers of eggs. Therefore, natural selection can occur more quickly in insects than in organisms that take longer to reach maturity.

Insects and People

Since insects are so abundant, it is not surprising that they affect our lives in many ways. Some insects, such as grasshoppers, boll weevils, and corn earworms, compete with humans for food by eating crops. In fact, nearly every crop plant has some insect pest. Other insects spread diseases by biting humans or domesticated animals. Some fleas carry plague; female *Anopheles* mosquitoes transmit *Plasmodium,* the protozoan that causes malaria; and flies transmit the bacterium *Salmonella typhi,* which causes typhoid fever. Termites, shown in Figure 39-2a, attack the wood in buildings, and some moths consume wool clothing and carpets.

Despite the problems some insects cause, it would be a serious mistake to think that the world would be better off without any insects. Insects play vital roles in almost all terrestrial and freshwater environments. They serve as food for numerous species of fish, birds, and other animals. Many kinds of insects, such as the beetle shown in Figure 39-2b, are essential for the cross-pollination of plants. It is estimated that insects pollinate 40 percent of the world's flowering plants, including many of those cultivated as food for humans and livestock. Insects also manufacture a number of commercially valuable products, including honey, wax, silk, and shellac. We tend to think of termites as destructive pests because of their effects on buildings, but by feeding on decaying wood, they also help recycle nutrients needed to maintain a healthy forest. Other insects recycle the nutrients contained in animal carcasses.

THE GRASSHOPPER

In this section, the grasshopper will be used to demonstrate some of the details of insect structure and function. As you read, remember that these details are not shared by all insects. The diversity of the insect world is so great that no typical insect exists.

External Structure

The major features of an adult grasshopper's external structure are illustrated in Figure 39-3. The body of a grasshopper clearly shows the three insect tagmata. The most anterior tagma, the head, bears the mouthparts. It also has a pair of unbranched antennae as well as simple and compound eyes.

The middle tagma, the thorax, is divided into three parts: the prothorax, mesothorax, and metathorax. The **prothorax** attaches to the head and bears the first pair of walking legs. The **mesothorax** bears the forewings and the second pair of walking legs. The **metathorax** attaches to the abdomen and bears the hindwings and the large jumping legs. A springlike mechanism inside the jumping legs stores mechanical energy when the legs are flexed. Release of this mechanism causes the legs to extend suddenly, launching the grasshopper into the air and away from danger. A flexible joint at the base of each leg provides the legs with great freedom of motion. Spines and hooks on the legs enable the grasshopper to cling to branches and blades of grass.

The leathery forewings cover and protect the membranous hindwings when the grasshopper isn't flying. Although the forewings help the grasshopper glide during flight, the hindwings actually propel it through the air. The wings are powered by muscles attached to the inside of the exoskeleton in the thorax. Note that insect wings develop as outgrowths from the epidermal cells that produce the exoskeleton. Unlike the wings of birds and bats, the wings of insects did not evolve from legs.

The segments in the most posterior tagma, the abdomen, are composed of upper and lower plates that are joined by a tough but flexible sheet of exoskeleton. The same flexible sheet also connects the segments to one another. The exoskeleton is covered by a waxy cuticle that is secreted by the cells of the epidermis. The rigid exoskeleton supports the grasshopper's body, and the cuticle retards the loss of body water. Both structures are adaptations for a terrestrial life.

internetconnect

SCiLINKS
NSTA

TOPIC: Grasshoppers
GO TO: www.scilinks.org
KEYWORD: HM765

FIGURE 39-3

The external anatomy of a grasshopper shows features that are characteristic of most insects: a body consisting of a head, thorax, and abdomen; a pair of unbranched antennae; three pairs of jointed legs; and two pairs of wings.

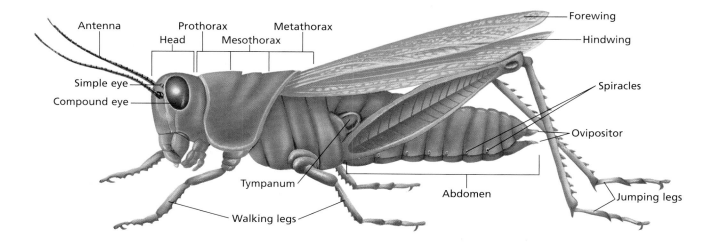

Feeding and Digestion

Grasshoppers feed on plants. The mouthparts of grasshoppers, shown in Figure 39-4a, are modified for cutting and chewing leaves and blades of grass. The **labrum** and **labium** are mouthparts that function like upper and lower lips, respectively. They hold the food in position so that the sharp-edged mandibles can tear off edible bits. Behind the mandibles are the maxillae, which also help hold and cut the food.

The mouthparts of other insects are specialized for the types of food they eat, as you can see in Figures 39-4b and 39-4c. For example, mosquitoes have long, thin mouthparts that fit together to form a needle-like tube, which the females use to pierce the skin of a larger animal and suck up blood. The mouthparts of many flies, in contrast, are soft, spongelike lobes that soak up fruit juices and other liquids.

The structures that make up the digestive tract of a grasshopper are visible in Figure 39-5. Food that enters the mouth is moistened by saliva from the **salivary** (SAL-uh-VER-ee) **glands.** The moistened food then passes through the esophagus and into the crop for temporary storage. From the crop, food passes into the gizzard, where sharp, chitinous plates shred it. The shredded mass then enters a portion of the digestive tract called the **midgut.** There, the food is bathed in enzymes secreted by the **gastric ceca** (SEE-kuh), which are pockets that branch from the digestive tract. Nutrients are absorbed into the coelom through the wall of the midgut. Undigested matter travels into the posterior section of the digestive tract, the **hindgut,** and leaves the body through the anus.

Circulation, Respiration, and Excretion

Nutrients and other materials are transported through the body of a grasshopper by an open circulatory system like that of the crayfish. Hemolymph flows through a large dorsal vessel called the **aorta** (ay-OHR-tuh), which is shown in Figure 39-5. The muscular heart, which is located in the abdomen and thorax, pumps the hemolymph forward through the aorta and into the part of the coelom nearest the head. The hemolymph then percolates through the coelom toward the abdomen and reenters the heart through small pores along its length.

Unlike most other animals, insects do not use their circulatory system to transport oxygen and carbon dioxide. Instead, they exchange these gases with the environment by pumping air deep into their body through a complex network of air tubes called tracheae. Recall from Chapter 38 that tracheae are also used for this purpose in some spiders. In grasshoppers, air enters the tracheae through spiracles located on the sides of the thorax and abdomen. You can see the tracheae in Figure 39-5 and the spiracles in Figure 39-3. The ends of the tracheae branch near the cells of the body and are filled with fluid. Oxygen diffuses into the cells from this fluid while carbon dioxide diffuses in the reverse direction. Air can be pumped in and out of the tracheae by the movements of the abdomen and wings.

Another anatomical structure shared by insects and spiders is Malpighian tubules, which are excretory organs that collect water

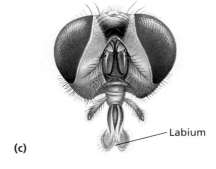

FIGURE 39-4

Insect mouthparts are adapted for different functions in different species. Mouthparts are used for biting and chewing in grasshoppers (a), piercing and sucking in mosquitoes (b), and sponging and lapping in houseflies (c).

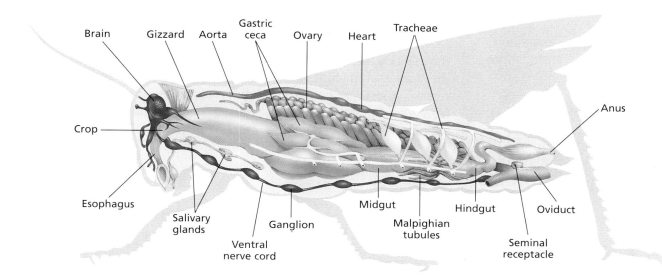

Brain Gizzard Aorta Gastric ceca Ovary Heart Tracheae

Crop

Anus

Esophagus

Salivary glands Ganglion Midgut Malpighian tubules Hindgut Oviduct

Ventral nerve cord Seminal receptacle

FIGURE 39-5

The major internal organs of a female grasshopper are seen in this cutaway side view.

and cellular wastes from the hemolymph. As Figure 39-5 shows, the Malpighian tubules in insects are attached to the digestive tract at the junction between the midgut and the hindgut. In insects that live in dry environments, the Malpighian tubules return most of the water to the hemolymph, producing a very concentrated mixture of wastes that is deposited in the hindgut and leaves the body with the feces. This is another method by which insects are adapted for life on land.

Neural Control

The grasshopper's central nervous system consists of a brain and a ventral nerve cord with ganglia located in each body segment. Nerves extend from the brain to the antennae, eyes, and other organs of the head. The antennae contain sensory structures that respond to both touch and smell. Look again at Figure 39-4a, and you can see that the three simple eyes are arranged in a row just above the base of the antennae. The simple eyes function merely to sense the intensity of light. Two bulging compound eyes, which are composed of hundreds of individual light detectors and lenses, allow the grasshopper to see in several directions at once. In addition to sensing light intensity, the compound eyes can detect movement and form images.

Other nerves extend from each of the ganglia to the muscles and sensory structures in the thorax and abdomen. One such structure is a sound-sensing organ called the **tympanum** (TIM-puh-nuhm). The tympanum is a large, oval membrane that covers an air-filled cavity on each side of the first abdominal segment. Sounds cause the tympanum to vibrate, and the vibrations are detected by nerve cells that line the cavity. Tympana are also found in many other insects that use sound in communication, such as crickets, katydids, and cicadas. In addition, sensory hairs like those described for crayfish in Chapter 38 are distributed over an insect's body. At the base of each hair is a nerve cell that is activated if the hair is touched or moved by vibration.

Reproduction

Grasshoppers have separate sexes, as do all insects. During mating, the male deposits sperm into the female's seminal receptacle, where they are stored until the eggs are released by the ovaries. After release, the eggs are fertilized internally. The last segment of the female's abdomen forms a pointed organ called an **ovipositor** (OH-vuh-PAHZ-uht-uhr), which you can see in Figure 39-3. The female grasshopper uses her ovipositor to dig a hole in the soil, where she lays the fertilized eggs.

DEVELOPMENT

After hatching from the egg, a young insect must undergo several molts before it reaches its adult size and becomes sexually mature. Only silverfish and a few other insects go through this process without any change in body form. The majority of insects undergo some type of change in form as they develop into adults. This phenomenon of developmental change in form is called **metamorphosis** (MET-uh-MOHR-fuh-suhs). There are two main kinds of metamorphosis in insects: incomplete and complete.

Incomplete Metamorphosis

In **incomplete metamorphosis,** illustrated in Figure 39-6, a nymph hatches from an egg and gradually develops into an adult. A **nymph** is an immature form of an insect that looks somewhat like the adult, but it is smaller, and its wings and reproductive organs are undeveloped. The nymph molts several times. With each molt, the wings become larger and more fully formed. The final molt transforms the nymph into an adult that can reproduce and, in most species, fly. Insects that undergo incomplete metamorphosis include grasshoppers, mayflies, dragonflies, and termites. Several other examples are listed in Table 39-1 on pages 762–763.

Complete Metamorphosis

In **complete metamorphosis,** an insect undergoes two stages of development between the egg and the adult. In both of those stages, the insect looks substantially different from its adult form. Figure 39-7 illustrates complete metamorphosis in the monarch butterfly. A wormlike larva, commonly called a caterpillar, hatches from the egg. The larva has three pairs of jointed legs on the thorax and several pairs of nonsegmented legs on the abdomen. The larva eats almost constantly, growing large on a diet of milkweed leaves. Thus, it is the larval stage of most insects that causes the most damage to plants.

The monarch larva molts several times as it grows. In the last larval stage, it develops bands of black, white, and yellow along its body. It continues to feed, but soon finds a sheltered spot and hangs upside down. Its body becomes shorter and thicker. Its

FIGURE 39-6

In incomplete metamorphosis, shown here in a grasshopper, a nymph hatches from an egg and molts several times before becoming an adult. Nymphs resemble adults but are not sexually mature and lack functional wings.

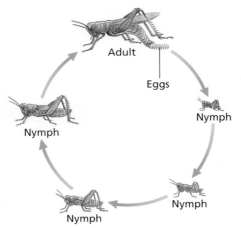

Adult

Eggs

Nymph

Nymph

Nymph

Nymph

exoskeleton then splits down the dorsal side, as shown in Figure 39-7, and falls off, revealing a green pupa. A **pupa** (PYOO-puh) is a stage of development in which an insect changes from a larva to an adult. The pupa of butterflies is enclosed in a protective case called a **chrysalis** (KRIS-uh-luhs). Moth pupae are enclosed in a case called a **cocoon.** Inside the pupa, the larval tissues break down, and groups of cells called imaginal disks develop into the wings and other tissues of the adult. When metamorphosis is complete, the pupa molts into a sexually mature, winged butterfly. Most insects go through complete metamorphosis. Table 39-1 lists several examples besides butterflies and moths, such as beetles, mosquitoes, and bees.

Importance of Metamorphosis

In a life cycle based on complete metamorphosis, the larval and adult stages often fulfill different functions, live in different habitats, and eat different foods. Therefore, the larvae and adults do not compete for space and food. For example, mosquito larvae live in fresh water and feed by filtering small food particles out of the water. When they become adults, the mosquitoes leave the water and feed on plant sap or the blood of terrestrial animals.

Metamorphosis also enhances insect survival by helping insects survive harsh weather. For instance, most butterflies and moths spend the winter as pupae encased in chrysalises or cocoons, which are often buried in the soil.

─┤ **Eco 🌲 Connection** ├─

Biological Control of Insects

Humans have been competing with insects for food since the invention of agriculture. To limit the damage that insects do to our food crops, we have developed a variety of poisons that kill a broad range of insects. However, these poisons have some serious drawbacks: they kill beneficial as well as harmful insects; they persist in the environment, accumulating in animals at higher levels in the food web; and they select for strains of insects that are resistant to the poisons. These drawbacks have led scientists to develop biological controls of insect pests.

One type of biological control is the use of natural predators or parasites that attack specific kinds of insects. For example, the bacterium *Bacillus thuringiensis* is used to control cabbage worms, tomato worms, and other moth larvae.

Biological control also includes methods that interfere with the reproduction of insects. In the sterile-male approach, for instance, large numbers of male insects sterilized by radiation are introduced into an area. The females lay eggs that never develop, so the next generation is smaller. Used over several generations, this technique can nearly eliminate some pest species in selected areas.

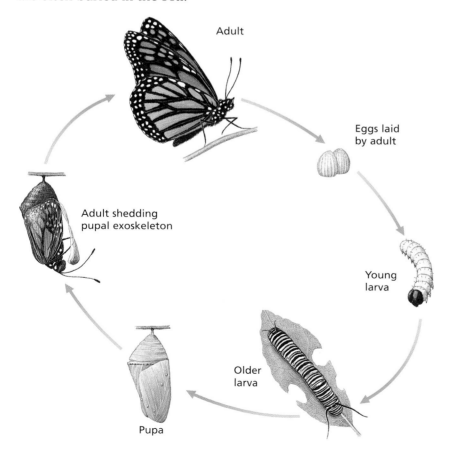

Adult

Eggs laid by adult

Adult shedding pupal exoskeleton

Young larva

Pupa

Older larva

FIGURE 39-7

In complete metamorphosis, shown here in the monarch butterfly, a larva hatches from an egg and goes through several molts before becoming a pupa, which then develops into an adult. Neither the larva nor the pupa resembles the adult.

DEFENSE

Insects have many defensive adaptations that increase their chances for survival. Some adaptations provide a passive defense. One form of passive defense that is frequently used by insects is camouflage, which was discussed in Chapter 21. Camouflage enhances survival by making it difficult for predators to recognize an insect. Insects often resemble parts of the plants on which they feed or hunt for food. For example, many varieties of stick insects and mantises look so much like twigs or leaves that they are easy to overlook unless they move.

Other defensive adaptations of insects are more aggressive, such as the venomous stingers of female bees and wasps. One of the most elaborate adaptations is that of the bombardier beetle, which defends itself by spraying a hot stream of a noxious chemical. The beetle can even rotate an opening on its abdomen to aim the spray at an attacker.

Insects that defend themselves by being dangerous or poisonous or by tasting bad often have bold, bright color patterns that make them clearly recognizable and warn predators away. This type of coloration is known as **warning coloration.** In some cases, several dangerous or poisonous species have similar patterns of warning coloration. For example, many species of stinging bees and wasps display a pattern of black-and-yellow stripes. This adaptation, in which a member of one dangerous species mimics the warning coloration of another, is called **Müllerian** (myoo-LER-ee-uhn) **mimicry.** Figure 39-8 shows that the black-and-yellow stripes of bees and wasps are also shared by some species of flies, which lack stingers and are therefore harmless. Mimicry of this type, in which a harmless species mimics the warning coloration of a dangerous species, is called **Batesian** (BAYTZ-ee-uhn) **mimicry.** Both Müllerian and Batesian mimicry encourage predators to avoid all similarly marked species.

FIGURE 39-8

Batesian mimicry is shown by the harmless syrphid fly, *Arctophila* (a), which looks very similar to the stinging bumblebee, *Bombus* (b).

(a)

(b)

SECTION 39-1 REVIEW

1. What are the major characteristics of the class Insecta?

2. What are some adaptations that have allowed insects to become successful?

3. List two ways insects are harmful to society and two ways they are beneficial.

4. State the function of each of the following parts of a grasshopper: labrum, tympanum, ovipositor.

5. What are the differences between incomplete and complete metamorphosis?

6. **CRITICAL THINKING** The monarch butterfly and the viceroy butterfly have similar bright colors and markings, and birds generally avoid eating both butterflies. If monarchs were distasteful to birds but viceroys were not, what type of defensive mechanism would viceroys exhibit?

INSECT BEHAVIOR

One reason for the success of insects is their ability to engage in complex behaviors. This ability is made possible by insects' jointed appendages, elaborate sense organs, and relatively complex brains. Insects are capable of interpreting sensory information to escape from predators, find food and mates, and communicate with one another.

OBJECTIVES

▲

Name three ways insects communicate, and give an example of each.

●

Describe the social organization of honeybees.

■

Explain how honeybees communicate information about the location of food.

COMMUNICATION

One of the most common forms of communication among insects is chemical communication involving pheromones. A **pheromone** (FER-uh-MOHN) is a chemical released by an animal that affects the behavior or development of other members of the same species through the sense of smell or taste. Pheromones play a major role in the behavior patterns of many insects. For example, you may have noticed ants, like those in Figure 39-9, marching along a tightly defined route on the ground. The ants are following a trail, of pheromones left by the ants that preceded them. Such trails are often laid down by ants that have found a source of food as they make their way back to the nest. As other ants follow the trail, they too deposit pheromones, so the trail becomes stronger as more ants travel along it. Pheromones are also used by honeybees to identify their own hives and to recruit other members of the hive in attacking animals that threaten the hive.

Some insects secrete pheromones to attract mates. The female silkworm moth, for example, can attract males from several kilometers away by secreting less than 0.01 µg of a pheromone. Sensory hairs on the large antennae of a male moth make it exquisitely sensitive to the pheromone.

Many insects communicate through sound. Male crickets produce chirping sounds by rubbing a scraper located on one forewing against a vein on the other forewing. They make these sounds to attract females and to warn other males away from their territories. Each cricket species produces several calls that differ from those of other cricket species. In fact, because many species look similar, entomologists often use a cricket's calls rather than its appearance to identify its species. Mosquitoes communicate through sound, too. Males that are ready to mate fly directly to the buzzing

FIGURE 39-9

These leaf-cutter ants, *Atta colombica*, are following a pheromone trail as they carry sections of leaves to their underground nest.

sounds produced by females. A male senses the buzzing by means of sensory hairs on his antennae that vibrate only at the frequency produced by females of the same species.

Insects may also communicate by generating flashes of light. Fireflies, for example, use light to find mates. Males emit flashes in flight, and females flash back in response. Each species of firefly has its own pattern of flashes, which helps males find females of the same species.

BEHAVIOR IN HONEYBEES

Some insects, such as certain species of bees, wasps, ants, and termites, live in complex colonies. In these colonies, some individuals gather food, others protect the colony, and others reproduce. Insects that live in such colonies are called **social insects.** The division of labor among social insects creates great interdependence and a heightened need for communication. This section will look at the behavioral adaptations of one well-studied species of social insect, the honeybee.

As you read about the complex behaviors of honeybees, keep in mind that these behaviors are neither taught nor learned. Instead, they are genetically determined. That is, the behaviors of honeybees are programmed by instructions stored in their genes. Genetically determined behavior is called **innate behavior.**

A honeybee colony consists of three distinct types of individuals, which are illustrated in Figure 39-10: worker bees, the queen bee, and drones. **Worker bees** are sterile females that make up the vast majority of the hive population, which may reach more than 80,000. The workers perform all the duties of the hive except reproduction. The **queen bee** is the only fertile female in the hive, and her only function is to reproduce. **Drones** are males that develop from unfertilized eggs. Their sole function is to deliver sperm to the queen. Their mouthparts are too short to obtain nectar from flowers, so the workers must feed them. The number of drones in the hive may reach a few hundred during the summer, but when the honey supply begins to run low, the workers kill the drones and clear them from the hive.

Worker Bees

Worker bees perform many functions at different times during their brief lifetime, which lasts about six weeks. After making the transition from pupa to adult, workers feed honey and pollen to the queen, drones, and larvae. During this stage the workers are called nurse bees. They secrete a high-protein substance known as **royal jelly,** which they feed to the queen and youngest larvae.

After about a week, worker bees stop producing royal jelly and begin to secrete wax, which they use to build and repair the honeycomb. During this stage they may also remove wastes from the hive, guard the hive, and fan their wings to circulate air through the hive.

FIGURE 39-10

In a honeybee colony, worker bees perform the work of the hive, while drones and the queen are involved exclusively with reproduction.

Worker bee

Drone

Queen bee

The workers spend the last weeks of their life gathering nectar and pollen. A number of structural adaptations aid them in this work. Their mouthparts are specialized for lapping up nectar, and their legs have structures that serve as pollen packers, pollen baskets, and pollen combs.

The sterile workers do not use their ovipositors for egg laying. Instead, these structures are modified into barbed stingers that the workers use to protect the hive. When a worker bee stings an animal, the stinger and attached venom sac are left behind in the victim as the bee flies away. The worker, having lost part of its body and much of its hemolymph, dies a day or two later. Wasps also have stingers that are modified ovipositors. Unlike honeybees, they can sting many times because their stinger is not barbed.

The Queen Bee

The queen bee develops from an egg identical to those that develop into the workers. The differences between the queen and the workers result from the continuous diet of royal jelly that the queen is fed throughout her larval development. In addition, the queen herself secretes a pheromone called the **queen factor** that prevents other female larvae from developing into queens.

The queen's role is to reproduce. Within a few days after she completes metamorphosis and emerges as an adult, she flies out of the hive and mates in the air with one or more drones. During mating, millions of sperm are deposited in the queen's seminal receptacle, where they will remain for the five or more years of her life. Although the queen mates only once, she may lay as many as a million eggs each year.

When the hive becomes overcrowded, the queen stops producing the queen factor and leaves the hive. As she leaves, she secretes a swarming pheromone that induces about half of the workers in the hive to follow her and form a swarm. Eventually the swarm finds another location for a new hive. Meanwhile, in the old hive, the remaining workers begin feeding royal jelly to other larvae. When a new queen emerges, she produces the queen factor, and in response, the workers destroy the other developing queens. The new queen departs on a mating flight, and the cycle begins again.

The Dances of the Bees

When honeybees leave the hive and find a source of pollen and nectar, how do they communicate the location of this food source to other workers in the hive? An Austrian biologist, Karl von Frisch (1886–1982), spent 25 years answering this question. His careful experimentation earned him a Nobel Prize in 1973.

To study bees, von Frisch built a glass-walled hive and placed feeding stations stocked with sweetened water near the hive. He noted that "scout bees" returning from the feeding stations would perform a series of dancelike movements in the hive. As shown in Figure 39-11a, the scout bee would circle first to the right and then to the left, a behavior that von Frisch called the **round dance.** After

Quick Lab

Interpreting Nonverbal Communication

Materials pencil, paper, wrapped candy pieces

Procedure

1. Choose one member of your group to play the part of the "scout" bee. The others in the group will be the "worker" bees.

2. Your teacher will secretly tell the scout bee where a piece of candy is located. The scout bee will develop a method of nonverbal communication to let the worker bees know where the candy is hidden. The scout bee may not point to the candy. Use Figure 39-11 as a guide to developing your method of communication.

3. When the candy has been located, the scout will hide another piece of candy and select a new scout. The new scout will develop a different way to tell the group where the candy is located. Repeat the procedure until everyone in your group has been a scout.

Analysis

1. How effective were each of your scout's methods for showing the location of the candy?

2. Did the worker bees improve their ability to find the candy after several trials?

3. List and describe some types of nonverbal communication that humans use.

(a) ROUND DANCE

(b) WAGGLE DANCE

FIGURE 39-11

Honeybees use two types of dances to convey information about food sources. (a) The round dance indicates that a food source is nearby but gives no information about its direction or distance. (b) The waggle dance is performed on a vertical surface in the hive when the food source is distant. The angle of the straight run part of the dance indicates the direction of food, while the duration of the dance and number of waggles indicate the food's distance from the hive.

many observations, von Frisch concluded that the round dance told other worker bees that a food source was near the hive, but it did not inform them of the exact location of the food.

Von Frisch also observed that when the food source was far from the hive, the scout bees would perform another type of dance on a vertical surface inside the hive. He called this dance the **waggle dance** because the scout bees waggled their abdomens from side to side. As you can see in Figure 39-11b, the pattern of the waggle dance is like a figure eight. The scout bee makes a circle in one direction, then a straight run while waggling her abdomen, and then another circle in the opposite direction from the first. Numerous experiments by von Frisch showed that the direction of food is indicated by the angle of the straight run on the vertical surface. Straight up, for example, indicates a direction toward the sun. The distance to the food source is indicated by the duration of the dance and the number of waggles on each run.

Altruistic Behavior

When worker bees sting an intruder to defend the colony, they cause their own deaths, as you learned earlier. This behavior is an example of **altruistic** (AL-troo-IS-tik) **behavior,** which is the aiding of other individuals at one's own risk or expense. The stinging of honeybees is an innate behavior. You might think that the genes directing this behavior would eventually be eliminated from the population, since dead bees can't reproduce. However, this does not happen.

To understand why evolution has selected for altruistic behavior in honeybees, you must focus not on the selection of individual bees, but rather on the selection of genes they possess. Remember that worker bees are sterile. Therefore, they cannot pass on their own genes by reproducing. However, they can pass on some of their genes by helping a closely related individual reproduce. By defending the colony, a worker bee increases the chances that the queen bee will survive. If the queen survives, she will produce more workers who will share many of the same genes. Thus, by behaving altruistically, a worker can cause more of her genes to be propagated in the population. This mechanism of increasing the propagation of one's own genes by helping a closely related individual reproduce is called **kin selection.**

SECTION 39-2 REVIEW

1. Name three ways insects communicate, and give an example of each.

2. What is a pheromone?

3. What determines whether a fertilized honeybee egg will develop into a worker or a queen?

4. How do honeybees behave when their hive is overcrowded?

5. How do honeybees convey information about the direction and distance of a food source that is far from the hive?

6. **CRITICAL THINKING** Current research indicates that a queen honeybee mates with drones from another hive rather than from her own hive. In what way might this behavior benefit the honeybee colony?

SUMMARY/VOCABULARY

39-1 ■ The insect body is divided into three tag-mata: the head has mandibles and one pair of unbranched antennae; the thorax has three pairs of jointed legs and, in many species, one or two pairs of wings; the abdomen has 9 to 11 segments but neither wings nor legs in adults.

■ Insects live in almost every terrestrial and freshwater environment. Factors responsible for their success include their ability to fly, exoskeleton, jointed appendages, small size, and short life span.

■ Insects negatively affect humans by competing for food, transmitting diseases, and destroying buildings and other manufactured products. However, insects are also beneficial: they serve as food for other animals, pollinate flowers, make valuable products such as honey, and recycle nutrients.

■ The mouthparts of an insect are specialized for tearing and cutting solid food or for sucking or soaking up liquid food.

■ Insects have an open circulatory system that transports nutrients through the body. Gas exchange occurs by means of air-filled tracheae that reach deep into the body.

Malpighian tubules remove cellular wastes from the hemolymph while conserving water.

■ Insect sensory structures include simple and compound eyes, sound-sensing tympana in some species, and sensory hairs on the antennae and other body parts.

■ Most insects go through a metamorphosis. In incomplete metamorphosis, a nymph hatches from an egg and resembles the adult but has undeveloped reproductive organs and no wings. The nymph molts several times to become an adult. In complete metamorphosis, a wormlike larva hatches from an egg and molts several times before becoming a pupa. The pupa molts to produce the adult, which resembles neither the larva nor the pupa.

■ Insects can defend themselves by using camouflage, stinging, or releasing noxious chemicals. Insects that are dangerous or taste bad often have warning coloration that makes them recognizable to predators. The warning coloration of a dangerous species may be mimicked by other species.

Vocabulary

aorta (766)	gastric cecum (766)	mesothorax (765)	ovipositor (768)
Batesian mimicry (770)	hindgut (766)	metamorphosis (768)	prothorax (765)
chrysalis (769)	incomplete metamorphosis	metathorax (765)	pupa (769)
cocoon (769)	(768)	midgut (766)	salivary gland (766)
complete metamorphosis (768)	labium (766)	Müllerian mimicry (770)	tympanum (767)
entomology (762)	labrum (766)	nymph (768)	warning coloration (770)

39-2 ■ Insects communicate by releasing pheromones and by producing sounds and flashes of light.

■ Honeybees live in complex colonies consisting mostly of sterile female workers that perform all duties except reproduction. Each colony also contains one fertile queen bee and a few hundred male drones.

■ Honeybees communicate the direction and distance to food sources by performing dances inside the hive.

■ In defending the colony, worker bees show altruistic behavior toward their close relatives in the colony. By doing so, they increase the propagation of their own genes.

Vocabulary

altruistic behavior (774)	kin selection (774)	queen factor (773)	social insect (772)
drone (772)	pheromone (771)	round dance (773)	waggle dance (774)
innate behavior (772)	queen bee (772)	royal jelly (772)	worker bee (772)

REVIEW

Vocabulary

1. Choose the term that does not belong in the following group, and explain why it does not belong: egg, larva, pupa, labium.
2. What is the function of the spiracles on a grasshopper?
3. Name the three tagmata that make up the body of an insect.
4. Define *innate behavior,* and give an example.
5. What is a chrysalis?

Multiple Choice

6. Adaptations responsible for the success of insects include (a) jointed appendages (b) the ability to fly (c) short life spans (d) all of the above.
7. The mouthparts of a grasshopper are specialized for (a) sucking fluids (b) lapping up liquids (c) cutting and tearing (d) filter feeding.
8. A female grasshopper uses her ovipositor to (a) store sperm from a male (b) inject venom (c) hold food in position during feeding (d) dig holes in the soil and lay eggs.
9. An insect's legs and wings are attached to its (a) head (b) thorax (c) abdomen (d) labrum.
10. The function of the gastric ceca is to (a) secrete digestive enzymes (b) secrete saliva (c) store undigested food (d) remove cellular wastes.
11. The immature form of an insect that undergoes incomplete metamorphosis is called a (a) drone (b) pupa (c) caterpillar (d) nymph.
12. Metamorphosis benefits insect species by (a) ensuring that different developmental stages fulfill the same functions (b) increasing competition between larvae and adults (c) promoting survival during harsh weather (d) all of the above.
13. Bees perform the round dance to inform other bees of (a) the presence of food near the hive (b) the distance to a food source from the hive (c) the direction of a food source from the hive (d) the type of food they have located.
14. The substance called queen factor (a) causes female larvae to develop into queen bees (b) causes worker bees to form swarms (c) prevents female larvae from becoming sexually mature (d) attracts drones.
15. Altruistic behavior is (a) behavior that benefits oneself at the expense of others (b) the aiding of other individuals at one's own risk or expense (c) behavior that is always genetically determined (d) none of the above.

Short Answer

16. How has the small size of insects contributed to their success?
17. Name three characteristics that entomologists use to divide insects into orders.
18. What are three ways that insects cause harm to human society?
19. What is a tympanum, and where is it located on a grasshopper?
20. How is the origin of wings in insects different from that in birds and bats?
21. What is the difference between camouflage and warning coloration?
22. How do crickets produce sounds? What functions do these sounds serve?
23. What three types of individuals make up a honeybee society?
24. When a worker bee stings to defend the hive, it loses its stinger and dies. Explain how such behavior has been selected in honeybees.
25. Identify the structures labeled *A* through *F* in the diagram below.

CRITICAL THINKING

1. Farmers who use an insecticide to control insect pests often find that strains of insects resistant to the insecticide rapidly appear. How do these insecticide-resistant strains develop? Why does this happen so quickly among insects?

2. Insects and crustaceans both belong to the phylum Arthropoda and share many characteristics. As you learned in Chapter 38, the largest crustacean, the Japanese spider crab, has a leg span of 4 m. In contrast, the largest insects, such as the atlas moth, have a wingspan of only about 25 cm. Why are the largest crustaceans so much bigger than the largest insects?

3. You learned in Chapter 37 that squids and other cephalopods have a closed circulatory system, which supports their active lifestyle by circulating blood quickly through their bodies. Many insects, such as dragonflies and bees, are also very active, but all insects have an open circulatory system. How can insects maintain active lifestyles while having an open circulatory system?

4. During their lives, worker bees move from first feeding and caring for larvae inside the hive to later gathering nectar and defending the hive. Why do you think this sequence is more advantageous for the hive than the reverse sequence might be?

5. What characteristics may have helped insects survive the major climatic changes that led to the extinction of the dinosaurs and many other species about 65 million years ago?

6. Worker honeybees guard the entrance to their hive, allowing nestmates to enter but turning away intruder bees. The graph below plots the percentage of bees turned away versus the genetic relatedness of the guards and the intruders. A genetic relatedness of 1.0 means that a guard and an intruder are genetically identical. Are guards more likely to turn away bees with a high or a low genetic relatedness? How might a guard determine the genetic relatedness of a bee that enters the hive?

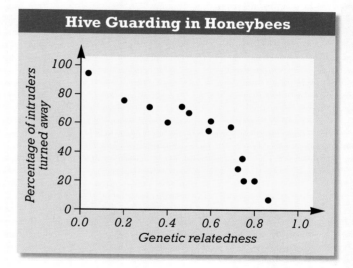

Hive Guarding in Honeybees

EXTENSION

1. Read "Pretty Poison" in *Audubon*, September/October 1999, on page 159. Explain how the monarch butterfly becomes toxic to bird predators. Describe the migration of the monarch butterfly.

2. Read "Child Care Among the Insects" in *Scientific American,* January 1999, on page 72. Why do some insects risk their own lives to protect their young? Describe how the male giant water bug takes care of his young.

3. Select any insect that lives in your area. Using a field guide, identify the insect. Make a drawing that shows the insect's characteristics. Use your library and other sources to find information on the insect's food sources, economic importance, and distribution.

4. Use your school library or public library to research the topic of sociobiology. Prepare a written report on what sociobiologists mean by *altruistic behavior* and how they explain such behavior in insect societies.

Anatomy of a Grasshopper

OBJECTIVES

- Examine the external and internal anatomy of a grasshopper.
- Infer function from observation of structures.

PROCESS SKILLS

- relating structure and function
- observing

MATERIALS

- safety goggles
- gloves
- preserved grasshopper (1 for each student)
- dissection tray
- forceps
- fine dissection scissors, with pointed blades
- hand lens or dissecting microscope
- blunt probe
- sharp probe
- dissection pins

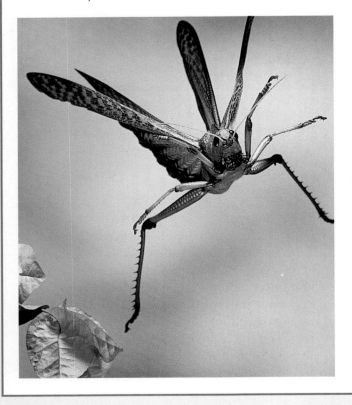

Background

1. List the distinguishing characteristics of insects.
2. In this investigation, you will dissect a grasshopper to observe its external and internal structure. To which order of insects do grasshoppers belong?
3. What characteristics of the grasshopper place it into this order?

PART A Observing the External Anatomy of the Grasshopper

1. **CAUTION Wear safety goggles and gloves during this investigation. Keep your hands away from your eyes and face when working with preserved specimens.** Using forceps, hold a preserved grasshopper under running water to gently but thoroughly remove excess preservative. Then place the grasshopper in a dissection tray.
2. Use a hand lens to observe the grasshopper's parts. While referring to Figure 39-3, identify the head, thorax, and abdomen. Note how the thorax and abdomen are divided into segments.
3. Use forceps to spread out and examine both pairs of wings. Notice that the forewings are narrow and the hindwings are wide. Observe how the hindwings fold fanlike against the body.
4. Observe the legs. Grasp one of each pair of legs and notice how the legs are divided into segments. Gently bend the legs to observe their normal range of motion.
5. Examine the 11 segments of the abdomen. On abdominal segment 1, find the tympanum. Then, along each side of abdominal segments 1–8, locate the spiracles, which look like small dots. Gently touch the abdomen with a blunt probe to find the flexible membrane that connects the segments to one another.
6. While referring to Figure 39-4a, examine the grasshopper's head. Find the two antennae, two compound eyes, and three simple eyes. Use a sharp probe to push apart the mouthparts. Locate and identify the mandibles, maxillae, labium, and labrum. Note that each maxilla has a segmented feeler called a palpus and that the labium has two palpi.

PART B Observing the Internal Anatomy of the Grasshopper

7. ◆ CAUTION **Dissecting instruments can cut you. Always cut in a direction away from your face and body.** Using scissors, snip off the grasshopper's legs, wings, and antennae at their bases. Pin the body to the dissection tray. Then use the scissors to make a shallow cut just above the spiracles through the exoskeleton along both sides of the thorax and abdomen.

8. As you remove the exoskeleton, look at its underside, where the heart and aorta may be attached. Also look for muscles attached to the inside of the exoskeleton. Find and remove any fatty tissue (which your teacher can help you identify) that may hide other organs.

9. If your grasshopper is a female, look for its ovaries, which may contain elongated eggs. Refer to Figure 39-5 to see what the ovaries look like. If your grasshopper is a male, examine the ovaries and eggs in the female grasshopper of another student. Remove the ovaries and eggs (if present) from one side of the abdomen to uncover the digestive tract.

10. Make a table in your lab report like the one shown. As you observe each of the structures listed in the table, fill in the function of that structure.

11. Referring to Figure 39-5, look for the organs of the digestive tract: esophagus, crop, gizzard, midgut, hindgut, and anus. Find the salivary glands and the gastric ceca, which are also parts of the digestive system.

12. On the surface of the midgut and hindgut, look for the Malpighian tubules, which are tiny tubes that connect to the digestive tract.

13. Locate and identify the brain, ventral nerve cord, and ganglia.

14. Carefully cut away and remove the organs of the digestive system to expose some parts of the respiratory system. Referring to Figure 39-5, locate and identify tracheae that run along the dorsal and ventral parts of the body, as well as other tracheae that connect them. The larger tracheae lead to spiracles in the abdomen. Look also for swollen tracheae, called air sacs, which increase the volume of air drawn into the abdomen when the grasshopper breathes.

15. ◆ ◆ Dispose of your specimen according to the directions from your teacher. Then clean up your materials and wash your hands before leaving the lab.

FUNCTION OF GRASSHOPPER STRUCTURES

Structure	Function
Esophagus	
Crop	
Gizzard	
Midgut	
Hindgut	
Salivary glands	
Gastric ceca	
Malpighian tubules	
Tracheae	
Spiracles	

Analysis and Conclusions

1. How do you think the membrane between segments helps the grasshopper in its movements?
2. How does the function of the stiff, leathery forewings differ from that of the more delicate hindwings?
3. Trace the path of food through the grasshopper's digestive tract.
4. To what system do the Malpighian tubules belong?
5. Why is the circulatory system of the grasshopper described as an open circulatory system?
6. Compared with invertebrates such as flatworms and earthworms, grasshoppers are highly responsive to environmental stimuli. What are some structural adaptations of the grasshopper that make this responsiveness possible?

Further Inquiry

1. Prepare an illustrated chart that compares and contrasts the characteristics of grasshoppers, beetles (order Coleoptera), and butterflies (order Lepidoptera). What trait of each kind of insect is reflected in the name of its order? Include other traits in your chart.
2. The fruit fly *Drosophila* is an insect that, unlike the grasshopper, undergoes complete metamorphosis. Research the life cycles of the grasshopper and the fruit fly, and make a chart that compares and contrasts their life cycles.

CHAPTER 40

ECHINODERMS AND INVERTEBRATE CHORDATES

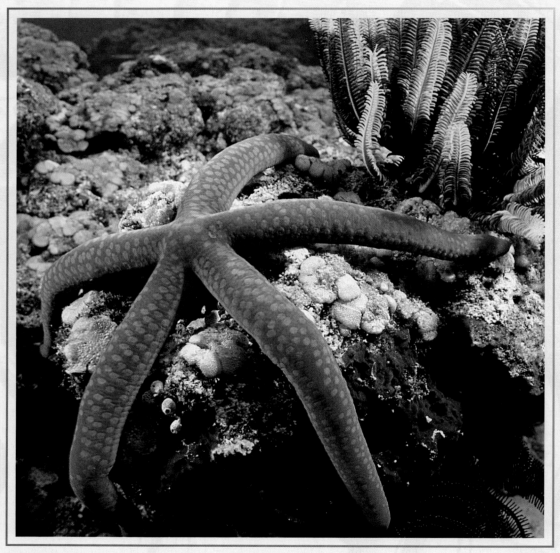

This blue sea star, Linckia laevigata, *shows the pentaradial symmetry of most echinoderms.*

FOCUS CONCEPT: *Evolution*

As you read, note the unique structural features of echinoderms and think about how echinoderms are similar to their closest relatives, the chordates.

40-1 *Echinoderms*

40-2 *Invertebrate Chordates*

ECHINODERMS

*The phylum Echinodermata (ee-KIE-noh-duhr-MAH-tuh) is a group of invertebrates that includes sea stars, sand dollars, sea urchins, and sea cucumbers. The members of this phylum, called **echinoderms,** inhabit marine environments ranging from shallow coastal waters to ocean trenches more than 10,000 m deep. They vary in diameter from 1 cm to 1 m and often are brilliantly colored.*

SECTION

40-1

OBJECTIVES

▲

Discuss the evolutionary origin of echinoderms.

●

List the characteristics that distinguish echinoderms from other phyla.

■

Name representative species in each echinoderm class.

◆

Explain how the water-vascular system aids in movement and feeding.

▲

Describe sexual and asexual reproduction in the sea star.

CHARACTERISTICS

Echinoderms are radially symmetrical animals. Like cnidarians and ctenophores, which are also radially symmetrical, echinoderms have no head or any other sign of cephalization. Unlike cnidarians and ctenophores, however, adult echinoderms develop from bilaterally symmetrical larvae. A few examples of echinoderm larvae are illustrated in Figure 40-1. This feature of development indicates that echinoderms almost certainly evolved from bilaterally symmetrical ancestors.

The fossil record of echinoderms dates back to the Cambrian period, more than 500 million years ago. Early echinoderms from this period appear to have been sessile, and biologists believe these animals evolved radial symmetry as an adaptation to a sessile existence. Echinoderms later evolved the ability to move from place to place. Today the vast majority of echinoderm species can move by crawling slowly along the ocean bottom, and only about 80 species are sessile.

Echinoderms are deuterostomes, which makes them different from all of the other invertebrates you have studied so far. Recall from Chapter 34 that deuterostomes are coelomates whose embryos

FIGURE 40-1

Notice the bilateral symmetry in these echinoderm larvae. The larvae develop into radially symmetrical adults.

SEA STAR LARVA
(bipinnaria)

BRITTLE STAR LARVA

SEA URCHIN LARVA

have radial cleavage, whose anus forms near the blastopore, and whose mesoderm arises from outpockets of the endoderm. Because they develop as deuterostomes, echinoderms are more closely related to chordates, which are discussed in the second part of this chapter, than to other invertebrates.

Most echinoderms have a type of radial symmetry called **pentaradial symmetry,** in which the body parts extend from the center along five spokes. In addition to their pentaradial symmetry, echinoderms have three other major characteristics that are not shared by any other phylum. (1) They have an endoskeleton composed of calcium carbonate plates known as **ossicles.** The ossicles may be attached to spines or spicules that protrude through the skin. The name *echinoderm* means "spiny skin." (2) They have a **water-vascular system,** which is a network of water-filled canals inside their body. (3) They have many small, movable extensions of the water-vascular system called **tube feet,** which aid in movement, feeding, respiration, and excretion. The water-vascular system and tube feet will be discussed in more detail.

CLASSIFICATION

Taxonomists divide the 7,000 species of echinoderms into six classes, five of which will be described here: Crinoidea (kri-NOID-ee-uh), Asteroidea (AS-tuh-ROID-ee-uh), Ophiuroidea (OH-fee-yoor-OID-ee-uh), Echinoidea (EK-uh-NOID-ee-uh), and Holothuroidea (HOH-loh-thuh-ROID-ee-uh).

Class Crinoidea

Members of the class Crinoidea, called crinoids (KRI-NOIDS), include the sea lilies and feather stars, which are shown in Figure 40-2. The name *crinoid* means "lily-like." Sea lilies most closely resemble the fossils of ancestral echinoderms from the Cambrian period. They are sessile as adults, remaining attached to rocks or the sea bottom by means of a long stalk. Feather stars, in contrast, can swim or crawl as adults, although they may stay in one place for long periods. In

FIGURE 40-2

This sea lily, *Cenocrinus* (a), and these feather stars, *Oxycomanthus bennetti* (b), are members of the class Crinoidea. Notice their adaptations for filter feeding.

(a)

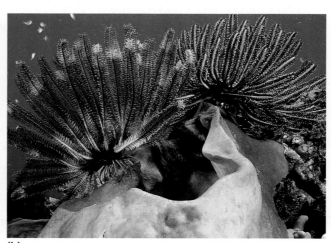

(b)

both types of crinoids, five arms extend from the body and branch to form many more arms—up to 200 in some feather star species. Sticky tube feet located at the end of each arm filter small organisms from the water. The tube feet also serve as a respiratory surface across which crinoids exchange oxygen and carbon dioxide with the water. Cilia on the arms transport trapped food to the crinoid's mouth at the base of the arms. The mouth faces up in crinoids, while in most other echinoderms the mouth faces toward the sea bottom.

Class Ophiuroidea

The 2,000 species of basket stars and brittle stars make up the largest echinoderm class, Ophiuroidea, which means "snake-tail." Members of this class are distinguished by their long, narrow arms, which allow them to move more quickly than other echinoderms. As you can see in Figure 40-3, the thin, flexible arms of basket stars branch repeatedly to form numerous coils that look like tentacles. Brittle stars, so named because parts of their arms break off easily, can regenerate missing parts.

Basket stars and brittle stars live primarily on the bottom of the ocean, often beneath stones or in the crevices and holes of coral reefs. They are so numerous in some locations that they cover the sea floor. Some species feed by raking in food with their arms or gathering it from the ocean bottom with their tube feet. Others trap suspended particles with their tube feet or with mucous strands located between their spines.

Class Echinoidea

The class Echinoidea consists of about 900 species of sea urchins and sand dollars. *Echinoidea* means "spinelike," a description that applies especially well to many of the sea urchins, such as the ones shown in Figure 40-4. In both sea urchins and sand dollars, the internal organs are enclosed within a compact, rigid endoskeleton called a **test.**

The spherical sea urchins are well adapted to life on hard sea bottoms. They use their tube feet for locomotion and feed by scraping algae from hard surfaces with the five teeth that surround their mouth. The teeth and the muscles that move them are part of a complex jawlike mechanism called Aristotle's lantern. The spines that protrude from the test may be short and flat, long and thin, or wedge-shaped, depending on the species. In some sea urchins, the spines are barbed, while in others, they are hollow and contain a venom that is dangerous to predators as well as swimmers.

Sand dollars live along seacoasts. As their name implies, they are usually found in sandy areas and have the flat, round shape of a silver dollar. Their shape is an adaptation for shallow burrowing. The short spines on a sand dollar are used in locomotion and burrowing, and they help clean the surface of the body. Sand dollars use their tube feet to capture food that settles on or passes over their body.

FIGURE 40-3

The basket star, *Oreaster reticulatus,* has long, flexible arms with many coiled branches.

internet**connect**

SC*I*LINKS
NSTA

TOPIC: Echinoidea
GO TO: www.scilinks.org
KEYWORD: HM783

FIGURE 40-4

The long, sharp spines that cover these sea urchins, *Strongylocentrotus,* provide protection against most predators.

FIGURE 40-5

Tentacles around the mouth of this sea cucumber collect food and bring it to the animal's mouth. Five rows of tube feet that run along the body are evidence of the sea cucumber's penta-radial symmetry.

internetconnect

SCI*LINKS*

NSTA

TOPIC: Asteroidea
GO TO: www.scilinks.org
KEYWORD: HM784

Class Holothuroidea

Sea cucumbers belong to the class Holothuroidea. Most of these armless echinoderms live on the sea bottom, where they crawl or burrow into soft sediment. The ossicles that make up their endoskeleton are very small and are not connected to each other, so their bodies are soft. Modified tube feet form a fringe of tentacles around the mouth. When these tentacles are extended, as shown in Figure 40-5, they resemble the polyp form of some cnidarians. That explains the name of this class, which means "water polyp." A sea cucumber uses its tentacles to sweep up sediment and water. It then stuffs its tentacles into its mouth and cleans the food off them.

Class Asteroidea

The sea stars, or starfish, belong to the class Asteroidea, which means "starlike." Sea stars live in coastal waters all over the world. They exist in a variety of colors and shapes, two of which are shown in Figure 40-6. Sea stars are economically important because they prey on oysters, clams, and other organisms that humans use as food.

FIGURE 40-6

Sea stars are found on rocky coastlines worldwide. One of the more colorful varieties is the African sea star, *Protoreaster linckii* (a). The sunflower star, *Pycnopodia helianthoides* (b), can have up to two dozen arms.

(a)

(b)

STRUCTURE AND FUNCTION OF ECHINODERMS

The sea star will be used to demonstrate some of the details of echinoderm structure and function. As you read about how echinoderms carry out life functions, consider how they differ from the other groups of invertebrates you have studied.

External Structure

As you can see in Figure 40-7, the body of a sea star is composed of several arms that extend from a central region. Sea stars typically have five arms, but in some species, such as the one shown in Figure 40-6b, there may be as many as 24. Two rows of tube feet run along the underside of each arm. The body is often flattened.

In echinoderms, the side of the body where the mouth is located is referred to as the **oral surface.** The side of the body that is opposite from the mouth is called the **aboral** (A-BOHR-uhl) **surface.** In sea stars, the oral surface is on the underside of the body.

The body of a sea star is usually covered with short spines that give the animal a rough texture. Surrounding each spine in many sea stars are numerous tiny pincers called **pedicellariae** (PED-uh-suh-LAR-ee-ee), which are shown in Figure 40-7. Pedicellariae help keep the body surface free of foreign objects, including algae and small animals that might grow on the sea star or damage its soft tissues. Pedicellariae are found in sea stars and some sea urchins.

FIGURE 40-7

Sea stars have a number of structural features that are unique to the phylum Echinodermata. Their pentaradial symmetry is indicated by their five arms, each of which contains a division of their internal organ systems. The water-vascular system consists of a network of canals connected to hundreds of tube feet. The inset shows that the sea star's exterior is dotted with short spines, pincerlike pedicellariae, and skin gills.

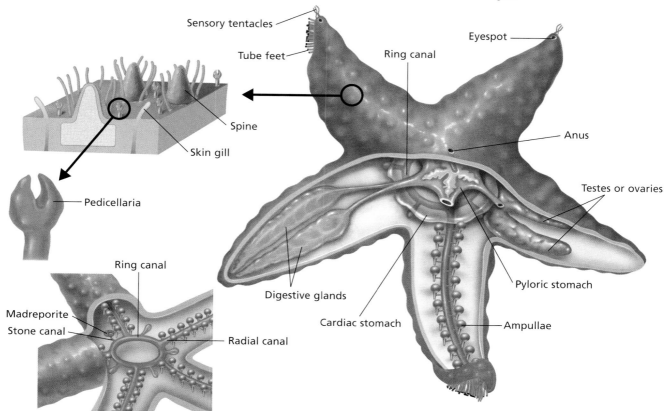

Sensory tentacles

Tube feet

Spine

Skin gill

Pedicellaria

Ring canal

Madreporite

Stone canal

Radial canal

Eyespot

Ring canal

Anus

Testes or ovaries

Digestive glands

Cardiac stomach

Pyloric stomach

Ampullae

Word Roots and Origins

ampulla

form the Latin *ampulla,*
meaning "flask"

Water-Vascular System

The water-vascular system is a network of water-filled canals that are connected to the tube feet. Use Figure 40-7 to follow the path of water through the water-vascular system. Water enters the system through small pores in the **madreporite** (MAD-ruh-POHR-IET), a sievelike plate on the aboral surface. Water then passes down the **stone canal,** a tube that connects the madreporite to the **ring canal,** which encircles the mouth. Another tube, the **radial canal,** extends from the ring canal to the end of each arm. The radial canals carry water to the hundreds of hollow tube feet. Valves prevent water from flowing back into the radial canals from the tube feet.

The upper end of each tube foot is expanded to form a bulblike sac called an **ampulla** (AM-PYU-luh). Contraction of muscles surrounding the ampullae forces water into the tube feet, causing them to extend. Contraction of muscles lining the tube feet forces water back into the ampullae and shortens the tube feet. In this way, the sea star uses water pressure to extend and withdraw its tube feet. In many species, small muscles raise the center of each tube foot's disklike end, creating suction when the tube feet are pressed against a surface. These coordinated muscular contractions enable sea stars to climb slippery rocks and capture prey.

Feeding and Digestion

The sea star's mouth is connected by a short esophagus to the **cardiac stomach,** which the sea star can turn inside out through its mouth when it feeds. The cardiac stomach transfers food to the **pyloric stomach,** which connects to a pair of digestive glands in each arm. The cardiac stomach, pyloric stomach, and digestive glands break down food with the help of the enzymes they secrete. Nutrients are absorbed into the coelom through the walls of the digestive glands, and undigested material is expelled through the anus on the aboral surface.

Most sea stars are carnivorous, feeding on mollusks, worms, and other slow-moving animals. When a sea star captures a bivalve mollusk, such as a clam, it attaches its tube feet to both halves of the clamshell and exerts a steady pull, as Figure 40-8 shows. Eventually, the clam's muscles tire and the shell opens slightly. The sea star then inserts its cardiac stomach into the clam and digests the clam's soft tissues while they are still in the shell. The sea star then withdraws the stomach, containing the partially digested food, back into its body, where the digestive process is completed.

Other Body Systems

Like other echinoderms, the sea star has no circulatory, excretory, or respiratory organ systems. Fluid in the coelom bathes the organs and distributes nutrients and oxygen. Gas exchange and waste excretion take place by diffusion through the thin walls of the tube feet and through the **skin gills,** hollow tubes that project from the coelom lining to the exterior. You can see the skin gills in the inset in Figure 40-7, on the previous page.

FIGURE 40-8

This sea star, *Asterias rubens,* is prying open the shell of a clam to feed on the clam's soft tissues.

The nervous system in sea stars is primitive. Since echinoderms have no head, they also have no brain. The nervous system consists mainly of a **nerve ring** that circles the mouth and a **radial nerve** that runs from the nerve ring along the length of each arm. The nerve ring and radial nerves coordinate the movements of the tube feet. If the radial nerve in one arm is cut, the tube feet in that arm lose coordination. If the nerve ring is cut, the tube feet in all arms become uncoordinated and the sea star cannot move. Sea stars also have a nerve net near the body surface that controls the movements of the spines, pedicellariae, and skin gills. The end of each arm has an eyespot that responds to light and several tentacles that respond to touch. The tube feet also respond to touch, and other touch-sensitive and chemical-sensitive cells are scattered over the surface of the sea star's body.

Reproduction and Development

Most sea star species have separate sexes, as do most other echinoderms. Each arm of the sea star contains a pair of ovaries or testes. Females produce up to 200 million eggs in one year. Fertilization occurs externally, when the eggs and sperm are shed into the water. Each fertilized egg develops into a bilaterally symmetrical, free-swimming larva called a **bipinnaria** (BIE-pin-AR-ee-uh). After about two months, the larva settles to the bottom, and metamorphosis begins. During metamorphosis the larva develops into a pentaradially symmetrical adult.

Echinoderms have remarkable powers of regeneration. Sea stars can regenerate arms from the central region of their body, even if they lose all of their arms. The process of regeneration is very slow, taking as long as a year. Sea stars use their regenerative ability as a defensive mechanism, automatically shedding an arm at its base when the arm is captured by a predator. As you can see in Figure 40-9, some sea stars can even regenerate a complete, new individual from a detached arm, as long as the arm is attached to a portion of the central region. Certain species reproduce asexually by splitting their body through the central region. The two parts that are formed then regenerate the missing structures.

FIGURE 40-9

As long as a sea star retains part of its central region, it can regenerate any arms it loses. The sea star shown here, a member of the genus *Echinaster*, is regenerating five new arms.

SECTION 40-1 REVIEW

1. Why are echinoderms thought to have evolved from bilaterally symmetrical ancestors?

2. What are the characteristics that distinguish echinoderms from other phyla?

3. Name the representative species in each class of echinoderms.

4. Explain how a sea star extends and withdraws its tube feet.

5. How do sea stars reproduce asexually?

6. **CRITICAL THINKING** How would a sea star's ability to feed be affected if the sea star lost the water in its water-vascular system?

SECTION

OBJECTIVES

▲

List the major characteristics
of chordates.

●

Describe the structure
of lancelets.

■

Describe the structure
of tunicates.

INVERTEBRATE CHORDATES

The phylum Chordata (kohr-DAHT-uh) includes all of the vertebrates, or animals with backbones. It also includes two groups of animals that lack backbones and are therefore invertebrates. The development of chordates is similar to the development of echinoderms, suggesting that these two phyla descended from a common ancestor.

CHARACTERISTICS

All animals with a backbone are vertebrates, and they make up one of the subphyla in the phylum Chordata, whose members are called chordates. Chordates are so named because they have a notochord, a stiff but flexible rod of cells that runs the length of the body near the dorsal surface. The notochord is illustrated in Figure 40-10. The stiffness of the notochord provides a resistance against which the body muscles can exert force when they contract. The flexibility of the notochord allows the body to bend from side to side as well as up and down. Some kinds of chordates retain the notochord throughout their life. In most vertebrates, however, the notochord is present in embryos but becomes greatly reduced when the vertebral column, or backbone, develops. In adult mammals, the notochord persists only as small patches of tissue between the bones of the vertebral column.

You learned in Chapter 34 that in addition to a notochord, all chordates have the following three characteristics during some stage of their life: (1) a dorsal nerve cord, (2) pharyngeal pouches, and (3) a postanal tail. These characteristics are also illustrated in Figure 40-10. Unlike the ventral nerve cords of invertebrates such as

FIGURE 40-10

All chordates have a notochord, a dorsal nerve cord, pharyngeal pouches, and a postanal tail during at least some stage of their life.

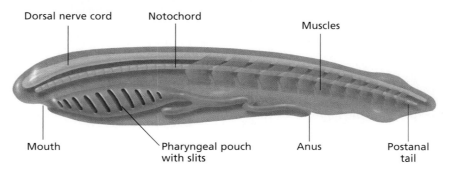

Dorsal nerve cord   Notochord   Muscles

Mouth   Pharyngeal pouch with slits   Anus   Postanal tail annelids and arthropods, the dorsal nerve cord of a chordate is a hollow tube. In vertebrates, the anterior end of the nerve cord enlarges during development to form the brain, and the posterior end forms the spinal cord. The brain receives information from a variety of complex sensory organs, many of which are concentrated at the anterior end of the body. The pharyngeal pouches are out-pockets in the pharynx, the portion of the digestive tract between the mouth and the esophagus. In aquatic chordates, the pharyngeal pouches became perforated by slits and evolved first into filter-feeding structures and later into gill chambers. In terrestrial chordates, the pouches evolved into a variety of structures, including the jaws, inner ear, and tonsils. The notochord or backbone extends into the postanal tail, and muscles in the tail can cause it to bend. The postanal tail provides much of the propulsion in many aquatic chordates. Invertebrates in other phyla lack this form of propulsion, because the anus, if present, is located at the end of the body.

EVOLUTION AND CLASSIFICATION

Like echinoderms, chordates are deuterostomes. This similarity provides evidence that echinoderms and chordates likely evolved from a common ancestor. The phylum Chordata is divided into three subphyla: Vertebrata, Cephalochordata (SEF-uh-loh-kohr-DAHT-uh), and Urochordata (YUR-uh-kohr-DAHT-uh). Members of the subphylum Vertebrata, the vertebrates, constitute more than 95 percent of all chordate species. They will be considered in detail in Chapters 41–45. Members of the other two subphyla live only in the ocean. They are the closest living relatives of the early animals from which all chordates evolved.

Subphylum Cephalochordata

The subphylum Cephalochordata contains about two dozen species of blade-shaped animals known as lancelets. Figure 40-11 shows that lancelets look much like the idealized chordate drawn in Figure 40-10. They retain their notochord, dorsal nerve cord,

FIGURE 40-11

(a) The lancelet *Branchiostoma lanceolatum* lives with most of its body buried in the sand. (b) Even as adults, lancelets clearly show all four chordate characteristics.

(a)

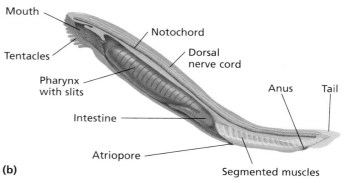

(b)

Mouth
Tentacles
Pharynx with slits
Intestine
Atriopore
Notochord
Dorsal nerve cord
Anus
Tail
Segmented muscles

(a)

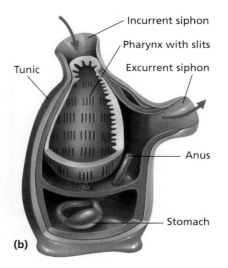

Incurrent siphon

Pharynx with slits

Tunic

Excurrent siphon

Anus

Stomach

(b)

FIGURE 40-12

Most adult tunicates, such as *Polycarpa auranta* (a), are sessile filter feeders. A drawing of a tunicate's internal structure (b) shows its enlarged pharynx with slits, the only chordate characteristic retained by adult tunicates.

pharyngeal pouches, and postanal tail throughout their life. Lancelets live in warm, shallow waters and use their muscular tail to wriggle backward into the sand. Only their anterior end protrudes from the sand. Lancelets use cilia to draw water into their pharynx through their mouth. Food particles in the water are trapped as the water passes through the numerous slits in the pharynx. The food enters the intestine to be digested, while the water leaves the body through an opening called the **atriopore** (AY-tree-oh-POHR).

Lancelets can swim weakly, powered by the coordinated contraction of muscles that run the length of their body. If you look closely at Figure 40-11, you can see that these muscles are arranged as a series of repeating segments. Body segmentation is another common feature of chordates. As you learned in Chapters 37 and 38, annelids and arthropods also have segmented bodies. However, animals in those phyla probably evolved body segmentation independently of chordates.

Subphylum Urochordata

The 2,000 species in the subphylum Urochordata are commonly called tunicates because their bodies are covered by a tough covering, or tunic. Tunicates are also called sea squirts because they squirt out a stream of water when touched. As adults, most tunicates are sessile, barrel-shaped animals that live on the sea bottom. They may be solitary or colonial. As you can see in Figure 40-12, tunicates are adapted for filter feeding. Propelled by the beating of cilia, water enters the body through an incurrent siphon, passes through slits in the pharynx, and exits through an excurrent siphon. Food that is filtered by the pharynx moves into the stomach. Undigested material leaves via the anus, which empties into the excurrent siphon. Tunicates are hermaphrodites. Sperm and eggs are released through the excurrent siphon into the surrounding water, where fertilization occurs.

Adult tunicates bear little resemblance to the idealized chordate shown in Figure 40-10. Although they do have a pouchlike pharynx with slits, they have no notochord, dorsal nerve cord, or postanal tail. Larval tunicates, however, possess all four chordate characteristics, but they lose most of them during metamorphosis.

SECTION 40-2 REVIEW

1. What are the four major characteristics of chordates?

2. Why are chordates and echinoderms thought to have evolved from a common ancestor?

3. How do vertebrates differ from the members of the other subphyla of chordates?

4. What evidence of body segmentation do lancelets display?

5. Which of the chordate characteristics do tunicates retain as adults?

6. CRITICAL THINKING In tunicates, the anus empties into the excurrent siphon. What is the advantage of this anatomical arrangement?

SUMMARY/VOCABULARY

40-1

- Most echinoderms develop from free-swimming, bilaterally symmetrical larvae into bottom-dwelling adults with penta-radial symmetry.

- Echinoderms have an endoskeleton made of ossicles, which may be attached to spines or spicules that protrude through the skin. They also have a water-vascular system, which includes many movable extensions called tube feet.

- The class Crinoidea includes sea lilies and feather stars, which are filter feeders that catch small organisms with their sticky tube feet.

- The class Ophiuroidea consists of basket stars and brittle stars, fast-moving echinoderms with long, flexible arms.

- The class Echinoidea includes sea urchins and sand dollars, whose internal organs are enclosed inside a rigid endoskeleton called a test. Many sea urchins have long spines.

- The class Holothuroidea is made of sea cucumbers, armless echinoderms with soft bodies.

- The class Asteroidea consists of sea stars, which have from 5 to 24 arms. Two rows of tube feet run along the underside of each arm.

- The water-vascular system of a sea star consists of a network of canals that connect to bulblike ampullae. Contraction of muscles surrounding the ampullae extends the tube feet, while contraction of muscles lining the tube feet makes the tube feet retract.

- Sea stars can turn one of their stomachs inside out through their mouth to feed on prey they have captured. After the food is partially digested outside the body, it is brought inside, where digestion is completed.

- Sea stars lack circulatory, excretory, and respiratory organ systems, and they have no head or brain. They use skin gills for gas exchange and waste excretion. Most have separate sexes.

Vocabulary

aboral surface (785)	madreporite (786)	pentaradial symmetry (782)	skin gill (786)
ampulla (786)	nerve ring (787)	pyloric stomach (786)	stone canal (786)
bipinnaria (787)	oral surface (785)	radial canal (786)	test (783)
cardiac stomach (786)	ossicle (782)	radial nerve (787)	tube foot (782)
echinoderm (781)	pedicellaria (785)	ring canal (786)	water-vascular system (782)

40-2

- Chordates have a notochord, a stiff but flexible rod of cells that runs the length of the body near the dorsal surface. In one group of chordates, the vertebrates, the notochord is largely replaced by the vertebral column, or backbone.

- Other defining characteristics of chordates are a dorsal nerve cord, pharyngeal pouches, and a postanal tail. These characteristics are not present at all life stages in all chordates.

- Like echinoderms, chordates are deuterostomes, which suggests that echinoderms and chordates evolved from a common ancestor.

- Animals in the subphylum Cephalo-chordata are called lancelets. These blade-shaped animals live partially buried in the sand, but they can swim from place to place. They retain all of the major chordate characteristics throughout their life.

- Animals in the subphylum Urochordata are called tunicates. Tunicate larvae have all of the major chordate characteristics, but they lose most of them when they develop into adults. Most tunicate adults are sessile.

Vocabulary

atriopore (790)

REVIEW

Vocabulary

1. What is pentaradial symmetry?
2. Distinguish between an oral surface and an aboral surface.
3. What term is used for the endoskeleton in members of the class Echinoidea?
4. What are pedicellariae?
5. Distinguish between a notochord and a dorsal nerve cord.

Multiple Choice

6. Scientists believe that the earliest adult echinoderms were (a) bilaterally symmetrical and sessile (b) bilaterally symmetrical and capable of moving about (c) radially symmetrical and sessile (d) radially symmetrical and capable of moving about.
7. Echinoderms lack all of the following organ systems except (a) a respiratory system (b) an excretory system (c) a circulatory system (d) a digestive system.
8. The class of echinoderms whose members most closely resemble the fossils of ancestral echinoderms is (a) Asteroidea (b) Crinoidea (c) Echinoidea (d) Holothuroidea.
9. The class Ophiuroidea consists of (a) sea cucumbers (b) sea stars (c) basket stars and brittle stars (d) sea urchins and sand dollars.
10. The endoskeleton of an echinoderm is composed of calcium carbonate plates referred to as (a) tests (b) ossicles (c) bipinnaria (d) pedicellariae.
11. In a sea star, gas exchange and excretion of wastes take place by diffusion through the walls of the (a) skin gills (b) atriopore (c) radial canals (d) pharynx.
12. When the muscles surrounding the ampullae of a sea star contract, the sea star's (a) stomach turns inside out (b) stomach retracts (c) tube feet retract (d) tube feet extend.
13. A sea star's nervous system does not include (a) a nerve ring (b) a nerve net (c) a brain (d) radial nerves.
14. Echinoderms and chordates are believed to have evolved from a common ancestor because both groups (a) are deuterostomes (b) are bilaterally symmetrical (c) have radially symmetrical larvae (d) have a postanal tail.
15. Adult tunicates have (a) a dorsal nerve cord (b) a pharynx with slits (c) a notochord (d) all of the above.

Short Answer

16. Trace the path of water through the water-vascular system of a sea star.
17. For what functions do echinoderms use their tube feet?
18. Contrast the ways that sea urchins and sand dollars are adapted to their environment.
19. Why are sea stars of economic importance to humans?
20. How does the sea cucumber transport food to its mouth?
21. Summarize the process of feeding and digestion in the sea star.
22. How have pharyngeal pouches become modified through evolution in aquatic chordates? How have they become modified in terrestrial chordates?
23. What is the significance of the notochord and the postanal tail to aquatic chordates?
24. Why are members of the subphylum Urochordata called tunicates?
25. Identify the structures labeled *A–F* in the diagram below.

CRITICAL THINKING

1. Sea cucumbers and sea lilies are relatively sessile animals. Their larvae, however, are capable of swimming. What advantage do swimming larvae provide for these echinoderms?

2. Commercial oyster farmers used to remove sea stars from their oyster beds, chop them in half, and throw them back into the water. Was this a good way to protect the oysters from sea stars? If your answer is yes, explain why. If your answer is no, explain why not and describe a better method.

3. Scientists have found many echinoderm fossils from the Cambrian period, but they have found few fossils of other species that must have lived during the Cambrian period. What might explain the large number of fossilized echinoderms?

4. Sea urchin eggs, or roe, are highly prized in Japan for sushi. In trying to supply the Japanese market for this delicacy, divers have nearly wiped out sea urchin populations in some areas of California. What steps could be taken to reestablish sea urchin populations in those areas?

5. Great populations of plankton rise to the surface of the ocean at night and return to the ocean depths during the day. Basket stars are also active at night, when they uncoil their thin, flexible arms. During the day, basket stars curl up and become a compact mass. Why do you think basket stars uncoil their arms at night and coil up during the day?

6. Neoteny is a phenomenon in which larvae become sexually mature while retaining larval characteristics. The term has been used to help explain the evolution of vertebrates from ancestral chordates. Use what you know about tunicates to support this hypothesis.

7. The two curves below show relative changes in the populations of two mollusk species (A and B) in a coastal area over time. At the time indicated by the dotted line, a species of sea star that preys on both A and B was introduced to the area. Which mollusk species is the preferred prey of the sea stars? Why did the population of the other mollusk species also decline in size after the sea stars were introduced? Explain your answers.

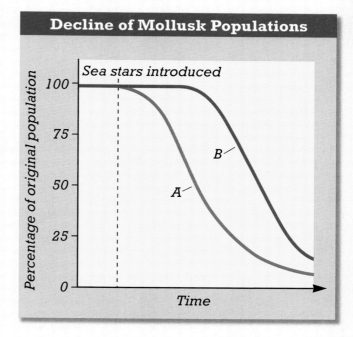

Decline of Mollusk Populations

Sea stars introduced

Percentage of original population — 100, 75, 50, 25, 0

A *B*

Time

EXTENSION

1. Read "Universe in a Puddle" in *Life,* April 1998, on page 52. Describe some of the adaptations that tidal pool organisms have that help them survive the crashing and pounding of incoming tides.

2. Write a short paper on a species of echinoderms that is not discussed in the chapter. Focus on the particular adaptations that enable the species you have selected to survive in its environment.

3. Research several species of sea urchins that have very different types of spines. Why and how might these differences have evolved? Report on why you think sea urchin spines have different forms. Mention in your report the mechanisms that predators use to get past these spines.

Comparing Echinoderms

- Compare the structure of two types of echinoderms.
- Infer function from the observation of structures.

- using dissection instruments and techniques
- observing

- preserved sea star
- preserved sea urchin
- sea urchin test
- dissection tray
- fine dissection scissors with pointed blades
- hand lens or dissecting microscope
- forceps
- blunt probe
- sharp probe
- dissection pins
- gloves (optional)
- 100 mL beaker
- household bleach
- Petri dish

Background

1. List the major characteristics of echinoderms.
2. Which feature of echinoderms gives their phylum its name?
3. To which classes of echinoderms do sea stars and sea urchins belong?
4. What is pentaradial symmetry?

PART A Observing the External Anatomy of a Sea Star

1. **CAUTION Put on safety goggles, gloves, and a lab apron.** Using forceps, hold a preserved sea star under running water to gently but thoroughly remove excess preservative. Then place the sea star in a dissection tray.

2. What evidence can you find that indicates that the sea star has pentaradial symmetry?

3. Make a table in your lab report like the one shown on the next page. As you observe each of the structures listed in the table, fill in the function of that structure.

4. While referring to Figure 40-7, find the madreporite on the aboral surface of your sea star. Record the madreporite's position and appearance.

5. Use a hand lens to examine the sea star's spines. Describe their size and shape. Are they distributed in any recognizable pattern on the surface of the sea star? Are they covered by tissue or exposed? Are they movable or fixed?

6. Are pedicellariae present? What is their location and arrangement? Draw one as it appears under the hand lens or dissecting microscope.

7. Use the dissecting microscope to look for small skin gills. If any are present, describe their location and structure.

8. Now examine the sea star's oral surface. Find the mouth, and describe its location and structure. Use forceps or a probe to gently move aside any soft tissues. What structures are found around the mouth?

9. Locate the tube feet. Describe their distribution. Using a dissecting microscope, observe and then draw a single tube foot.

PART B Observing the Internal Anatomy of a Sea Star

10. Using scissors and forceps, carefully cut the body wall away from the aboral surface of one of the sea star's arms. Start near the end of the arm and work toward the center. The internal organs may stick to the inside

of the body wall, so use a sharp probe to gently separate them from the body wall as you cut. Be careful
not to damage the madreporite.

11. While referring to Figure 40-7, find the digestive
glands in the arm you have opened. Describe their
appearance. If you have dissected carefully, you should
be able to find a short, branched tube that connects
the digestive glands to the pyloric stomach. If you
cannot find the digestive glands or this tube, repeat
step 10 on one of the other arms and look for them
there.

12. Cut the tube that connects the digestive glands to the
pyloric stomach, and move the digestive glands out of
the arm. Look for the testes or ovaries. If your specimen is an immature animal, these organs may be
small and difficult to find.

13. Locate the two rows of ampullae that run the length
of the arm. What is the relationship between the
ampullae and the tube feet, which you observed on
the oral surface?

14. Carefully remove the body wall from the aboral surface of the central region of the sea star. Try to avoid
damaging the underlying structures. Locate the pyloric
stomach and the cardiac stomach. How does a sea
star use its cardiac stomach during feeding?

15. Remove the stomachs and find the canals of the
water-vascular system: stone canal, ring canal, and
radial canals. In which direction does water move
through these canals?

16. CAUTION   Bleach is a highly corrosive
agent. If you get it on your skin or clothing, wash it off at the sink while calling to your
teacher. If you get it in your eyes, immediately
flush it out at the eyewash station while calling
to your teacher. Cut a 1 cm cross section out of the
middle of one of the arms. Using forceps, transfer the
section to a small beaker containing enough bleach to
cover it. The bleach will eat away the soft tissues,
exposing the endoskeleton.

17. After about 10–15 minutes, use the forceps to carefully transfer the endoskeleton to a Petri dish containing tap water. Observe the endoskeleton under
a dissecting microscope. Can you find individual
ossicles?

FUNCTION OF SEA STAR STRUCTURES

Structure	Function
Madreporite	
Pedicellaria	
Skin gill	
Tube foot	
Digestive gland	
Ampulla	
Ossicle	

PART C   Observing the Anatomy of a Sea Urchin

18. Using forceps, hold a preserved sea urchin under running water to remove excess preservative. Then place
the sea star in a dissection tray. What evidence can
you find that indicates that the sea urchin has pentaradial symmetry?

19. Observe the sea urchin's spines. Answer the same
questions for the sea urchin's spines that you
answered for the sea star's spines in step 5.

20. Examine the sea urchin's oral surface. Find the mouth
and use a sharp probe to explore the structures
around the mouth. How does the sea urchin's mouth
differ from the sea star's?

21. Examine the sea urchin test. What might be the function of the rows of small pores on the test? What
might be the function of the small bumps on the test?

22. Dispose of the specimens according to
the directions from your teacher. Then
clean up your materials and wash your hands before
leaving the lab.

Analysis and Conclusions

1. What features are shared by sea stars and sea
urchins?

2. What are some of the structural differences between
sea stars and sea urchins?

Further Inquiry

Observe how living sea stars move in a saltwater aquarium. Add some live mussels, and observe the feeding
behavior of the sea stars.

unit 9

VERTEBRATES

❝ *Nature discloses the secrets of her past with the greatest reluctance. We paleontologists weave our tales from fossil fragments poorly preserved in incomplete sequences of sedimentary rocks. Most fossil mammals are known only from teeth—the hardest substance in our bodies— and a few scattered bones.* **❞**

From "History of the Vertebrate Brain," from *Ever Since Darwin: Reflections in Natural History,* by Stephen Jay Gould. Copyright © 1973, 1974, 1975, 1976, 1977 by the American Museum of Natural History; copyright © 1977 by Stephen Jay Gould. Reprinted by permission of *W. W. Norton & Company, Inc.*

internet**connect**

SCiLINKS
NSTA
National Science Teachers Association *sci*LINKS Internet resources are located throughout this unit.

Opossums are the only North American marsupial mammals.

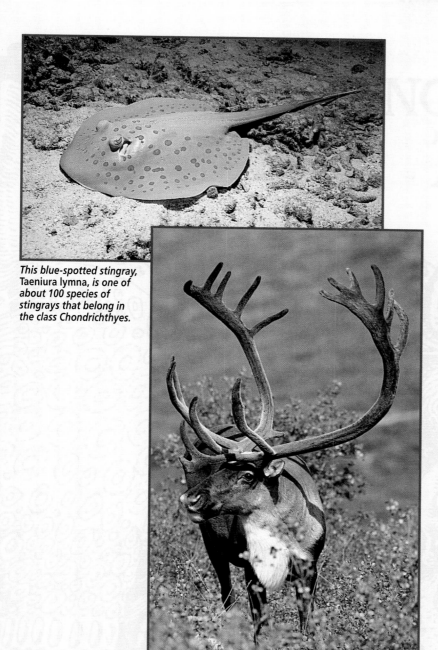

This blue-spotted stingray, Taeniura lymna, is one of about 100 species of stingrays that belong in the class Chondrichthyes.

These colorful rainbow lorikeets, also known as brush-tongued parrots, can be found in eastern Australia, where they feed on eucalyptus flowers.

Antlers, such as those on this caribou, are bony outgrowths that are shed each winter.

Flap-necked chameleon

CHAPTER 41

FISHES

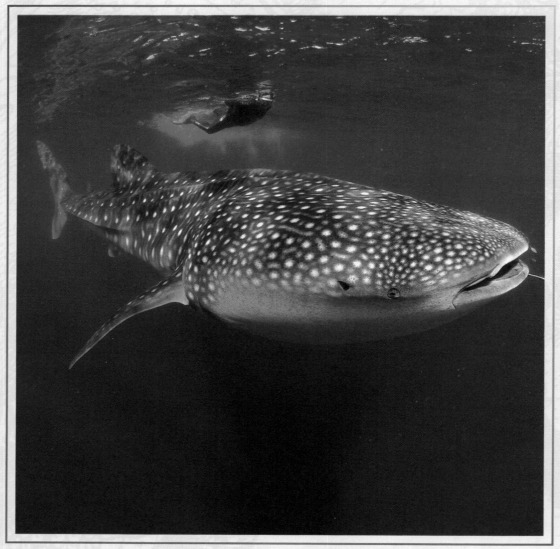

The whale shark lives in a saltwater environment, for which it has special organs and biochemical adaptations.

FOCUS CONCEPT: *Structure and Function*

As you read the chapter, focus on the adaptations that allow fishes to survive and reproduce in aquatic environments.

Introduction to Vertebrates

Although the vertebrates are not the largest or most abundant group of animals, they are the most familiar to us. This is partly because we are vertebrates. Vertebrates are an important part of our diet. In many parts of the world, vertebrates, not machines, perform the hard work of pulling plows and hauling heavy loads. We have also taken vertebrates into our homes as pets.

CHARACTERISTICS

Vertebrates are one subphylum within the phylum Chordata. Like other chordates, vertebrates have, at some stage of life, a notochord, a dorsal hollow nerve cord, pharyngeal pouches, and a post-anal tail. Vertebrates are a distinct group because they have three characteristics that distinguish them from other chordates. First, vertebrates have vertebrae, bones or cartilage that surround and protect the dorsal nerve cord. The vertebrae form the **vertebral column,** or spine. Second, vertebrates have a **cranium,** or skull, that protects the brain. Third, all vertebrates have an endoskeleton composed of bone or cartilage.

Classification

Today there are about 45,000 species of vertebrates. They occupy all but the most extreme terrestrial habitats. More than 24,000 vertebrate species are fishes. Fishes are found in a wide range of water habitats. The major groups of vertebrates are summarized below.

- **Lampreys and Hagfishes** (class Agnatha)—These fishes have elongated, eel-like bodies, and they lack jaws, paired fins, and bone. There are about 80 species.
- **Sharks, Rays, and Skates** (class Chondrichthyes)—These predatory fishes have jaws and paired fins. Their skeleton is made of cartilage, not bone, and their skin is covered by a unique kind of scale. There are about 800 species.
- **Bony Fishes** (class Osteichthyes)—Most familiar fishes, such as guppies, salmon, bass, and catfish, are bony fishes. All have jaws, and most species have a skeleton composed of bone. This group comprises two main lineages: the ray-finned fishes and the lobe-finned fishes. There are over 23,000 species of bony fishes.

FIGURE 41-1

This phylogenetic tree shows the evolutionary relationships among vertebrates.

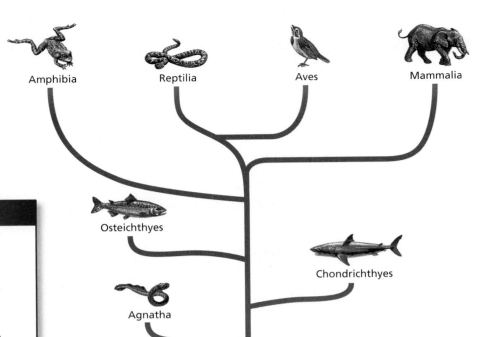

Quick Lab

Analyzing a Phylogenetic Tree

Materials paper, pencil

Procedure

1. Draw the phylogenetic tree shown on this page on your paper.

2. Using the information on pp. 799 and 800, determine the key characteristics that distinguish each vertebrate group. Indicate these evolutionary changes on the branches of the tree to make a diagram of the relationship that exists among vertebrates. Begin at the bottom of the tree with the key characteristics that distinguish vertebrates from other chordates.

Analysis What characteristics are shared by all vertebrates? What key characteristic separates the classes Chondrichthyes and Osteichthyes? What adaptations lead to the divergence of mammals? Which two groups of vertebrates share the most recent common ancestor?

- **Amphibians** (class Amphibia)—Frogs, toads, and salamanders belong to this group. Their skin is thin and is permeable to gases and water. Most species lay their eggs in water and pass through an aquatic larval stage.

- **Reptiles** (class Reptilia)—This group includes turtles, crocodiles, alligators, lizards, and snakes. The skin of reptiles is dry and scaly. The eggs of reptiles protect the embryo from drying out and can be laid on land. There are about 6,000 species.

- **Birds** (class Aves)—Birds are characterized by adaptations that enable flight, including feathers, hollow bones, and a unique respiratory system. There are over 10,000 species.

- **Mammals** (class Mammalia)—Humans, cats, mice, and horses are among the members of this group. All mammals have hair and nurse their young with milk. There are about 4,400 species. Figure 41-1 shows the relationships among the major groups of living vertebrates.

EVOLUTION

Most biologists think that vertebrates originated about 550 million years ago, shortly after the first chordates appear in the fossil record. The oldest known vertebrate fossils are those of jawless fishes. They appear in the fossil record starting a little over 500 million years ago. Most early jawless fishes did not have paired fins. Their bodies were covered with heavy, bony scales, but their skeletons were composed of cartilage. Figure 41-2 shows an artist's reconstruction of one of these fishes.

Jawless fishes were the only vertebrates for more than 50 million years, and they diversified into many evolutionary lines. By about 350 million years ago, most of these lines had become extinct. The survivors became the ancestors of today's jawless fishes (class Agnatha).

Origin of Jaws

About 440 million years ago, the first fishes with jaws and paired fins appeared. Paired fins increased their stability and maneuverability, and jaws allowed them to seize and manipulate prey. Jaws are thought to have evolved from the first pair of **gill arches,** the skeletal elements that support the pharynx. Figure 41-3 shows three possible stages in this transformation.

The first fishes to have paired fins and jaws were the acanthodians (AY-kan-THOH-dee-uhnz), or spiny fishes, in the class Acanthodii. Acanthodians became extinct about 270 million years ago. Modern fishes—the sharks and rays (class Chondrichthyes) and the bony fishes (class Osteichthyes)—make their first appearance in the fossil record about 400 million years ago.

FIGURE 41-2

Early jawless fishes, such as this *Pharyngolepis,* lacked paired fins and probably fed on small invertebrates. Most species of early jawless fishes were less than 15 cm (6 in.) in length.

FIGURE 41-3

Jaws are thought to have developed from the gill arches of early jawless fishes. These figures represent hypothesized stages of evolution.

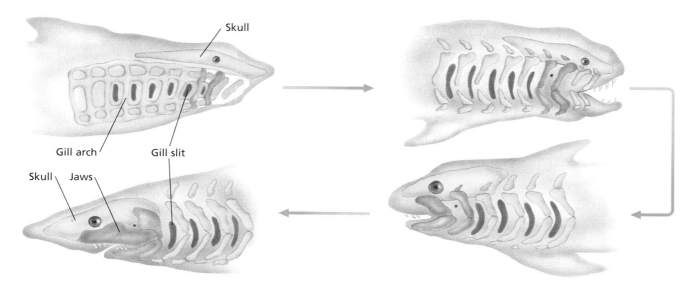

Skull

Gill arch · Gill slit

Skull · Jaws

SECTION 41-1 REVIEW

1. What are three characteristics of vertebrates?

2. Which group of modern vertebrates contains the jawless fishes?

3. Name two differences between the first fishes and modern bony fishes.

4. Explain why scientists think that the early jawless fishes were probably awkward swimmers.

5. List the function of jaws.

6. **CRITICAL THINKING**   Explain why scientists think that the vertebrates evolved from chordates in the sea.

SECTION

OBJECTIVES

Identify three problems
faced by all fishes.

Describe the feeding behavior of
lampreys and hagfishes.

Identify two characteristics
of cartilaginous fishes.

Describe how sharks detect prey.

Describe reproduction in
cartilaginous fishes, and contrast it
with reproduction in jawless fishes.

Eco Connection

Hagfish Depletion

Hagfishes have recently become
economically important. Most "eel-
skin" products, such as wallets, are
actually made from the tanned skin
of hagfishes. The demand for these
products is so high that hagfish
populations in some parts of the
world have been almost wiped out
by overfishing.

JAWLESS FISHES, SHARKS, AND RAYS

*T*he term fish *generally refers to three distinct classes of living vertebrates: Agnatha, jawless fishes; Chondrichthyes, cartilaginous fishes; and Osteichthyes, bony fishes. Fishes are the most numerous and widespread of all vertebrates.*

LIFE IN THE WATER

The body plan of a fish makes it well-suited to live in a water environment. A streamlined shape and a muscular tail enable most fishes to move rapidly through the water. Paired fins allow fishes to maneuver right or left, up or down, and backward or forward. Unpaired fins on the back and belly increase stability. In addition, most fishes secrete a mucus that reduces friction as they swim.

Most of the tissues in a fish's body are denser than water. By controlling the amount of gas in their bodies, many fishes can regulate their vertical position in the water. Some fishes also store lipids, which are less dense than water and therefore help them to float.

Fishes need to absorb oxygen and rid themselves of carbon dioxide. However, scales on fishes limit diffusion through the skin. Instead, most exchanges between water and blood take place across the membranes of gills—the internal respiratory organs of fishes.

Homeostasis

The concentration of solutes in a fish's body usually differs from the concentration of solutes in the water in which the fish swims. The body of a freshwater fish has a higher concentration of solutes than the surrounding water does, so the fish tends to gain water through osmosis and lose ions, such as sodium and chloride ions, through diffusion. Most saltwater fishes contain lower concentrations of solutes than their surroundings do. Thus, saltwater fishes tend to lose water and gain ions.

Like all organisms, fishes must also rid themselves of the waste products produced by metabolism. The kidneys and gills play important roles in maintaining homeostasis in the tissues and in getting rid of metabolic wastes. The kidneys filter the blood and help regulate the concentration of ions in the body. The gills release wastes, such as carbon dioxide and ammonia, and either absorb or release ions, depending on whether the fish lives in fresh water or in salt water.

Sensory Functions

A prominent adaptation present in nearly all fishes is the **lateral line system.** This system consists of a row of sensory structures that run the length of the fish's body on each side and that are connected by nerves to the brain. The lateral line system detects vibrations in the water, such as those caused by a fish swimming nearby. Most fishes also have highly developed senses of smell and sight. Hearing is an important sense for some fishes, and some species can detect electrical currents.

CLASS AGNATHA

The only existing jawless fishes are the 80 species of hagfishes and lampreys that compose the class Agnatha. Figure 41-4 shows an example of both types of jawless fishes. Their skin has neither plates nor scales. Hagfishes and lampreys have an eel-like body, a cartilaginous skeleton, and unpaired fins. The notochord remains throughout life. Hagfishes have small eyes that are beneath the skin, while lampreys have large eyes. Hagfishes lack vertebrae and are unique among vertebrates in that their body fluids have nearly the same ion concentration as sea water. Hagfishes live only in the oceans. Many lampreys live permanently in fresh water, and all species reproduce in fresh water.

Hagfishes

Hagfishes are bottom dwellers in cold marine waters. They feed on small invertebrates or on dead and dying fish. Because the hagfish lacks jaws, it cannot bite, but within its mouth are two movable plates and a rough tonguelike structure that it uses to pinch off chunks of flesh. Hagfishes often burrow into the body of a dead fish through the gills, skin, or anus. Once inside, they eat the internal organs. Hagfishes can tie their bodies into knots to evade capture. They also secrete bad-tasting slime to discourage predators. Hagfishes usually remain hidden in mud burrows on the ocean floor.

Lampreys

About half the species of lampreys are free-living and do not feed as adults. The other half are parasites as adults and feed on the blood and body fluids of other fishes. Once a suitable host is located, a lamprey uses its disk-shaped mouth to attach to the host. Then it scrapes a hole in the host with its rough tongue and secretes a chemical that keeps the host's blood from clotting. The lamprey feeds on the blood and fluids that leak from the wound. After feeding, the lamprey drops off. The host may recover, bleed to death, or die from an infection.

Some lamprey species spend most of their adult lives in the ocean. Others live in rivers or lakes and never enter salt water. All lampreys breed in fresh water, usually choosing a shallow stream

FIGURE 41-4

Hagfishes (a) and lampreys (b) are modern jawless fishes. What feature can you see on the lamprey and hagfish that would prevent them from swimming as well as bony fishes and sharks?

(a)

(b)

Modeling a Shark Adaptation

Materials 8 cm dialysis tubing, 8 cm length of string (2), 100 mL salt solution (5 percent), 250 mL beaker, 10 mL distilled water, scale, graduated cylinder

Procedure

1. Tightly tie one end of the dialysis tubing with string. Place 10 mL of distilled water inside the dialysis tubing, and tie the other end of the tube tightly with string.

2. Record the initial weight of the filled tube.

3. Add the filled dialysis tubing to a beaker filled with 100 mL of salt solution.

4. After 10 minutes, remove the tubing from the beaker, blot the outside, and reweigh it. Record your observations.

Analysis Explain the reason for the change in the weight of the tube, if any. Are sharks likely to lose or gain ions? What physical structures of a shark play a key role in maintaining ionic homeostasis in sharks?

FIGURE 41-5

These teethlike placoid scales are found on the skin of cartilaginous fishes. What advantage might they give a shark in swimming?

with a gravel bottom. They scrape out a small nest in the gravel, and the female releases eggs while the male releases sperm. Fertilization occurs outside the body of either parent. This type of fertilization is known as **external fertilization.** The eggs hatch into small larvae that closely resemble an amphioxus, or lancelet. The larvae eventually transform into adults.

CLASS CHONDRICHTHYES

Sharks, skates, and rays belong to the class Chondrichthyes. Because the fishes in this class have skeletons composed of cartilage, they are also called cartilaginous fishes. **Cartilage** is a flexible, lightweight material made of cells surrounded by tough fibers of protein. Sharks, skates, and rays differ from lampreys and hagfishes in that they have movable jaws, skeletons, and paired fins. Almost all of the approximately 800 species of sharks, skates, and rays live in salt water. All species are carnivores and some are scavengers. They eat many different kinds of foods, including fishes, seals, aquatic invertebrates, and plankton. The skin of cartilaginous fishes is covered with **placoid** (PLA-koyd) **scales**—small, toothlike spines that feel like sandpaper. Placoid scales, shown in Figure 41-5, probably reduce turbulence of the water flow and thus increase swimming efficiency.

Sharks

The largest sharks, the whale shark (up to 18 m, or 59 ft, long) and the basking shark (up to 15 m, or 49 ft, long), feed on plankton. Sharks swim in a side-to-side pattern created by the motion of their asymmetrical tail fin. Just behind a shark's head are paired **pectoral** (PEK-tuh-ruhl) **fins,** which jut out from the body like the wings of a plane. Figure 41-6 shows the external structure and internal anatomy of a shark.

The mouth of a typical shark has 6 to 20 rows of teeth that point inward. When a tooth in one of the front rows breaks or wears down, a replacement moves forward to take its place. One shark may use more than 20,000 teeth over its lifetime. The structure of each species' teeth is adapted to that species' feeding habits. Sharks that feed primarily on large fish or mammals have big, triangular teeth with sawlike edges that hook and tear flesh.

Sharks use several senses to locate prey. Their ability to detect chemicals—that is, their sense of smell—is particularly acute. Paired nostrils on the snout have specialized nerve cells that connect with the **olfactory** (awl-FAK-tuh-ree) **bulbs** of the brain, where the information from the nostrils is analyzed. Water entering the nostrils is continuously monitored for chemicals. Sharks also have a well-developed lateral line system. Their vision is keen, even at low levels of light. They are also extremely sensitive to electrical fields, such as those generated by the muscular contractions of animals.

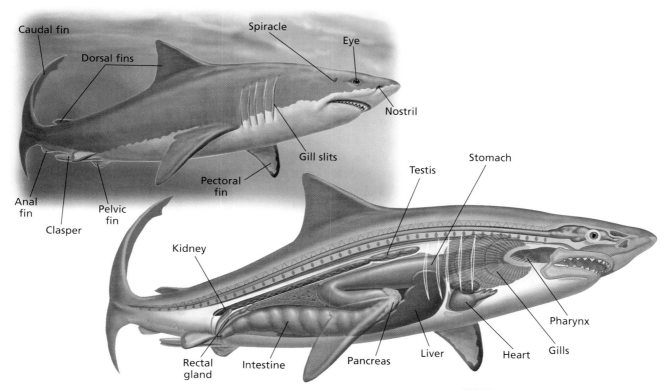

Caudal fin
Spiracle
Eye
Dorsal fins
Nostril
Gill slits
Anal fin
Pelvic fin
Clasper
Pectoral fin
Testis
Stomach
Kidney
Pharynx
Rectal gland
Intestine
Pancreas
Liver
Heart
Gills

FIGURE 41-6

A streamlined shape allows the shark to slip through the water with little resistance. The shark's powerful caudal fin propels it forward, and the paired fins help steer and stabilize it. The shark's internal anatomy includes organs for digestion, reproduction, and maintaining homeostasis. Note how the rectal gland is connected to the lower part of the intestine. This makes the disposal of excess salts easier.

Sharks detect these fields by means of sensitive receptors located in small pits scattered over their head. Tests have shown that sharks can find and capture prey using only their sensitivity to electrical fields. Evaluating and integrating information from all these different senses requires a large and complex brain. Sharks have the largest brain—for their body size—of any fishes.

Rays and Skates

Rays and skates have flattened bodies with paired winglike pectoral fins and, in some species, whiplike tails. Rays have diamond- or disk-shaped bodies, while most skates have triangular bodies. Most rays and skates are less than 1 m (3.3 ft) long. Rays and skates are primarily bottom dwellers. Their flat shape and coloration camouflage them on the ocean floor. Most rays and skates feed on mollusks and crustaceans. Figure 41-7 shows an example of a ray.

Adaptations of Cartilaginous Fishes

In cartilaginous fishes, gas exchange occurs in the gills, which lie behind the head. Efficient gas exchange requires a continuous flow of water across the gills. Some fast-swimming sharks are able to push water through their mouth, over their gills, and out of their gill slits by swimming alone. However, most sharks and rays pump water over their gills by expanding and contracting their mouth cavity and pharynx. When lying on the bottom, rays and skates cannot bring in water through their mouth, which is located on the ventral surface of their body, so instead, they draw water in through their spiracles, which are two large openings on the top of the head, just behind the eyes.

FIGURE 41-7

This blue-spotted stingray, *Taeniura lymna,* is an example of a bottom dweller. This stingray was photographed in the Red Sea near Egypt.

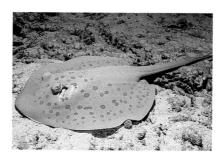

Instead of releasing ammonia, cartilaginous fishes use energy to convert ammonia into a compound called urea, which is much less toxic. Sharks retain large amounts of urea in their blood and tissues, thus raising the concentration of solutes in their body to at least the same level as that found in sea water. As a result, sharks do not need to drink. Because the concentration of sodium and chloride in the body of a shark is less than the concentration found in sea water, these ions still diffuse into the body across the gills and are absorbed with food. The **rectal gland,** located in the posterior portion of the intestine, removes excess sodium and chloride ions from the blood and releases them into the rectum for elimination.

Cartilaginous fishes maintain their position in the water in two ways. First, because a fish generates lift, or upward force, as it swims, it can remain at the same level in the water, counteracting the tendency to sink, as long as it keeps moving. Some open-water sharks rely entirely on this method, but it does use up a lot of energy. Second, many cartilaginous fishes store large amounts of low-density lipids, usually in the liver. A shark's lipid-filled liver may account for 25 percent of its mass. Lipids give sharks buoyancy by reducing the overall density of the body. Because continuous swimming is not necessary, less energy is used.

Reproduction in Cartilaginous Fishes

Cartilaginous fishes differ from jawless fishes in that fertilization occurs inside the body of the female. This type of fertilization is called **internal fertilization.** During mating, the male transfers sperm into the female's body with modified pelvic fins called **claspers.** In a few species of sharks and rays, the females lay large yolky eggs right after fertilization. The young develop within the egg, are nourished by the yolk, and hatch as miniature versions of the adults. The eggs of many species develop in the female's body, and the young are born live. In some of these species, the mother nourishes the developing sharks while they are in her body. No cartilaginous fishes provide parental care for their young after birth or hatching.

SECTION 41-2 REVIEW

1. What is the function of the lateral line in fishes?

2. How do parasitic lampreys feed?

3. Name two characteristics shared by all cartilaginous fishes.

4. A shark can locate and capture a fish buried in the gravel at the bottom of its tank. Describe at least two senses that the shark might be using to find the fish.

5. Define the terms *internal fertilization* and *external fertilization.*

6. CRITICAL THINKING When sea lampreys invaded the Great Lakes, they devastated populations of their hosts. In lakes where sea lampreys have lived for a long time, host populations have not declined. Using what you know about co-evolution, explain this difference.

BONY FISHES

Of the 24,000 known species of fishes, about 95 percent are in the class Osteichthyes—the bony fishes. Bony fishes account for most of the vertebrates living in fresh water and in salt water. In this section you will study some of the adaptations of this very large and successful group.

OBJECTIVES

▲
List three characteristics of bony fishes.

●
Distinguish between ray-finned fishes and lobe-finned fishes.

■
Trace the flow of blood through a fish's heart.

◆
Explain how gills function in respiration.

▲
Describe the function of the swim bladder.

●
Compare and contrast reproduction in bony fishes with reproduction in cartilaginous fishes.

CHARACTERISTICS

The bony fishes are characterized by three key features:
- **Bone**—This material is typically harder and heavier than cartilage. The skeletons of most bony fishes contain bone.
- **Lungs or swim bladder**—Early bony fishes had **lungs,** internal respiratory organs in which gas is exchanged between the air and blood. Only a few species of bony fishes have lungs today. Most bony fishes have a **swim bladder,** a gas-filled sac that is used to control buoyancy. The swim bladder is thought to have evolved from the lungs of the early bony fishes.
- **Scales**—The body of a bony fish is usually covered with scales. Scales protect the fish and help reduce water resistance.

Biologists divide the bony fishes into two main groups: lobe-finned fishes and ray-finned fishes.

Lobe-Finned Fishes

The **lobe-finned fishes** have fleshy fins that are supported by a series of bones. Only seven species of lobe-finned fishes exist today, six species of lungfishes and one species of coelacanth. Lungfishes, which exchange gases through lungs and gills, live in shallow tropical ponds that periodically dry up. They burrow into the mud and cover themselves with mucus to stay moist until the pond refills. Lobe-finned fishes are important because extinct lobe-finned fishes are ancestors of amphibians and all other terrestrial vertebrates.

Ray-Finned Fishes

Ray-finned fishes have fins that are supported by long, segmented, flexible bony elements called rays. Rays probably evolved from scales. In contrast to lobe-finned fishes, ray-finned fishes do not have fins with a central bony axis. Ray-finned fishes are diverse in appearance, behavior, and habitat. Ray-finned fishes include most familiar fishes, such as eels, yellow perch, trout, salmon, guppies, bass, herring, and darters.

EXTERNAL ANATOMY

Figure 41-8 shows the external anatomy of a yellow perch, a bony fish that is common in the Great Lakes and in other freshwater lakes of the eastern United States and Canada. The yellow perch, like all bony fishes, has distinct head, trunk, and tail regions. On each side of the head is the **operculum** (oh-PERK-yoo-LUHM), a hard plate that opens at the rear and covers and protects the gills.

Fins

The fins of the yellow perch are adapted for swimming and navigating through the water. The **caudal fin** extends from the tail. It moves from side to side and amplifies the swimming motion of the body. Two **dorsal fins,** one anterior and one posterior, and a ventral **anal fin** help keep the fish upright and moving in a straight line. The fish uses paired **pelvic fins** and pectoral fins to navigate, stop, move up and down, and even back up. The pelvic fins also orient the body when the fish is at rest. The fins are supported by either rays or spines. Rays are bony yet flexible, while spines are bony and rigid.

Skin

The skin of the yellow perch is covered with scales. Scales are thin, round disks of a bonelike material that grow from pockets in the skin. As Figure 41-8 shows, scales overlap like roof shingles. They all point toward the tail to minimize friction as the fish swims. Scales grow throughout the life of the fish, adjusting their growth pattern to the food supply. The scales grow quickly when food is abundant and slowly when it is scarce. In fishes that live in habitats with annual variations in food availability, the resulting growth rings give a good approximation of the fish's age.

FIGURE 41-8

The external features of the yellow perch, *Perca flavescens,* are representative of bony fishes. Note the growth rings on the scales shown in the inset. They indicate the fish's approximate age.

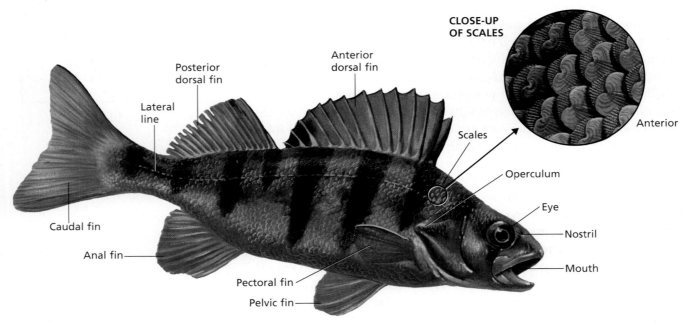

CLOSE-UP
OF SCALES

Posterior
dorsal fin

Anterior
dorsal fin

Lateral
line

Scales

Anterior

Operculum

Caudal fin

Eye

Nostril

Anal fin

Mouth

Pectoral fin

Pelvic fin

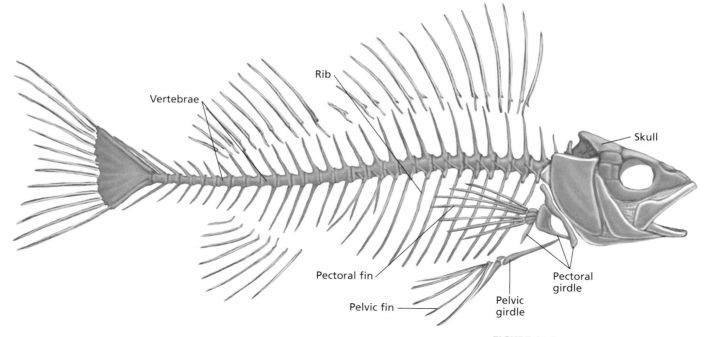

Vertebrae

Rib

Skull

Pectoral fin

Pelvic fin

Pelvic girdle

Pectoral girdle

FIGURE 41-9

The skeleton of *Perca flavescens* is similar to that of other bony fishes. The general structure of the vertebrae, rib cage, and fins is found in many fishes.

INTERNAL ANATOMY

The major parts of a fish's skeleton, shown in Figure 41-9, are the skull, spinal column, pectoral girdle, pelvic girdle, and ribs. The spinal column is made up of many bones, called the vertebrae, with cartilage pads between each. The spinal column also partly encloses and protects the spinal cord. The **pectoral girdle** is the attachment point for the pectoral fins. The **pelvic girdle** is the attachment point for the pelvic fins. In a human skeleton, the pectoral girdle is the shoulder and its supporting bones, while the pelvic girdle is the hips. A fish's skull is composed of a large number of bones (far more than are in the human skull) and is capable of a wide range of movements. Figure 41-9 shows the skeleton of a bony fish.

Digestive System

Most bony fishes are generalized carnivores. The jaws of predatory fishes are lined with many sharp teeth that point inward to keep prey from escaping. Strong muscles operate the jaws, which are hinged to allow the mouth to open wide.

Figure 41-10 shows the internal anatomy of a bony fish. Food passes from the mouth into the pharynx, or throat cavity, and then moves through the **esophagus** to the stomach. The **stomach** secretes acid and digestive enzymes that begin to break down food. From the stomach, food passes into the **intestine,** where digestion is completed and nutrients are absorbed. The **liver,** located near the stomach, secretes **bile,** which helps break down fats. The **gallbladder** stores bile and releases it into the intestine. The **pancreas,** also located near the stomach, releases digestive enzymes into the intestine. The lining of the intestine is covered with fingerlike extensions called villi that increase the surface area for absorption of digested foods. Undigested material is then eliminated through the **anus.**

internet**connect**

SC*L*INKS

NSTA

TOPIC: Anatomy of a bony fish
GO TO: www.scilinks.org
KEYWORD: HM809

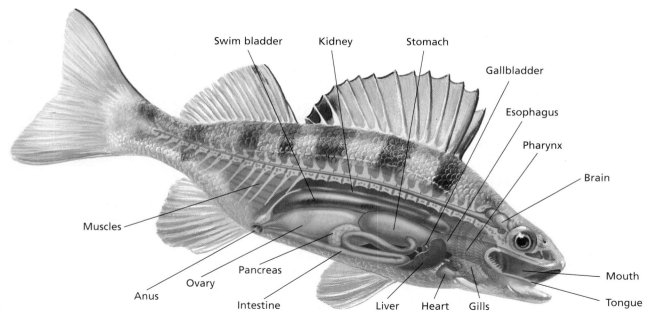

Swim bladder   Kidney   Stomach

Gallbladder

Esophagus

Pharynx

Brain

Muscles

Mouth

Anus   Ovary   Pancreas   Intestine   Liver   Heart   Gills   Tongue

FIGURE 41-10

The internal anatomy of a bony fish, such as this perch, is a model for the arrangement of organs in all vertebrate descendants of fish. Food passes first from the mouth through the esophagus, then to the stomach and intestines. Finally, undigested waste is eliminated through the anus. Digestion of protein occurs in the stomach, and absorption of nutrients occurs in the intestine.

Circulatory System

The circulatory system of a fish delivers oxygen and nutrients to the cells of the body. It also transports wastes produced by metabolism—carbon dioxide and ammonia—to the gills and kidneys for elimination. The circulatory system consists of a heart, blood vessels, and blood. The heart pumps blood through **arteries** to small, thin-walled vessels, called **capillaries,** in the gills. There the blood picks up oxygen and releases carbon dioxide. From the gills, the blood then travels to the body tissues, where nutrients and wastes are exchanged. The blood returns to the heart through **veins.**

The heart of a bony fish has four chambers in a row, as you can see in Figure 41-11. Deoxygenated blood from the body empties into a collecting chamber called the **sinus venosus.** Next, blood moves into the larger **atrium.** Contraction of the atrium speeds up the blood and drives it into the muscular **ventricle,** the main pumping chamber of the heart. Contraction of the ventricle provides most of the force that drives the blood through the circulatory system. The final chamber is the **conus arteriosus.** It has an elastic wall and usually contains valves to prevent blood from flowing back into the ventricle. The conus arteriosus smooths the flow of blood from the heart.

FIGURE 41-11

A fish's heart is a series of four chambers that act in sequence to move blood through the body, transporting oxygen to the cells and wastes to organs for elimination. Note the thickness of the muscle in the ventricle. Why would the ventricle muscle be so much thicker than the other muscles of the heart?

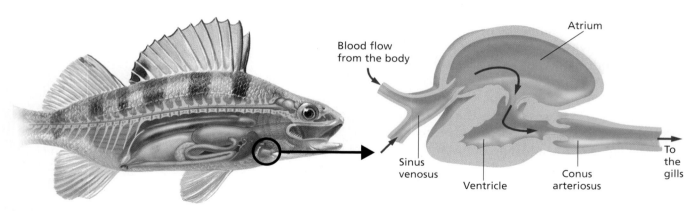

Blood flow from the body

Atrium

Sinus venosus   Ventricle   Conus arteriosus   To the gills

Respiratory and Excretory Systems

The large surface area of a fish's gills allows for rapid gas exchange. Gills are supported by four sets of curved bones on each side of the fish's head. Each gill has a double row of thin projections, called gill filaments. In most bony fishes, water is taken into the mouth and pumped over the gills, where it flows across the gill filaments before exiting behind the operculum. As you can see in Figure 41-12, water flows away from the head while blood flows toward the head. This arrangement is known as **countercurrent flow.** Countercurrent flow allows more oxygen to diffuse into the gills than would be possible if blood and water flowed in the same direction.

A fish's kidneys filter dissolved chemical wastes from the blood. The resulting solution, called **urine,** contains ammonia, ions such as sodium and chloride, and water. Urine is carried from the kidneys through a system of ducts to the **urinary bladder,** where it is stored and later expelled. By varying the amount of water and salts in the urine, the kidneys help regulate the water and the ion balance.

As blood flows through the gill filaments, ammonia generated by metabolism diffuses from the blood into the water passing over the gills and is removed from the body. The gills also regulate the concentration of ions in the body. Recall that saltwater fishes have lower ion concentrations than sea water has. Therefore, they lose water through osmosis and gain ions, such as sodium and chloride ions. Saltwater fishes make up for this water loss by excreting very little urine and by drinking sea water, but this increases their internal concentration of sodium and chloride ions. Both kinds of ions are actively transported out through the gills. Freshwater fishes tend to gain water and lose ions. They respond by producing large amounts of urine and actively transporting sodium and chloride ions in through the gills.

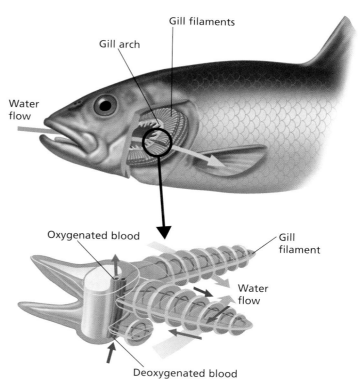

Gill filaments
Gill arch
Water flow
Oxygenated blood
Gill filament
Water flow
Deoxygenated blood

FIGURE 41-12

The gills are located directly behind the head and beneath the operculum. The gill filaments provide the organism with a large surface area, thus enabling gas exchange to occur quickly.

Swim Bladder

Most bony fishes have a swim bladder. This thin-walled sac in the abdominal cavity contains a mixture of oxygen, carbon dioxide, and nitrogen obtained from the bloodstream. Fish adjust their overall density by regulating the amount of gas in the swim bladder, enabling them to move up or down in the water.

Nervous System

The nervous system of a bony fish includes the brain and spinal cord, nerves that lead to and from all parts of the body, and various sensory organs. The major sensory organs are connected directly

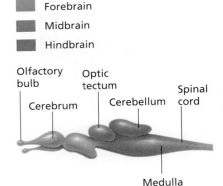

■ Forebrain
■ Midbrain
■ Hindbrain

Olfactory
bulb
Optic
tectum
Spinal
cord
Cerebrum
Cerebellum
Medulla

FIGURE 41-13

The fish brain, like the shark brain, has a well-developed medulla to coordinate muscle control.

FIGURE 41-14

This male ringtailed cardinal fish, *Apogon aureus*, is carrying fertilized eggs in its mouth. This behavior lowers losses of eggs to predators and contributes to the success of the species.

with the brain via **cranial nerves.** The fish brain is illustrated in Figure 41-13. The most anterior part of the brain, the forebrain, contains the very prominent olfactory bulbs, which process information on smell. The forebrain, which includes the **cerebrum,** has areas that integrate sensory and other types of information from other areas of the brain. Behind the forebrain lies the midbrain, which is dominated by the **optic tectum.** The optic tectum receives and processes information from the fish's visual, auditory, and lateral line systems. The optic tectum is also involved in turning an animal's body toward or away from a stimulus. The most posterior division of the brain is the hindbrain, which contains the **cerebellum** (SER-uh-BEL-uhm) and the **medulla oblongata** (muh-DUL-uh AHB-lawn-GAHT-uh). The cerebellum helps coordinate motor output. The medulla oblongata helps control some body functions and acts as a relay station for stimuli from sensory receptors throughout the fish's body.

From the medulla oblongata, the spinal cord extends the length of the body and carries nerve impulses to and from the brain. **Spinal nerves** connect the spinal cord with the internal organs, muscles, and sense organs.

REPRODUCTION

Eggs are produced by ovaries in the female, and sperm are produced by the testes in the male. Eggs and sperm are released through an opening behind the anus. Fertilization in most species takes place externally. Mortality among the eggs and young fishes is often very high. Many species of fishes lay large numbers of eggs to ensure that at least a few individuals survive to become adult fish.

Some bony fishes bear live young. Using a modified anal fin, the male inserts sperm into the female, and fertilization is internal. The female carries the eggs in her body until the young are born. Other species care for the young as shown in Figure 41-14.

The reproductive, or **spawning,** behavior of bony fishes varies widely. Some species build crude nests from plants, sticks, and shells. Many species migrate to warm, protected shallow water to spawn. For example, adult salmon migrate back to fresh water to spawn.

SECTION 41-3 REVIEW

1. Describe two characteristics of bony fishes.

2. Identify the two kinds of lobe-finned fishes.

3. What is the function of the ventricle in the fish's heart?

4. What is countercurrent flow, and how does it relate to respiration in fishes?

5. Why is laying a large number of eggs an adaptation of some fishes?

6. **CRITICAL THINKING** Bottom-dwelling fish often lack a swim bladder. Explain the adaptive advantage of this.

SUMMARY/VOCABULARY

41-1
- Vertebrates are chordates and have a notochord, pharyngeal pouches, a dorsal nerve cord, and a post-anal tail at some stage of life.
- Vertebrates have vertebrae, a cranium, and an endoskeleton.
- Vertebrates are classified into seven classes: jawless fishes (class Agnatha); sharks and rays (class Chondrichthyes); bony fishes (class Osteichthyes); amphibians (class Amphibia); reptiles (class Reptilia); birds (class Aves); and mammals (class Mammalia).
- The oldest known vertebrates are jawless fishes.

Vocabulary

cranium (799)　　　gill arch (801)　　　vertebral column (799)

41-2
- Fishes have streamlined bodies and most have paired fins. Fishes float by means of a swim bladder or lipids in the body.
- Fishes use gills for respiration in water. The kidney and the gills help them maintain homeostasis.
- Living jawless fishes lack paired fins and jaws and have a notochord throughout life.
- Many lampreys are external parasites that feed on other fishes. Hagfishes feed on invertebrates or on dead or dying fishes.
- Sharks, rays, and skates are cartilaginous fishes.
- Sharks can smell, see, and detect electrical fields to detect prey. Rays and skates are flattened bottom-dwellers.

Vocabulary

cartilage (804)　　　internal fertilization (806)　　　olfactory bulb (804)　　　placoid scale (804)
clasper (806)　　　lateral line system (803)　　　pectoral fins (804)　　　rectal gland (806)
external fertilization (804)

41-3
- The characteristics of bony fishes are scales on the body, lungs or a swim bladder, and bone in the skeleton.
- Fishes use their fins for propulsion, maneuvering, and stability.
- The digestive system of a fish consists of a mouth, pharynx, esophagus, stomach, intestine, liver, gallbladder, pancreas, and anus.
- The fish heart has a sinus venosus, atrium, ventricle, and conus arteriosus.
- The main parts of a fish's brain are optic tectum, olfactory bulbs, the cerebrum, the medulla oblongata, and the cerebellum.
- Fertilization is external in most bony fishes and is internal in some species.

Vocabulary

anal fin (808)　　　countercurrent flow (811)　　　medulla oblongata (812)　　　spawning (812)
anus (809)　　　cranial nerve (812)　　　operculum (808)　　　spinal nerves (812)
artery (810)　　　dorsal fin (808)　　　optic tectum (812)　　　stomach (809)
atrium (810)　　　esophagus (809)　　　pancreas (809)　　　swim bladder (807)
bile (809)　　　gallbladder (809)　　　pectoral girdle (809)　　　urinary bladder (811)
capillary (810)　　　intestine (809)　　　pelvic fin (808)　　　urine (811)
caudal fin (808)　　　liver (809)　　　pelvic girdle (809)　　　vein (810)
cerebellum (812)　　　lobe-finned fish (807)　　　ray-finned fish (807)　　　ventricle (810)
cerebrum (812)　　　lung (807)　　　sinus venosus (810)
conus arteriosus (810)

REVIEW

Vocabulary

In each set of terms below, choose the term that does not belong, and explain why it does not belong.

1. atrium, ventricle, sinus venosus, gill
2. cerebrum, cerebellum, operculum, optic tectum
3. internal fertilization, lung, placoid scale, rectal gland
4. cranium, vein, capillary, artery
5. stomach, liver, pancreas, swim bladder

Multiple Choice

6. Which of the following is *not* a characteristic of the first fishes? (a) bony plates on body (b) jaws (c) no paired fins (d) cartilaginous skeleton
7. The spinal column (a) protects the spinal cord (b) anchors limb muscles (c) protects the lateral line (d) collects sensory information.
8. One characteristic found in lampreys but not in hagfishes is (a) a notochord (b) paired fins (c) vertebrae (d) a cranium.
9. Which of the following is true of sharks and rays? (a) They have placoid scales. (b) Most species live in fresh water. (c) They have lungs. (d) They do not have a lateral line system.
10. Which of the following is not a way to control buoyancy? (a) the swim bladder (b) a fat-filled liver (c) continuous swimming (d) the rectal gland
11. The lateral line system (a) keeps fish moving in a straight line (b) initiates migration (c) detects vibrations (d) acts as camouflage.
12. Sharks use claspers to (a) increase maneuverability (b) startle other fish (c) transfer sperm while mating (d) hold on to prey while feeding.
13. The esophagus of a fish (a) creates buoyancy (b) fertilizes eggs (c) carries food from the mouth to the stomach (d) holds wastes moving from the stomach to the anus.
14. A fish's ventricle (a) pumps blood through the body (b) collects blood returning to the heart (c) facilitates gas exchange through diffusion (d) carries oxygen through the capillaries.
15. Bony fishes that live in fresh water (a) lose water (b) gain sodium and chloride ions (c) store urea (d) produce large amounts of urine.

Short Answer

16. Name the three classes of fishes, and give a representative of each.
17. What is the advantage to lungfishes of having both lungs and gills?
18. Why do all scales point toward a fish's tail?
19. Explain how bony fishes living in salt water and fresh water maintain their salt and water balance. How do sharks and rays prevent water loss?
20. What is the function of the rectal gland in sharks and rays?
21. Trace the flow of blood through the heart of a fish.
22. Many female sharks and rays retain the eggs inside their body, and some may even provide nutrition for the developing young. Explain why natural selection might have favored this behavior.
23. A shark replaces lost and worn teeth throughout its life. Why is this ability advantageous? How is this pattern of tooth replacement different from that of humans?
24. Describe as many functions of gills as possible. Be sure to include respiratory and excretory functions in your answer.
25. Identify each lettered structure in the figure below.

CRITICAL THINKING

1. Neoteny is a phenomenon in which larvae become sexually mature but still retain larval characteristics. The term has been used to explain in part the evolution of vertebrates from ancestral chordates. Use what you know about tunicates to test this hypothesis.

2. Sharks have a large corkscrew-shaped structure in the intestine called a spiral valve. How might this organ function in digestion?

3. In a famous set of experiments, A. J. Kalmijn studied the ability of sharks to find prey. He showed that a shark could locate and capture a stationary fish buried in the sand at the bottom of its tank. When the fish was enclosed in electrical insulation and then buried, however, the shark could not locate it. From this information alone, can you conclude that the shark is using only its electrical sense to locate the buried fish? Explain your answer.

4. Saltwater fishes drink more water and produce much less urine than freshwater fishes do. How do you account for this difference?

5. Cod and many other ocean fishes lay eggs near the surface of the water. The male largemouth bass scoops out a nest in a lake or river bottom and waits for a female to deposit her eggs. What hypothesis would you make regarding the relative number of cod and bass eggs? Explain your answer.

6. Many species of fishes that live deep in the ocean, where there is little or no light, are luminescent. What might be the advantages of such an adaptation?

7. Many fish are able to regulate their internal ion concentration as they go from a saltwater environment to a freshwater environment. Study the chart below, which shows the excreted ion concentration of a fish as it travels from one body of water to another. Is the fish traveling from fresh water to salt water or salt water to fresh water? Explain your reasoning.

Effect of Environment on Ion Excretion

Excreted ion concentration

Distance traveled

EXTENSION

1. Scientists are investigating an unexplained aspect of shark biology: sharks rarely get cancer. Use library resources or an on-line database to research this phenomenon. Gather information on how scientists are studying sharks' resistance to cancer. Also gather information on shark-cartilage dietary supplements. How has the popularity of shark-cartilage affected shark populations?

2. Read "Relax, It's Only a Piranha" in *Smithsonian*, July 1999, on page 42. Why does the author believe that the piranha has an undeserved and mistaken reputation for viciousness? How do piranhas usually feed? Describe the environmental conditions that led to the legendary voracious reputation that piranhas have.

3. Study the anatomy of any fish other than a yellow perch. Identify the operculum, vertebral column, and each fin. Label the internal organs. Compare the internal anatomy of your fish with that of the fish shown in Figure 41-10. What conclusions can you draw about habitat and behavior on the basis of the fish's structure?

Exploring the Fish Heart

OBJECTIVES

- Simulate the action of a fish heart.
- Compare the structure and efficiency of a fish heart with those of the hearts of other vertebrates.

MATERIALS

- computer with CD-ROM drive
- CD-ROM *Interactive Explorations in Biology: Human Biology*

Background

This Interactive Investigation allows you to examine the action of a fish heart. Complex animals such as fishes require a uniform system of oxygen and nutrient distribution throughout their body. They also require a way to rid themselves of waste products, such as urea and carbon dioxide. The heart and the system of veins and arteries work together to provide these functions. The fish heart is a muscular tube with valves and chambers. It pumps blood to the gills and then throughout the body. The blood travels in a single loop, so that only deoxygenated blood enters the heart. Because the fish heart must pump blood through the fish's body in one cycle, it is less efficient than a human heart, which pumps blood first to the lungs, then to the heart, and finally to the rest of the body. Single-cycle pumping is considered to be less efficient than double-cycle pumping because it does not deliver as much oxygen and nutrients to the body's tissues.

Prelab Preparation

1. Start up the program Evolution of the Heart. Click the Topic Information button. Read the focus questions and review the three key concepts: the circulatory system, the heart, and the pulmonary vein.

2. Click the word *File* at the top left of the screen, and select Interactive Exploration Help. Listen to the instructions for operating the exploration. Click the Exploration button at the bottom right of the screen to begin the exploration. You will see an animated drawing like the one below.

VARIABLE

Type of heart: *allows you to select one of five hearts: fish, primitive amphibian, advanced amphibian, reptile, or mammal*

FEEDBACK METERS

Efficiency: *the efficiency with which the heart delivers oxygen and nutrients to the body's tissues*

Delivery Rate: *how rapidly the blood is pumped*

Separation: *the degree of separation of oxygenated blood and deoxygenated blood*

Procedure

Create a table like the one below for recording your data.

PART A The Fish Heart

First you will investigate the shape of the fish heart and its efficiency in pumping blood through the fish body.

1. Click the Interactive Explorations button (the one with the "magnifying glass" icon) at the top right of the screen. A fish heart is displayed with its efficiency, delivery rate, and separation in the feedback meters on the bottom left of the screen.
2. Note the route that blood travels through the fish heart. How does the blood complete the circuit? What is the efficiency of the fish heart? What is the delivery rate? Record this information in your data table.
3. Why is the separation in the feedback meter so low? Why does the lack of separation not matter in a single-cycle heart? Would this affect a two-cycle heart?

PART B The Primitive Amphibian Heart

4. Move the pointer to the primitive amphibian icon and click it. Has the shape of the heart changed significantly? How has the route of blood flow through the body changed?
5. How have the feedback meters changed? Did the amount of separation change from the fish heart?

PART C The Advanced Amphibian Heart

6. Move the pointer to the advanced amphibian icon and click it. What significant change occurs that separates it from the primitive amphibian heart?
7. Note the changes in the feedback meters. How did the change in the heart architecture change the readings on the feedback meters?

PART D The Reptile Heart

8. Move the pointer to the reptile icon and click it. What changes did you see take place?
9. Do the changes in the feedback meter indicate an improvement for the reptile's heart over the advanced amphibian's heart? Explain your answer.
10. Compare the reptile data with the fish heart data. Is the reptile heart better than the fish heart? Are the reptile data uniformly better than the fish heart data? Explain any inconsistencies.

PART E The Mammal Heart

11. Move the pointer to the mammal icon and click it. Record the feedback meter readings in the table you made. How do these changes compare with the readings from the other hearts?
12. What is the major advancement in the structure of the mammalian heart over the other animal hearts?

Analysis and Conclusions

1. What advantage does the fish's heart have over the reptilian and amphibian hearts? Explain the reason for the difference.
2. What advantage do the reptilian and amphibian hearts have over a fish's heart? How is this advantage improved on in the mammalian heart?

Further Investigation

Click the Navigation button and then click the Readings button. Click the "book" icon to the left of the article titled "The Beat Goes On." Prepare a report summarizing how successful scientists have been in producing artificial hearts.

COMPARISON OF VERTEBRATE HEARTS

Animal	Efficiency rate	Delivery rate	Separation

AMPHIBIANS

Amphibians, such as this southern leopard frog (Rana pipiens), are thought to have been the first vertebrates on land. Many amphibians still live part or all of their life in water.

FOCUS CONCEPT: *Structure and Function*

As you read, note the adaptations of amphibians that enable them to live on land and in water.

ORIGIN AND EVOLUTION OF AMPHIBIANS

About 370 million years ago, the first amphibians evolved from lobe-finned bony fishes and became the first vertebrates to live on land. The name amphibian *comes from the Greek words meaning "double" and "life" and reflects the fact that many amphibians spend part of their life on land and part in water.*

SECTION
42-1
OBJECTIVES

▲

Describe two similarities between amphibians and lobe-finned fishes.

●

List three characteristics of *Ichthyostega.*

■

List the major characteristics of living amphibians.

◆

Name the three orders of living amphibians, and give an example of each.

ADAPTATION TO LAND

According to one hypothesis, aquatic vertebrates first moved onto land as shallow pools of water began drying up, leaving these amphibian ancestors without water. Vertebrates adapted to land, according to this hypothesis, as a way to escape shrinking pools and move to those that still contained water. This hypothesis is no longer widely accepted because, as many critics have pointed out, it is unlikely that all the complex land-dwelling adaptations shown by amphibians would have evolved merely for short periods of over-land travel. It is more likely that the ancestors of amphibians left the water to escape predation and competition and to gain access to the resources that were becoming abundant on land. At that time, oceans, lakes, rivers, and ponds supported a tremendous number and variety of fishes. Food and space were limited, and the numerous species of fishes competed intensely for them. On land, however, there were no vertebrates, and terrestrial invertebrates such as insects, a promising food source, were beginning to diversify.

Characteristics of Early Amphibians

Scientists have long recognized that amphibians evolved from lobe-finned fishes. The groups share many anatomical similarities, including features of the skull and vertebral column. Also, the bones in the fin of a lobe-finned fish are similar in shape and position to the bones in the limb of an amphibian. Figure 42-1 shows a crossopterygian (kraw-SEP-te-RIJ-ee-uhn), an extinct lobe-finned fish that is thought to be closely related to amphibians. This fish probably lived in shallow water and used its sturdy pelvic and pectoral fins to move along the bottom and to support its body while resting.

The oldest known amphibian fossils date from about 370 million years ago. *Ichthyostega* is the best known early amphibian. Like

FIGURE 42-1

Early lobe-finned fishes, such as this crossopterygian, are thought to be the immediate ancestors of the first land vertebrates.

FIGURE 42-2

Ichthyostega had well-developed limbs and is thought to have been a crawler on land, but it still had an overall fishlike body.

Ichthyostega, which is shown in Figure 42-2, all of the early amphibians had four strong limbs, which developed from the fins of their fish ancestors. The forelimbs of amphibians (and all other terrestrial vertebrates) are homologous to the pectoral fins of fishes, and the hind limbs are homologous to the pelvic fins. The early amphibians also breathed air with lungs. As you learned in Chapter 41, lungs arose early in the history of fishes and are found in the descendants of these early fishes—including terrestrial vertebrates.

Although the early amphibians showed several adaptations for life on land, such as sense organs for detecting airborne scents and sounds, they probably spent most of their time in the water. For example, *Ichthyostega* had a large tail fin and lateral-line canals on its head. Its teeth were large and sharp, indicating a diet of fish, not insects. In addition, some of the early amphibians appear to have had gills like those of fishes. An unusual characteristic of the early amphibians is the number of toes on their feet. Most present-day terrestrial vertebrates have five toes on each foot. However, *Ichthyostega* had seven toes on each hind foot (no fossils of its front feet have been discovered), while *Acanthostega,* another early amphibian, had eight toes per foot. Apparently, the five-toed characteristic had not yet occurred.

Diversification of Amphibians

During the late Devonian period and the Carboniferous period (360 million to 286 million years ago), amphibians split into two main evolutionary lines. One line included the ancestors of modern amphibians, and the other line included the ancestors of reptiles. Amphibians have been a diverse, widespread, and abundant group since this early diversification.

Today there are about 4,500 species of amphibians, belonging to three orders. The largest order, with more than 3,900 species, is Anura, which comprises the frogs and toads. The order Urodela contains about 400 species of salamanders. And the third order, Apoda, consists of about 160 species of caecilians, which are legless, wormlike, tropical amphibians. Figure 42-3 shows the phylogenetic relationships between these three groups.

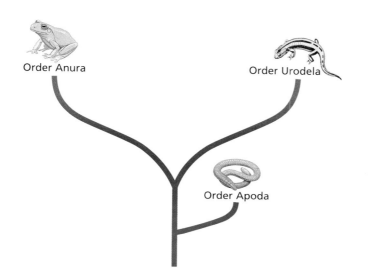

Order Anura

Order Urodela

Order Apoda

FIGURE 42-3

This phylogenetic tree represents the evolutionary relationships among the amphibians.

internet**connect**

SCiLINKS
NSTA

TOPIC: Frogs
GO TO: www.scilinks.org
KEYWORD: HM821

MODERN AMPHIBIANS

Modern amphibians share several key characteristics:

- Most change from an aquatic larval stage to a terrestrial adult form. This transformation is called metamorphosis.
- Most have moist, thin skin with no scales.
- Feet, if present, lack claws and often are webbed.
- Most use gills, lungs, and skin in respiration.
- Eggs lack multicellular membranes or shells. They are usually laid in water or in moist places and are usually fertilized externally.

Order Anura

Anurans (frogs and toads) are found worldwide except in polar climates and a few isolated oceanic islands. They live in a variety of habitats, from deserts and tundra to tropical rain forests. Figure 42-4 shows two examples of anurans. The term *toad* is commonly used for any anuran that has rough, bumpy skin, while the term *frog* commonly refers to anurans having smooth, moist skin. These

FIGURE 42-4

Anurans include toads and frogs such as the plains spadefoot toad (a), *Scaphiopus bombifrons,* which can be found throughout the United States, and the White's tree frog (b), *Litoria caerulea,* which is common in Australia.

(a)

(b)

FIGURE 42-5

The flatwoods salamander (a), *Ambystoma cingulatum,* and the spotted salamander (b), *Ambystoma maculatum,* are members of the order Urodela. *A. cingulatum,* which lives only in Florida, is an endangered species; *A. maculatum* can be found from eastern Canada to eastern Texas.

terms are general descriptions, however, and do not refer to any specific groups of anurans. Many anurans spend at least part of their life in water, and some species are permanently aquatic. However, many other species live and reproduce on land.

Anurans are characterized by a body adapted for jumping. Long, muscular legs provide power for the jump. The anuran body is compact, with a short, rigid spine and strong forelimbs that help absorb the shock of landing. The word *anuran* means "tailless" and reflects the fact that no adult anuran has a tail.

Adult anurans are carnivores that feed on any animal they can capture. Some frogs have a sticky tongue that can be extended to catch prey. Many species of anurans return to water to reproduce. In nearly all species, eggs are fertilized externally. The fertilized eggs hatch into swimming, tailed larvae called **tadpoles.**

Order Urodela

Salamanders have elongated bodies, long tails, and moist skin. Except for a few aquatic species, they have four limbs. The smallest salamanders are only a few centimeters long, while the largest reach lengths of 1.5 m (4.5 ft). Like anurans, salamander species range from fully aquatic to permanently terrestrial. Terrestrial salamanders usually live in moist places, such as under logs and stones. Larval and adult salamanders are carnivores. They are active mainly at night. Figure 42-5 shows two representative salamanders.

Most salamander species live in North America and Central America. There are very few species in Africa and South America, several species are found in Asia and in Europe, and there are no species found in Australia. With more than 300 species, the lungless salamanders (family Plethodontidae) are the largest group of salamanders. As their name suggests, these salamanders lack lungs. They absorb oxygen and release carbon dioxide through their skin.

Like most anurans, many salamanders lay their eggs in water, and the eggs hatch into swimming larval forms. Other species can reproduce in moist land environments. Eggs laid on land usually hatch into miniature adult salamanders and do not pass through a

(a)

(b)

(a)

(b)

free-living larval stage. Most salamander species have a type of internal fertilization by which females pick up sperm packets deposited by males. In some terrestrial species, the female stays with the eggs until they hatch, which can take up to several weeks.

Order Apoda

The common name used to refer to members of the order Apoda is caecilian (see-SIL-yuhn). Caecilians are a highly specialized group of legless amphibians that resemble small snakes, as you can see in Figure 42-6. Caecilians average about 30 cm (12 in.) in length, but some species reach lengths of 1.5 m (4.5 ft). Because they have very small eyes that are located beneath the skin or even under bone, caecilians often are blind. Caecilians are rarely seen, and little is known about their ecology and behavior. Most species burrow in the soil, but some species are aquatic. All species have teeth in their jawbones that enable them to catch and consume prey. They eat worms and other invertebrates, which they detect by means of a chemosensory tentacle located on the side of their head. All species are thought to have internal fertilization. Some species lay eggs, which the female guards until they hatch. In a few species, the young are born alive. Caecilians live in tropical areas of Asia, Africa, and South America.

SECTION 42-1 REVIEW

1. Explain the most likely reason that aquatic vertebrates evolved from an aquatic existence to a land-based existence.

2. What characteristics suggest that lobe-finned fishes are the ancestors of amphibians?

3. What features of *Ichthyostega* suggest that it spent most of its time in water?

4. What is metamorphosis?

5. Give two examples of modern amphibians, and name the order to which each belongs.

6. **CRITICAL THINKING** Fossils of *Ichthyostega* and other early amphibians do not indicate the presence of lungs. Explain why scientists think the early amphibians had lungs.

OBJECTIVES

Relate the structure of amphibian skin to the types of habitats in which amphibians can survive.

Identify three adaptations for life on land shown by the skeleton of a frog.

Describe the pattern of blood flow through an amphibian's heart.

Describe how a frog fills its lungs with air.

Explain the function of each organ of an amphibian's digestive system.

Compare the amphibian's nervous system with that of a bony fish.

CHARACTERISTICS OF AMPHIBIANS

As you have already seen, terrestrial vertebrates face challenges that are far different from those faced by aquatic vertebrates. In this section, you will learn about some of the ways amphibians meet the challenges of living on land.

EXTERNAL COVERING

The skin of an amphibian serves two important functions—respiration and protection. The skin is moist and permeable to gases and water, allowing rapid diffusion of carbon dioxide and water. Numerous **mucous glands** supply a lubricant that keeps the skin moist in air. This mucus is what makes a frog feel slimy. The skin also contains glands that secrete foul-tasting or poisonous substances that provide protection from predators.

However, the same features that allow efficient respiration also make amphibians vulnerable to dehydration, the loss of body water. Therefore, amphibians live mainly in wet or moist areas on land. Many species are active at night, when loss of water through evaporation is reduced. Although some species of frogs and toads survive in deserts, they spend most of their life in moist burrows deep in the soil. Only after heavy rains do these amphibians come to the surface to feed and reproduce.

INTERNAL ANATOMY

While water supports the body of an aquatic vertebrate against the force of gravity, terrestrial vertebrates must rely on the support of their strong internal skeleton. The vertebrae of the spine interlock and form a rigid structure that can bear the weight of the body. Strong limbs support the body during walking or standing. The forelimbs attach to the pectoral girdle (the shoulder and supporting bones), while the hind limbs attach to the pelvic girdle (the "hips"). The pectoral and pelvic girdles transfer the body's weight to the limbs. The cervical vertebra at the anterior end of the spine allows neck movement.

The frog skeleton in Figure 42-7 shows several specializations for absorbing the forces created by jumping and landing. In most terrestrial vertebrates, there are two bones in the lower hind limb, the tibia and the fibula, and two bones in the lower forelimb, the ulna and the radius. In frogs, the bones of the lower forelimb are fused into a single bone, the radio-ulna. The bones of the lower hind limb are fused into the tibiofibula. Frogs have few vertebrae, and the vertebrae at the posterior end of the spine are fused into a singe bone called the urostyle.

Heart and Circulatory System

The circulatory system of an amphibian, illustrated in Figure 42-8, is divided into two separate loops. The **pulmonary circulation** carries deoxygenated blood from the heart to the lungs, then returns the oxygenated blood to the heart. The **systemic circulation** carries oxygenated blood from the heart to the muscles and organs of the body and brings deoxygenated blood back to the heart. All other terrestrial vertebrates also have a "double-loop" circulatory pattern. This pattern of circulation provides a significant advantage over the "single-loop" circulation of a fish—faster blood flow to the body. In a fish, the blood loses some of its force as it passes through the narrow capillaries of the gills, and blood flow slows as a result. The lungs of an amphibian also contain narrow capillaries that slow blood flow. But after passing through the capillaries of the lung, blood returns to the heart to be pumped a second time before circulating to the body.

FIGURE 42-7

The skeleton of the frog absorbs shocks when the frog jumps. The urostyle and the two bones of the pelvic girdle extend outward to meet the sacral vertebra. This structure absorbs the shock for the long leg bones when the frog lands.

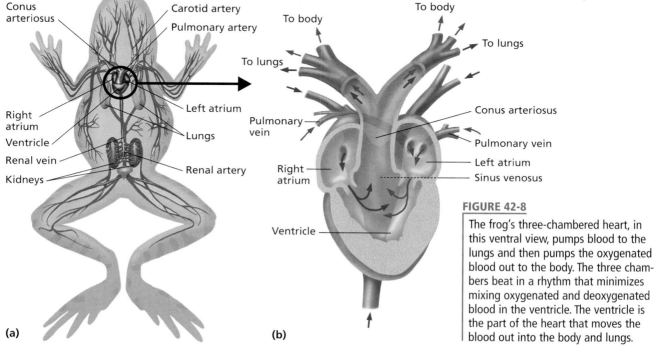

(a) (b)

FIGURE 42-8

The frog's three-chambered heart, in this ventral view, pumps blood to the lungs and then pumps the oxygenated blood out to the body. The three chambers beat in a rhythm that minimizes mixing oxygenated and deoxygenated blood in the ventricle. The ventricle is the part of the heart that moves the blood out into the body and lungs.

(a)

Nostril
opens

Floor of
mouth
drops

(b)

Nostril
closes

Floor of
mouth
rises

(c)

Nostril
closes

Floor of
mouth
drops

(d)

Nostril
opens

Floor of
mouth
rises

Frogs breathe by creating pressure that forces air into their lungs. When the floor of the frog's mouth drops, air capacity increases in the frog's mouth (a), and air rushes in. When the nostril is closed and the mouth floor rises, the air is forced into the lungs of the frog (b). The elasticity of the lungs and the use of muscles force the air back out (c). Then the nostril opens and the mouth floor rises again, forcing air out the nostril (d).

The three-chambered heart of an amphibian reflects the division of the circulatory system into pulmonary and systemic circulation. Deoxygenated blood from the body first enters the sinus venosus, a collecting chamber on the dorsal right side of the heart, indicated by the dashed line in Figure 42-8. From the sinus venosus, blood moves into the right atrium. Oxygenated blood from the lungs enters the left atrium, and contraction of the atria forces the deoxygenated and oxygenated blood into the single ventricle, the main pumping chamber of the heart. Although the ventricle is not divided, its spongy, irregular interior surface and the coordinated contractions of the atria keep the oxygenated and deoxygenated blood from mixing. Ventricular contraction expels both kinds of blood into the conus arteriosus, which directs deoxygenated blood to the lungs and oxygenated blood to the body. A valve within the conus arteriosus prevents mixing of oxygenated and deoxygenated blood.

Respiration

Larval amphibians respire, or exchange carbon dioxide and oxygen, through their gills and skin. Most adult amphibians lose their gills during metamorphosis, but they can respire in two ways: through the lungs and through the skin.

Respiration through the lungs is called **pulmonary respiration.** Amphibians ventilate their lungs with a unique mechanism that pumps air into the lungs; this is called positive-pressure breathing. For example, a frog breathes by changing the volume and pressure of air in its mouth while either opening or closing its nostrils, as shown in Figure 42-9. Both inhalation and exhalation involve a two-step process during which the floor of the frog's mouth is raised and lowered. The frog controls the direction of air flow by opening or closing its nostrils. Because amphibians have a small surface area in the lungs for gas exchange, respiration through the skin, or **cutaneous respiration,** is very important to most aquatic and terrestrial amphibians.

Digestive System

All adult amphibians are carnivorous. Because most amphibians are small, insects and other arthropods are their most commonly consumed prey. Larger amphibians sometimes eat mice, snakes, fish, and other amphibians. Many amphibian larvae, such as those of frogs, are herbivorous, feeding on algae or bacteria. The larvae of some species, such as those of salamanders, are carnivorous, and some feed on the larvae of other species.

The amphibian digestive system includes the pharynx, esophagus, stomach, liver, gallbladder, small intestine, large intestine, and cloaca. Figure 42-10 shows the digestive system of a frog. The elastic esophagus and stomach allow an amphibian to swallow large amounts of food. Once food reaches the stomach, tiny glands in the stomach walls secrete gastric juices that help break down, or digest, the food. A muscle called the pyloric sphincter at the lower end of the stomach relaxes, which allows digested food to move into the small intestine. The upper portion of the small intestine is called the **duodenum** (DOO-oh-DEE-nuhm). The coiled middle portion of the small intestine is the **ileum** (IL-ee-uhm). A membrane resembling plastic wrap, called the **mesentery,** holds the small intestine in place. Inside the small intestine, digestion is completed and the released nutrients pass through capillary walls into the bloodstream, which carries them to all parts of the body.

The lower end of the small intestine leads into the large intestine. Here indigestible wastes are collected and pushed by muscle action into a cavity called the cloaca (kloh-AY-kuh). Waste from the kidneys and urinary bladder, as well as either eggs or sperm from the gonads, also passes into the cloaca. Waste materials exit the body through the **vent.**

Other glands and organs aid in the digestion process. The liver produces bile, which is stored in the gallbladder. Bile helps break down fat into tiny globules that can be further digested and absorbed. A gland called the pancreas, located near the stomach, secretes enzymes that enter the small intestine and help break down food into products that can be absorbed by the blood.

FIGURE 42-10

The frog digestive system is shown in ventral view. Notice how the short small intestine is an adaptation for a carnivorous diet. Recall that the shark and perch also have short intestines.

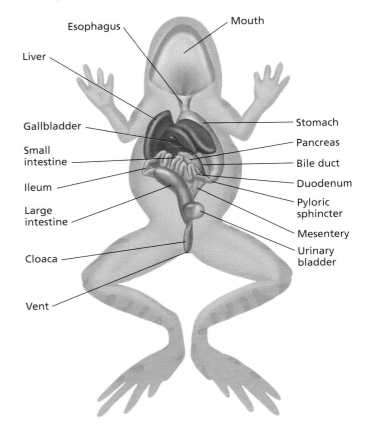

Esophagus · Mouth
Liver ·
Gallbladder ·
Small intestine ·
Ileum ·
Large intestine ·
Cloaca ·
Vent ·
· Stomach
· Pancreas
· Bile duct
· Duodenum
· Pyloric sphincter
· Mesentery
· Urinary bladder

Excretory System

The kidneys are the primary excretory organs. One kidney lies on either side of the spine against the dorsal body wall. The kidneys filter nitrogenous wastes from the blood. These wastes, flushed from the body with water, are known as urine. Urine flows from the kidneys to the cloaca through tiny tubes called urinary ducts. From the cloaca, it flows into the urinary bladder, which branches from the ventral wall of the cloaca. For many terrestrial amphibians, the urinary bladder serves as a water-storage organ. During dry periods, water can be reabsorbed from the urine in the bladder.

Like the larvae of fishes, most amphibian larvae excrete the nitrogen-containing wastes as ammonia. Because ammonia is very toxic, it must be removed from the body quickly or diluted with large amounts of water in the urine. To conserve water, adult amphibians transform ammonia into urea, a less-toxic substance that can be excreted without using as much water. Although this transformation uses energy, it helps save water. During metamorphosis, larval amphibians change from excreting ammonia to excreting urea.

Nervous System

Use the diagram in Figure 42-11 to find the main components of the amphibian nervous system. An amphibian's brain is about the same size as that of a similarly sized fish. The olfactory lobes, which are the center of the sense of smell, are larger in amphibians than in fish, and they lie at the anterior end of the brain. Notice that behind the

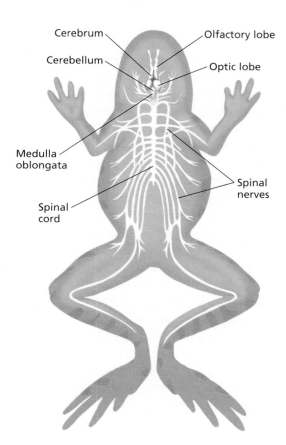

FIGURE 42-11

This diagram shows the frog's nervous system in ventral view. The brain of the frog is sufficiently developed to cope with both land and water environments.

olfactory lobes are the long lobes of the cerebrum, the area of the brain that integrates behavior and is responsible for learning. The optic lobes, which process information from the eyes, lie behind the cerebrum. The cerebellum, a small band of tissue that lies at a right angle to the long axis of the brain, is the center of muscular coordination and is not as well developed in amphibians as it is in other tetrapods. The medulla oblongata lies at the back of the brain and joins the spinal cord. It controls some organ functions, such as heart rate and respiration rate. There is continuous communication among most areas of the brain. Ten pairs of cranial nerves extend directly from the brain. The spinal cord conducts signals from all parts of the body to the brain and from the brain back to the body. Encased in protective bony vertebrae, the spinal cord extends down the back. As in fishes, the spinal nerves branch from the spinal cord to various parts of the body.

Sense Organs

Some sense organs work as well in air as in water, but others do not. For example, the lateral line system, used by fishes to detect disturbances in the water, works only in water. Thus, while larval amphibians have a lateral line, it is usually lost during metamorphosis. Only a few species of aquatic amphibians have a lateral line as adults. The senses of smell, sight, and hearing are well developed in most amphibians. All amphibians have eyes, and visual information is often important in hunting and in avoiding predators. The eyes are covered by a transparent, movable membrane called a **nictitating** (NIK-ti-tayt-eeng) **membrane.** Sound receptors are located in the inner ear, which is embedded within the skull. Sounds are transmitted to this organ by the **tympanic** (tim-PAN-ik) **membrane,** or eardrum, and the **columella** (CAHL-yoo-MEL-uh), a small bone that extends between the tympanic membrane and the inner ear. Sounds first strike the tympanic membrane, which is usually located on the side of the head, just behind the eye. Vibrations of the tympanic membrane cause small movements in the columella that are transmitted to the fluid-filled inner ear. In the inner ear, the sound vibrations are converted to nervous impulses by sensitive hair cells. These nervous impulses are then transmitted to the brain through a nerve.

Word Roots and Origins

nictitating

from the Latin *nictare,* meaning "to wink"

SECTION 42-2 REVIEW

1. Why do most amphibians live in wet or moist habitats?

2. Describe two features of a frog's skeleton that are adaptations for jumping.

3. Trace the flow of blood through a frog's heart.

4. Explain how a frog moves air into and out of its lungs.

5. What is the function of the large intestine in amphibians?

6. CRITICAL THINKING Which sense organ of a terrestrial amphibian resembles the fish's lateral line in function? Explain your answer.

▲

Describe the life cycle of a frog.

●

Describe the changes that occur during metamorphosis in frogs.

■

Identify two examples of parental care in amphibians.

internet**connect**

SC**LINKS**
NSTA

TOPIC: Life cycle of frogs
GO TO: www.scilinks.org
KEYWORD: HM830

Word Roots and Origins

amplexus

from the Latin *amplexus,*
meaning "embrace"

REPRODUCTION IN AMPHIBIANS

One of the biggest differences between aquatic and terrestrial life-forms is their method of reproduction. Most amphibians depend on water for reproduction. They lay their eggs in water and spend the early part of their lives as aquatic larvae.

LIFE CYCLE

Consider the life cycle of a wood frog, illustrated in Figure 42-12. The reproductive system of the male frog includes two bean-shaped testes located near the kidneys. During the breeding season, sperm cells develop in the testes and pass through tubes to the kidneys and urinary ducts. During mating, sperm leave the body through the cloacal opening. In female frogs, a pair of large, lobed ovaries containing thousands of tiny immature eggs lie near the kidneys. During the breeding season, the eggs enlarge, mature, and burst through the thin ovarian walls into the body cavity. Cilia move the eggs forward into the funnel-like openings of the oviducts. As the eggs pass down the oviducts, they are coated with a protective jellylike material. The eggs exit by the cloaca to the external environment, where they are fertilized.

Courtship and Fertilization

In the first warm days of spring in the temperate zones, frogs emerge from hibernation. They migrate in great numbers to ponds and slow-moving streams. Males call to attract females of their own species and to warn off other males. Each species has its own mating call. The frog's croak is produced by air that is driven back and forth between the mouth and the lungs, vibrating the vocal folds. Male frogs have vocal sacs that amplify their calls. The female responds only to the call from a male of the same species.

When a female approaches, the male frog climbs onto her back. He grasps her firmly in an embrace called **amplexus** (am-PLEKS-UHS), which is shown in Figure 42-12a. The male clings to the female, sometimes for days, until she lays her eggs. When the female finally releases her eggs into the water, the male frog discharges his sperm over them, and direct external fertilization takes place. The frogs then separate and resume their solitary lives. Courtship behavior and fertilization often vary from one species to another.

(a) (b) (c) (d)

FIGURE 42-12

The life cycle of the wood frog, *Rana sylvatica,* begins with mating (a). The male frog holds the female frog in amplexus, and when she releases her eggs, he releases his sperm on the eggs. When the eggs hatch, a tadpole is released (b). One of the first developments of metamorphosis is the growth of hind legs (c). When the tadpole completes metamorphosis, a small adult (d) emerges from the water onto the land.

Metamorphosis

Within a few days of fertilization, the eggs hatch into tadpoles. A newly hatched tadpole lives off yolk stored in its body. It gradually grows larger and develops three pairs of gills. Eventually, the tadpole's mouth opens, allowing it to feed. The tadpole grows and slowly changes from an aquatic larva into an adult. This process of change is called metamorphosis. Legs grow from the body, and the tail and gills disappear. The mouth broadens, developing teeth and jaws, and the lungs become functional.

Biologists have long studied the process of metamorphosis and regeneration to learn what controls such dramatic physical changes. Increasing levels of a hormone called thyroxine, which circulates throughout the bloodstream, stimulate metamorphosis.

The life cycles of many amphibians are similar to that of the wood frog. But there are a variety of alternative reproductive patterns among amphibians. For example, many amphibians do not lay their eggs in water. They select a moist place on land, such as under a rock, inside a rotting log, or in a tree. One or both parents may even construct a nest for the eggs. A number of frog species make a nest of mucus, whipping it into a froth by kicking their hind legs. And not all amphibians undergo metamorphosis. Some salamanders remain in the larval stage for their entire life. Other amphibians bypass the free-living larval stage and hatch from the egg as a small version of the adult.

FIGURE 42-13

Rhinoderma darwinii male frogs exhibit parental care by holding the maturing eggs and larvae in their vocal sacs. This frog has already released his offspring, whose tails are still visible. Not all frogs express parental care in this way, and some frogs express no parental behavior at all.

PARENTAL CARE

Parental care is common among amphibians. Eggs and larvae are vulnerable to predators, but parental care helps increase the likelihood that some offspring will survive. Most often, one parent (often the male) remains with the eggs, guarding them from predators and keeping them moist until they hatch. The male Darwin's frog *(Rhinoderma darwinii)* takes the eggs into his vocal sacs, where they hatch and eventually undergo metamorphosis. The young frogs climb out of the vocal sacs and emerge from the male's mouth, as shown in Figure 42-13. Female gastric-brooding frogs of Australia swallow their eggs, which hatch and mature in the stomach. The eggs and tadpoles are not digested because the stomach stops producing acid and digestive enzymes until the young pass through metamorphosis and are released. There are two species of gastric-brooding frogs. Both appear to have become extinct within the last two decades. Females of some species of frogs, such as *Eleutherodactylus,* sit on their eggs until they hatch, not to provide warmth but to prevent the eggs from dessicating. The female normally lays the eggs in the leaves of trees or bushes, where they may dry up.

SECTION 42-3 REVIEW

1. What is the function of the male frog's call?

2. Describe the changes that occur during metamorphosis.

3. What role does thyroxine play in metamorphosis?

4. How does the female gastric-brooding frog care for her eggs?

5. Why is standing water not always required for amphibian reproduction?

6. **CRITICAL THINKING** How does the parental care of a female gastric-brooding frog help her offspring survive? How might her behavior reduce her likelihood of survival?

SUMMARY/VOCABULARY

42-1
- Amphibians evolved from lobe-finned fishes about 370 million years ago.
- *Ichthyostega* and the other early amphibians had lungs and four legs. They were predominantly aquatic, they had a lateral line and a fishlike tail fin, and some had gills.
- Modern amphibians are divided into three orders: Anura (frogs and toads), Urodela (salamanders), and Apoda (caecilians).

- Anurans are found on all continents except Antarctica, and they have large hind legs for jumping and a strong skeleton.
- Salamanders have four legs and a tail. They are found mainly in North America and Central America.
- Caecilians are legless tropical amphibians that resemble earthworms.

Vocabulary
tadpole (822)

42-2
- Amphibians respire through their lungs and skin. Mucous glands produce slimy mucus that helps retain moisture.
- The skeleton of an amphibian supports the body against the pull of gravity. The spine and limbs are strong so that they can bear the body's weight.
- The amphibian pulmonary circuit carries blood between the heart and lungs. The systemic circuit carries blood to the body and returns it to the heart.
- The heart of an amphibian consists of the sinus venosus, two atria, one ventricle, and the conus arteriosus. Although the ventricle is not divided, deoxygenated and oxygenated blood mix little in the heart.

- Larval amphibians respire with gills and through their skin. Adult amphibians respire with the lungs and the skin. Amphibians pump air into their lungs by raising and lowering the floor of their mouth cavity.
- In amphibians, food passes through the mouth, esophagus, stomach, small intestine, large intestine, and cloaca. The kidneys remove wastes from the blood. Adult amphibians eliminate nitrogenous wastes as urea.
- The brain of a frog has large optic lobes that process visual information, large olfactory lobes that control the sense of smell, a cerebrum that integrates behavior and controls learning, a cerebellum that coordinates movement, and a medulla oblongata that controls the heart and respiration rate.

Vocabulary

columella (829)	ileum (827)	nictitating membrane (829)	systemic circulation (825)
cutaneous respiration (827)	mesentery (827)	pulmonary circulation (825)	tympanic membrane (829)
duodenum (827)	mucous gland (824)	pulmonary respiration (826)	vent (827)

42-3
- Most amphibians lay their eggs in water and have an aquatic larval stage.
- Male frogs call to attract females. Females of some species can distinguish the species of the caller and determine his size.
- The male frog grasps the female and fertilizes her eggs as they are released.

- The hormone thyroxine triggers metamorphosis. During metamorphosis, the tadpole loses its tail and gills and grows legs and lungs.
- Many amphibians show parental care, guarding their eggs and keeping them moist, and some take them into their body to develop.

Vocabulary
amplexus (830)

REVIEW

Vocabulary

Explain the difference between each pair of related terms.

1. systemic circulation, pulmonary circulation
2. amplexus, metamorphosis
3. ileum, cloaca
4. conus arteriosus, sinus venosus
5. pulmonary respiration, cutaneous respiration

Multiple Choice

6. Which of the following is not a characteristic of *Ichthyostega*? (a) tail fin (b) four limbs (c) lungs (d) pelvic fins
7. The forelimbs of vertebrates evolved from which structures in lobe-finned fishes? (a) pelvic fins (b) pectoral fins (c) pectoral girdle (d) anal fin
8. Amphibians must lay eggs in water primarily because the eggs (a) need oxygen from water (b) are not laid in nests (c) do not have multicellular membranes and a shell (d) need protection from predators.
9. Metamorphosis must take place before amphibians are able to (a) swim (b) live on land (c) feed themselves (d) respire with gills.
10. Salamanders differ from frogs in that they have (a) aquatic larvae (b) four limbs (c) a tail (d) moist skin.
11. The frog's ventricle pumps (a) only oxygenated blood (b) only deoxygenated blood (c) only blood returning from the lungs (d) both oxygenated and deoxygenated blood.
12. Adult amphibians release their nitrogenous wastes in the form of (a) urea (b) uric acid (c) guanine (d) ammonia.
13. Bile is a fluid that (a) aids in circulation (b) lubricates skin (c) breaks down fats into globules (d) aids in respiration.
14. The frog's tympanic membranes are (a) eardrums (b) mouth parts (c) eyelids (d) vocal folds.
15. Which of the following is true of reproduction in most frogs? (a) female calls to attract male (b) eggs surrounded by tough shell (c) fertilization is external (d) fertilization is internal

Short Answer

16. Identify and describe the major characteristics of amphibians.
17. Explain why scientists no longer favor one early theory of why vertebrates moved from water to land. What is the most likely reason to explain why vertebrates moved from water to land?
18. Identify two of *Ichthyostega's* adaptations for life on land.
19. Although frogs do not have watertight skin, some species can survive in deserts. Explain how frogs survive such dry conditions.
20. Salamanders in the family Plethodontidae have no lungs. Explain how these salamanders respire.
21. Outline the route of blood flow through the body of a frog, beginning with the ventricle. How does this route differ from the circulatory system of a fish?
22. What functions do the tympanic membrane and columella perform?
23. What kind of information can a female frog get from a male frog's call?
24. Why are the nitrogenous wastes of an adult amphibian and its larvae different?
25. Look at the diagram of a frog's heart shown below. Identify the structures indicated by the letters. In which structures would you find deoxygenated blood? In which structures would you find oxygenated blood?

CRITICAL THINKING

1. There are usually many ecological differences between a frog and its tadpoles. Describe some of these differences. Explain why such differences might have been favored by natural selection.

2. As you learned in Chapter 39, insects also undergo metamorphosis. Compare metamorphosis in insects with metamorphosis in amphibians.

3. Charles Darwin noticed that frogs and toads are often absent from oceanic islands, such as the Galápagos Islands, even though they may be found on the nearby mainland. Darwin conducted some experiments that showed that frogs' eggs cannot tolerate exposure to salt water. What hypothesis do you think Darwin was trying to test? Explain your answer.

4. In the brains of amphibians, the largest parts are the olfactory lobes and the optic lobes, the centers of smell and sight. This is very important to amphibians in hunting prey and avoiding predators. In what other biological process is the capacity for hearing important? Explain why hearing must then be especially distinctive.

5. The female gastric-brooding frogs of Australia do not produce stomach acid or digestive enzymes while brooding their young in their stomachs until the tadpoles have completed metamorphosis and leave. If the mother frog does not eat during this period, from where does she get her energy? What other types of frogs must live off the same energy source during similar periods of fasting?

6. When tadpoles undergo metamorphosis, their bodies begin to produce an enzyme that converts ammonia into urea. The time that a tadpole takes to produce this enzyme varies among species. In the graph below, the rate of enzyme production in metamorphosis is shown for a species that inhabits a desertlike environment and a species that inhabits a forest environment. Which curve represents which frog? Explain your answer.

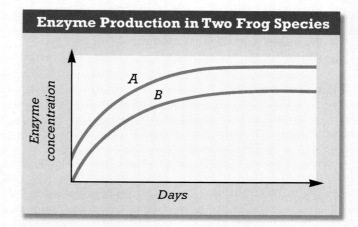

Enzyme Production in Two Frog Species

EXTENSION

1. Read "Having Their Toxins and Eating Them, Too" in *BioScience,* December 1999, on page 945. Answer the following question from the section titled "A Frog One Doesn't Kiss": Where does the family Dendrobatidae of poison-Dart frogs acquire the toxins found in their skin?

2. Research human uses of the skin secretions of frogs. Find out how South American Indians use the skin secretions of frogs in the family Dendrobatidae. What are some potential medical uses of skin secretions of frogs? Write a report describing what you have learned.

3. Read "Are Pathogens Felling Frogs?" in *Science,* April 30, 1999, on page 728. Frog deformities have been blamed on pollution in the past. What does new data from Australia now suggest may be the real cause of frog deformities and die-offs?

Observing Live Frogs

OBJECTIVES

- Observe the behavior of a frog.
- Explain how a frog is adapted to life on land and in water.

PROCESS SKILLS

- observing
- relating structure to function
- recognizing relationships

MATERIALS

- live frog in a terrarium
- aquarium half-filled with dechlorinated water
- live insects (crickets or mealworms)
- 600 mL beaker

Background

1. What does *amphibious* mean?
2. Describe how amphibians live part of their life on land and part in water.
3. What are some major characteristics of amphibians?

PART A Observing the Frog in a Terrarium

1. Observe a live frog in a terrarium. Closely examine the external features of the frog. Make a drawing of the frog in your lab report. Label the eyes, nostrils, tympanic membranes, front legs, and hind legs. The tympanic membrane, or eardrum, is a disklike membrane behind each eye.

2. In your lab report, make a table similar to the one on the facing page to note all your observations of the frog in this investigation.

3. Watch the frog's movements as it breathes air with its lungs. Record your observations in your data table.

4. Look closely at the frog's eyes, and note their location. Examine the upper and lower eyelids as well as a third transparent eyelid called a nictitating membrane. The upper and lower eyelids do not move. The nictitating membrane moves upward over the eye. This eyelid protects the eye when the frog is underwater and keeps the eye moist when the frog is on land.

5. Study the frog's legs. Note in your data table the difference between the front and hind legs.

6. Place a live insect, such as a cricket or a mealworm, in the terrarium. Observe how the frog reacts.

7. Gently tap the side of the terrarium farthest from the frog, and observe the frog's response.

PART B Observing the Frog in an Aquarium

8. **CAUTION You will be working with a live animal. Handle it gently and follow instructions carefully.** Frogs are slippery. Do not allow the frog to injure itself by jumping from the lab bench to the floor. Place a 600 mL beaker in the terrarium. Carefully pick up the frog and examine its skin. How does it feel? The skin of a frog acts as a respiratory organ, exchanging oxygen and carbon dioxide with the air or water. A frog also takes in and loses water through its skin.

9. Place the frog in the beaker. Cover the beaker with your hand, and carry it to a freshwater aquarium. Tilt the beaker and gently submerge it beneath the surface of the water until the frog swims out of the beaker.

OBSERVATIONS OF A LIVE FROG

Characteristic	Observation
Breathing	
Eyes	
Legs	
Response to food	
Response to noise	
Skin texture	
Swimming behavior	
Skin coloration	

10. Watch the frog float and swim in the aquarium. How does the frog use its legs to swim? Notice the position of the frog's head.

11. As the frog swims, bend down and look up into the aquarium so that you can see the underside of the frog. Then look down on the frog from above. Compare the color on the dorsal and ventral sides of the frog. When you are finished observing the frog, your teacher will remove the frog from the aquarium.

12. Record your observations of the frog's skin texture, swimming behavior, and skin coloration in your data table.

13. Clean up your materials and wash your hands before leaving the lab.

Analysis and Conclusions

1. From the position of the frog's eyes, what can you infer about the frog's field of vision?

2. How does the position of the frog's eyes benefit the frog while it is swimming?

3. How does a frog hear?

4. How can a frog take in oxygen while it is swimming in water?

5. Why must a frog keep its skin moist while it is on land?

6. How are the hind legs of a frog adapted for life on land and in water?

7. What adaptive advantage do frogs have in showing different coloration on their dorsal and ventral sides?

8. What features provide evidence that an adult frog has an aquatic life and a terrestrial life?

9. What adaptations does the frog display in order to eat? What senses are involved in catching prey?

10. What movement does the frog make in order to breathe?

Further Inquiry

Observe other types of amphibians, or do research to find out how they are adapted to life on land and in water. How do the adaptations of other types of amphibians compare with those of the frog you observed in this investigation?

CHAPTER 43

REPTILES

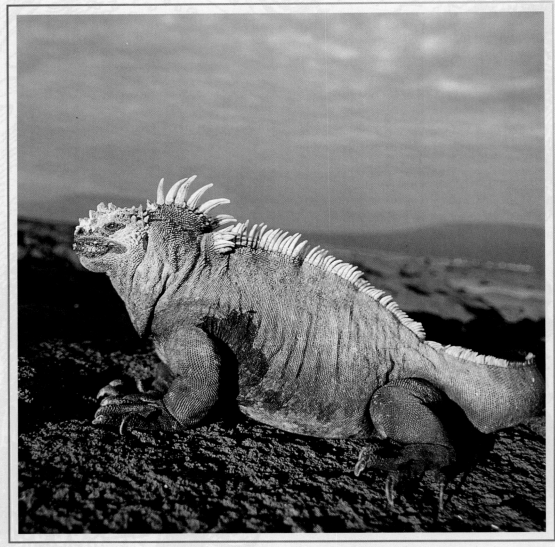

A marine iguana, Amblyrhynchus cristatus, of the Galápagos Islands warms itself by basking on a rock. These are the only marine lizards in the world, and they feed exclusively on seaweed.

FOCUS CONCEPT: *Structure and Function*

As you read the chapter, compare reptiles' structural and functional adaptations for living on land with those of amphibians.

ORIGIN AND EVOLUTION OF REPTILES

The reptiles (class Reptilia) appeared more than 300 million years ago. They are one of the largest and most evolutionarily successful groups of terrestrial vertebrates. In this chapter, you will study the diversity of reptiles and learn about some of the characteristics that make the reptiles a successful group.

HISTORY OF REPTILES

From studies of fossils and comparative anatomy, biologists infer that reptiles arose from amphibians. The oldest known fossils of reptiles were found in deposits from the early Carboniferous period (360 million to 286 million years ago) and are about 350 million years old. The earliest reptiles were small, four-legged vertebrates that resembled lizards and had teeth adapted for eating insects. The abundance of insects at the time may have been one reason the early reptiles flourished.

Age of Reptiles

The reptiles diversified rapidly, and by the Permian period (286 million to 245 million years ago) they had become the dominant land vertebrates. The Mesozoic era (245 million to 65 million years ago) is often called the Age of Reptiles because nearly all of the large vertebrates on Earth were reptiles during that time. On land, the most famous and spectacular reptiles, the **dinosaurs,** appeared and evolved into a great variety of forms during the Mesozoic era. Dinosaurs are known for the great size of some species. One of the largest dinosaurs, *Brachiosaurus,* measured 23 m (75.4 ft) long, stood 12 m (39.4 ft) tall, and weighed more than 77,000 kg (169,400 lb). In other words, *Brachiosaurus* was as long as a tennis court, as tall as a four-story building, and heavier than 10 elephants. Although the size of some dinosaurs has captured our imagination, many species were small, some no larger than a chicken.

Over 300 genera of dinosaurs have been identified. Their fossils have been discovered on all continents, even Antarctica, which had a much milder climate during the Mesozoic era than it does today. Dinosaurs were adapted to a wide range of environments and to different ways of life. Some reconstructions of dinosaurs are shown in Figure 43-1 on the following page.

SECTION

OBJECTIVES

Identify and describe three groups of reptiles that lived during the Mesozoic era.

Describe the asteroid-impact hypothesis to explain the extinction of the dinosaurs.

Describe the structure of the amniotic egg, and explain the functions of its parts.

Contrast the skin of reptiles with that of amphibians.

Word Roots and Origins

dinosaur

from the Greek *deinos,* meaning "terrible," and the Greek *sauros,* meaning "lizard"

FIGURE 43-1

Brachiosaurus, shown in (a), and related dinosaurs were herbivores that probably used their long necks to reach vegetation in the treetops. *Deinonychus,* shown in (b), and other carnivores walked on their hind legs and used sharp claws to rip apart prey. *Triceratops,* shown in (c), had body armor and horns to defend itself against meat-eating dinosaurs, but it was a plant eater. Scientists believe *Triceratops* may have roamed in great herds across western North America.

Reptilian success during the Mesozoic era was not limited to terrestrial habitats. Several groups of reptiles, including the ichthyosaurs and plesiosaurs, lived in the oceans. Ichthyosaurs, illustrated in 43-2b, were sleek aquatic reptiles that resembled modern bottlenose dolphins. Plesiosaurs had long, flexible necks and compact bodies. Mesozoic reptiles called pterosaurs, shown in Figure 43-2a, evolved the ability to fly. There are no flying reptiles today.

Extinction of Dinosaurs

Although the fossil record provides many clues about what dinosaurs were like, paleontologists who study dinosaurs still have many unanswered questions. For example, why did the dinosaurs become extinct 65 million years ago, at the end of the Cretaceous period? Many species of aquatic and terrestrial organisms besides the dinosaurs became extinct at this time.

Most scientists think that a catastrophic cosmic event was responsible for the mass extinction. Supporters of this hypothesis—called the **asteroid-impact hypothesis**—suggest that a huge asteroid hit the Earth, sending so much dust into the atmosphere that the amount of sunlight reaching the Earth's surface was greatly reduced. The reduced sunlight caused severe climatic changes that led to the mass extinction. According to this hypothesis, the dinosaurs would have become extinct very quickly, perhaps even within a few months.

The asteroid-impact hypothesis was first proposed in 1980 by Luis Alvarez, a Nobel Prize–winning physicist, and his son Walter, a geologist. They noted that sediments from the end of the Cretaceous period contain unusually high concentrations of iridium. Iridium is a metal that is very rare in the Earth's crust but more abundant in asteroids and other extraterrestrial bodies. Other scientists discovered that some sediments from this time contain quartz crystals that have been deformed by a powerful force, such as that resulting from the collision of a large asteroid with Earth. Further evidence for this hypothesis was provided by the discovery of the likely site of impact, a crater located on the Yucatan Peninsula in southern Mexico. The crater dates from the end of the Cretaceous period and is about 180 km (110 mi) across.

(a)

(b)

FIGURE 43-2

The smallest pterosaurs, such as the one in (a), were only the size of sparrows, while the largest were about the size of a small airplane, with wingspans of 12 m (about 39 ft). Like dolphins, ichthyosaurs, as in (b), were probably fast swimmers and fed on fish.

SUCCESS OF REPTILES

Representatives of the four modern orders of reptiles—turtles and tortoises, lizards and snakes, tuataras, and crocodilians—survived the mass extinction of the Cretaceous period. These four orders of reptiles have diversified to more than 6,000 species. Reptiles successfully occupy a variety of terrestrial and aquatic habitats on all continents except Antarctica. Figure 43-3 shows the evolutionary relationships between modern reptiles and birds.

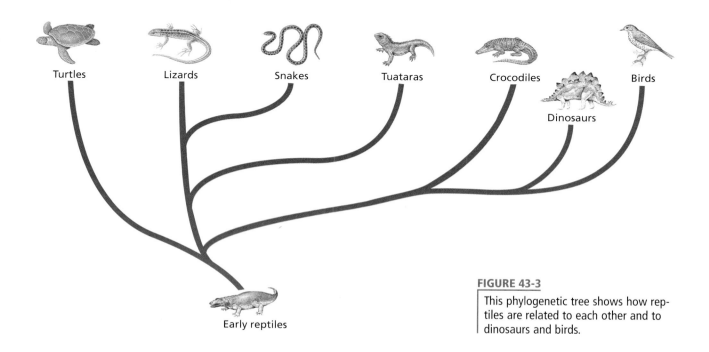

Turtles   Lizards   Snakes   Tuataras   Crocodiles   Dinosaurs   Birds

Early reptiles

FIGURE 43-3

This phylogenetic tree shows how reptiles are related to each other and to dinosaurs and birds.

The Amniotic Egg

Although amphibians were the first vertebrates to successfully invade land, they could not make a full transition to terrestrial life. They still require water in their environment to reproduce. Reptiles are considered the first fully terrestrial vertebrates because they do not need to reproduce in water, as most amphibians do. Reptiles produce **amniotic eggs,** which encase the embryo in a secure, self-contained aquatic environment. Amniotic eggs provide more protection for the developing embryo than the jellylike eggs of amphibians.

Figure 43-4 shows the internal structure of the amniotic egg, including its four specialized membranes: the amnion, yolk sac, allantois, and chorion. The egg is named for the **amnion** (AM-nee-AHN), the thin membrane enclosing the fluid in which the embryo floats. The **yolk sac** encloses the yolk, a fat-rich food supply for the developing embryo. The **allantois** (uh-LAN-toh-wis) stores the nitrogenous wastes produced by the embryo. Because it contains many blood vessels, the allantois also serves as the embryo's "lung," exchanging carbon dioxide for oxygen from the environment. The **chorion** (KOR-ee-AHN) surrounds all the other membranes and helps protect the developing embryo. Protein and water needed by the embryo are contained in the **albumen** (al-BYOO-muhn). You are familiar with albumen as the egg white in a chicken's egg. In most reptiles, the tough outer shell provides protection from physical damage and limits the evaporation of water from the egg.

The amniotic egg first evolved in reptiles, but it also occurs in mammals and birds. The presence of this feature is strong evidence that reptiles, birds, and mammals evolved from a common ancestor. The eggs of some reptiles and nearly all mammals lack shells, and the embryo develops within the mother's body.

FIGURE 43-4

This amniotic egg at an early stage of development shows a chick embryo and the four major membranes. The porous shell allows the exchange of oxygen and carbon dioxide.

FIGURE 43-5

The skin of the spiny lizard *Sceloporus poinsetti* protects it from the rugged terrestrial environment and from water loss.

Watertight Skin

Because amphibians exchange gases through their skin, the skin must be moist and thin enough to allow rapid diffusion. A drawback of this kind of skin is that it cannot be watertight, and one problem amphibians face on land is the loss of body water through evaporation. Reptiles, like the lizard shown in Figure 43-5, are covered by a thick, dry, scaly skin that prevents water loss. This scaly covering develops as surface cells fill with **keratin,** the same protein that forms your fingernails and hair. Lipids and proteins in the skin help make the skin watertight. The tough skin of a reptile not only helps conserve body water but also protects the animal against infections, injuries, and the wear and tear associated with living in terrestrial environments.

internet**connect**

SC*i*LINKS. NSTA

TOPIC: Amniotic egg
GO TO: www.scilinks.org
KEYWORD: HM843

Respiration and Excretion

All reptiles have lungs for gas exchange. Thus, all of the tissues involved in gas exchange are located inside the body, where they can be kept moist in even the driest environments. The excretory system of reptiles also helps them conserve body water. Snakes, lizards, and other land-dwelling reptiles excrete nitrogenous wastes in the form of uric acid. Uric acid is much less toxic than ammonia or urea. Thus, it requires little water for dilution, and reptiles lose only small amounts of water in their urine.

SECTION 43-1 REVIEW

1. Describe three kinds of Mesozoic reptiles, not including dinosaurs.

2. Why is the presence of iridium in sediments from the end of the Cretaceous period an important piece of evidence supporting the asteroid-impact hypothesis?

3. Explain the significance of the amniotic egg for reproduction on land.

4. Describe the functions of the chorion and the allantois in the amniotic egg.

5. What are two differences between the skin of an amphibian and the skin of a reptile?

6. CRITICAL THINKING   If it were shown that dinosaurs disappeared slowly over many millions of years, would this contradict or support the asteroid-impact hypothesis? Explain your answer.

Dinosaurs Are Extinct—But Why?

The following excerpt is from *The Dinosaur Heresies,* by Robert T. Bakker.

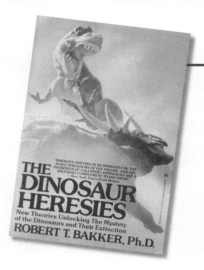

A very well-preserved segment of fossil history . . . permits a computation of how long the average species and genus of dinosaur lasted. And that can be compared with the rates of change computed for warm-blooded animals on the one hand and cold-blooded on the other. Rates of evolutionary change must somehow be linked to the metabolic rate of any given organism. When metabolism is very high, the high physical costs of its living must drive the animal to be an aggressive competitor or predator. And the rapid reproduction typical of warm-blooded animals tends to fill habitats to overcrowded levels much more quickly than the more leisurely breeding schedules characteristic of cold-bloods. An ecological community full of warm-blooded species is therefore a tough environment where the resident species jostle one another for food and water, breeding sites and burrows, all year round. In this sort of environment, the average species will not last long in terms of geological time before it is driven to extinction either by a new species, or by a combination of old species, or by an adverse change of climate.

Clams, by contrast, with their low metabolism, move around very little to accomplish the tasks of their adult lives. It is consequently not surprising that species of clams last much longer than warm-blooded species. Crocodiles and turtles are far more active than clams, but are still sluggish compared to the fully warm-blooded mammals. If dinosaurs resembled cold-blooded reptiles metabolically, their rate of evolutionary change would very nearly match that found in crocodiles or large turtles. But if the dinosaurs' metabolism was heated, then the average life span of one of their species or genera would have to be short, like a mammal's.

One of the best places to study the rate of evolutionary changes in dinosaurs is in the Late Cretaceous deltas of Wyoming, Montana, and Alberta. There the changes through the last ten million years of the dinosaurs' history can be followed. As might be expected, the turtles and crocodiles show very little change in these strata. The genera representing these cold-bloods hold on through formation after formation. But what about the dinosaurs here? Their evolutionary pace stands out as quite different. New species and genera kept appearing and eliminating older ones at quite a brisk tempo, geologically speaking. The average genus of dinosaur lasted for only a fraction of the time of that of the average crocodile. . . .

One part of the orthodox story does appear to be unassailable, an ineradicable fact safe from even the wildest heretic: Dinosaurs are indeed all extinct. The fact of their extinction is the cornerstone underlying the orthodox belief that dinosaurs were maladapted failures.

Dinosaurs are incontrovertibly dead. But that does not prove what orthodoxy believes about them. Paradoxically, the extinction of the dinosaurs is strong evidence that their biology was heated to levels far above those of typical reptiles. The basic principle is simple: The higher the metabolic needs of a group of species, the more vulnerable it is to sudden and catastrophic extinction.

Reading for Meaning
What is Bakker's explanation for the extinction of the dinosaurs?

Read Further
Bakker follows the text excerpted here by describing the best natural design for avoiding extinction. Explain what you think that design might be, and name some existing animals that are similar to that design.

CHARACTERISTICS OF REPTILES

Reptiles live in many different kinds of habitats and show a great deal of diversity in size and shape. Think of the differences between a snake and a turtle or between a lizard and a crocodile. In this section, we will look at some of the anatomical, physiological, and behavioral characteristics of reptiles.

SECTION

43-2

OBJECTIVES

▲

Describe the pattern of blood flow through the heart of a lizard.

Compare the lungs of reptiles with those of amphibians.

Identify three senses of reptiles.

Contrast endothermy with ectothermy.

Explain the differences between oviparity, ovoviviparity, and viviparity.

CIRCULATORY SYSTEM

The circulatory system of a reptile, like those of all terrestrial vertebrates, is composed of two loops. The pulmonary loop carries deoxygenated blood from the heart to the lungs and returns oxygenated blood to the heart. The systemic loop transports oxygenated blood to the tissues of the body, where oxygen and nutrients are unloaded and carbon dioxide is picked up, and returns deoxygenated blood to the heart.

Heart Structure and Function

In lizards, snakes, tuataras, and turtles, the heart has two atria and a single ventricle partially divided by a wall of tissue called a **septum.** In crocodiles, there are two atria and two separate ventricles. The sinus venosus and the conus arteriosus, which are major structures in the heart of a fish, are much smaller in reptiles. In fact, the sinus venosus is absent in some species. When it is present, it collects blood from the body and channels it into the right atrium. The conus arteriosus forms the base of the three large arteries exiting from the reptilian heart.

Because the ventricle is not completely divided (except in crocodiles), it might seem that deoxygenated and oxygenated blood would mix. However, recent studies have shown that blood mixing does not occur when a reptile is active. Deoxygenated and oxygenated blood are kept separate during contraction of the heart by the actions of the heart valves and the movement of the septum and ventricular walls.

Pumping blood through lungs requires energy. Under some conditions, it is advantageous for a reptile to divert blood away from the lungs to conserve energy. For example, an inactive reptile needs so little oxygen that it may go a long time without breathing. Similarly, aquatic reptiles do not breathe while they are underwater.

internetconnect

SCI**LINKS**
NSTA

TOPIC: Reptiles
GO TO: www.scilinks.org
KEYWORD: HM845

FIGURE 43-6

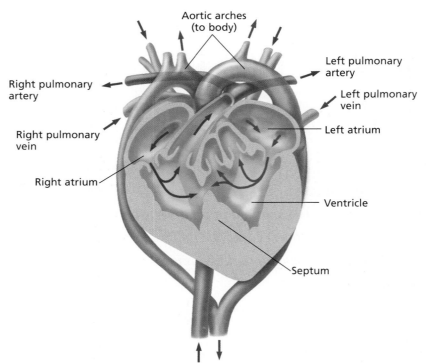

FIGURE 43-6
The turtle's heart, shown in cross section, has a partially divided ventricle, unlike an amphibian's three-chambered heart or a crocodile's four-chambered heart. Because the flow of blood through a turtle's heart is asynchronous, deoxygenated blood and oxygenated blood pass through the upper part of the ventricle at different times and so do not mix.

Aortic arches (to body)

Right pulmonary artery

Left pulmonary artery

Left pulmonary vein

Right pulmonary vein

Left atrium

Right atrium

Ventricle

Septum

By constricting the pulmonary arteries, a reptile's blood flow through the heart can be redirected to send some deoxygenated blood back to the body instead of to the lungs. Bypassing the lungs may also help a reptile raise its body temperature quickly—warm blood from the skin can be directed to the organs deep within the body. The reptilian heart has a degree of circulatory flexibility that the hearts of birds and mammals do not. Instead of being a handicap, this flexibility is actually well suited to reptilian physiology and activity patterns. Figure 43-6 shows a schematic diagram of the heart of a turtle. Compare this diagram with the illustrations of the three-chambered heart of a frog (Figure 42-8) and the two-chambered heart of a fish (Figure 41-11).

RESPIRATION

The lungs of reptiles are large, and they are often divided internally into several chambers. The lining of the lungs may be folded into numerous small sacs called **alveoli.** Alveoli greatly increase the internal surface area of the lungs, thus increasing the amount of oxygen that can be absorbed. In most snakes, only the right lung actively functions. It is elongated and may be half as long as the body. The left lung is either reduced to a small nonfunctional sac or absent entirely.

A reptile fills its lungs by expanding its rib cage. This expansion reduces the pressure within the thorax and draws air into the lungs. When the ribs return to their resting position, pressure within the thorax increases and air is forced out of the lungs. Similar movements help you to breathe.

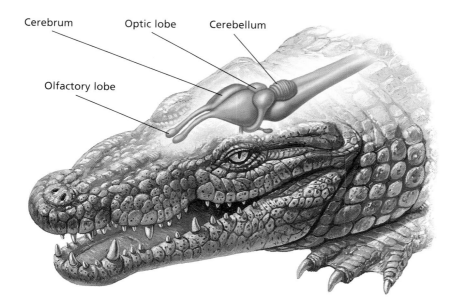

Cerebrum   Optic lobe   Cerebellum

Olfactory lobe

NERVOUS SYSTEM

The brain of a reptile is about the same size as that of an amphibian of the same size. However, the reptilian cerebrum is much larger. This region of the brain is involved in controlling and integrating behavior. Because vision is an important sense for most reptiles, the optic lobes, which receive input from the eyes, are large. Figure 43-7 shows the structure of a crocodile's brain.

Most reptiles rely on their sense of sight to detect predators and prey. The eyes of reptiles are usually large, and many species have keen vision. Hearing is also an important sense. As in amphibians, sound waves first strike the tympanum, or eardrum, and are transmitted to the inner ear through the movements of a small bone called the columella. The inner ear contains the receptors for sound. Snakes lack a tympanum and are sensitive only to low-frequency sounds. They are able to detect ground vibrations, which are transmitted to the columella by the bones of the jaw.

Jacobson's organ is a specialized sense organ located in the roof of the mouth of reptiles. Jacobson's organ is sensitive to odors. Like the snake shown in Figure 43-8, reptiles use their tongue to gather chemicals from the environment. These chemicals are transferred to the Jacobson's organ when the tongue is drawn back into the mouth. Jacobson's organ is found in all reptiles except crocodiles and most turtles, but it is highly developed in lizards and snakes.

Pit vipers, such as rattlesnakes, copperheads, and water moccasins, are able to detect the heat given off by warm-bodied prey, such as mammals and birds. These snakes have one heat-sensitive pit below each eye, as shown in Figure 43-8. Input from these pits allows a snake to determine the direction of and distance to a warm object.

THERMOREGULATION

The control of body temperature is known as **thermoregulation.** Vertebrates regulate their body temperature in two different ways. An **ectotherm** warms its body by absorbing heat from its surroundings. It has a slow metabolism that produces little heat. Reptiles, fishes, and amphibians are ectotherms. In contrast, **endotherms,** such as mammals and birds, have a rapid metabolism, which generates heat needed to warm the body. Most endotherms have insulation, such as hair, feathers, or fat, to retain the heat. The body temperatures of many aquatic ectotherms, such as fishes and amphibians, remain close to the temperature of their surroundings. When active, however, terrestrial ectotherms, such as lizards and snakes, usually keep their body temperatures about the same as the body temperatures of endotherms.

Reptiles regulate their body temperature by controlling how much heat they absorb. For example, when a lizard emerges from its nest after a cool night, its body temperature is low and must be raised before it can become active. The lizard warms itself by basking in the sun, as shown in Figure 43-9a. The lizard's warm blood is diverted from the skin to the interior of the body. The lizard continues to bask until it is warm enough to become active. As the graph in Figure 43-9b shows, a lizard can maintain its body temperature within a narrow range by using a variety of behaviors and body positions, despite variations in air temperature.

Advantages and Limitations of Ectothermy

Ectotherms require very little energy because their metabolism is very slow, and they also need only about one-tenth as much food as an endotherm of the same size. Ectotherms cannot live in very cold climates, and they can survive temperate climates only by becoming dormant during the coldest months. Furthermore, ectotherms can run or swim at maximum speed only for short periods of time. Ectothermic metabolism cannot provide enough energy for sustained exertion.

FIGURE 43-9

(a) A lizard regulates its body temperature throughout the day, basking to warm and seeking shade to prevent overheating. If its body temperature rises too high, the lizard may pant to accelerate heat loss. The graph in (b) shows an early-morning increase in the lizard's body temperature. The body temperature fluctuates only slightly during the remainder of the day despite wide fluctuations in ground temperature.

(a)

(b)

REPRODUCTION AND PARENTAL CARE

There are three patterns of reproduction among reptiles. The differences between these three patterns lie in how long the eggs remain within the female and in how she provides them with nutrition.

In **oviparity,** the female's reproductive tract encloses each egg in a tough protective shell. The female then deposits the eggs in a favorable place in the environment. Oviparity is characteristic of most reptiles, all birds, and three species of mammals.

Once released from the female's body, an egg is particularly vulnerable to predators and to environmental hazards. One way to reduce exposure to these hazards is to retain the eggs within the female's body for a time. This strategy is called **ovoviviparity.** The eggs may be laid shortly before hatching, or they may hatch within the female's body. The eggs absorb water and oxygen from the female, but they receive no nutrition other than the yolk.

In **viviparity,** a shell does not form around the egg, and the young are retained within the female's body until they are mature enough to be born. Nutrients and oxygen are transferred from mother to embryo through a structure called the **placenta.** The placenta forms from the membranes within the egg, and it brings blood vessels from the embryo near the vessels of the mother. Viviparity is the reproductive pattern shown by most mammals, but it is also found in a few species of lizards and snakes.

Many reptiles provide no care for their eggs or young. However, some species of lizards and snakes guard and warm the eggs until they hatch. Crocodiles and alligators provide the greatest amount of parental care. A female crocodilian, for example, builds a nest for her eggs. She remains nearby while the eggs incubate, guarding against nest-robbing predators. After the young hatch, they produce a high-pitched yelp, which summons the mother. She then breaks open the nest and carries the hatchlings to the water in her mouth, as shown in Figure 43-10. The mother crocodile may protect her young for a year or more.

Word Roots and Origins

ovoviviparous

from the Latin *ovum*, meaning "egg," the Latin *vivus*, meaning "alive," and the Latin *parere*, meaning "to bring forth"

FIGURE 43-10

Reptiles generally provide no care for their young, but the hatchlings are usually able to fend for themselves as soon as they emerge from the shell. Crocodiles and alligators, however, care for their young for up to two years. The female crocodile in the photograph is transporting her baby in her mouth.

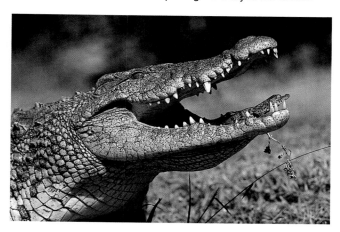

SECTION 43-2 REVIEW

1. Describe how the heart of a lizard differs from the heart of a crocodile.

2. Explain how a reptile inflates its lungs.

3. What is the function of the Jacobson's organ?

4. Compare ectothermy with endothermy.

5. Contrast oviparity with viviparity.

6. **CRITICAL THINKING** Describe which of the three patterns of reproduction in reptiles best serves to protect the eggs from predators. Explain your answer.

▲

Compare the anatomy of turtles with that of other reptiles.

●

Describe how crocodilians capture prey.

■

Explain two antipredator defenses of lizards.

◆

Describe two ways snakes subdue their prey.

▲

Identify two characteristics of tuataras.

FIGURE 43-11

The Galápagos tortoise, *Geochelone gigantops,* shown in (a), is protected from predators by its high domed carapace. The green sea turtle, *Chelonia mydas,* shown in (b), is streamlined for life in the sea.

MODERN REPTILES

*M*odern reptiles are classified into four orders: Chelonia, Crocodilia, Squamata, and Rhynchocephalia. As different as two species of reptile—such as a turtle and a snake—appear to be, all species of modern reptiles share the following characteristics: an amniotic egg; internal fertilization of eggs; dry, scaly skin; respiration through lungs; and ectothermic metabolism.

ORDER CHELONIA

The order Chelonia consists of about 250 species of turtles and tortoises. The term *tortoise* is generally reserved for the terrestrial members of the order, such as the Galápagos tortoise shown in Figure 43-11a. *Turtle* usually refers to chelonians that live in water, such as the green sea turtle shown in Figure 43-11b.

The earliest known turtle fossils, which are more than 200 million years old, show that ancient chelonians differed little from today's turtles and tortoises. This evolutionary stability may be the result of the continuous benefit of the basic turtle design—a body covered by a shell. The shell consists of fused bony plates. The **carapace** is the top, or dorsal, part of the shell, and the **plastron** is the lower, or ventral, portion. In most species, the vertebrae and ribs are fused to the inner surface of the carapace. Turtles are also distinctive in that the pelvic and pectoral girdles lie within the ribs instead of outside the ribs, as they do in all other terrestrial vertebrates. Unlike other reptiles, turtles have a sharp beak instead of teeth.

(a)

(b)

Turtles and tortoises live in a variety of habitats. Some species are permanently aquatic, some are permanently terrestrial, and some spend time both on land and in the water. The differing demands of these habitats are reflected in the shells and limbs of turtles. For example, water-dwelling turtles usually have a stream-lined, disk-shaped shell that permits rapid turning in water, and their feet are webbed for swimming. Many tortoises have a domed carapace into which they can retract their head, legs, and tail as a means of protection from predators. Their limbs are sturdy and covered with thick scales. The limbs of marine turtles, which spend their entire lives in the ocean, have evolved into flippers for swimming and maneuvering.

Reproduction

All turtles and tortoises lay eggs. The female selects an appropriate site on land, scoops out a hole with her hind limbs, deposits the eggs, and covers the nest. She provides no further care for the eggs or the hatchlings. Marine turtles often migrate long distances to lay their eggs on the same beach where they hatched. For example, Atlantic green sea turtles travel from their feeding grounds off the coast of Brazil to Ascension Island in the South Atlantic—a distance of more than 2,000 km (1,242 mi). These turtles probably rely on several environmental cues, possibly even the Earth's magnetic field and the direction of currents, to find this tiny island.

ORDER CROCODILIA

The living reptiles most closely related to the dinosaurs are the crocodilians, order Crocodilia. This group is composed of about 21 species of large, heavy-bodied, aquatic reptiles. In addition to crocodiles and alligators, the order includes the caimans and the gavial. Figure 43-12 shows some examples of crocodilians.

Crocodilians live in many tropical and subtropical regions of the world. Alligators live in China and the southern United States. Caimans are native to Central America and South America, but they have been introduced into Florida.

FIGURE 43-12

Crocodiles, such as genus *Crocodylus,* shown in (a), are found in Africa, Asia, and the Americas. The gavial, *Gavialis gangeticus,* shown in (b), is a croco-dilian with an extremely long and slender snout adapted for seizing and eating fish. Gavials live only in India and Burma.

(a)

(b)

All crocodilians are carnivorous. They feed on fish and turtles, and on land animals that come to the water to feed or drink. Crocodilians capture their prey by lying in wait until an animal approaches and then attacking swiftly. A crocodilian can see and breathe while lying quietly submerged in water. A valve at the back of the throat prevents water from entering the air passage when a crocodilian feeds underwater.

ORDER SQUAMATA

The order Squamata consists of about 5,500 species of lizards and snakes. A distinguishing characteristic of this order is an upper jaw that is loosely joined to the skull. Squamates are the most structurally diverse of the living reptiles, and they are found worldwide.

Lizards

There are about 3,000 species of living lizards. Common lizards include iguanas, chameleons, and geckos. Lizards live on every continent except Antarctica. Figure 43-13 shows some examples of lizards. Most lizards prey on insects or on other small animals. A few of the larger species, such as the chuckwalla and desert iguana of the southwestern United States, feed on plants. The Komodo dragon feeds on prey as large as goats and deer. Only two species of lizards are venomous. They are the Gila monster of the southwestern United States and northern Mexico and the related beaded lizard of southern Mexico.

Most lizards rely on agility, speed, and camouflage to elude predators. If threatened by a predator, some lizards have the ability to detach their tail. This ability is called **autotomy.** The tail continues to twitch and squirm after it detaches, drawing the predator's attention while the lizard escapes. The lizard grows a new tail in several weeks to several months, depending on the species.

Most lizards are small, measuring less than 30 cm (12 in.) in length. The largest lizards belong to the monitor family (Varanidae). Like snakes, monitors have deeply forked tongues that pick up airborne particles and transfer them to the Jacobson's organ in the roof of the mouth.

FIGURE 43-13

The largest of all monitors is the Komodo dragon, *Varanus komodoensis,* of Indonesia, shown in (a). The Komodo dragon can grow to 3 m long (10 ft). A colorful gecko, genus *Phelsuma,* is shown in (b). The gecko has specialized structures on the pads of its fingers and toes that allow it to cling to almost any surface.

(a)

(b)

(a)

(b)

Snakes

There are about 2,500 species of snakes, and like lizards, they are distributed worldwide. Figure 43-14 shows some examples of snakes. The most obvious characteristic of snakes is the lack of legs, which affects all other aspects of their biology. What was the selective pressure that caused snakes to evolve leglessness? One possibility is that the ancestors of snakes were terrestrial but lived in thick vegetation, where legs were a hindrance to rapid movement.

The graceful movements of snakes are made possible by their unique anatomy. A snake has a backbone of 100 to 400 vertebrae, and a pair of ribs are attached to each vertebra. These bones provide the framework for thousands of muscles. The muscles manipulate not only the skeleton but also the snake's skin, causing the overlapping scales to extend and contract.

Capturing and Consuming Prey

A snake may just seize and swallow its prey. However, many snakes employ one of two methods for killing: constriction or injection of venom. Snakes that are **constrictors** wrap their bodies around prey. A constrictor suffocates its prey by gradually increasing the tension in its coils, squeezing a little tighter each time the prey breathes out. This technique is used both by large snakes, such as boas, pythons, and anacondas, and by smaller snakes, such as gopher snakes and king snakes.

Some snakes inject their prey with a toxic venom in one of three different ways. The snakes with fangs in the back of the mouth, such as the boomslang and twig snakes of Africa, bite the prey and use grooved teeth in the back of the mouth to guide the venom into the puncture. Cobras, kraits, and coral snakes are elapids. **Elapid** snakes inject poisons through two small, fixed fangs in the front of the mouth. **Vipers** inject venom through large, mobile fangs in the front of the mouth. Rattlesnakes, copperheads, and water moccasins are examples of vipers. When a viper strikes, these hinged fangs swing forward from the roof of the mouth and inject venom more deeply than can the fangs of elapids.

FIGURE 43-14

The Gaboon viper, *Bitis gabonica*, shown in (a), injects a toxic venom to kill its prey before it begins the process of swallowing. The boa constrictor, *Constrictor constrictor*, shown in (b), suffocates its prey.

Quick Lab

Demonstrating Muscle Contractions

Materials plastic drinking straw, small ball of modeling clay

Procedure Make a small ball of clay slightly smaller than the opening of the drinking straw. Find a way to get the ball of clay into the middle of the straw.

Analysis How is this model similar to the feeding mechanism of a snake? If you used a ball of clay that was larger than the opening of the drinking straw, what problems would you encounter? Why is the size of larger prey not a problem for snakes?

FIGURE 43-15

This series of photographs shows a snake, *Dasypeltis scabra,* swallowing a bird's egg. Prey is often larger than the diameter of the snake's head, so the process of swallowing can take an hour or more.

Once killed, the prey must be swallowed whole because a snake's curved, needlelike teeth are not suited for cutting or chewing. Several features of a snake's skull enable it to swallow an animal larger in diameter than its head, as shown in Figure 43-15. The upper and lower jaws are loosely hinged and move independently, and can open to an angle of 130 degrees. In addition, a snake's lower jaw, palate, and parts of its skull are joined by a flexible, elastic ligament that allows the snake's head to stretch around its prey.

ORDER RHYNCHOCEPHALIA

FIGURE 43-16

Unlike most reptiles, the endangered tuataras, such as the one shown, are most active at low temperatures.

The order Rhynchocephalia (RING-koe-suh-FAY-lee-uh) is an ancient one that contains only two living species, the tuataras of the genus *Sphenodon.* Today tuataras inhabit only a few small islands of New Zealand. The Maoris of New Zealand named the tuataras for the conspicuous spiny crest that runs down the animal's back, which you can see in Figure 43-16. The word *tuatara* means "spiny crest" in the Maori language. Tuataras resemble large lizards and grow to about 60 cm (24 in.) in length. They usually hide in a burrow during the day and feed on insects, worms, and other small animals at night.

Since arriving in New Zealand about 1,000 years ago, humans have radically changed the landscape and introduced predators such as rats and cats, which feed on tuataras and their eggs. As a result, tuataras have disappeared from most of their original range.

SECTION 43-3 REVIEW

1. Where do tuataras live, and what do they feed on?

2. Describe the structure of a turtle's shell.

3. How does the position of a crocodile's eyes and nostrils relate to its hunting behavior?

4. What is autotomy? How does it help a lizard escape predators?

5. How does a constrictor kill its prey?

6. **CRITICAL THINKING** Describe the costs of autotomy for a lizard.

SUMMARY/VOCABULARY

43-1
- All reptiles produce amniotic eggs in which the embryo is surrounded by two protective membranes, the chorion and the amnion. The yolk sac provides food for the embryo, and the allantois stores its wastes.
- Reptiles conserve water by having a dry, scaly watertight skin and by eliminating their nitrogenous wastes as uric acid.
- During the Mesozoic period, most large

vertebrates were reptiles. The dinosaurs lived at this time, as did the aquatic plesiosaurs and ichthyosaurs and the flying pterosaurs.
- Dinosaurs became extinct about 65 million years ago, at the end of the Cretaceous period. Most scientists think that the collision of a large asteroid with Earth caused this extinction.

Vocabulary

albumin (842)	amniotic egg (842)	chorion (842)	yolk sac (842)
allantois (842)	asteroid-impact	dinosaur (839)	
amnion (842)	hypothesis (840)	keratin (843)	

43-2
- Lizards, turtles, snakes, and tuataras have a heart with two atria and one partially divided ventricle. Crocodiles have a four-chambered heart, as mammals do.
- Reptiles inflate their lungs by expanding the ribs, drawing in air by decreasing abdominal pressure.
- A reptile's brain is about the same size as the brain of an amphibian, but it has a much larger cerebrum.
- The Jacobson's organ detects chemicals picked up by the tongue.
- All living reptiles are ectotherms. Ectotherms warm their body mainly by absorb-

ing heat from their surroundings.
- Reptiles can keep their body temperature fairly constant by moving into and out of the sun.
- Ectotherms require very little food, but they cannot live in cold climates or be active when temperatures are low.
- Many reptiles lay shelled eggs. This is called oviparity. Some species transfer nutrients and oxygen to the developing embryos through a placenta. This strategy is called viviparity. Some species retain the eggs inside the female's body. This is called ovoviviparity.

Vocabulary

alveolus (846)	Jacobson's organ (847)	placenta (849)	thermoregulation (848)
ectotherm (848)	oviparity (849)	septum (845)	viviparity (849)
endotherm (848)	ovoviviparity (849)		

43-3
- Living reptiles are classified into four orders: Rhynchocephalia, Chelonia, Crocodilia, and Squamata.
- All turtles (order Chelonia) have a shell composed of bony plates. The vertebrae and ribs are fused to the interior surface of the shell. Turtles are mainly aquatic, while tortoises are terrestrial. All species lay eggs.
- Crocodilians (order Crocodilia) are large aquatic or semiaquatic carnivores. This

group includes crocodiles, alligators, caimans, and the gavial.
- Lizards and snakes belong to the largest order of reptiles (order Squamata). Most lizards are small, agile, and feed on insects.
- Some snakes kill their prey by constriction, suffocating it with their coiled body. Some species kill by injecting venom. Snakes can swallow objects larger than their head because they have a very flexible skull.

Vocabulary

autotomy (852)	constrictor (853)	plastron (850)	viper (853)
carapace (850)	elapid (853)		

REVIEW

Vocabulary

1. Briefly contrast elapids with vipers and give one example of each.
2. What is the function of the septum in the heart?
3. Which reptiles have a carapace and plastron?
4. The term *placenta* is most closely associated with which of the following terms: *oviparity, viviparity, ovoviviparity?* Explain your answer.
5. Use a dictionary to find the meanings of the following Greek roots: *endo-, ecto-, -therm.* Relate these roots to the meaning of the terms *ectotherm* and *endotherm*.

Multiple Choice

6. The membrane that encloses the fluid around a reptilian embryo is the (a) amnion (b) yolk sac (c) allantois (d) chorion.
7. The food supply within the egg is contained within the (a) amnion (b) yolk sac (c) allantois (d) chorion.
8. Which of the following is not true of dinosaurs?
   (a) They lived during the Mesozoic era.
   (b) They became extinct at the end of the Cretaceous period.
   (c) They were all large.
   (d) They lived on all continents.
9. Evidence for the asteroid-impact hypothesis of dinosaur extinction includes all of the following, except (a) sediments rich in iridium from the end of Cretaceous period (b) quartz crystals with blast damage (c) lack of dinosaur fossils from the early Permian period (d) remains of a large impact crater in Mexico.
10. Which of the following is true of the heart of a crocodile?
    (a) It has one ventricle.
    (b) Its atrium is partially divided by a septum.
    (c) It doesn't allow mixing of deoxygenated and oxygenated blood.
    (d) It only pumps deoxygenated blood.
11. The Jacobson's organ is most like our sense of (a) smell (b) hearing (c) sight (d) touch.
12. The two basic parts of a turtle's shell are the (a) septum and amnion (b) carapace and plastron (c) chorion and allantois (d) keratin and columella.
13. All of the following reptiles belong to the order Crocodilia, except (a) alligators (b) tuataras (c) caimans (d) gavial.
14. The ability to lose its tail and grow a new one helps a lizard (a) reduce its need for food (b) hide from predators (c) escape from predators (d) capture prey.
15. Long legless bodies may have arisen as an adaptation that helped snakes (a) absorb oxygen through their skin (b) move through thick vegetation (c) catch prey (d) swallow large animals.

Short Answer

16. What problem of life on land was solved by the evolution of the amniotic egg?
17. Describe how the structure of a turtle's heart allows for flexibility in blood circulation.
18. Explain the purpose of a lizard's ability to lose its tail and grow a new one.
19. Explain why it is inaccurate to call reptiles coldblooded.
20. What is the major benefit of ectothermy?
21. Describe two senses, other than vision and hearing, that reptiles use to find prey.
22. Describe the parental care of crocodilians.
23. Describe three ways snakes inject venom.
24. How has the settling of New Zealand by humans affected the tuataras?
25. The following diagram shows five parts of the amniotic egg, indicated by A, B, C, D, and E. Name and define the function of these parts.

CRITICAL THINKING

1. When a female leatherback turtle comes up on a beach to lay eggs, she first digs a deep hole, lays her eggs, and covers them with sand. Next she crawls about 100 m and digs another hole. This time she lays no eggs but just covers the hole with sand. Suggest a possible explanation for this behavior.

2. Why is it advantageous for a snake to kill its prey, either through constriction or venom, before trying to eat it.

3. The skin of a basking lizard is usually dark. As the lizard warms, the skin lightens. Suggest a functional explanation for this change. (Hint: Consider how this change might affect the lizard's absorption of heat.)

4. Fossil evidence collected in Alaska suggests that some dinosaurs were year-round residents of areas subject to freezing temperatures and long periods of darkness. Does this evidence of arctic dinosaurs support or contradict the hypothesis that the extinction of dinosaurs was due to the intense cold produced by a cloud of debris in the atmosphere? Explain your answer.

5. Many viviparous snakes and lizards live in cold climates. Why might viviparity be advantageous in such environments?

6. Luis and Walter Alvarez first proposed the asteroid-impact hypothesis after the discovery of abnormally high levels of iridium in sediments from the end of the Cretaceous period. According to the Alvarezes, what was the source of the iridium? High iridium levels were initially discovered at one site in Italy. Since then, high levels have been found at more than 100 sites around the world, all dating from the end of the Cretaceous period. Explain how the worldwide distribution of iridium is important evidence for the asteroid-impact hypothesis.

7. Examine the photo of the inside of a turtle's carapace. In cartoons, turtles often crawl out of their shell. Could a real turtle do this? What do you see in the photo that would indicate whether a real turtle could crawl out of its shell?

EXTENSION

1. Read "A Dinosaur with Altitude" in *Time*, November 15, 1999, on page 96. Describe the dinosaur that paleontologists say may be the tallest dinosaur ever. How have they come to this conclusion?

2. Read "Snake Charmer" in *National Wildlife*, February–March 1999, on page 36. Explain why Dr. D. Bruce Means believes we should care about the fate of the eastern diamondback rattlesnake.

3. Use a library or on-line database to research an endangered species of reptile, such as Kemp's ridley turtle. Prepare a report describing the conditions that threaten the survival of the species and the efforts being made to save it (if any).

4. Observe the behavior of a small lizard kept in a terrarium. Keep a log of your observations, noting differences in behavior at various times of day and before and after feeding.

Observing Color Adaptation in Anoles

OBJECTIVES

- Observe live anoles.
- Test whether background color stimulates color change in anoles.

PROCESS SKILLS

- observing
- hypothesizing
- experimenting
- organizing data
- analyzing data

MATERIALS

- glass-marking pencil
- 2 large clear jars with wide mouths and lids with air holes
- 2 live anoles
- 6 shades each of brown and green construction paper, ranging from light to dark (2 swatches of each shade)

Background

1. Anoles include 250–300 species of lizards in the genus *Anolis.*
2. Anoles can change color, ranging from brown to green, and are sometimes mottled.

3. Anoles live in shrubs, grasses, and trees. Describe some ways in which the ability to change color might be an advantage to anoles.
4. Light level, temperature, and other factors, such as whether the anole is frightened or whether it has eaten recently, can affect color. When anoles are frightened, they usually turn a dark grey or brown and are unlikely to respond to other stimuli.
5. Anoles can change color within a few minutes.

Procedure

1. Observe the anoles in two terraria, and discuss the purpose of this investigation with your partners. Develop a hypothesis that describes a relationship between anole skin color and background color. Write your hypothesis in your lab report.
2. Obtain swatches of construction paper in at least six different shades of green and brown. You will need two swatches of paper in each color.
3. Obtain two clear jars. Label one jar "Anole 1," and label the other jar "Anole 2."
4. **CAUTION You will be working with live animals. Handle them gently and follow instructions carefully.** Select two anoles of the same color from the terraria. Plan your actions and cooperate with a partner to transfer one anole into each labeled jar. Anoles will run fast and are easily frightened. Carefully pick them up and place the animals in separate jars. Do not pick up anoles by their tails. Grasp them gently behind the head. Quickly and carefully place a lid with air holes on each jar.
5. Gently place the jar with Anole 1 on a swatch of construction paper that most closely matches the anole's color. Try not to jostle the anole in the jar, and move the jar as little and as gently as possible. Repeat this procedure for Anole 2. Both anoles should closely match the color of the swatch.

6. When you have obtained and matched two anoles to closely matching colors, label the back of the pieces of paper "Initial Color of Anole 1" and "Initial Color of Anole 2," respectively. Replace the swatches underneath the jars after you have labeled them. The anoles should stay in their respective jars until the end of this investigation.

7. Using the given setup and the remaining swatches of colored construction paper, devise a control experiment to test whether background color stimulates color change in the anole.

8. In your lab report, list the independent variable and the dependent variables that you intend to use in your experiment. Describe how you will vary the independent variable and how you will measure changes in your dependent variable.

9. In your lab report, describe the control you will use in your experiment.

10. Create a data table similar to the one below to record your experimental observations for your lab report. For example, the table below is designed to record any change in anole skin color on four different background colors and the time it took for each change to take place. Design your data table to fit your own experiment. Remember to allow plenty of space to write your observations.

11. Have your experiment approved by your teacher before conducting it. As you conduct your experiment, be sure to record all of your data and observations in your lab report.

12. Attach your color swatches to your lab report, or include a color-coded key so that others reading your report will be able to understand how you measured initial color and color changes in your anoles. Be sure the color that most closely represents the initial color of both anoles is clearly indicated in your lab report.

13. Clean up your materials and wash your hands before leaving the lab.

Analysis and Conclusions

1. What effect, if any, did changes in the independent variable have on the dependent variable in your experiment?

2. Do your data support your hypothesis? Explain.

3. Can you think of any sources of error in your experiment?

4. Was your experiment a controlled experiment? If yes, describe your control and why you think a control is necessary for your experiment.

5. Were there any uncontrolled variables in your experiment, such as loud noises, bright light, or sudden movements, that could have affected your experiment? Describe how you might be able to improve your methods.

Further Inquiry

Design an experiment that tests the effects of temperature on anole skin color.

DATA TABLE *OBSERVING ANOLES*								
	Color 1		Color 2		Color 3		Color 4	
	Change	Time	Change	Time	Change	Time	Change	Time
Anole 1								
Anole 2								

BIRDS

Young birds, such as this owl, depend on their parents for food and protection.

FOCUS CONCEPT: *Structure and Function*
As you read, note the characteristics of birds that are adaptations for flight.

44-1 **Origin and Evolution of Birds**

44-2 **Characteristics of Birds**

44-3 **Classification**

Origin and Evolution of Birds

Birds belong to the class Aves, which, with about 9,700 species, is the largest class of terrestrial vertebrates. Birds are also the most recently evolved group of vertebrates, having appeared only about 150 million years ago. Among living vertebrates, only birds and bats can fly. The bodies of birds are well adapted to flight.

CHARACTERISTICS

Birds are so distinctive that it is difficult to mistake one for any other kind of vertebrate. Seven important characteristics of birds are described below.

- **Feathers**—Feathers are unique to birds, and all birds have them. Like hair, feathers are composed mainly of the versatile protein keratin. Feathers are essential for flight, and they insulate a bird's body against heat loss.
- **Wings**—A bird's forelimbs are modified into a pair of wings. Feathers cover most of the surface area of the wing.
- **Lightweight, rigid skeleton**—The skeleton of a bird reflects the requirements of flight. Many of the bones are thin-walled and hollow, making them lighter than the bones of nonflying animals. Air sacs from the respiratory system penetrate some of the bones. Because many bones are fused, the skeleton is rigid and can resist the forces produced by the strong flight muscles.
- **Endothermic metabolism**—A bird's rapid metabolism supplies the energy needed for flight. Birds maintain a high body temperature of 40–41°C (104–106°F). The body temperature of humans, by contrast, is about 37°C, or 98.6°F.
- **Unique respiratory system**—A rapid metabolism requires an abundant supply of oxygen, and birds have the most efficient respiratory system of any terrestrial vertebrates. The lungs are connected to several sets of air sacs, an arrangement that ensures that oxygen-rich air is always in the lungs.
- **Beak**—No modern bird has teeth, but the jaws are covered by a tough, horny sheath called a beak.
- **Oviparity**—All birds lay amniotic eggs encased in a hard, calcium-containing shell. In most species, the eggs are incubated in a nest by one or both parents.

Identify and describe seven characteristics of birds.

List three similarities between birds and dinosaurs.

Describe the characteristics of *Archaeopteryx*.

Summarize the two main hypotheses for the evolution of flight.

FIGURE 44-1

This phylogenetic tree shows the phylogenetic relationships between various terrestrial vertebrates. Note how birds, dinosaurs, and crocodiles evolved from a common ancestor, which split off very early from the other terrestrial vertebrates.

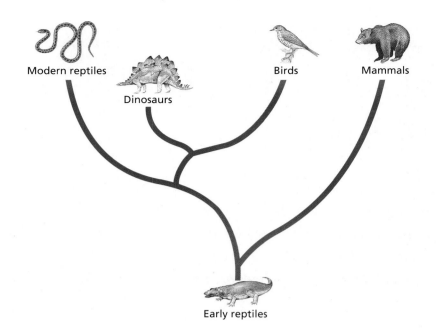

Modern reptiles

Dinosaurs

Birds

Mammals

Early reptiles

EVOLUTION

Scientists have long recognized the large number of similarities between birds and some dinosaurs. Three of these similarities include a flexible S-shaped neck, a unique ankle joint, and hollow bones. Birds are thought to have evolved from small, fast-running carnivorous dinosaurs during the Jurassic period (208–144 million years ago). Figure 44-1 shows the relationships between birds and other terrestrial vertebrates.

The oldest known bird fossils belong to the species *Archaeopteryx lithographica* and date from the late Jurassic period, about 150 million years ago. In the fossil in Figure 44-2a, the impressions of feathers are clearly visible. Feathers covered *Archaeopteryx*'s forelimbs, forming wings, and covered its body and tail as well. Like modern birds, *Archaeopteryx* had hollow bones and a **furcula** (FUR-kyuh-luh), the fused collarbones commonly called a wishbone. However, *Archaeopteryx* also had several characteristics of its dinosaur ancestors, including teeth, claws on its forelimbs, and a long, bony tail. Figure 44-2b shows an artist's conception of what an *Archaeopteryx* might have looked like.

Based on certain key similarities with modern birds, most scientists think that *Archaeopteryx* could fly. The furcula plays an important role in flight by helping to stabilize the shoulder joint.

Origin of Flight

The evolution of a flying animal from nonflying ancestors entails many changes in anatomy, physiology, and behavior. According to one hypothesis, the ancestors of birds were tree dwellers that ran along branches and occasionally jumped between branches and trees. Wings that allowed these animals to glide from tree to tree evolved. Once gliding was possible, the ability to fly by flapping the wings evolved. Another hypothesis draws on the fact that the

Word Roots and Origins

archaeopteryx

from the Greek *archaios,* meaning "ancient," and *pteryx,* meaning "wing"

(a)

(b)

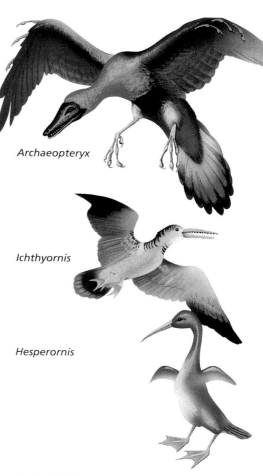

Archaeopteryx

Ichthyornis

Hesperornis

dinosaurs most closely related to birds were terrestrial and states that the evolution of birds must have occurred on the ground, not in the trees. Wings may have originally served to stabilize the animals as they leapt after prey. Or they may have been used for trapping or knocking down insect prey. Over generations, the wings became large enough to allow the animal to become airborne.

Evolution After *Archaeopteryx*

A number of recent discoveries show that by the early Cretaceous period (144–65 million years ago), birds had already begun diversifying. *Sinornis,* a 140-million-year-old specimen discovered in China in 1987, had some key features of modern birds, including a shortened, fused tail and a wrist joint that allowed the wings to be folded against the body. The diversification of birds continued throughout the Cretaceous period. Figure 44-2 shows three birds from the late Cretaceous period.

Only two of the modern orders of birds had appeared by the end of the Cretaceous period. Birds survived the asteroid impact that is thought to have wiped out the dinosaurs and underwent a dramatic and rapid radiation shortly afterward. By about 40 million years ago, most of the modern orders of birds had originated.

FIGURE 44-2

In this fossil of *Archaeopteryx lithographica* (a), one can see the link between birds and dinosaurs. These artist's renderings (b) of three extinct birds are based on fossil evidence. *Archaeopteryx* is the oldest bird; it still had claws on its wings. *Ichthyornis* had strongly developed wings and was about 21–26 cm (8–10 in.) in length. *Hesperornis* lacked a keel, had small wings, and was considered flightless, but its well-developed legs made it a strong swimmer.

SECTION 44-1 REVIEW

1. List two unique features of a bird's skeleton.

2. What are two functions of feathers?

3. Describe two characteristics shared by *Archaeopteryx* and modern birds.

4. Name two differences between *Archaeopteryx* and modern birds.

5. Summarize the two major hypotheses for the evolution of flight.

6. **CRITICAL THINKING** Modern birds lack teeth. Form a hypothesis to explain why this characteristic might have evolved.

OBJECTIVES

▲

Describe the structure of a contour feather.

●

Identify two modifications for flight seen in a bird's skeletal system.

■

Contrast the function of the gizzard with that of the crop.

◆

Trace the movement of air through the respiratory system of a bird.

▲

Explain the differences between altricial and precocial young.

CHARACTERISTICS OF BIRDS

A number of unique anatomical, physiological, and behavioral adaptations enable birds to meet the aerodynamic requirements of flight. For example, natural selection has favored a lightweight body and powerful wing muscles that give birds their strength.

FEATHERS

Feathers are modified scales that serve two primary functions: providing lift for flight and conserving body heat. Soft, fluffy **down feathers** cover the body of nestling birds and provide an insulating undercoat in adults. **Contour feathers** give adult birds their streamlined shape and provide coloration and additional insulation. **Flight feathers** are specialized contour feathers on the wings and tail. Birds also have dust-filtering bristles near their nostrils.

The structure of a feather combines maximum strength with minimum weight. Feathers develop from tiny pits in the skin called **follicles.** A **shaft** emerges from the follicle, and two **vanes,** pictured in Figure 44-3a, develop on opposite sides. At maturity, each vane has many branches, called **barbs.** The barbs in turn have many projections, called **barbules,** equipped with microscopic hooks, as shown in Figure 44-3b. The hooks interlock and give the feather its sturdy but flexible shape.

Feathers need care. In a process called **preening,** birds use their beaks to rub their feathers with oil secreted by a **preen gland,** located at the base of the tail. Birds periodically molt, or shed, their feathers. Birds living in temperate climates usually replace their flight feathers (called major molt) during the late summer.

FIGURE 44-3

Bird feathers usually have a shaft, with two vanes growing out either side of the shaft. The vanes consist of barbs and barbules that interlock by means of hooks. Feathers are made of keratin, an insoluble protein that is highly resistant to enzyme digestion by bacteria. Keratin is also the protein that makes up fingernails, claws, hair, and scales.

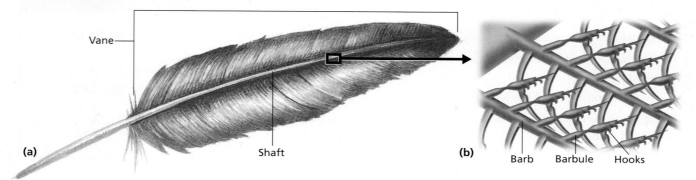

(a) Vane — Shaft

(b) Barb   Barbule   Hooks

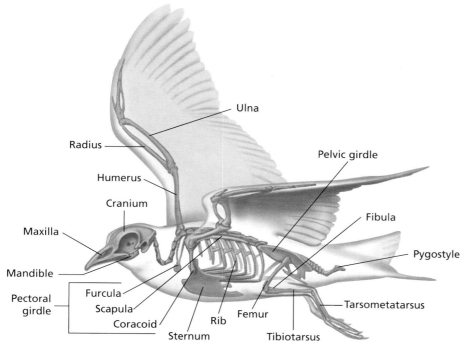

Ulna

Radius

Humerus

Cranium

Maxilla

Mandible

Pectoral girdle

Furcula

Scapula

Coracoid

Sternum

Rib

Femur

Tibiotarsus

Pelvic girdle

Fibula

Pygostyle

Tarsometatarsus

FIGURE 44-4
The avian skeleton is well adapted for flight. The bones are air-filled, making them light but strong. The skeleton is arranged to support the large muscles necessary for flight.

SKELETON AND MUSCLES

The avian skeleton combines lightness with strength. The bones are thin and hollow. Many bones are fused, so the skeleton is more rigid than the skeleton of a reptile or mammal. The rigid skeleton provides stability during flight. Note in Figure 44-4 the fused bones of the trunk and hip vertebrae and the pectoral and pelvic girdles. The large, keeled **sternum,** or breastbone, is an attachment point for flight muscles. The humerus, ulna, and radius, along with the pectoral girdle and the sternum, support the wing. The **pygostyle** (PIE-GUH-stiel), the terminal fused vertebrae of the spine, supports the tail feathers, which also play an important role in flight. The tail provides additional lift and aids in steering and braking.

Flight involves a series of complex wing movements, each one using a different set of muscles. On the downstroke the wings cut forward and downward through the air. During upstroke, they move upward and backward. These movements are made possible by large, powerful flight muscles. In some birds, flight muscles account for 50 percent of the body weight.

Quick Lab

Comparing Wing Structures

Materials photocopies of different birds featuring their wings, ruler

Procedure Examine each sheet of birds and their wings. Compare the structure and shape of the wings. Measure the wingspan relative to the bird's body length. Record your observations.

Analysis Predict the type of habitat in which each bird lives. How does the shape of the wing relate to the bird's niche? Explain why the type of wings each bird has might make the bird unsuccessful if it were introduced into a much different environment.

METABOLISM

Birds are endothermic; that is, they generate heat to warm the body internally. Rapid breathing and digestion of large quantities of food support the high metabolic rate necessary to generate this heat. Birds, unlike reptiles, cannot go for long periods without eating. To help conserve body heat they fluff out their feathers. Aquatic birds have a thin layer of fat that provides additional insulation.

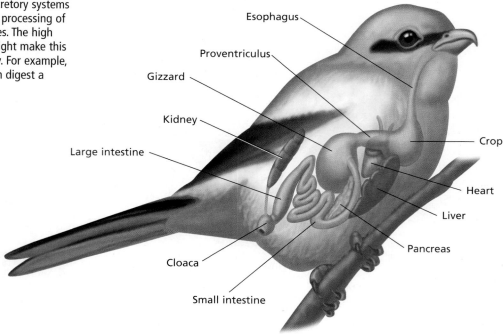

FIGURE 44-5

A bird's digestive and excretory systems are adapted for the rapid processing of food and metabolic wastes. The high energy requirements of flight make this efficient system necessary. For example, the carnivorous shrike can digest a mouse in three hours.

Esophagus

Proventriculus

Gizzard

Kidney

Large intestine

Cloaca

Small intestine

Crop

Heart

Liver

Pancreas

Word Roots and Origins

proventriculus

from the Greek *pro,* meaning "before," and the Latin *ventriculus,* meaning "stomach"

Digestive and Excretory Systems

The high amount of energy required to fly and regulate body heat is obtained by a quick and efficient digestive system, as illustrated in Figure 44-5. Because birds do not have teeth, they are not able to chew their food. Instead, food passes from the mouth cavity straight to the esophagus. An enlargement of the esophagus called the **crop** stores and moistens food. Food then passes to the two-part stomach. In the first chamber, the **proventriculus** (PROH-ven-TRIK-yuh-luhs), acid and digestive enzymes begin breaking down the food. Food then passes to the **gizzard,** the muscular portion of the stomach, which kneads and crushes the food. The gizzard often contains small stones that the bird has swallowed. These aid in the grinding process. Thus, the gizzard performs a function similar to that of teeth and jaws. Raptors, such as hawks and eagles, have modified systems for digesting protein. The crop and gizzard may be reduced or modified.

From the stomach, food passes into the small intestine. Here bile from the liver and enzymes made in the pancreas and intestine further break down the food. The nutrients are then absorbed into the bird's bloodstream. Passage of food through the digestive system of a bird is usually very rapid. For instance, a thrush can eat blackberries, digest them, and excrete the seeds 45 minutes later.

The avian excretory system is efficient and lightweight. Unlike other vertebrates, most birds do not store liquid waste in a urinary bladder. The two kidneys filter a nitrogenous waste called uric acid from the blood. Concentrated uric acid travels through ducts called ureters to the cloaca, where it mixes with undigested matter from the intestines and is then eliminated. Bird droppings are a mixture of feces and uric acid.

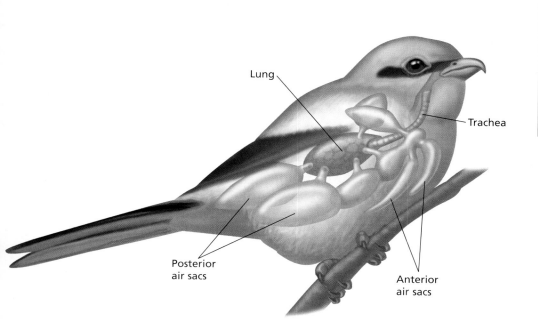

FIGURE 44-6

The unique architecture of the bird's respiratory system provides a virtual one-way flow of air. This highly efficient system of air flow allows birds to maintain the high metabolic rate necessary for flight. It also enables birds to function at high altitudes, where other animals would suffer from the lower levels of oxygen.

Lung

Trachea

Posterior air sacs

Anterior air sacs

Respiratory System

The high metabolic rate of birds requires large amounts of oxygen. Yet some birds migrate thousands of miles at altitudes as high as 7,000 m (23,000 ft), where oxygen levels are very low. An elaborate and highly efficient respiratory system meets these oxygen needs. Air enters the bird's body through paired nostrils located near the base of the beak. The air passes down the trachea and enters the two primary bronchi. From the bronchi, some of the air moves to the lungs. However, about 75 percent of the air bypasses the lungs and flows directly to posterior air sacs, shown in Figure 44-6. Nine sacs extend from the lungs, in most birds, occupying a large portion of the bird's chest and abdominal cavity. These sacs also extend into some of the long bones. Thus, the air sacs not only function in respiration but also greatly reduce the bird's density.

Gas exchange does not occur in the air sacs. Their function is to store air. When the bird exhales, the carbon dioxide–rich air from its lungs is forced into the anterior air sacs, and the oxygen-rich air in the posterior air sacs is forced into the lungs. This way, the bird has oxygenated air in its lungs during both inhalation and exhalation.

Circulatory System

Like crocodiles and mammals, birds have a heart with two separate ventricles. Deoxygenated blood is always kept separate from oxygenated blood. In comparison with reptiles and most other vertebrates, most birds have a rapid heartbeat. A hummingbird's heart beats about 600 times a minute. An active chickadee's heart beats 1,000 times a minute. In contrast, the heart of the larger, less active ostrich averages 70 beats per minute, or about the same rate as a human heart. Avian red blood cells have nuclei.

Nervous System and Sense Organs

Relative to their body size, birds have large brains. The most highly developed areas of the bird's brain are those that control flight-related functions, such as the cerebellum, which coordinates movement. The cerebrum is also large. It controls complex behavior patterns, such as navigation, mating, nest building, and caring for the young. The large optic lobes receive and interpret visual stimuli.

Keen vision is necessary for taking off, landing, spotting landmarks, hunting, and feeding. Most birds have good color vision that aids them in finding food. In most species, the eyes are large and are located near the sides of the head, giving the bird a wide field of vision. Birds that have eyes located near the front of the head have better binocular vision, meaning they can perceive depth in the area where the visual fields of the two eyes overlap.

Hearing is important to songbirds and to nocturnal species, such as owls, which rely on sounds to help them locate their prey. Though birds lack external ears, owls have feathers shaped to create a trough around their ear openings, which helps direct sound into the ear. The sense of smell is also developed in many birds.

REPRODUCTION

In the male bird, sperm is produced in two testes that lie anterior to the kidneys. Sperm passes through small tubes called **vasa deferentia** into the male's cloaca. During mating, the male presses his cloaca to the female's cloaca and releases sperm. Most females have a single ovary located on the left side of the body. The ovary releases eggs into a long funnel-shaped **oviduct,** where they are fertilized by sperm. Fertilized eggs move down the oviduct, where they receive a protective covering and a shell. The egg passes out of the oviduct and into the cloaca. From the cloaca, it is expelled from the bird.

Nest Building and Parental Care

Birds usually lay their eggs in a nest. Nests hold the eggs, conceal young birds from predators, provide shelter from the elements, and sometimes serve to attract a mate. Most birds build nests in sheltered, well-hidden spots—from holes in the ground to treetops. Woodpeckers, for example, nest in a hole they have drilled in a tree. Orioles suspend their nests from branches, well beyond the reach of predators. And barn swallows build a saucer of mud on the beam of a building. Birds construct their nests from almost any available material. Twigs, grasses, feathers, and mud are the most common materials used.

One or both parents incubate, or warm, the eggs by sitting on them and covering them with a thickened, featherless patch of skin on the abdomen called a **brood patch.** Once the eggs hatch, the young usually receive extensive parental care. Birds have two methods of rearing young. Those that lay many eggs and incubate

Eco Connection

DDT and Bird Eggs

DDT is a pesticide that was widely used on crops until the 1970s. DDT was banned because of the harm it was causing to birds. DDT causes thinning of birds' egg shells, decreasing survival rates of the birds' offspring. This caused a significant drop in the numbers of raptors, brown pelicans, and other pelicans. The thinning of the eggs was so significant that even the weight of an incubating parent could crush the eggs. With the banning of DDT in the United States, populations of the affected birds have increased.

A Hemispheric Strategy: A Single Vast Wildlife Reserve

The numbers of shorebirds—such as sandpipers, plovers, and curlews—are declining worldwide, but people in North America and elsewhere are working to preserve and protect these valuable species. To do this, researchers must first determine shorebird populations and map their migratory routes. To appreciate the magnitude of the job, you should know that more than 40 North American shorebird species breed in the Arctic and migrate to wintering sites in Central and South America, an annual round trip of 12,000 to 25,000 km.

Today the work of preserving shorebirds has been greatly advanced and simplified through the use of computer technology. One group that uses computers in this work is the International Shorebird Survey (ISS). Migrating shorebirds recognize no national boundaries, so any strategy for preserving them must be international. The International Shorebird Survey was established in 1974 and consists of both volunteers and professional researchers. The volunteers record information on populations, habitat characteristics, weather conditions, and human activity. Researchers use computers to identify relationships among these variables. Complex methods of analysis have revealed much about the migratory habits of shorebirds—their velocity, altitude, flight path, and gathering sites, for example. Computers have also helped researchers identify significant trends, such as a 70 percent to 80 percent drop in the population of sanderlings and short-billed dowitchers.

Another organization that uses computers in its work of preserving shorebirds is the Western Hemisphere Shorebird Reserve Network (WHSRN). As an international group of conservation organizations, the Western Hemisphere Shorebird Reserve Network has identified more than 90 sites where significant numbers of shorebirds breed, feed, and rest. The organization has proposed that these sites be recognized internationally as a single vast wildlife reserve whose boundaries are, in effect, defined by the migrating birds.

Shorebirds congregate in a few strategic sites, making them especially vulnerable to human activity. Replacing one beach or wetland with a housing development can have serious effects on the population of a species that depends on that site. However, humans must also develop a strategy for the survival of the congregation sites. The hemispheric wildlife reserve is the basis of such a strategy.

Shorebird populations are likely to need ongoing analysis, sometimes for new reasons. For example, possible consequences of global warming, such as changes in weather patterns and sea level, could affect shorebird habitats drastically. Thus computer technology will continue to facilitate the work of international conservation organizations and individuals who devote themselves to preserving and protecting shorebirds.

Delaware Bay, located between Delaware and New Jersey, is a staging site for shorebirds that migrate between South America and the Arctic. Up to 80 percent of the population of red knots feed and rest at this site. Preservation of the bay is critical to the species.

FIGURE 44-7

This yellow warbler cares for its young by feeding and protecting them.

them for long periods hatch **precocial** (pree-KOH-shuhl) young. These young birds are active as soon as they hatch. The mother provides warmth and protection, but the newly hatched birds can walk, swim, and feed themselves. Ducks, quail, and other ground-nesting species produce precocial offspring. Birds that lay only a few eggs that hatch quickly produce **altricial** (al-TRI-shuhl) young. These birds hatch blind, naked, and helpless, as shown in Figure 44-7. They depend on both parents for several weeks. The parents keep the young warm and feed them. The young of woodpeckers, hawks, pigeons, parrots, warblers, and many aquatic birds are altricial.

MIGRATION

Each year, thousands of bird species exploit the spring and summer food resources of temperate regions. Then, when temperatures drop and the food supply dwindles, they travel to warmer climates. The seasonal movement of animals from one habitat to another habitat is called migration. Many of the birds that nest in the United States and Canada during the spring and summer fly south in the fall to spend the winter in Mexico, Central America, the Caribbean, or South America. For example, the blackburnian warbler is a small songbird that nests in forests of the northeastern United States and southern Canada but winters in Central and South America.

How do birds manage to navigate thousands of kilometers across varied terrains to the same spot year after year? **Ornithologists**—biologists who study birds—have learned that birds rely on a variety of cues to help them navigate. Some species monitor the position of the stars or the sun. Others rely on topographical landmarks, such as mountains. The Earth's magnetic field, changes in air pressure due to altitude, and low-frequency sounds may also provide information to migrating birds.

Many species migrate thousands of kilometers and must rely on their fat reserves in order to complete the journey. To prepare for their migration, some birds, such as blackpoll warblers, eat so much food before their journey that their weight nearly doubles.

internet connect

SCI LINKS
NSTA

TOPIC: Migration of birds
GO TO: www.scilinks.org
KEYWORD: HM870

SECTION 44-2 REVIEW

1. **Distinguish between vanes, barbs, and barbules.**

2. **What is the function of the keeled sternum?**

3. **In what way does the gizzard compensate for the lack of teeth in birds?**

4. **What are the functions of the anterior and posterior air sacs?**

5. **Ground-nesting birds often produce precocial young. How might this improve the odds of survival for the young?**

6. **CRITICAL THINKING** How do you think the destruction of tropical rain forests affects populations of birds in the United States? Explain your answer.

CLASSIFICATION

Birds are the most widespread terrestrial vertebrates. Their ability to navigate over long distances and their many adaptations for flight enable them to migrate to and inhabit virtually any environment. Their anatomical diversity reflects the diversity of places they inhabit.

DIVERSITY

By looking closely at a bird's beak and feet, you can infer many things about where it lives and how it feeds. Hawks and eagles have powerful beaks and clawed talons that help them capture and tear apart their prey. Swifts have a tiny beak that opens wide like a catcher's mitt to snare insects in midair. Because swifts spend most of their lives in flight, their feet are small and adapted for infrequent perching. The feet of flightless birds, on the other hand, are modified for walking and running. Some examples of the variety of bird beaks and feet are shown in Figure 44-8.

(a)

(b)

(c)

(d)

internetconnect

TOPIC: Classification of birds
GO TO: www.scilinks.org
KEYWORD: HM871

FIGURE 44-8

The cardinal (a), *Cardinalis cardinalis,* has a short, strong beak for cracking seeds and feet that enable it to perch on small tree branches. The kestrel (b), *Falco sparverius,* has a beak that enables it to tear flesh and talons that enable it to grip and kill prey. The calliope hummingbird (c), *Stellula calliope,* has a long, thin beak that enables it to extract nectar from flowers. The northern shoveler duck (d), *Anas clypeata,* has a flat beak that enables it to shovel mud while searching for food.

FIGURE 44-9

This mute swan, *Cygnus olor,* is able to take off from water and fly at very high speeds despite its great weight. Weighing up to 23 kg (50 lb), mute swans are the heaviest flying birds. Swans are monogamous, meaning they mate for life. While the female incubates the eggs, the male helps guard the nest.

FIGURE 44-10

The parrot pictured below is a lesser sulfur-crested cockatoo, *Cacatua sulphurea.* Parrots range in length from 8 cm (3 in.) to over 91 cm (3 ft). The earliest fossils of parrots indicate that they have existed as a group for at least 20 million years. Like most parrots, these cockatoos nest in holes in trees, and they usually lay only two eggs per year. Because of their low reproductive rate and destruction of habitat, many species have become extinct or endangered.

Most taxonomists divide the 10,000 species of living birds into 29 orders. Taxonomists have traditionally used morphological evidence from beaks, feet, plumage, bone structure, and musculature to classify birds. Technological advances in the analysis of blood proteins, chromosomes, and DNA have also been used. Despite the introduction of these new methods, the relationships among the 29 orders of birds are still not well resolved. Following are 12 of the most familiar orders of living birds.

Order Anseriformes

Swans, geese, and ducks—commonly called waterfowl—belong to this order of 160 species. Found worldwide, members of this order are usually aquatic and have webbed feet for paddling and swimming. Waterfowl feed on a variety of aquatic and terrestrial foods, ranging from small invertebrates and fish to grass. The bill is typically flattened. The young are precocial, and parental care is usually provided by the female. A mute swan is shown in Figure 44-9.

Order Strigiformes

This order contains the owls, the nocturnal counterparts to the raptors. Owls are predators that have a sharp, curved beak and sharp talons or claws. As you can see in the figure on page 860, owls also have large, forward-facing eyes that provide improved vision at night. Owls rely on their keen sense of hearing to help locate prey in the dark. There are about 180 species of owls, and they are found throughout the world.

Order Apodiformes

Hummingbirds and swifts belong to this order. All of the roughly 420 species are small, fast-flying, nimble birds with tiny feet. Swifts pursue insects and capture them in flight. Hummingbirds, by contrast, feed on nectar, which they lap up with a very long tongue. The long, narrow bill of a hummingbird can reach deep into a flower to locate nectar. Swifts have a worldwide distribution, but hummingbirds live only in the Western Hemisphere.

Order Psittaciformes

This order includes the parrots and their relatives, the parakeets, budgerigars, cockatoos, and cockatiels. Most of the roughly 360 species in this order live in the tropics. Parrots are characterized by a strong, hooked beak that is often used for opening seeds or slicing fruits. Their upper mandible is hinged on the skull and movable. Unlike most birds, parrots have two toes that point forward and two toes that point toward the rear, an adaptation for perching and climbing. They are vocal birds, and many species gather in large, noisy flocks. Parrots have long been prized as pets because of their colorful plumage and intelligence and because some species can be taught to mimic human speech. However, excessive collecting for the pet trade and habitat destruction now threaten many parrot species with extinction. Figure 44-10 shows a cockatoo.

Order Piciformes

This diverse group of tree-dwelling birds contains woodpeckers, honeyguides, and toucans. All members of this order nest in tree cavities. Like parrots, they have two forward-pointing toes and two that point to the rear. There are about 350 species found throughout the world except in Australia. The diversity of foods consumed by these birds is reflected in the diversity of their bills. Woodpeckers, which drill holes into trees to capture insects, have strong, sharp, chisel-like bills. Toucans feed mainly on fruit, which they pluck with a long bill, as shown in Figure 44-11.

Order Falconiformes

Known as raptors, the members of this order have a sharp, curved beak and sharp talons. Raptors include ospreys, hawks, falcons, vultures, and eagles. The 310 or so species of raptors are distributed throughout the world. Most species are diurnal (daytime) hunters with keen vision. Vultures, however, feed on dead animals and use their sense of smell to detect the odor of decomposing flesh.

Order Passeriformes

This large order contains about 5,700 species—more than half the total number of bird species—and includes most of the familiar North American birds. Robins, warblers, blue jays, and wrens are just some of the birds belonging to this group. In most birds, three toes point forward and one points backward. Passerines have this same arrangement of toes, but the rear toe is enlarged and particularly flexible to provide a better grip on branches. Passerines are sometimes called perching birds. Passerines feed on a variety of foods, including nectar, seeds, fruit, and insects.

Many passerines are called songbirds because the males produce long, elaborate, and melodious songs. Male birds sing to warn away other males and to attract females. The song is produced in the structure known as the **syrinx** (SIR-inks), which is located at the base of the bird's trachea. By regulating the flow of air through the syrinx, birds can generate songs of great range and complexity.

Order Columbiformes

This globally distributed group contains about 310 species of pigeons and doves. Figure 44-12 shows a mourning dove. These birds usually are plump-breasted and have relatively small heads; short necks, legs, and beaks; and short, slender bills. Most feed on fruit or grain. The crop, which in most other birds is used to store food, secretes a nutritious milklike fluid called **crop milk.** Both sexes produce crop milk to feed their young. Columbiform birds usually lay a clutch of two eggs, which hatch after a two-week incubation period. The young usually leave the nest two weeks after hatching. Another member of this order is the now-extinct dodo of Mauritius, an island in the Indian Ocean.

FIGURE 44-11

Toucans, such as this keel-billed toucan, *Ramphastos sulfuratus,* mate once per year, usually laying two to four eggs. The male and female toucans take turns sitting on the eggs. The eggs usually hatch after about 15 days of incubation.

FIGURE 44-12

The adult mourning dove, *Zenaida macroura,* stands about 30 cm (12 in.) tall and nests in trees or bushes. Mourning doves breed throughout North America. They winter as far south as Panama.

Order Ciconiiformes

This group of long-necked, long-legged birds includes 120 species of herons, storks, ibises, and egrets. They tend to have a long, flexible neck and a long bill. Many are wading birds, and they feed on fish, frogs, and other small prey in shallow water. Some members of this order grow to be quite large. The marabou stork of Australia, for example, can be more than 1.5 m (59 in.) in height. Figure 44-13 shows a great blue heron, a common species in North America. The order has a worldwide distribution.

Order Galliformes

Members of this group, which includes turkeys, pheasants, chickens, grouse, and quails, are commonly called fowl. These terrestrial birds are usually plump-bodied and may have limited flying ability. Grains form a large part of the diet of many fowl, and all species have a large, strong gizzard. Some are also an important part of the human diet. The young are precocial. There are about 260 species distributed worldwide.

Order Sphenisciformes

Penguins are a unique group of flightless marine birds. All 17 species live in the Southern Hemisphere. The penguin's wedge-shaped wings have been modified into flippers, and the feet are webbed. Underwater, penguins flap their flippers to propel themselves forward—they "fly" through the water. Most species have a thick coat of insulating feathers and a layer of fat beneath the skin, enabling them to live in polar conditions. Penguins maintain this fat layer by consuming large quantities of fish and krill.

Order Struthioniformes

Only the ostrich, the world's largest bird, belongs to this order. Ostriches can attain a height of nearly 3 m and weigh 150 kg. Ostriches cannot fly, but they are specialized as high-speed runners. Propelled by their long, strong legs, ostriches can reach speeds of 55 km per hour. Each foot has only two toes. Reduction in the number of toes is common in running animals—horses have just one toe per foot, for instance. Ostriches are native to Africa.

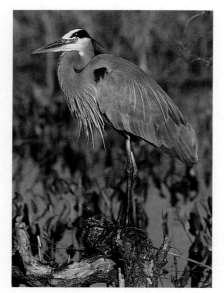

FIGURE 44-13

The great blue heron, *Ardea herodias,* uses its spearlike beak to stab fish, frogs, and other prey. Young herons must be taught how to hunt. Scientists have learned that young herons often miss their intended prey and must also learn what is and is not food.

Word Roots and Origins

syrinx

from the Greek *syrinx,* meaning "reed" or "pipe"

SECTION 44-3 REVIEW

1. Name two birds mentioned in this section, and describe how their beaks are suited to their way of life.

2. Identify the order to which each of the following birds belongs: eagle, robin, goose, penguin.

3. Name two similarities between raptors and owls. Name one difference.

4. What is crop milk? What types of birds produce it?

5. What is the function of the syrinx?

6. **CRITICAL THINKING** Penguins have a large, keeled sternum, but ostriches do not. Provide an explanation for this difference.

SUMMARY/VOCABULARY

44-1 ■ Seven characteristics of birds are: feathers; wings; a lightweight, rigid flight skeleton; a respiratory system involving air sacs; endothermy; a beak instead of teeth; and oviparity.

■ Birds evolved from small, carnivorous dinosaurs during the Jurassic period. The oldest known bird is *Archaeopteryx lithographica.*

■ There are two hypotheses for the origin of flight in birds. One hypothesis is that flight began in the trees, with organisms progressing from jumping to gliding and flying. The second hypothesis is that birds began on the ground. Wings initially served as stabilizers or as "nets" for capturing insects. Feathers may have been used for heat regulation.

■ Birds diversified after *Archaeopteryx,* a process that accelerated when the dinosaurs were wiped out.

Vocabulary

furcula (862)

44-2 ■ Feathers function in insulation and in flight. Down feathers provide insulation; contour feathers provide insulation and coloration and contribute most of the surface area of the wings and tail.

■ Many of the bones in a bird's skeleton are hollow; many are also fused.

■ The crop stores food. The two parts of the stomach are the proventriculus and the gizzard.

■ Birds lack a urinary bladder and excrete their nitrogenous waste as uric acid.

■ The lungs of a bird are connected to several air sacs that store air but do not participate in gas exchange.

■ The cerebellum, cerebrum, and optic lobes of the bird's brain are large.

■ All birds lay hard-shelled eggs. The eggs are usually laid in a nest and cared for by the parents.

■ Many birds migrate using a variety of environmental cues to guide their migration.

Vocabulary

altricial (870)	down feather (864)	precocial (870)	shaft (864)
barb (864)	flight feather (864)	preen gland (864)	sternum (865)
barbule (864)	follicle (864)	preening (864)	vane (864)
brood patch (868)	gizzard (866)	proventriculus (866)	vasa deferentia (868)
contour feather (864)	ornithologist (870)	pygostyle (865)	
crop (866)	oviduct (868)		

44-3 ■ The feet and beak of a bird reflect its way of life.

■ There are 29 orders of living birds, but scientists do not agree on the relationships among these orders.

■ The majority of the world's birds belong to the order Passeriformes. Many are songbirds.

■ Swifts and hummingbirds belong to the order Apodiformes. Parrots and relatives belong to the order Psittaciformes. Woodpeckers and toucans belong to the order Piciformes. Raptors belong to the order Falconiformes.

■ Pigeons and doves belong to the order Columbiformes. Chickens and turkeys, belong to the order Galliformes. Owls are nocturnal hunters and belong to the order Strigiformes. Ducks, geese, and swans belong to the order Anseriformes.

■ The herons and egrets belong to the order Ciconiiformes. Penguins belong to the Sphenisciformes, and the ostrich is in the order Struthioniformes.

Vocabulary

crop milk (873)   syrinx (873)

REVIEW

Vocabulary

1. Differentiate between the terms *altricial* and *precocial.*
2. What are the differences between a barb and a barbule?
3. What are the differences between the furcula and the sternum?
4. Explain the difference between a crop and a gizzard.
5. Describe the differences between migration and preening.

Multiple Choice

6. Which of the following characteristics of *Archaeopteryx* is not shared by modern birds? (a) long tail (b) feathers (c) teeth (d) furcula
7. One similarity between birds and dinosaurs is (a) the presence of feathers (b) the lack of teeth (c) the structure of the ankle joint (d) size.
8. The function of the preen gland is to (a) produce digestive enzymes (b) produce an oily substance used to condition the feathers (c) release scents that help attract mates (d) control salt balance in the body.
9. The bone that supports the tail feathers is the (a) pelvic girdle (b) pygostyle (c) ulna (d) furcula.
10. Gas exchange in birds takes place in the (a) anterior air sacs (b) posterior air sacs (c) syrinx (d) lungs.
11. The structure that grinds food, aided by stones swallowed by the bird, is the (a) gizzard (b) proventriculus (c) crop (d) small intestine.
12. The excretory system of a bird (a) lacks a urinary bladder (b) excretes nitrogenous wastes as ammonia (c) stores large amounts of water (d) has only one kidney.
13. Birds that produce altricial young (a) abandon their newly hatched chicks immediately (b) lay only a few eggs at a time (c) usually build nests on the ground (d) incubate their eggs for a long period of time.
14. A cue that is believed to aid birds in navigation during their annual migrations is (a) the Earth's magnetic field (b) weather (c) cloud formations (d) phases of the moon.
15. Crop milk is produced by birds in the order (a) Ciconiiformes (b) Galliformes (c) Columbiformes (d) Falconiformes.

Short Answer

16. Summarize the evidence that *Archaeopteryx* could fly.
17. What characteristics did *Archaeopteryx* share with its dinosaur ancestors?
18. Contrast the function of down feathers with that of contour feathers.
19. What function does the crop serve in digestion?
20. How do air sacs increase respiratory efficiency in birds?
21. Why is binocular vision important to some birds?
22. Many birds migrate long distances over the ocean. What types of cues might these birds use to guide their movements?
23. Owls and raptors often coexist. Would you expect these two types of birds to compete? Explain your answer.
24. Explain why birds migrate.
25. Look at the diagram below of a bird's skeleton. Identify the following structures: pelvic girdle, furcula, sternum, femur, humerus, ulna, and tibiotarsus.

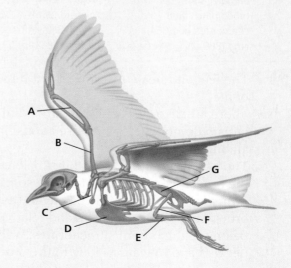

CRITICAL THINKING

1. What factors might explain why birds live in the Arctic but reptiles do not?
2. From studying the circulatory system of birds, you know that the right and left sides of a bird's heart are completely separated. This means that the oxygenated blood is never mixed with the deoxygenated blood. Why is this complete separation in the heart necessary?
3. Cowbirds lay their eggs in the nests of other birds. The young cowbirds hatch slightly earlier than the other birds do, and the cowbird hatchlings are slightly larger. Why might these distinctions be advantageous for the young cowbirds?
4. Although many species of temperate-zone birds migrate to the tropics to escape winter, some species remain behind. What benefits might these birds gain from not migrating?
5. From an evolutionary point of view, explain why the young of some birds, such as ducks and quail, are precocial.
6. The graph at right shows the results of an experiment on magpies in which the clutch size, that is, the number of eggs in the nest, was manipulated. Based on these data, determine whether the following statements are true or false.

   a. The greater the clutch size is, the greater the number of surviving offspring.
   b. More offspring died in nests containing eight eggs than in nests containing five eggs.
   c. Nests with nine eggs produced the fewest number of surviving offspring.

7. Drawing on data similar to that shown in the graph above, the ecologist David Lack argued that natural selection would favor intermediate clutch sizes. Explain the logic behind Lack's argument.

EXTENSION

1. Bird-watching is a fascinating and interesting hobby practiced by millions of Americans. From your library or bookstore, obtain a field guide to the birds in your area, and borrow a pair of binoculars. Take a long walk and try to locate as many birds as you can. Be sure to keep a notebook of the birds you find, including species, date sighted, location, and habits.
2. Many of the world's bird species have become extinct in the last 2,000 years. Three examples are the Carolina parakeet, the passenger pigeon, and the dodo. Using library resources or an on-line database, collect information on one of these extinct species. Find out as much as you can about its ecology and former distribution and about what caused it to become extinct. Write a report that summarizes your findings.
3. Read "Clown-Faced Hoarders" in *Audubon*, September–October 1999, on page 158. Describe the unique way acorn woodpeckers have of working together and storing food for the winter.

Comparing Feather Structure and Function

OBJECTIVES

- Observe a quill feather, a contour feather, and a down feather.
- Compare the structure and function of different kinds of feathers.

PROCESS SKILLS

- observing
- relating structure to function
- comparing and contrasting

MATERIALS

- 1 quill feather
- 1 contour feather
- 1 down feather
- unlined paper
- prepared slide of a contour feather
- compound light microscope
- prepared slide of a down feather

Background

1. List several distinguishing characteristics of birds.
2. How do birds differ from other vertebrates?
3. What are the functions of feathers?

Procedure

1. In your lab report, make a table like the one on the next page. Record your observations of each kind of feather in your data table.
2. Examine a quill feather. Hold the base of the central shaft with one hand and gently bend the tip of the feather with your other hand. Be careful not to break the feather. Next hold the shaft and wave the feather in the air. Record your observations concerning the structure of the quill feather. Relate your observations to the feather's possible function.

Flight feather

3. Examine the vane of the feather. Does the vane appear to be a solid structure? Include a description of the quill feather's vane structure under "Structure of feather" in your data table.
4. Make a drawing of the quill feather. Label the shaft, vanes, and barbs. Compare your feather with the figure above.
5. Examine a contour feather. Make a sketch of the contour feather in your data table. Label the shaft, vanes, and barbs on your sketch. Does the feather resemble the one in the figure on the next page?
6. Describe the structure of the contour feather under "Structure of feather" in your data table.
7. Examine a prepared slide of a contour feather under low power. Note the smaller barbs, called barbules, extending from each of the barbs.
8. How might you observe the region between the barbs? Locate the tiny hooks at the end of each barbule. Note the arrangement of the hooks on adjacent barbs. Why do you think the hooks are so small? Make a labeled drawing of the hooks in your lab report.
9. Examine the down feather and sketch it in your data table. How does your down feather compare with the figure on the next page?
10. Describe the structure of the down feather in your data table. Do you notice a difference in the structure of the contour and down feathers?

COMPARISON OF FEATHERS

Type of feather	Sketch of feather	Structure of feather	Function of feather
Quill feather			
Contour feather			
Down feather			

Contour feather

Down feather

11. Examine the prepared slide of the down feather under low power. Locate the barbs and barbules. Switch your microscope to high power, and make a labeled drawing of the down feather in your lab report. Does it resemble the one in the figure above?

12. Clean up your materials and wash your hands before leaving the lab.

Analysis and Conclusions

1. What is the function of the shaft? What is the function of the vanes and barbs?
2. How do hooks increase the strength and air resistance of a feather?
3. How is the structure of the quill feather related to its function of aiding flight?
4. Based on your observations, why might down feathers be more effective at keeping a bird warm than the other two feather types you observed?
5. Based on your observations of the structure and function of the feathers, how do you expect to see these feathers oriented on a bird? Explain how orientation of the feather affects the function of the feather.
6. What evolutionary pressure(s) would have caused the evolution of these different types of feathers?

Further Inquiry

Each of the feather types you have examined has a specific structure and function. Review your observations, and try to think of features that account for the efficiency of the three types of feathers.

CHAPTER 45

MAMMALS

These young opossums depend on their mother to provide them with nourishment from her mammary glands—a unique mammalian trait.

FOCUS CONCEPT: *Stability and Homeostasis*

As you read the chapter, note the ways mammals meet the demands of their rapid metabolism.

45-1 **Origin and Evolution of Mammals**

45-2 **Characteristics of Mammals**

45-3 **Mammalian Classification**

ORIGIN AND EVOLUTION OF MAMMALS

*T*here are about 4,400 species in the class Mammalia. Mammals are classified into more than 20 orders, one of which includes humans. Mammals live on every continent and in every ocean. Some mammals have the ability to fly, while others are exclusively aquatic.

KEY CHARACTERISTICS

Six important characteristics of mammals are listed below.

- **Endothermy**—Like birds, mammals produce body heat internally through metabolism. Mammals keep their body temperature high and nearly constant by controlling their metabolism and regulating the loss of heat through the body surface.
- **Hair**—All mammals have hair. The main function of hair is to insulate the body against heat loss. Most mammals (humans and whales are obvious exceptions) are covered with a thick coat of hair. Hair color also serves to camouflage a mammal from predators or a predator from being seen by its prey.
- **Completely divided heart**—Like crocodiles and birds, mammals have a four-chambered heart with two completely separate ventricles. Separate ventricles keep deoxygenated blood from diluting oxygenated blood and allow more efficient pumping of blood through both circuits of the circulatory system.
- **Milk**—Female mammals produce milk to feed their offspring. Milk is a nutritious fluid that contains fats, protein, and sugars. It is produced by the **mammary glands,** which are modified sweat glands located on the thorax or abdomen.
- **Single jawbone**—The lower jaw of a reptile is composed of several bones, but the lower jaw of a mammal is composed of a single bone. This characteristic is particularly important for identifying mammalian fossils because many of the other characteristics of mammals, such as hair and mammary glands, do not fossilize or leave traces on the skeleton.
- **Specialized teeth**—Teeth in different parts of a mammal's jaws are modified for different functions. Those at the front of the jaw are used for biting, cutting, or seizing prey, while those along the sides of the jaw are used for crushing, grinding, or slicing. The teeth of most reptiles are uniform in size and shape, regardless of where they are located in the mouth.

internet**connect**

SCLINKS
NSTA

TOPIC: Mammals
GO TO: www.scilinks.org
KEYWORD: HM881

FIGURE 45-1

This *Dimetrodon* is an example of a synapsid. Note the sail-like structure on its back. Scientists think that it was probably filled with blood vessels and that it acted as a temperature-regulating device that could absorb heat during the day. *Dimetrodon* could grow up to 3.5 m (11 ft) in length.

internet **connect**

SCI **LINKS**
NSTA

TOPIC: Therapsids
GO TO: www.scilinks.org
KEYWORD: HM882

ANCESTORS OF MAMMALS

The ancestors of mammals first appeared on Earth more than 300 million years ago. At that time, a major evolutionary split occurred in the terrestrial vertebrates, producing two groups of animals. Members of the first group gave rise to dinosaurs, birds, and all the living reptiles. Members of the second group, known as **synapsids,** include mammals and their closest relatives. Mammals are the only surviving synapsids. Early synapsids can be distinguished by the structure of their skull. There is a single opening in the outer layer of the skull just behind the eye socket. This same type of skull is found in all later synapsids, including mammals, although often in a highly modified form.

The first synapsids were only about 50 cm (20 in.) in length and resembled modern lizards. By the early Permian period (286–245 million years ago), an assortment of large synapsids, some of which reached 4 m (13 ft) in length and weighed more than 200 kg (440 lb), had appeared. Figure 45-1 shows a reconstruction of a carnivorous synapsid known as *Dimetrodon.* In most reptiles, teeth throughout the jaw are uniform in size and shape. But in many of the early carnivorous synapsids, including *Dimetrodon,* the teeth are specialized to a small degree, with long stabbing teeth in the front of the mouth and smaller teeth toward the back.

Therapsids

Among the synapsids that appeared later in the Permian period were the **therapsids,** the group that gave rise to mammals. Figure 45-2 shows a rendering of a therapsid. Therapsids were the most

FIGURE 45-2

Lycaenops was a carnivorous therapsid. Its legs supported its body more directly than did those of the early synapsids. The repositioning of the legs also improved its speed, making it a better predator.

abundant terrestrial vertebrates during the late Permian period. They survived through the Triassic period (245–208 million years ago) and into the Jurassic period (208–144 million years ago).

The evolution of mammals from therapsids involved changes in anatomy, physiology, ecology, and behavior. The rich and unusually complete fossil record of therapsids preserves many transitional forms that bridge the gap between therapsids and mammals. By studying these fossils, scientists can follow the anatomical changes that occurred during this transition and infer when some of the physiological, ecological, and behavioral changes must have happened.

Many of the features we associate with mammals evolved first among therapsids. For example, many therapsids had teeth differing in size, shape, and function, depending on their position in the jaw. The limbs of mammals are positioned directly beneath the body, as were the limbs of many therapsids. Some therapsids were probably endothermic, and some may have had hair.

Early Mammals

The first mammals and the first dinosaurs appeared at about the same time, during the Triassic period, and the dinosaurs had an important influence on the evolution of mammals for more than 150 million years. Figure 45-3 shows a reconstruction of an early mammal. The early mammals were about 10 cm (4 in.) long and

FIGURE 45-3

The first mammals, such as this *Eozostrodon*, had to compete with the larger, dominant dinosaurs. These first mammals functioned at night, when dinosaurs were probably less active.

20–30 g (0.5 oz) in mass, or about the size of a mouse. Fossil skeletons show that early mammals had large eye sockets, which suggests that these creatures probably were active at night. Their teeth indicate that they probably fed on insects. By hiding during the day, mammals would have avoided predation by dinosaurs, and by feeding on insects, they would not have competed with dinosaurs for food. Although there is no direct evidence of mammary-gland development in early mammals, scientists infer from similarities of mammary tissue among different mammalian orders that mammary glands were present as early as the late Triassic period.

During this time, dinosaurs filled the majority of terrestrial habitats. Mammals remained small and probably were neither abundant nor diverse. By the end of the Jurassic period, at least five orders of mammals had evolved. And by the middle of the Cretaceous period (144–65 million years ago), the three main groups to which modern mammals belong had appeared. The first group, the **monotremes,** are oviparous, that is, they lay eggs. The second group is the **marsupials.** Marsupials are viviparous, which means they give birth to live young, but the period of development within the mother is short. **Placental mammals,** the third group, are also viviparous, but the young are born at a much later stage of development than are marsupial offspring. As they develop inside the mother's uterus, placental young are nourished through a structure called the placenta.

Diversification of Mammals

The dinosaurs became extinct about 65 million years ago, at the end of the Cretaceous period. This opened up many new habitats and resources to mammals, and mammals took over many of the ecological roles previously fulfilled by dinosaurs. For example, during the Jurassic and Cretaceous periods, most of the large terrestrial carnivores and herbivores were dinosaurs. Today, nearly all large terrestrial carnivores (lions, tigers, and wolves, for example) and herbivores (elephants, giraffes, cattle, and horses, for example) are mammals.

SECTION 45-1 REVIEW

1. How does hair help a mammal maintain its body temperature?

2. Identify two differences between the jaw of a mammal and the jaw of a reptile.

3. What is one characteristic shared by mammals and the early synapsids?

4. List two characteristics of therapsids.

5. Why was it advantageous for the early mammals to be nocturnal?

6. **CRITICAL THINKING** Scientists think that mammals were rare during the time of the dinosaurs because there are few fossils of mammals from that time period. However, the early mammals were very small, and their fossils are very fragile. How might these factors influence estimates of the abundance of early mammals?

CHARACTERISTICS OF MAMMALS

*M*ammals inhabit a wide range of habitats on land and in the water. They can survive in some of the coldest and hottest environments on Earth. Adaptations have enabled mammals to inhabit such diverse environments.

SECTION

45-2

OBJECTIVES

▲

Describe the advantage of endothermy in mammals.

●

Describe two features of the mammalian respiratory and circulatory systems that help sustain a rapid metabolism.

■

Describe two mammalian adaptations for digesting plants.

◆

• **C**ompare and contrast reproduction in monotremes, marsupials, and placental mammals.

ENDOTHERMY

Endotherms generate heat internally by breaking down food, while ectotherms absorb most of their heat from their surroundings. Endothermy determines many of the capabilities of mammals. For instance, mammals can live in cold climates and be active. Perhaps more important, their rapid metabolism provides mammals with the energy to perform strenuous activities for long periods of time. As a general rule, ectotherms are not capable of sustained activity because they tire quickly.

The organ systems of mammals also differ from the organ systems of ectotherms. Figure 45-4 shows the internal anatomy of a typical mammal.

FIGURE 45-4

The organs and organ systems of modern mammals have a high demand for energy. The mammalian heart efficiently pumps oxygenated blood throughout the body, delivering nutrients that fuel the high-energy requirements of endothermy.

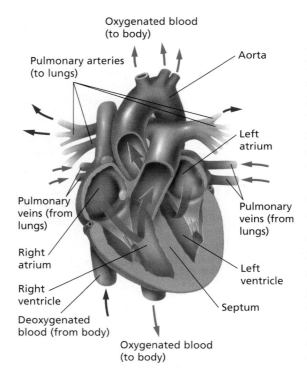

Oxygenated blood
(to body)

Pulmonary arteries
(to lungs)

Aorta

Left
atrium

Pulmonary
veins (from
lungs)

Pulmonary
veins (from
lungs)

Right
atrium

Left
ventricle

Right
ventricle

Septum

Deoxygenated
blood (from body)

Oxygenated blood
(to body)

FIGURE 45-5

The red arrows show the path of oxygenated blood through the heart, and the blue arrows show the path of deoxygenated blood. As you can see, the ventricle is completely divided by a septum. As a result, the blood pumped to the body contains a higher percentage of oxygen than results from blood pumped by a reptilian or fish heart.

Because of its faster metabolism, a mammal needs more oxygen and food than does a reptile of the same size. Heat is constantly escaping from a mammal's body through its skin and exhaled air. Because producing heat requires so much energy, mammals need to limit their loss of body heat to the environment. Hair and fat layers serve as insulation for most mammals. For example, mammals that live in very cold climates usually have a very thick coat of hair. Large tropical mammals, such as elephants, have very little hair.

Circulatory System

The structure of the mammalian heart helps ensure the efficient flow of blood throughout the body. As you can see in Figure 45-5, the heart has two atria and two completely separated ventricles. Note that oxygenated and deoxygenated blood never mix. Recall that in the heart of a lizard or turtle, deoxygenated blood and oxygenated blood can mix when the animal is inactive. However, mammals have such a high demand for oxygen that they cannot tolerate the dilution of oxygenated blood by deoxygenated blood.

Respiratory System

The respiratory system of a mammal is adapted for efficient gas exchange. The lungs are large and contain millions of alveoli, the small chambers in which gas exchange occurs. Compared with the lung of a reptile, the lung of a mammal has a much larger surface area available for gas exchange. For example, the internal surface area of a pair of human lungs is about 140 m^2 (1,500 ft^2). Another adaptation that contributes to the efficiency of respiration is the **diaphragm,** a sheet of muscle below the rib cage. Contraction of the diaphragm during inhalation helps draw air into the lungs.

Feeding and Digestion

For most mammals, the breakdown of food begins with chewing in the mouth. Other vertebrates simply swallow their food whole or in large pieces. Chewing speeds up digestion by breaking food into small pieces that can be more easily digested by enzymes. Most mammals have specialized teeth for gripping and holding food, and for chewing. Chisel-like **incisors** cut. Pointed **canines** grip, puncture, and tear. **Premolars** shear, shred, cut, or grind. **Molars** grind, crush, or cut. Variations in the size and shape of teeth among different mammalian species reflect differences in diet. For instance, notice the differences between the teeth of a carnivore and those of a herbivore, as shown in Figure 45-6.

Baleen whales, such as the blue whale, do not have teeth. Instead they have **baleen,** thin plates of fingernail-like material that hang from the roof of the mouth. As a baleen whale swims, it gulps huge quantities of water. Then it closes its mouth and pushes the water through the baleen. Shrimp and other small invertebrates are trapped in the baleen and then swallowed.

Adaptations for Digesting Plants

Plants can be difficult to digest because they contain large amounts of cellulose, which is a polymer of glucose, and no vertebrates produce enzymes to break down cellulose. However, some mammals can digest cellulose with the aid of microorganisms. Cows, sheep, goats, giraffes, and many other hoofed mammals have a large stomach with four chambers. The first chamber, known as the **rumen** (ROO-muhn), contains symbiotic bacteria and other microorganisms. After plant material is chewed and swallowed, it enters the rumen. Microorganisms then begin to break down the cellulose. The food is further digested in the rumen, then regurgitated, chewed again, and swallowed again (a cow chewing its cud is actually rechewing partially digested food). Food may be regurgitated and swallowed several times. Microorganisms that live in the rumen break down cellulose into small molecules that are eventually absorbed into the animal's bloodstream when the food reaches the small intestine.

In horses, rodents, rabbits, and elephants, microorganisms that live in the **cecum** (SEE-kuhm) complete digestion of the food. The cecum is a large sac that branches from the small intestine and acts as a fermentation chamber. Food passes through the stomach and small intestine before entering the cecum. The human appendix is a vestigial cecum. Mammals with a cecum do not chew cud.

NERVOUS SYSTEM AND SENSE ORGANS

The brain of a mammal is about 15 times heavier than the brain of a similarly sized fish, amphibian, or reptile. Enlargement of one part of the brain, the cerebrum, accounts for most of this size increase. In mammals, the cerebrum is the largest part of the brain. The cerebrum's surface is usually folded and wrinkled, which greatly increases its surface area without increasing its volume. The cerebrum evaluates input from the sense organs, controls movement, and initiates and regulates behavior. It is also involved in memory and learning. Humans have the highest brain-to-body-size ratio.

Like other terrestrial vertebrates, mammals depend on five major senses: vision, hearing, smell, touch, and taste. The importance of each sense often depends on the mammal's environment. For instance, most bats, which are active at night, rely on sound rather than vision for navigating and finding food. Using a process called **echolocation** (EK-oh-loh-KAY-shuhn), these bats emit high-frequency sound waves, which bounce off objects, and then they analyze the returning echoes to determine the size, distance, direction, and speed of the objects.

FIGURE 45-6

Carnivores, such as this lion, have large, sharp incisor and canine teeth that are able to cut and tear flesh. Herbivores, such as the zebra, have flat teeth that are useful for grinding grass and grain, which are the staples of their diet.

Word Roots and Origins

cecum

from the Latin *intestinum caecum*, meaning "blind intestine"

REPRODUCTION

Each main group of mammals—monotremes, marsupials, and placental mammals—has a unique reproductive pattern. A female monotreme typically lays one or two large eggs that have thin leathery shells and incubates them with her body heat. The developing embryo is nourished by the yolk within the egg. At hatching, a monotreme is very small and only partially developed. Its mother protects it and feeds it milk from her mammary glands until it is ready to survive on its own.

Marsupials are characterized by a very short period of development within the mother's uterus. Newborn marsupials emerge from the uterus after they have completed enough development to be able to survive outside the uterus. The newborn offspring of a kangaroo, for example, is only 2 to 3 cm (1 in.) long. Figure 45-7 shows a marsupial soon after birth. The newborn crawls into the mother's pouch, located on her abdomen, and attaches to a nipple. The newborn's development and growth then continue in the pouch.

Placental mammals, the group that includes cats, dogs, humans, and most other familiar mammals, give birth to their young after a much longer period of development. During this period, the mother provides nourishment and oxygen to her developing offspring through the placenta. The placenta begins to form shortly after fertilization, when the fertilized egg attaches to the lining of the uterus. Extensions from the chorion, the outer membrane surrounding the egg, grow into the lining of the uterus, and blood vessels from the uterus surround these extensions. When completely formed, the placenta contains tissue and blood vessels from both the mother and the offspring. Nutrients and oxygen diffuse from the mother's blood into the blood of the offspring, and carbon dioxide and other wastes diffuse from the offspring into the mother's blood.

Newborn mammals are nourished with milk from the mother's mammary glands. Young mammals are dependent on the mother for food and care.

FIGURE 45-7

Marsupials, such as this young kangaroo, are born soon after conception and must crawl into their mother's pouch for the rest of their development. The level of development is so low that many marsupials are born before separation of the heart ventricle is complete. Other organs not yet completed include lungs, kidneys, and major nerves.

SECTION 45-2 REVIEW

1. A mammal eats about 10 times as much food as a lizard of the same size. Explain this difference.

2. How does the heart of a mammal differ from the heart of a lizard?

3. What is the function of the rumen in hoofed mammals?

4. Bats, which are active only at night, often have very large ears. Why might large ears be advantageous to a bat?

5. Identify one difference and one similarity between the reproductive patterns of monotremes and marsupials.

6. **CRITICAL THINKING** What sort of ecological relationship exists between a cow and the microorganisms living in its rumen? Explain your answer.

Gorillas in the Mist

This excerpt is from *Gorillas in the Mist,* by Dian Fossey.

During the early days of the study at Kabara, it was difficult to establish contacts because the gorillas were not habituated or accustomed to my presence and usually fled on seeing me. I could often choose between two different kinds of contacts: obscured, when the gorillas didn't know I was watching them, or open contacts, when they were aware of my presence.

Obscured contacts were especially valuable in revealing behavior that otherwise would have been inhibited by my presence. The drawback to this method was that it contributed nothing toward the habituation process. Open contacts, however, slowly helped me win the animals' acceptance. This was especially true when I learned that imitation of some of their ordinary activities such as scratching and feeding or copying their contentment vocalizations tended to put the animals at ease more rapidly than if I simply looked at them through binoculars while taking notes. I always wrapped vines around the binoculars in an attempt to disguise the potentially threatening glass eyes from the shy animals. With gorillas, as is often the case with humans, direct staring constitutes a threat.

Not only was it necessary to get the gorillas accustomed to the blue-jeaned creature who had become a part of their daily lives, it was also very necessary for me to know and recognize the particular animals of each group as the amazing individuals they were. Just as George Schaller had done some seven and a half years before me, I relied heavily upon "noseprints" for identification purposes. There is a tendency for the gorillas of each group to resemble one another, especially within matrilineal lines. As no two humans have exactly the same

fingerprints, no two gorillas have the same "noseprint"—the shape of the nostrils and the outstanding troughs seen on the bridges of their noses. Since the gorillas initially were unhabituated, I had to use binoculars, but even from a distance I could quickly make sketches of noseprints seen on the more curious group members peeking back at me from partially hidden positions in the dense vegetation. These sketches proved invaluable at a time when close-up photography was out of the question. Also, I would have needed a third hand in order to manage a camera, binoculars, and note taking, not to mention carrying on with the imitative routine of feeding, scratching, and vocalizing needed to relax the gorillas as well as to arouse their curiosity.

Reading for Meaning

What do you think Fossey means when she says the gorillas "were not habituated"?

Read Further

Gorillas in the Mist tells about Dian Fossey's experiences during 13 years she spent observing African mountain gorillas in their natural habitat. How did her growing understanding of the gorillas help her become almost a part of their community?

▲

Name the orders of mammals, and give an example of each.

●

Describe two differences between marsupials and monotremes.

■

Distinguish between artiodactyls and perissodactyls.

◆

Identify two orders whose members are aquatic, and describe one adaptation for aquatic life shown by each order.

FIGURE 45-8

The duckbill platypus (a) and the spiny anteater (b) are two of the three species in the order Monotremata. The platypus's scientific name is *Ornithorhynchus anatinus,* and the anteater's scientific name is *Tachyglossus aculeatus.*

MAMMALIAN CLASSIFICATION

The roughly 4,400 species of mammals are divided into more than 20 orders. One order contains the monotremes, one order contains marsupials, and the remaining orders contain placental mammals.

ORDER MONOTREMATA

Monotremes are the only egg-laying mammals. Just three species exist, one platypus and two anteaters, or echidna, and they have a very restricted distribution. Monotremes live only in Australia and New Guinea. Figure 45-8 shows an example of a platypus and an echidna. Monotremes are considered to be the most primitive of all the mammals, as is illustrated in the phylogenetic tree in Figure 45-9.

The duckbill platypus is adapted to life in water. It has waterproof fur, webbed feet, and a flattened tail that aids in swimming. Its most distinctive characteristic is its flat, sensitive, rubbery muzzle, which it uses to root for worms, crayfish, and other invertebrates in soft mud. The female platypus digs a den in the bank of a river or stream to lay her eggs. She curls around the eggs to protect and incubate them. After hatching, the newborns lick milk from nippleless mammary glands on the mother's abdomen.

Echidnas are terrestrial. They have a coat of protective spines and a long snout for probing into anthills and termite nests. Echidnas incubate their eggs in a pouch on the belly.

(a)

(b)

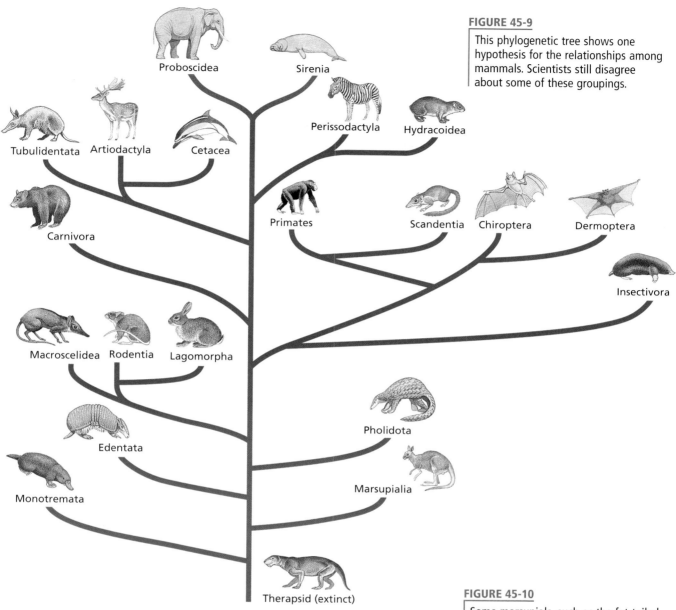

FIGURE 45-9

This phylogenetic tree shows one hypothesis for the relationships among mammals. Scientists still disagree about some of these groupings.

Proboscidea

Sirenia

Tubulidentata Artiodactyla Cetacea

Perissodactyla Hydracoidea

Carnivora

Primates

Scandentia Chiroptera Dermoptera

Insectivora

Macroscelidea Rodentia Lagomorpha

Pholidota

Edentata

Marsupialia

Monotremata

Therapsid (extinct)

FIGURE 45-10

Some marsupials, such as the fat-tailed dunnart, eat insects and small vertebrates. The marsupial line split from the placental-mammal line during the late Jurassic or early Cretaceous periods.

ORDER MARSUPIALIA

About 280 marsupial species exist today, inhabiting Australia, New Guinea, and the Americas. The United States has only one marsupial species, the Virginia opossum. Figure 45-10 shows an example of a marsupial.

These unique mammals evolved during a long period of isolation. Recall that Australia and New Guinea drifted away from the other continents more than 40 million years ago. At that time, placental mammals were apparently rare in the region. According to the fossil record, marsupials once dominated South America; they were gradually displaced by placental mammals, and many species became extinct.

FIGURE 45-11

These porcupines are members of the order Rodentia. The range of the North American porcupine, *Erithizon dorsatum,* on the left, extends from Canada to northern Mexico. The Brazilian porcupine, *Coendou prehensilis,* on the right, has a prehensile tail that enables it to maintain a firm grip on tree branches.

Quick Lab

Comparing Gestation Periods

Materials paper, pencil

Procedure

1. Make a table of gestation periods for different mammals. Make three columns labeled "Mammal," "Gestation period," and "Offspring per pregnancy."

2. Fill in your table with the following data:

Bat, 210 days, 1 offspring

Gerbil, 19–21 days, 4–7 offspring

Horse, 332–342 days, 1 offspring

Monkey, 226–232 days, 1 offspring

Squirrel, 44 days, 3 offspring

Rabbit, 31 days, 3–6 offspring

Whale, 420–430 days, 1 offspring

Wolf, 63 days, 4–5 offspring

Analysis

1. State a generalization about the relationship of the length of the gestation period to the number of offspring per pregnancy.

2. Propose a hypothesis to explain this relationship.

3. Rearrange your table, if necessary, to show this relationship more clearly.

PLACENTAL MAMMALS

Placental mammals are a diverse group that comprises at least 18 orders. Ninety-five percent of all mammal species are placental mammals. They live on land, in water, and in the air.

Order Rodentia

Rodentia, the largest mammalian order, includes more than 1,800 species, or about 40 percent of all placental mammals. Rodents flourish on every continent except Antarctica and are adapted to a wide range of habitats. Squirrels, marmots, chipmunks, gophers, muskrats, mice, rats, and porcupines are rodents. Rodents have only two pairs of incisors, which continue to grow as long as the rodent lives. Rodent incisors are sharp, an adaptation for the rodent's diet of hard seeds, twigs, roots, and bark. As a rodent gnaws, the back surface of the tooth wears away faster than the front surface, maintaining the tooth's chisel-like edge. Rodents also have a very high reproductive capacity. Figure 45-11 shows two examples of rodents.

Order Edentata

The order Edentata is made up of about 30 living species, including anteaters, armadillos, and sloths. These mammals are found in southern North America, Central America, and South America. The name of this order means "toothless." However, only anteaters are completely toothless; armadillos and sloths have teeth, although the teeth are peglike and lack enamel. Most edentates feed on insects, which they capture with a long, sticky tongue. Their powerful front paws have large, sharp claws, which they use to rip open anthills and termite nests. Armadillos supplement their insect diet with small reptiles, frogs, mollusks, and carrion. Sloths, on the other hand, are herbivores; their continuously growing teeth are an adaptation for grinding plants.

Order Lagomorpha

About 70 species make up the order Lagomorpha, which includes rabbits, hares, and pikas. Lagomorphs are found worldwide. They differ from rodents in that they have a double row of upper incisors, with two large front teeth backed by two smaller ones. Lagomorph teeth continue to grow throughout the animal's lifetime. Such teeth are an adaptation to the lagomorph's herbivorous diet.

Order Insectivora

The order Insectivora consists of about 390 species of shrews, hedgehogs, and moles. Insectivores are usually small animals with a high metabolic rate. Insectivores are found in North America, Africa, Europe, and Asia. Most have long, pointed noses that enable them to probe in the soil for insects, worms, and other invertebrates. They have teeth adapted for grasping and piercing their prey.

Insectivores are adapted to life on the ground, in trees, in water, and underground. Shrews, for example, feed on the surface of the ground, catching insects with their sharp teeth. Moles, on the other hand, burrow underground. They have stout limbs for digging, small eyes, and no external ears.

Order Primates

Recall from Chapter 17 that humans belong to the order Primates. The 235 species of living primates are classified as either prosimians, which include lemurs, tarsiers, and lorises, or anthropoids, which include monkeys, apes, and humans. Most primates are omnivores and have teeth suited for a varied diet. Primates have particularly large brains, which make possible the complex behaviors characteristic of this group.

Primates vary greatly in size and weight. The smallest primates weigh tens of grams, while the largest primate, the gorilla, *Gorilla gorilla,* can weigh 140–180 kg (300–400 lb). Most primates have two forward-facing eyes, a feature that enables depth perception. All primates have grasping hands and, with one notable exception, grasping feet, and many primates also have a grasping tail. The grasping feet, hands, and tail are excellent adaptations for life in the trees. Because of the wide range of body sizes and adaptations, primates live in a variety of habitats. The rhesus monkey, *Macaca mulatta,* is a tree-living species that is native to India. The gorilla, which is too large to climb trees, lives on the ground in the mountainous areas of Africa.

Order Chiroptera

This order includes bats, the only mammals that can fly. There are more than 900 species of bats, and they live throughout the world, except in polar environments. A bat's wing is a modified front limb with a skin membrane that stretches between extremely long finger bones to the hind limb. A bat's wingspan can measure up to 1.5 m (4.5 ft). The bat's clawed thumb sticks out from the top edge of the wing. Bats use their thumbs for walking, climbing, and grasping. Figure 45-12 shows an example of a bat.

Most bats use echolocation for navigation and have small eyes and large ears. Most feed on insects. However, some tropical bats feed on fruit or flower nectar and do not use echolocation. These bats, sometimes called "flying foxes," have large eyes and a keen sense of smell.

FIGURE 45-12

Peter's epauletted fruit bat is a member of the order Chiroptera, the only flying mammals. The physics of the bat's wing in flight gives the bat more lift in relation to its body weight than most birds have. This enables bats to remain airborne at slower speeds than birds are capable of.

Order Carnivora

The 274 living species of the order Carnivora are distributed world-wide. Dogs, cats, raccoons, bears, hyenas, otters, seals, and sea lions are some well-known carnivores. Most of the species eat meat, which explains the name of the order. Carnivores generally have long canine teeth, strong jaws, and clawed toes, which they use for seizing and holding prey. Most have keen senses of sight and smell, which aid in hunting. Skeletal adaptations, such as long limbs, enable terrestrial carnivores to run quickly. Aquatic carnivores, such as sea lions, seals, and walruses, have streamlined bodies for efficient swimming and are known as **pinnipeds.** Pinnipeds propel themselves through the water and steer with their flattened, paddlelike forelimbs and hind limbs. Although pinnipeds spend much of their time in the sea feeding, they return to land to sleep and to give birth. Some scientists think that pinnipeds should be in their own order—Pinnipedia.

Pinnipeds are generally larger than land carnivores, weighing 90–3,600 kg (198–7,920 lb). Pinnipeds spend a large part of their life in cold water, so their large size serves to help maintain endothermy. Perhaps one of the most impressive feats of pinnipeds is their diving ability. Pinnipeds generally can dive to depths of 100 m (330 ft), and some species can dive to 400 m (1,313 ft). Most pinnipeds can remain underwater for up to five minutes, and some species can remain submerged for up to an hour.

Order Artiodactyla

Ungulates (UHN-gyoo-luhts) are mammals with hooves. Ungulates with an even number of toes make up the order Artiodactyla. Deer, elk, bison, moose, cattle, sheep, goats, pigs, and camels are artiodactyls (AHRT-ee-oh-DAK-tuhls). About 210 species belong to this order. Artiodactyls are native to every continent except Antarctica and Australia. They are fast runners and use speed as their major defense.

Most artiodactyls are herbivores, although pigs are omnivores. Their molars tend to be large and flat, for grinding plant material. As you learned in the last section, artiodactyls have a storage chamber in the stomach, called the rumen, in which bacteria and other microorganisms break down cellulose. This mutualistic relationship with microorganisms enables artiodactyls to extract nutrients efficiently from plants. Figure 45-13 shows an example of an artiodactyl.

Order Perissodactyla

Ungulates with an odd number of toes make up the order Perissodactyla, which includes about 17 living species. Horses, zebras, rhinoceroses, and tapirs are examples of perissodactyls (PER-is-oh-DAK-tuhls). Most species are native to Africa and Asia. However, some species of tapirs live in Central and South America. Figure 45-14 shows a tapir.

Like artiodactyls, perissodactyls have adaptations that help them digest the cellulose found in plant material. Members of this

FIGURE 45-13

This caribou is a member of the order Artiodactyla. Artiodactyls are native to all continents except Australia and Antarctica. The first domesticated artiodactyls were probably sheep and goats.

FIGURE 45-14

Although this tapir, *Tapirus bairdi,* looks like a pig, it is a member of the order Perissodactyla, making it more closely related to the horse and rhinoceros. This is another example of convergent evolution.

FIGURE 45-15

Most cetaceans, like this killer whale, *Orcinus orca*, live in the oceans, but some species of dolphins live in freshwater lakes and rivers.

order have a cecum, instead of a rumen, in which microorganisms break down cellulose, releasing nutrients that the perissodactyl can absorb.

Order Cetacea

The order Cetacea includes 90 species of whales, dolphins, and porpoises. Cetaceans (se-TAY-shuhns) are distributed worldwide. Cetaceans have fishlike bodies with forelimbs modified as flippers. They lack hind limbs but have broad, flat tails that help propel them through the water. Cetaceans breathe through blowholes located on the top of the head. They are completely hairless, except for a few bristles on the snout. A thick layer of blubber below the skin provides insulation. Like bats, cetaceans navigate and find prey by using echolocation.

Cetaceans are exclusively aquatic and even give birth underwater, but they evolved from land-dwelling mammals. Cetaceans are divided into two groups: toothed whales and baleen whales. Toothed whales include sperm whales, beluga whales, narwhals, killer whales, dolphins, and porpoises. They can have from 1 to 100 teeth, and they prey on fish, squid, seals, and other whales. Figure 45-15 shows a killer whale. Baleen whales, such as blue whales, lack teeth and filter invertebrates from the water with a mesh of baleen that hangs from the roof of the mouth.

Order Sirenia

The order Sirenia is made up of four species of manatees and dugongs. These large herbivores inhabit tropical seas, estuaries, and rivers. Their front limbs are flippers modified for swimming. Like whales (order Cetacea), sirenians lack hind limbs but have a flattened tail for propulsion. Although manatees and dugongs superficially resemble whales, they are more closely related to elephants. The similarities between whales and sirenians came about through convergent evolution. Figure 45-16 shows the only sirenian found in North America, the manatee.

Word Roots and Origins

ungulate

from the Latin *ungula,* meaning "hoof"

FIGURE 45-16

This manatee, *Trichechus manatus,* or sea cow, is one of three species of manatee. Sirenian fossils that date to 50 million years ago have been found.

TABLE 45-1   *Minor Orders of Mammals*

Order	Characteristic	Example
Macroscelidea	ground-dwelling insectivores with long, flexible snouts; 15 species found only in Africa	elephant shrew
Pholidota	insectivores with protective scales composed of fused hair; resemble reptiles; found in Africa and southern Asia	pangolin
Tubulidentata	nearly hairless insectivores with piglike bodies and long snouts; found in southern Africa	aardvark
Scandentia	squirrel-like omnivores that live on ground and in trees; feed on fruit and small animals; found in tropical Asia	tree shrew
Dermoptera	only two species exist; glide in air using a thin membrane stretched between their limbs; found only in parts of Asia	flying lemur
Hyracoidea	small rabbitlike herbivores; 7 species found only in Africa	hyrax

Order Proboscidea

Members of the order Proboscidea are characterized by a boneless, trunked nose, or proboscis. Only two species of this order exist today, the Asian elephant and the African elephant. Mammoths are an extinct member of this order. Elephants are the largest land animals alive today. The African elephant, the larger of the two species, can reach 6,000 kg (13,200 lb). To sustain such a large body, an elephant must feed on plants for up to 18 hours a day. Elephants use the trunk to gather leaves from high branches. They have modified incisors, called tusks, for digging up roots and for stripping bark from branches. The large, jagged molars, which can grow up to 30 cm (1 ft) long, are used for grinding plant material.

Elephants have one of the longest gestation periods of any animal. A female calf takes 20 months to develop, and a male calf takes 22 months to develop. Female elephants can continue to have calves until the age of 70, and elephants can live to be 80 years old.

The 12 orders just described include most of the familiar placental mammals. The six remaining orders contain just 1 percent of the mammalian species. These orders are summarized in Table 45-1.

SECTION 45-3 REVIEW

1. List any five orders of placental mammals, and name an example of each order.

2. Where would you go to find both monotremes and marsupials?

3. What is unusual about the incisors of rodents?

4. Name two differences between artiodactyls and perissodactyls.

5. What are some feeding adaptations of whales?

6. **CRITICAL THINKING** The pouch of the marsupial mole opens toward the rear of the body. How would such a pouch aid in the survival of this burrowing animal's young?

SUMMARY/VOCABULARY

 45-1
- Six key characteristics of mammals are endothermy; a fully divided heart; hair; milk production by females; a single jawbone; and complex, diverse teeth.
- Mammals belong to a group called synapsids. Synapsids have a skull with one opening behind the eye socket.
- Synapsids called therapsids gave rise to mammals. Therapsids had complex teeth and legs positioned beneath their body.
- Mammals first appeared about 225 million years ago. During the time of the dinosaurs they remained small and lacked diversity. After the extinction of dinosaurs, mammals evolved rapidly.

Vocabulary

mammary gland (881)	monotreme (884)	synapsid (882)	therapsid (882)
marsupial (884)	placental mammal (884)		

 45-2
- Mammals are endothermic.
- Endothermy expands the range of habitats mammals can occupy and facilitates sustained, strenuous activity. It also requires abundant supplies of food and oxygen.
- The heart of a mammal has two atria and two ventricles.
- Mammals have large lungs with a large internal surface area.
- Mammals, unlike most vertebrates, chew their food to begin its breakdown. Mammals have incisors, canines, premolars, and molars.
- Some hoofed mammals digest cellulose with the aid of microorganisms that live in the rumen. Elephants, rodents, and horses digest cellulose with the aid of microorganisms living in the cecum.
- Mammals have much larger brains than most other vertebrates.
- Monotremes lay eggs. Marsupials give birth to partially developed young that continue development in the mother's pouch. Placental mammals give birth to fully developed young.

Vocabulary

baleen (886)	diaphragm (886)	incisor (886)	premolar (886)
canine (886)	echolocation (887)	molar (886)	rumen (887)
cecum (887)			

 45-3
- There are at least 20 orders of mammals. Eighteen contain placental mammals. The other orders are monotremes and marsupials.
- Edentates—the sloths, anteaters, and armadillos—have either small teeth or no teeth. Rodents have two continuously growing incisors. Lagomorphs, such as rabbits, have four continuously growing incisors. Insectivores, such as shrews, are small and are adapted for eating invertebrates.
- Primates, including apes, monkeys, and humans, have very large brains and complex behaviors. Bats (order Chiroptera) are the only flying mammals. Carnivores, such as lions, are meat eaters. Deer, cattle, and sheep (order Artiodactyla) are hoofed mammals with an even number of toes. Hoofed mammals with an odd number of toes, such as rhinoceroses, belong to the order Perissodactyla. Whales and dolphins (order Cetacea) are exclusively aquatic and lack hind limbs. Elephants (order Proboscidea) have a long, prehensile nose called a trunk. Manatees and dugongs (order Sirenia) are large aquatic herbivores.

Vocabulary

pinniped (894)	ungulate (894)

REVIEW

Vocabulary

Explain the differences in meaning between each pair of terms.

1. rumen, cecum
2. ventricle, diaphragm
3. baleen, incisor
4. monotreme, placental mammal
5. canine, molar

Multiple Choice

6. Which of the following characteristics is present in all synapsids? (a) hair (b) placenta (c) skull with one opening behind the eye socket (d) endothermic metabolism

7. Which of the following is not true of therapsids? (a) may have been endothermic (b) gave rise to mammals (c) died out after dinosaurs (d) legs were positioned beneath the body

8. Evidence that early mammals were active at night includes the fossils of mammals with (a) a single jawbone (b) large eye sockets (c) a four-chambered heart (d) mammary glands.

9. After the dinosaurs became extinct, mammal species flourished because (a) many new habitats were suddenly available to them (b) the climate became warmer and wetter (c) the reptiles had undergone adaptive radiation (d) the reptiles had become endothermic.

10. The diaphragm allows mammals to (a) carry the young inside the uterus (b) have a divided ventricle (c) provide nourishment for their young (d) breathe efficiently.

11. Which of the following is not part of the mammalian heart? (a) conus arteriosus (b) septum (c) ventricle (d) atrium

12. Marsupials differ from monotremes in that marsupials (a) lay eggs (b) carry developing young in a pouch (c) live only in Australia (d) nourish their newborns with milk from mammary glands.

13. Which of these mammals is a marsupial? (a) kangaroo (b) duckbill platypus (c) lion (d) echidna

14. The order Chiroptera is made up of (a) toothless mammals (b) marine mammals (c) flying mammals (d) arboreal mammals.

15. Baleen whales feed on (a) fish (b) marine mammals (c) invertebrates (d) algae.

Short Answer

16. Name and describe two characteristics common to all mammals.

17. Describe two benefits of endothermy for mammals.

18. The ventricles of the mammalian heart are completely separated. How does this help a mammal maintain a constant body temperature?

19. Describe how specialized teeth aid mammals in digesting food.

20. Mammals cannot produce enzymes that break down cellulose, yet many mammals eat plants. Describe two mammalian adaptations for digesting plants.

21. In a famous study conducted 200 years ago, the Italian scientist Lazzaro Spallanzani showed that a blinded bat could still fly and capture insects. A bat whose ears had been plugged with wax could neither fly nor hunt. Explain Spallanzani's observations.

22. How is reproduction in reptiles and monotremes similar? How is it different?

23. Whales have only a few hairs on their snout, yet they are able to live in the coldest oceans. How do they retain their body heat in such environments?

24. How do the teeth of rodents differ from those of lagomorphs?

25. Examine the two skulls below. Which is mammalian? Justify your answer.

CRITICAL THINKING

1. Evaluate this statement by the paleontologist Robert Bakker: "Dinosaurs suppressed the evolutionary potential of mammals, not the other way around."

2. Mammals that live in very cold environments are usually larger than members of the same species that live in warmer climates. Propose a functional explanation for this. (Hint: Consider the effect that increasing size has on volume and surface area.)

3. Mice give birth only 21 days after mating. Why might this characteristic make mice ideal laboratory animals for experiments dealing with mammalian development and heredity?

4. Sloths are arboreal edentates that spend most of their lives hanging upside down from tree branches in the tropical forests of Central and South America. Most sloths have green algae growing in tiny pits in their hair. How might this be an advantage for the sloth? What advantage might the green algae gain by colonizing the sloth's fur?

5. In recent years, surgeons have tried transplanting baboon and pig hearts into humans. Explain why surgeons tried these hearts rather than a turtle's heart.

6. When performing surgery on animals such as cows, veterinarians try not to puncture the stomach because of the danger of infection. Explain what is meant by this statement. Why would it be unwise to completely sterilize the inside and outside of the animal?

7. The metabolic rates of two groups of sheep were measured as the amount of oxygen consumed per hour. One group was sheared before the experiment and the other was not. Explain the results shown below. How do these results support the theory that hair is an evolutionary advantage for endotherms?

Sheep-Shearing Experiment

Metabolic rate ($L O_2$ per kg of body weight)

100

50

Unshorn   Shorn

EXTENSION

1. Choose a nondomesticated mammal species, and write a report on its classification; habitat; morphology; life cycle; and adaptations for feeding, defense, and reproduction. Discuss its evolution if the information is available. You may wish to visit a zoo to observe the mammal. If possible, include labeled drawings or photographs of the mammal.

2. Read "Mind of a Dog" in *New Scientist*, March 4, 2000, on page 22. How long does dog mitochondrial DNA evidence suggest that humans have lived with dogs? Why does the author think dogs are particularly well suited to living with human society?

3. Obtain a live mammal, such as a mouse, hamster, or gerbil, from a pet store or your school. Get instructions on the care and feeding of the mammal. Then observe the mammal for at least 3 weeks. Take notes on its feeding and sleeping behavior. Share what you learn with your class.

Mammalian Characteristics

OBJECTIVES

- Observe examples of mammals.
- Examine the distinguishing characteristics of mammals.

PROCESS SKILLS

- observing
- inferring

MATERIALS

- hand lens or stereomicroscope
- microscope slide of mammalian skin
- compound light microscope
- mirror
- selection of vertebrate skulls (some mammalian, some nonmammalian)
- field guide to mammals

Background

1. List the distinguishing characteristics of mammals.
2. Define the term *endothermy.*
3. Mammalian skin is characterized by cutaneous glands, such as sebaceous glands and sweat glands, that develop as ingrowths from the epidermis into the dermis.

PART A Mammalian Hair and Skin

1. Use a hand lens to examine several areas of your skin that appear to be hairless. Record your observations in your lab report.
2. Compare the amount of hair on humans with the amount on other mammals that you have seen or read about. What role does hair or fur play in endothermy? What other roles does hair (or whiskers) play in mammals?
3. Examine a slide of mammalian skin under low power. Notice the glands in the skin.
4. Identify the sebaceous glands and the sweat glands in the skin. Sweat glands are found only in mammals, but some mammals do not have them or have few of them. What mechanism for cooling might these other animals have? Which other glands are unique to mammals?

PART B Mammalian Reproduction

5. Look at the photographs of mammals on this page. What characteristics do these animals share?
6. Name the two kinds of mammals represented in the photographs on this page.

PART C Mammalian Mouth and Teeth

7. Use a mirror to look in your mouth, and identify the four kinds of mammalian teeth. Count how many of each you have on one side of your lower jaw.

8. Look at the skulls of several mammals. Identify the four kinds of teeth in each skull, and count them as you counted your own. How are the four types of teeth different from yours?

9. Look at the skulls of several nonmammalian vertebrates. Describe the teeth in each one, and compare them with mammalian teeth.

10. Breathe with your mouth closed. Do you feel a flow of air into your mouth? You have a hard palate (the roof of your mouth) that separates your mouth from your nose.

11. Look again at the different skulls. In which vertebrates do you see a hard palate? What is an advantage of having a hard palate?

12. Compare the jaws of the mammalian skulls with those of the nonmammalian skulls. Notice how the upper jawbone and the lower jawbone connect in each skull. Is there a similarity in the mammalian jaws that distinguishes them from the nonmammalian jaws? Explain.

13. Create a data table, similar to the model below, to record your observations for your lab report. For example, the table below is designed to record observations of differences that you will find among the animal skulls. Remember to allow plenty of space to record your observations.

PART D Vertebrate Diversity

14. Use a field guide to find out more about the following mammal orders: Cetacea, Edentata, Philodota, and Chiroptera. Answer the following questions about these mammals in your lab report:

a. Cetaceans, such as whales and dolphins, are marine mammals. Except for a few bristles, cetaceans are hairless. Why do you think cetaceans are classified as mammals? How do they survive without hair or fur?

b. Some mammals—including some members of Edentata (anteaters and armadillos) and Philodota (pangolins)—lack teeth. What characteristics do these animals share with other mammals?

c. Like many birds, chiropterans (bats) have wings, fly, and are endotherms. What characteristics distinguish these mammals from birds?

Analysis and Conclusions

1. List the characteristics that distinguish mammals from other vertebrates.

2. List several characteristics you observed that most mammals share.

3. Birds are also endotherms. What structure in birds serves the same function as hair in mammals? Explain.

4. Compare the data you collected on the teeth from different animal skulls with the diet of each of those animals. How does the type of teeth that they have help with the particular diet that each animal has?

Further Inquiry

Find out how mammalian brains are different from the brains of other vertebrates. What adaptive advantage might these differences provide mammals?

OBSERVATIONS OF ANIMAL SKULLS

Animal	Mammal?	Number of incisors	Number of canines	Number of premolars	Number of molars	Hard palate?	Jaw

unit 10

HUMAN BIOLOGY

internetconnect

SCILINKS National Science Teachers Association *sci*LINKS Internet resources are located throughout this unit.

66 *The human body is marvelous. It can move freely, act deliberately, and survive under the most variable conditions. Its construction is complex and its requirements many.* 99

From "Exploring Man," from *Behold Man: A Photographic Journey of Discovery Inside the Body,* by Lennart Nilsson in collaboration with Jan Lindberg. English translation copyright © 1974 by Albert Bonniers Förlag, Stockholm. Reprinted by permission of *Little, Brown and Company.*

Near-perfect coordination of the many organ systems enables humans to play soccer and carry out daily activities.

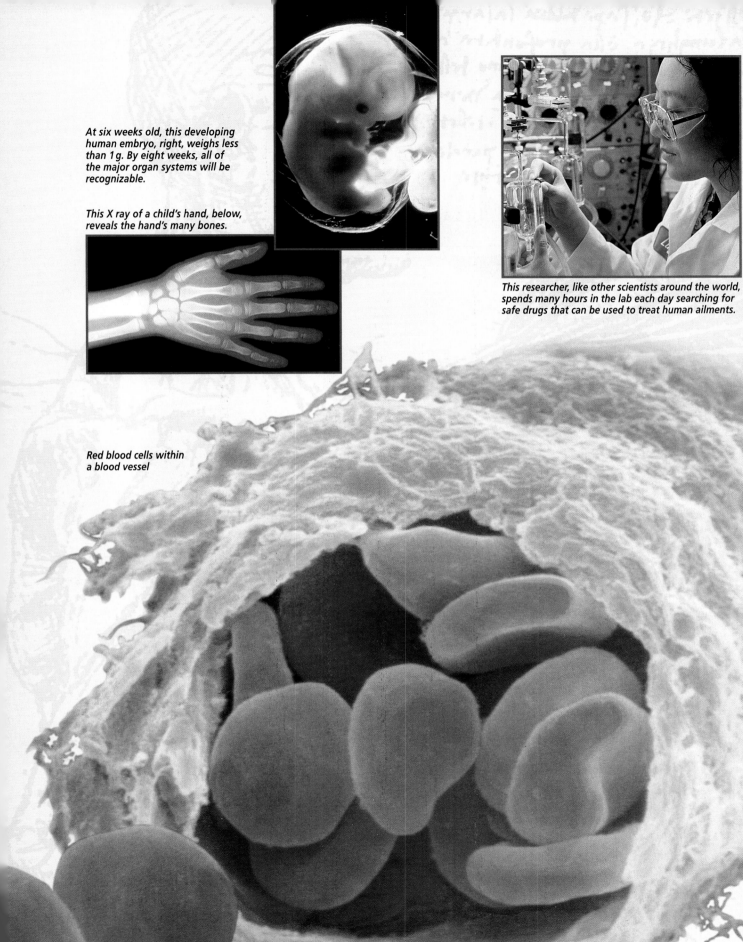

At six weeks old, this developing human embryo, right, weighs less than 1 g. By eight weeks, all of the major organ systems will be recognizable.

This X ray of a child's hand, below, reveals the hand's many bones.

This researcher, like other scientists around the world, spends many hours in the lab each day searching for safe drugs that can be used to treat human ailments.

Red blood cells within a blood vessel

SKELETAL, MUSCULAR, AND INTEGUMENTARY SYSTEMS

This X ray shows a color-enhanced image of the human skull, mandible, teeth, and neck.

FOCUS CONCEPT: *Structure and Function*

As you read about bones, muscles, and skin, note how their structures are related to their functions in the human body.

THE HUMAN BODY PLAN

SECTION

46-1

*T*he human body begins to take shape during the earliest stages of embryonic development. While the embryo is a tiny hollow ball of dividing cells, it begins forming the tissues and organs that compose the human body. By the end of its third week, the human embryo has bilateral symmetry and is developing vertebrate characteristics that will support an upright body position.

OBJECTIVES

▲

List and describe the four types of tissues that make up the human body.

●

Explain how tissues, organs, and organ systems are organized.

■

Summarize the functions of the primary organ systems in the human body.

◆

Name and locate four human body cavities, and describe the organs that each contains.

BODY TISSUES

In Chapter 4 you learned that a tissue is a collection of cells that are similar in structure and that work together to perform a particular function. The human body has four main types of tissues: muscle, nervous, epithelial, and connective.

Muscle Tissue

Muscle tissue is composed of cells that can contract. Every function that muscle tissue performs—from creating a facial expression to keeping the eyes in focus—is carried out by groups of muscle cells that contract in a coordinated fashion. The human body has three types of muscle tissue: skeletal, smooth, and cardiac. **Skeletal muscle** moves the bones in your trunk, limbs, and face. **Smooth muscle** handles body functions that you cannot control consciously, such as the movement of food through your digestive system. **Cardiac muscle,** found in your heart, pumps blood through your body. Figure 46-1a, on the following page, shows cells of skeletal muscle tissue.

Nervous Tissue

Nervous tissue contains cells that receive and transmit messages in the form of electrical impulses. These cells, called **neurons** (NOO-rahnz), are specialized to send and receive messages from muscles, glands, and other neurons throughout the body. Nervous tissue makes up your brain, spinal cord, and nerves. It is also found in parts of sensory organs, such as the retina in your eye. Nervous tissue provides sensation of the internal and external environment, and it integrates sensory information. Coordination of voluntary and involuntary activities and regulation of some body processes are also accomplished by nervous tissue. Figure 46-1b, on the following page, shows cells of nervous tissue.

internet**connect**

SC*LINKS*
NSTA

TOPIC: Tissues
GO TO: www.scilinks.org
KEYWORD: HM905

(a) MUSCLE TISSUE

(b) NERVOUS TISSUE

(c) EPITHELIAL TISSUE

(d) CONNECTIVE TISSUE

FIGURE 46-1

These four drawings show representative cells of the four main types of tissues in the human body: (a) muscle tissue, (b) nervous tissue, (c) epithelial tissue, and (d) connective tissue.

Epithelial Tissue

Epithelial (ep-uh-THEE-lee-uhl) **tissue** consists of layers of cells that line or cover all internal and external body surfaces. Each epithelial layer is formed from cells that are tightly bound together, providing a protective barrier for these surfaces. Epithelial tissue is found in various thicknesses and arrangements, depending on where it is located. For example, the epithelial tissue that lines blood vessels is a single layer of flattened cells through which substances can easily pass, but the epithelial tissue that lines the windpipe consists of a layer of cilia-bearing cells and mucus-secreting cells that act together to trap inhaled particles. The most easily observed epithelial tissue, the body's outer layer of skin, consists of sheets of dead, flattened cells that cover and protect the underlying living layer of skin. Figure 46-1c shows cells of epithelial tissue.

Connective Tissue

Connective tissue binds, supports, and protects structures in the body. Connective tissues are the most abundant and diverse of the four types of tissue, and include bone, cartilage, tendons, fat, blood, and lymph. These tissues are characterized by cells that are embedded in large amounts of an intercellular substance called **matrix.** Matrix can be solid, semisolid, or liquid. Bone cells are surrounded by a hard, crystalline matrix containing the mineral calcium. The cells in cartilage, tendons, and fat are surrounded by a semisolid fibrous matrix. Blood and lymph cells are suspended in a liquid matrix. Figure 46-1d shows cells of connective tissue.

ORGANS AND ORGAN SYSTEMS

An organ consists of various tissues that work together to carry out a specific function. The stomach, a saclike organ in which food is mixed with digestive enzymes, is composed of the four types of tissues. A single organ, such as the stomach, usually does not function in isolation. Rather, groups of organs interact in an organ system. For example, in the digestive system, the stomach, small intestine, liver, and pancreas all work together to break down food into molecules the body can use for energy. Table 46-1 lists the body's organ systems and names their major structures and functions. As you study the table, think about the ways in which the different organ systems work together to function in an efficient, integrated manner.

TABLE 46-1 **Summary of Organ Systems**

System	Major structures	Functions
Skeletal	bones	provides structure; supports and protects internal organs
Muscular	muscles (skeletal, cardiac, and smooth)	provides structure; supports and moves trunk and limbs; moves substances through body
Integumentary	skin, hair, nails	protects against pathogens; helps regulate body temperature
Cardiovascular	heart, blood vessels, blood	transports nutrients and wastes to and from all body tissues
Respiratory	air passages, lungs	carries air into and out of lungs, where gases (oxygen and carbon dioxide) are exchanged
Immune	lymph nodes and vessels, white blood cells	provides protection against infection and disease
Digestive	mouth, esophagus, stomach, liver, pancreas, small and large intestines	stores and digests food; absorbs nutrients; eliminates waste
Excretory	kidneys, ureters, bladder, urethra, skin, lungs	eliminates waste; maintains water and chemical balance
Nervous	brain, spinal cord, nerves, sense organs, receptors	controls and coordinates body movements and senses; controls consciousness and creativity; helps monitor and maintain other body systems
Endocrine	glands (such as adrenal, thyroid, and pancreas), hypothalamus	maintains homeostasis; regulates metabolism, water and mineral balance, growth and sexual development, and reproduction
Reproductive	ovaries, uterus, mammary glands (in females), testes (in males)	produces ova and milk in females, sperm in males, and offspring after fertilization

Cranial cavity

Spinal cavity

Thoracic cavity

Diaphragm

Abdominal cavity

FIGURE 46-2

The human body has four main cavities that house and protect delicate internal organs.

Integration of Organ Systems

An even higher level of organization is the integration of organ systems. Each organ system has organs associated with it according to the organ's primary function. However, the boundaries are not always well defined. For example, nearly all of the juices produced by the pancreas are designed to aid in digestion. But because the pancreas produces vitally important hormones, it is also considered a component of the endocrine system. Each organ system carries out its own specific function, but for the organism to survive, the organ systems must work together. For example, nutrients from the digestive system are distributed by the circulatory system. The efficiency of the circulatory system depends on nutrients from the digestive system and oxygen from the respiratory system. An organism, whether it is a worm, a bird, or a human, is much more than an assembly of tissues. It is an integrated, whole being.

BODY CAVITIES

Many organs and organ systems in the human body are housed in compartments called body cavities. These cavities protect delicate internal organs from injuries and from the daily wear and tear of walking, jumping, or running. The body cavities also permit organs such as the lungs, the urinary bladder, and the stomach to expand and contract while remaining securely supported. As shown in Figure 46-2, the human body has four main body cavities, each of which contains one or more organs. The **cranial cavity** encases the brain. The **spinal cavity,** extending from the cranial cavity to the base of the spine, surrounds the spinal cord.

The two main cavities in the trunk of the human body are separated by a wall of muscle called the **diaphragm** (DIE-uh-FRAM). The upper compartment, or **thoracic** (thoh-RAS-ik) **cavity,** contains the heart, the esophagus, and the organs of the respiratory system—the lungs, trachea, and bronchii. The lower compartment, or **abdominal** (ab-DAHM-uh-nuhl) **cavity,** contains organs of the digestive, reproductive, and excretory systems.

SECTION 46-1 REVIEW

1. Name the four types of tissues in the human body, and give an example of each.

2. How do muscle tissue and nervous tissue differ?

3. How are bone, cartilage, tendons, fat, blood, and lymph tissues structurally similar?

4. How are tissues, organs, and organ systems organized in the body?

5. Locate the thoracic and abdominal cavities, and describe the organs each cavity contains. What structure separates these cavities from each other?

6. **CRITICAL THINKING** Describe how the skeletal, muscular, nervous, respiratory, and circulatory systems function in a person swimming laps in a pool.

SKELETAL SYSTEM

The adult human body consists of approximately 206 bones, which are organized into an internal framework called the **skeleton.** *Because the human skeleton is an internal structure, biologists refer to it as an endoskeleton. The variation in size and shape among the bones that make up the skeleton reflects their different roles in the body.*

THE SKELETON

As shown in Figure 46-3, the human skeleton is composed of two parts—the axial skeleton and the appendicular skeleton. The bones of the skull, ribs, spine, and sternum form the **axial skeleton.** The bones of the arms and legs, along with the scapula, clavicle, and pelvis, make up the **appendicular** (AP-uhn-DIK-yuh-luhr) **skeleton.**

OBJECTIVES

▲

Distinguish between the axial skeleton and the appendicular skeleton.

●

Explain the function and structure of bones.

■

Summarize how bones develop and elongate.

◆

List three types of joints, and give an example of each.

▲

Describe a common disorder that affects the skeletal system.

Cranium
Maxilla
Mandible
Cervical vertebrae
Clavicle
Scapula
Sternum
Ribs
Humerus
Lumbar vertebrae
Radius
Ulna
Pelvis
Carpals
Metacarpals
Phalanges
Sacral vertebrae
Pubis
Femur
Patella
Tibia
Fibula
Tarsals
Metatarsals
Phalanges

Cervical vertebrae (7)

Thoracic vertebrae (12)

Lumbar vertebrae (5)

Sacral vertebrae (5)

Coccyx

(a) HUMAN SKELETON

(b) HUMAN SPINE

FIGURE 46-3

(a) The skeleton is the framework on which the rest of the body is built. (b) Like a stack of segmented tubes, the vertebrae of the spinal column offer strong protection for the spinal cord, yet they permit the trunk to bend and twist.

The bones that make up the skeleton function in a variety of ways. Bones provide a rigid framework against which muscles can pull, give shape and structure to the body, and support and protect delicate internal organs. Notice, for example, that the ribs curve to form a cage that contains the heart and lungs. Similarly, bones in the skull form the cranium, a dome-shaped case that protects the brain. Bones also store minerals, such as calcium and phosphorus, which play vital roles in important metabolic processes. In addition, the internal portion of many bones produces red blood cells and certain types of white blood cells.

BONE STRUCTURE

Despite their number and size, bones make up less than 20 percent of the body's mass. The reason for their having relatively little mass can be better understood by looking at bone structure. Bones are not dry, rigid structures, as they may appear in a museum exhibit. They are moist, living tissues. As shown in Figure 46-4, a long bone consists of a porous central canal surrounded by a ring of dense material. The bone's surface is covered by a tough membrane called the **periosteum** (PER-ee-AHS-tee-uhm). This membrane contains a network of blood vessels, which supply nutrients, and nerves, which signal pain.

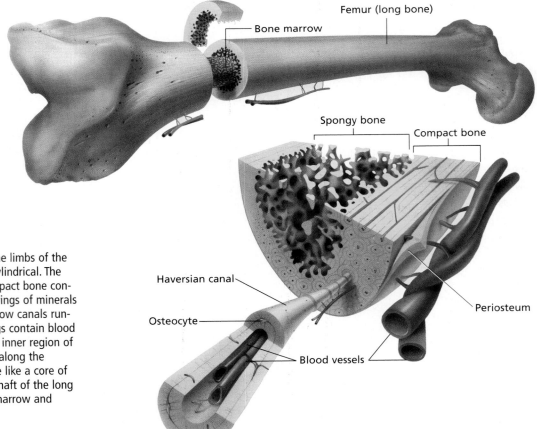

Femur (long bone)

Bone marrow

Spongy bone

Compact bone

Haversian canal

Osteocyte

Blood vessels

Periosteum

FIGURE 46-4

Long bones, found in the limbs of the body, are hollow and cylindrical. The outer shell of hard compact bone consists of closely packed rings of minerals and protein fibers. Narrow canals running through these rings contain blood vessels and nerves. The inner region of spongy bone stretches along the length of the long bone like a core of rigid lace. The central shaft of the long bone contains yellow marrow and blood vessels.

(a) COMPACT BONE

Mineral rings (lamellae)

Osteocytes

Periosteum

Vein

Artery

Haversian canals

(b) HAVERSIAN CANAL

Under the periosteum is a hard material called **compact bone.** A thick layer of compact bone enables the shaft of the long bone to endure the large amount of stress it receives upon impact with a solid object. In the cross section shown in Figure 46-5a, notice that compact bone is composed of cylinders of mineral crystals and protein fibers called lamellae. In the center of each cylinder is a narrow channel called a **Haversian** (huh-VER-shuhn) **canal,** as shown in Figure 46-5b. Blood vessels run through interconnected Haversian canals, creating a network that carries nourishment to the living bone tissue. Several layers of protein fibers wrap around each Haversian canal. Embedded within the gaps between the protein layers are living bone cells called **osteocytes** (AHS-tee-uh-SIETS).

Inside the compact bone is a network of connective tissue called **spongy bone.** Although its name suggests that it is soft, this tissue is hard and strong. As shown in Figure 46-4, spongy bone has a lattice-work structure that consists of bony spikes. It is arranged along points of pressure or stress, making bones both light and strong.

Many bones also contain a soft tissue called **bone marrow,** which can be either red or yellow. Red bone marrow—found in spongy bone, the ends of long bones, ribs, vertebrae, the sternum, and the pelvis—produces red blood cells and certain types of white blood cells. Yellow bone marrow fills the shafts of long bones. It consists mostly of fat cells and serves as an energy reserve. It can also be converted to red bone marrow and produce blood cells when severe blood loss occurs.

Injury and Repair

Despite their strength, bones will crack or even break if they are subjected to extreme loads, sudden impacts, or stresses from unusual directions. The crack or break is referred to as a **fracture.** If circulation is maintained and the periosteum survives, healing will occur even if the damage to the bone is severe.

FIGURE 46-5

The cross section in (a) shows the internal structure of compact bone. A micrograph of a Haversian canal (380×) surrounded by lamellae in compact bone is shown in (b).

Eco Connection

Bones of Lead

Millions of Americans have been exposed to lead in the environment. Following exposure to lead, the kidneys excrete most of the metal. But 7 to 10 percent of the remaining lead in the body is stored in bone and can stay there for a lifetime. The rapid bone uptake of lead acts as a detoxifying mechanism. But lead is not permanently locked in bone. As people age, bone degeneration may occur, releasing lead into the bloodstream. Even very small concentrations of lead in the bloodstream can cause damage to kidneys, which in turn can cause high blood pressure.

The United States has outlawed the addition of lead to gasoline, water pipes, and paint. As a result, people who are now under age 25 may not accumulate as much lead in their bones as people from earlier generations.

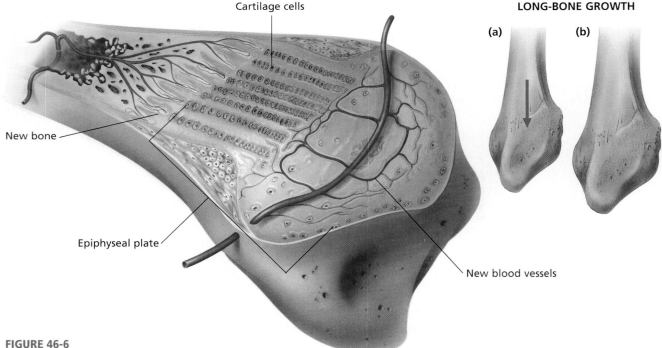

Cartilage cells

LONG-BONE GROWTH

(a)   (b)

New bone

Epiphyseal plate

New blood vessels

FIGURE 46-6

The epiphyseal plate, found at the ends of long bones, such as the femur shown above, is the site of bone elongation. This region is rich with cartilage cells, which divide, enlarge, and push older cells toward the middle of the bone shaft. As older cells move back, they are replaced by new bone cells, forming new regions of bone. A long bone (a) will grow in length, circumference, and density in this manner, as shown in (b).

BONE DEVELOPMENT

Most bones develop from cartilage, a tough but flexible connective tissue. In the second month of fetal development, much of the skeleton is made of cartilage. During the third month, osteocytes begin to develop and release minerals that lodge in the spaces between the cartilage cells, turning the cartilage to bone. The process by which cartilage slowly hardens into bone as a result of the deposition of minerals is called **ossification** (AHS-uh-fuh-KAY-shuhn). Most fetal cartilage is eventually replaced by bone. However, some cartilage remains, lending flexibility to the areas between bones, at the end of the nose, in the outer ear, and along the inside of the trachea.

A few bones, such as some parts of the skull, develop directly into hard bone without forming cartilage first. In these cases, the osteocytes are initially scattered randomly throughout the embryonic connective tissue but soon fuse into layers and become flat plates of bone. In the skull, suture lines can be seen where the plates of bone meet.

Bone Elongation

Bones continue to develop after a person's birth. Between early childhood and late adolescence, bone cells gradually replace the cartilage in long bones of limbs, such as the arms and legs. Bone elongation takes place near the ends of long bones in an area known as the **epiphyseal** (EP-uh-FIZ-ee-uhl) **plate.** As shown in Figure 46-6, the epiphyseal plate is composed of cartilage cells that divide and form columns, pushing older cells toward the middle of the bone. As these older cells die, they are replaced by new bone cells.

Growth continues until bone has replaced all the cartilage in the epiphyseal plate. At this point, bones no longer elongate, and a person is considered to have reached full height.

JOINTS

The place where two bones meet is known as a **joint.** Three kinds of joints are found in the human body—fixed, semimovable, and movable. Examples of these joints are shown in Figure 46-7.

Joint Function

Fixed joints prevent movement. They are found in the skull, where they securely connect the bony plates and permit no movement of those bones. A small amount of connective tissue in a fixed joint helps absorb impact to prevent the bones from breaking.

Semimovable joints permit limited movement. For example, semimovable joints hold the bones of the vertebral column in place and allow the body to bend and twist. The vertebrae of the spine are separated by disks of cartilaginous tissue. These tough, springy disks compress and absorb shocks that could damage the fragile spinal cord. Semimovable joints are also found in the rib cage, where long strands of cartilage connect the upper seven pairs of ribs to the sternum, allowing the chest to expand during breathing.

Most of the joints in the body are **movable joints.** These joints enable the body to perform a wide range of movements and activities. Movable joints include hinge, ball-and-socket, pivot, saddle, and gliding joints. An example of a **hinge joint** is found in the elbow, which allows you to move your forearm forward and backward, like a hinged door. An example of a **ball-and-socket joint** is the shoulder joint, which enables you to move your arm up, down, forward, and backward, as well as to rotate it in a complete circle. The joint formed by the top two vertebrae of your spine is an example of a **pivot joint;** it allows you to turn your head from side to side, as when shaking your head "no." The **saddle joint,** found at the base of each thumb, allows you to rotate your thumbs and helps you grasp objects with your hand. Finally, **gliding joints** allow bones to slide over one another. Examples are the joints between the small bones of your foot, which allow your foot to flex when you walk.

Joint Structure

Joints, such as the knee, are often subjected to a great deal of pressure and stress, but their structure is well suited to meet these demands. As in all movable joints, the parts of the bones that come in contact with each other are covered with cartilage, which protects the bones' surface from friction. Tough bands of connective tissue, called **ligaments,** hold the bones of the joint in place. The surfaces of the joints that are subjected to a great deal of pressure are lined with tissue that secretes a lubricating substance called

Fixed joint
Pivot joint
Semimovable joints
Hinge joint
Saddle joint
Ball-and-socket joint
Gliding joint

FIGURE 46-7

In addition to fixed joints and semimovable joints, the human body has five types of movable joints: pivot, hinge, saddle, ball-and-socket, and gliding.

FIGURE 46-8

The knee is a movable joint formed by the ends of the femur and the fibula. Many cordlike ligaments stabilize the joint, especially during movement. Pads of cartilage protect the ends of bones and act as shock absorbers. Like many joints in the body, the knee is a synovial joint. It contains membranes that secrete synovial fluid, which lubricates and nourishes the tissues inside the joint.

Cartilage

Ligament

Fibula

Femur

Patella

Synovial fluid

Tibia

synovial (sih-NOH-vee-uhl) **fluid.** Synovial fluid helps protect the ends of bones from damage by friction. Figure 46-8 shows the internal structures of the synovial knee joint.

Sometimes these protective structures are not enough to prevent a joint from becoming injured. Of all the joints in the body, the knee joint is the most susceptible to injury because it carries the body's weight and relies on many ligaments for stability.

The term *arthritis* is used to describe several types of disorders that cause painful, swollen joints. There are two forms of arthritis that affect joints. **Rheumatoid arthritis** develops when the immune system begins to attack body tissues. The joints become inflamed, swollen, stiff, and deformed. **Osteoarthritis** is a degenerative joint disease in which the cartilage covering the surface of bone becomes thinner and rougher. As a result, bone surfaces rub against each other, causing severe discomfort.

SECTION 46-2 REVIEW

1. Name the two main parts of the human skeleton, and list the bones that form them.

2. What are five functions of bones?

3. How do compact bone and spongy bone differ in structure and function?

4. When do most of the bones in the body begin to ossify? When does this process end?

5. What are the three major types of joints in the human body? Describe the function of each type and give an example.

6. CRITICAL THINKING What is the advantage of a cartilaginous skeleton during prenatal development?

MUSCULAR SYSTEM

*M*uscles make up the bulk of the body and account for about one-third of its weight. Their ability to contract not only enables the body to move, but also provides the force that pushes substances, such as blood and food, through the body. Without the muscular system, none of the other organ systems would be able to function.

SECTION

46-3

OBJECTIVES

▲

Distinguish between the three types of muscle tissues.

●

Describe the structure of skeletal muscle fibers.

■

Explain how skeletal muscles contract.

◆

Explain how muscles move bones.

MUSCLE TYPES

A muscle is tissue that can contract in a coordinated fashion and includes muscle tissue, blood vessels, nerves, and connective tissue. Recall that the human body has three types of muscle tissues: skeletal, smooth, and cardiac.

Skeletal muscle is responsible for moving parts of the body, such as the limbs, trunk, and face. Skeletal muscle tissue is made up of elongated cells called **muscle fibers.** Each muscle fiber contains many nuclei and is crossed by light and dark stripes, called **striations,** as shown on the following page in Figure 46-10a. Skeletal muscle fibers are grouped into dense bundles called **fascicles.** A

Frontalis
Trapezius
Deltoid
Pectoralis major
Triceps brachii
Biceps brachii
Latissimus dorsi
Abdominal muscles
Gluteus maximus
Sartorius
Biceps femoris
Rectus femoris
Gastrocnemius
Achilles tendon

FIGURE 46-9

Skeletal muscle tissue is shown in these diagrams of some of the major muscles in the human body.

(a) SKELETAL MUSCLE TISSUE

(b) SMOOTH MUSCLE TISSUE

(c) CARDIAC MUSCLE TISSUE

FIGURE 46-10

These light micrographs show the three types of muscle tissue. Skeletal muscle tissue (a) has a striped appearance when viewed under a microscope (430✕). Smooth muscle tissue (b) is found in the digestive tract, the uterus, the bladder, and the blood vessels (400✕). Cardiac muscle tissue (c) is found only in the heart (270✕). Its interconnected fibers allow impulses to spread rapidly.

group of fascicles are bound together by connective tissue to form a muscle. Because their contractions can usually be consciously controlled, skeletal muscles are described as **voluntary muscles.**

Smooth muscle forms the muscle layers found in the walls of the stomach, intestines, blood vessels, and other internal organs. Individual smooth muscle cells are spindle-shaped, have a single nucleus, and interlace to form sheets of smooth muscle tissue, as shown in Figure 46-10b. Notice that smooth muscle lacks the striations found in skeletal muscle tissue. Smooth muscle fibers are surrounded by connective tissue, but the connective tissue does not unite to form tendons as it does in skeletal muscles. Because most of its movements cannot be consciously controlled, smooth muscle is referred to as **involuntary muscle.**

Cardiac muscle, shown in Figure 46-10c, makes up the walls of the heart. Cardiac muscle shares some characteristics with both skeletal muscle and smooth muscle. As with skeletal muscle, cardiac muscle tissue is striated; as with smooth muscle, it is involuntary and each cell has one nucleus. A bundle of specialized muscle cells in the upper part of the heart sends electrical signals through cardiac muscle tissue, causing the heart to rhythmically contract and pump blood throughout the body.

MUSCLE STRUCTURE

A muscle fiber is a single, multinucleated muscle cell. A muscle may be made up of hundreds or even thousands of muscle fibers, depending on the muscle's size. Although muscle fibers make up most of the muscle tissue, a large amount of connective tissue, blood vessels, and nerves are also present. Like all body cells, muscle cells are soft and easy to injure. Connective tissue covers and supports each muscle fiber and reinforces the muscle as a whole.

The health of a muscle depends on a sufficient nerve and blood supply. Each skeletal muscle fiber has a nerve ending that controls its activity. Active muscles use a lot of energy and therefore require a continuous supply of oxygen and nutrients, which are supplied by arteries. Muscles produce large amounts of metabolic waste that must be removed through veins.

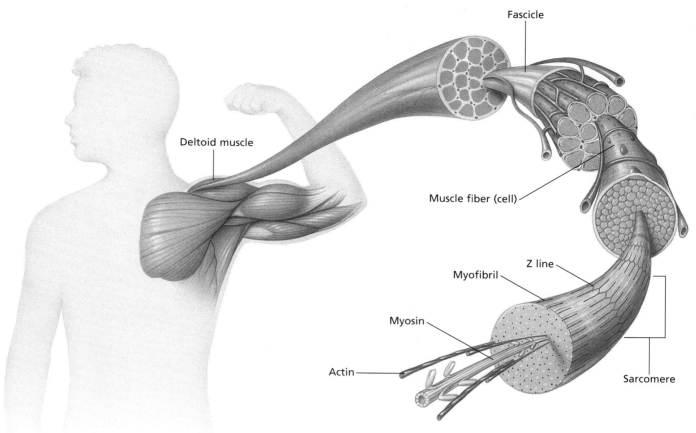

Fascicle

Deltoid muscle

Muscle fiber (cell)

Z line

Myofibril

Myosin

Actin

Sarcomere

FIGURE 46-11

Skeletal muscles consist of densely packed groups of elongated cells, called fascicles, that are held together by connective tissue. Muscle fibers consist of protein filaments called myofibrils. Two types of filaments are found in muscle fibers—actin and myosin. The complementary structures of actin and myosin interact to contract and relax muscles.

A muscle fiber, such as the one shown in Figure 46-11, consists of bundles of threadlike structures called **myofibrils** (MIE-oh-FIE-bruhlz). Each myofibril is made up of two types of protein filaments—thick ones and thin ones. Thick filaments are made of the protein **myosin** (MIE-uh-suhn), and thin filaments are made of the protein **actin.** Myosin and actin filaments are arranged to form an overlapping pattern, which gives muscle tissue its striated appearance. Thin actin filaments are anchored at their endpoints to a structure called the **Z line.** The region from one Z line to the next is called a **sarcomere** (SAHR-kuh-MIR).

Muscular Contraction

The sarcomere is the functional unit of muscle contraction. When a muscle contracts, myosin filaments and actin filaments interact to shorten the length of a sarcomere. Myosin filaments have extensions shaped like oval "heads." Actin filaments look like a twisted strand of beads. When a nerve impulse stimulates a muscle fiber to contract, the heads at the end of the myosin filaments attach to points between the beads of the actin filaments. The myosin heads then bend inward, pulling the actin filaments with them. The myosin heads then let go, bend back into their original position, attach to a new point on the actin filament, and pull again. This action shortens the length of the

FIGURE 46-12

In a relaxed muscle, the actin and myosin filaments overlap. During a muscle contraction, the filaments slide past each other and the zone of overlap increases. As a result, the length of the sarcomere shortens.

sarcomere. The synchronized shortening of sarcomeres along the full length of a muscle fiber causes the whole fiber, and hence the muscle, to contract. Figure 46-12 shows the structures of the sarcomere.

Like all cellular activities, muscle contraction requires energy, which is supplied by ATP. This energy is used to detach the myosin heads from the actin filaments. Because myosin heads must attach and detach a number of times during a single muscle contraction, muscle cells must have a continuous supply of ATP. Without ATP, the myosin heads would remain attached to the actin filaments, keeping a muscle permanently contracted.

Muscle contraction is an all-or-none response—either the fibers contract or they remain relaxed. How, then, are you able to contract your muscles tightly enough to lift a dumbbell or gently enough to lift a pen? The force of a muscle contraction is determined by the number of muscle fibers that are stimulated. As more fibers are activated, the force of the contraction increases.

Some muscles, such as the muscles that hold the body in an upright position and maintain posture, are nearly always at least partially contracted. However, prolonged contraction may cause the muscle to use up all its available energy, become overly tired, and begin to cramp. To prevent this from happening, the nervous system automatically stimulates different muscle fibers alternately in the muscle, allowing some to be at rest while others are working to maintain the body's posture.

MUSCULAR MOVEMENT OF BONES

Generally, skeletal muscles are attached to one end of a bone, stretch across a joint, and are fastened to the end of another bone. Muscles are attached to the outer membrane of bone, either directly or by a tough fibrous cord of connective tissue called a **tendon.** For example, as shown in Figure 46-13, one end of the large biceps muscle in the arm is connected by tendons to the radius and ulna in the forearm, while the other end of the muscle is connected to the scapula in the shoulder. When the biceps muscle contracts, the forearm flexes upward while the scapula remains stationary. The point where the muscle attaches to the stationary bone—in this case, the scapula—is called the **origin.** The point where the muscle attaches to the moving bone—in this case the bones in the forearm—is called the **insertion.**

Most skeletal muscles are arranged in opposing pairs. One muscle in a pair moves a limb in one direction; the other muscle moves it in the opposite direction. Muscles move bones by pulling them, not by pushing them. For example, when the biceps muscle contracts, the elbow bends. The biceps muscle is known as a **flexor,** a muscle that bends a joint. Contraction of the triceps muscle in the upper arm straightens the limb. The triceps muscle is an example of an **extensor,** a muscle that straightens a joint. To bring about a smooth movement, one muscle in a pair must relax while the opposing muscle contracts.

FIGURE 46-13

Skeletal muscles, such as the biceps and triceps muscles in the upper arm, are connected to bones by tendons. (a) When the biceps muscle contracts, the elbow bends. (b) When the triceps muscle contracts, the elbow straightens.

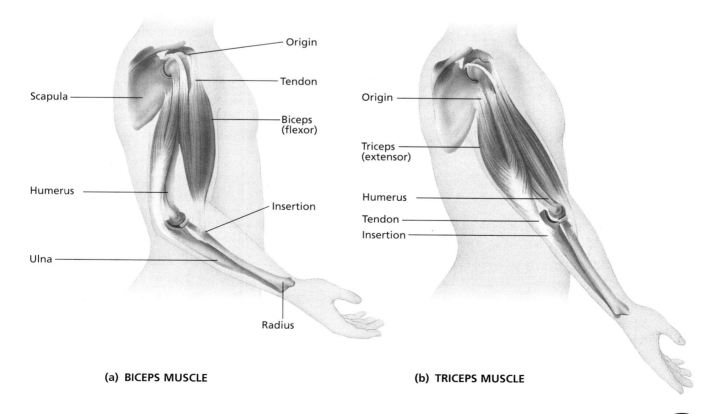

(a) BICEPS MUSCLE

(b) TRICEPS MUSCLE

MUSCLE FATIGUE

Muscle cells store glycogen, which is used as a source of energy after blood-delivered glucose is exhausted. The breakdown of glycogen releases large amounts of energy, but sometimes even those reserves are used up, especially in athletes who participate in sports that require sustained exertion. During prolonged and vigorous exertion, fat molecules are utilized for energy. Fat molecules contain a greater concentration of potential energy than any other molecule in the body. When energy availability fails to keep pace with its use, muscle fatigue sets in and controlled muscle activity ceases, even though the muscle may still receive nerve stimulation to move. **Muscle fatigue** is the physiological inability of a muscle to contract. Muscle fatigue is a result of a relative depletion of ATP. When ATP is absent, a state of continuous contraction occurs. An example of depletion of ATP is when a marathon runner collapses during a race, suffering from severe muscle cramps.

Oxygen Debt

Oxygen is used during cellular respiration in the synthesis of ATP. Large amounts of oxygen are needed to maintain the rate of maximum ATP production required to sustain strenuous exercise. However, after several minutes of exertion, the circulatory system and the respiratory system are not able to bring in enough oxygen to meet the demands of energy production. Oxygen levels in the body become depleted. This temporary lack of oxygen availability is called **oxygen debt.** Oxygen debt leads to an accumulation of metabolic wastes in the muscle fibers. The presence of this waste produces the soreness you may experience after prolonged exercise. Oxygen debt is what causes an athlete to spend a minute or two in rapid, deep breathing after strenuous exercise, as the athletes shown in Figure 46-14 are doing. The oxygen debt is repaid quickly as additional oxygen becomes available, but muscle soreness may persist until all of the metabolic wastes that have accumulated in the muscle fibers are carried away or converted.

internetconnect

SCI
LINKS.
NSTA

TOPIC: Muscle fatigue
GO TO: www.scilinks.org
KEYWORD: HM920

FIGURE 46-14

These athletes are in the process of repaying their oxygen debts. Oxygen debt occurs frequently after strenuous, sustained exertion.

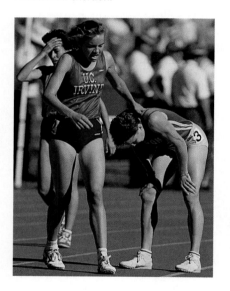

SECTION 46-3 REVIEW

1. What are the three main types of muscle tissues found in the body, and what are their functions?

2. Why is smooth muscle referred to as involuntary muscle?

3. What is a muscle fiber? Why does it appear striated?

4. What are actin and myosin, and how are they organized in a muscle? How do they interact during a muscle contraction?

5. How do muscle pairs work together to move a limb?

6. **CRITICAL THINKING** Rigor mortis is a condition in which all the body muscles become rigid shortly after a person dies. Why does rigor mortis develop?

Looking Inside the Human Body

In 1895, the development of X-ray equipment provided physicians a way to look inside the body at images of dense tissue, such as bones. Modern imaging techniques rely on computers. For example, computerized tomography (CT) uses a focused beam of low-dose X rays to obtain cross-sectional images of structures in the body. Tomography is the X-ray technique used to image only a specific "slice" or plane of tissue. Computerized tomography can differentiate tissues of various densities. Another technology, magnetic resonance imaging (MRI), creates images of soft tissues by using radio waves emitted by the nuclei of hydrogen atoms activated by a magnetic scanner.

Still another and newer imaging technology is positron emission technology, or PET. Positrons are positively charged particles that result from the disintegration of radioisotopes. Michael M. TerPogossian and his colleagues at Johns Hopkins suggested using short-lived radioisotopes in medical research in 1966. They then developed scanners to detect the positrons released by radioisotopes that had been injected into a patient's bloodstream. As electronic and computer technology improved, biomedical engineers redesigned scanning equipment to create three-dimensional images from the positron emissions. Positron emission technology is often used in evaluating brain metabolism. It is also used to map areas of the brain involved in memory, sensation, perception, speech, and information processing. In addition, positron emission technology provides clues to the physiological and neurochemical basis of medical psychiatric disorders, such as depression.

A new holographic imaging system combines images obtained by computerized tomography or magnetic resonance scanners and displays an accurate three-dimensional image of the anatomical structures being viewed. A holograph is a method of photography that uses laser light. A three-dimensional image is produced when the holograph is viewed under visible light. The transparent but solid-seeming image floats in front of the holographic film and can be moved around or reversed so that it can be studied from all sides. Computer point-and-click methods allow viewers to focus on specific areas of the image. Physicians can make surgical plans by studying the actual appearance of a patient's organs, as shown in the 3-D PET scan of a brain that highlights the verbal center in (a). Compare the 3-D PET scan with the X ray of the same part of the body in (b). The X ray may not be as helpful as the 3-D PET scan is when a physician must diagnose an illness or injury of the brain.

Some of the newest techniques are interactive. On the Internet, for example, medical students and researchers can view a "Visible Man" made up of thousands of computerized tomography cross sections. They can use the images to test theories or study the relationships of various anatomical structures. An explosion in technology has provided medicine with new techniques, such as virtual reality. Virtual reality is a computer simulation of a system that allows the user to perform operations on the system and that shows the effects of those operations. Doctors are beginning to use virtual reality to navigate through a patient's computerized tomography images when planning for surgery or other treatments.

(a) 3-D PET SCAN

(b) X RAY

46-4

Describe the functions of the skin.

Distinguish between the two layers that form the skin.

Compare the structure of hair with that of nails.

Identify two types of glands found in the skin, and describe their functions.

INTEGUMENTARY SYSTEM

The integumentary system, consisting of the skin, hair, and nails, acts as a barrier to protect the body from the outside world. It also functions to retain body fluids, protect against disease, eliminate waste products, and regulate body temperature.

SKIN

The skin is one of the human body's largest organs. Subjected to a lifetime of wear and tear, the layers of skin are capable of repairing themselves. Skin contains sensory devices that monitor the external environment, and mechanisms that rid the body of wastes. The skin is composed of two layers—the epidermis and the dermis.

Epidermis

The **epidermis,** or outer layer of skin, is composed of many sheets of flattened, scaly epithelial cells. Its layers are made of mostly dead cells. These cells are exposed to the dangers of the external environment. Scraped or rubbed away on a daily basis, they are replaced by new cells made in the rapidly dividing lower layers. The cells of the epidermis are filled with a protein called **keratin,** which gives skin its rough, leathery texture and its waterproof quality.

There is a great variety in skin color among humans. The color of skin is mainly determined by a brown pigment called **melanin** (MEL-uh-nin), which is produced by cells in the lower layers of the epidermis. Melanin absorbs harmful ultraviolet radiation. The amount of melanin produced in skin depends on two factors: heredity and the length of time the skin is exposed to ultraviolet radiation. Increased amounts of melanin in a person's skin occurs in response to injury of the skin by ultraviolet radiation. All people, but especially people with light skin, need to minimize exposure to the sun and protect themselves from its ultraviolet radiation, which can damage the DNA in skin cells and lead to deadly forms of skin cancer.

Dermis

The **dermis,** the inner layer of skin, is composed of living cells and many kinds of specialized structures, such as sensory neurons, blood vessels, muscle fibers, hair follicles, and glands. Sensory neurons make it possible for you to sense many kinds of conditions and signals from the environment, such as heat and pressure. Blood vessels provide nourishment to the living cells and help regulate body

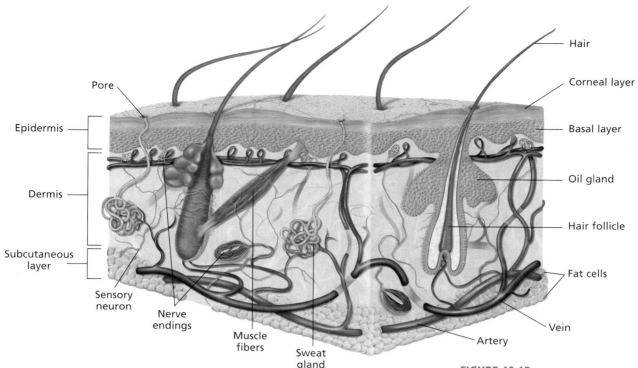

temperature. Tiny muscle fibers attached to hair follicles contract and pull hair upright when you are cold or afraid, producing what are commonly called goose bumps. Glands produce sweat, which helps cool your body, and oil, which helps soften your skin. A layer of fat cells lies below the dermis. These cells act as energy reserves; add a protective, shock-absorbing layer; and insulate the body against heat loss. Study the structures of the skin in Figure 46-15.

Nails and Hair

Nails, which protect the ends of the fingers and toes, form from nail roots under skin folds at their base and sides. As new cells form, the nail grows longer. Like hair, nails are composed primarily of keratin. The nail body is about 0.5 mm (0.02 in.) thick, and growth continues throughout life. Nails grow at about 1 mm (0.04 in.) per week. Nails rest on a bed of tissue filled with blood vessels, giving the nails a pinkish color. The structure of a fingernail can be seen in Figure 46-16.

Changes in the shape, structure, and appearance of the nails may be an indicator of a disease somewhere in the body. They may turn yellow in patients with chronic respiratory disorders, or they may grow concave in certain blood disorders.

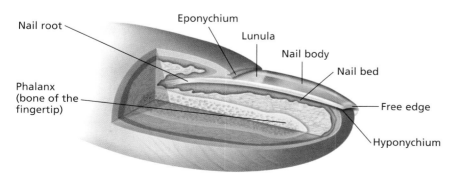

FIGURE 46-16

This illustration of the structure of a fingernail shows that the nail root, from which the nail is constantly regenerated, is protected well beneath the surface of the finger, next to the bone of the fingertip.

FIGURE 46-17

Skin acts as a temperature-controlling device. It contains millions of sweat glands that secrete microscopic droplets of water. The water droplets help cool the body when its temperature rises, such as after a rigorous workout.

Hair, which protects and insulates the body, is produced by a cluster of cells at the base of deep dermal pits called **hair follicles.** The shaft of the hair that extends beyond the skin is composed of dead, keratin-filled cells that overlap like roof shingles. Glands associated with hair follicles secrete oil, which prevents hair from drying out and breaking off. Most individual hairs grow for several years and then fall out. However, hair on the scalp can grow continuously for many years.

Hair color is the result of the presence of the pigment melanin in the hair shaft. Black, brown, and yellow variants of melanin combine in an almost infinite number of proportions to determine an individual's hair color. Hair color is influenced by hereditary factors and may vary over different areas of the body.

Glands

The skin contains **exocrine glands,** glands that release secretions through ducts. The main exocrine glands of the skin are the sweat glands and the oil glands.

The skin functions as an excretory organ by releasing excess water, salts, and urea through the **sweat glands.** By releasing excess water, the skin also helps regulate body temperature. When the body's temperature rises, circulation increases, and the skin becomes warm and flushed, as shown in Figure 46-17. The sweat glands then release sweat. As the water in sweat evaporates, the skin is cooled.

Oil glands, found in large numbers on the face and scalp, secrete a fatty substance known as **sebum.** Oil glands are usually connected by tiny ducts to hair follicles. Sebum coats the surface of the skin and the shafts of hairs, preventing excess water loss and lubricating and softening the skin and hair. Sebum is also mildly toxic to some bacteria. If the ducts of oil glands become clogged with excessive amounts of sebum, dead cells, and bacteria, the skin disorder **acne** can result. The production of sebum is controlled by hormones. During adolescence, high levels of sex hormones increase the activity of the skin's oil glands, often resulting in skin eruptions called acne. Although it is difficult to prevent, acne can sometimes be controlled with meticulous skin care.

SECTION 46-4 REVIEW

1. What are the names and functions of the two layers of skin?

2. What is melanin? Why can sunbathing be considered dangerous?

3. Why is the dermis considered the living layer of skin?

4. In what two ways are hair and nails similar?

5. What are the functions of the two types of exocrine glands found in the dermis?

6. **CRITICAL THINKING** Why are third-degree burns—which destroy the epidermis and dermis of the skin—over large regions of the body often fatal?

SUMMARY/VOCABULARY

 46-1
- A tissue is a collection of cells that work together to perform a particular function.
- The human body has four main types of tissue: muscle, nervous, epithelial, and connective.
- An organ consists of various tissues that work together to carry out a specific function.

- An organ system is a group of organs interacting to perform a life process.
- Many organs and organ systems in the human body are housed in body cavities.

Vocabulary

abdominal cavity (908)
cardiac muscle (905)
connective tissue (906)
cranial cavity (908)

diaphragm (908)
epithelial tissue (906)
matrix (906)
muscle tissue (905)

neuron (905)
nervous tissue (905)
skeletal muscle (905)
smooth muscle (905)

spinal cavity (908)
thoracic cavity (908)

 46-2
- The human skeleton is composed of the axial skeleton (skull, ribs, spine, and sternum) and the appendicular skeleton (arms and legs, scapula, clavicle, and pelvis).
- Bones support muscles and organs, give structure to the body, protect internal organs, store minerals, and manufacture blood cells.
- Bones are made up of minerals, protein fibers, and cells called osteocytes. Most

consist of compact and spongy bone and may contain bone marrow.
- Most bones develop from cartilage through a process called ossification.
- Bone elongation occurs near the ends of long bones, at the epiphyseal plate.
- The human body has three types of joints—fixed, semimovable, and movable.

Vocabulary

appendicular skeleton (909)
axial skeleton (909)
ball-and-socket joint (913)
bone marrow (911)
compact bone (911)
epiphyseal plate (912)
fixed joint (913)

fracture (911)
gliding joint (913)
Haversian canal (911)
hinge joint (913)
joint (913)
ligament (913)
movable joint (913)

ossification (911)
osteoarthritis (914)
osteocyte (911)
periosteum (910)
pivot joint (913)
rheumatoid arthritis (914)
saddle joint (913)

semimovable joint (913)
skeleton (909)
spongy bone (911)
synovial fluid (914)

 46-3
- The human body has three types of muscle tissues—skeletal muscle, smooth muscle, and cardiac muscle.
- Skeletal muscles consist of groups of muscle fibers that contain threadlike myofibrils. Each myofibril is made up of two types of protein filaments, thin actin filaments and thick myosin filaments.

- A sarcomere is the fundamental unit of a muscle contraction. During a muscle contraction, myosin and actin filaments interact to shorten the length of a sarcomere.
- Most skeletal muscles are arranged in opposing pairs.

Vocabulary

actin (917)
extensor (919)
fascicle (915)
flexor (919)
insertion (919)

involuntary muscle (916)
muscle fatigue (920)
muscle fiber (915)
myofibril (917)
myosin (917)

origin (919)
oxygen debt (920)
sarcomere (917)
striation (915)
tendon (919)

voluntary muscle (916)
Z line (917)

46-4 ■ Skin, hair, and nails act as barriers that protect the body from the environment.

■ Skin is composed of two layers: the epidermis (composed of dead, keratin-filled cells) and the dermis (composed of living cells and a variety of structures).

■ Hair and nails are composed of the protein keratin; they grow from a bed of rapidly dividing cells.

■ Sweat glands produce sweat, which evaporates and helps cool the body. Oil glands secrete sebum, which helps soften the skin and prevents hair from drying out.

Vocabulary

acne (924)	exocrine gland (924)	melanin (922)	sebum (924)
dermis (922)	hair follicle (924)	oil gland (924)	sweat gland (924)
epidermis (922)	keratin (922)		

REVIEW

Vocabulary

1. What is epithelial tissue?
2. Distinguish between compact bone and spongy bone.
3. Describe the components of a sarcomere.
4. Describe how skeletal muscle, smooth muscle, and cardiac muscle differ.
5. What is the difference between the epidermis and the dermis?

Multiple Choice

6. The thoracic cavity contains the (a) brain (b) organs of the digestive system (c) organs of the respiratory system (d) spine.
7. The cells of connective tissue are embedded in a substance called (a) marrow (b) matrix (c) synovial fluid (d) keratin.
8. The periosteum is a membrane that (a) covers the bone (b) produces red blood cells (c) contains marrow (d) protect the ends of long bones.
9. During ossification (a) cartilage replaces bone cells (b) bones become more porous (c) bone replaces cartilage (d) marrow is produced.
10. Hinge joints allow (a) gliding movement (b) circular movement (c) no movement (d) back-and-forth movement.
11. Cardiac muscle is (a) voluntary muscle (b) involuntary muscle (c) a type of smooth muscle (d) found in the lungs.
12. Actin and myosin are types of protein found in (a) cartilage (b) bone cells (c) hair and nails (d) muscle cells.
13. Red bone marrow (a) acts as an energy reserve (b) cushions the ends of bones (c) produces red and white blood cells (d) contains melanin.
14. The bones of a joint are held in place by (a) tendons (b) the epiphyseal plate (c) sarcomeres (d) ligaments.
15. The dermis (a) contains nerves and blood vessels (b) contains keratin (c) is the top layer of skin (d) is made up of dead cells.

Short Answer

16. Identify the structure in the figure below. Describe the components of this structure, and explain how it changes during a muscle contraction.

17. What is the relationship between cells and organ systems?

18. What is a body cavity? What organs are found in the abdominal cavity?

19. What are five functions of the skeletal system?

20. Explain the role Haversian canals play in compact bone.

21. What is red bone marrow? Where is it produced and what is its function?

22. Describe the cause and symptoms of the disease rheumatoid arthritis.

23. Compare the functions of tendons and ligaments.

24. What substance prevents the hair and skin from drying out? Where is this substance produced?

25. What is melanin? What is its role in the body?

CRITICAL THINKING

1. Young thoroughbred horses that are raced too early in life have an increased risk of breaking the bones in their legs. What can you infer about the process of ossification in horses?

2. Red bone marrow produces red blood cells. How are these cells transported to the rest of the body?

3. During a normal birth, a baby passes through the mother's pelvis. A woman's pelvis has a larger diameter and is more oval-shaped than a man's pelvis. In addition, a newborn's skull bones are not completely ossified. How are these skeletal properties advantageous to the birthing process?

4. The walls of blood vessels are encircled by a single layer of smooth muscle. The walls of the stomach and small intestine have a layer of circular smooth muscle and a layer of longitudinal smooth muscle. How do these muscle arrangements reflect the functions of each structure?

5. Oil glands secrete an oily substance that helps keep the skin soft and flexible. They also secrete fatty acids, which help kill bacteria. How can their function be affected if you wash your skin too frequently?

6. Examine the drawing of epithelial cells below. The flat epithelial cells of the skin overlap each other much like shingles on a roof do. How does this arrangement enable these cells to perform their protective function?

EXTENSION

1. The knee is a joint covered by the patella, or kneecap. Find out what function the kneecap serves. Research and write a report about an athlete who has suffered an injury to the patella. Report the cause of and treatment for the injury.

2. Read "Musical Muscles" in *Discover*, August 1999, on page 25. What are vocal cords? How do vocal cords make sound? Describe the damage that singers often do to their vocal cords. What is the condition called, and how is it treated?

3. Choose a form of exercise, such as running, cycling, or weight training. Write a report about the types of skills that are necessary for the exercise and the long-term effects it has on the body.

Dehydrating and Demineralizing Bone

OBJECTIVES

- Determine the amount of water and minerals in bone.
- Identify structures in bone cells.

PROCESS SKILLS

- observing
- identifying
- calculating

MATERIALS

- safety goggles
- lab apron
- gloves
- bones (2)
- drying oven
- balance
- specimen tag
- tongs
- 250 mL beaker
- wax pencil
- gauze, circular piece
- hot pad
- 500 mL beakers (2)
- 300 mL of 1 M hydrochloric acid
- glass plate or parafilm
- prepared bone slides
- compound microscope
- lens paper
- resealable plastic bag
- permanent marker

Background

1. Dehydration is the process of removing the water from a substance.
2. Demineralization is the process of removing the minerals from a substance.

TABLE A DEHYDRATION OF BONE

Mass before drying	Mass after drying	Percentage of bone mass lost

PART A Dehydrating a Bone

1. In your lab report, prepare a data table similar to Table A.
2. Put on safety goggles, a lab apron, and gloves. Wear this protective gear during all parts of this investigation.
3. Obtain a bone from your teacher. Test the flexibility of the bone by trying to bend and twist it.
4. Place the bone on a balance. Measure the mass of the bone to the nearest 0.1 g, and record it in your data table. Then use a permanent marker to write the initials of each member of your group on a specimen tag, and tie the tag to the bone.
5. Place the bone in a drying oven at 100°C for 30 minutes. While the bone is in the oven, complete Part C.
6. **CAUTION Do not touch hot objects with your bare hands. Use insulated gloves and tongs as appropriate.** Using tongs, remove the bone from the oven and place it on a heatproof pad to cool for 10 minutes.
7. Use tongs to place the cooled bone on the balance. Measure the mass of the bone to the nearest 0.1 g, and record it in your data table.
8. Use the equation below to calculate the percentage of the bone's mass that was lost during heating.

Percentage mass lost =

$$\frac{\text{mass before heating} - \text{mass after heating}}{\text{mass before heating}} \times 100$$

PART B Demineralizing a Bone

9. In your lab report, prepare a data table similar to Table B.
10. Obtain a second bone from your teacher. Test the flexibility of the bone by trying to bend and twist it.

TABLE B DEMINERALIZATION OF A BONE

Mass before demineralizing	Mass after demineralizing and drying	Percentage of bone mass lost

11. Place the bone on a balance. Measure the mass of the bone, and record it in your data table.

12. ⚠ CAUTION **Glassware is fragile. Notify your teacher promptly of any broken glass or cuts. Do not clean up broken glass or spills unless your teacher tells you to do so.** Using a wax pencil, label a 500 mL beaker "1 M HCl." Also label the beaker with the initials of all group members. Place a piece of gauze in the bottom of the beaker.

13. ☠ CAUTION **If you get an acid on your skin or clothing, wash it off at the sink immediately while calling to your teacher.** Place the bone on top of the gauze in the beaker, and add enough 1 M HCl to cover the bone. Use a glass plate or parafilm to cover the beaker.

14. Place the beaker under a fume hood, and allow the bone to soak in the acid until it softens and becomes spongy. This should take 5–7 days. Periodically use tongs to test the hardness of the bone. *Note: Do not touch the bone with your fingers while it is soaking in acid. Rinse the tongs with water thoroughly each time you finish testing the bone.*

15. When the bone becomes spongy, use tongs to carefully remove it from the beaker, and rinse it under running water for two minutes.

16. After the bone has been thoroughly rinsed, test the bone for hardness by twisting and bending it with your fingers. *Note: Be sure you are wearing gloves.*

17. Then use a permanent marker to write the initials of each member of your group on a specimen tag, and tie the tag to the bone. Place the bone in a drying oven at 100°C for 30 minutes.

18. ⚠ CAUTION **Do not touch hot objects with your bare hands. Use insulated gloves and tongs as appropriate.** Using tongs, remove the bone from the oven and place it on a heat-proof pad to cool for 10 minutes.

19. Use tongs to place the cooled bone on the balance. Measure the mass of the bone to the nearest 0.1 g, and record it in your data table.

20. Use the equation below to calculate the percentage of the bone's mass that was lost through demineralization and dehydration.

Percentage of mass lost =

$$\frac{\text{mass before demineralizing} - \text{mass after demineralizing and drying}}{\text{mass before demineralizing}} \times 100$$

PART C Observing Prepared Slides of Bone

21. ⚡ Using a compound light microscope, focus on a prepared slide of bone using low power, and then switch to high power. Locate a Haversian canal, the darkly stained circle in the center of a set of lamellae. Find the darkly stained osteocytes between the lamellae.

22. In your lab report, draw and label the following bone structures: Haversian canal, lamella, osteocyte.

Analysis and Conclusions

1. What effect did water loss have on the bone? What effect did mineral loss have on the bone?

2. Why did you have to dehydrate the bone before measuring its mass in Part B?

3. What percentage of bone is water? What percentage of bone is mineral?

4. If you were to prepare a slide using the dehydrated and demineralized bone, what do you think it would look like?

5. What happened when the demineralized bone was dried? Why do you think this happened?

6. If a person's diet lacked calcium, how could this affect his or her bones?

Further Inquiry

Research the differences in the amount and distribution of compact bone and spongy bone among bones from various parts of the human skeleton. Discover whether there are any other differences in the internal structure of different types of bones.

CHAPTER 47

CIRCULATORY AND RESPIRATORY SYSTEMS

This photograph shows the air sacs of a human lung. (SEM 780×)

FOCUS CONCEPT: *Structure and Function*

As you read, note how the structural features of the organs in the circulatory and respiratory systems are related to the transport and exchange of materials.

THE CIRCULATORY SYSTEM

*M*ost of the cells in the human body are not in direct contact with the external environment. The circulatory system acts as a transport service for these cells. Two fluids move through the circulatory system: blood and lymph. The blood, heart, and blood vessels form the **cardiovascular system.** The lymph, lymph nodes, and lymph vessels form the **lymphatic system.** The cardiovascular system and lymphatic system collectively make up the **circulatory system.**

THE HEART

The central organ of the cardiovascular system is the heart, the muscular organ that pumps blood through an intricate network of blood vessels. The heart beats more than 2.5 billion times in an average life span. Yet this organ that does so much work is slightly larger than a fist. The heart lies within the thoracic (chest) cavity, behind the sternum (breastbone) and between the two lungs. A tough, saclike membrane called the **pericardium** surrounds the heart and secretes a fluid that reduces friction as the heart beats.

Notice in Figure 47-1 that a **septum** vertically divides the heart into two sides. The right side pumps blood to the lungs, and the left side pumps blood to the other parts of the body. Each side of the heart is divided into an upper and lower chamber. Each upper chamber is called an **atrium,** and each lower chamber is called a **ventricle.**

OBJECTIVES

▲

Describe the structure and function of the human heart.

●

Trace the flow of blood through the heart and body.

■

Distinguish between arteries, veins, and capillaries in terms of their structure and function.

◆

Distinguish between pulmonary circulation and systemic circulation.

▲

Describe the functions of the lymphatic system.

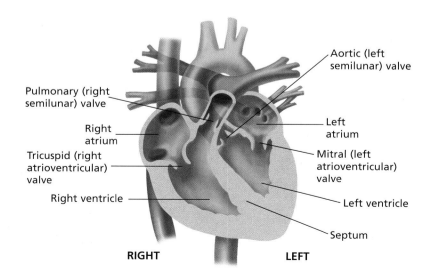

Pulmonary (right semilunar) valve

Right atrium

Tricuspid (right atrioventricular) valve

Right ventricle

Aortic (left semilunar) valve

Left atrium

Mitral (left atrioventricular) valve

Left ventricle

Septum

RIGHT   **LEFT**

FIGURE 47-1

The septum prevents mixing of blood from the two sides of the heart, and the valves ensure that blood flows in only one direction.

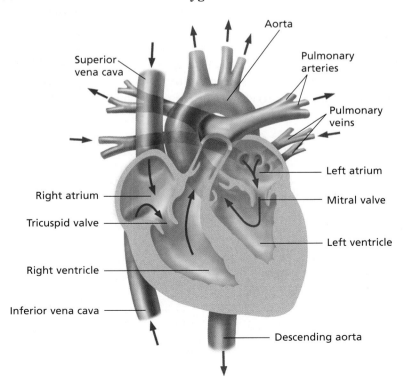

Quick Lab

Determining Heart Rate

Materials stopwatch or clock with second hand

Procedure

1. Have your partner find the pulse in your wrist and count your heartbeats for 15 seconds while you are seated. Calculate your resting heart rate in beats per minute.

2. Have your partner count your heartbeats for 15 seconds while you are standing. Calculate your heart rate in beats per minute.

3. Have your partner count your heartbeats for 15 seconds while you are lying down. Calculate your heart rate in beats per minute.

Analysis What causes your pulse? What causes the change in your heart rate in each position?

A one-way valve separates each atrium from the ventricle beneath it. These valves are called **atrioventricular** (AY-tree-oh-ven-TRIH-kyuh-luhr) **(AV) valves.** They consist of flaps of tissue that open in only one direction. The AV valve on the right side is called the **tricuspid valve.** The **mitral valve,** also called the bicuspid valve, is on the left. As the ventricles pump, blood pressure closes the AV valves, preventing blood from flowing backward from the ventricles to the atria.

From the ventricles, blood flows out of the heart into large vessels. A **semilunar** (semee-LOON-uhr) **(SL) valve** separates the ventricles from these large vessels on each side of the heart. The SL valve on the right side is known as the **pulmonary valve,** and the SL valve on the left side is known as the **aortic valve.** The SL valves prevent blood from flowing back into the ventricles when the heart relaxes.

Circulation in the Heart

Refer to Figure 47-2 to trace the path of the blood as it circulates through the heart. Blood returning to the heart from parts of the body other than the lungs has a high concentration of carbon dioxide and a low concentration of oxygen. This deoxygenated blood enters the right atrium. Notice in Figure 47-2 that the flow of blood on the right side of the heart is illustrated with a blue arrow representing deoxygenated blood, which has a deep bluish-red color.

The right atrium pumps the deoxygenated blood into the right ventricle. The muscles of the right ventricle contract and force the blood into the pulmonary arteries, which lead to the lungs. In the lungs, the carbon dioxide diffuses out of the blood and oxygen diffuses into the blood. The oxygenated blood returns to the left

FIGURE 47-2

Trace the path of blood through the heart. Which side of the heart contains deoxygenated blood? Notice that illustrations of a heart are drawn as if the heart were in a person facing you, that is, the left side of the heart is shown on the right as you face it, and the right side of the heart is on the left as you face it.

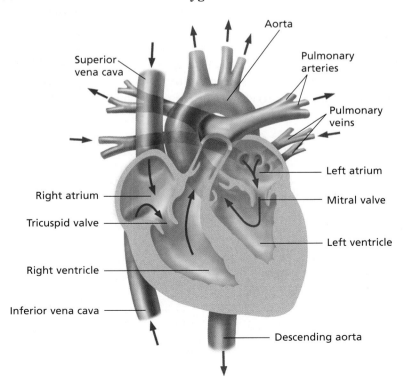

Labels on figure: Aorta, Pulmonary arteries, Superior vena cava, Pulmonary veins, Left atrium, Mitral valve, Right atrium, Tricuspid valve, Left ventricle, Right ventricle, Inferior vena cava, Descending aorta

atrium of the heart. Notice in Figure 47-2 that the flow of blood on the left side of the heart is illustrated with a red arrow representing oxygenated blood, which has a bright red color.

The oxygenated blood is then pumped into the left ventricle. Contraction of the muscular walls of the left ventricle force the blood into a large blood vessel called the **aorta.** From the aorta, blood is transported to all parts of the body except the lungs. The left ventricle is the thickest chamber of the heart because it has to do the most work to pump blood to all parts of the body.

Control of the Heartbeat

The heart consists of muscle cells that contract in waves. When the first group of cells are stimulated, they in turn stimulate neighboring cells. Those cells then stimulate more cells. This chain reaction continues until all the cells contract. The wave of activity spreads in such a way that the atria and the ventricles contract in a steady rhythm. The first group of heart-muscle cells that get stimulated lie in an area of the heart known as the sinoatrial node, shown in Figure 47-3.

The **sinoatrial** (SIEN-oh-AY-tree-uhl) **(SA) node** is a group of specialized heart-muscle cells located in the right atrium. These muscle cells spontaneously initiate their own electrical impulse and contract. The SA node is often called the **pacemaker** because it regulates the rate of contraction of the entire heart. The electrical impulse initiated by the SA node subsequently reaches another special area of the heart, known as the **atrioventricular (AV) node.** The AV node is located in the septum between the atria, as shown in Figure 47-3. The AV node relays the electrical impulse to the muscle cells that make up the ventricles. As a result, the ventricles contract a fraction of a second after the atria, completing one full heartbeat. In an average adult at rest, the heart beats about 70 times each minute.

A heartbeat has two phases. Phase one, called **systole** (SIS-tohl), occurs when the ventricles contract, closing the AV valves and opening the SL valves to pump blood into the two major vessels that exit the heart. Phase two, called **diastole** (DIE-a-stohl), occurs when the ventricles relax, allowing the back pressure of the blood to close the SL valves and opening the AV valves. The closing of these two heart valves results in the characteristic *lubb dup* sound we call a heartbeat. If one of the valves fails to close properly, some blood may flow backward, creating a different sound, which is known as a heart murmur.

Blood Vessels

The circulatory system is known as a closed system because the blood is contained within either the heart or the blood vessels at all times. This type of system differs from an open system, in which blood leaves the vessels and circulates within tissues throughout the organism's body. The blood vessels that are part of the closed circulatory system of humans form a vast network to help keep the blood flowing in one direction.

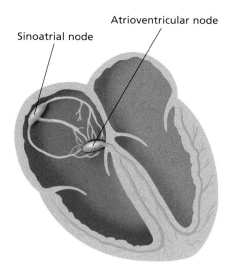

Sinoatrial node

Atrioventricular node

FIGURE 47-3

Two areas of specialized tissue, known as nodes, control the heartbeat. A person whose SA node is defective can have an operation to implant an artificial pacemaker. An artificial pacemaker can also help a defective AV node. Why is the term *artificial pacemaker* appropriate?

FIGURE 47-4

Notice the thick muscular layer of an artery. The layers of the artery wall are separated by elastic tissue. This tissue provides strength, preventing systolic pressure from bursting the artery.

FIGURE 47-5

The diameter of a capillary is so small that red blood cells must move single file through these vessels, as shown in this photograph (1,200×). All exchange of nutrients and waste between blood and cells occurs across the thin walls of the capillaries.

Arteries and Blood Pressure

Each beat of the heart forces blood through blood vessels. The large, muscular vessels that carry blood away from the heart are called **arteries.** As shown in Figure 47-4, the thick walls of the arteries have three layers: an inner endothelial layer, a middle layer of smooth muscle, and an outer layer of connective tissue. This structure gives arteries a combination of strength and elasticity, which allows them to stretch as pressurized blood enters from the heart. You can feel this stretching of arteries—it is your pulse.

Contraction of the heart propels the blood through the arteries with considerable force. The force that blood exerts against the walls of a blood vessel is known as **blood pressure.** Blood pressure is always highest in the two main arteries that leave the heart. It is usually measured in the artery that supplies blood to the arm. To measure blood pressure, a trained person inflates a cuff that is placed around a person's arm, temporarily stopping the flow of blood through the artery. Connected to the cuff is a gauge containing a column of mercury (Hg) that rises as the pressure in the cuff increases. The trained person then releases the air in the cuff slowly while listening to the artery with a stethoscope and watching the column of mercury. The first sounds of blood passing through the artery mean that the ventricles have pumped with enough force to momentarily overcome the pressure exerted by the cuff. This is known as the **systolic pressure,** or the pressure of the blood when the ventricles contract. In a normal adult, the systolic pressure is about 120 mm of Hg for males and 110 mm of Hg for females. Continuing to release the air in the cuff, the trained person next listens for the disappearance of sound, which indicates a steady flow of blood through the artery in the arm. At this point, the pressure of the blood is sufficient to keep the arteries open constantly even with the ventricles relaxed. This is known as **diastolic pressure.** In a normal adult, the diastolic pressure is about 80 mm of Hg for males and 70 mm of Hg for females.

High blood pressure, or **hypertension,** is a leading cause of death in many countries. Blood pressure that is higher than normal places a strain on the walls of the arteries and increases the chance that a vessel will burst. Because people with chronic high blood pressure often display no external symptoms, hypertension is sometimes referred to as the silent killer.

Capillaries and Veins

Recall that when the left ventricle contracts, it forces blood into the aorta, the body's largest artery. From the aorta, blood travels through a network of smaller arteries, which in turn divide and form even smaller vessels, called **arterioles.** The arterioles branch into a network of tiny vessels, called **capillaries.** A capillary is shown in Figure 47-5.

The network formed by capillaries is so extensive that all of the approximately 100 trillion cells in the body lie within about 125 μm of a capillary. This close association between capillaries and cells allows for rapid exchange of materials. Capillary walls are only one cell thick; gases and nutrients can diffuse through these thin walls. Wherever the concentration of oxygen or nutrients is higher in the blood than in the surrounding cells, the substance diffuses from the blood into the cells. Wherever the concentrations of carbon dioxide and wastes are higher in the cells than in the blood, these substances diffuse from the cells into the blood.

Blood flows through capillaries that merge to form larger vessels called **venules** (VEN-yoolz). Several venules in turn unite to form a **vein,** a large blood vessel that carries blood to the heart. Veins returning deoxygenated blood from the lower parts of the body merge to form the **inferior vena cava.** Veins returning deoxygenated blood from the upper parts of the body merge to form the **superior vena cava.** Refer back to Figure 47-2 and locate the inferior vena cava and the superior vena cava.

As you can see in Figure 47-6, although the walls of the veins are composed of three layers, like those of the arteries, they are thinner and less muscular. By the time blood reaches the veins, it is under much less pressure than it was in the arteries. With less pressure being exerted in the veins, the blood could flow backward and disrupt the pattern of circulation. To prevent that, valves in the veins help keep the blood flowing in one direction. Many veins pass through skeletal muscle. When these muscles contract, they are able to squeeze the blood through the veins. When these muscles relax, the valves can close, thus preventing the blood from flowing backward. Figure 47-7 shows the structure of a valve in a vein.

FIGURE 47-6

Like an artery, a vein has three layers. Notice the outer layer of connective tissue, the middle layer of smooth muscle, and the inner layer of endothelial tissue. Compare this figure with Figure 47-4. How do the three layers in a vein compare with those in an artery?

PATTERNS OF CIRCULATION

The English scientist William Harvey (1578–1657) first showed that the heart and the blood vessels form one continuous, closed system of circulation. He also reasoned that this system consists of two primary subsystems: **pulmonary circulation,** in which the blood travels between the heart and lungs, and **systemic circulation,** in which the blood travels between the heart and all other body tissues.

Pulmonary Circulation

Deoxygenated blood returning from all parts of the body except the lungs enters the right atrium, where it is then pumped into the right ventricle. When the right ventricle contracts, the deoxygenated blood is sent through the pulmonary artery to the lungs. The pulmonary artery is the only artery that carries deoxygenated blood. The pulmonary artery branches into two smaller arteries, with one artery going to each lung. These arteries branch into arterioles and then into capillaries in the lungs.

In the lungs, carbon dioxide diffuses out of the capillaries and oxygen diffuses into the capillaries. The oxygenated blood then

FIGURE 47-7

This figure shows the structure of the valves in veins. Many veins have valves to keep the blood flowing in one direction. If these valves fail to close properly, some blood can leak backward and expand a weak area of the vein. This results in a condition known as varicose veins.

FIGURE 47-8

The pulmonary circulation between the heart and the lungs involves the pulmonary arteries and the pulmonary veins. Deoxygenated blood flows from the right side of the heart to the lungs. Oxygenated blood is returned to the left side of the heart from the lungs. This is the opposite of systemic and coronary blood flow, in which oxygen-rich blood flows from the heart and oxygen-poor blood is returned to the heart.

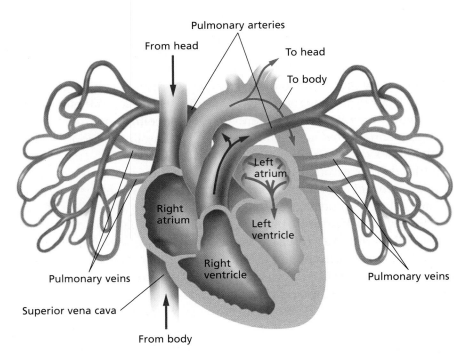

FIGURE 47-9

Notice three subsystems of systemic circulation. Other subsystems transport blood between the heart and the head, arms, organs, and legs.

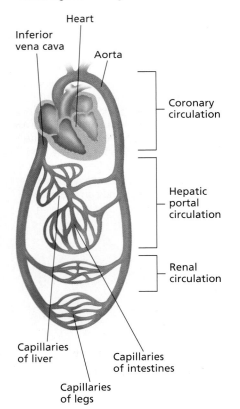

flows into venules, which merge into the **pulmonary veins** that lead to the left atrium of the heart. The pulmonary veins are the only veins that carry oxygenated blood. From the left atrium, blood is pumped into the left ventricle and then to the body through the aorta, supplying the cells with oxygen. In Figure 47-8, trace the path blood takes as it passes through pulmonary circulation.

Systemic Circulation

Systemic circulation is the movement of blood between the heart and all parts of the body except the lungs. Trace the path blood follows in systemic circulation in Figure 47-9. Notice that oxygenated blood is pumped out of the left ventricle and into the aorta. From the aorta, blood flows into other subsystems of systemic circulation.

Coronary circulation is one subsystem of systemic circulation that supplies blood to the heart itself. The heart muscle is thick, and oxygen and nutrients must be supplied to each cell. If the blood supply to the heart is reduced or cut off, muscle cells will die. This can happen when an artery is blocked by a blood clot or by **atherosclerosis** (ATH-uhr-oh-skler-OH-sis), a disease characterized by the buildup of fatty materials on the interior walls of the coronary artery. If either type of blockage reduces the flow of blood to the heart muscle cells, a heart attack will result.

Renal circulation, another subsystem of systemic circulation, supplies blood to the kidneys. Nearly one-fourth of the blood that is pumped into the aorta by the left ventricle flows to the kidneys. The kidneys filter waste from the blood.

Hepatic portal circulation is a subsystem of systemic circulation. Nutrients are picked up by capillaries in the small intestine and are transported by the blood to the liver. Excess nutrients are stored in the liver for future needs. The liver receives oxygenated blood from a large artery that branches from the aorta.

LYMPHATIC SYSTEM

In addition to the cardiovascular system, the circulatory system also includes the lymphatic system. One function of the lymphatic system is to return fluids that have collected in the tissues to the bloodstream. Fluids diffuse through the capillary walls just as oxygen and nutrients do. Some of these fluids pass into cells, some return to the capillaries, and some remain in the intercellular spaces.

Excess fluid in the tissues moves into the tiny vessels of the lymphatic system; this fluid is called **lymph.** Lymph vessels merge to form larger vessels. The lymph vessels are similar in structure to capillaries, and the larger lymph vessels are similar in structure to veins. However, an important difference exists between blood vessels and lymph vessels. As you learned earlier, blood vessels form a complete circuit so that blood passes from the heart to all parts of the body and then back again to the heart. In contrast, lymph vessels form a one-way system that returns fluids collected in the tissues back to the bloodstream. In addition, the lymphatic system has no pump like the heart. Like the blood in veins, lymph must be moved through the vessels by the squeezing of skeletal muscles. Like veins, the larger lymph vessels have valves to prevent the fluid from moving backward.

Notice in Figure 47-10 that lymph vessels form a vast network that extends throughout the body. The lymph that travels in these vessels is a transparent yellowish fluid, much like the liquid part of the blood. As the lymph travels through these vessels on its way to the heart, it passes through small organs known as lymph nodes. Notice in Figure 47-10 that lymph nodes are like beads on a string. These nodes filter the lymph as it passes, trapping foreign particles, microorganisms, and other tissue debris. Lymph nodes also store **lymphocytes,** white blood cells that are specialized to fight disease. When a person has an infection, the nodes may become inflamed, swollen, and tender because of the increased number of lymphocytes.

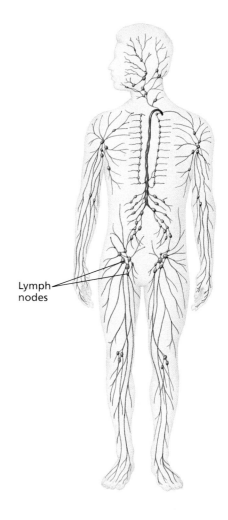

Lymph nodes

FIGURE 47-10

Like the cardiovascular system, the lymphatic system forms a vast network. Concentrated in certain regions of this network are lymph nodes that contain some of the disease-fighting cells of the immune system.

SECTION 47-1 REVIEW

1. Identify the structure that prevents blood from mixing between the left and right sides of the heart. Explain what prevents blood from flowing from the ventricles backward into the atria.

2. Identify the structure that controls the heartbeat, and describe the process by which it regulates the heartbeat.

3. Outline the path that blood follows in pulmonary circulation.

4. Compare the lymphatic system with the cardiovascular system.

5. In which blood vessels would you expect to find the lowest average blood pressure? Explain your answer.

6. CRITICAL THINKING Some babies are born with a hole in the septum between the two atria. Based on what you know about blood flow through the heart, explain why this condition would be harmful to the baby.

On the Motion of the Heart

This excerpt is from William Harvey's anatomical essay *On the Motion of the Heart and Blood in Animals*. It was first presented in 1628.

The study of medicine in Harvey's time normally consisted of studying the works of ancient Greek doctors and philosophers, not direct observation. Harvey's work as a physician and anatomist was revolutionary because he actually observed the action of the heart and the movement of blood in live animals.

When the chest of a living animal is laid open and the capsule that immediately surrounds the heart is slit up or removed, the organ is seen now to move, now to be at rest; there is a time when it moves, and a time when it is motionless.

These things are more obvious in the colder animals, such as toads, frogs, serpents, small fishes, crabs, shrimps, snails, and shell-fish. They also become more distinct in warm-blooded animals, such as the dog and hog, if they be attentively noted when the heart begins to flag, to move more slowly, and, as it were, to die: the movements then become slower and rarer, the pauses longer, by which it is made much more easy to perceive and unravel what the motions really are, and how they are performed. In the pause, as in death, the heart is soft, flaccid, exhausted, lying, as it were, at rest.

In the motion, and interval in which this is accomplished, three principal circumstances are to be noted:

1. That the heart is erected, and rises upwards to a point, so that at this time it strikes against the breast and the pulse is felt externally.

2. That it is everywhere contracted, but more especially towards the sides so that it looks narrower, relatively longer, more drawn together. The heart of an eel taken

out of the body of the animal and placed upon the table or the hand, shows these particulars; but the same things are manifest in the hearts of all small fishes and of those colder animals where the organ is more conical or elongated.

3. The heart being grasped in the hand, is felt to become harder during its action. Now this hardness proceeds from tension, precisely as when the forearm is grasped, its tendons are perceived to become tense and resilient when the fingers are moved.

4. It may further be observed in fishes, and the colder blooded animals, such as frogs, serpents, etc., that the heart, when it moves, becomes of a paler color, when quiescent of a deeper blood-red color.

From these particulars it appears evident to me that the motion of the heart consists in a certain universal tension—both contraction in the line of its fibres, and constriction in every sense.

Reading for Meaning

Because *On the Motion of the Heart and Blood in Animals* was written in Latin in the seventeenth century and was translated into English in 1910, the language is very old-fashioned. Rewrite the last paragraph of this passage, paraphrasing it in simple, modern language.

Read Further

In Harvey's time, knowledge about an animal's internal anatomy came from direct observation. Observations of human anatomy and physiology were rare because the observation techniques were injurious and often fatal. What equipment and techniques are used today in modern hospitals to make observations of human anatomy and physiology that are not invasive or harmful to the patient? How are these techniques used in the diagnosis of illness or disease?

BLOOD

Blood is a liquid connective tissue that constitutes the transport medium of the cardiovascular system. The two main functions of the blood are to transport nutrients and oxygen to the cells and to carry carbon dioxide and other waste materials away from the cells. Blood also transfers heat to the body surface and plays a major role in defending the body against disease.

OBJECTIVES

▲

List the components of blood.

●

Distinguish between red blood cells, white blood cells, and platelets in terms of their structure and function.

■

Summarize the process of blood clotting.

◆

Explain what determines the compatibility of blood types for transfusion.

COMPOSITION OF BLOOD

Blood is composed of a liquid medium and blood solids. Blood solids consist of red blood cells, white blood cells, and platelets. The liquid makes up about 55 percent of the blood, and blood solids make up the remaining 45 percent. A healthy adult has about 4 to 5 L of blood in his or her body.

Plasma

Plasma, the liquid medium, is a sticky, straw-colored fluid that is about 90 percent water. Cells receive nourishment from dissolved substances carried in the plasma. These substances, which may include vitamins, minerals, amino acids, and glucose, are absorbed from the digestive system and transported to the cells. Plasma also carries hormones and brings wastes from the cells to the kidneys or the lungs to be removed from the body.

Proteins are carried in the plasma and have various functions. Some of the proteins in the plasma are essential for the formation of blood clots. Another protein, called albumin, plays an important role in the regulation of osmotic pressure between plasma and blood cells and between plasma and tissues. Other proteins, called antibodies, help the body fight disease.

Red Blood Cells

Red blood cells, or **erythrocytes** (uh-RITH-ruh-siets), shown in Figure 47-11, transport oxygen to cells in all parts of the body. Red blood cells are formed in the red marrow of bones. Red blood cells synthesize large amounts of an iron-containing protein called **hemoglobin.** Hemoglobin is the molecule that actually transports oxygen and, to a lesser degree, carbon dioxide. During the formation of a red blood cell, its cell nucleus and organelles disintegrate. The mature red blood cell becomes little more than a membrane sac containing hemoglobin.

FIGURE 47-11

Notice that a mature red blood cell (RBC) is disk-shaped and is concave on both sides (5,250×). A red blood cell is little more than a cell membrane filled with hemoglobin. How is this structure related to its function?

Because red blood cells lack nuclei, they cannot divide and they have a limited survival period, usually 120 to 130 days. Of the more than 30 trillion red blood cells circulating throughout the body at one time, 2 million disintegrate every second. To replace them, new ones form at the same rate in the red marrow of bones. Some parts of the disintegrated red blood cells are recycled. For example, the iron portion of the hemoglobin molecule is carried in the blood to the marrow, where it is reused in new red blood cells.

White Blood Cells

White blood cells, or **leukocytes** (LOO-kuh-siets), help defend the body against disease. They are formed in the red marrow, the lymph nodes, and the spleen. White blood cells are larger than red blood cells and significantly less plentiful. Each cubic millimeter of blood normally contains about 4 million red blood cells and 7,000 white blood cells. White blood cells can squeeze their way through openings in the walls of blood vessels and into the intercellular fluid. In that way, white blood cells can reach the site of infection and help destroy invading microorganisms.

Notice in Figure 47-12 that a white blood cell has a very different structure from that of a red blood cell. For instance, a white blood cell may be irregularly shaped and may have a rough outer surface. There are other differences between red blood cells and white blood cells as well. In contrast with the short-lived red blood cells, white blood cells may function for years. And while there is only one type of red blood cell, there are several types of white blood cells.

The white blood cell shown in Figure 47-12 is the type of white blood cell known as a **phagocyte** (FA-guh-siets). Phagocytes are cells that engulf invading microorganisms. Locate the microorganisms that are being engulfed by the phagocyte in Figure 47-12. Another type of white blood cell produces **antibodies.** Antibodies are proteins that help destroy substances, such as bacteria and viruses, that enter the body and can cause disease. When a person has an infection, the number of white blood cells can double.

FIGURE 47-12

Some white blood cells, like the phagocyte shown in blue, engulf and destroy invading microorganisms.

(a)

(b)

FIGURE 47-13

Inactive platelets, such as the yellow object shown in (a), derive their name from the fact that they look like little plates (7,410×). Platelets are colorless and contain chemicals that are involved in the clotting process. (b) The platelets change shape during the clotting process. When activated, the platelets settle and spread on the substrate (4,900×).

Platelets

Platelets are essential to the formation of a blood clot. A blood clot is a mass of interwoven fibers and blood cells that prevents excess loss of blood from a wound. Platelets are not whole cells. They are fragments of very large cells that were formed in the bone marrow. As you can see in Figure 47-13a, platelets get their name from their platelike structure. Platelets lack a nucleus and have a life span of 7 to 11 days. A cubic micrometer of blood may contain as many as half a million platelets.

When a blood vessel tears or rips, platelets congregate at the damaged site, sticking together and forming a small plug. The vessel constricts, slowing blood flow to the area. Then special clotting factors are released from the platelets. These factors begin a series of chemical reactions that occur at the site of the bleeding. The last step in this series brings about the production of a protein called **fibrin.** Fibrin molecules consist of long, sticky chains. As you can see in Figure 47-14, these chains form a net that traps red blood cells, and the mass of fibrin and red blood cells hardens into a clot, or scab.

FIGURE 47-14

Long, sticky threads of fibrin trap blood cells and other materials to form a network to stop bleeding. This is comparable to placing a small piece of tissue paper over a cut. The fibers in the tissue paper act like fibrin to form a network to stop the bleeding. (5,000×)

BLOOD TYPES

Blood type is determined by the type of antigen present on the surface of the red blood cells. An **antigen** is a protein or carbohydrate that acts as a signal, enabling the body to recognize foreign substances that enter the body. Antigens that are normally present in a person's body provoke no response. However, when foreign antigens enter the body, cells respond by producing antibodies. In fact, the word *antigen* is an abbreviation for "antibody-generating substance."

Blood from the human population is classified into four groups, based on the antigens on the surface of the red blood cell. Physicians learned of the differences by observing what happened when blood samples from different patients were mixed. In the early 1900s, Karl Landsteiner wanted to find out why some blood transfusions caused no problems, while others led to complications and even death for the recipient. Using blood taken from his laboratory

internet**connect**

SC*LINKS*

NSTA

TOPIC: Blood types
GO TO: www.scilinks.org
KEYWORD: HM941

FIGURE 47-15

Notice that there is no agglutination of red blood cells in the slide in (a), where blood samples from two people with the same blood type were mixed (20×). Compare this with the slide in (b), where blood samples from two people with different blood types were mixed (20×).

(a)

(b)

workers, Landsteiner made observations similar to those you see in Figure 47-15. He noticed that mixing blood samples from two people sometimes resulted in the cells clumping together, or agglutinating. However, at other times no clumping or agglutination occurred when blood samples were mixed. Landsteiner reasoned that clumping occurred when blood samples of two different blood types were mixed.

When samples of two different blood types are mixed together, reactions occur between the antigens on the red blood cells and the antibodies in the plasma, causing the cells to agglutinate. When samples of the same blood type are mixed, no reaction occurs and the blood cells do not agglutinate. Landsteiner's observations led to the classification of human blood by blood types. Blood typing involves identifying the antigens in a sample. Three of the most important human antigens are called A, B, and Rh. The A-B-O system of blood typing, described below, is based on the A and B antigens.

A-B-O System

The A-B-O system is a means of classifying blood by the antigens located on the surface of the red blood cells and the antibodies circulating in the plasma. As shown in Table 47-1, an individual's red blood cells may carry an A antigen, a B antigen, both A and B antigens, or no antigen at all. These antigen patterns are called blood types A, B, AB, and O, respectively.

Notice in Table 47-1 that an individual with type A blood also has anti-B antibodies against type B blood. If type B blood is given to a recipient with type A blood, the recipient's anti-B antibodies will

TABLE 47-1   *Blood Types, Antigens, and Antibodies*

Blood types	Antigen on the red blood cells	Antibodies in the plasma	Can get blood from	Can give blood to
A	A	anti-B	O, A	A, AB
B	B	anti-A	O, B	B, AB
AB	A and B	none	A, B, AB, O	AB
O	none	anti-A, anti-B	O	A, B, AB, O

react with the B antigens on the donated red blood cells and the blood will agglutinate. In addition, the donor's type B blood has anti-A antibodies. Their presence will compound the antigen-antibody reaction in the recipient. The net result will be agglutinated blood that will block the flow of blood through the vessels. For this reason, transfusion recipients must receive blood that is compatible with their own. Based on the information in Table 47-1, why can a person with type AB blood receive blood from any of the four types?

Rh System

An antigen that is sometimes present on the surface of red blood cells is the **Rh factor,** named after the rhesus monkey in which it was first discovered. Eighty-five percent of the United States' population is Rh-positive (Rh$^+$), meaning that Rh antigens are present. People who do not have Rh antigens are called Rh-negative (Rh$^-$).

If an Rh$^-$ person receives a transfusion of blood that has Rh$^+$ antigens, antibodies will react with the antigen and agglutination will occur. The most serious problem with Rh incompatibility occurs during pregnancy. If the mother is Rh$^-$ and the father is Rh$^+$, the child may inherit the dominant Rh$^+$ allele from the father. The blood supplies of the mother and the fetus are separated during pregnancy, but during delivery, a small amount of the fetus's Rh$^+$ blood may reach the mother's bloodstream. If this happens, the mother will develop antibodies to the Rh factor. If a second Rh$^+$ child is conceived later, the mother's antibodies can cross the placenta and attack the blood of the fetus. This condition is called erythroblastosis fetalis. The fetus may die as a result of this condition, or if the child is born alive, he or she may need an immediate transfusion of Rh$^+$ blood.

To prevent this condition, an Rh$^-$ mother of an Rh$^+$ child can be given antibodies to destroy any Rh$^+$ cells that have entered her bloodstream from the fetus. These antibodies must be administered to the mother within three days after the birth of her first Rh$^+$ child. By destroying any Rh$^+$ cells in her bloodstream, any danger to a second child is prevented because the mother will not make any antibodies against the blood cells of the Rh$^+$ fetus.

Quick Lab

Identifying Offspring

Materials pencil, paper

Procedure Two babies are believed to have been swapped at birth in error. Blood samples were taken from each of the parents and babies. The following results were obtained from the blood samples:

Family 1: mother, type B; father, type O; baby, type A

Family 2: mother, type O; father, type A; baby, type O

Design a chart or data table that correctly pairs the biological parents with their baby.

Analysis Are the babies with the correct biological parents? How do you know?

SECTION 47–2 REVIEW

1. What is plasma? Name at least one major function of plasma.

2. Distinguish between the three solid components of the blood.

3. Identify the stages and structures involved in the clotting process.

4. Explain why a pregnant woman should know her blood type and the blood type of her baby's father.

5. Which blood type, in terms of the A-B-O and Rh antigens, can be donated to all others? Why?

6. **CRITICAL THINKING** Why do you think some people turn pale when they are frightened?

SECTION

47-3

OBJECTIVES

▲

Trace the passage of air from the environment to the bloodstream.

●

Describe how gases are exchanged in the lungs.

■

Contrast the ways that oxygen and carbon dioxide are transported in the bloodstream.

◆

Summarize the skeletal and muscular changes that occur during breathing.

▲

Describe how the rate of breathing is controlled.

THE RESPIRATORY SYSTEM

You have read how the blood transports oxygen from the lungs to cells and carries carbon dioxide from the cells to the lungs. It is the function of the respiratory system to transport gases to and from the cardiovascular system. The respiratory system involves both external respiration and internal respiration.

__External respiration__ is the exchange of gases between the atmosphere and the blood. __Internal respiration__ is the exchange of gases between the blood and the cells of the body. In Chapter 7, you learned how aerobic respiration involves the use of oxygen to break down glucose in the cell. In this section, you will examine the structures and mechanisms that carry oxygen to the cells for use in aerobic respiration and that eliminate the carbon dioxide that is produced by the same process.

THE LUNGS

The lungs are the site of gas exchange between the atmosphere and the blood. Notice in Figure 47-16 that the right lung has three divisions, or lobes. It is slightly heavier than the two-lobed left lung. The lungs are located inside the thoracic cavity, bounded by the rib cage and the diaphragm. Lining the entire cavity and encasing the lungs are pleura, membranes that secrete a slippery fluid that decreases friction from the movement of the lungs during breathing.

The Passage of Air

Refer to Figure 47-16 to trace the path air follows from the atmosphere to the capillaries in the lungs. External respiration begins at the mouth and at the nose. Air filters through the small hairs of the nose and passes into the nasal cavity, located above the roof of the mouth. In the nasal cavity, mucous membranes warm and moisten the air, which helps prevent damage to the delicate tissues that form the respiratory system. The walls of the nasal cavity are also lined with cilia. These cilia trap particles that are inhaled and are eventually swept into the throat, where they are swallowed.

SUMMARY/VOCABULARY

 ■ The circulatory system consists of the cardio-vascular system and the lymphatic system.

■ The human heart is located in the thoracic cavity and has two atria and two ventricles.

■ Heartbeat is initiated by the sinoatrial (SA) node, also known as the pacemaker. A heartbeat has two phases: systole and diastole.

■ Blood vessels include arteries, capillaries, and veins. Arteries are thick, muscular vessels that transport blood away from the heart. Arteries branch into smaller vessels known as arterioles and capillaries.

■ Capillaries merge to form venules, which then collect into veins. Veins return blood to the heart.

■ Pulmonary circulation involves blood flow between the heart and the lungs.

■ Systemic circulation includes the heart, the kidneys, the liver, and all other organs, including skin and muscle.

■ The lymphatic system returns intercellular fluid to the heart. Fluid in the lymphatic system is called lymph.

Vocabulary

aorta (933)
aortic valve (932)
arteriole (934)
artery (934)
atherosclerosis (936)
atrioventricular (AV) node (933)
atrioventricular valve (932)
atrium (931)
blood pressure (934)

capillary (934)
cardiovascular system (931)
circulatory system (931)
coronary circulation (936)
diastole (933)
diastolic pressure (934)
hepatic portal circulation (936)
hypertension (934)
inferior vena cava (935)
lymph (937)

lymphatic system (931)
lymphocyte (937)
mitral valve (932)
pacemaker (933)
pericardium (931)
pulmonary circulation (935)
pulmonary valve (932)
pulmonary vein (936)
renal circulation (936)
semilunar valve (932)

septum (931)
sinoatrial (SA) node (933)
superior vena cava (935)
systemic circulation (935)
systole (933)
systolic pressure (934)
tricuspid valve (932)
vein (935)
ventricle (931)
venule (935)

 ■ Blood is composed of plasma, red blood cells, white blood cells, and platelets. Red blood cells transport oxygen. White blood cells help defend the body against disease. Platelets help form blood clots.

■ Human blood can be grouped into four types: A, B, AB, and O. In addition, blood is either Rh-positive or Rh-negative.

Vocabulary

antibody (940)
antigen (941)
blood type (941)

erythrocyte (939)
fibrin (941)
hemoglobin (939)

leukocyte (940)
phagocyte (940)
plasma (939)

platelet (941)
Rh factor (943)

 ■ Oxygen enters the bloodstream through the lungs.

■ The epiglottis prevents food from entering the trachea during swallowing. The larynx contains the vocal cords.

■ Oxygen and carbon dioxide are exchanged between the alveoli and blood and between blood and the cells.

■ Nearly all the oxygen in the body is transported by hemoglobin. The level of carbon dioxide in the blood determines the rate of breathing, which is controlled by the brain.

■ During inspiration, the thoracic cavity expands, pulling air into the lungs. During expiration, the thoracic cavity gets smaller, forcing air out of the lungs.

Vocabulary

alveolus (945)
bronchiole (945)
bronchus (945)

epiglottis (945)
expiration (948)
external respiration (944)

inspiration (947)
internal respiration (944)

larynx (945)
trachea (945)

REVIEW

Vocabulary

1. Distinguish between systolic pressure and diastolic pressure.
2. What do the pulmonary arteries and the aorta have in common? How are they different?
3. What do the pulmonary veins and the inferior vena cava have in common? How are they different?
4. What do arteries, veins, and capillaries have in common?
5. Identify the solid components of the blood.

Multiple Choice

6. The wall that divides the heart vertically is the (a) ventricle (b) pericardium (c) septum (d) atrium.
7. During systole, blood moves from the (a) ventricles to the atria (b) atria to the veins (c) atria to the ventricles (d) ventricles to the arteries.
8. Pulmonary circulation involves movement of blood between the heart and the (a) lungs (b) brain (c) liver (d) kidneys.
9. One of the functions of the lymphatic system is that it (a) interacts with the respiratory system (b) helps the body fight infection (c) consists of a series of two-way vessels (d) transports intercellular fluid away from the heart.
10. One function of plasma is to (a) carry substances that nourish cells (b) aid in the formation of blood clots (c) carry the majority of the oxygen supply of the blood (d) defend against disease.
11. The function of fibrin is to (a) transport oxygen (b) destroy invading microorganisms (c) stimulate the production of antibodies (d) help form a blood clot.
12. A person who has no antigens present on the red blood cells has blood type (a) AB Rh$^+$ (b) O Rh$^-$ (c) A Rh$^+$ (d) O Rh$^+$.
13. During internal respiration, gases are (a) exchanged between the atmosphere and the blood (b) exchanged between the blood and the cells (c) produced by the heart (d) warmed and moistened.
14. Gases diffuse (a) from an area of high concentration to an area of low concentration (b) from an area of low concentration to an area of high concentration (c) directly from the cells to the air passages (d) from the alveoli to the cells.
15. Cilia (a) move air molecules (b) moisten the air passages (c) sweep foreign particles into the stomach (d) sweep particles out of the air passages.

Short Answer

16. Describe the route of blood through the heart. Include circulation through the lungs, and specify whether the artery or the vein carries oxygenated blood.
17. What are two major roles of the lymphatic system?
18. What structure do red blood cells lack that limits their life span?
19. A child is about to be born to parents who are both Rh$^-$. Given their Rh status, what concerns might the parents have about the health of their child ? Explain your answer.
20. How are human vocal sounds produced?
21. What is one factor that stimulates the brain stem to increase the breathing rate?
22. Describe three differences between white blood cells and red blood cells.
23. Describe the movement of the diaphragm and the rib muscles during inspiration and expiration.
24. How are the structures of alveoli and capillaries related to their function?
25. List the part of the heart denoted by each letter in the diagram below.

RIGHT   LEFT

CRITICAL THINKING

1. A person with anemia has too few red blood cells. The most common symptom is a lack of energy. Why would anemia cause this symptom?

2. Polio is a disease that paralyzes muscles by affecting the nerves that make them move. Before the polio vaccine was developed, many people who had polio died because they could not breathe. Some of the survivors had to be placed in an "iron lung" that breathed for them. From what you know about the respiratory system, explain why people stricken with polio could no longer breathe on their own.

3. Even a small increase or decrease in blood volume has an effect on blood pressure. When an accident victim suffers significant blood loss, the person is transfused with plasma rather than whole blood. Why is plasma effective in meeting the immediate threat to life?

4. Explain how the lymphatic system moves lymph through the body without the aid of a pumping organ like that of the cardiovascular system.

5. Calculate the number of times a person's heart will beat if the person lives 75 years. Assume that the average heart beats 70 times per minute. Assuming that the heart of an overweight person beats an additional 10 beats per minute, explain why being overweight can put additional strain on the heart.

6. One function of the cardiovascular system is to help maintain a uniform body temperature. Explain how the constant circulation of blood throughout the body can accomplish this task.

7. Copy the blood-type table below on a sheet of paper. Fill in the missing information for each type.

Blood Types, Antigens, and Antibodies

Blood types	Antigen on the red blood cells	Antibodies in the plasma	Can get blood from	Can give blood to
A		anti-B	O, A	A, AB
B	B		O, B	B, AB
AB	A and B	none	A, B, AB, O	
O	none	anti-A, anti-B		A, B, AB, O

EXTENSION

1. Read "The Beat Goes On" in *Popular Science*, March 2000, on page 62. Describe the port-access mitral valve repair/replacement method of heart surgery. What is the major advantage of this kind of surgery?

2. Using the library or on-line references, research work that has been done about developing and implanting an artificial heart. Write a paper about the operation, the likely candidates for the operation, the number of people who have received an artificial heart, and some of the outcomes of these operations.

3. Carbon monoxide is an odorless gas that is extremely poisonous. Find out how this gas affects the respiratory and circulatory systems. What symptoms would a victim of carbon monoxide inhalation exhibit?

4. Using the library or an on-line data base, research a respiratory ailment, such as cystic fibrosis or emphysema. Write a report that includes information on the people who are most likely to get the disease. What are the causes, and what are the typical outcomes?

Tidal Volume, Expiration Volume, and CO₂ Production

OBJECTIVES

- Use indirect measurement to determine lung capacity.
- Determine the effect of exercise on breathing rate and CO_2 production.

PROCESS SKILLS

- measuring
- hypothesizing
- collecting data
- analyzing data
- experimenting

MATERIALS

- safety goggles
- 1 L bromothymol indicator solution
- drinking straws
- 100 mL Erlenmeyer flasks, 2 per group
- 100 mL graduated cylinders
- marker
- plastic wrap
- spirometer
- stopwatch or clock with second hand

Background

1. A spirometer is an instrument used to measure the volume of air a person can breathe.
2. Examine the diagram of a spirometer on the right. Compare the diagram with the spirometer you will be using to complete this investigation. Note that the marking pen creates a line that can be compared with the scale on the left side to measure liters of air.
3. Tidal volume is the volume of air you inhale or exhale during a single, normal breath.
4. Lung capacity is the available volume of your lungs. Total lung capacity is 5 to 6 L. What factors might increase or reduce lung capacity?
5. Expiratory reserve volume is the amount of air remaining in the lungs after a normal exhalation.
6. Vital capacity is the maximum amount of air that can possibly be inhaled or exhaled.

7. Carbon dioxide is soluble in water. You can determine the relative amount of CO_2 in your breath at rest and after exercise by using an indicator to react with the CO_2. Higher CO_2 levels will react with the indicator solution faster.

PART A Tidal Volume, Expiratory Volume, and Vital Capacity

1. Make a data table in your notebook like one shown on the next page.
2. Place the tube of the spirometer near your mouth, and inhale a normal breath. Hold your nose, then exhale a normal breath into the spirometer and take a reading. Record your data in the table.
3. Measure your expiratory reserve volume by first breathing a normal breath and exhaling normally. Then put the spirometer tube to your mouth as you forcefully exhale whatever air is left in your lungs. Be sure to force out as much air as possible. Record your data in the table.

SPIROMETER

	Average for young adult males	Average for young adult females	Average for athletes	Your readings
Tidal volume	500 mL			
Expiratory reserve volume	100 mL			
Vital capacity	4,600 mL			

4. The table includes values for young adult males. The average volume for young adult females is 20–25 percent lower than that of males. Calculate the average volumes for young adult females. Athletes can have volumes that are 30–40 percent greater than the average for their gender. Calculate the average volume for an athlete.

PART B Breathing Rate and CO_2 Production

5. Discuss the purpose of this part of the investigation with your partners. You will use bromothymol blue as an indicator of the CO_2 you bubble into each flask. Develop a hypothesis that describes a relationship between air volume exhaled during rest or exercise and the volume of CO_2 exhaled.

6. CAUTION **Wear safety goggles at all times during this procedure. If you get the indicator solution on your skin or clothing, wash it off at the sink while calling to your teacher. If you get the indicator solution in your eyes, immediately flush it out at the eyewash station while calling to your teacher.**

7. Label the two flasks as 1 and 2.

8. Add 100 mL of indicator solution to each flask. Cover the mouth of each flask with plastic wrap.

9. Remove the plastic wrap from flask 1. Blow gently through one straw into flask 1 until the solution turns a yellowish color, exhaling slowly so that the solution does not bubble up. Be careful not to inhale the solution or get it in your mouth.

10. Record on your Part B Data Table the time in seconds that it took to see a color change in flask 1.

11. Exercise by jogging in place or doing jumping jacks for 2 min. Immediately blow gently through a new straw into flask 2 until the solution becomes the same yellowish color as the solution in flask 1.

12. In your Part B Data Table, record the amount of time in seconds that it took to get the same yellow color in flask 2 as you got in flask 1.

13. Calculate the difference in the amount of time it took to see a color change in the two flasks. What can you infer about the amount of CO_2 you exhaled before and after exercise?

14. Clean up your materials. Pour the solutions down the sink, and rinse the sink thoroughly with water. Wash your hands before leaving the lab.

Analysis and Conclusions

1. How did your tidal volume compare with that of your classmates?

2. What are the independent and dependent variables in Part B of the Investigation? How did you vary the independent variable and measure changes in the dependent variable?

3. Why were the flasks covered with plastic wrap?

4. Do your data support your hypothesis from Part B? Explain your answers.

5. How do you know whether you produced more carbon dioxide before or after you exercised? Support your answer with evidence from this lab.

6. What were some of the possible sources of error in your experiment?

PART B *DATA TABLE*

Time for color change in flask 1	
Time for color change in flask 2	
Difference in time between flask 1 and flask 2	

Further Inquiry

Design an experiment to determine whether exercise affects heart rate in the same way it affects breathing rate and tidal volume.

INFECTIOUS DISEASES AND THE IMMUNE SYSTEM

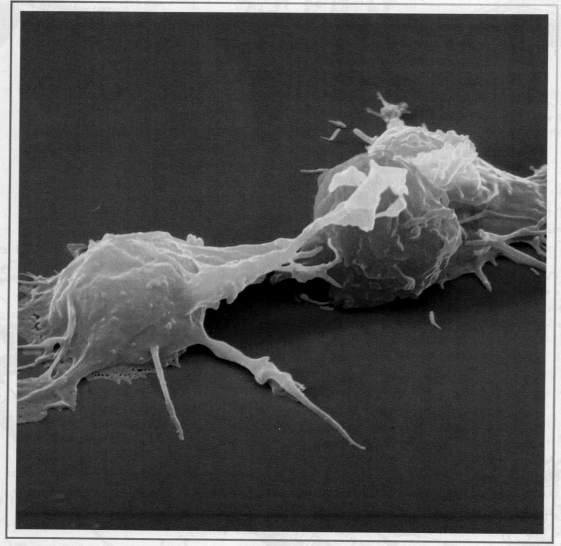

Two natural killer cells, which are defensive cells in the body, are attacking a cancer cell (shown in red). They will kill the cancer cell by puncturing its membrane (SEM 14,900×).

FOCUS CONCEPT: *Stability and Homeostasis*

As you read, identify ways to prevent, diagnose, treat, and cure diseases.

48-1 *Nonspecific Defenses*

48-2 *Specific Defenses: The Immune System*

48-3 *AIDS*

NONSPECIFIC DEFENSES

*T*he human body is continuously exposed to pathogens, such as viruses and bacteria. When one of these pathogens enters the body and begins to multiply, it causes an **infectious disease.** In this section, you will examine the body's nonspecific defenses, which are the first lines of protection against invading pathogens.

SECTION

48-1

OBJECTIVES

▲

Summarize Koch's postulates for identifying a disease-causing agent.

●

Describe how the skin and mucous membranes protect the body against pathogens.

■

Describe the steps of the inflammatory response.

◆

Identify the white blood cells involved in a nonspecific response, and describe their functions.

▲

Explain the functions of interferon and fever.

DISEASE TRANSMISSION

Robert Koch (1843–1910), a German physician, was the first scientist to establish a step-by-step procedure for identifying the particular pathogen responsible for a disease. In the 1870s, Koch was studying anthrax, a disease of cattle that can spread to humans. Koch observed that cattle with anthrax had swarms of bacteria in their blood. He hypothesized that these bacteria caused anthrax.

To test his hypothesis, Koch isolated bacteria from a cow with anthrax and grew the bacteria in a laboratory culture. Then he inoculated a healthy cow with bacteria from the culture. This cow developed anthrax, and Koch found that its blood contained the same kind of bacteria as the blood of the first cow. He concluded that these bacteria caused anthrax. The steps that Koch developed for determining the cause of a given disease, known as **Koch's postulates,** are listed in Figure 48-1.

Scientists have used Koch's postulates to identify thousands of pathogens. Human diseases are caused by bacteria, viruses, protists, fungi, and invertebrates. Each kind of pathogen affects the body differently. Among humans, pathogens can spread in five

Koch's Postulates
1. The suspected pathogen must occur in the body of an animal with the disease and not occur in the body of a healthy animal.
2. The suspected pathogen should be isolated and grown in a laboratory culture.
3. If a healthy animal is inoculated with this culture, the animal should develop the disease.
4. The pathogen from the second animal should be isolated and grown in the laboratory. It should be the same as the pathogen isolated from the first animal.

FIGURE 48-1

The bacterium that causes anthrax, *Bacillus anthracis* (SEM 6,700×), was identified as a pathogen by means of Koch's postulates.

TABLE 48-1 *Some Human Diseases and Their Means of Transmission*

Disease	Pathogen	Principal means of transmission
AIDS	HIV (human immunodeficiency virus)	sexual intercourse, contaminated syringes
Common cold	any of 100 viruses	air currents, person-to-person contact
Malaria	protozoan parasites of genus *Plasmodium*	mosquitoes
Measles (rubeola)	paramyxovirus	air currents, person-to-person contact
Botulism	*Clostridium botulinum* (bacterium)	contaminated food

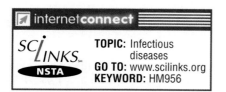

internetconnect

SCiLINKS
NSTA

TOPIC: Infectious diseases
GO TO: www.scilinks.org
KEYWORD: HM956

main ways—through air, food, water, person-to-person contact, and the bites of animals. Some pathogens are transmitted in only one way, while others may be transmitted in several ways. Table 48-1 lists some human pathogens, the diseases they cause, and their means of transmission.

SKIN AND MUCOUS MEMBRANES

The body's nonspecific defenses protect the body against any pathogen, regardless of its identity. Most pathogens must enter the body to cause disease. The skin, with its tough keratin shield, serves as a physical barrier to pathogens—as long as it remains intact. Any break in the skin may permit pathogens to enter the body. Extensive damage to the skin can be life threatening. A victim of severe burns, for example, is especially vulnerable to infections. Such a person must be thoroughly bandaged and treated with antibiotics until the skin has healed.

The skin continuously releases sweat, oils, and waxes, all of which contain chemicals that are toxic to many bacteria and fungi. Sweat, for example, contains the enzyme lysozyme, which can destroy the cell walls of bacteria. However, if all of the bacteria living on the skin were removed, harmful infections of the skin could occur because some of these bacteria inhibit the growth of pathogens.

Mucous membranes are epithelial tissues that protect the interior surfaces of the body that may be exposed to pathogens. Mucous membranes line the respiratory and digestive systems, the urethra, and the vagina. Mucous membranes serve as a barrier and secrete **mucus,** a sticky fluid that traps pathogens. The mucous membranes of the respiratory tract are covered with many beating cilia, as shown in Figure 48-2. These cilia constantly sweep mucus and pathogens up to the pharynx, where they are swallowed and forced into the stomach. Most swallowed pathogens are destroyed in the stomach by strong acids secreted by the stomach lining.

FIGURE 48-2

The passages of the respiratory system are lined with cells covered with beating cilia. Pathogens that become trapped in mucus secreted by these cells are swept upward, away from the lungs (5,325×).

THE INFLAMMATORY RESPONSE

Any pathogen that penetrates the skin or a mucous membrane will stimulate another nonspecific defense mechanism called the **inflammatory response,** which is summarized in Figure 48-3. Whenever an injury occurs, such as a cut or a splinter, some damaged cells release chemical messengers. One kind of chemical messenger is called histamine (HIS-tuh-MEEN). **Histamine** increases blood flow to the injured area and increases the permeability of the surrounding capillaries. As a result, fluids and white blood cells pass through capillary walls to the injured area. The changes caused by histamine result in redness, swelling, warmth, and pain—the familiar symptoms of inflammation.

If blood vessels have been damaged by the injury, platelets and clotting proteins initiate the blood-clotting process, sealing off the surrounding tissues and preventing pathogens from invading the rest of the body. To combat the pathogens that may have already entered through the wound, the body relies on white blood cells.

The chemical signals released by injured cells attract white blood cells to the site of the injury. Pus, the thick, whitish or yellowish fluid that often accumulates in wounds, contains dead pathogens and white blood cells. The presence of pus is a sign that white blood cells have arrived at the injury and are fighting pathogens.

Among the white blood cells that are involved in an inflammatory response are phagocytes. Phagocytes, as you learned in Chapter 5, are white blood cells that engulf pathogens by phagocytosis. The most common type of phagocyte, constituting 50 to 70 percent of the white blood cells in the body, is the **neutrophil** (NOO-truh-fil). Neutrophils circulate freely through blood vessels, and they

FIGURE 48-3

A small cut in the skin triggers an inflammatory response. (a) Injured cells release chemical alarm signals as pathogens enter through the cut. (b) In response, nearby capillaries swell and become leakier. The area around the wound swells and becomes warm. Phagocytes arrive to attack the pathogens. (c) Phagocytes destroy the pathogens, and the cut begins to heal.

(a)

(b)

(c)

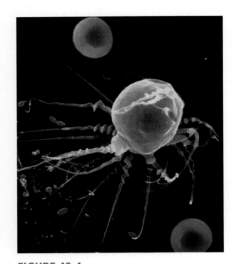

FIGURE 48-4

This macrophage is using cytoplasmic extensions to capture bacteria (shown in purple). (SEM 17,400×)

Word Roots and Origins

macrophage

from the Greek *makros,*
meaning "long," and *phagein,*
meaning "to eat"

can squeeze between the cells in the wall of a capillary to reach the site of an infection. Once there, neutrophils engulf and destroy any pathogens they encounter. Another type of phagocyte is the **macrophage** (MA-kroh-FAYJ), shown in Figure 48-4. Macrophages consume and destroy any pathogens they encounter. They also rid the body of worn-out cells and cellular debris. Some macrophages are stationed in the tissues of the body, awaiting pathogens, while others move through the tissues and seek out pathogens.

Natural killer cells are large white blood cells that, unlike phagocytes, attack the cells that have been infected by pathogens, not the pathogens themselves. Natural killer cells are particularly effective in killing cancer cells and cells infected with a virus. A natural killer cell punctures the cell membrane of its target cell, allowing water to rush into the cell, causing the cell to burst.

OTHER NONSPECIFIC DEFENSES

Interferon (in-tuhr-FEER-AHN) is a protein that inhibits the reproduction of viruses. It is produced in small amounts by cells that are infected by a virus. Interferon stimulates neighboring cells to produce an enzyme that inhibits the synthesis of viral proteins. This prevents viruses from reproducing within these cells. Scientists are investigating whether interferon can be used to treat viral diseases and cancer.

Fever is an elevation in body temperature above the normal 37°C (99°F). Fever is not a disease; it is a sign that the body is responding to an infection. Some pathogens trigger fever, as do chemical signals released by macrophages. Research suggests that a moderate fever stimulates the body's defense mechanisms. It suppresses the growth of some bacteria and may promote the action of white blood cells. However, high fevers are harmful. High temperatures can inactivate cellular enzymes in the body. In general, body temperatures greater than 39°C (103°F) are considered dangerous, and those greater than 41°C (105°F) are often fatal.

SECTION 48-1 REVIEW

1. How did Koch test his hypothesis about the cause of anthrax?

2. What chemical defenses does the skin use against pathogens?

3. What role does increased permeability of capillaries play in the inflammatory response?

4. How do natural killer cells differ from macrophages?

5. What is the function of interferon?

6. **CRITICAL THINKING** In many cases, not all of Koch's postulates can be applied to determine the cause of a human disease. Explain why.

SPECIFIC DEFENSES: THE IMMUNE SYSTEM

Although the nonspecific defenses usually keep pathogens from entering and becoming established in the body, pathogens occasionally break through these defenses and begin to multiply. In response, the body's specific defenses are called into action. Unlike the nonspecific defenses, the specific defenses act against one particular pathogen.

THE IMMUNE SYSTEM

The body's specific defenses are part of the immune system, one of the major organ systems you studied in Chapter 46. The **immune system** has the job of fighting off invading pathogens and preventing the growth and spread of cancers. The immune system consists of several organs and the white blood cells found in these organs, as well as white blood cells in the blood and lymph. The organs of the immune system are scattered throughout the body; they include the bone marrow, thymus, lymph nodes, tonsils, adenoids, and spleen.

Each organ of the immune system plays a different role in defending the body against pathogens. Bone marrow, the soft material found inside long bones, such as the femur, manufactures the billions of new white blood cells needed by the body every day. Some newly produced white blood cells remain in the bone marrow to mature and specialize, while others travel to the **thymus** (THIE-muhs), a gland in the upper part of the chest just above the heart, to mature. Lymph nodes are located throughout the body along the vessels of the lymphatic system and contain large numbers of white blood cells. Lymph nodes filter pathogens from the lymph and expose them to white blood cells. The **spleen**, a fist-sized organ located just behind the stomach, filters pathogens from the blood. It is stocked with white blood cells that respond to the trapped pathogens. Figure 48-5, on the next page, shows the organs of the immune system.

The white blood cells of the immune system are known as lymphocytes (LIM-foh-SIETZ). As their name implies, these white blood cells accumulate in the lymph and lymph nodes, but lymphocytes are also found in the spleen and blood. There are two main types of lymphocytes: B cells and T cells. **B cells** are produced in the bone marrow and complete their development there. **T cells** are also produced in the bone marrow, but they mature after traveling to the thymus.

OBJECTIVES

▲

Identify and describe the components of the immune system.

●

Explain the functions of the three kinds of T cells.

■

Describe the actions of B cells in an immune response.

◆

Explain how a vaccine works.

▲

Contrast *allergy* with *autoimmune disease*.

FIGURE 48-5

The organs of the immune system produce lymphocytes and filter pathogens from the blood and lymph.

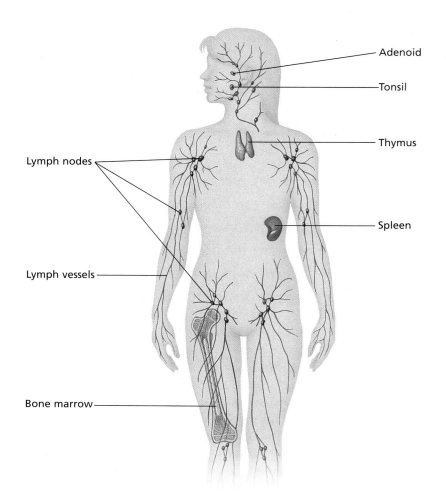

Adenoid

Tonsil

Thymus

Lymph nodes

Spleen

Lymph vessels

Bone marrow

RECOGNIZING PATHOGENS

Lymphocytes are the body's specific defenses. When the body is invaded by a pathogen, lymphocytes launch an attack known as an **immune response** to eliminate the pathogen. In order to respond to a pathogen, however, lymphocytes must be able to recognize it as a foreign invader and distinguish it from the cells of the body. Any substance that the immune system recognizes as a potential pathogen and that provokes an immune response is known as an **antigen** (AN-tuh-jin). A wide variety of substances can be antigens, including pathogens or parts of pathogens, bacterial toxins, insect venom, and pollen.

How do lymphocytes identify antigens? Every lymphocyte has receptor proteins scattered over the surface of its cell membrane. These receptor proteins recognize and bind to antigens that match their particular three-dimensional shape, as shown in Figure 48-6. The surface of a bacterial cell, for instance, can be covered with many different kinds of molecules—including proteins and polysaccharides—each of which can function as an antigen and cause lymphocytes to react. All of the receptors on an individual lymphocyte are the same shape and thus bind to the same antigen.

Word Roots and Origins

antigen

From the Greek *anti-*, meaning "against," and *-genes,* meaning "born"

FIGURE 48-6

The receptor proteins on the surface of lymphocytes have a complex, three-dimensional structure. The receptors can fit onto, and thus bind, molecules on pathogens that have a complementary shape.

The body can defend itself against an enormous number of different pathogens because the immune system makes millions of different kinds of lymphocytes, each carrying uniquely shaped receptors. The specificity of the immune system is due to the specificity of the antigen receptors on the lymphocytes. For example, when a cold virus invades the body, lymphocytes whose receptor molecules match the antigens of the cold virus are activated to counterattack. Lymphocytes with different-shaped receptors, such as those that recognize an influenza (flu) virus, do not respond.

IMMUNE RESPONSE

An immune response is a two-pronged assault on a pathogen. One arm of the immune response, the **cell-mediated immune response,** involves T cells. The other arm involves mainly B cells and is called the **humoral** (HYOO-muh-ruhl) **immune response.** Both parts of the immune response are controlled by a type of T cell called a **helper T cell.**

The first step in an immune response occurs when a macrophage engulfs and destroys a pathogen. The macrophage then displays fragments of the pathogen's antigens on the surface of its own cell membrane. When a helper T cell with a receptor matching this antigen encounters the macrophage, the macrophage releases a cytokine called interleukin-1 (IN-tuhr-LOO-kin), which in turn triggers the helper T cell to release a second cytokine, called interleukin-2.

Cell-Mediated Immune Response

Interleukin-2 stimulates the helper T cells and two other types of T cells—cytotoxic T cells and suppressor T cells—to rapidly divide. **Cytotoxic** (SIE-toh-TAHK-sik) **T cells** combat the pathogen by destroying any of the body's cells that have been infected by the

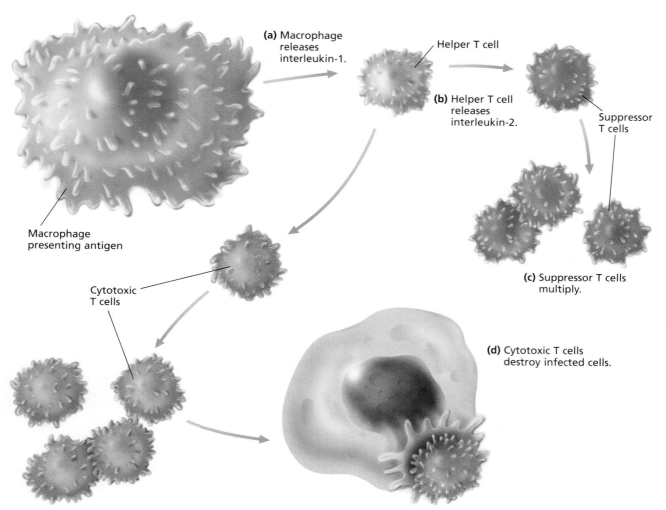

(a) Macrophage releases interleukin-1.

Helper T cell

(b) Helper T cell releases interleukin-2.

Suppressor T cells

Macrophage presenting antigen

(c) Suppressor T cells multiply.

Cytotoxic T cells

(d) Cytotoxic T cells destroy infected cells.

FIGURE 48-7

The cell-mediated immune response involves macrophages, helper T cells, cytotoxic T cells, and suppressor T cells. (a) The macrophage releases interleukin-1, which stimulates the helper T cell. (b) The helper T cell then releases interleukin-2. In response, cytotoxic T cells and suppressor T cells begin to divide. (c) Suppressor T cells divide slowly. Their role is to shut down the immune response. (d) Cytotoxic T cells destroy infected cells by puncturing their cell membranes.

pathogen. Cells that have been invaded by a pathogen are recognizable because they usually have some of the pathogen's antigens on their surface. Cytotoxic T cells attach to these antigens. Like natural killer cells, cytotoxic T cells kill by puncturing the cell membrane of their target. Cytotoxic T cells can also kill cancer cells and attack parasites and foreign tissues, such as those received during an organ transplant. **Suppressor T cells** help to shut down the immune response after the pathogen has been cleared from the body. Figure 48-7 illustrates the cell-mediated immune response.

Humoral Immune Response

Interleukin-2 and antigen presentation by a macrophage or T cell stimulate B cells to divide and differentiate into plasma cells. **Plasma cells** are highly specialized cells that produce defensive proteins and secrete them into the blood. These defensive proteins are identical to the plasma cell's antigen receptors and are known as **antibodies.** Antibodies are Y-shaped molecules. The two arms of each Y are identical, and they recognize and attach to the same antigen. One plasma cell can make up to 30,000 antibody molecules per second.

Antibodies bind to specific pathogens but do not destroy them directly. Instead, they either inactivate the pathogen or trigger its destruction by the nonspecific defenses. For example, by attaching

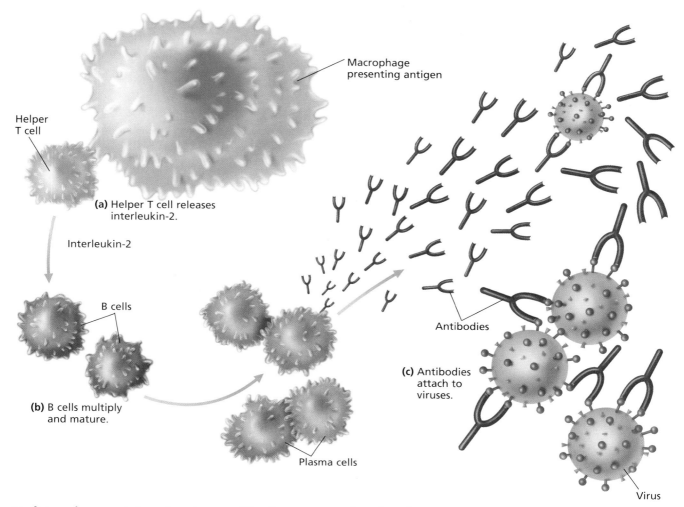

Macrophage presenting antigen

Helper T cell

(a) Helper T cell releases interleukin-2.

Interleukin-2

B cells

(b) B cells multiply and mature.

Plasma cells

Antibodies

(c) Antibodies attach to viruses.

Virus

to the surface proteins of a virus, antibodies prevent the virus from entering a cell, thereby blocking its reproduction. Antibodies also cause pathogens to clump together, which facilitates phagocytosis by macrophages. Figure 48-8 summarizes the humoral immune response.

Primary and Secondary Immune Responses

After an infection has been overcome, the immune response is shut down and most of the participating cells die. However, some B cells and T cells remain, often throughout the individual's life, as memory cells. **Memory cells** are the body's long-term protection against reinfection by a specific pathogen. Because of memory cells, you cannot get most diseases more than once. If you are exposed to a pathogen a second time, memory cells immediately recognize it and begin to divide rapidly. They eliminate the pathogen before it can produce disease. The first time the body encounters an antigen, the immune response is called a **primary immune response.** The response of memory cells to a subsequent infection by the same pathogen is called a **secondary immune response.** As you can see in Figure 48-9 on the next page, a secondary immune response is much faster and more powerful, producing many more antibodies. Keep in mind that memory cells only protect against a pathogen that the immune system has already encountered.

FIGURE 48-8

The humoral immune response involves the activation of B cells and the production of antibodies. (a) After encountering a macrophage, a helper T cell releases interleukin-2. This stimulates rapid division by B cells. (b) After dividing for five days, mature B cells differentiate into antibody-secreting plasma cells. (c) Antibodies bind to free antigen particles and cause antigens such as bacteria and viruses to clump.

Primary and Secondary Immune Responses

FIGURE 48-9

Compare the production of antibodies during the primary and secondary immune responses.

IMMUNITY AND VACCINATION

A person who is resistant to a specific pathogen is said to have **immunity** to it. One way to acquire immunity is to be infected by the pathogen and to survive the disease it causes. Another, safer way is through vaccination. Vaccines contain pathogens or toxins that have been modified so that they can no longer cause disease. Vaccines produce immunity because they contain antigens that stimulate an immune response, resulting in the production of memory cells. Thus, a vaccine prepares the immune system to fight off a pathogen should it ever appear in its disease-causing form.

Among the diseases that have been controlled through the use of vaccines are polio, measles, mumps, tetanus, and diphtheria. An intensive worldwide vaccination campaign has eliminated smallpox. Sometimes the protection provided by vaccination wears off over time. That's why doctors recommend periodic booster shots to restore immunity against some diseases, such as tetanus and polio.

ALLERGIES

Sometimes the immune system reacts to otherwise harmless antigens in ways that can be harmful. This inappropriate reaction to a harmless substance is called **allergy.** Antigens that can trigger allergic reactions include pollen, animal dander (flakes of skin), dust mites, food, and fungal spores. Allergic reactions are characterized by watery eyes, wheezing, and sneezing. Many of the symptoms of allergy result from the release of histamine by cells that are exposed to the antigen. Drugs called antihistamines help counteract the effects of histamine and can relieve the symptoms of allergies. For most people, allergies are irritating and inconvenient but not life threatening. However, some people experience severe reactions that can be fatal.

Quick Lab

Organizing the Immune Response

Materials paper, pencil

Procedure Create a diagram or a flowchart that outlines the steps involved in a cell-mediated immune response. Label the cells and the steps.

Analysis What are helper T cells? How is a cell-mediated response different from a humoral response?

TABLE 48-2	Autoimmune Diseases and Their Target Tissues	
Disease	**Tissues affected**	**Symptoms**
Systemic lupus erythematosus	connective tissue throughout the body	facial skin rash, painful joints, fever, fatigue, kidney problems, weight loss
Type 1 diabetes	insulin-producing cells in pancreas	excessive urine production, blurred vision, weight loss, fatigue, irritability
Graves' disease	thyroid	weakness, irritability, heat intolerance, increased sweating, weight loss, insomnia
Rheumatoid arthritis	joints	painful, crippling inflammation of the joints

AUTOIMMUNE DISEASES

Lymphocytes that recognize and react to the body's own cells are usually eliminated during development, before they become functional. This prevents an attack directed at the body's own tissues. However, in rare cases the immune system does respond to the body's own cells, attacking them as if they were pathogens. Such a disorder is called an **autoimmune** (AW-toh-i-MYOON) **disease.** For example, multiple sclerosis is an autoimmune disease of the nervous system that affects mainly young adults. In this disease, T cells attack and slowly destroy the insulating material that covers nerves. Although the severity of multiple sclerosis varies from individual to individual, the damage may progress to a point at which nerve transmission is interrupted. In severe cases, paralysis, blindness, and even death can result. Scientists are still searching for the causes of multiple sclerosis and other autoimmune diseases. Table 48-2 lists several autoimmune diseases and describes their effects on the body.

internet**connect**

SC*LINKS*

NSTA

TOPIC: Autoimmune diseases
GO TO: www.scilinks.org
KEYWORD: HM965

SECTION 48-2 REVIEW

1. Describe the functions of the spleen and of the bone marrow.

2. Contrast the functions of helper T cells with those of cytotoxic T cells.

3. What is the role of B cells in an immune response? How do B cells depend on T cells?

4. Explain how a vaccine stimulates immunity to a disease.

5. Name one similarity and one difference between autoimmune diseases and allergies.

6. **CRITICAL THINKING** A friend tells you that because he has just recovered from a cold, he now cannot get the flu. Is your friend right? Explain your answer.

Development of a Vaccine

HISTORICAL PERSPECTIVE

The vaccinations you received as a child were unknown in the 1700s. At that time, the diseases that are controlled today plagued children and adults, as they had for centuries. The odds were great that one or more children in a family would not live to be 10 years old. Today, however, in developed countries, it is rare for a child to die of any disease before the age of 10. A major reason is the use of vaccines.

A Dreaded Disease

Before the 1800s, a disease known as smallpox often reached epidemic proportions throughout the world. Thousands of people died of smallpox annually, and thousands of others were disfigured for life by deep scars.

It had long been observed that people who survived smallpox were thereafter immune to it. Thus the practice of inoculating a person with a mild form of smallpox had developed. But there were grave risks. When the disease was contracted in this way, there was still a risk that the symptoms would become severe, and many died as a result.

One Man's Plan

Edward Jenner, a British physician, was investigating cowpox. He had heard that milkmaids seemed to be immune to smallpox and that because of their contact with cows, they often contracted cowpox, a relatively harmless disease. It was also widely known at the time that milkmaids who had cowpox were immune to smallpox. Jenner saw a

Edward Jenner

connection between these observations and came to the conclusion that there was a safer way to immunize against smallpox—by using cowpox. All Jenner needed was an opportunity to test his hypothesis.

In 1796, a milkmaid named Sarah Nelmes contracted cowpox, and Jenner had his chance. He took matter from a cowpox sore on Sarah's hand and injected it into James Phipps, an 8-year-old boy. Two months later, Jenner inoculated the boy with material taken from a sore of a smallpox patient. James

remained healthy. In fact, James never got smallpox, even after Jenner repeatedly inoculated him with smallpox material. Jenner named the procedure *vaccination*, after the Latin word *vacca*, which means "cow." (Note that Jenner's methods were acceptable by the ethical standards of his time, but they would not be permitted today.)

In London, Jenner sought volunteers for further tests, but no one was willing to take the risk. Jenner tried to convince the Royal Society, the foremost scientific society of his day, to publish his results. When the group refused, he published, at his own expense, a 64-page book, *An Inquiry into the Causes and Effects of the Variolae Vaccinae, a Disease Known by the Name of Cow Pox*, in which he described his work and its results:

> *I have proceeded in an inquiry founded on experiment and I shall continue to prosecute this inquiry, encouraged by the pleasing hope of its becoming essentially beneficial to mankind.*

Roadblocks and Rewards

Although other doctors had verified Jenner's results, the new procedure was not initially accepted by the medical community. Also, some of the few physicians who did use the vaccine used cowpox material contaminated with smallpox viruses, which confused the results. Jenner was able to prove that those experiments were flawed and thus gained acceptance for his conclusions. He worked actively for vaccination, and soon the procedure was used worldwide.

Much still remained to be done; many doctors who vaccinated for smallpox used improper methods. Still, the importance of Jenner's work became evident as the death rate from smallpox fell, and Jenner began to receive honors and awards. A Royal Jennerian Society was created to ensure that the vaccination process was used throughout London. Parliament twice voted to give Jenner monetary rewards, and statues were erected in his honor in London and Gloucester.

A Medical Success Story

For almost a hundred years, the use of cowpox matter to create immunity against smallpox was the only vaccination procedure. It wasn't until 1881 that a vaccine for another disease was produced. The French scientist Louis Pasteur was able to grow a weakened form of the cholera bacteria, and he inoculated chickens with these bacteria, immunizing them against the disease.

The vaccination for smallpox has been so successful that it is no longer necessary. The last smallpox case was reported in 1977 in Somalia. The disease is now declared eradicated worldwide.

Today's Search

Most children in the United States are routinely vaccinated against numerous diseases at an early age, so few American lives are cut short by measles, diphtheria, tetanus, or polio. But problems remain. For a number of deadly diseases, such as AIDS, malaria, schistosomiasis, and African sleeping sickness, no vaccine has yet been produced. For other diseases, such as influenza, vaccination provides only short-term immunity, and frequent re-vaccination is required. However, new vaccines made using DNA technology may soon be introduced into medical practice and may help to solve these problems.

Most of today's vaccines work by introducing into the patient weakened or dead bacteria or viruses that stimulate an immune

Edward Jenner described the results of his work in the Inquiry, *published at his own expense in 1798.*

response. New approaches, which immunize by using a DNA carrier, may lead to the prevention of diseases such as influenza, hepatitis, malaria, and AIDS. These DNA vaccines are easily stored, which would greatly facilitate their delivery to developing countries, bringing us even closer to a day when other deadly diseases will follow smallpox into extinction.

Jenner used matter taken from cowpox lesions like these as a vaccine against smallpox. He included this drawing of Sarah Nelmes's hand in the Inquiry.

SECTION

OBJECTIVES

▲

Describe the course
of HIV infection.

●

Identify four ways HIV
is transmitted.

■

Describe how HIV's rate
of evolution affects the
development of vaccines
and treatments.

AIDS

*T*he *immune system normally provides very effective
protection against infectious diseases. Its importance to our
health is dramatically illustrated by the diseases in which the
immune system malfunctions. The most deadly of these
diseases is AIDS, or acquired immunodeficiency syndrome.
AIDS was first recognized as a disease in 1981, and since
then it has killed more than 300,000 Americans.*

HIV AND AIDS

AIDS is a disease in which the immune system loses its ability to
fight off pathogens and cancers. As you learned in Chapter 24, AIDS
is caused by the human immunodeficiency virus, or HIV, a type of
retrovirus. Recall that retroviruses contain RNA, not DNA, as their
genetic material. Like other viruses, HIV cannot reproduce outside
a cell. HIV can invade several kinds of cells, including macrophages, but its main targets are helper T cells. HIV enters a cell by
binding to a receptor called CD4 and one other receptor on the
cell's membrane. An infected helper T cell manufactures large numbers of new virus particles, as shown in Figure 48-10.

Course of the Disease

HIV begins to reproduce within the body shortly after infection.
The presence of large numbers of viruses stimulates the immune
system to launch a vigorous attack. At this point, which usually
occurs within a month or so of infection, the individual often experiences a short flulike illness, with fever, fatigue, body aches, and
swollen lymph nodes.

This first battle is the beginning of a long-term struggle between
HIV and the immune system. HIV continues to replicate rapidly, but
the immune system keeps the virus in check, and the infected person usually feels well and appears healthy. This stage of HIV infection can last for as little as two years, but typically lasts for 10
years or longer.

For reasons that are not well understood, HIV eventually gets
the upper hand in its battle with the immune system. The number
of helper T cells in the body begins to decline gradually, as shown
in Figure 48-11.

The reduction in helper T cells is disastrous for the infected person. Helper T cells play a crucial role as the "commanders" of the

FIGURE 48-10

This image shows particles of HIV
escaping through the membrane of
an infected T cell. (TEM 117,000×)

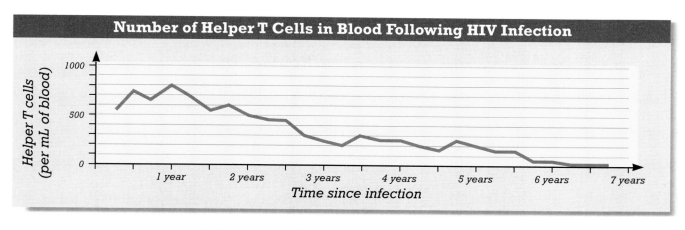

Number of Helper T Cells in Blood Following HIV Infection

Helper T cells (per mL of blood)

1000

500

0

1 year 2 years 3 years 4 years 5 years 6 years 7 years

Time since infection

immune response, activating both cytotoxic T cells and B cells. As the number of helper T cells falls, the immune system becomes weaker, and the infected individual becomes vulnerable to a variety of cancers and diseases that a healthy immune system would normally defeat. These diseases are called **opportunistic infections,** and they usually strike only people with weakened immune systems. When the number of helper T cells in the blood falls below 200/mL (a normal amount is 600/mL–700/mL), the individual is said to have AIDS. AIDS is the last stage of HIV infection. Few individuals live more than two years after being diagnosed with AIDS, usually dying from opportunistic infections or cancer.

Transmission

HIV is transmitted by the transfer of body fluids containing HIV or HIV-infected cells. The most common means of infection is sexual intercourse with an infected person. HIV-infected cells are found in semen and vaginal secretions, and infection can occur through vaginal, oral, or anal intercourse. Use of a latex condom during sex greatly reduces the likelihood of transmission but does not eliminate it completely. It is important to remember that people who have been infected with HIV but have not developed AIDS can still transmit the virus.

The second most common means of infection is through the use of syringes and hypodermic needles that have been contaminated with blood containing HIV. People who inject intravenous drugs, such as heroin, and who share syringes or hypodermic needles with others are at very high risk of infection. During the early years of the AIDS epidemic, a number of individuals were infected by receiving HIV-contaminated blood transfusions. Donated blood is now tested for the presence of antibodies to HIV, and people who may have been exposed to the virus are discouraged from donating, so the likelihood of being infected through a transfusion is very low.

You cannot be infected with HIV through casual contact, such as by shaking hands with an infected person or by handling an object used by an infected person. HIV is apparently not transmitted through the air, in water, or on toilet seats. There is no evidence that it can be spread through the bites of arthropods, such as mosquitoes, fleas, and ticks.

FIGURE 48-11

Once HIV begins to destroy the immune system, the number of helper T cells in the blood falls dramatically.

internet**connect**

SC*LINKS*
NSTA

TOPIC: AIDS
GO TO: www.scilinks.org
KEYWORD: HM969

FIGURE 48-12

According to the World Health Organization, more than 34.3 million people are infected with HIV. This graph shows estimates of the number of HIV-infected people in each region of the world.

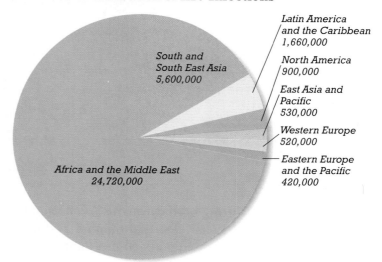

Worldwide Distribution of HIV Infections

South and South East Asia
5,600,000

Latin America and the Caribbean
1,660,000

North America
900,000

East Asia and Pacific
530,000

Western Europe
520,000

Eastern Europe and the Pacific
420,000

Africa and the Middle East
24,720,000

Although most early cases of AIDS were diagnosed in the United States and Western Europe, AIDS is now a worldwide problem. Figure 48-12 shows the estimated numbers of HIV-infected people in different parts of the world.

Treatments and Vaccines

Scientists trying to create vaccines for HIV must contend with its very rapid rate of evolution. The genes that code for the virus's surface proteins mutate frequently. As a result, new variants of the virus with slightly different surface proteins are constantly appearing. To produce effective immunity, a vaccine against HIV must stimulate the immune system to respond to many variants of the virus. Although several vaccines against HIV are under development or being tested, none have yet proven effective.

HIV quickly becomes resistant to drugs used against it. To avoid this problem, scientists have begun treating patients with three antiviral drugs. Even if the virus evolves resistance to one drug, it is unlikely to become simultaneously resistant to three drugs. Scientists have already observed some encouraging results from this treatment. However, it is important to note that there is currently no cure for HIV infection.

SECTION 48-3 REVIEW

1. Name two kinds of cells that HIV can infect.

2. How does the immune system respond to the first appearance of HIV in the body?

3. Why is the risk of becoming infected with HIV through a blood transfusion extremely low?

4. Name two ways that HIV apparently cannot be transmitted.

5. How does HIV's rapid rate of evolution affect the development of a vaccine?

6. **CRITICAL THINKING** Explain the difference between HIV infection and AIDS.

CHAPTER 48 REVIEW

SUMMARY/VOCABULARY

 48-1
- Robert Koch developed four basic steps, known as Koch's postulates, for identifying the particular pathogen responsible for a disease.
- The skin is a nonspecific defense that helps keep pathogens out of the body. Mucous membranes line vulnerable interior surfaces of the body and serve as a barrier to pathogens.

- A break in the skin will trigger another non-specific defense, called the inflammatory response, characterized by swelling, redness, raised temperature, and pain.
- Neutrophils and macrophages are phagocytes that engulf and destroy pathogens and cellular debris. Natural killer cells destroy infected cells.

Vocabulary

fever (958)
histamine (957)
infectious disease (955)
inflammatory response (957)
interferon (958)
Koch's postulates (955)
macrophage (958)
mucous membrane (956)
mucus (956)
natural killer cell (958)
neutrophil (957)

 48-2
- The immune system consists of the spleen, tonsils, adenoids, lymph nodes, thymus, bone marrow, and white blood cells called lymphocytes.
- An antigen is any substance that can stimulate a response from the immune system. Lymphocytes have receptor proteins on their cell membrane that allow them to recognize antigens.
- The immune system's reaction to a pathogen is called an immune response.

- The immune response is controlled by helper T cells.
- Helper T cells activate the division of B cells to give rise to plasma cells, which produce and secrete defensive proteins called antibodies.
- An allergy is an extreme reaction by the immune system to a harmless antigen. An autoimmune disease is an attack on the cells of the body by the immune system.

Vocabulary

allergy (964)
antibody (962)
antigen (960)
autoimmune disease (965)
B cell (959)
cell-mediated immune response (961)
cytotoxic T cell (961)
helper T cell (961)
humoral immune response (961)
immune response (960)
immune system (959)
immunity (964)
memory cell (963)
plasma cell (962)
primary immune response (963)
secondary immune response (963)
spleen (959)
suppressor T cell (962)
T cell (959)
thymus (959)

 48-3
- Acquired immunodeficiency syndrome (AIDS) is caused by the human immunodeficiency virus (HIV). HIV enters and reproduces inside helper T cells.
- HIV and the immune system fight a long battle, which the immune system eventually loses.

- Most AIDS patients die of opportunistic diseases or cancers.
- HIV is transmitted mainly through sexual intercourse and the use of HIV-contaminated hypodermic needles or syringes.

Vocabulary

opportunistic infection (969)

REVIEW

Vocabulary

1. Distinguish between a primary immune response and a secondary immune response.
2. Describe the function of interferon.
3. Contrast a neutrophil with a B cell.
4. Using a dictionary, find the meaning of the word *opportunistic*. Relate the meaning of this word to the action of opportunistic infections.
5. Explain the relationship between T cells and B cells.

Multiple Choice

6. Robert Koch (a) established procedures for identifying the cause of disease (b) identified specific neurotoxins (c) discovered interferon (d) pioneered the process of vaccination.
7. Pathogens can be (a) bacteria (b) viruses (c) invertebrates (d) any of the above.
8. Nonspecific defenses include the (a) primary immune response (b) secondary immune response (c) inflammatory response (d) T cells.
9. The skin acts as a defense against infection by (a) forming a physical barrier to pathogens (b) engulfing and digesting pathogens (c) forming blood clots (d) producing antibodies.
10. The primary immune response involves (a) the recognition of antigens (b) release of antibodies by macrophages (c) a general reaction to all pathogens (d) the action of cilia lining the air passages.
11. Antibodies are produced by (a) helper T cells (b) plasma cells (c) suppressor T cells (d) macrophages.
12. Cytotoxic T cells (a) are directly stimulated by macrophages (b) attack infected cells (c) mature in the bone marrow (d) help shut down the immune response.
13. Which of the following is *not* true of autoimmune diseases?
    (a) An example is Type 1 diabetes.
    (b) They are a type of cancer.
    (c) They target the body's cells.
    (d) They can be fatal.
14. HIV is transmitted through (a) infected food or water (b) sexual contact that involves the exchange of body fluids (c) intravenous injections with contaminated syringes (d) both b and c.
15. HIV (a) infects only macrophages (b) has DNA as its genetic material (c) can be eliminated with antibiotics (d) replicates in helper T cells.

Short Answer

16. What steps must be followed to prove that a particular pathogen is responsible for a disease?
17. Look at the diagram shown below.
    a. Identify the cell labeled *1*.
    b. What is the function of the structure labeled *2*?
    c. What process is illustrated by this diagram?

18. How does the function of the mucous membranes compare with that of the skin?
19. Describe the steps of an inflammatory response.
20. What is the function of the thymus?
21. Describe the primary immune response.
22. What functions do antibodies serve?
23. What are memory cells, and what is their role in providing immunity against disease?
24. What white blood cells are involved in the inflammatory response?
25. What problem have scientists encountered in trying to develop a vaccine against HIV?

CRITICAL THINKING

1. Many people take fever-reducing drugs as soon as their temperature exceeds 37°C (99°F). Why might it not be a good idea to immediately reduce a fever with drugs? What are the benefits of taking fever-reducing drugs?

2. Scientists created an effective vaccine for smallpox but have not been able to do so for AIDS. What does this suggest about the rate of evolution of the smallpox virus?

3. Cytotoxic T cells attack and destroy some kinds of cancer cells. What can you conclude about the surface proteins of these cancer cells?

4. A government agency is reviewing two proposals for HIV research, but it can fund only one. Suppose you are asked to provide input. Which proposal would you recommend that the agency fund? You should consider not only the likely effectiveness of the treatment but also the likely side effects. Explain how you made your choice. **Proposal 1**: Develop a drug that interferes with protein synthesis. **Proposal 2:** Develop a substance that binds to CD4 receptors on helper T cells.

5. Look at the graph shown below. It shows the amount of HIV in the blood of an infected person. Answer the following questions about the graph:
   a. What caused the peak in viral concentration at point *a*?
   b. Why did the level of virus drop between points *a* and *b*?
   c. Describe what is happening to both the virus and the immune system at points *c* and *d*.

Virus Concentration in HIV Infection

EXTENSION

1. Read "Granting Immunity" in *Scientific American*, March 2000, on page 15. Why are some parents becoming uncooperative about obtaining vaccines for their children? At what age should a person have the chicken pox vaccine?

2. Use the *Physicians' Desk Reference* (PDR) at your local library to research the large numbers of specialized antibiotics made by drug companies. To summarize what you have learned, make a large chart on poster board using the following headings: brand name of the drug, generic name of the drug, uses of the drug, company that manufactures the drug, and disease the drug controls. Select five or six antibiotics, and fill in the appropriate information on the chart.

3. During the early stages of the AIDS epidemic, many hemophiliacs became infected with HIV after using infected clotting factor. Using library resources or an on-line database, research this aspect of the AIDS epidemic. Why do hemophiliacs need clotting factor? How was it produced, and how did this lead to contamination with HIV? What changes have been made in the production of clotting factor to reduce the risk of infection?

Simulating Disease Transmission

OBJECTIVES

■ Simulate the transmission of a disease.
■ Determine the original carrier of the disease.

PROCESS SKILLS

■ organizing data
■ analyzing data
■ identifying
■ modeling

MATERIALS

■ lab apron
■ safety goggles
■ disposable gloves
■ dropper bottle of unknown solution
■ large test tube
■ indophenol indicator

Background

1. What are the five main ways that human diseases can be transmitted?
2. How does a cold or flu spread from person to person?
3. How does the body fight invading viruses?
4. Why has the transmission of HIV become a great concern worldwide?
5. Why is a person with AIDS less able to combat infections than a person who does not have AIDS?

PART A   Simulating the Transmission of a Disease

1. This investigation will involve the class in a simulation of disease transmission. After the simulation, you will try to identify the original infected person in the closed class population.

2. In your lab report, construct a data table similar to Table A.

3. **CAUTION Put on a lab apron, goggles, and disposable gloves.**

4. **CAUTION If you get any solution used in this investigation on your skin or clothing, wash it off at the sink while calling to your**

TABLE A   LIST OF PARTNERS' NAMES

Round number	Partner's name
1	
2	
3	

teacher. **If you get any solution used in this investigation in your eyes, immediately flush your eyes with water at the eyewash station while calling to your teacher.** You have been given a dropper bottle of unknown solution and a clean test tube. The solution in the dropper bottle represents the pathogens that you carry. Handle the unknown solution with care because it is not simply water.

5. When your teacher says to begin, transfer three dropperfuls of your solution to your clean test tube. Then replace the lid on the dropper bottle and do not re-open it until Part B of this investigation.

6. Select one person to be your partner. Let one partner pour the contents of his or her test tube into the other partner's test tube. Then pour half the solution back into the first test tube. You and your partner now share pathogens of any possible transmittable disease that either of you might have had. Record the name of your first partner (Round 1) in your data table in your lab report.

7. For Round 2, wait for your teacher's signal, and then find a different partner and exchange solutions in the same manner as you did in step 6. Record the name of your second partner (Round 2) in your lab report. Do not exchange solutions with the same person more than once. Repeat this procedure again for Round 3.

8. After all rounds are finished, your instructor will ask you to add one dropperful of indophenol indicator to your test tube to see if the fluids in your test tube have become infected. Infected solutions will be colorless or light pink. All uninfected solutions will appear blue. Record the outcome of your tests in your lab report.

TABLE B PATH OF DISEASE TRANSMISSION

Name of infected person	Names of infected person's partners		
	Round 1	Round 2	Round 3

PART B Tracing the Source of the Disease

9. If you are an infected person, give your name to your teacher. As names of infected people are written on the chalkboard or on the overhead projector, record them in your lab report in a table similar to Table B shown above.

10. Try to trace the original source of the infection, then determine the transmission route of the disease. In your table, cross out the names of all the uninfected partners in Rounds 1, 2, and 3. There should be only two people in Round 1 who were infected. One of these people was the original carrier.

11. Draw a diagram that shows the transmission route of the disease through all three rounds. Your diagram may look something like the chart below. Include your diagram in your lab report.

Transmission Route

12. In your diagram, insert the names of the two people in Round 1 who were infected and the names of their partners in Rounds 2 and 3.

13. To test whether a person was the original disease carrier, pour a sample from his or her dropper bottle into a clean test tube and add indophenol indicator.

14. Clean up your materials and wash your hands before leaving the lab.

Analysis and Conclusions

1. What might the clear fluid in each student's dropper bottle represent?
2. Does the simulated disease have any apparent symptoms?
3. What chemical is added to the test tubes when the rounds are completed?
4. What color indicates a positive result?
5. What color indicates a negative result?
6. Who was the original disease carrier?
7. After the three rounds, how many students were infected? Express this as a percentage of the number of students in the class.
8. If an epidemic occurred in your community, how might public-health officials work to stop the spread of the disease?

Further Inquiry

A public-health official is sent to investigate an outbreak of a new disease. Devise an experiment to allow the official to determine whether the disease has been caused by the passing of pathogens from person to person or by environmental conditions.

CHAPTER 49

DIGESTIVE AND EXCRETORY SYSTEMS

This is a scanning electron micrograph of a filtration membrane in the human kidney. (SEM 3060×)

FOCUS CONCEPT: *Structure and Function*

As you read, notice how the structure of each digestive and excretory organ relates to its function.

NUTRIENTS

Carrots, fish, eggs, hamburgers, blackberries, cow's milk—the human body is able to convert each of these foods into nutrients that body cells need to function, grow, and replicate. In this section you will learn what nutrients the human body needs and how it uses those nutrients to carry out life processes.

SIX BASIC FOOD INGREDIENTS

All of the different foods in the world contain at least one of six basic ingredients: carbohydrates, proteins, lipids, vitamins, minerals, and water. These ingredients, called **nutrients,** are the chemical substances necessary for organisms to grow and function properly. Four of these nutrients—carbohydrates, proteins, fats, and vitamins—are organic compounds because they contain the elements carbon, hydrogen, and oxygen. The two remaining nutrients—minerals and water—are inorganic compounds.

Few foods contain all six nutrients. In fact, most foods contain a concentration of just one or two. Nutritionists classify foods into four groups—meat, milk, fruits and vegetables, and breads and cereals—based on nutrient similarity.

Carbohydrates

Carbohydrates are organic compounds composed of carbon, hydrogen, and oxygen in a ratio of about two hydrogen atoms to one oxygen atom and one carbon atom. Carbohydrates are broken down in aerobic respiration to provide most of the body's energy. Although proteins and fats also supply energy, the body most easily uses the energy provided by carbohydrates. Carbohydrates contain sugars that are quickly converted into the usable energy ATP, while proteins and fats must go through many chemical processes before the body can obtain energy from them.

The fructose and glucose (also known as dextrose) in fruit and honey are simple sugars, or monosaccharides. These sugars can be absorbed directly into the bloodstream and made available to cells for use in aerobic respiration. Sucrose (cane sugar), maltose, and lactose (milk sugar) are disaccharides. Disaccharides are sugars that consist of two chemically linked monosaccharides. These disaccharides must be converted into monosaccharides before they can be used by the body for energy. Disaccharides are split into two

SECTION

49-1

OBJECTIVES

▲

List the four organic nutrients needed by the human body.

●

Identify foods containing each of the organic nutrients.

■

Explain the importance of inorganic mineral nutrients.

◆

Summarize the functions that the six nutrients perform in the body.

▲

Explain why water is a vital nutrient.

internet**connect**

SC*i*LINKS
NSTA

TOPIC: Nutrients
GO TO: www.scilinks.org
KEYWORD: HM977

SUCROSE

+

Water (H₂O)

GLUCOSE   FRUCTOSE

FIGURE 49-1

The hydrolysis, or digestion, of a disaccharide, such as sucrose, requires water and an enzyme. When sucrose is digested, two monosaccharides are formed—glucose and fructose. These monosaccharides are then transported through cell membranes to be used by cells.

FIGURE 49-2

The combination of legumes with seeds or grains and the combination of grains with milk products furnish all the essential amino acids.

monosaccharides in a process called hydrolysis. Figure 49-1 shows how sucrose is hydrolyzed to produce glucose and fructose.

The carbohydrates that require the longest digestion time are polysaccharides. Polysaccharides are complex molecules that consist of many monosaccharides bonded together. The starch found in rice, corn, and many other grains and vegetables is a polysaccharide made up of long chains of glucose molecules. During digestion, the body chemically breaks down these long chains into individual glucose units, which then can be absorbed by the blood and carried to the tissues.

Many foods we get from plants contain cellulose, a polysaccharide that the body cannot break down into individual component sugars. Cellulose, the substance that forms the walls of plant cells, is nevertheless an extremely important part of the human diet. Although indigestible, it provides fiber that aids in human digestion. Cellulose stimulates contractions of the smooth muscles that line the organs of the digestive system. These contractions help move the food along.

Proteins

Proteins are the major structural and functional material of body cells. Proteins from food help the body to grow and to repair tissues. Proteins consist of long chains of amino acids. The human body uses about 20 kinds of amino acids to construct the proteins it needs. The body manufactures many of these amino acids, but it cannot produce all of them in the quantities that it needs. Amino acids that the body produces are called nonessential amino acids because you do not have to get them from your food. Amino acids that must be obtained from food are called essential amino acids. Ten amino acids are essential to children and teenagers, while only eight are essential to adults. The two additional amino acids needed by children are involved in growth.

Most of the foods we get from plants do not contain all the essential amino acids. Eating certain combinations of two or more plant products, such as those shown in Figure 49-2, can supply all the essential amino acids. Vegetarians who do not eat animal

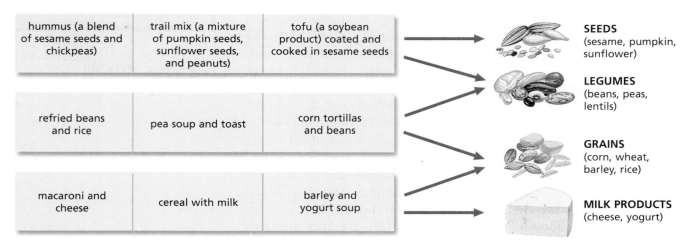

hummus (a blend of sesame seeds and chickpeas)	trail mix (a mixture of pumpkin seeds, sunflower seeds, and peanuts)	tofu (a soybean product) coated and cooked in sesame seeds	**SEEDS** (sesame, pumpkin, sunflower)
refried beans and rice	pea soup and toast	corn tortillas and beans	**LEGUMES** (beans, peas, lentils)
macaroni and cheese	cereal with milk	barley and yogurt soup	**GRAINS** (corn, wheat, barley, rice) **MILK PRODUCTS** (cheese, yogurt)

products get their proteins by eating combinations of two or more plant products or by combining seeds or grains with legumes. Most animal products, such as eggs, milk, fish, poultry, and beef, contain all the essential amino acids.

Lipids

Lipids are organic compounds that contain more carbon and hydrogen atoms than oxygen atoms. Lipids include triglycerides, commonly known as fats. Fats are organic molecules that the body uses to obtain energy and to build cell membranes and other cell parts. The body stores excess fat from the diet in special tissues under the skin and around the kidneys and liver. Excess carbohydrates may be converted to fat for storage.

Why does the human body store fat? The answer is that stored fats are beneficial unless they are excessive. A light layer of body fat beneath the skin provides insulation in cold weather. Fat surrounding vulnerable organs, such as the kidneys and liver, acts as protective padding. And most important, fat reserves are a source of energy. While you cannot live off just your body fat, the body can use its fat for energy, especially when carbohydrates are unavailable.

To use fats, the body must first break down each fat molecule into glycerol and fatty acids. The glycerol molecule is the same in all fats, but the fatty acids differ in both structure and composition. The body converts some fatty acids to other fatty acids, depending on which one the body needs at the time.

Scientists classify fats as saturated or unsaturated, based on structural differences in their fatty acids. A saturated fatty acid has all its carbon atoms connected by single bonds and thus contains as many hydrogen atoms as possible. An unsaturated fatty acid has at least one double bond between carbon atoms. If there are two or more double bonds, the fatty acid is called polyunsaturated. How many double bonds are shown in the structure of a fatty acid in Figure 49-3? In general, animal fats are saturated and plant oils are unsaturated. However, some vegetable oils, such as palm oil and coconut oil, are composed primarily of saturated fats.

FIGURE 49-3

The structure of linoleic acid, a fatty acid in margarine, is shown in this figure. Is this fatty acid saturated, unsaturated, or polyunsaturated?

Linoleic acid

TABLE 49-1 *Food Sources of Vitamins*

Vitamins	Best sources	Essential for	Deficiency diseases and symptoms
Vitamin A (carotene; fat soluble)	fish-liver oils, liver and kidney, green and yellow vegetables, yellow fruit, tomatoes, butter, egg yolk	growth, health of the eyes, and functioning of the cells of the skin and mucous membranes	retarded growth, night blindness, susceptibility to infections, changes in skin, defective tooth formation
Vitamin B$_1$ (thiamin; water soluble)	meat, soybeans, milk, whole grains, legumes	growth; carbohydrate metabolism; functioning of the heart, nerves, muscles	beriberi—loss of appetite and weight, nerve disorders, and faulty digestion
Vitamin B$_2$ (riboflavin; water soluble)	meat, fowl, soybeans, milk, green vegetables, eggs, yeast	growth, health of the skin and mouth, carbohydrate metabolism, functioning of the eyes, red blood cell formation	retarded growth, dimness of vision, inflammation of the tongue, premature aging, intolerance to light
Vitamin B$_3$ (niacin; water soluble)	meat, fowl, fish, peanut butter, potatoes, whole grains, tomatoes, leafy vegetables	growth; carbohydrate metabolism; functioning of the stomach, intestines, and nervous system	pellagra—smoothness of the tongue, skin eruptions, digestive disturbances, and mental disorders
Vitamin B$_6$ (pyridoxine; water soluble)	whole grains, liver, fish	coenzymes for metabolic reactions	dermatitis, nervous disorders
Vitamin B$_{12}$ (cyanocobalamin; water soluble)	green vegetables, liver	preventing pernicious anemia	a reduction in number of red blood cells
Vitamin C (ascorbic acid; water soluble)	fruit (especially citrus), tomatoes, leafy vegetables	growth, strength of the blood vessels, development of teeth, health of gums	scurvy—sore gums, hemorrhages around the bones, and tendency to bruise easily
Vitamin D (calciferol; fat soluble)	fish-liver oil, liver, fortified milk, eggs, irradiated foods	growth, calcium and phosphorus metabolism, bones and teeth	rickets—soft bones, poor development of teeth, and dental decay
Vitamin E (tocopherol; fat soluble)	wheat-germ oil, leafy vegetables, milk, butter	normal reproduction	anemia in newborns
Vitamin K (naphthoquinone; fat soluble)	green vegetables, soybean oil, tomatoes	normal clotting of the blood, liver functions	hemorrhages

Vitamins

Vitamins are complex organic molecules that serve as coenzymes. Vitamins activate the enzymes and help them function. For example, vitamin B$_1$, or thiamin, is essential to the functioning of two enzymes that catalyze the first step in aerobic respiration. Because vitamins generally cannot be synthesized by the body, a diet should include the proper daily amounts of all vitamins. Like enzymes, coenzymes can be reused many times. Thus only small quantities of vitamins are needed in the diet. Table 49-1 summarizes the sources of the vitamins and their functions.

Vitamins dissolve in either water or fat. The fat-soluble vitamins include vitamins A, D, E, and K. The water-soluble vitamins are vitamins C and the B vitamins. Fat-soluble vitamins are absorbed and stored like fats. As with fats, the body can amass a reserve of fat-soluble vitamins. Unpleasant physical symptoms and even death can result from storing too much or having too little of a particular vitamin. Continual large doses of vitamin A, for example, can result in severe nausea and a yellow skin color. Because the body cannot store water-soluble vitamins, it excretes surplus amounts in urine.

The only vitamin that the body can synthesize in large quantities is vitamin D. This synthesis involves the conversion of cholesterol to vitamin D by intestinal enzymes and sunlight. People who do not spend a lot of time in the sun can get their vitamin D from food. With the exception of vitamin D, human beings must obtain the vitamins they need from food sources and vitamin supplements.

Minerals

Minerals are inorganic substances required for the normal functioning of the body. Some minerals, such as calcium, magnesium, and iron, are drawn from the soil and become part of plants. Animals that feed on plants extract the minerals and incorporate them into their bodies. Table 49-2 lists the primary sources and functions of a few of the minerals considered most essential to human beings. Iron, for example, is necessary for the formation of red blood cells, while potassium maintains the body's acid-base balance and aids in growth. Both are found in certain fruits and vegetables; iron is also found in meats. Iodine—found in seafood, water, and iodized salt—is needed for hormone production by the thyroid gland. Minerals are excreted through the skin in perspiration and through the kidneys in urine.

TABLE 49-2 *Food Sources of Minerals*

Minerals	Source	Essential for
Calcium salts	milk, whole-grain cereals, vegetables, meats	deposition in bones and teeth; functioning of heart, muscles, and nerves
Iodine	seafoods, water, iodized salt	thyroid gland secretion
Iron salts	leafy vegetables, liver, meats, raisins, prunes	formation of red blood cells
Magnesium salts	vegetables	muscle and nerve action
Phosphorus salts	milk, whole-grain cereals, vegetables, meats	deposition in bones and teeth; formation of ATP and nucleic acid
Potassium salts	vegetables, citrus fruits, bananas, apricots	maintaining acid-base balance; growth; nerve action
Sodium salts	table salt, vegetables	blood and other body tissues; nerve action

TABLE 49-3 *Sources of Water Balance in Humans*

Source of water	Water gain (mL/day)	Water loss (mL/day)
Ingested in liquid	1,500 (60%)	
Ingested in food	750 (30%)	
Derived from metabolism	250 (10%)	
Evaporation		900 (36%)
Urine		1,500 (60%)
Feces		100 (4%)
Total gain	2,500 (100%)	
Total loss		2,500 (100%)

Water

Water accounts for over half of your body weight. Most of the reactions that maintain life can take place only in water. Water makes up over 90 percent of the fluid part of the blood, which carries essential nutrients to all parts of the body. It is also the medium in which waste products are dissolved and carried away from body tissues.

Water also helps regulate body temperature. It absorbs the heat released in cellular reactions and distributes the heat throughout the body. When the body needs to cool, perspiration—a water-based substance—evaporates from the skin, and heat is drawn away from the body.

Usually the water lost through your skin and kidneys is easily replaced by drinking water or consuming moist foods. If excess water is lost and not replenished, water moves from intercellular spaces to the blood by osmosis. Eventually, water will be drawn from the cells themselves. As a cell loses water, the cytoplasm becomes more concentrated until, finally, the cell can no longer function. This condition is referred to as **dehydration.** Humans can die if they lose as much as 12 percent of their body water. Table 49-3 summarizes sources of water gain and loss for the average person in the United States. The statistics vary according to the person's location and level of activity.

SECTION 49-1 REVIEW

1. Differentiate between organic nutrients and inorganic nutrients.

2. What are the primary functions performed by proteins?

3. Describe three benefits of a normal distribution of body fat.

4. Explain why water is a vital nutrient.

5. Explain the function of indigestible cellulose in digestion.

6. CRITICAL THINKING   What do you think the consequences might be of a diet of only water, brown rice, and fruits?

DIGESTIVE SYSTEM

*B*efore your body can use the nutrients in the food you consume, the nutrients must be broken down physically and chemically. This process of breaking down food into molecules the body can use is called **digestion.**

THE GASTROINTESTINAL TRACT

Digestion occurs in the **gastrointestinal tract,** or digestive tract, which begins at the mouth and winds through the body to the anus. The gastrointestinal tract, shown in Figure 49-4, is a long, winding tube that is divided into several distinct organs. These organs, such as the stomach and small intestine, carry out the digestive process. Located along the gastrointestinal tract are other organs that aid in digestion. These organs, such as the liver and pancreas, are not part of the gastrointestinal tract, but they deliver secretions into the tract through ducts. As you read, locate each of the structures of the digestive system in Figure 49-4.

SECTION

49-2

OBJECTIVES

▲

List the major organs of the digestive system.

●

Distinguish between mechanical digestion and chemical digestion.

■

Relate the structure of each digestive organ to its function in mechanical digestion.

◆

Identify the source of each major digestive enzyme, and describe the function of the enzyme.

▲

Summarize the process of absorption in both the small and large intestine.

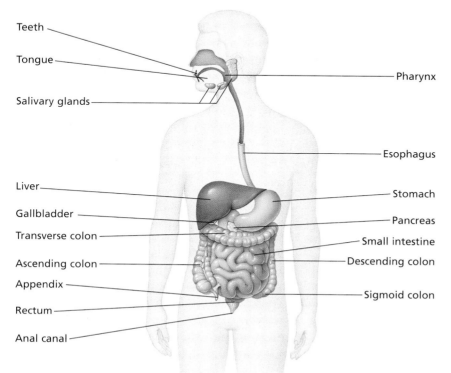

Teeth
Tongue
Salivary glands
Pharynx
Esophagus
Liver
Stomach
Gallbladder
Pancreas
Transverse colon
Small intestine
Ascending colon
Descending colon
Appendix
Rectum
Sigmoid colon
Anal canal

FIGURE 49-4

Notice that the gastrointestinal tract is basically a long tube with an opening at each end. Although food never passes through the liver and pancreas, these two organs are part of the digestive system because they secrete enzymes that break down food.

FIGURE 49-5

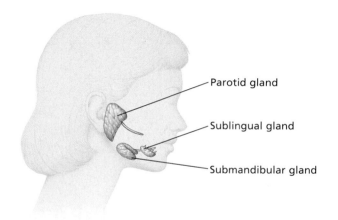

Parotid gland

Sublingual gland

Submandibular gland

Mouth

When you take a bite of food, you begin the mechanical phase of digestion. In the mechanical phase, the body physically breaks down chunks of food into small particles. Mechanical digestion increases the surface area of food on which digestive enzymes can act. **Incisors**—sharp, flat front teeth—cut the food. Then the broad, flat surfaces of **molars,** or back teeth, grind it up. The tongue helps keep the food between the chewing surfaces of the upper and lower teeth by manipulating it against the **hard palate,** the bony, membrane-covered roof of the mouth. This structure is different from the **soft palate,** an area located just behind the hard palate. The soft palate is made of folded membranes and separates the mouth cavity from the nasal cavity.

While the mechanical phase of digestion is occurring, the chemical phase of digestion also takes place. Chemical digestion involves a change in the chemical nature of the nutrients. Preparations for chemical digestion begin even before the first bite of food is taken. The mouth starts to water—that is, the salivary glands increase their production of **saliva** (suh-LIE-vuh), a mixture of water, mucus, and a digestive enzyme called salivary amylase. Besides the many tiny salivary glands located in the lining of the mouth, there are three more pairs of larger salivary glands. Locate the three sets of salivary glands in Figure 49-5.

The mucus in the saliva softens and lubricates food and helps hold the food together. The salivary amylase begins the chemical digestion of carbohydrates by breaking down some starch into the disaccharide maltose.

Esophagus

After food has been thoroughly chewed, moistened, and rolled into a **bolus,** or ball, it is forced into the pharynx by swallowing action. The pharynx, an open area that begins at the back of the mouth, serves as a passageway for both air and food. As Figure 49-6 shows, during swallowing, a flap of tissue called the **epiglottis** (ep-uh-GLAHT-is) prevents food from entering the trachea, or windpipe. Instead, the bolus passes into the esophagus, a muscular tube approximately 25 cm long that connects the pharynx with the stomach. The esophagus has two muscle layers: a circular layer that wraps

FIGURE 49-6

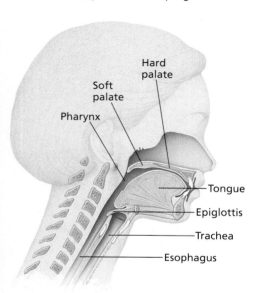

Soft palate

Hard palate

Pharynx

Tongue

Epiglottis

Trachea

Esophagus

around the esophagus and a longitudinal layer that runs the length of the tube. As you can see in Figure 49-7, alternating contractions of these muscle layers push the bolus through the esophagus and into the stomach. This series of rhythmic muscular contractions and relaxations is called **peristalsis.**

Stomach

The **stomach,** an organ involved in both mechanical and chemical digestion, is located in the upper left side of the abdominal cavity, just below the diaphragm. It is an elastic bag that is J-shaped when full and that lies in folds when empty. You have probably heard your stomach "growl" when it has been empty for some time. These sounds are made by the contraction of smooth muscles that line the stomach.

The walls of the stomach have several layers of smooth muscle. As you can see in Figure 49-8, there are three layers of muscle—a circular layer, a longitudinal layer, and a diagonal layer. Together, these muscles twist and turn the stomach. When nothing is present in the stomach, the growling sound is the result. When food is present, the muscles churn the contents of the stomach. This churning helps the stomach carry out mechanical digestion.

The inner lining of the stomach is a thick, wrinkled mucous membrane composed of epithelial cells. This membrane is dotted with small openings called gastric pits. **Gastric pits,** which are shown in Figure 49-9, are the open ends of gastric glands that release secretions into the stomach. Some of these glands secrete mucus, some secrete digestive enzymes, and still others secrete hydrochloric acid. The mixture of these secretions forms the acidic digestive fluid.

Muscle relaxed
Circular muscle
Bolus of food
Longitudinal muscle
Muscles contracted
Bolus of food
Muscles relaxed

FIGURE 49-7

Peristalsis is so efficient at moving materials down the esophagus that you can drink while standing on your head. The smooth muscles move the water "up" the esophagus, against the force of gravity.

Esophagus
Longitudinal muscle
Diagonal muscle
Small intestine
Circular muscle

FIGURE 49-8

Each of the muscle layers of the stomach is oriented in a different direction. This allows the stomach to twist and turn in a variety of ways to thoroughly mix food.

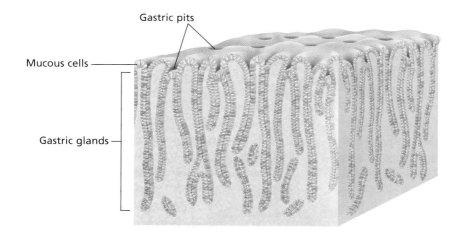

Gastric pits
Mucous cells
Gastric glands

FIGURE 49-9

Because of the hydrochloric acid that the gastric glands secrete, the pH of the stomach is normally between 1.5 and 2.5, making it by far the most acidic environment in the body. Mucous cells lining the stomach wall protect the organ from damage.

CHEMICAL DIGESTION

internet**connect**

SCi**LINKS**
NSTA

TOPIC: Chemical
digestion
GO TO: www.scilinks.org
KEYWORD: HM986

Gastric fluid carries out chemical digestion in the stomach. An inactive stomach secretion called pepsinogen is converted into a digestive enzyme called **pepsin** at a low pH. Chemical digestion starts in the stomach when pepsin splits complex protein molecules into shorter chains of amino acids called peptides. The presence of hydrochloric acid in the stomach not only ensures the low pH needed for the pepsinogen to transform into pepsin, but also dissolves minerals and kills bacteria that enter the stomach along with food.

The mucus secreted in the stomach is vital to the survival of this organ. Mucus forms a coating that protects the lining from hydrochloric acid and prevents pepsin from digesting the proteins that make up the stomach tissue. In some people, the mucous coating of the stomach tissue breaks down, allowing digestive enzymes to eat through part of the stomach lining. The lesion, or sore, that results is called an **ulcer.** Scientists have recently discovered that the breakdown of the mucous layer is often caused by bacteria. These bacteria secrete toxins that destroy the epithelial cells that form the mucous layer.

Formation of Chyme

The **cardiac sphincter** (SFINK-tuhr) is a circular muscle located between the esophagus and the stomach. Food enters the stomach when the cardiac sphincter opens. After the food enters the stomach, the cardiac sphincter closes to prevent the food from reentering the esophagus. Food usually remains in the stomach for three to four hours. During this time, muscle contractions in the stomach churn the contents, breaking up food particles and mixing them with gastric fluid. This process forms a mixture called **chyme** (KIEM), a pastelike substance containing various nutrients. Chyme usually contains fats, sugars, starches, vitamins, minerals, peptides, and proteins that were not broken down by the pepsin.

Peristalsis forces chyme out of the stomach and into the small intestine. The **pyloric** (pie-LOR-ik) **sphincter,** a circular muscle between the stomach and the small intestine, regulates the flow of chyme. Each time the pyloric sphincter opens, about 5 to 15 mL (about 0.2 to 0.5 oz) of chyme moves into the small intestine, where it mixes with secretions from the liver and pancreas.

Liver

The **liver** is a large organ located to the right of the stomach and in the upper right area of the abdominal cavity, just below the diaphragm, as shown in Figure 49-10. The liver performs numerous functions in the body, including storing glycogen and breaking down toxic substances, such as alcohol. The liver also secretes bile, which is vital in the digestion of fats. Though it is not a digestive enzyme, bile breaks fat globules into small droplets, forming a

FIGURE 49-10

The liver is the body's largest internal organ, weighing about 1.5 kg (3 lb). If a small portion is surgically removed because of disease or injury, the liver regenerates the missing section.

Diaphragm

Liver

Stomach

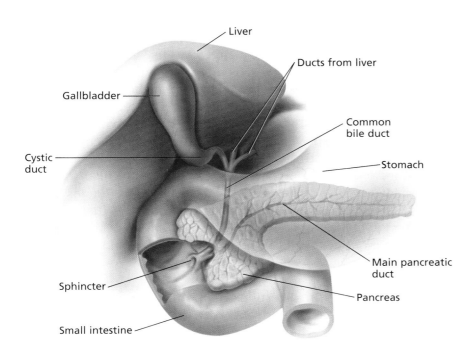

Liver
Ducts from liver
Gallbladder
Common bile duct
Cystic duct
Stomach
Sphincter
Main pancreatic duct
Pancreas
Small intestine

FIGURE 49-11

Cholesterol deposits known as gallstones can form in the ducts leading from the liver and gallbladder to the small intestine. If the gallstones interfere with the flow of bile, they must be removed, along with the gallbladder in most cases.

milky fluid in which fats are suspended. This process exposes a greater surface area of fats to the action of digestive enzymes and prevents small fat droplets from rejoining into large globules.

The bile secreted by the liver passes through a Y-shaped duct, as shown in Figure 49-11. The bile travels down one branch of the Y, the hepatic duct, and then up the other branch, the cystic duct, to the **gallbladder,** a saclike organ that stores and concentrates bile. When chyme is present in the small intestine, the gallbladder releases bile through the common bile duct into the small intestine.

Pancreas

As you can see in Figure 49-12, the pancreas is an organ that lies behind the stomach, against the back wall of the abdominal cavity. As part of the digestive system, the pancreas secretes pancreatic fluid, which contains digestive enzymes that help complete the breakdown of nutrients in the chyme. This pancreatic fluid enters the small intestine through the pancreatic duct, which joins the common bile duct just before it enters the intestine.

Pancreatic fluid contains sodium bicarbonate, which changes the pH of the chyme from an acid to a base. Many enzymes in the pancreatic fluid are activated by the higher pH. These enzymes hydrolyze disaccharides into monosaccharides, fats into fatty acids and glycerol, and proteins into amino acids.

Small Intestine

If you could stretch the small intestine to its full length, you would find that it is nearly 7 m (about 21 ft) long. The duodenum, the first section of this coiled tube, makes up only the first 25 cm (about

FIGURE 49-12

Most of the pancreas looks like the salivary glands of the mouth region. Like the salivary glands, the pancreas secretes amylases to digest carbohydrates. Other digestive enzymes are secreted by the pancreas to break down nutrients in the chyme.

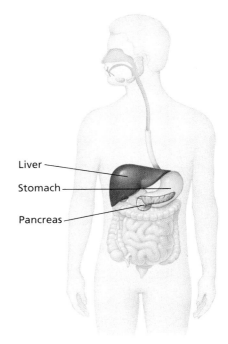

Liver
Stomach
Pancreas

10 in.) of that length. The **jejunum** (jee-JOO-nuhm), the middle section, is about 2.5 m (about 8 ft) long. The ileum, which makes up the remaining portion of the small intestine, is approximately 4 m (about 13 ft) in length. As you can see in Figure 49-13, the entire length of the small intestine lies coiled in the abdominal cavity.

The secretions from the liver and pancreas enter the duodenum, where they continue the chemical digestion of chyme. When the secretions from the liver and pancreas, along with the chyme, enter the duodenum, they trigger intestinal mucous glands to release large quantities of mucus. This mucus protects the intestinal wall from protein-digesting enzymes and the acidic chyme. Glands in the mucous lining of the small intestine release enzymes that complete digestion by breaking down peptides into amino acids, disaccharides into monosaccharides, and fats into glycerol and fatty acids.

Absorption

The end products of digestion—amino acids, monosaccharides, glycerol, and fatty acids—are absorbed into the circulatory system through blood and lymph vessels in the lining of the small intestine. The structure of this lining provides a huge surface area for absorption to take place. In **absorption,** the end products of digestion are transferred into the circulatory system. The highly folded lining of the small intestine is covered with millions of fingerlike projections called **villi,** which are shown in Figure 49-14. The cells covering the villi, in turn, have extensions on their cell membranes called **microvilli.** The folds, villi, and microvilli give the small intestine a surface area of about 250 m^2 (about 2,685 ft^2), or roughly the area of a tennis court. Nutrients are absorbed through this surface by means of diffusion and active transport.

Inside each of the villi are capillaries and tiny lymph vessels called **lacteals** (lak-TEE-uhls). Locate the lacteals in Figure 49-14.

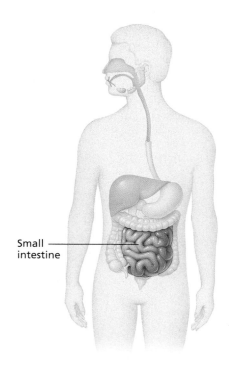

Small intestine

FIGURE 49-13

Although the small intestine is nearly 7 m long, only the first 25 cm is involved in digesting food. The rest is involved in the absorption of the digested products, including monosaccharides, amino acids, glycerol, and fatty acids.

FIGURE 49-14

Villi, as shown in the SEM (137×) and the diagram, expand the surface area of the small intestine to allow greater absorption of nutrients.

Capillaries

Villus

Lacteal

Glycerol and fatty acids enter the lacteals, which carry them through the lymph vessels and eventually to the bloodstream through lymphatic vessels near the heart. Amino acids and monosaccharides enter the capillaries and are carried to the liver. The liver neutralizes many toxic substances in the blood and removes excess glucose, converting it to glycogen for storage. The filtered blood then carries the nutrients to all parts of the body.

LARGE INTESTINE

After absorption in the small intestine is complete, peristalsis moves the remaining material on to the large intestine. The **large intestine,** or **colon,** is the final organ of digestion. Study Figure 49-15 to identify the four major parts of the colon: ascending colon, transverse colon, descending colon, and sigmoid colon. The sigmoid colon leads into the very short, final portions of the large intestine called the rectum and the anal canal.

Most of the absorption of nutrients and water is completed in the small intestine. About 9 L (about 9.5 qt) of water enters the small intestine daily, but only 0.5 L (about 0.53 qt) of water is present in the material that enters the large intestine. In the large intestine, only minerals and vitamins produced by bacteria that live in the colon, as well as most of the remainder of the water, are absorbed. Slow contractions move the material in the large intestine toward the rectum. Distension of the colon initiates reflex contractions which move the material out of the body. As this matter moves through the intestine, the absorption of water solidifies the mass. The solidified material is called **feces.**

As the fecal matter solidifies, cells lining the large intestine secrete mucus to lubricate the intestinal wall. This lubrication makes the passing of the feces less abrasive. Mucus also binds together the fecal matter, which is then eliminated through the anus.

FIGURE 49-15

This X ray shows the large intestine, or colon. Identify the four major regions of the colon in the X ray.

SECTION 49-2 REVIEW

1. Describe the gastrointestinal tract.

2. Name one structure involved in the mechanical phase of digestion, and explain its function in mechanical digestion.

3. Trace the route of bile, noting where it is produced, where it is stored, and how it functions in digestion.

4. Explain how the structure of the small intestine is related to the function of absorption.

5. Compare the process of chemical digestion with the process of mechanical digestion, and list the organs involved in each.

6. **CRITICAL THINKING** Which of the six basic nutrients might a person need to restrict after an operation to remove the gallbladder? Explain your answer.

Food Poisoning

The following excerpt is from "Family Reunion," a chapter in *Eleven Blue Men and Other Narratives of Medical Detection,* by Berton Roueché, published in 1954.

Botulism is a true but atypical form of food poisoning. Its methodical approach, its excessive lethality, and the predominantly neural cast of its clinical features all are unpleasantly peculiar. Even its history is unusual. Ordinary food poisoning, in common with many other ailments, is probably as old as mankind. Its beginnings go back to the first butcher with an infected finger, the first cook with a streptococcic cough, the first imprudent assumption of the first man rash enough to eat mushrooms.

Botulism is of far less fundamental origin. It is, in fact, one of the very few diseases for whose existence man has nobody to blame but himself. Like carbon-monoxide poisoning, and alcoholism, and the bends, botulism is essentially, if inadvertently, a product of human ingenuity. *Clostridium botulinum,* though plethorically abundant throughout the world, is not among man's natural antagonists. The organism is incapable of establishing itself in any living plant or animal. Its home is soil and earthy dust, its food is inanimate matter, and although it is able to exist in a dormant, sporal state almost indefinitely in almost any environment, it can mature and multiply and manufacture its vigorous venom only in the total absence of oxygen. Because of these physiological quirks, the toxin of *Clostridium botulinum,* under normal conditions, is safely out of human reach. It is dissipated deep in the earth.

Exactly when botulism seized its first victim is unknown, but it could hardly have been more than eight or ten thousand years ago, when man ceased to subsist exclusively on fresh food. Freshly gathered food, along with everything else on the face of the earth, is exposed to the intrusion of dust-borne botulinus spores, but it is also exposed to the spore-stunting sweep of air. Botulism came into being when man made the otherwise triumphant discovery that prompt deoxidation would make numerous foods more or less permanently resistant to decay.

Reading for Meaning

How is botulism a result of human ingenuity?

Interpret the writer's meaning when he says that *Clostridium botulinum* is "plethorically abundant."

In the last paragraph, this excerpt explains how the botulism toxin first came into contact with humans. Explain what the writer means by "prompt deoxidation" of food.

Read Further

In an article more recent than this one, what new information might be included about how current methods of food handling help prevent food poisoning?

Use your school library or an on-line database to investigate infant botulism. How does infant botulism relate to sudden infant death syndrome (SIDS)?

URINARY SYSTEM

*T*he body must rid itself of the waste products of cellular activity. The process of removing metabolic wastes, called **excretion,** is just as vital as digestion in maintaining the body's internal environment. Thus, the urinary system not only excretes wastes but also helps maintain homeostasis by regulating the content of water and other substances in the blood.

SECTION

49-3

OBJECTIVES

▲

Define the term *excretion,* and list the functions of each of the major excretory organs.

●

Identify the major parts of the kidney.

■

Relate the structure of a nephron to its function.

◆

Explain how the processes of filtration, reabsorption, and tubular secretion help maintain homeostasis.

▲

Name the main parts of the urinary system.

KIDNEYS

The main waste products that the body must eliminate are carbon dioxide, from cellular respiration, and nitrogenous compounds, from the breakdown of proteins. The lungs excrete most of the carbon dioxide, and nitrogenous wastes are eliminated by the kidneys. The excretion of water is necessary to dissolve wastes and is closely regulated by the kidneys, the main organs of the urinary system.

Humans have two kidneys, bean-shaped excretory organs each about the size of a clenched fist. The kidneys are located in the small of the back, one behind the stomach and the other behind the liver. Together they regulate the chemical composition of the blood.

Structure

Figure 49-16 shows the three main parts of the kidney. The **cortex,** the outermost portion of the kidney, makes up about a third of the

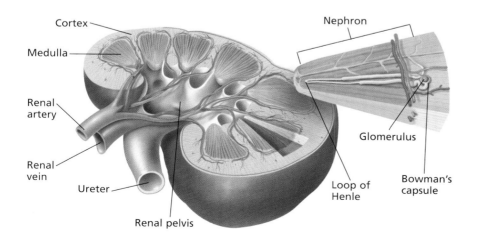

Cortex
Medulla
Renal artery
Renal vein
Ureter
Renal pelvis
Nephron
Glomerulus
Loop of Henle
Bowman's capsule

FIGURE 49-16

The outer region of the kidney, the cortex, contains structures that filter blood brought by the renal artery. The inner region, or medulla, consists of structures that carry urine, which empties into the funnel-shaped renal pelvis. The renal vein transports the filtered blood back to the heart.

kidney's tissue mass. The **medulla** is the inner two-thirds of the kidney. The **renal pelvis** is a funnel-shaped structure in the center of the kidney. Also notice in Figure 49-16 that blood enters the kidney through a renal artery and leaves through a renal vein. The renal artery transports nutrients and wastes to the kidneys. The nutrients are used by kidney cells to carry out their life processes. One such process is the removal of wastes brought by the renal artery.

The most common mammalian metabolic waste is **urea** (yoo-REE-uh), a nitrogenous product made by the liver. Nitrogenous wastes are initially brought to the liver as **ammonia,** a chemical compound of nitrogen so toxic that it could not remain long in the body without harming cells. The liver removes ammonia from the blood and converts it into the less harmful substance urea. The urea enters the bloodstream and is then removed by the kidneys.

Nephrons

The substances removed from the blood by the kidneys—toxins, urea, water, and mineral salts—form an amber-colored liquid called **urine.** Urine is made in structures called **nephrons** (NEF-rahns), the functional units of the kidney.

Take a close look at the structure of the nephron, shown in Figure 49-17. Each kidney consists of more than a million nephrons. If they were stretched out, the nephrons from both kidneys would extend for 80 km (50 mi). As you read about the structure of a nephron, locate each part in Figure 49-17.

FIGURE 49-17

Notice the close association between a nephron of the kidney and capillaries of the circulatory system. Initially, fluid passes from the glomerulus, which is made of a capillary network, into a Bowman's capsule of the nephron. As the fluid travels through the nephron, nutrients that passed into the Bowman's capsule are removed and returned to the bloodstream. All that normally remains in the nephron are waste products, which form the urine that passes out of the kidney.

Each nephron has a cup-shaped structure, called a **Bowman's capsule,** that encloses a bed of capillaries. This capillary bed, called a **glomerulus** (glo-MER-yoo-luhs), receives blood from the renal artery. High pressure forces fluids from the blood through the capillary walls and into the Bowman's capsule. The material filtered from the blood then flows through the **renal tubule,** a long tube with permeable walls. The renal tubule consists of three parts: the proximal convoluted tubule, the loop of Henle, and the distal convoluted tubule. Blood remaining in the glomerulus then flows through a network of capillaries that wraps around these three parts of the renal tubule. The long and winding course of both the renal tubule and the surrounding capillaries provides a large surface area for the exchange of materials.

As the filtrate flows through a nephron, its composition is modified by the exchange of materials among the renal tubule, the capillaries, and the extracellular fluid. Various types of exchanges take place in the different parts of the renal tubule. To understand how the structure of each part of the nephron is related to its function, we will examine the three major processes that take place in the nephron: filtration, reabsorption, and secretion. Figure 49-18 shows the site of each of these processes in the nephron.

Filtration

Materials from the blood are forced out of the glomerulus and into the Bowman's capsule during a process called **filtration.** Blood in the glomerulus is under relatively high pressure. This pressure forces water, urea, glucose, vitamins, and salts through the thin capillary walls of the glomerulus and into the Bowman's capsule. About one-fifth of the fluid portion of the blood filters into the Bowman's capsule. The rest remains in the capillaries, along with proteins and cells that are too large to pass through the capillary walls. In a healthy kidney, the filtrate—the fluid that enters the nephron—does not contain large protein molecules.

Word Roots and Origins

glomerulus

from the French *glomérule,* meaning "a compact cluster"

FIGURE 49-18

Color-coded arrows indicate where in the nephron filtration, reabsorption, and secretion occur.

Reabsorption and Secretion

The body needs to retain many of the substances that were removed from the blood by filtration. Thus, as the filtrate flows through the renal tubule, these materials return to the blood by being selectively transported through the walls of the renal tubule and entering the surrounding capillaries. This process is called **reabsorption.** Most reabsorption occurs in the proximal convoluted tubule. In this region, about 75 percent of the water in the filtrate returns to the capillaries by osmosis. Glucose and minerals, such as sodium, potassium, and calcium, are returned to the blood by active transport. Some additional reabsorption occurs in the distal convoluted tubule.

When the filtrate reaches the distal convoluted tubule, some substances pass from the blood into the filtrate through a process called **secretion.** These substances include wastes and toxic materials. The pH of the blood is adjusted by hydrogen ions that are secreted from the blood into the filtrate.

Formation of Urine

The fluid and wastes that remain in the distal convoluted tubule form urine. The urine from several renal tubules flows into a collecting duct. Notice in Figure 49-19 that the urine is further concentrated in the collecting duct by the osmosis of water through the wall of the duct. This process allows the body to conserve water. In fact, osmosis in the collecting duct, together with reabsorption in other parts of the tubule, returns to the blood about 99 of every 100 mL (about 3.4 oz) of water in the filtrate.

FIGURE 49-19

The sodium chloride that is actively transported out of the loop of Henle makes the extracellular environment surrounding the collecting duct hypertonic. Thus, water moves out of the collecting duct by osmosis into this hypertonic environment, increasing the concentration of urine.

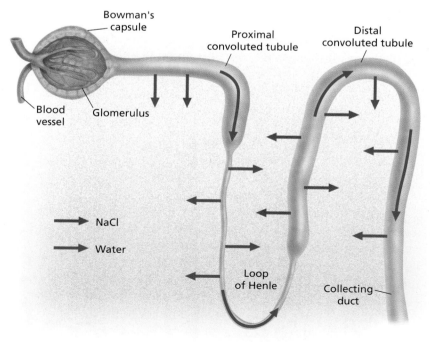

FORMATION OF URINE

The Loop of Henle

The function of the **loop of Henle** (HEN-lee) is closely related to that of the collecting duct. Water moves out of the collecting duct because the concentration of sodium chloride is higher in the fluid surrounding the collecting duct than it is in the fluid inside the collecting duct. This high concentration of sodium chloride is created and maintained by the loop of Henle. Notice in Figure 49-19 that cells in the wall of the loop actively transport negatively charged chloride ions from the filtrate to the fluid between the loops and the collecting duct. Positively charged sodium ions follow the chloride ions into the fluid. This ensures that the sodium chloride concentration of the fluid between the loops and the collecting duct remains high and thus promotes the reabsorption of water from the collecting duct.

Elimination of Urine

Urine from the collecting ducts flows through the renal pelvis and into a narrow tube called a **ureter** (yoo-REET-uhr). A ureter leads from each kidney to the **urinary bladder,** a muscular sac that stores urine. Muscular contractions of the bladder force urine out of the body through a tube called the **urethra** (yoo-REE-thruh). Locate the ureters, urinary bladder, and urethra in Figure 49-20.

At least 500 mL (17 oz) of urine must be eliminated every day because this amount of fluid is needed to remove potentially toxic materials from the body and to maintain homeostasis. A normal adult eliminates from 1.5 L (1.6 qt) to 2.3 L (2.4 qt) of urine a day, depending on the amount of water taken in and the amount of water lost through respiration and perspiration.

Kidney

Ureter

Urinary bladder

Urethra

 Quick Lab

Analyzing Kidney Filtration

Materials disposable gloves, lab apron, and safety goggles, 20 mL of test solution, 3 test tubes, filter, beaker, 15 drops each of biuret and Benedict's solution, 2 drops IKI solution, 3 pipets, wax marker pen

Procedure

1. Put on your gloves, lab apron, and safety goggles.

2. Put 15 drops of the test solution into each of the test tubes. Label the test tubes "Protein," "Starch," and "Glucose."

3. Add 15 drops of biuret solution to the test tube labeled "Protein." Record your observations.

4. Add 15 drops of Benedict's solution to the test tube labeled "Glucose." Record your observations.

5. Add two drops of IKI solution to the test tube labeled "Starch." Record your observations.

6. Discard the tested solutions, and rinse your test tubes as your teacher directs.

7. Pour the remaining test solution through a filter into a beaker. Using the test solution from the beaker, repeat steps 3–5.

Analysis Which compounds passed through the filter paper? If some did not, explain why. How does the filtration of this activity resemble the activity of the kidney?

FIGURE 49-20

Urine trickles from each kidney through a ureter to the urinary bladder, where it is stored until it is eliminated from the body through the urethra.

TABLE 49-4	*Waste Substances and Excretion Sites*
Substance excreted	**Excreting organ(s)**
Nitrogenous waste	kidneys, skin (a small amount in sweat)
Water	kidneys, skin, lungs
Salts	kidneys, skin (in sweat)
Carbon dioxide	lungs
Spices	lungs, kidneys

The Excretory System

The kidneys are the primary organs of the excretory system. They play a vital role in maintaining the homeostasis of body fluids. While kidney failure is an immediate, life-threatening situation, there are other organs that are involved in the excretion of metabolic waste.

As you know, the lungs are the primary site of carbon dioxide excretion. The lungs carry out detoxification, altering harmful substances so that they are not poisonous. The lungs are also responsible for the excretion of the volatile substances in onions, garlic, and other strong spices. These strong spices are frequently detectable on a person's breath.

While the kidneys control the salt composition of the blood, some salt is excreted through perspiration. A person working in extreme heat may lose water through perspiration at the rate of 1 L per hour. This loss of water represents a loss of about 10 to 30 g of salt per day.

Table 49-4 summarizes some waste substances and the organ(s) that excrete them. Notice that undigested food is not in the table of substances excreted by the body. Undigested food is not excreted in the scientific sense; it is eliminated, meaning it is expelled as feces from the body without ever passing through a membrane or being subjected to metabolic processes. The term *excretion* is correctly used only to indicate those substances that must pass through a membrane to leave the body.

internet**connect**

SCI**LINKS** NSTA

TOPIC: Excretory system
GO TO: www.scilinks.org
KEYWORD: HM996

SECTION 49-3 REVIEW

1. Define and describe *excretion.*

2. Explain the function of an organ other than the kidney that is involved in excretion.

3. Name and describe each structure of the renal tubule.

4. Contrast the function of filtration with the function of reabsorption.

5. Given the definition of excretion, why do you think the large intestine is not classified as a major excretory organ?

6. **CRITICAL THINKING**   Explain why a high concentration of protein in the urine may indicate damaged kidneys.

SUMMARY/VOCABULARY

 49-1
- The human body needs six nutrients—carbohydrates, proteins, lipids, vitamins, minerals, and water—to grow and function.
- Carbohydrates provide most of the body's energy. Monosaccharides are quickly processed by the body. Cellulose cannot be digested but is needed for fiber.
- Proteins help the body grow and repair tissues. Amino acids must be obtained from foods.

- Lipids are used to build cell membranes.
- Vitamins act as coenzymes. The body can synthesize vitamin D.
- Minerals are inorganic substances that are needed in small amounts.
- Water helps regulate body temperature and transports nutrients and wastes.

Vocabulary

dehydration (982)	mineral (981)	nutrient (977)	vitamin (980)

 49-2
- Mechanical digestion involves the breaking of food into smaller particles. Chemical digestion involves changing the chemical nature of the food substance.
- The mouth, teeth, and tongue carry out mechanical digestion. Chemical digestion of carbohydrates occurs in the mouth.
- The esophagus is a passageway through which food passes by peristalsis.
- The stomach has layers of muscles that churn the food to assist in mechanical

digestion. Pepsin in the stomach begins the chemical digestion of proteins.
- Bile assists in the mechanical digestion of lipids. Enzymes secreted by the pancreas complete the digestion of the chyme.
- The digested nutrients are absorbed through the villi of the small intestine.
- The large intestine absorbs water from the undigested mass. The undigested mass is eliminated as feces through the anus.

Vocabulary

absorption (988)	feces (989)	jejunum (988)	peristalsis (985)
bolus (984)	gallbladder (987)	lacteal (988)	pyloric sphincter (986)
cardiac sphincter (986)	gastric fluid (986)	large intestine (989)	saliva (984)
chyme (986)	gastric pit (985)	liver (986)	soft palate (984)
colon (989)	gastrointestinal tract (983)	microvillus (988)	stomach (985)
digestion (983)	hard palate (984)	molar (984)	ulcer (986)
epiglottis (984)	incisor (984)	pepsin (986)	villus (988)

 49-3
- The kidneys are the main organs of the urinary system. Reabsorption and secretion occur in the proximal and distal convoluted tubules and the loop of Henle. Nutrients are removed from the nephron

and returned to the blood. The filtrate is called urine.
- The urine passes through a ureter and is stored in the urinary bladder until it is eliminated through the urethra.

Vocabulary

ammonia (992)	glomerulus (993)	renal pelvis (992)	ureter (995)
Bowman's capsule (993)	loop of Henle (995)	renal tubule (993)	urethra (995)
cortex (991)	medulla (992)	secretion (994)	urinary bladder (995)
excretion (991)	nephron (992)	urea (992)	urine (992)
filtration (993)	reabsorption (994)		

REVIEW

Vocabulary

For each set of terms below, choose the one that does not belong, and explain why it does not belong.

1. carbohydrate, protein, fat, mineral
2. pharynx, epiglottis, bolus, esophagus
3. cardiac sphincter, gastric pits, medulla, pyloric sphincter
4. absorption, filtration, secretion, reabsorption
5. nephron, ileum, glomerulus, renal tubule

Multiple Choice

6. The primary function of carbohydrates is to (a) break down molecules (b) aid in digestion (c) supply the body with energy (d) regulate the flow of chyme.
7. Cellulose (a) builds body tissue (b) is a monosaccharide (c) is used for energy (d) aids in digestion.
8. Proteins consist of (a) catalysts (b) enzymes (c) amino acids (d) polysaccharides.
9. The body needs vitamins because they (a) supply it with energy (b) serve as coenzymes (c) function as enzymes (d) act as hormones.
10. Dehydration is best prevented by (a) inhaling air (b) drinking water (c) not drinking water (d) perspiring.
11. The epiglottis is important because it (a) prevents food from going down the trachea (b) separates the pharynx from the nasal cavity (c) is the passage through which food travels to the stomach (d) regulates the flow of chyme.

12. The gallbladder (a) creates bile (b) stores urine (c) stores, concentrates, and secretes bile (d) is made up of nephrons.
13. During absorption, the lacteals absorb (a) glycogen (b) glycerol and fatty acids (c) amino acids and monosaccharides (d) lactose.
14. Organs involved in the excretion process include the (a) kidneys and stomach (b) liver and pancreas (c) nephron and glomerulus (d) kidneys and lungs.
15. During secretion in the kidney, substances move from (a) filtrate to blood (b) blood to blood (c) blood to filtrate (d) filtrate to filtrate.

Short Answer

16. Why can consuming a great deal of saturated fat be harmful?
17. Briefly explain the synthesis of vitamin D in the body.
18. What role does bile play in digestion?
19. In what two ways do the liver and pancreas differ from other digestive organs?
20. How is mechanical digestion carried out by the stomach?
21. Why does the body convert ammonia into urea?
22. Explain the difference between water-soluble and fat-soluble vitamins.
23. What processes occur in the nephron that maintain homeostasis?
24. List the structures of a nephron.
25. Examine the diagram of the kidney. Name each of the indicated structures.

CRITICAL THINKING

1. In some countries many children suffer from a type of malnutrition called kwashiorkor. They have swollen stomachs and become increasingly thin until they die. Even when given rice and water, these children still die. What type of nutritional deficiency might these children have?

2. Some people cannot drink milk because they are unable to digest lactose, the sugar in milk. Doctors think this inability involves specific areas of the digestive system. What do you think these areas are?

3. Why is it important that the large intestine reabsorb water and not eliminate it?

4. When the kidneys stop functioning, urea builds up in the blood and poisons the body. A person with kidney failure will eventually die if the urea is not somehow removed. For the urea to be removed, the patient must be attached to an artificial kidney, also called a dialysis machine. Using your understanding of how a normal kidney functions, suggest a design for the major components of a dialysis machine.

5. A person has a small intestine that has villi but lacks microvilli. Would you expect this person to be underweight or overweight? Explain your answer.

6. The loop of Henle functions to conserve water by reabsorbing it. Its length varies among mammal species. Would you expect the loop of Henle of an animal like the beaver, which lives in a watery environment, to be longer or shorter than that found in humans? Explain your answer.

7. Look at the pictures of the teeth of different animals. What can you tell about the human diet by comparing the teeth of humans with those of the other animals shown here?

EXTENSION

1. Bring the label from a cereal box to class. Compare the "percent daily value" of vitamins and minerals on your label with those on labels brought in by other students.

2. Use the library and on-line sources for information about diets that claim to reduce the chances of a heart attack and cancer. Write a brief report summarizing a few of these articles.

3. Read "Fire in the Belly" in *Time*, April 26, 1999, on page 108. What is heartburn? What does heartburn have to do with the heart? What are the most common foods that cause heartburn?

4. Use library references to research kidney diseases and disorders. Write and illustrate a report focusing on the causes of these illnesses, their symptoms, and their treatment.

5. Look at your library's reference books that describe the cultures and customs of other nations. Find information relating to eating habits for at least five different countries. How do these customs differ from those in America? Investigate at least one nation or area where food is scarce. What are some of the causes and consequences of widespread food shortages?

Modeling Human Digestion

OBJECTIVES

- Test a model of digestion in the human stomach.

PROCESS SKILLS

- modeling
- observing
- predicting
- inferring

MATERIALS

- safety goggles
- lab apron
- glass-marking pencil
- 5 test tubes with stoppers
- test-tube rack
- scalpel
- cooked egg white
- balance
- 10 mL graduated cylinder
- 1% pepsin solution
- 0.2% hydrochloric acid
- 1% sodium bicarbonate
- distilled water
- red and blue litmus paper
- lined paper
- disposable gloves

Background

1. How is food changed from the chunks you chew with your teeth to the chyme absorbed in your small intestine?
2. What type of organic compound does the enzyme pepsin digest?

PART A Setting Up

1. Label five test tubes 1, 2, 3, 4, and 5, and place them in a test-tube rack.
2. CAUTION **Always cut in a direction away from your body.** Use a scalpel to cut a firm, cooked egg white into fine pieces.
3. Using the balance, measure and place equal amounts (about 6 g) of the fine egg white sample into each test tube, as shown in the illustration above.
4. CAUTION **Put on safety goggles and a lab apron. If you get hydrochloric acid solution on your skin or clothes, wash it off at the sink while calling to your teacher. If you get any solutions in this investigation in your eyes, immediately flush them out at the eyewash station while calling to your teacher.** Use a clean graduated cylinder to add the solutions listed below to the test tubes. Rinse the cylinder between additions so that you do not contaminate the samples.
   - test tube 1—10 mL of water
   - test tube 2—10 mL of pepsin solution
   - test tube 3—10 mL of hydrochloric acid
   - test tube 4—5 mL of pepsin solution and 5 mL of sodium bicarbonate solution
   - test tube 5—5 mL of pepsin and 5 mL of hydrochloric acid

DEGREE OF DIGESTION OF EGG WHITE UNDER VARYING CONDITIONS

Test tube number	Contents	pH	Degree of digestion
1	egg white 10 mL water		
2	egg white 10 mL 1% pepsin solution		
3	egg white 10 mL 0.2% hydrochloric acid solution		
4	egg white 5 mL 1% pepsin solution 5 mL 1% sodium bicarbonate solution		
5	egg white 5 mL 1% pepsin solution 5 mL 0.2% hydrochloric acid solution		

5. Stopper and gently shake each test tube.

6. In your lab report, make a data table like the one shown above. Fill in the first column with the test-tube numbers. Under the heading "Contents," fill in a description of the contents of each test tube, as shown.

7. Predict which test tube will show the most digestion after 48 hours. Explain your reasoning.

8. Label your test-tube rack with your initials. Store the test-tube rack for 48 hours at room temperature. Leave a note on the rack cautioning others not to spill the acids or bases.

9.   Clean up your lab materials and wash your hands before leaving the lab.

PART B Recording the Results

10. After 48 hours, measure the pH of each solution with red and blue litmus paper. Record your results in the data table you created in your lab report.

11. Look for the egg white in each test tube. In your data table, describe the degree to which the egg white has broken down and dissolved in each test tube.

12. Clean up your lab materials and wash your hands before leaving the lab.

Analysis and Conclusions

1. What conditions caused the greatest digestion of cooked egg white?

2. Which test tube best modeled the chemical composition in the human stomach?

3. What information do test tubes 1, 2, and 3 give you? What do they control?

4. Compare test tubes 4 and 5. What can you conclude about the effects of the chemical environment on the activity of pepsin?

5. List some other foods that pepsin is likely to digest.

6. Do you think that pepsin would digest butter? Explain your answer.

Further Inquiry

Design an experiment to test the digestion of a food containing carbohydrates, such as a potato or an apple.

CHAPTER 50

NERVOUS SYSTEM AND SENSE ORGANS

This color-enhanced magnetic-resonance imaging (MRI) of the head shows a living brain and spinal cord in cross section.

FOCUS CONCEPT: *Stability and Homeostasis*

As you read, notice how the nervous system functions to ensure that other body systems work together in an efficient and coordinated manner.

CENTRAL NERVOUS SYSTEM

*Mental and physical activity and many aspects of homeostasis are controlled by the **nervous system,** a complex network of cells that communicate with one another. Within this communications network, a carefully organized division of labor exists so that each component of the nervous system operates effectively. As a result, a football player can weave through opposing tacklers, an architect can create an original design, and you can read and understand the words on this page.*

ORGANIZATION

The nervous system is composed of neurons, specialized cells that transmit information throughout the body. A neuron, such as the one shown in Figure 50-1, demonstrates the relationship between structure and function in living systems. The **axon,** a threadlike projection of the cell body, enables the neuron to transmit signals rapidly over relatively long distances in the body. Other structures projecting from the cell body allow the neuron to receive signals from other neurons. You will examine the structure and function of neurons more closely later in this chapter.

SECTION

50-1

OBJECTIVES

▲

Identify the two main organs of the central nervous system.

●

Summarize the functions of the cerebrum, brain stem, and cerebellum.

■

Describe how the central nervous system is protected from injury.

◆

Describe the structure of the spinal cord.

▲

Distinguish between sensory receptors, motor neurons, and interneurons.

Cell body

Axon

FIGURE 50-1

Neurons transmit information through-out the body in a combination of chemical and electrical signals. This stellate neuron is named for its starlike shape (SEM, 26,000×).

The central nervous system includes the brain and spinal cord, shown in orange. The peripheral nervous system, shown in violet, includes all other nervous tissue in the body.

Word Roots and Origins

corpus callosum

from the Latin *corpus,* meaning "body," and *callosus,* meaning "thick and hard"

The nervous system includes two major divisions: the central nervous system and the peripheral nervous system. The brain and spinal cord make up the **central nervous system,** shown in orange in Figure 50-2. The spinal cord carries messages from the body to the brain, where they are analyzed and interpreted. Response messages are then passed from the brain through the spinal cord and to the rest of the body.

The **peripheral nervous system,** shown in violet in Figure 50-2, consists of the neurons that are not included in the brain and spinal cord. Some peripheral neurons collect information from the body and transmit it *toward* the central nervous system. These are called **afferent neurons.** Other peripheral neurons transmit information *away* from the central nervous system. These are called **efferent neurons.**

BRAIN

The human brain is responsible for overseeing the daily operations of the human body and for interpreting the vast amount of information it receives. The adult human brain weighs an average of 1.4 kg, or about 2 percent of total body weight. Despite its relatively small mass, the brain contains approximately 100 billion neurons. Functioning as a unit, these neurons make up the most complex and highly organized structure on Earth. Because of the brain's complex nature, much remains to be learned about how it functions, but scientists have uncovered a good deal of information about the brain's many functions.

You may realize that the brain is responsible for many of the qualities that make each individual unique—thoughts, feelings, emotions, talents, memories, and the ability to process information. It is important to understand, however, that much of the brain is dedicated to running the body. For example, the brain is responsible for maintaining homeostasis by controlling and integrating the various systems that make up the body. Through painstaking trial-and-error study of the brain, scientists have established how and where various functions are localized in the brain.

Cerebrum

The largest portion of the human brain consists of the cerebrum (SER-uh-bruhm). The **cerebrum,** which is easily identified by its highly folded outer layer, is composed of two **cerebral hemispheres,** as shown in Figure 50-3a. The cerebral hemispheres are connected by the **corpus callosum** (KOR-puhs kuh-LOH-suhm), a heavy band of the axons of many neurons. The corpus callosum lies deep in the central groove that separates the right hemisphere from the left hemisphere. Other deep grooves separate each hemisphere into four lobes: the frontal, parietal (puh-RIE-uh-tuhl), temporal, and occipital (ahk-SIP-i-tuhl) lobes, as shown in Figure 50-3b.

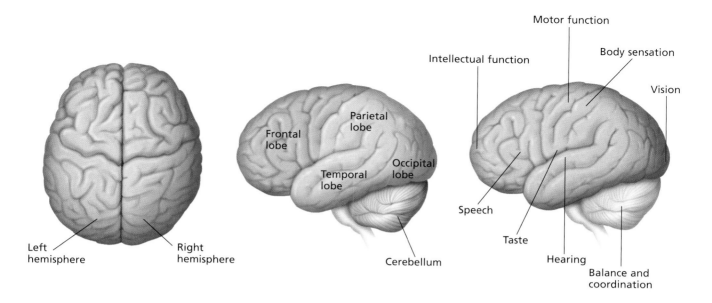

(a) TOP OF BRAIN

(b) LOBES OF THE LEFT HEMISPHERE

(c) LEFT HEMISPHERE FUNCTIONAL AREAS

The folded outer layer of the cerebral hemispheres is called the **cerebral cortex.** In humans, the cerebral cortex is a sheet of neurons about 2 to 4 mm (0.75 to 1.5 in.) thick. Scientists estimate that it contains nearly 10 percent, or about 10 billion, of the brain's total number of neurons. The surface area of the cerebral cortex is too large to lie smoothly over the lower structure of the brain. The folds, or convolutions, accommodate the surface area of the cortex within the limits of the interior of the skull.

The cerebral cortex is very important in sensory processing and in motor responses. As shown in Figure 50-3c, separate areas of the cerebral cortex control auditory, visual, body sensation, and motor processing. For example, an area of the cortex in the occipital lobe, at the rear of the brain, is essential for processing visual information. The area of the cortex that interprets touch information from all parts of the body lies in a band across the top of the brain, in the parietal lobe. Some functions are not localized in a symmetrical way in the brain. In right-handed individuals, cortical areas and other brain centers involved in speech and language production are located primarily in the left hemisphere. Brain centers involved in processing spatial information and in certain kinds of reasoning are located primarily in the right hemisphere. In left-handers, there is some variation in the location of functions.

Below the wrinkled surface of the cerebral cortex lies the **white matter,** which is composed of the axons of cortical neurons. These axons link specific regions of the cortex with each other and with other neural centers. There is a great degree of crossover of axons in the spinal cord and brain. That is, many impulses originating in the right half of the body are processed in the left half of the brain, and vice versa.

FIGURE 50-3

(a) A view of the top of the brain shows the left and right cerebral hemispheres. (b) Each cerebral hemisphere of the brain has four lobes. (c) Control centers for various functions are located in different areas of the brain.

internetconnect

SC*i*LINKS

NSTA

TOPIC: Central nervous system
GO TO: www.scilinks.org
KEYWORD: HM1005

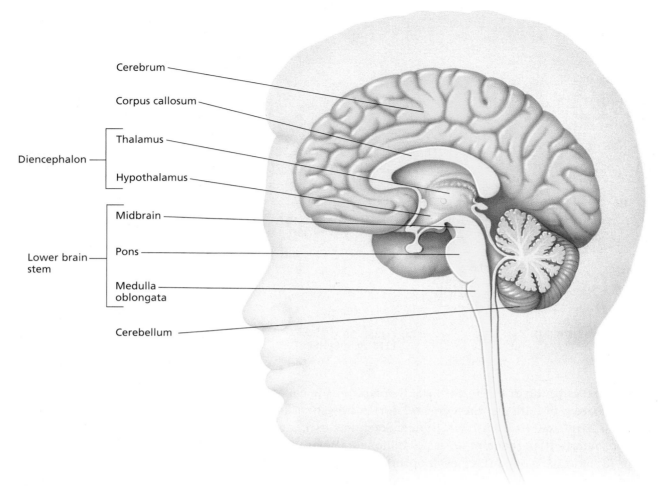

Cerebrum

Corpus callosum

Diencephalon — Thalamus

Hypothalamus

Midbrain

Lower brain — Pons
stem

Medulla
oblongata

Cerebellum

FIGURE 50-4

A side view through the center of the brain shows the right hemisphere. The wrinkled cerebral cortex is visible along the front, rear, and top of the brain, where it rolls into the deep groove separating the two hemispheres. The structures lying below the cerebrum are shown in cross section.

Upper Brain Stem—Diencephalon

Below the cerebrum, the **brain stem** links the cerebrum with the spinal cord. The upper part of the brain stem, the **diencephalon** (DIE-uhn-SEF-uh-lahn), contains important relay centers for information entering and exiting the brain. The upper relay center, the **thalamus** (THAL-uh-muhs), shown in Figure 50-4, directs most incoming sensory signals to the proper region of the cerebral cortex. The hypothalamus, located just below the thalamus, is linked to several other parts of the brain. The hypothalamus is very important in maintaining homeostasis, and it both directly and indirectly controls much of the body's hormone production.

Parts of the diencephalon and the cerebrum are included in an important group of connected brain centers called the **limbic system.** The limbic system includes the thalamus, the hypothalamus, some deeper parts of the cerebral cortex, and centers in the temporal lobes. The limbic system plays an important role in emotion, memory, and motivation, among other things. Scientists have tried to determine the functions of the different parts of the limbic system by observing problems associated with damage to its various regions. For example, people with damage to certain limbic areas may display inappropriate emotional responses, such as rage in response to a trivial, irritating stimulus.

Lower Brain Stem

Below the diencephalon, the brain stem narrows. This region of the brain stem has three main divisions: the midbrain, the pons, and the medulla oblongata.

The **midbrain** is an important relay center for visual and auditory information. The **pons** serves as a relay center between the neurons of the cerebral hemispheres and those of the cerebellum. The **medulla oblongata** (mi-DUHL-uh AHB-lahn-GAHT-uh) contains neurons that serve as both a relay center and a control center. Also within the medulla oblongata are centers that control various homeostatic activities, including heart rate and respiration rate.

Lying throughout the brain stem is a diffuse network of neurons called the **reticular formation.** The reticular formation helps to control respiration and circulation and serves as a filtering system for incoming sensory signals. The reticular formation separates signals that demand attention from those that are unimportant. Some of this function of the reticular formation is modified by learning. For example, a person can learn to sleep through the noise of a radio or television but awaken at the sound of a doorbell.

Cerebellum

Just below the occipital lobes of the cerebral hemispheres lies the **cerebellum** (SER-uh-BEL-uhm), a region of the brain that plays a vital role in the coordination of muscle action, particularly the timing of muscle contractions. As Figure 50-4 shows, the surface of the cerebellum is very highly folded, giving it a striated appearance. The cerebellum receives sensory impulses from muscles, tendons, joints, eyes, and ears, as well as input from other brain centers. It processes information about body position and controls posture by keeping skeletal muscles in a constant state of partial contraction. The cerebellum coordinates rapid and ongoing movements. It acts together with brain stem motor centers and with the section of cerebral cortex that is responsible for motor responses. Nerve impulses are sent down through the spinal cord and stimulate or inhibit the contraction of skeletal muscles.

Protection

The delicate neurons of the brain and spinal cord are surrounded by three protective layers called the **meninges** (muh-NIN-JEEZ). The outer layer, the **dura mater** (DU-ruh MAYT-uhr), consists of connective tissue, blood vessels, and neurons. The middle layer, the **arachnoid** (uh-RAK-NOYD) **layer,** is elastic and weblike. The thin inner layer, the **pia mater** (PIE-uh MAYT-uhr), adheres to the brain and spinal cord and contains many blood vessels and neurons.

A clear liquid called **cerebrospinal** (SER-uh-BROH-SPIE-NUHL) **fluid** provides a cushion that protects the brain and spinal cord from injury. Cerebrospinal fluid separates the middle and inner meninges and fills four interconnected **ventricles,** or cavities, in the brain. Within the ventricles, cerebrospinal fluid acts as a transport medium for substances that are important to brain function.

FIGURE 50-5

The spinal cord, shown in cross section, carries information toward and away from the brain. Sensory information from the body enters the spinal cord through the dorsal roots. Instructions to the body's many motor neurons exit the spinal cord through the ventral roots.

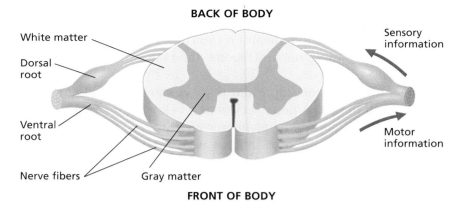

BACK OF BODY

White matter

Dorsal root

Ventral root

Nerve fibers

Gray matter

Sensory information

Motor information

FRONT OF BODY

Spinal Cord

The **spinal cord** is a column of nerve tissue that starts in the medulla oblongata and runs down through the vertebral column. The spinal cord is composed of an outer sheath of white matter. As it does in the brain, the white matter contains primarily the axons of neurons. The white matter surrounds a rigid inner core of gray matter, which is composed of the cell bodies of neurons.

Thirty-one pairs of spinal nerves, part of the peripheral nervous system, originate in the spinal cord and branch out to both sides of the body. Recall that neurons have long axons that enable them to transmit signals rapidly. When bundled together, these axons form a **nerve.** Each spinal nerve consists of a dorsal root and a ventral root. The dorsal roots, shown in Figure 50-5, contain neurons that carry signals to the central nervous system from various kinds of sensory receptor neurons. A **sensory receptor** is a neuron that is specialized to detect a stimulus, such as pressure or heat.

The ventral roots, also shown in Figure 50-5, contain the axons of **motor neurons,** which are neurons that contact and carry information to muscles and glands. Within the spinal cord and elsewhere in the body are **interneurons,** which are neurons that connect other neurons to each other.

SECTION 50-1 REVIEW

1. Name the two organs that make up the central nervous system.

2. How do the functions of the cerebral hemispheres, cerebellum, and brain stem differ?

3. Explain the difference between sensory receptors and motor neurons.

4. How are the brain and spinal cord protected from injury?

5. What are the gray matter and white matter in the spinal cord composed of?

6. **CRITICAL THINKING** Strokes result in the death of neurons in the brain. How can a doctor tell what areas of the brain have been affected in a person who has had a stroke?

PERIPHERAL NERVOUS SYSTEM

The workings of your brain may be largely a mystery to you. You are undoubtedly more familiar with the workings of your peripheral nervous system. In the peripheral nervous system, 12 pairs of cranial nerves connect the brain with the head and neck and 31 pairs of spinal nerves connect the central nervous system with the rest of the body.

▲

Name the two divisions of the peripheral nervous system and describe their function.

●

Distinguish between the somatic nervous system and the autonomic nervous system.

■

Distinguish between the sympathetic division and the parasympathetic division.

◆

Describe a spinal reflex.

SENSORY DIVISION

The **sensory division** of the peripheral nervous system is composed of sensory receptors and the interneurons that connect them to the central nervous system. Sensory receptors acquire information from the external and internal environments of the body. Spinal and cranial nerves enable the flow of sensory information to the central nervous system. You will learn more about the processing of sensory information in Section 50-4.

MOTOR DIVISION

The **motor division** of the peripheral nervous system allows the body to react to the sensory information. The motor division is composed of two independent systems—the somatic nervous system and the autonomic nervous system.

Somatic Nervous System

The **somatic nervous system** of the motor division consists of motor neurons that control the movement of skeletal muscles. The somatic system is said to be voluntary—that is, skeletal muscles can be moved at will. The somatic system can also operate automatically, as it does when you maintain your balance.

One important function of the peripheral nervous system is the relay of signals in **reflexes,** which are involuntary and often self-protective movements. The patellar reflex, which depends on one of the simplest neural circuits in the human body, is shown in Figure 50-6.

Word Roots and Origins

somatic

from the Greek *somatikos,* meaning "of the body"

FIGURE 50-6

In the patellar reflex, a sensory neuron (red) with a receptor that detects stretch in the quadriceps muscle sends signals to the spinal cord. The axon of the sensory neuron is split. One branch (green) stimulates motor neurons in the quadriceps, causing the muscle to contract and extend the leg. The other branch (blue) stimulates an interneuron which inhibits motor neurons in the hamstrings.

When the tendon below the patella is tapped sharply, a sensory receptor, shown in red, in the attached quadriceps muscle sends an impulse to the spinal cord. This impulse activates a motor neuron, shown in green, that leads back to the quadriceps muscle, causing the muscle to contract. The impulse also activates an interneuron, shown in blue, that has an inhibitory, or calming, effect on the motor neurons of the hamstrings in the lower thigh. The contraction of the quadriceps coupled with the relaxation of the hamstrings extends the lower leg. This type of reflex is a true **spinal reflex;** that is, it involves only neurons in the body and spinal cord, and completely bypasses the brain. Many of the body's involuntary actions, however, originate in a second subdivision of the motor division of the peripheral nervous system—the autonomic nervous system.

Autonomic Nervous System

The **autonomic nervous system** of the motor division consists of nerves that control the body's internal conditions by affecting smooth muscles, both in blood vessels and in organs. The main function of the autonomic nervous system is the control of respiration, heartbeat, and other functions involved in homeostasis. Stimulation and inhibition of body systems are the responsibility of two different subdivisions of the autonomic system—the sympathetic division and the parasympathetic division—as shown in Figure 50-7.

A major function of the **sympathetic division** is the shunting of blood from one part of the body to another. The sympathetic division of the autonomic nervous system is activated by conditions

internetconnect

SC**LINKS**
NSTA

TOPIC: Peripheral nervous system
GO TO: www.scilinks.org
KEYWORD: HM1010

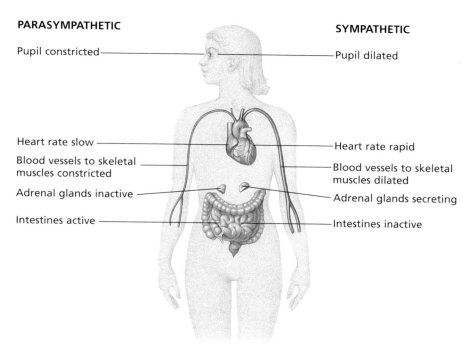

PARASYMPATHETIC

Pupil constricted

Heart rate slow

Blood vessels to skeletal muscles constricted

Adrenal glands inactive

Intestines active

SYMPATHETIC

Pupil dilated

Heart rate rapid

Blood vessels to skeletal muscles dilated

Adrenal glands secreting

Intestines inactive

FIGURE 50-7

In the autonomic nervous system, the sympathetic division readies the body to respond to stress or danger. Activation of the parasympathetic division conserves energy and restores homeostasis.

of physical or emotional stress. For example, the threat of a physical attack would cause your sympathetic division to redirect the flow of blood away from your digestive organs and toward your heart and skeletal muscles. This is often called the "fight-or-flight" response. As Figure 50-7 shows, the sympathetic division stimulates activities that consume large amounts of energy.

The **parasympathetic division** of the autonomic nervous system controls the internal environment during routine conditions. After a threat of danger has passed, nerves from the parasympathetic division signal organs to revert to normal levels of activity. Blood flow to the heart and skeletal muscles is decreased and their function slows. The action of the parasympathetic division induces the body to conserve energy. Under normal conditions, both systems usually are activated to some degree. The balance of actions of the sympathetic division and the parasympathetic division of the autonomic nervous system help the body maintain homeostasis.

SECTION 50-2 REVIEW

1. Name the two main divisions of the peripheral nervous system.

2. Name two types of neurons in the peripheral nervous system.

3. Name the parts of the nervous system that are involved in a spinal reflex.

4. How do the somatic nervous system and the autonomic nervous system differ?

5. Which division of the autonomic nervous system is involved in "fight-or-flight" reactions in response to danger?

6. CRITICAL THINKING Most organs in the body are stimulated by both the sympathetic division and the parasympathetic division of the autonomic nervous system. Explain how this helps maintain homeostasis.

SECTION

OBJECTIVES

Describe the structure
of a neuron.

Summarize the electrical
and chemical conditions
of resting potential.

Describe the electrical
and chemical changes that occur
during an action potential.

Describe the role of
neurotransmitters in transmitting
a signal across a synapse.

TRANSMISSION OF NERVE IMPULSES

The ability of the nervous system to monitor and respond to the environment, both external and internal, depends on the transmission of signals within a neuron and from one neuron to another. The transmission of a signal along the axon of a neuron is known as an **action potential.** *The transmission of action potentials depends on electrochemical energy— electrical energy that is generated as charged chemical substances move into and out of neurons.*

NEURON STRUCTURE

Figure 50-8 shows the morphology of a typical neuron. The nucleus of a neuron, along with most of its organelles, is located in the cell body. Extending out from the cell body in different directions are membrane-covered extensions called dendrites. **Dendrites** receive action potentials from other neurons. The axon is a long, membrane-bound projection that transmits the action potentials away from the cell body. A neuron may have a single axon or branching axons that contact several other neurons. The end of the axon is called the **axon terminal.** It may lie near a muscle, a gland, or the dendrite or cell body of another neuron.

The axons of most neurons are covered with a lipid layer known as the **myelin** (MIE-uh-lin) **sheath.** The myelin sheath both insulates the axon much like the rubber coating of an electrical cord and speeds up transmission of action potentials through the axon. In the peripheral nervous system, myelin is produced by cells called **Schwann cells,** which surround the axon. Gaps in the myelin sheath along the length of the axon are known as the **nodes of Ranvier** (RAHN-vee-ay).

As Figure 50-8 shows, neurons do not touch each other. Instead a small gap, called a **synaptic cleft,** is present between the end of the axon of one neuron and the dendrite or cell body of another neuron. In most neurons, electrical activity in the neuron causes the release of chemicals into the synaptic cleft. These chemicals, called **neurotransmitters,** in turn elicit electrical activity in a second neuron. Thus, the signalling activity of the nervous system is composed of electrical activity *within* neurons and chemical flow

Word Roots and Origins

synapse

from the Greek *synaptein,* meaning "to fasten together"

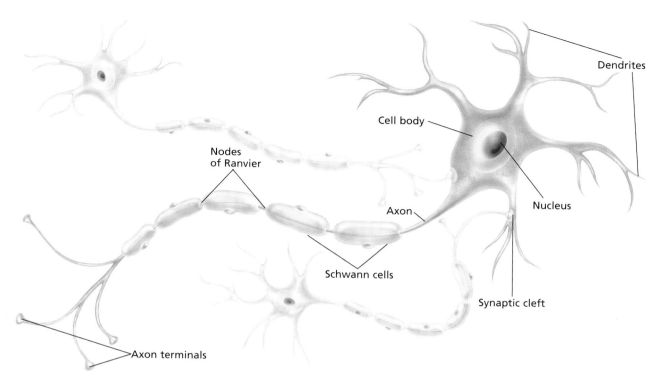

Dendrites

Cell body

Nodes of Ranvier

Nucleus

Axon

Schwann cells

Synaptic cleft

Axon terminals

between neurons. Neurons form numerous interconnections that in turn form circuits in the same way that telephone lines interconnect to form circuits. These neural circuits form complex networks throughout the body, just as telephone circuits form networks that extend throughout the world.

NEURON FUNCTION

Nearly 200 years ago, scientists discovered that when an electrical current is passed through a muscle removed from a dead animal, the muscle will contract just as it did in life. Scientists have learned that electricity stimulates neurons that affect muscle cells. Neuron function is dependent on electrical activity.

Neurons have an electrical charge different from the extracellular fluid that surrounds them. A difference in the electrical charge between two locations is called a **potential.** In neurons, potentials are produced by a complex interplay of several different ions. The movement of these ions is affected by their ability to pass through the cell membrane, their concentrations inside and outside of the cell, and their charge.

Resting Potential

A neuron is at rest when it is not receiving or transmitting a signal. In a neuron at rest, the concentration of large, negatively-charged proteins and potassium, K^+, ions is greater inside the cell than outside. In contrast, the concentration of sodium, Na^+, ions is greater outside the cell than inside. This imbalance of Na^+ and K^+ ions is, in

FIGURE 50-8

Neurons are separated from other neurons by small gaps. Some neurons have many other neurons contacting their multiple dendrites. A long axon, which carries action potentials, extends from the cell body of the neuron. Most axons are covered by a fatty insulating layer called the myelin sheath.

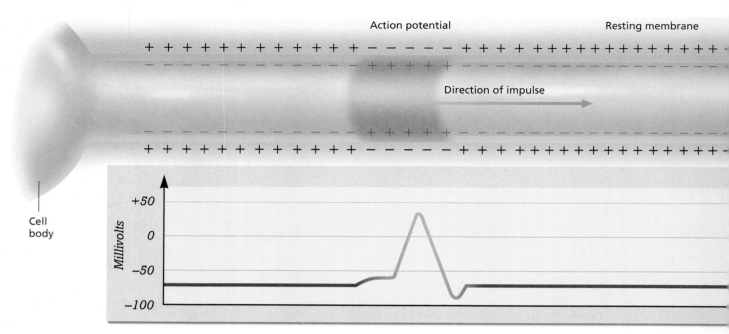

Action potential　　　　　　　　　　　Resting membrane

Direction of impulse

Cell body

Millivolts

+50

0

−50

−100

FIGURE 50-9

In the resting state, the interior of a neuron is negatively charged with respect to the extracellular fluid. The passage of an action potential over the membrane of the axon reverses this polarity, making the interior of the axon positively charged for a brief time. A graph shows the change in voltage during an action potential. The charge of the interior of the neuron rapidly switches from negative to positive, and then immediately reverses, the interior regaining its negative charge.

part, due to the action of the sodium-potassium pump. Recall from Chapter 5 that the sodium-potassium pump actively moves Na^+ out of cells while moving K^+ in.

The cell membrane is permeable to some ions but not to others. Na^+ ions do not readily diffuse through the membrane, and they accumulate outside the cell. The negatively charged proteins remain inside because they are too large to exit. K^+ ions, however, pass freely through the membrane and tend to diffuse out of the cell, down their concentration gradient. This exit of positively charged potassium ions, coupled with the retention of negatively charged protein ions, eventually causes the interior of the neuron to become negatively charged with respect to the exterior. This charge difference is called the **resting potential** of the membrane. In animal neurons, the resting potential is about −70 millivolts.

Action Potential

When a dendrite or the cell body of a neuron is stimulated, a sudden change occurs in the permeability of its cell membrane. At the point where it is stimulated, the cell membrane becomes permeable to Na^+ ions. The rush of Na^+ ions into the cell opens voltage gated channels in the membrane that allow even more Na^+ ions to diffuse rapidly from the outside of the membrane to the inside of the neuron. Remember from Chapter 5 that gated channels control the passage of ions through a cell membrane. As a result of the inward diffusion of Na^+ ions, the interior of the neuron's cell body becomes more positively charged than the outer surface. The interior, once negatively charged, is now positively charged. The exterior, once positively charged, is now negatively charged with respect to the interior. This reversal of polarity across the membrane begins an action potential. The action potential starts at the point where the cell body of the neuron joins the axon.

Voltage gated channels exist along the entire length of the axon. As the first small segment of the axon becomes positively charged, the rise in voltage opens channels in the adjacent segment of axon membrane. As before, Na⁺ ions enter, driving the voltage in a positive direction and opening channels in the next segment of the axon. In this way, a wave of positive charge passes down the membrane of the axon like a flame burning down a length of rope. Axon potentials travel in one direction only—away from the cell body, where they begin, and toward the axon terminal.

Shortly after they open, the gated channels for Na⁺ ions close. Then voltage gated channels for K⁺ ions open. The result is an abrupt outward flow of K⁺ ions. The outer surface again becomes positively charged, and the inner surface regains its negative charge. This signals the end of the action potential. The neuron cannot generate another action potential until the resting membrane potential is restored. This period, during which the neuron cannot fire, is called the **refractory period.**

After the action potential, the concentration of Na⁺ inside the cell is abnormally high, and the concentration of K⁺ inside the cell is abnormally low. The sodium-potassium pump reestablishes the original concentrations of Na⁺ ions and K⁺ ions on both sides of the membrane. Na⁺ ions are actively pumped out across the cell membrane, while K⁺ ions are actively pumped in across the membrane. Thus, the original ion concentrations are restored, and the neuron is ready for the next action potential. This restoration of resting potential comes at a price. Recall from Chapter 5 that the sodium-potassium pump requires energy in order to function. Neurons need a continuous supply of ATP to keep the sodium-potassium pump operating. In fact, neurons consume a great deal of energy in the body.

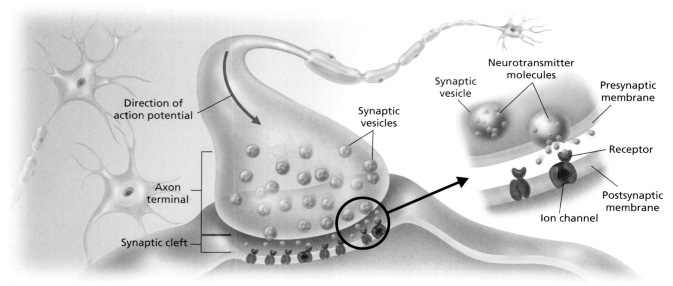

FIGURE 50-10

Neurotransmitter molecules are released into the synaptic cleft by the presynaptic neuron. These molecules bind at receptors in the postsynaptic membrane, opening ion channels. Positive ions entering through these channels cause the resting membrane potential of the postsynaptic neuron to rise. If it rises sufficiently, the postsynaptic neuron will generate an action potential, continuing the signal.

Neurotransmitter Function

When an action potential reaches the axon terminal, vesicles that are stored in the axon terminal and that contain neurotransmitters fuse with the presynaptic membrane. As Figure 50-10 shows, the fusion releases neurotransmitter molecules into the synaptic cleft. These molecules diffuse across the short distance of the synaptic cleft and bind to receptor molecules embedded in the postsynaptic membrane.

The interaction of neurotransmitter molecules and receptor molecules changes the permeability of the postsynaptic membrane by affecting chemically-gated ion channels. The opening of Na^+ channels in the postsynaptic membrane causes the neuron to become more positive in charge. If this positive change of the membrane potential is great enough, a new action potential is generated in the receiving neuron, effectively continuing the electrical signal.

On the other hand, if a sufficient number of Na^+ channels in the postsynaptic membrane fail to open, or if other channels open, allowing the rush of negatively charged ions in, the membrane potential of the receiving neuron will not rise appreciably or will become more negative. No new action potential will be generated in the receiving neuron, and the nervous signal will terminate.

SECTION 50-3 REVIEW

1. Describe the structure of a neuron.

2. What is the resting potential of the membrane?

3. How is a signal in the nervous system transmitted between adjacent neurons?

4. Why does the nervous system consume a large amount of energy?

5. Describe two possible effects that neurotransmitters may have at a synapse.

6. **CRITICAL THINKING** What functional advantage does a neuron with several dendrites have over a neuron with only one dendrite?

SENSORY SYSTEMS

Human experience is affected by both internal and external stimuli. Humans are able to distinguish among many different types of stimuli by means of a highly developed system of sense organs. Sensory systems represent an integration of the functions of the peripheral nervous system and the central nervous system. The sensory division of the peripheral nervous system gathers information about the body's internal conditions and the external environment. Sensory systems translate light, sound, temperature, and other aspects of the environment to electrical signals and transmit these signals, in the form of action potentials, to the central nervous system, where they are interpreted.

OBJECTIVES

▲

List five types
of sensory receptors.

●

Describe the structure
of the eye and the roles of
rods and cones in vision.

■

Identify the parts of the ear
responsible for hearing and for
maintaining balance.

◆

Explain how taste and smell
are detected.

RECEPTORS AND SENSE ORGANS

A sensory receptor is a neuron that is specialized to detect a stimulus. There are many kinds of sensory receptors, and they can be categorized on the basis of the types of stimuli they respond to.

- *Mechanoreceptors* respond to movement, pressure, and tension.
- *Photoreceptors* respond to variations in light.
- *Chemoreceptors* respond to chemicals.
- *Thermoreceptors* respond to changes in temperature.
- *Pain receptors* respond to tissue damage.

Sensory receptors are found in high concentrations in the **sense organs**—the eyes, ears, nose, mouth, and skin—and in fewer numbers, throughout the rest of the body. When a particular sense organ receives appropriate stimulation, its sensory receptors convert the stimulus into electrical signals that are sent to specific regions of the brain. The action potentials generated by the different sense organs are electrically similar, but the regions of the brain where they are interpreted vary according to the type of stimulus.

As you learned in Section 50-1, the brain has a specific region for each sense. Thus, signals received by the auditory region of the temporal lobe may be interpreted as sounds regardless of whether a sound wave was the original stimulus.

Word Roots and Origins

tympanic

from the Greek *tympanon,* meaning "drum"

HEARING AND BALANCE

The ear is specialized for two functions: detecting sound and maintaining balance. Sound is transmitted as vibrations of a substance; for humans, usually the substance is air. Sound is directed by the fleshy structure of the external ear into the ear itself, where the vibrations are translated into action potentials.

As shown in Figure 50-11, the **auditory canal** connects the external ear with the **tympanic** (tim-PAN-ik) **membrane,** also called the eardrum. Vibrations in the air passing through the auditory canal cause the tympanic membrane to vibrate. Air pressure in the chamber beyond the tympanic membrane, the middle ear, can be regulated and balanced by the amount of air allowed to enter the middle ear through the Eustachian tube. The **Eustachian** (yoo-STAY-kee-uhn) **tube** is an opening to the throat that enables you to equalize the pressure on both sides of your tympanic membrane whenever you experience a sudden change in atmospheric pressure, such as when you take off in an airplane. By swallowing, you allow air to enter the middle ear through the Eustachian tube. This air is under the same pressure as the air pressing against the tympanic membrane on the exterior side. Thus, the air pressure is equalized and you no longer feel pressure on the tympanic membranes in your ears.

Vibrations of the tympanic membrane are transmitted to three small bones of the middle ear: the hammer, the anvil, and the stirrup. The stirrup transfers the vibrations to a membrane called the **oval window,** which separates the middle ear from the inner ear. The inner ear contains the **cochlea** (KAHK-lee-uh), a coiled tube consisting of three fluid-filled chambers that are separated by membranes. The middle chamber contains the **organ of Corti,** which is the organ of

FIGURE 50-11

Sound waves, which are vibrations in the air, cause the tympanic membrane to move back and forth. This motion causes the small bones of the middle ear to move as well, transferring vibrations to the oval window. Mechanoreceptors in the inner ear translate these vibrations to action potentials, which travel through the auditory nerve to auditory processing centers in the brain.

FIGURE 50-12

Hair cells are arranged in orderly rows in the organ of Corti in the cochlea. In this damaged section, the hair cells in the top and center rows are relatively intact. Many of the hair cells of the bottom row, however, are frayed and bent. Four clusters of hair cells (the third, sixth, ninth, and tenth from the left) have been completely destroyed.

hearing. The organ of Corti rests on the bottom membrane in the cochlea and contains sensory receptors known as hair cells. Vibrations of fluid in the cochlea move the bottom membrane and cause these hair cells to bend against a second membrane, which covers them like a roof. This movement stimulates the hair cells to produce action potentials. These action potentials travel along the auditory nerve to the auditory region of the brain stem, then to the thalamus, and finally to the auditory cortex, where they are interpreted as sound.

Different pitches stimulate different parts of the cochlea. Normally, the human ear can detect sounds ranging from 16 to 20,000 cycles per second. If the human ear could hear sounds lower than 16 cycles per second, it would pick up sounds generated by the flow of blood through the vessels and the movement of food through the digestive system.

The hair cells that line the cochlea are a delicate and vulnerable part of the ear. Repeated or sustained exposure to loud noise destroys the neurons of the organ of Corti. Once destroyed, the hair cells are not replaced, and the sound frequencies interpreted by them are no longer heard. Figure 50-12 shows rows of hair cells in a damaged section of the organ of Corti. Damage is most apparent in the bottom row of hair cells. Hair cells that respond to high frequency sound are very vulnerable to destruction, and loss of these neurons typically produces difficulty understanding human voices. Much of this type of permanent hearing loss is avoidable by reducing exposure to loud noises in the environment, such as industrial and machinery noise, gunfire, and loud music.

Balance is maintained with the help of mechanoreceptors in the three **semicircular canals** of the inner ear, shown in Figure 50-11. These canals are filled with fluid, and their interiors are lined with hair cells that have tiny particles of calcium carbonate on top of them. When the head moves, the hair cells are bent by the action of gravity on the calcium carbonate particles. The brain decodes the degree and direction of bend of the hair cells, interpreting the motion and the orientation of the head in space.

FIGURE 50-13

Light entering the eye travels through the cornea, pupil, and the clear lens to the retina, which contains millions of photoreceptors. Activation of these specialized sensory receptors sends a signal through the optic nerve to the optic centers of the brain—first to the thalamus and eventually to the visual cortex in the occipital lobe.

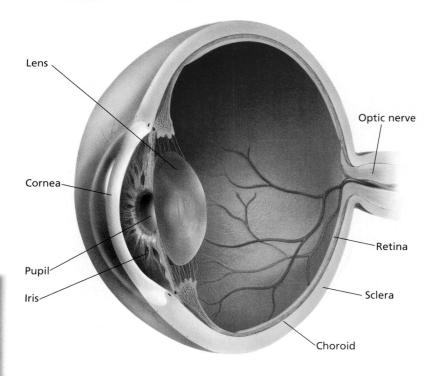

Lens · Optic nerve · Cornea · Retina · Pupil · Sclera · Iris · Choroid

Quick Lab

Observing a Lens

Materials beaker, water, piece of newspaper, 4 drops cooking oil

Procedure

1. Observe the newspaper through the sides of an empty beaker. Fill the beaker with water, and observe the newspaper through the water. Note any difference in print size.

2. Add four drops of oil to the top of the water. Place the newspaper under the glass, and observe the print size through the oil drops and the water.

Analysis Infer why the print size changes when the newspaper is viewed through water. What structure of the eye does the oil on the water represent?

VISION

The eyes are specialized organs that function by receiving light and transmitting signals to visual processing areas of the brain. The eye is basically a hollow sphere filled with a clear fluid. The structures of the eye, shown in Figure 50-13, act together to focus light on the **retina,** the light-sensitive inner layer of the eye.

Light passes first through a clear, protective layer called the **cornea.** Light then passes through the **pupil,** the opening to the interior of the eye. The pupil becomes larger when light is dim and smaller when light is bright. These involuntary responses are controlled by muscles in the pigmented **iris** that surrounds the pupil.

After light passes through the pupil, it travels through a convex crystalline structure called the **lens.** Attached to the lens are muscles that adjust the lens's shape to bend the rays of the incoming light. This bending focuses the complete image formed by the light onto the retina.

Lying deep within the retina are rods and cones, photoreceptors that translate light energy into electrical signals that can be interpreted by the brain. There are nearly 125 million **rods** in a single retina. Rods contain rhodopsin, a light-sensitive pigment that allows the rods to respond to dim light. The 7 million **cones** in the retina are stimulated by bright light. The cones initiate the production of sharp images and respond to different colors. Humans have three kinds of cones. Each type of cone contains a pigment that absorbs different wavelengths of light. When the signals from these three kinds of cones are integrated, a person is able to see all the colors in the visible spectrum. Colorblindness, which is the inability to distinguish certain colors, is caused by a chemical disorder in the cones.

Each photoreceptor responds to light from a single location in the visual field. Signals from the stimulated photoreceptors in the deepest layer of the retina travel to neurons on the surface of the retina. From these neurons, millions of axons, which form the optic nerve, exit the eye. The **optic nerve** carries visual information in the form of action potentials from the retina to the thalamus. Visual information is ultimately processed in the cortex of the occipital lobe.

TOPIC: The senses
GO TO: www.scilinks.org
KEYWORD: HM1021

TASTE AND SMELL

Specialized chemoreceptors allow humans to perceive variations in tastes and odors. The chemoreceptors for taste are clustered in the **taste buds.** Most of the 10,000 taste buds are embedded between bumps called **papillae** (puh-PIL-ee) on the tongue; additional taste buds are found on the roof of the mouth and in the throat.

Chemicals from food dissolved in saliva enter a taste bud through a small opening and stimulate a signal in the neurons that line the inner surface of the taste buds. As Figure 50-14 shows, taste signals travel through a relay in the brain stem, then to the thalamus and finally to the cortex, where they are interpreted.

Other chemicals in the environment are perceived by receptors in the nasal passages. Specialized chemoreceptors called **olfactory** (ahl-FAK-tuh-ree) **receptors** are located in the olfactory epithelium of the nasal passage, as shown in Figure 50-14. These cells lie within the mucous lining of the epithelium. The binding of molecules in the air to specific receptor molecules in the olfactory receptors

FIGURE 50-14

Taste and smell are chemical senses. Sensory receptors in the mouth and nasal passage bind molecules from the environment, initiating neural signals that travel to the brain.

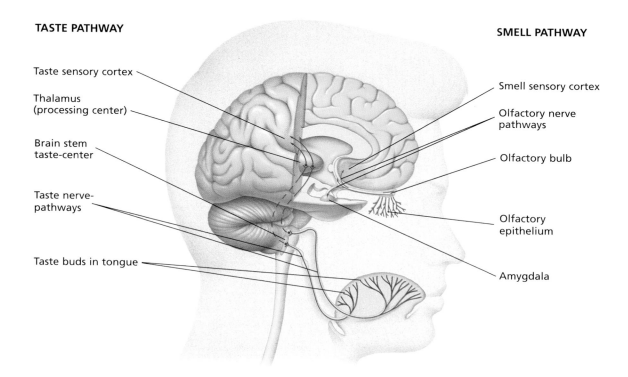

TASTE PATHWAY

Taste sensory cortex

Thalamus (processing center)

Brain stem taste-center

Taste nerve-pathways

Taste buds in tongue

SMELL PATHWAY

Smell sensory cortex

Olfactory nerve pathways

Olfactory bulb

Olfactory epithelium

Amygdala

stimulates the receptors. Signals from olfactory receptors travel to the olfactory bulb, a structure of the limbic system, then to olfactory areas of the cortex and to the **amygdala,** another limbic structure important in emotion, memory, and eating behavior.

OTHER SENSES

Mechanoreceptors located throughout the skin make it possible to sense touch, pressure, and tension. In humans, the receptors for touch are concentrated in the face, tongue, and fingertips. Body hair also plays an important role in the ability to sense touch. Large numbers of mechanoreceptors are found in the skin at the base of the hair follicles.

Two types of specialized thermoreceptors monitor temperature. Cold receptors are most sensitive to temperatures below 20°C. Heat receptors respond to temperatures between about 30°C and 45°C.

Pain receptors are sensory neurons located in the base of the epidermis and throughout the interior of the body. Pain receptors are stimulated by mechanical, thermal, electrical, or chemical energy. The type and number of pain receptors vary at different locations throughout the body. For example, the hands and mouth have a high concentration of pain receptors.

Sensory input from the surface of the body goes to the spinal cord in a very orderly way, as shown in Figure 50-15. Sensory input from the shoulders enters upper dorsal root sections of the spinal cord, while sensory input from the lower body enters the dorsal roots of the lower spinal cord. Damage to a specific section of the spinal cord results in sensory problems limited to a well-defined area of the body. This is an example of how function is mapped throughout the nervous system. In the brain, specific areas of the sensory cortex and motor cortex likewise correspond to specific body parts, and damage to specific areas of the cortex results in isolated problems, such as the loss of sensation in part of a hand.

FIGURE 50-15

Specific dorsal roots of the spinal cord carry sensory information from certain parts of the skin and body.

SECTION 50-4 REVIEW

1. Distinguish between chemoreceptors and mechanoreceptors.

2. How are sound vibrations transmitted through the ear?

3. Explain the role of rods and cones in the perception of images by humans.

4. What mechanisms do the senses of taste and smell have in common?

5. What is the importance of the high concentration of pain receptors in the hands?

6. **CRITICAL THINKING** Why might an injury to the lower spinal cord cause a loss of sensation in the legs?

■ The central nervous system (CNS) includes the brain and spinal cord.

■ Main divisions of the brain include the cerebrum and the brain stem—including the diencephalon—and the cerebellum. The cerebral cortex forms the outer layer of the cerebrum.

■ The cerebellum coordinates muscle action and helps the body maintain its balance.

■ The lower brain stem has three main sections—the midbrain, the pons, and the medulla oblongata.

■ Thirty-one pairs of spinal nerves each consist of a dorsal root containing sensory neurons and a ventral root containing motor neurons.

Vocabulary

afferent neuron (1004)
arachnoid layer (1007)
axon (1003)
brain stem (1006)
central nervous system (1004)
cerebellum (1007)
cerebral cortex (1005)

cerebral hemispheres (1004)
cerebrospinal fluid (1007)
cerebrum (1004)
corpus callosum (1004)
diencephalon (1006)
dura mater (1007)
efferent neuron (1004)
interneuron (1008)

limbic system (1006)
medulla oblongata (1007)
meninges (1007)
midbrain (1007)
motor neuron (1008)
nerve (1008)
peripheral nervous system (1004)

pia mater (1007)
pons (1007)
reticular formation (1007)
sensory receptor (1008)
spinal cord (1008)
thalamus (1006)
ventricle (1007)
white matter (1005)

50-2 ■ The peripheral nervous system (PNS) links the central nervous system and the rest of the body. The PNS is composed of a sensory division and a motor division.

■ The motor division of the PNS is divided into the somatic nervous system and the autonomic nervous system.

■ The somatic nervous system controls skele-tal muscles and is under voluntary control.

■ In a reflex, a signal is routed from sensory neurons, through the spinal cord and out through motor neurons.

■ In autonomic control of internal conditions, the sympathetic division and the parasympathetic division have largely opposite effects.

Vocabulary

autonomic nervous system (1010)
motor division (1009)

parasympathetic division (1011)
reflex (1009)

sensory division (1009)
somatic nervous system (1009)

spinal reflex (1010)
sympathetic division (1010)

 ■ A neuron consists of a cell body, dendrites, and an axon. The transmission of a signal through a neuron is called an action potential.

■ In a neuron at rest, K⁺ ions are concentrated inside the membrane while Na⁺ ions are concentrated outside the cell membrane. The inside of the cell membrane has a negative charge relative to the outside.

■ During an action potential, the polarity of the membrane is reversed briefly as Na⁺ ions diffuse into the neuron and K⁺ ions diffuse out of the neuron through gated channels.

■ When an action potential reaches the presynaptic membrane of the next neuron, neurotransmitter molecules diffuse across the synapse, where they can either stimulate or inhibit the start of an action potential in the postsynaptic neuron.

Vocabulary

action potential (1012)
axon terminal (1012)
dendrite (1012)

myelin sheath (1012)
neurotransmitter (1012)
node of Ranvier (1012)

potential (1013)
refractory period (1015)
resting potential (1014)

Schwann cell (1012)
synaptic cleft (1012)

50-4 ■ Sensory receptors include mechano-receptors, photoreceptors, chemorecep-tors, thermoreceptors, and pain receptors.

■ The eye receives light through the pupil. The lens focuses this light on the retina, which is composed of photoreceptors. The optic nerve that exits at the back of the retina carries a signal to the brain.

■ In the ear, vibrations pass through the aud-itory canal, the tympanic membrane, the bones of the middle ear, the oval window, and the cochlea of the inner ear. Hair cells in

the organ of Corti produce signals that travel through the auditory nerve to the brain.

■ Hair cells in the semicircular canals of the inner ear monitor the body's position in space.

■ Stimulation of neurons that line the inner surface of a taste bud initiates signals that travel to the brain, where they are inter-preted as taste. Likewise, olfactory recep-tors in the nasal passage transmit signals to the brain, where they are interpreted as odor.

Vocabulary

amygdala (1022)	Eustachian tube (1018)	organ of Corti (1019)	rod (1020)
auditory canal (1018)	iris (1020)	oval window (1018)	semicircular canal (1019)
cochlea (1018)	lens (1020)	papilla (1021)	sense organ (1017)
cone (1020)	olfactory receptor (1021)	pupil (1020)	taste bud (1021)
cornea (1020)	optic nerve (1021)	retina (1020)	tympanic membrane (1018)

REVIEW

Vocabulary

1. Explain the relationship between the auto-nomic nervous system, the sympathetic divi-sion, and the parasympathetic division.
2. Where is the hypothalamus located with respect to the thalamus?
3. Explain the relationship between the resting potential of the membrane and the action potential.
4. The word *pons* means "bridge." How is this related to the function of the pons in the brain?
5. What do the terms *afferent* and *efferent* mean with respect to neurons?

Multiple Choice

6. The central nervous system consists of (a) the brain and spinal cord (b) 31 pairs of spinal nerves (c) the cranial nerves (d) the peripheral nervous system.
7. The cerebral cortex (a) is located deep in the brain (b) is the folded outer covering of the brain (c) is the lobed, highly folded structure located at the back of the brain (d) contains the reticular formation.
8. The thalamus (a) lies below the medulla oblongata in the brain stem (b) controls

homeostasis (c) directs sensory information to the proper regions of the cerebral cortex (d) is important in maintaining balance.

9. The cerebellum is important in (a) coordinat-ing motor responses and maintaining posture (b) controlling hormone levels and maintain-ing homeostasis (c) protecting the brain and spine (d) processing olfactory and taste information.
10. In a spinal reflex, the signal travels (a) imme-diately to the brain (b) to the spinal cord and then to the brain (c) to the spinal cord and out to a muscle (d) directly to a sense organ.
11. When a neuron is at resting potential, (a) the outside is negatively charged (b) the inside is negatively charged (c) both sides are equally charged (d) the polarity across the mem-brane reverses.
12. Neurotransmitters (a) diffuse across the membrane, carrying charge with them (b) diffuse across the synaptic cleft and open channels on the postsynaptic neuron (c) are transported across the synaptic cleft and close channels in the postsynaptic neuron (d) do not work at the synaptic cleft.
13. Sensory receptors (a) link interneurons with motor neurons (b) are found only in the spine (c) are found only in the brain (d) respond to stimuli.

14. Photoreceptors are stimulated by (a) heat (b) pressure (c) chemicals (d) light.
15. Mechanoreceptors are stimulated by (a) heat (b) pressure (c) chemicals (d) light.

Short Answer

A B C D E

16. List the part of the neuron denoted by each letter in the diagram above.
17. What are two functions of cerebrospinal fluid?
18. What is the relationship between afferent neurons, interneurons, and efferent neurons?
19. How does the autonomic nervous system work to maintain homeostasis?
20. What are the roles of the three sections of the lower brain stem?
21. At resting potential, what ions do not readily cross the cell membrane of the neuron?
22. What role does the sodium-potassium pump play in the restoration of the membrane potential?
23. What event triggers release of neurotransmitter molecules?
24. What are dendrites and what function do they play in signaling in neurons?
25. What is the role of the ear in maintaining balance?
26. What are rods and cones, and how do their functions differ?

CRITICAL THINKING

1. Epilepsy affects one of every 200 Americans. Brain neurons normally produce small bursts of action potentials in varying patterns. During an epileptic seizure, large numbers of brain neurons send rapid bursts of action potentials simultaneously. The body of an individual having a seizure may grow rigid and jerk or convulse. From what you know about the brain's control of muscles and posture, how might you explain these symptoms?
2. Synesthesia is a puzzling phenomenon in which one type of sensory input is interpreted by the brain as another type. For example, a person hearing music might associate certain notes with certain colors. What may be happening in the central nervous system to produce this effect?
3. An imbalance of electrolytes, the ion-containing fluids of the body, can impair transmission of nerve signals. Why might this be so?
4. Look at the diagram below of the brain of a fish. How does the cerebrum differ from that of a human? The fish's brain has large olfactory bulbs. What does this tell you about the relative importance of the sense of smell to the fish?

Cerebrum

Olfactory bulbs

EXTENSION

1. Read "Why We Cry" in *Current Science,* February 11, 2000, on page 8. Describe the three kinds of tears that humans produce. Do any other animals cry tears? Explain the following comment by the writer: "Contrary to common belief, recent studies show that people don't weep while they're feeling a strong emotion."

2. Research the way general anesthetics work. Then write a short report in which you discuss a specific anesthetic, the effect of the anesthetic on the brain, and the effect of body weight and the passage of time on the action of an anesthetic.

Sheep's Eye Dissection

OBJECTIVES

- Describe the main external and internal structures of a sheep's eye.
- Name the various structures associated with sight.

PROCESS SKILLS

- observing
- identifying
- comparing and contrasting

MATERIALS

- safety goggles
- disposable gloves
- lab apron
- preserved sheep's eye
- dissection tray
- scalpel
- tweezers
- fine scissors
- blunt probe

Background

1. The sheep's eye is very similar to the human eye, as shown in the diagram below. The wall of the eyeball is made up of three layers. The outer layer, the sclera, is a tough tissue that forms the white of the eye. At the front of the eye, the sclera becomes thin and transparent to form the cornea.

2. The middle layer, the choroid, is dark and rich with blood vessels. At the front of the eye behind the cornea, the choroid is modified into the iris and the ciliary body. The pigment in the doughnut-shaped iris determines the color of the eye. The opening in the center of the iris is the pupil. What is the function of the pupil?

3. The inner layer, the retina, is sensitive to light. What are the sensory receptor neurons in the retina called?

4. Directly behind the iris is the elastic, transparent lens. The suspensory ligament attaches the ciliary muscle, the main part of the ciliary body, to the lens. This ring of muscle changes the shape of the lens to focus on near and far objects.

5. The lens and its suspensory ligament divide the eye into two chambers. The large vitreous chamber extends from the retina to the lens and ligaments. It is filled with a gelatinous mass, the vitreous humor. This vitreous humor helps to maintain the shape of the eye and hold the retina in place. The second chamber, which extends from the iris to the cornea, is subdivided into two parts, the anterior and posterior chambers. The anterior chamber extends from the cornea to the iris; the posterior chamber from the iris to the suspensory ligament. Both chambers contain aqueous humor, a watery substance that bathes the front part of the eye.

6. In the retina, the nerves from the rods and cones bundle together at the optic nerve. The region of the retina where its nerve fibers and blood vessels enter the optic nerve is the small optic disk, which contains no rods or cones. Why is the optic disk also called the blind spot?

7. A very short distance away is a yellowish spot, the fovea. It is the site of sharpest vision because it has a high concentration of photoreceptors.

Ciliary body
Ciliary muscle
Retina
Choroid
Sclera
Fovea
Optic nerve
Optic disk
Lens
Pupil
Cornea
Iris
Anterior chamber
Posterior chamber
Vitreous chamber

Procedure

1.   Put on safety goggles, gloves, and a lab apron.

2. Locate the six main muscles on the outside of the eye, as shown in the diagram below. These

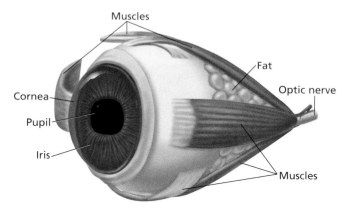

Muscles

Fat

Optic nerve

Cornea

Pupil

Iris

Muscles

muscles move the eye in various directions. Use a scalpel to carefully cut the muscles near the eye. This will expose the sclera.

3. Observe the fatty tissue that cushions the eye in its socket, especially around the optic nerve. This fatty tissue helps to prevent shock. With a tweezer and scalpel, remove the fatty tissue. This will expose the optic nerve more fully.

4. Using a scalpel, carefully cut the sclera about 1 cm behind the cornea. Using fine scissors, extend the cut to make a flap that you can lift, as shown in the diagram below.

Incision line

Fat

Optic nerve

Scleral flap

Edge of cornea

Blood vessels of choroid

Incision line

5. With forceps, carefully remove the sclera in this area and observe the dark choroid layer immediately below the sclera.

6. Next, use a scalpel to make an incision through the eye. Following along the incision you made in step 4, cut almost completely around the eye. You have separated the eye into an anterior and a posterior portion.

7. In the posterior section, observe the whitish retina. It is probably shriveled and may have fallen into the vitreous chamber.

8. In the anterior section, use a blunt probe to expose the lens. In a preserved eye, the lens is no longer clear.

9. In the anterior section, also locate the ciliary muscle and as many other structures as possible.

10. When you have finished your dissection, remove the specimen from the dissecting tray. Dispose of your materials according to the directions from your teacher.

11. Clean up your work area and wash your hands before leaving the lab.

Analysis and Conclusions

1. How is the lens different from the other structures of the eye?
2. How do the nature of the sclera and choroid change as they reach the front part of the eye?
3. How does the vitreous chamber differ from the anterior and posterior chambers?
4. What would be the result of the cornea becoming cloudy during an animal's lifetime?
5. Sometimes the retina of the eye becomes detached. Why is it important that the retina be reattached, if possible?

Further Inquiry

You see light if the vision center of your cerebrum is stimulated electrically. Scientists are trying to find out which brain cells are involved in forming images in our brains. How might scientists someday use this knowledge to help blind people see?

ENDOCRINE SYSTEM

The neurotransmitter dopamine is one of many amino acid–based compounds that act as chemical messengers in the body.

FOCUS CONCEPT: *Stability and Homeostasis*

As you read, examine the various ways that the endocrine system helps the body maintain homeostasis and stability.

51-1 *Hormones*

51-2 *Endocrine Glands*

51-3 *Feedback Mechanisms*

HORMONES

The **endocrine** *(EN-duh-KRIN)* **system** *consists of glands that transmit chemical messengers throughout the body. These chemical messengers, called* **hormones** *(HOHR-MOHNZ), circulate in the bloodstream and affect many types of body cells. In this section, you will learn about hormones and mechanisms of their action.*

OBJECTIVES

▲

Compare exocrine glands with endocrine glands.

●

Contrast amino acid–based hormones with steroid hormones.

■

Describe two ways that hormones affect their target cells.

◆

Distinguish hormones from prostaglandins.

TYPES OF GLANDS

A gland is an organ that consists of cells that secrete materials into other regions of the body. The body contains two types of glands: exocrine glands and endocrine glands. **Exocrine** (EK-suh-KRIN) **glands** secrete nonhormonal chemicals into ducts, which transport the chemicals to specific locations inside and outside the body. Sweat glands, mucous glands, salivary glands, and other digestive glands are examples of exocrine glands. **Endocrine glands** are ductless glands that are located throughout the body. Endocrine glands secrete hormones into the bloodstream through the fluid that surrounds their cells. You will learn more about endocrine glands in Section 51-2.

TYPES OF HORMONES

Hormones are compounds that are secreted in small amounts into the bloodstream and that influence the activity of distant cells. Hormones diffuse into the blood, which is their vehicle for transportation to various cells throughout the body. Hormones can be grouped into two general categories based on their structure: amino acid–based hormones and steroid, or lipid, hormones. **Amino acid–based hormones,** such as epinephrine (adrenaline), include proteins, peptides, amino acids, and other forms that are derived from amino acids. **Steroid** (STER-OYD) **hormones,** such as estrogen and testosterone, are lipids that the body synthesizes from cholesterol.

These two general classes of hormones differ significantly in their physical, and therefore chemical, properties. Thus, their mechanisms of action on body cells are also different. As you will see, mechanisms of hormone action depend on the way that hormones interact with cells that they affect.

internet**connect**

SCLINKS.
NSTA

TOPIC: Glands
GO TO: www.scilinks.org
KEYWORD: HM1029

Word Roots and Origins

hormone

from the Greek *hormon,* meaning "to excite"

HORMONE ACTION

The body produces many hormones, and each hormone affects only specific cells, called **target cells.** Target cells have receptors that recognize and bind to specific hormones. **Receptors** are proteins that are located both inside the cytoplasm and on the surface of a target cell. When a hormone binds to a receptor on its target cell, it triggers events that lead to changes within the cell.

Amino Acid–Based Hormones

Because most amino acid–based hormones cannot diffuse passively across the membranes of their target cells, a two-messenger system is commonly required for the action of most of these hormones. Amino acid–based hormones identify their target cells by their attraction to receptor proteins that are embedded in the target cell membrane. The hormone acts as a **first messenger** by binding to a specific receptor on the surface of its target cell. This forms a **hormone-receptor complex,** which activates a second messenger located inside the target cell. A **second messenger** relays and amplifies the hormone signal. Figure 51-1 shows how, in many cases, the hormone-receptor complex indirectly activates an enzyme that converts molecules of ATP to cyclic AMP (c-AMP) inside the cell. Cyclic AMP acts as a second messenger by indirectly activating other enzymes and proteins in the target cell. Thus, c-AMP initiates a chain of biochemical events that leads to functional changes within the target cell.

Steroid Hormones

Steroid hormones do not act through cell surface receptors. Instead, they diffuse through the membranes of their target cells and bind to receptors in the cytoplasm. The newly formed hormone-receptor complexes cause the cells to activate existing enzymes or to initiate synthesis of new enzymes or proteins. Figure 51-2 illustrates how a hormone-receptor complex binds to DNA inside the nucleus of a target cell. Once bound to DNA, the hormone-receptor complex activates transcription of mRNA. By activating mRNA transcription, steroid hormones stimulate production of new proteins, which cause changes in the target cell.

internetconnect

SCLINKS
NSTA

TOPIC: Hormones
GO TO: www.scilinks.org
KEYWORD: HM1030

FIGURE 51-1

(a) An amino acid–based hormone acts as a first messenger by binding to receptor proteins located on the target cell membrane. (b) The hormone-receptor complex indirectly activates an enzyme that converts ATP to cyclic AMP. (c) Cyclic AMP indirectly activates other enzymes that cause changes in the target cell.

Amino acid–based hormone

Hormone-receptor complex

Receptor protein   Cytoplasm   Cell membrane   Nucleus

(a) FIRST-MESSENGER ACTION

Enzyme

Cyclic AMP

ATP

(b) SECOND-MESSENGER ACTION

Enzymes

Cyclic AMP   Cellular changes

(c) CELLULAR RESPONSES

(a) STEROID ENTERS CELL

Steroid hormone

Cell membrane

Cytoplasm

Nucleus

Receptor protein

(b) COMPLEX FORMS

Hormone-receptor complex

(c) TRANSCRIPTION OCCURS

mRNA

(d) NEW PROTEIN FORMS

New protein

FIGURE 51-2

(a) Steroid hormones diffuse through the target cell membrane. (b) Once inside the target cell, the hormone binds to a receptor protein. (c) The newly formed hormone-receptor complex enters the nucleus of the target cell and binds to DNA, activating mRNA transcription. (d) Genes are activated, mRNA is transcribed, and new proteins are synthesized.

PROSTAGLANDINS

Prostaglandins (PRAHS-tuh-GLAN-dinz), a group of hormonelike lipids, also regulate cell activities. Unlike hormones, prostaglandins are not produced by specific endocrine glands. Instead, these chemicals are produced in small quantities by many cells throughout the body. Rather than being transported through the blood to distant regions of the body, prostaglandins act locally. Their effects include relaxation of smooth muscles that line air passageways and blood vessels, regulation of blood pressure, contraction of the intestinal walls and the uterus, and stimulation of the body's inflammatory response to infection.

SECTION 51-1 REVIEW

1. Compare exocrine glands with endocrine glands.

2. What are hormones, and what do they do?

3. Explain the differences in the way amino acid–based hormones and steroid hormones affect their target cells.

4. How are hormones transported throughout the body?

5. Compare prostaglandins with hormones.

6. **CRITICAL THINKING** Why are nonendocrine messengers not considered to be hormones?

ENDOCRINE GLANDS

OBJECTIVES

▲

List the major endocrine glands and hormones found in the body.

●

Discuss the relationship between the hypothalamus and the pituitary gland.

■

Describe the function of each endocrine gland.

*E*ndocrine glands, shown in Figure 51-3, are located throughout the body and regulate many of its vital processes. This section discusses the hormones that each endocrine gland produces and their effects on the body.

PITUITARY GLAND

The **pituitary** (puh-TOO-uh-TER-ee) **gland,** shown in Figure 51-4, secretes hormones that affect other glands and organs. The two lobes of the pituitary gland are regulated by the hypothalamus, a structure of the nervous system, also shown in Figure 51-4. The hypothalamus links the nervous system to the endocrine system. **Neurosecretory** (NOO-roh-SEE-kret-ohr-ee) **cells** of the hypothalamus produce hormones that either are stored in the pituitary gland or regulate the pituitary's activity. The hypothalamus and the pituitary gland are the primary regulators of the endocrine system.

Posterior Pituitary

Two amino acid–based hormones—oxytocin and antidiuretic hormone—are produced by neurosecretory cells whose axons extend into the posterior pituitary lobe, as shown in Figure 51-4. These hormones are transported down these axons into the posterior pituitary, where they are stored for eventual release into the bloodstream. Signaling through these neurons, the hypothalamus also regulates the secretion of these hormones from the posterior pituitary.

Oxytocin (AHK-see-TOH-sin) stimulates contraction of the uterus—a structure of the female reproductive system—during childbirth and flow of breast milk from the mammary glands during nursing. **Antidiuretic** (AN-tie-die-yoo-RET-tik) **hormone (ADH)** helps regulate the concentration of solutes in the blood by controlling the amount of water excreted by the kidneys. When the concentration of solutes in the blood increases, the hypothalamus signals the posterior pituitary to secrete ADH. ADH causes tubules in the kidneys to reabsorb water into the blood. Thus, the kidneys produce urine with a high solute concentration. Hypothalamic receptors detect the subsequent decrease in the concentration of solutes in the blood and stop signaling the posterior pituitary to release ADH.

Anterior Pituitary

Neurosecretory cells also produce and secrete **releasing hormones,** which stimulate endocrine cells of the anterior pituitary

FIGURE 51-3

Endocrine glands are located throughout the body. All of these glands contain cells that secrete hormones. The hypothalamus is a part of the nervous system that regulates the pituitary gland.

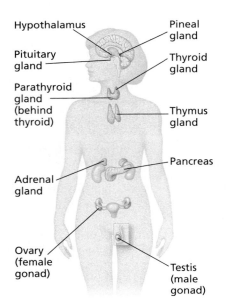

Hypothalamus

Pineal gland

Pituitary gland

Thyroid gland

Parathyroid gland (behind thyroid)

Thymus gland

Pancreas

Adrenal gland

Ovary (female gonad)

Testis (male gonad)

lobe to produce and secrete hormones. Other hypothalamic neurosecretory cells produce **release-inhibiting hormones,** which inhibit production and secretion of anterior-pituitary hormones. Releasing hormones and release-inhibiting hormones are produced in response to various stimuli that are processed by the nervous system. There is at least one releasing hormone for each anterior-pituitary hormone. As shown in Figure 51-4, a specialized system of blood vessels connects the hypothalamus with the anterior pituitary. Neurosecretory cells release hormones into the anterior pituitary through blood vessels.

Some anterior pituitary hormones, such as prolactin and growth hormone, are regulated by the hypothalamus through both a releasing hormone and a release-inhibiting hormone. **Growth hormone (GH)** controls skeletal and muscular growth. **Prolactin** (proh-LAK-tin) **(PRL)** stimulates and sustains production of breast milk during lactation. PRL-releasing hormone stimulates PRL production and secretion, whereas PRL release-inhibiting hormone stops PRL secretion. Releasing hormones also regulate production and secretion of other hormones—luteinizing hormone, follicle-stimulating hormone, adrenocorticotropic hormone, and thyroid-stimulating hormone—in the anterior pituitary that stimulate other endocrine glands. Table 51-1 lists eight hormones that are secreted by the pituitary gland.

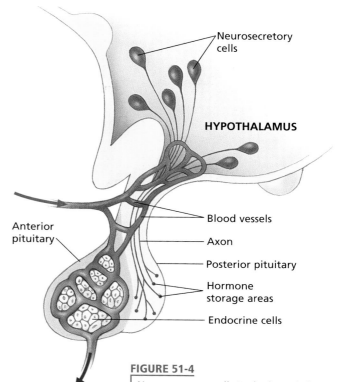

FIGURE 51-4

Neurosecretory cells in the hypothalamus produce hormones that affect the pituitary gland. The hypothalamus regulates the posterior pituitary through axons and the anterior pituitary through blood vessels. (Blood vessels in the posterior pituitary have been omitted to show axon projections.)

TABLE 51-1 *Hormones Secreted by the Pituitary Gland*

Hormone	Target	Function
Adrenocorticotropic hormone (ACTH)	adrenal cortex	stimulates secretion of cortisol and aldosterone by the adrenal cortex
Antidiuretic hormone (ADH)	kidney tubules	stimulates reabsorption of water by kidneys, reducing the concentration of solutes in the blood
Follicle-stimulating hormone (FSH)	ovaries in females; testes in males	stimulates egg production in females; stimulates sperm production in males
Growth hormone (GH)	muscle and bone	regulates development of muscles and bones
Luteinizing hormone (LH)	ovaries in females; testes in males	stimulates progesterone and estrogen production; initiates ovulation in females; stimulates testosterone production
Oxytocin	mammary glands and uterine muscles	initiates uterine contractions during childbirth; stimulates flow of milk from breasts during lactation
Prolactin (PRL)	mammary glands	stimulates milk production in breasts during lactation
Thyroid-stimulating hormone (TSH)	thyroid gland	regulates secretion of the thyroid hormones—thyroxine and triiodothyronine

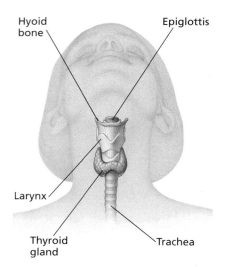

Hyoid bone

Epiglottis

Larynx

Thyroid gland

Trachea

FIGURE 51-5

The thyroid gland is located under the larynx and on the trachea.

Quick Lab

Observing Solubilities

Materials 100 mL beakers (4), water, gelatin, cooking oil, vitamin A or E capsules, dissecting pin, measuring spoon

Procedure

1. Put 75 mL of water into a beaker. Place 2.5 g of gelatin (protein) into the beaker, and swirl the solution. Does the gelatin dissolve? Record your observations.

2. Put 75 mL of oil into a clean beaker. Repeat the procedure in step 2 using oil instead of water.

3. Repeat steps 2 and 3 using the contents of a vitamin capsule (fat) instead of gelatin.

Analysis Which substance is fat soluble? Which substance is water soluble? What type of substance can diffuse through a cell membrane? Relate the solubilities of hormones to whether or not they enter their target cells or work outside them.

THYROID GLAND

The two lobes of the **thyroid** (THIE-ROYD) **gland** are located near the lower part of the larynx, as shown in Figure 51-5. **Thyroid-stimulating hormone (TSH)** regulates the thyroid gland. Release of TSH from the anterior pituitary is regulated by both a releasing hormone and a release-inhibiting hormone. When stimulated by TSH, the thyroid gland produces and secretes the hormones **thyroxine** (thie-RAHK-sin) and **triiodothyronine** (TRIE-ie-oh-DOH-THIE-roh-NEEN). Both of these hormones are derived from the same amino acid and are synthesized with iodine atoms. The thyroid hormones help maintain normal heart rate, blood pressure, and body temperature. They stimulate enzymes that are associated with glucose oxidation and oxygen consumption, generating heat and increasing cellular metabolic rates. They also promote carbohydrate usage over fat usage for energy.

The thyroid gland is important to human development. It also produces **calcitonin** (KAL-sih-TOH-nin), a hormone that stimulates the transfer of calcium ions from blood to bone, where they can be used to generate bone tissue.

Abnormal thyroid activity can be detrimental to the body's metabolism. Overproduction of the thyroid hormones is called **hyperthyroidism** (HIE-puhr-THIE-royd-izm). Symptoms of hyperthyroidism include overactivity; weight loss; and high blood pressure, heart rate, and body temperature. Hyperthyroidism can be treated with medication or by surgical removal of part of the thyroid gland. Thyroid-hormone deficiency is known as **hypothyroidism** (HIE-poh-THIE-royd-izm). Symptoms of hypothyroidism include growth retardation, lethargy, weight gain, and low heart rate and body temperature. It can also cause **cretinism** (KREET-uhn-IZ-uhm), a form of mental retardation, during fetal and childhood development. If hypothyroidism is caused by iodine deficiency, then **goiter** (GOY-tuhr), or swelling of the thyroid gland, results. Hypothyroidism can be treated with supplementary thyroxine.

ADRENAL GLANDS

One **adrenal** (uh-DREE-nuhl) **gland** is located above each kidney, as shown in Figure 51-6. Each adrenal gland has an inner core, the medulla, and an outer layer, the cortex. The medulla and cortex function as separate endocrine glands. Medullary hormone secretion is controlled by the nervous system, whereas the anterior pituitary regulates cortical hormone secretion.

Adrenal Medulla

The adrenal medulla produces two amino acid–based hormones: **epinephrine** (EP-i-NEF-rin) and **norepinephrine** (NOHR-ep-i-NEF-rin) **(NE),** also known as adrenaline (uh-DREN-uh-lin) and noradrenaline (NOR-uh-DREN-uh-lin), respectively. These hormones orchestrate the nervous system's reaction to stress and its "fight-or-flight" response to danger. When a person is stressed, the medulla secretes epinephrine and NE into the bloodstream. These hormones cause the liver to break down glycogen into glucose, raising the level of glucose, which is oxidized for additional energy, in the blood. The results include enlargement of the bronchial tubes, dilation of the pupils, and an increase in heart rate. As the heart beats faster, surface blood vessels constrict, blood pressure rises, and more blood circulates to the muscles, brain, and heart.

Adrenal Cortex

The adrenal cortex responds to **adrenocorticotropic** (uh-DRE-noh-KOHR-ti-koh-TROH-pik) **hormone (ACTH),** which is secreted by the anterior pituitary. Stress causes the hypothalamus to secrete ACTH-releasing hormone. ACTH then stimulates the adrenal cortex to produce the steroid hormones **cortisol** (KOHRT-uh-SAWL), which regulates metabolism of carbohydrates and proteins, and **aldosterone** (al-DAHS-tuh-ROHN), which helps maintain the salt-and-water balance in the body by affecting the kidneys.

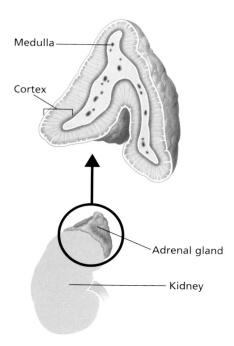

FIGURE 51-6

The adrenal glands, located above each kidney, consist of an inner medulla and an outer cortex. Epinephrine and norepinephrine are produced in the medulla, while cortisol and aldosterone are produced in the cortex.

GONADS

Gonads—the ovaries in females and the testes in males—are gamete-producing organs that also produce a group of steroid sex hormones. **Sex hormones** regulate body changes that begin at puberty. **Puberty** (PYOO-buhr-tee) is the adolescent stage during which the sex organs mature and secondary sex characteristics, such as facial hair, appear. During puberty in males, sperm production begins, the voice deepens, the chest broadens, and hair grows on the body and face. In females, the menstrual cycle begins, the breasts grow, and the hips widen. When secreted by the anterior pituitary, **luteinizing** (LOO-tee-in-IZE-ing) **hormone (LH)** and **follicle-stimulating** (FOL-uh-kuhl) **hormone (FSH)** stimulate secretion of sex hormones from the gonads.

In females, LH and FSH stimulate secretion of **estrogen** (ES-truh-jen) and **progesterone** (proh-JES-tuh-ROHN) from the ovaries. In preparation for a possible pregnancy, these sex hormones cause the monthly release of an egg by an ovary and buildup of the uterine lining. Estrogen also regulates female secondary sex characteristics. In males, LH stimulates the testes to secrete a group of sex hormones called **androgens** (AN-druh-jenz). **Testosterone** (tes-TAHS-tuh-ROHN) is an androgen that regulates male secondary sex characteristics. Along with FSH, testosterone also stimulates sperm production. You will learn more about the gonads and the sex hormones in Chapter 52.

FIGURE 51-7

A cross section of pancreatic tissue shows the islets of Langerhans (lightly colored region). These endocrine cells are surrounded by exocrine cells that produce digestive fluids. (LM 315×)

PANCREAS

The pancreas mostly contains exocrine cells, but specialized cells in the pancreas called the **islets of Langerhans** (LANG-uhr-HANZ) function together as an endocrine gland. Shown in Figure 51-7, these endocrine cells secrete two amino acid–based hormones that regulate the level of sugar in the blood. **Insulin** (IN-suh-lin) lowers the blood sugar level by stimulating body cells, especially muscles, to absorb glucose. In contrast, **glucagon** (GLOO-kuh-gahn) stimulates release of glucose into the bloodstream by liver cells.

Insulin deficiency causes **diabetes mellitus** (die-uh-BEET-eez muh-LIET-uhs), a condition of abnormally high blood glucose concentration. Type I diabetes is a severe childhood disorder in which insulin-producing islet cells die. Type I generally is treated with daily injections of insulin into the blood, and sometimes is treated with islet cell transplant. Type II diabetes usually occurs after age 40, and it is more common and less severe than type I. Type II is caused by insufficient insulin or unresponsive target cell receptors. Although type II is hereditary, its onset correlates with obesity, and type II often can be controlled through exercise and diet. In people with diabetes, excess glucose inhibits water reabsorption by the kidneys, producing large amounts of urine. Thus, dehydration and kidney damage can result. Lack of insulin can also cause nausea and rapid breathing, possibly leading to oxygen deficiency, circulatory and nervous system failure, diabetic coma, or even death.

TABLE 51-2	*Summary of Endocrine Glands and Their Functions*	
Glands	**Hormone**	**Function**
Adrenal glands		
Cortex	aldosterone	maintains salt-and-water balance
	cortisol	regulates carbohydrate and protein metabolism
Medulla	epinephrine, norepinephrine	initiate body's response to stress and the "fight-or-flight" response to danger
Ovaries	estrogen	regulates female secondary sex characteristics
	progesterone	maintains growth of uterine lining
Pancreas (islets of Langerhans)	glucagon	stimulates release of glucose
	insulin	stimulates absorption of glucose
Parathyroid glands	parathyroid hormone	increases blood calcium concentration
Pineal gland	melatonin	regulates sleep patterns
Pituitary gland	see Table 51-1	see Table 51-1
Testes	androgens (testosterone)	regulate male secondary sex characteristics
Thymus gland	thymosin	stimulates T-cell formation
Thyroid gland	thyroxine, triiodothyronine	increase cellular metabolic rates

Excessive insulin causes **hypoglycemia** (HIE-poh-glie-SEE-mee-uh), a disorder in which glucose is stored, rather than being properly delivered to body cells. This leads to a lowered blood glucose concentration and subsequent release of glucagon and epinephrine. Symptoms of hypoglycemia include lethargy, dizziness, nervousness, overactivity, and in extreme cases, unconsciousness and death.

OTHER ENDOCRINE GLANDS

There are several other glands in the endocrine system, including the thymus gland, the pineal gland, and the parathyroid glands. There are also specialized digestive endocrine cells. The endocrine glands and their functions are listed in Table 51-2.

The **thymus** (THIE-muhs) **gland,** located beneath the sternum and between the lungs, consists mostly of T-cells and plays a role in the development of the immune system. The thymus gland secretes **thymosin** (THIE-moh-sin), an amino acid–based hormone that stimulates formation of T-cells, which help defend the body from pathogens.

The **pineal** (PIEN-ee-uhl) **gland** is located near the base of the brain, as shown in Figure 51-8. It secretes the hormone melatonin. **Melatonin** (mel-uh-TOH-nin) concentrations increase sharply at night and decrease dramatically during the day. This cyclic release of melatonin indicates that it helps regulate sleep patterns.

As Figure 51-9 shows, the four **parathyroid glands** are embedded in the back of the thyroid gland, two in each lobe. These glands secrete **parathyroid hormone,** which increases the concentration of calcium ions in the blood. A proper balance of calcium ions is necessary for normal bone growth, muscle tone, and neural activity.

Endocrine cells within the walls of some digestive organs also secrete a variety of hormones that help digest food. When food is eaten, endocrine cells in the stomach lining secrete **gastrin** (GAS-trin), a hormone that stimulates other stomach cells to release digestive enzymes and hydrochloric acid. Endocrine cells of the small intestine release **secretin** (si-KREE-tin), a hormone that stimulates the release of various digestive fluids from the pancreas and bile from the liver.

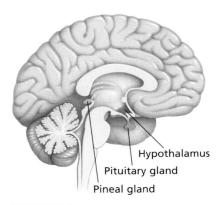

FIGURE 51-8

The pineal gland, located near the base of the brain, secretes the hormone melatonin at night.

FIGURE 51-9

The four parathyroid glands are embedded in the dorsal side of the thyroid gland. They secrete a hormone that regulates the concentration of calcium ions in the blood.

SECTION 51-2 REVIEW

1. List six endocrine glands and their functions.

2. What is a releasing hormone?

3. Describe the effects of two releasing hormones on the pituitary gland.

4. Explain why the pineal gland is considered the "biological clock" of the body and why the pituitary gland is considered the "master gland" of the body.

5. Describe the malfunctions that cause Type I and Type II diabetes.

6. **CRITICAL THINKING** Why might overactive parathyroid glands cause bone problems?

▲

Define the terms *feedback mechanism* and *antagonistic hormones.*

●

Distinguish positive feedback from negative feedback.

■

Explain the role of negative feedback mechanisms in maintaining homeostasis.

◆

Give examples of negative feedback in the endocrine system.

FEEDBACK MECHANISMS

*T*he endocrine system uses feedback mechanisms to respond and adjust to changes that occur in and outside the body. In a **feedback mechanism,** the last step in a series of events controls the first step.

HOMEOSTASIS

Recall that homeostasis is defined as a stable internal environment. The endocrine system plays an important role in the maintenance of homeostasis because it affects the activities of cells, tissues, and organs throughout the body. For example, glucagon and insulin together maintain a balanced blood glucose concentration. These hormones are considered **antagonistic hormones** because their actions have opposite effects. Figure 51-10 illustrates how an increase in glucose concentration following glucagon secretion is counteracted by insulin secretion.

To maintain homeostasis, hormone secretion must be tightly regulated. One example of hormone regulation was discussed in Section 51-2: ADH secretion is controlled by hypothalamic receptors that detect the concentration of solutes in the blood. More-common types of endocrine control are **feedback mechanisms,** which are illustrated in Figure 51-11. Most hormone systems use **negative feedback,** in which release of an initial hormone stimulates release or production of other hormones or substances that subsequently inhibit further release of the initial hormone. In **positive feedback,** release of an initial hormone stimulates release or production of other hormones or substances, which stimulate further release of the initial hormone. For example, although LH regulates estrogen production by the ovaries, increased estrogen concentrations stimulate a surge in LH secretion prior to ovulation.

FIGURE 51-10

Working in opposition, glucagon and insulin maintain a balanced blood glucose concentration. These antagonistic hormones oppositely affect the amount of glucose in the blood.

Negative Feedback

Positive Feedback

NEGATIVE FEEDBACK MECHANISMS

Negative feedback mechanisms in the body involve interactions of the nervous, endocrine, and circulatory systems. In negative feedback, the final step in a series of events inhibits the initial signal in the series. To understand negative feedback, consider a home heating system that is controlled by a thermostat, as illustrated in Figure 51-12. When the room temperature drops below a set point, the thermostat activates the heater to produce heat. When room temperature returns to the set point, the thermostat shuts off the heater.

Negative feedback mechanisms help maintain hormone concentrations at a certain range. A good example of negative feedback in the endocrine system is the hypothalamus–anterior-pituitary–testis system discussed in Section 51-2. The hypothalamus secretes LH-releasing hormone, which stimulates secretion of LH from the anterior pituitary. LH is released into the bloodstream and is transported throughout the body. LH binds to its target cells in the testes, forming hormone-receptor complexes that stimulate c-AMP production, which leads to testosterone secretion into the bloodstream. Testosterone binds to its target cells, some of which are the hypothalamic neurosecretory cells that produce LH-releasing hormone. If the testosterone concentration is higher than normal, then secretion of LH-releasing hormone will be inhibited.

Another example of negative feedback in the endocrine system is the regulation of the concentration of the thyroid hormones in the blood. When the hypothalamus detects low concentrations of thyroxine and triiodothyronine, it secretes TSH-releasing hormone into the anterior

FIGURE 51-11

In negative feedback, a secondary substance (A) inhibits production of its initial stimulating substance (B). In positive feedback, a secondary substance (A) stimulates production of its initial stimulating substance (B).

FIGURE 51-12

Negative feedback mechanisms inhibit the original signal as its products build up.

FIGURE 51-13

The thyroid hormones regulate cellular metabolic rates through a negative feedback mechanism. Low concentrations of the thyroid hormones stimulate production and secretion of TSH-releasing hormone from the hypothalamus; high concentrations inhibit TSH-releasing hormone but stimulate TSH release-inhibiting hormone.

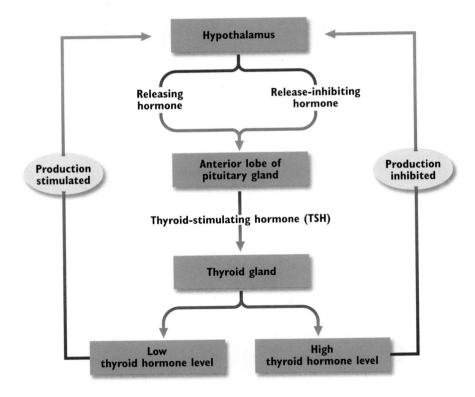

pituitary, as Figure 51-13 illustrates. The anterior pituitary then secretes TSH into the bloodstream. TSH stimulates the thyroid gland to secrete thyroxine and triiodothyronine, whose target cells include hypothalamic neurosecretory cells that produce TSH-releasing hormone and TSH release-inhibiting hormone. When the hypothalamus detects increasing concentrations of the thyroid hormones in the blood, it stops secreting TSH-releasing hormone and begins to secrete TSH release-inhibiting hormone into the anterior pituitary. Thus, the anterior pituitary no longer secretes TSH, and the thyroid gland no longer secretes thyroxine and triiodothyronine. As a result, the concentration of the thyroid hormones in the blood decreases. When the concentration again drops to a certain point, the cycle is repeated.

SECTION 51-3 REVIEW

1. Explain why glucagon and insulin are antagonistic hormones.

2. Explain what might happen to the level of glucose circulating in the blood if the production of insulin were controlled by a positive, rather than a negative, feedback mechanism.

3. How do feedback mechanisms help maintain homeostasis?

4. What would happen if a thermostat operated under a positive feedback mechanism?

5. How would lack of dietary iodine affect the negative feedback mechanism that controls the level of the thyroid hormones?

6. CRITICAL THINKING Why is it important to carefully control the dose of thyroxine administered to a person with hypothyroidism?

CHAPTER 51 REVIEW

· SUMMARY/VOCABULARY

- Endocrine glands produce and secrete hormones that affect distant target cells.
- Amino acid–based hormones bind to receptors on their target cells, activating a second messenger.

- Steroid hormones diffuse through the membranes of their target cells and bind to cytoplasmic receptors.
- Prostaglandins are hormonelike lipids that affect nearby cells.

Vocabulary

amino acid–based hormone (1029)
endocrine gland (1029)
endocrine system (1029)
exocrine gland (1029)
first messenger (1030)
hormone-receptor complex (1030)
hormone (1029)
prostaglandin (1031)
receptor (1030)
second messenger (1030)
steroid hormone (1029)
target cell (1030)

- The hypothalamus links the nervous system to the endocrine system by regulating the pituitary gland.
- Releasing hormones and release-inhibiting hormones secreted by the hypothalamus regulate the anterior-pituitary hormones.
- The thyroid gland secretes hormones that regulate metabolism.
- The adrenal glands help regulate metabolism and the body's responses to stress and danger.

- The gonads secrete sex hormones that are responsible for body changes that begin at puberty.
- The islets of Langerhans of the pancreas secrete hormones that regulate the blood glucose level.
- Other endocrine glands include the thymus gland, the pineal gland, the parathyroid glands, and endocrine cells of the digestive system.

Vocabulary

adrenal gland (1034)
adrenocorticotropic hormone (1035)
aldosterone (1035)
androgens (1035)
antidiuretic hormone (1032)
calcitonin (1034)
cortisol (1035)
cretinism (1034)
diabetes mellitus (1036)
epinephrine (1034)
estrogen (1035)
follicle-stimulating hormone (1035)
gastrin (1037)
glucagon (1036)
goiter (1034)
gonads (1035)
growth hormone (1033)
hyperthyroidism (1034)
hypoglycemia (1037)
hypothyroidism (1034)
insulin (1036)
islets of Langerhans (1036)
luteinizing hormone (1035)
melatonin (1037)
neurosecretory cell (1032)
norepinephrine (1034)
oxytocin (1032)
parathyroid gland (1037)
parathyroid hormone (1037)
pineal gland (1037)
pituitary gland (1032)
progesterone (1035)
prolactin (1033)
puberty (1035)
release-inhibiting hormone (1033)
releasing hormone (1032)
secretin (1037)
sex hormones (1035)
testosterone (1035)
thymosin (1037)
thymus gland (1037)
thyroid gland (1034)
thyroid-stimulating hormone (1034)
thyroxine (1034)
triiodothyronine (1034)

51-3

- Feedback mechanisms help maintain homeostasis.
- In negative feedback, the final step in a series inhibits the first step.

- In positive feedback, the final step in a series stimulates the first step.

Vocabulary

antagonistic hormone (1038)
feedback mechanism (1038)
negative feedback (1038)
positive feedback (1038)

REVIEW

Vocabulary

For each set of terms below, choose the one that does not belong and then explain why it does not belong.

1. insulin, prostaglandin, thyroxine, GH
2. oxytocin, prolactin, epinephrine, ADH
3. cortisol, parathyroid hormone, epinephrine, aldosterone
4. aldosterone, estrogen, progesterone, testosterone
5. thyroid gland, liver, adrenal glands, pineal gland

Multiple Choice

6. The endocrine system (a) affects only the nervous system (b) helps maintain homeostasis (c) affects only the reproductive system (d) primarily uses positive feedback.
7. In a negative feedback system, the end product (a) inhibits the first step (b) inhibits the last step (c) stimulates the first step (d) stimulates the last step.
8. Steroid hormones (a) bind to receptors on a target cell (b) convert ATP to cyclic AMP (c) diffuse through the target cell membrane (d) activate a second messenger.
9. Cyclic AMP is produced by a cell in response to (a) estrogen (b) amino acid–based hormones (c) testosterone (d) steroid hormones.
10. Which of the following organs does not contain endocrine cells? (a) stomach (b) pancreas (c) small intestine (d) liver
11. Diabetes mellitus can be caused by (a) insufficient insulin (b) lack of insulin receptors (c) obesity (d) all of the above.
12. The interaction of the hypothalamus and the pituitary gland demonstrates (a) the relationship between the nervous system and the endocrine system (b) the relationship between the endocrine system and the digestive system (c) that energy from the hypothalamus transports glucose (d) the involvement of the pituitary gland in prostaglandin production.
13. Prostaglandins are (a) lipids (b) hormones (c) endocrine glands (d) proteins.

14. Oxytocin (a) is secreted by the posterior pituitary (b) controls the amount of water excreted in the urine (c) increases the calcium ion concentration in the blood (d) regulates secondary sex characteristics.
15. Which of the following is both an exocrine gland and an endocrine gland? (a) the thyroid gland (b) the pancreas (c) the thymus gland (d) the pituitary gland

Short Answer

16. Describe the interaction of a steroid hormone and its target cell.
17. Why is positive feedback not an efficient way to control hormone levels?
18. What would be the consequence if the pituitary gland secreted too little ADH?
19. Explain why frequent urination is a symptom of diabetes.
20. How does gastrin help digestion?
21. Describe two ways in which the endocrine system and the nervous system are similar.
22. How does the endocrine system help the immune system?
23. Name two antagonistic hormones besides insulin and glucagon.
24. How do LH and FSH help regulate secondary sex characteristics in males and females?
25. Identify and describe the type of feedback mechanism operating in the diagram shown below.

CRITICAL THINKING

1. Why might damage to the pituitary gland be considered far more serious than damage to one of the other endocrine glands?

2. A number of different hormones secreted by various endocrine glands help regulate the blood glucose concentration. Based on your knowledge of the importance of glucose, hypothesize why glucose should be controlled by several hormones rather than just one hormone.

3. Severe structural abnormalities result from gigantism, a condition of extremely rapid growth, and from pituitary dwarfism, a condition of slowed growth. Based on your knowledge of the endocrine system, suggest what causes these disorders.

4. Suppose that a friend tells you that he or she has recently experienced some of the warning signs of diabetes mellitus. What other conditions could cause symptoms that are similar to those of diabetes?

5. The graph shown at right illustrates the change in the blood glucose level before and after eating. According to the graph, what happens after food is eaten?

6. Which hormones are primarily responsible for the changes in blood glucose level shown in the graph?

7. Referring to the graph, identify and explain the type of feedback mechanism that enables the body to adjust the blood glucose level after eating.

Blood Glucose Level

Blood glucose level (mg/100 mL)

Food ingestion

Time (in hours)

EXTENSION

1. The connection between melatonin and sleep patterns has kindled interest in this hormone. Check the library and on-line references for information about other uses that have been proposed for melatonin.

2. Read "Hormone Helps Ring Internal Alarm Clock" in *Science News*, January 9, 1999, on page 22. Describe the hormones that control waking from sleep. What did the researchers conclude was the primary factor that set the neurological timer to prepare the body to awaken?

3. Read "Is Leptin a 'Thrifty' Hormone in Muscle and Fat?" in *Science*, March 10, 2000, on page 1739. Explain the "thrifty genotype" proposition as an evolutionary mechanism that prepares a body for times of famine. How does this hypothesis explain why many people who live in developed countries struggle with obesity?

4. Check the library and on-line references for information about disorders of the endocrine system, such as Addison's disease, diabetes mellitus, Cushing's syndrome, and pituitary gigantism and dwarfism. Describe the symptoms and treatments for these and other disorders of the endocrine system.

5. Read "Hormone Recall" in *New Scientist*, September 18, 1999, on page 12. Investigate evidence presented in the article that estrogen is involved in memory and cognitive circuits in the brain. Also investigate the evidence that hormone replacement therapy protects the brains of postmenopausal women against diseases such as Alzheimer's.

Observing the Effects of Thyroxine on Frog Metamorphosis

OBJECTIVES

- Observe the effects of the hormone thyroxine on the development of tadpoles.

PROCESS SKILLS

- observing
- measuring
- comparing and contrasting
- organizing data
- inferring

MATERIALS

- safety goggles
- protective gloves
- lab apron
- glass-marking pencil
- six 600 mL beakers
- pond water
- 10 mL graduated cylinder
- 0.01% thyroxine solution
- strained spinach
- graph paper marked in 1 mm squares
- Petri dish
- small fish net
- 9 tadpoles with budding hind legs
- 3 pencils in different colors

Background

1. What is a hormone?
2. What is metamorphosis?
3. Describe the stages of frog development.
4. What are the effects of thyroxine in humans?
5. What effects do you predict the hormone thyroxine will have on tadpole growth and development?

PART A Setting Up the Experiment

1. In your lab report, make a data table similar to the one shown on the facing page.
2. Use a glass-marking pen to label three beakers A, B, and C. Also write your initials on the beakers.

3. Add 500 mL of pond water to each beaker.
4. **CAUTION Put on a lab apron and safety goggles. If you get thyroxine on your skin or clothing, rinse with water while calling to your teacher. If you get thyroxine in your eyes, immediately flush them with water at the eyewash station while calling to your teacher.**
5. Use a graduated cylinder to measure 10 mL of thyroxine solution. Add the 10 mL of solution to beaker A. Measure and add 5 mL of thyroxine solution to beaker B.
6. Add equal amounts (about 1 mL) of strained spinach to beakers A, B, and C.
7. Place a sheet of graph paper, ruled side up, under a Petri dish.
8. **CAUTION You will be working with live animals. Handle them with care and follow directions carefully.** Catch a tadpole with a fish net and place the tadpole in the Petri dish. Measure the tadpole's total length, tail length, and body length in millimeters by counting the number of squares that it covers on the graph paper. Then place the tadpole in beaker A.

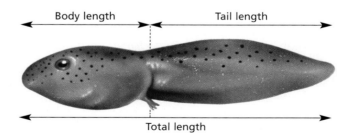

Body length | Tail length

Total length

9. Repeat step 8 with two more tadpoles. Average the total length, tail length, and body length of the three tadpoles that you placed in beaker A. In your data table, record the average measurements under the column labeled "Beaker A."

10. Repeat step 8 with three more tadpoles, this time placing the tadpoles in beaker B. Average the total length, tail length, and body length of the three tadpoles. Record your average measurements in your data table under "Beaker B."

11. Repeat step 8 with three more tadpoles. Place these three tadpoles in beaker C. Average the total length, tail length, and body length of the three tadpoles. Record your average measurements in your data table under "Beaker C." You should have measured a total of nine tadpoles and placed three in each beaker.

12. Clean up your materials and wash your hands before leaving the lab.

Part B Observing the Effects of Thyroxine on Tadpoles

13. Feed the tadpoles 1 mL of spinach every other day. Be careful not to overfeed the tadpoles. Change the water in the beakers every 4 days, adding thyroxine solution in the original amounts to beakers A and B. Label the beakers, and do not mix up the tadpoles during the water changes.

14. Measure the tadpoles once a week for 3 weeks and average the length of the tadpoles in each beaker. Record the average lengths in your data table.

15. Calculate the average growth-per-week for each set of three tadpoles. For example, the average growth in total length during the second week is equal to the average total length at the end of week 2 minus the average total length at the end of week 1. Record your values in the appropriate spaces of your data table.

16. Graph your data using a different colored pencil for the tadpoles in each beaker. Label the horizontal axis "Time in weeks," and label the vertical axis "Length in centimeters." You should have three graphs. Each graph should include the changes in average total length, average tail length, and average body length for one group of tadpoles.

17. Clean up your materials and wash your hands before leaving the lab.

Analysis and Conclusions

1. Did this investigation include a control group? If so, describe it. If not, suggest a possible control that you could have used.

2. Why are three tadpoles used for each beaker rather than just one?

3. According to the data that you collected in this investigation, what is the effect of thyroxine on tadpole metamorphosis?

4. Which concentration of thyroxine solution caused the greatest visible change in the tadpoles?

5. How do average body length and tail length change during metamorphosis?

Further Inquiry

Iodine is needed to produce thyroxine. Design—but do not conduct—an experiment that shows the effect of adding iodine to water that contains tadpoles. NOTE: Iodine is a highly poisonous substance.

MEASUREMENT OF TADPOLE GROWTH

	Beaker A			Beaker B			Beaker C		
	Average total length	Average tail length	Average body length	Average total length	Average tail length	Average body length	Average total length	Average tail length	Average body length
Initial									
End of week 1									
End of week 2									
End of week 3									

REPRODUCTIVE SYSTEM

This is a photograph of a fetus. Notice the umbilical cord and the placenta, through which oxygen and nutrients are passed from the mother to the fetus.

FOCUS CONCEPT: *Structure and Function*

As you read this chapter, notice how the structures of the male and female reproductive systems are adapted for fertilization and development.

MALE REPRODUCTIVE SYSTEM

*R*ecall from Chapter 51 that the gonads—testes and ovaries—are endocrine glands that secrete sex hormones. However, the primary function of the gonads is not to produce hormones but to produce and store gametes—sperm and eggs. Other organs in the male reproductive system prepare sperm for the possible fertilization of an egg.

OBJECTIVES

▲

Describe the structure of a human sperm.

●

Identify the major parts of the male reproductive system.

■

Describe the function of each part of the male reproductive system.

◆

Trace the path that sperm follow in leaving the body.

FORMATION OF SPERM

Males begin to produce sperm during puberty, the adolescent stage of development when changes in the body make reproduction possible. At this time, the concentration of the hormone testosterone is high enough to stimulate sperm production. Recall from Chapter 51 that testosterone is the main androgen (male sex hormone) produced by the testes. The **testes** (TES-teez) are the gamete-producing organs of the male reproductive system. A male will continue to produce sperm as long as his testosterone level is high enough—usually for most of his life.

In Chapter 8, you learned that the formation of gametes in humans involves the process of meiosis. Recall that meiosis results in a reduction of the number of chromosomes from the diploid ($2n$) number to the haploid ($1n$) number. As cells that produce sperm within the testes undergo meiosis, their chromosome number drops from 46 to 23. Four sperm cells result from each cell that begins meiosis. The immature sperm that result from meiosis then undergo significant changes. These changes prepare the sperm for passage through the female reproductive system.

The structure of a mature sperm is shown in Figure 52-1. Notice that a mature sperm consists of three regions—a head, a midpiece, and a tail. The tip of the head region contains enzymes. During fertilization, these enzymes help the sperm penetrate the protective layers that surround an egg cell. Also located in the head region are the 23 chromosomes that will be delivered to the egg. The midpiece is packed with mitochondria. Remember from Chapter 6 that mitochondria are the sites of aerobic respiration and ATP production. These mitochondria supply the energy that is required for sperm to reach an egg. The tail consists of a single, powerful flagellum that propels the sperm.

FIGURE 52-1

A mature sperm is an elongated cell with three distinct parts, all of which are enclosed by a cell membrane.

Tail

Midpiece

Mitochondria

Head

Nucleus

Enzymes

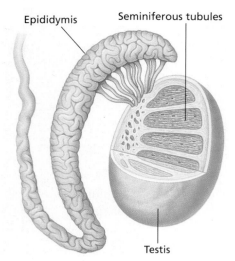

Epididymis   Seminiferous tubules

Testis

FIGURE 52-2

Sperm are formed continuously within the seminiferous tubules, which make up the bulk of each testis. Cells in the tissue that surrounds the seminiferous tubules secrete testosterone, which stimulates the production of sperm. Before leaving the body, sperm mature and are stored in each epididymis.

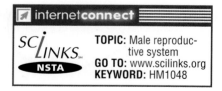

MALE REPRODUCTIVE STRUCTURES

The male reproductive system contains two egg-shaped testes. Each testis, which is about 4 cm (1.5 in.) long and 2.5 cm (1 in.) in diameter, has about 250 compartments. As shown in Figure 52-2, these compartments contain many tightly coiled tubules, called **seminiferous** (SEM-uh-NIF-uhr-uhs) **tubules.** Each seminiferous tubule is approximately 80 cm (32 in.) long. If all of the tubules in both testes were stretched out end to end, they would extend about 500 m (1,640 ft). Sperm form through meiosis in the specialized lining of this extensive network of tubules.

The testes develop within the abdominal cavity. Before a male is born, the testes leave this cavity and descend into an external sac called the **scrotum** (SKROHT-uhm). The temperature within the scrotum is about 3°C cooler than the temperature inside the abdomen. The slightly cooler temperature of the scrotum is necessary for the development of normal sperm.

Path of Sperm Through the Male Body

Mature sperm move through and past several other male reproductive structures, some of which further prepare the sperm for a possible journey through the female reproductive system. Figure 52-3 shows the path taken by sperm as they exit the body.

Sperm move from the seminiferous tubules to the **epididymis** (EP-uh-DID-i-mis), a long, coiled tubule that is closely attached to each testis. Within each epididymis, a sperm matures and gains the ability to swim as its flagellum completes development. Although most sperm remain stored in each epididymis, some leave the epididymis and pass through the **vas deferens** (vas DEF-uh-RENZ), a duct that extends from the epididymis. Smooth muscles that line each vas deferens contract to help move sperm along as they exit the body. Each vas deferens enters the abdominal cavity, where it loops around the urinary bladder and merges with the urethra. Recall from Chapter 49 that the urethra is the duct through which urine exits the urinary bladder. Thus, in a male, both urine and sperm exit the body through the urethra.

In the urethra, sperm mix with fluids that are secreted by three exocrine glands—the seminal vesicles, bulbourethral glands, and the prostate gland. Recall from Chapter 51 that exocrine glands deliver their products through ducts. Ducts that extend from the seminal vesicles, bulbourethral glands, and the prostate gland connect with the urethra. These glands secrete fluids that nourish and protect the sperm. Together, sperm and these secretions form a fluid called **semen** (SEE-muhn). Semen has a high concentration of fructose. Sperm break down fructose by aerobic respiration to obtain energy that they need for movement. To increase sperm survival, semen also contains alkaline fluids that help neutralize the acidic environment of the female's vagina. To help sperm move

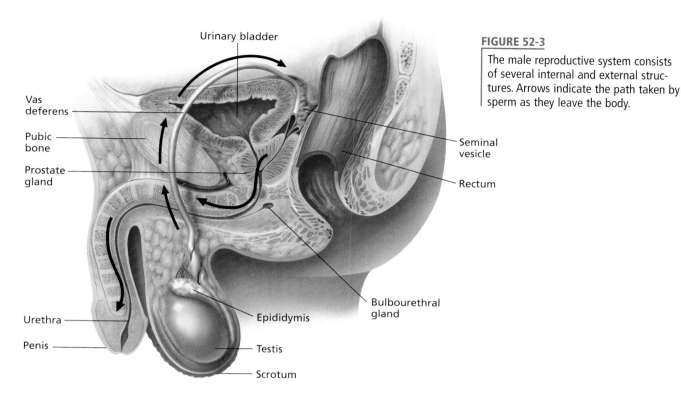

Vas deferens

Pubic bone

Prostate gland

Urethra

Penis

Epididymis

Testis

Scrotum

Bulbourethral gland

Seminal vesicle

Rectum

FIGURE 52-3

The male reproductive system consists of several internal and external structures. Arrows indicate the path taken by sperm as they leave the body.

through the female reproductive system, semen also contains prostaglandins that stimulate contractions of smooth muscles that line the female reproductive tract.

Delivery of Sperm

The urethra passes through the **penis,** the organ that deposits sperm in the female reproductive system. When a male becomes sexually aroused, spongy tissue in the penis fills with blood. This causes the penis to become erect, enabling it to deposit sperm. Semen is forcefully expelled from the penis by contractions of the smooth muscles that line the urethra. This process is called **ejaculation** (ee-JAK-yoo-LAY-shun). Each ejaculation expels 3–4 mL (0.10–0.14 fl oz) of semen. Sperm make up only 10 percent of this volume. Fluids that are secreted by the seminal vesicles, bulbourethral glands, and the prostate gland make up the other 90 percent. Even so, 300–400 million sperm leave the male body during a single ejaculation. Still, only a few sperm reach the site of fertilization. Most sperm are killed by the acidic environment of the female reproductive tract.

SECTION 52-1 REVIEW

1. What parts make up a mature sperm? What does each part contain?

2. Which structures in a male produce fluids that mix with sperm to form semen?

3. What is the function of the testes? the epididymis?

4. Describe the composition of semen.

5. Trace the path that sperm take in exiting the body.

6. CRITICAL THINKING Why are so many sperm produced by the male reproductive system?

SECTION

OBJECTIVES

▲

Compare eggs with sperm.

●

Identify the major parts of the female reproductive system.

■

Describe the function of each part of the female reproductive system.

◆

Describe the menstrual cycle and explain how it is regulated.

FEMALE REPRODUCTIVE SYSTEM

*L*ike the testes, the female gonads—ovaries—are endocrine glands that produce gametes. The female reproductive system prepares the female gametes—eggs—for possible fertilization. It also contains structures that enable fertilization to occur and that house and nourish a developing baby.

FORMATION OF EGGS

A female is born with more than 400,000 eggs in her **ovaries** (OH-vuh-reez), the gamete-producing organs of the female reproductive system. When a female is born, her eggs are immature and cannot be fertilized. Typically, a female will release 300–400 mature eggs during her lifetime, averaging one egg about every 28 days from the time she reaches puberty to about age 50. Thus, fewer than 1 percent of a female's eggs reach maturity.

Like sperm formation, the formation of eggs involves meiosis. Unlike in sperm production—in which four sperm result from each cell that begins meiosis—only one egg results from each cell that undergoes meiosis. All immature eggs begin meiosis, but the process is stalled in prophase I until the female reaches puberty, when levels of the sex hormones become high enough to complete the maturation of the eggs. Regulated by these hormones, 10–20 immature eggs resume meiosis every 28 days. However, typically only one mature egg is released each time. A mature egg, or **ovum** (OH-vuhm), shown in Figure 52-4, is about 75,000 times larger than a sperm and is visible to the unaided eye. Meiosis II is not completed unless a sperm fuses with the egg. If the ovum is fertilized, it completes the final meiotic division. Only one cell retains most of the cytoplasm, which provides nutrients that are needed for the egg's survival through the early stages of development. Deprived of cytoplasm, the other three meiotic cells die.

FIGURE 52-4

This ovum is being approached by a single sperm. Notice the tremendous size difference between the egg and the sperm. (SEM 1225×)

FEMALE REPRODUCTIVE STRUCTURES

The female reproductive system contains two almond-shaped ovaries that are located in the lower abdomen. Eggs mature near the surface of the ovaries, which are about 3.5 cm (1.4 in.) long and 2 cm (0.8 in.) in diameter. An ovum is released into the abdominal cavity, where it is swept by cilia into the opening of a nearby **fallopian** (fuh-LOH-pee-uhn) **tube,** or uterine tube. This narrow passageway leads to the uterus, as shown in Figure 52-5. The **uterus** (YOOT-uhr-uhs) is a hollow, muscular organ about the size of a fist. If an egg is fertilized, it will develop in the uterus. The lower entrance to the uterus is called the **cervix** (SUHR-viks). A sphincter muscle in the cervix controls the opening to the uterus. Leading from the cervix to the outside of the body is a muscular tube called the **vagina** (vuh-JIE-nuh). The vagina receives sperm from the penis; it is also the channel through which a baby passes during childbirth. The external structures of the female reproductive system are collectively called the **vulva** (VUHL-vuh). The vulva includes the **labia** (LAY-bee-uh), folds of skin and mucous membranes that cover and protect the opening to the female reproductive system.

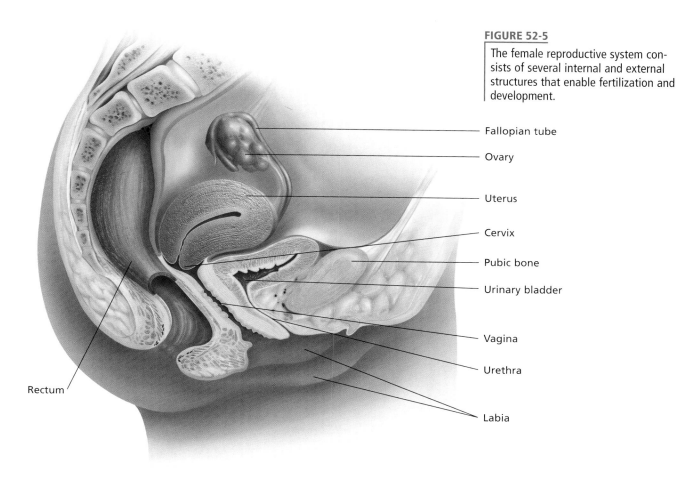

FIGURE 52-5

The female reproductive system consists of several internal and external structures that enable fertilization and development.

Fallopian tube

Ovary

Uterus

Cervix

Pubic bone

Urinary bladder

Vagina

Urethra

Labia

Rectum

FIGURE 52-6

During the 28-day menstrual cycle, an egg matures and is released by an ovary, and the uterus prepares for a possible pregnancy. The events of the menstrual cycle are regulated by hormones that are produced by the anterior pituitary and the ovaries.

PREPARATION FOR PREGNANCY

Each month, the female reproductive system prepares for a possible pregnancy by undergoing a series of changes called the **menstrual** (MEN-struhl) **cycle.** For most women, the menstrual cycle lasts about 28 days. During this time, an egg matures and enters a fallopian tube, where it is able to fuse with a sperm. If the egg does not fuse with a sperm, the egg degenerates. The menstrual cycle has four stages: the follicular phase, ovulation, the luteal phase, and menstruation. These stages are regulated by hormones secreted by the endocrine system. Figure 52-6 summarizes the stages of the menstrual cycle.

Follicular Phase

An immature egg cell completes its first meiotic division during the **follicular** (fuh-LIK-yoo-luhr) **phase.** This phase begins when the hypothalamus secretes a releasing hormone that stimulates the anterior lobe of the pituitary gland to secrete follicle-stimulating hormone (FSH). FSH stimulates cell division in a **follicle,** a layer of cells that surrounds an immature egg. Follicle cells supply nutrients to the egg. They also secrete estrogen, which stimulates mitotic divisions of cells in the lining of the uterus, causing the lining to thicken. The follicular phase lasts approximately 14 days. During this time, the estrogen level in the blood continues to rise until it reaches a peak and the egg moves to the surface of the ovary. The elevated estrogen level stimulates the anterior pituitary to secrete luteinizing hormone (LH), which initiates the next stage of the menstrual cycle (a positive feedback mechanism).

Ovulation

The sharp rise in the level of LH that occurs midway through the menstrual cycle causes the follicle to rupture and release its egg at that time. The release of an egg from a ruptured follicle is called **ovulation** (AHV-yoo-LAY-

Luteinizing hormone (LH)

Follicle-stimulating hormone (FSH)

Estrogen

Progesterone

Developing follicle | Ovulation | Corpus luteum

Follicular phase | Luteal phase

0   7   14   21   28

Menstruation   *Days of cycle*

shuhn). Following ovulation, an egg is swept into a fallopian tube, where it travels toward the uterus awaiting fertilization. The egg has enough stored nutrients to survive about 48 hours.

Luteal Phase

The cells of the ruptured follicle grow larger and fill the cavity, forming a new structure called a **corpus luteum** (KOHR-puhs LOOT-ee-uhm). Thus, this stage of the menstrual cycle is called the **luteal** (LOOT-ee-uhl) **phase.** The corpus luteum begins to secrete large amounts of progesterone and estrogen. Progesterone stimulates growth of blood vessels and storage of fluids and nutrients in the lining of the uterus. This causes the uterine lining to become even thicker. In addition, increased levels of estrogen and progesterone cause the pituitary gland to stop secreting LH and FSH (a negative feedback mechanism). The luteal phase lasts about 14 days. During this time, estrogen and progesterone levels in the blood rise, while the FSH and LH levels drop.

Menstruation

If an egg is fertilized, the resulting zygote attaches to the lining of the uterus, where it will develop for the next nine months. A hormone that is produced early in pregnancy stimulates the corpus luteum to continue producing estrogen and progesterone, and the thickened lining of the uterus is maintained. If the egg is not fertilized, the corpus luteum stops producing sex hormones. Without estrogen and progesterone to maintain the thickened uterine lining, the lining begins to slough off. In the last stage of the menstrual cycle, called **menstruation** (men-STRAY-shuhn), the lining of the uterus and blood from ruptured blood vessels are discharged through the vagina. Menstruation lasts about five days at the beginning of the follicular phase.

Menstruation continues in most women until about age 50. By then, most of a woman's follicles have either matured and ruptured or degenerated. Without follicles, the ovaries cannot secrete enough estrogen and progesterone to continue the menstrual cycle, and menstruation ceases. This stage is called **menopause** (MEN-uh-PAHZ).

internet**connect**

SCI**LINKS**

NSTA

TOPIC: Female reproductive system
GO TO: www.scilinks.org
KEYWORD: HM1053

SECTION 52-2 REVIEW

1. What are the main female reproductive organs?

2. How are eggs and sperm similar? How are they different?

3. Where does fertilization occur?

4. What is ovulation? When does it occur?

5. How do high levels of estrogen and progesterone during the luteal phase of the menstrual cycle affect the uterus?

6. CRITICAL THINKING What might happen if more than one egg were simultaneously released from the ovaries?

OBJECTIVES

▲

Describe the processes of fertilization, cleavage, and implantation.

●

Summarize the changes that take place during the development of an embryo.

■

List the three stages of pregnancy, and describe each stage.

FIGURE 52-7

Several sperm surround this ovum, but only one will be able to fertilize it. (SEM 1165×)

GESTATION

*A new individual is produced when a sperm fertilizes an egg, resulting in the formation of a zygote. During the nine-month period of **gestation** (jes-TAY-shuhn), a series of changes transforms a single cell into a complex organism made of trillions of cells—a human.*

FERTILIZATION

Recall that with one ejaculation, a male releases hundreds of millions of sperm into the vagina of a female. Once sperm are released, they swim through the vagina, cervix, and uterus, and, finally, up the fallopian tubes. If ovulation occurs anytime from 72 hours before to 48 hours after ejaculation, sperm may encounter an egg in one of the fallopian tubes. Fertilization occurs when a sperm and an egg fuse and form a zygote.

An egg in a fallopian tube is encased in a jellylike substance and surrounded by a layer of cells from the follicle of the ovary. As shown in Figure 52-7, several sperm may attach to an egg and attempt to penetrate its outer layers. Recall from Section 52-1 that the head of a sperm contains digestive enzymes. These enzymes break down an egg's outer layers and enable the cell membrane that surrounds the head of the sperm to fuse with the egg's cell membrane. The sperm's nucleus and midpiece then enter the cytoplasm of the egg. The tail of the sperm remains outside the egg. Usually only one sperm is successful in penetrating an egg. Changes that occur in an egg's cell membrane after a sperm enters the egg help keep other sperm from penetrating the egg.

After a sperm enters an egg, its nucleus fuses with the egg's nucleus. The diploid cell that results from this fusion is called a zygote. Recall that each gamete contains 23 chromosomes, the haploid ($1n$) number. Thus, fusion of a sperm nucleus and an egg nucleus causes a zygote to have 46 chromosomes, the diploid ($2n$) number.

Cleavage and Implantation

Immediately following fertilization and while still in the fallopian tube, the zygote begins a series of mitotic divisions known as cleavage. The resulting cells do not increase in size during these cell divisions. Cleavage produces a ball of cells called a **morula** (MOHR-yoo-luh), which is not much larger than the zygote. Cells of the morula divide and release a fluid, resulting in a blastocyst. A **blastocyst** (BLAS-toh-SIST) is a ball of cells with a large, fluid-filled cavity.

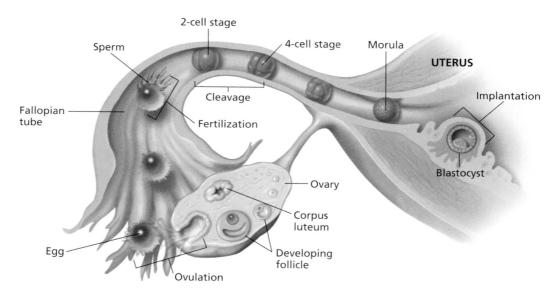

Labels in figure:
- 2-cell stage
- Sperm
- 4-cell stage
- Morula
- UTERUS
- Fallopian tube
- Cleavage
- Implantation
- Fertilization
- Ovary
- Blastocyst
- Corpus luteum
- Egg
- Developing follicle
- Ovulation

As shown in Figure 52-8, the morula has become a blastocyst by the time it reaches the uterus. In the uterus, the blastocyst attaches to the thickened uterine lining. The blastocyst then releases an enzyme that breaks down the epithelial tissue that lines the uterus and burrows into the thickened lining. The process in which the blastocyst burrows and embeds itself into the lining of the uterus is called **implantation** (IM-plan-TAY-shun). Pregnancy begins at implantation, which occurs about six days after fertilization.

PREGNANCY

After implantation, the blastocyst slowly takes on the recognizable features of a human infant. This nine-month period of development is called gestation, or **pregnancy.** Pregnancy is divided into three equal periods, or **trimesters.** Significant changes occur during each trimester.

First Trimester

The most dramatic changes in human development take place during the first trimester. Throughout the first two to three weeks following fertilization, a developing human embryo resembles the embryos of other animals. The embryo develops from the mass of cells on the inner surface of the blastocyst. At first, all of the cells in the mass look alike. But the cells soon reorganize, first into two and then into three distinct types of cells, forming the primary germ layers: the ectoderm, mesoderm, and endoderm. Different parts of the body develop from each of the primary germ layers. The nervous system and the epidermis of the skin develop from the ectoderm. Muscle tissue, connective tissue, and organs develop from the mesoderm. The linings of the digestive, respiratory, and urinary tracts develop from endoderm, as do glands, such as the liver, pancreas, thyroid, and thymus.

Quick Lab

Summarizing Vocabulary

Materials pencil, paper, dictionary

Procedure Write and define the following list of words: *ovary, ovum, follicle, gestation, morula, blastocyst, amnion, chorion, umbilical, uterus, corpus,* and *luteum.*

Analysis Do any of the meanings of the words surprise you? Explain. How does knowing the roots and meanings of the words help you remember them?

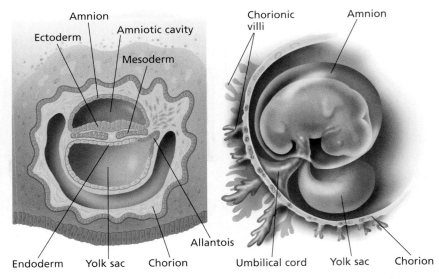

(a) 9-DAY BLASTOCYST   **(b) 16-DAY EMBRYO**   **(c) 4-WEEK EMBRYO**

FIGURE 52-9

(a) An embryo develops from the mass of cells on one side of a blastocyst. (b) The primary germ layers develop by the third week of pregnancy, and the four embryonic membranes form. (c) By the end of the first month of pregnancy, all of the embryonic membranes are formed.

Four membranes that aid the development of the embryo also form during the first trimester. One of these membranes, called the amnion (AM-nee-uhn), forms the fluid-filled **amniotic** (AM-nee-AHT-ik) **sac,** which surrounds the developing embryo. The fluid in the amniotic sac cushions the embryo from injury and keeps it moist. A second membrane forms the yolk sac. Although it does not contain yolk, the yolk sac is an important structure because it is where the first blood cells and reproductive cells originate. A third membrane, called the allantois (uh-LAN-toh-is), forms near the yolk sac. The fourth membrane, called the chorion (KOHR-ee-AHN), surrounds all of the other membranes. As shown in Figure 52-9, one side of the chorion forms many small, fingerlike projections called **chorionic villi** (KOHR-ee-AHN-ik VIL-IE), which extend into the uterine lining. Blood vessels that form within the chorionic villi originate in the allantois.

Together, chorionic villi and the portion of the uterine lining that they invade form a close-knit structure called the placenta. A human placenta is about 15–20 cm (6–8 in.) in diameter and about 2.5 cm (1 in.) thick. Nutrients, gases, pathogens, drugs, and other substances pass from the mother to the fetus through the placenta. The developing fetus is attached to the placenta by the **umbilical** (uhm-BIL-i-kuhl) **cord,** which contains arteries and veins that carry blood between the fetus and the placenta. As Figure 52-10 shows, blood from the mother and fetus never mixes. Instead, materials are exchanged by diffusion.

By this time, had the egg not been fertilized, the corpus luteum would have stopped producing sex hormones, and menstruation would have followed. A developing placenta begins to secrete a hormone called **human chorionic gonadotropin (HCG)** early in the second week after fertilization. In the early stages of pregnancy, HCG stimulates the corpus luteum to continue producing sex hormones, and thus the uterine lining and the embryo are retained. As the placenta grows, it begins to secrete large amounts of progesterone and estrogen, which take over maintenance of the uterine lining from hormones that were produced by the corpus luteum. Continued production of estrogen and progesterone throughout pregnancy prevents the release of FSH and LH, and eggs are not ovulated.

The brain, the spinal cord, and the rest of the nervous system begin to form in the third week. The heart begins to beat at 21 days, and it develops a smooth, rhythmic beat at 28 days. By the fifth week, human features, including arms, legs, eyes, ears, and the digestive system have begun to develop. At six weeks, the fingers and toes form, and the brain shows signs of activity. The embryo also begins to move, although it is so small that the mother cannot feel it. From eight weeks until birth, the developing child is called a **fetus** (FEET-uhs). The fetus is only about 5 cm (2 in.) long when the first trimester ends, but all of its organ systems have begun to form.

Second Trimester

During the second trimester, the mother's abdomen begins to swell as her uterus enlarges. The fetus's heartbeat can be heard, its skeleton begins to form, and a layer of soft hair grows over its skin. At this time, the fetus also begins to wake and sleep. The mother may feel the fetus move about. The fetus swallows, hiccups, sucks its thumb, and makes a fist. It also kicks its feet and curls its toes. By the end of the second trimester, the fetus is about 32 cm (12.6 in.) long, and its eyes are open.

Third Trimester

In the third trimester, the fetus grows quickly and undergoes changes that will enable it to survive outside the mother. The fetus can see light and darkness through the mother's abdominal wall,

FIGURE 52-10

About two weeks after fertilization, chorionic villi form and the placenta begins to develop. The placenta and umbilical cord function as the lifeline between an embryo and its mother.

and it can react to music and loud sounds. During the last half of this trimester, the fetus develops fat deposits under its skin. These fat deposits, which make the fetus look rounded and less wrinkled, insulate the body so that it can maintain a steady body temperature.

Birth

Birth occurs about 270 days after fertilization. Prostaglandins that are produced by the fetal membranes, along with hormones that are produced by the fetus and the mother, initiate childbirth. High levels of estrogen, prostaglandins, and oxytocin, a hormone that is secreted by the pituitary gland, cause the smooth muscles that line the uterus to contract. The amniotic sac breaks, and its fluid flows out through the vagina. This is called "breaking water." Muscles in the cervix and the vagina relax, enabling the cervix and vagina to enlarge and allowing the fetus to pass through them. The muscular contractions and other events that lead up to childbirth are called **labor.**

During childbirth, strong contractions of the uterus push a fetus out through the cervix, through the vagina, and from the body, as shown in Figure 52-11. The placenta, the amnion, and the uterine lining, collectively called **afterbirth,** are expelled from the mother's body about 10 minutes after the baby is born. Following birth, the newborn baby's lungs expand for the first time as the baby cries and begins to breathe on its own. At this time, the umbilical cord is tied and cut. The umbilical arteries and veins close off within 30 minutes after birth. This and other changes in the baby's blood vessels lead to completion of cardiopulmonary and renal circulation, allowing the baby to function independent of the mother. The newborn baby's respiratory and excretory systems soon become fully functional.

FIGURE 52-11

During childbirth, the fetus passes through the greatly enlarged cervix and vagina.

Placenta

Umbilical cord

Uterus

Vagina

SECTION 52-3 REVIEW

1. What is the process of implantation?

2. What is a blastocyst?

3. How is a fetus nourished during development?

4. Summarize the events of human development that occur during the first trimester of pregnancy.

5. What changes occur in a fetus during the third trimester of pregnancy?

6. **CRITICAL THINKING** Why is it important for a pregnant woman to eat healthy foods, to avoid unhealthy substances, and to follow her doctor's advice?

CHAPTER 52 REVIEW

SUMMARY/VOCABULARY

52-1
- Sperm form in the seminiferous tubules of the testes. Meiosis reduces the number of chromosomes in sperm to 23.
- A mature sperm consists of a head, which contains the nucleus and chromosomes; a midpiece that contains mitochondria; and a tail, which consists of a flagellum.
- The testes are contained in the scrotum, where the cooler temperature allows normal sperm development.
- Sperm take the following path to exit the body: seminiferous tubules of the testes → epididymis → vas deferens → urethra.
- Fluids that are secreted by various exocrine glands are mixed with sperm to produce semen.

Vocabulary

ejaculation (1049)	penis (1049)	semen (1048)	testes (1047)
epididymis (1048)	scrotum (1048)	seminiferous tubules (1048)	vas deferens (1048)

52-2
- Eggs form in the ovaries. Meiosis reduces the chromosome number in eggs to 23.
- A female is born with all of the eggs that she will ever produce.
- Starting at puberty, one egg matures (completes meiosis) approximately every 28 days during the menstrual cycle.
- The menstrual cycle consists of four phases: follicular phase, ovulation, luteal phase, and menstruation.
- In the follicular phase, FSH causes a follicle to grow in an ovary. Estrogen produced by the follicle causes an egg to mature and stimulates the buildup of the uterine lining.
- Ovulation occurs midway through the menstrual cycle, when LH causes the follicle to rupture and release its egg.
- In the luteal phase, the follicle becomes a corpus luteum. The corpus luteum secretes progesterone, which stimulates further buildup of the uterine lining.
- Menstruation, the discharge of the uterine lining, occurs when a corpus luteum stops secreting progesterone and estrogen.

Vocabulary

cervix (1051)	follicular phase (1052)	menstrual cycle (1052)	ovum (1050)
corpus luteum (1053)	labia (1051)	menstruation (1053)	uterus (1051)
fallopian tube (1051)	luteal phase (1053)	ovary (1050)	vagina (1051)
follicle (1052)	menopause (1053)	ovulation (1052)	vulva (1051)

52-3
- Fertilization occurs in a fallopian tube.
- Pregnancy begins when a blastocyst implants itself in the lining of the uterus.
- The three primary germ layers—the ectoderm, mesoderm, and endoderm—form early in embryonic development.
- Four membranes—the amnion, yolk sac, allantois, and chorion—also form early in embryonic development.
- Part of the chorion and part of the lining of the uterus form the placenta, through which nutrients, gases, and other substances pass by diffusion to the fetus from the mother.
- From the eighth week until birth, a developing human is known as a fetus.
- During childbirth, contractions of the uterus initiated by prostaglandins and oxytocin push the baby from the mother's body through the vagina.

Vocabulary

afterbirth (1058)	fetus (1057)	implantation (1055)	trimester (1055)
amniotic sac (1056)	gestation (1054)	labor (1058)	umbilical cord (1056)
blastocyst (1054)	human chorionic	morula (1054)	
chorionic villi (1056)	gonadotropin (1056)	pregnancy (1055)	

REVIEW

Vocabulary

1. Name the male and female gamete-producing organs.
2. What is the difference between sperm and semen?
3. Explain the relationships between the following: the menstrual cycle, menstruation, and menopause.
4. Which two structures form the placenta?
5. What is the difference between an embryo and a fetus?

Multiple Choice

6. The correct pathway for sperm is from the (a) testes to the vas deferens to the epididymis (b) epididymis to the urethra to the vas deferens (c) urethra to the vas deferens to the testes (d) testes to the epididymis to the vas deferens.
7. One similarity between a sperm and an egg is their (a) chromosome number (b) size (c) ability to move quickly (d) role in producing hormones.
8. Which of the following is not a function of the uterus? (a) house the developing fetus (b) help produce eggs (c) provide protection for an embryo (d) aid the birth of the baby.
9. Follicle-stimulating hormone (a) promotes contractions of the uterine muscles (b) is secreted by the follicle (c) is secreted by the pituitary gland (d) stimulates the development of the placenta.
10. During menstruation (a) the egg moves into the fallopian tube (b) the corpus luteum develops (c) the uterine lining is discharged (d) the egg matures.
11. Fertilization takes place in the (a) vagina (b) cervix (c) uterus (d) fallopian tube.
12. The embryonic membranes that help form the placenta and umbilical cord are (a) the amnion and yolk sac (b) the chorion and allantois (c) the chorion and yolk sac (d) the amnion and chorion.
13. Which of the following organs develops from ectoderm? (a) brain (b) liver (c) heart (d) lungs

14. The placenta is the (a) site of yolk development (b) site of nutrient and gas exchange between the mother and the fetus (c) structure that protects the fetus from injury (d) tip of the uterus.
15. By the end of the first trimester (a) the fetus can suck its thumb (b) the brain of the fetus is fully developed (c) the fetus uses its lungs to breathe (d) all of the organs of the fetus have begun to form.

Short Answer

16. Describe the structure of a mature human sperm cell.
17. How is semen formed?
18. How are sperm formation and egg formation similar?
19. Use the graph shown below to answer the following questions:
    (a) What phase of the menstrual cycle is occurring during the period labeled *A*?
    (b) What phase of the menstrual cycle is occurring at the period labeled *B*?
    (c) When during the menstrual cycle does ovulation usually occur?
    (d) When during the menstrual cycle is fertilization most likely to occur?
    (e) When during the menstrual cycle is the estrogen level highest?
    (f) When during the menstrual cycle does the progesterone level start to fall?

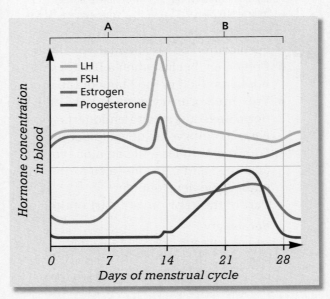

20. Where are eggs produced?
21. Which part of the menstrual cycle does not occur if implantation occurs? Why is this important?
22. How does a sperm penetrate an egg during fertilization?
23. How does the developing fetus receive nourishment?
24. What role does the amnion play in human development?
25. What changes does the cervix undergo during childbirth?

CRITICAL THINKING

1. Why are sperm able to survive as long as they do in the female, even though they have very little cytoplasm to provide nutrients?
2. What do you think might happen if more than one sperm were able to penetrate the cell membrane of an egg?
3. A human female produces on average only one mature egg every 28 days. In contrast, a female salmon lays 50 million eggs at each spawning. Hypothesize why there is such a great difference in egg production between the two species.
4. Women who smoke tobacco, drink alcoholic beverages, or consume other drugs or harmful substances during pregnancy give birth to infants who are often addicted to drugs, have severe birth defects, or develop learning disabilities and behavioral disorders. Why is this so?
5. About 20 years ago, a large number of women who took a tranquilizer called thalidomide early in pregnancy gave birth to babies with serious limb defects. Other mothers who took the drug later on in pregnancy had normal children. What does this tell you about the sequence of development in a fetus?
6. What is the fetus doing in the photograph below? Suggest an adaptive advantage for this activity.

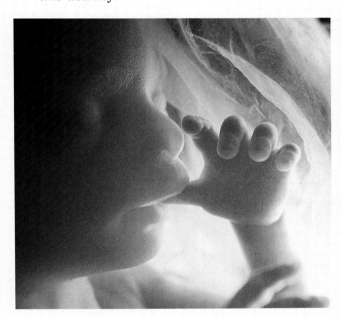

EXTENSION

1. Concerned about the rapid increase in the world's population, several countries are attempting to reach zero population growth (ZPG). These countries have encouraged women to have fewer children or have instituted laws that limit the number of children that each woman may have. Check on-line references to identify one such country, and prepare a report summarizing what measures the country has taken to attain ZPG.

2. Read "Why We Don't Lay Eggs" in *New Scientist,* June 12, 1999, on page 12. Prepare a report on the origin of ERVs in the human placenta. Include in your report how ERVs are involved in protecting the fetus.
3. Research some of the physical and hormonal causes of infertility. Write a report describing the conditions, and explain how medical science is helping couples overcome infertility.

Observing Embryonic Development

OBJECTIVES

- Identify the stages of early animal development.
- Describe the changes that occur during early development.
- Compare the stages of human embryonic development with those of echinoderm embryonic development.

PROCESS SKILLS

- observing
- comparing and contrasting
- making drawings
- drawing conclusions

MATERIALS

- prepared slides of sea-star development, including
  unfertilized egg
  zygote
  2-cell stage
  4-cell stage
  8-cell stage
  16-cell stage
  32-cell stage
  64-cell stage
  blastula
  early gastrula
  middle gastrula
  late gastrula
  young sea-star larva
- compound light microscope
- paper and pencil

Background

1. Most members of the animal kingdom (including sea stars and humans) begin life as a single cell—the fertilized egg, or zygote. How does a fertilized egg become a completely developed organism?

2. The early stages of development are quite similar in different species. Cleavage follows fertilization. During cleavage, the zygote divides many times without growing. The new cells migrate and form a hollow ball of cells called a blastula. The cells then begin to organize into the three primary germ layers: endoderm, mesoderm, and ectoderm. During this process, the developing organism is called a gastrula.

3. The early stages of mammalian development are difficult to study because mammalian eggs are tiny and are not produced in great numbers. In addition, mammalian embryos develop within the mother's body. In the laboratory, it is difficult to replicate the internal conditions of the mother's body. Because the early stages of echinoderm development are similar to those of human development, and because echinoderm development is easier to study in the laboratory than human development, you will observe the early developmental stages of an echinoderm—the sea star—in this investigation.

2-cell stage

4-cell stage

8-cell stage

64-cell stage

Blastocyst

4. As development continues, the cells continue to specialize as they become part of specific tissues and complex structures. Ectoderm forms the epidermis and nerve tissue. Mesoderm forms muscle, connective tissue, and vascular organs. Endoderm forms the lining of the digestive, urinary, and respiratory tracts.

5. Similarities and differences in early stages of development reflect evolutionary relationships between species.

Procedure

1. Obtain a set of prepared slides that show sea-star eggs at different stages of development. Choose slides labeled unfertilized egg, zygote, 2-cell stage, 4-cell stage, 8-cell stage, 16-cell stage, 32-cell stage, 64-cell stage, blastula, early gastrula, middle gastrula, late gastrula, and young sea-star larva. (Note: *Blastula* is the general term for the embryonic stage that results from cleavage. In mammals, a blastocyst is a modified form of the blastula.)

2. Examine each slide using a compound light microscope. Using the microscope's low-power objective first, focus on one good example of the developmental stage listed on the slide's label. Then switch to the high-power objective, and focus on the image with the fine adjustment.

3. In your lab report, draw a diagram of each developmental stage that you examine (in chronological order). Label each diagram with the name of the stage it represents and the magnification used. Record your observations as soon as they are made. Do not redraw your diagrams. Draw only what you see; lab drawings do not need to be artistic or elaborate. They should be well organized and include specific details.

4. Compare your diagrams with the diagrams of human embryonic stages shown at left.

5. Clean up your materials and wash your hands before leaving the lab.

Analysis and Conclusions

1. Compare the size of the sea-star zygote with that of the blastula. At what stage does the embryo become larger than the zygote?

2. At what stage do all of the cells in the embryo not look exactly like each other?

3. How do cell shape and size change during successive stages of development?

4. Do the cell nuclei stay the same size, get larger, or get smaller as the stages progress?

5. Compare the number of chromosomes in a fertilized sea-star egg with the number of chromosomes in one cell of each of the following phases: 2-cell stage, blastula, gastrula, and adult stage.

6. From your observations of changes in cellular organization, why do you think the blastocoel (the space in the center of the hollow sphere of cells of a blastula) is important during embryonic development?

7. Label the endoderm and ectoderm in your drawing of the late gastrula stage. What do these two tissue types eventually develop into?

8. How are the symmetries of a sea-star embryo and a sea-star larva different from the symmetry of an adult sea star? Would you expect to see a similar change in human development?

9. What must happen to the sea-star gastrula before it becomes a mature sea star?

10. How do your drawings of sea-star embryonic development compare with those of human embryonic development? Based on your observations, in what ways do you think sea-star embryos could be used to study early human development?

11. Describe one way that the cleavage of echinoderms and mammals is alike.

12. Describe two ways that the cleavage of echinoderms and mammals is different.

13. Why are sea-star eggs a good choice for the study of embryonic development in humans?

Further Inquiry

Using the procedure that you followed in this investigation, compare embryonic development in other organisms with embryonic development in sea stars. Which types of organisms would you expect to develop similarly to sea stars? Which types of organisms would you expect to develop differently from sea stars?

DRUGS

This color-enhanced micrograph (SEM, 6000×) shows a liver affected by the disease cirrhosis. The deep blue central cavity is a blood vessel. Fibers and clumps of scar tissue surrounding the blood vessel have replaced much of the liver's normal cellular architecture.

FOCUS CONCEPT: *Stability and Homeostasis*

As you read, note how certain drugs affect the body's ability to maintain homeostasis.

ROLE OF DRUGS

As biologists explore the structure and function of the various systems that make up the human body, they discover the complex series of chemical reactions that form the basis of each life process. Understanding the chemistry of the body has enabled scientists to alter it by administering naturally occurring or laboratory-synthesized chemicals called drugs. *The wise use of drugs can alleviate suffering by curing or controlling many kinds of diseases. But the unwise use of drugs can cause great harm because many drugs taken for nonmedical purposes have the potential to destroy human lives.*

DRUG USE AND ADMINISTRATION

A **drug** is a chemical compound that affects the structure of a body part or the functioning of a biological process. There are thousands of different drugs, and they affect many different parts of the body. Some drugs are synthesized in laboratories, while other drugs are derived from natural sources. Many drugs are refined from plant or animal tissue. For example, *Rauwolfia serpentina* is a plant native to India and neighboring countries. Ancient Hindu writings describe use of the plant's roots as a remedy for snakebites, insomnia, and psychotic behavior. The modern drug reserpine, which is used to control blood pressure, is extracted from the roots of *Rauwolfia serpentina*.

A drug can be introduced into the body in a variety of ways. Drugs taken orally, in pill or liquid form, are absorbed by the small intestine and then enter the bloodstream. Drugs can also be injected directly into the bloodstream or muscle tissue or under the skin. Other methods of administering drugs include inhaling the drug, placing the drug under the tongue, inserting it in the rectum in the form of a suppository, or applying the drug to the skin.

The method of administering a drug depends on its chemical nature and the organ to be treated. For example, because insulin is a protein, if it were taken orally, it would be digested in the stomach and would therefore be useless. Thus, insulin is injected under the skin, where it can diffuse into the bloodstream for transport throughout the body. In contrast, drugs used to treat respiratory problems are often administered by inhalation so that they can reach their destination quickly.

SECTION
53-1

OBJECTIVES

▲

Define the term *drug*.

●

Name four ways that a drug can be administered.

■

List five common types of prescription and nonprescription drugs.

◆

Describe the potential consequences of a drug interaction.

▲

Describe the consequences of the overuse of a drug.

internetconnect

SC**LINKS** NSTA

TOPIC: Drugs
GO TO: www.scilinks.org
KEYWORD: HM1065

MEDICAL USE

Drugs classified as **prescription drugs** cannot be obtained unless they are prescribed by a physician or dentist. The physician or dentist specifies the **dose,** that is, the amount of the drug to be taken and the number of times per day that the drug should be taken. Thousands of prescription drugs are currently available to treat a variety of diseases and disorders.

Nonprescription drugs, also called over-the-counter (OTC) drugs, can be purchased without a prescription and are available at pharmacies and supermarkets. A quick look at the shelves in a supermarket will show the variety of nonprescription drugs that are available. Such drugs are used to relieve pain, treat minor skin infections, reduce stomach acidity, and alleviate symptoms of a cold or flu.

The labels on nonprescription drugs contain information regarding correct usage. These drugs are safe for most people when taken in the recommended dose but can be dangerous if too much is taken. More than 100 children in the United States die each year from accidental overdoses of aspirin, and even children's vitamins are harmful in large doses. Certain precautions may be stated on the drug's label. For example, aspirin labels caution against giving aspirin to children or teenagers who have flulike symptoms or chickenpox because of the possibility of their developing Reye's syndrome, an often fatal condition. Pregnant women and nursing mothers should consult their physician before using any drug, even nonprescription drugs, because many drugs can cross the placenta or enter a mother's milk and can affect a fetus or a young child.

TABLE 53-1	*Common Types of Prescription and Nonprescription Drugs*	
Drug type	**Medical use**	**Mode of action**
Antacids, acid reducers	heartburn, indigestion, ulcer	neutralize excess stomach acid or slow its production
Antibiotics	bacterial infection	kill or prevent growth of infectious bacteria
Antidepressants	mental depression	increase activity in some neurons in the brain
Anti-inflammatory and non-narcotic pain medications	arthritis; headache; injury to bone, joint, or muscle	reduce inflammatory response (swelling, redness, pain) to injury; relieve pain
Antihistamines	allergy, cold, influenza	reduce allergic response (excess fluid in tissue, contraction of bronchi, dilation of capillaries)
Blood pressure medications	hypertension	dilate blood vessels or cause excretion of water, which reduces blood volume
Decongestants	asthma, cold, influenza	dilate nasal passages and bronchi
Hormone replacements	diabetes mellitus, hypothyroidism, post-menopausal hormone loss	restore normal levels of hormones

Drug Interactions

Table 53-1 lists several common types of drugs. You may have taken one or more of these kinds of drugs. Have you ever taken more than one drug at the same time? Many people do, particularly the elderly and those with chronic diseases. For example, a person with a heart ailment might take a drug to reduce blood clotting, a drug to reduce high cholesterol levels, and a drug to regulate heart function. Although simultaneous use of more than one drug is common, some combinations of drugs are inappropriate because of the chemical interactions between them. In such cases, one drug might add to the effect of the other drug, resulting in symptoms of overdose, or one drug might cancel the effectiveness of the other drug. For example, the commonly prescribed antibiotic tetracycline is rendered inactive in the presence of calcium. Therefore, taking tetracycline within an hour of taking a chewable antacid containing calcium will impair the drug's effectiveness. Similarly, some antibiotics interfere with the action of birth-control pills.

In some cases, drug interactions can lead to more-serious problems and can even cause death. A commonly used antihistamine combined with an often-prescribed antifungal drug can cause an irregular heartbeat and even a heart attack. A physician or pharmacist must closely monitor anyone who is taking more than one drug simultaneously. And a prescribing physician must be informed of the name and dose of *any* drugs—prescription or nonprescription—that a patient is taking or has taken in the past few weeks.

Drug Overuse

Overuse of both prescription drugs and nonprescription drugs can lead to serious problems. Continual use of acetaminophen, a common nonprescription pain medication, can damage the liver. Large doses of magnesium-containing antacids can interfere with the functioning of the heart and kidneys. Anyone who is taking any drug for an extended period of time should consult a doctor.

The problems of drug overuse are not confined to damage to the body. The overuse and misuse of antibiotics have resulted in strains of bacteria that are resistant to these drugs. For example, some strains of the organism, shown in Figure 53-1, that causes the lung disease tuberculosis, are resistant to all antibiotics currently in use.

FIGURE 53-1

Some strains of the common pathogen *Mycobacterium tuberculosis* are resistant to antibiotics.

SECTION 53-1 REVIEW

1. What is a drug?

2. Describe four ways that a drug can be administered.

3. Explain why doctors ask patients to list all the medications they are taking.

4. Name five commonly used types of drugs.

5. What problem has the overuse of antibiotics produced?

6. **CRITICAL THINKING**   Colds, flu, and 90 percent of sore throats are caused by viruses. Why would taking an antibiotic be useless in these cases?

OBJECTIVES

▲

Describe the effects
of nicotine on the body.

●

List three diseases that
can result from smoking
or chewing tobacco.

■

Explain what can happen
to the fetus of a pregnant
woman who smokes.

◆

Distinguish between a stimulant
and a depressant.

▲

Define *blood alcohol
concentration,* and name
three factors that affect it.

●

Explain what can happen
as a result of excessive
alcohol consumption.

SOCIAL DRUGS

*T*wo drugs that are often used by people in a social context are nicotine, found in all tobacco products, and alcohol. The leaves of the tobacco plant, Nicotiana tabacum, *are dried and crushed, then smoked in cigarettes, cigars, and pipes. Tobacco is also chewed and snuffed. Ethanol—the alcohol found in beer, wine, liquor, and certain other beverages—comes from the anaerobic respiration of sugars in fruits and grains. Both tobacco and alcohol have gained wide social acceptance, but that acceptance has come at a great price.*

TOBACCO

Nicotine, the major drug found in tobacco, is a stimulant. A **stimulant** is a drug that increases the activity of the central nervous system. When tobacco is inhaled, nicotine is absorbed into the bloodstream through the lining of the mouth and through the lungs. Nicotine is quickly transported throughout the body, penetrating the brain, all other organs, and, in pregnant women, the fetus.

Effects of Tobacco

Nicotine increases blood pressure and heart rate while decreasing the oxygen supply to body tissues and the blood supply to the hands and feet. Nicotine is an addictive drug. In **addiction,** the user of a drug becomes dependent on the drug and cannot function comfortably without it. Nicotine is a poison—60 mg of nicotine is a lethal dose for an adult. But nicotine is not the only poison found in tobacco. There are more than 2,000 potentially toxic chemical compounds produced when tobacco is burned. Collectively, these are called tars.

Tars are complex mixtures of chemicals and smoke particles produced by burning tobacco. Tars paralyze the cilia that line the air passages. Remember from Chapter 47 that these cilia move particles out of the air passages and protect the passages from disease-causing microorganisms. Tars irritate the nose, throat, trachea, and bronchial tubes, causing sore throat and coughing. Eventually, tars settle in the lungs. The result is a reduction in breathing capacity and increased susceptibility to infections. The lungs of a smoker look much different from those of a nonsmoker due to the accumulation of tars, as shown in Figure 53-2.

FIGURE 53-2

The blackened appearance of a smoker's lung is the result of years of tar accumulation. Contrast the smoker's lung (left) with the healthy lung (right).

Hazards of Long-Term Tobacco Use

Figure 53-3 illustrates the hazards of tobacco use. Notice how many parts of the body can be affected by tobacco. As it circulates in the bloodstream, nicotine can affect the performance of nearly every system in the body. The system that is most affected is the cardio-vascular system. Approximately 25 percent of all heart attacks are associated with the use of tobacco.

The causal relationship between smoking and lung cancer is well established. As you read in Chapter 11, lung cancer is one of the deadliest forms of cancer. More than 90 percent of all lung cancer deaths can be attributed to smoking. Many smokers contract **chronic bronchitis** (brahn-KIET-is), an inflammation of the bronchi and bronchi-oles, or **emphysema** (EM-fuh-SEE-muh), a degenerative lung disease. In emphysema, the alveoli lose their elasticity and eventually rupture, reducing the surface area available for gas exchange in the lungs.

Users of smokeless tobacco, such as chewing tobacco and snuff, have a higher rate of lip, gum, and mouth cancer than people who

FIGURE 53-3

The health risks associated with smoking extend to many parts of the body.

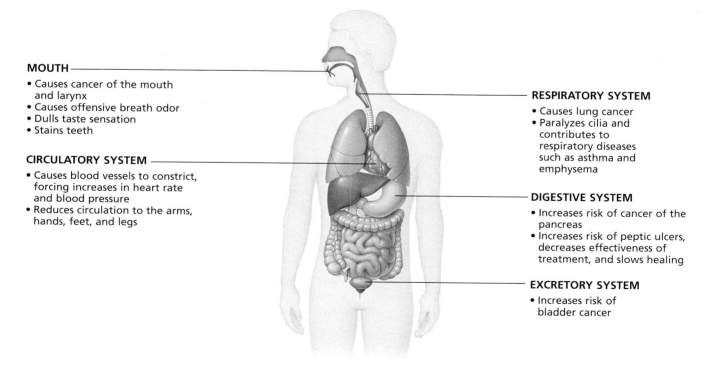

MOUTH
- Causes cancer of the mouth and larynx
- Causes offensive breath odor
- Dulls taste sensation
- Stains teeth

CIRCULATORY SYSTEM
- Causes blood vessels to constrict, forcing increases in heart rate and blood pressure
- Reduces circulation to the arms, hands, feet, and legs

RESPIRATORY SYSTEM
- Causes lung cancer
- Paralyzes cilia and contributes to respiratory diseases such as asthma and emphysema

DIGESTIVE SYSTEM
- Increases risk of cancer of the pancreas
- Increases risk of peptic ulcers, decreases effectiveness of treatment, and slows healing

EXCRETORY SYSTEM
- Increases risk of bladder cancer

do not use smokeless tobacco. Tobacco-induced cancers can also occur far from the respiratory system. Smoking is associated with cancers of the bladder and pancreas and may be associated with other types of cancer as well. Cancers associated with smoking likely result from the effects of tars on body tissues.

The consequences of smoking during pregnancy are serious. Pregnant women who smoke are twice as likely as nonsmoking mothers to suffer miscarriages. Their babies tend to have lower birth weights than babies of nonsmokers and are twice as likely to die in the first few months of life. The infants of nursing mothers who smoke may have concentrations of nicotine in their blood as high as those of their mothers.

Tobacco even affects nonsmokers. Tobacco smoke released by cigarettes or exhaled by a smoker is called **secondhand smoke.** Laboratory studies have shown that people exposed to secondhand smoke are at risk for the same diseases as people who smoke. Researchers have recently found that exposure to secondhand smoke increases the risk of sudden infant death syndrome in infants up to the age of 12 months.

ALCOHOL

Ethanol is the alcohol found in beer, wine, and mixed drinks. Alcohol is generally a **depressant,** a drug that decreases the activity of the central nervous system. Following consumption, alcohol is immediately absorbed by the stomach and intestines, where it enters the bloodstream and is transported to the brain and other organs.

Effects of Alcohol

Alcohol increases circulation to the skin, resulting in decreased blood flow to internal organs and a net drop in body temperature. Alcohol increases excretion of water by the kidneys and can result in dehydration if the fluid is not replaced. The greatest and most immediate effects of alcohol, however, occur in the brain.

Alcohol affects different classes of neurons in the brain at different times as a person drinks. This accounts for the wide spectrum of behaviors associated with alcohol consumption. Behavioral excitability and an increased respiration rate are often seen immediately after a person begins to drink. As drinking continues, judgment and coordination are significantly impaired, speech becomes slurred, and reaction time lengthens. Respiration rate slows after the initial increase, and high doses of alcohol can cause death by respiratory failure.

The severity of all of these effects depends largely on **blood alcohol concentration (BAC),** a measurement of the amount of alcohol in the blood. As shown in Figure 53-4, BAC can be determined by a breath test, which measures alcohol vapors given off by the lungs. Table 53-2 illustrates the relationship between body

FIGURE 53-4

A Breathalyzer is an instrument that estimates blood alcohol concentration from alcohol vapors released by the lungs.

TABLE 53-2 Blood Alcohol Concentration (in mg of alcohol per mL of blood) and Its Effects

| Drinks per hour | Body weight in pounds | | | | | | | | Result |
	100	120	140	160	180	200	220	240	
1	0.04	0.03	0.03	0.02	0.02	0.02	0.02	0.02	impairment
2	0.06	0.06	0.05	0.05	0.04	0.04	0.03	0.03	impairment
3	0.11	0.09	0.08	0.07	0.06	0.06	0.05	0.05	intoxication
4	0.15	0.12	0.11	0.09	0.08	0.08	0.07	0.06	intoxication
5	0.19	0.16	0.13	0.12	0.11	0.09	0.09	0.08	intoxication
6	0.23	0.19	0.16	0.14	0.13	0.11	0.10	0.09	intoxication
7	0.26	0.22	0.19	0.16	0.15	0.13	0.12	0.11	severe intoxication
8	0.30	0.25	0.21	0.19	0.17	0.15	0.14	0.13	severe intoxication

One drink is 1 oz of 80 proof (40%) liquor, 12 oz of 4.5% beer, or 4 oz of 12% wine.

weight, rate of alcohol consumption, and BAC values. A BAC level of 0.30 or greater produces unconsciousness, and a BAC of 0.50 can be fatal. The BAC can be affected by factors other than body weight, such as gender—BAC rises more rapidly in female drinkers—and the ratio of lean body mass to fat. Food in the stomach slows the absorption of alcohol, so a person who drinks on an empty stomach will have a higher BAC than a person of similar weight who drinks the same amount but has recently eaten.

Drivers who have consumed alcohol are much more likely to be involved in motor-vehicle accidents than are sober drivers. In fact, alcohol is a factor in nearly 50 percent of all fatal crashes involving young people, and alcohol-related motor-vehicle accidents are the leading cause of death among people 15 to 24 years of age. You can see in Table 53-3 that many tragedies stem from the impaired judgment that invariably results from drinking.

Like other drugs, alcohol can contribute to serious and even fatal drug interactions. For example, when alcohol is combined with another depressant, such as a tranquilizer or a narcotic analgesic, the cumulative effects of the two drugs can slow the cardiac and respiratory systems to the point of causing death.

TABLE 53-3 Alcohol-Related Tragedies

Alcohol is a factor in the following:

- 70 percent of all murders
- more than 50 percent of all suicides
- more than 50 percent of all drownings
- more than 50 percent of all fire-related deaths
- 50 percent of all arrests
- nearly 50 percent of all fatal car accidents involving young people

Quick Lab

Graphing Tobacco Use

Materials graph paper, poster board, pencil, colored markers or pencils, ruler

Procedure

1. Examine the following table, which lists the percentage of students who said on national surveys that they smoked.

Grade	1991	1994	1998
8th	14.3%	18.4%	19.1%
10th	20.9%	25.4%	27.6%
12th	28.3%	31.2%	35.1%

2. Using a different color for each grade, graph each grade on the same set of axes. Put the year along the x-axis and the percentage along the y-axis.

3. Using the data in the graph and the table, design a poster to help prevent a teenager from smoking.

Analysis Analyze the resulting graph. What trends do you notice?

FIGURE 53-5

This child shows some of the abnormalities associated with fetal alcohol syndrome. The forehead is narrow, the wide-set eyes have a shallow crease in the upper eyelid, the upper lip is thin, and the span from the upper lip to the nose is long and lacks a central groove.

Word Roots and Origins

cirrhosis

from the Greek *kirrhos,* meaning "tawny-colored"

Hazards of Long-Term Alcohol Use

People who consume alcohol in large amounts over long periods of time are more likely than nonusers to suffer from high blood pressure and some forms of heart disease. Excessive alcohol use can irritate the lining of the stomach. The most serious result of long-term or inappropriate use of alcohol is **alcoholism,** the addiction to alcohol.

In alcoholics, alcohol takes the place of nutritious foods, causing metabolic disorders. Long-term use of alcohol is associated with the degeneration of neurons in the peripheral nervous system as well as irreversible damage to the brain. Chronic alcohol use forces the liver to use alcohol as an energy source. Eventually, liver cells become unable to function properly, and they accumulate fat deposits. As a result, the liver enlarges. This **fatty liver** is a condition that occurs in 75 percent of all alcoholics. If the drinker abstains from alcohol, the liver can return to normal functioning. If drinking continues, however, the drinker may develop **alcoholic hepatitis** (HEP-uh-TIET-is), an inflammation of the liver, or even **cirrhosis** (suh-ROH-sis), a condition in which normal liver tissue is replaced by scar tissue. Locate the scar tissue in the liver shown in the first illustration in this chapter, on page 1064. Cirrhosis causes severe impairment of liver function and is often fatal.

Like many other drugs, alcohol passes through the placenta and thus can affect a fetus. Children born to women who drink during pregnancy, such as the child shown in Figure 53-5, may suffer from fetal alcohol syndrome. **Fetal alcohol syndrome (FAS)** is a cluster of physical and mental disabilities associated with exposure of the developing fetus to alcohol. Babies that exhibit FAS are small and have an abnormally formed head. They lack normal motor coordination, grow slowly, and may be mentally retarded. Mild degrees of FAS in children often go undiagnosed and may exhibit themselves as behavioral, intellectual, or motor problems.

The severity of FAS seems to be related to the amount of alcohol a pregnant woman drinks and when, during her pregnancy, drinking occurs. There is no established safe level of alcohol intake during pregnancy; researchers think that fetal brain damage occurs at very low levels of alcohol exposure. Moreover, the fetus may be vulnerable to serious damage very early in development, even before a woman realizes that she is pregnant.

SECTION 53-2 REVIEW

1. In what ways does nicotine affect the body?

2. How do tars contribute to a smoker's increased susceptibility to colds and infections?

3. What factors influence blood alcohol concentration in a drinker?

4. How does a stimulant drug differ from a depressant drug?

5. What are some of the effects of fetal alcohol syndrome?

6. **CRITICAL THINKING** Why does alcohol, a single drug, have a wide range of effects on a user?

ABUSE OF DRUGS

When used correctly, both prescription and nonprescription drugs can be beneficial. However, many drugs are abused, that is, taken for nonmedical reasons. Drug abuse includes taking a drug in doses greater than prescribed or for a longer time than recommended, as well as taking a drug that is obtained illegally or without a doctor's prescription.

DRUG ADDICTION

Addiction to a drug involves physiological changes in neurons, especially those in the brain. Studies have shown that physical addiction results in changes in body and brain chemistry that in turn create a demand for a steady or increasingly large supply of the drug. The drive to consume greater and greater amounts of a drug is all too familiar to alcoholics and abusers of many other drugs.

Tolerance

As a person becomes addicted to a drug, his or her body may become less responsive to the drug. The addict has developed **tolerance,** which means that increasingly large amounts of the drug are needed to attain the sensation previously achieved with a smaller dose. This rise in the **effective dose,** the dose that results in the desired feeling, is a deadly situation for users of some drugs, particularly depressant drugs. As tolerance increases, the addict must take higher and higher doses of the drug, approaching the lethal dose. The **lethal dose** of a drug is the amount of drug that will cause the user to die, and it does not change as tolerance builds.

If the drug supply is cut off, the addict will go through **withdrawal,** a physical and mental response to the lack of the drug. The symptoms of withdrawal vary, depending on the drug being used and the duration of use. Symptoms may include nausea, headache, insomnia, breathing difficulties, depression, mental instability, and seizures. Withdrawal from addiction to some depressant drugs, such as alcohol and barbiturates, can be life threatening. Addicts undergoing withdrawal are often hospitalized so that their responses can be monitored. Although drug users develop an emotional dependence on a drug, tolerance and withdrawal are physiological effects of drug use. Figure 53-6 shows what happens in neurons of a person addicted to cocaine. The excitatory effect sought by users of cocaine is probably due to the drug's action on neurons that use the neurotransmitters **dopamine** and norepinephrine, NE.

SECTION
53-3

OBJECTIVES

▲

Define the term *tolerance.*

●

Explain the physical basis of drug addiction.

■

Describe the process of withdrawal.

◆

Identify five types of psychoactive drugs.

▲

List one example of each type of drug, and describe how each affects the body.

Word Roots and Origins

tolerance

from the Latin *tolerare,* meaning "to bear"

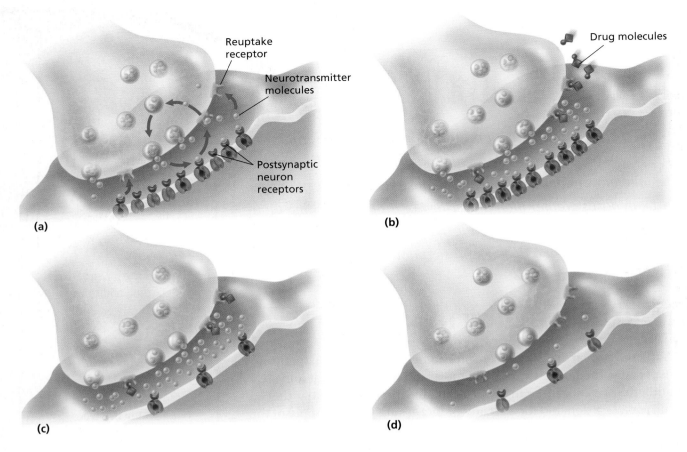

Reuptake
receptor

Neurotransmitter
molecules

Postsynaptic
neuron
receptors

(a)

Drug molecules

(b)

(c)

(d)

FIGURE 53-6

(a) At a normal NE synapse, neurotransmitter molecules are removed by reuptake receptors. (b) Cocaine and certain other drugs bind at reuptake receptors, blocking them. Neurotransmitter molecules remain in the synaptic cleft. (c) The overstimulated postsynaptic neuron reduces its number of receptors over time to normalize firing. (d) When the drug is removed, the number of neurotransmitter molecules drops to normal—a level too low to stimulate the altered postsynaptic neuron normally.

Neural Changes

Recall from Chapter 50 that when an axon terminal receives a signal—an action potential—it releases molecules of neurotransmitter into the synaptic cleft. In dopamine and NE neurons, and in many other kinds of neurons, neurotransmitter molecules are removed from the synaptic cleft when they bind to reuptake receptors on the presynaptic (neurotransmitter-releasing) neuron, as shown in Figure 53-6a. **Reuptake receptors** are molecular transporters that move neurotransmitter molecules back into the presynaptic neuron. Cocaine acts by binding at these presynaptic reuptake receptors, stopping their function. As a result, a large number of neurotransmitter molecules collect in the synaptic cleft, as shown in Figure 53-6b. These excess neurotransmitter molecules in the synapse excite the postsynaptic neuron to an abnormal degree, increasing firing rate. This excitatory response in dopamine and NE neurons in the brain provides the sensation sought by the drug user.

In response to this chronic surplus of neurotransmitter, the postsynaptic (neurotransmitter-receiving) neurons reduce their number of neurotransmitter receptors over time, as shown in Figure 53-6c. This response is the body's attempt to restore homeostasis in these neurons. As you can see in Figure 53-6d, when the drug is removed, the number of neurotransmitter molecules in the synaptic cleft decreases. (They are taken up by the presynaptic neuron, as is normal.) However, this now-normal level of neurotransmitter is not sufficient to stimulate the postsynaptic neuron, with its now-reduced number of receptors, and transmission of the signal is disrupted.

DRUGS OF ABUSE

Drugs that affect the functioning of the central nervous system are known as **psychoactive drugs.** Psychoactive drugs are often addictive, and possession of many types of psychoactive drugs is illegal. Table 53-4 lists the broad categories of frequently abused drugs; all groups but one, the steroids, are primarily psychoactive.

TABLE 53-4	**Common Drugs of Abuse**	
Drug	**Short-term effects**	**Dangers of use**
Depressants • Alcohol • Barbiturates • Tranquilizers • Nonbarbiturate sleeping drugs	temporary sense of well-being, impaired judgment, impaired sensory perception, loss of motor control, confusion, sedation	emotional depression, liver damage, brain and peripheral nerve damage, respiratory failure (Withdrawal from alcohol or barbiturates can cause death; withdrawal should be medically supervised.)
Narcotics • Codeine • Heroin • Morphine • Synthetic opiates	temporary feeling of euphoria, impaired reflexes, impaired sensory perception, sedation	coma, respiratory failure
Stimulants • Amphetamines • Caffeine • Cocaine/crack cocaine	temporary feeling of exhilaration and energy, distorted thoughts, irritability, anxiety, restlessness, insomnia, elevated blood pressure, increased heart rate	sleep disturbances, irregular heartbeat; with amphetamines and cocaine, paranoia, delusions, hallucinations, loss of coordination, permanent brain damage, respiratory paralysis, cardiac arrest
Hallucinogens • Amphetamine-like drugs • Ecstasy (MDMA) • Marijuana/hashish • LSD • Mescaline/peyote • PCP (phencyclidine) • Psilocybe mushrooms	temporary dreamlike sense of detachment from surroundings, sensory distortion, hallucinations, delusions, anxiety, slurred speech, numbness, bizarre or violent behavior	mental depression, "flashbacks," paranoia, genetic damage; with marijuana, amotivational syndrome
Inhalants • Aerosol propellants • Alkyl nitrates • Anesthetic gases • Solvents in glue, paint, correction fluid, marking pens, gasoline additives	disorientation, confusion, memory loss; with anesthetic gases, sedation	severe permanent brain damage, hearing loss, limb spasms, bone marrow damage, liver and kidney damage, cardiac arrest; with anesthetic gases, respiratory failure
Anabolic steroids	increase of muscle mass, fluid retention, insomnia, depression	cancer, liver disease, stunted growth, heart disease, heart attack

Marijuana

One of the hallucinogens listed in Table 53-4 is marijuana, which comes from the flowers, leaves, and seeds of *Cannabis sativa,* the hemp plant. The active ingredient in marijuana is 9-tetrahydro-cannabinol, or THC. When smoked, or when heated and then eaten, marijuana produces feelings of disorientation in space and time. Continual use of marijuana can lead to addiction and a suppressed activity level referred to as **amotivational syndrome.**

Cocaine

One of the illegal stimulants listed in Table 53-4 is cocaine. Cocaine is a white powder that is extracted from the leaves of the coca plant, *Erythroxylon coca.* Cocaine is generally inhaled, although it can be injected. Crack cocaine is a smokable form of the drug. Cocaine is a powerful stimulant that raises heart rate, blood pressure, and body temperature. A single dose of cocaine can cause a heart attack. Cocaine is one of the most addictive drugs known.

Opium

Figure 53-7 shows the poppy plant, *Papaver somniferum,* from which the resinous extract opium is obtained. Opium is used to make morphine and codeine, prescription drugs used to alleviate pain. Heroin, an illegal drug, is a semisynthetic, more potent form of morphine. Morphine, codeine, heroin, and similar synthetic drugs are known as narcotics. A **narcotic** is a pain-relieving drug that also induces sedation and sleep. Tolerance and addiction to narcotics occur rapidly.

Narcotics work by mimicking natural painkillers that are produced by the body. Natural painkillers include a class of neurotransmitters known as **enkephalins** (en-KEF-uh-linz). When enkephalins bind to receptor proteins in spinal neurons, they block action potentials from reaching the brain, where they would be interpreted as pain. Narcotics bind to the same receptor sites that enkephalins bind to, triggering and amplifying the body's own pain-blocking system.

At times, morphine is used under medical supervision when the intensity or duration of pain is too much for a person to bear. However, keep in mind that pain plays an important role in the body. Pain makes you aware of some damage that has occurred to a body part or of some malfunction that has occurred in a physiological process. In effect, pain can tell you that an organ system is not operating at its normal level of performance—something that is critical for good health.

FIGURE 53-7

Several narcotic drugs are made from the resin of the opium poppy.

SECTION 53-3 REVIEW

1. Name five types of psychoactive drugs.

2. What is tolerance to a drug?

3. How does withdrawal affect the body?

4. Explain how cocaine affects NE neurons.

5. Why is drug addiction considered a physical problem in addition to being a psychological problem?

6. **CRITICAL THINKING** Why are long-term drug users, who have built a large degree of tolerance, endangered by their effective dose?

SUMMARY/VOCABULARY

53-1 ■ A drug is a chemical compound that affects either the structure of a body part or the functioning of a physiological process. A drug can be introduced into the body orally, by injection, by being placed under the tongue, through inhalation, or by application to the skin.

■ Prescription drugs are prescribed by a doc-

tor or dentist. Nonprescription drugs can be purchased without a prescription.

■ Taking more than one drug at the same time can cause a harmful drug interaction.

■ Overuse of prescription drugs can lead to serious problems. Overuse of antibiotics has fostered the evolution of increasing numbers of resistant bacteria.

Vocabulary

dose (1066)   drug (1065)   nonprescription drug (1066)   prescription drug (1066)

53-2 ■ Tobacco contains more than 2,000 potentially toxic chemical compounds, including nicotine and tars. Nicotine is an addictive stimulant drug that increases the heart rate and decreases blood flow to the hands and feet.

■ Tars paralyze the cilia lining the respiratory passages.

■ Health problems associated with tobacco use include lung, lip, mouth, gum, bladder, and pancreatic cancers; chronic bronchitis; emphysema; heart attacks; and health problems in babies of smokers.

■ Alcohol is a depressant drug that affects

multiple organ systems. Alcohol interferes with normal brain function. Impairment caused by alcohol depends on the amount consumed; the person's body weight, gender, rate of consumption, and ability to metabolize alcohol; and the amount of food in the person's stomach.

■ Health problems associated with prolonged, excessive alcohol consumption include high blood pressure, heart disease, fatty liver, alcoholic hepatitis, cirrhosis, and fetal alcohol syndrome. Alcohol can lead to the addiction known as alcoholism.

Vocabulary

addiction (1068)
alcoholic hepatitis (1072)
alcoholism (1072)
blood alcohol concentration (1070)

chronic bronchitis (1069)
cirrhosis (1072)
depressant (1070)
emphysema (1069)

fatty liver (1072)
fetal alcohol syndrome (1072)
nicotine (1068)

secondhand smoke (1070)
stimulant (1068)
tar (1068)

53-3 ■ Drug abuse can lead to addiction, in which the body undergoes physiological changes that result in a need for the drug.

■ Drug addiction results in tolerance as the addict's body becomes less responsive to the drug. During withdrawal, an addict will experience both physical and mental reactions to the lack of the drug.

■ Cocaine is an extremely addictive stimulant drug that causes repeated stimulation of

NE neurons. Crack cocaine is a smokable form of the drug.

■ Marijuana is a hallucinogen that produces feelings of disorientation in space and time. Prolonged use of marijuana can lead to amotivational syndrome.

■ Morphine, codeine, and heroin are narcotics derived from opium. Narcotics are powerful painkillers that mimic the body's natural painkillers.

Vocabulary

amotivational syndrome (1076)
dopamine (1073)

effective dose (1073)
enkephalin (1076)
lethal dose (1073)

narcotic (1076)
psychoactive drug (1075)
reuptake receptor (1074)

tolerance (1073)
withdrawal (1073)

REVIEW

Vocabulary

1. Define the term *drug*.
2. Identify two respiratory diseases caused by tobacco.
3. Identify two diseases caused by alcohol.
4. What is blood alcohol concentration, and what are some factors that affect it?
5. Describe the relationship between addiction, tolerance, and withdrawal.

Multiple Choice

6. Drugs can be administered (a) orally (b) by injection (c) by inhalation (d) all of the above.
7. Tars (a) cause an increase in heart rate (b) are stimulants (c) paralyze cilia (d) are neurotransmitters.
8. Emphysema is (a) a degenerative lung disease (b) a form of cancer (c) an inflammation of the throat (d) a result of chewing tobacco.
9. Alcohol is a (a) stimulant (b) depressant (c) narcotic (d) steroid.
10. BAC specifically measures (a) the rate at which a person has been drinking (b) a person's genetic ability to metabolize alcohol (c) the amount of alcohol in a person's blood (d) the time at which a person was drinking.
11. Fetal alcohol syndrome can cause (a) low birth weight (b) heart defects (c) learning difficulties (d) all of the above.
12. Enkephalins are (a) natural painkillers (b) illegal drugs (c) stimulants (d) synthetic narcotics.
13. Addiction (a) occurs when the body becomes dependent on a drug (b) occurs when the supply of a drug is stopped (c) is easily reversed when the supply of a drug is stopped (d) is caused only by illegal drugs.
14. Depressants include (a) cocaine (b) barbiturates (c) nicotine (d) amphetamines.
15. Narcotics cause (a) an increased heart rate (b) increased alertness (c) decreased alertness (d) lung damage.

Short Answer

16. Describe a situation in which a nonprescription drug could be dangerous.
17. Describe the harmful effects of secondhand smoke.
18. What are some of the harmful effects of smoking during pregnancy?
19. Describe the specific effects of alcohol on the cells of the liver.
20. In what ways are mental capabilities diminished as BAC increases?
21. What are some potential effects of long-term, excessive alcohol use?
22. What is the relationship between fatty liver and cirrhosis?
23. What are psychoactive drugs?
24. In the figure below, explain what has just occurred in (a).
25. In the figure below, explain what has just occurred in (b).

(a)

(b)

CRITICAL THINKING

1. Alcohol is primarily a depressant drug. How do you explain the fact that consumption of alcohol sometimes results in a carefree attitude and a feeling of elation?

2. If you are given a 10-day course of an antibiotic for a bacterial infection and you take the medicine for only five days, how might the infectious bacteria respond?

3. Some infants are born addicted to a drug. Explain how this is possible.

4. Why is tolerance a deadly problem for long-term addicts of some drugs?

5. The table below shows typical blood alcohol concentration values for individuals of different weights. Use the table to answer the following.

   a. What is the blood alcohol concentration of a 140 lb person who has consumed three drinks in one hour?

   b. How many drinks would a 200 lb person have to consume in an hour to equal the BAC of a 140 lb person who consumed three drinks in an hour?

   c. At what weight (among those shown on the table) does a person's BAC rise most rapidly?

Blood Alcohol Concentration (in mg of alcohol per mL of blood) and Its Effects

Drinks per hour	100	120	140	Body weight in pounds 160	180	200	220	240	Results
1	0.04	0.03	0.03	0.02	0.02	0.02	0.02	0.02	impairment
2	0.06	0.06	0.05	0.05	0.04	0.04	0.03	0.03	impairment
3	0.11	0.09	0.08	0.07	0.06	0.06	0.05	0.05	intoxication
4	0.15	0.12	0.11	0.09	0.08	0.08	0.07	0.06	intoxication
5	0.19	0.16	0.13	0.12	0.11	0.09	0.09	0.08	intoxication
6	0.23	0.19	0.16	0.14	0.13	0.11	0.10	0.09	intoxication
7	0.26	0.22	0.19	0.16	0.15	0.13	0.12	0.11	severe intoxication
8	0.30	0.25	0.21	0.19	0.17	0.15	0.14	0.13	severe intoxication

EXTENSION

1. In the 1960s, many pregnant women in Europe took the prescription drug thalidomide. Many of the women gave birth to children with severe deformities. In the United States this drug was not available because it had not undergone the lengthy testing required for approval. Find out what is required before a drug is made available to the public in the United States.

2. Investigate and report on the resources available in your local community for treating addiction to both social drugs and illegal drugs.

3. Read "Of Two Minds About Marijuana" in *Discover*, November 1999, on page 26. Why, according to the article, do schizophrenics have a higher rate of marijuana abuse than the general population? Explain why researchers say marijuana is not suitable to treat brain disorders.

CHAPTER 53

INTERACTIVE EXPLORATION

Exploring a Model of Cocaine Addiction

OBJECTIVES

- Simulate the effects of cocaine use on a synapse in the brain.
- Observe the effect of cocaine use on the number of receptors in a synapse.

MATERIALS

- computer with CD-ROM drive
- CD-ROM *Interactive Explorations in Biology: Human Biology*

Background

This interactive exploration enables you to learn about the physical basis of drug addiction by exploring the consequences of exposure of a neuron to cocaine. The exploration presents an animated diagram of a single neural synapse in a "pleasure center" in the human brain. You will explore the consequences of introducing cocaine into a normal neural synapse.

Prelab Preparation

1. Load and start the program Drug Addiction. Click the Topic Information button on the Navigation Palette. Read the focus questions, and review these concepts: The Synapse, Neurotransmitters, Transporters, Neuromodulators, Desensitization, and Addiction.
2. Now click the word *File* at the top left of the screen, and select Interactive Exploration Help. Listen to the instructions that explain the operation of the exploration. Click the Exploration button at the bottom right of the screen to begin the exploration. You will see an animated diagram like the one below.

Procedure
PART A   Normal Synapse

First you will investigate how the synapse works when no cocaine is present.

1. Before beginning the simulation, record the number of receptors in the post-synaptic neuron. As the simulation runs, observe what happens to the Pleasure

FEEDBACK METERS

a Addiction Meter: *the number of receptors in the synapse*

b Pleasure Meter: *the number of receptors firing*

VARIABLES

c Frequency of Use: *changes the frequency at which cocaine is taken*

d Dosage: *varies the cocaine dosage from 0 to 5 g*

Meter and the Addiction Meter. Record the highest and lowest levels reached on the Pleasure Meter.

2. Click the Start button to begin the simulation. Observe what happens when neurotransmitter molecules (the blue spheres) are released into the synapse. For the purpose of this demonstration, each contact with a receptor on the other side of the synapse "fires" the postsynaptic neuron, producing a sensation of pleasure. Note carefully that in the normal synapse, the neurotransmitter molecules are recycled by the presynaptic neuron so that they do not accumulate in the synapse.

3. Allow the simulation to run for 3 to 4 minutes, noting any changes in the number of receptors (recorded by the Addiction Meter) and in the postsynaptic neuron's firing rate (recorded by the Pleasure Meter). End the simulation by clicking the Stop button.

4. Record the number of receptors in the postsynaptic neuron at the end of the simulation. Did the number of receptors change during the simulation? Explain why or why not.

PART B Data Collection

Now you will explore the effects of cocaine on the synapse.

5. Click the Reset button to clear the simulation.

6. Slide the Dosage indicator to 1 g and the Frequency of Use indicator to Weekly.

7. On a separate sheet of paper, create a six-column table like the one shown below.

8. Record the number of postsynaptic receptors in your table in the column labeled Addiction Meter: Start. Record the postsynaptic neuron firing rate in the column labeled Pleasure Meter: Start.

9. Click the Start button. For each dose of cocaine, you will see a burst of red spheres, representing cocaine,

enter the synapse. What happens to the red spheres after they enter the synapse?

10. Based on what happens to the red spheres, explain why cocaine induces pleasurable sensations.

11. The simulation will run until five doses have been taken, which should require about 5 minutes. At the end of the simulation, record in your table the number of receptors and the postsynaptic neuron's firing rate.

12. How does the number of receptors in the synapse change with repeated cocaine doses?

13. Is this dose large and frequent enough to cause addiction? Explain your answer.

14. What was the highest level reached by the Pleasure Meter? Compare this level with the highest level reached without cocaine use, and account for the difference.

15. Explain how the simulation you carried out in Part A serves as a control for this simulation.

16. Click the Reset button to clear the simulation. Set the Frequency of Use Indicator at Weekly, but slide the Dosage indicator to 2 g. Repeat steps 8–14. How do the results of this simulation differ from those obtained with a 1 g dose?

Analysis and Conclusions

1. Based on your results, can you conclude that cocaine can be taken at a safe dose, at which addiction does not occur? Explain your answer.

2. Explain why people who are addicted to cocaine require higher and higher doses to produce pleasure.

Further Investigation

Selective serotonin reuptake inhibitors (SSRIs) constitute a relatively new class of antidepressants. Read about SSRIs, and write a short description of how they work; include names of specific drugs and the subclasses of serotonin receptors they target.

TABLE A *CHANGES IN RECEPTOR NUMBER AND FIRING RATE AFTER COCAINE USE*

	Addiction Meter: Start	Addiction Meter: End	Change in receptor number	Pleasure Meter: Start	Pleasure Meter: End	Change in firing rate
No drug (control)						
1 g cocaine/week						
2 g cocaine/week						

It is your responsibility to protect yourself and other students by conducting yourself in a safe manner while in the laboratory. You will avoid accidents in the laboratory by following directions, handling materials carefully, and taking your work seriously. Read the following general safety guidelines before attempting to work in the laboratory. Make sure that you understand all safety guidelines before entering the laboratory. If necessary, ask your teacher for clarification of laboratory rules and procedures.

General Guidelines for Laboratory Safety

Do not perform experiments not specifically assigned by your teacher. Do not attempt any laboratory procedure without your teacher's direction, and do not work in the laboratory by yourself.

Familiarize yourself with the investigation and all safety precautions before entering the lab. Be aware of the potential hazards of the required materials and procedures. Ask your teacher to explain any parts of an investigation that you do not understand before you begin.

Before beginning work, tie back long hair, roll up loose sleeves, and put on any required personal protective equipment as directed by your teacher. Avoid or confine loose clothing that could knock things over, catch on fire, or absorb chemical solutions. Nylon and polyester fabrics burn and melt more readily than do cotton fabrics. Do not wear open-toed shoes, sandals, or canvas shoes in the laboratory.

Always wear a lab apron and safety goggles. Wear this equipment even if you are not working on an experiment at the time. Laboratories contain chemicals that can damage your clothing, skin, and eyes. If your safety goggles cloud up or are uncomfortable, ask your teacher for help. Lengthening the strap slightly, washing the goggles with soap and warm water, or using an anti-fog spray may help alleviate the problems.

Do not wear contact lenses in the lab. Even if you are wearing safety goggles, chemicals could get between contact lenses and your eyes and cause irreparable eye damage. If your doctor requires that you wear contact lenses instead of glasses, then you should wear eye-cup safety goggles—similar to goggles that are worn for underwater swimming—in the lab. Ask your doctor or your teacher how to use eye-cup safety goggles to protect your eyes.

Know the location of all safety and emergency equipment used in the laboratory. Ask your teacher where the nearest eyewash stations, safety blankets, safety shower, fire extinguisher, first aid kit, and chemical spill kit are located.

Immediately report any accident, incident, or hazard—no matter how trivial—to your teacher. Any incident involving bleeding, burns, fainting, chemical exposure, or ingestion should also be reported immediately to the school nurse or to a physician.

In case of fire, alert the teacher and leave the laboratory. Standard school fire safety procedures should be followed.

Do not fool around in the lab. Take your lab work seriously and behave appropriately in the laboratory. Be aware of your classmates' safety as well as your own at all times.

Do not have or consume food or drink in the laboratory. Do not store food in the laboratory. Keep your hands away from your face. Do not apply cosmetics in the laboratory. Some hair-care products and nail polish are highly flammable.

Keep your work area neat and uncluttered. Have only books and other materials that are needed to conduct the experiment in the laboratory.

Clean your work area at the conclusion of each lab period as your teacher directs. Broken glass, chemicals, and other laboratory waste products should be disposed of in separate special containers. Dispose of waste materials as directed by your teacher.

Wash your hands with soap and water after each lab period. Also wash your hands before each lab period to avoid contamination.

Key to Safety Symbols and Their Precautions

Before you begin working in the laboratory, familiarize yourself with the following safety symbols that are used in this textbook and the guidelines that you should follow when you see these symbols.

EYE SAFETY

- **Wear approved safety goggles as directed.** Goggles should always be worn in the laboratory, especially when you are working with a chemical or a solution, a heat source, or a mechanical device.

- **In case of eye contact, do the following:** Go to an eyewash station immediately, and flush your eyes (including under the eyelids) with running water for at least 15 minutes. Hold your eyelids open with your thumb and fingers, and roll your eyeball around. While doing this, have another student notify your teacher.

- **Do not wear contact lenses in the laboratory.** Chemicals can be drawn up under the contact lens and into the eye. If you must wear contacts, tell your teacher. You must also wear approved eye-cup safety goggles to protect your eyes.

- **Do not look directly at the sun through any optical device or lens system or reflect direct sunlight to illuminate a microscope.** Such actions concentrate light rays to an intensity that can severely burn your retina, possibly causing blindness.

HAND SAFETY

- **Do not cut objects while holding them in your hand.** Dissect specimens in a dissecting tray.

- **Wear protective gloves when working with an open flame, chemicals, solutions, or wild or unknown plants.**

SAFETY WITH GASES

- **Do not inhale any gas or vapor unless directed to do so by your teacher.** Do not breathe pure gases.

- **Handle materials prone to emit vapors or gases in a well-ventilated area.** This work should be done in an approved chemical fume hood.

SHARP-OBJECT SAFETY

- **Use extreme care when handling all sharp and pointed instruments, such as scalpels, sharp probes, and knives.**

- **Do not use double-edged razor blades in the laboratory.**

- **Do not cut objects while holding them in your hand.** Cut objects on a suitable work surface. Always cut in a direction away from your body.

CLOTHING PROTECTION

◆ **Wear an apron or laboratory coat at all times in the laboratory to prevent chemicals or solutions from contacting skin or clothes.**

ANIMAL CARE AND SAFETY

◆ **Do not touch or approach wild animals.** When working in the field, be aware of poisonous or dangerous animals in the area.

◆ **Always obtain your teacher's permission before bringing any animal (including pets) into the school building.**

◆ **Handle animals only as your teacher directs.** Mishandling or abusing any animal will not be tolerated.

HEATING SAFETY

◆ **Be aware of any source of flames, sparks, or heat (open flames, electric heating coils, hot plates, etc.) before working with flammable liquids or gases.**

◆ **When heating chemicals or reagents in a test tube, do not point the test tube toward anyone.**

◆ **Avoid using open flames.** If possible, work only with hot plates that have an "On-Off" switch and an indicator light. Do not leave hot plates unattended. Do not use alcohol lamps. Turn off hot plates and open flames when they are not in use.

◆ **Know the location of laboratory fire extinguishers and fire-safety blankets.**

◆ **Use tongs or other appropriate, insulated holders when heating objects.** Heated objects often do not appear to be hot. Thus, do not pick up an object with your hand if it could be warm.

◆ **Keep flammable substances away from heat, flames, and other ignition sources.**

HYGIENIC CARE

◆ **Keep your hands away from your face and mouth while working in the laboratory.**

◆ **Wash your hands thoroughly before leaving the laboratory.**

◆ **Remove contaminated clothing immediately.** If you spill caustic substances on your skin or clothing, use the safety shower or a faucet to rinse. Remove affected clothing while under the shower, and call to your teacher. (It may be temporarily embarrassing to remove clothing in front of your classmates, but failing to rinse a chemical off your skin could cause permanent damage.)

◆ **Launder contaminated clothing separately.**

◆ **Use the proper technique demonstrated by your teacher when handling bacteria or similar microorganisms.** Do not open Petri dishes to observe or count bacterial colonies.

PLANT SAFETY

◆ **Do not ingest any plant part used in the laboratory (especially commercially sold seeds).** Do not touch any sap or plant juice directly. Always wear gloves.

◆ **Wear disposable polyethylene gloves when handling any wild plant.**

◆ **Wash hands thoroughly after handling any plant or plant part (particularly seeds).** Avoid touching your face and eyes.

◆ **Do not inhale or expose yourself to the smoke of any burning plant.** Smoke contains irritants that can cause inflammation in the throat and lungs.

◆ **Do not pick wildflowers or other wild plants unless otherwise directed by your teacher.**

GLASSWARE SAFETY

◆ **Inspect glassware before use; do not use chipped or cracked glassware.** Use heat-resistant glassware for heating materials or storing hot liquids.

◆ **Do not attempt to insert glass tubing into a rubber stopper without specific instruction from your teacher.**

◆ **Immediately notify your teacher if a piece of glassware breaks. Do not attempt to clean up broken glass.**

CHEMICAL SAFETY

◆ **Always wear appropriate protective equipment.** Eye goggles, gloves, and a lab apron or lab coat should always be worn when working with any chemical or chemical solution.

◆ **Do not taste, touch, or smell any substance or bring it close to your eyes, unless specifically instructed to do so by your teacher.** If you are directed by your teacher to note the odor of a substance, do so by waving the fumes toward you with your hand. Do not pipette any substance by mouth; use a suction bulb as directed by your teacher.

◆ **Always handle chemicals and solutions with care.** Check the labels on bottles, and observe safety procedures. Do not return unused chemicals or solutions to their original containers. Return unused reagent bottles or containers to your teacher.

◆ **Do not mix any chemicals unless specifically instructed to do so by your teacher.** Two harmless chemicals can be poisonous if combined.

◆ **Do not pour water into a strong acid or strong base.** The mixture can produce heat and splatter.

◆ **Report any spill immediately to your teacher.** Do not clean up spills yourself unless your teacher instructs you otherwise.

PROPER WASTE DISPOSAL

◆ **Clean and decontaminate all work surfaces and personal protective equipment after each lab period as directed by your teacher.**

◆ **Dispose of all sharp objects (such as broken glass) and other contaminated materials (biological or chemical) in special containers as directed by your teacher.**

ELECTRICAL SAFETY

◆ **Do not use equipment with frayed electrical cords or loose plugs.**

◆ **Fasten electrical cords to work surfaces with tape.** This will prevent tripping and will ensure that equipment cannot fall off the table.

◆ **Do not use electrical equipment near water or with wet hands or clothing.**

◆ **Hold the rubber cord when you plug in or unplug equipment. Do not touch the metal prongs of the plug, and do not unplug equipment by pulling on the cord.**

MEASUREMENT

Scientists throughout the world use the Système International d'Unités, or International System of Measurements. It is usually referred to simply as SI. You will often use SI units to express the measurements that you will make in the laboratory. Most measurements in this book are expressed in SI units.

SI is a decimal system; that is, all relationships between SI units are based on powers of 10. Most units have a prefix that indicates the relationship of that unit to a base unit. For example, the SI base unit for length is the meter. A meter equals 100 centimeters (cm), or 1,000 millimeters (mm). A meter also equals 0.001 kilometers (km). Table 1 summarizes the prefixes and abbreviations that are commonly used to represent SI units.

TABLE 1   SI PREFIXES

Prefix	Abbreviation	Factor of base unit
giga	G	1,000,000,000
mega	M	1,000,000
kilo	k	1,000
hecto	h	100
deka	da	10
deci	d	0.1
centi	c	0.01
milli	m	0.001
micro	μ	0.000001
nano	n	0.000000001

SI Units

BASE UNITS

Seven fundamental quantities are represented by base units in SI. These base units include familiar quantities, such as length, mass, and time. These base quantities, their units, and their abbreviations are given in Table 2.

TABLE 2   SI BASE UNITS

Base quantity	Unit	Abbreviation
Length	meter	m
Mass	kilogram	kg
Time	second	s
Electric current	ampere	A
Thermodynamic temperature	kelvin	K
Amount of substance	mole	mol
Luminous intensity	candela	cd

DERIVED UNITS

The base units in Table 2 cannot be used to express measurements such as the surface area of a wildlife preserve or the speed of a running cheetah. Therefore, other important quantities, such as area, volume, and velocity, are expressed in derived units. Derived units are mathematical combinations of one or more base units.

TABLE 3   EXAMPLES OF SI DERIVED UNITS

Derived quantity	Unit	Abbreviation
Area	square meter	m^2
Volume	cubic meter	m^3
Mass density	kilogram per cubic meter	kg/m^3
Specific volume	cubic meter per kilogram	m^3/kg
Velocity	meter per second	m/s
Celsius temperature	degree Celsius	°C

Table 3 lists some derived units that you may encounter in your study of biology.

Like base units, derived units also can be expressed using prefixes. In the lab, you will often express volume measurements in cubic centimeters (cm^3). Graduated cylinders are calibrated in milliliters or cubic centimeters. A square meter equals 10,000 square centimeters (cm^2). Large area measurements are often expressed in hectares (ha). A hectare equals 10,000 square meters (m^2).

UNITS ACCEPTED FOR USE WITH SI

Certain units of measure that are not SI units are still acceptable for use with SI units. They are the units of time—minute, hour, and day; a unit of volume—liter; and a unit of mass—metric ton. These units are listed in Table 4.

TABLE 4 EXAMPLES OF UNITS ACCEPTED FOR USE WITH SI

Unit	Abbreviation	Value in SI units
Minute	min	1 min = 60 s
Hour	h	1 h = 3,600 s
		1 h = 60 min
Day	d	1 d = 24 h
Liter	L	1 L = 0.001 m³
Metric ton	t	1 t = 1,000 kg

Equivalent Measurements and Conversions

Conversion between SI units requires a conversion factor. For example, to convert from meters to centimeters, you need to know the relationship between meters and centimeters.

$$1 \text{ cm} = 0.01 \text{ m} \quad \text{or} \quad 1 \text{ m} = 100 \text{ cm}$$

If you needed to convert a lab measurement of 15.5 centimeters to meters, you could do either of the following:

$$15.5 \text{ cm} \times \frac{1 \text{ m}}{100 \text{ cm}} = 0.155 \text{ m}$$

or

$$15.5 \text{ cm} \times \frac{0.01 \text{ m}}{1 \text{ cm}} = 0.155 \text{ m}$$

The following are some measurement equivalents for length, area, mass, and volume.

LENGTH
1 kilometer (km)	= 1,000 m
1 meter (m)	= base unit of length
1 centimeter (cm)	= 0.01 m
1 millimeter (mm)	= 0.001 m
1 micrometer (μm)	= 0.000001 m

AREA
square kilometer (km²)	= 100 ha
1 hectare (ha)	= 10,000 m²
1 square meter (m²)	= 10,000 cm²
1 square centimeter (cm²)	= 100 mm²

MASS
1 kilogram (kg)	= base unit of mass
1kg	= 1,000 grams (g)
1 gram (g)	= 0.001 kg
1 milligram (mg)	= 0.001 g
1 microgram (μg)	= 0.000001 g

LIQUID VOLUME
1 kiloliter (kL)	= 1,000 L
1 liter (L)	= base unit of liquid volume
1 milliliter (mL)	= 0.001 L
1 mL	= 1 cm³

NOTE: When measuring liquid volume in a graduated cylinder, read the measurement at the bottom of the meniscus, or curve.

TEMPERATURE
In this textbook, the Celsius scale is used to express temperature measurements. In Celsius, 0° is the freezing point of water, and 100° is the boiling point of water. You can use the scale shown below to convert between the Celsius scale and the Fahrenheit scale.

°F (Fahrenheit)
0 10 20 30 40 50 60 70 80 90 100 110 120 130 140 150 160 170 180 190 200 210 220 230

−20 −10 0 10 20 30 40 50 60 70 80 90 100 110
°C (Celsius)
Freezing point of water   Boiling point of water

Parts of the Compound Light Microscope

- The **eyepiece** magnifies the image, usually 10×.

- The **low-power objective** further magnifies the image, up to 4×.

- The **high-power objectives** further magnify the image, from 10× to 43×.

- The **nosepiece** holds the objectives and can be turned to change from one objective to another.

- The **body tube** maintains the correct distance between the eyepiece and the objectives. This is usually about 25 cm (10 in.), the normal distance for reading and viewing objects with the naked eye.

- The **coarse adjustment** moves the body tube up and down in large increments to allow gross positioning and focusing of the objective lens.

- The **fine adjustment** moves the body tube slightly to bring the image into sharp focus.

- The **stage** supports a slide.

- The **stage clips** secure the slide in position for viewing.

- The **diaphragm** (not labeled), located under the stage, controls the amount of light that is allowed to pass through the object being viewed.

- The **light source** provides light for viewing the image. It can be either a light reflected with a mirror or an incandescent light from a small lamp. NEVER use reflected direct sunlight as a light source.

- The **arm** supports the body tube.

- The **base** supports the microscope.

EYEPIECE

BODY TUBE

NOSEPIECE

HIGH-POWER OBJECTIVE

LOW-POWER OBJECTIVE

STAGE CLIPS

STAGE

LIGHT SOURCE

BASE

ARM

COARSE ADJUSTMENT

FINE ADJUSTMENT

Proper Handling and Use of the Compound Light Microscope

1. Carry the microscope to your lab table using both hands, one supporting the base and the other holding the arm of the microscope. Hold the microscope close to your body.

2. Place the microscope on the lab table at least 5 cm (2 in.) from the edge of the table.

3. Check to see what type of light source the microscope has. If the microscope has a lamp, plug it in, making sure that the cord is out of the way. If the microscope has a mirror, adjust it to reflect light through the hole in the stage.

   CAUTION If your microscope has a mirror, do not use direct sunlight as a light source. Using direct sunlight can damage your eyes.

4. Adjust the revolving nosepiece so that the low-power objective is in line with the body tube.

5. Place a prepared slide over the hole in the stage, and secure the slide with the stage clips.

6. Look through the eyepiece, and move the diaphragm to adjust the amount of light that passes through the specimen.

7. Now look at the stage at eye level, and slowly turn the coarse adjustment to raise the stage until the objective almost touches the slide. Do not allow the objective to touch the slide.

8. While looking through the eyepiece, turn the coarse adjustment to lower the stage until the image is in focus. Never focus objectives downward. Use the fine adjustment to attain a sharply focused image. Keep both eyes open while viewing a slide.

9. Make sure that the image is exactly in the center of your field of vision. Then switch to the high-power objective. Focus the image with the fine adjustment. Never use the coarse adjustment at high power.

10. When you are finished using the microscope, remove the slide. Clean the eyepiece and objectives with lens paper, and return the microscope to its storage area.

Procedure for Making a Wet Mount

1. Use lens paper to clean a glass slide and coverslip.

2. Place the specimen that you wish to observe in the center of the slide.

3. Using a medicine dropper, place one drop of water on the specimen.

4. Position the coverslip so that it is at the edge of the drop of water and at a 45° angle to the slide. Make sure that the water runs along the edge of the coverslip.

5. Lower the coverslip slowly to avoid trapping air bubbles.

6. If a stain or solution will be added to a wet mount, place a drop of the staining solution on the microscope slide along one side of the coverslip. Place a small piece of paper towel on the opposite side of the coverslip.

7. As the water evaporates from the slide, add another drop of water by placing the tip of the medicine dropper next to the edge of the coverslip, just as you would if you were adding stains or solutions to a wet mount. If you have added too much water, remove the excess by using the corner of a paper towel as a blotter. Do not lift the coverslip to add or remove water.

Imagine that you could watch what happens within a plant cell during photosynthesis or that you could observe how drug use changes the human nervous system. You cannot do these things in a conventional laboratory exercise, but you can in an Interactive Exploration. By using the *Interactive Explorations in Biology* CD-ROMs, you can explore biological processes that are important to both human biology and cell biology. The instructions on these two pages describe how to use the CD-ROMs.

Using the CD-ROM
Interactive Explorations in Biology: Human Biology

1. Obtain the CD-ROM *Interactive Explorations in Biology: Human Biology* from your teacher. Load the disc into the CD-ROM drive as directed by your teacher.

2. An icon for the CD-ROM will appear on the screen. Click it, and then click the icon labeled "Start Explorations."

3. After a few moments, the title screen will appear. Click the button labeled "Menu" at the bottom right of the screen.

4. The computer will then display the menu screen, which lists all the Interactive Explorations on the disc. Select the Interactive Exploration that you would like to run, and click on its title.

5. After a few moments, the computer will display a screen containing a column of buttons along the right edge. This column is the Navigation Palette, and the buttons it contains enable you to access the various features found in each Interactive Exploration. To begin, click the top button of the column. This button displays a magnifying glass and is labeled "Interactive Investigation."

6. If you have questions about an Interactive Exploration, you can play the instructions for operating the Interactive Exploration by clicking the File menu at the top of the screen and selecting "Interactive Exploration Help." You may also refer to the User's Guide for additional information or help.

Using the CD-ROM
Interactive Explorations in Biology: Cell Biology and Genetics

1. Obtain the CD-ROM *Interactive Explorations in Biology: Cell Biology and Genetics* from your teacher. Load the disc into the CD-ROM drive as directed by your teacher.

2. An icon for the CD-ROM will appear on the screen. Click it, and then click the icon labeled "Start Explorations."

3. After a few moments, the title screen will appear. Click the button labeled "Menu" at the bottom right of the screen.

4. The computer will then display the menu screen, which lists all the Interactive Explorations on the disk. Select the Interactive Exploration that you would like to run, and click on its title.

5. After a few moments, the computer will display the Interactive Exploration and play a short narration that describes the problem you will be studying. (To shut off this narration, select "Sound Off" from the Sound menu at the top right of the screen.) After this brief narration has played, the Interactive Exploration is ready to run.

6. If you have questions about an Interactive Exploration, you can play the instructions for operating the Interactive Exploration by clicking the Help menu at the top of the screen, and selecting "How to Use This Exploration." Clicking the Help button on the Navigation Palette will call up instructions on how to use the features of the Navigation Palette. You may also refer to the User's Guide.

FEEDBACK METER: Displays a response to changes in variables

VARIABLES: Conditions that you can change in the Exploration

The classification of organisms in this textbook is based on the six-kingdom system described in Chapter 18. Not all groups are shown, and numbers of species are approximate. Also, since the division of the kingdoms Eubacteria and Archaebacteria into phyla is controversial, only broad, generally recognized groups are presented for these two kingdoms. As you read about the groups below that comprise the six kingdoms, bear in mind that the classification of organisms changes as new information about the evolutionary relationships among organisms is uncovered.

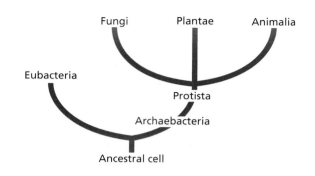

KINGDOM EUBACTERIA

Typically unicellular; prokaryotic: without membrane-bound organelles or a nucleus; nutrition mainly by absorption, but some are photosynthetic or chemosynthetic; includes anaerobic and aerobic species; reproduction usually by fission or budding; about 5,000 species have been recognized, but there are undoubtedly many thousand more

CYANOBACTERIA

Photosynthetic bacteria surrounded by a gooey, deeply pigmented covering; photosynthetic mechanism is very similar to that in plants; some species can fix nitrogen; had an important effect on life's evolution because photosynthesis by early cyanobacteria raised the oxygen content of the atmosphere; common on land and in the ocean; some early species were probably ancestors of chloroplasts in some kinds of protists: *Anabaena, Oscillatoria, Spirulina*

Salmonella

SPIROCHETES

Long, spiral cells with flagella originating at each end; aerobic and anaerobic heterotrophs; move with corkscrew-like motion; parasitic, symbiotic, or free-living; responsible for several serious diseases, including syphilis (*Treponema pallidum*) and Lyme disease (*Borrelia burgdorferi*)

PROTEOTIC BACTERIA

A large, metabolically and ecologically diverse group of Gram-negative bacteria; includes anaerobes and aerobes, heterotrophs and autotrophs; free-living, symbiotic, and parasitic species; many species are of great ecological or medical significance; examples include nitrogen-fixing *Azotobacter* and *Rhizobium*, pathogens such as *Rickettsia rickettsii* (Rocky Mountain spotted fever), *Salmonella typhi* (typhoid), and *Vibrio cholerae* (cholera), and intestinal symbionts such as *Escherichia coli*

GRAM-POSITIVE BACTERIA

A group of predominantly Gram-positive bacteria; heterotrophic; anaerobic and aerobic species; many can form endospores to resist unfavorable environmental conditions: *Streptococcus, Staphylococcus, Lactobacillus, Bacillus, Clostridium*

CHLAMYDIAE

A small group of obligate intracellular parasites that infect endothermic hosts; heterotrophic; cell walls do not have peptidoglycan; *Chlamydia trachomatis* causes chlamydia, one of the most common sexually transmitted diseases in humans

KINGDOM ARCHAEBACTERIA

Methanosarcina

Anaerobic and aerobic prokaryotes that are bio-chemically distinct from eubacteria; many species are adapted to environments with extreme tempera-tures, acidity, or salt content; differ from eubacteria in structure of cell membrane and cell wall; RNA polymerase and ribosomal RNA sequences are simi-lar to those in eukaryotes, suggesting that archae-bacteria are more closely related to eukaryotes than to eubacteria; undergo asexual reproduction only; fewer than 100 named species, divided into three broad groups

METHANOGENS

Anaerobic methane producers; most species use carbon dioxide as a carbon source; found in soil, swamps, and the digestive tract of animals, particularly grazing mammals such as cattle; also inhabit the human large intestine; produce nearly 2 trillion kg (2 billion tons) of methane gas annually: *Methanococcus, Methanosarcina*

THERMOACIDOPHILES

Inhabit very hot environments that are often very acidic; some species can tolerate temperatures of 110°C (230°F); require sulfur; nearly all are anaer-obes: *Sulfolobus, Pyrodictium*

EXTREME HALOPHILES

Live in environments with very high salt content, including the Dead Sea and the Great Salt Lake; nearly all are aerobic; all are Gram-negative: *Heliobacterium, Halococcus*

KINGDOM PROTISTA

A catchall kingdom for the eukaryotes that are not plants, fungi, or animals; the most structurally diverse kingdom; unicellular and multicellular repre-sentatives; all have a membrane-bound nucleus; nearly all have chromosomes, mitochondria, and internal compartments; many have chloroplasts; most have cell walls; reproduce sexually and asexu-ally; more than 60,000 living species

PHYLUM SARCODINA

Heterotrophic, unicellular protists that move and feed with flexible cytoplasmic extensions called pseudopods; aquatic (fresh and salt water) and ter-restrial forms; most are free-living, but a few are par-asitic; undergo asexual and sexual reproduction: amoebas, radiolarians, foraminiferans (*Entamoeba, Amoeba*); several hundred living species

PHYLUM CILIOPHORA

Very complex single cells; heterotrophic; have rows of cilia and two types of cell nuclei: ciliates (*Didinium, Paramecium, Stentor, Vorticella*); about 8,000 species

PHYLUM ZOOMASTIGINA

Mostly unicellular; heterotrophic; all have at least one flagellum: zoomastigotes (*Giardia, Leishmania, Trichonympha, Trypanosoma*); about 2,500 species

PHYLUM SPOROZOA

Unicellular, heterotrophic, spore-forming parasites of animals; have complex life cycles with asexual and sexual stages; nonmobile as adults; *Plasmodium* is responsible for malaria, which kills more than 2 mil-lion people each year: sporozoans (*Plasmodium, Toxoplasma*); about 6,000 species

PHYLUM MYXOMYCOTA

Heterotrophic; stream along as a multinucleate mass of cytoplasm; when dry or starving, can give rise to spores that start a new individual in a more favor-able environment: plasmodial slime molds (*Physarum*); about 450 species

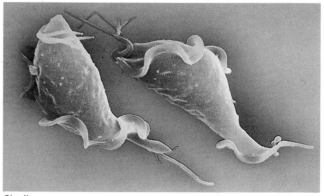
Giardia

PHYLUM ACRASIOMYCOTA

Heterotrophic, amoeba-shaped cells that aggregate into a moving mass called a slug when deprived of food; cells within the slug retain their membranes and do not fuse; a slug produces spores that form new amoebas elsewhere: cellular slime molds (*Dictyostelium*); about 65 species

PHYLUM OOMYCOTA

Heterotrophic, unicellular parasites or decomposers; cell walls composed of cellulose, not chitin as in fungi; asexual and sexual reproduction: water molds, white rusts, downy mildews (*Phytophthora, Plasmopara*); about 580 species

PHYLUM CHYTRIDIOMYCOTA

Funguslike, heterotrophic decomposers and parasites with cell walls of chitin; most are unicellular; gametes and zoospores have a single, posterior flagellum; live in water and the soil: chytrids (*Allomyces*); about 750 species (some scientists place this group within the kingdom Fungi)

PHYLUM CHLOROPHYTA

Unicellular, colonial, and multicellular algae; all are photosynthetic; have chlorophylls *a* and *b;* use starch to store food; contain chloroplasts very similar to those of plants; most scientists think that plants descended from this group: green algae (*Chlamydomonas, Chlorella, Oedogonium, Spyrogyra, Ulva, Volvox*); about 7,000 species

PHYLUM PHAEOPHYTA

Multicellular and photosynthetic; nearly all are marine; contain chlorophylls *a* and *c* and fucoxanthin, the source of their brownish color; store food as laminarin: brown algae (*Fucus, Laminaria, Postelsia, Sargassum*); about 1,500 species

PHYLUM RHODOPHYTA

Almost all are multicellular; all are photosynthetic; most are marine; contain chlorophyll *a* and phycobilins; chloroplasts probably evolved from symbiotic cyanobacteria: red algae (*Porphyra*); about 4,000 species

PHYLUM BACILLARIOPHYTA

Unicellular photosynthetic inhabitants of fresh and salt water; secrete a unique shell made of opaline silica that resembles a box with a lid; chloroplasts resemble those of brown algae; contain chlorophylls *a* and *c* and fucoxanthin; important component of plankton: diatoms; more than 11,500 species

PHYLUM DINOFLAGELLATA

Unicellular and aquatic; heterotrophic and autotrophic species; mostly marine; body is enclosed within two cellulose plates; most have two flagella; contain chlorophylls *a* and *c* and carotenoids: dinoflagellates (*Gonyaulax, Noctiluca*); about 1,100 species

PHYLUM CHRYSOPHYTA

Photosynthetic, usually aquatic, and often colonial; two flagella at the end of each cell; golden brown color imparted by carotenoid pigments; can form durable cysts to survive adverse environmental conditions: golden algae; about 850 species

PHYLUM EUGLENOPHYTA

Unicellular; cells lack a cell wall and are surrounded by a flexible protein covering called pellicle; both photosynthetic and heterotrophic species; asexual reproduction; most live in fresh water; chloroplasts are similar to those of green algae and are thought to have evolved from the same symbiotic bacteria: euglenoids (*Euglena*); about 1,000 species

KINGDOM FUNGI

Eukaryotic heterotrophs with nutrition by absorption; all but yeasts are multicellular; nearly all are terrestrial; body is typically composed of filaments (called hyphae) and is multinucleate, with incomplete divisions (called septa) between cells; cell walls are made of chitin; asexual or sexual reproduction; about 100,000 species

PHYLUM ASCOMYCOTA

Hyphae usually have perforated septa; fusion of hyphae leads to formation of densely interwoven mass that contains characteristic microscopic reproductive structures called asci; terrestrial, marine, and freshwater species: brewer's and baker's yeasts, molds, morels, truffles (*Neurospora, Saccharomyces, Candida*); more than 60,000 species

PHYLUM BASIDIOMYCOTA

Hyphae usually have incomplete septa; reproduction is typically sexual; fusion of hyphae leads to the formation of a densely interwoven reproductive structure (mushroom) with characteristic microscopic, club-shaped structures called basidia; terrestrial: mushrooms, toadstools, shelf fungi, rusts, smuts; about 25,000 species

PHYLUM ZYGOMYCOTA

Usually lack septa; fusion of hyphae leads directly to formation of a zygote, which divides by meiosis when it germinates; terrestrial or parasitic: bread molds (*Pilobolus, Rhizopus*); about 660 species

Amanita muscaria

KINGDOM PLANTAE

Multicellular, eukaryotic, autotrophic, terrestrial organisms with tissues and organs; cell walls contain cellulose; chlorophylls *a* and *b* are present and are localized in plastids; all have alternation of generations between diploid sporophyte and haploid gametophyte; about 270,000 species

PHYLUM BRYOPHYTA

Small and usually found in moist environments; most lack vascular tissues; gametophyte is the dominant generation; gametophyte lacks roots, stems, and leaves and is anchored to a substrate by projections called rhizoids: mosses (*Sphagnum*); about 10,000 species

PHYLUM HEPATOPHYTA

Gametophyte is dominant, usually small, and grows close to the ground; gametophyte lacks stomata, vascular tissue, roots, stems, and leaves; sporophyte is inconspicuous and dependent on the gametophyte: liverworts (*Marchantia*); about 6,500 species

PHYLUM ANTHOCEROPHYTA

Gametophyte is the dominant generation; usually small and flat; stoma are present on sporophyte; lack vascular tissue, roots, stems, and leaves; contain a single chloroplast per cell: hornworts (*Anthoceros*); about 100 species

PHYLUM PSILOTOPHYTA

Vascular system present; seedless; no roots or leaves; gametophyte is small and independent; sporophyte is dominant and has small leaves: whisk ferns (*Psilotum*); about 10 species

PHYLUM LYCOPHYTA

Vascular system present; sporophyte is dominant and mosslike; has roots, stems, and leaves; gametophyte is small and independent; seedless: club mosses (*Lycopodium, Selaginella*); about 1,000 species

PHYLUM SPHENOPHYTA

Vascular system present; gametophyte is small and independent; sporophyte is dominant; roots are present; seedless: horsetails (*Equisetum*); 15 species

PHYLUM PTEROPHYTA

Vascular system present; gametophyte is small and independent; sporophyte generation is dominant; has roots, stems, and leaves; seedless: ferns (*Salvinia*); about 12,000 species

PHYLUM CYCADOPHYTA

Palmlike gymnosperms; vascular system present; male and female cones produced on different trees; naked seeds; sporophyte is dominant; tropical and subtropical: cycads (*Cycas*); about 100 species

PHYLUM CONIFEROPHYTA

Gymnosperms that produce cones; vascular system lacks vessels; leaves are usually needles or scales; typically evergreen; sporophyte is dominant; ovules are exposed at time of pollination; pollen is dispersed by wind: pines, spruces, firs, redwoods, cypresses, yews; about 550 species

PHYLUM GNETOPHYTA

Specialized gymnosperms; vascular system contains water-conducting vessels; seeds are naked; sporophyte dominant: gnetophytes (*Ephedra, Welwitschia*); about 70 species

PHYLUM GINKGOPHYTA

Deciduous, gymnosperm tree; vascular system is present; has fanlike leaves; sporophyte is dominant; produces conelike male reproductive structures and uncovered seeds on different individuals: the ginkgo, *Ginkgo biloba*, is the only living species

PHYLUM ANTHOPHYTA

Angiosperms; vascular system present; sporophyte is dominant, ovules are fully enclosed by ovary, gametophyte greatly reduced after fertilization, ovary and seed mature to become fruit; flowers are reproductive structures: flowering plants (*Aster, Prunus, Quercus, Zea*); about 240,000 species

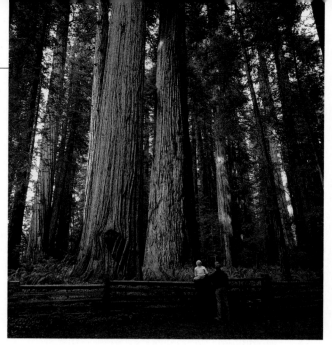

Redwoods

Class Monocotyledones

Embryo has one cotyledon; flower parts in threes; leaf veins are parallel; vascular bundles are scattered through stem tissue: grasses, sedges, lilies, irises, palms, orchids; around 70,000 species

Class Dicotyledones

Embryo has two cotyledons; flower parts in fours or fives; leaves have netlike veins; vascular bundles in orderly arrangement in stems: roses, maples, elms, cactuses; about 170,000 species

KINGDOM ANIMALIA

Multicellular, eukaryotic, heterotrophic organisms; nutrition mainly by ingestion; most have specialized tissues, and many have organs and organ systems; no cell walls or chloroplasts; sexual reproduction predominates; both aquatic and terrestrial forms; more than 1 million species

PHYLUM PORIFERA

Typically asymmetrical; lack tissues and organs; body wall consists of two cell layers penetrated by numerous pores; internal cavity is lined with unique food-filtering cells called choanocytes; adults are sessile; mostly marine; sexual and asexual reproduction: sponges; about 10,000 species

PHYLUM CNIDARIA

Radially symmetrical and gelatinous; most have distinct tissues; baglike body of two cell layers; marine and freshwater species: hydras, jellyfishes, corals, sea anemones (*Hydra, Obelia*); about 10,000 species

Class Hydrozoa

Most have both polyp and medusa stages in life cycle; usually colonial: hydras, Portuguese men-of-war; about 3,700 species

Class Scyphozoa

Exclusively marine; medusa stage is usually dominant: jellyfishes; about 200 species

Class Anthozoa

Marine; solitary or colonial; medusa stage absent: sea anemones, corals, sea fans; about 6,100 species

PHYLUM CTENOPHORA

Transparent, gelatinous marine animals resembling jellyfishes; radially symmetrical; propelled by cilia: comb jellies; about 100 species

PHYLUM PLATYHELMINTHES

Body flat and ribbonlike, without true segments; bilaterally symmetrical acoelomates; organs present; three germ layers: flatworms (*Dugesia, Planaria, Schistosoma*) more than 18,000 species

Class Turbellaria

Mostly free-living aquatic or terrestrial forms: planarians (*Dugesia*); about 4,500 species

Class Trematoda

Internal parasites with mouth at anterior end; often have complex life cycle with alternation of hosts: human blood flukes (*Schistosoma*), human liver fluke (*Chlonorchis sinensis*); about 9,000 species

Class Cestoda

Extremely specialized internal parasites; hooked scolex for attaching to host: tapeworms (*Taenia*); about 5,000 species

PHYLUM ROTIFERA

Small, wormlike or spherical animals; bilaterally symmetrical and transparent; pseudocoelomates; almost all live in fresh water: rotifers; about 1,750 species

PHYLUM NEMATODA

Typically tiny, parasitic, unsegmented worms; body slender and elongated; pseudocoelomates with one-way gut; includes important human parasites such as *Ascaris,* pinworms, hookworms, *Trichinella*, and *Wuchereria*: roundworms; more than 80,000 species

PHYLUM MOLLUSCA

Soft-bodied animals with a true coelom; usually two-part body plan consisting of head-foot and visceral mass; visceral mass is covered by mantle; protostomes; most have a unique rasping tongue called a radula; terrestrial, freshwater, and marine: clams, snails, octopuses, squids, mussels, slugs; more than 110,000 species

Class Cephalopoda

Foot modified into tentacles; closed circulatory system: squids, octopuses, nautiluses; over 600 species

Class Bivalvia

Two shells connected by a hinge; no radula; large, wedge-shaped foot: clams, oysters, scallops; more than 10,000 species

Class Gastropoda

Visceral mass twisted during development; head, distinct eyes, and tentacles usually present: snails, slugs, whelks; about 90,000 species

Class Polyplacophora

Elongated body and reduced head: chitons; about 600 species

PHYLUM ANNELIDA

Serially segmented worms; bilaterally symmetrical; protostomes: annelids; about 15,000 species

Class Polychaeta

Fleshy outgrowths called parapodia extend from segments; marine; many bristles: sandworms

Class Oligochaeta

Head not well developed; no parapodia; terrestrial and freshwater forms: earthworms

Class Hirudinea

Body flattened; no parapodia; usually suckers at both ends; many are external parasites: leeches

PHYLUM ARTHROPODA

Segmented bodies with paired, jointed appendages; bilaterally symmetrical coelomates; chitinous exoskeleton; protostomes; aerial, terrestrial, and aquatic forms: arthropods; about 1 million species

Subphylum Chelicerata

Distinguished by absence of antennae and presence of chelicerae; all appendages are unbranched; four pairs of walking legs; body has two regions (cephalothorax and abdomen); predominantly terrestrial

Class Merostomata

Cephalothorax covered by protective "shell"; sharp spike on tail: horseshoe crabs (*Limulus*); 4 species

Class Pycnogonida

Small, marine predators or parasites; usually four pairs of legs but sometimes five or six pairs: sea spiders; about 1,000 species

Class Arachnida

Terrestrial; book lungs and tracheae for respiration: spiders, scorpions, ticks, mites; about 70,000 species

Lone star tick

Subphylum Crustacea

Two pairs of antennae; chewing mandibles; appendages with two branches; predominantly aquatic: crayfish, lobsters, crabs, shrimps, sowbugs; about 40,000 species

Subphylum Uniramia

Have antennae, mandibles, and unbranched appendages

Class Chilopoda

Body flattened and consisting of 15 to 170 or more segments; one pair of legs attached to each segment; carnivorous: centipedes; about 2,500 species

Class Diplopoda

Elongated body of 15 to 200 segments; two pairs of legs per segment; primarily herbivorous: millipedes; about 10,000 species

Class Insecta

Body has three regions—head, thorax, and abdomen; three pairs of legs, all attached to thorax; usually two pairs of wings: insects; about 750,000 described species, but millions more may exist

Order Thysanura: silverfishes
Order Ephemeroptera: mayflies
Order Odonata: dragonflies, damsel flies
Order Orthoptera: grasshoppers, cockroaches, walking sticks, praying mantises, crickets
Order Isoptera: termites
Order Dermaptera: earwigs
Order Anoplura: sucking lice
Order Hemiptera: true bugs—water striders, water boatmen, back swimmers, bedbugs, squash bugs, stink bugs, assassin bugs
Order Homoptera: cicadas, aphids, leaf hoppers, scale insects
Order Neuroptera: ant lions, lacewings
Order Coleoptera: beetles—ladybugs, fireflies, boll weevils
Order Lepidoptera: butterflies and moths
Order Diptera: flies, mosquitoes, gnats, midges
Order Siphonaptera: fleas
Order Hymenoptera: bees, ants, wasps, hornets

PHYLUM ECHINODERMATA

Deuterostomes; adults are radially symmetrical with five-part body plan; most forms have a water vascular system with tube feet for locomotion; marine: echinoderms; about 7,000 species

Class Crinoidea

Mouth faces upward and is surrounded by many arms: sea lilies, feather stars; about 600 species

Class Asteroidea

Body usually has five arms and double rows of tube feet on each arm; mouth directed downward: sea stars; about 1,500 species

Class Ophiuroidea

Usually has five slender, delicate arms or rays: brittle stars, basket stars; about 2,000 species

Class Echinoidea

Body spherical, oval, or disk-shaped; arms lacking but five-part body plan still apparent: sea urchins, sand dollars; about 900 species

Class Holothuroidea

Elongated, thickened body with tentacles around the mouth: sea cucumbers; about 1,500 species

PHYLUM HEMICHORDATA

Wormlike relatives of chordates; deuterostomes; body in three regions: acorn worms; about 90 species

PHYLUM CHORDATA

Bilaterally symmetrical; deuterostomes; coelom present; have a notochord, a dorsal nerve cord, pharyngeal slits, and a tail at some stage of life; aquatic and terrestrial; more than 47,000 species

Subphylum Urochordata

Body with saclike covering, or tunic, in adults; larvae are free-swimming and have nerve cord and notochord; marine: tunicates; about 2,000 species

Subphylum Cephalochordata

Small and fishlike with a permanent notochord; filter feeders: lancelets (*Branchiostoma*); about 25 species

Subphylum Vertebrata

Most of the notochord is replaced by a spinal column composed of vertebrae that protect the dorsal nerve cord; recognizable head containing a brain: vertebrates; about 45,000 species

Class Agnatha

Freshwater or marine eel-like fishes without jaws, scales, or paired fins; cartilaginous skeleton: lampreys, hagfishes; about 80 species

Class Chondrichthyes

Fishes with jaws and paired fins; gills present; no swim bladder; cartilaginous skeleton: sharks, rays, skates; about 800 species

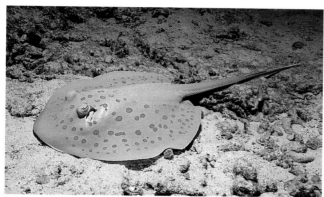
Blue-spotted stingray

Class Osteichthyes

Freshwater and marine fishes with gills attached to gill arch; jaws and paired fins; bony skeleton; most have swim bladder: bony fishes; about 23,000 species

Class Amphibia

Freshwater or terrestrial; gills present at some stage; skin is often slimy and lacking scales; eggs typically laid in water and fertilized externally: amphibians; about 4,500 species

Order Apoda: caecilians
Order Urodela: salamanders and newts
Order Anura: frogs and toads

Class Reptilia

Terrestrial or semiaquatic vertebrates; breathe with lungs at all stages; body covered by scales; most species lay amniotic eggs covered with a protective shell; fertilization internal: reptiles; about 6,000 species

Order Rhynchocephalia: tuataras
Order Chelonia: turtles and tortoises
Order Crocodilia: alligators, crocodiles, gavials, caimans
Order Squamata: lizards and snakes

Class Aves

Body covered with feathers; forelimbs modified into wings; four-chambered heart; endothermic; lay shelled, amniotic eggs: birds; about 10,000 species

Order Gaviiformes: loons
Order Pelecaniformes: pelicans, cormorants, ganets
Order Ciconiiformes: herons, bitterns, egrets, storks, spoonbills, ibises
Order Anseriformes: ducks, geese, swans
Order Falconiformes: hawks, falcons, eagles, kites, vultures
Order Galliformes: pheasants, turkeys, quails, partridges, grouse

Order Gruiformes: cranes, coots, gallinules, rails
Order Charadriiformes: snipes, sandpipers, plovers, gulls, terns, auks, puffins, ibises
Order Procellariiformes: albatrosses, petrels
Order Columbiformes: pigeons and doves
Order Psittaciformes: parrots, parakeets, macaws, cockatoos
Order Cuculiformes: cuckoos, roadrunners
Order Strigiformes: owls
Order Caprimulgiformes: goatsuckers, whippoor-wills, nighthawks
Order Apodiformes: swifts, hummingbirds
Order Coraciiformes: kingfishers
Order Sphenisciformes: penguins
Order Piciformes: woodpeckers, sapsuckers, flickers, toucans, honeyguides
Order Passeriformes: robins, bluebirds, sparrows, warblers, thrushes
Order Struthioniformes: ostriches

Class Mammalia

Hair on at least part of body; young nourished with milk secreted by mammary glands; endothermic; breathe with lungs: mammals; about 4,400 species

Order Monotremata: duckbill platypuses and spiny anteaters
Order Marsupialia: opossums, kangaroos, koalas, wallabies
Order Insectivora: moles and shrews
Order Chiroptera: bats
Order Edentata: armadillos, sloths, anteaters
Order Pholidota: pangolins
Order Rodentia: squirrels, woodchucks, mice, rats, muskrats, beavers
Order Lagomorpha: rabbits, hares, pikas
Order Carnivora: bears, weasels, mink, otters, skunks, lions, tigers, wolves, seals
Order Cetacea: whales, porpoises, dolphins
Order Sirenia: sea cows, dugongs, manatees
Order Proboscidea: elephants
Order Pinnipedia: seals, sea lions, walruses
Order Perissodactyla: tapirs, rhinoceroses, horses, zebras
Order Artiodactyla: hippopotamuses, camels, llamas, deer, giraffes, cattle, sheep, goats
Order Primates: monkeys, lemurs, gibbons, orangutans, gorillas, chimpanzees, humans
Order Macroscelidea: elephant shrews
Order Scandentia: tree shrews
Order Hyracoidea: hyraxes
Order Dermoptera: flying lemurs
Order Tubulidentata: aardvark

GLOSSARY

Phonetic Key

Capital letters indicate primary stress. Small caps indicate secondary stress.

Sound symbol	Key word(s)	Phonetic respelling
a	map	MAP
ay	face day	FAYS DAY
ah	father cot	FAH-thuhr KAHT
aw	caught law	KAWT LAW
ee	eat ski	EET SKEE
e	wet rare	WET RER
oy	boy foil	BOY FOYL
ow	out now	OWT NOW
oo	shoot suit	SHOOT SOOT
u	book put	BUK PUT
uh	sun cut	SUHN KUHT
i	lip	LIP
ie	tide sigh	TIED SIE
oh	over coat	OH-vuhr KOHT
yoo	yule globule	YOOL GLAH-byool
yu	cure	KYUR
uhr	paper fern	PAY-puhr FUHRN
k	card kite	KAHRD KIET
s	cell sit	SEL SIT
y	yes	YES
j	job	JAHB
g	got	GAHT
zh	pleasure	PLE-zhuhr

Each page number provided indicates where the word is defined and not necessarily where it is first used. Remember to refer to the index for more page numbers if further investigation is needed.

A

abdomen a posterior segment of an animal that usually houses the organs of digestion and excretion (748)

abiotic factor any nonliving component of an ecosystem (368)

aboral surface the surface opposite the mouth on an echinoderm (785)

abscisic acid a hormone in plants that helps regulate the growth of buds and the germination of seeds (651)

abscission zone the area at the base of a leaf petiole where the leaf breaks off from the stem (651)

absorption in digestion, the movement of nutrients to the circulatory system (988)

accessory pigment a pigment that absorbs light energy and transfers energy to chlorophyll *a* in photosynthesis (113)

acclimation the process of an organism's adjustment to an abiotic factor (370)

acetyl coenzyme A (acetyl CoA) the compound that reacts with oxaloacetic acid in the first step of the Krebs cycle (134)

acid any substance that increases the concentration of hydrogen (H+) ions when added to a water solution (41)

acne an inflammatory disorder of the sebaceous glands characterized by skin lesions in the form of pimples, blackheads, and sometimes cysts (924)

acoelomate an animal with no coelom, or body cavity (686)

acquired immune deficiency syndrome (AIDS) a group of diseases resulting from a viral disruption of the immune system (968)

actin one of the two protein filaments in a muscle cell that function in contraction (79)

actinomycete a member of a class of bacteria characterized as rod-shaped monerans that form branched filaments (472)

activation energy amount of energy required for a chemical reaction to start and to continue on its own (36)

active transport the movement of a substance across a cell membrane against a concentration gradient; requires the cell to expend energy (101)

acyclovir an antiviral drug (498)

adapt in populations, to change genetically over generations to become more suited to the environment (288)

adaptation an inherited trait that increases an organism's chance of survival in a particular environment (288)

adaptive radiation an evolutionary pattern in which many species evolve from a single ancestral species (292)

addiction a dependency on a drug (1068)

adductor muscle the muscle with which a bivalve closes its shell (728)

adenine a nitrogen-containing base that is a component of a nucleotide (185)

adenosine diphosphate (ADP) a substance involved in energy metabolism formed by the breakdown of adenosine triphosphate (116)

adenosine triphosphate (ATP) a molecule present in all living cells and acting as an energy source for metabolic processes (54)

adhesion the attractive force between unlike substances (51)

adrenal gland an endocrine gland located on the top of a kidney (1034)

adrenaline epinephrine; a hormone secreted by the adrenal medulla that raises the level of glucose in the blood, increases the heartbeat, and raises blood pressure (1034)

adrenocorticotropic hormone a hormone that stimulates the adrenal cortex (1035)

aerobic respiration the process in which cells make ATP by breaking down organic compounds, with oxygen as the final electron acceptor (133)

afferent neuron a neuron that conducts impulses toward the central nervous system (1008)

aflatoxin a toxic fungal poison that causes liver cancer; found as contaminants in peanuts and corn; produced by species of *Aspergillus* (551)

afterbirth the remains of the placenta and the amnion, expelled from the mother's body following birth (1058)

agar a gel-like base for culturing microbes; extracted from the cell walls of red algae (531)

age structure the distribution of individuals among different ages in a population (382)

alcoholic fermentation the process by which pyruvic acid is converted to ethyl alcohol; the anaerobic action of yeast on sugars (129)

alcoholism the disease of addiction to ethanol (1072)

aldosterone a hormone that helps maintain water and salt balance (1035)

algae autotrophic protists (5)

allantois in amniotic eggs, the membranous sac that contains many blood vessels; in humans, a membrane surrounding the embryo that becomes the umbilical cord (842)

allele an alternative form of a gene (169)

allele frequency the percentage of an allele in a gene pool (300)

allergen a usually harmless antigen in the environment that is capable of inducing an allergic reaction (964)

allergy immune reaction to an allergen (964)

alternation of generations a sexual life

cycle in plants and algae involving two or more phases (581)

altricial referring to birds that, at hatching, are immature and in need of parental care (870)

altruistic behavior sacrifice by one individual that results in a benefit for another individual (774)

alveolus one of the tiny air sacs found in the lungs (945)

amebic dysentery a sometimes fatal disease caused by an amoeba that enters the body in contaminated food or water (513)

amebocyte in sponges, an amoebalike cell that moves through the body cells, supplying nutrients, removing wastes, and transporting sperm during sexual reproduction (694)

amino acid a carboxylic acid with an amino group; one of 20 monomers that form proteins (56)

amino acid–based hormones a group of hormones that includes proteins, peptides, amino acids, and other forms derived from amino acids (1029)

ammonification in the nitrogen cycle, the formation of ammonia compounds (423)

amniocentesis a procedure used in fetal diagnosis in which fetal cells are removed from the amniotic fluid (232)

amnion one of four membranes of an amniotic egg; surrounds and protects the embryo (842)

amniotic egg the four-membrane egg of a terrestrial vertebrate (842)

ampulla a bulblike sac at the base of the tube foot of an echinoderm that functions in movement (786)

anal pore in protozoa, an opening from which wastes are eliminated (514)

analogous structure in evolution, structures in more than one organism that have similar appearance and function, but different embryological origin (290)

anaphase a phase of mitosis and meiosis in which the chromosomes separate (150)

androgen a hormone secreted by the testes that controls secondary sex characteristics (1035)

angiosperm a flowering plant (581)

annelid a bilaterally symmetrical, segmented worm, such as an earthworm or a leech (733)

annual ring a yearly growth ring in a woody plant (611)

antenna a sensory appendage on the head of an arthropod (748)

anterior the front end of a bilaterally symmetrical organism (670)

anther the microsporangium of an angiosperm in which pollen grains are produced (166)

antheridium in plants, algae, and fungi a reproductive structure that produces gametes by mitosis (625)

anthropoid primate one of a subgroup of primates that includes monkeys and apes (320)

antibiotic a chemical that can inhibit the growth of some bacteria (472)

antibody a protein produced by B cells that binds to antigens (940)

anticodon a region of tRNA consisting of three bases complementary to the codon of mRNA (195)

antidiuretic hormone a hormone that helps regulate solute concentration in the blood (1033)

antigen a substance that stimulates an immune response (960)

anus the posterior opening of the digestive tract (809)

aorta the largest artery in the human body; carries blood from the left ventricle to systemic circulation (932)

aortic valve the semilunar valve on the left side of the heart (932)

aphotic zone the ocean layer that receives no light (431)

apical dominance a plant growth pattern in which branches near the shoot tip are shorter than branches farther from the shoot tip (649)

apical meristem the growing region at the tips of stems and roots in plants (602)

appendage any complex part or organ extending from the body (743)

appendicular skeleton in vertebrates, the bones that form the limbs (909)

aqueous solution a solution in which water is the solvent (40)

arachnid an arthropod with four pairs of walking legs; a spider, scorpion, mite, or tick (751)

arachnoid membrane the middle layer of the three sacs that surround the brain and spinal cord (1007)

archaebacterium a prokaryotic organism distinguished from other prokaryotes by the composition of the cell membranes and walls (467)

archegonium in seedless plants, a reproductive structure that produces a single egg by mitosis (625)

arteriole a branch of an artery that gives rise to capillaries (934)

artery a vessel that carries blood away from the heart to the body's organs (934)

arthropod segmented animal with jointed appendages and an exoskeleton (742)

artificial selection breeding of organisms by humans for specific phenotypic characteristics (292)

ascocarp the fruiting body of an ascomycete (548)

ascogonium a gamete-producing structure in ascomycetes (548)

ascospore one of eight haploid cells in an ascus (548)

ascus a spore sac that forms on the surface of an ascocarp (548)

asexual reproduction the production of offspring that does not involve the union of gametes (156)

asteroid-impact hypothesis the hypothesis that the extinction of the dinosaurs was caused by the impact of a huge asteroid (840)

asthma a chronic respiratory condition characterized by recurring attacks of wheezing, coughing, and labored breathing (1066)

atherosclerosis a disease characterized by the buildup of fatty materials on the interior walls of the arteries (936)

atom the simplest particle of an element that retains all the properties of that element (32)

atomic number the number of protons in an atom (32)

ATP synthase an enzyme that catalyzes the synthesis of ATP from ADP and phosphate (116)

atrioventricular node a group of nerves in the heart that functions in the heartbeat (933)

atrioventricular valve a one-way valve separating each atrium from the ventricle beneath it (931)

atrium an anterior chamber of the heart (931)

attenuated strain refers to a preparation of a virus for a vaccine in which the virus is incapable of causing disease under normal circumstances (497)

auditory canal the tube through which air enters the ear (1018)

australopithecine early hominid from the genus *Australopithecus* (325)

autoimmune disease a disorder in which the immune system attacks the organism's own cells (965)

autonomic nervous system a division of the peripheral nervous system that controls the involuntary actions that regulate the body's internal environment (1010)

autosome a chromosome that is not a sex chromosome (146)

autotomy the ability of an organism to deliberately drop a body part, most often to escape a predator (852)

autotroph an organism that uses energy to synthesize organic molecules from inorganic substances (10)

auxin a plant hormone that regulates cell elongation (647)

axial skeleton the backbone, skull, and associated bones of vertebrates (909)

axon in a neuron, an elongated extension that carries impulses away from the cell body (1003)

azidothymidine (AZT) an antiviral drug that inhibits the reverse transcriptase of retroviruses, such as HIV (498)

B

B cell a lymphocyte that produces antibodies in response to antigens (959)

bacillus a rod-shaped bacterium (470)

bacteriophage a virus that infects bacteria (491)

baleen one of the keratinous plates that function to filter food from water in some whales (886)

ball-and-socket joint allows movement in all directions, as in the shoulder (913)

barb a branch of a vane in the feather of a bird (864)

barbule a branch of a barb in the feather of a bird (864)

base any substance that increases the concentration of hydroxide (OH^-) ions when added to a water solution (42)

base unit one of seven fundamental units of SI measurement that describe length, mass, time, and other quantities (23)

base-pairing rule the rule stating that in DNA, cytosine pairs with guanine and adenine pairs with thymine and in RNA, adenine pairs with uracil (187)

basidiocarp the fruiting body of a basidiomycete (547)

basidium a specialized club-shaped reproductive structure that forms on the gills of mushrooms (547)

benign tumor an abnormal but non-threatening cell mass (211)

benthic zone the ocean bottom (431)

biennial a plant having a two-year life cycle (658)

bilateral symmetry in animals, a body plan in which the left and right sides mirror each other (670)

bile a yellowish fluid secreted by the liver that functions as a fat emulsifier in digestion (809)

binary fission an asexual cell division of prokaryotes that produces identical offspring (148)

binomial nomenclature a system of naming organisms that uses the genus name and a species identifier (339)

biochemical pathway a series of chemical reactions in which the product of one reaction is consumed in the next reaction (111)

biodiversity the number and variety of organisms in a given area during a specific period of time (448)

biogenesis the theory that living organisms come only from other living organisms (261)

biogeochemical cycle the process by which materials necessary for organisms are circulated through the environment (420)

biogeography study of the geographical distribution of fossils and living organisms (281)

biological species concept the principle that defines a species as those organisms that can produce offspring together (310)

bioluminescence the production of light by means of a chemical reaction in an organism (702)

biomass the dry weight of organic material in an ecosystem (415)

biome a geographic area characterized by specific kinds of plants and animals (424)

biosphere the area on and around Earth where life exists (363)

biotic factor a living component of an ecosystem (368)

bipedalism the ability to walk upright on two legs (319)

bipinnaria the larva of echinoderms (787)

birth rate the number of births occurring in a period of time (381)

bivalve an aquatic mollusk with a shell divided into two halves connected by a hinge, such as a clam, oyster, or scallop (728)

blade the broad, flat portion of a typical leaf (616)

blastocoel the central cavity of a blastula (683)

blastopore a depression formed when cells of the blastula move inward (344)

blastula a hollow ball of cells formed when a zygote undergoes repeated cycles of cell division (344)

blight a disease of plants characterized by quickly developing decay and discoloring of leaves, stems, and flowers (535)

blood alcohol concentration (BAC) a measurement of the amount of alcohol in a person's blood (1071)

blood pressure the force that blood exerts against the walls of a blood vessel (934)

blood type a specific characteristic of the blood of an individual; A, B, AB, or O, depending on the type of antigen present on the surface of the red blood cell (941)

bolting the rapid lengthening of internodes caused by gibberellic acid (658)

bone marrow the soft tissue in the center and ends of long bones where blood cells are produced (911)

book lung in the abdomen of an arachnid, an organ for gas exchange with parallel folds that resembles the pages of a book (752)

botany the scientific study of plants (561)

Bowman's capsule cup-shaped structure of the nephron of a kidney which encloses the glomerulus and in which filtration takes place (991)

brain stem the region of the brain that lies posterior to the cerebrum and that connects the cerebrum to the spinal cord (1007)

broad-spectrum antibiotic an antibiotic that is able to affect a wide variety of organisms (479)

bronchiole a small tube that branches from the bronchi within the lungs (945)

bronchus one of the two branches of the trachea that enter the lungs (945)

bryophyte a plant that has no vascular tissue and does not form true roots, stems, and leaves (583)

bud a structure that develops on the stem at the point of attachment of each leaf (609)

bud scale a modified leaf that forms a protective covering for a bud until it opens (609)

budding in fungi, a form of asexual reproduction in which a part of a cell pinches off to produce an offspring cell (544)

buffer chemical that neutralizes small amounts of acids or bases added to a solution (42)

C

calcitonin a hormone that stimulates removal of calcium from the blood (1036)

Calvin cycle a biochemical pathway of photosynthesis in which CO_2 is converted into carbohydrate (117)

CAM crassulacean acid metabolism; a biochemical pathway in certain plants in which CO_2 is incorporated into organic acids at night and released for fixation in the Calvin cycle during the day (119)

cancer the uncontrolled growth of cells (211)

canopy layers of treetops that shade the forest floor (429)

capillarity the reaction of a liquid surface with a solid; capillarity allows water to creep up the interior of a narrow vessel (51)

capillary the smallest vessel in the blood vessel network (810)

capsid the protein covering a virus (488)

capsule in mosses, a sporangium that produces spores; in bacteria, a protective layer of polysaccharides around the cell wall (475)

carageenan a substance found in the cell walls of red algae that is used commercially as a smoothing agent (531)

carapace a tough covering over the cephalothorax of some crustaceans; the dorsal part of a turtle's shell (748, 850)

carbohydrate an organic compound present in the cells of all living things and a major organic nutrient for humans (55)

carbon cycle process in which carbon is cycled through the biosphere (421)

carbon fixation the incorporation of carbon dioxide into organic compounds (117)

carcinogen a cancer-causing substance (212)

carcinoma a malignant tumor that grows in body tissues (211)

cardiac muscle the involuntary muscle of the heart (905)

cardiac sphincter a circular muscle located between the esophagus and the stomach (986)

cardiac stomach in an echinoderm, the stomach closer to the mouth (786)

cardiovascular system the blood, the heart, and the blood vessels (931)

carnivore a consumer that eats other consumers (416)

carotenoid a light-absorbing compound that functions as an accessory pigment in photosynthesis (113)

carrier protein a protein that transports specific substances across a biological membrane (99)

carrying capacity the number of individuals of a species that an ecosystem is capable of supporting (385)

cartilage a strong, flexible connective tissue (804)

cast a type of fossil formed when sediments fill in the cavity left by a decomposing organism (279)

catalyst a chemical that reduces the amount of activation energy needed for a reaction but is not a reactant (36)

caudal fin in fishes, a fin extending from the tail that moves from side to side and amplifies the swimming motions (808)

cause and effect a relationship between two variables in which a change in one variable leads to a change in the other (444)

cecum a sac usually found at the beginning of the large intestine (887)

cell a membrane-bound structure that is

the basic unit of life (11)

cell cycle the events of cell division; includes interphase, mitosis, and cytokinesis (149)

cell differentiation the change in morphology, physiology, or function of a cell in relation to its neighboring cells (209)

cell junction connection between cells that holds them together as a unit (667)

cell-mediated response part of an immune response involving a T-cell attack on an antigen (961)

cell membrane the lipid bilayer that forms the outer boundary of a cell (59)

cell plate a membrane that divides newly forming plant cells following mitosis (151)

cell theory the theory that all living things are made up of cells, that cells are the basic units of organisms, and that cells come only from existing cells (69)

cell wall a rigid structure that surrounds the cells of plants, fungi, many protists, and most bacteria (82, 468, 543)

cellular respiration the process in which cells make ATP by breaking down organic compounds (127)

cellular slime mold individual haploid cells that move about like amoebas; member of the phylum Acrasiomycota (534)

central nervous system the brain and the spinal cord (1003)

centriole a structure that appears during mitosis in animal cells (150)

centromere a region of the chromosome where the two sister chromatids are held together and which is the site of attachment of the chromosome to the spindle fibers during mitosis (146)

centrosome a dark body containing a centriole in animal cells but not in plant cells; spindle fibers radiate from the centrosome in preparation for mitosis (150)

cephalization concentration of nerve tissue and sensory organs at the anterior end of an organism (670)

cephalopod a free-swimming, predatory mollusk with a circle of tentacles extending from the head; an octopus, squid, cuttlefish, or chambered nautilus (730)

cephalothorax in arachnids and some crustaceans, a body part formed by the fusion of the head with the thorax (748)

cerebellum a posterior portion of the brain that controls movement and muscle coordination (1007)

cerebral cortex the folded outer layer of the cerebrum that controls motor and sensory activities (1005)

cerebral ganglion one of a pair of nerve-cell clusters that serve as a brain at the anterior end of some invertebrates (771)

cerebrospinal fluid a watery substance that provides a cushion that protects the brain and spinal cord (1007)

cerebrum the anterior portion of the brain where higher brain functions occur (1004)

character displacement evolution of anatomical differences that reduce competition between similar species (401)

chelicera a pincerlike mouthpart of some arthropods (745)

cheliped in arthropods, a claw used to capture food and for defense (748)

chemical bond a chemical attachment between atoms (33)

chemical reaction the process of breaking chemical bonds, forming new bonds, or both (33)

chemiosmosis a process in chloroplasts and mitochondria in which the movement of protons down their concentration gradient across a membrane is coupled to the synthesis of ATP (116)

chemoautotroph an organism that synthesizes organic compounds using chemicals instead of light (473)

chemosynthesis the production of carbohydrates through the use of energy from inorganic molecules instead of light (271)

chemotropism plant growth in response to a chemical (654)

chitin a carbohydrate that forms part of the arthropod exoskeleton (736)

chlorofluorocarbons (**CFCs**) a class of industrial chemicals found to be destroying the ozone layer in the upper atmosphere (443)

chlorophyll a class of light-absorbing pigments used in photosynthesis (113)

chloroplast a plastid containing chlorophyll; the site of photosynthesis (83)

chordate an animal that, at some stage of its life cycle, has a dorsal nerve cord, a notochord, and pharangeal pouches, such as mammals, birds, reptiles, amphibians, fish, and some marine lower forms (788)

chorion the outer membrane surrounding an embryo (842)

chorionic villi fingerlike projections of the chorion that extend into the uterine lining (1056)

chorionic villi sampling a procedure involving the analysis of the chorionic villi to diagnose fetal genotypes (232)

chromatid one of two identical parts of a chromosome (146)

chromatin the DNA and proteins in the nucleus of a nondividing cell (80)

chromosome DNA and protein in a coiled, rod-shaped form that occurs during cell division (81)

chromosome map a diagram of allele positions on a chromosome (224)

chronic bronchitis an inflammation of the bronchi and bronchioles (1069)

chrysalis the outer covering of a butterfly pupa (769)

chyme the mixture formed in the stomach from digested food particles and gastric fluid (986)

chytrid an aquatic protist characterized by gametes and zoospores with a single, posterior flagellum (536)

cilium a short, hairlike organelle that extends from a cell and functions in locomotion or in the movement of substances across the cell surface (80)

circulatory system the system that distributes oxygen and nutrients to cells in all parts of the body (675)

cirrhosis a condition in which normal liver tissues are replaced by scar tissue (1072)

citric acid a six-carbon compound formed in the Krebs cycle (134)

cladistics a system of phylogenetic classification using shared derived characters and the recency of ancestry is the sole criterion for grouping taxa (345)

clasper in fishes, a structure that transfers sperm into the female's body (806)

class in taxonomy, a group of related orders (338)

cleavage the divisions of the zygote immediately following fertilization (683)

cleavage furrow the area of the cell membrane that pinches in and eventually separates the dividing cell (151)

clitellum a noticeable swelling around the sex organs of an earthworm during reproduction (735)

cloaca in animals, such as birds, amphibians, and reptiles, a common chamber into which the digestive, reproductive, and excretory systems enter (718)

clone an offspring produced by asexual production (639)

cloning vector a carrier used to clone a gene and transfer it from one organism to another (240)

closed circulatory system a system in which blood is contained within vessels as in the human circulatory system (675)

cnidarian a phylum of animals with radially symmetrical bodies, a saclike internal cavity, tentacles, and nematocysts, such as jellyfish, hydras, sea anemones, and corals (696)

cnidocyte a stinging cell of a cnidarian (697)

coacervate a cell-like droplet formed from dissimilar substances (268)

coccus sphere-shaped bacterium (470)

cochlea a coiled tube in the inner ear that is filled with fluid and lined with hair-like cells that translates the mechanical energy from sound into nerve impulses (1018)

cocoon the outer covering of a moth pupa; a chrysalis (769)

codominance an inheritance relationship in which neither of two alleles of the same gene totally masks the other (176)

codon a group of three sequential nitrogen bases of an mRNA molecule (193)

coelom a body cavity formed within the mesoderm (685)

coenocytic referring to filaments without internal cross walls (543)

coevolution the mutual evolution of two different species interacting with each other (291)

cohesion the attraction of like molecules to each other (51)

cohesion-tension theory states that water is able to move up the stem xylem due to the strong attraction of water molecules to each other (613)

collar cell a cell lining the inside of sponges that circulates water; also called a choanocyte (693)

collenchyma plant tissue made up of elongated cells with unevenly thickened, flexible walls (599)

colloblast a cell on the tentacles of a ctenophore that secretes a sticky substance that binds to the organism's prey (702)

colon the large intestine (989)

colonial algae algae that have a structure that consists of groups of cells behaving in a coordinated manner (526)

colonial organism a collection of genetically identical cells that live together in a closely connected group (87)

columella a bone that transmits sounds from the eardrum to the inner ear (829)

commensalism an ecological relationship in which one organism benefits and the other neither benefits nor is harmed (402)

community all the populations in one area (363)

compact bone the layer of bone just beneath the periosteum that gives the bone its strength (911)

companion cell a specialized plant cell that helps control the movement of sugars through sieve tubes (601)

competitive exclusion the local extinction of a species due to competition (400)

complete dominance an inheritance relationship in which one allele is completely dominant over the other; both Bb and BB have the same phenotype (176)

compound eye an eye composed of many light detectors, each with its own lens (743)

compound leaf a type of leaf in which the blade is divided into leaflets (616)

compound light microscope an instrument that magnifies small objects so they can be seen easily using two or more lenses (21)

concentration a measurement of the amount of solute dissolved in a fixed amount of solvent (40)

concentration gradient the difference in concentration of a substance across space (95)

condensation reaction a chemical reaction, also called dehydration synthesis, in which one molecule of water is produced (53)

cone a photoreceptor within the retina that can produce sharp images and distinguish colors; in gymnosperms, a seed-bearing structure (588, 1020)

conformer an organism that does not regulate its internal environment (370)

conidium a spore produced during asexual reproduction in ascomycetes (544)

conjugation the union of two protists to exchange genetic material (477)

conjugation bridge in certain algae and fungi, a passageway for the transfer of the genetic information from one organism to another (477)

connective tissue body tissue that supports and holds body structures together (906)

conservation biology a branch of biology concerned with preserving biodiversity in natural areas (452)

constrictor snake that kills its prey by constriction and suffocation (853)

consumer a heterotroph that obtains energy from organic molecules made by other organisms (416)

contour feather a feather that provides coloration, insulation, and a streamlined shape to adult birds (864)

contractile vacuole an organelle in protists that expels water (97)

control group in an experiment, a group or individual that serves as a standard of comparison with another group or individual to which it is identical except for one factor (17)

controlled experiment a test of variables using a comparison of a control group with an experimental group (17)

conus arteriosus in fishes and frogs, the final chamber of the heart (810)

convection cell a regional pattern of rising and falling air (441)

convergent evolution the process by which unrelated species become more similar as they adapt to the same kind of environment (292)

coral reef a rocklike formation in warm, shallow seas composed of the skeletons of corals (432)

cork cambium the lateral meristem of a plant; produces cork (602)

cornea protective layer that covers the iris and pupil of the eye (1020)

coronary circulation a subsystem of systemic circulation that supplies blood to the heart (936)

corpus callosum the structure formed by nerve fibers connecting the cerebral hemispheres of the brain (1004)

corpus luteum the structure that forms from the ruptured follicle in the ovary at ovulation (1053)

correlation a relationship between two variables in which both variables change together (444)

cortex in plants, a mature ground tissue located just inside the epidermis; in animals, the outermost portion of an organ such as the kidney (605, 991)

cortisol a hormone that regulates certain phases of carbohydrate and protein metabolism (1035)

cotyledon a seed leaf in a plant embryo (592)

countercurrent flow in gills of fishes, an arrangement whereby water flows away from the head and blood flows toward the head (811)

covalent bond a bond that forms when two atoms share one or more pairs of electrons (33)

coxal gland in some arachnids, an organ that removes wastes and discharges them at the base of the legs (752)

C₃ plant a plant that fixes carbon exclusively through the Calvin cycle, named for the three-carbon compound that is initially formed (119)

C₄ plant a plant that incorporates CO_2 into four-carbon compounds (119)

cranial cavity the area in which the brain rests (908)

cranial nerve one of the 12 nerves of the head that relay information between the brain and the muscular and sensory structures in the head (811)

cretinism a form of mental retardation caused by hypothyroidism (1034)

crista a fold of the inner membrane of mitochondria (77)

crop in earthworms, a structure that stores soil; in birds, a structure that stores food (734, 766, 866)

crop milk a nutritious milklike fluid secreted by the crop of pigeons and doves to feed their young (873)

cross-pollination a reproductive process in which pollen from one plant is transferred to the stigma of another plant (166)

crossing-over the exchange of genes by reciprocal segments of homologous chromosomes during meiosis (153)

crustacean an arthropod with mandibles and branched appendages; examples include shrimps, barnacles, crabs, and pill bugs (746)

crustose a type of lichen that grows as a layer on rocks and trees (549)

cultivar a combination of the words *cultivated* and *variety* for a food plant that has a specific distinguishing characteristic, such as Thompson Seedless grapes (561)

cutaneous respiration in some animals, the exchange of gases through the skin (827)

cuticle in plants and insects, a waxy covering that prevents desiccation; in parasitic roundworms, a noncellular layer that protects the worm from the host's digestive and immune systems (600, 715)

cyanobacteria photosynthetic unicellular prokaryotes (271)

cyst a resistant, thick-walled structure that encloses and protects a dormant organism (714)

cytokine a chemical signal between cells of the immune system (957)

cytokinesis the division of the cytoplasm of one cell into two new cells (149)

cytokinins plant hormones that promote cell division (651)

cytolysis the bursting of a cell (99)

cytoplasm the region of a cell between the cell membrane and the nucleus (75)

cytoplasmic streaming the circular motion of the cytoplasm (512)

cytosine a nitrogen-containing base; a pyrimidine of DNA and RNA (185)

cytoskeleton a network of long protein strands in the cytosol that helps maintain the shape and size of a eukaryotic cell (79)

cytosol the gelatinlike aqueous fluid that bathes the organelles on the inside of the cell membrane (75)

cytotoxic T cell a type of T cell that destroys infected body cells (961)

D

day-neutral plant a plant unaffected by day length (656)

death rate or **mortality rate** the number

of deaths occurring in a period of time (381)

debt-for-nature swap a conservation strategy in which a developing country takes steps to preserve its biodiversity in exchange for a reduction in its foreign debt (450)

decapod a crustacean with five pairs of legs, such as shrimps, crayfish, and lobsters (747)

deciduous referring to trees that lose their leaves at the end of the growing season (589)

decomposer an organism that obtains nutrients from dead plants and animals (416)

dehydration the condition resulting from excessive water loss (982)

deletion a mutation in which a segment of DNA breaks off of a chromosome (225)

denitrification a final step in the nitrogen cycle, during which nitrogen gas is returned to the atmosphere (423)

density-dependent factor a variable related to the density of a population that affects population size (386)

density-independent factor a variable that affects population size regardless of population density (386)

dental formula the number, kind, and placement of teeth that are specific for a particular kind of animal (320)

deoxyribonucleic acid (DNA) a double-helix-shaped nucleic acid (7)

dependent variable the responding variable in an experiment (18)

depressant a drug that decreases the activity of the central nervous system (1070)

derived character a feature that evolved only within the group under consideration, such as the feathers of birds (345)

dermal tissue system one type of plant tissue system, which forms the outer covering of plants (600)

desert an area where rainfall averages less than 25 cm per year (416)

determinate cleavage a process in which each cell develops into a specific part of the gastrula (684)

detritivore a consumer that feeds on dead plants and animals (416)

deuterostome an organism in which the blastopore develops into the anus and the coelom arises by enterocoely and whose embryo has indeterminate cleavage (684)

development the process by which an organism grows (12)

diabetes mellitus a disorder of glucose metabolism caused by insufficient insulin (60)

diaphragm a sheet of muscle below the rib cage that functions in inspiration and expiration (886)

diastole a phase in the heartbeat during which the ventricles relax and the blood flows in from the atria (933)

diastolic pressure the pressure maintained in the blood when the ventricles are relaxed (934)

diatom an abundant component of phytoplankton; member of phylum Bacillariophyta (532)

dicot an angiosperm with two cotyledons, net venation, and flower parts in fours or fives (580)

diencephalon in the brain, an area below the cerebral hemisphere that contains the thalamus and the hypothalamus (1006)

differentiation a process in which the cells of a multicellular individual become specialized during development (209)

diffusion the process by which molecules move from an area of greater concentration to an area of lesser concentration (95)

digestion breaking down food into usable molecules (983)

dihybrid cross a cross between individuals that involves the pairing of contrasting traits (177)

dimorphism the existence of distinct, genetically determined forms of the same species, such as male and female forms (544)

dinosaur one of a great variety of terrestrial reptilian forms during the Mesozoic era 245 million to 65 million years ago (839)

dipeptide a formation from two amino acids bonded together by means of a condensation reaction (57)

diploid a cell that contains both chromosomes of a homologous pair (147)

disaccharide a double sugar formed from two monosaccharides (56)

dispersion the spatial distribution of individuals in a population (380)

disruptive selection a type of natural selection in which individuals with two extreme forms of a trait have an advantage (307)

dissociation the separating of a molecule into simpler molecules, atoms, radicals, or ions (41)

divergent evolution the process of two or more related species becoming more and more dissimilar (292)

division in taxonomy, a grouping of similar classes of plants (338)

DNA hereditary information in the form of a large molecule called deoxyribonucleic acid (7)

DNA fingerprint a pattern of bands made up of specific fragments from an individual's DNA (243)

DNA polymerase an enzyme that binds to the separated strands of DNA and assembles each strand's complement in replication (188)

domain in the three-domain system of classification, one of three broad groups that all living things fall into on the basis of rRNA analysis (350)

dominant referring to an allele that masks the presence of another allele for the same characteristic (168)

donor gene a specific gene that is isolated from another organism and spliced into a plasmid (240)

dormancy a state of decreased metabolism (370)

dorsal the top of a bilaterally symmetrical animal (670)

dorsal nerve cord a neural tube dorsal to the notochord (673)

double fertilization in plants, the process in which two types of cell fusion take place in the embryo sac (633)

down feather one of the soft, fluffy feathers that cover the body of nesting birds and help insulate adult birds (864)

Down syndrome a disorder caused by an extra twenty-first chromosome and characterized by a number of physical and mental abnormalities (231)

drone a male bee that develops from an unfertilized egg and functions only to fertilize eggs from the queen (772)

drug any chemical taken into the body that alters the normal processes of either the mind or the body (1065)

Duchenne muscular dystrophy a form of muscular dystrophy that weakens and progressively destroys muscle tissue (229)

duodenum the first section of the small intestine (827)

dura mater the outermost of the three sacs that enclose the brain and spinal cord (1007)

E

echinoderm a radially symmetrical marine invertebrate with an endoskeleton, a water-vascular system, and tube feet, such as a sea star, a sea urchin, or a sea cucumber (781)

echolocation a method of navigation similar to sonar in which the sound produced bounces off an object used by bats and cetaceans (887)

ecology the study of the relationship between organisms and their environment (359)

ecosystem all the biotic and abiotic components of an environment (363)

ecotourism a form of tourism that helps local people make money from an intact ecosystem; tourists pay for nature guides, food, and lodging to tour the ecosystem (451)

ectoderm the outermost of the three germ layers of the gastrula that develops into the epidermis and epidermal tissues, the nervous system, external sense organs, and the mucous membranes lining the mouth and anus (683)

ectoparasite a parasite that lives on a host but does not enter the host's body (399)

ectoplasm the region in the cytoplasm located directly inside the cell membranes (512)

ectothermic referring to an animal whose body temperature is determined by the environment (848)

efferent neuron a neuron that conducts impulses away from the central nervous system (1008)

ejaculation contractions of the smooth muscles surrounding the urethra by which semen is forcefully expelled (1049)

elapid a venomous snake with two small, fixed fangs in the front of the mouth (853)

El Niño a disruption of the normal air and water circulation patterns in the Pacific Ocean, leading to unusual weather in many parts of the world (442)

electron a particle with a negative electric charge that orbits the nucleus of an atom (32)

electron microscope an instrument that uses a beam of electrons rather than a beam of light to enlarge the image of an extremely small object so that it can be seen (22)

electron transport chain molecules in the thylakoid membrane or inner mitochondrial membrane that uses some of the energy in electrons to pump protons across the membrane (115)

element a substance that ordinarily cannot be broken down chemically to form simpler kinds of matter (31)

elephantiasis a condition of swollen lymphatic vessels in the limbs caused by a parasitic filarial worm (718)

embryo sac in plants, a megagametophyte containing seven cells and eight nuclei (630)

emigration the movement of individuals out of a population (304)

emphysema a degenerative lung disease (1069)

endocrine gland a ductless gland that secretes hormones into the blood (1029)

endocrine system a system of glands that transmit chemical messages throughout the body (1029)

endocytosis the process by which a cell surrounds and engulfs substances (103)

endoderm the innermost of the three germ layers of the gastrula and develops into the epithelium of the pharynx, respiratory tract, digestive tract, bladder, and urethra (683)

endodermis in plants, a specialized layer of cells that regulates substances entering the center of the root (605)

endoparasite a parasite that lives inside the host's body (399)

endoplasm the region in the cytoplasm found in the interior of the cell (512)

endoplasmic reticulum a system of membranous tubules and sacs in eukaryotic cells that functions as a path along which molecules move from one part of the cell to another (77)

endoskeleton an internal skeleton (909)

endosperm a tissue in angiosperms that provides food for the developing embryo (579)

endospore a dormant bacterial cell enclosed by a tough coating (475)

endosymbiosis a mutually beneficial relationship between one organism and another that lives within it; the hypothesis of endosymbiosis relating to the evolution of eukaryotes that holds that chloroplasts and mitochondria evolved from endosymbiotic bacteria (132)

endotherm an animal that generates its own body heat through metabolism (848)

endotoxin a substance that causes a poison reaction; a compound that makes up part of the cell wall of Gram-negative bacteria (479)

enhancer a region adjacent to a eukaryotic gene that must be activated if the gene is to be expressed (208)

enkephalin a neurotransmitter that blocks pain messages to the brain (1076)

enteric bacteria Gram-negative heterotrophic bacteria that inhabit animal intestinal tracts (473)

enterocoely the process of mesoderm formation in deuterostomes in which the coelom forms in folded mesoderm (685)

entomology the study of insects (762)

environmental science a field of study that uses biological principles to look at the relationships between humans and the Earth (440)

enzyme a catalyst, usually a protein, in living systems (37)

ephedrine a decongestant drug derived from *Ephedra,* a genus of desert shrubs (590)

epidermis a layer of cells that forms a continuous sheet over the outer surface of a plant or animal (696)

epididymis coiled tube on each testis where sperm complete their development (1048)

epiglottis a flap of tissue that covers the trachea (945)

epiphyseal plate the site of bone elongation at the ends of long bones (912)

epiphyte a plant that grows on other plants (429)

epithelial tissue tissue composed of cells that create a solid sheet that covers a body part (906)

equilibrium a state that exists when the concentration of a substance is the same throughout a space (95)

erosion the loss of soil that is caused by wind or water (822)

erythrocyte a red blood cell (939)

esophagus a tube connecting the mouth or pharynx to the stomach or crop (734)

estrogen hormone that helps regulate the menstrual cycle (1035)

estuary an aquatic biome found where freshwater streams and rivers flow into the sea; where the tides meet a river current (433)

ethephon a synthetic chemical that breaks down to release ethylene gas; used to ripen fruit (650)

ethylene a gaseous hormone produced by various parts of plants and released into the air (650)

eubacteria the lineage of prokaryotes that includes all contemporary bacteria except archaebacteria (348)

euchromatin the uncoiled form of chromatin (206)

euglenoid flagellated unicellular algae; many are photosynthetic (533)

eukaryote a cell that contains a nucleus and membrane-bound organelles (72)

eustachian tube a canal that connects the middle ear to the mouth cavity (1018)

eutrophication the increase of nutrients in an environment (472)

evenness the number of individual organisms that belong to each species in a given area (449)

evolution all the changes that have formed life on Earth from its earliest beginnings to the diversity that characterizes it today (8)

excretion the process of removing metabolic wastes (991)

excurrent siphon a tube through which water exits the mantle cavity of a bivalve (729)

exergonic reaction a chemical reaction that involves a net release of free energy (36)

exocrine gland a gland that secretes non-hormonal chemicals through a duct (1029)

exocytosis a process in which a vesicle inside a cell fuses with the cell membrane and releases its contents to the external environment (104)

exon coding region of a eukaryotic gene (206)

exoskeleton the hard external covering of some invertebrates that provides protection and support (675)

exotoxin a toxic protein secreted by pathogenic bacteria (478)

expiration the process in which air is forced out of the lungs (948)

exponential growth a model of population growth in which the birth and death rates are constant (384)

extensor a muscle that straightens a joint (919)

external fertilization the union of gametes outside the bodies of the parents, as in many fishes and amphibians (804)

external respiration the exchange of gases between the atmosphere and the blood (948)

extinction the dying out of a species (281)

extreme halophile an archaebacterium that lives in very high salt concentrations (468)

eyespot a localized region of pigment in some invertebrates and protozoa that detects changes in the quantity and quality of light (508)

F

facilitated diffusion a process in which substances move down their concentration gradient across the cell membrane with the assistance of carrier proteins (99)

facultative anaerobe an organism that can metabolize with or without oxygen (476)

FAD flavin adenine dinucleotide; a compound that accepts electrons during redox reactions (134)

fallopian tube a tube through which eggs move from the ovary to the uterus (1051)

family in taxonomy, a group of related genera (338)

fascicle a dense bundle of skeletal muscle fibers (916)

fatty acid a monomer that is part of most lipids (58)

feces waste materials that pass through the anus or cloacal opening (989)

feedback mechanism (positive or negative) a series of events in which the last step controls the first (1038)

fermentation a process in which cells make a limited amount of ATP by converting glucose into another organic compound, such as lactic acid or ethyl alcohol, in the absence of oxygen (129)

fertilizer a compound that provides plants with essential mineral nutrients like nitrogen and phosphorus (564)

fetal alcohol syndrome a condition characterized by growth and developmental defects affecting some children born to women who drink alcohol during pregnancy (1072)

fetus referring to a developing human from the end of the eighth week until birth (1057)

F_1 generation the offspring of cross-pollinated P_1 generation plants (166)

F_2 generation the offspring of self-pollinated F_1 generation plants (166)

fibrin the long, sticky threads that function in blood clotting (941)

fibrous root system a mat of threadlike roots that spread out below the surface of the soil to maximize exposure to water and minerals and to anchor the plant firmly to the soil (603)

filament in flowers, the structure that supports the anther (629)

filamentous alga an alga that has a slender, rod-shaped thallus composed of rows of cells joined end to end (526)

filarial worm one of a variety of parasitic roundworms that cause elephantiasis in humans and heartworm disease in dogs (717)

filter feeding the method by which a sessile organism screens food out of the surrounding water (694)

filtration the process in the kidney in which materials from the blood are forced out of the glomerulus into Bowman's capsule (993)

first messenger a hormone that activates a second messenger inside its target cell (1030)

fission a type of asexual reproduction in which the organism splits in two and regenerates the parts missing on each new half to produce two whole organisms (711)

fitness a measurement of the ability of a species to respond to the pressures of natural selection; the ability of individuals to survive to propagate their genes (288)

fixed joint a place where two bones meet but movement does not occur, as in the skull (913)

flagellum a hairlike structure made up of microtubules that function in locomotion (80)

flame cell in a flatworm, a cell that collects excess body water and transfers it to the excretory system(710)

flatworm the common name for any of the dorso ventrally flattened worms of the phylum Platyhelminthes, such as a planarian, fluke, and a tapeworm (709)

flavin adenine dinucleotide see FAD

flexor a muscle that bends a joint (919)

flight feather a specialized contour feather on the wing or tail of a bird (864)

fluid mosaic model a model of cell mem-

brane structure representing the dynamic nature of membrane lipids and proteins (75)

fluke a leaf-shaped parasitic flatworm (711)

flyway the route followed by migratory birds (453)

foliose lichen a type of lichen that lives on soil surfaces, where it forms a mat-like growth (549)

follicle a pit in the skin in which hair or a feather develops; a structure surrounding an immature egg in an ovary (864)

follicle stimulating hormone (FSH) a gonadotropin that stimulates sperm production and causes cells around an immature egg to form a follicle (1035)

follicular phase the stage in which an immature egg completes its first meiotic division (1052)

food chain pathway beginning with producers along which energy is transferred from trophic level to trophic level (417)

food web the interconnected food chains in an ecosystem (417)

foraminifera an ancient group of shelled sarcodines found in oceans (513)

fossil the remains or traces of a once-living organism (279)

fracture a crack or break in a bone (911)

fragmentation in fungi, a form of asexual reproduction in which individual cells are released that act like spores (544)

frame shift mutation a mutation that results in the misreading of the code during translation because of a change in the reading frame (226)

free energy the energy in a system available for work (35)

frond the mature leaf of a fern (588)

fruit a mature plant ovary; a modified flower part that encloses a seed or seeds (563)

fruiting body spore-bearing structure of a slime mold during reproduction (534)

fruticose a shrublike lichen (549)

fucoxanthin a carotenoid pigment that is one of the primary pigments found in diatoms and brown algae (531)

functional group a structural building block that determines the characteristics of a chemical compound (53)

fundamental niche the full range of conditions that a species can tolerate and resources it can use (371)

fungi imperfecti or **deuteromycota** a group of fungi whose sexual phase has not been discovered (549)

furculum the fused collarbones in a bird's skeleton; the "wishbone" (862)

G

gallbladder the saclike organ in vertebrates that is connected to the liver that stores bile (809)

gametangium in algae and fungi, a gamete chamber (525)

gamete a reproductive cell (153)

gametocyte an undifferentiated cell that develops into a gamete (517)

gametophyte in plants and algae, a multi-cellular structure that produces

gametes (529)

ganglion a mass of nerve cells (726)

gasohol an alternative fuel made from alcohol from fermented grains mixed with gasoline (567)

gastric cecum a pocket that branches from the digestive tract and secretes enzymes (766)

gastric fluid a liquid secreted by gastric glands in the stomach (986)

gastric pit the open end of gastric glands through which secretions are released into the stomach (985)

gastrin a hormone that stimulates the stomach to secrete digestive enzymes (1037)

gastrodermis in cnidarians, the layer of cells surrounding the gastrovascular cavity (696)

gastrointestinal tract the digestive tract from the mouth to the anus (983)

gastropod a mollusk that has one or no shell and moves by gliding on a muscular foot; examples include snails, slugs, and nudibranchs (727)

gastrovascular cavity a digestive chamber with a single opening found in cnidarians, ctenophores, and flatworms (696)

gastrula the cup-shaped embryo formed as the blastula folds inward (683)

gel electrophoresis technique used to separate nucleic acids or proteins by size and charge (244)

gemmule an asexual reproductive structure produced by some freshwater sponges (695)

gene a segment of DNA that contains coding for a polypeptide or protein; a unit of hereditary information (7)

gene clone an exact copy of a gene (240)

gene expression the transcription of DNA into RNA and then into proteins (202)

gene flow the movement of genes into or out of a population (305)

gene pool all the genes for all of the traits in a population (300)

gene therapy treatment of a genetic disorder by introducing a healthy gene into a cell (246)

generalist a species with a broad niche that can tolerate a wide range of conditions and can use a variety of resources (372)

generative cell in a pollen grain, the cell that forms two sperm (632)

genetic code triplets of nucleotides in mRNA that determine the sequence of amino acids in protein (193)

genetic counseling the process of informing a couple about their genetic makeup, which has the potential to affect their offspring (231)

genetic disorder a disease that has a genetic basis (228)

genetic diversity the amount of genetic variation within a population or species (449)

genetic drift a shift in allele frequencies in a population due to chance (305)

genetic engineering a form of applied genetics in which scientists directly manipulate genes (238)

genetic marker a short section of DNA

that indicates the presence of an allele that codes for a trait (228)

genetic screening an examination of a person's genetic makeup (231)

genetics the field of biology devoted to understanding how traits are passed from parents to offspring (164)

genome the complete genetic material contained in an individual (203)

genomic library a set of thousands of DNA pieces cut by a specific restriction enzyme (241)

genotype the genetic makeup of an organism (172)

genotypic ratio the probable ratio of genotypes produced by a cross (175)

genus in taxonomy, a group of similar species (338)

geographic isolation the physical separation of populations (310)

germ cell mutation a change in the DNA of a sex cell (224)

germ layer a specific layer of cells in an embryo from which specific organ systems are derived (671)

germinate in plants, sprout; the seed embryo begins to grow (588)

gestation the length of a normal pregnancy (1054)

giardiasis an illness characterized by severe diarrhea and intestinal cramps caused by a protozoan parasite (507)

gibberellin a plant hormone that, among other actions, stimulates bolting and cessation of dormancy (650)

gill in mushrooms, one of the radiating rows on the underside of the cap; in animals, an organ specialized for the exchange of gases with water (802)

gizzard a muscular region of the digestive tract in birds that crushes food (734, 866)

gliding joint a joint that allows bones to slide over one another, as in foot bones that flex in walking (913)

glomerulus a cluster of capillaries that receives blood from the renal artery and that is enclosed in Bowman's capsule (993)

glucagon a hormone that raises the blood glucose level (1036)

glycolysis a pathway in which glucose is oxidized to pyruvic acid (127)

glycoprotein a molecule of protein with attached sugar chains (489)

Golgi apparatus a system of membranes in eukaryotic cells that modifies proteins for export by the cell (78)

gonad the organ that produces gametes and some sex hormones (1035)

G_0 phase a phase of the cell cycle in which the cell is not dividing and its DNA is not replicating (149)

G_1 phase the first period of interphase, in which the cell doubles in size (149)

G_2 phase the final period of interphase, in which the cell undergoes rapid growth and prepares mitosis (149)

grafting a technique in which a portion of one plant is inserted into and grows with the root or shoot of another (640)

Gram-negative bacterium a bacterium that stains pink with Gram stain and that usually has an outer covering on its cell wall (471)

Gram-positive bacterium a bacterium that stains purple with Gram stain and that usually lacks an outer covering on its cell wall (471)

Gram stain a series of dyes that stain bacteria either purple or pink according to the chemistry of the bacterial cell wall (471)

granum a stack of thylakoids in a chloroplast (112)

gravitropism a plant growth response to gravity (654)

great ape a gibbon, orangutan, gorilla, or a chimpanzee (320)

green gland an excretory organ of some crustaceans that helps regulate the solute concentration of the hemolymph (750)

greenhouse effect warming of the Earth due to the insulating effect of gases in the atmosphere, such as carbon dioxide and water vapor (361)

gross primary productivity the rate at which energy is produced in an ecosystem (415)

ground water water found in the soil or in underground formations of porous rock (421)

ground-tissue system one type of plant-tissue system, made up of parenchyma, collenchyma, and sclerenchyma (601)

growth factor protein that regulates the rate and sequence of the events of cell division (212)

growth hormone a hormone secreted by the anterior lobe of the pituitary gland that regulates skeletal and muscular growth (1033)

growth rate the amount by which a population's size changes in a given time (383)

growth regulator a hormone that stimulates or inhibits plant growth (647)

growth retardant a chemical that retards plant growth (651)

guanine a nitrogen-containing base that is a component of a nucleotide (185)

guard cell one of two cells bordering a stoma, each of which has flexible cell walls that regulate gas and water exchange (618)

gullet the structure that forms food vacuoles that circulate throughout the cytoplasm of the *Paramecium* (514)

gut digestive tract (676)

gymnosperm a seed plant whose seeds are not enclosed by an ovary (581)

H

habitat the physical area in which an organism lives (368)

half-life the period of time in which half of a radioactive substance decays (265)

haploid having only one chromosome of each homologous pair (147)

hard palate the bony roof of the mouth (984)

Hardy-Weinberg principle of genetic equilibrium the stability of gene frequencies across generations (302)

Haversian canal a channel containing nerves and blood vessels making up

compact bone (911)

hay fever a pollen allergy that results in sneezing, a running nose, and watering eyes (572)

head-foot one of the two regions of the mollusk body consisting of the head and the foot (726)

heartwood the darker wood in the center of a tree (611)

heartworm disease a disease of the heart and large arteries in dogs caused by a filarial worm (718)

helicase an enzyme that separates DNA strands before replication (188)

helper T cell a type of T cell that coordinates the immune response (961)

hemocoel the hemolymph-filled space or body cavity some invertebrates (727)

hemoglobin the oxygen-carrying pigment in red blood cells (939)

hemolymph the fluid that is circulated through the body of an animal with an open circulatory system (766)

hemophilia a trait in which the blood lacks a protein that is essential for clotting (229)

hepatic portal circulation the system of blood movement through the digestive tract and liver (936)

herb a flowering, vascular seed plant that lacks a woody stem; a plant part used to add flavor to food (563)

herbaceous plant an annual plant that is nonwoody (580)

herbivore a consumer that eats primary producers (398)

heredity the transmission of traits from parents to their offspring (165)

heterocyst a cell of cyanophytes that fixes atmospheric nitrogen (472)

heterospory a phenomenon in which two types of spores are produced by an individual plant (627)

heterotroph an organism that obtains organic food molecules by eating other organisms or their by-products (10)

heterozygous referring to a gene pair in which the two alleles do not code for the same trait (173)

hilum a scar along the edge of a plant seed marking where the seed was attached to the ovary wall (636)

hindgut the colon and rectum of some invertebrates (766)

hinge joint allows movement back and forth like a hinged door, as in the elbow (913)

histamine a kind of cytokine that causes an inflammatory response to an injury resulting in redness, swelling, warmth, and pain (957)

histone a protein molecule that DNA wraps around during chromosome formation (145)

holdfast the part of an algal thallus that anchors it to a substrate (529)

homeobox a specific DNA sequence within a homeotic gene that regulates patterns of development (209)

homeostasis the stable internal conditions of a living thing (6)

homeotic gene a gene that controls the development of a specific adult structure (209)

hominid a subgroup of primates that

includes modern humans and their bipedal ancestors (319)

homologous chromosome one of a pair of morphologically similar chromosomes (146)

homologous features similar features that originated in a shared ancestor (289)

homospory a phenomenon in which all spores look alike and produce similar gametophytes (626)

homozygous referring to a gene pair in which the two alleles code for the same trait (173)

hookworm a parasitic roundworm that feeds on its host's blood by cutting into the intestinal wall (716)

hormone a chemical secreted by an endocrine gland that specifically influences the activity of distant cells (1029)

host an organism that supports a parasite (399)

human chorionic gonadotropin (HCG) a hormone secreted by the placenta that stimulates the corpus luteum (1056)

Human Genome Project worldwide scientific collaboration to determine the nucleotide sequence of the entire human genome (246)

human immunodeficiency virus (HIV) the virus that causes AIDS (488)

humoral immune response an arm of the immune response that involves mainly B cells and antibodies (961)

hunter-gatherer lifestyle a nomadic way of life in which food is found by hunting animals and gathering uncultivated plants, fruits, and shellfish (388)

Huntington's disease a human genetic disorder caused by a dominant allele resulting in involuntary movements, mental deterioration, and eventual death (228)

hydrogen bond a weak chemical bond between the hydrogen atom in one molecule and a negatively-charged region of another molecule (50)

hydrolysis the splitting of a molecule through reaction with water (54)

hydrophilic referring to the molecular attraction to water (58)

hydrophobic referring to the molecular repulsion of water (58)

hypertension high blood pressure (934)

hyperthyroidism overproduction of thyroid hormones (1034)

hypertonic describing a solution whose solute concentration is higher than that inside a cell (96)

hypha the vegetative filament of a fungus (543)

hypocotyl a stemlike area in plants between the cotyledons and radicle (636)

hypoglycemia overproduction of insulin (1036)

hypothesis a statement that can be tested experimentally (17)

hypothyroidism thyroid hormone deficiency (1034)

hypotonic describing a solution whose solute concentration is lower than that inside a cell (96)

I

icosahedron a polyhedron or a capsid of a virus with 20 triangular faces (489)

ileum the middle portion of the small intestine (827)

immigration the movement of individuals into a population (366)

immune response a reaction of the body against a foreign substance (960)

immune system a body system that has the job of fighting off invading pathogens and preventing the growth and spread of cancers (959)

immunity resistance to a specific pathogen (964)

implantation the process by which the newly fertilized egg in the blastocyst stage imbeds itself into the lining of the uterus (1055)

inactivated vaccine a vaccine that has been treated so that its component microorganisms no longer have the ability to cause disease (497)

inbreeding mating with relatives (387)

incisor a chisel-like tooth used for biting and cutting (984)

incomplete dominance an inheritance relationship that occurs when both alleles influence the phenotype (176)

incurrent siphon a tube through which water enters the mantle cavity of a bivalve (729)

independent assortment during meiosis, the random distribution of genes from different chromosomes to the gametes (154)

independent variable an experimentally manipulated variable (18)

indeterminate cleavage a pattern of development in which the functional destiny of each cell is not determined early in the development of the embryo (685)

indoleacetic acid (IAA) an auxin produced in actively growing regions of plants (647)

inducer in the *lac* operon, the molecule that binds to repressor molecules and induces gene expression (205)

infectious disease a disease caused by a pathogen that can be transmitted from one individual to another (496)

inferior vena cava the large vein carrying blood from the lower part of the body (935)

inflammatory response a response in which white blood cells engulf foreign substances and body temperature rises (957)

insertion the attachment point of a tendon to a moving bone (919)

inspiration the process of taking air into the lungs (947)

insulin a hormone that lowers the blood glucose level (1036)

integral protein a protein imbedded in the bilayer of the cell membrane (74)

integument in plants, one or two outer layers of the ovule; in animals, the outer covering (628)

intercalary meristem a region of plant tissue that allow grass leaves to quickly regrow (958)

interferon a protein produced by the

---

body that inhibits the reproduction of viruses (958)

intermediate host the host from which the larvae of a parasite derive their nourishment (713)

internal fertilization fertilization in which sperm fuses with an egg inside the female's body (806)

internal respiration the exchange of gases between the blood and the cells of the body (944)

interneuron a neuron that connects with another neuron (1008)

internode one of the different segments of a stem (609)

interphase a period of cell growth and development that precedes eukaryotic cell nuclear division (149)

intertidal zone an area along ocean shorelines that is repeatedly covered and uncovered by ocean tides (431)

intestine the part of the body where digestion is completed and nutrients are absorbed (809)

intron a section of a structural gene that does not code for an amino acid and is excised before translation (206)

inversion a mutation that occurs when a chromosome piece breaks off and reattaches in reverse orientation (225)

invertebrate an animal without a backbone (667)

involuntary muscle a muscle whose movement cannot be consciously controlled (916)

ion an atom or a compound with a net electrical charge (34)

ion channel a membrane protein that provides a passageway across the cell membrane through which an ion can diffuse (100)

ionic bond a bond formed by electrical attraction between two oppositely charged ions (34)

islets of Langerhans specialized cells in the pancreas that secrete two hormones, insulin and glucagon (1036)

isomer one of two or more compounds that differ in structure but not in molecular composition (55)

isopod a crustacean with seven pairs of identical legs; examples include sow bugs and pill bugs (745)

isotonic describing a solution whose solute concentration equals that inside a cell (97)

isotope one of multiple forms of a chemical element that has a different number of neutrons than other atoms of that element (264)

J

Jacobson's organ one of two pits in the mouth of a snake that contain nerves which are extremely sensitive to odors (847)

jejunum the middle section of the small intestine (988)

joint the place where two bones meet (913)

K

karyotype a picture of an individual's chromosomes (147)

keratin a protein that forms hair, bird feathers, human fingernails, and the horny scales of reptiles (843)

kidney an excretory organ in which wastes are filtered from the blood (678)

kilocalorie a unit of energy equal to 1,000 calories; the amount of heat needed to raise the temperature of 1 kg of water by 1° C (130)

kin selection a mechanism for increasing the propagation of one's own genes by helping a closely related individual reproduce (774)

kinetochore a disk-shaped protein found in the centromere region of a chromosome and attaches the chromosomes to the mitotic spindle (150)

kinetochore fiber a spindle fiber that extends from the centrosome at one pole of the cell to a chromatid during mitosis (150)

kingdom in taxonomy, a group of similar phyla or divisions (338)

Koch's postulates the steps that Robert Koch, a Nobel Prize–winner in 1905 for his work on tuberculosis, formulated for determining the cause of a given disease (955)

Krebs cycle a series of biochemical reactions that release carbon dioxide and result in the formation of ATP (133)

L

labium an insect mouthpart that functions like a lower lip (766)

labor the muscular contractions of the uterus and other events that lead to birth (1058)

labrum an insect mouthpart that functions like an upper lip (766)

lac **operon** DNA segment that codes for the regulatory enzymes for lactose metabolism in *E. coli* (203)

lacteal a tiny lymph vessel (989)

lactic acid fermentation the process by which pyruvic acid is converted to lactic acid (129)

laminarin a type of polysaccharide with glucose units linked differently from those in starch (531)

large intestine an organ of digestion in which water is reabsorbed (989)

larva an immature form of an organism that is morphologically distinct from that of an adult (695)

larynx the voice box that houses the vocal cords (945)

lateral line system a row of sensory structures that run the length of the body of a fish (803)

lateral meristem in plants, a growing region that increases the diameter of roots and stems (602)

law of independent assortment law stating that pairs of genes separate independently of one another in meiosis (168)

law of segregation law stating that pairs of genes separate in meiosis and each gamete receives one gene of a pair (168)

law of superposition a law that states that successive layers of rock or soil were deposited on top of one another and the lowest level is oldest (280)

layering the process of causing roots to form on a stem (640)

leaflet one of the divisions of a blade (616)

legume any plant of the family Leguminosae, such as a bean, a pea, or a lentil (412)

lens a convex crystalline structure in the eye that focuses light on the retina (1020)

leukemia a progressive, malignant disease of the blood-forming organs (211)

leukocyte a white blood cell (940)

lichen a symbiotic association between fungi and green algae (549)

life expectancy how long, on average, an individual is expected to live (381)

ligament a connective tissue in a joint (913)

light reactions the initial reactions in photosynthesis, including the absorption of light by photosystems I and II, the passage of electrons along the electron transport chains, the production of NADPH and O_2, and the synthesis of ATP through chemiosmosis (112)

limbic system a group of clusters of neurons in the brain that helps regulate the emotions (1006)

limiting factor biotic or abiotic factor that restrains the growth of a population (385)

linkage group the group of genes, located on the same chromosome, that are usually inherited together (222)

lipid a kind of organic compound that is insoluble in water, such as fats and steroids (58)

liver organ that performs vital metabolic processes including filtration of blood, secretion of bile, and conversion of sugars into glycogen (986)

lobe-finned fish a fish having paddlelike fins with fleshy bases (807)

logistic growth a model of population growth in which birth and death rates vary with population size and are equal at the carrying capacity (385)

long-day plant a plant that flowers when exposed to day lengths longer than the plant's critical length (656)

loop of Henle in the kidney, the part of the nephron that maintains a high concentration of sodium chloride in the surrounding fluid (993)

lung the respiratory organ where gas exchange occurs (678)

luteal phase the menstrual stage in which the corpus luteum develops (1053)

luteinizing hormone (LH) a hormone that stimulates ovulation and androgen secretion by the corpus luteum (1035)

lymph the fluid of the lymphatic system (937)

lymphatic system a series of one-way vessels that carry intercellular fluid from tissues to the bloodstream (931)

lymphocyte a type of white blood cell occurring in two primary forms, T cells and B cells (959)

lymphoma a tumor in the tissues that form blood cells (211)

lysis the disintegration of a cell by disruption of the plasma membrane (493)

lysosome an organelle containing digestive enzymes, existing primarily in animal cells (79)

lytic cycle the replication process of viruses that results in the destruction of the host cell (492)

M

macromolecule a very large organic molecule composed of many smaller molecules (53)

macronucleus in *Paramecia,* the larger of the two types of nuclei (514)

macronutrient an element used by plant cells in relatively large amounts (606)

macrophage a large white blood cell that engulfs pathogens and cellular debris (961)

madreporite a sievelike plate on the aboral surface of an echinoderm through which water enters the water-vascular system (786)

malignant tumor a cancerous mass of cells (211)

Malpighian tubule the main excretory organ of most insects and some myriapods and arachnids (752)

mammary gland one of the milk-secreting glands of mammals (881)

mandible a movable mouthpart that usually functions in chewing (745)

mantle the epidermal layer of mollusks (726)

mantle cavity a space between the mantle and the visceral mass in mollusks (726)

map unit a unit in chromosome mapping equal to a 1 percent occurrence of crossing-over (224)

marsupial a mammal that carries its young in a pouch (884)

mass a fundamental property of an object generally regarded as equivalent to the amount of matter in the object (31)

mass extinction one of the brief periods of time during which large numbers of species disappeared (281)

mass number the sum of the protons and the neutrons in an atom (265)

mastax a muscular organ that breaks up food in rotifers (718)

matter anything that occupies space and has mass (10)

maxilla a head appendage in arthropods that is used to manipulate food (748)

maxilliped a thoracic appendage in arthropods that is used to manipulate food and to detect touch and chemicals (748)

medulla the innermost portion of an organ such as the kidney (992)

medulla oblongata in fish, the posterior brain lobes that regulate the internal organs; in humans, a part of the brain stem (812, 1007)

medusa a free-swimming, bell-shaped stage in the life cycle of a cnidarian (696)

megagametophyte female gametophyte (628)

megasporangium structure that produces megaspores (628)

megaspore a spore produced by meiosis in a megasporangium (627)

megaspore mother cell a diploid cell in the ovule that undergoes meiosis to produce four haploid megaspores (630)

meiosis the process of nuclear division that reduces the number of chromosomes in a cell by half (148)

melatonin a hormone that probably regulates sleep patterns (1037)

memory cell a specialized white blood cell that protects the body from reinfection by a specific pathogen (963)

meninges the three protective membranes that surround the brain and spinal cord (1007)

menopause the cessation of the menstrual cycle (1053)

menstrual cycle the monthly changes in the female reproductive system (1052)

menstruation the release of the uterine lining, blood, and an unfertilized egg at the end of the menstrual cycle (1053)

meristem the growing region in plants (602)

merozoite an asexually produced stage in the life cycle of some parasitic sporozoan protozoans that disperse and infect additional cells (517)

mesentery a fanlike membrane that holds the digestive organs in place (827)

mesoderm a layer of cells in the gastrula that gives rise to muscles and to interior body linings (683)

mesoglea in cnidarians, the jellylike material located between the epidermis and the gastrodermis (696)

mesophyll in leaves, the tissue where photosynthesis occurs (616)

mesothorax the middle segment of an insect's thorax (765)

messenger RNA (mRNA) the type of RNA that carries genetic information from the nucleus to the ribosomes (191)

metabolism the sum of all chemical processes in living things (10)

metamorphosis a major change in form that occurs as a larval animal develops into an adult (768)

metaphase the second phase of mitosis, during which all the chromosomes move to the cell's equator (150)

metastasis the spread of cancer cells beyond their original site (211)

metathorax the most posterior segment of an insect's thorax (765)

methanogen a bacterium that produces methane during anaerobic respiration (468)

microfilament a polymer chain of the protein actin; the smallest strand in the cytoskeleton (79)

micronucleus in *Paramecia*, the smaller of the two nuclei; involved in sexual reproduction (515)

micronutrient an element used by plants in relatively small amounts (606)

microsphere a type of microscopic droplet enclosed by a membrane composed of organic molecules (268)

microsporangium structure that produces microspores (628)

microspore a spore produced by meiosis in a microsporangium (627)

microspore mother cell diploid cell in the pollen sac that undergoes meiosis to produce four haploid microspores (631)

microtubule a hollow tube of protein that constitutes the largest strand in the cytoskeleton (79)

microvillus one of the extensions of membranes covering the villi (688)

midbrain the section of the brain stem, which acts as a relay between the cerebrum and cerebellum (709)

midgut the stomachlike region of some invertebrates (766)

migratory bird a bird that overwinters in the tropics and then travels to temperate areas to breed and raise its offspring (453)

mimicry a defense in which one organism resembles another that is dangerous or poisonous (398)

mineral an inorganic solid formed in the Earth (981)

mitochondrial matrix the space inside the inner membrane of a mitochondrion (133)

mitochondrion the organelle that is the site of aerobic respiration in eukaryotic cells (76)

mitosis eukaryotic nuclear division (148)

mitotic spindle the array of spindle fibers that serve to divide the chromatids during nuclear division (150)

mitral valve bicuspid valve; the atrioventricular valve on the left side of the heart (932)

molar a flattened tooth used to grind and crush (984)

mold a type of fossil formed from an impression of the shape or tracks of an organism; in fungi, a mass of tangled filaments of cells, such as the fungus that grows on bread (279)

molecular genetics the study of the structure and function of chromosomes and genes (169)

molecule a chemical structure composed of one or more atoms (34)

mollusk an invertebrate with a soft, unsegmented body often enclosed in a hard shell containing calcium carbonate; examples include snails, clams, and squids (725)

molting the process of shedding an exoskeleton or other outer layer on an animal (744)

monocot an angiosperm with a single cotyledon, parallel veins, and flower parts in multiples (592)

monohybrid cross a cross between individuals that involves one pair of contrasting traits (174)

monomer a repeated, single-molecule unit in a polymer (53)

monosaccharide a simple sugar such as fructose or glucose (55)

monosomy a condition in a diploid cell in which one chromosome of one pair is missing as a result of nondisjunction during meiosis (231)

monotreme egg-laying mammal (884)

morphogenesis the change in form of an organism resulting from cell differentiation (209)

morphology the study of the internal and external structure and form of an organism (309)

morula a ball of cells produced by cleavage of the zygote (1054)

motor division a division of the peripheral nervous system that allows the body to react to the brain's interpretation of sensory information (1009)

motor neuron a neuron that carries impulses from the spinal cord to muscle cells (1004)

mouth pore the structure at the oral groove into which the *Paramecium* sweeps food (514)

movable joint enables the skeleton to move where bones come together to perform a wide range of activities (913)

M phase mitosis; the phase of cell division in which the nucleus divides (148)

mucous membrane the mucus-secreting epithelial tissue lining of the interior surfaces of the body (956)

mucus a thick, slimy fluid produced by the mucous membranes (956)

multicellular organism a living thing that consists of more than one cell (6)

multiple fission a form of cell division that results in a number of identical individuals (507)

muscle fatigue the physiological inability of a muscle to contract (920)

muscle fiber a skeletal muscle cell that runs the length of the muscle and contains many nuclei (916)

muscle tissue the body tissue that enables movement (905)

mutagen an environmental factor that damages DNA (212)

mutation a change in DNA (189)

mutualism a form of symbiosis in which both organisms benefit from living together (402)

mycelium a mat of interwoven hyphae (543)

mycology the study of fungi (543)

mycorrhiza a symbiotic association between fungi and plant roots (549)

myofibril a contracting thread in a skeletal muscle (917)

myosin the thick protein filament of a sarcomere (917)

N

NAD+ nicotinamide adenine dinucleotide; an organic molecule that accepts electrons during redox reactions (128)

NADP+ nicotinamide adenine dinucleotide phosphate; an organic molecule that accepts electrons during redox reactions (115)

naphthalene acetic acid (NAA) synthetic auxin used to promote root formation on stem and leaf cuttings (648)

narcotic a drug derived from opium that relieves pain and induces sleep (1076)

nastic movement a type of plant movement that is independent of the direction of the stimuli (654)

natural killer cell a large white blood cell that attacks pathogen-infected cells and cancer cells (958)

natural selection the process by which organisms with favorable variations reproduce at higher rates than those without such variations (284)

nauplius the free-swimming larva of most crustaceans (746)

nematocyst a stinging organelle in the cnidocytes of cnidarians (697)

nephridium tubule through which some invertebrates eliminate wastes (735)

nephron the functional unit of the kidney (992)

neritic zone the ocean subarea over the continental shelf (431)

nerve a strand of axons through which impulses travel (1008)

nerve net a diffuse web of interconnected nerve cells in the nervous system of cnidarians (697)

nerve ring a nerve that encircles the central region of an echinoderm (787)

nervous tissue a type of animal tissue that conducts electrical impulses (905)

net primary productivity the rate at which biomass accumulates in an ecosystem (415)

net venation in plant leaves, the repeated branching of veins to form a network of smaller veins (592)

neuron a cell that transmits electrical signals (668)

neurosecretory cells cells of the hypothalamus that produce and secrete hormones (1032)

neutron a subatomic particle with no electric charge (32)

neutrophil a large leukocyte containing a lobed nucleus and many cytoplasmic granules (957)

niche the way of life of a species (371)

nicotine a toxic, addictive alkaloid derived from tobacco and one of the major contributors to the harmful effects of smoking; used as an insecticide (1068)

nictitating membrane a third membrane that can cover the eyeball (829)

nitrification the process in the nitrogen cycle by which nitrites and nitrates are produced (423)

nitrogen-containing base a DNA nucleotide containing nitrogen, a sugar molecule, and a phosphate group (185)

nitrogen cycle the pathway that nitrogen follows within an ecosystem (422)

nitrogen fixation the process by which gaseous nitrogen in the air is converted into ammonia (251)

nitrogen-fixing bacteria bacteria that live in the roots of legumes and convert atmospheric nitrogen into ammonia (423)

node the end of the internode where one or more leaves are attached (609)

nondisjunction the failure of homologous chromosomes to separate during meiosis or the failure of sister chromatids to separate during mitosis (225)

nonutilitarian value the intrinsic value of biodiversity apart from any human use or economic value (451)

nonvascular plant a plant that lacks vascular tissue and true roots, stems, and leaves (581)

norepinephrine (noradrenaline) a chemical that is a hormone in the endocrine system and is a neurotransmitter in the nervous system (1035)

notochord a flexible rod of tissue found in the dorsal part of chordates (673)

nuclear envelope a double membrane that surrounds the nucleus of a eukaryotic cell (80)

nuclear matrix the nuclear skeleton, a shape-maintaining protein (80)

nuclear pore a small hole in the nuclear envelope through which substances pass between the nucleus and the cytoplasm (81)

nucleic acid an organic molecule, DNA or RNA, that stores and carries important information for cell function (59)

nucleolus the structure in which ribosomes are synthesized and partially assembled; found in most nuclei (81)

nucleotide a monomer of DNA and RNA, consisting of a nitrogen base, a sugar, and a phosphate group (59)

nucleus in an atom, the core of protons and neutrons; in a eukaryotic cell, the organelle that contains most of the DNA and directs most of the cell's activities (32)

nutrient a chemical substance an organism needs to grow and function properly (977)

nyctinastic movement plant movement in response to the daily cycle of light and temperature (655)

nymph an immature form of an insect (768)

O

obligate aerobe an organism that requires oxygen (476)

obligate anaerobe an organism that requires the absence of oxygen (476)

obligate intracellular parasite a parasite that requires a host cell in order to reproduce (491)

oceanic zone one of two subareas of the pelagic zone (432)

ocular lens in a microscope, the lens in the eyepiece (21)

olfactory lobe the brain region that interprets smell (812)

olfactory nerve the nerve that carries impulses from olfactory receptors in the nasal passage to the brain (721)

omnivore an animal that eats both plants and animals (416)

oncogene a gene that induces cancer or other uncontrolled cell proliferation; a mutated or activated proto-oncogene that is associated with the development of tumor cells (213)

oogenesis the production of mature egg cells (155)

oogonium a unicellular gametangium that produces eggs (528)

open circulatory system a system in which the circulatory fluid is not contained entirely within vessels (675)

operator a sequence of DNA to which a repressor binds to prevent mRNA synthesis from the adjacent gene; characteristically composed of one or more

palindromic sequences (204)

operculum in fish, a hard plate attached to each side of the head that covers gills and is open at the rear (808)

operon a unit of DNA common in bacteria and phages consisting of clusters of regulated genes (204)

opportunistic infection an infection that does not normally cause disease but becomes pathogenic if the patient's immune system is weakened (969)

optic nerve the nerve that transmits signals from the retina of the eye to the brain (1021)

optic tectum an area of the fish brain that receives and processes information from the fish's visual, auditory, and lateral line systems (812)

oral groove a funnel-like structure used by ciliates for feeding (514)

oral surface the surface of an echinoderm where the mouth is located (785)

order in taxonomy, a group of similar families (338)

organ several types of body tissues that together perform a function (86)

organelle one of several formed bodies with a specialized function that is suspended in the cytoplasm and found in eukaryotic cells (71)

organ of Corti in the ear, the middle fluid-filled chamber of the cochlea; the organ of hearing (1019)

organ system a group of organs that interact to perform a set of related tasks (8)

organic compound a compound that is derived from living things and contains carbon (52)

origin attachment point of a tendon to a stationary bone (919)

osculum an opening at the top of a sponge through which water leaves the sponge (693)

osmosis the diffusion of water across a selectively permeable membrane (96)

ossicle one of the small calcium carbonate plates that make up the endoskeleton of an echinoderm (782)

ossification process by which cartilage is converted to bone (912)

osteoarthritis degenerative joint disease (914)

osteocyte a living bone cell (911)

oval window the membrane that separates the middle ear from the inner ear (1018)

ovary an egg-producing gonad of a female (1050)

oviparous referring to organisms that produce eggs that hatch outside the body of the mother (849)

ovipositor in many female insects, a structure at the end of the abdomen used for laying eggs (768)

ovoviviparous referring to organisms that produce eggs that hatch inside the body of the mother (849)

ovulation menstrual stage in which the ovarian follicle ruptures and releases an egg (1052)

ovule the megasporangium of a flowering plant (630)

ovum a female gamete or an egg (1050)

oxaloacetic acid a four-carbon compound that combines with acetyl CoA in the Krebs cycle to produce citric acid (134)

oxidation reaction a chemical reaction in which a reactant loses one or more electrons, becoming more positive in charge (37)

oxygen debt a temporary lack of oxygen availability due to exertion (920)

oxytocin a hormone that stimulates uterine contractions during childbirth (1032)

ozone a molecule composed of three atoms of oxygen; ozone in the upper atmosphere shields the Earth from ultraviolet radiation (271)

P

P₁ a strain obtained through self-pollination (166)

pacemaker the sinoatrial node that regulates the contraction of the heart (933)

palisade mesophyll in plants, a layer of mesophyll directly beneath the upper epidermis where most photosynthesis takes place (616)

pancreas the organ that lies behind the stomach and produces and secretes insulin, glucagon, and digestive enzymes (809)

papilla bumps of tissue on the tongue, between which are embedded taste buds (1021)

parallel venation in plants, the arrangement of several main veins parallel to each other (616)

parapodium one of the fleshy appendages on each side of most segments in a polychaete annelid (733)

parasite an organism that obtains its nutrition at the expense of another (399)

parathormone a hormone that regulates the levels of calcium ions and phosphate ions in the blood (1037)

parathyroid gland a gland that secretes hormones that regulate calcium and phosphate ions in the blood (1037)

parenchyma in plants, the living tissue of the ground system, consisting of cells with thin cell walls (599)

passive transport the movement of substances across a cell membrane without the use of cell energy (95)

pathogen an organism that causes disease (250)

pathology the scientific study of disease (804)

pectoral fin a fin located on the side of a fish body just behind the head (804)

pedicellaria one of many pincerlike structures on the surface of certain echinoderms (785)

pedigree a diagram of the genetic history of an individual; can show how a trait is inherited over several generations (227)

pedipalp in arachnids, an appendage that aids in chewing (753)

pellicle a rigid protein covering of some unicellular organisms (514)

pelvic fin in fishes, one of the paired fins positioned in the ventral, posterior portion of the body (808)

pelvis the hipbones (319)

penicillin antibiotic drug that combats bacteria by interfering with bacterial cell-wall synthesis (479)

pentaradial symmetry body symmetry in which body parts extend from the center along five spokes (782)

pepsin digestive enzyme of the stomach (986)

peptide bond a covalent bond between two amino acids (57)

peptidoglycan a protein-carbohydrate compound found in the cell walls of bacteria (468)

pericardium the tough saclike membrane that surrounds the heart (931)

pericycle in plants, the outermost cylinder of cells in the central vascular area (606)

periosteum the tough outer membrane of a bone; the point where tendons attach muscles to bones (910)

peripheral nervous system the network of nerves that connects the central nervous system with all parts of the body (1004)

peripheral protein a protein attached to the interior or exterior surface of the cell membrane (74)

peristalsis a series of rhythmic muscular contractions that force food through the digestive system (985)

permafrost in the tundra, a permanently frozen layer of ground (425)

pesticide a chemical used to control insects (564)

petal one of the leaf-shaped parts of the corolla of a flower, usually brightly colored and conspicuous (629)

petiole in leaves, the structure that attaches blade and stem (616)

PGA phosphoglycerate; a three-carbon molecule formed in the first step of the Calvin cycle (117)

PGAL glyceraldehyde phosphate; a three-carbon molecule formed in the second step of the Calvin cycle that can leave the cycle and be used to make other organic compounds (118)

phagocyte a cell that engages in phagocytosis (104)

phagocytosis a type of endocytosis in which a cell engulfs large particles or whole cells (103)

pharyngeal pouch a small outpocket of the anterior gut in a chordate (673)

pharynx in flatworms, a muscular tube that leads to the gastrovascular cavity; in animals with a digestive tract, the part of the tract between the mouth and the esophagus (710)

phenotype the external appearance of an organism that is determined by the individual's genotype (172)

phenotype frequency a ratio stating the number of times a specific phenotype occurs in a population in a single generation (175)

phenylketonuria (PKU) a genetic disorder in which the body cannot metabolize phenylalanine (232)

pheromone a chemical released by an animal that affects the behavior or development of other animals (771)

phloem in plants, the specialized tissue in the vascular system that transports dissolved sugars (580)

phospholipid a complex lipid having two fatty acids joined by a molecule of glycerol (58)

photic zone the layer of the ocean that receives light (431)

photoautotroph an organism that uses sunlight as an energy source (476)

photoperiodism a plant response to changes in day length (656)

photosynthesis the conversion of light energy into chemical energy stored in organic compounds (10, 111)

photosystem in plants, a unit of several hundred chlorophyll molecules and carotenoid pigment molecules in the thylakoid membrane (114)

phototropism plant growth in response to light (652)

pH scale a numeric range that quantifies the relative concentrations of hydronium ions and hydroxide ions in a solution (42)

phycobilin a pigment in red algae capable of absorbing the wavelengths of extremely dim light, allowing red algae to exist in very deep water (531)

phylogeny the evolutionary history of a species or taxonomic group (339)

phylum in taxonomy, a group of similar classes (338)

phytochrome a pigment in plants that monitors changes in day length (657)

phytoplankton a photosynthetic, aquatic microorganism (525)

pia mater the innermost layer of the three sacs that surround the brain and spinal cord (1007)

pigment in plants, a compound that absorbs light and imparts color (112)

pilus an appendage that bacteria use to attach to objects (475)

pineal gland endocrine gland that secretes melatonin (1037)

pinocytosis a type of endocytosis in which a cell engulfs solutes or fluids (103)

pinworm roundworm parasite that lives in the lower intestine of humans but causes no serious disease (717)

pioneer species the first species to colonize a new habitat (406)

pistil a plant structure formed of fused carpels (629)

pith the plant tissue located in the center of the stem (606)

pituitary gland the endocrine gland suspended directly below the brain that secretes several different regulatory hormones (1032)

pivot joint allows movement from side to side and up and down, as in the top two vertebrae of the spine (913)

placenta the organ that nourishes unborn young (884)

placental mammal an animal that nourishes its young through a placenta inside the mother's body (884)

placoid scale a toothlike spine found on shark skin (804)

plankton the abundant small plant and animal organisms that drift or swim weakly near the surface of a body of water (432)

plant growth regulator a hormone that affects growth (421)

planula a free-swimming, ciliated larva of cnidarians (700)

plasma the liquid component of blood (939)

plasma cell a differentiated B cell that produces antibodies and secretes them into the blood (962)

plasmid a single ring of extrachromosomal DNA in bacteria (240)

plasmodial slime mold a member of phylum Myxomycota; a multinucleate mass of cytoplasm that engulfs food by phagocytosis (534)

plasmodium the multinucleate cytoplasm of a slime mold surrounded by a membrane that moves as a mass (517)

plasmolysis the shrinking or wilting of a walled cell in a hypertonic environment (98)

plastid an organelle of plant cells that contains starch, fats, or pigments (83)

plastron the ventral portion of a turtle shell (850)

platelet a partial cell needed to form blood clots (941)

plumule in plants, the structure composed of the epicotyl plus any embryonic leaves (636)

point mutation the change of a single nitrogen-containing base within a codon (225)

polar body one of two small cells produced and discarded during each of the two meiotic divisions that yield the haploid egg (156)

polar compound a compound with one side having a negative charge and the other side a positive charge (49)

polar nucleus in plants, a nucleus that migrates to the center of the cell during embryo-sac formation (630)

pollen grain the microgametophyte of seed plants (628)

pollen tube a structure that grows from a pollen grain, down which the sperm travels to the eggs (628)

pollination the transfer of pollen from an anther to a stigma of a flower of the same species (166)

pollinator an animal that carries pollen, such as insects, birds, or bats (402)

pollution an alteration of the natural environment producing a condition that is harmful to living organisms (825)

polygenic trait a trait controlled by multiple genes (229)

polymer a compound consisting of repeated linked monomers (53)

polymerase chain reaction (PCR) technique used to quickly make many copies of selected segments of DNA (245)

polyp a sessile, vase-shaped stage in the life cycle of a cnidarian (696)

polypeptide a long chain of several amino acids (57)

polysaccharide a complex carbohydrate composed of three or more monosaccharides (56)

pons a segment of the brain stem (1007)

population all the members of a species that live in the same area and make up a breeding group (363)

population density the number of individuals in a population in a given area at a specific time (380)

population genetics the study of evolution from a genetic point of view (299)

posterior the back or dorsal side of an organism (670)

postzygotic isolation a barrier to successful breeding that occurs after fertilization, such as the production of nonviable or sterile offspring (311)

power of magnification in a microscope, the factor of enlargement (22)

precocial referring to birds that, when hatched, are physically active and relatively mature (870)

preen gland the oil-secreting gland of a bird (864)

preening in birds, the act of grooming their feathers with oil secreted by the preen gland (864)

prehensile grasping, as in a primate's hand, foot, or tail (320)

premolar a tooth used to shear, shred, and grind (886)

pre-mRNA a form of mRNA that contains introns and exons (207)

pressure-flow hypothesis an explanation of the movement of sugars in the phloem of plants (612)

prezygotic isolation a barrier to successful breeding that occurs before fertilization, such as differences in mating time or behavior (311)

primary electron acceptor a molecule in the thylakoid membrane that accepts the electrons that chlorophyll *a* loses in the light reactions (115)

primary growth the tissue produced by apical meristems in plants (602)

primary host the host from which the adults of a parasite derive their nourishment and in which sexual reproduction occurs (712)

primary immune response an immunological response that occurs when an antigen is encountered for the first time (963)

primary succession the process of sequential replacement of populations in an area that has not previously supported life (406)

primate a member of the order Primates, the mammalian order that includes humans (320)

primer an artificially made single-stranded sequence of DNA required for the initiation of replication (245)

prion a glycoprotein particle implicated in diseases with long incubation periods (490)

probability the number of times an event is expected to happen divided by the number of opportunities for an event to happen (173)

probe a radioactive segment of DNA used in DNA fingerprinting (244)

producer an autotrophic organism that captures energy to make organic molecules (415)

product a compound formed by a chemical reaction (36)

progesterone a steroid hormone secreted by the corpus luteum of the ovary that stimulates the uterine lining to prepare for the implantation of a fertilized egg; produced by the placenta during pregnancy (1035)

proglottid one of the many body sections of a tapeworm; contains reproductive organs (713)

prokaryote a unicellular organism that lacks a nucleus and membrane-bound organelles (72)

prolactin a hormone that stimulates and maintains milk production (1033)

promoter a nucleotide sequence on a DNA molecule that, when attached to an RNA polymerase molecule, will initiate transcription of a specific structural gene (192)

prophage an intracellular bacteriophage that is harmless to the host cell (494)

prophase the first stage of mitosis and meiosis, characterized by condensation of chromosomes (150)

prosimian primate a suborder of modern primates that includes lemurs, lorises, and tarsiers (320)

prostaglandin a hormonelike chemical messenger that functions as a cell regulator (1031)

protease inhibitor an antiviral drug that interferes with the synthesis of viral capsids during viral replication; in combination with AZT has shown some promise in treating patients infected with HIV (498)

protein an organic compound composed of one or more chains of polypeptides, which in turn are formed from amino acids (56)

protein synthesis the formation of proteins using information coded on DNA and carried by RNA (193)

prothorax the most anterior segment of an insect's thorax (765)

proton a subatomic particle with a positive charge (32)

proto-oncogene oncogene precursor that controls a cell's growth and differentiation (214)

protostome an organism in which the blastopore develops into the mouth and the coelom arises by schizocoely and whose embryo has determinate cleavage (684)

protozoan a single-celled, eukaryotic protist that is able to move independently (84)

proventriculus the first of two chambers in the stomach of a bird (866)

provirus a viral DNA molecule produced by reverse transcriptase (495)

pseudocoelom in animals, a cavity between the mesoderm and the endoderm (686)

pseudoplasmodium a group of cells that act together as a unit to form a sporangium (534)

pseudopodium a retractile, temporary cytoplasmic extension that functions in movement in certain ameboid organisms (512)

psychoactive drug a chemical compound that affects the central nervous system (1075)

puberty a stage of human life when the

sex organs mature and secondary sex characteristics appear (1035)

pulmonary artery the artery that carries deoxygenated blood from the heart to the lungs (935)

pulmonary circulation the movement of blood between the heart and the lungs (935)

pulmonary respiration a type of respiration involving lungs, in which air is inhaled and exhaled by changing the volume and pressure of air in the mouth (826)

pulmonary vein the vein that carries oxygenated blood from the lungs to the heart (936)

punctuated equilibrium a theory that speciation occurs during brief periods of rapid genetic change (312)

Punnett square a model used to establish the probabilities of the results of a genetic cross (174)

pupa a stage in which an insect that goes through complete metamorphosis changes from a larva to an adult (769)

pupil the opening in the eye that allows light to enter (1020)

purine an organic molecule that has a double ring of carbon and nitrogen atoms (186)

pyloric sphincter the valve that separates the stomach from the small intestine (986)

pyloric stomach in a sea star, the stomach that is connected to the digestive glands (786)

pyrenoid a small protein structure found within the chloroplasts of certain algae that stores starch (525)

pyrimidine an organic molecule that has a single ring of carbon and nitrogen atoms (186)

pyruvic acid a three-carbon molecule that is the end product of glycolysis (128)

Q

quadrupedal able to walk on four limbs (324)

queen bee the only fertile female in a hive of honeybees (772)

queen factor a pheromone secreted by a queen bee that prevents other female larvae from developing into fertile females (773)

quinine a drug used to treat malaria (399)

R

radial canal the portion of a sea star's water-vascular system that runs the length of each arm (786)

radial cleavage in deuterostomes, the division of cells parallel to or at right angles to the polar axis of a fertilized egg (684)

radial nerve a nerve that runs along the length of each arm of a sea star (787)

radial symmetry in animals, an arrangement of body parts around a central axis (670)

radicle in plants, the embryonic root (636)

radioactive dating a method of determining the age of an object by measuring the amount of a specific radioactive isotope it contains (264)

radioactive decay the release of particles or radiant energy by the unstable nuclei of some isotopes (265)

radioactive isotope an isotope with an unstable nucleus (265)

radula a rough, tonguelike structure used in feeding by many mollusks (726)

ray-finned fish a fish with fins supported by several flexible bones rather than a single bony axis (807)

reabsorption a process in the kidney by which materials return to the blood from the nephron (994)

reactant a compound or atom involved in a chemical reaction (36)

realized niche the range of resources and conditions a species actually uses or can tolerate at optimal efficiency; smaller than fundamental niche (372)

receptacle the swollen tip of a branch that is the base of a flower (629)

receptor site the area of a cell membrane where antigen attachment takes place (492)

recessive referring to an allele that is masked by the presence of another allele for the same characteristic (168)

recombinant DNA a DNA segment from at least two different organisms (241)

rectal gland in fishes, a gland that removes excess sodium and chloride ions from the blood and releases them into the rectum for elimination (806)

red tide discoloration of sections of the ocean caused by a population explosion of certain dinoflagellates; contains a poisonous alkaloid produced by the dinoflagellates (528)

redox reaction a reduction-oxidation reaction in which electrons are transferred between atoms (37)

reduction reaction a chemical reaction in which a reactant gains one or more electrons, becoming more negative in charge (37)

regeneration the regrowth of missing body parts (695)

regulator an organism that uses energy to control its internal environment (370)

regulator gene a genetic unit that regulates or suppresses the activity of one or more structural genes (205)

releasing hormones hormones secreted by the hypothalamus that stimulate the anterior pituitary (1033)

release-inhibiting hormone hormones secreted by the hypothalamus that inhibit the anterior pituitary (1033)

renal circulation a subsystem of the systemic circulation that involves the movement of blood through the kidneys (936)

renal pelvis the central structure of the kidney (992)

renal tubule a long tube with permeable walls in a nephron (993)

replication the process by which DNA copies itself during interphase (188)

replication fork the points at which the DNA strands separate during replication (188)

repressor in the *lac* operon, a protein that inhibits an operator and thus stops gene expression (204)

reproduction the production of new offspring (7)

reproductive isolation the inability of formerly interbreeding organisms to produce offspring (311)

resolution the power of a microscope to show detail (21)

resource partitioning among similar species, a pattern of resource use in which species reduce their use of shared resources (401)

restoration biology the science of reversing major changes in ecosystems and replacing missing ecosystem components (452)

restriction enzyme a protein that recognizes specific sequences in a DNA molecule and cuts it into pieces (239)

reticular formation a network of nerve fibers running through the brain stem and the thalamus (1007)

retina the light-sensitive inner layer of the eye (1020)

retrovirus a virus, such as HIV, that contains RNA and reverse transcriptase, (490)

reverse transcriptase an enzyme that makes DNA from an RNA template (490)

RFLP analysis restriction fragment length polymorphism; the method for preparing a DNA fingerprint (244)

Rh factor a type of antigen found in the blood that may cause complications during some pregnancies (943)

rheumatoid arthritis an immune-system disorder causing painful joints (914)

rhizoid a rootlike structure attaching a gametophyte to soil, rock, or tree bark; a rootlike structure that anchors fungal hyphae to a solid substance (546)

rhizome the underground stem of a fern sporophyte (588)

ribonucleic acid (RNA) a nucleic acid composed of a single strand and distinguished from DNA by containing ribose and uracil (59)

ribose the five-carbon sugar in RNA (190)

ribosomal RNA (rRNA) the type of RNA found in a ribosome (191)

ribosome an organelle that functions in the synthesis of proteins (77)

ribozyme a type of RNA that is able to act as an enzyme (270)

ring canal the portion of a sea star's water-vascular system that encircles the mouth (786)

RNA polymerase the primary transcription enzyme (192)

root cap a shield covering the apical meristem (604)

root crop a plant grown for the nutrients it stores in its roots or modified underground stems (563)

root hair an extension of the epidermal cells (604)

rotifer a small, aquatic invertebrate with a crown of cilia surrounding its mouth (718)

rough endoplasmic reticulum the portion of the endoplasmic reticulum that contains attached ribosomes (76)

roundworm a worm in the phylum Nematoda with a long, slender body that tapers at both ends, such as hookworms and pinworms (715)

royal jelly a high-protein substance secreted by worker bees and fed to the queen and the youngest larvae (772)

RuBP ribulose bisphosphate; a five-carbon carbohydrate that combines with CO_2 to form two molecules of PGA in the first step of the Calvin cycle (117)

rumen the storage chamber in the stomach of artiodactyls, such as the antelope and the bison (887)

--- **S** ---

saddle joint type of joint found at the base of each thumb; allows grasping and rotation (913)

saliva a watery fluid secreted into the mouth; moistens food and begins digestion (984)

saprophyte an organism that feeds on dead organic material (476)

sapwood lighter-colored wood near the outside of a tree trunk active in transporting sap; tissue of the secondary xylem (611)

sarcoma a tumor growing in bone or muscle tissue (211)

sarcomere the basic contractile unit of skeletal and cardiac muscle that is the portion of the myofibril between two adjacent Z lines (917)

saturated solution a solution in which no more solute can dissolve (40)

savanna subtropical or tropical grassland with scattered trees and shrubs (428)

scanning electron microscope a microscope that produces an enlarged image of the surface of an object with a beam of electrons rather than light (22)

schistosomiasis a disease caused by a parasitic blood fluke of the genus *Schistosoma* (713)

schizocoely the method of coelom formation in protostomes that involves splitting the embryonic mesoderm into two layers (685)

sclerenchyma the tissue of the ground system that supports and strengthens the plant (600)

scolex a knob-shaped organ bearing hooks and suckers; lies at the anterior end of a tapeworm (713)

scrotum an external sac of skin that contains the testes (1048)

second messenger a chemical signal that relays a message from a cell's surface to its interior (1030)

secondary compound a poisonous, irritating, or bad-tasting substance synthesized by plants as a defense mechanism (398)

secondary growth the tissue produced by lateral meristems of plants (602)

secondary immune response the response to a subsequent infection by the same pathogen (963)

secondary succession the sequential replacement of populations in a disrupted habitat (406)

sediment dust, sand, or mud deposited over time by wind or water (279)

seed a plant embryo enclosed in a protective coat (579)

seed coat the protective structure of a plant seed (636)

seed plant a plant that produces seeds for reproduction (581)

segmentation division of a body into units (675)

selectively permeable membrane a membrane that keeps out some molecules but allows others to pass through (73)

self-pollination pollination involving the same flower, flowers on the same plant, or two genetically identical plants (166)

semen a fluid formed from sperm and various exocrine secretions (1048)

semicircular canal a structure in the inner ear that helps maintain balance (1019)

semilunar valve valve that separates the ventricles from the large vessels on each side of the heart (932)

semimovable joint a joint that allows limited movement, as in vertebrae (913)

seminal receptacle a structure on a female or hermaphrodite that receives sperm (735)

seminiferous tubules the location of sperm formation in the testes (1048)

sense organ an organ that contains sensory neurons which detect external stimuli (1017)

sensory division a division of the peripheral nervous system that acquires information from the external and internal environments of the body (1009)

sensory neuron a neuron that transmits impulses from sensory receptors to the central nervous system (1004)

sensory receptor a neuron that detects a stimulus (1009)

sepal a modified leaf that protects a young flower (629)

septum a wall dividing hyphae into cells; a thick wall that divides an organ, such as the heart (931)

sessile referring to an organism that attaches firmly to a surface and does not move (694)

seta one of the external bristles on annelids (733)

sex chromosome a chromosome that determines sex (146)

sex-influenced trait a trait that is influenced by the presence of male or female sex hormones (229)

sex-linkage the presence of a gene on a sex chromosome (222)

sexual reproduction the production of offspring from the combination of genetic material from two parent organisms (156)

sexual selection the preferential choice of a mate based on a specific phenotypic trait (308)

shaft the center of a bird feather (864)

short-day plant a plant that flowers when exposed to day lengths shorter than the plant's critical length (656)

sieve plate a region at the end of a sieve tube member through which compounds move from cell to cell (601)

sieve tube structure formed by stacked sieve tube members (601)

sieve tube member the conducting cell of angiosperm phloem (601)

simple leaf a leaf with only one blade (616)

single-allele trait a trait controlled by a single allele (228)

sink the place where a plant stores or uses sugars (613)

sinoatrial node the nerve tissue in the right atrium that regulates the contraction rate of the heart (933)

sinus venosus in fishes and amphibians, a collecting chamber for deoxygenated blood (810)

siphon on a clam, a tube through which water enters or leaves the body (729)

SI Système International d'Unités (International System of Measurements) the scientific standard of measurement which employs a set of units that describe length, mass, time and other attributes of matter (23)

skeletal muscle voluntary muscle, attached to bones by tendons, that moves parts of the body (905)

skeleton the bones of an animal body that form its internal framework (909)

skin gill one of many hollow tubes that project from the surface of a sea star, through which gas exchange and excretion take place (785)

smooth endoplasmic reticulum the portion of the endoplasmic reticulum that lacks attached ribosomes (76)

smooth muscle elongated, spindle-shaped involuntary muscles (except cardiac muscles) (905)

sodium-potassium pump a carrier protein that actively transports K^+ ions into and Na^+ ions out of cells (101)

soft palate a soft area made of folded membranes that separates the mouth cavity from the nasal cavity (984)

solar tracking the phototropism of leaves or flowers as they follow the sun's movement across the sky (653)

solute a substance dissolved in a solution (40)

solution a mixture in which one or more substances are uniformly dissolved in another substance (40)

solvent in a solution, the substance in which a solute is dissolved (40)

somatic mutation a mutation that occurs in a body cell (224)

somatic nervous system the division of the peripheral nervous system that controls skeletal muscles (1009)

sorus a cluster of sporangia in ferns (627)

source the place where sugars are made in a plant (613)

spawning the egg-laying behavior of some bony fishes (812)

specialist a species with a narrow niche that can tolerate a narrow range of conditions and can use only a few specific resources (372)

specialization the differentiation of a cell for a particular function (667)

speciation the formation of a new species (309)

species a group of organisms of a single type that are capable of producing fertile offspring in the natural environment (338)

species-area effect a pattern of species distribution in which larger areas contain more species than smaller areas do (404)

species diversity an index combining the number and relative abundance of different species in a community (403)

species identifier the second part of a species name; humans are known by genus name *Homo* and by species identifier *sapiens*; specific epithet (339)

species name the two-part scientific name of a species composed of the genus and the species identifier (339)

species richness the number of different species in a community (403)

spermatid in meiosis, a haploid cell that develops into a mature sperm cell (156)

spermatogenesis the production of sperm cells (155)

S phase the second period of interphase during which replication of DNA occurs (132)

spicule one of the small, spike-shaped particles of calcium carbonate or silicon dioxide that make up the skeleton of some sponges (693)

spinal cavity the area that surrounds and protects the spinal cord (908)

spinal cord a column of nerve tissue running through the vertebral column (1008)

spinal nerve a nerve connection between the spinal cord and an organ or muscle (812)

spinal reflex a muscular reaction to a stimulus that is initiated by the neurons of the spinal cord instead of the brain (1009)

spindle fiber one of the microtubules that extend across a dividing eukaryotic cell; assists in the movement of chromosomes (150)

spinneret the structure through which fluid from the silk gland of spiders passes (752)

spiracle an external opening of a trachea in an insect, myriapod, or spider (752)

spiral cleavage in protostomes, the division of cells in a spiral arrangement (684)

spirillum spiral-shaped eubacteria (470)

spirochete Gram-negative, spiral-shaped, heterotrophic bacterium (472)

spleen the largest lymphatic organ in the body; serves as a blood reservoir, disintegrates old red blood cells, and produces lymphocytes and plasmids (959)

sponge a sessile, aquatic invertebrate in the phylum Porifera with no true tissues or organs (693)

spongin the network of protein fibers making up the simple skeleton of some sponges (693)

spongy bone the lacy network of connective tissue in the center of a bone (911)

spongy mesophyll a mesophyll of irregularly shaped cells surrounded by air spaces that allow oxygen, carbon dioxide, and water to diffuse into and out of the leaf (616)

spontaneous generation an early and now disproved hypothesis that living organisms develop from nonliving material (261)

sporangiophore in some fungi, an upright hypha that produces sporangia (544)

sporangiospore in fungi, a specialized hypha supporting a sporangium (544)

sporangium a spore-bearing sac in plants, algae, and fungi (544)

spore a resistant reproductive cell of some organisms, such as certain plants, protists, and fungi (535)

sporophyte one of the diploid generation of land plants that produce spores (581)

sporozoite a sporozoan that has been released from the oocyst and is ready to penetrate a new host cell (517)

springwood in woody plants, secondary xylem with cells that are wide and thin walled; the first wood of a growing season (611)

stabilizing selection a type of natural selection in which the average form of a trait causes an organism to have an advantage in reproduction (306)

stamen the structure in the flower of plants that produces pollen (629)

staphylococcus eubacterium occurring in grapelike clusters (470)

start codon the codon AUG which engages a ribosome to start translating an mRNA molecule (194)

steroid a lipid in which the molecule is composed of four carbon rings (74)

steroid hormones a class of hormones synthesized from cholesterol (1030)

sticky end the single-stranded end of a double-stranded DNA fragment that can form base pairs with another sticky end of a DNA fragment cut by the same enzyme (240)

stigma an expanded apex of a pistil, supported by the style; the part of the pistil that receives pollen (166)

stimulant a drug that increases the activity of the central nervous system (1068)

stipe in some algae, the stemlike region of a thallus (531)

stolon the horizontal hypha of some fungi (546)

stoma one of many small pores usually located on the underside of a leaf; aids in gas exchange (119)

stomach an organ that prepares food for absorption by both physical and chemical activities (985)

stone canal part of the water-vascular system in sea stars that connects the madreporite with the ring canal (786)

stop codon causes the ribosome to stop translating mRNA; UAA, UAG, UGA (194)

stratum in geology, a layer of soil or rock in a cross section of the Earth (280)

streptococcus Gram-positive eubacterium occurring in chains (470)

strobilus a conelike structure of sporangia-bearing leaves (587)

stroma in plants, the solution that surrounds the thylakoids in a chloroplast (112)

structural gene a gene that codes for a

product, such as an enzyme, protein, or RNA, rather than serving as a regulator (204)

style in plants, a stalklike structure of the ovary (629)

subspecies varieties of animal species that occur in different geographical areas (339)

substitution a point mutation in which one nucleotide in a codon is replaced with a different nucleotide (225)

substrate a part, substance, or element that lies beneath and supports another; the reactant in any enzyme-catalyzed reaction (57)

succession the predictable, sequential replacement of populations in an ecosystem (406)

sulfa drug an antibiotic drug that combats bacteria by inhibiting bacterial cell metabolism (479)

summerwood in woody plants, secondary xylem cells that are small and thick walled and that are produced in hot, dry summers (611)

superior vena cava the large vein carrying blood from the upper part of the body (935)

suppressor T cell a type of T cell that shuts down the immune response after the pathogen has been eliminated (961)

survivorship curve the graph of a species' mortality-rate data (382)

swim bladder in bony fishes, a gas-filled sac that is used to control bouyancy (807)

swimmeret one of 10 bilaterally paired appendages on the abdomen of a crayfish (748)

swimmer's itch a condition characterized by minor skin irritation and swelling, caused by a small, brown fluke that usually lives in fresh water (713)

symbiosis the relationship between different species living in close association with one another (397)

sympathetic division the part of the autonomic nervous system that controls internal organs during conditions of high stress or increased activity (1010)

synapsis the pairing of homologous chromosomes during meiosis (153)

synovial joint a joint filled with synovial fluid (914)

syrinx the vocal organ of birds (873)

systematics systematic taxonomy; taxonomic organization of living things in the context of evolution (342)

systemic circulation the movement of blood between the heart and all parts of the body except the lungs (935)

systole the phase of the heartbeat in which the ventricles contract and force blood into the arteries (933)

systolic pressure pressure of the blood when the ventricles contract (934)

T

tagma in arthropods, a structure composed of several segments that have fused to perform specific functions (744)

taiga forested biome characterized by

cone-bearing evergreen trees (426)

tapeworm a parasitic flatworm that lives in the vertebrate intestine (713)

taproot the organ that results when the primary root grows downward and becomes the largest root (603)

tar a sticky mixture of chemicals and particles from tobacco (1068)

target cell the specific cell affected by a hormone (1029)

taste bud a structure in which chemoreceptors for taste are clustered (1021)

taxonomy the science of grouping organisms according to their presumed evolutionary relationships (337)

T cell a thymus-derived lymphocyte that helps stimulate an immune response against an antigen and can attack certain antigens (499)

tegument a continuous sheet of fused cells that covers the external surface of a fluke or tapeworm and protects the worm from the host's digestive and immune systems (712)

telophase the final stage of mitosis during which a nuclear membrane forms around each set of new chromosomes (151)

telson a flat, paddlelike projection at the posterior end of many crustaceans (748)

temperate referring to a nonvirulent virus, rarely causing disease; moderate, not subject to prolonged extremes of hot or cold (493)

temperate deciduous forest a forest characterized by trees that shed their leaves in the fall (426)

tendon a tough, solid band of connective tissue that supports and connects body parts (919)

tendril a specialized leaf found in many vines that takes on a coiled appearance (615)

tentacle a flexible appendage with which an animal feels its environment or grasps objects (696)

termination signal a specific sequence of nucleotides that marks the end of a gene in eukaryotes (192)

test the shell, or hardened covering, of some invertebrates (783)

test cross the crossing of an individual of unknown genotype with a homozygous recessive individual to determine the unknown genotype (175)

testis the gamete-producing gonad of a male (1047)

testosterone a hormone that regulates male secondary sex characteristics and the production of sperm cells (1035)

tetracycline an antibiotic drug that combats bacteria by interfering with bacterial protein synthesis (479)

tetrad a group of two homologous chromosomes during meiosis (153)

thalamus the brain structure that directs incoming sensory impulses to the proper region of the cerebral cortex (1006)

thallus the body of an alga (525)

theory a broad and comprehensive statement of what is believed to be true, supported by considerable experimental evidence resulting from many tests of related hypotheses (19)

thermoacidophile an archaebacterium that lives only in hot, acid places (468)

thermoregulation control of body temperature (848)

thigmotropism a plant's growth response to touching a solid object, as in the tendrils of vines that coil when they touch an object (653)

thoracic cavity the upper ventral cavity of the human body, containing the heart, lungs, and esophagus (908)

thorax in insects and some crustaceans, the part of the body between the head and the abdomen; in mammals, the part of the body between the neck and the abdomen (748)

thylakoid a flattened, membranous sac inside a chloroplast; contains most of the components involved in the light reactions of photosynthesis (83)

thymine a nitrogen-containing base, one component of a nucleotide (185)

thymosin a hormone produced in the thymus gland that stimulates the differentiation of T cells (1037)

thymus gland endocrine gland involved in immune-system development (1037)

thyroid gland the endocrine gland that secretes thyroxine (1034)

thyroxine a thyroid hormone that increases metabolism (1034)

tissue in most multicellular organisms, a group of similar cells that carry out a common function (86)

tissue culture the growing of living cells in a controlled medium (640)

tolerance a lessening response to a drug as a result of physical addiction (1073)

tolerance curve a graph of an organism's tolerance to a range of an environmental variable (369)

topsoil the uppermost layer of soil (822)

torpor a state of stupor (556)

torsion a process occurring during the larval development of gastropods in which the visceral mass twists 180° in relation to the head (727)

toxin a chemical substance, usually biological in origin, that is harmful to the normal functioning of cells (478)

toxoplasmosis a disease caused by a sporozoan that can cause serious harm to fetuses and newborns and can cause flulike symptoms in adults (517)

trachea in insects, myriapods, or spiders, one of a network of air tubes; in vertebrates, the tube that connects the pharynx to the lungs (752, 945)

tracheid a long, thick wall with tapering ends, forming part of the xylem tissue of plants (601)

trait in genetics, a category within which alternate characteristics, such as height and eye color, can be observed (165)

transcription the process in which RNA is made from DNA (191)

transcription factor one of the additional proteins bound to enhancers and RNA polymerase that regulate transcription (208)

transduction in viruses, the process in which genetic material is transferred from one cell to another (477)

transfer RNA (tRNA) the type of RNA that carries amino acids from the cytoplasm to the ribosomes (191)

transformation a process of direct transfer of nucleic acid from one bacterium to another (477)

transgenic organism a host organism that has received recombinant DNA (242)

translation the process of converting the genetic code in RNA into the amino acid sequence that makes up a protein (194)

translocation a mutation in which a broken piece of chromosome attaches to a nonhomologous chromosome; movement of organic molecules in plant tissues (225)

transmission electron microscope a microscope that transmits a beam of electrons rather than light through a thinly sliced specimen (22)

transpiration the evaporation of water through stomata (421)

trichinosis a disease caused by a parasitic roundworm of the genus *Trichinella;* characterized by muscle pain and stiffness (717)

triglyceride a lipid made of three fatty-acid molecules and one glycerol molecule (58)

trimester one of three divisions of pregnancy (1055)

trisomy a chromosomal anomaly in which an individual has an extra chromosome in any of the chromosome pairs (231)

trisomy 21 a human congenital disorder caused by trisomy of chromosome 21 due to the failure of the sister chromatids to separate during mitosis or the failure of homologous chromosomes to separate during meiosis (see Down syndrome) (231)

trochophore a free-swimming, ciliated larva of most mollusks and some annelids (725)

trophic level a feeding level in an ecosystem (417)

tropical rain forest a biome near the equator characterized by large amounts of rain and sunlight (429)

tropism plant movement toward or away from an environmental stimulus (652)

trypanosomiasis any of the forms of sleeping sickness or Chagas' disease (516)

tube cell the cell of a pollen grain that contains the tube nucleus (631)

tube foot one of many small, flexible, fluid-filled tubes that project from the body of an echinoderm and are used in locomotion, feeding, gas exchange, and excretion (782)

tumor an abnormal mass of cells (211)

tumor-suppressor gene a gene that suppresses tumor formation but when mutated causes a loss in cell function, resulting in tumor formation (213)

tundra a biome of low-growing vegetation that forms a continuous belt across North America, Europe, and Asia (425)

turgor pressure water pressure within a plant cell (98)

tympanic membrane the eardrum (1018)

tympanum a sound-sensing membrane on each side of the abdomen of an insect (767)

typhlosole in an earthworm, an infolding of the intestinal wall (734)

U

umbilical cord blood vessels that connect the placenta to the fetus (1056)

ungulate a hoofed mammal (894)

unicellular gametangium a single-celled gamete holder (321)

unicellular organism a living thing composed of one cell (6)

uniformitarianism a principle that states that the geological structure of Earth resulted from cycles of observable processes and that these processes operate continuously (284)

upwelling cold water rising from the ocean floor bringing organic material and nutrients (442)

uracil a nitrogen-containing base found in RNA (190)

urban ecology a new environmental field wherein people are challenged to increase biodiversity even in the most heavily developed areas (458)

urea product of the liver's conversion of ammonia that is eliminated by the kidneys (992)

ureter a narrow tube through which urine flows from the renal pelvis to the urinary bladder (995)

urethra the tube through which urine flows from the urinary bladder out of the body (995)

urinary bladder a muscular sac that stores urine (995)

urine a liquid containing nitrogenous wastes that have been removed from the blood (995)

uropod the most posterior appendage on many crustaceans (748)

uterus a female reproductive structure where eggs are stored or fertilized or where development of the young occurs (1051)

utilitarian value a way of relating the importance of biodiversity in terms of the economic benefits biodiversity provides to humans (451)

V

vaccine a solution containing a harmless version of a virus, bacterium, or toxin that causes an immune response when introduced to the body (250)

vacuole a fluid-filled organelle that stores enzymes or metabolic wastes in a plant cell (82)

vane the projection on either side of a bird's feather (864)

variety a further division or subset of species (339)

vascular cambium the lateral meristem in a plant that produces additional vascular tissue (602)

vascular plant a plant that has xylem and phloem (581)

vascular tissue system the system that includes the xylem and phloem tissues of plants (601)

vas deferens a duct through which sperm leave the epididymis (1048)

vasopressin a hormone that helps control the amount of water excreted by the kidneys (1033)

vegetable food derived from any part of soft plants (563)

vegetative propagation asexual reproduction in plants (639)

vein a vessel carrying blood to the heart (934)

venation the arrangement of veins in a leaf (616)

vent in amphibians and reptiles, the opening through which waste and eggs or sperm exit the body (827)

ventral the bottom of a bilaterally symmetrical organism (670)

ventricle a lower, and the most muscular, chamber of the heart (931)

venule a small vessel in the network of veins (935)

vernalization the requirement that some seeds or spores be exposed to cold before they can germinate (658)

vertebra one of the repeating bony units of the backbone (677)

vertebrate an animal with a backbone (667)

vesicle a membrane-bound sac in a eukaryotic cell that contains materials involved in endocytosis, exocytosis, or transport within the cell (103)

vessel in plants, a structure formed by stacked vessel elements; in animals, a tubular conducting structure for blood or other body fluid (601)

vessel element an elongated, water-conducting plant cell wall with slanting ends and holes through which water can pass (601)

vestigial referring to a functionless structure that was functional in an ancestral species (290)

villus one of the small projections lining the small intestine (988)

viper venomous snake with two large, mobile fangs at the front of the mouth (853)

viroid a short, single strand of RNA that causes disease in plants (490)

virology the study of viruses (487)

virulent disease-causing and highly infectious (492)

virus a nonliving infectious particle composed of a nucleic acid and a protein coat (486)

visceral mass the central region of a mollusk, located between the head-foot and the mantle (726)

visible spectrum the portion of sunlight perceived by the human eye as various colors (112)

vitamin complex organic molecule that serves as a coenzyme; one of the basic six nutrients (980)

viviparous referring to organisms that carry and nourish the young inside the body before birth (849)

voluntary muscle a muscle whose movement can be consciously controlled (916)

vulva the external part of the female reproductive system (1051)

W

warning coloration a bold, bright color pattern that makes dangerous, poisonous, or bad-tasting animals clearly recognizable and warns predators away (770)

water cycle the movement of water between the ground, the atmosphere, and bodies of water (420)

water mold a funguslike organism composed of branching filaments of cells, found in freshwater systems (535)

water-vascular system a network of water-filled canals in echinoderms (782)

wavelength the distance between crests in a wave (113)

withdrawal a reaction to the lack of a drug (1073)

woody tissue in plants, tissue that is formed from several layers of xylem, usually concentrated in the center of the stem (580)

worker bee a sterile female bee that makes up the majority of the beehive population (772)

X

xylem the vascular tissue in plants that transfers water and minerals from the roots to the leaves (580)

X-linked gene a gene found on the X chromosome (222)

Y

yeast unicellular fungus whose colonies resemble those of bacteria; known as the microorganisms that make bread rise (543)

Y-linked gene a gene found on the Y chromosome (222)

yolk sac in amniote eggs, the membrane that encloses the yolk and supplies the embryo with food (842)

Z

Z line boundary of a sarcomere; point of anchor for thin actin filaments (917)

zooplankton microscopic animal organisms that drift in bodies of water worldwide; represent a basic level of feeding relationships (507)

zoospore a flagellated spore (527)

zygosporangium in fungi, fused gametangia in conjugation (547)

zygospore the protective structure that results when the wall surrounding a zygote thickens (527)

zygote the diploid cell that results from the fusion of gametes (1054)

INDEX

swamp, 468, **468**
swamp gas, 517
swan, 872
sweat gland, 924, **924**
sweet potato, 607
swift, 871–872
swim bladder, 807, 811
swimmeret, 748, *t* 749
swimmer's itch, 713
sycamore, 427, 572
symbiosis, 397, 701, **701**
symmetry, of animal bodies, 670–671, **671**, 674
sympathetic division, of autonomic nervous system, 1010–1011, **1011**
synapsid, 882, **882**
synapsis, 153
synaptic cleft, 1012, **1013**, 1016, **1016**, 1074, **1074**
synovial joint, 914, **914**
syphilis, 472
syrinx, 873
syrphid fly, **770**
Systemae Naturae, 340, **341**
systematics, 342–345, **343–344**
systemic circulation, 825–826, 935–936, **936**
systemic lupus erythematosus, *t* 965
systole, 933
systolic pressure, 934

T

tadpole, 831, **831**
tagmata, 744, 746, 761
taiga, *t* 425, 426, **426**
tailbone, vestigial, 290
tapeworm. *See* Cestoda
tapir, 894, **894**
taproot, 603, **603, 605**
target cell, 1029
tars, 1068, **1069**
tarsier, 320, **320**, 893
taste, 887, 1021, **1021**
taxol, 399, *t* 564
taxonomy, 337, 669. *See also* classification
 cladistics, 345–346, **346**
 history of, 337–341
 Linnaeus's system of, 337–341
 phylogenetic, 342–346
 systematic, 342–345, **343–344**
Tay-Sachs disease, *t* 230
T cell, 499, 959, 961–963, **962–963**
teeth, 984
 of mammals, 881, 886–887
 of shark, 804
tegument, 712–713. *See also* integument
telson, 748
temperate deciduous forest, 424, **424,** *t* 425, 426–427, **427**
temperate grassland, **416,** 424, **424,** *t* 425, 427, **427**
temperate virus, 493–495
temperature. *See also* body temperature
 changes in environment, 368–369, **369**
 effect on photosynthesis, 120, **120**

moderation by water, 51
 tolerance curve, 369, **369**
temporal lobe, 1004, **1005**
tendon, 906, 919, **919**
tendril, 615, **615,** 653
tentacle, 696, **696, 709,** 730, **730**
teredo, 730
terminal bud, 609
termination signal, 192
termite, **507,** 763, **764,** 768
Terpogossian, Michael, 921
terrestrial ecosystem, 424–429
Tertiary period, *t* 280
test
 of echinoids, 783
 of sarcodines, 513, **513**
testcross, 175, **175**
testis, 155–156, 1047–1048
 hormones produced by, 1035, *t* 1036
 of hydra, **699,** 700
testosterone, 230, **298,** 1035, *t* 1036, 1047, **1048**
tetanus, 476, 478, *t* 478
 vaccine, 964
tetracycline, 479, *t* 479, 1067
tetrad, 153–154
9-tetrahydrocannabinol. *See* THC
Tetrahymena, t 509
thalamus, 1006, **1006**
thalloid, 584, **584**
thallus, 525–526
THC, 1076
theory, 19
therapsid, 882–883, **883**
thermal pollution, 462–463
thermoacidophile, 468
thermophile, 476
thermoreceptor, 1017, 1022
thermoregulation, in reptiles, 848, **848**
thiamin. *See* vitamin B₁
thiarubrin-A, 614
thigmonastic movement, 654–655, **654**
thigmotropism, 653, *t* 653
thoracic cavity, 908, **908,** 931, 948
thorax, of arthropods, 748, 761, 765, **765**
thorium-230, *t* 266
thorn, 608
thrush, 866
thumb, opposable, 320
thylakoid, 83, **83,** 112, **112, 114,** 115, 474
thymine, 185, **186,** 190, **190**
thymosin, *t* 1036, 1037
thymus gland, 959, *t* 1036, 1037
thyroid gland, 1034, **1034,** *t* 1036
thyroid stimulating hormone (TSH), *t* 1033, 1034
thyroxine, 831, 1034, *t* 1036, 1040, **1040**
 in frog metamorphosis, 1044–1045
Thysanura (bristle-tailed insects), *t* 762
tibiofibula, 825, **825**
tick, 364–365, **364, 400,** 745, 751, 753, **753**
tidal volume, 952–953
tiger, 397
Tilman, David, 405

tinea cruris, *t* 551
tinnitus, 1017
tissue, 86–87, 667, 672, 905–906
tissue culture, plant, 640, **640,** 651
tissue plasminogen activator, *t* 249
toad, 820–822, **821,** 824
tobacco, **119,** 399, 572, 656, 1068–1070, **1069.** *See also* smoking
 effects of, 1068, **1069**
 hazards of long-term use of, 1069–1070, **1069**
tobacco mosaic virus, 487, 504–505
tocopherol. *See* vitamin E
tolerance, drug, 1073
tomato, 648, 650, 656
 genetically engineered, **238,** 251–252, 251
tomato worm, 773
Tømmervik, Hans, 447
tongue, 1021
 of snake, **847**
tonsils, 959
tooth decay, 472, *t* 478
toothed whale, 895
toothpaste, *t* 566
topoisomerase-1 inhibitor, 213
torsion, 727, **727**
tortoise, **278,** 841, 850–851
 Galápagos, 850, **850**
toucan, 429, 873, **873**
Tournefort, Joseph, 341
toxin, 478
Toxoplasma, t 509, 517, **517**
toxoplasmosis, 517, **517**
T phage, 491
trachea (insect), 752, 766
trachea (vertebrate), 945
tracheid, 601, **601**
trait, 165
 variations in population, 299–300, **299–300**
tranquilizer, *t* 1075
transcription, 191–192, **191,** 200–201, 203, 1031, **1031**
 control after, 207, **207**
transcription factor, 208, **208**
transduction, 477, *t* 477
transfer RNA (tRNA), 191–192, 194–195, **194–195, 269**
transformation, in bacteria, 477, *t* 477
transfusion, 38–39, 969
transgenic organism, 242
translation, 194–195, **195,** 203
translocation, 225, **225,** 612
transmission electron microscope, 22, **22**
transpiration, **420,** 421, 613, 655
transport
 active, 101–104
 passive, 95–100
transposon, 171
transverse colon, 989, **989**
tree fern, 588, **588**
tree frog, **578**
tree shrew, *t* 896
Trematoda (flukes), 709, 711–713, **711–712**
Treponema, 472
Triassic period, *t* 280, 883
triceps muscle, 919, **919**

Triceratops, **840**
Trichinella, 717, **717**
trichinosis, 717–718
Trichonympha, **507,** *t* 509
Trichophyton, t 551
tricuspid valve, 932, **932**
triglyceride, 58
triiodothyronine, 1034
Trilobita (trilobytes), **279,** 745, **745**
triple bond, 52, **53**
trisomy-21. *See* Down syndrome
tRNA. *See* transfer RNA
trochophore, 725, **725,** 729, 736
trophic level, 417–419, **417**
tropical rain forest, 9, **9, 414,** 416, 422, 424, **424,** *t* 425, 429–430, **429,** 450, **570,** 571, **578**
tropic hormone, 1034
tropism, 652–654, *t* 653
trout, 807
true bug, *t* 762
truffle, 552, **552**
Trypanosoma, t 509, 516
trypanosomiasis, 516, **516**
tsetse fly, 516
TSH. *See* thyroid stimulating hormone
tuatara, 841, 845. *See also* Rhynchocephalia
tube cell, 631–632
tube foot, 782–784, **784,** 786
tube nucleus, 631
tuber, 608, **608,** *t* 639
tuberculosis, 476, *t* 478, 957, 1067, **1067**
tube worm, 469
Tubulidentata (ground-dwelling insectivores), *t* 896
tumor, 211, 213
tumor-suppressor gene, 213–214, **214**
tundra, 425–426, **425,** *t* 425
tunicate. *See* Urochordata
Turbellaria (flatworms), 709–711, **710.** *See also* planarian
turgor pressure, 98, 654, **654**
Turkana boy (fossil), 328
turkey, 873
Turner's syndrome, 231
turnip, 563, 607
turtle. *See* Chelonia
twig snake, 853
twins, identical, 344, 685
tympanic membrane, 829, 1018, **1018**
tympanum, 767, 847
typhlosole, 734
typhoid fever, 763

u

ulcer, 986, *t* 1066
ultraviolet radiation, 361, 443, 922
Ulva, 526, **526,** 529, **529**
umbilical cord, 1056, **1057,** 1058
ungulate, 894
unicellular organism, 5–6, **5,** 13, **30,** 72, 87, 667–668
uniformitarianism, 284

CREDITS

ILLUSTRATION

Abbreviation Code

AT = Alexander & Turner; SB = Sally J. Bensusen/Visual Science Studio; KC = Kip Carter; BH = Barbara Hoopes-Ambler; RH = Robert Hynes; BJ = Bridgette James; JK = John Karapelou; KK = Keith Kasnot; GK = George Kelvin; CK = Christy Krames; JL = Joe LeMonnier; MCA = Morgan-Cain & Associates; PG = Precision Graphics; SR = Steve Roberts; WAA = Wildlife Art Agency; MW = Michael Woods; SW = Sarah Woodward

All Safety Symbols were designed by Michael Helfenbein/Evolution Design.

xi KK; **xiv** MW; **Chapter 1:** 16, 21, 26 MCA; **Chapter 2:** 31–37, 42, 44, 46 MCA; **Chapter 3:** 49–50, 52–56 MCA; **57** (t) MCA; (b) Robert Margulies/MMA; **58–59, 62** MCA; **Chapter 4:** 70, 74–79, 83 MCA; **86** JK; **91** MCA; **Chapter 5:** 95, 97, 99, 102–104, 106–108 MCA; **Chapter 6:** 112–117, 120, 122–124 MCA; **Chapter 7:** 127–129, 133–137, 140–141 MCA; **Chapter 8:** 145 PG/MCA; **148** T Narashima; **149–151** MCA; **154** (t) MCA; (b) PG; **155** (t) MCA; (b) PG; **159** MCA; **Chapter 9:** 166 MW; **167** PG/(flowers) MW; **169** MCA; **174** (t) (spot) MW; (graphics) MCA; **174** (b) (spot) BH; (graphics) MCA; **175** (spot) BH; (graphics) MCA; **176–178** (spots) PG; (graphics) MCA; **180** MCA; **Chapter 10:** 185–186, 188, 190–191 MCA; **194** GK; **195, 199** MCA; **Chapter 11:** 204–205, 207–208 MCA; **210** (spots) SR/WAA; (graphics) MCA; **214, 216–217, 219** MCA; **Chapter 12:** 221 (spots) SR/WAA; (graphics) MCA; **222** MCA; **223** (t) (spots) SR/WAA; (graphics) MCA; **223** (b) JL; **224** (spots) SR/WAA; (graphics) MCA; **225–227, 231** MCA; **232** CK; **235–236** MCA; **Chapter 13:** 239–241, 244–245 MCA; **250** SD/David Fischer; **255** MCA; **Chapter 14:** 261–263, 265, 267 Mellander; **269, 272** MCA; **274** Mellander; **275** MCA; **Chapter 15:** 281 MW; **285** (map) MCA/Mountain High Map Resources; **286** Doug Schneider; **287** (spots) MW; (graphics) MCA; **289** JK; **291** SW; **282** BH; **294** (spots) MW; (graphics) MCA; **295–296** MCA; **Chapter 16:** 299, 301 (spots) PG; (graphics) MCA; **305** MCA; **307** (spots) PG; (graphics) MCA; **311** MCA; **312** (spots) MW; (graphics) MCA; **309** Doug Schneider; **314** PG; **315** MCA; **Chapter 17:** 321 JK; **326** Chris Forsey; **328** MCA; **330** David Fischer; **333–335** MCA; **Chapter 18:** 338 MCA; **343** (spots) BH; (graphics) MCA; **344** SW; **346** (spots) BH; (graphics) MCA; **350, 352** MCA; **353** MW; **354** Pond & Giles; **Chapter 19:** 361 MCA; **362, 364** BH; **367, 369–370** MCA; **371** (t) MW; (b) MCA; **372, 374–375** (MCA); **Chapter 20:** 381–382, 384–386, 389, 392–394 MCA; **Chapter 21:** 400 MCA; **401** RH; **404, 410** MCA; **411** Cecile Duray-Bito; **Chapter 22:** 416 MCA; **417** (spots) MW; (graphics) MCA; **418** (t) (spots) MW; (graphics) MCA; **418** (b) PG; **420–422** RH, (graphics) MCA; **424** MCA; **431** JL; **437** (spots) MW; (graphics) MCA; **Chapter 23:** 441–442, 444 David Uhl Illustration; **445** BJ/WAA; **448** BH; **449** BH; **450, 453–454, 457, 460–461** MCA; **Chapter 24:** 471, 482 MCA; **Chapter 25:** 488 MCA; **489** MCA; **491** MCA; **492** GK; **493** MCA; **494** (t) GK, (b) MCA; **502** GK; **503** MCA; **Chapter 26:** 510 MCA; **513** Claire Booth/CBMI; **514–515** MCA; **518** SB; **Chapter 27:** 528 (t) Henry Hill/John Edwards & Associates; (b) MCA; **529** Andrew Grivas; **533, 538** MCA; **539** Andrew Grivas; **Chapter 28:** 543 MCA; **546–547** MW; (zooms, graphics) MCA; **548** MCA; **554** MW; (zoom) MCA; **555** MCA; **Chapter 29:** 574 Ian Milnes/WAA; **Chapter 30:** 579 MW; **581** (spots) Cy Baker/WAA; (graphics) MCA; **582** (spots) MW; (graphics) MCA; **590** Stansbury, Ronsaville, Wood, Inc.; **592** Cy Baker/WAA; (graphics) MCA; **594** MCA; **Chapter 31:** 599, 601 MCA; **609** Stansbury, Ronsaville, Wood, Inc.; **612, 617** MCA; **Chapter 32:** 625–627, 629–631, 633, 635** MW; **636** (l) (c) SW; (r) MW; **638** SW; **Chapter 33:** 647 RH, 657** (spots) RH; (graphics) MCA; **Chapter 34:** 669 AT; **671** (tl) RH; (tc) MCA; (tr) BJ/WAA; **671** (b) AT; **672** (spots) BH; (graphics) MCA; **676** BH; **677, 679** KC; **682** SW; **683** (t) SW, (b) SW/MCA; **685–686, 689** MCA; **690–691** CK; **Chapter 35:** 694–696 SW; **697, 699** MCA; **700** SW; **704–705** MCA; **Chapter 36:** 710 AT; **712** David DeGasperis, **713** MCA; **714** JK; **718** AT; **721** MCA; **Chapter 37:** 725 AT; **726** (t) SW; (c) MCA; **727, 729** AT;

734 Cynthia Turner; **738** AT; **739** MCA; **Chapter 38:** 743 MCA; **745** (spots) SR/WAA; (graphics) MCA; **746** AT; **748** SB; **749,** SR/WAA Walter Stuart; **756** SB; **757** MCA; **758** SR/WAA; **Chapter 39:** 762–763 (spots) SR/WAA; **765** PG; **766** SR/WAA; **767** PG; **768** SR/WAA; **769** BJ/WAA; **772** PG; **774** BJ/WAA; **776** PG; **777** MCA; **Chapter 40:** 781, 785, 788–790, 792 AT; **793** MCA; **Chapter 41:** 800 (spots) BH; (graphics) MCA; **801** BH; (b) Laurie O'Keefe; **805** KC; **808** BH; **809, 810** (t) (br) KC; **811** KC; **812** Todd Buck/HS; **814** BH; **815–816** MCA; **Chapter 42:** 819 PG; **820** Peg Gerrity/HS; **821** (spots) MW; (graphics) MCA; **825** PG, (silhouettes & heart) KC; **826** PG; **827** KC; **828** PG; (silhouette) KC; **834** KC; **835** MCA; **Chapter 43:** 840 BH; **841** (t) BH; (b) (dinosaurs) Chris Forsey; (animals) Pond & Giles; (graphics) MCA; **842, 846** KC; **847** (head) BH; (brain) KC; **848** MCA; **856** KC; **Chapter 44:** 862 (dinosaurs) Chris Forsey; (animals) Pond & Giles; (graphics) MCA; **863** PG; **864** (l) RH; (r) MCA; **865–867** KC; **876** KC; **877** MCA; **Chapter 45:** 882 BH; **883** Howard Friedman; **885** KC; **886** E. Alexander/AT; **891** (graphics) MCA; **898** BH; **899** MCA; **Chapter 46:** 906 KK; **908** KK; (silhouette) JK; **909** JK; **910, 911** (l) 912 KK; **913–915, 917** KK; **918** MCA; **919** KK, (silhouette) JK; **923** (t) MCA; (b) CK; **926** MCA; **Chapter 47:** 931–932 KC; **933** CK; **934, 935** (t) Walter Stuart; **935** (b) 936 CK; **937, 945** JK; **946** MCA; **947** KC; **950** KC; **952** MCA; **Chapter 48:** 957 CK; **960** JK; **961–964, 969–970, 972–973** MCA; **Chapter 49:** 978 (t) (bl) MCA; (br) MW; **979** (spot) MW, (graphics) MCA; **983–984** JK; **985** (t) CK, (c) KK/CK; (b) MCA; **986** JK; **987** (t) KK/CK; (b) JK; **988** (t) JK; (r) MCA; **991** KK/CK; **992–994** MCA; **995** JK; **998** KK/CK; **999** BH; **Chapter 50:** 1004 JK; **1005** CK; **1006** JK; **1008** CK; **1010** MCA; **1011** JK; **1013, 1014–1015, 1016** MCA; **1018, 1020** KK; **1021–1022** JK; **1025** (t) MCA, (b) Todd Buck; **1026–1027** KC; **Chapter 51:** 1030–1031 MCA; **1032** JK; **1033** Tonya Hines; **1034** JK; **1035** CK; **1037** JK; **1038–1040, 1043** MCA; **1044** AT; **Chapter 52:** 1047–1048 MCA; **1049, 1051** KK; **1052** MCA; **1055–1057** CK; **1058** C. Turner/AT; **1060, 1062** MCA; **Chapter 53:** 1069 JK; **1074, 1078, 1080** MCA; **1091, 1092** MCA

PHOTOGRAPHY

Abbreviation Code

AA = Animals, Animals; BPA = Biophoto Associates; BPS = Biological Photo Service; CB = Corbis-Bettmann; ES = Earth Scenes; FH = Fran Heyl Associates; GH = Grant Heilman Photography; HRW = Holt, Rinehart and Winston staff photograph; JS/FS = Jeff Smith/FOTOSMITH; MP = Minden Pictures; NASC = National Audubon Society Collection; OSF = Oxford Scientific Films; PA = Peter Arnold, Inc.; PH = Phototake NYC; PR = Photo Researchers; RLM = Robert & Linda Mitchell; SPL = Science Photo Library; SS = Science Source; TSI = Tony Stone Images; VU = Visuals Unlimited

Cover: © Manfred Danegger/Okrpai/Photo Researchers, Inc. © Michael Fogden/DRK Photo; **iv** (t) © Tim Fitzharris; (b) © Flip Nicklin/MP; **v** © BPA/SS/PR; **vi** © Mark Joseph/ TSI; **vii** AA/© Anup & Manuj Shah; **viii** © Oliver Meckes/MPI-Túbingen; **ix** (t) © John Kaprielian/PR; (b) © Neil McDaniel/PR; **x** © Kevin Schafer/Martha Hill; **xi** © U.H.B. Trust/TSI; **xiii** © Cornell University Photography; **Unit 1:** 2 © E.R. Degginger; **3** (tl) © Tony Stone Imaging/TSI; (tc) © Luiz C. Marigo/PA; (tr) © Frans Lanting/MP; (b) © Tim Davis/TSI; **Chapter 1:** 4 © Art Wolfe; **5** © Philip Sze/VU; **6** © Carolina Biological Supply/PH; **7** (t) © Dan Guravich/NASC/PR; (b) © Pr. Stanley Cohen/SPL/PR; **8** (l) © Jim Brandenburg/MP; (r) © Steve Kaufman/PA; **9** © Gunter Ziesler/PA; **10** © Alfred Pasieka/PA; **11** © Runk/Schoenberger/GH; **12** (t) © Stephen J. Krasemann/NASC/PR; (b) © Dr. K.S. Kim/PA; **13** © A. Kerstitch/VU; **15** © Sinclair Stammers/SPL/PR; **16** © Barry Dowsett/SPL/PR; **19** © Agence France Presse/CB; © Will & Demi McIntyre/PR; **22** (t) © E. White/VU; (b) © Jerome Paulin/VU; **27** (t) © Oliver Meckes/SS/PR; (b) © CNRI/SPL/PR; **28** © JS/FS; **Chapter 2:** 30 © Alfred Pasieka/PA; **38** (bkgnd) © Superstock/

Mark Romine; courtesy of the American Red Cross; **39** (t) courtesy of the American Red Cross; (b) © Larry Mulvehill/SS/PR; **41** © Harvey Lloyd/PA; **Chapter 3:** 48 © Fred Bavendam/TSI; **51** © William Hopkins; **60** (bkgnd) Geoff Tompkison/SPL/PR; © UPI/CB; **Unit 2:** 66–67 (bkgnd) © BPA/PR; **66** © FH; **67** (white blood cells) © Don Fawcett/E. Shelton/PR; (t) © Barry L. Runk/Rannels/GH; (cr) © FH; (br) © Don W. Fawcett/VU; **Chapter 4:** 68 © Dr. Gopal Murti/PH; **70** ©Barry L. Runk/Rannels/GH; **71** (tl) © Dr. David Scott/CNRI/PH; (tc) © David Scharf/PA; (tr) © Meckes/Ottawa/SS/PR; (b) © Dr. Patricia Schultz/PA; **72** © John Cardmore/BPS/TSI; **77** © Don W. Fawcett/VU; **78** © R. Bolender–D. Fawcett/VU; **79** (t) © R. Bolender–D. Fawcett/VU; (b) © Pr. Jan de May/PH; **80** (t, bl, br) © David M. Phillips/VU; **81** © Don Fawcett/VU; **82** (t) © BPA/SS/PR; (b) © Dr. Jeremy Burgess/SPL/SS/PR; **83** PR; **84** (bkgnd) © Superstock/Mark Romine; © CB; **85** (l) RLM; (r) © K. Talaro/VU; **88** © Roland Burke/PA; **90** © Don W. Fawcett/VU; **92** © Sergio Purtell/FOCA; **93** © Runk/Schoenberger/GH; **Chapter 5:** 94 © FH; **97** © M. Abbey/VU; **98** (t) © Runk/Schoenberger/GH; (b) © David M. Phillips/VU; **104** © Prof. Birgit H. Satir; **Chapter 6:** 110 © Arthur C. Smith III/GH; **119** © Dr. Jeremy Burgess/SS/PR; **Chapter 7:** 126 © Frans Lanting/MP; **130** © John Colwell/GH; **132** © From THE LIVES OF CELLS by Lewis Thomas. © Used by permission of Bantam Books, a division of Bantam Doubleday Dell Publishing Group, Inc.; (b) © BPA/SS/PR; **142** WARD'S Natural Science; **Chapter 8:** 144 © CNRI/SPL/PR; **146** © Gunther F. Bahr/AFIP/TSI; **151** (t) © David M. Phillips/VU; (b) © R. Calentine/VU; **152** (bkgnd) Geoff Tompkison/SPL/PR; © CNRI/PH; **156** © Jerome Wexler/PR; **158** © David M. Phillips/VU; **160** © John D. Cunningham/VU; **Unit 3:** 162 © Schafer & Hill/TSI; **163** (t) © Mark Joseph/TSI; (c) © David Scharf; (b) © James H. Robinson; **Chapter 9:** 164 © James H. Robinson; **170** (bkgnd) © Superstock/Mark Romine; © AP/Wide World Photos; **171** © Gregory G. Dimijian/PR; **172** (l) © Jane Grushow/GH; (r) © Christian Grzimek, OKAPIA/PR; **176** © Larry Lefever/GH; **Chapter 10:** 184 © Tony Stone Imaging/TSI; **187** © Rosalind Franklin/SS/PR; **198** © Dr. Gopal Murti/PH; **200-202** JS/FS; **Chapter 11:** 202 © David Scharf; **206** © Professor Oscar Miller/SPL/PR; **210** © Oliver Meckes/PR; **211** (l) © Bob Thomason/TSI; (r) © Martin M. Rotker/SS/PR; **212** © Tom Tracy/TSI; **213** (bkgnd) Geoff Tompkison/SPL/PR; James King-Holmes/SPL/PR; **Chapter 12:** 220 © BPA/SS/PR; **232** © CNRI/PH; **234** © Gopal Murti/CNRI/PH; **Chapter 13:** 238 © Agricultural Research Service, USDA; **243** © Mark Joseph/TSI; **247** from GENETHICS by David Suzuki and Peter Knudston © 1989 by New Data Enterprises and Peter Knudston. Reprinted by permission of Harvard University Press; **248** © University of Florida; **251** AA/© Zig Leszczynski; **252** © Agricultural Research Service, USDA; **254** © Courtesy of Cellmark Diagnostics, Germantown, Md; **256** © Sergio Purtell/FOCA; **Unit 4:** 258–259 (bkgnd) Iconographic Encyclopedia of Science, Art and Literature (1851); **258** (l) © Tui DeRoy/Bruce Coleman, Inc.; (r) © CB; **259** (tl) © Nanci Kahn/Institute of Human Origins; (tr) Smithsonion Institution (b) © Cabisco/VU; **Chapter 14:** 260 © Douglas Peebles; **266** © Kenneth Garrett; **268** © Sidney Fox/VU; **271** (t) © Henry C. Aldrich, U. of Florida; (b) © Stanley Awramik/BPS/TSI; **276** © WARD'S Natural Science; **Chapter 15:** 278 © Tui DeRoy/Bruce Coleman, Inc.; **279** © RLM; **282** (bkgnd) Geoff Tompkison/SPL/PR; **284** © Bridgeman/Art Resource, NY; **290** (t) AA/© Joe McDonald; (b) © Runk/Schoenberger/GH; **291** © Stephen Dalton/PR; **292** AA/© Fritz Prenzel; **Chapter 16:** 298 © Art Wolfe/TSI; **300** © HRW photo/Sam Dudgeon; **302** © Art Wolfe/TSI; **303** (t) The cover from THE FLAMINGO'S SMILE: Reflections in Natural History by Stephen Jay Gould. © 1985 by Stephen Jay Gould. Reprinted by permission of W. W. Norton & Company, Inc.; (b) © Paula Lerner/Woodfin Camp & Associates; **305** AA/© Ralph A. Reinhold; **308** © Art Wolfe/TSI; **310** © Tom McHugh, Steinhart Aquarium/PR; **311** (t) AA/© Zig Leszczynski; (b) © Barry L. Runk/GH; **Chapter 17:** 318 © Enrico Ferorelli/Institute of Human Origins; **320** (t) © Frans Lanting/MP; (b) © Adam Jones/PR; **322** (bkgnd) © Superstock/Mark Romine; © Des & Jen Bartlett/National Geographic Image Collection; **323** (t) © E. R.